Lecture Notes in Computer Science

Edited by G. Goos and J. Hartmanis

140

Automata, Languages and Programming

Ninth Colloquium
Aarhus, Denmark
July 12–16, 1982

Edited by M. Nielsen and E.M. Schmidt

Springer-Verlag
Berlin Heidelberg New York 1982

Editors
Mogens Nielsen
Erik Meineche Schmidt
Computer Science Department, Aarhus University
Ny Munkegade, DK-8000 Aarhus C, Denmark

CR Subject Classifications (1981): E 2, F 1, F 2.2, F 3, F 4, G 2.1

ISBN 3-540-11576-5 Springer-Verlag Berlin Heidelberg New York
ISBN 0-387-11576-5 Springer-Verlag New York Heidelberg Berlin

Printed in Germany

Printing and binding: Beltz Offsetdruck, Hemsbach/Bergstr.
2145/3140-543210

9th International Colloquium on

Automata, Languages and Programming

ICALP 82

July 12-16, 1982

Aarhus, Denmark

TABLE OF CONTENTS

LOCALITY IN MODULAR SYSTEMS

R.J.R. Back and H. Mannila
Department of Computer Science
University of Helsinki

ABSTRACT

Modularity of programs is studied from a semantic point of view. A simple model of modular systems and modularization mechanisms is presented, together with correctness criteria for modular systems. A concept of locality of modular systems is defined; it is a property which "good" modular decompositions should have. The locality of certain kinds of modularization mechanisms is studied, and the results are applied to parameterless procedures.

1. INTRODUCTION

Modularity is one of the most important concepts in computer science. It is the key to mastering the complexity of large programs and is therefore central in the theory of programming. There is quite an extensive body of research on specific modularization mechanisms, such as procedures, processes and abstract data types. Modularity in itself, in abstraction, has not been equally well investigated. The most notable studies in this direction are those by Parnas (e.g. /4,5,6/), in which he discusses general principles for program modularization, covering such aspects as the appropriate choice of program modules and abstraction levels, gives different explications of the notion of hierarchicality and discusses the loss of transparency when using abstraction. The incorporation of abstract data types in recent programming languages such as Ada and Modula has somewhat renewed the interest in basic modularization principles (see e.g. /3/).

It is our belief that the concept of modularity, as a general principle for organizing programs, can be studied in abstraction, and that one can derive nontrivial properties which well-modularized systems should have. The present paper reports on one way of approaching this problem. We study modular systems from a semantic point of view, by giving a semantic model of modular systems and defining a notion of correctness for such systems. Our basic concern is to characterize modularization mechanisms in which the correctness of a modular system can be established by checking for each module separately that it satisfies its specification, provided all modules it uses satisfy their specification. Such modularization mechanisms will be called *local*. We will give a precise definition of this property within the framework of our semantic model and then discuss the conditions under which modularization mechanisms are local.

A semantic approach, as opposed to a syntactic approach within some fixed formal system, is chosen for a number of reasons. It allows us to study properties of modular systems without being too much distracted by questions of expressibility within a specific formal system. The theory can also be developed with a minimum of assumptions. A small disadvantage of this approach is that we in some situations are forced to give semantic definitions of concepts (like terms, declarations and hierarchicality) which are rather syntactic in flavour.

2. DECLARATION MECHANISMS

The main problem in the approach we have chosen is to find a simple semantic model for modular systems. We want to describe semantically modular system like the following one:

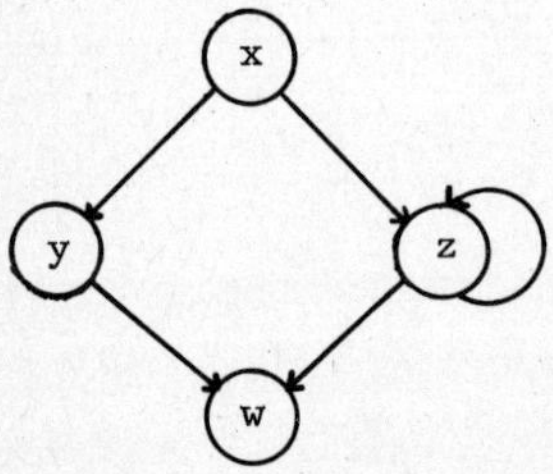

DCL: x: A(y,z)
y: B(w)
z: C(z,w)
w: D

dependency graph module declarations

Figure 1. An example modular system

The left hand side describes the way in which the modules x, y, z and w depend on each other. We see that module x uses both modules y and z, that both y and z use module w (sharing), that module z also uses itself (recursion) and that module w does not use any other modules. The right hand side shows schematically the way in which such a modular system usually would be declared, by associating an implementation A(y,z) with x, B(w) with y and so on. The dependency of e.g. x on y and z is indicated by the free occurences of the names y and z in the implementation A(y,z) of x.

The declaration DCL above will define a meaning for each module x, y, z and w. What exactly this meaning is depends on the application at hand. If we are declaring procedures, then A(y,z), B(w), C(z,w) and D would be procedure bodies, and the meaning of x, y, z and w would be some kind of state transformations. If again we were declaring (abstract) data types, then the meanings could be algebras. It is our intention here to abstract away from the specific choice of meaning for modules and study only those properties which are common to all modular systems, independently of what the meanings of the modules are assumed to be. We therefore simply postulate that a set Obj of possible meanings of modules is given. The elements of Obj are referred to as *objects*.

We will also postulate a set of module names or *variables* Var. The declaration DCL above can now be understood as a syntactic way of associating with each variable x, y, z and w some specific object in Obj. Such an association will be called an *environment*. More precisely, and environment on X in Obj, $X \subseteq$ Var, is a function e from X to Obj. We write $Env_{Obj}(X) = X \rightarrow Obj$ for the set of all environments on X in Obj. The declaration DCL then defines some specific environment e in $Env_{Obj}(X)$, where $X = \{x,y,z,w\}$. (The subscript Obj will henceforth be dropped when it is clear from the context what the set of objects is.)

Let us consider the declaration x: A(y,z) a little closer. We may assume that the meaning of A is a function $a:Obj \times Obj \rightarrow Obj$, such that if o_y is the meaning of y and o_z the meaning of z, o_y and $o_z \in Obj$, then $a(o_y,o_z)$ is the meaning of x. In other words, if $e \in Env(X)$ is the environment determined by DCL, then we should have

$$\begin{aligned} e(x) &= a(e(y),e(z)), \\ e(y) &= b(e(w)), \\ e(z) &= c(e(z),e(w)) \text{ and} \\ e(w) &= d, \end{aligned} \tag{1}$$

where b, c and d are, respectively, the meanings of B, C and D. We assume that there is an environment e which does satisfy this condition. In case there are more than one such environment, we assume that the modularization mechanism prescribes on of these as the one determined by the declaration.

The above discussion suggests that a semantic model of modular systems like the one above can be built out of the following ingredients:

(i) a set of module names (x,y,z and w) and their dependency graph,

(ii) for each module name a corresponding object function (a,b,c and d),

(iii) a rule for determining which of the environments satisfying (1) is the intended environment.

We will in fact simplify (i) and (ii), in order to make the semantics more manageable. Rather than using the object function a above, we use an environment function $a':Env(Y) \rightarrow Obj$, such that $a'(e) = a(e(y),e(z))$, for any $e \in Env(Y)$, where $Y = \{y,z,w\}$ is the set of all variables which some module is dependent on. This means that all functions in the modular system will have the same domain. It also means that the dependency graph can be ignored: the dependency of e.g. x on y will be shown be the fact that for some environments $e_1,e_2 \in Env(Y)$ agreeing on z and w but not on y, we have $a'(e_1) \neq a'(e_2)$. (We thus replace a syntactic notion of module dependency by a semantic dependency notion.)

The above view of module declarations will be formalized as follows. First, a *term* on X, $X \subseteq$ Var, is a function $t:Env(X) \rightarrow Obj$. Let Trm(X) be a set of *permitted* terms on X (in general, not every term will be permitted in building a modular system). A *declaration* of X using Y, $X,Y \subseteq$ Var, is a function $d:X \rightarrow Trm(Y)$ (X is the set of variables declared by d and Y is the set of variables used by d). Let Dcl(X,Y) be a set of *permitted* declarations of X using Y (again, not every declaration need to be permitted).

If $Y \subseteq X$, then the declarations in Dcl(X,Y) are said to be *self-contained*. Finally, a *solution function* for a set Dcl(X,Y) of self-contained declarations is a function $*:\mathrm{Dcl}(X,Y) \to \mathrm{Env}(X)$ which satisfies the condition

$$d^*(x) = d(x)(d^*|Y),$$

for any $d \in \mathrm{Dcl}(X,Y)$, where we write d^* for $*(d)$ and $d^*|Y$ is the restriction of d^* to Y. This is essentially a formalization of condition (iii) above.

A *declaration mechanism* for Obj determines which terms and declarations are permitted and how declarations are solved. We define a declaration mechanism as a triple, $D = (\mathrm{Trm},\mathrm{Dcl},*)$, where for each $X,Y \subseteq \mathrm{Var}$

$$\mathrm{Trm}(X) \subseteq \mathrm{Env}(X) \to \mathrm{Obj},$$
$$\mathrm{Dcl}(X,Y) \subseteq X \to \mathrm{Trm}(Y) \text{ and}$$
$$*:\mathrm{Dcl}(X,Y) \to \mathrm{Env}(X),\ Y \subseteq X.$$

We write $\mathrm{Trm}_D(X)$ for the set of terms on X permitted by D, $\mathrm{Dcl}_D(X,Y)$ for the set of declarations permitted by D and $*_D$ for the solution function prescribed by D. Also, when neccessary, we write Obj_D for the objects of D and $\mathrm{Env}_D(X)$ for the environments of D.

3. MODULARIZATION MECHANISMS

Modularizing a program implies that each module is given a *specification*, which describes for other modules what they may expect it to do. As we are only concerned with the semantics of modular systems, we will here simply identify a specification with the set of all objects satisfying it, i.e. a specification will be a subset of Obj. The set Obj is itself a specification, the *trivial* specification, which is satisfied by every object in Obj. The empty set is an *inconsistent* specification, which is not satisfied by any object. A *specification language* is a set Spc of specifications containing the trivial specification, i.e. $\mathrm{Spc} \subseteq P(\mathrm{Obj})$ and $\mathrm{Obj} \in \mathrm{Spc}$.

A set of modules Z, $Z \subseteq \mathrm{Var}$, is specified by a *requirement* on Z, which is a function $r:Z \to \mathrm{Spc}$, assigning to each variable in Z some specification in Spc. We write $\mathrm{Req}_{\mathrm{Spc}}(Z) = Z \to \mathrm{Spc}$ for the set of all requirements on Z. (The subscript Spc will usually be omitted.) A requirement $r \in \mathrm{Req}(Z)$ is said to be *satisfiable*, if $r(z) \neq \phi$ for every $z \in Z$. For $r \in \mathrm{Req}(Z)$, we denote by r^X the set of all environments in Env(X) which satisfy r, i.e. r^X is the set

$$r^X = \{e \in \mathrm{Env}(X) \mid e(z) \in r(z) \text{ for all } z \in X \cap Z\}.$$

(Note that r only constrains environments on variables which are both in X and Z.)

A *modularization mechanism* is a pair $M = (D,\mathrm{Spc})$, where $D = (\mathrm{Dcl},\mathrm{Trm},*)$ is a declaration mechanism, determining what declarations are permitted and how they are solved, and Spc is a specification language, determining how modules are specified. A *modular system* in M is a pair $m = (d,r)$, where d is a declaration in Dcl(X,Y) and r is a requirement in $\mathrm{Req}_{\mathrm{Spc}}(Z)$, X,Y and $Z \subseteq \mathrm{Var}$. The system m is said to be self-contained, if d is self-contained. We write

$$\mathrm{Mod}_M(X,Y,Z) = \mathrm{Dcl}_D(X,Y) \times \mathrm{Req}_{Spc}(Z)$$

for the set of all modular systems of M *declaring* X, *using* Y and *specifying* Z. We do not assume that each variable declared or used in a modular system is in fact specified. Variables not explicitly specified can be understood as being implicitly specified by the trivial specification.

4. AN EXAMPLE

We will illustrate the definitions above by describing a simple modularization mechanism, the declaration of constants (a more realistic example will be given in section 10). Integer constant declarations, in the form they appear in e.g. Ada, are probably among the simplest of declaration mechanisms. We define a declaration mechanism C for the set of integers Int, Int = min .. max, where min is the smallest and max is the biggest integer allowed (we use a .. b to denote the integer range from a to b). An enviroment e in $\mathrm{Env}_{Int}(X)$, where X is a finite set of variables, associates with each $x \in X$ an integer $e(x) \in \mathrm{Int}$.

A declaration mechanism for integers is a triple $C = (\mathrm{Trm}_C, \mathrm{Dcl}_C, *_C)$, defined as follows. First, $\mathrm{Trm}_C(Y)$ is the set of all functions $t:\mathrm{Env}_{Int}(Y) \to \mathrm{Int}$ which can be defined by arithmetical expressions. An expression like x + 2*y defines a function $t \in \mathrm{Trm}_C(Y)$ in the obvious way: $t(e) = e(x) + 2*e(y)$, for any $e \in \mathrm{Env}_{Int}(Y)$ $(x,y \in Y)$.

A declaration $d \in \mathrm{Dcl}_C(X,Y)$ associates with each $x \in X$ an arithmetical expression $d(x) \in \mathrm{Trm}_C(Y)$. No recursion is allowed in $\mathrm{Dcl}_C(X,Y)$. Solutions are calculated in the obvious way. A simple example of a declaration is

$$\begin{aligned} x &= y + z \\ y &= z - w + 1 \\ z &= 2*w \\ w &= 3. \end{aligned} \tag{2}$$

This declaration is self-contained, as the variables used (y,z,w) form a subset of the variables declared (x,y,z,w). The solution of (2) is the environment x = 10, y = 4, z = 6 and w = 3.

Specifications of integers are sets of integers. One simple choice of a specification language would be to take all integer ranges a .. b. Such specifications are used in Ada, where we can e.g. write

subtype small *is* integer *range* 1 .. 10 ;
y : *constant* small := z - w + 1 .

We can turn declaration (2) above into a modular system by adding specifications for some variables. The requirement $x \in 1 .. 20$, $y \in 1 .. 10$ is e.g. satisfied by the solution of declaration (2).

Recursive constant declarations are also conceivable. In a LISP system with lazy evaluation one could allow a declaration like x = cons(0,x), which can be understood as defining the infinite list (0,0,0,...).

5. CORRECTNESS OF SELF-CONTAINED MODULAR SYSTEMS

We now consider the question of correctness of modular systems. Let M be a self-contained modularization mechanism and let $m = (d,r) \in Mod_M(X,Y,Z)$, $Y \subseteq X$. We say that m is *globally correct*, if $d^* \in r^X$ (i.e. every object $d^*(x)$ satisfies its specification $r(x)$). Note that global correctness only restricts the value of d for variables in $X \cap Z$.

The modular system m is said to be *locally correct*, if r is satisfiable and $d(x)[r^Y] \subseteq r(x)$ for all $x \subseteq X$, where $d(x)[r^Y]$ is the image of r^Y under $d(x)$.

The global correctness of a modular system m = (d,r) is the "real" correctness criterion. It says that the actual behaviour of the modular system (i.e. d^*) satisfies the requirement r given for it. Local correctness considers each module in isolation, requiring that this module satisfies its specification, if each module it uses satisfies its specification. Local correctness has the advantage that the declaration need not be solved (d^* need not be computed) in order to establish local correctness.

There is no a priori relationship between global and local correctness of modular systems, i.e. neither one needs to imply the other. An example of a globally correct modular system which is not locally correct is the constant declaration (2) in the previous section, together with the requirement r: $x \in 1 .. 10$, $y \in 1 .. 10$, $z \in 5 .. 8$ and $w \in 3 .. 3$. This modular system is globally correct, since the solution of the declaration is x = 10, y = 4, z = 6 and w = 3, which satisfies the requirement r. The system is not locally correct, as the specifications are too wide. For example, the environment e: y = 10, z = 6 and w = 3 is permitted by r, i.e. $e \in r^Y$, where $Y = \{y,z,w\}$. But d(x)(e) = 16, which does not belong to the specification r(x) = 1 .. 10.

On the other hand, local correctness does not necessarily imply global correctness. A simple example is the declaration x = cons(0,x) from the previous section. We could choose as specification for x the set of all finite lists. The modular system is then obviously locally correct, as cons(0,x) is finite for any finite list x. However, the system is not globally correct, as the solution of the declaration is the infinite list (0,0,0,...).

6. LOCALITY OF MODULAR SYSTEMS

As the examples show, a modular system can be locally correct and yet not be globally correct and vice versa. However, if local correctness of a modular system implies its global correctness, then the latter can be established without having to solve the declaration, by establishing the local correctness of the modular system. This means that there is a strong decomposition of the modular system, as its (global) correctness can be established by local arguments only, by considering each declared module in turn and checking it against its own specification and the specifications of the modules it uses. This strong decomposition property is the main theme of our study and is captured by the following definition.

Let $M = (D,Spc)$ be a modularization mechanism and let $d \in Dcl_D(X,Y)$. The declaration d is *local* in M, if for any $Z \subseteq Var$ and any requirement $r \in Req(Z)$ we have

$$(d,r) \text{ locally correct} \Rightarrow (d,r) \text{ globally correct.}$$

The modularization mechanism M is said to be *local* if all its declarations are local.

Let us define the approximation ordering $\leq$ between specifications by $s \leq s'$ if and only if $s \supseteq s'$, for all $s,s' \in Spc$. This is obviously a partial ordering, with the specifications ordered according to their information content. A set theoretically smaller specification is stronger (contains more information) than a larger one, as it allows fewer alternatives. (This ordering of specifications is also used by Scott in his topologically oriented approach to denotational semantics /7/.)

The partial order $\leq$ is extended to Req(X) in the usual way: for $e,e' \in Req(X)$, $e \leq e'$ iff $e(x) \leq e'(x)$ for all $x \in X$.

A specification language Spc is said to be *complete*, if for any $o \in Obj$, $\{o\}$ is a specification in Spc. This means that each object in Obj can be uniquely characterized by a specification in Spc, and consequently that each environment can be uniquely characterized by a requirement. Especially, for $d \in Dcl(X,Y)$, $Y \subseteq X$, the solution d^* is characterized by the requirement $r^* \in Req(X)$, where $r^*(x) = \{d^*(x)\}$ for all $x \in X$.

Let $d \in Dcl(X,Y)$, where $Y \subseteq X$. Define the *local requirement set* R_d of d by

$$R_d = \{r \in Req(X) \mid (d,r) \text{ is locally correct}\}.$$

$(R_d,\leq)$ is a partially ordered set. The following theorem gives a simple characterization of locality in modular systems with a complete specification language.

Theorem 1. Let M be a modularization mechanism with a complete specification language and let d be a self-contained declaration in M. Then d is local if and only if r^* (as defined above) is the greatest element in the local requirement set R_d of d. (For proofs of theorems and lemmas, see /1/.)

7. DECLARATIONS WHICH ARE NOT SELF-CONTAINED

To define global correctness for declarations which are not self-contained, we need to introduce some notation and additional assumptions. For each object $o \in Obj$ we define the corresponding *constant term* $o_X:Env(X) \rightarrow Obj$ by $o_X(e) = o$, for all $e \in Env(X)$. We will assume that Trm(X) contains o_X for all $o \in Obj$ and $X \subseteq Var$.

Similarly, we can extend any environment $e \in Env(X)$ to a declaration $e_Y:X \rightarrow Trm(Y)$, $Y \subseteq Var$, by defining $e_Y(x) = e(x)_Y$ for each $x \in X$. We assume that Dcl(X,Y) contains e_Y for each $e \in Env(X)$ and $Y \subseteq Var$. The solution of e_Y is, of course, e.

Given two declarations $d_1 \in Dcl(X_1,Y)$ and $d_2 \in Dcl(X_2,Y)$, where $X \cap Y = \phi$, we define their *sum* $d_1 + d_2:X_1 \cup X_2 \rightarrow Y$ by

$$(d_1 + d_2)(z) = \begin{cases} d_1(z), & \text{if } z \in X_1 \\ d_2(z), & \text{if } z \in X_2. \end{cases}$$

Again we assume that under the assumptions above, $d_1 + d_2$ is an element of the set $Dcl(X_1 \cup X_2, Y)$.

Global correctness of modular systems in which the declarations are not self-contained is now defined as follows. Let $m = (d,r)$ be a modular system in $Mod(X,Y,Z)$, where $Y - X \neq \phi$. We say that m is *globally correct*, if for any $e \in r^{Y-X}$, the self-contained modular system $(d + e_{Y-X}, r)$ is globally correct. Local correctness and locality are defined as before.

It turns out that only self-contained declarations are in fact relevant, when studying the locality of a modularization mechanism.

Theorem 2. A modularization mechanism M is local if and only if all self-contained declarations of M are local.

8. LOCALITY OF HIERARCHICAL SYSTEMS

In this section we study hierarchically organized modular systems and show that such systems are always local. Let D be a declaration mechanism and let $d \in Dcl(X,Y)$, $X,Y \subseteq Var$. Let $z_1, z_2 \in X \cup Y$. We say that z_1 *depends* on z_2 (*in* d), if there exists environments $e,e' \in Env(Y)$ such that $e(y) = e'(y)$ for all $y \in Y-\{z_2\}$ and $d(z_1)(e) \neq d(z_1)(e')$. If z_1 depends on z_2 in d, we write $z_2 \; dep_d \; z_1$. (Note the direction here; the relation should be understood as saying that z_2 is needed to determine z_1.)

Consider as an example the constant declaration

$$x_1 = 1 + x_2 * x_3$$
$$x_2 = 0.$$

By definition, $x_3 \; dep_d \; x_1$ will hold, even though $x_1 = 1$ for all values of x_3. The definition of dependency thus considers the declarations locally, one by one, and not globally. (On the other hand, in $x_1 = 1 + 0 * x_3$, x_1 does not depend on x_3.)

Let d be as above and let dep_d^+ be the transitive closure of dep_d. The declaration d is said to be *hierarchical*, if dep_d^+ is well-founded, and *recursive*, if for some $z \in X$ we have $z \; dep_d^+ \; z$. It is easy to see that for finite X, $d \in Dcl(X,Y)$ is hierarchical if and only if d is not recursive. (For infinite X this does not necessarily hold.)

A declaration mechanism is *hierarchical*, if it permits only hierarchical declarations. A declaration $d \in Dcl(X,Y)$ is *finite*, if X is finite. A declaration mechanism is again finite, if it permits only finite declarations (i.e. $Dcl(X,Y) \neq \phi$ only for finite X).

Lemma 1. Any finite, hierarchical and self-contained declaration has a unique solution.

Theorem 3. Finite hierarchical self-contained declarations are local.

Combining theorems 2 and 3 gives the following result.

Corollary 1. Finite hierarchical declaration mechanisms are local.

9. LOCALITY OF RECURSIVE SYSTEMS

We now turn our attention to recursive declaration mechanisms. Let the set of objects Obj form a complete partial order, with approximation ordering $\sqsubseteq$ and the bottom element $\perp$. Then $Env(X) = X \to Obj$ is also a cpo, with the induced ordering $e \sqsubseteq e'$ if and only if $e(x) \sqsubseteq e'(x)$ for all $x \in X$, and the bottom element $\perp$, where $\perp(x) = \perp$ for all $x \in X$.

A declaration mechanism $D = (Trm, Dcl, *)$ for Obj is said to be *continuous*, if $Trm(X)$ is the set of all continuous functions $t: Env(X) \to Obj$ and for all $d \in Dcl(X,Y)$, $Y \subseteq X$, d^* is the least fixed point of the continuous function $d_0: Env(X) \to Env(X)$, where $d_0(e)(x) = d(x)(e)$ for all $e \in Env(X)$ and $x \in X$. A continuous declaration mechanism permits recursive declarations, with a least fixed point semantics used to determine the solution of such declarations.

Let $Spc \in P(Obj)$ be a specification language for Obj. A specification $s \in Spc$ is said to be *continuous*, if $(s, \sqsubseteq)$ is a cpo with the bottom element of Obj as bottom. The specification language Spc is continuous, if each specification in it is continuous. Finally, a modularization mechanism $M = (D, Spc)$ is continuous, if D is a continuous declaration mechanism and Spc is a continuous specification language for the objects of D. We now have the following result about the locality of modularization mechanisms permitting recursive declarations.

Theorem 4. Any self-contained continuous modularization mechanism is local.

Proof. Let $M = (D, Spc)$ be a continuous modularization mechanism. Let $d \in Dcl(X,Y)$, $Y \subseteq X$. Let $r \in Req(Z)$ be such that (d,r) is locally correct. We may assume that $Z = X$, since any $x \in X-Z$ can be seen as specified by the trivial specification Obj, and any $x \in Z-X$ is unnecessary and does not affect locality. We must show that (d,r) is globally correct. By local correctness we have $d(x)[r^X] \subseteq r(x)$ for all $x \in X$. Therefore, if $e \in r^X$, then for all $x \in X$, $d(x)(e) \in r(x)$. By the definition of d_0 we have that $d_0(e)(x) = d(x)(e)$, so $d_0(e)(x) \in r(x)$ for all x, i.e. $d_0(e) \in r^X$. We thus have that $e \in r^X \Rightarrow d_0(e) \in r^X$, for any $e \in Env(X)$.

The continuity of Spc means that $\perp \in s$ for each $s \in Spc$. Therefore $\perp \in r^X$ for each $r \in Req(X)$, as $\perp(x) = \perp \in r(x) \in Spc$ for each $x \in X$. It is also easily seen that r^X is chain closed, as each specification in Spc is chain closed. Thus r^X is a cpo, with bottom element $\perp$.

Combining these two results shows that $\perp \in r^X$, so $d_0(\perp) \in r^X$, so $d_0^2(\perp) \in r^X$ etc., i.e. $d_0^i(\perp) \in r^X$ for any $i \geq 0$. As d_0 is continuous, it is monotonic, so we have in fact an ascending chain $\perp \sqsubseteq d_0(\perp) \sqsubseteq d_0^2(\perp) \sqsubseteq \dots$ in r^X. As r^X is a cpo we have that $\sup d_0^i(\perp) \in r^X$. By continuity of D we know that

$$d^* = \sup d_0^i(\perp) \in r^X,$$

i.e. $d^* \in r^X$, so (d,r) is globally correct. Thus d is local and the modularization mechanism M is local. □

Using theorem 2, we get the following result.

Corollary 2. Any continuous modularization mechanism is local.

10. AN APPLICATION: PROCEDURE DECLARATIONS

We will apply the results derived above to study the locality of (parameterless) procedure declarations. A parameterless procedure essentially defines a state transformation, where a state, in its simplest form, can be understood as an assignement of values to program variables. Let us assume that all procedures work in the same state space Σ. Let $\Sigma_\perp$ stand for the set $\Sigma \cup \{\perp\}$; the meaning of a procedure can then be taken as a function $f:\Sigma \to \Sigma_\perp$. Here $f(\sigma) = \perp$ indicates that the procedure does not terminate for initial state σ. Thus, as objects we take the set $Obj = \Sigma \to \Sigma_\perp$.

A procedure is usually specified by giving pre- and postconditions for it. A precondition corresponds here to some set $U \subseteq \Sigma$, while a postcondition can be understood as a function $W:\Sigma \to P(\Sigma)$. Let (U,W) be such a pre-postcondition pair. We define the sets

$$PC(U,W) = \{f \in Obj \mid f(\sigma) = \perp \text{ or } f(\sigma) \in W(\sigma) \text{ for each } \sigma \in U\} \text{ and}$$
$$TC(U,W) = \{f \in Obj \mid f(\sigma) \in W(\sigma) \text{ for each } \sigma \in U\}.$$

The set PC(U,W) is the set of all state transformations which are *partially correct* with respect to (U,W), while TC(U,W) is the set of all state transformations which are *totally correct* with respect to (U,W). Let P be the set of all specifications PC(U,W) and T the set of all specifications TC(U,W), for (U,W) a pre-postcondition pair. Then both P and T are specification languages for Obj (in both cases the trivial specification is given by (ϕ,W), for any W).

A declaration mechanism D = (Trm,Dcl,*) can be built for Obj by choosing as terms all state transformations that can be described by while programs, with possible calls on parameterless recursive procedures. If Dcl(X,Y) permits only hierarchical declarations, then the solution function * is unique (lemma 1). If recursive declarations are allowed, then we take as approximation ordering the usual ordering induced into $\Sigma \to \Sigma_\perp$ by the ordering of the flat cpo $\Sigma_\perp$ (for further details see e.g. /2/). Allowing only while programs guarantees that all terms will be continuous. The solution is taken to be the least fixed point of the declaration, as described in section 9, so the declaration mechanism will be continuous.

A declaration mechanism for parameterless procedures permitting only hierarchical declarations will be local, by corollary 1. In case of declaration mechanisms permitting recursion, by theorem 4 the locality depends on whether the specification language is continuous or not. A check of this reveals that P is continuous but T is not. Thus recursive procedure declarations with partial correctness specifications are local. In case of total correctness specifications this is not the case. A simple counterexample is the declaration p = p, p a procedure identifier, with p specified by (Obj,W), where $W(\sigma) = Obj$ for all $\sigma \in Obj$. This specification says that p always terminates. This system is locally but not globally correct.

Summarizing, we have the following result about locality of procedure declarations:

	partial correctness	total correctness
hierarchical declarations	local	local
recursive declarations	local	not local

11. COMPOSING DECLARATIONS

We showed in section 8 that hierarchical declarations are always local. Here we generalize this result and show that hierarchical composition of arbitrary declarations preserves locality. We also give a representation theorem for declarations, essentially showing that any declaration is a hierarchical composition of its minimal recursive components (a precise definition of these notions is given below).

Let X_i and Y_i be finite sets of variables, $i = 1,\ldots,n$, and assume that the sets X_i are pairwise disjoint. Let $d_i \in Dcl(X_i,Y_i)$, $i = 1,\ldots,n$. Let $X = \cup_i X_i$ and $Y = \cup_i Y_i$. We define the *composition* $\Sigma_i d_i$ of the declarations d_i to be a declaration $d \in Dcl(X,Y)$ such that $d(x) = d_i'(x)$, if $x \in X_i$, where d_i' is the extension of d_i to $Dcl(X_i,Y)$ defined by $d_i'(z)(e) = d_i(z)(e|Y_i)$, for all $z \in X_i$ and $e \in Env(Y)$.

Composition of declarations is intended to model top-down/bottom-up program construction. We think of the whole program as being built in successive stages, each stage either declaring variables used in previous stages (top-down development) or adding new declarations using variables declared in previous stages (bottom-up development).

Let $d = \Sigma_i d_i$ be a composition of declarations. Let ρ_0 be the binary relation on $\{1,\ldots,n\}$ defined by $i \rho_0 j$ iff $X_i \cap Y_j \neq \phi$ and $i \neq j$. Let ρ be the transitive closure of ρ_0. We say that d is a *hierarchical composition,* if ρ is well-founded.

This is a rather strong requirement for hierarchical composition. We view the declarations d_i as black boxes, i.e. we do not make any assumptions about their internal connections, and connect these boxes non-recursively. An alternative approach would be to use the relation $tdep_d$ and only require that no cycle in the composition contains elements from different sets X_i. This would mean that the internal connections of the boxes are taken into account. A third way would be to set $i \rho_0 j$ iff there exists $x \in X_i$ and $y \in Y_j$ such that $x\ tdep_d\ y$. The definition above is, however, quite simple and seems to be closest to the idea of top-down/bottom-up program development.

<u>Theorem 5</u>. A hierarchical composition of local declarations is local.

Let d Dcl(X,Y), where X and Y are finite sets of variables and let dep_d^* be the reflexive and transitive closure of the dependency relation of d. Define an equivvalence relation $\equiv_d$ on X by $x \equiv_d y$ if and only if $x\ dep_d^*\ y$ and $y\ dep_d^*\ x$. Let

$$X = X_1 \cup X_2 \cup \ldots \cup X_n,\ n \geq 1,$$

be the partition induced by $\equiv_d$. (If we view (X, dep_d) as a directed graph, then the sets X_i are exactly the strongly connected components of X.) Define sets $Y_i \subseteq Y$, $i = 1,\ldots,n$, by

$$Y_i = \{y \in Y \mid y\ dep'_d\ x \text{ for some } x \in X_i\}.$$

The *minimal recursive components* of d are the declarations $d_i \in Dcl(X_i, Y_i)$ defined by $d_i(x)(e) = d(x)(e')$ for all $x \in X_i$ and $e \in Env(Y_i)$, where e' is any environment of Y such that $e'|Y_i = e$.

Lemma 2. The minimal recursive components are well-defined and unique.

Let $d \in Dcl(X,Y)$, and let X_i and Y_i be defined as above. We say that d is *tight*, if $Y = \cup_i Y_i$. If d is not tight, then there is some $y \in Y$ such that no $x \in X$ uses y, i.e. y is not needed in order to determine the solution of d. We have the following decomposition theorem.

Theorem 6. Each finite tight declaration is the hierarchical composition of its minimal recursive components.

Corollary 3. Any finite and tight non-local declaration has a non-local minimal recursive component.

12. CONCLUDING REMARKS

The previous sections have outlined a strictly semantical treatment on modularization mechanisms. The results fall into two different categories. The first one presents a semantic model for modular systems, modularization mechanisms, correctness of modular systems and gives an explication of the locality property. The other category contains an analysis of the locality of hierarchical and recursive modular systems.

Our work has concentrated on the semantic aspects of modularity, within a rather simple framework. The adequacy of this framework for the analysis of modularization mechanisms in real programming languages has not yet been thoroughly investigated. Certain extensions of the model are obviously needed in the case of a real programming language, e.g. it becomes necessary to study many-sorted modularization mechanisms (i.e. there may be many different sorts of objects). Also, the special characteristics of actual modularization mechanisms, such as procedures, processes and data types, need to be taken into account.

ACKNOWLEDGEMENT

We would like to thank Pekka Orponen and Henry Tirri for fruitful discussions on the themes treated in this paper. This research has been supported by the Academy of Finland.

REFERENCES

1. Back, R.J.R & H. Mannila: A semantic approach to program modularity, University of Helsinki, Department of Computer Science, Series C, to appear.

2. De Bakker, J.W.: Mathematical Theory of Program Correctness, Prentice-Hall 1980.

3. Habermann, A.N. & D.E. Perry: Well-formed system composition, Research report CMU-CS-80-117, Carnegie-Mellon University, 1980.

4. Parnas, D.L.: On the criteria to be used in decomposing systems into modules. Communications of the ACM 15, 2, 1053-1058, 1972.

5. Parnas, D.L.: On a "buzzword": hierarchical structure, Proceedings of the IFIP Congress -74, 336-339, North-Holland, 1974.

6. Parnas, D.L. & D.P. Siewiorek: Use of the concept of transparency in the design of hierarchically structured systems, Communications of the ACM 18, 7, 401-408, 1975.

7. Scott, D.: Lectures on a mathematical theory of computation, Technical monograph PRG-19, Oxford University Computing Laboratory, 1981.

On-the-Fly Garbage Collection:
New Algorithms Inspired by Program Proofs

Mordechai Ben-Ari

Department of Computer Sciences
School of Mathematical Sciences
Tel Aviv University
69978 Ramat Aviv
Israel

1. Introduction

In (2) an algorithm was presented for on-the-fly garbage collection. This algorithm (henceforth called the DLMSS algorithm) is one of the most difficult concurrent programs ever studied. It has been the subject of two formal proofs ((3) and (5)). The proofs are extremely complex; it would be difficult to check them mechanically. The informal proof of the algorithm for the same problem given by Kung and Song (6) is even longer and more complex.

We looked for and found a new algorithm for on-the-fly garbage collection. The criterion that the algorithm was to satisfy is that the correctness proof should be elementary. Neither the algorithm nor the invariants used in the proof are much simpler than DLMSS; however, each step in the verification of the invariants is almost trivial and could be mechanically checked.

Our algorithm is probably better than DLMSS in that it uses two colors instead of three (four colors are used in (6)). Our algorithm is probably worse than DLMSS in that an implementation might be less efficient. Neither point is to us as important as the simplicity of the proof. A significant point in favor of our algorithm is that it is robust to the seemingly innocent variation that introduces a bug into DLMSS.

The new algorithm was then used to develop other algorithms which may be significantly better in practice. The simplicity of the correctness proof was crucial: a new idea for modifying the algorithm could be easily checked to see if the proof could be similarly modified. One variation of the algorithm attempts to minimize the number of non-garbage nodes that must be marked. The second variation is an incremental garbage collector.

2. On-the-Fly Garbage Collection

We follow the model of the problem from (2). (A survey article on garbage collection was recently published by Cohen (1).) In a system such as a LISP interpreter, pointer manipulations can cause certain nodes to become inaccessible from a designated root. Such nodes, called garbage, must be identified and recycled by linking them to a list of free nodes. Thus we have two actors in the system. The <u>mutator</u> is that part of the system doing "useful" work and the <u>collector</u>

is that part of the system that recycles the garbage. An on-the-fly garbage collector is a program that allows concurrent execution of the mutator and the collector.

Garbage collection is done by a two-phase algorithm. First the collector marks all nodes accessible from the root and then it appends to the free list all unmarked (and hence inaccessible) nodes. We are given an array of nodes, each of which has a field that contains a color: black or white and a fixed number of fields that contain pointers (indexes) to other nodes. Some of the nodes are designated as roots. In (2) it is shown that by considering both the pointer to the free list and the special cell NIL to be roots then the only mutator instruction that modifies the data structure is one which chooses two accessible nodes i and k and causes k to become a son (say the j'th) of i. Of course, if some node l was previously the j'th son of i, it could happen that l is no longer accessible from any root. The task of the collector is to identify these garbage nodes and append them to the free list.

Following (2), we abstract the problem by omitting all other details of the mutator's program as well as the (straightforward) details of the pointer manipulations required to implement the free list. A further abstraction is to ignore the synchronization that must be done when the mutator attempts to remove a node from an empty free list. If the removal is done from one end of the list and appending at the other, this should happen infrequently and any convenient synchronization primitive can be used.

The computational environment that the algorithms are directed to is a real-time system where we assume that a microprocessor is dedicated to garbage collection. Thus the mutator contribution to garbage collection must be minimized while collector time is essentially free. Similarly, scratch memory is very limited and no queues or stacks are maintained to shorten transversal of the data structure. This contrasts with (6): they even require the mutator to enqueue the nodes that it marks. We do not assume the existence of indivisible atomic operations beyond Load and Store.

3. The Algorithm

The algorithm is given as fragments of an Ada program. The line numbers on the executable statements are used in the proof.

```
-- The data structure.
     type Hue is (White,Black);
     type Index is new Integer range 1..Number_of_Nodes;
     subtype Roots is Index range 1..Number_of_Roots;
     type Sons is new Integer range 1..Number_of_Sons;
     type Node is record
          Son: array(Sons) of Index;
          Color: Hue := White;
          end record;
     M: array(Index) of Node;     -- M is initialized so that all nodes are linked
                                  -- on the free list and all links not so used are
                                  -- pointing to the root NIL.
```

```
-- The mutator.
     -- The mutator executes the following pair of instructions at its discretion.
     -- The mutator ensures that both R and T point to  nodes accessible from a root.

a0   M(R).Son(S) := T;
a1   M(T).Color  := Black;

-- The collector.
     -- The collector executes procedure Marking_Phase and then collects white
     -- nodes and appends them to the free list.

c0   Marking_Phase;
c1   for I in Index loop
c2        if M(I).Color = White
c3             then Append_to_Free(I);
c4             else M(I).Color := White;
c5        end if;
c6   end loop;

     procedure Marking_Phase is
          Black_Count, Old_Black_Count: Integer := 0;
b0   begin

          -- Blacken the roots.
b1   for I in Roots loop
b2        M(I).Color := Black;
b3   end loop;

b4   Main: loop
          -- Propagate the coloring.
b5   for I in Index loop
b6        if M(I).Color = Black
b7             then for J in Sons loop
b8                  M( M(I).Son(J) ).Color := Black;
b9                  end loop;
b10       end if;
b11  end loop;

          -- Count the number of Black nodes.
b12  Black_Count := 0;
b13  for I in Index loop
b14       if M(I).Color = Black
b15            then Black_Count := Black_Count + 1;
b16       end if;
b17  end loop;

          -- Repeat main loop if more Black nodes than before.
b18  if Black_Count > Old_Black_Count
b19       then Old_Black_Count := Black_Count;
b20       else exit;
b21  end if;

b22  end loop Main;
b23  end Marking_Phase;
```

Remark: The algorithm can be made more efficient by repeating the propagation loop b5-b11 until no new nodes are colored (as in the DLMSS algorithm) and only then proceeding to count the black nodes.

4. The Safety of the Algorithm

In this section we prove that the following safety property holds: when Marking_Phase terminates then all white nodes are garbage. Once this has been shown, the proof of the correctness of the algorithm is straightforward. The safety property will be proven by the method of invariants of concurrent programs ((7), (8)). We attach invariants to points in the program and then show that execution of an instruction of either process preserves the truth of the invariant. We use explicit propositions for the locations of the program counters (4) though auxiliary variables could also be used (8).

So as not to obscure the main ideas, the exposition will be limited to the critical facets of the proof. A mechanically verifiable proof would need all sorts of trivial invariants (e.g., Marking_Phase does not change the data structure) and elementary transformations of our invariants (e.g., the invariants we give for line b8 have counterparts at other points in the loop b5-b11 with appropriate adjustments of the indices).

The following propositions are used in the proof.

b8(i,j) iff the collector is at b8 and I=i and J=j.

BW(i,j,k) iff M(i).Son(j) = k and M(i).Color = Black and M(k).Color = White and M(i) is accessible from a root.

In words: k is a white j'th son of an accessible black node i.

a1(r,s,t) iff the mutator is at a1 and R=r and S=s and T=t.

In words: the mutator has made t the s'th son of r but has not yet colored node t.

We also use the following notation:

Blacks = |{i| M(i).Color = Black} |

This is the number of black nodes in the data structure and may be larger than Black_Count, the number of black nodes that the collector has counted.

(i,j) << (i',j') : Lexicographical order on nodes and sons.

Lemma 1: The following formula is invariant.

b8(i,j) and (Blacks = Old_Black_Count) -->

forall (r,s,t) ((r,s) << (i,j) and BW(r,s,t) --> a1(r,s,t)).

Proof (Informal): The existence of a triple such that BW(r,s,t) and (r,s) << (i,j) can occur if after the collector has passed (i,j) the mutator executes the assignment but not the coloring. Since the mutator always "covers its tracks" immediately, at most one such triple can be in existence. Note that once a white node has been colored black, then Blacks = Old_Black_Count is false and the invariant trivially holds. Thus we do not care if coloring (by either the mutator or the collector) introduces new black nodes and hence possibly new triples (u,v,w) such that BW(u,v,w).

Proof (Formal): During the initial execution of the collector loop b5-b11, there are no values (r,s) such that (r,s) << (1,1). Assume now as an induction hypothesis that the invariant is true. It could be falsified only if 1) both the antecedent and the consequent are false and the execution of an instruction "suddenly" makes the antecedent true (without simultaneously making the consequent true); or, 2) both are true and the execution of an instruction "suddenly" makes the consequent false (without falsifying the antecedent).

Let us look at the invariant in the following equivalent form.

forall (r,s,t) ((b8(i,j) and (Blacks = Old_Black_Count) and
(r,s) << (i,j) and BW(r,s,t)) --> a1(r,s,t)).

We now show that neither 1) nor 2) can occur for any possible step of either process. Consider first the collector. 1) If BW(r,s,t) becomes true for (r,s) << (i,j) because the collector blackens r then Blacks = Old_Black_Count is simultaneously falsified. If BW(r,s,t) becomes true because (r,s,t) is (i,j,k) and (i,j) is incremented, then k is blackened and Blacks = Old_Black_Count is falsified. Thus in both cases, we have failed to make the antecedent true. 2) The collector cannot affect the truth of a1(r,s,t).

Now for the mutator. 1) As for the collector, if the mutator blackens a node then the invariant trivially holds. The mutator can make the antecedent true by executing the assignment at a0 but that makes the consequent a1(r,s,t) true also. 2) The mutator can falsify the consequent (when the antecedent is true for (r,s,t)) only by falsifying Blacks = Old_Black_Count (and BW(r,s,t)). □

In (2), the authors note that they originally had the mutator execute its instructions in the opposite order -- first coloring the node and then executing the pointer assignment. Woodger then found a bug by a scenario in which the mutator is suspended for a long period of time between the coloring and the assignment. The coloring can thus be lost by a complete execution of the collector which whitens all nodes. In our solution, exchanging the mutator's instructions cannot lead to a bug. Informally, the collector visits each node at least twice. Woodger's scenario shows that the collector may not mark an accessible node on the first visit. But if the mutator attempts to fool the collector a second time, it must first mark the target node -- defeating the scenario.

Lemma 2: The following formula is invariant:

b8(i,j) and(Blacks = Old_Black_Count) -->
(exists (r,s,t) ((r,s) << (i,j) and BW(r,s,t)) -->
exists (u,v,w) ((u,v) >=>= (i,j) and BW(u,v,w))).

Proof: As in the proof of the previous lemma, any coloring will falsify Blacks = Old_Black_Count and preserve the invariant. If BW(r,s,t) for (r,s) << (i,j) and the (u,v) promised by the consequent happens to be (i,j) then execution of a cycle of the collector could falsify the consequent but only if it simultaneously falsifies Blacks = Old_Black_Count.

So suppose that an assignment of the mutator causes BW(r,s,t) to become true for (r,s) << (i,j) and that forall (u,v,w) ((u,v) >=>= (i,j) --> not BW(u,v,w)), thus falsifying the invariant.

But the mutator ensures that M(t) is accessible before the execution of this instruction. Since the roots are black and M(t).Color = White, there is a triple (r',s',t') such that BW(r',s',t') and (incidently) there is a path from t' to t (or possibly t = t'). By the previous paragraph, we assume that (r',s') >=>= (i,j) is not true. (r,s) == (r',s') means that the invariant was false before executing this step -- contradicting the induction hyposthesis. The only possibility left is (r',s') << (i,j) and (r',s') ≠≠ (r,s) but this contradicts Lemma 1 since it is not possible that a1(r,s,t) and a1(r',s',t') for distinct triples. □

Safety now follows from the fact that if Blacks > Old_Black_Count at b12 then Black_Count > Old_Black_Count at b18 since the mutator can only make more black nodes, not fewer. Thus if we exit the main loop, it is only because we left b12 with Blacks = Old_Black_Count. Then Lemma 2 implies that there are no triples such that BW(u,v,w), otherwise we would have (u,v) >>(Number_of_Nodes,Number_of_Sons) which is not possible. Since all roots are black, we can conclude that all white nodes are garbage. More formally, we would deduce from Lemma 2 the following.

Lemma 3: The following formula is invariant:

b12 and (Blacks = Old_Black_Count) --> not exists (i,j,k) (BW(i,j,k)).

Then, to relate the number of black nodes to Black_Count, we need Lemma 4.

Lemma 4: The following formula is invariant:

b18 and (Blacks = Old_Black_Count) -->
    Black_Count = Old_Black_Count and not exists (i,j,k) (BW(i,j,k))
and
b18 and (Blacks > Old_Black_Count) -->
    Black_Count > Old_Black_Count.

Proof: The first half follows from Lemma 3 since if there are no BW(i,j,k) then all accessible nodes are black and thus the mutator cannot change the number of black nodes during the execution of b12-b17. The second half is trivial. □

Lemma 5: The following formula is invariant:

b23 --> forall (i) ((M(i).Color = White) --> M(i) is garbage).

Proof: By Lemma 4, we exit Marking_Phase if and only if there are no triples (i,j,k) such that BW(i,j,k). Since the roots are black, there are no accessible nodes. □

Lemma 5 is the central fact needed to prove the correctness of the algorithm. We now turn to modifications of the basic algorithm.

5. A More Efficient Algorithm

One problem that most garbage collection algorithms have in common is that they spend a lot of time coloring non-garbage. This can be inefficient if the application contains large data structures which are modified only occasionally. The next algorithm that we describe is designed to be efficient in this situation. It goes as follows (ignoring for now the synchronization considerations).

Initially, all nodes are accessible and black. When the mutator is about to redirect an edge, it colors the old target white. This is intended to mean that the node is suspected of being garbage. Since this node may be the root of a subgraph of garbage nodes, the collector propagates the white coloring as far as possible. Then the collector applies the marking algorithm above and collects and blackens the remaining white nodes.

In the worst case (where some white node points to each root) this algorithm is no improvement, but hopefully if only a small set of nodes is accessible from each suspected node, the marking phase will converge rapidly. As an implementation note, it should be possible to identify situations which will not produce garbage and refrain from marking them as suspected. For example, a LISP Cons -- removing a node from the free list, directing it to two accessible nodes and returning a pointer -- cannot produce garbage.

The algorithm sketched is not correct. The mutator may continue to whiten suspected nodes while the collector is blackening nodes. There are two possible bugs: 1) if the collector is convinced that all accessible nodes are now black, it may collect a new white node which is actually accessible; 2) if the mutator created several garbage nodes by the redirection, only the first "suspected" node will be collected and its descendents will be lost. We need to be able to temporarily ignore the mutator's accusations without losing track of them. For this we introduce the color gray.

```
    type Hue is (White,Gray,Black);
        -- Initial Color is Black.
    -- The mutator.
a0  M( M(R).Son(S) ).Color := Gray;
a1  M(R).Son(S) := T;
    -- The collector.
c0  for I in Index loop
c1      if M(I).Color = Gray          -- Make gray nodes white.
c2          then M(I).Color := White;
c3      end if;
c4  end loop;

    -- Propagate the white color to descendents as long as possible.
c5  Propagate_White;
```

```
New_Marking_Phase;
for I in Index loop
     if M(I).Color = White
          then Append_to_Free(I);
          M(I).Color := Black;
     end if;
end loop;
```

New_Marking_Phase is like Marking_Phase except that b6 and b14 become:

```
if M(I).Color >= Gray then
```

Informally what is happening is as follows. Whatever is garbage at the start of Propagate_White must be a gray node or a descendent of a gray node and will be whitened and collected. New_Marking_Phase treats black and gray as the "same" color. If the mutator generates a garbage node during a collector cycle, it will remain as such until the next cycle. Since it is not accessible, it will not be blackened and hence will remain suspicious for the next cycle of the collector. If the mutator colors an accessible node gray, the node will not be collected because it is not white and no nodes are whitened during New_Marking_Phase.

The formal proof of the safety of this algorithm is similar to that of the original algorithm, except that wherever Black is mentioned, "Gray or Black" should be used.

6. Incremental Garbage Collection

If we delete the call to Propagate_White in the previous algorithm (or limit the propagation to a fixed depth), the algorithm becomes a good candidate for an incremental garbage collector. Very few nodes are whitened and hence the marking phase converges rapidly to recover a few nodes. Unfortunately, if we do not propagate the white color, then garbage nodes can be lost.

There is a simple solution to this problem. Once the collector has decided that a set of white nodes is garbage, it simply grays their sons -- for they are also suspect and should be checked on the next cycle. Make sure that you never gray a white node -- otherwise, a garbage node pointing to itself will never be collected. The proof of the safety of this algorithm is identical to that of the previous section, though to prove that all garbage nodes are collected a slightly more complicated proof would be needed.

```
    -- The collector.
for I in Index loop
if M(I).Color = Gray
     then M(I).Color := White;
end if;
end loop;

for I in Index loop
     if M(I).Color = White then
          for J in Sons loop
               if M(I).Color ≠ White then M(I).Color := Gray end if;
          end loop;
     end if;
end loop;
```

```
New_Marking_Phase;
for I in Index loop
if M(I).Color = White
     then Append_to_Free(I);
     M(I).Color := Black;
end if;
end loop;
```

7. Conclusion

New algorithms for on-the-fly garbage collection have been presented. The basic algorithm has a correctness proof that is much simpler than that of the DLMSS algorithm. In (2), the color gray is introduced so that what we call BW(i,j,k) will always be false. Later this was found to be untenable and the invariants underwent modifications until correct ones were found. Rather than tinker with the invariants, we took the opportunity to look for changes in the algorithm which would keep the invariants simple. We do not claim to have synthesized the algorithm from the proof but do claim to have developed a good algorithm by setting simplicity of the proof as the primary goal.

This simplicity has paid off since we are able to obtain other improved algorithms whose proofs are immediate modifications of the original proof. Much work needs to be done investigating the performance of this and other on-the-fly garbage collection algorithms.

Acknowledgments: I would like to thank Tmima Olshansky for noting that the algorithm is impervious to Woodger's scenario. I am grateful to Amir Pnueli for his assistance in the formulation of the proofs.

8. References

(1) J. Cohen. Garbage collection of linked data structures. *Computing Surveys* 13(3), 1981, 341-367.

(2) E.W. Dijkstra, L. Lamport, A.J. Martin, C.S. Scholten and E.F.M. Steffens. On-the-fly garbage collection: an exercise in cooperation. *Communications ACM* 21(11), 1978, 966-975.

(3) N. Francez. An application of a method for analysis of cyclic programs. *IEEE Transactions on Software Engineering* SE-4(5), 1978, 371-378.

(4) N. Francez and A. Pnueli. A proof method for cyclic programs. *Acta Informatica* 9(1978), 133-157.

(5) D. Gries. An exercise in proving parallel programs correct. *Communications ACM* 20(12), 1977, 921-930.

(6) H.T. Kung and S.W. Song. An efficient parallel garbage collection system and its correctness proof. *IEEE Symp. Found. Comp. Sci.* 1977, 120-131.

(7) L. Lamport. Proving the correctness of multiprocess programs. *IEEE Transactions on Software Engineering* SE-3, 1977, 125-143.

(8) S. Owicki and D. Gries. An axiomatic proof technique for parallel programs I. *Acta Informatica* 6(1976), 319-340.

ALGEBRAIC SPECIFICATIONS FOR PARAMETRIZED DATA TYPES WITH MINIMAL PARAMETER AND TARGET ALGEBRAS

J.A. Bergstra
Department of Computer Science
University of Leiden
Wassenaarseweg 80
2300 RA Leiden, The Netherlands

J.W. Klop
Department of Computer Science
Mathematical Centre
Kruislaan 413
1098 SJ Amsterdam, The Netherlands

ABSTRACT

We conceive a parametrized data type as a partial functor φ: ALG $(\Sigma) \rightarrow$ ALG (Δ), where Δ is a signature extending Σ and ALG (Σ) is the class of minimal Σ-algebras which serve as parameters.

We focus attention on one particular method of algebraically specifying parametrized data types: finite specifications with conditional equations using auxiliary sorts and functions provided with initial algebra semantics.

We introduce the concept of an effective parametrized data type. A satisfactory adequacy result is then obtained: each effective parametrized data type possesses a finite algebraic specification under initial semantics.

INTRODUCTION

The mathematical theory of parametrized data types was initially investigated in ADJ [15], [8], LEHMANN & SMYTH [12], KAPHENGST & REICHEL [11] and EHRICH [7]. Central topics in these studies are specification methods and the correctness problem for specifications and parameter passing mechanisms.

Reading through the growing literature on parametrized data types one observes small but important differences between the basic definitions used by various authors; these variations resulting from differences in aims as well as from differences concerning the general points of view.

Obviously this situation entails a difficulty for the theoretical development of the subject. Rather than aiming at a unified theoretical framework it is our intention to consider one single specification method and to investigate that one in depth. This method is: initial algebra specifications with conditional equations using auxiliary sorts and functions.

The relevance of our results should not only be measured against the importance of the specification method that we analyze; it also indicates a style of investigating specification mechanisms for data types in general. The main idea is to connect specification methods to recursion theoretic concepts; similar results for abstract data type specification were obtained in BERGSTRA & TUCKER [4] and [5].

A parametrized data type will be a partial functor φ: ALG$(\Sigma) \rightarrow$ ALG(Δ), for some signatures Σ,Δ with $\Sigma \subseteq \Delta$. Here ALG(Γ) denotes the class of all minimal algebras of signature Γ. (Remark on terminology: BURSTALL & GOGUEN [6] call $A \in ALG(\Gamma)$ an algebra 'without junk'.)

Further, φ is called persistent if $\varphi(A)$ is an expansion of A for all $A \in Dom(\varphi)$. Apart from the requirement that parameter algebras be minimal these definitions correspond to the original ones in ADJ [15].

All the constructions and arguments in the sequel will be modulo isomorphism of the minimal algebras we are dealing with. (Alternatively, one may consider $ALG(\Sigma)$, the class of minimal Σ-algebras, as consisting of term algebras, i.e. quotients of the free term algebra over Σ.) In this way we get around the difference between 'persistent' and 'strongly persistent' from ADJ [15]. For generalizations of our results however, a more sophisticated approach of this issue will be required.

Keeping in mind that the application of a parametrized data type on a parameter algebra is to be effectively performed in a computational process, the following class of effective parametrized data types seems to be of intrinsic importance. A parametrized data type φ is called effective iff there exists a computable transformation (γ,ε) that transforms a finite input specification (Σ',E') for a parameter algebra A into a finite specification $(\gamma(\Sigma',E'), \varepsilon(\Sigma',E')) = (\Sigma'',E'')$ for a target algebra $\varphi(A)$. In both cases the specifications are allowed to use auxiliary sorts and functions.

An attractive transformation mechanism for specifications is the following one:

$$(\gamma(\Sigma',E'), \varepsilon(\Sigma',E')) = (\Sigma' \cup \Gamma, E' \cup E)$$

for some fixed finite specification (Γ,E). If such (Γ,E) can be found, the parametrized data type φ is said to have a finite algebraic specification .

Our main interest is the following question: to what extent are algebraic specifications available for effective parametrized data types. For this question we are interested in parametrized data types with a domain consisting of semi-computable algebras only, because other algebras have no finite specification. We are then able to prove the following adequacy theorem (where $SCA(\Sigma)$ denotes the class of semi-computable Σ-algebras):

THEOREM 3.1. *Let* φ: $ALG(\Sigma) \to ALG(\Delta)$ *be a persistent parametrized data type such that* $Dom(\varphi) = ALG(\Sigma,E) \cap SCA(\Sigma)$ *for some finite* E. *Then* φ *is effective iff it has a finite algebraic specification.*

The proof is quite involved and uses a detour via an auxiliary notion, viz. that of a (effectively) continuous parametrized data type. A continuous parametrized data type φ can be represented by an element F in the Graph model $P\omega$ for the λ-calculus; an effectively continuous one by a recursively enumerable $F \in P\omega$. Now it turns out that a parametrized data type has a (finite) algebraic specification iff it is (effectively) continuous.

For further information about parametrized data types the reader is referred to [9], [10] and [16].

1. SPECIFICATION OF PARAMETER AND TARGET ALGEBRAS

In this section we will collect several definitions of preliminary notions and some facts about them.

1.1. Algebras. The concepts of signature Σ, Σ-algebra, Σ-term are supposed known. $Ter_s(\Sigma)$ is the set of Σ-terms of sort $s \in \Sigma$. A closed term contains no variables. $Ter^c(\Sigma)$ is the set of closed Σ-terms. An equation (of sort s) is an expression of the form $\tau = \tau'$ where $\tau,\tau' \in Ter_s(\Sigma)$. A closed equation is an equation between closed terms. A conditional equation is a construct of the form $\tau_1 = \tau_1' \wedge \ldots \wedge \tau_k = \tau_k' \rightarrow \tau = \tau'$ where $\tau_i, \tau_i' \in Ter_{s_i}(\Sigma)$, $i = 1,\ldots,k$ and $\tau,\tau' \in Ter_s(\Sigma)$ for some s_i, s.

The free term algebra $T(\Sigma)$ is obtained by taking as domains A_s the sets $Ter_s^c(\Sigma)$ and interpreting functions and constants 'by themselves'.

A Σ-algebra A is minimal if it has no proper Σ-subalgebras. If $\Gamma \supseteq \Sigma$ and A is some Γ-algebra, then $A|_\Sigma$ is the reduct of A of signature Σ which results by forgetting sorts, constants and functions not named in Σ. By $\langle A\rangle_\Sigma$ we denote the minimal Σ-subalgebra of $A|_\Sigma$. If $A|_\Sigma = \langle A\rangle_\Sigma = B$, we write $(A)_\Sigma = B$ and call A an enrichment of B.

With $ALG(\Sigma)$ we denote the class of minimal Σ-algebras. For a set E of conditional equations, $ALG(\Sigma,E)$ denotes the class of algebras $A \in ALG(\Sigma)$ with $A \models E$.

To each $A \in ALG(\Sigma)$ we can associate the congruence $\equiv_A$, that is the set of all closed equations true in A. Note that $A \cong T(\Sigma)/\equiv_A$.

If $K \subseteq ALG(\Sigma)$, then $I(K)$ denotes the initial algebra of K, if it exists. (This is the algebra A from which all $B \in K$ are homomorphic images; A is determined up to isomorphism.)

1.2. Recursion theory and coding. We use the notation W_z (of ROGERS [13]) for recursively enumerable (r.e.) subsets of ω; $z \in \omega$ is called an r.e. -index for $V = W_z$.

Often we will use a bijective and effective coding $\ulcorner\ \urcorner : S \rightarrow \omega$ for a set S of syntactic constructs, e.g. $S = Ter^c(\Sigma)$. Decoding $\llcorner\ \lrcorner : \omega \rightarrow S$ is given by the inverse function. It is left to the reader to give a detailed construction of $\ulcorner\ \urcorner$. If $T \subseteq S$, then $\ulcorner T \urcorner = \{\ulcorner t \urcorner \mid t \in T\}$; likewise $\llcorner A \lrcorner$, for $A \subseteq \omega$, is defined.

Let $A \in ALG(\Sigma)$. Then A is called semi-computable iff $\ulcorner \equiv_A \urcorner$ is r.e. (iff $\exists z\ \ulcorner \equiv_A \urcorner = W_z$). The set of semi-computable minimal Σ-algebras is denoted by $SCA(\Sigma)$.

Let $\ulcorner\ \urcorner$: $TER^c(\Sigma) \times Ter^c(\Sigma) \rightarrow \omega$ be a bijective coding of all closed Σ-equations, with $\llcorner\ \lrcorner$ as decoding function. Now an arbitrary $\llcorner W_z \lrcorner$ need not yet be a congruence; it is after closure under logical derivability: $\overline{\llcorner W_z \lrcorner}$.
Coding again it is not hard to see that $\ulcorner \overline{\llcorner W_z \lrcorner} \urcorner = W_{c(z)}$ for some recursive $c : \omega \rightarrow \omega$. So $W_{c(z)}$ codes a congruence, for all $z \in \omega$. (See also the diagram in section 1.3.)

1.3 Initial algebra specifications. Let $A \in ALG(\Sigma)$, and $\Sigma' \supseteq \Sigma$. Then (Σ',E') is a specification of A using auxiliary sorts and functions if $A = (I(ALG(\Sigma',E')))_\Sigma$. For brevity we will use the notation: $(\Sigma',E')_{\Sigma} = A$. To employ in diagrams, we use the alternative notation: $(\Sigma',E') \xrightarrow{\Sigma} A$.

Note that $I(ALG(\Sigma',E'))$ always exists. However, $(I(ALG(\Sigma',E')))_{\Sigma}$ is not for all (Σ',E') and $\Sigma' \supseteq \Sigma$ defined (see the definition of enrichment in 1.1). Note that if E' is finite, $I(ALG(\Sigma',E')) \in SCA(\Sigma')$. In fact we have:

1.3.1 LEMMA. $A \in SCA(\Sigma) \Leftrightarrow A = (\Sigma',E')_{\Sigma}$ *for some* $\Sigma' \supseteq \Sigma$ *and finite* E'.

This is proved in BERGSTRA & TUCKER [3]. In fact it is proved there that from an r.e.-index z for $\lceil \equiv_A \rceil$ one can uniformly find a finite (Σ',E') specifying A; see the diagram below.

Finite specifications (Σ',E') for A can be thought of as 'indices' just like z is an r.e.-index for $\equiv_A$ ($= \lfloor W_z \rfloor$) after coding. Indeed, the following diagram asserts that both kinds of indices can effectively be translated into each other:

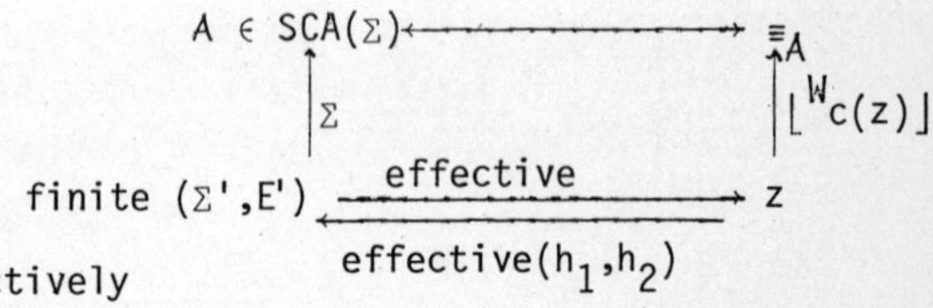

2. PARAMETRIZED DATA TYPES, DESCRIPTIONS AND SPECIFICATIONS

In this section we explain our definition of a parametrized data type, and explain what it means for a parametrized data type to be: effectively given, algebraically specified, continuous or effectively continuous.

2.1. A parametrized data type is a partial functor φ: $ALG(\Sigma) \to ALG(\Delta)$ where $\Sigma \subseteq \Delta$, which satisfies the following condition: for each $A \in Dom(\varphi)$ there is a surjective homomorphism α: $A \to \varphi(A)|_{\Sigma}$.

If, moreover, for each $A \in Dom(\varphi)$ we have: $A \cong \varphi(A)|_{\Sigma}$ then φ is persistent.

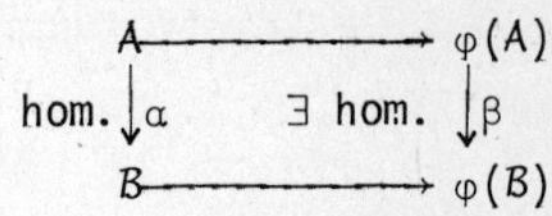

2.2. φ is effectively given (φ is effective) if $Dom(\varphi) \subseteq SCA(\Sigma)$ and there is a pair (γ,ε) of computable operations, acting on finite specifications, that produces a specification $(\gamma(\Sigma',E'), \varepsilon(\Sigma',E'))$ of $\varphi(A)$ for each specification (Σ',E') of some $A \in Dom(\varphi)$.

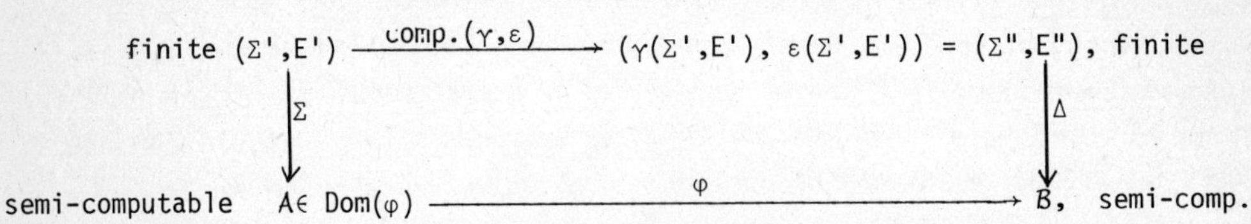

In a different notation: $\varphi((\Sigma',E')_{\Sigma}) = (\gamma(\Sigma',E'), \varepsilon(\Sigma',E'))_{\Delta}$.

2.3. φ has an algebraic specification if there is a specification (Γ,E) such that for

all $A \in \mathrm{Dom}(\varphi)$ this diagram commutes:
If (Γ,E) is finite, then φ has a finite algebraic specification; in that case $\varphi \upharpoonright \mathrm{SCA}(\Sigma)$ is effectively given with

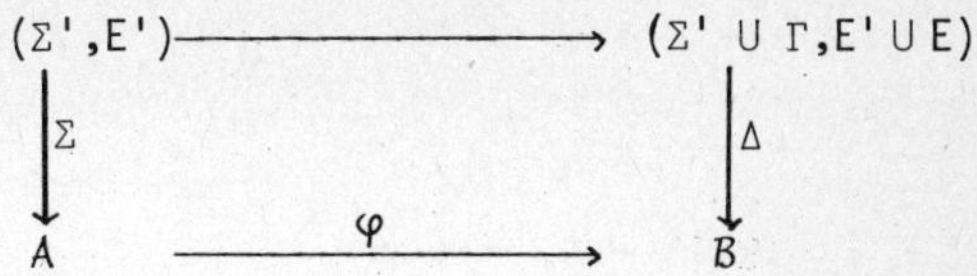

$\gamma(\Sigma',E') = \Sigma'\cup\Gamma$ and $\varepsilon(\Sigma',E') = E'\cup E$. Here it is required that $\Sigma'\cap\Gamma \subseteq \Sigma$.

<u>Notation</u>: $\varphi \subseteq (\Gamma,E)^{\Sigma}_{\Delta}$; so the diagram states: $(\Gamma,E)^{\Sigma}_{\Delta}\,(\Sigma',E')_{\Sigma_{\Sigma}} = (\Sigma'\cup\Gamma,E'\cup E)_{\Delta}$. Note the following composition rule (with $\Gamma'\cap\Gamma = \Delta$): $(\Gamma',F)^{\Delta}_{\Pi}\circ(\Gamma,E)^{\Sigma}_{\Delta} = (\Gamma'\cup\Gamma,F\cup E)^{\Sigma}_{\Pi}$.

2.4. <u>Representing parametrized data types in reflexive domains</u>

Let $\ulcorner\ \urcorner\Gamma$ be a bijective coding of closed Γ-equations, and $\llcorner\ \lrcorner\Gamma$ the corresponding decoding. We will omit the Γ when no confusion is likely to arise. For a parametrized data type φ: $\mathrm{ALG}(\Sigma) \to \mathrm{ALG}(\Delta)$, let

$\ulcorner\mathrm{Dom}(\varphi)\urcorner = \{\ulcorner\equiv_A\urcorner^{\Sigma} \mid A \in \mathrm{Dom}(\varphi)\}$ and

$\ulcorner\mathrm{Range}(\varphi)\urcorner = \{\ulcorner\equiv_B\urcorner^{\Delta} \mid B \in \mathrm{Range}(\varphi)\}$.

The mapping $\overline{\varphi} : \ulcorner\mathrm{Dom}(\varphi)\urcorner \to \ulcorner\mathrm{Range}(\varphi)\urcorner$ is introduced by $\overline{\varphi}(\ulcorner\equiv_A\urcorner) = \ulcorner\equiv_{\varphi(A)}\urcorner$. (See diagram.)

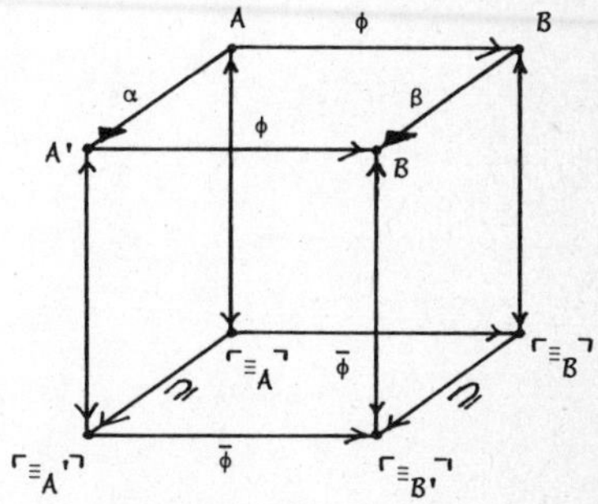

<u>A reflexive domain</u>. The Graph model $P\omega$ is the structure consisting of the powerset of ω and an application operator $\cdot$ on it. Application is defined as follows: for $A,B \in P\omega$,

$A\cdot B = \{m \mid \exists\, n \in \omega\ (n,m) \in A \ \&\ D_n \subseteq B\}$ where $(\ ,\ )$: $\omega \times \omega \to \omega$ is a bijective and effective pairing function and D_n is the finite set with 'canonical index' n defined as follows: $D_0 = \emptyset$; if $n = 2^{a_1} + \ldots + 2^{a_k}$, $a_1 < \ldots < a_k$, then $D_n = \{a_1,\ldots,a_k\}$.

A mapping F: $P\omega \to P\omega$ is <u>continuous</u> if for all $X \in P\omega$:
$F(X) = \bigcup\{F(D_n) \mid D_n \subseteq X\}$. For the next Lemma, see SCOTT [12].

2.4.1. <u>LEMMA</u> *Let* F: $P\omega \to P\omega$. *Then:* F *is continuous* $\Longleftrightarrow \exists F \in P\omega\ \forall X \in P\omega\ \ F(X) = F\cdot X$.

2.4.2. <u>DEFINITION</u>. (i) The parametrized data type φ is <u>continuous</u> if $\overline{\varphi}$ is the restriction to $\ulcorner\mathrm{Dom}(\varphi)\urcorner$ of some continuous mapping F: $P\omega \to P\omega$. (ii) Moreover, φ is called <u>effectively continuous</u> if $\overline{\varphi}$ is the restriction of a continuous F which is represented in $P\omega$ by an r.e. element $F \in P\omega$. (I.e. F is an <u>enumeration operator</u>, in the sense of ROGERS [13].) (iii) Write RE for the set of r.e. subsets of P . Let φ: RE $\to$ RE . Then φ is called <u>effective</u> if for some computable f: $\forall z\ \ \varphi(W_z) = W_{f(z)}$.

We need the following version of the Theorem of Myhill and Shepherdson (see ROGERS [13]), as stated in SCOTT [14]:

2.4.3. <u>THEOREM</u>. *If* Φ: RE $\to$ RE *is effective, then for some r.e. element* F of $P\omega$:
$\forall X \in \mathrm{RE}\ \ \ \Phi(X) = F\cdot X$.

Consequently Φ as in the Theorem can be extended to a continuous operator (viz. $\lambda X.\ F \cdot X$). On the other hand of course: if $F \in RE$, then $\lambda X \in RE\ \ F\cdot X$ is effective.

3. SPECIFICATION THEOREMS

The main result of this paper is Theorem 3.1 which essentially asserts that effective parametrized data types have finite specifications, provided their domain is reasonably well-behaved. We expect that 3.1(ii)$\Longleftrightarrow$(iii) will have many generalizations; for instance, in BERGSTRA & KLOP [2] the condition that input algebras are minimal is removed. Other specification methods, such as working with requirements (see EHRIG [9]) or with final algebras, lead to similar questions.

Theorems 3.2 and 3.3 provide exact characterizations of the persistent parametrized data types that can be specified, without any condition on the domains involved.

3.1. THEOREM. *Let* φ: ALG(Σ) $\to$ ALG(Δ) *be a persistent parametrized data type with* Dom(φ) = ALG(Σ,E) $\cap$ SCA(Σ), *for some finite E. Then the following are equivalent:*
(i) φ *is effectively continuous;*
(ii) φ *possesses a finite algebraic specification* ;
(iii) φ *is effective.*

3.2. THEOREM. *Let* φ: ALG(Σ) $\to$ ALG(Δ) *be a persistent parametrized data type. Then the following are equivalent:*
(i) φ *is continuous;*
(ii) φ *has an algebraic specification.*

3.3. THEOREM. *Let* φ: ALG(Σ) $\to$ ALG(Δ) *be a persistent parametrized data type. Then the following are equivalent:*
(i) φ *is effectively continuous;*
(ii) φ *has a finite algebraic specification.*

The structure of the proofs is displayed in the diagrams on the following page.

4. PROVING CONTINUITY

We will now prove (iii) $\Rightarrow$ (i) of Theorem 3.1.and (ii) $\Rightarrow$ (i) of Theorems 3.2, 3.3. First the easier two implications:

4.1. Proof of Theorem 3.2 (ii) $\Rightarrow$ (i). Let $\lceil\ \rceil$ and $\lfloor\ \rfloor$ be bijective coding and decoding functions for closed Σ-equations, and likewise $\llbracket\ \rrbracket, \lfloor\!\lfloor\ \rfloor\!\rfloor$ for closed Γ-equations.

Suppose that φ has a specification, say (Γ,F). So $\varphi(A) = (\Gamma,F)^{\Sigma}_{\Delta}\ (A)$, for $A \in \mathrm{Dom}(\varphi)$. Noting that $A = (\Sigma,\equiv_A)_\Sigma$, we have $\varphi(A) = (\Gamma,F)^{\Sigma}_{\Delta}\ (\Sigma,\equiv_A)_\Sigma = (\Gamma \cup \Sigma, F\cup\equiv_A)_\Delta$.

Now let $A = \{(n,m) \mid F \cup \lfloor D_n \rfloor \vdash \lfloor\!\lfloor m \rfloor\!\rfloor\}$, $A \in P\omega$. Then for $A \in\ \mathrm{Dom}(\varphi)$:

$$A \cdot \lceil\equiv_A\rceil\ = \{m \mid \exists D_n \subseteq \lceil\equiv_A\rceil\ (n,m) \in A\} = \{m \mid \exists D_n \subseteq \lceil\equiv_A\rceil\ F \cup \lfloor D_n \rfloor \vdash \lfloor\!\lfloor m \rfloor\!\rfloor\} =$$
$$\{m \mid F \cup \equiv_A\ \vdash \lfloor\!\lfloor m \rfloor\!\rfloor\} = \{\llbracket e \rrbracket \mid F \cup \equiv_A \vdash\ e\} = \{\llbracket e \rrbracket \mid (\Gamma\cup\Sigma\ , F\cup\equiv_A)_\Delta\ \models\ e\} = \llbracket \equiv_{\varphi(A)} \rrbracket = \overline{\varphi}(\lceil\equiv_A\rceil).$$

Hence φ is continuous (by Def. 2.4.2. and Lemma 2.4.1.) □

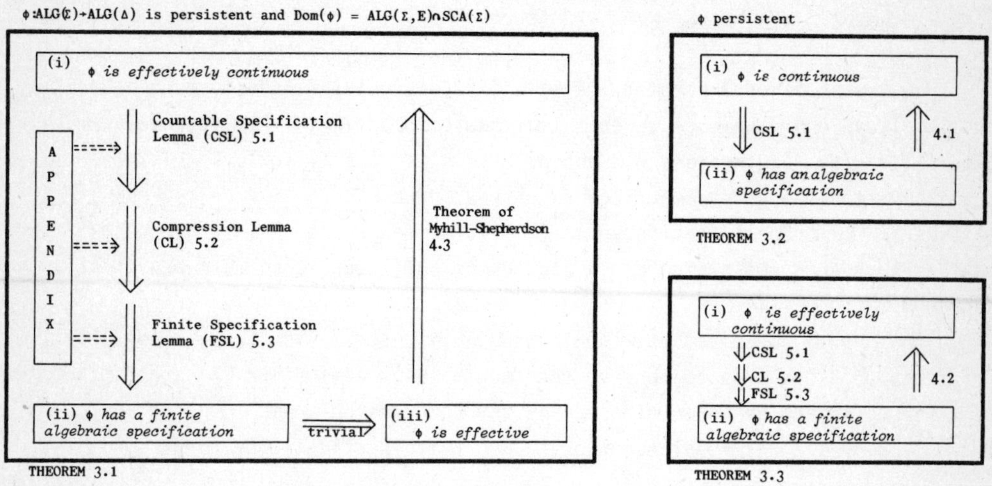

4.2. Proof of Theorem 3.3 (ii) ⇒ (i). If in the above proof F is finite, then obviously A is r.e. Hence φ is effectively continuous. □

4.3. Proof of Theorem 3.1 (iii) ⇒ (i). Let (γ,ε) be an effective transformation of specifications that describes φ. Consider $\overline{\varphi}$. We will construct an effective operator (see 2.4.2) δ: RE → RE that extends $\overline{\varphi}$. Then it follows by the Theorem of Myhill & Shepherdson (2.4.3) that δ can be extended to an enumeration operator (2.4.2 (ii)), which immediately implies that φ is effectively continuous.

In order to define δ, consider the domain $ALG(\Sigma,E) \cap SCA(\Sigma)$ of φ. Let $W_{d(z)}$ be the coded congruence of an algebra in $ALG(\Sigma,E) \cap SCA(\Sigma)$ which is generated by W_z (cfr. $W_{c(z)}$ in diagram in 1.3; there $E = \emptyset$). To be precise, let d be a recursive function such that for all z:

$$W_{d(z)} = \{e \mid e \text{ is a closed } \Sigma\text{-equation } \& \ E \cup \lfloor W_z \rfloor \vdash e\} .$$

Such a function d exists because E is finite.

Further, let (h_1,h_2) be as in the diagram in 1.3, and let $(\Sigma'(z), E'(z)) = (h_1(d(z)), h_2(d(z))$. Now define:

$$\delta(W_z) = \{\ulcorner e \urcorner \mid (\gamma(\Sigma'(z),E'(z)), \varepsilon(\Sigma'(z),E'(z))) \vdash e, \ e \text{ is a closed } \Delta\text{-equation}\}$$
$$= W_{g(z)} \quad \text{for an appropriate computable function } g.$$

One easily verifies that δ is an effective operator, Morover, δ extends $\overline{\varphi}$: let $A \in \mathrm{Dom}(\varphi)$ and $\lceil \equiv_A \rceil = W_z$. Then $W_z = W_{d(z)}$ and thus $(\Sigma'(z),E'(z) \xrightarrow{\Sigma} A$ and $(\Upsilon(\Sigma'(z),E'(z)),\ \varepsilon(\Sigma'(z),E'(z))) \xrightarrow[\Delta]{} \varphi(A)$ which implies $W_{g(z)} = \llbracket \equiv_{\varphi(A)} \rrbracket$. Hence $\delta(W_z) = \overline{\varphi}(\lceil \equiv_A \rceil)$. □

5. THREE SPECIFICATION LEMMA'S

Since the proof of Theorem 3.1 (ii) ⇒ (iii) is trivial and since Theorem 3.1 (i) ⇒ (ii) follows from the more general implication 3.3 (i) ⇒ (ii), it remains to establish (i) ⇒ (ii) for Theorems 3.2 and 3.3. This is done as follows.

Given a continuous parametrized data type φ, we have an $F \in P\omega$ representing φ . Now the Countable Specification Lemma (5.1) transforms this F into a countable specification E_F for φ consisting of closed conditional equations. This proves already Theorem 3.2 (i) ⇒ (ii).

If moreover φ is effectively continuous, F is r.e. . Then the Finite Specification Lemma (5.3) is able to convert the countable specification E_F into a finite one; but first E_F has to be 'preprocessed' by the Compression Lemma (5.2) to an E_F' containing only closed conditional equations $e \to e'$ with precisely one condition.

5.1. <u>COUNTABLE SPECIFICATION LEMMA</u>. *Let* φ: ALG(Σ) → ALG(Δ) *be a persistent and continuous parametrized data type. Then* φ *has a specification* (Δ,E) *with* E *containing closed conditional equations only.*

If moreover φ *is effectively continuous, then* E *can be taken to be an r.e. set.*

PROOF. Let φ be continuous. Let $F \in P\omega$ represent $\overline{\varphi}$(i.e. F extends $\overline{\varphi}$).
Let $\lceil\ \rceil$, $\lfloor\ \rfloor$, $\llbracket\ \rrbracket$ and $\lfloor\!\lfloor\ \rfloor\!\rfloor$ be as in 4.1.
Now there is a nice correspondence between $(m,n) \in F$ and closed conditional equations as follows: to each $(m,n) \in F$ we associate the conditional equation

$$e_{(m,n)} = \bigwedge \lfloor D_m \rfloor \to \lfloor\!\lfloor n \rfloor\!\rfloor .$$

These closed conditional equations turn out to be the desired specification:

$$(*)\ \ \varphi \subseteq (\Delta,E_F)^{\Sigma}_{\Delta} \qquad \text{where} \qquad E_F = \{e_{(m,n)} \mid (m,n) \in F\} .$$

We will now prove that (*) indeed holds. In order to do so, we need a proposition expressed in the following claim. There the following notation is used: if E is a set of conditional equations, E^o is the set of all closed equations logically derivable from E.

<u>CLAIM</u>. *Let* φ,F *and* E_F *be as above. Then:* (i) $A \in \mathrm{Dom}(\varphi) \Rightarrow (E_F \cup \equiv_A)^o \subseteq \equiv_{\varphi(A)}$,

(ii) *if* φ *is persistent:*

$$A \in \mathrm{Dom}(\varphi) \Rightarrow (E_F \cup \equiv_A)^o = \equiv_{\varphi(A)} .$$

<u>Proof of the claim</u> .

(i) is obvious from the construction of E_F .

(ii) It suffices to show that $\varphi(A) \models E_F \cup \equiv_A$. That $\varphi(A) \models \equiv_A$ is obvious since $(\varphi(A))_\Sigma$ is a homomorphic image of A. Also $\varphi(A) \models E_F$; for, let $e_{(m,n)} \in E_F$. Assume $\varphi(A) \models \bigwedge \lfloor D_m \rfloor$. Then also $(\varphi(A))_\Sigma \models \bigwedge \lfloor D_m \rfloor$. By persistency $A = (\varphi(A))_\Sigma$, hence $A \models \bigwedge \lfloor D_m \rfloor$. Now $A \models \bigwedge \lfloor D_m \rfloor \Leftrightarrow \lfloor D_m \rfloor \subseteq \equiv_A \Leftrightarrow D_m \subseteq \lceil \equiv_A \rceil \Rightarrow n \in [\![\equiv_{\varphi(A)}]\!] \Leftrightarrow [\![n]\!] \in \equiv_{\varphi(A)} \Leftrightarrow \varphi(A) \models [\![n]\!]$. Therefore $\varphi(A) \models \bigwedge \lfloor D_m \rfloor \rightarrow [\![n]\!]$ ($= e_{(m,n)}$), which proves the claim.

So if φ is persistent, then for $A \in \mathrm{Dom}(\varphi)$:

$$(\Delta,E_F)^\Sigma_\Delta\ (\Sigma,\equiv_A)_\Sigma = (\Delta,E_F \cup \equiv_A)_\Delta = (\Delta,(E_F \cup \equiv_A)^0)_\Delta = \text{(by the claim)}$$
$$(\Delta,\equiv_{\varphi(A)})_\Delta = \varphi(A).$$

Now (*) follows by the Standard Application Lemma (App. 7.2). □

In the next two lemma's the concept $(\Gamma',E') \trianglerighteq (\Gamma,E)$ (the specification (Γ',E') <u>is a lifting of</u> (Γ,E)) is employed. The precise definition and the statement of the 'Lifting Lemma' are given in the Appendix. The intuitive idea is simply that a lifting (Γ',E') of (Γ,E) is some kind of extension of the specification (Γ,E) such that they specify the same parametrized data types:

$$(\Gamma',E') \geq (\Gamma,E) \Rightarrow (\Gamma',E')^\Sigma_\Delta = (\Gamma,E)^\Sigma_\Delta \ .$$

(In fact we must slightly more precise - see the Appendix.)

5.2. <u>COMPRESSION LEMMA</u>. *Let* (Γ,E) *be a specification with* E *containing closed conditional equations only. Then there is a lifting* (Γ',E') *of* (Γ,E) *with* E' *containing closed conditional equations of the form* $e \rightarrow e'$ *only.*

Moreover, if E *is r.e. then so is* E'.

<u>PROOF</u>. Consider the following extension $\Gamma \cup \Delta$ of Γ : the signature Δ has <u>sorts</u> NAT , LINK; <u>functions</u> S: NAT $\rightarrow$ NAT, L: NAT $\times$ NAT $\rightarrow$ LINK; <u>constants</u> $0 \in$ NAT. We use the abbreviation $\underline{k}$ for the term $S^k(0)$ of sort NAT ($k \in \omega$).

Let $E = \{s_1 = t_1 \wedge \ldots \wedge s_{m_i} = t_{m_i} \rightarrow s_i' = t_i' \mid i \in \omega\}$ be a (not necessarily effective) enumeration of E, for some function $i \mapsto m_i$. We may suppose $m_i \geq 1$ (by prefixing a dummy condition if necessary).

Consider e_i: $s_1 = t_1 \wedge \ldots \wedge s_{m_i} = t_{m_i} \rightarrow s_i' = t_i'$ ($m_i \geq 1$). We will replace e_i by the set E_i of $m_i + 1$ conditional equations each having only one condition:

$$s_1 = t_1 \rightarrow L(\underline{i},\underline{0}) = L(\underline{i},\underline{1}), \ldots, s_{m_i} = t_{m_i} \rightarrow L(\underline{i},\underline{m_i - 1}) = L(\underline{i},\underline{m_i})$$
$$L(\underline{i},\underline{0}) = L(\underline{i},\underline{m_i}) \rightarrow s_i' = t_i'$$

(Note that using these conditional equations:
$s_1 = t_1 \wedge \ldots \wedge s_{m_i} = t_{m_i} \rightarrow L(\underline{i},\underline{0}) = L(\underline{i},\underline{1}) = L(\underline{i},\underline{2}) = \ldots = L(\underline{i},\underline{m_i}) \rightarrow s_i' = t_i'$.)

Now (Γ',E') will be $(\Gamma \cup \Delta, \bigcup_{i \in \omega} E_i)$. The verification that indeed $(\Gamma',E') \trianglerighteq (\Gamma,E)$ is left to the reader. If E is r.e., it is not hard to see that E' is r.e. too.

5.3. <u>FINITE SPECIFICATION LEMMA</u>. *Let* (Γ,E) *be a specification with* E *an r.e. set of conditional equations of the form* $e \to e'$. *Then* (Γ,E) *has a lifting* (Γ',E') *with* E' *finite.*

<u>PROOF</u>. Let $E = \cup\{E^{(s,t)} \mid s,t \in \underline{sorts}(\Gamma)\}$ where $E^{(s,t)}$ contains only conditional equations of the form $\tau_1^s = \tau_2^s \to \tau_3^t = \tau_4^t$. Since E is r.e., there are recursive functions $g_i^{(s,t)}$ $(i=1,\ldots,4;\ s,t \in \underline{sorts}(\Gamma))$ such that

$$E^{(s,t)} = \{\lfloor g_1^{(s,t)}(n)\rfloor = \lfloor g_2^{(s,t)}(n)\rfloor \to \lfloor g_3^{(s,t)}(n)\rfloor = \lfloor g_4^{(s,t)}(n)\rfloor \mid n \in \omega\}\ .$$

We define an algebra E as follows. Let Γ^* be a disjoint copy of Γ: for each $s,f,c \in \Gamma$ we have s^*, f^*, $c^* \in \Gamma^*$. We extend $*$ in the obvious way to $Ter(\Gamma)$. Now Σ_E consists of Γ^* augmented by a sort NAT, a constant 0, a function S: NAT $\to$ NAT and for each $s,t \in \underline{sorts}(\Gamma)$ functions $G_i^{(s,t)}$:NAT $\to s^*$ $(i=1,2)$ and $G_i^{(s,t)}$:NAT $\to t^*$ $(i=3,4)$. We write $\underline{k}$ for $S^k(0)$.

E is the minimal algebra specified by the recursive set of closed Σ_E-equations

$$\{G_i^{(s,t)}(\underline{k}) = \lfloor g_i^{(s,t)}(k)\rfloor^* \mid k\in\omega; s,t \in \underline{sorts}(\Gamma)\}\ .$$

E is computable and, therefore, by Lemma 1.3.1 it has a <u>finite</u> specification (Δ,F).

Now let for each $s \in \underline{sorts}(\Gamma)$ a homomorphism h_s be given satisfying the finite set of equations

$$H = \begin{cases} h^s(c^*) = c \\ h^s(f^*(x_1,\ldots,x_k)) = f(h^{s_1}(x_1),\ldots,h^{s_k}(x_k)) \end{cases}$$

(for all constants c and functions f of Γ).

Finally, define $\mathbb{E} = \{e^{(s,t)} \mid s,t \in \underline{sorts}(\Gamma)\}$ where $e^{(s,t)}$ is the conditional equation

$$h^s(G_1^{(s,t)}(x)) = h^s(G_2^{(s,t)}(x)) \to h^t(G_3^{(s,t)}(x)) = h^t(G_4^{(s,t)}(x)).$$

Then, if $(\Gamma',E') = \{\Gamma \cup \Delta \cup \{h^s \mid s \in \underline{sorts}(\Gamma)\}, \mathbb{E} \cup F \cup H\}$, we have $(\Gamma',E') \trianglerighteq (\Gamma,E)$. The routine verification is left to the reader. □

6. PROOF OF THEOREM 3.2 (i) ⇒ (ii) AND 3.3 (i) ⇒ (ii).

Clearly 3.2 (i) ⇒ (ii) is a consequence of the Countable Specification Lemma (CSL) 5.1.

The other implication requires some argument. Let φ: ALG(Σ) $\to$ ALG(Δ) be persistent and effectively continuous. According to CSL 5.1 it has a specification (Δ,E) with E r.e. and containing closed conditional equations only. According to the Compression Lemma (5.2) this specification can be lifted to a specification (Γ,F) with F r.e. and containing closed conditional equations of the form $e \to e'$ only.

Then, using the Finite Specification Lemma (5.3), (Γ,F) is lifted to (Γ',F') with F' finite. By transitivity of lifting, $(\Gamma',F') \trianglerighteq (\Delta,E)$.

Finally, by the Lifting Lemma (App. 7.4) we may conclude from $\varphi \subseteq (\Delta,E)^{\Sigma}_{\Delta}$ to $\varphi \subseteq (\Gamma',F')^{\Sigma}_{\Delta}$, i.e. φ possesses a finite specification. □

7. APPENDIX: LIFTINGS OF SPECIFICATIONS (proofs deleted: see [1])

7.1. JOINT EXPANSION LEMMA. *Let* $A_i \in ALG(\Sigma_i)$, $i = 0,1,2$, *be such that* $\Sigma_1 \cap \Sigma_2 = \Sigma_0$ *and* $(A_1)_{\Sigma_0} = A_0 = (A_2)_{\Sigma_0}$.

Then there is a unique joint expansion $A_1 \sqcup A_2 \in ALG(\Sigma_1 \cup \Sigma_2)$ *of* A_1, A_2 *such that* $(A_1 \sqcup A_2)_{\Sigma_i} = A_i$, $i = 1,2$.

The next Lemma is intended to simplify a verification that some specification indeed specifies a parametrized data type φ.

7.2. STANDARD APPLICATION LEMMA. *Suppose that* φ: $ALG(\Sigma) \to ALG(\Delta)$ *is a persistent parametrized data type. Then the following is a sufficient condition for* $\varphi \subseteq (\Gamma,E)^{\Sigma}_{\Delta}$: *for all* $A \in Dom(\varphi)$, $\varphi(A) = (\Gamma,E)^{\Sigma}_{\Delta}\ (\Sigma,\equiv_A)_{\Sigma}$.

7.3. DEFINITION. Let (Γ',E') and (Γ,E) be two specifications. We say that (Γ',E') is a lifting of (Γ,E), notation: $(\Gamma',E') \trianglerighteq (\Gamma,E)$, if the following three conditions are satisfied:

(i) $\Gamma' \supseteq \Gamma$,

(ii) $\overline{E'} \supseteq E$ ($\overline{}$ denotes the closure under logical derivability),

(iii) each $A \in ALG(\Gamma,E)$ can be expanded to an algebra $A' \in ALG(\Gamma',E')$. (I.e. $(A')_{\Gamma} = A$.)

The important property of liftings is the following.

7.4. LIFTING LEMMA. *Let* φ: $ALG(\Sigma) \to ALG(\Delta)$ *be a persistent parametrized data type. Let* $\Sigma \subseteq \Delta \subseteq \Gamma$ *and assume* $(\Gamma',E') \trianglerighteq (\Gamma,E)$. *Then:*

$$\varphi \subseteq (\Gamma,E)^{\Sigma}_{\Delta} \Rightarrow \varphi \subseteq (\Gamma',E')^{\Sigma}_{\Delta} \quad . \qquad (*)$$

Note here that the requirement that φ is persistent, turns the statement $(*)$ into one weaker than the statement $(\Gamma,E)^{\Sigma}_{\Delta} \subseteq (\Gamma',E')^{\Sigma}_{\Delta}$.

REFERENCES

[1] BERGSTRA, J.A. & J.W. KLOP, *Algebraic specifications for parametrized data types with minimal parameter and target algebras*, Mathematical Centre, Department of Computer Science Research Report IW 183, Amsterdam 1981.

[2] BERGSTRA, J.A. & J.W. KLOP, *Initial algebra specifications for parametrized data types*, Mathematical Centre, Department of Computer Science Research Report IW 186, Amsterdam 1981.

[3] BERGSTRA, J.A. & J.V. TUCKER, *Algebraic specifications of computable and semi-computable data structures*, Mathematical Centre, Department of Computer Science Research Report IW 115, Amsterdam 1979.

[4] BERGSTRA, J.A. & J.V. TUCKER, *A characterization of computable data types by means of a finite equational specification method*, Proc. 7th ICALP, Springer LNCS Vol. 85, 1980.

[5] BERGSTRA, J.A. & J.V. TUCKER, *Initial and final algebra semantics for data type specifications: two characterization theorems*, Mathematical Centre, Department of Computer Science Research Report IW 131, Amsterdam 1980.

[6] BURSTALL, R.M. & J.A. GOGUEN, *An informal introduction to specifications using* CLEAR, Lecture notes for the International Summer School on theoretical foundations of programming methodology, Munich 1981.

[7] EHRICH, H.D., *On the theory of specification, implementation and parametrization of abstract data types*. Research Report Dortmund 1978.

[8] EHRIG, H.E., H.-J. KREOWSKI, J.W. THATCHER, E.G. WAGNER & J.B. WRIGHT, *Parameterized data types in algebraic specification languages*, Proc. 7th ICALP, Springer LNCS Vol. 85, 1980.

[9] EHRIG, H., *Algebraic theory of parameterized specifications with requirements*, in Proc. of CAAP81, Springer LNCS, Vol. 112.

[10] GANZINGER, H., *Parameterized specifications: parameter passing and optimizing implementation*. Report TUM-18110. Technische Universität München, August 1981.

[11] KAPHENGST, H. & H. REICHEL, *Algebraische Algorithmentheorie*, VEB Robotron, Dresden WIB, 1971.

[12] LEHMANN, D.J. & M.B. SMYTH, *Data types*, Proc. 18th IEEE Symposium on Foundations of Computing, Providence R.I. November 1977.

[13] ROGERS jr., H., *Theory of recursive functions and effective computability*, McGraw-Hill, 1967.

[14] SCOTT, D.S., *Lambda calculus and recursion theory*, in Proc. Third Scandinavian Logic Conf., Ed. S. Kanger, North Holland Studies in Logic and the Foundations of Mathematics, Vol. 82, 1975.

[15] THATCHER, J.W., E.G. WAGNER & J.B. WRIGHT, *Data type specification: parameterization and the power of specification techniques*, Proc. SIGACT 10th Annual Symp. on Theory of Computing, pp. 119-132, May 1978.

[16] WIRSING, M., *An analysis of semantic models for algebraic specifications*, Lecture Notes for the International Summer School on theoretical foundations of programming methodology, Munich 1981.

A modification of the λ-calculus as a base for functional programming languages

K.J. Berkling
Institut für
Informationssystemforschung
GMD-Bonn

E. Fehr
Lehrstuhl für
Informatik II
RWTH Aachen

Abstract

Church´s λ-calculus is modified by introducing a new mechanism, the lambda-bar operator "#", which neutralizes the effect of one preceeding λ-binding. This operator can be used in such a way that renaming of bound variables in any reduction sequence can be avoided, with the effect that efficient interpreters with comparatively simple machine organization can be designed.
Any semantic model of the pure λ-calculus also serves as a model for this modified reduction calculus, which guarantees smooth semantical theories.
The Berkling Reduction Language BRL is a new functional programming language based upon this modification.

Introduction

Functional (applicative) programming languages, such as LISP, Turner´s KRC, Plotkin´s PCF, etc. , are in general based upon Church´s lambda-calculus. Although operational and denotational semantics of the λ-calculus are by now well understood, most of the existing implementations of the λ-calculus are inconsistent extensions or incomplete versions of the λ-calculus.

The reason for this is mainly the fact that β-conversions with preceeding tests on variable conflicts and appropriate renaming is highly inefficient, when implemented on or simulated by a machine. LISP - machines and related implementations for other functional programming languages introduce dynamic binding, call by value mode, problems with functional arguments and/ or do not completely reduce all input terms (Mc Gowan [7], Fehr [5]).They gain satisfactory implementations at the price of either inconsistent semantical theories or at least very complicated denotational descriptions (Gordon [6]),which violate the semantic of the underlying λ-calculus.

Backus introduced in [1] a new functional language which avoids variable conflicts by using special combinators instead of λ-terms to express the control structure. Although the combinatorial theory is equivalent to the λ-calculus, there are two drawbacks : First, there is no possibility for the programmer to name his objects in his programs, which results in a rather obscure programming style. Second, the implementation of the full combinatory theory is about as complex as the implementation of the λ-calculus, which led Backus the usage of only a restricted set of combinators. He does not allow for example combinators of higher functional types, because this could not be expressed in his algebra of programs.

Berkling has introduced in [3] a reduction language BRL which is an extension of the λ-calculus not only by a certain set of base operations, such as conditionals, arithmetical - , boolean - , and list operations, but also by an unbinding mechanism lambda-bar "#", which neutralizes the effect of one preceeding lambda-binding. For example #x occurs free in λx.#x but bound in λx.λx.#x . The effect of this extension is that β-conversion can be performed without renaming of variables by systematically using the lambda-bar mechanism. As a result machine models of the BRL or related languages based upon this extension have an uncomplicated machine structure and run very efficiently as compared to lambda-calculus machines. The BRL-machine was first simulated by Homes [8] and then a hardware-model built together with Kluge [10] started operating in 1978, and has since then shown a satisfactory performance.

De Bruijn introduced earlier in [4] a variant of the λ-calculus which is completely equivalent to the modification by Berkling, who independently developed it in [2]. De Bruijn uses an implementation of this mechanism in his AUTOMATH-project and shows that it is very efficient for automatic formula manipulation.
The semantical effect of the lambda-bar operation on the lambda-calculus was until now not very clear, since there existed only the syntactical and operational description of it. In this paper we want to give a denotational semantics to it and give a proof that it is a consistent extension of the λ-calculus.

1. A short introduction to BRL

As in most functional programming languages there is only one syntactical category, the expressions, in the Berkling Reduction Language. In this paper we do not mention every feature of BRL but rather point out the different ways of forming new expressions from given ones.

(i) "simple expressions" in BRL are built up from variables and constants using arithmetical, logical and list operations, as well as conditionals.

e.g.
- (3.1415 * (radius * radius))
- 4.3 : 3.7
- _if_ x>0 _then_ 1 _else_ _if_ x=0 _then_ 0 _else_ -1

(ii) "abstractions" can be produced from any expression e and identifier x by writing :

" _sub_ x _in_ e , " which is a sugared version of the lambda-expression " $\lambda x.e$ " and denotes a function with formal parameter x , which substitutes a given argument at each free occurrence of x in e.

e.g.
- _sub_ radius _in_ (3.1415 * (radius * radius))
- _sub_ r _in_ _sub_ h _in_ (((3.1415 * (r * r)) * h)

(iii) "combinations" are made of two arbitrary expressions f and g where one takes the function part and the other one takes the argument part. The corresponding BRL-expression just reads :

" _apply_ f _to_ g " , again a sugared version of the λ-expression " (f g) ".

e.g. - _apply_ _sub_ r _in_ (3.1 * (r * r)) _to_ 24.3 .

During an execution, the above expression will be reduced in the first step to (3.1 * (24.3 * 24.3)) and in the next step to its value 1830.319 . To illustrate the effect of the unbinding mechanism # , consider the λ-expression : ($\lambda x.\lambda y.x\ y$). Due to the fact that y occurs free in the argument and bound in the function body, a renaming say ($\lambda x.\lambda z.x\ y$) has to be performed before β-reduction can reduce the term to $\lambda z.y$.

The corresponding expression in BRL reads :

apply _sub_ x _in_ _sub_ y _in_ x _to_ y .

After one step of reduction it turns into _sub_ y _in_ #y .

The formal rule corresponding to β-reduction will be presented in the next section.

(iv) "recursive expressions" are introduced explicitly into BRL although one could use the expression corresponding to the Y-operator of the λ-calculus. For any expression e and variable f we can build the BRL expression. " rec f : e " , which corresponds to an equation f = e or to the λ-expression (Y λf.e) .
Consider the definition of the factorial as an example :

- rec fac : sub n in if (n=1) then 1
  else (n * apply fac to (n-1))

(v) Other concepts of BRL are convenient operations for tree manipulations, for pattern matching and some facilities to save function definitions. They will not be presented in this paper, but can be looked at in Hommes/Schlütter [9].

A very nice feature of the BRL-machine is that when working at a terminal, program development runs interactively and long subexpressions are automatically reduced to one symbol, which can be easily expanded using the cursor.

2. Syntax and conversion rules of the reduction-calculus :

In this chapter we want to give a formal description of the lambda- calculus modification which is the support for BRL. In order to ease an immediate comparison to the λ-notation we shall use pure λ-terms rather then BRL-expressions.
Definition 1 (Syntax) : Let X be a denumerable set of variables, then the set T of reduction terms is given inductively by :

(i) $\#^n x \in T$ for all $x \in X$, $n \in \mathbb{N}$, $n \geqslant 0$
(ii) $(t_1\ t_2) \in T$ for all $t_1, t_2 \in T$
(iii) $\lambda x.t \in T$ for all $x \in X$ ■

In (i) the ysmbols $\#^n$ could be read as " the n-fold application of # ", which reduces to the identity in the case of $n = 0$.
As indicated in the introduction, the β-conversion will systematically make use of the unbinding operation # (lambda-bar).
This principle is formalized by the meta-constructors Π^+ and Π^- , which augment and decrement the unbindings of particular variables.
Definition 2 (Π^+) : Let $x \in X$, $n \in \mathbb{N}$, and $t \in T$.
The reduction term $\Pi^+ \#^n x\ t$ is given by induction on the structure of t :

(i) $$\Pi^+ \#^n x\ \#^m y = \begin{cases} \#^{m+1} y & \text{if } x = y \text{ and } m \geqslant n \\ \#^m y & \text{otherwise} \end{cases}$$

(ii) $\pi^{+} \#^{n}x\ (t_1\ t_2) \quad = \quad (\pi^{+} \#^{n}x\ t_1\ \pi^{+} \#^{n}x\ t_2)$

(iii) $$\pi^{+} \#^{n}x\ \lambda y.t = \begin{cases} \lambda y.\ \pi^{+} \#^{n+1}x\ t & \text{if } x = y \\ \lambda y.\ \pi^{+} \#^{n}x\ t & \text{if } x \neq y \end{cases}$$ ■

<u>Defintion 3 (π^{-})</u> : Let x,n and t as above. The reduction term $\pi^{-} \#^{n}x\ t$ is inductively given by :

(i) $$\pi^{-} \#^{n}x\#^{m}y = \begin{cases} \#^{m-1}y & \text{if } x = y \text{ and } m > n \\ \#^{m}y & \text{otherwise} \end{cases}$$

(ii) $\pi^{-} \#^{n}x\ (t_1\ t_2) \quad = \quad (\pi^{-} \#^{n}x\ t_1\ \pi^{-} \#^{n}x\ t_2)$

(iii) $$\pi^{-} \#^{n}x\ \lambda y.t = \begin{cases} \lambda y.\ \pi^{-} \#^{n+1}x\ t & \text{if } x = y \\ \lambda y.\ \pi^{-} \#^{n}x\ t & \text{if } x \neq y \end{cases}$$ ■

Now the substitution operator $\$^{v}_{s}\ t$, which substitutes s for v in t can be defined without using the notions of free and bound occurrences of variables.

<u>Definition 4 (\$)</u> : Let v be $\#^{n}x$ for some $n \in \mathbb{N}$, $x \in X$, and let $s, t \in T$. The reduction term $\$^{v}_{s}\ t$ is inductively defined by :

(i) $$\$^{v}_{s}\ \#^{m}y = \begin{cases} s & \text{if } v = \#^{m}y, \text{ i.e. } m = n \text{ and } x = y \\ \#^{m}y & \text{otherwise} \end{cases}$$

(ii) $\$^{v}_{s}\ (t_1\ t_2) \quad = \quad (\$^{v}_{s}\ t_1\ \$^{v}_{s}\ t_2)$

(iii) $$\$^{v}_{s}\ \lambda y.t = \begin{cases} \lambda y.\ \$^{\#v}_{\pi^{+}ys}\ t & \text{if } x = y \\ \lambda y.\ \$^{v}_{\pi^{+}ys}\ t & \text{if } x \neq y \end{cases}$$

The only reduction rule in this calculus is corresponding to the β-conversion of the λ-calculus, but as clashes of variables cannot occur, all redexes can be reduced without a prior renaming.

<u>Definition 5 ($\underset{\beta'}{\rightarrow}$)</u> : Let again $x \in X$ and let t and s be arbitrary reduction terms, then

$$(\lambda x.\ t\ s) \underset{\beta'}{\rightarrow} \pi^{-}\ x\ \$^{x}_{\pi^{+}xs}\ t$$ ■

This definition shows clearly the protection mechanism of the lambda-bar operator : If one thinks about the above reduction rule operationally, one realizes that in the first step, one could obtain t' from t by replacing each occurrence of x in t by the term s in which all variables of the form $\#^n x$ were transformed into $\#^{n+1}$ The second step somehow reverses this by changing each occurrence of $\#^{n+1}x$ in t' into $\#^n x$, with the effects that indeed s was substituted for x in t and furthermore, occurrences of $\#^{n+1}x$ in t are now changed into $\#^n x$ which reflects that one unbinding of x in t has become superfluous due to the disappearance of λx in front of t . A detailed description of the reduction calculus can be found in Berkling [2] , where another simplification which uses only one variable is presented too.

3. Denotational semantics and consistency proof

In this section we show that the reduction calculus as introduced above has a neat denotational semantics in any model of the λ-calculus, as for example the $P\omega$-model by Scott [12] , Scott's D_∞ [11], or any other.
Let for the rest of this paper M be such a model and let φ denote the retraction from M onto $[M \to M]$, the set of continuous functions from M to M.
In our analysis environments ρ will be mappings from $\bigcup_{n \in \mathbb{N}} \{\#^n x \mid x \in X\}$ to M .
In a first step we shall model the effect of Π^+ and Π^- on environments, following a suggestion by one of the referees.

Definition 6 ($\Pi^+_{n,x}$, $\Pi^-_{n,x}$) : Let $x \in X$, $n \in \mathbb{N}$. The operators $\Pi^+_{n,x}$ and $\Pi^-_{n,x}$ on environments are given by :

a) $$\Pi^+_{n,x}(\rho)(\#^k y) = \begin{cases} \rho(\#^{k+1}x) & \text{if } x = y \text{ and } k \geq n \\ \rho(\#^k y) & \text{if } x \neq y \text{ or } k < n \end{cases}$$

b) $$\Pi^-_{n,x}(\rho)(\#^k y) = \begin{cases} \rho(\#^{k-1}x) & \text{if } x = y \text{ and } k > n \\ \rho(\#^k y) & \text{if } x \neq y \text{ or } k \leq n \end{cases}$$

Another useful definition serves to modify an environment such that one protection is neglected, and a new value is given to unprotected occurrences of x .

Definition 7 ($\rho[x\#m]$) : For $x \in X$, $m \in M$ and an environment ρ let $\rho[x\#m]$ be a new environment given by :

$$\rho[x\#m](\#^k y) = \begin{cases} \rho(\#^k y) & \text{if } x \neq y \\ m & \text{if } x = y \text{ and } k = 0 \\ \rho(\#^{k-1}x) & \text{if } x = y \text{ and } k > 0 \end{cases}$$ ∎

The next lemma shows how $\Pi^+_{n,x}$ and $\Pi^-_{n,x}$ commute with $[y\#m]$.

Lemma 8 : Let $n,k \in \mathbb{N}$, $x,y \in X$, $m \in M$ and ρ be an environment. Then the following holds :

a) $$\Pi^+_{n,x}(\rho)\,[y\#m] = \begin{cases} \Pi^+_{n+1,x}\,(\rho[y\#m]) & \text{if } x = y \\ \Pi^+_{n,x}\,(\rho[y\#m]) & \text{if } x \neq y \end{cases}$$

and

b) $$\Pi^-_{n,x}(\rho)\,[y\#m] = \begin{cases} \Pi^-_{n+1,x}\,(\rho[y\#m]) & \text{if } x = y \\ \Pi^-_{n,x}\,(\rho[y\#m]) & \text{if } x \neq y \end{cases} .$$

Proof Both results can be shown by considering all cases and using the definitions. ■

Now we can elegantly formulate the denotational semantics of the reduction terms.

Definition 9 (semantics $[\![\;]\!]$) : The semantics with respect to ρ of a reduction term t in the model M is given inductively by :

(i) $[\![v]\!]\,\rho = \rho\,(v)$ for each $v = \#^n x$, $n \in \mathbb{N}$, $x \in X$

(ii) $[\![(t_1\,t_2)]\!]\,\rho = \varphi\,([\![t_1]\!]\,\rho)\,([\![t_2]\!]\,\rho)$

(iii) $[\![\lambda x.t]\!]\,\rho \doteq \varphi^{-1}(m \mapsto [\![t]\!]\,\rho\,[x\#m])$

■

This definition exhibits the fact that our reduction calculus is semantically a clear extension of the λ-calculus, because terms without occurrences of $\#$ obtain exactly the usual λ-semantics. Before proving that this semantic definition is compatible with the β'-reduction, we have to show in several lemmas, how the two meta-constructors Π^+ and Π^- as well as the substitution operator $ behave on the semantical level.

Lemma 10 : Let $n \in \mathbb{N}$, $x \in X$, $t \in T$, and ρ be an environment,

$[\![\Pi^+\,\#^n x\ t]\!]\,\rho = [\![t]\!]\,\Pi^+_{n,x}(\rho)$.

Proof (induction on the structure of t) :

(i) $$[\![\Pi^+\#^n x\#^k y]\!]\,\rho = \begin{cases} [\![\#^{k+1}y]\!] & \text{if } x = y \text{ and } k \geq n \\ [\![\#^k y]\!]\,\rho & \text{otherwise} \end{cases}$$

$$= \Pi^+_{n,x}(\rho)\,(\#^k y) \quad \text{by def. 6(a)}$$

$$= [\![\#^k y]\!]\,\Pi^+_{n,x}(\rho) \quad \text{by def. 9(i)}$$

(ii) By definition 2. (ii) Π^+ distributes to both components of the combination, thus the induction hypothesis is applicable.

(iii) $$[\![\Pi^+ \#^n x\ \lambda y.t]\!]\ \rho = \begin{cases} [\![\lambda y.\ \Pi^+ \#^{n+1} x\ t]\!]\ \rho & \text{if } x = y \\ [\![\lambda y.\ \Pi^+ \#^n x\ t]\!]\ \rho & \text{if } x \neq y \end{cases}$$

by def. 2. (iii)

$$= \begin{cases} \varphi^{-1}(m \mapsto [\![\Pi^+ \#^{n+1} x\ t]\!]\ \rho\ [y\#m]) & \text{if } x = y \\ \varphi^{-1}(m \mapsto [\![\Pi^+ \#^n x\ t]\!]\ \rho\ [y\#m]) & \text{if } x \neq y \end{cases}$$

by def. 9 (iii)

$$= \begin{cases} \varphi^{-1}(m \mapsto [\![t]\!]\ \Pi^+_{n+1,x}(\rho[y\#m]) & \text{if } x = y \\ \varphi^{-1}(m \mapsto [\![t]\!]\ \Pi^+_{n,x}(\rho[y\#m]) & \text{if } x \neq y \end{cases}$$

by ind. hyp.

$$= \quad \varphi^{-1}(m \mapsto [\![t]\!]\ \Pi^+_{n,x}(\rho)[y\#m]) \qquad \text{by lemma 8a)}$$

$$= \quad [\![\lambda y.t]\!]\ \Pi^+_{n,x}(\rho)$$

■

<u>Lemma 11</u> : Let n , x , t and ρ be as above.

$$[\![\Pi^- \#^n x\ t]\!]\ \rho \quad = \quad [\![t]\!]\ \Pi^-_{n,x}(\rho) \quad .$$

<u>Proof</u> (induction on the structure of t) :

(i) $$[\![\Pi^- \#^n x\ \#^k y]\!]\ \rho = \begin{cases} [\![\#^{k-1} y]\!]\ \rho & \text{if } x = y \text{ and } k > n \\ [\![\#^k y]\!]\ \rho & \text{otherwise} \end{cases}$$

by def. 3. (i)

$$= [\![\#^k y]\!]\ \Pi^-_{n,x}(\rho) \qquad \text{by def. 6(b) and 9 (i)}$$

(ii) follows by distributivity of Π^- and induction hypothesis

(iii) $$[\![\Pi^- \#^n x\ \lambda y.t]\!]\ \rho = \begin{cases} [\![\lambda y.\ \Pi^- \#^{n+1} x\ t]\!]\ \rho & \text{if } x = y \\ [\![\lambda y.\ \Pi^- \#^n x\ t]\!]\ \rho & \text{if } x \neq x \end{cases}$$

by def. 3. (iii)

$$= \begin{cases} \varphi^{-1}(m \mapsto [\![\Pi^{-} \ \#^{n+1}x \ t]\!] \ \rho \ [y\#m]) & \text{if } x = y \\ \varphi^{-1}(m \mapsto [\![\Pi^{-} \ \#^{n}x \ t]\!] \ \rho \ [y\#m]) & \text{if } x \neq y \end{cases}$$

by def. 9 (iii)

$$= \begin{cases} \varphi^{-1}(m \mapsto [\![t]\!] \ \Pi^{-}_{n+1,x}(\rho[y\#m])) & \text{if } x = y \\ \varphi^{-1}(m \mapsto [\![t]\!] \ \Pi^{-}_{n,x}(\rho[y\#m]) & \text{if } x \neq y \end{cases}$$

$$= \quad \varphi^{-1}(m \mapsto [\![t]\!] \ \Pi^{-}_{n,x}(\rho)[y\#m]) \qquad \text{by lemma 8b}$$

$$= \quad [\![\lambda y.\ t]\!] \ \Pi^{-}_{n,x}(\rho)$$

■

<u>Lemma 12</u> : Let x , m , and ρ be as above.

$$\Pi^{+}_{o,x}(\rho[x\#m]) \quad = \rho$$

<u>Proof</u> :

$$\Pi^{+}_{o,x}(\rho[x\#m])\ (\#^{k}y) \quad = \begin{cases} \rho[x\#m]\ (\#^{k}y) & \text{if } x \neq y \\ \rho[x\#m]\ (\#^{k+1}x) & \text{if } x = y \end{cases}$$

$$= \begin{cases} \rho(\#^{k}y) & \text{if } x \neq y \\ \rho(\#^{k}y) & \text{if } x = y \end{cases}$$

$$= \quad \rho(\#^{k}y)$$

■

<u>Lemma 13</u> : Let $v = \#^{n}x$ for some $n \in \mathbb{N}$, $x \in X$ and let $s, t \in T$, and ρ be an environment.

$$[\![\$^{v}_{s}\ t]\!] \ \rho = [\![t]\!] \ \rho \ [v \mid [\![s]\!] \ \rho]$$

<u>Proof</u> (induction on the structure of t).

(i) $$[\![\$^{v}_{s}\ \#^{m}y]\!] \ \rho \quad = \begin{cases} [\![s]\!] \ \rho & \text{if } v = \#^{m}y \\ [\![\#^{m}y]\!] \ \rho & \text{otherwise} \end{cases}$$

$$= \quad [\![\#^{m}y]\!] \ \rho \ [v \mid [\![s]\!] \ \rho] \quad .$$

(ii) immediate by the induction hypothesis and distributivity of \$.

(iii) $[\![\$^{v}_{s}\ \lambda y.\ t]\!]\ \rho = \begin{cases} [\![\lambda y.\ \$^{\#v}_{\Pi^+ ys}\ t]\!]\ \rho & \text{if } x = y \\ [\![\lambda y.\ \$^{v_+}_{\Pi^+ ys}\ t]\!]\ \rho & \text{if } x \neq y \end{cases}$ by definition 4. (iii)

$= \begin{cases} \varphi^{-1}(m \mapsto [\![\$^{\#v}_{\Pi^+ ys}\ t]\!]\ \rho\ [y\#m]) & \text{if } x = y \\ \varphi^{-1}(m \mapsto [\![\$^{v}_{\Pi^+ ys}\ t]\!]\ \rho\ [y\#m]) & \text{if } x \neq y \end{cases}$ by definition 9. (iii)

$= \begin{cases} \varphi^{-1}(m \mapsto [\![t]\!]\ \rho\ [y\#m]\ [^{\#v}\,|\,[\![\Pi^+ ys]\!]\ \rho\ [y\#m]]) & \text{if } x = y \\ \varphi^{-1}(m \mapsto [\![t]\!]\ \rho\ [y\#m]\ [^{v}\,|\,[\![\Pi^+ ys]\!]\ \rho\ [y\#m]]) & \text{if } x \neq y \end{cases}$ by ind. hyp.

$= \begin{cases} \varphi^{-1}(m \mapsto [\![t]\!]\ \rho\ [y\#m]\ [^{\#v}\,|\,[\![s]\!]\ \Pi^+_{o,y}(\rho[y\#m])]) & \text{if } x = y \\ \varphi^{-1}(m \mapsto [\![t]\!]\ \rho\ [y\#m]\ [^{v}\,|\,[\![s]\!]\ \Pi^+_{o,y}(\rho[y\#m])]) & \text{if } x \neq y \end{cases}$ by lemma 10

$= \begin{cases} \varphi^{-1}(m \mapsto [\![t]\!]\ \rho\ [y\#m]\ [^{\#v}\,|\,[\![s]\!]\ \rho\,]) & \text{if } x = y \\ \varphi^{-1}(m \mapsto [\![t]\!]\ \rho[y\#m]\ [v\,|\,[\![s]\!]\ \rho\,]) & \text{if } x \neq y \end{cases}$ by lemma 12

$= \varphi^{-1}(m \mapsto [\![t]\!]\ \rho\ [v\,|\,[\![s]\!]\ \rho][y\#m])$ because $v = \#^n x$

$= [\![\lambda y.t]\!]\ \rho\ [v\,|\,[\![s]\!]\ \rho]$

■

<u>Lemma 14</u> : Let x , m , and ρ be as above.

$$\rho[x\#m] = \Pi^-_{o,x}(\rho)[x\,|\,m]$$

<u>Proof</u> :

$$\rho[x\#m](\#^k y) = \begin{cases} \rho(\#^k y) & \text{if } x \neq y \\ m & \text{if } x = y \text{ and } k = 0 \\ \rho(\#^{k-1} x) & \text{if } x = y \text{ and } k > 0 \end{cases}$$ by def. 7

$$= \Pi^-_{o,x}(\rho)\ [x\,|\,m]$$ by def. 6 (b)

■

Lemma 15 : Let $n \in \mathbb{N}$ and $x \in X$. Then

$$\Pi^{+}_{n,x}(\Pi^{-}_{n,x}(\rho)) = \rho \qquad \text{for all environments } \rho \quad .$$

Proof immediate by definition 6

■

We can now prove our main theorem, which ensures the consistency of the β' conversion with the rules of the λ-calculus.

Theorem 16 :

$$[\![(\lambda x.s)]\!] \rho \quad = \quad [\![\Pi^{-} x \ \$^{x}_{\Pi^{+}xs} \ t]\!] \rho$$

Proof :

$$[\![\Pi^{-} x \ \$^{x}_{\Pi^{+}xs} \ t]\!] \rho \ = \ [\![\$^{x}_{\Pi^{+}xs} \ t]\!] \ \Pi^{-}_{o,x} \ (\rho) \qquad \text{by lemma 11}$$

$$= [\![t]\!] \ \Pi^{-}_{o,x}(\rho)[x \mid [\![\Pi^{+}xs]\!] \ \Pi^{-}_{o,x}(\rho)] \qquad \text{by lemma 13}$$

$$= [\![t]\!] \ \rho \ [x\#[\![\Pi^{+}xs]\!] \ \Pi^{-}_{o,x}(\rho)] \qquad \text{by lemma 14}$$

$$= [\![t]\!] \ \rho \ [x\#[\![s]\!] \ \Pi^{+}_{o,x}(\Pi^{-}_{o,x}(\rho))] \qquad \text{by lemma 10}$$

$$= [\![t]\!] \ \rho \ [x\#[\![s]\!] \ \rho] \qquad \text{by lemma 15}$$

$$= \varphi(\varphi^{-1}(m \mapsto [\![t]\!] \ \rho \ [x\#m])) \ ([\![s]\!] \ \rho)$$

$$= \varphi([\![\lambda x.\ t]\!] \ \rho) \ ([\![s]\!] \ \rho) \qquad \text{by def. 9 (iii)}$$

$$= [\![(\lambda x.\ t\ s)]\!] \ \rho \qquad \text{by def. 9 (ii)}$$

■

Now we can make a last observation, which guarantees that β′-conversion is also complete.

<u>Theorem 17</u> : Let $t \in T$. If t has a normal-form t' then $t \xrightarrow[\beta']{*} t'$.

<u>Proof</u> : Consider t as a term of Church′s λ-calculus and let u be a normal form of t , which is derived from t by outside-in reductions. Any β-reduction during this sequence has a corresponding β' -reduction in a sequence starting also from t . Furthermore, after each β-reduction in the first sequence and β' -reduction in the second sequence both corresponding terms have the same abstract syntax. Hence, the term corresponding to u is in normal-form and was reached from t by β' -reductions.

∎

This concludes our formal treatment of the reduction calculus.

<u>Concluding remarks</u> :

The aim of functional programming is to design a clear system which includes transparent computer architecture, for a neatly defined language, and a profound metatheory to support program-verification.

The BRL is a suggestion for such a language, where a transparent computer architecture already exists and this paper makes the full theory of λ-calculus available for a program verification system.

References

[1] Backus, J. : "Can Programming Be Liberated from the von Neumann Style ?", CACM 21 (8), pp. 613-641, (1978)

[2] Berkling, K. J. : "A symmetric complement to the Lambda calculus", Interner Bericht ISF-76-7, GMD, D-5205 St. Augustin 1, 1976

[3] Berkling, K.J. : "Reduction languages for reduction machines", Interner Bericht ISF-76-8, GMD, D-5205 St. Augustin 1, 1976

[4] De Bruijn, N.G.: "Lambda-calculus notation with nameless dummies, a tool for automatic formula manipulation", Indag. Math. 34

[5] Fehr, E. : "The lambda-semantics of LISP", Schriften zur Informatik und Mathematik, Bericht Nr. 72, RWTH Aachen, Mai 1981

[6] Gordon, M. : "Operational reasoning and denotational semantics" Stanford Artificial Intelligence Laboratory, Memo AIM-264, 1975

[7] Mc Gowan, C.: "The modified SECD-machine" Second ACM Symposium on Theory of Computing, 1970

[8] Hommes, F. : "The internal structure of the reduction machine", Interner Bericht ISF-77-3, GMD, D-5205 St. Augustin 1, 1977

[9] Hommes, F. /Schlütter, H. : " Reduction machine system. User´s guide" GMD-ISF, D-5205 St. Augustin 1, 1979

[10] Kluge, W.E. : "The architecture of a reduction language machine hardware model," Interner Bericht ISF-79-3, GMD, 5205 St. Augustin-1, 1979

[11] Scott, D. : "Continuous lattices", Proc. of Dalhousie Conf., Springer LNM No. 274, pp. 97-134, 1972

[12] Scott, D. : "Data types as lattices", SIAM J. Computing, Vol. 5.3, 1976

[13] Turner, D.A. : "A new Implementation Technique for Applicative Languages", Software-Practice and Experience, Vol. 9, 31-49, (1979)

On the Power of Nondeterminism in Dynamic Logic

Piotr Berman[1], Joseph Y. Halpern[1,2], Jerzy Tiuryn[3]

1. Laboratory for Computer Science, M.I.T., Cambridge, MA02139
2. Aiken Computation Laboratory, Harvard University, Cambridge, MA02138
3. Institute of Mathematics, Warsaw University, Warsaw

1. Introduction

The question of whether nondeterminism supplies more expressive power in First-Order Regular Dynamic Logic (DL) was first raised in [Har]. Research into related problems has yielded both positive and negative results. The answer is affirmative in the quantifier-free case [MW], in the propositional case [HR], and in the case of a first-order language without equality [Hal]. By way of contrast, if r.e. programs are allowed instead of regular programs, deterministic and nondeterministic r.e. DL coincide [MT].

In this paper we extend the techniques of [HR] and [Hal] to show that DL, even with equality in the language, is indeed more expressive than its deterministic counterpart (DDL). We do this by considering the DL formula SEARCH(x,y) which says "y is a descendant of x" when interpreted over treelike structures. We show that for any DDL formula p we can find an infinite binary treelike structure $\mathbf{A_p}$ in which all the programs mentioned in p are equivalent to loop-free programs (cf. Theorem 2). From this we can deduce that p is equivalent to a first-order formula in $\mathbf{A_p}$. However, we can show that SEARCH is not equivalent to a first-order formula in $\mathbf{A_p}$, and hence is not equivalent to p.

The proof involves combinatorial arguments and an analysis of the behavior of multiheaded finite automata operating on finite binary trees, and is quite delicate. This is not too surprising in view of the fact that in any structure with a copy of the integers and a successor (for example, a structure with a unary function f such that for some x, we have x, f(x), f(f(x)), ... all distinct) it is easy to show that deterministic **while**-programs have the power of Turing machines, so DL and DDL are equivalent. The same is also clearly true in any finite domain (where both DL and DDL reduce to first-order logic.)

We give all the basic definitions in section 2 and prove our results in section 3.

2. Basic Definitions

We first give a brief description of the syntax and semantics of DL and DDL. The reader is referred to [Har] for more details.

Syntax: Just as in first-order predicate calculus, we have predicate symbols P, Q, ... and function symbols f, g, ..., each with an associated arity, variables x_0, x_1, ..., and logical symbols $\exists$, $\neg$, and $\vee$. We will always assume that one of the predicate symbols in the language is the binary predicate symbol "=" (equality), which gets its standard interpretation. (Note this was not the case in [Hal].) We use x and y as metavariables ranging over variables. As usual in DL, we do not distinguish between variables and constants. DL also uses a few special symbols, namely :=, ;, *, ∪, ?, and <> (pronounced "diamond").

Terms are formed exactly as in first-order predicate calculus. Formulas and programs are defined inductively:

1. Any formula of first-order predicate calculus with equality is a formula.
2. <variable> := <term> is a (basic) program.
3. If p, q are formulas, and α is a program, then $p \vee q$, $\neg p$, $\exists x p$, and $\langle\alpha\rangle p$ are formulas.
4. If α and β are programs, then $\alpha;\beta$, $\alpha \cup \beta$, and α^* are programs.
5. If p is a quantifier-free formula of predicate calculus, p? is a program.

Semantics: A *state* (A,σ) consists of two parts: A is a *structure* which consists of a domain A and an interpretation of all the function and predicate symbols over this domain, and σ is a *valuation* which assigns values in the domain to all the variables. A^{Var} denotes the set of valuations on the structure A.

For any structure A, we can define ρ_A, a mapping from programs to binary relations on A^{Var} which describes the input-output behavior of programs in structure A, and $\models$, a relation between states and formulas (which defines the states for which the formula is "true"), by induction:

1. For p a formula of first-order predicate calculus with equality, $(A,\sigma) \models p$ is defined as usual.

2. For basic programs of the form $x:=t$, $\rho_A(x:=t) = \{(\sigma,\sigma[x/d]): d \in A \text{ is the value of term t in } (A,\sigma)\}$, where $\sigma[x/d]$ is the valuation such that $\sigma[x/d](y) = \sigma(y)$ if $y \neq x$ and $\sigma[x/d](x) = d$.

3. For programs α, β and formula p

$$\rho_A(\alpha \cup \beta) = \rho_A(\alpha) \cup \rho_A(\beta)$$
$$\rho_A(\alpha;\beta) = \rho_A(\alpha) \circ \rho_A(\beta)$$
$$= \{(\sigma,\sigma'): \exists \sigma'' [(\sigma,\sigma'') \in \rho_A(\alpha) \;\&\; (\sigma'',\sigma') \in \rho_A(\beta)]\}$$
$$\rho_A(p?) = \{(\sigma,\sigma): (A,\sigma) \models p\}.$$
$$\rho_A(\alpha^*) = \bigcup_{n \geq 0} \rho_A(\alpha^n) \quad (\text{where } \alpha^0 = \mathit{true?})$$

4. For formulas p, q and program α

$$(A,\sigma) \models \neg p \text{ iff } (A,\sigma) \not\models p$$
$$(A,\sigma) \models p \vee q \text{ iff } (A,\sigma) \models p \text{ or } (A,\sigma) \models q$$
$$(A,\sigma) \models \exists x p \text{ iff for some } d \in A, (A,\sigma[x/d]) \models p$$
$$(A,\sigma) \models \langle\alpha\rangle p \text{ iff for some } \sigma' \text{ with } (\sigma,\sigma') \in \rho_A(\alpha), (A,\sigma') \models p.$$

A *loop-free* program is a DL program in which the construct * does not appear. We have the following lemma, due to Pratt [Pr].

Lemma 1: Any DL formula involving only loop-free programs is equivalent to a first-order formula.

Proof: It is clearly sufficient to prove the result for formulas of the form $<\alpha>p$, where p is a first-order formula; this can be done by a straightforward induction on the structure of programs. ∎

Nondeterminism occurs in DL through the constructs * and ∪. We can eliminate the nondeterminism by allowing * and ∪ to appear only in the contexts

$$p?;\alpha \cup \neg p?;\beta \quad \text{and} \quad (p?;\alpha)^*;\neg p?,$$

which we abbreviate respectively as **if** p **then** α **else** β **fi** and **while** p **do** α **od**. We leave it to the reader to check that this restriction leaves us with a deterministic set of programs, which we call the **while**-programs. The restriction of DL to formulas only involving **while**-programs is called DDL.

Definition: Let $\alpha^{\leq k}$ be an abbreviation for $\alpha^0 \cup ... \cup \alpha^k$, and let $\alpha^{(k)}$, the kth *approximation of* α, be the program which results by replacing each occurrence of * in α by $\leq k$. It is easy to see that $\alpha^{(k)}$ is loop-free and that for *any* structure A, we have $\rho_A(\alpha) = \cup_k \rho_A(\alpha^{(k)})$.

The following lemma is straightforward to prove:

Lemma 2: If α is equivalent to $\alpha^{(k)}$ in A (i.e. $\rho_A(\alpha) = \rho_A(\alpha^{(k)})$) and B is elementarily equivalent to A, then α is equivalent to $\alpha^{(k)}$ in B.

3. Main Results

Let s, t be unary function symbols, and $\Sigma = \{s,t\}$. We define a sequence of structures $A_1, A_2, ...$ where

$$A_n = \{v \in \Sigma^*: |v| \leq n\} \quad \text{(where } |v| \text{ denotes the length of v as a string in } \Sigma^*)$$

$$s_{A_n}(v) = sv \quad \text{if } |v| < n \qquad t_{A_n}(v) = tv \quad \text{if } |v| < n,$$

$$= v \quad \text{if } |v| = n; \qquad = v \quad \text{if } |v| = n.$$

We assume all other function and predicate symbols have trivial interpretations in A_n (i.e. the function symbols are all interpreted as projection on the first coordinate, while the predicates are all identically true).

We can think of A_n as a full binary tree of depth n, where s means "go left" and t means "go right". Note we are deliberately using s and t here both as functions and elements of the domain. A_2 is shown below:

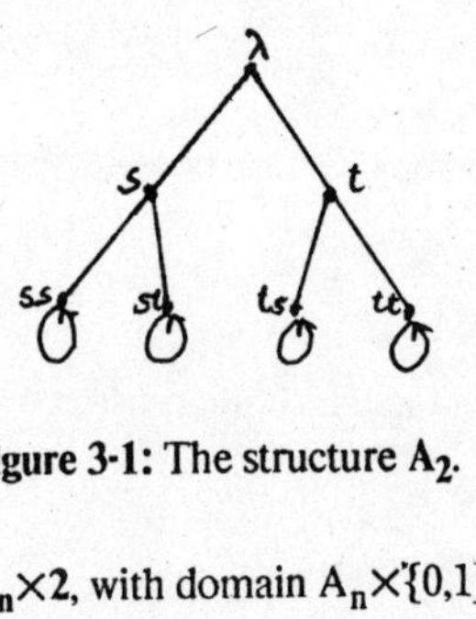

Figure 3-1: The structure A_2.

We will also use auxiliary structures $A_n \times 2$, with domain $A_n \times \{0,1\}$, where

$s_{A_n\times 2}(\langle v,i\rangle) = \langle s_{A_n}(v),i\rangle$ and $t_{A_n\times 2}(\langle v,i\rangle) = \langle t_{A_n}(v),i\rangle$, for $i = 0,1$.

Again all other functions and predicates are trivial. We can view $A_n\times 2$ as a union of two copies of A_n.

We will be interested in the behavior of deterministic flowchart schemes on these structures. We will assume that the only assignment statements which appear in these flowcharts are *basic* assignments of the form $x{:=}y$, $x{:=}s(x)$, or $x{:=}t(x)$, while the only tests are of the form $x{=}y?$, since it is easy to see that any flowchart running over A_n or $A_n\times 2$ can be simulated by one meeting the above restrictions. Since a DDL flowchart can be associated with a deterministic flowchart in an obvious way, our results will apply to DDL programs as well.

Starting in a given state, a flowchart executes a (possibly infinite) sequence of *steps*, each one being a basic assignment or a test. Thus it makes sense to talk about the mth step executed by flowchart α in state (A_n, σ), although we do not give a formal definition here.

We simultaneously define $Val(m,i,\alpha,A,\sigma)$ and $\tau(m,i,\alpha,A,\sigma)$ to be the value (resp. term) computed for the variable x_i on the mth step of the execution of flowchart α in state (A,σ).

$$
\begin{aligned}
Val(0,i,\alpha,A,\sigma) &= \sigma(x_i) \\
Val(m+1,i,\alpha,A,\sigma) &= Val(m,j,\alpha,A,\sigma) && \text{if the } m+1^{th} \text{ step is } x_i{:=}x_j \\
&= s_A(Val(m,i,\alpha,A,\sigma)) && \text{if the } m+1^{th} \text{ step is } x_i{:=}s(x_i) \\
&= t_A(Val(m,i,\alpha,A,\sigma)) && \text{if the } m+1^{th} \text{ step is } x_i{:=}t(x_i) \\
&= Val(m,i,\alpha,A,\sigma) && \text{if the } m+1^{th} \text{ step is a test}
\end{aligned}
$$

To define τ, we use the *symbolic inputs* $z_0,z_1,\ldots$, which act as placeholders for the variables $x_0, x_1, \ldots$

$$
\begin{aligned}
\tau(0,i,\alpha,A,\sigma) &= z_i \\
\tau(m+1,i,\alpha,A,\sigma) &= \tau(m,j,\alpha,A,\sigma) && \text{if the } m+1^{th} \text{ step is } x_i{:=}x_j \\
&= sv && \text{if the } m+1^{th} \text{ step is } x_i{:=}s(x_i),\ v=\tau(m,i,\alpha,A,\sigma), \\
& && \quad \textit{and} \text{ the value of } x_i \text{ changes as a result of this assignment} \\
& && \quad \text{(i.e. if } Val(m+1,i,\alpha,A,\sigma) \neq Val(m,i,\alpha,A,\sigma)) \\
&= tv && \text{if the } m+1^{th} \text{ step is } x_i{:=}t(x_i),\ v=\tau(m,i,\alpha,A,\sigma), \\
& && \quad \text{and } Val(m+1,i,\alpha,A,\sigma) \neq Val(m,i,\alpha,A,\sigma) \\
&= \tau(m,i,\alpha,A,\sigma) && \text{otherwise}
\end{aligned}
$$

Note that if $\tau(m,i,\alpha,A_n,\sigma) = vz_j$, where $v \in \Sigma^*$ and z_j is a symbolic input, then $Val(m,i,\alpha,A_n,\sigma) = v\sigma(x_j)$.

Definitions: We define $\mathcal{T}(\alpha,A,\sigma)$, $\mathcal{T}(\alpha,A,Z)$, $\mathcal{T}(\alpha,A)$, which are respectively, the set of nontrivial terms generated by α in structure A in a single valuation σ, over a set of valuations $Z \subseteq A^{Var}$, and over all the valuations in A^{Var} as follows:

$$
\begin{aligned}
\mathcal{T}(\alpha,A,\sigma) &= \bigcup_{m,i} \{\tau(m,i,\alpha,A,\sigma)\} - \{z_1,z_2,\ldots\}, \\
\mathcal{T}(\alpha,A,Z) &= \bigcup_{\sigma\in Z} \mathcal{T}(\alpha,A,\sigma), \text{ for } Z \subseteq A^{Var}, \\
\mathcal{T}(\alpha,A) &= \mathcal{T}(\alpha,A,A^{Var}). \ \blacksquare
\end{aligned}
$$

We can think of a flowchart α operating on A as a multiheaded finite automaton; each head corresponds to one of the variables mentioned in α. The initial location of the head corresponding to x_i is given by $\sigma(x_i)$; in general its location at time m is given by Val(m,i,α,A,σ). The next theorem essentially says that a deterministic multiheaded finite automaton cannot examine all the nodes of a binary tree.

Theorem 1: For every flowchart α there is a polynomial p_α such that for all n,

$$|\mathcal{T}(\alpha,A_n)| \leq p_\alpha(n).$$

Proof: The strategy of the proof is to show we can simulate α by a flowchart α' such that all variables in α' which are involved in tests are restricted to the leftmost branch of the tree. It is then relatively straightforward to show that flowcharts such as α' satisfy the theorem.

To make these ideas precise we need the following definitions:

Definitions: Let Var(α) be the set of variables mentioned in the flowchart α. Let G_α, the *general variables* of α, be the smallest subset of Var(α) satisfying

(a) If there is an instruction $x:=t(x)$ in the flowchart α then $x \in G_\alpha$.
(b) If $x \in G_\alpha$ and there is an instruction in α of the form $(x=y)?$, $(y=x)?$, or $y:=x$, then $y \in G_\alpha$.

Note that if G_1 and G_2 both satisfy (a) and (b) then so does $G_1 \cap G_2$; thus G_α is well defined.

The *counters* of α are the variables in the set $C_\alpha = \mathrm{Var}(\alpha) - G_\alpha$.

We will be particularly interested in valuations in which the counters are restricted to the leftmost branch of the tree. Thus we define σ to be a *proper valuation* for flowchart α in A_n (resp. $A_n \times 2$) if

$$\forall x \in C_\alpha\ \sigma(x) \in \{s^k : k \leq n\} \quad (\text{resp. } \sigma(x) \in \{\langle s^k,0\rangle : k \leq n\}).$$

Finally we define

$\mathrm{Proper}(\alpha,A) = \{\sigma \in A^{\mathrm{Var}} : \sigma \text{ is a proper valuation for } \alpha\}$, and
$\mathcal{T}_c(\alpha,A) = \mathcal{T}(\alpha,A,\mathrm{Proper}(\alpha,A))$. ∎

With these definitions in hand we can state three lemmas from which the proof of Theorem 1 follows immediately:

Lemma 3: For any flowchart α there is a flowchart α' such that

$$\forall n\ \mathcal{T}(\alpha,A_n) \subseteq \mathcal{T}_c(\alpha',A_n).$$

Lemma 4: For every flowchart α there is a flowchart α' such that everv test of α' involves only counters and

$$\forall n\ \mathcal{T}_c(\alpha,A_n) \subseteq \mathcal{T}_c(\alpha',A_n).$$

Lemma 5: If every test of flowchart α involves only counters, there is a polynomial p_α such that

$$\forall n \ |\mathcal{T}_c(\alpha,A_n)| \leq p_\alpha(n).$$

Lemma 3 is straightforward; we can simply pad α to an equivalent α' such that $C_{\alpha'} = \emptyset$. (For example, if $Var(\alpha) \subseteq \{x_1,...,x_k\}$, we can simply prefix α by **if** $x_1=x_1$ **then** $x_1:=x_1$ **else** $x_1:=t(x_1);...;x_k:=t(x_k)$ **fi**.) Lemma 5 is similar to [Hal, Lemma 3] and is proved in Appendix 1; Lemma 4 is proved in Appendix 2. ∎

For $n > 0$ and $w \in \Sigma^n$, let $A_{n,w}$ be the infinite treelike structure shown below, consisting of copies of A_n attached at w:

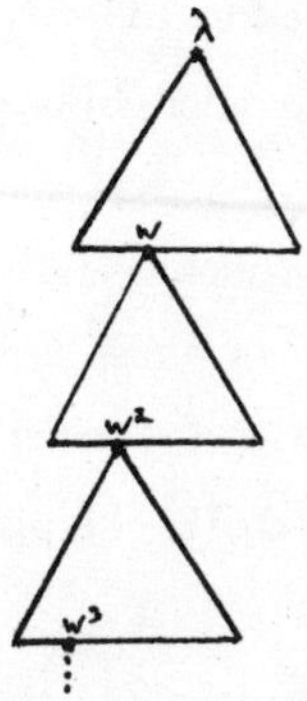

Figure 3-2: The structure $A_{n,w}$.

More precisely, if $n > 0$ and $|w|=n$, define $A_{n,w}$ to be the structure with

$$A_{n,w} = \{vw^m \in \Sigma^*: m \geq 0, |v| \leq n\},$$

$$s_{A_{n,w}}(v) = sv \quad \text{if } sv \in A_{n,w} \qquad t_{A_{n,w}}(v) = tv \quad \text{if } tv \in A_{n,w}$$
$$= v \quad \text{otherwise} \qquad\qquad = v \quad \text{otherwise}$$

and all other functions and predicates trivial.

Theorem 2: For every finite set of flowcharts $\{\alpha_1,...,\alpha_k\}$ there exist $n > 0$, $w \in \Sigma^n$ such that for some constant c, every halting computation of α_i in $A_{n,w}$ has at most c steps for $i = 1,...,k$.

The existence of suitable n and w will be shown by a counting argument based on Theorem 1. The following lemma provides a basis for this counting.

Lemma 6: For every flowchart α there is another flowchart α' such that if $w \in \Sigma^n$ and $wz_1 \notin \mathcal{T}(\alpha',A_n)$ then there is a constant c such that every halting computation of α in $A_{n,w}$ has at most c steps.

Proof: It is convenient to view the set $A_{n,w}$ as a union of *blocks*, $B_1, B_2,...$, where $B_i = \{vw^i: |v| \leq n\}$. Each B_i is essentially a copy of A_n. For a flowchart α and a valuation $\sigma \in A_{n,w}^{Var}$, we say that a block B_i is *accessible* with respect to σ if for some $x \in Var(\alpha)$, we have $\sigma(x) \in B_i \cup B_{i-1}$. A block which is not accessible is said to be *remote.*

The program α' simulates the behavior of α as long as no value of a variable in Var(α) is in a remote block. More precisely, we will have a family of mappings, $f_{n,w}$: $A_{n,w}^{Var} \to A_n^{Var}$. If x $\in$ Var(α) and the value of x at some step of the computation of α in state $(A_{n,w},\sigma)$ is vw^m, $|v| \leq n$, then the value of x at the corresponding step in the computation of α' in state $(A_n, f_{n,w}(\sigma))$ is v. In particular we define $f_{n,w}(\sigma)$ on Var(α) so that this is true at the beginning of the computation. The simulation halts if the computation of α enters a remote block (i.e. we halt at the mth step of the simulation if for some x$\in$Var(α), Val(m,i,α,$A_{n,w}$,σ) is in some remote block).

In order to simulate in A_n the computation performed by α in the infinite structure $A_{n,w}$, we use $f_{n,w}(\sigma)$ to encode some information about the relative positions of blocks which are accessible with respect to σ; namely, given two accessible blocks B_i and B_j, we encode whether or not $i=j+1$. Since the number of accessible blocks is at most 2|Var(α)|, this information is easy to encode. At every step of the simulation and for every x$\in$Var(α) we will also keep track of which block contains the value of x. Finally, we can assume without loss of generality that x_1, $x_2 \notin$ Var(α) (otherwise just rename variables) and use these variables to store the values λ and w, respectively (i.e. we will set $f_{n,w}(\sigma)(x_1) = \lambda$, $f_{n,w}(\sigma)(x_2) = w$, and ensure that α' never changes these values.)

The rules of the simulation are simple. Whenever we encounter a test (x=y)?, we first check that x and y currently have values in the same block according to our encoding. If they do, we perform the test. Otherwise we just take the result of the test to be *false*. After every assignment of the form x:=s(x) or x:=t(x) we must check if the value of x is w (by testing if $x=x_2$). If not, we just continue the simulation. If x=w and the value of x has just entered a remote block (according to the code), we halt the simulation; otherwise we set x to λ and continue the simulation. Of course, after each assignment statement we update the encoding if necessary.

It is easy to see that if α enters a remote block during its computation in state $(A_{n,w},\sigma)$, then α' generates the term wz_1 when run in state $(A_n, f_{n,w}(\sigma))$. This corresponds to "traversing" an accessible block. Now suppose $wz_1 \notin \mathcal{T}(\alpha', A_n)$. Then for all $\sigma \in A_{n,w}^{Var}$, no computation of α can ever enter a remote block. Since for any valuation there are at most 2|Var(α)| accessible blocks, and each block has 2^{n+1}-1 elements, it follows that the variables in Var(α) can take on at most $d = 2^{n+2}|Var(\alpha)|$ distinct values. If α has d' instructions, it is easy to see that every halting computation of α has at most $c = d^{Var(\alpha)}d'$ steps. ∎

Returning to the proof of Theorem 2, given flowcharts $\{\alpha_1,..., \alpha_k\}$, find the corresponding $\{\alpha_1',...,\alpha_k'\}$ by Lemma 6. From Theorem 1 it follows that there are polynomials $p_1,...,p_k$ such that for all n,

$|\mathcal{T}(\alpha_i', A_n)| \leq p_i(n)$, i = 1,...,k.

Thus by choosing n sufficiently large (i.e. such that $2^n > p_1(n)+...+p_k(n)$), we can find $w \in \Sigma^*$ such that $wz_1 \notin \cup_i \mathcal{T}(\alpha_i', A_n)$. By Lemma 6 again, it follows that Theorem 2 holds for this choice of n and w. ∎

Corollary: For any finite set of **while**-programs $\{\alpha_1,..., \alpha_k\}$ there exist $n > 0$, $w \in \Sigma^n$, and $c > 0$ such that $\alpha_i^{(c)}$ is equivalent to α in $A_{n,w}$ for $i = 1,...,k$.

Proof: The **while**-programs $\alpha_1,...,\alpha_k$ can clearly be simulated by flowcharts $\beta_1,..,\beta_k$; note that since we are restricting our attention to structures $A_{n,w}$ we can replace all the instructions in the **while**-programs which are inconsistent with the signature <s,t,=> by trivial instructions of the form x=x? or x:=y. We can now apply Theorem 2 to $\beta_1,...,\beta_k$ to find an appropriate n, w, and c. Because β_i simulates α_i in $A_{n,w}$, it follows that if a computation of the program α_i in $A_{n,w}$ does not diverge, then no **while**-loop can be executed more than c times. Thus $\alpha_i^{(c)}$ is equivalent to α in $A_{n,w}$ for $i = 1,...,k$. ∎

Now we are ready to prove our main result. In [Hal] it was shown that the formula

$$<(x:=s(x) \cup x:=t(x))^*>P(x)$$

is not expressible in DDL without equality. Here we show that the formula

$$\text{SEARCH}(x,y) = <(x=s(x) \cup x:=t(x))^*> (x=y),$$

is not expressible in DDL, even with equality. SEARCH(x,y) intuitively says that we can reach y starting from x by applying s and t (nondeterministically), and thus, in the case of treelike structures, x is a descendant of y.

Theorem 3: DDL is less expressive than DL. In particular, the formula SEARCH(x,y) is not equivalent to any DDL formula.

Proof: Suppose SEARCH(x,y) were equivalent to some DDL formula p. Let $\alpha_1,...,\alpha_k$ be the **while**-programs which appear in p. By the Corollary to Theorem 2, there exists $n > 0$ and $w \in \Sigma^n$ such that $\alpha_i^{(c)}$ is equivalent to α in $A_{n,w}$ for $i = 1,...,k$. Choose **B** elementarily equivalent to $A_{n,w}$, but with B uncountable. (Such a **B** exists by the upward Löwenheim-Skolem Theorem; cf. [En].) By Lemma 2, $\alpha_1,...,\alpha_k$ are still equivalent to $\alpha_1^{(c)},...,\alpha_k^{(c)}$ respectively in **B**. Let p' be the formula that results by replacing each α_i by $\alpha_i^{(c)}$. Thus in both $A_{n,w}$ and **B** we have $p \equiv p'$. But by Lemma 1 (since $\alpha_i^{(c)}$ is loop-free), there is a first-order formula p" with $p' \equiv p''$.

Now $A_{n,w} \models \exists x \forall y \text{SEARCH}(x,y)$ (take x to be the root of the tree), so $A_{n,w} \models \exists x \forall y p''$. But $A_{n,w}$ and **B** are elementarily equivalent, so $\mathbf{B} \models \exists x \forall y p''$, and hence $\mathbf{B} \models \exists x \forall y \text{SEARCH}(x,y)$. This is a contradiction, since **B** is uncountable. ∎

Appendix 1

Proof of Lemma 5: Let $U = \{\sigma \in \text{Proper}(\alpha,A_n): \sigma(x) = \lambda \text{ for } x \notin C_\alpha\}$. Then we claim that

$$\mathcal{T}_c(\alpha,A_n) = \mathcal{T}(\alpha,A_n,U)$$

Since $U \subseteq \text{Proper}(\alpha,A_n)$, we clearly have $\mathcal{T}_c(\alpha,A_n) \stackrel{\text{def}}{=} \mathcal{T}(\alpha,A_n,\text{Proper}(\alpha,A_n)) \supseteq \mathcal{T}(\alpha,A_n,U)$. For the opposite inclusion, suppose $\sigma_1 \in \text{Proper}(\alpha,A_n)$. Choose $\sigma_2 \in U$ such that for all $x \in C_\alpha$, $\sigma_1(x) = \sigma_2(x)$. Now we claim $\mathcal{T}(\alpha,A_n,\sigma_1) \subseteq \mathcal{T}(\alpha,A_n,\sigma_2)$. To see this, note that the sequence of instructions executed by α depends only on variables involved in tests, and hence by hypothesis only on members of C_α. Thus the same sequence of instructions gets executed by α in both (A_n,σ_1) and (A_n,σ_2). But the initial value of a variable in valuation σ_2 is a prefix of its value in σ_1, so in general more terms will be generated by α in state (A_n,σ_2). For example, if $x_i \in G_\alpha$ and $\sigma_1(x_i) = st$, then in state (A_n,σ_1) we will generate exactly those terms of the form vz_i with $|v| \leq n\text{-}2$ which were generated in (A_n,σ_2). This proves the desired inclusion.

Let $|C_\alpha| = h$. Then $|U| = (n+1)^h$, so it is enough to show that there exists a polynomial p'_α such that for any valuation $\sigma \in U$

$$|\mathcal{T}(\alpha,A_n,\sigma)| \leq p'_\alpha(n).$$

Given a valuation in U, we can view α as a finite state machine whose current state depends on the values of the counters (since these are the only variables involved in tests) and the instruction currently being executed. Hence either the computation loops or halts after at most $c(n+1)^h$ steps, where c is the number of instructions in α. If it halts, then our problem is trivial. If it loops, each cycle in the loop consists of at most $c(n+1)^h$ steps. Thus it certainly suffices to show that only a linear number of cycles can generate new terms.

Consider the sequence of assignments performed in a cycle as a straightline program β. On the structure $A_\omega = \Sigma^*$, β is equivalent to the program $x_1{:=}v_1x_{i_1}; x_2{:=}v_2x_{i_2}; \ldots ; x_k{:=}v_kx_{i_k}$, where $\{v_1,\ldots,v_k\} \subseteq \Sigma^*$. Define $f: \{1,\ldots,k\} \rightarrow \{1,\ldots,k\}$ via $f(j) = i_j$. Assume $i_1,\ldots,i_k$ are all distinct. (The general case is similar; we omit it here.) Since f is simply a permutation on k elements, it follows that for all j we have $f^{k!}(j) = j$. Thus $\beta^{k!}$ is equivalent to $x_1{:=}w_1x_1; \ldots ; x_k{:=}w_kx_k$, where $\{w_1,\ldots,w_k\} \subseteq \{v_1,\ldots,v_k\}^{k!}$. If $w_i \neq \lambda$, then n executions of $\beta^{k!}$ will yield a term on x_i longer than n. Thus in structure A_n, β will stop generating new terms after k!n cycles.

These arguments show we can take $p'_\alpha(n) \leq ck!(n+1)^{h+1}$, and $p_\alpha(n) \leq ck!(n+1)^{2h+1}$. ∎

Appendix 2

Proof of Lemma 4: We would like to simulate the computation of a flowchart which tests general variables by another flowchart whose tests involve only counters. We will do this by induction on the *activity of the flowchart,* which essentially corresponds to the number of general variables which are involved in tests.

Definitions:

The *offspring* of symbolic input z_i in the mth step of computation of α in state (A,σ) are the values derived from z_i at this step:

$$Off(m,\alpha,A,\sigma,z_i) = \{Val(m,j,\alpha,A,\sigma) : \tau(m,j,\alpha,A,\sigma) = vz_i\}$$

For $U \subseteq \{z_1,z_2,...\}$ we define

$$Off(m,\alpha,A,\sigma,U) = \bigcup_{z \in U} Off(m,\alpha,A,\sigma,z)$$

Symbolic input z_i is active in the computation of α in state (A,σ) iff $x_i \in G_\alpha$ and some offspring of z_i is involved in a test; that is

$$\exists m,h,j \text{ (the } m^{th} \text{ step of } \alpha \text{ in } (A,\sigma) \text{ is } x_h=x_j? \text{ or } x_j=x_h?, \text{ and } Val(m,h,\alpha,A,\sigma) \in Off(m,\alpha,A,\sigma,z_i)).$$

Value $a \in A$ *is active in the* m^{th} *step* of the computation of α in (A,σ) if it is the offspring of some active symbolic input; i.e. $a \in Off(m,\alpha,A,\sigma,z_i)$, where z_i is active. We then define

$$Act(m,\alpha,A,\sigma) = \{a \in A: a \text{ is active in the } m^{th} \text{ step of computation of } \alpha \text{ in } (A,\sigma)\},$$

$$Act(\alpha) = \max_m \max_n \max_\sigma |Act(m,\alpha,A_n,\sigma)|.$$

Note that if $Act(\alpha) = 0$ then only counters of α are involved in tests.

Finally we define $\mathcal{T}_c(\alpha,A,k)$, the *terms of activity k generated by α over the structure* A by

$$\mathcal{T}_c(\alpha,A,k) = \{\tau(m,i,\alpha,A,\sigma) \in \mathcal{T}_c(\alpha,A): \forall m' \le m\ (|Act(m',\alpha,A,\sigma)| \le k)\}. \quad \blacksquare$$

The rest of our proof will be devoted to proving the following claim:

$$(*) \quad \forall i\ \forall \alpha\ \exists \alpha_i\ \forall n\ [Act(\alpha_i) = 0 \text{ and } \mathcal{T}_c(\alpha,A_n \times 2,i) \subseteq \mathcal{T}_c(\alpha_i,A_n)]$$

Since for any flowchart β and for all n we have $\mathcal{T}_c(\beta,A_n) \subseteq \mathcal{T}_c(\beta,A_n \times 2) \subseteq \mathcal{T}_c(\beta,A_n \times 2,|G_\beta|)$, it follows that (*) is sufficient to prove Lemma 5: we simply take α' to be $\alpha_{|G_\alpha|}$.

We prove (*) by induction on i.

Base case: Let α_0 be α with all tests involving general variables removed. To see this works, define $\pi : A_n \times 2 \to A_n$ via $\pi(\langle v,i \rangle) = v$. If m is the first step of the computation in state $(A_n \times 2,\sigma)$ such that a test involving a general variable is performed, then for $m' < m$ and any j

$$\pi(Val(m',j,\alpha,A_n \times 2,\sigma)) = Val(m',j,\alpha,A_n,\pi \circ \sigma) = Val(m',j,\alpha_0,A_n,\pi \circ \sigma), \quad \text{and}$$

$$\mathcal{T}(m',j,\alpha,A_n \times 2,\sigma) = \mathcal{T}(m',j,\alpha,A_n,\pi \circ \sigma) = \mathcal{T}(m',j,\alpha_0,A_n,\pi \circ \sigma).$$

Hence $\mathcal{T}_c(\alpha,A_n \times 2,0) \subseteq \mathcal{T}_c(\alpha_0,A)$.

Inductive step: Now we assume that (*) is true for k. We make the following

Definitions:

$Act_0(m,\alpha,A_n\times 2,\sigma) = Act(m,\alpha,A_n\times 2,\sigma) \cap (A_n\times\{0\})$
$Act_1(m,\alpha,A_n\times 2,\sigma) = Act(m,\alpha,A_n\times 2,\sigma) \cap (A_n\times\{1\})$
The computation of α in state $(A_n\times 2,\sigma)$ is *within the (k,i) limitation up to the mth step* iff
$\forall m' \leq m\ (|Act(m',\alpha,A_n\times 2,\sigma| \leq k+1, |Act_0(m',\alpha,A_n\times 2,\sigma)| \leq k, |Act_1(m',\alpha,A_n\times 2,\sigma)| \leq i)$
$\mathcal{T}(\alpha,A_n\times 2,\sigma,k,i) = \{\tau(m,h,\alpha,A_n\times 2,\sigma) \in \mathcal{T}_c(\alpha,A_n\times 2)$: the computation of α in $A_n\times 2,\sigma)$ is within the (k,i) limitation up to the mth step$\}$
$\mathcal{T}_c(\alpha,A_n\times 2,k,i) = \cup(\{\tau(m,h,\alpha,A_n\times 2,\sigma) \in \mathcal{T}(\alpha,A_n\times 2,\sigma,k,i): \sigma\in Proper(\alpha,A_n\times 2)\})$ ∎

We will prove

(**) $\forall i\ \forall\alpha\ \exists\alpha_i\ \forall n\quad \mathcal{T}_c(\alpha,A_n\times 2,k,i) \subseteq \mathcal{T}_c(\alpha_i,A_n\times 2,k,0)$.

This suffices to complete the proof as can be seen from the following inclusions:

$\mathcal{T}_c(\alpha,A_n\times 2,k+1) \subseteq \mathcal{T}_c(\alpha,A_n\times 2,k,k+1)$ (see below for details)
$\subseteq \mathcal{T}_c(\alpha_{k+1},A_n\times 2,k,0)$ (by (**))
$\subseteq \mathcal{T}_c(\alpha_{k+1},A_n,k)$ (by definition)
$\subseteq \mathcal{T}_c(\beta,A_n)$, for some β with $Act(\beta)=0$ (by (*))

The first inclusion (which is in fact an equality) can be shown as follows:

Suppose $\tau(m,i,\alpha,A_n\times 2,\sigma) \in \mathcal{T}_c(\alpha,A_n\times 2,k+1)$. We want to show $\tau(m,i,\alpha,A_n\times 2,\sigma) \in \mathcal{T}_c(\alpha,A_n\times 2,k,k+1)$. If $|Act_0(m',\alpha,A_n\times 2,\sigma)| \leq k$ for all $m'\leq m$, we are done. And if $|Act_1(m',\alpha,A_n\times 2,\sigma)| \leq k$ for all $m'\leq m$, let κ be the automorphism on $A_n\times 2$ defined by $\kappa(\langle v,i\rangle) = \langle v,1-i\rangle$. Then it is easy to check that

$$\tau(m,i,\alpha,A_n\times 2,\sigma) = \tau(m,i,\alpha,A_n\times 2,\kappa\circ\sigma) \in \mathcal{T}_c(\alpha,A_n\times 2,k,k+1),$$

since for all $m'\leq m$, $|Act_0(m',\alpha,A_n\times 2,\kappa\circ\sigma)| = |Act_1(m',\alpha,A_n\times 2,\sigma)| \leq k$. Finally, note that one of these two cases must obtain since if $|Act_j(m',\alpha,A_n\times 2,\sigma)| = k+1$, then for all $m''\geq m'$, $|Act_j(m'',\alpha,A_n\times 2,\sigma)| = 0$.

To prove (**) we again proceed by induction on i.

Base case: Given α, we want to find α_1 such that for all n,

$\mathcal{T}_c(\alpha,A_n,k,1) \subseteq \mathcal{T}_c(\alpha_1,A_n,k,0)$.

We will in fact construct α_1 and a family of mappings

$f_n : Proper(\alpha,A_n\times 2) \rightarrow Proper(\alpha_1,A_n\times 2)$

such that α_1 in state $(A_n\times 2,f_n(\sigma))$ will simulate the computation of α in $(A_n\times 2,\sigma)$ up to the first step m for which $Act_1(m,\alpha,A_n\times 2,\sigma)$ has more than one element. The flowchart α_1 will have the same set of general variables as α but it will use extra counters in such a way as to ensure that it never has to test any values from $A_n\times\{1\}$. In particular we will have

$\mathcal{T}(\alpha,A_n\times 2,\sigma,k,1) \subseteq \mathcal{T}(\alpha_1,A_n\times 2,f_n(\sigma),k,0)$.

The mapping f_n is defined as follows. For all $x \in Var(\alpha)$, $\sigma(x) = f_n(\sigma)(x)$. Moreover, α_1 uses additional counters (not used by α) to encode information about α. The first thing we encode is whether the number of initial active values (of α in state $(A_n \times 2,\sigma)$) which are in $A_n \times \{1\}$ is zero, one, or greater than one. (That is, we choose some $x \notin Var(\alpha)$ and set $f_n(\sigma)(x)$ to λ, s, or ss, depending on which situation holds.) If it is one, we use additional counters to encode the length of the (first component of the) active value, and the names of the variables which initially have this value.

The flowchart α_1 simply simulates the instructions of α one by one, updating the encoding after each of them and halting when the code indicates that there is more than one value in $A_n \times \{1\}$. The crucial point is that α_1 can do the simulation without ever performing a test involving a value from $A_n \times \{1\}$. If it encounters such a test, it assumes the result to be *true* if both variables involved are in $A_n \times \{1\}$ and *false* if only one of them is. This works because when α_1 runs in state $(A_n \times 2, f_n(\sigma))$, then there is at most one active value in $A_n \times \{1\}$ throughout its computation. Note that the number of such values can increase only after an an assignment of the form $x:=s(x)$ or $x:=t(x)$, and that only if both x and another variable y have the same active value in $A_n \times \{1\}$, and the length of that value is less than n; thus the code can be updated easily. This completes the proof of the base case.

Inductive Step: We will now assume (*) for k and (**) for i to prove

(***) $\forall \alpha\ \exists \alpha_{i+1}\ \forall n\ \ \mathcal{T}_c(\alpha, A_n \times 2, k, i+1) \subseteq \mathcal{T}_c(\alpha_{i+1}, A_n \times 2, k, 0)$.

We use a simulation similar to that in the base case. The flowchart α_{i+1} will use all the variables in $Var(\alpha)$ and some extra counters. Again we will have functions f_n encoding information about the general variables of α on the counters so that α_{i+1} will be able to perform tests on the counters instead of performing them on the general variables.

However, the information to be encoded is much more complex than in the base case, since there is more that one active value in $A_n \times \{1\}$. Nevertheless, we will be able to encode (and keep track of) the relationships between these values because, as we shall show, the number of different relationships we can encounter is polynomial. The following claim is a precise formulation of the last statement.

Definition: For a flowchart β, $V_{\beta,n} = \{v: \exists z(vz \in \mathcal{T}_c(\beta, A_n)\}$.

Claim: For every flowchart α, there is a flowchart β such that $Act(\beta)=0$ and for all n, m, σ, if the mth step of the computation of α in $(A_n \times 2,\sigma)$ is within the (k,i) limitation, then either

(a) $\forall a \in Act_1(m,\alpha,A_n \times 2,\sigma)\ \exists \langle v,1\rangle \in Act_1(0,\alpha,A_n \times 2,\sigma)\ \exists b \in V_{\beta,n}\ \ a=\langle bv,1\rangle$, or
(b) $\exists \langle v,1\rangle\ \forall a \in Act_1(m,\alpha,A_n \times 2,\sigma) \exists b_1,\ldots,b_{i+2} \in V_{\beta,n}\ \ a=\langle b_1 \ldots b_{i+2} v,1\rangle$.

We can use the flowchart β provided by the claim to encode the relationships between the values generated by α. By Lemma 5, $|\mathcal{T}_c(\beta,A_n)| \leq p_\beta(n)$. Moreover, the proof in Appendix 1 shows that every term in $\mathcal{T}_c(\beta,A_n)$ can be written as $\tau(m,h,\beta,A_n,\sigma)$, where $m \leq p_\beta(n)$ and $\sigma(x)=\lambda$ for $x \notin C_\beta$. Thus we can encode a term in $\mathcal{T}_c(\beta,A_n)$ by a tuple (m,h,σ) using only a bounded number of counters. (Note the only information we need to encode about σ is the values it gives to variables in C_β, which we can just copy into some of the additional counters.) A word $b \in V_{\beta,n}$ is encoded by the corresponding term from $\mathcal{T}_c(\beta,A_n)$; a string of the form $b_1b_2...b_{i+2}$ is encoded via the corresponding sequence of terms.

Because our encoding is so natural, it is not hard to write a subroutine COMP which, given any two pairs of encodings will decide if they represent the same term, and another subroutine UPDA to update encodings. Using these subroutines we can construct the flowchart α_{i+1} required for (***). We leave the proof of the claim and the construction α_{i+1} to the full paper.

Acknowledgments: We would like to thank Albert Meyer for many valuable discussions, and helpful comments on previous drafts of this paper. This research was supported in part by NSF Grant MCS80-10707. The second author was also partially supported by a grant from the National Science and Engineering Research Council of Canada.

References

[En] Enderton, H. B. *A Mathematical Introduction to Logic.* Academic Press, 1972.

[HR] J. Y. Halpern and J. Reif, The propositional dynamic logic of deterministic, well-structured programs, *in* "Proc. of the 22nd FOCS", October, 1981, pp. 322-334. A revised version appears as MIT/LCS/TM-198, 1981; to appear in *Theoretical Computer Science.*

[Hal] J. Y. Halpern, On the expressive power of dynamic logic, II, MIT/LCS/TM-204.

[Har] D. Harel, *First-Order Dynamic Logic,* Lecture Notes in Computer Science, 68, Springer-Verlag, N.Y., 1979.

[MT] A. R. Meyer and J. Tiuryn, A note on equivalences among logics of programs, to appear *in* "Proceedings of the IBM Conference on Logics of Programs", (ed. D. Kozen), Lecture Notes in Computer Science series (1982).

[MW] A. R. Meyer and K. Winklmann, On the expressive power of dynamic logic, *in* "Proc. of the 11th STOC", May, 1979, pp. 167-175. A revised version appears as MIT/LCS/TM-157, February, 1980.

[Pr] V. R. Pratt, Semantical considerations of Floyd-Hoare logic. *in* "Proc. of the 17th FOCS", October, 1976, pp. 109-121.

EQUIVALENCE AND MEMBERSHIP PROBLEMS FOR REGULAR TRACE LANGUAGES

A. Bertoni°^ - G. Mauri°* - N. Sabadini°

°) Istituto di Cibernetica - Università di Milano

^) Istituto di Matematica - Università della Calabria

*) Istituto di Matematica - Università di Udine

1. INTRODUCTION

Trace languages were introduced by Mazurkiewicz [8] as a tool for describing the behaviour of concurrent program schemes, at the same abstraction level as usual languages describe the behaviour of sequential program schemes. In the latter case, a program scheme is unfolded into a set of words (a language), everyone of which is a linearly ordered set of symbols occurrences, representing occurrences of actions (events) in the program scheme.

In the concurrent case, imposing a linear (temporal) ordering on occurrences of actions may be an arbitrary restriction: in fact, two concurrent actions can take place in any order, or even at the same time. Hence, a partial ordering suits better our purposes: roughly speaking, a trace may be defined as a partially ordered set of symbols occurrences.

From an algebraic point of view, a trace is an element of a free partially commutative monoid (f.p.c.m.) [1], representing the set of all the "sequential" executions of the actions in the trace that are compatible with the concurrency structure. Such a definition provides us with an algebra of traces similar to that of strings, and allows to extend the formal language theory to the case of trace languages: in particular, a Chomsky-like classification for trace languages may be given [10].

An extensive analysis of regular trace languages has been carried out by Szijárto [10], E. Knuth [6] and Bertoni, Mauri and Sabadini [1], [2]. More precisely, in [6] the relations between regular trace languages and Petri nets are investigated, while in [10] a careful analysis of algebraic and closure properties of regular trace languages is carried out; finally, in [2], after defining some interesting subclasses of regular trace languages, among which recognizable and deterministic ones, it is shown that an analogous of Kleene's theorem does not hold for regular trace languages; more precisely, it can be shown that regular trace languages extend the notion of languages recognizable by k-tape non deterministic automata. Furthermore, some results on asymptotic densities for such subclasses have been given.

In this paper, we are interested in the recursive decidability and in the computational complexity of the classical membership and equivalence problems for regular trace languages. We will show that the membership problem for regular trace languages is a polynomial one, while the uniform membership problem is NP-complete.

As far as the equivalence problem is concerned, we will give an undecidability result for the general case, while for the particular case where the concurrency relation is transitive, it turns out that the equivalence can be decided.

2. TRACE LANGUAGES

In this section, the basic definitions and facts about trace languages and the algebraic structure supporting them, i.e. free partially commutative monoids, will be recalled. In the following, the reader will be supposed to be acquainted with the standard notions of automata and language theory (as exposed for example in [5]). Here, we will only recall the definition of shuffle product between languages.

Def.2.1 - Let Σ be a finite alphabet; the <u>shuffle product</u> $\|$ between two languages $L_1, L_2 \subseteq \Sigma^*$ is recursively defined by:

a) $L \| \emptyset = \emptyset \| L = \emptyset$

b) $L \| \{\varepsilon\} = \{\varepsilon\} \| L = L$, being ε the empty word;

c) $\{aw\} \| \{bu\} = (\{a\}.(\{w\} \| \{bu\})) \cup (\{b\}.(\{aw\} \| \{u\}))$, for $a,b \in \Sigma$ and $u,w \in \Sigma^*$

d) $(L_1 \cup L_2) \| L_3 = ((L_1 \| L_3) \cup (L_2 \| L_3))$ and $L_1 \| (L_2 \cup L_3) = ((L_1 \| L_2) \cup (L_1 \| L_3))$

First of all, taking into account the characterization of the concurrency, or independency, relation among actions given by Petri [9], we can define:

Def.2.2 - A <u>concurrent alphabet</u> is a pair $<\Sigma,C>$, where:

a) $\Sigma = \{\sigma_1, \sigma_2, \ldots, \sigma_n\}$ is a finite alphabet;

b) $C \subseteq \Sigma \times \Sigma$ is a symmetric and irreflexive relation, the concurrency relation.

Now, the following definition allows us to consider as being equivalent sequences of actions that differ only for the order in which adjacent concurrent actions are executed.

Def.2.3 - The <u>free partially commutative monoid</u> (f.p.c.m.) generated by a given concurrent alphabet $<\Sigma,C>$ is the quotient structure $F(\Sigma,C) = \Sigma^*/\equiv_C$, where $\equiv_C$ is the least congruence on Σ^* such that $C \subseteq \equiv_C$.

As usual, the congruence class of the word $w \in \Sigma^*$ is denoted by $[w]_C$, the composition on $F(\Sigma,C)$ is defined by $[w]_C \cdot [v]_C = [w.v]_C$ and the identity is the class $[\varepsilon]_C = \{\varepsilon\}$, being ε the empty string.

Def.2.4 - A <u>trace</u> on a concurrent alphabet $<\Sigma,C>$ is any element $t \in F(\Sigma,C)$; a <u>trace language</u> is any subset $T \subseteq F(\Sigma,C)$.

Example - Let $\Sigma = \{a,b,c,d,e\}$ and $C = \{\{a,b\},\{b,d\},\{e,d\}\}$. An example of trace is the set:

$$t = \{abcdeab, abcdeba, abcedab, abcedba, abcebda, bacdeab, bacdeba, bacedab, bacedba, bacebda\}$$

A trace t may be represented in a synthetic way as a graph, corresponding to a partial ordering relation between the symbols appearing in any word of t.

More precisely, let $t = [x_1 x_2 \ldots x_{|t|}]_C$ ($x_i \in \Sigma$ for $1 \leq i \leq |t|$). Then, we define an ordering relation $<<$ in the set $\{x_1,\ldots,x_{|t|}\}$, where equal symbols with different indexes are considered as different (or, equivalently, in the set of indexes $V = \{1,\ldots,|t|\}$), as follows:

$<<$ is the reflexive and transitive closure of the relation R defined as follows:

$$x_i R x_j \quad \text{iff} \quad (i<j \wedge \sim x_i C x_j)$$

The graph representation of the trace t in the above example is:

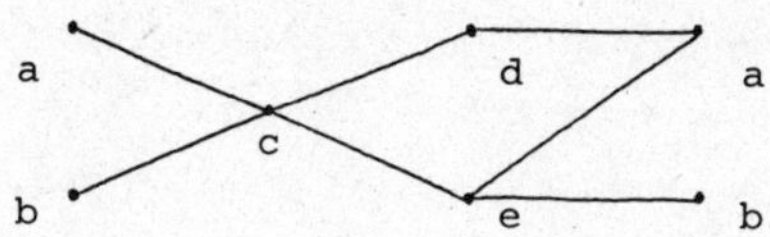

Now, given a language $L \subseteq \Sigma^*$, it is possible to associate with it a trace language as follows.

Def.2.5 - Given a language L on a finite alphabet Σ and a concurrency relation C on Σ, the set $[L]_C = \{[w]_C / w \in L\}$ is the <u>trace language generated by L under C</u>.

The above definition allows us to extend the Chomsky hierarchy for languages to trace languages [8]. In particular, regular trace languages are defined by:

Def.2.6 - A trace language T is <u>regular</u> iff there is a regular language $L \subseteq \Sigma^*$ such that $T = [L]_C$.

Analogous definitions have been given for context-free, context-sensitive and type 0 languages [10].

Now, we observe that, for a given trace language being regular, Def.2.6 requires the existence of a regular language L containing <u>at least</u> one word for every trace; if we impose that L contains <u>exactly</u> one word for every trace and hence that there exists a finite automaton that choose an <u>unique</u> sequentialization for every trace, we obtain the following (proper, as shown in [2]) subclass:

Def.2.7 - A trace language T is <u>deterministic</u> iff there exist a regular language L such that:

a) $T = [L]_C$

b) $x \in L \Rightarrow \#([x]_C \cap L) \leq 1$.

3.THE MEMBERSHIP PROBLEM FOR REGULAR TRACE LANGUAGES

Let us consider a concurrent alphabet $<\Sigma,C>$ and a regular trace language T. The <u>membership problem</u> for T may be defined as follows:

<u>PROBLEM</u> (MPRTL):

Instance: A word $x \in \Sigma^*$

Question: $[x]_C \in T$?

The following theorem shows that MPRTL can be solved in polynomial time.

Th.3.1 - Given a concurrent alphabet $<\Sigma,C>$ and a regular trace language T, the membership problem for T can be solved in time $O(|x|^{\alpha})$, where $|x|$ is the length of the input word x, and α is the cardinality of the greatest clique of C (which is,obviously, a maximal clique).

To prove this statement, we need previously to prove some lemmas. In the following, we will suppose that $T = [L_G]_C$, where L_G is the language generated by the regular grammar $G = <V_N,\Sigma,P,S>$.

Lemma 3.1 - Given a trace $t \in F(\Sigma,C)$, we have:

$t \in T = [L_G]_C$ iff $S \in Q(t)$, where:

$$Q(t) = \{A \;/\; A \in V_N \wedge \exists y([y]_C = t \wedge A \overset{*}{\underset{G}{\Rightarrow}} y)\}$$

The proof of this lemma is obvious; it allows us to reduce the membership problem (MP) to verifying if $S \in Q(t)$. Furthermore, $Q(t)$ may be recursively defined as follows, where the symbol t denotes ambiguously both a trace and a representative in it.

Lemma 3.2 - Given a trace $t \in F(\Sigma, C)$, let us define:

$$\vartheta(t) = \underline{\text{if}}\ |t|=1\ \underline{\text{then}}\ \{A/\ A \Rightarrow t\}\ \underline{\text{else}} \bigcup_{t=at', a\in\Sigma} \{A/\ A \Rightarrow aB \in P \wedge B \in \vartheta(t')\}$$

Then $\vartheta(t) = Q(t)$.

Proof - By induction on the length of t, we have:

a) for $|t|=1$, the assert obviously holds;

b) let $|t|>1$. Then:

$A \in \vartheta(t)$ iff there are a,B such that $A \Rightarrow aB$, $B \in \vartheta(t')$, $at'=t$.

Since $|t'| < |t|$, by induction hypothesis we have that $\vartheta(t') = Q(t')$.

Hence, $A \in \vartheta(t)$ iff there are a,B,y such that:

$$A \Longrightarrow aB,\ B \overset{*}{\Longrightarrow} y,\ [y]_C = t',\ at' = t.$$

Since $A \underset{G}{\overset{*}{\Longrightarrow}} ay$ and $[ay]_C = a.[y]_C = t$ hold, we can conclude:

$$A \in \vartheta(t) \text{ iff } \exists y (A \underset{G}{\overset{*}{\Longrightarrow}} y \wedge [y]_C = t) \text{ iff } A \in Q(t).$$

Our task is now that of implementing the above recursive definition by a polynomial time algorithm.

Def.3.1 - A trace p is said to be a <u>prefix</u> (a <u>suffix</u>) of a trace t, $p \triangleleft_l t$ (resp. $p \triangleleft_r t$), iff $\exists \alpha (t=p\alpha)$ (resp. $\exists \alpha (t=\alpha p)$).

It is easy to verify that there is a one to one correspondence among the set of prefixes and suffixes of a given trace t: in fact, the concatenation in a partially commutative monoid satisfies the cancellation laws, so that if p is a prefix of t, there exists a unique p' such that $p.p'=t$ and, conversely, for every suffix p' there exists an unique p such that $p.p'=t$. Hence, if we denote by I_l and I_r respectively the cardinalities of such sets, we have $I_r=I_l$. Furthermore, we have:

Lemma 3.3- Let α be the cardinality of a greatest maximal clique of the relation C. Then:

$$I_l(t) \leqslant \left(\frac{|t|}{\alpha} + 1\right)^{\alpha} \qquad (|t| \to +\infty)$$

Proof - Given the trace $t = [x_1 \ldots x_{|t|}]_C$, let us consider the poset of indexes $V = \{1, \ldots, |t|\}$ ordered by <<. By definition of <<, every prefix of t is specified by an ideal of V, i.e. a subset $I \subseteq V$ such that:

$$x \in I \wedge y << x \Longrightarrow y \in I.$$

Let q be the greatest cardinality of any antichain in $\langle V, << \rangle$. Since, given an antichain $\{j_1, \ldots, j_k\}$ the corresponding set of symbols

$\{x_{j_1},\ldots,x_{j_K}\}$ is a clique in C, we have $q \leq \alpha$.

Now, a theorem of Dilworth [3] guarantees the existence of a partition of V into exactly q chains $\{C_1,\ldots,C_q\}$. Since every ideal of V may be expressed as union of ideals of the chains C_i (one for every chain, possibly the empty ideal), the total number of order ideals of V will be bounded by $\prod_{j=1}^{q}(l_j+1)$, being l_j the length of the chain C_j.

Since $l_1+l_2+\ldots+l_q=|t|$, it follows:

$$\prod_{j=1}^{q}(l_j+1) \leq \left(\frac{|t|}{q}+1\right)^q \leq \left(\frac{|t|}{\alpha}+1\right)^{\alpha}$$

We can now prove the theorem.

Proof of Th.3.1 (outline):

By lemma 3.2, we can build up the set Q(t) by a recursion which computes Q(p), for every suffix p of t, by calling all the Q(p') such that ap'=p, for $a\in\Sigma$; this would imply, by a naive algorithm, an exponential number of procedure callings, but, by Lemma 3.3, the suffixes of t are at most $O(|t|^{\alpha})$, and this in turn makes it possible to perform the whole computation in time $O(|t|^{\alpha})$, by a dynamic programming technique. Finally, to test if $S\in Q(t)$ (see Lemma 3.1) requires a constant time.

4. THE UNIFORM MEMBERSHIP PROBLEM FOR REGULAR TRACE LANGUAGES

For the membership problem, the concurrent alphabet and the language are given a priori, and the instance of the problem consists only of the word we want test for its membership to the language. In the case where even the alphabet and the language are given as variable parameters of the problem, we have the <u>uniform membership problem for regular trace languages</u>:

<u>PROBLEM</u> (UMPRTL)

Instance: A concurrent alphabet $<\Sigma,C>$, a regular grammar G and a word $x\in\Sigma^*$.

Question: $[x]_C \in T = [L_G]_C$?

This problem is a difficult one, as stated by the following:

Th.4.1 - The Uniform Membership Problem for Regular Trace Languages is NP-complete.

Proof - First of all, let us show that the UMPRTL belongs to the class NP [4].

In fact, we have:

$$[x]_C \in [L_G]_C \quad \text{iff} \quad \exists z([z]_C = [x]_C \wedge z \in L_G).$$

Hence, we can proceed as follows:

a) All the words $y\in[x]_C$ are generated. It is easy to see that this step may be accomplished in non deterministic polynomial time. In fact, it may be reduced to the problem of generating all the permutations of the indexes $\{1,\dots,n\}$, where n is the lenght of the given word x, that are compatible with the ordering << as defined in section 2.

b) For every y obtained in the step a), a test is carried out to verify whether $y \in L_G$; but this amounts to solve an instance of the membership problem for regular languages in the usual sense, a polynomial time task.

We have now to prove that the UMP for regular trace languages is NP-hard; the proof is obtained by showing that a well-known NP-complete problem, the Hamiltonian Circuit Problem, can be polinomially reduced to it. The Hamiltonian Circuit Problem is defined as follows:

PROBLEM (HCP)
Instance: a graph $\langle V,E\rangle = G$
Question: is there an Hamiltonian circuit in G ?

Now, given an instance $\langle\{v_1,\dots,v_n\},E\rangle = G$ of the HC problem, we can (polynomially) construct the set $\mathcal{R}_G$ of all the paths in G. $\mathcal{R}_G$ is a regular set. Furthermore, we define the concurrency relation on V by $C = V\times V - I$. It is easy to see that:

G admits an Hamiltonian circuit iff $[v_1\dots v_n]_C \in [\mathcal{R}_G]_C$

so completing the reduction.

5. THE EQUIVALENCE PROBLEM FOR REGULAR TRACE LANGUAGES

The third problem we will treat is the <u>equivalence problem for regular trace languages (EPRTL)</u>. Let $\langle\Sigma,C\rangle$ be a concurrent alphabet; then we can define:

<u>PROBLEM</u> (EPRTL)
Instance: Two regular languages L_1,L_2 on Σ.
Question: $[L_1]_C = [L_2]_C$?

The following negative result can be stated:

Th.5.1 - The Equivalence Problem for Regular Trace Languages is recursively undecidable.

The proof is given by reducing the equivalence problem for 2-tape non deterministic finite state automata, that is known to be recursively undecidable [11], to EPRTL. Hence, we must give some definitions and preliminary lemmas.

Def.5.1 - A 2-tape non deterministic finite state automaton (2-ndfsa) is a 6-uple $M = \langle Q_1, Q_2, \Sigma, \delta, q_o, F\rangle$, where:

- Q_1 and Q_2 are disjoint finite sets of states, with Q_1 controlling the first tape and Q_2 the second one;
- Σ is a finite alphabet;
- $q_o \in Q_1 \cup Q_2$ is the initial state;
- $F \subseteq Q_1 \cup Q_2$ is the set of accepting states;
- $\delta : ((Q_1 \cup Q_2) \times \Sigma) \longrightarrow 2^{(Q_1 \cup Q_2)}$ is the transition function.

Without loss of generality, in the following we will suppose that the alphabet Σ is partitioned into two disjoint alphabets Σ_1 and Σ_2 for the two tapes.

Def.5.2 - Given a 2-ndfsa M, the language L(M) accepted by M is defined by:

$$L(M) = \{(u,v)/u \in \Sigma_1^* \wedge v \in \Sigma_2^* \wedge \exists q(q \in F \wedge q \in \delta((u,v),q_o)\}$$

The trace language T(M) accepted by M is defined by:

$$T(M) = \{[xy]_C / x \in \Sigma_1^* \wedge y \in \Sigma_2^* \wedge (x,y) \in L(M)\}$$

where the concurrency relation C on Σ is defined by:

$$xCy \wedge yCx \quad \text{iff} \quad x \in \Sigma_1 \wedge y \in \Sigma_2 .$$

Lemma 5.1 - Given a 2-ndfsa $M = \langle Q_1, Q_2, \Sigma, \delta, q_o, F\rangle$, the trace language T(M) is regular.

Proof (outline) - We can construct the following one-tape non deterministic automaton: $M' = \langle Q_1 \cup Q_2 \cup \{q_T\}, \Sigma, \tilde{\delta}, q_o, F\rangle$, where $q_T \notin Q_1 \cup Q_2$ is a trap state and $\tilde{\delta}$ is defined as:

$$q' \in \tilde{\delta}(\sigma,q) \quad \text{iff} \quad (q \in Q_1 \wedge \sigma \in \Sigma_1 \wedge q' \in \delta(\sigma,q)) \vee (q \in Q_2 \wedge \sigma \in \Sigma_2 \wedge q' \in \delta(\sigma,q))$$

$$q_T \in \tilde{\delta}(\sigma,q) \quad \text{iff} \quad (q \in Q_1 \wedge \sigma \in \Sigma_2) \vee (q \in Q_2 \wedge \sigma \in \Sigma_1)$$

$$q_T \in \tilde{\delta}(\sigma,q_T) \quad \text{for every } \sigma \in \Sigma .$$

Now, let us call accepting scanning every word $z \in (\Sigma_1 \cup \Sigma_2)^*$ such that the 2-ndfsa M, by reading sequentially the symbols of z starting from the initial state, reaches an accepting state. Then, given the pair $(x,y) \in \Sigma_1^* \times \Sigma_2^*$, it is easy to prove that, for $z \in x \| y$, we have:

a) if z is not an accepting scanning, then $\tilde{\delta}(z,q_o) = \{q_T\}$

b) if z is an accepting scanning, then $\tilde{\delta}(z,q_o) \cap (Q_1 \cup Q_2) \subseteq \delta((x,y),q_o)$

c) $(Q_1 \cup Q_2) \cap \bigcup_{z \in x \| y} \tilde{\delta}(z,q_o) = \delta((x,y),q_o)$

It is easy to see that this implies that the trace language accepted by M coincides with the one accepted by M', hence it is regular.

The converse does not hold, i.e. there are regular trace languages on the concurrent alphabet $(\Sigma_1 \cup \Sigma_2, C)$, with C defined as in Def.5.2, such that cannot be accepted by any 2-ndfsa.

The proof of Th.5.1 immediately follows from Lemma 5.1 and from the fact that the equivalence problem for 2-ndfsa is undecidable.

Despite the negative result proved, for a non trivial subclass of concurrent alphabets the EPRTL turns out to be decidable.

Th.5.2 - Let $<\Sigma, C>$ be a concurrent alphabet with C transitive; then, given two regular trace language $[L_1]_C$ and $[L_2]_C$, the equivalence between them can be decided.

To prove the theorem, first we remark that, being C transitive, it generates a partition of Σ into a set of disjoint subsets $\Sigma_1, \dots, \Sigma_n$. Now, given an automaton $M = <Q, \Sigma, \delta, q_o, F>$, we define:

$$N(M) = \{q'jq'' / \exists x (x = \alpha\sigma' z \sigma'' k)$$

where:

a) $\sigma', \sigma'' \notin \Sigma_j \wedge z \in \Sigma_j^*$ $\qquad (j=1,\dots,n)$;

b) $\begin{cases} \delta(q_o, \alpha\sigma') = q' \\ \delta(q', z) = q'' \\ \delta(q'', \sigma'' k) = q_F \qquad (q_F \in F) \end{cases}$

It is easy to show that N(M) may be effectively constructed. Furthermore, we pose:

$L_{q'q''}$:= the language accepted by M with initial state q' and final state q";

$P_{q'jq''}$:= the Parikh language [10] defined by $[L_{q'q''} \cap \Sigma_j^*]_C$

and state the following lemma:

Lemma 5.2 - Given two automata M_1 and M_2, the following statements are equivalent:

a) $[L_1]_C = [L_2]_C$

b) $\forall j, q_1', q_2', q_1'', q_2''\ (q_1'jq_1'' \in N(M_1) \wedge q_2'jq_2'' \in N(M_2) \Longrightarrow P_{q_1'jq_1''} = P_{q_2'jq_2''})$

Since the equivalence problem for Parikh languages is decidable, this proves the theorem; the proof of the lemma will not be given for lack of space.

On the other hand, there is another class of concurrency relations for which the EPRTL is undecidable:

Th.5.3 - Let $<\Sigma, C>$ be a concurrent alphabet such that the graph of C contains the pattern:

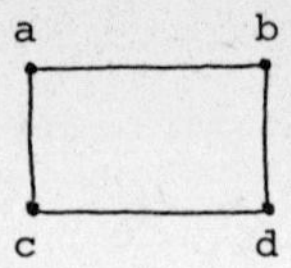

(edges between the nodes a and d or b and c must be explicitly excluded). Then, the equivalence problem for regular trace languages on it is undecidable.

Proof (outline) - Without loss of generality, we can assume that $\Sigma = \{a,b,c,d\}$ and that C is given exactly by the previous graph. Let us consider the alphabets

$$\Sigma_1 = \{\sigma_1, \ldots, \sigma_n\} \quad \text{and} \quad \Sigma_2 = \{\rho_1, \ldots, \rho_m\}$$

with a concurrency relation C' defined as in Def.5.2. The EPRTL in this case is undecidable by Th.5.1.

Given two regular trace languages $[L_1]_{C'}$ and $[L_2]_{C'}$ on $<\Sigma_1 \cup \Sigma_2, C'>$, we construct two languages $[L'_1]_C$ and $[L'_2]_C$ by substituting every σ_j with the string $a^j c$ and every ρ_i with the string $b^i d$.

Since it may be proved that:

$$[L_1]_{C'} = [L_2]_{C'} \Longleftrightarrow [L'_1 \cap R]_C = [L'_2 \cap R]_C$$

where $R = \{ac, a^2c, \ldots, a^nc, bd, \ldots, b^md\}^*$, the decidability of the right equality would imply the decidability of the left one, a contradiction .

REFERENCES

[1] Bertoni,A.,Brambilla,M.,Mauri,G.,Sabadini,N., An application of the theory of free partially commutative monoids : asymptotic densities of trace languages,Lect.Not.Comp.Sci.,118,Springer, 1981.

[2] Bertoni,A.,Mauri,G.,Sabadini,N.,A hierarchy of regular trace languages and some combinatorial applications,Second World Conference on Mathematics at the Service of Men,Las Palmas,1982.

[3] Dilworth,R.P.,A decomposition theorem for partially ordered sets,Ann.of Math.51,1950,pp.161-166.

[4] Garey,M.,Johnson,D.J.,Computers and intractability,Freeman and Co, San Francisco,1979.

[5] Hopcroft,J.E.,Ullman,J.D.,Formal languages and their relations to automata, Addison Wesley,Reading Mass.,1969.

[6] Knuth,E.,Petri Nets and regular trace languages, Univ. of Newcastle upon Tyne,Comp.Lab.,ASM/47,1978.

[7] Lallement,G.,Semigroups and combinatorial applications,J.Wiley and Sons, New York,1979.

[8] Mazurkiewicz,A.,Concurrent program schemes and their interpretations, DAIMI,PB 78,Aarhus University,1977.

[9] Petri,C.A.,Non sequential processes,ISF Rep.77/01,GMD Bonn,1977.

[10] Szijarto,M.,Trace languages and closure operations,Automata Theoretic Letters,1979/2,Dept.of numerical and computer math., L.Eotvos University, Budapest,1979.

[11] Fisher,P.C.,Rosenberg,A.L.,Multitape non writing automata,J.C.S.S., 2,1968,pp.88-101.

This research has been supported by Ministero della Pubblica Istruzione and by Communication and Programming Project of Università di Milano and Honeywell Information Systems Italia.

ON THE POWER OF CHAIN RULES IN CONTEXT FREE GRAMMARS

by

Norbert Blum

Fachbereich 1o
Angewandte Mathematik
und Informatik
Universität des Saarlandes
6600 Saarbrücken
West Germany

Abstract:

For all $n \geq 2$, we construct a context-free language L_n for which we prove the following:

a) L_n has a cfg of size $O(n)$
b) Any chain rule free cfg for L_n has size $\Omega(n \log \log n)$.

I. Introduction and Definitions

A context-free grammer (cfg) G is a 4-tuple (V_T, V_N, P, S) where V_T is a finite set of terminal symbols, V_N a finite set of nonterminal symbols disjoint from V_T, P a finite set of productions, and S, the distinguished symbol, is a member of V_N. The productions are of the form $A \rightarrow \alpha$, where $A \in V_N$, $\alpha \in (V_N \cup V_T)^*$. L(G) denotes the context-free language (cfl) generated by G.

A cfg G is in Chomsky normal form (Cnf) if each rule is of the form

i) $A \rightarrow BC$ with $B, C \in V_N$
ii) $A \rightarrow a$ with $a \in V_T$
iii) $S \rightarrow \varepsilon$ ε is the empty word

Furthermore, if $S \rightarrow \varepsilon$ is in P, then $B, C \in V_N \setminus \{S\}$ in i) above.

The size $|G|$ of a cfg $G = (V_T, V_N, P, S)$ is defined by:

$$|G| := \sum_{\substack{A\to\alpha \\ \text{in } P}} lg(A\alpha).$$

$lg(A\alpha)$ is the length of the string $A\alpha$.
A production $A \to \varepsilon$ is called ε-rule.
A production $A \to B$ in a cfg with $B \in V_N$ is called <u>chain rule</u>.
A cfg $G = (V_T, V_N, P, S)$ is called <u>chain rule free</u>, if in P no chain rule and no ε-rule exists.

It is well known that for each cfg $G = (V_T, V_N, P, S)$ a cfg $G' = (V_T, V_N, P', S)$ exists such that $L(G) = L(G')$ and G' is chain rule free [H, p.1o1-1o2]. The proof is constructive and the transformation can enlarge the size of G' by a factor $|G|$. But it is not known if there is a family $\{L_n \mid n \in N\}$ of cfl's, L_n is generated by a cfg G_n of size $O(n)$ and no chain rule free cfg G_n' with $L(G_n') = L_n$ has size $O(n)$. We prove that chain rules really help.

II. The results

Let $L_n = \{a_i b_j \mid 1 \le i < j \le n\}$. The following cfg G_n generates L_n.

$G_n = (V_T, V_N, P, S)$ with:

$$V_T = \{a_i, b_j \mid i \in \{1,2,...,n-1\},\ j \in \{2,3,...,n\}\}$$

$$V_N = \{S, B_i \mid i \in \{2,,,.n\}\}$$

$$\begin{aligned} P = \{S &\to a_i B_{i+1} & 1 \le i < n, \\ B_i &\to B_{i+1} & 2 \le i < n, \\ B_i &\to b_i & 2 \le i \le n\} \end{aligned}$$

It holds: $|G_n| = 7n-9$. G_n is not chain rule free.

We can illustrate the language L_n as in figure 1.

We prove that any chain rule free cfg for L_n has size $\Omega(n \log \log n)$. Since for each chain rule free cfg G there exists a cfg G' in Cnf with $L(G') = L(G)$ and $|G'| \le 5|G|$ it suffices to prove:

Theorem 1:

Let $n \geq 2$. For each cfg G'_n in Cnf with $L(G'_n) = L_n$ the number of productions $T(n)$ satisfies

$$T(n) \geq \max\{1, 1/4\ n \log \log n\}$$

and hence

$$|G'_n| \geq \max\{2, 1/2\ n \log \log n\}$$

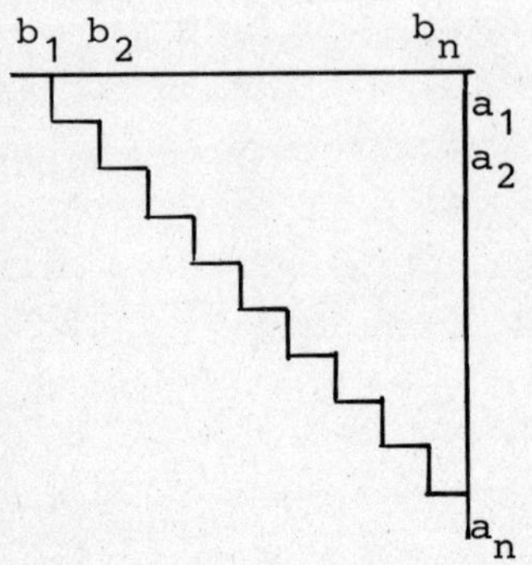

figure 1

The idea of the proof is the following:

In each stage, we count productions and isolate certain subproblems, such that the following holds:

(1) The subproblems are disjoint. This means that no production used in any subproblem helps in any other subproblem.

(2) The productions counted cannot be used to generate any word in any of the isolated subproblems.

Proof:

Let $A = \{a_1, a_2, \ldots, a_{n-1}\}$, $B = \{b_2, b_3, \ldots, b_n\}$.

A cfg G'_n in Cnf with $L(G'_n) = L_n$ and minimal number of productions looks like:

$G'_n = (V_T, V_N, P, S)$ with

$$
\begin{aligned}
V_T &= A \cup B \\
V_N &= \{A_1, A_2, \ldots, A_q, B_1, B_2, \ldots, B_p, S\} \\
P &= \{S \to A_{i_1} B_{j_1} \\
&\quad \vdots \qquad\qquad i_e \in \{1,\ldots,q\},\ j_e \in \{1,\ldots,p\} \\
&\quad \qquad\qquad\quad \forall\, e \in \{1,\ldots,r\}, \\
&\quad S \to A_{i_r} B_{j_r} \\
&\quad A_i \to a_\nu \qquad a_\nu \in \alpha_i \subseteq A \qquad \forall\, i \in \{1,\ldots,q\}, \\
&\quad B_j \to b_\mu \qquad b_\mu \in \beta_j \subseteq B \qquad \forall\, j \in 1,\ldots,p\}\}
\end{aligned}
$$

It holds: $|G'_n| = 3r + 2 \sum_{i=1}^{q} |\alpha_i| + 2 \sum_{j=1}^{p} |\beta_j|$

We prove the theorem by induction.

For $2 \le k \le 2^{16}$ the assertion trivially holds since $1/4\ k \log\log k \le k$.

Assume the assertion holds $\forall\, k\colon 2 \le k < n$

Consider the following figure:

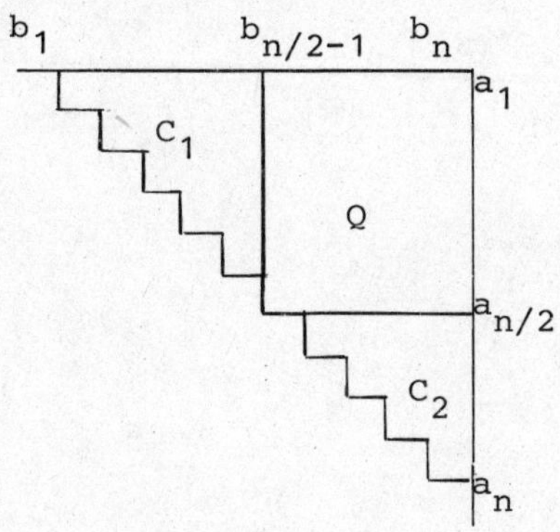

figure 2

Clearly, a production $B_j \to b_\ell$, $\ell > n/2$ cannot help to generate a word in C_1. If there exists a production $B_j \to b_\mu$, $\mu \le n/2$ then if we use the production $B_j \to b_\ell$ to generate a word $a_i b_\ell \in C_2$ then we can also generate the word $a_i b_\mu$; but $a_i b_\mu \notin L_n$. Hence the production $B_j \to b_\ell$ cannot help to generate a word in C_2 if a production $B_j \to b_\mu$, $\mu \le n/2$, exists. An analogous consideration can be done for productions of type $A_i \to a_\ell$, $\ell \le n/2$. It is clear that a production $S \to A_iB_j$ with $\alpha_i \subseteq \{a_1,\ldots,a_{n/2}\}$ and $\beta_j \subseteq \{b_{n/2+1},\ldots,b_n\}$ cannot help to generate a word in C_1 or C_2.

In the following we distinguish three cases.

Case 1: There exist n/4 productions $B_j \to b_\ell$, $\ell > n/2$, for which a production $B_j \to b_\mu$ exists, $\mu \le n/2$, or there exist n/4 productions $A_i \to a_\ell$, $\ell \le n/2$, for which a production $A_i \to a_\nu$, $\nu > n/2$ exist.

Case 2: Case 1 is not fulfilled but there exist n/4 productions $S \to A_iB_j$ with $\alpha_i \subseteq \{a_1,\ldots,a_{n/2}\}$ and $\beta_j \subseteq \{b_{n/2+1},\ldots,b_n\}$.

Case 3: Case 1 and case 2 are not fulfilled.

This idea is laid out more precisely in the following:

Let $\mathfrak{A}_1 = \{\alpha_i \mid 1 \le i \le s,\ \exists\, a_\ell, a_\kappa \in \alpha_i\colon \ell \le n/2 \text{ and } \kappa > n/2\}$

$\mathfrak{A}_2 = \{\alpha_i \mid 1 \le i \le s,\ \forall\, a_\ell \in \alpha_i \text{ holds } \ell \le n/2\}$

$\mathcal{B}_1 = \{\beta_j \mid 1 \le j \le t,\ \exists\, b_\ell, b_\kappa \in \beta_j\colon \ell \le n/2 \text{ and } \kappa > n/2\}$

$\mathcal{B}_2 = \{\beta_j \mid 1 \le j \le t,\ \forall\, b_\ell \in \beta_j \text{ holds } \ell > n/2\}$

$\forall\, \alpha_i \in \mathfrak{A}_1$ let $c_i = |\{a_\ell \in \alpha_i \mid \ell \le n/2\}|$

$$c := \sum_{\alpha_i \in \mathfrak{A}_1} c_i$$

$\forall\, \beta_j \in \mathcal{B}_1$ let $d_i = |\{b_\ell \in \beta_j \mid \ell > n/2\}|$

$$d := \sum_{\beta_j \in \mathcal{B}_1} d_j$$

d and c, respectively, correspond to the productions which we count in case 1.

Case 1: $c \ge n/4$ or $d \ge n/4$

w.l.o.g. let be $d \ge n/4$

Since all these productions cannot help to generate a word in C_1 or C_2 and all productions which are used to generate a word in C_1 (C_2) cannot be used to generate a word in C_2 (C_1) it holds:

$$\begin{aligned} T(n) &\geq 2\ T(n/2) + n/4 \\ &\geq 2 \cdot 1/4\ n/2 \log\log n/2 + n/4 \\ &= 1/4(n \log\log n/2 + n) \\ &\geq 1/4\ n \log\log n \quad \text{(since } n > 4) \end{aligned}$$

<u>Case 2:</u> $c < n/4$, $d < n/4$ and the number of productions in P of the form $S \to A_iB_j$, $\alpha_i \in \mathfrak{A}_2$, $\beta_j \in \mathfrak{B}_2 \geq n/4$

Then it holds:

$$\begin{aligned} T(n) &\geq 2\ T(n/2) + n/4 \\ &\geq 1/4\ n \log\log n \end{aligned}$$

<u>Case 3:</u> $c < n/4$, $d < n/4$ and the number of productions in P of the form $S \to A_iB_j$, $\alpha_i \in \mathfrak{A}_2$, $\beta_j \in \mathfrak{B}_2 < n/4$

In this case we don't easily get a recursion inequality for T(n). The following property is very useful for deriving a recursion inequality for T(n).

Let $\beta = \{b_{\ell_1},\ldots,b_{\ell_\kappa}\} \subseteq \{b_{n/2+1},\ldots,b_n\}$, $\ell_1 < \ell_2 < \ldots < \ell_\kappa$. Then β induces the language L_κ in the following way:

Define $\alpha = \{a_{\ell_1},\ldots,a_{\ell_\kappa}\}$, and

$L'_\kappa = \{a_ib_j \mid i < j,\ a_i \in \alpha,\ b_j \in \beta\}$. Clearly $L'_\kappa = L_\kappa$, up to the names of terminal symbols. Analogously the set α induces the language L_κ.

It is clear that a production $B_i \to b_{\ell_j}$, $2 \leq j \leq \kappa$, ($A_i \to a_{\ell_j}$, $1 \leq j \leq \kappa-1$) cannot help to generate a word in L'_κ , if the production $B_i \to b_{\ell_1}$ ($A_i \to a_{\ell_\kappa}$) exists.

$$\text{Let } \overline{A} = \{a_j \mid j \leq n/2,\ a_j \notin \alpha_i\ \forall\ \alpha_i \in \mathfrak{A}_1\}$$

$$\overline{B} = \{b_j \mid j > n/2,\ b_j \notin \beta_i\ \forall\ \beta_i \in \mathfrak{B}_1\}$$

Since $c < n/4$ and $d < n/4$ we have $|\overline{A}| > n/4$ and $|\overline{B}| > n/4$. Now we define partitions $\mathfrak{A}_3$ of $\overline{A}$ and $\mathfrak{B}_3$ of $\overline{B}$. Let $\mathfrak{A}_3 = \{\overline{\alpha}_{\kappa_1},\ldots,\overline{\alpha}_{\kappa_t}\}$ and $\mathfrak{B}_3 = \{\overline{\beta}_{\ell_1},\ldots,\overline{\beta}_{\ell_s}\}$ where $\overline{\alpha}_{\kappa_i}$ (and $\overline{\beta}_{\ell_i}$) are defined in the following way:

Let be $a_{\kappa_i} \in \overline{A} \setminus \bigcup_{j=1}^{i-1} \overline{\alpha}_{\kappa_j}$ such that $\forall\, a_\ell \in \overline{A} \setminus \bigcup_{j=1}^{i-1} \overline{\alpha}_{\kappa_j}$ holds $\ell \le \kappa_i$.

Then $\overline{\alpha}_{\kappa_i} := \{a_\nu \in \overline{A} \setminus \bigcup_{j=1}^{i-1} \overline{\alpha}_{\kappa_j} \mid \exists\, \alpha_\mu \in \mathfrak{A}_2 \colon a_{\kappa_i}, a_\nu \in \alpha_\mu\}$

Let be $b_{\ell_i} \in \overline{B} \setminus \bigcup_{j=1}^{i-1} \overline{\beta}_{\ell_j}$ such that $\forall\, b_\kappa \in \overline{B} \setminus \bigcup_{j=1}^{i-1} \overline{\beta}_{\ell_j}$ holds $\kappa \ge \ell_i$.

Then $\overline{\beta}_{\ell_i} := \{b_\nu \in \overline{B} \setminus \bigcup_{j=1}^{i-1} \overline{\beta}_{\mu_j} \mid \exists\, \beta_\mu \in \mathfrak{B}_2 \colon b_{\ell_i}, b_\nu \in \beta_\mu\}$

$\overline{\alpha}_{\kappa_i}$ is constructed in such a way that for all $a_\nu \in \overline{\alpha}_{\kappa_i}$ there exist productions $A_\mu \to a_\nu$ and $A_\mu \to a_{\kappa_i}$ with $\alpha_\mu \in \mathfrak{A}_2$. Hence we can count $|\overline{\alpha}_{\kappa_i}|$ productions which cannot help to generate a word in $L'_{|\overline{\alpha}_{\kappa_i}|}$. An analogous property holds for $\overline{\beta}_{\ell_i}$.

Now we consider how a word $a_{\kappa_i} b_{\ell_j}$, $1 \le i \le t$, $1 \le j \le s$ can be generated. For each such word there exist a production $S \to A_\nu B_\mu$ and productions $A_\nu \to a_{\kappa_i}$, $B_\mu \to b_{\ell_j}$ and $\alpha_\nu \in \mathfrak{A}_2$, $\beta_\mu \in \mathfrak{B}_2$.

By construction of $\mathfrak{A}_3$ and $\mathfrak{B}_3$, for distinct such words, the productions of the form $S \to A_\nu B_\mu$ must be distinct. Since the number of productions of the form $S \to A_i B_j$, $\alpha_i \in \mathfrak{A}_2$, $\beta_j \in \mathfrak{B}_2$ is $< n/4$ it holds: $s < 1/2\sqrt{n}$ or $t < 1/2\sqrt{n}$.

Let w.l.o.g. $s < 1/2\sqrt{n}$. Let $\forall\, i \in \{1,\ldots,s\}\colon n_i := |\overline{\beta}_{\ell_i}|$. Define $T(1) := 1$.

For $1 \le i \le s$ we can count n_i productions $B_\mu \to b_\nu$ with $b_\nu \in \overline{\beta}_{\ell_i}$, which cannot be used to generate a word in any of the following languages:

(1) the words in C_1 of figure 2, since $\forall\, b_\nu \in \overline{\beta}_{\ell_i}$ holds: $\nu > n/2$

(2) L'_{n_i}, since for all productions $B_\mu \to b_\nu$, which we count, there exists the production $B_\mu \to b_{\ell_i}$

(3) L'_{n_j}, $1 \le j \le s$, $j \ne i$, since $\overline{\beta}_{\ell_i} \cap \overline{\beta}_{\ell_j} = \phi$

(4) L'_m, where L'_m is the language induced by
$\tilde{B} := b_{n/2+1},\ldots,b_n \quad \bigcup_{i=1}^{s} \overline{\beta}_{\ell_i}$, $|\tilde{B}| = m$, since $\tilde{B} \cap \overline{\beta}_\ell = \phi$.

We have $\sum_{i=1}^{s} n_i > n/4$. Hence the following holds:

$$T(n) \ge T(n/2) + T(m) + \sum_{i=1}^{s} T(n_i) + 1/4\, n$$

with $m + \sum_{i=1}^{s} n_i = n/2$, $m < n/4$, $s < 1/2\,\sqrt{n}$.

Since $T(\ell) = 1$ for $1 \le \ell \le 4$ we can enlarge the $n_j < 4$ to the cost of the biggest n_ℓ's. Hence we have

$$T(n) \ge T(n/2) + T(m) + \sum_{i=1}^{s} T(\overline{n}_i) + 1/4\, n$$

with $m + \sum_{i=1}^{s} \overline{n}_i = n/2$, $m < n/4$, $s < 1/2\,\sqrt{n}$, $\overline{n}_i \ge 4\ \forall\, i \in \{1,\ldots,s\}$

and hence by induction hypothesis

$$T(n) \ge 1/4\ (n/2 \log\log n/2 + m \log\log m + \sum_{i=1}^{s} \overline{n}_i \log\log \overline{n}_i + n)$$

with $m + \sum_{i=1}^{s} \overline{n}_i = n/2$, $m < n/4$, $s < 1/2\,\sqrt{n}$, $\overline{n}_i \ge 4\ \forall\, i \in \{1,\ldots,s\}$

Since $p \log\log p \ge 2\ p/2 \log\log p/2$ we get by halving the biggest $\overline{n}_\ell$'s

$$T(n) \ge 1/4\ (n/2 \log\log n/2 + m \log\log m + \sum_{i=1}^{1/2\sqrt{n}} m_i \log\log m_i + n)$$

with $m + \sum_{i=1}^{1/2\sqrt{n}} m_i = n/2$, $m < n/4$, $m_i \ge 4$, $\forall\, i \in \{1,\ldots,1/2\sqrt{n}\}$

Since the function $f(x) = x \log\log x$ is convex for $n > 4$, we have:

$$T(n) \geq 1/4 \; (n/2 \log\log n/2 + m \log\log m + 1/2\sqrt{n} \; (\frac{n/2-m}{1/2\sqrt{n}}) \cdot \log\log (\frac{n/2-m}{1/2\sqrt{n}}) + n)$$

Hence

$$T(n) \geq 1/4 \; (n/2 \log\log n/2 + m \log\log m + (n/2-m) \log\log (\frac{n-2m}{\sqrt{n}}) + n)$$

<u>Case 1:</u> $m < \frac{n-2m}{\sqrt{n}} \Rightarrow m < \sqrt{n}$

$$\begin{aligned}
\Rightarrow T(n) &\geq 1/4 \; (n/2 \log\log n/2 + n/2 \log\log (\sqrt{n}-2) - \sqrt{n} \log\log \sqrt{n} + n) \\
&\geq 1/4 \; (n/2 \log\log n/2 + n/2 \log\log (\sqrt{n}-2) + 3/4\, n) \\
&= 1/4 \; (n/2 \log\log n/2 + n/2 \; (\log\log (\sqrt{n}-2) + \log 2) + n/4) \\
&= 1/4 \; (n/2 \log\log n/2 + \log\log (n-4\sqrt{n}+4) + n/4) \\
&\geq 1/4 \; (n \log\log n/2 + n/4) \quad \text{(since } n > 48) \\
&\geq 1/4 \; n \log\log n \quad \text{(since } n > 128)
\end{aligned}$$

<u>Case 2:</u> $m > \frac{n-2m}{\sqrt{n}}$

$$\begin{aligned}
\Rightarrow T(n) &\geq 1/4 \; (n/2 \log\log n/2 + n/2 \log\log \frac{n-2m}{\sqrt{n}} + n) \\
&\geq 1/4 \; (n/2 \log\log n/2 + n/2 \log\log 1/2 \sqrt{n} + n) \\
&\quad \text{(since } m < n/4) \\
&= 1/4 \; (n/2 \log\log n/2 + n/2 \log 1/2 \log n/4 + n) \\
&= 1/4 \; (n/2 \log\log n/2 + n/2 \log\log n/4 + n/2) \\
&\geq 1/4 \; (n \log\log n/4 + n/2) \\
&\geq 1/4 \; n \log\log n \quad \text{(since } n > 128)
\end{aligned}$$

□

Next we prove that the lower bound is strict.

<u>Theorem 2:</u>

There exists a cfg $G'_n = \{V_T, V_N, P, S\}$ in Cnf with $L(G'_n) = L_n$ and

$|G'_n| \leq 11/2\ n \log \log n$

Proof:

Let $\alpha_i = \{a_{i\sqrt{n}+\ell} \mid 1 \leq \ell \leq \sqrt{n}\}$ $0 \leq i \leq \sqrt{n} - 1$

$\beta_i = \{b_{i\sqrt{n}+\ell} \mid 1 \leq \ell \leq \sqrt{n}\}$ $0 \leq i \leq \sqrt{n} - 1$

Let the following productions be in P:

$S \rightarrow A_i B_j$ $0 \leq i < j \leq \sqrt{n} - 1$

$A_i \rightarrow a_j$ $a_j \in \alpha_i$

$B_i \rightarrow b_j$ $b_j \in \beta_i$

With the production above, we can generate the words in the hatched region of figure 3.

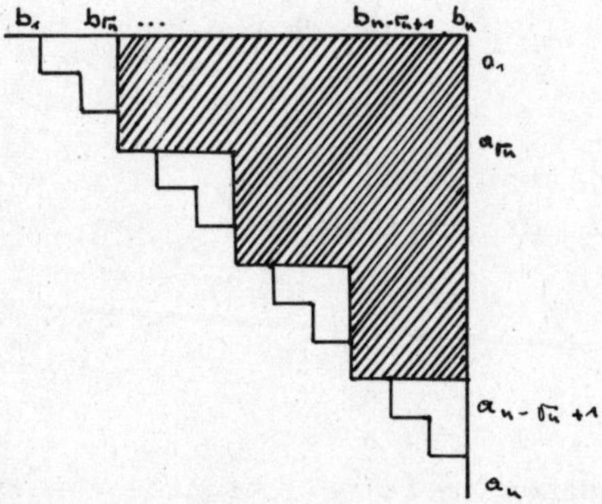

figure 3

Thus the only productions we still have to add to P are those for generating words which are not in the hatched region of figure 3. Those words separate in $\sqrt{n}$ disjoint subproblems of size $\sqrt{n}$.

Let G(n) be the size of G'_n. Then we have by the construction above:

$$G(n) \leq \sqrt{n} \cdot G(\sqrt{n}) + 11/2\ n$$
$$\leq 11/2\ n \log \log n \quad \square$$

Open questions:

We have proved:

$\nexists$ c $\forall$ cfg G $\exists$ cfg G' chain rule free such that

$L(G') = L(G)$ and $|G'| \leq c\ |G|$

more exactly:

$\forall$ n $\in$ N $\exists$ cfg G with $|G| = 7n$ and $\forall$ cfg G' chain rule free with $L(G') = L(G)$ it holds $|G'| = \Omega$ (n log log n).

There exists always a large gap between this lower bound and the best known upper bound, which can square the size of the grammar.

Kurt Mehlhorn mentioned the following question:

$\forall$ V_T $\exists$ c $\forall$ cfg $G = (V_T, V_N, P, S)$ $\exists$ cfg G' chain rule free such that $L(G) = L(G')$ and $|G'| \leq c\ |G|$, i.e. c can depend on V_T.

Acknowledgement: I'd like to thank Kurt Mehlhorn for focussing my attention on a conjecture of Yehudai that any cfg in Cnf for L_n has size Ω (n log n) [Y].

References:

[H] Harrison, M.A.: Introduction to formal language theory, Addison-Wesley (1978)

[Y] Yehudai, A.: On the complexity of grammer and language problems, Dissertation, Berkeley (1977)

EXTENDED CHOMSKY-SCHÜTZENBERGER THEOREMS

Franz-Josef Brandenburg

Institut für Informatik, Universität Bonn

Wegelerstr. 6, 5300 Bonn, Federal Republic of Germany

ABSTRACT

The operations of a homomorphic equality and an inverse homomorphic equality are introduced. These operations are obtained from n-tuples of homomorphisms, incorporating the notion of an equality set. For one-tuples they are a homomorphism and an inverse homomorphism. Homomorphic equality and inverse homomorphic equality operations provide simple and uniform characterizations of the recursively enumerable sets in terms of the regular sets, and of classes $H(L \wedge MR)$ in terms of L. These characterizations resemble the Chomsky-Schützenberger theorem for context-free languages.

INTRODUCTION

A great deal of activity in formal language theory aims at studying classes of languages specified in terms of certain closure properties. Particularly interesting are characterizations of a class L as the smallest class containing certain generators G and closed under certain operations, and minimal representations of each language in L in terms of the operations and the generators. A classical result of the latter type is the Chomsky-Schützenberger theorem for context-free languages, which asserts that each context-free language can be obtained from a special Dyck set by applying an inverse homomorphism, the intersection with a regular set, and a (nonerasing) homomorphism. For the recursively enumerable sets an analogous result has been proved in [13] with a special equality set as a generator. Based on the notion of an equality set simple representations of other important classes of languages have been developed thereupon. See [2,7,1o,11,13,15].

Here we use equality sets as the inherent part of a mapping, called homomorphic equality, and its inverse, called inverse homomorphic equality. These operations are obtained by combining several homomorphisms aiming at the same target, and they are canonical extensions of homomorphisms and inverse homomorphisms, respectively. Now the recursively enumerable sets can be represented in terms of the regular sets by two homomorphic equality operations (of just three homomorphisms) and by an extended Chomsky-Schützenberger theorem, which uses inverse homomorphic equality operations instead of inverse homomorphisms. Analogously, the class $H(L \wedge MR)$ is obtained from a class L in the nonerasing case, where MR is a specific class introduced in [4]. Classes of the form $H(L \wedge MR)$ have been studied in [1,4,5]. For well-behaved L they are a trio and closed under intersection.

In a concise set notation our results are as follows:

$$RE = \widehat{HEQ}_1(HEQ_2(REG)) = \hat{H}(HEQ_2^{-1}(REG)) = \hat{H}(HEQ_2^{-1}(\{o,1\}^*) \wedge REG).$$

$$H(L \wedge MR) = HEQ_1(HEQ_3(L)) = H(HEQ_3^{-1}(L) \wedge REG).$$

PRELIMINARIES

It is assumed that the reader is familiar with the basic concepts from formal language theory. Some of the concepts that are most important for this paper are reviewed and notation is established.

Recall that a homomorphism (between free monoids) is a mapping h from Σ^* into Δ^* such that $h(xy) = h(x)h(y)$ for all $x,y \in \Sigma^*$. h is nonerasing, if $h(a) \neq \lambda$ for each $a \in \Sigma$, where λ denotes the empty string.

Our central notions are built from finite sets of homomorphisms.

<u>DEFINITION</u>. Let $h_1,\ldots,h_n$ be homomorphisms from Σ^* into Δ^*. For each string $w \in \Sigma^*$ define

$$\langle heq; h_1,\ldots,h_n\rangle(w) = \begin{cases} h_1(w), & \text{if } h_1(w) = \ldots = h_n(w), \\ \text{undefined, otherwise.} \end{cases}$$

$\langle heq; h_1,\ldots,h_n\rangle$ is called a <u>homomorphic equality</u> (of $h_1,\ldots,h_n$). It is a <u>nonerasing homomorphic equality</u>, if at least one homomorphism h_i is nonerasing.

A homomorphic equality $\langle heq; h_1,\ldots,h_n\rangle$ is a mapping from Σ^* into Δ^*, which is pointwise extended to languages. It is a <u>partial</u> mapping, which is total if and only if $n=1$ or $h_i = h_j$ for all h_i,h_j. In this case the embedded equality test is meaningless, and $\langle heq; h_1,\ldots,h_n\rangle = h_1$ is a homomorphism. Hence, a homomorphic equality is an extension of a homomorphism.

DEFINITION. For homomorphisms $h_1,\ldots,h_n$ from Σ^* into Δ^* and $y \in \Delta^*$ define

$$\langle heq^{-1};\ h_1,\ldots,h_n\rangle(y) = \{w \in \Sigma^* \mid \langle heq;\ h_1,\ldots,h_n\rangle(w) = y\}.$$

$\langle heq^{-1};\ h_1,\ldots,h_n\rangle$ is called an inverse homomorphic equality (of $h_1,\ldots,h_n$).

Note that if $n=1$ or $h_i = h_j$ for all h_i,h_j, then $\langle heq^{-1};\ h_1,\ldots,h_n\rangle = h_1^{-1}$ is an inverse homomorphism, so that an inverse homomorphic equality is an extension of an inverse homomorphism.

The interrelations between the homomorphisms $h_1,\ldots,h_n$ and their homomorphic equality and inverse homomorphic equality can be interpreted as follows: $\langle heq;\ h_1,\ldots,h_n\rangle(w)$ is defined if and only if w has a common homomorphic descendant under $h_1,\ldots,h_n$, and $\langle heq^{-1};\ h_1,\ldots,h_n\rangle(y)$ is the collection of all common homomorphic ancestors of y under $h_1,\ldots,h_n$. Hence, for each string w, $\langle heq;\ h_1,\ldots,h_n\rangle(w) = h_1(w) \cap\ldots\cap h_n(w)$ and $\langle heq^{-1};\ h_1,\ldots,h_n\rangle(w) = h_1^{-1}(w) \cap\ldots\cap h_n^{-1}(w)$. These relations cannot be transferred to languages, since the inclusions $\langle heq;\ h_1,\ldots,h_n\rangle(L) \subseteq h_1(L) \cap\ldots\cap h_n(L)$ and $\langle heq^{-1};\ h_1,\ldots,h_n\rangle(L) \subseteq h_1^{-1}(L) \cap\ldots\cap h_n^{-1}(L)$ are generally proper.

DEFINITION. For homomorphisms $h_1,\ldots,h_n$ from Σ^* into Δ^* define the equality set of $h_1,\ldots,h_n$ by $Eq(h_1,\ldots,h_n) = \{w \in \Sigma^* \mid h_1(w) = \ldots = h_n(w)\}$. A language L such that $L = Eq(h_1,\ldots,h_n)$ is called an n-fold equality set.

n-fold equality sets have been studied in detail in [7]. They are canonical extensions of (two-fold) equality sets, which have been investigated in a number of recent papers. See, e.g., [2,7-13,15]. Further generalizations of n-fold equality sets appear in [9].

The following expressions are obvious from the definitions.

LEMMA 1. For each language L, homomorphisms $h_1,\ldots,h_n$, and each $i=1,\ldots,n$,

$$\langle heq;\ h_1,\ldots,h_n\rangle(L) = h_i(Eq(h_1,\ldots,h_n) \cap L) = \bigcap_{i=1}^{n} (h_i(Eq(h_1,\ldots,h_n) \cap L)),$$ and

$$\langle heq^{-1};\ h_1,\ldots,h_n\rangle(L) = Eq(h_1,\ldots,h_n) \cap h_i^{-1}(L) = Eq(h_1,\ldots,h_n) \cap (\bigcap_{i=1}^{n} h_i^{-1}(L)).$$

It is important to note that each homomorphism h_i appears twice in different situations. First it contributes to the definition of an equality set and then it functions as a homomorphism resp. as an inverse homomorphism. This connection is significant, and it distinguishes a homomorphic equality and an inverse homomorphic equality from the independent use of a homomorphism resp. an inverse homomorphism and the intersection with an equality set.

For brevity we shall use a set theoretic notation.

NOTATION. Let L be a class of language. Let $H(L) = \{h(L) \mid L \in L$ and h is a nonerasing homomorphism$\}$, and $\hat{H}(L) = \{h(L) \mid L \in L$ and h is a homomorphism$\}$. Let $HEQ_n(L) = \{\langle heq; h_1,\ldots,h_n\rangle(L) \mid L \in L$ and $\langle heq; h_1,\ldots,h_n\rangle$ is a nonerasing homomorphic equality of n homomorphisms$\}$, and $\widehat{HEQ}_n(L) = \{\langle heq; h_1,\ldots,h_n\rangle(L) \mid L \in L$ and $\langle heq; h_1,\ldots,h_n\rangle$ is a homomorphic equality of n homomorphisms$\}$. Let $H^{-1}(L) = \{h^{-1}(L) \mid L \in L$ and h is a homomorphism$\}$, and let $HEQ_n^{-1}(L) = \{\langle heq^{-1}; h_1,\ldots,h_n\rangle(L) \mid L \in L$ and $\langle heq^{-1}; h_1,\ldots,h_n\rangle$ is an inverse homomorphic equality of n homomorphisms$\}$.

Note that $H(L) = HEQ_1(L)$, $\hat{H}(L) = \widehat{HEQ}_1(L)$, and $H^{-1}(L) = HEQ_1^{-1}(L)$ for all classes L. Furthermore, $H(H(L)) = H(L)$, and similarly for $\hat{H}$ and H^{-1}, which means that H, $\hat{H}$ and H^{-1} are idempotent operators on classes of languages. However, HEQ_n, $\widehat{HEQ}_n$ and HEQ_n^{-1} are not idempotent for $n \geq 2$.

DEFINITION. A class of languages L is closed under nonerasing homomorphism, if $H(L) \subseteq L$. Similarly define the closure under homomorphism, inverse homomorphism, etc. L is closed under (nonerasing resp. inverse) homomorphic equality, if for every $n \geq 1$, $\widehat{HEQ}_n(L) \subseteq L$ ($HEQ_n(L) \subseteq L$ resp. $HEQ_n^{-1}(L) \subseteq L$).

We now return to a formulation of the Chomsky-Schützenberger theorem.

DEFINITION. A trio is a class of languages containing a nonempty language and closed under nonerasing homomorphism, inverse homomorphism, and intersection with regular sets (which in our set notation is denoted by $\wedge REG$). A full trio is a trio closed under homomorphism. For a class of languages L let $M(L)$ ($\hat{M}(L)$) denote the smallest (full) trio containing L. If L consists of a single language L, we write $M(L)$ ($\hat{M}(L)$) and call it a (full) principal trio with (trio) generator L.

Recall that a (full) trio is characterized by a single application of each trio operation such that $M(L) = H(H^{-1}(L) \wedge REG)$ and $\hat{M}(L) = \hat{H}(H^{-1}(L) \wedge REG)$, where REG denotes the class of regular sets. The Chomsky-Schützenberger theorem for context-free languages thus says that the class of context-free languages CFL is a (full) principal trio with e.g. the Dyck set D_2 as a generator, i.e., $CFL = H(H^{-1}(D_2) \wedge REG) = \hat{H}(H^{-1}(D_2) \wedge REG)$. Other examples of full principal trios are the classes of regular sets, of linear context-free languages, and of recursively enumerable sets, whose generators are, e.g., $\{\lambda\}$, $\{ww^R \mid w \in \{a,b\}^*\}$, and $\{w \in \{a,b,\bar{a},\bar{b}\}^* \mid g(w) = h(w)$ with $g(a)=h(\bar{a})=a$, $g(b)=h(\bar{b})=b$, and g,h erase, otherwise$\}$, respectively. More results on trios can be found in [14].

NOTATION. Let RE denote the class of all recursively enumerable sets, and let REG denote the class of all regular sets.

REPRESENTATIONS OF THE RECURSIVELY ENUMERABLE SETS

Here we characterize the class of recursively enumerable sets RE in terms of the class of regular sets REG and homomorphic equality and inverse homomorphic equality operations.

First notice that the regular sets are not preserved under homomorphic equality and inverse homomorphic equality. For example, if $g(a) = a$, $g(b) = b$, $g(c) = \lambda$, $h(a) = \lambda$, $h(b) = a$, and $h(b) = b$, then $\langle heq; g,h\rangle (\{a\}^*\{b\}^*\{c\}^*) = \{a^n b^n \mid n \geq o\}$ and $\langle heq^{-1}; g,h\rangle (\{a\}^*\{b\}^*) = \{a^n b^n c^n \mid n \geq o\}$. On the other hand, it can be shown that the language $\{a^{2^n} \mid n \geq o\}$ cannot be obtained from any context-free language by a single application of a homomorphic equality or by a composition of inverse homomorphic equality operations. See [9].

<u>THEOREM 1</u>. For every recursively enumerable set L there exist homomorphisms g, h, h_1, h_2, and regular sets Q and R such that

$$L = g(\langle heq; h_1, h_2\rangle (Q)) \quad \text{and} \quad L = h(\langle heq^{-1}; h_1, h_2\rangle (R)).$$

Thus,

$$\mathit{RE} = \widehat{HEQ}_1(\widehat{HEQ}_2(\mathit{REG})) \quad \text{and} \quad \mathit{RE} = \hat{H}(HEQ_2^{-1}(\mathit{REG})).$$

<u>Proof</u>. The proof is a modification of the proof of theorem 2.1 in [2], using a triplicate encoding of instantaneous descriptions. In detail, let L be accepted by a Turing machine M. For any $w \in L$ there exists a sequence of instantaneous descriptions $ID_o, ID_1, \ldots, ID_t$ making up an accepting computation of M. Encode each such sequence into a string of the form of U (cf. (*) on p. 731 in [2]).

$$U = [\overline{\overline{ID_o\#}}, \overline{ID_o}\#, ID_1\#]\,[\overline{ID_o}\#, ID_1\#, ID_2\#] \ldots\ldots [ID_{i-1}\#, ID_i\#, ID_{i+1}\#] \ldots\ldots [ID_{t-1}\#, ID_t\#, \overline{\overline{ID_t\#}}].$$

Let h_1 be the projection onto the first and second components, and let h_1 erase symbols whose first component is double barred. Accordingly, let h_2 be the projection onto the second and third components erasing symbols whose third component is double barred. Let Q be a regular set which controls the proper format of U, and in particular the barring and the fact that substrings $[ID_{i-1}\#, ID_i\#, ID_{i+1}\#]$ represents three successive instantaneous descriptions. Let $R = h_1(Q)$. Then $Q = h_1^{-1}(R) \cap h_2^{-1}(R)$, which is the reason for the choice of the format of U. Let the homomorphisms g and h retrieve w from the strings $h_1(U)$ and U, i.e., from the substring with $\overline{ID_o}$. Then $L = g(h_1(Eq(h_1,h_2) \cap Q)) = h(Eq(h_1,h_2) \cap h_1^{-1}(R))$, and we obtain the representations from above. []

Employing the techniques developed in Theorem 4.6 in [2], Theorem 1 can be sharpened to a nonerasing version, such that h_1 and h_2 are nonerasing homomorphisms.

THEOREM 2. For every recursively enumerable set L there exist homomorphisms g, h, h_1, h_2, where h_1, h_2 are nonerasing, and regular sets Q and R such that

$$L = g(\langle heq;\ h_1,h_2\rangle\ (Q)) \qquad \text{and} \qquad L = h(\langle heq^{-1};h_1,h_2\rangle(R)),\ \text{i.e.,}$$

$$RE = \widehat{HEQ}_1(HEQ_2(REG)) \qquad \text{and} \qquad RE = \hat{H}(HEQ_2^{-1}(REG)).$$

Next we develop an extended Chomsky-Schützenberger theorem for the recursively enumerable sets, and we show that e.g. the language $\{o,1\}^*$ is a generator of the recursively enumerable sets under the operations of homomorphism, inverse homomorphic equality and intersection with regular sets.

THEOREM 3. For every recursively enumerable set L there exist homomorphisms h, h', h" , where h', h" may be nonerasing, and a regular set S such that

$$L = h(\langle heq^{-1};\ h',h''\rangle(\{o,1\}^*)\ \cap S).$$

Hence, $\qquad RE = \hat{H}(\ HEQ_2^{-1}(\{o,1\}^*)\ \wedge\ REG).$

Proof. Let $L = h(\langle heq^{-1};h_1,h_2\rangle(R))$, where h, h_1, h_2 and R are as in Theorem 1 or Theorem 2. Let $S = h_1^{-1}(R)$. For each symbol a_i let $f(a_i) = o\,1^i\,o$, and define $h' = f\bullet h_1$ and $h'' = f\bullet h_2$. Then $Eq(h_1,h_2) = Eq(h',h'')$ and $\langle heq^{-1};h',h''\rangle(\{o,1\}^*)\ \cap\ S\ =\ \langle heq^{-1};h_1,h_2\rangle(R)$. []

From Lemma 1 it is clear that the class of recursively enumerable sets is closed under homomorphic equality and inverse homomorphic equality. Theorem 1 now characterizes this class as the smallest such class.

THEOREM 4. The class of recursively enumerable sets is the smallest class containing the regular sets and closed under homomorphic equality. It is the smallest class containing the regular sets and closed under inverse homomorphic equality and homomorphism. Furthermore, it is the smallest full trio that is closed under inverse homomorphic equality.

A related result has appeared in [4], which charaterizes the class of recursively enumerable sets in terms of homomorphic duplication and intersection. A homomorphic duplication is also based on n-tuples of homomorphisms and defined by the concatenation of the individual homomorphic images, i.e., $h_1(w)h_2(w)\dots h_n(w)$. See [1,4].

THE NONERASING CASE

Here we restrict ourselves to nonerasing homomorphic equality operations. From a class of languages $\mathcal{L}$ we now obtain characterizations of the class $H(\mathcal{L} \wedge \mathcal{MR})$ that parallel the previous results for the class of recursively enumerable sets.

First we must specify the classes $\mathcal{MR}$ and $H(\mathcal{L} \wedge \mathcal{MR})$. $\mathcal{MR}$ is the class MULTI-RESET from [4]. It can be defined, e.g., by nondeterministic real-time acceptors whose working tapes are three or more reset tapes [4], or two or more Post tapes [7], or a k-head Post tape with $k \geq 3$ [7]. Alternatively, $\mathcal{MR}$ is the smallest trio containing all 3-fold equality sets [7]. Moreover, $\mathcal{MR}$ contains all k-fold equality sets for $k \geq 1$, it is a principal trio and closed under intersection and Kleene star. See [1,4,7].

For a class $\mathcal{L}$, $H(\mathcal{L} \wedge \mathcal{MR}) = \{h(L_1 \cap L_2) \mid L_1 \in \mathcal{L}, L_2 \in \mathcal{MR}$, and h is a nonerasing homomorphism$\}$. Classes of the form of $H(\mathcal{L} \wedge \mathcal{MR})$ have been investigated in [1,4,5]. In general, these classes have good closure properties. For example, if $\mathcal{L}$ is a trio, then $H(\mathcal{L} \wedge \mathcal{MR})$ is an intersection closed trio [5].

Using the aforementioned properties of $\mathcal{MR}$, Lemma 1, the set identity $f(X) \cap Y = f(X \cap f^{-1}(Y))$, and the fact that $H(\mathcal{L} \wedge \mathcal{MR})$ is closed under inverse homomorphism, if $\mathcal{L}$ is so closed, we can add to the closure properties of $H(\mathcal{L} \wedge \mathcal{MR})$.

<u>THEOREM 5</u>. Let $\mathcal{L}$ be a class of languages and closed under inverse homomorphism. Then the class $H(\mathcal{L} \wedge \mathcal{MR})$ is closed under nonerasing homomorphic equality and under inverse homomorphic equality.

It is convenient to have a machine characterization for classes $H(\mathcal{L} \wedge \mathcal{MR})$. Therefore we introduce preset k-head Post machines, which are used as a technical tool and programmed in an appropriate way.

<u>DEFINITION</u>. A <u>preset</u> k-<u>head</u> <u>Post</u> <u>machine</u> <u>with</u> <u>base</u> B is a nondeterministic acceptor with a one-way input tape, a finite state control, and a working tape. The working tape is scanned left-to-right by k read-only heads. The contents of the working tape is preset by any member of the base. In each move M nondeterministically changes states, it visits a new square on the input tape (so that it runs in real time) and new squares with some of its heads on the working tape. M blocks whenever the symbols read on these squares do not correspond to an instruction. M accepts an input string w, if there exists a working tape $y \in B$ and a sequence of moves such that M reads w on the input tape and reads y with each head on the working tape and enters an accepting state. Let L(M,B) denote the <u>language</u> accepted by M with base B. (For formal definitions see [9]).

In their behaviour preset k-head Post machines closely resemble k-head Post machines (see [7]), and it is readily seen that each preset k-head Post machine with a regular base can be simulated by a k-head Post machine, and vice versa. Hence, preset k-head Post machines with regular bases define exactly the class MR.

LEMMA 2. Let M be a preset k-head Post machine with base B. Then there exist homomorphisms $h, h_1, \ldots, h_k$, where h is nonerasing, and a regular set R such that

$$L(M,B) = h(\langle heq^{-1}; h_1, \ldots, h_k \rangle (B) \cap R).$$

Proof. The proof follows the usual method in AFL theory [14]. Encode each sequence of instructions of an accepting computation of M into a string c over symbols of k+2 tuples, such that h retrieves the input w from c, h_i models the actions of the ith head on the working tape, such that $h_i(c)$ represents the contents of the working tape and $h_i(c) = h_j(c)$ for $1 \leq i,j \leq k$, and the regular set R models the finite state control of M and controls the proper format of c. Let C be the set of all such c. Then $C = Eq(h_1, \ldots, h_k) \cap R \cap h_1^{-1}(B)$, $h(C) = L(M,B)$, and $h_1(C)$ is the set of all working tapes, which together with some input have an accepting computation of M. (See Theorem 3.4 in [7] and Theorem 6.2 in [9] for more details). []

Next we construct preset k-head Post machines with only three heads, which behave in a special way.

LEMMA 3. Let $L = f^{-1}(L_1) \cap L_2$, where $L_1 \subseteq \Sigma^*$, $L \subseteq \Gamma^*$, and $L_2 \in MR$. Then there exists a preset 3-head Post machine M with base B such that $L(M,B) = L$, $B = g^{-1}(f^{-1}(L_1))$ for some nonerasing homomorphism g, and for every $w \in L(M,B)$ there exists a unique $y \in B$ such that there is an accepting computation of M on w with working tape y, $w = g(y)$, and the first head on the working tape moves uniformly at every step or at every fifth step.

Proof. Let M_1 be the three head Post machine from Theorem 4.7 and Lemma 4.6 in [7] with $L(M_1) = L_2$. Augment the working tape of M_1 by two extra channels, which in accepting computations contain the input string w and its homomorphic image $f(w)$ in compressed form. The compression is in accordance with the movements of the first head on the working tape, which, moreover, checks the properness of these channels symbol by symbol. Let the homomorphism g retrieve w from these channels. Then $L = L(M,B)$, and M and B satisfy all the claimed properties. []

Combining Lemmas 1-3 we can characterize the classes $H(L \wedge MR)$ in terms of an extended Chomsky-Schützenberger theorem with inverse homomorphic equality operations of three homomorphisms, and in terms of L-based preset 3-head Post machines.

<u>THEOREM 6</u>. Let L be a class of languages that is closed under inverse homomorphism. Then $H(L \wedge MR) = H(HEQ_3^{-1}(L) \wedge REG)$,

and it is the smallest class containing L and closed under inverse homomorphic equality, nonerasing homomorphism, and intersection with regular sets.

For a characterization of the classes $H(L \wedge MR)$ in terms of nonerasing homomorphic equality we reconsider the proofs of Lemma 2 and Lemma 3. The constructions for Lemma 3 enable us to overcome the two remaining difficulties, namely, to retrieve an input string from the working tape, and to make a homomorphism of the homomorphic equality nonerasing.

<u>THEOREM 7</u>. Let L be a class of languages that is closed under inverse homomorphism and intersection with regular sets. Then

$$H(L \wedge MR) = HEQ_1(HEQ_3(L)),$$

and it is the smallest class containing L and closed under nonerasing homomorphic equality.

<u>Proof</u>. Let $L = h(L_1 \cap L_2)$ with $L_1 \in L$, $L_2 \in MR$, and some nonerasing homomorphism h. Let $L_1 \cap L_2 = L(M,B)$, where M and B are as in Lemma 3. Applying Lemma 2 we can express the set of sequences of instructions of accepting computations by $C = Eq(h_1,h_2,h_3) \cap R \cap h_1^{-1}(B)$ and $L(M,B) = g(h_1(C))$. However, the homomorphism h_1 is not nonerasing. Let $C \subseteq \Phi^*$ for some alphabet Φ, and let Φ_5 be the compression of five symbols of Φ into a new symbol. Let the homomorphism α be the decompression. Since the first head on the working tape of M moves at least at every fifth step and h_1 models the actions of this head, now $h_1 \cdot \alpha$ is a nonerasing homomorphism. Since $C = \alpha(\alpha^{-1}(C))$, now $L(M,B) = g(\langle heq; h_1\alpha, h_2\alpha, h_3\alpha\rangle(L_1'))$ and $L = h \cdot g(\langle heq; h_1\alpha, h_2\alpha, h_3\alpha\rangle(L_1'))$, where $L_1' = \alpha^{-1} h_1^{-1} g^{-1}(L_1) \cap \alpha^{-1}(R) \in L$. Hence, $H(L \wedge MR) \subseteq HEQ_1(HEQ_3(L))$. The remaining part of the proof follows easily from Theorem 5. []

Finally we consider principal trios L and the principality of $H(L \wedge MR)$ in terms of nonerasing homomorphism, inverse homomorphic equality, and intersection with regular sets.

Let the language G be a trio generator of a class L. Let $G \subseteq \Sigma^*$ and let $o,1 \notin \Sigma$. Let G' be obtained by "padding" G with o's and 1's. Formally, let π be a homomorphism from $(\Sigma \cup \{o,1\})^*$ into Σ^* with $\pi(a) = a$ for $a \in \Sigma$ and $\pi(o) = \pi(1) = \lambda$. Define $G' = \pi^{-1}(G)$. Clearly, G' is a new trio generator of L.

THEOREM 8. Let L be a principal trio with generator G, i.e., $L = H(H^{-1}(G) \wedge REG)$. Then $H(L \wedge MR) = H(HEQ_3^{-1}(G') \wedge REG)$.

Proof. If $L = f_o(f_1(f_2^{-1}(G) \cap R_1) \cap L_2) \in H(L \wedge MR)$, then there is $L_3 \in MR$ and $L = f_o f_1(f_2^{-1}(G) \cap L_3) \in H(L \wedge MR)$. Let $f_2^{-1}(G) \cap L_3 = L(M,B)$, where M is a preset 3-head Post machine with base B from Lemma 3. Applying Lemma 2 we can express the set of sequences of instructions of accepting computations of M by $C = Eq(h_1,h_2,h_3) \cap R \cap h_1^{-1}(B)$, such that $L(M,B) = h(C)$ for some nonerasing homomorphism h. If $c \in C$ describes a computation of M on an input w with working tape y, then $h_1(c) = y$, and y contains $f_2(w)$ on one of its "new channels". Let $\Sigma' = \{b_u \mid u \in \Sigma^* \text{ and } |u| \leq \max\{|f_2(a)| \mid a \in \Gamma\}\}$ be the set of symbols occurring on this channel, and let Δ be the set of symbols occurring on the remaining channels, such that $\Delta \times \Sigma'$ is the working tape alphabet of M. Let γ be a homomorphism from $(\Delta \times \Sigma')^*$ into $(\Sigma \cup \{o,1\})^*$ with $\gamma(a_i,b_u) = o1^i ou$. Thus γ encodes the first components and decompresses the second components. Then $Eq(h_1,h_2,h_3) = Eq(h_1\gamma,h_2\gamma,h_3\gamma)$ and $C = Eq(h_1\gamma,h_2\gamma,h_3\gamma) \cap R \cap h_1^{-1}(\gamma^{-1}(G' \cap \gamma(\Delta\times\Sigma')^*))$. Hence, $C = \langle heq^{-1};h_1\gamma,h_2\gamma,h_3\gamma\rangle(G') \cap R \cap h_1^{-1}(\gamma^{-1}(\gamma(\Delta \times \Sigma')^*))$, and $L = g_o(\langle heq^{-1};g_1,g_2,g_3\rangle(G') \cap R_2)$ for appropriate homomorphisms $g_o,\ldots,g_3$, where g_o is nonerasing, and a regular set R_2. []

Our characterizations can be applied to some important classes of languages, and we obtain extended Chomsky-Schützenberger theorems for these classes.

Let BNP be a specific class of languages from [6]. BNP is, e.g., the smallest intersection closed trio containing the class of linear-context-free languages LIN. See [1,5,6]. Let $PAL = \{w w^R \mid w \in \{a,b\}^*\}$, and let $PAL' = \pi^{-1}(PAL)$ with π as above. Note that PAL and PAL' are trio generators of LIN.
Let Q be the class of quasirealtime languages from [3]. Q is the smallest intersection closed trio containing the class of context-free languages CFL. Let D_2 be the Dyck set (over the pairs $(a,\bar{a})$ and $(b,\bar{b})$), and let $D_2' = \pi^{-1}(D_2)$. Note that D_2 and D_2' are trio generators of CFL.

COROLLARY 1. (1) $MR = HEQ_1(HEQ_3(REG)) = H(HEQ_3^{-1}(\{o,1\}^*) \wedge REG)$, and MR is the smallest class containing the regular sets and closed under nonerasing homomorphic equality, and is the smallest trio that is closed under inverse homomorphic equality.

(2) $BNP = HEQ_1(HEQ_3(LIN)) = H(HEQ_3^{-1}(PAL') \wedge REG)$, and BNP is the smallest class containing the linear context-free languages and closed under nonerasing homomorphic equality, and it is the smallest trio containing the linear context-free languages and closed under inverse homomorphic equality.

$$(3) \qquad \mathcal{Q} = \mathrm{HEQ}_1(\mathrm{HEQ}_3(\mathit{CFL})) = \mathrm{H}(\mathrm{HEQ}_3^{-1}(\mathrm{D}_2') \wedge \mathit{REG}),$$

and $\mathcal{Q}$ is the smallest class containing the context-free languages and closed under nonerasing homomorphic equality, and is the smallest trio containing the context-free languages and closed under inverse homomorphic equality.

Finally, note that a related characterization of the class $\mathrm{H}(L \wedge MR)$ can be obtained from a class L by using the operations of nonerasing homomorphic duplication and intersection. See [1,4]. Hence, in the framework of trios, the operations of nonerasing homomorphic equality, of inverse homomorphic equality and nonerasing homomorphism, and of nonerasing homomorphic duplication and intersection are equivalent in the sense that they characterize the class $\mathrm{H}(L \wedge MR)$ in terms of L.

REFERENCES

1. R.V. Book, Simple representations of certain classes of languages. J. Assoc. Comput. Mach. 25 (1978), 23-31.

2. R.V. Book and F.J. Brandenburg, Equality sets and complexity classes. SIAM J. Comput. 9 (198o), 729-743.

3. R.V. Book and S.A. Greibach, Quasi-realtime languages. Math. Systems Theory 4 (197o), 97-111.

4. R.V. Book, S.A. Greibach, and C. Wrathall, Reset machines. J. Comput. System Sci. 19 (1979), 256-276.

5. R.V. Book and M. Nivat, Linear languages and the intersection closure of classes of languages. SIAM J. Comput. 7 (1978), 167-177.

6. R.V. Book, M. Nivat, and M. Paterson, Reversal-bounded acceptors and intersections of linear languages. SIAM J. Comput. 3 (1974), 283-295.

7. F.J. Brandenburg, Multiple equality sets and Post machines. J. Comput. System Sci. 21 (198o), 292-316.

8. F.J. Brandenburg, Unary multiple equality sets: the languages of rational matrices. Inform. Contr. (in press).

9. F.J. Brandenburg, Homomorphic equality operations on languages. Habilitationsschrift, Universität Bonn (1981).

1o. K. Culik II, A purely homomorphic characterization of recursively enumerable sets. J. Assoc. Comput. Mach. 26 (1979), 345-35o.

11. K. Culik II and H.A. Maurer, On simple representations of language families. RAIRO Theoret. Informatics 13 (1979), 241-25o.

12. J. Engelfriet and G. Rozenberg, Equality sets and fixed point languages. Inform Contr. 43 (1979), 2o-49.

13. J. Engelfriet and G. Rozenberg, Fixed point languages, equality languages and representations of recursively enumerable languages. J. Assoc. Comput. Mach. 27 (198o), 499-518.

14. S. Ginsburg, "Algebraic and automata-theoretic properties of formal languages". North-Holland, Amsterdam, 1975.

15. A. Salomaa, Equality sets for homomorphisms of free monoids. Acta Cybernetica 4 (1978), 127-139.

Real Time Agents

Luca Cardelli
Dept. of Computer Science
University of Edinburgh
JCMB The King's Buildings
Edinburgh EH9 3JZ, Scotland

Introduction

This paper is inspired by Milner's approach to synchronous processes, as reported in (Milner 82). The main differences are the use of a dense time domain and a dense-nondeterminism operator. Milner has shown that many of the characteristics of concurrent processes can be modelled and, more importantly, manipulated in an algebraic framework tailored to synchronous discrete interaction. Although much can be done in a discrete-time model by reducing the grain of discreteness to the desired level, we think it is interesting to see what can be gained in a dense-time framework and what additional difficulties arise.

At an appropriate level of abstraction there are entities which act and influence each other's behaviour through a <u>continuous interaction</u>. These entities are called here <u>agents</u> and their interactions are assumed to happen in <u>real time</u> (we use real numbers as a standard example of dense order). Agents progress by performing <u>actions</u>. Actions are denoted by the letters a,b,c and d, and the set of all the actions is A. Actions can be performed concurrently, so we denote by $a \cdot b$ (or simply ab) the simultaneous occurrence of the actions a and b. We also admit a <u>neutral</u> action 1, so that $(A, \cdot, 1)$ is an abelian monoid.

Communication between agents can be modelled by requiring A to be a commutative group $(A, \cdot, 1, \bar{\ })$. A successful communication between two agents is represented by the matching of two complementary actions a and $\bar{a}$. The fact that $a\bar{a} = 1$ means that communication involves exactly two agents, that the respective communication capabilities are consumed during the process and that an external observer is unable to tell which communication took place (he can only observe 1). Note that communication here means simple synchronisation, without passage of values.

The central idea in real time agents is the explicit use of time information when expressing the behaviour of agents. Time is assumed to be dense, i.e. for every two instants t',t" it is always possible to find an instant t such that $t' < t < t"$. We shall formalise the idea of <u>observing</u> a real time system <u>during</u>

intervals of time (i.e. not observing at time instants) and we want to rule out the possibility of observing zero-length actions. Hence the variables denoting time will range over a dense domain $\mathbb{K}$ (for Kronos) = $\mathbb{R}^+$, that is the set of strictly positive real numbers. The letters t,u,v will range over $\mathbb{K}$.

Deterministic Agents

We first examine agents which are deterministic, in the informal sense that every agent has a unique possible development in time. A formal property corresponding to the idea of determinism will be examined later.

We begin with a very simple set of operators to build agents. Our initial operator signature consists of: a constant $\mathbb{1}$ representing the neutral agent always performing the neutral action 1; a unary prefix operator $a[t]:$ which represents the act of performing the action a for an interval of time t; and the binary infix operator X representing the synchronous composition (coexistence) of two agents. An agent (denoted by p,q,r,s) is an expression over the signature $\Sigma^D = \{\mathbb{1}, a[t]:, X\}$ (where D stands for deterministic). The set of agents P^D is the free algebra over Σ^D.

Now we specify how our agents behave, by defining a set of binary relations $\xrightarrow[t]{a}$ (for $a \in A$ and $t \in \mathbb{K}$) over P^D. We read $p \xrightarrow[t]{a} q$ as "p moves to q performing a for an interval t", or "p takes t to move under a to q". The reduction rules for deterministic agents are as follows:

$$(\mathbb{1} \rightarrow) \qquad \mathbb{1} \xrightarrow[t]{1} \mathbb{1}$$

$$(a[\,] \rightarrow) \qquad a[t]:p \xrightarrow[t]{a} p \qquad\qquad (X \rightarrow) \qquad \frac{p \xrightarrow[t]{a} p' \qquad q \xrightarrow[t]{b} q'}{p\,X\,q \xrightarrow[t]{ab} p'\,X\,q'}$$

$$(a[\,]a[\,] \rightarrow) \qquad a[t+u]:p \xrightarrow[t]{a} a[u]:p$$

Rule $(\mathbb{1} \rightarrow)$ asserts that $\mathbb{1}$ moves under 1 for an arbitrary interval t to produce $\mathbb{1}$ again. Rule $(a[\,] \rightarrow)$ says that $a[t]:p$ takes t to move under a to p, with $t>0$. Rule $(a[\,]a[\,] \rightarrow)$ has to do with the density of time; it says that after an interval t, $a[t+u]:p$ has only reached $a[u]:p$. Note that it is possible to split actions at arbitrary points, but this is done consistently so that the final outcome remains the same. Rule $(X \rightarrow)$ gives meaning to the coexistence of two agents: if p takes t to move under a to p' and q takes t to move under b to q', then $p\,X\,q$ takes t (the same t) to move under $a{\cdot}b$ to $p'\,X\,q'$. Note that if q has form $b[t+u]:q''$, we can use $(a[\,]a[\,] \rightarrow)$ to get a t-derivation of q, so that we can use $(X \rightarrow)$.

This set of operational rules enjoys two fundamental properties:

<u>Lemma 1</u> (Density Lemma) $p \xrightarrow[t+u]{a} r \Rightarrow \exists q.\ p \xrightarrow[t]{a} q,\ q \xrightarrow[u]{a} r$

Proof: Induction on the structure of the derivation of $p \xrightarrow[t+u]{a} r$ □

<u>Lemma 2</u> (Persistency Lemma) $\forall p,t.\ \exists p_1,a_1,t_1 \dots p_n,a_n,t_n.$

$$\textstyle\sum_i t_i = t \quad \text{and} \quad p \xrightarrow[t_1]{a_1} p_1 \dots \xrightarrow[t_n]{a_n} p_n$$

Proof: Induction on the structure of p. The case p=p'Xp" needs the density lemma□

We shall abandon the persistency lemma later, but density is fundamental for all the different signatures we shall study. When adding a new operator to our signature, most of the results for the old signature extend to the new one, provided that density is preserved.

Agents will be observed by considering the sequences of actions they can perform. If the agents p and q are in the relation $p \xrightarrow[t]{a} q$, and q and r are in the relation $q \xrightarrow[u]{b} r$, then we can consider the composition of the relations $\xrightarrow[t]{a}$ and $\xrightarrow[u]{b}$ (denoted $\xrightarrow[t]{a} \circ \xrightarrow[u]{b}$) so that p and r are in the relation $p\ (\xrightarrow[t]{a} \circ \xrightarrow[u]{b})\ r$.

<u>Definition 1</u> $\xrightarrow[t]{a} \circ \xrightarrow[u]{b} \ = \ \left\{(p,r) \,\middle|\, \exists q.\ (p,q) \in \xrightarrow[t]{a} \text{ and } (q,r) \in \xrightarrow[u]{b}\right\}$ □

We write $\xrightarrow[(t_1 \dots t_n)]{(a_1 \dots a_n)}$ for $\xrightarrow[t_1]{a_1} \circ \dots \circ \xrightarrow[t_n]{a_n}$ $(n>0)$. Moreover a sequence of actions is denoted by $\hat{a} = (a_1 \dots a_n)$ with $\#\hat{a} = n$, and a sequence of time intervals by $\hat{t} = (t_1 \dots t_n)$ with $\#\hat{t} = n$ and $\sum\hat{t} = \sum_{1 \leq i \leq n} t_i$.

We want to observe actions in such a way that, for example, the sequences $\xrightarrow[(1,1)]{(a,a)}$ and $\xrightarrow[(2)]{(a)}$ are indistinguishable. This can be done by considering <u>similar</u> sequences in the following informal sense:

$\xrightarrow[(2,2,2,2)]{(a,b,b,b)}$ is similar to $\xrightarrow[(1,1,3,3)]{(a,a,b,b)}$; $\xrightarrow[(1,2)]{(a,b)}$ is not similar to $\xrightarrow[(2,1)]{(a,b)}$.

<u>Definition 2</u> Similarity is the least equivalence relation, $\triangleq$, between relations $\xrightarrow[\hat{t}]{\hat{a}}$ such that:

(i) If $a_1 = \dots = a_n = b_1 = \dots = b_m$ and $\sum\hat{t} = \sum\hat{u}$ then $\xrightarrow[\hat{t}]{\hat{a}} \triangleq \xrightarrow[\hat{u}]{\hat{b}}$

(ii) If $\xrightarrow[\hat{t}']{\hat{a}'} \triangleq \xrightarrow[\hat{u}']{\hat{b}'}$ and $\xrightarrow[\hat{t}'']{\hat{a}''} \triangleq \xrightarrow[\hat{u}'']{\hat{b}''}$ then $\xrightarrow[\hat{t}']{\hat{a}'} \circ \xrightarrow[\hat{t}'']{\hat{a}''} \triangleq \xrightarrow[\hat{u}']{\hat{b}'} \circ \xrightarrow[\hat{u}'']{\hat{b}''}$ □

We can also talk about sequences which are <u>finer</u> than other sequences:

<u>Definition 3</u> $\xrightarrow[\hat{t}]{\hat{a}}$ is finer than $\xrightarrow[\hat{u}]{\hat{b}}$ when $\xrightarrow[\hat{t}]{\hat{a}} \leqslant \xrightarrow[\hat{u}]{\hat{b}}$, where $\leqslant$ is the least relation satisfying:

(i) $\xrightarrow[(t_1 \dots t_n)]{(a \dots a)} \leqslant \xrightarrow[\sum_i t_i]{a}$

(ii) If $\xrightarrow[\hat{t}']{\hat{a}'} \leqslant \xrightarrow[\hat{u}']{\hat{b}'}$ and $\xrightarrow[\hat{t}'']{\hat{a}''} \leqslant \xrightarrow[\hat{u}'']{\hat{b}''}$ then $\xrightarrow[\hat{t}']{\hat{a}'} \circ \xrightarrow[\hat{t}'']{\hat{a}''} \leqslant \xrightarrow[\hat{u}']{\hat{b}'} \circ \xrightarrow[\hat{u}'']{\hat{b}''}$ □

<u>Theorem 1</u> $\leqslant$ is a partial order over the relations $\xrightarrow[\hat{t}]{\hat{a}}$. Moreover:

(i) If $\xrightarrow[\hat{t}]{\hat{a}} \leqslant \xrightarrow[\hat{u}]{\hat{b}}$ then $\xrightarrow[\hat{t}]{\hat{a}} \simeq \xrightarrow[\hat{u}]{\hat{b}}$

(ii) If $\xrightarrow[\hat{t}]{\hat{a}} \simeq \xrightarrow[(u)]{\hat{u}(b)}$ then $\xrightarrow[\hat{t}]{\hat{a}} \leqslant \xrightarrow[(u)]{\hat{u}(b)}$

(iii) The greatest lower bound of two similar sequences exists and is unique.

Proof: Directly from the definitions □

The density lemma implies the following:

<u>Lemma 3</u> (Refinement Lemma) If $p \xrightarrow[\hat{t}]{\hat{a}} q$ and $\xrightarrow[\hat{u}]{\hat{b}} \leqslant \xrightarrow[\hat{t}]{\hat{a}}$ then $p \xrightarrow[\hat{u}]{\hat{b}} q$ □

The following abbreviation will be used:

<u>Definition 4</u> $p \xrightarrow[\hat{t}]{\hat{a}}{}^{s} q$ if there exists $\xrightarrow[\hat{t}']{\hat{a}'} \simeq \xrightarrow[\hat{t}]{\hat{a}}$ such that $p \xrightarrow[\hat{t}']{\hat{a}'} q$ □

Informally, the behaviour of agents is given by their reduction chain, and we want to regard as equivalent agents which have the "same" reduction chains (i.e. which perform the "same" actions) even if they are syntactically different as members of P^D. After having defined a congruence relation $\sim$ over P^D so that $p \sim q$ iff they perform the same actions, we can then take the equivalence class of p in $P^D/\sim$ as the semantics of p.

We are going to define the following equivalence: p is equivalent to q iff whenever p can reduce under a single action $\xrightarrow[t]{a}$ to p', then q can reduce by a <u>similar</u> sequence $\xrightarrow[t]{a}{}^{s}$ to some q' equivalent to p', and vice versa. This equivalence is called <u>smooth</u> <u>equivalence</u> because it ignores the "density" of individual actions and only considers their coarse result. We first define a formula $\mathbb{D}(\approx)$ parametrically in an arbitrary relation over P^D:

<u>Definition 5</u> $\mathbb{D}(\approx) \;=\; p \approx q$ iff $\forall a \in A, \forall t \in \mathbb{K}$.

$$\text{both } p \xrightarrow[t]{a} p' \;\Rightarrow\; \exists q'.\; q \xrightarrow[t]{a}{}^{s} q' \text{ and } p' \approx q'$$

$$\text{and } q \xrightarrow[t]{a} q' \;\Rightarrow\; \exists p'.\; p \xrightarrow[t]{a}{}^{s} p' \text{ and } p' \approx q' \quad \square$$

<u>Definition 6</u> Smooth equivalence ($\sim$) is the maximal fixpoint of the equation $\mathbb{D}(\approx) = \approx$ in the lattice of binary relations over P^D □

<u>Theorem 2</u> (Park's Induction Principle (Park 81))

$$p \sim q \quad \text{iff} \quad \exists R \subseteq P^D \times P^D. \quad \text{(i)} \; (p,q) \in R$$

$$\text{(ii)} \; R \subseteq \mathbb{D}(R) \quad \square$$

Condition (ii) can be written more explicitely as:

$$(p,q) \in R \Rightarrow \begin{array}{l} (ii')\ \forall p \xrightarrow[t]{a} p'.\ \exists (p',q') \in R.\ q \xrightarrow[t]{a}{}^{s} q' \\ (ii'')\ \forall q \xrightarrow[t]{a} q'.\ \exists (p',q') \in R.\ p \xrightarrow[t]{a}{}^{s} p' \end{array}$$

Theorem 3

(i) $\sim$ is an equivalence relation.

(ii) $\sim$ is a congruence with respect to $\Sigma^D = \{\mathrm{1l},\ a[t]:,\ X\}$.

(iii) $P^D/\sim$ is a Σ^D-algebra.

Proof: (i) is easily verified.

(ii) We have to show that for every Σ^D-context $C(x)$: $p \sim q \Rightarrow C(p) \sim C(q)$.

It is enough to show (using Park's induction) that:

(1) $p \sim q \Rightarrow a[t]:p \sim a[t]:q$

(2) $p \sim q \Rightarrow p\,X\,r \sim q\,X\,r$ and $r\,X\,p \sim r\,X\,q$

For (1) take $R = \{(a[t]:p,\ a[t]:q) \mid p \sim q\} \cup \sim$, and proceed by Park's induction and analysis of the structure of the derivations. For (2), similarly, take $R = \{(p\,X\,r,\ q\,X\,r) \mid p \sim q\} \cup \sim$ (and symmetrically in the second case). Note that the density lemma is required.

(iii) This is a standard algebraic result, based on (ii) □

We can now investigate the equivalence ($\sim$) of agents. The following laws hold:

(X 1l)	$p\ X\ \mathrm{1l} \sim p$	(1[]1l)	$1[t]: \mathrm{1l} \sim \mathrm{1l}$
(X)	$p\ X\ q \sim q\ X\ p$	(a[]a[])	$a[t]:a[u]:p \sim a[t+u]:p$
(XX)	$p\ X\ (q\ X\ r) \sim (p\ X\ q)\ X\ r$	(a[]X)	$a[t]:p\ X\ b[t]:q \sim ab[t]:(pXq)$

All the laws can be proved smoothly by Park's induction. Both the congruence property for X and the factorisation law (a[]X) depend only on the density lemma; whenever we modify our signature we need only to make sure that the density lemma still holds.

The following results tell us that the above set of laws is rich and consistent:

Theorem 4 (Soundness) Let us denote by $\equiv$ the congruence defined by the set of laws (X 1l) ... (a[]X). We say that p is convertible to q iff $p \equiv q$. Then:

$$p \equiv q \Rightarrow p \sim q$$

Proof: Induction on the derivation of $p \equiv q$, using the fact that $\sim$ is a congruence and the laws are valid □

Theorem 5 (Normal Forms) Let $S_{i \leq n}\ a_i[t_i]:p$ abbreviate $a_1[t_1]:\ldots a_n[t_n]:p$ (for $n \geq 0$). An agent is in sequence form if it has the form $S_{i \leq n}\ a_i[t_i]: \mathrm{1l}$.

An agent is in <u>normal form</u> if it is in sequence form $S_{i\leq n}\ a_i[t_i]: 1\!1$ with both $(n>0 \Rightarrow a_n \neq 1)$ and $(n\geq 2 \Rightarrow \forall i<n.\ a_i \neq a_{i+1})$. Then:

(i) Every agent is convertible to a sequence form.

(ii) Every sequence form is convertible to a normal form.

(iii) Every agent has a unique normal form.

Proof: Simple inductions on the structure of terms □

<u>Theorem 6</u> (Completeness)

$$p \sim q \quad \Rightarrow \quad p \equiv q$$

Proof: First prove that for p',q' in normal form, $p' \sim q' \Rightarrow p' \equiv q'$ by induction on the structure of p' and q' (this is easy because of the simple structure of normal forms: we even have $p' \sim q' \Rightarrow p' = q'$). In general, by the normal form theorem, p and q have respective normal forms p' and q' (so that $p \equiv p'$ and $q \equiv q'$). By soundness $p' \sim p \sim q \sim q'$. So by the first part of the proof $p' \equiv q'$. Hence $p \equiv p' \equiv q' \equiv q$ □

We said that our agents are deterministic: this can be stated formally in the following way:

<u>Theorem 7</u> (Determinism)

Vertical determinism: $p \xrightarrow[t]{a} q$ and $p \xrightarrow[u]{b} r$ implies $a = b$

Horizontal determinism:

(i) If $p \xrightarrow[\hat{t}]{\hat{a}} q$, $p \xrightarrow[\hat{u}]{\hat{b}} r$ and $\xrightarrow[\hat{t}]{\hat{a}} \simeq \xrightarrow[\hat{u}]{\hat{b}}$ then $q = r$

(ii) If $p \sim q$, $p \xrightarrow[\hat{t}]{\hat{a}} p'$, $q \xrightarrow[\hat{u}]{\hat{b}} q'$ and $\xrightarrow[\hat{t}]{\hat{a}} \simeq \xrightarrow[\hat{u}]{\hat{b}}$ then $p' \sim q'$

Proof: Structural induction on the left hand side of the arrows, plus in each case a simple lemma about the corresponding structure of the action and the right hand side of the arrow □

In this formal sense our agents are completely deterministic, and we can also see that it is possible to introduce two orthogonal kinds of nondeterminism. This will be done in the next section.

<u>Nondeterministic Agents</u>

Let us now extend our signature by the following operators. A constant 0 representing an agent with no actions; when a system reaches the state 0, a catastrophe occurs and time ceases to flow, hence 0 is called a disaster. A unary prefix operator a(t): performing the action a for a positive interval of length <u>at most</u> t; we say that a(t): introduces horizontal continuous nondeterminism in the sense

that arrows can be stretched horizontally according to the duration of a(t):.
A binary infix operator + representing the choice between two behaviours; we say that + introduces vertical discrete nondeterminism. We can imagine the behaviour of an agent as a (discontinuous) trajectory on the plane, with time on the x axis and the action monoid on the y axis; this explains the sense of the adjectives "horizontal" and "vertical".

The operational semantics is as follows. There are no axioms for 0. The agent a(t):p takes time $v \leq t$ to move under a to p, and a(t+u):p takes time $v \leq t$ to move under a to p + a(u):p. Hence a(t):p can choose at any move to shorten its life span by some amount; moreover at any point in time it can stop its a-action and start executing p. As for +, if p takes t to move under a to p', then p+q may move under a to p' taking time t, or else if q takes u to move under b to q', then p+q may move under b to q' taking time u.

$$(a()\rightarrow) \quad a(t):p \xrightarrow[v]{a} p \qquad v \leq t$$

$$(a()a()\rightarrow) \quad a(t+u):p \xrightarrow[v]{a} p+a(u):p \qquad v \leq t$$

$$(+\rightarrow) \quad \frac{p \xrightarrow[t]{a} p'}{p+q \xrightarrow[t]{a} p'} \qquad \frac{q \xrightarrow[u]{b} q'}{p+q \xrightarrow[u]{b} q'}$$

Applying the same definition of smooth equivalence to the new extended signature Σ (freely generating the new set of agents P), we obtain the following laws:

(+0)	$p + 0 \sim p$	(a()+)	$a(t+u):p \sim a(t+u):p + a(t):p$
(+p)	$p + p \sim p$	(a()a())	$a(t+u):p \sim a(t):(p + a(u):p)$
(+)	$p + q \sim q + p$	(X0)	$p \times 0 \sim 0$
(++)	$p + (q + r) \sim (p + q) + r$	(X+)	$p \times (q + r) \sim (p \times q) + (p \times r)$
(1()𝟙)	$1(t):𝟙 \sim 𝟙$		

The density lemma is still valid (we must abandon the persistency lemma because of 0) and $\sim$ is a congruence. However the set of laws above is not complete, we lack the distributivity of a(t): over X and laws relating a(t): to a[t]:.

Laws relating a(t): and X are called <u>factorisation theorems</u> (the restriction operator $\lceil B$ used below is explained in the next section; the laws (FT2) and (FT4) hold also with all the $\lceil B$ elided):

(FT1) $(a(t):p \times b(t):q)\lceil B \sim 0$ if $ab \notin B$

(FT2) $(a(t):p \times b(t):q)\lceil B \sim (ab(t):(p \times q))\lceil B$

if either $\forall u<t.\ (p\times(q+b(u):q))\lceil B \sim (p\times q)\lceil B$
or $\forall u<t.\ \exists v\leq u.\ (p\times(q+b(u):q))\lceil B \sim (p\times q+a(v):(p\times b(v):q))\lceil B$
and either $\forall u<t.\ ((p+a(u):p)\times q)\lceil B \sim (p\times q)\lceil B$

$$\begin{aligned}
&\text{or } \forall u<t.\ \exists v\leq u.\ ((p+a(u):p)Xq)\lceil B \sim (pXq+a(v):(pXb(v):q))\lceil B \\
&\text{and either } \forall u<t.\ ((p+a(u):p)X(q+b(u):q))\lceil B \sim (pXq)\lceil B \\
&\text{or } \forall u<t.\ \exists v\leq u.\ ((p+a(u):p)X(q+b(u):q))\lceil B \sim (pXq+a(v):pXb(v):q)\lceil B \\
&\text{and either } \forall u<t.\ (pXq+a(u):pXb(u):q)\lceil B \sim (pXq)\lceil B \\
&\text{or } \forall u<t.\ \exists v\leq u.\ (pXq+a(u):p+b(u):q)\lceil B \sim ((p+a(v):p)X(q+b(v):q))\lceil B
\end{aligned}$$

(FT3) $(a(t):p \ X \ b[t]:q)\lceil B \sim 0 \qquad \text{if } ab \notin B$

(FT4) $(a(t):p \ X \ b[t]:q)\lceil B \sim (ab[t]:(pXq))\lceil B$

$$\begin{aligned}
&\text{if } \forall u<t.\ (a(u):p \ X \ b[u]:q)\lceil B \sim (p \ X \ b[u]:q)\lceil B \\
&\text{and } \forall u<t.\ \exists v\leq u.\ (a(u):p \ X \ b[u]:q)\lceil B \sim ((p+a(v):p) \ X \ b[u]:q)\lceil B
\end{aligned}$$

These laws constitute a major departure from the equational style we have observed so far, and may be an indication that we have not chosen the best possible set of primitive operators. On the other hand they seem to reflect rather faithfully the complex relationships between a synchronous deterministic world (1l, a[t]:, X) and an asynchronous nondeterministic one (0, a(t):, +), and we could not devise a simpler formulation. The factorisation theorems can usually be much simplified in practical situations (e.g. replacing "$\forall u<t$" by "$\forall u$"), and they turn out to be very useful in proving <u>equational</u> laws of interesting derived operators, as we shall see later.

<u>Communication</u>

The <u>restriction</u> operator $\lceil B$, for $B \subseteq A$ and $1 \in B$ is used to extract a subset of the possible actions of an agent, inhibiting the rest of the actions.

$$(\lceil \rightarrow) \qquad \frac{p \xrightarrow[t]{a} q}{p\lceil B \xrightarrow[t]{a} q\lceil B} \qquad \text{if } a \in B$$

Thus $p\lceil B$ can only perform actions which are in B, and this can force some communication event inside p. The action 1 is never inhibited by definition: it represents the possible anonymous occurrence of a communication event inside p.

The <u>delabelling</u> operator $p\backslash\alpha$ is a particular case of restriction. We assume here that A is generated by a set of atomic actions $\alpha, \beta, \gamma \ldots$. Then $p\backslash\alpha$ is the restriction of p to the set of all the actions of A not containing α or $\bar{\alpha}$ as prime factors.

We also need a way of renaming actions, so that we can easily set up communication channels. The most general form of renaming is called a <u>morphism</u> $p\{\phi\}$ where $\phi: A \rightarrow A$ is a monoid homomorphism:

$$(\{\phi\} \rightarrow) \qquad \frac{p \xrightarrow[t]{a} p'}{p\{\phi\} \xrightarrow[t]{\phi(a)} p'\{\phi\}}$$

We write $\{\alpha_i/\beta_i\}$ for the unique monoid morphism renaming the generators β_i to α_i and leaving the other generators unchanged.

We omit the laws for restriction and morphism, because they are not significantly different from those of (Milner 82).

Recursion

A recursive definition facility will now be introduced in our language. Its general form for a single recursive definition is:

$x \Leftarrow r$

where x is a variable and r is a context, i.e. a term possibly containing variables. We have the operational rule:

$$(\Leftarrow) \qquad \frac{r \xrightarrow[t]{a} p}{x \xrightarrow[t]{a} p}$$

To satisfy a definition like $x \Leftarrow 1\!\!1 + a[t]:x$, it is sufficient to find a p such that $p \sim 1\!\!1 + a[t]:p$ because all our laws are valid up to equivalence. In fact it is easy to show that $(\Leftarrow)$ implies $x \sim p$. But we still need to specify which particular x we want, when several of them are available, like in the definition $x \Leftarrow x$. To avoid this problem we restrict our admissible definitions to those having a unique solution up to equivalence; thus there is no doubt about which x we mean. In general we use sets of definitions, to take mutual recursion into account.

Definition 7 A definition set is a set of pairs $\{(x_i, r_i)\}$, written $\{x_i \Leftarrow r_i\}$ or $\hat{x} \Leftarrow \hat{r}$, where x_i are variables and r_i are contexts. A 1-step expansion of a definition set $\hat{x} \Leftarrow \hat{r}$ is obtained by replacing $x_i \Leftarrow r_i$ by $x_i \Leftarrow r_i\{r_j/x_j\}$ (for some i and j) in $\hat{x} \Leftarrow \hat{r}$. A finite expansion $\hat{x} \Leftarrow \hat{r}'$ of $\hat{x} \Leftarrow \hat{r}$ is an expansion obtained by a finite number of 1-step expansions □

Definition 8 A variable x is guarded in a context r if all the occurrences of x are in subterms of r of the form a[t]:r' or a(t):r'. A context r is guarded if all its variables are guarded. A definition set $\{x_i \Leftarrow r_i\}$ is guarded if there is a finite expansion $\{x_i \Leftarrow r_i'\}$ such that each r_i' is guarded □

In order to have unique solutions for our definition sets, we need to exclude definition sets which expand indefinitely but only approach a finite limit (i.e. such that the duration of their infinite chains of actions is finite). Definition sets which can expand for the same duration as their solutions are persistent.

Definition 9 A definition set $\{x_i \Leftarrow r_i\}$ is persistent if whenever $\hat{p} \sim \hat{r}\{\hat{p}/\hat{x}\}$ then for all j, $p_j \xrightarrow[t]{a} q_j$ implies that there exists a finite expansion r^o_j of r_j such that $r^o_j \xrightarrow[t]{a}{}^s r'_j$ with $r'_j\{\hat{p}/\hat{x}\} \sim q_j$ □

Every persistent definition set is guarded, and every finite guarded definition set is persistent, but there are infinite guarded definition sets which are not persistent (e.g. $\{Z_n \Leftarrow 1[n]:Z_{n/2} \mid n \in \mathbb{K}\}$).

Theorem 10 (Recursion Theorem)

Every persistent definition set $\hat{x} \Leftarrow \hat{r}$ has a unique solution up to $\sim$, i.e.:

$$p_i \sim r_i\{\hat{p}/\hat{x}\} \quad \text{and} \quad q_i \sim r_i\{\hat{q}/\hat{x}\} \quad \Rightarrow \quad p_i \sim q_i$$

Proof: Let $\approx\; = \{(C\{\hat{p}/\hat{x}\}, C\{\hat{q}/\hat{x}\}) \mid C \text{ is a context}\}$. By Park's induction:

(i) $p_i \approx q_i$ (take $C = x_i$)

(ii) $C\{\hat{p}/\hat{x}\} \xrightarrow[t]{a} P$ may hold because either $C \xrightarrow[t]{a} C'$ with $P = C'\{\hat{p}/\hat{x}\}$ (then also $C\{\hat{q}/\hat{x}\} \xrightarrow[t]{a} Q = C'\{\hat{q}/\hat{x}\}$, and $Q \approx P$), or x_j is not guarded in C and $p_j \xrightarrow[t]{a} P$. In the latter case, $\hat{r}$ is persistent and there is a finite expansion r^o_j with $r^o_j \xrightarrow[t]{a}{}^s r'_j$ and $r'_j\{\hat{p}/\hat{x}\} \sim P$. Then also $r^o_j\{\hat{q}/\hat{x}\} \xrightarrow[t]{a}{}^s r'_j\{\hat{q}/\hat{x}\}$, and since $q_j \sim r_j\{\hat{q}/\hat{x}\} \sim r^o_j\{\hat{q}/\hat{x}\}$, we have $q_j \xrightarrow[t]{a}{}^s Q \sim r'_j\{\hat{q}/\hat{x}\}$. Hence $C\{\hat{q}/\hat{x}\} \xrightarrow[t]{a}{}^s Q$ with $Q \approx P$ □

Indefinite Actions and Delays

We now use recursion and nondeterministic guards to define actions of indefinite duration in time (a.p):

$$a.p \Leftarrow a(1):(p + a.p)$$

The particular choice of unit delay above makes no difference, as we have:

$$\begin{aligned} a(t):(p + a.p) &\sim a(t):(p + a.p + a.p) && \text{by } (+p) \\ &\sim a(t):(p + a.p + a(1):(p + a.p)) && \text{by definition of a.p} \\ &\sim a(t+1):(p + a.p) && \text{by } (a()+) \\ &\sim a(1):(p + a.p + a(t):(p + a.p)) && \text{by } (a()+) \end{aligned}$$

$$a.p \sim a(1):(p + a.p) \sim a(1):(p + a.p + a.p)$$

Hence $a.p \sim a(t):(p + a.p)$ for any t, by the recursion theorem.

Moreover a.p enjoys the laws:

(1.0)	$1.0 \sim \mathbb{1}$	(a.)	$a.p \sim a.(p + a.p)$
(1.𝟙)	$1.\mathbb{1} \sim \mathbb{1}$	(a.Xb.)	$a.p \times b.q \sim ab.(p \times q + a.p \times q + p \times b.q)$

Note the importance of the law (a.Xb.); it allows us to equationally factorise actions in horizontally nondeterministic agents, which we could not do for the "a(t):" operator. The first three laws can be proved easily by the recursion theorem. Law (a.Xb.) is proved using the factorisation theorems, thereby demonstrating some of their power:

$$
\begin{array}{lll}
a.p \; X \; b.q & \sim \; a(1):(p + a.p) \; X \; b(1):(q + b.q) & \text{by definition of } a.p \\
& \sim \; ab(1):((p + a.p) \; X \; (q + b.q)) & (\ast) \\
& \sim \; ab(1):(p X q + a.p X q + p X b.q + a.p X b.q) & \text{by } (X+)
\end{array}
$$

$$
\begin{array}{l}
ab.(p X q + a.p X q + p X b.q) \\
\qquad ab(1):(p X q + a.p X q + p X b.q + ab.(p X q + a.p X q + p X b.q))
\end{array}
$$

Hence $a.p X b.q \sim ab.(p X q + a.p X q + p X b.q)$ by the recursion theorem. The step leading to $(\ast)$ uses a factorisation theorem (FT2); the four hypotheses of the theorem can be verified as follows (using the fact that $a.p \sim a(t):(p + a.p)$ and $b.q \sim b(t):(q + b.q)$):

$$
\begin{array}{ll}
(1) & (p + a.p) \; X \; (q + b.q + b(t):(q + b.q)) \sim (p + a.p) \; X \; (q + b.q) \\
(2) & (p + a.p + a(t):(p + a.p)) \; X \; (q + b.q) \sim (p + a.p) \; X \; (q + b.q) \\
(3) & (p+a.p+a(t):(p+a.p)) \; X \; (q+b.q+b(t):(q+b.q)) \sim (p+a.p) \; X \; (q + b.q) \\
(4) & (p+a.p) \; X \; (q+b.q) + a(t):(p+a.p) \; X \; b(t):(q+b.q) \sim (p+a.p) \; X \; (q+b.q)
\end{array}
$$

A closely related operator to a.p is <u>indefinite</u> <u>delay</u>:

$$d_a p \Leftarrow p + a.p$$

where the agent p may be activated immediately, or delayed indefinitely by an action a. The following laws can all be easily derived from the properties of a.p:

$$
\begin{array}{ll}
d_a 0 \sim \mathbb{K}_a & \qquad \text{where } \mathbb{K}_a \Leftarrow a[1]: \mathbb{K}_a \\
d_a \mathbb{K}_a \sim \mathbb{K}_a & \\
d_a(d_a p) \sim d_a p & \\
d_a p \; X \; d_b q \sim d_{ab}(d_a p \; X \; d_b q) & \\
d_a p \; X \; d_b q \sim d_{ab}(d_a p X q + p X d_b q) &
\end{array}
$$

<u>An Asynchronous Rising Edge Counter</u>

We now discuss an example of application of non deterministic guards. Suppose we have a boolean signal represented as $tt[t_1]:ff[t_2]:tt[t_3]:ff[t_4]: \ldots$, where the length of the intervals t_i is completely arbitrary. The problem consists in counting the number of rising edges (i.e. transitions from ff to tt) which have occurred in the signal at any given time. It is pretty well evident that there can be no solution using deterministic guards, as any proposal would be bound to fail on some input waveforms.

The counter has two states: Low_n and $High_n$, and n is increased at any passage from Low to High (for simplicity n is not supplied as an explicit output).

$$Low_n \Leftarrow ff(1):Low_n + tt(1):High_{n+1}$$
$$High_n \Leftarrow ff(1):Low_n + tt(1):High_n$$

Note how the guards tt and ff are programmed to last as long as their corresponding non synchronised inputs. Again, we first prove that the "1"s used in the definition are not significative using the technique shown in the previous section:

$$Low_n \sim ff(t):Low_n + tt(1):High_{n+1} \sim ff(1):Low_n + tt(t):High_{n+1}$$
$$High_n \sim ff(t):Low_n + tt(1):High_n \sim ff(1):Low_n + tt(t):High_n$$

The following equivalences state the correctness of the counter; they can be proved using (FT3) and (FT4):

$$(Low_n \times \overline{ff}[t]:p)\backslash ff \sim 1[t]:(Low_n \times p)\backslash ff$$
$$(High_n \times \overline{tt}[t]:p)\backslash tt \sim 1[t]:(High_n \times p)\backslash tt$$
$$(Low_n \times \overline{tt}[t]:p)\backslash tt \sim 1[t]:(High_{n+1} \times p)\backslash tt$$
$$(High_n \times \overline{ff}[t]:p)\backslash ff \sim 1[t]:(Low_n \times p)\backslash ff$$

Descriptive Operators

Some operators can be introduced just to talk about the properties of agents. In order to talk about synchrony we can introduce synchronisation operators Γ_t, designed to "impose" a clock of period t on an otherwise unsynchronised agent.

$$(\Gamma_t \rightarrow) \quad \frac{p \xrightarrow[t]{a} q}{\Gamma_t p \xrightarrow[t]{a} \Gamma_t q} \qquad\qquad (\Gamma_{t+u} \rightarrow) \quad \frac{\Gamma_t p \xrightarrow[u+v]{a} q}{\Gamma_t p \xrightarrow[u]{a} a[v]:q}$$

Rule $(\Gamma_t \rightarrow)$ says that $\Gamma_t p$ can perform "t-ticks" only if p can, i.e. p must be synchronisable to a clock of period t, otherwise $\Gamma_t p$ will stop. Rule $(\Gamma_{t+u} \rightarrow)$ is introduced to preserve the density lemma.

Definition 10 An agent is t-synchronous if $p \sim \Gamma_t p$.
An agent is non-synchronous if it is not t-synchronous for any t □

The definition of t-synchrony intends to capture the idea that all the "significant changes" (i.e. transitions from an a-action to a different b-action) in a t-synchronous agent occur at instants which are divisors of t. For example $p \Leftarrow a[2]:b[2]:p$ is 2-synchronous, 1-synchronous etc., but it is not 3-synchronous, 4-synchronous etc. because p cannot produce any action longer than 2.

An example of a non-synchronous agent is provided by a "bouncing ball" agent $p_n \Leftarrow a[1/n]:b[1/n]:p_{n+1}$ which changes its output at a faster and faster rate.

If we eliminate the nondeterministic guard "a(t):" from our signature, and we replace "a[t]:" by "a[1]:" (abbreviated "a:"), then all the agents which can be expressed are 1-synchronous. The set of 1-synchronous agents correspond exactly to the Synchronous CCS calculus (Milner 82), in the sense that the same set of laws holds.

Finally we can try to characterise some form of asynchronous behaviour by the following operator, which stretches by arbitrary amounts all the actions of an agent:

$$(\Delta\rightarrow) \qquad \frac{p \xrightarrow[t]{a} q}{\Delta p \xrightarrow[t+u]{a} \Delta q}$$

<u>Definition 11</u> An agent is <u>asynchronous</u> if $p \sim \Delta p$ $\square$

Note that this definition allows us to make a subtle distinction between non-synchronous or non t-synchronous agents (which are deterministic) and asynchronous ones (which are completely nondeterministic) and that many other behaviours lie in between.

Acknowledgements

I would like to thank Matthew Hennessy, Robin Milner and Gordon Plotkin for helpful discussions and comments.

References

(Cardelli 80) L.Cardelli: "Analog processes". Proc. 9th Symposium on Mathematical Foundations of Computer Science. Lecture Notes in C.S. n.88, Springer-Verlag.

(Hennessy 80) M.Hennessy, R.Milner: "On observing nondeterminism and concurrency". Proc. ICALP 80. Lecture Notes in C.S. n.85, Springer-Verlag.

(MacQueen 79) D.MacQueen: "Models for distributed computing". Report n.351, IRIA.

(Milner 80) R.Milner: "A calculus of communicating systems". Lecture Notes in C.S. n.92, Springer-Verlag.

(Milner 82) R.Milner: "Calculi for synchrony and asynchrony". Internal report (to appear), Dept of Computer Science, University of Edinburgh.

(Plotkin 81) G.D.Plotkin: "A structural approach to operational semantics". Report DAIMI FN-19, Dept. of Computer Science, University of Aarhus.

(Park 81) D.M.Park: "Concurrency and automata on infinite sequences". Proc. GI Conference.

MACHINE INDUCTIVE INFERENCE AND LANGUAGE IDENTIFICATION

John Case

Computer Science Department
State University of New York at Buffalo
4226 Ridge Lea Road
Amherst, New York 14226

Christopher Lynes

Computer Science Department
Courant Institute
New York University
New York, New York 10012

Abstract. We show that for some classes $\mathcal{L}$ of recursive languages, from the characteristic function of any L in $\mathcal{L}$ an approximate decision procedure for L with no more than n + 1 mistakes can be (uniformly effectively) inferred in the limit; whereas, in general, a grammar (generation procedure) with no more than n mistakes cannot; for some classes an infinite sequence of perfectly correct decision procedures can be inferred in the limit, but single grammars with finitely many mistakes cannot; and for some classes an infinite sequence of decision procedures each with no more than n + 1 mistakes can be inferred, but an infinite sequence of grammars each with no more than n mistakes cannot. This is true even though decision procedures generally contain more information than grammars. We also consider inference of grammars for r.e. languages from arbitrary texts, i.e., enumerations of the languages. We show that for any class of languages $\mathcal{L}$, if some machine, from arbitrary texts for any L in $\mathcal{L}$, can infer in the limit an approximate grammar for L with no more than 2·n mistakes, then some machine can infer in the limit, for each language in $\mathcal{L}$, an infinite sequence of grammars each with no more than n mistakes. This reduction from 2·n to n is best possible. From these and other results we obtain and compare several natural, inference hierarchies. Lastly we show that if we restrict ourselves to recursive texts, there is a machine which, for any r.e. language, infers in the limit an infinite sequence of grammars each with only finitely many mistakes. We employ recursion theoretic methods including infinitary and ordinary recursion theorems.

Background.

M. Gold in his seminal paper [Go 67] investigated the problem of algorithmically synthesizing (in the limit) decision procedures for arbitrary recursive languages given enumerations of their characteristic functions. Gold showed, for example, that there _is_ an algorithm for effecting such a synthesis for the entire class of primitive recursive (hence also context sensitive) languages but _not_ for the entire class of recursive languages. Gold briefly mentioned the connection of his work to machine inductive inference in general. L. and M. Blum in [BB 75] consider this latter problem. They are concerned, among other things, with algorithmically synthesizing in the limit programs for arbitrary recursive functions f, where a number x may represent a particular scientific experiment and f(x) the corresponding experimental result. [BB 75] contains several computational complexity characterizations of the power of machines to correctly synthesize programs. The work of J. Case and C. Smith [CS 78,82] was largely inspired by [BB 75], the possibility of more flexibility in the notion of "synthesis in the limit", and the fact that physicists sometimes employ practical but anomalous explanations, explanations which fail to correctly predict the outcome of a few experiments but which are otherwise correctly predictive. More specifically:

Definition. (i) An inductive inference machine (abbr: IIM) is an algorithmic device which takes as its input the values of a function f in the order f(0), f(1), f(2),... and which from time to time returns a program (i.e., an index in a fixed acceptable gödel numbering [Ro 58, MY 78]).

(ii) N denotes the set of natural numbers 0, 1, 2,... Suppose $a \in N \cup \{*\}$. An IIM M EX^a-identifies a function f iff M fed f outputs a non-empty, finite sequence of programs the last of which explains f except at up to a anomalous points, i.e., computes f except at up to a points if $a \in N$ (except at up to finitely many points if $a = *$).

(iii) An IIM M BC^a-identifies f iff M fed f outputs an infinite sequence of programs $p_0, p_1, p_2, \ldots$ such that the programs in all but an initial segment of the sequence behaviourally correctly predict f up to a anomalous points, i.e., for all but finitely many i, p_i computes f except at up to a points.

(iv) Let $\mathcal{S}$ range over classes of recursive functions.
$EX^a = \{\mathcal{S} \mid (\exists M)(\forall f \in \mathcal{S})[M\ EX^a\text{-identifies } f]\}$.

(v) $BC^a = \{\mathcal{S} \mid (\exists M)(\forall f \in \mathcal{S})[M\ BC^a\text{-identifies } f]\}$.

Case and Smith [CS 78,81] in a sense justified physicists' use of anomalous explanations by showing that $EX^0 \subset EX^1 \subset \ldots \subset EX^* \subset BC^0 \subset BC^1 \subset \ldots \subset BC^*$, where "$\subset$" denotes proper containment. For example, let $\mathcal{S}$ = {f| for all but finitely many i, f(i) is a program which computes f except perhaps at one point}; $\mathcal{S}$ is non-empty by the Kleene recursion theorem [Ro 67], and clearly $\mathcal{S} \in BC^1$ as witnessed by the IIM which on input f(0), f(1), f(2),... just outputs that same sequence; it is shown in [CS 78,82] that $\mathcal{S} \notin BC^0$. EX^0-identification is just Gold's [Go 67] notion of identification in the limit as extended slightly in [BB 75]. EX^*-identification was first defined in [BB 75] (see also [Mi 76]) where it was called a.e.-identification. In [BB 75] it was announced that $EX^0 \subset EX^*$. J. Barzdin [Ba 74], acting on an important observation of J. Feldman [Fe 72], independently and earlier defined BC^0; he called it GN^∞ and showed that $EX^0 \subset BC^0$. The proof in [CS 78,82] that $(BC^0 - EX^*) \neq \emptyset$ was done in collaboration with L. Harrington who also showed in [CS 82] the surprising result that $\mathcal{R}$, the entire class of recursive functions, is in BC^*.

J. Steel first noted in [CS 78,82] that $EX^* \subseteq BC^0$. Extensions of [CS 78,82] in various directions appear in [Ch 81 & 82, CN 82, Da 82, Sm 81].

R. Wiehagen in [Wi 77] (see also [FW 79, KW 80]) considered the problem of synthesizing in the limit (type 0) grammars (i.e., generation procedures or, equivalently, acceptor Turing machines [HU 79]) for arbitrary recursive languages given enumerations of their characteristic functions. We extend his identification criterion as follows:

Definition. (i) $A \oplus B = (A-B) \cup (B-A)$. $A =^a B$ means $card(A \oplus B) \leq a$ if $a \in N$ (is finite if $a = *$). $\mathcal{R}_{0,1}$ denotes the class of recursive characteristic functions. An IIM M $EXGEN^a$-identifies $f \in \mathcal{R}_{0,1}$ iff M fed f outputs a non-empty, finite sequence of programs the last of which generates a set $=^a$ $f^{-1}(1)$, the set of which f is the characteristic function.

(ii) W_p = the r.e. set generated by program p [Ro 67]. M $BCGEN^a$-identifies $f \in \mathcal{R}_{0,1}$ iff M fed f outputs an infinite sequence of programs $p_0, p_1, p_2, \ldots$ such that for all but finitely many i, $W_{p_i} =^a f^{-1}(1)$.

(iii) $EXGEN^a = \{\mathcal{S} \subseteq \mathcal{R}_{0,1} \mid (\exists M)(\forall f \in \mathcal{S})$ [M $EXGEN^a$-identifies f]$\}$.

(iv) $BCGEN^a = \{\mathcal{S} \subseteq \mathcal{R}_{0,1} \mid (\exists M)(\forall f \in \mathcal{S})$ [M $BCGEN^a$-identifies f]$\}$.

Wiehagen's notion is just $EXGEN^0$. He announces in [Wi 77] that $EX^0_{0,1} \subset EXGEN^0$, i.e., IIMs can be more nearly general purpose if they are to synthesize grammars rather than decision procedures. A proof of this result appears in [FW 79].

Gold in [Go 67] cites the work of psycholinguists as indicating that children are seemingly rarely informed of their grammatical errors; hence, their formal exposure to language consists in receiving some enumeration of utterances in the language without much information about the non-elements of the language. This led him to consider algorithmic synthesis (in the limit) of grammars for arbitrary r.e. languages given texts, i.e., enumerations of those languages. We extend his definitions as follows. $\mathcal{E}$ denotes the class of r.e. languages $\subseteq N$. The restriction to languages $\subseteq N$ is without loss of generality. A text for $L \in \mathcal{E}$ is a sequence t of *s and numbers such that $(range(t) - \{*\}) = L$. The *s are a device from [BB 75] for handling gaps and finite sets, especially the empty set.

Definition. (i) M $TXTEX^a$-identifies $L \in \mathcal{E}$ iff M, fed any text for L, outputs a non-empty, finite sequence of programs the last of which generates a set $=^a$ L.

(ii) M $TXTBC^a$-identifies $L \in \mathcal{E}$ iff M, fed any text for L, outputs an infinite sequence of programs $p_0, p_1, p_2, \ldots$ such that, for all but finitely many i, $W_{p_i} =^a L$.

(iii) We let $\mathcal{L}$ range over subsets of $\mathcal{E}$.

$TXTEX^a = \{\mathcal{L} \mid (\exists M)(\forall L \in \mathcal{L})$[M $TXTEX^a$-identifies L]$\}$.

(iv) $TXTBC^a = \{\mathcal{L} \mid (\exists M)(\forall L \in \mathcal{L})[M\ TXTBC^a\text{-identifies } L]\}$.

Gold's criterion of language learning is just our $TXTEX^0$. Osherson and Weinstein [OW 82a & b] independently define our criteria $TXTEX^*$, $TXTBC^0$, and $TXTBC^*$. In [OW 82b] they establish the interrelations between these, $TXTEX^0$, and many other important criteria. [OW 82a] contains an interesting discussion of Gold's paradigm [Go 67] for language learning and the role it has played in evaluating contemporary theories of natural language [Pi 79, WC 80]. Wexler [We 82] provides an interesting critique of this discussion.

Gold [Go 67] proved that no class in $TXTEX^0$ can contain all finite languages and at least one infinite language; hence, for example, not even the class of regular languages can be $TXTEX^0$-identified. This suggested to Gold that the classes in $TXTEX^0$ are small. He considered essentially two plausible, alternate conclusions. One was that the possible natural languages are a much smaller class than previously thought. Of course this was based on his taking the absence of any superset of the class of regular languages in $TXTEX^0$ as a measure of smallness of its classes. Arguing against this Angluin [An 80a & b] defines a natural class of languages called the <u>pattern languages</u> and shows that while this class <u>is</u> in $TXTEX^0$, it is incomparable to both the class of regular languages and the class of context free languages. Hence, the classes in $TXTEX^0$ aren't necessarily small compared to low level Chomsky hierarchy classes, they just divide up the set of strings quite differently. In [An 81] Angluin studies natural $TXTEX^0$-identifiable sub-regular classes called the k-reversible languages and presents efficient algorithms for inferring them. In another direction Wiehagen [Wi 77, KW 80] demonstrated that in a strong sense there are large classes in $TXTEX^0$. He exhibited a class in $TXTEX^0$ that contains a self-referential finite variant of each r.e. language.

Gold's alternative, plausible conclusion was that children are being given additional information in some perhaps subtle way. Wexler [We 82] suggests a plausible form for such additional information but one which may be difficult to formalize mathematically. Freivald and Wiehagen [FW 79] consider some rather restricted but nonetheless mathematically formalized and interesting cases of algorithmic synthesis with additional information. For example, they consider the case of inferring single decision procedures in the limit given the characteristic functions and the additional information of grammars for the languages.

<u>Results</u>.

If I is EX^a or BC^a, we write $I_{0,1}$ to denote $(I \cap \{\mathcal{S} \mid \mathcal{S} \subseteq \mathcal{R}_{0,1}\})$. We sometimes (ambiguously) write $\mathcal{R}_{0,1}$ for the class of recursive languages and identify a recursive set with its characteristic function. If I is $TXTEX^a$ or $TXTBC^a$, we write $I_{0,1}$ to denote $(I \cap \{\mathcal{L} \mid \mathcal{L} \subseteq \mathcal{R}_{0,1}\})$.

Theorem 1. Let $\mathcal{L} = \{L \in \mathcal{R}_{0,1} \mid L \neq \emptyset$ and $W_{\mu x[x \in L]} = L\}$. Then $\mathcal{L} \in (\mathrm{TXTEX}^0_{0,1} - \bigcup\{\mathrm{BC}^n_{0,1} \mid n \in N\})$.

Hence, for some class of recursive languages, grammars can be synthesized in the limit from arbitrary text, but, for no n, can an infinite sequence of decision procedures each with no more than n anomalies be synthesized in the limit from the characteristic functions. This theorem immediately yields Wiehagen's result that $(\mathrm{EXGEN}^0 - \mathrm{EX}^0) \neq \emptyset$; our proof employs the recursion theorem and turns out to resemble the proof of one direction of Theorem 5 in [FW 79]. This theorem also yields Wiehagen's result as a corollary.

One might think that since it's easier to synthesize grammars than decision procedures (in the limit), it would also be easier to synthesize grammars than <u>slightly incorrect</u> decision procedures. Surprisingly, this is <u>not</u> so, as shown by the next theorem, which we prove by the recursion theorem. ϕ_p denotes the partial recursive function computed by program p.

Theorem 2. Let $\mathcal{S} = \{f \in \mathcal{R}_{0,1} \mid [(\exists x)[f(x) = 1]$ and $\phi_{\mu x[f(x) = 1]} =^{n+1} f]\}$. Then $\mathcal{S} \in (\mathrm{EX}^{n+1}_{0,1} - \mathrm{EXGEN}^n)$.

Hence, for <u>some</u> classes of recursive languages, decision procedures with n + 1 mistakes can be algorithmically synthesized in the limit, but grammars with only n mistakes cannot!

Corollary 3. Let $\mathcal{S} = \{f \in \mathcal{R}_{0,1} \mid [(\exists x)[f(x) = 1]$ and $\phi_{\mu x[f(x) = 1]} =^{*} f]\}$. Then $\mathcal{S} \in (\mathrm{EX}^{*}_{0,1} - \bigcup\{\mathrm{EXGEN}^n \mid n \in N\})$.

Intuitively the mechanisms responsible for Theorem 2 are indeterminacy in whether approximate decision procedures will have singularities (points of divergence) and, when they do, that the gap left by the singularity is greater in information content than the complement of the language, i.e., the gap left by the grammars. Much more subtle mechanisms are responsible for the next two theorems. The first shows that for <u>some</u> classes of recursive languages, an <u>infinite</u> sequence of completely correct decision procedures can be synthesized in the limit but <u>single</u> grammars with an unbounded finite set of mistakes cannot!

Theorem 4. Let $\mathcal{S} = \{f \in \mathcal{R}_{0,1} \mid$ there are infinitely many x such that f(x) = 1 and for all but finitely many such x, $\phi_x = f\}$. Then $\mathcal{S} \in (\mathrm{BC}^0_{0,1} - \mathrm{EXGEN}^*)$.

Our proof of this theorem employs Case's operator recursion theorem [Ca 74], an infinitary recursion theorem involving infinite sequences of self (and other) referential programs. This proof technique applied to machine inductive inference was first developed in [CS 78] and has subsequently been used in [CS 82, Sm 81, Da 82].

Our next theorem shows that for <u>some</u> class of recursive languages, an infinite sequence of <u>decision procedures</u> each with up to n + 1 mistakes can be synthesized in the limit, but an infinite sequence of grammars each with up to n mistakes cannot. It too is proved by the operator recursion theorem.

<u>Theorem 5</u>. Let $\mathcal{S} = \{f \in \mathcal{R}_{0,1} \mid$ there are infinitely many x such that f(x) = 1 and, for all but finitely many such x, $\phi_x =^{n+1} f\}$. Then $\mathcal{S} \in (BC^{n+1}_{0,1} - BCGEN^{n})$.

To obtain some of our hierarchy results about text criteria we employ the following Lemma which was suggested by Lemma B in [OW 82b].

<u>Lemma 6</u>. Suppose without loss of generality M, fed any text, outputs an infinite <u>sequence</u> of not necessarily distinct programs. Suppose for a language L ($\subseteq$ N) and set of programs Y, that, for all texts t for which (range(t) - {*}) = L, M fed t outputs past some point only programs in Y. Then there is a finite initial segment of text σ such that range(σ) $\subseteq$ (L $\cup$ {*}) and, for all t extending σ for which range(t) $\subseteq$ L $\cup$ {*}, M fed t outputs, past σ, only programs in Y.

The following proposition generalizes to all text criteria a result of Gold [Go 67] mentioned earlier. It is proved by a simple application of Lemma 6.

<u>Proposition 7</u>. No class which contains an infinite (r.e.) set and all its finite subsets can be $TXTBC^{*}$-identified.

<u>Corollary 8</u>. Let $\mathcal{S}$ = the class of all (characteristic functions of) primitive recursive languages. Then $\mathcal{S} \in (EX^{0}_{0,1} - TXTBC^{*})$.

<u>Theorem 9</u>. Let $\mathcal{S}$ be as in Theorem 4. Then $\mathcal{S} \in (TXTBC^{0}_{0,1} - TXTEX^{*})$.

Theorem 9 is a corollary of Theorem 4. Osherson and Weinstein independently showed that $(TXTBC^{0} - TXTEX^{*}) \neq \emptyset$ by other means.

If M $EXGEN^{*}$-identifies $\mathcal{S}$, then M' $BCGEN^{0}$-identifies $\mathcal{S}$, where M' on f runs M on f and if p is M's current last output, M' putputs p' which is p patched (perhaps needlessly) to be assuredly correct on what's been seen so far of f. Clearly, then, $EXGEN^{*} \subseteq BCGEN^{0}$. Osherson and Weinstein [OW 82b] prove the sharply contrasting result (generalized in Corollary 11 below) that the class of co-finite languages is in $(TXTEX^{*} - TXTBC^{0})$. Intuitively a text for L doesn't supply direct information about the complement of L which we ostensibly need to do the patching. Our next theorem shows though that, for each <u>uniform</u> bound on the number of anomalies with (intuitively) half the information available, exactly one-half the anomalies can be patched! The proof of the left to right direction is by Lemma 6.

Theorem 10. $\mathrm{TXTEX}^m \subseteq \mathrm{TXTBC}^n$ iff $m \leq 2\cdot n$. Moreover, the class of languages which differ from N by no more than $2\cdot n + 1$ elements is in $(\mathrm{TXTEX}_{0,1}^{2\cdot n+1} - \mathrm{TXTBC}^n)$.

Corollary 11. Let $\mathcal{L}$ be the class of co-finite sets. Then $\mathcal{L} \in (\mathrm{TXTEX}_{0,1}^{*} - \bigcup\{\mathrm{TXTBC}^n \mid n \in N\})$.

Theorems 1, 2, 4, 5, 9, and 10 and Corollaries 3, 8, and 11, together with Harrington's result [CS 82] that $\mathcal{R} \in \mathrm{BC}^*$ and the obvious positive containment relations, yield the following corollary. " → " stands for "is a subset of".

Corollary 12. Inclusion relations not implicit in the following diagram do not hold.

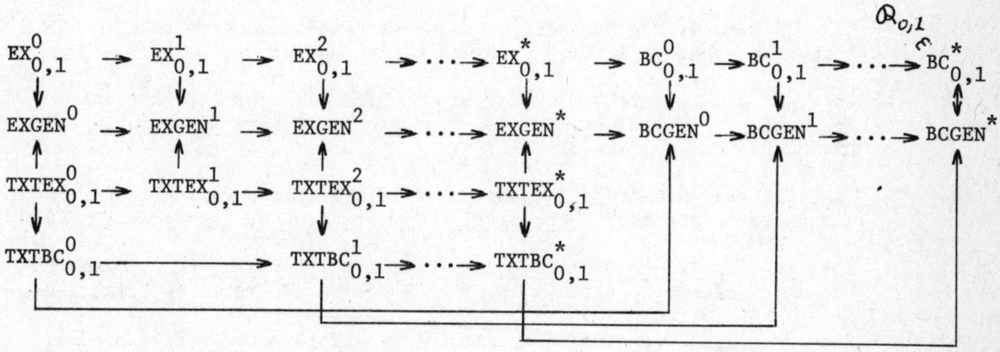

We briefly consider the problem of inferring in the limit grammars from <u>recursive</u> texts. If I is EX^a or BC^a, then RECTXTI-<u>identification</u> is just like TXTI-identification except the texts are restricted to being recursive. Wiehagen [Wi 77] notes that $\mathrm{RECTXTEX}^0 = \mathrm{TXTEX}^0$. In fact an effectivized variant of Lemma 6 can be used (much as in Theorem 2 in [BB 75]) to show that $\mathrm{RECTXTEX}^a = \mathrm{TXTEX}^a$. The following theorem, together with Proposition 7 and Corollary 8, shows that sometimes a tremendous gain can be made in inferring power from the additional information that the text is recursive. It complements Gold's result that $\mathcal{E}$ can be TXTEX^0-identified from <u>primitive</u> recursive text.

Theorem 13. $\mathcal{E} \in \mathrm{RECTXTBC}^*$.

In a later paper we will consider the problems of inferring decision procedures from text, of text identification with additional information (including restricted texts), and of text identification by new criteria suggested by combining ideas from [OW 82b] and [CS 78,82].

Acknowledgement. This research was supported in part by NSF grant #MCS-8010728.

References.

[An 80a] Angluin, D., "Finding patterns common to a set of strings," J. of Computer and System Sciences, 21 (1980), 46-62.

[An 80b] Angluin, D., "Inductive inference of formal languages from positive data," Information and Control, 45, 117-135, 1980.

[An 81] Angluin, D., "Inference of Reversible Languages," J. of the ACM, to appear.

[Ba 74] Barzdin, J., "Two theorems on the limiting synthesis of functions," Latvii gosudarst. Univ. ucenye Zapiski, 210, 82-88 (Russian), 1974.

[BB 75] Blum, L. and M. Blum, "Toward a mathematical theory of inductive inference," Information and Control, 28, 125-155, 1975.

[Ca 74] Case, J., "Periodicity in generations of automata," Math. Systems Theory, 8, 15-32, 1974.

[CN 82] Case, J. and S. Ngo Manguelle, "Refinements of inductive inference by Popperian machines I, II," Kybernetika, to appear.

[CS 78] Case, J. and C. Smith, "Anomaly hierarchies of mechanized inductive inference," Proceedings 10th ACM Symposium on Theory of Computing, San Diego, Calif., pp. 314-319, 1978.

[CS 82] Case, J. and C. Smith, "Comparison of identification criteria for machine inductive inference," Theoretical Computer Science, to appear.

[Ch 81] Chen, K. J., Tradeoffs in Machine Inductive Inference, Ph.D. Dissertation, Computer Science Department, SUNY at Buffalo, Amherst, New York, 1981.

[Ch 82] Chen, K. J., "Tradeoffs in the inductive inference of nearly minimal size programs," Information and Control, to appear in the special issue devoted to papers presented at the Workshop on Recursion Theory in Computer Science held at Purdue University, 1981.

[Da 82] Daley, R., "On the error correcting power of pluralism in inductive inference," preprint.

[Fe 72] Feldman, J., "Some decidability results on grammatical inference and complexity," Information and Control, 20, 244-262, 1972.

[FW 79] Freivald, R. and R. Wiehagen, "Inductive inference with additional information," Electronische Informationsverarbeitung und Kybernetik, 15, 179-185, 1979.

[Go 67] Gold, M., "Language identification in the limit," Information and Control, 10, 447-474, 1967.

[HU 79] Hopcroft, J. and J. Ullman, Introduction to Automata Theory, Languages, and Computation, Addison-Wesley, Reading, Massachusetts, 1979.

[KW 80] Klette, R. and R. Wiehagen, "Research in the theory of inductive inference by GDR mathematicians -- a survey," Information Sciences, 22, 149-169, 1980.

[MY 78] Machtey, M. and P. Young, An Introduction to the General Theory of Algorithms, North-Holland, New York, 1978.

[Mi 76] Minicozzi, E., "Some natural properties of strong-identification in inductive inference," Theoretical Computer Science, 2, 345-360, 1976.

[OW 82a] Osherson, D. and S. Weinstein, "A note on formal learning theory," Cognition, 11 (1982), 77-88.

[OW 82b] Osherson, D. and S. Weinstein, "Criteria of language learning," preprint.

[Pi 79] Pinker, S., "Formal models of language learning," Cognition, 7 (1979), 217-283.

[Ro 58] Rogers, H., "Gödel numberings of the partial recursive functions," J. of Symbolic Logic, 23, 331-341, 1958.

[Ro 67] Rogers, H., Theory of Recursive Functions and Effective Computability, McGraw-Hill, New York, 1967.

[Sm 81] Smith, C., "The power of parallelism for automatic program synthesis," Proceedings of the 22nd FOCS Conference, Nashville, Tennessee, October, 1981 (to appear revised in J. of the ACM).

[We 82] Wexler, K., "On extensional learnability," Cognition, 11 (1982), 89-95.

[WC 80] Wexler, K. and P. Culicover, Formal Principles of Language Acquisition, MIT Press, Cambridge, Massachusetts, 1980.

[Wi 77] Wiehagen, R., "Identification of Formal Languages," Lecture Notes in Computer Science, 53, 571-579, 1977.

APPROXIMATIONS OF INFINITARY OBJECTS

G. COMYN
M. DAUCHET

U.E.R. D'I.E.E.A. - INFORMATIQUE - UNIVERSITE DE LILLE-I
59655 - VILLENEUVE D'ASCQ Cédex
(France)

ABSTRACT.- *We compare metric approximations with ordered ones and define on infinitary CPO's a new metric such that both are bijectively related.
We extend this construction to functional spaces and prove that convergence for our metric implies pointwise convergence and uniform convergence for increasing sequences. Finally we prove that decidable elements in infinitary computable CPO's are effective limits of computable Cauchy sequences in recursive metric spaces.*

INTRODUCTION.-

A theory of approximation in complete ordered sets (CPO's) has been elaborated in various papers : In [15] SCOTT studied infinite objects as limits of finite ones; later was this kind of approximation used in the definition of computation domains [12], [14],[15]. In the area of algebraic semantics, infinite objects such as words [2], trees [11] were studied from a double point of view : infinite trees for example can be viewed as lub's of directed sequences and as limits of Cauchy sequences of finite trees. Hence it is quite natural to study the relationship between metric and order structure : It has been already proved that a metrizable topology (Cantor-topology in [14], Lawson-topology in [7]) can be defined on a CPO. PLOTKIN [13] informed us recently of a result which implies the completeness of any infinitary CPO equipped with any metric inducing a Lawson topology on it. More generally, some of the results presented in this paper might have been obtained by a topological approach.

Nevertheless our point of view is purely metric : in a first section, we define on infinitary (i.e. ω-algebraic and consistently complete) CPO's a metric from a numbering of the finitary basis. In fact this metric doesn't depend on the choice of the numbering (Theorem 1) and is equivalent to the metric used in [2],[11] on infinite words and infinite trees built on finite alphabets. An important result is a bijection between metric and order completions (Theorem 2). In a third section we extend these properties to functional spaces and prove (Theorem 3) that the convergence for our metric implies the pointwise convergence on the basis and the uniform convergence (Theorem 4) for increasing sequences of CPO-continuous functions. Finally we particularize these results to effective domains [8],[17],[15] and recursive metric spaces [9],[10] and characterize (Theorem 5) the decidable elements of any effective domain as limits of effective Cauchy sequences.

I - BACKGROUND AND NOTATIONS.

In this first section, we recall some notions and define notations which will be used in this paper.

I.A.- INFINITARY CPO

Let D be a partially ordered set with a minimal element $\perp$; $\Delta \subseteq D$, $\Delta \neq \emptyset$, is said to be *directed* if every finite subset in Δ is bounded in Δ . D is a CPO iff every directed subset Δ , $\Delta \subseteq D$, has a lub. $b \in D$ is *finitary* if $b \leq \text{lub}\,\Delta$, Δ directed, implies that $b \leq x$ for an x in Δ .

$B \subseteq D$ is a *basis* for D if, for any $x \in D$, $\exists\, \Delta \subseteq B$, Δ directed, such that $x = \text{Lub}\,\Delta$; A basis B is *finitary* if any $b \in B$ is finitary.

Let B^∞ be the set of ideals defined from the basis B ; it is well known [1] that B^∞ is the order-completed set and that generally B^∞ differs from D . The CPO's we consider are those which are (isomorphic to) the order-completion of their finitary basis : Such CPO's will be denoted B^∞ and their elements called *infinitary*.

Let B^ω be the set of lub's of strictly ascending chains; let us notice :

<u>PROPERTY</u> 1.- *Let* D *be a* CPO *and* B *be a finitary basis of* D

a) B *is unique*

b) $B^\omega = B^\infty - B$.

This property gives a characterization of the finitary elements which cannot be lub's of infinite increasing chains : So are they called "finite approximation" by SCOTT [16] (finite amount of information) in contrast with the "limits of approximations" (infinite amount of information) which are in B^ω.

Eventually we define an *infinitary CPO* D as follows :

(i) D is (isomorphic to) the order-completion B^∞ of its finitary and countable basis B .

(ii) For any b,c in B , lub(b,c) is defined (in B as can be easily proved) whenever $\{b,c\}$ is bounded in B .

It is easy to verify that any infinitary CPO is ω-algebraic [17] and consistently complete [12] , and conversely. Moreover for any (b,c) in $B \times B$, glb(b,c) is defined but is not necessarily in B .

Many examples of infinitary CPO's can be chosen in the papers dealing with semantic domains : $\mathbb{N}$ with the "flat" order; Σ^∞ , the set of finite and infinite words [2] defined over an alphabet Σ ; $M^\infty(F,E)$, the complete F-magma whose finitary basis is the free F-magma $M(F,E)$ [11]; the set F of functions from $\mathbb{N}$ into $\mathbb{N}$ equipped with the graph-inclusion; finally, the set of intervals with real end-points is an infinitary CPO whose finitary basis is the set of open intervals whose end-points are rational.

I.B.- METRIC COMPLETION

Let (B,d) be a set equipped with a metric d ; the definition of a Cauchy sequence (x_i) can be formulated as follows : There is a function ψ (sometimes called a regulator of convergence) such that for any n :

$$\forall\ p \geq \psi(n)\ ,\ \forall\ q \geq \psi(n)\ ,\ d(x_p,x_q) < \frac{1}{n}$$

The metric space (B,d) can be isometrically embedded into a complete metric space $\bar{B}$ (of equivalence classes of Cauchy sequences in B) unique up to isometry and such that B is dense in it.

We define now a metric such that both completed spaces B^∞ and $\bar{B}$ get in bijection.

II - A METRIC DEFINED ON A CPO.

II.A.- Let $\phi : \mathbb{N} \to B$ be a numbering of the finitary basis B of B^∞ ; i.e. a surjective mapping; let us define the symmetrical difference between infinitary elements of B^∞ by :

$$x \mathbin{\Delta} x' = \{b \in B \mid b \leq x \ \ \&\ \ b \nleq x' \ \ \underline{\text{or}}\ \ b \leq x' \ \ \&\ \ b \nleq x\}$$

Define a mapping $d : B^\infty \times B^\infty \to \mathbb{R}$ by :

$$d_\phi(x,y) = \frac{1}{1+\mu n[\phi(n) \in x \mathbin{\Delta} y]} \qquad x,y \in B^\infty$$

with $\mu n[\phi(n) \in x \mathbin{\Delta} y] = +\infty$ if $x \mathbin{\Delta} y = \emptyset$ (i.e. $x = y$). It can be seen that d is quite different from WEIHRAUCH's metric [15].

<u>PROPOSITION</u> 1.- d_ϕ *is an ultrametric.*

Sketch of the proof : - $d_\phi(x,y)$ iff $x = y$ } obvious.
- $d_\phi(x,y) = d_\phi(y,x)$ }
- $d_\phi(x,y) \leq \mathrm{Max}\{d_\phi(x,z)\ ,\ d_\phi(y,z)\}$ $\qquad x,y,z \in B^\infty$

Let n be such that $\phi(n) \le x$ & $\phi(n) \not\le y$

- $\phi(n) \le z$ implies $\phi(n) \in y \,\Delta\, z$ and so $n \ge \mu i[\phi(i) \in y \,\Delta\, z]$
- $\phi(n) \not\le z$ implies $\phi(n) \in x \,\Delta\, z$ and so $n \ge \mu i[\phi(i) \in x \,\Delta\, z]$

Finally $\mu n[\phi(n) \in x \,\Delta\, y] \ge \mathrm{Min}\{\mu n[\phi(n) \in x \,\Delta\, z] \,,\ \mu n[\phi(n) \in y \,\Delta\, z]\}$.

Let us prove now that the topological properties of the metric space (B^{∞}, d_{ϕ}) do not depend on the choice of the numbering :

THEOREM 1.- *Let* i *be the identity on* B *;* $\bar{B}_{\phi}$ *and* $\bar{B}_{\phi'}$ *the complete spaces for* d_{ϕ} *and* $d_{\phi'}$ *respectively; then the canonical extension* $\bar{i} : \bar{B}_{\phi} \to \bar{B}_{\phi'}$ *is biuniformly continuous.*

It is easy to define two functions A and $A' : \mathbb{N} \to \mathbb{N}$ such that $A(i)$ and $A'(i) \underset{i\to\infty}{\longrightarrow} +\infty$ and :

$$\begin{cases} \mu i[\phi(i) \in a \,\Delta\, b] \ge A(n) \Longrightarrow \mu i[\phi'(i) \in a \,\Delta\, b] \ge n \\ \mu i[\phi'(i) \in a \,\Delta\, b] \ge A'(n) \Longrightarrow \mu i[\phi(i) \in a \,\Delta\, b] \ge n \end{cases}$$

Let $(b_i)_{i\in\mathbb{N}}$ be a Cauchy sequence for the metric d_{ϕ} :

$$\forall \varepsilon \,,\ \exists m : \forall p \ge m \,,\ \forall q \ge m \,,\ d_{\phi}(b_p, b_q) \le \varepsilon \,.$$

$$\Longrightarrow \forall n \,,\ \exists m : \forall p \ge m \,,\ \forall q \ge m \,,\ \mu i[\phi(i) \in b_p \,\Delta\, b_q] \ge A(n)$$

$$\Longrightarrow \mu i[\phi'(i) \in b_p \,\Delta\, b_q] \ge n$$

Every d_{ϕ}-Cauchy sequence is also a $d_{\phi'}$-Cauchy sequence (and conversely by an identical proof).

So is the function $\bar{i}$:

$$\bar{i}(\lim_{d_{\phi}} b_j) = \lim_{d_{\phi'}} (i(b_j)) \quad \text{well defined.}$$

The uniform continuity results from the definition of the functions $A(n)$ and $A'(n)$ independently on the elements of the sequences.

So are d_{ϕ} and $d_{\phi'}$ uniformly equivalent. Therefore we shall write d instead of d_{ϕ} and $\bar{B}$ instead of $\bar{B}_{\phi}$ when no ambiguity arises.

II.B.- COMPARISON WITH OTHER METRICS.

The spaces Σ^{∞} and $M^{\infty}(F,E)$ are often studed from a metric point of view, with the following metrics extended to the complete spaces :

$$\underset{u,v\,\in\,\Sigma^*}{\delta_1(u,v)} = \begin{cases} 0 \text{ if } u = w \\ \dfrac{1}{\mu n[u[n] \ne v[n]]} \end{cases} \qquad \underset{u,v\,\in\,M(F,E)}{\delta_2(u,v)} = \begin{cases} 0 \text{ if } u = v \\ \dfrac{1}{\mu n[\pi_n(u) \ne \pi_n(v)]} \end{cases}$$

where $\pi_n(t)$, $t \in M(F,E)$, is the truncation of the tree t at depth n .
We prove in [3] and [4] that :

PROPOSITION 2.- *The metrics* d *and* δ_1 *are equivalent whenever* $\mathrm{Card}(\Sigma)$ *is finite.*

PROPOSITION 3.- *The metrics* d *and* δ_2 *are equivalent whenever* $\mathrm{Card}(F)$ *and* $\mathrm{Card}(E)$ *are finite.*

Nevertheless our metric d is not equivalent to the Baire-metric on the space of functions from $\mathbb{N}$ into $\mathbb{N}$ as proved in the following example :

$$\text{Let } f_n(x) = \begin{cases} n & \text{if } x = 0 \\ 0 & \text{if } x \neq 0 \end{cases}$$

The sequence (f_n) is not convergent for the Baire metric but it is easy to see that (f_n) converges for our metric to the function f defined by :

$$f(x) = \begin{cases} \text{undefined if } x = 0 \\ 0 \quad \text{else} \end{cases}$$

Whereas the set F of functions from $\mathbb{N}$ to $\mathbb{N}$ is not compact for the Baire metric, the following property :

PROPERTY 2.- *The* d*-complete space* $\bar{B}$ *is compact*

results from the :

LEMMA.- *The topology induced by* d *is the Lawson-topology on* B^∞.

and from the compactness of the Lawson-topology.

II.c.- We prove now that there is a bijective map between the complete spaces B^∞ and $\bar{B}$; more precisely :

THEOREM 2.- *Let* $i : (B,\leq) \to (B,d)$ *be the identity ;* B *the finitary basis of the infinitary CPO* B^∞ . *Then :*

(i) i *extends uniquely to* $\hat{\imath} : B^\infty \to \bar{B}$ *defined by*

$$\hat{\imath}(\mathrm{lub}\ b_j) = \lim_{j\to\infty} i(b_j)$$

where (b_j) *is an increasing chain in* B .

(ii) $\hat{\imath}$ *is bijective.*

Sketch of the proof :

a) We have to prove first that $\hat{\imath}$ is well defined; we use the following lemma whose proof is easy :

<u>LEMMA.</u>- *For any* a,b,c *in* B^∞ , $a \le b \le c \Longrightarrow d(a,b) \le d(a,c)$

Let (b_j) be an increasing chain in B ; this chain has a lub b in the CPO B^∞ . So is the sequence $(d(b_j,b))_{i\in\mathbb{N}}$ decreasing by the preceding lemma ; as B is finitary, it can be proved that there is no $n \in \mathbb{N}$ such that $\min_{i\in\mathbb{N}} d(b,b_i) > 1/n$. So is the sequence (b_i) convergent and therefore a Cauchy-sequence.

b) $\hat{\imath}$ in onto : we have to prove that any Cauchy sequence (b_i) in B converges to an $a \in B^\infty$; Let us define a directed sequence (a_i) as follows :

$$a_i = \text{lub}\{\phi(m) \mid m \le i \ \& \ \phi(m) \le b_{\psi(i)}\}$$

By our hypothesis on B , a_i is in B for any $i \in \mathbb{N}$; moreover (a_i) is increasing.
Let $a = \text{lub } a_i$, $a \in B^\infty$. We prove that $a = \lim b_i$; more precisely that :

$$\forall i \ , \ i \ge \psi(n) \Longrightarrow \mu j[\phi(j) \in b_i \,\Delta\, a_n] \ge n$$

By proposition 1 , $\mu j[\phi(j) \in b_i \,\Delta\, a_n] \ge \text{Min}\{n_0,n_1\}$ with :

$$n_0 = \mu j[\phi(j) \in b_i \,\Delta\, b_{\psi(n)}] \text{ and } n_1 = \mu j[\phi(j) \in a_n \,\Delta\, b_{\psi(n)}]$$

$i \ge \psi(n) \Longrightarrow n_0 \ge n$ since (b_i) is a Cauchy sequence and $n_1 \ge n$ by definition of the directed sequence (a_i). So is a the limit of the Cauchy sequence (b_i).

c) $\hat{\imath}$ is one-to-one . Let $a = \text{lub } a_i$, $b = \text{lub } b_i$ $a,b \in B^\infty$ (a_i) and (b_i) increasing chains in B .
Let us prove that $d(\hat{\imath}(a),\hat{\imath}(b)) = 0$ implies $a = b$:
$\lim_{n\to\infty} d(a_n,b_n) = 0$ by continuity of d , and so :
$\forall n_0$, $\exists k(n_0)$ such that $k \ge k(n_0)$ implies $\forall n$,
$n \le n_0 \Longrightarrow \phi(n) \not\in a_k \,\Delta\, b_k$. Let n_0 such that $\phi(n_0) = a_j$
$\Longrightarrow \exists k(n_0)$ such that $k \ge k(n_0) \Longrightarrow a_j \not\in a_k \,\Delta\, b_k$ and particularly with $k \ge \text{Sup}\{k(n_0),j\}$, $\phi(n_0) \not\le a_k$ & $a_j \le b_k$.

Thus it can be found, for any j , an integer k such that :

$$a_j \le b_k$$

Similarly, we obtain for any j an integer k such that $b_j \le a_k$, and finally $a = b$.

We point out that (i) in Theorem 2 is not true if (b_j) is directed. Nevertheless the completions by increasing chains an directed sets [5] lead to the same infinitary spaces.

Obviously $\hat{\imath}$ cannot be continuous since the separation properties of $\bar{B}$ and B^∞ as topological spaces are quite different.

III - FUNCTIONAL SPACES.

III.A.- It is well known [12] that the space $[B^\infty \to B'^\infty]$ of continuous functions has a basis whose elements are the step-functions defined by :

$$(b,b')(x) = \begin{cases} b' & \text{if } x \geq b \\ \perp & \text{else} \end{cases} \qquad b \in B \text{ , } b' \in B'$$

Using the results of [12] it is easy to prove that :

PROPERTY 3.- $[B^\infty \to B'^\infty]$ *is an infinitary CPO.*

The finitary basis $[B \to B']$ is the closure of the set $\{(b,b') | b \in B \text{ , } b' \in B'\}$ by finite conditional lub. By construction, $[B \to B']^\infty$ is isomorphic to $[B^\infty \to B'^\infty]$: An obvious corollary of the theorem 2 is then the following :

COROLLARY.- $[B^\infty \to B'^\infty]$ *and* $[\overline{B \to B'}]$ *can be settled in bijection by* $\hat{\imath}$ *defined as in Theorem 2.*

III.B.- CONVERGENCE PROPERTIES.

We give only our main results : A more extensive paper dealing with convergence properties is being redacted.

a) Let us prove first that the convergence for our metric is equivalent to the pointwise convergence on the basis; more precisely :

THEOREM 3.- *Let* $e : \mathbb{N} \to [B \to B']$ *be a numbering of the finitary basis for the infinitary CPO* $[B^\infty \to B'^\infty]$; *let* ϕ *and* ϕ' *be numberings of* B *and* B' *respectively. Let* (f_n) *be a sequence in* $[B^\infty \to B'^\infty]$ *and* $g \in [B^\infty \to B'^\infty]$; *then*

$$d_e(f_n,g) \underset{n\to\infty}{\longrightarrow} 0 \quad \textit{iff} \quad d_{\phi'}(f_n(x),g(x)) \underset{n\to\infty}{\longrightarrow} 0 \quad \textit{for any } x \textit{ in } B .$$

The following lemma is very important in our proof :

LEMMA.- $\forall f,g \in [B^\infty \to B'^\infty]$, $b' \in f(b) \Delta g(b) \iff (b,b') \in f \Delta g$, $b \in B$, $b' \in B'$

REMARK.- It is worth noting that the d_e-convergence does not imply the pointwise convergence on B^∞ and illustrated by the following example : Let B^∞ the $\mathbb{N} \cup \{+\infty\}$ equipped with the arithmetic order and (f_n) defined by :

$$f_n(x) = \begin{cases} 0 & \text{if } x \leq n \\ 1 & \text{else} \end{cases}$$

It can be seen that (f_n) d_e-converges to f defined by $f(x) = 0$ for any x, but $\lim_{n\to\infty} f_n(\infty) = 1 \neq f(\infty)$.

b) The d_e-convergence doesn't imply the uniform convergence; but we have the :

THEOREM 4.- *Let* $(g_i)_{i\in\mathbb{N}}$ *be an increasing sequence in* $[B^\infty \to B'^\infty]$ *, which* d_e*-converges to an* $f \in [B^\infty \to B'^\infty]$ *; then* (g_i) *converges uniformly to* f.

The proof is an obvious adaptation of DINIS's Theorem.

IV - INFINITARY COMPUTABLE OBJECTS.

Let us extend now the Theorem 2 to the "computable" completed spaces associated to B^∞ and $\bar{B}$; for we have to define what a "computable extension" of a finitary basis is.

IV.A.- INFINITARY COMPUTABLE CPO'S

As in [8] , a numbering $\phi : \mathbb{N} \to B$ is *effective* iff both following conditions are verified :

1) the predicate $[\{\phi(x),\phi(y)\}$ bounded$]$ is recursive,
2) the graph of the lub is recursive.

The completion B^∞ of a basis B having an effective numbering is an effectively given domain [17] ; the subset $COMP(B^\infty)$ of computable elements is called an effective domain in [8] ; $COMP(B^\infty)$ is called an *infinitary computable CPO* whenever B has the properties of a finitary basis. KANDA [8] proved that the computable elements can be characterized by the following properties :

a) if $\phi(w_z)$ is directed, $lub(\phi(w_z)) \in COMP(B^\infty)$, w_z being the recursively enumerable set whose Gödel number is z , $w_z \subseteq \mathbb{N}$.
b) $\forall x$, $x \in COMP(B^\infty) \Longrightarrow \exists z$ such that $x = lub(\phi(w_z))$

A numbering ϕ^∞ of $COMP(B^\infty)$ can easily be built (directed numbering in [8]; single-valued numbering in [6]).

Furthermore we shall say that $\phi^\infty(y) \in COMP(B^\infty)$ is *decidable* iff the set $\{x \in \mathbb{N} | [\phi(x) \leq \phi^\infty(y)]\}$ is recursive : This definition extends the usual definition of recursive subsets of $\mathbb{N}$.

Let us recall that [8] $COMP(B^\infty)$ is the set of semi-decidable elements of B^∞ , every semi-decidable (computable) element $\phi^{\infty}(y)$ being characterized by the property :

$$\{x | x \in \mathbb{N} \ \& \ \phi(x) \leq \phi^{\infty}(y)\} \quad \text{is r.e.}$$

IV.B.- RECURSIVE METRIC SPACES

As in ([10],[9]) a metric space (E,d) is called *recursive* if there is a countable subset $D \subset E$ effectively enumerated by ϕ and such that :

1) E is complete
2) D is dense on E
3) $\delta : \mathbb{N}^2 \to \mathbb{R}$ defined by $\delta(n,n') = d(\phi(n),\phi(n'))$ is recursive.

It is easy to verify that $(\bar{B},d)$, with an effective numbering of B , is a recursive metric space.

Let us define now an effective Cauchy sequence (b_i) in B as follows :

1) $\exists\, \Theta$ recursive such that $b_i = \phi(\Theta(i))$, $i \in \mathbb{N}$
2) $\exists\, \psi$ recursive such that : $\forall\, n,n',p[n \geq \psi(p), n' \geq \psi(p) \Longrightarrow d(b_n,b_{n'}) < \frac{1}{p}]$

It is easy to see that effective versions of Theorem 1 and propositions 1 and 2 can be done; we try to obtain an effective version of Theorem 2.

IV.C.- DECIDABILITY AND LIMITS OF EFFECTIVE CAUCHY SEQUENCES.

Our main result on computability is the following :

THEOREM 5.- *Let* $COMP(B^{\infty})$ *be an infinitary computable CPO.* $x \in COMP(B^{\infty})$ *is decidable iff* x *is limit of an effective Cauchy sequence in* B .

Sketch of the proof :

1) First we prove that any effective Cauchy sequence converges to a decidable element in $COMP(B^{\infty})$.

   Let (b_i) be an effective Cauchy sequence whose recursive regulator is ψ ; let (a_i) be the directed sequence defined in Theorem 2 :

$$a_i = \text{lub}\{\phi(m) | m \leq i \ \& \ \phi(m) \leq b_{\psi(i)}\}$$

   We have to prove that $a = \text{lub}\{a_i | i \in \mathbb{N}\}$ is decidable.

The following lemma can be easily proved.

LEMMA 1.- $\phi(n) \leq b_{\psi(n')}$ *iff* $\phi(n) \leq a_{n'}$ *for every* $n \leq n'$.

This lemma implies :

<u>LEMMA 2</u>.- $\phi(n) \leq a$ *iff* $\phi(n) \leq a_n$.

First, $\phi(n) \leq a_n \Longrightarrow \phi(n) \leq a$ by definition of a .

Conversely, $\phi(n) \not\leq a_n \Longrightarrow \phi(n) \not\leq a$

It results from the lemma 1 :

$$\begin{aligned} \phi(n) \not\leq a_n &\Longrightarrow \phi(n) \not\leq b_{\psi(n)} \\ &\Longrightarrow \forall n' \quad (n' > n \Longrightarrow \phi(n) \not\leq b_{\psi(n')}) \end{aligned}$$

The lemma 1 implies :

$$\begin{aligned} &\forall n' \quad (n' > n \Longrightarrow \phi(n) \not\leq a_{n'}) \\ &\Longrightarrow \forall n' , \ \phi(n) \not\leq a_{n'} \text{ since } (a_i) \text{ is increasing} \\ &\Longrightarrow \phi(n) \not\leq a \end{aligned}$$

The lemma 2 gives the conclusion since the order relation on B is recursive.

2) Conversely, let us prove that any recursive element a is limit (effective) of an effective Cauchy sequence.

   Let (a_i) an increasing sequence such that $a = \text{lub}(a_i)$; let us define :

$$b_n = \text{lub}\{\phi(i) | i \leq n \ \& \ \phi(i) \leq a\}$$

   (b_i) is effective; it is easy to prove that (b_i) is Cauchy (his regulator is the identity) effective. On the other hand, $\text{lub}\{b_n | n \in \mathbb{N}\} = \text{lub}\{\phi(i) | \phi(i) \leq a\}$

$$\Longrightarrow a = \text{lub}\{b_n | n \in \mathbb{N}\}$$

   Furthermore, $\mu i[\phi(i) \in b_n \,\Delta\, a] > n \Longrightarrow d(a,b) < \frac{1}{1+n} \Longrightarrow a = \lim_{n\to\infty} b_n$ with (b_i) Cauchy effective. q.e.d.

A natural extension of this work is an effective version of the part III on functional spaces; for we are studying a definition of effective compactness and proving that $\text{COMP}(\bar{B})$ is effectively compact [3].

AKNOWLEDGMENT : The authors would like to thank G. PLOTKIN for helpful discussion and advices about Lawson topology and characterization of completeness.

REFERENCES

[1] G. BIRKOFF
LATTICE THEORY
3rd Ed., NEW YORK, 1967

[2] L. BOASSON, M. NIVAT
ADHERENCES OF LANGUAGES
JCSS 20, 1980, pp. 285-309

[3] G. COMYN
OBJETS INFINIS CALCULABLES
THESE D'ETAT, LILLE, Mars 1982

[4] G. COMYN, M. DAUCHET
OBJETS INFINITAIRES - APPROXIMATIONS DANS LES CPO's ET DANS LES ESPACES METRIQUES
Colloque A.F.C.E.T. "LES MATHEMATIQUES DE L'INFORMATIQUE", 16-18 Mars 1982, PARIS

[5] P.M. COHN
UNIVERSAL ALGEBRA
Harper and Row, NEW YORK, 1965

[6] H. EGLI, R. CONSTABLE
COMPUTABILITY CONCEPTS FOR PROGRAMMING LANGUAGES
TCS 2, 1976, pp. 98-105

[7] G. GIERZ, K.H. HOFMANN, K. KEIMEL, J.D. LAWSON, M. MISLOVE, D.S. SCOTT
A COMPENDIUM OF CONTINUOUS LATTICES
Springer Verlag, 1980

[8] A. KANDA
FULLY EFFECTIVE SOLUTIONS OF RECURSIVE DOMAIN EQUATIONS
Math. Foundations of Computer Science, 1979, OLOMOUC,
Lecture Notes in Computer Science, n° 74, pp. 326-336

[9] D. LACOMBE
QUELQUES PROCEDES DE DEFINITION EN TOPOLOGIE RECURSIVE
Constructivity in Mathematics, Proc. of the Colloquium Held at AMSTERDAM, 1957
Studies in Logic and the foundations of Mathematics, 1959, pp. 129-158

[10] Y. MOSCHOVAKIS
RECURSIVE METRIC SPACES
Fundamenta Mathematicae, LV, 1964, pp. 215-238

[11] M. NIVAT

INFINITE WORDS, INFINITE TREES, INFINITE COMPUTATIONS
Foundations of Computer Science III
Part 2 : Languages, Logic, Semantics
J.W. DE BAKKER (Ed.), J. VAN LEEUWEN (Ed.)
Mathematical Centre Tract, 1979, pp. 1-52

[12] G. PLOTKIN

$\mathbf{T}^{\omega}$ *AS A UNIVERSAL DOMAIN*
JCSS 17, 1978, pp. 209-236

[13] G. PLOTKIN

Personal Communication, LILLE, Mars 1982

[14] G. PLOTKIN

A POWERDOMAIN CONSTRUCTION
SIAM. J. Comput. 5 (Sept. 1976), pp. 452-487

[15] E. SCIORE, A. TANG

COMPUTABILITY THEORY IN ADMISSIBLE DOMAIN
Proc. of the 10 th ACM Symp. on the Theory of Computing
SAN DIEGO, California, Mai 1978, pp. 95-104

[16] D. SCOTT

LATTICE THEORY, DATA TYPES AND SEMANTICS
Symposium on formal Semantics of Programming Languages
Ed. by RANDALL RUSTIN, Sept. 1970
Prentice Hall, Inc. ENGLEWOOD CLIFFS, New Jersey

[17] M. SMYTH

EFFECTIVELY GIVEN DOMAINS
Theoretical Computer Science 5 , 1977, pp. 257-274

[18] K. WEIHRAUCH, U. SCHREIBER

METRIC SPACES DEFINED BY WEIGHTED ALGEBRAIC CPO's
FCT 79, Math. Research, Akademic Verlag, pp. 516-522

[19] G. WERNER

REPRESENTATION OF EFFECTIVELY COMPUTABLE LIMITS
Technical Report IT, LILLE-I, n° IT-3081

ON TEST SETS AND THE EHRENFEUCHT CONJECTURE *

Karel Culik II
Department of Computer Science
University of Waterloo
Waterloo, Ontario, Canada

Juhani Karhumäki
Department of Mathematics
University of Turku
Turku, Finland

ABSTRACT

Ehrenfeucht conjectured that each language over a finite alphabet Σ possesses a test set, that is a finite subset F of L such that any two morphisms on Σ^* agreeing on each string of F also agree on each string of L. We give a sufficient condition for a language L to guarantee that it has a test set. We also show that the Ehrenfeucht conjecture holds true if and only if every (infinite) system of equations (with finite number of variables) over a finitely generated free monoid has an equivalent finite subsystem. The equivalence and the inclusion problems for finite systems of equations are shown to be decidable. As an application we derive a result that for DOL languages the existence of a test set implies its effective existence. Consequently, the validity of the Ehrenfeucht conjecture for DOL languages implies the decidability of the HDOL sequence equivalence problem. Finally, we show that the Ehrenfeucht conjecture holds true for so-called positive DOL languages.

1. INTRODUCTION

Ehrenfeucht conjectured (Problem 108 in [14]) that for every language $L \subseteq \Sigma^*$ there exists a finite subset F of L such that for any pair (g,h) of morphisms on Σ^*, $g(x) = h(x)$ holds for each x in L if and only if $g(x) = h(x)$ holds for each x in F. Such a finite subset F has been called a test set for L in [9], where it has been shown that the Ehrenfeucht conjecture holds true for every language over a binary alphabet (for a new proof see [10]). It is clear from the arguments in [8] that a test set can be effectively constructed for each regular language and this has been extended to context-free languages in [1]. The effective existence of a test set for each language L in a family $\mathcal{L}$ clearly implies that the morphism equivalence problem for $\mathcal{L}$ is decidable, i.e. we can test whether for any given language L in $\mathcal{L}$ and any

* This work was carried out when the second author visited at the University of Waterloo and it was supported by Natural Science and Engineering Research Council of Canada, Grant A 7403.

two morphisms g and h the equation $g(x) = h(x)$ holds for all x in L.

After preliminaries we introduce in Section 3, as a generalization of the notion of the weighted difference from [9], the notion of the deviation of a string with respect to a language. Using this we give a sufficient condition for a language to possess a test set. More precisely, we show that every language with bounded prefix deviation and fair distribution of letters has a test set.

In Section 4 we consider the Ehrenfeucht conjecture in a little bit different light. Using the terminology of systems of equations over a free monoid the conjecture says that every (infinite) system of equations of certain very special form has an equivalent finite subsystem. Here we show a result which emphasizes the importance of the Ehrenfeucht conjecture from purely algebraic point of view, namely we show that it is equivalent to the following conjecture: Every (infinite) system of equations (with a finite number of variables) over a finitely generated free monoid has an equivalent finite subsystem. Moreover, with suitable definitions, we are able to show that if the Ehrenfeucht conjecture holds true for some family of languages (e.g. rational languages) then the above conjecture holds for the systems of equations of "the same type" (e.g. rational systems of equations), and vice versa.

In Section 5 we show, using a deep decidability result of Makanin [15], that the equivalence problem for finite systems of equations over a finitely generated free monoid is decidable. Among the applications of this result is the following surprising fact: For DOL (and even DTOL) languages the existence of a test set implies its effective existence. This, in turn, yields that the validity of the Ehrenfeucht conjecture implies the decidability of the well known HDOL sequence equivalence problem and also the DTOL sequence equivalence problem, cf. [4]. In fact, for the above results it is enough that the Ehrenfeucht conjecture holds for DOL and DTOL languages, respectively. We conclude this section with a result showing that a test set really exists for each positive DOL language.

This paper is a combination of the results of [6] and [7]. The detailed proofs of the results can be found therein, however, some of the most interesting are presented here, too.

2. PRELIMINARIES

Here we need only very basic properties of free monoids and formal languages. For unexplained notions we refer to [13]. For clarity we want to specify the following.

The length of a word x is denoted by $|x|$, while $|x|_a$ means the number of letters a in x. For a finite set A, $|A|$ denotes its cardinality. The notation ψ is used for the <u>Parikh mapping</u>. When x is a prefix of y or y is a prefix of x we write $x \text{ Pref } y$. $\text{Pref}(L)$ denotes the set of all prefixes of words of a language L.

We say that two morphisms $h, g : \Sigma^* \to \Delta^*$ are <u>equivalent</u> on a language L or

<u>agree</u> on a language L, in symbols $h \overset{L}{\equiv} g$, if $h(x) = g(x)$ for each x in L. If h(x) and g(x) are of the same length for each x in L then we say that h and g <u>agree lengthwise</u> on L. The set of all pairs of morphisms agreeing (resp. agreeing lengthwise) on a language L is denoted by $H(L)$ (resp. $H_\ell(L)$). We call a language L <u>rich</u> if $H(L) = \{(h,h) \mid h$ is a morphism$\}$. Let L be a language and x a word. We say that x is <u>morphically forced</u> by L if for all pairs (h,g) of morphisms $h \overset{L}{\equiv} g$ implies that $h(x) = g(x)$. A finite subset F of L is called a <u>test set</u> for L if, for any pair (h,g) of morphisms, $h \overset{F}{\equiv} g$ iff $h \overset{L}{\equiv} g$.

Our basic interest is in the following:

EHRENFEUCHT CONJECTURE: For every language over a finite alphabet there exists a test set.

A <u>DOL system</u> is a triple (Σ,h,x) where Σ is an alphabet, h is a morphism $\Sigma^* \to \Sigma^*$ and x is a nonempty word in Σ^*. A DOL system defines a <u>DOL sequence</u> when h is applied iteratively to x: $x, h(x), h^2(x), \ldots$ We call a DOL system <u>positive</u> if, for each (a,b) in $\Sigma\times\Sigma$, a occurs in h(b). For the basic properties of DOL systems as well as those of DTOL systems we refer to [17].

We shall also need some basic terminology concerning vectors over rational number $\mathbb{Q}$ and nonnegative integers $\mathbb{N}$. For two vectors z and z' in $\mathbb{Q}^t$, $z \leq z'$ means that z is componentwise smaller than or equal to z'. If $z \leq z'$ and $z \neq z'$ we write $z < z'$. By the absolute value of a vector $z = (z_1,\ldots,z_t)$ we mean the number $|z| = \sum_{i=1}^{t} |z_i|$. Let $M \subseteq \mathbb{Q}^t$. The <u>vector space</u> over $\mathbb{Q}$ generated by M is denoted by $\langle M \rangle$. When $M \subseteq \mathbb{N}^t$ we call an element z of M <u>minimal</u> (with respect to M) if there does not exist in M any element z' such that $z' < z$. The <u>set of minimal elements</u> of M is denoted by Min(M). If M is a finite set of numbers we denote by min(M) (resp. max(M)) the smallest (resp. the largest) element of M.

3. A SUFFICIENT CONDITION FOR THE EXISTENCE OF A TEST SET

In this section we define and study our central notion: deviation of a word with respect to a language. This notion is closely related to the notion of balance of a word with respect to two morphisms, cf. [4]. However, our new notion depends on the considered language only.

Let L be a language over $\{a_1,\ldots,a_t\}$. We define a subset of $\mathbb{N}^t$ induced by L, in symbols sp(L), by setting

$$sp(L) = \psi^{-1}(\langle\psi(L)\rangle \cap \mathbb{N}^t) .$$

Since $\psi(sp(L)))$ is a subtractive submonoid of the additive monoid $\mathbb{N}^t$ we have, see [12],

<u>Lemma 1.</u> For each language L over $\{a_1,\ldots,a_t\}$, $\psi(sp(L))$ is finitely generated submonoid of $(\mathbb{N}^t,+)$.

By Lemma 1, for each language L there exists a finite set β of vectors in $\mathbb{N}^t$, say $\beta=\{e_1,\ldots,e_p\}$, such that

$$\psi(sp(L)) = \{\sum_{i=1}^{p} n_i e_i \mid n_i \in \mathbb{N} \text{ for } i=1,\ldots,p\}.$$

Now, we state our basic definition.

<u>Definition 1.</u> Let L be a language over $\Sigma=\{a_1,\ldots,a_t\}$ and $w\in\Sigma^*$. The <u>deviation of w with respect to L</u>, in symbols $d_L(w)$ or briefly $d(w)$ when L is known, is the set

$$d_L(w) = \mathrm{Min}\,\{z \in \mathbb{N}^t \mid \psi(w) \in \psi(sp(L)) + z\}.$$

<u>Example 1.</u> Let $L=ab^*c$. Then $\psi(sp(L))=\{x\in\{a,b,c\}^* \mid |x|_a=|x|_c\}$, and, in terms of Lemma 1, $\psi(sp(L))=\{n(1,0,1)+m(0,1,0) \mid n,m\in\mathbb{N}\}$. Further for each proper prefix ab^i of a word in L, $d(ab^i)=\{(1,0,0)\}$.

Roughly speaking $d(w)$ tells how far w is from the language $sp(L)$. It follows from the König Infinite Lemma, see [13], that $d(w)$ is always finite. The relation between the deviation and the balance is as follows. Let $(h,g)\in H_\ell(L)$. Then for every word w we have

(1) $$|\beta_{h,g}(w)| \leq \min\{|z| \mid z\in d(w)\}\max\{|h(a)|, |g(a)| \mid a\in\Sigma\},$$

where $\beta_{h,g}(w)$ denotes the balance of w with respect to the pair (h,g). We also have

<u>Lemma 2.</u> Let L be a language and (h,g) a pair of morphisms in $H_\ell(L)$. If u and w are words such that $\psi(u)\in d_L(w)$, then $\beta_{h,g}(u)=\beta_{h,g}(w)$.

Our next simple observation is

<u>Theorem 1.</u> Every language L over $\{a_1,\ldots,a_t\}$ containing t linearly independent Parikh-vectors is rich.

Our second central definition is as follows.

<u>Definition 2.</u> Let L and L' be languages over the same alphabet. We say that L has <u>bounded prefix deviation with respect to L'</u> if there exists a constant C such that for every prefix w of a word in L

$$\min\{|z| \mid z\in d_{L'}(w)\} \leq C.$$

If the above is satisfied with $L=L'$ we say that L has <u>bounded prefix deviation</u>.

It follows from (1) that if L has bounded prefix deviation, then each pair (h,g) of morphisms in $H_\ell(L)$ has bounded balance on L. However, the bound depends on the pair. On the other hand, a pair of morphisms may have a bounded balance on such a language which has unbounded prefix deviation, cf. [7].

Our notions of the deviation and the bounded prefix deviation are generalizations of those of the weighted difference and the bounded prefix difference defined in [9]. We can also generalize some arguments of [9] to yield the following theorem. To be able to state it we still need one notion. We say that a language L has a fair distribution of letters if there exists a constant q such that every subword in L with the length at least q contains all letters of the alphabet of L.

Theorem 2. Every language L over $\{a_1,\dots,a_t\}$ with bounded prefix deviation and fair distribution of letters has a test set.

Proof. Let the prefix deviation of L be bounded by C and let q be a constant giving a fair distribution of letters for L. We first prove

Claim: There exists a constant N such that for any $uv \in \mathrm{pref}(L)$, with $|v| \geq N$, the following holds true: For any pair (h,g) in $H_\ell(L)$

$$\min\{|h(uv)|\ ,\ |g(uv)|\} \geq \max\{|h(u)|\ ,\ |g(u)|\}.$$

The claim is proved as follows. Let z be a vector in d(u) such that $|z| \leq C$. We start by showing that there exist a constant D and a vector z_1 in $\psi(sp(L))$ such that

$$z + Dy \geq z_1 \geq z\ , \tag{2}$$

where $y = (1,\dots,1)$, i.e. all of its components equal 1. According to Lemma 1 let $\psi(sp(L))$ be generated by $\{e_1,\dots,e_p\}$. We set $D = C + C\sum_{i=1}^{p}|e_i|$ and $z_1 = C\sum_{i=1}^{p} e_i$. Then

$$z + Dy > C(\sum_{i=1}^{p}|e_i|)\,y = |z_1|\,y > z_1$$

and

$$z < |z|\,y \leq Cy \leq z_1\ ,$$

where the last inequality follows since each letter a_i occurs in a word of L. Hence (2) has been established.

Now, let $N = Dq$. Since $|v| \geq N$, v contains as a sparse subword a word v' (i.e. v' is obtained from v by erasing some occurrences of letters in v) such that $\psi(v') \geq Dy$. Assuming, without loss of generality, that $|h(u)| \geq |g(u)|$ we should show that $|g(uv)| \geq |h(u)|$. For a vector x in $\mathbb{N}^t$ let $\overline{x}$ denote a word such that $\psi(\overline{x}) = x$. Then, by Lemma 2 and the above, we obtain

$$\begin{aligned}|g(uv)| - |h(u)| &= |g(\bar{z}v)| - |h(\bar{z})| \\ &\geq |g(\bar{z}v')| - |h(\bar{z})| \\ &\geq |g(\bar{z}\bar{y}^D)| - |h(\bar{z})| \\ &\geq |g(\bar{z}_1)| - |h(\bar{z}_1)| \\ &= 0 .\end{aligned}$$

Thus, the proof of the claim is completed and we return to the proof of the theorem.

We divide L into two parts F and $L - F$ by setting $F = \{w \in L \mid |w| \leq 3N\}$. Moreover, for every w in $L - F$ we choose a fixed decomposition

(3) $$w = u_1 \dots u_m \quad \text{with} \quad N \leq |u_j| \leq 2N .$$

For each such decomposition and for each $j = 1,\dots,m$ we define pairs (z_j,u_j), where z_j is a fixed vector in $d(u_1\dots u_{j-1})$ satisfying $|z_j| \leq C$. Such pairs are called <u>pieces</u>. Clearly, the number of different pieces is finite. We say that two pieces (z,x) and (z',x') <u>occur consecutively in L</u> if there exists in L a word w such that x and x' occur consecutively in its decomposition (3), say $x = u_k$ and $x' = u_{k+1}$, and moreover $z \in d(u_1\dots u_{k-1})$ and $z' \in d(u_1\dots u_k)$. Now, we choose a finite subset L' of L such that for any pair of pieces if they occur consecutively in L they occur consecutively in L'. Finally, we choose a finite subset F' of L such that $sp(F \cup L' \cup F') = sp(L)$.

We infer that $F \cup L' \cup F'$ is a test set for L. We should show that for any pair (h,g) of morphisms, $h \overset{F\cup L'\cup F'}{\equiv} g$ implies $h \overset{L}{\equiv} g$. Let $(h,g) \in H(F \cup L' \cup F')$ and $w \in L - F \cup L' \cup F'$. Let the decomposition of w according to (3) be $w = u_1\dots u_m$. Since $(h,g) \in H(F \cup L' \cup F')$ and $sp(L) = sp(F \cup L' \cup F')$, h and g agree lengthwise on L and therefore by the claim and the choice of (3)

$$\min\{|h(u_1\dots u_i)| , |g(u_1\dots u_i)|\} \geq \max\{|h(u_1\dots u_{i-1})| , |g(u_1\dots u_{i-1})|\}$$

for $i = 1,\dots,m$. Consequently, the choice of L' and the fact $h \overset{L'}{\equiv} g$ imply that if $h(u_1\dots u_{i-1})$ Pref $g(u_1\dots u_{i-1})$ then also $h(u_1\dots u_i)$ Pref $g(u_1\dots u_i)$. So we conclude inductively that $h(w) = g(w)$ which completes the proof of the theorem.

We note that not only the assumption that L has bounded prefix deviation but also the assumption that L has fair distribution of letters is essential for our above proof, i.e. for the piece construction. This is seen as follows.

<u>Example 1 (continued).</u> As we mentioned the language $L = ab^*c$ has bounded prefix deviation. However, the pairs (h_k,g_k) of morphisms, for $k \geq 1$, defined by

$$h_k : \begin{array}{l} a \to a(ba)^k \\ b \to ba \\ c \to ba \end{array} \qquad\qquad g_k : \begin{array}{l} a \to ab \\ b \to ab \\ c \to (ab)^k a \end{array}$$

show that the claim in the proof of Theorem 2 does not hold true. Despite of that we, of course, believe that the theorem is true without the assumption of fair distribution of letters. Indeed, $\{ac, abc\}$ is a test set for L.

Whether the assumptions of Theorem 2 imply the effective existence of a test set depends, of course, on how L is given. In the case of DOL languages we have the following result, see [7].

Theorem 3. Let L be a DOL language. The set sp(L) can be effectively found. Moreover, it is decidable whether L has bounded prefix deviation and fair distribution of letters, and if so, then a test set for L can be effectively found.

4. A GENERALIZATION OF THE EHRENFEUCHT CONJECTURE

We now show that the existence of a test set for a language of certain type is equivalent to the existence of an equivalent finite subsystem of equations for a system of equations of "the same type".

A system of equations over Σ^* with unknowns N is a binary relation $S \subseteq (N \cup \Sigma)^* \times (N \cup \Sigma)^*$. A pair $(u,v) \in S$ represents the equation $u = v$. A solution of an equation (or a system of equations) with n unknowns over Σ is an n-tuple from $(\Sigma^*)^n$. Formally, a solution of a system S is nothing but a morphism $h : (N \cup \Sigma)^* \to \Sigma^*$ such that $h(a) = a$ for each a in Σ and $h(u) = h(v)$ for each equation $u = v$ in S. Two systems of equations are called equivalent if they have exactly the same solutions.

We say that a system of equations is rational (regular) if N is finite and S is a rational (regular) relation, cf. [2]. Similarly we have algebraic (push down) systems of equations. A family of binary relations $\mathcal{R}$ is said to be morphically characterized by a family of languages $\mathcal{L}$ if the following holds: $R \in \mathcal{R}$ if and only if there exists two morphisms h and g and a language L in $\mathcal{L}$ such that $R = \{(h(w), g(w)) \mid w \in L\}$, or briefly $R = [h,g]L$.

It is well known (Nivat theorem) that the family of rational (regular) relations is morphically characterized by the family of rational (regular) languages, and the family of algebraic (push down) relations by the family of algebraic (context-free) languages.

Lemma 3. The family of all binary relations is morphically characterized by the family of all languages.

Let $\mathcal{L}$ be a family of languages. We say that a system of equations $S \subseteq (N \cup \Sigma)^* \times (N \cup \Sigma)^*$ is of type $\mathcal{L}$ (e.g. rational) if S belongs to the family of relations morphically characterized by $\mathcal{L}$, i.e. $S = [h,g]L$ for some L in $\mathcal{L}$ and some morphisms h and g. The discussion above justifies this terminology in the case of rational, algebraic and arbitrary systems of equations.

Now, we are ready to show the correspondence between the existence of test sets for languages of type $\mathcal{L}$ and the existence of equivalent finite subsystems for systems of equations of type $\mathcal{L}$.

Theorem 4. Let $\mathcal{L}$ be a family of languages. The following two conditions are equivalent:

(i) For each L in $\mathcal{L}$ there (effectively) exists a test set.

(ii) For each system of equations S of type $\mathcal{L}$ there (effectively) exists an equivalent finite subsystem (subset of S).

Proof. (ii) $\Rightarrow$ (i). Let $L \in \mathcal{L}$, $L \subseteq \Sigma^*$. Define $\overline{\Sigma} = \{\overline{a} \mid a \in \Sigma\}$, and a morphism $\mu : \Sigma^* \to \overline{\Sigma}^*$ by $\mu(a) = \overline{a}$ for each a in Σ.

Consider the system of equations $S = [I,\mu]L$, where I is the identity morphism. Clearly, for morphisms f and g, $f \overset{L}{\equiv} g$ iff $f \cup (g \circ \mu^{-1})$ is a solution of S (the union of two morphisms is defined in a natural way when the domains of the morphisms are disjoint). System S is of type $\mathcal{L}$, therefore, by (ii), there exists an equivalent finite subsystem S' of S. Let F be a finite subset of L such that $S' \subseteq [I,\mu]F$. Now, if $f \overset{F}{\equiv} g$, then $f \cup (g \circ \mu^{-1})$ is a solution of S', therefore it it also a solution of S and thus $f \overset{L}{\equiv} g$. Hence F is a test set for L.

(i) $\Rightarrow$ (ii). Let $S \subseteq (N \cup \Sigma)^* \times (N \cup \Sigma)^*$ be a system of equations of type $\mathcal{L}$. This means that there exist $L \in \mathcal{L}$, $L \subseteq \Delta^*$ for some alphabet Δ and morphisms $f,g : \Delta^* \to (N \cup \Sigma)^*$ such that $S = [f,g]L$. By (i), there exists a test set F for L. Consider the system S' of equations defined by $S' = [f,g]F$. Let h be a solution of S', i.e. $h(u) = h(v)$ for each $(u,v) \in S'$. This means $h \circ f \overset{L}{\equiv} h \circ g$ which, in turn, can be written as $h(u) = h(v)$ for each $(u,v) \in S$, i.e. h is also a solution of S. Thus every solution of the subsystem S' is a solution of the system S. Since the converse is obvious the system S and its finite subsystem S' are equivalent.

Finally, we observe that our constructions are effective, so if a test set for a language from $\mathcal{L}$ exists effectively, then also the finite subsystem S' exists effectively, and vice versa.

Now, we are ready to state the following conjecture and demonstrate its equivalence to the Ehrenfeucht conjecture.

Conjecture A. For each system of equations (with a finite number of variables) over a finitely generated free monoid there exists (noneffectively) an equivalent finite subsystem.

By Lemma 3 and Theorem 4 we have

Corollary 1. Conjecture A holds if and only if the Ehrenfeucht conjecture holds.

Since for each context-free language there effectively exists a test set, cf. [1], we have

Corollary 2. For every algebraic system of equations there effectively exists an equivalent finite subsystem.

Concerning Conjecture A we have the following two simple reduction results.

Theorem 5. Any system S of equations over Σ^* is equivalent to a system S', where constants occur only in the equations of the form $x_a = a$ with $a \in \Sigma$ and x_a is a variable.

To be able to state our second reduction result we need the following notion. Let S be a system of equations without constants. We say that a solution of S is nonsingular if all of its components are nonempty. We also say that two systems of equations are nonsingularly equivalent if they have exactly the same nonsingular solutions.

Theorem 6. If any system of equations without constants is nonsingularly equivalent to its finite subsystem, then Conjecture A holds.

We want to finish this section with the following discussion which, we believe, gives some intuitive support for the validity of the Ehrenfeucht conjecture. We start with some terminology.

Let $L \subseteq \Sigma^*$. The simplicity degree of L, in symbols sd(L), is defined by

$$sd(L) = \min \{|F| \mid F \subseteq \Sigma^*,\ L \subseteq F^*\} .$$

For a morphism $h : \Sigma^* \to \Delta^*$ the simplicity degree of h, in symbols sd(h), is defined by $sd(h) = sd(h(\Sigma))$. (Sometimes, e.g. in [16], the simplicity degree of h is called the rank of h.) It is clear that for any language L, $sd(L) \leq \min \{|\Sigma|, |L|\}$ and for any morphism h, $sd(h) \leq |\Sigma|$. Following [11] we call a language or a morphism simplifiable if its simplicity degree is strictly smaller than $|\Sigma|$. By a periodic language or morphism we mean a language or morphism having simplicity degree equal to 1. Finally, by an atomic morphism $h : \Sigma^* \to \Sigma^*$ we mean a morphism which is of the form $h(a) = ab$ for some $a \neq b$ and $h(c) = c$ for $c \neq a$ or of the form $h(a) = ba$ for some $a \neq b$ and $h(c) = c$ for $c \neq a$, and by a qausiatomic morphism a morphism which is a finite composition of atomic morphisms.

We have the result, cf. [6].

Theorem 7. For each λ-free morphism $h : \Sigma^* \to \Delta^*$ there exists a biprefix $f : \Sigma_1^* \to \Delta^*$ for some $\Sigma_1 \subseteq \Sigma$, a letter-to-letter morphism $c : \Sigma^* \to \Sigma_1^*$ and a quasiatomic morphism $\pi : \Sigma^* \to \Sigma^*$ such that $h = f \circ c \circ \pi$.

As an immediate consequence of Theorem 6 we obtain, among other things, the following known result, cf. e.g. [3],

Corollary 3. Let S be a nontrivial equation containing n variables and no constants. Then any solution of S is of the simplicity degree at most $n-1$.

Now, what happens if we have two independent nontrivial equations. Are solutions simplified by two? This is not the case. Indeed, the system $xyz = yzx$, $xzy = zyx$ is independent and, however, it has a (singular) solution $x=\lambda$, $y=a$, $z=b$. Even in the case when only nonsingular solutions are considered the answer to the above question is negative, as examplified the system $xyz = zyx$, $xzy = zxy$. This is also independent and it has a solution $x=z=a$, $y=b$.

So the question remains: Under which conditions all the solutions of an independent system of n equations are simplified by n? What we know is the following. Let S be a system of equations with n variables and without constants. For each s in S let first(s) be the set of first variables of s, i.e. if $s: xu = yv$, where x and y are variables, then first(s) $= \{x,y\}$. We define an <u>undirected graph G_S associated to S</u> as follows: the variables of S are the verticies of G_S, and there exists an edge between x and y if and only if first(s) $= \{x,y\}$ for some s in S. From [3] we can derive

<u>Theorem 8.</u> Let k be the cardinality of the largest component of G_S. Then any nonsingular solution of S is of the simplicity degree at most $n-k+1$. Especially, if G_S is connected, then any nonsingular solution of S is periodic.

Theorem 8 yields a sufficient condition, under which Conjecture A holds true.

5. THE EQUIVALENCE PROBLEM FOR SYSTEMS OF EQUATIONS OVER A FREE MONOID, AND APPLICATIONS

In this section we show that the equivalence of two finite systems of equations (with a finite number of unknowns) over Σ^* is decidable. Clearly, this result extends to all types of equations for which there effectively exists a finite subsystem, in particular, to algebraic systems of equations. We reduce these problems to the solvability of a system of equations shown decidable in [15]. Essential is the technique of translating the nonequality into several systems of equations shown in [5].

<u>Theorem 9.</u> The equivalence problem for finite systems of equations (with a finite number of variables) is decidable.

<u>Proof.</u> Given two systems $S_1, S_2 \subseteq (N \cup \Sigma)^* \times (N \cup \Sigma)^*$ we construct a finite number of systems $Z_1, \ldots, Z_n$ such that S_1 and S_2 are equivalent iff for $i = 1, \ldots, n$ no Z_i has a solution.

Let $S_1 = \{\alpha_j = \beta_j \mid j = 1, \ldots, r\}$ and $S_2 = \{\gamma_j = \delta_j \mid j = 1, \ldots, s\}$ where each $\alpha_j, \beta_j, \gamma_j, \delta_j \in (N \cup \Sigma)^*$. Clearly, systems S_1 and S_2 are equivalent iff either for some values of the unknowns and some $k \in \{1, \ldots, s\}$

(4) $$\alpha_j = \beta_j \quad \text{for} \quad j = 1,\ldots,r \quad \text{and} \quad \gamma_k \neq \delta_k$$

or for some values of the unknowns and some $k \in \{1,\ldots,r\}$

(5) $$\alpha_k \neq \beta_k \quad \text{and} \quad \gamma_j = \delta_j \quad \text{for} \quad j = 1,\ldots,s\,.$$

Like in [5] we translate (4), for each value of k, into a finite number of systems of equations, that is to say, we construct a finite number of new systems of equations in such a way that at least one of these has a solution iff (4) is satisfied for some values of the unknowns N.

For each $a \in \Sigma$ we define systems of equations with unknowns $N \cup \{x\}$ over Σ^* by

(6) $$S_1 \cup \{\gamma_k = \delta_k ax\}$$

and

(7) $$S_1 \cup \{\gamma_k ax = \delta_k\}\,.$$

Furthermore, for each pair $(a,b) \in \Sigma \times \Sigma$, $a \neq b$, we construct systems of equations with unknowns $N \cup \{x,y,z\}$ over Σ^* as follows:

(8) $$S_1 \cup \{\gamma_k = xay,\ \delta_k = xbz\}\,.$$

Note that, for each $k = 1,\ldots,s$, (6), (7) and (8) represent several systems each but altogether a finite number of systems. Symmetrically, we can translate (5) into a finite number of systems.

Using the result of Makanin [15] we can test for each of the systems, say $Z_1,\ldots,Z_n$, whether it has a solution. If at least one of them has a solution, then systems S_1 and S_2 are nonequivalent, otherwise they are equivalent.

Theorem 9 has some interesting corollaries.

Corollary 4. The equivalence problem for algebraic systems of equations is decidable.

Corollary 5. Given two finite languages L_1 and L_2, $L_1 \subseteq L_2$, it is decidable whether L_1 is a test set for L_2.

Corollary 6. The inclusion problem for finite and algebraic systems of equations is decidable.

Next we apply Corollary 5 to derive a rather surprising result, namely that the Ehrenfeucht conjecture implies the effective existence of test sets for DOL and DTOL languages, and thus also the decidability of some well known open problems, for example the HDOL sequence equivalence problem.

Theorem 10. For every DOL language L, the existence of a test set implies that a test set can be effectively found.

Proof. Let $L = L(G)$ where $G = (\Sigma, h, w)$ is a DOL system. Since L possesses a test set there exists the minimal $p > 0$ such that the set $\{w, \ldots, h^{p-1}(w)\}$ morphically forces $h^p(w)$, i.e. if for arbitrary morphisms f and g

$$f(h^k(w)) = g(h^k(w)) \quad \text{for} \quad k = 0, \ldots, p-1$$

then

$$f(h^p(w)) = g(h^p(w)) \, .$$

This minimal p can be found effectively, since by Corollary 5 we can test whether $\{w, h(w), \ldots, h^{p-1}(w)\}$ is a test set for the language $\{w, h(w), \ldots, h^p(w)\}$. We now show that for each $n \geq p$, the set $\{w, h(w), \ldots, h^{n-1}(w)\}$ morphically forces the word $h^n(w)$, which means that $\{w, h(w), \ldots, h^{p-1}(w)\}$ is a test set for L.

Assume that there exists $N > p$ such that $h^N(w)$ is not morphically forced by $\{w, h(w), \ldots, h^{N-1}(w)\}$, that is there exist morphisms α and β such that $\alpha(h^k(w)) = \beta(h^k(w))$ for $0 \leq k < N$ and $\alpha(h^N(w)) \neq \beta(h^N(w))$. Let $\gamma = \alpha \circ h^{N-p}$ and $\delta = \beta \circ h^{N-p}$. Morphisms γ and δ are equivalent on the set $\{w, h(w), \ldots, h^{p-1}(w)\}$ but $\gamma(h^p(w)) = \alpha(h^N(w)) \neq \beta(h^N(w)) = \delta(h^p(w))$, a contradiction with the choice of p.

Theorem 10 can be generalized to

Theorem 11. For every DTOL language L, the existence of a test set implies that a test set can be effectively found.

From theorems 9 and 10 we obtain

Corollary 7. If the Ehrenfeucht conjecture holds true, then for every DOL (DTOL) language there effectively exists a test set.

We also have the following reduction results, cf. [4].

Corollary 8. If the Ehrenfeucht conjecture holds true, then the following problems are decidable:

(i) Morphism equivalence on DOL languages, i.e. given a DOL system G and morphisms g and f, decide whether or not $g \overset{L(G)}{\equiv} f$?

(ii) HDOL sequence equivalence problem.

(iii) Morphism equivalence on DTOL languages.

(iv) DTOL sequence equivalence problem.

Actually, for the decidability results of Corollary 8 it is enough that the Ehrenfeucht conjecture holds for DOL and DTOL languages, respectively.

We conclude this section with a result showing that the Ehrenfeucht conjecture really holds true for a subclass of DOL languages. The proof of this result is quite cumbersome and here we only refer to [7].

Theorem 12. For each positive DOL language there effectively exists a test set.

Acknowledgement. The authors are grateful to C. Choffrut and the anonymous referee for very useful comments which helped to clarify the presentation of this paper. Moreover the second author wants to express his gratitude to the Academy of Finland for excellent working conditions.

REFERENCES

[1] Albert, J., Culik, K. II and Karhumäki, J., Test sets for context-free languages and algebraic systems of equations over a free monoid, Res. Rep. CS-81-16, Dept. of Comp. Science, University of Waterloo, Canada (1981).

[2] Berstel, J., Transductions and context-free languages, (B.G. Teubner, Stuttgart, 1979).

[3] Berstel, J., Perrin, D., Perrot, J.F. et Restivo, A., Sur le théorème du défaut, J. of Algebra 60, 169-180 (1979).

[4] Culik, K. II, Homomorphisms: Decidability, Equality and Test sets, in: R. Book, ed., Formal Language Theory, Perspectives and Open Problems, (Academic Press, New York 1980).

[5] Culik, K. II and Karhumäki, J., On the equality sets for homomorphisms on free monoids with two generators, R.A.I.R.O. Theoretical Informatics 14, 349-369 (1980).

[6] Culik, K. II and Karhumäki, J., Systems of equations over a free monoid and Ehrenfeucht conjecture, Res. Rep. CS-81-15, Dept. of Comp. Science, University of Waterloo, Canada (1981).

[7] Culik, K. II and Karhumäki, J., On the Ehrenfeucht Conjecture for DOL languages, R.A.I.R.O. Theoretical Informatics (to appear).

[8] Culik, K. II and Salomaa, A., On the decidability of homomorphism equivalence for languages, JCSS 17, 163-175 (1978).

[9] Culik, K. II and Salomaa, A., Test sets and checking words for homomorphism equivalence, JCSS 19, 379-395 (1980).

[10] Ehrenfeucht, A., Karhumäki, J. and Rozenberg, G., On binary equality languages and a solution to the Ehrenfeucht conjecture in the binary case, manuscript (1981).

[11] Ehrenfeucht, A. and Rozenberg, G., Simplification of homomorphisms, Information and Control 38, 289-309 (1978).

[12] Eilenberg, S. and Schützenberger, M.P., Rational sets in commutative monoids, J. of Algebra 13, 173-191 (1969).

[13] Harrison, M., Introduction to Formal Language Theory, (Addison-Wesley, Reading, Massachusetts, 1978).

[14] Karpinski, M., ed., New Scottish Book of Problems, in preparation.

[15] Makanin, G.S., The problem of solvability of equations in a free semigroup (in Russian), Matematiceskij Sbornik 103, 148-236 (1977).

[16] Perrin, D., Combinatorics on words, (Addison-Wesley, Reading, Massachusetts, to appear).

[17] Rozenberg, G. and Salomaa, A., The Mathematical Theory of L systems, (Academic Press, New York, 1980).

AN AUTOMATA-THEORETIC CHARACTERIZATION OF THE OI-HIERARCHY

Werner Damm Andreas Goerdt
Lehrstuhl für Informatik II, RWTH Aachen

1 INTRODUCTION

One of the main objects of formal language theory has been to provide tools and models for analyzing syntactical or semantical concepts of programming languages in an abstract setting. This paper provides an operational model for the run-time behaviour of programs involving recursively defined procedures on higher types much in the same way as the classical pushdown-automaton corresponds to parameterless recursive procedures.

The storage structure for the *level-n pushdown automata* providing this characterization - originally defined in [Mas] - can be described by

- a level-1 pushdown-store consists of a (classical) pushdown-list
- a level-(n+1) pushdown-store consists of a pushdown list of pairs (pushdown symbol, level-n pushdown store).

Figure 1 below gives a typical level-3 store.

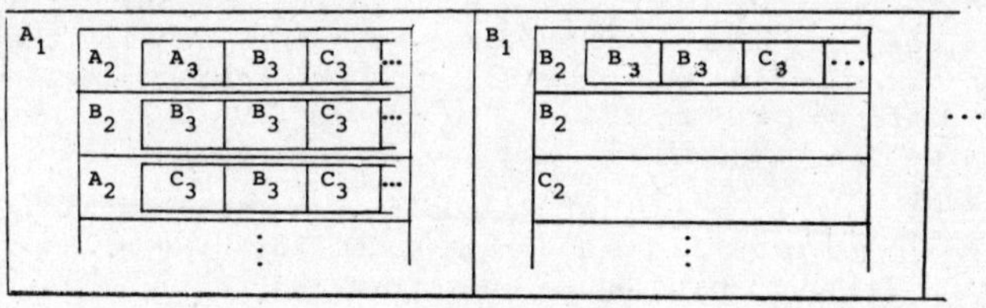

- figure 1 -

We denote by ex-pd the "undotted" version of the above store.

Reading on the storage structure is determined by its inductive definition: only the top pd-symbols of the pd-lists "on the top" are accessible, hence A_1, A_2 and A_3 for ex-pd. We choose to make the move of a level-n pda dependent on *all* of the n top symbols.

Popping at level j will delete - together with the top level-j pd-symbol - the top level-(n-j) - pd-store, in the example for j = 2 leading to

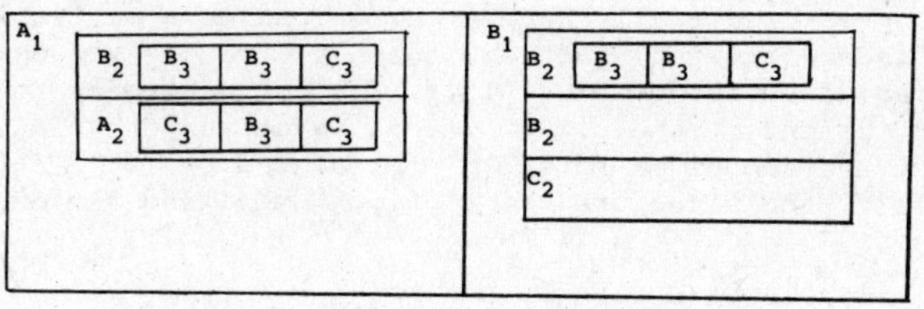

- figure 2 -

For the *push*-operation *at level j* a choice had to be made with respect to its implementation, since the top level-j pd-symbol in general (for $j < n$) will be "flagged" by a (n-j) pd-store. The crucial observation is, that the information stored in the "flag" has to be passed to all pushed symbols (and not just to the leftmost, say), hence pushing involves *copying*. The reader familiar with indexed grammars [Aho] will have noticed the similarity to the "flag-passing-mechanism" in non-index derivation steps. Figure 3 shows the store resulting from pushing C_2C_2 at level-2 on ex-pd.

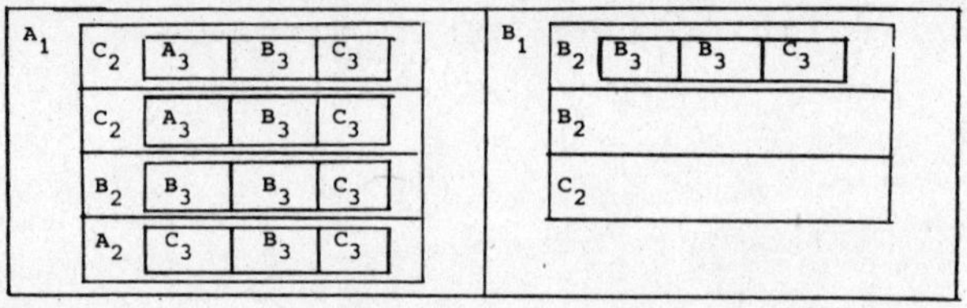

- figure 3 -

Clearly 2-pda's are equivalent (using any standard notion of acceptance) to the *indexed pushdown automata* of Duske et al., thus by theorem 2.2 in [PDS] they are equivalent to the *nested stack automata* [Aho] , i.e. they accept exactly the class of indexed-languages. This paper extends these automata-theoretic characterizations to the language families in the *OI-hierarchy* [Da 1 , ES, Wa] using n-pda's, thus lending more support to the claim, that the OI-hierarchy forms *the* natural extension of the Chomsky-hierarchy [Wa]. In particular it shows how to implement the combination of copying and parallel processing inherent in *level-n grammars* (which are generalized from *macro-grammars* [Fi] by allowing nonterminals to carry up to n levels of parameters) by superimposing pushdown lists.

The abstraction process leading from higher-type procedures to level-n grammars has been discussed in detail elsewhere ([Da 1, DF]) using a subset of finitely typed ALGOL 68 programs (see also [Kot] for the case $n = 1$). We note that a direct attempt to simulate the run-time behaviour of such programs on level-n pda's turned out to be extremly difficult and could only be proved for $n \geq 3$ by imposing additional restrictions on the programming language [Kle].

To our knowledge, the concept underlying n-pda's was first mentioned in [Gre] and then defined in [Mas] to provide an automata-model for *generalized indexed languages* (obtained by allowing flags to be flagged and iterating this process). Because of the similarity of structure - we will in fact use a notational variant of generalized indexed expressions as denotations for level-n pd-stores - accepting such languages on an n-pda is straightforward. The opposite inclusion - though only sketched in [Mas] - demands a series of normalizations and will be proved in detail elsewhere [Goe 2]. Finally, [DGu] characterizes level-n languages by *level-n stack-automata* which are obtained from stack-automata by increasing the complexity of the operations on the stack (rather than the storage-structure itself).

2 LEVEL-N PDA'S

We start the formal treatment of n-pda's by translating the intuitive pictures of the introduction into a mathematically handier notation. As a motivation, let us describe ex-pd in an "index-oriented" fashion: then A_1 can be viewed as a (base-level) nonterminal flagged by three flags f_1, f_2, f_3 corresponding to the three pd-lists in the second component of the top of ex-pd. We attach the flags as a list to the nonterminal; hence the top of ex-pd is represented by $A_1[f_1f_2f_3]$. Following this pattern, we "unfold" the structure of f_1, f_2, f_3 yielding the expression

$$\underbrace{A_1[A_2}_{\textit{topsymbols}}\underbrace{[A_3B_3C_3]}_{f_1}\underbrace{B_2[B_3B_3C_3]}_{f_2}\underbrace{A_2[C_3B_3C_3]}_{f_3}]$$

The reader can easily construct the full representation of ex-pd by concatenating the representation of its top and its bottom. Note, that the symbols accessible to the automaton appear as left "slope" of the expression. The following definition formalizes this notation.

2.1 Definition
Let Γ be a set of *pushdown-symbols* and $n \in \omega$. The $[n+1]$-set[1] $n\text{-}pds(\Gamma)$ of *level-n pushdown stores* is defined inductively by

$$n\text{-}pds(\Gamma)^{n+1} = \{e\}^{2}, \quad n\text{-}pds(\Gamma)^{j} = (\Gamma[\, n\text{-}pds(\Gamma)^{j+1}])^{*} \qquad \square$$

Intuitively, $pds \in n\text{-}pds(\Gamma)^{j}$ describes a level-n pd-store, where only the levels $\geq j$ are specified. Note that $pds \neq e$ has a unique decomposition $A[\,j{+}1\text{-}flag]\,j\text{-}rest$ with $A \in \Gamma$, $j{+}1\text{-}flag \in n\text{-}pds(\Gamma)^{j+1}$), $j\text{-}rest \in n\text{-}pds(\Gamma)^{j}$. We will identify $A[e]$ with A.

Let us now formalize the operations on the store.

2.2 Definition

(1) For $j \leq n+1$, $topsyms\colon n\text{-}pds(\Gamma)^{j} \to \Gamma^{n-j+1}$ is defined inductively by $topsyms(e)=e$, $topsyms(A[m{+}1\text{-}flag]\,m\text{-}rest) = A \cdot topsyms(m{+}1\text{-}flag)$ for $m \leq n$.

(2) For $j \leq n$, $pop_j : n\text{-}pds(\Gamma) \dashrightarrow n\text{-}pds(\Gamma)$ is defined inductively by
- $pop_j(e)$ is undefined
- $pop_1(A[\,m{+}1\text{-}flag]\,m\text{-}rest) = m\text{-}rest$
  $pop_{j+1}(A[\,m{+}1\text{-}flag]\,m\text{-}rest) = A[\,pop_j(m{+}1\text{-}flag)]\,m\text{-}rest$ for $m \leq n$.

(3) For $j \leq n$, $\alpha = \alpha(1)\cdot\ldots\cdot\alpha(r) \in \Gamma^{+}$, $push_j(\alpha) : n\text{-}pds(\Gamma) \dashrightarrow n\text{-}pds(\Gamma)$ is defined by[3]
- $push_1(\alpha)(e) = \alpha$, $push_{j+1}(\alpha)(e)$ is undefined
- $push_1(\alpha)(A[\,m{+}1\text{-}flag]\,m\text{-}rest) = \alpha(1)[\,m{+}1\text{-}flag]\cdot\ldots\cdot\alpha(r)[\,m{+}1\text{-}flag]\,m\text{-}rest$
  $push_{j+1}(\alpha)(A[\,m{+}1\text{-}flag]\,m\text{-}rest) = A[\,push_j(\alpha)(m{+}1\text{-}flag)]\,m\text{-}rest$ for $m \leq n$.

Since 2.2 captures exactly the possible operations of an n-pda, the formal definition of its syntax and semantics is now routine and can safely be skipped on first reading.

2.3 Definition (*syntax of n-pda's*)

(1) Let $POP := \{j\text{-}pop \mid j \in [n]\}$, $PUSH(\Gamma) = \{j\text{-}push(\alpha) \mid \alpha \in \Gamma^{+} \wedge j \in [n]\}$, and $TOPSYMS(\Gamma) = \bigcup_{l \in [n]} \Gamma^{l}$ (the list of accessible pd-symbols).

(2) A *level-n pushdown automaton* over a terminal alphabet Σ is a structure $A = (Q,\Sigma,\Gamma,\delta,q_0,Z)$ with
- Q is a finite set of *states*, $q_0 \in Q$ denoting the *initial state*
- Γ is a finite set of *pushdown-symbols* with $Z \in \Gamma$ as start symbol.
- the *transition function* δ maps $Q \times (\Sigma \cup \{e\}) \times TOPSYMS(\Gamma)$ into the finite subsets of $Q \times (PUSH(\Gamma) \cup POP)$ subject to $(q,j\text{-}push(\alpha)) \in \delta(p,a_e,topsyms)$ $\rightsquigarrow j \leq l(topsyms)+1$ and $(q,j\text{-}pop) \in \delta(p,a_e,topsyms) \rightsquigarrow j \leq l(topsyms)$

(3) The class of n-pda's over Σ will be denoted $n\text{-}PDA(\Sigma)$ $\square$

2.4 Definition (*semantic of n-pda's*)

Let $A \in n\text{-}PDA(\Sigma)$ as above.

(1) The set of *configurations* of A is $Con_A = Q \times \Sigma^{*} \times n\text{-}pds(\Gamma)^{1}$.

---

1 $[n]$ denotes $\{1,\ldots,n\}$; for any set I (of *sorts*), an I-*set* S is a family of sets $(S^{i} \mid i \in I)$.

2 e denotes the empty string

3 this case will not arise in 2.4

(2) A determines its *single step relation* $\vdash_A \subseteq Con_A \times Con_A$ by
$(p,w,pds) \vdash_A (q,v,pds')$ <u>iff</u>
- $\delta(p,a_e,topsyms(pds)) \ni (q,k\text{-}push(\alpha))$
<u>and</u> $a_e v = w$ <u>and</u> $pds' = push_k(\alpha)(pds)$

<u>or</u>
- $\delta(p,a_e,topsyms(pds)) \ni (q,j\text{-}pop)$
<u>and</u> $a_e v = w$ <u>and</u> $pds' = pop_j(pds)$

(3) The *language accepted by* A (with empty store) is defined by
$L(A) = \{w \in \Sigma^* \mid (q_o,w,Z) \vdash^*_A (q,e,e)\}$.

(4) The class of languages accepted by n-pda's over Σ is denoted n-$PDA(\Sigma)$. □

The usual techniques for pda's can be used to prove that acceptance by empty store, with final states, with final states and by empty store define the same class of languages. Rather than stating this exercise in automata-theory we give an example (which is simple enough to be used when trying out the constructions of section 3).

2.5 Example

The following 2-pda accepts $\{a^{2^m} \mid m \in \omega\}$ by generating $Z\underbrace{A...A}_{m\text{-times}}$ and then iteratively erasing A, 1-*pushing* Z Z (which causes duplication of the flags!), and if possible checking the input against the store. If m was guessed correctly, this will empty the store. Figure 5 lists all defined transitions. The automaton starts by *guessing*.

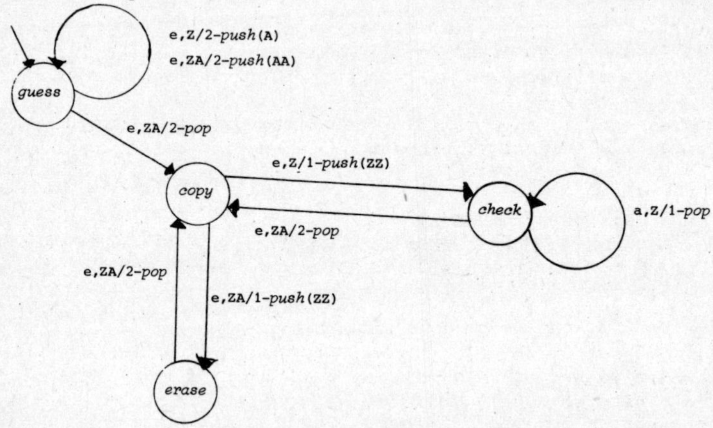

- figure 5 - □

While the above example is simple, it does illustrate the control of copying on lower levels by higher levels. Superimposing this idea to up to n-levels leads to the characteristic n-exponential growth of level-n languages.

We note that restricting the push-operation by just passing <u>one</u> copy of the associated flag still takes us outside the context-free languages (see [Goe 1] for an example of a restricted 2-pda recognizing $\{a^n b^n c^n \mid n \in \omega\}$).

We close this section by normalizing the length of the strings to be pushed. This will simplify the construction in the following section.

2.6 Lemma

Any n-pda A is equivalent to an n-pda A' which pushes only strings of length two.

proof:

apply the following transformations:

case 1: $\delta(q,a_e,A_1\cdot\ldots\cdot A_l) \ni (p,j\text{-}push(X))$
is replaced by
$\delta'(q,a_e,A_1\cdot\ldots\cdot A_l) \ni ([p,j\text{-}pop],j\text{-}push(XX))$
and $\delta'([p,j\text{-}pop],e,A_1\ldots X\ldots A_l) = \{(p,j\text{-}pop)\}$

case 2: $\delta(q,a_e,topsyms(pds)) \ni (p,j\text{-}push(\alpha))$ with $\alpha = A_1\ldots A_k$ and $k \geq 3$ is simulated using states $[p,\alpha,r]$ where r is counted downward from $k-1$ to 1 while outputting the corresponding length 2 substring of α. □

3 SIMULATING N-PDA'S BY LEVEL-N GRAMMARS

Let us start this section by showing how a level-2 grammar would generate the example language of 2.5.

3.1 Example

The grammar has three nonterminals *start*, *copy*, and *guess*. It starts by calling *guess* with the terminal symbol 'a' at first level and the symbol for the empty string at level O (hence *guess* expects two one-element lists as parameters). *guess* nondeterministically generates m calls of the *copy* functional, which applies its first argumentlist twice to its zero-level argument-list. The formal parameters at level 1 and level O are y_1 and y_o, respectively.

$start \rightarrow guess(a)(e) \qquad copy(y_1)(y_o) \longrightarrow y_1(y_1(y_o))$
$guess(y_1)(y_o) \rightarrow guess(copy(y_1))(y_o) \mid y_1(y_o)$ □

Again the example is typical in exhibiting the inherent copying power of higher level grammars: by successively applying j-level copy-functions to j-1-level-copy-functions (with j decreasing from n to 1) it is easy to generate functions with n-exponential growth. Note that copying has to be <u>explicitly</u> specified in higher-level grammars by double occurences of the same formal parameter.

The example is special in that it contains no *parallel* processing: both parameterlists have length 1. It is essentially the power of parallelism which will be exploited when simulating n-pda's.

We now briefly review the formal definition of level-n grammars. The concept of *level* of parameterlists is formalized by associating to each nonterminal a functional type over the base type l (denoting formal languages). The right-hand-sides of productions in a level-n grammar consist of finitely typed applicative terms over nonterminals, terminals, and formal parameters.

3.2 Definition

(1) The set of *derived types* over l is defined inductively by
$D^o := \{l\}$, $D^{n+1} := D^{n*} \times D^n$, $n\text{-}D := \bigcup_{m\leq n} D^m$.
Note that each $\tau \in D^n$ has a unique decomposition $(\alpha_n,\ldots,(\alpha_o,l)\ldots)$ with $\alpha_j \in D^{j*}$.

(2) For $\alpha = \alpha(1)\ldots\alpha(k) \in D^{n*}$ we let $y_\alpha = (y_{1,\alpha(1)},\ldots,y_{k,\alpha(k)})$ and $Y_\alpha = \{y_{j,\alpha(j)} \mid j \in [k]\}$. If τ is as above, the set of *formal parameters* of *type* τ is $Y^\tau := \bigcup_{j=o}^{n} Y_{\alpha_j}$.

(3) Let N,Y denote n-D-sets, and Σ an alphabet. The n-D-set $T_{\Sigma,N,Y}$ of applicative terms over Σ,N, and Y is the smallest n-D-set satisfying
- $e \in T^l$, $\Sigma \subset T^{(l,l)}$, $N^\tau \cup Y^\tau \subset T^\tau$ [5]
- $t_o \in T^{(\alpha,\tau)}$, $t \in T^\alpha \leadsto t_o t \in T^\tau$

(4) For $t \in T_{\Sigma,N,Y}$ and τ as above, we define $t\downarrow := t y_{\alpha_n}\ldots y_{\alpha_o}$.

---

[5] For any I-set S and $\alpha \in I^*$, $S^\alpha := S^{\alpha(1)} \times\ldots\times S^{\alpha(k)}$.

(5) A *level-n grammar* over a terminal alphabet Σ is a structure $G = (N,\Sigma,P,S)$ where
- N is a finite n-D-set of nonterminals and $S \in N^{l}$ is the *startsymbol*
- P is a finite set of productions of the form $A{\downarrow} \rightarrow t$ with $A \in N^{\tau}$ for some τ and $t \in T^{l}_{\Sigma,N,Y^{\tau}}$.

(6) The class of level-n grammars over Σ is denoted $n\text{-}N\lambda(\Sigma)$. □

Since terms can be uniquely decomposed according to their types, brackets will be omitted (except for examples to increase readability). Note that T_{Σ} is isomorphic to the *left-concatenation-algebra over* Σ^* , in particular, concatenation itself is not allowed to construct terms (c.f. [BD]) .

It is easy to check, that the example grammar complies to the above definition using the types *start* : l , *guess* : $((l,l),(l,l))$, *copy* : $((l,l),(l,l))$ and identifying $y_1 \equiv y_{1,(l,l)}, y_o \equiv y_{1,l}$.

We refer the reader to [Da 1] for a detailed discusion and motivation of this concept. Justified by the Chomsky-normalform result proved in [Da 1] (see section 4), we specialized the above definition by allowing only applicative rather than arbitrary typed λ-terms as rigth-hand-side of a production. To generate strings using such a grammar, simply apply the ALGOL 60 copy-rule to calls of nonterminals, where all actual parameters (down to level o) are supplied. The *level-n language generated by* $G, L(G)$, is the set of terminal strings derivable in this way from the start symbol. We will use the fact, that outside-in - derivations - which in this monadic case coincide with leftmost derivations - are sufficient to generate all trees in $L(G)$ [Da 1] .

It has been shown in [Da 1 , Da 2] that the classes $n\text{-}L_{OI}$ of level-n languages form an infinite hierarchy of substitution closed AFL's , which starts with the regular, context-free, and macro-languages.

We now give a precise definition of leftmost derivations in level-n grammars.

3.3 Definition

Let $G \in n\text{-}N\lambda(\Sigma)$ as above.

(1) The set of *sentential forms* of G is $T^{l}_{\Sigma,N}$. Note that each sentential form can be uniquely written as $w\gamma$ where $w \in \Sigma^*$, $\gamma \equiv A\gamma_m \dots \gamma_o$, $A \in N^{\tau}$ for some $\tau = (\alpha_m,\dots,(\alpha_o,l)\dots) \in n\text{-}D$, $\gamma_j \in T^{\alpha_j}_{\Sigma,N}$ for $j \in \{o,\dots,m\}$. If γ is as above, we denote by *head*(γ) its top nonterminal A and k-*list*(γ) its k-th parameterlist γ_k .

(2) The derivation relation $\Rightarrow_G \subseteq Sen_G \times Sen_G$ is defined by $w\gamma \Rightarrow_G sen$ iff there is a productuin $A{\downarrow} \rightarrow t$ in P s.t. $A = head(\gamma)$ and $sen = wt[y_{\alpha_m}/m\text{-}list(\gamma)] \dots [y_{\alpha_m}/o\text{-}list(\gamma)]$ [6] where A has type $(\alpha_m,\dots,(\alpha_o,l)\dots)$. It is easy to see that $sen \in Sen_G$.

(3) The OI-*language* generated by G is defined by $L_{OI}(G) = \{w \in \Sigma^* \mid S \overset{*}{\Rightarrow}_G we\}$. □

We now turn to encoding the n-pds structure as an applicative term. Clearly, since a single move of an n-pda depends on all topsymbols of the current pds and the current state, and leftmost-derivations in level-n grammars depend on the *head* nonterminal, this will have to encode the current state and topsymbols, hence we take N to be Q·TOPSYMS .

The principle of encoding a pds can then roughly be described by

---

6 For $s = (s_1,\dots,s_q) \in T^{\alpha}_{\Sigma,N,Y}$, $t[y_{\alpha}/s]$ denotes the term obtained from t by simultaneously substituting s_j for $y_{j,\alpha(j)}$ for all $j \in [q]$

- the "slope" of topsymbols is memorized in the *head* nonterminal
- the *rests* are memorized in the parameter*lists* in decreasing order.

Now clearly - because of the inductive definition of $n\text{-}pds(\Gamma)$ - the encoding has to cope with only "partially specified" n-pds', i.e. elements of $n\text{-}pds(\Gamma)^j$ for some $j > 1$. The problem of encoding such partially specified structures has been solved by encoding *all possible extensions* to an n-pds "in parallel" - i.e. in different parameter positions - in such a way, that a *particular* extension can be recovered by means of a *projection*, i.e. a production of the form $A\, y_{\alpha_m} \ldots y_{\alpha_0} \to y_{r,\alpha_r(k)} \downarrow$, hence by an extensive use of the parallelism inherent in level-n grammars. The following diagram captures this idea.

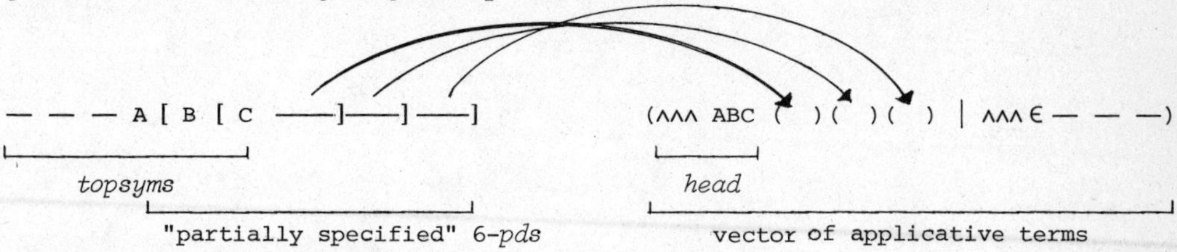

- figure 6 : the encoding of pds' -

In the above figure, ABC denotes the fully specified part of *topsyms*, with one possible extension being ΛΛΛ ABC . Note that the type of the nonterminals has to be defined in a way providing for the storage of all possible extensions in its argumentlists.

3.4 Construction

Let $A \in n\text{-}PDA(\Sigma)$ with states Q and pushdown-symbols Γ be in normalform according to 2.6.

(1) Let $k_j := |Q \cdot \Gamma^j|$ [7] and $nr_j : Q \cdot \Gamma^j \to [k_j]$ denote a bijective numbering with inverse w_j.

(2) The types needed can be defined inductively by $\tau_o := l$, $\tau_{j+1} := (\tau_j^{k_j}, \tau_j) \in D^{j+1}$ for $o \leqslant j < n$.

(3) The n-D-set of nonterminals is defined by $N^{\tau_o} := \{S\} \cup Q$, $N^{\tau_{j+1}} := Q\Gamma^{j+1}$ for $o \leqslant j < n$.

(4) For $1 \leqslant j \leqslant n$ we define the encoding $f_j : n\text{-}pds(\Gamma)^j \to T_N^{\tau_{j-1}^{k_{j-1}}}$ inductively by
- $f_j(e) = (w_{j-1}(1), \ldots, w_{j-1}(k_{j-1}))$ (= "all possibilities")
- for $l \leqslant n$ $f_j(A_j[\ldots A_l\ l\text{-}rest \ldots]\, j\text{-}rest)$
$= (w_{j-1}(1) A_j \ldots A_l f_l(l\text{-}rest) \ldots f_j(j\text{-}rest), \ldots$
$\ldots, w_{j-1}(k_{j-1}) A_j \ldots A_l f_l(l\text{-}rest) \ldots f_j(j\text{-}rest))$

(5) The coding of configurations into sentential forms is given by
$cd : Q \times n\text{-}pds(\Gamma) \to T_N^l \quad (q, pds) \mapsto pr^{nr_o(q)}(f_1(pds))$ [8] □

We pause in the formal construction to illustrate the encoding by an example.

3.5 Example

Consider the $3\text{-}pds$ pds = A[B[AB]B] . For simplicity assume $Q = \{q\}$, $\Gamma = \{A, B\}$. We take the numbering induced from the lexicographical ordering with $A < B$.
$f_1(pds) = q\ ABA\ f_3(B) f_2(B) f_1(e)$

---

[7] $|S|$ denotes the *cardinality* of S

[8] pr^j denotes the projection on the j-th component

$$= qABA(qAAB(all_3), qABB(all_3), qBAB(all_3), qBB(all_3))\,(qAB(all_2), qBB(all_2))\,(q)$$

$$\underbrace{\qquad\qquad}_{f_3(B)} \qquad \underbrace{\qquad\qquad}_{f_2(B)}$$

where $all_3(e) = (qAA, qAB, qBA, qBB)$ and $all_2 = f_2(e) = (qA, qB)$ □

3.6 Construction (cont.)

(6) In the following definition of the set of productions P we abbreviate $y_j \equiv y_{\tau_j k_j}$

(6.1) $\delta(p, a_e, A_1 \ldots A_l) \ni (q, j\text{-}push(BC))$ iff

$$pA_1 \ldots A_l{\downarrow} \rightarrow a_e qA_1 \ldots A_{j+1} BA_{j+1} \ldots A_l y_{l-1} \ldots y_j \quad (w_{j-1}(1)\, CA_{j+1} \ldots A_l y_{l-1} \ldots y_{j-1}, \ldots, w_{j-1}(k_{j-1}) CA_{j+1} \ldots A_l y_{l-1} \ldots y_{j-1}) y_{j-2} \ldots y_o \in P$$ [9]

(6.2) $\delta(p, a_e, A_1 \ldots A_l) \ni (q, l+1\text{-}push(BC))$ iff

$$pA_1 \ldots A_l{\downarrow} \rightarrow a_e qA_1 \ldots A_l B \quad (w_1(1)\, C(w_1(1), \ldots, w_1(k_1)), \ldots, w_1(k_1) C(w_1(1), \ldots, w_1(k_1))) y_{l-1} \ldots y_o \in P$$ [9]

(6.3) $\delta(p, a_e, A_1 \ldots A_l) \ni (q, j\text{-}pop)$ iff [9]

$$pA_1 \ldots A_l{\downarrow} \rightarrow a_e y_{nr_{j-1}(qA_1 \ldots A_{j-1}), \tau_{j-1}} y_{j-2} \ldots y_o \in P$$

(6.4) $S \rightarrow q_o Z(w_o(1), \ldots, w_o(k_o)) \in P$ (initial production)

$q \rightarrow e \in P$ (terminal productions)

Clearly the grammar G_A associated by the above construction to a level-n pda A is a level-n grammar. Note that G_A has the special property that $Sen_{G_A} \subseteq T_N^l$.

The equivalence of A and G_A rests on the following key lemma. Let, for a production $\pi \in P$, $\underset{\pi, G_A}{\Rightarrow}$ denote a derivationstep involving π .

3.7 Lemma

Let $pds \in n\text{-}pds(\Gamma) \setminus \{e\}, t \in Sen_{G_A}$, $a_e \in \Sigma \cup \{e\}$.

Then

$\exists\, pds' \in n\text{-}pds(\Gamma), q \in Q \quad (p, a_e w, pds) \vdash_A (q, w, pds') \wedge cd(p, pds') = t$

iff

$\exists \pi \in P \setminus \{\text{startproduction}, \text{terminal productions}\} \quad cd(p, pds) \underset{\pi, G_A}{\Rightarrow} a_e t$

proof:

The assertion is proved by considering the cases (6.1) to (6.3). □

By a simple induction on the length of the derivation- and/or computation sequence, we obtain as a corollary to the above lemma the correctness of construction 3.6.

3.7 Corollary

$L(A) = L(G_A)$ □

4 IMPLEMENTING LEVEL-N GRAMMARS BY N-PDA'S

Consider first the problem of encoding the set mT_N of those terms which only involve *monadic* application. Since the type of such terms is uniquely determined by their (functional) level, mT_N can be viewed as an [n]-set (where n is the maximal level of a nonterminal in N). The coding *mcd* of such a term into a generalized indexed expression can be explained by:

- The *head* nonterminal should be the leftmost symbol having no flag.
- By viewing application of t of type (l,l) to a string as concatenation, split $sen \in Sen_G$ into its factors $sen_1 \cdot \ldots \cdot sun_k \cdot e$ and concatenate the coding of the factors.

---

9 in case $a_e \equiv e$ we identify $a_e w$ and w

- Each factor can be pictured as

$$A(\underset{m}{—}(\underset{\uparrow}{mp_m}))(\underset{m-1}{—}(\underset{\uparrow}{mp_{m-1}}))\ldots(\underset{1}{—}(\underset{\uparrow}{mp_1})) \quad ,$$

level m m-1 ... 1

where the arrows point to the subexpressions of *minimal level*. Such a factor is - roughly - coded to $mp_1[\ldots mp_{m-1}[mp_m[A\ mcd(—_m)]mcd(—_{m-1})]\ldots mcd(—_1)]$.

4.1 Example

Let $sen = A_3(B_4(A_3)(\underset{\uparrow}{C_2}))(C_2(\underset{\uparrow}{A_1}))(A_3(\underset{\uparrow}{A_2})(\underset{\uparrow}{A_1})(e))$

where the first part $A_3(B_4(A_3)(C_2))(C_2(A_1))$ is sen 1 and $(A_3(A_2)(A_1)(e))$ is sen 2.

then $mcd(\text{sen } 2) = A_1[A_2[A_3]]$ and $mcd(\text{sen } 1) = A_1[C_2[A_3\ mcd(B_4(A_3))]mcd(C_2)]$

hence $mcs(\text{sen}) = A_1[C_2[A_3A_3[B_4]]C_2]A_1[A_2[A_3]]$. □

It was crucial for the extension of this encoding to observe, that sentential forms generated by level-n grammars in Chomsky-Normalform (CNF) have a characteristic feature, which makes a "linearization" into monadic terms possible. To explain this property, let us recall the following result.

4.2 Theorem

Let $m \geq 1$.

Any $G' \in n\text{-}N\lambda(\Sigma)$ is equivalent to a level-n grammar $G = (N,\Sigma,S,P)$ satisfying

- S is the only nonterminal of type l
- all $A \in N \setminus \{S\}$ have *exactly one* parameter at the lowest level
- all $A \in N \setminus \{S\}$ use only *nonempty* parameterlists
- all productions in P are of one of the following forms

(1a) $Ay_{1,l} \rightarrow ay_{1,l}$ (1b) $Ay_{1,l} \rightarrow y_{1,l}$

(2a) $Ay_{1,l} \rightarrow BCy_{1,l}$

(2b) $Ay_{\alpha_m}\ldots y_{1,l} \rightarrow B(B_1y_{\alpha_m},\ldots,B_ky_{\alpha_m})y_{\alpha_{m-1}}\ldots y_l$

(3) $A\!\downarrow\ \rightarrow B\!\downarrow$ with *type* A = *type* B

(4a) $A(y_{1,(l,l)},y_{2,(l,l)})(y_{1,l}) \rightarrow y_{1,(l,l)}(y_{2,(l,l)}(y_{1,l}))$

(4b) $Ay_{\alpha_m}\ldots y_{1,l} \rightarrow y_{1,\alpha_m(1)}(y_{2,\alpha_m(2)}y_{\alpha_{m-1}},\ldots,y_{k,\alpha_m(k)}y_{\alpha_{m-1}})y_{\alpha_{m-2}}\ldots y_{1,l}$ and $m \geq 2$

(5) $Ay_{\alpha_m}\ldots y_{1,l} \rightarrow y_{j,\alpha_m(j)}y_{\alpha_{m-1}}\ldots y_{1,l}$

(6) $Ay_{\alpha_m}\ldots y_{1,l} \rightarrow B(C_1,\ldots,C_k)y_{\alpha_m}\ldots y_{1,l}$

(7) $S \rightarrow Ae$

proof:

specialize the Chomsky normalform theorem 7.3 in [Da 1] to the monadic case as in the proof of 7.17. □

The following two features of such a grammar G will be exploited:

- all sentential forms can be uniquely decomposed into factors as above (i.e. function application at the base level can be viewed as concatenation)
- G passes all actual parameterlists only as a whole (cases (1),(2),(6)) except for possibly decomposing its highest level parameterlist.

The second property induces a characteristic of G's sentential forms which allows for a coding into monadic applicative terms: parameters belonging to the *same nonterminal* and occuring at the *same fuctional level* differ at most in their headnonterminal.

4.3 Example

The following expression satisfies the above "symmetric-list property":

$sym \equiv A_3(B_3(C_3(E_2),D_3(E_2)),F_3(C_3(E_2),\ D_3(E_2)))(G_2(H_1),K_2(H_1))(e)$

The expression can be restructured without loosing information by combining the differing topsymbols into one nonterminal:

$A_3(\underline{B_3F_3}(\underline{C_3D_3}(\underset{\uparrow}{E}_2)))(\underline{G_2K_2}(\underset{\uparrow}{H}_1))(e)$. Coding this monadic term yields

$H_1[E_2[A_3\ \underline{B_3\ F_3}\ \underline{C_3\ D_3}]\ \underline{G_2\ K_2}]$. □

We now formalize the above concept of *symmetric terms* (which generalizes the notion developped by Fisher [Fi]) and prove that (the nonterminal part of) a sentential form of G is a symmetric term.

4.4 Definition

Let N an n-D-set. Denote the maximal arity occuring in a type of a nonterminal in N by M . Let $I = \{\alpha \in \bigcup_{m \in [n]} D^{m*} \mid l(\alpha) \leqslant M\}$.

(1) The set SL_N of *symmetric lists over* N is the smallest set $SL \subseteq \bigcup_{\alpha \in I} T^{\alpha}_N$
- $N^{\alpha} \subseteq SL$ for $\alpha \in I$
- $A_1,\dots,A_r \in N$ and $\overline{t}_m,\dots,\overline{t}_k \in SL$
  $\curvearrowright$ $(A_1\overline{t}_m\dots\overline{t}_k,\dots,A_r\overline{t}_m\dots\overline{t}_k) \in SL$.

(2) The set ST_N of *symmetric terms over* N is the smallest set $ST \subseteq T^{l}_{\Sigma,N}$ satisfying
- $e \in ST$
- $(slist) \in SL^{(l,l)}$, $t \in ST$ $\curvearrowright$ $slist\ t \in ST$ □

4.5 Lemma

Let $G = (N,\Sigma,P,S) \in n\text{-}N\lambda(\Sigma)$ be in Chomsky-Normalform.
Then

$$S \overset{+}{\Rightarrow}_G w\,A\,\overline{t}_m\dots\overline{t}_o \curvearrowright A\,\overline{t}_m\dots\overline{t}_o \in ST_N$$

proof:

The proof proceeds by induction on the length of the derivation. The base step is trivial. The induction step is proved by considering cases (1) to (6) in 4.2 for the last derivation step. □

Now that we have established the symmetric-list-property for a sufficiently rich class of terms.,let us combine the two conceptual transformation described above into a formal definition of the encoding of symmetric terms into pushdown-expressions.

4.6 Definition

Let N denote a finite n-D-set.

(1) Denote the maximal arity occuring in a type of a nonterminal in N by M . We define the set Γ_N by
$\Gamma_N = \{\underline{A_1\dots A_l} \mid 1 \leqslant l \leqslant M\ ,\ \mathit{level}\ A_1 = \dots = \mathit{level}\ A_l\} \cup \{Z\}$

(2) The *minimal parameter* of a symmetric list, $\mathit{mp} : SL_N \to \Gamma_N$ is defined inductively by
- $\mathit{mp}(A_1,\dots,A_l) = \underline{A_1\dots A_l}$
- $\mathit{mp}(A_1\overline{t}_m\dots\overline{t}_k,\dots,A_l\overline{t}_m\dots\overline{t}_k) = \mathit{mp}(\overline{t}_k)$

(3) We need an auxiliary function ': $n\text{-}pds(\Gamma_N) \to n\text{-}pds(\Gamma_N)$ defined by

$$A_1[A_2[\dots[A_m\,m\text{-}rest]\dots]\,2\text{-}rest]\,1\text{-}rest \mapsto \begin{cases} A_2[\dots[A_m\,m\text{-}rest]\dots]\,2\text{-}rest & \text{iff } 1\text{-}rest \equiv e \\ \text{undefined otherwise.} \end{cases}$$

(4) The coding of symmetric lists $\mathit{slcd} : SL_N \to n\text{-}pds(\Gamma_N)$ is defined inductively by
- $\mathit{slcd}(A_1,\dots,A_l) = \underline{A_1\dots A_l}$
- $\mathit{slcd}(A_1\overline{t}_m\dots\overline{t}_k,\dots,A_l\overline{t}_m\dots\overline{t}_k) =$
  $\mathit{mp}\ \overline{t}_k[\mathit{mp}\ \overline{t}_{k-1}\dots\mathit{mp}\ \overline{t}_m[\underline{A_1\dots A_l}\ \mathit{slcd}\ \overline{t}_m{}']\dots\mathit{slcd}\ \overline{t}_k{}']$.

(5) The coding $\mathit{stcd} : ST_N \to n\text{-}pds(\Gamma_N)^1$ of symmetric terms is defined by

- $stcd(e) = e$
- $stcd(\text{slist } t) = slcd(\text{slist})\cdot stcd(t)$ □

We now describe the simulation of G's productions following the numbering in 4.2. Note that the simulation of rules like (4 b) demands the decomposition of complex symbols and in general copying of some part of the store. A simulation of a production will be completed if the automaton reaches again its "normal" state q .

4.7 Construction

Let $G = (N,\Sigma,P,S) \in n\text{-}N\lambda(\Sigma)$ in Chomsky normalform. We define $A_G = (Q,\Sigma,\Gamma_N,\delta,q_o,Z) \in n\text{-PDA}(\Sigma)$ by

- $Q = \{q_o, q\}$

  $\cup \{[q,\pi],[q,\pi,\gamma],[p,\pi,\gamma] \mid \pi \in P$ is a type-(4 a) production, $\gamma = \underline{A_1A_2} \in \Gamma_N\}$

  $\cup \{[q,\pi],[q,\pi,\gamma],[p,\pi,\gamma] \mid \pi \in P$ is a type-(4 b) production, $\gamma = \underline{A_1 \ldots A_l} \in \Gamma_N$, level $A_1 > 1$ and l is the length of the top-level parameterlist in $\pi\}$

  $\cup \{[q,\pi] \mid \pi \in P$ is a type-(5) production$\}$

- δ is defined by

(1a) - production in P iff $\delta(q,a,A) \ni (q,1\text{-}pop)$

(1b) - production in P iff $\delta(q,e,A) \ni (q,1\text{-}pop)$

(2a) - production in P iff $\delta(q,e,A) \ni (q,1\text{-}push(BC))$

(2b) - production in P iff $\delta(q,e,A_1\ldots A_mA) \ni (q,m{+}1\text{-}push(B\ \underline{B_1\ldots B_k}))$
for all $A_j \in \Gamma_N$.

(3) - production in P iff $\delta(q,e,A_1\ldots A_mA) \ni (q,m{+}1\text{-}push(B))$
for all $A_j \in \Gamma_N$.

(4a) - production in P iff $\delta(q,e,A_1A) \ni ([q,\pi],2\text{-}pop)$
for all $A_1 \in \Gamma_N$ ("erase A")

and

(i) $\delta([q,\pi],e,\underline{BC}) \ni (q,\underline{BC})$ for all $\underline{BC} \in \Gamma_N$

(ii) $\delta([q,\pi],e,A_1\ldots A_l\underline{DE}) \ni ([q,\pi,\underline{DE}], l{+}1\text{-}push(E))$
("decompose and store $\underline{DE}$ in finite control to recall D")
$\delta([q,\pi,\underline{DE}],e,A_1\ldots A_lE) \ni ([p,\pi,\underline{DE}],1\text{-}push(A\ A))$
("copy;memorize copying by changing state")
$\delta([p,\pi,\underline{DE}],e,A_1\ldots A_lE) \ni (q,l{+}1\text{-}push(D))$
("replace the 'incorrect' E by the 'correct' D"
for all $n > l \geq 1, A_j \in \Gamma_N, \underline{DE} \in \Gamma_N$.

(4b) - production in P iff $\delta(q,e,A_1\ldots A_mA) \ni ([q,\pi], m{+}1\text{-}pop)$
for all $A_j \in \Gamma_N$ ("erase A")

and

(i) $\delta([q,\pi],e,A_1\ldots A_{m-1}\underline{A_1\ldots A_k}) \ni (q,m\text{-}push(A_1\underline{A_2\ldots A_k}))$
for all $A_j \in \Gamma_N, \underline{A_1\ldots A_k} \in \Gamma_N$ ("decompose")

(ii) $\delta([q,\pi],e,A_1\ldots A_l\underline{B_1\ldots B_k}) \ni ([q,\pi,\underline{B_1\ldots B_k}],l{+}1\text{-}push(\underline{B_2\ldots B_k}))$
("decompose and store in finite control to recall B_1")
$\delta([q,\pi,\underline{B_1\ldots B_k}],e,A_1\ldots A_l\underline{B_2\ldots B_k}) \ni ([p,\pi,\underline{B_1\ldots B_k}],m\text{-}push(A_mA_m))$
("copy at level m; memorize copying by changing state")
$\delta([p,\pi,\underline{B_1\ldots B_k}],e,A_1\ldots A_l\underline{B_2\ldots B_k}) \ni (q,l{+}1\text{-}push(B_1))$
("replace 'incorrect' $\underline{B_2\ldots B_k}$ by the 'correct' B_1")
for all $n > l \geq m$, $A_j \in \Gamma_N, \underline{B_1\ldots B_k} \in \Gamma$

(5) - production in P iff $\delta(q,e,A_1\ldots A_mA) \ni ([q,\pi],m{+}1\text{-}pop)$
and $\delta([q,\pi],e,A_1\ldots A_l\underline{B_1\ldots B_k}) \ni (q,l{+}1\text{-}push(B_j))$
for all $n > l \geq m{-}1, \underline{B_1\ldots B_k} \in \Gamma_N$

(6) - production in P iff $\delta(q,e,A_1\ldots A_mA) \ni ([q,\pi],m{+}1\text{-}push(\underline{C_1\ldots C_k}))$
and $\delta([q,\pi],e,A_1\ldots A_m\underline{C_1\ldots C_k}) \ni (q,m{+}2\text{-}push(B))$
for all $A_j \in \Gamma_N$

(7) - production in P iff $\delta(q_o,e,Z) \ni (q,1\text{-}push(A))$ □

The correctness of 4.7 is due to the following key Lemma:

4.8 Lemma

Let $G = (N,\Sigma,P,S) \in n\text{-}N\lambda(\Sigma)$ be in Chomsky-Normalform, and let $t \in ST_N$, $pds \in n\text{-}pds(\Gamma_N)^1, v,w \in \Sigma^*$. Then

$\exists s \in ST_N \quad t \underset{G}{\Rightarrow} vs$ and $pds = stcd(s)$

iff

$(q,vw,stcd(t)) \overset{+}{\vdash}_{A_G} (q,w,pds)$

without entering q in intermediate computation steps

proof:

by considering the cases (1a) to (7) □

4.9 Corollary

$L_{OI}(G) = L(A_G)$ □

5 CONCLUSION

Though is was "obvious" to "insiders", that the level-n pds - which circulated in unformalized versions prior to the knowledge of Maslov's papers - just had to be *the* automata model fitting to level-n languages, the complexity of the encodings in both directions shows, how far apart both concepts are. We hope that the technics develloped in establishing

5.1 Theorem

$\forall n \geq 1 \qquad n\text{-}\mathcal{L}_{OI}(\Sigma) = n\text{-}\mathcal{PDA}(\Sigma)$ □

will turn out to be useful in further applications, e.g. reducing the equivalence problem of level-n schemes [Da 1] to that of deterministic n-pda's (c.f. [Cou], [Gal] for the case $n = 1$).

ACKNOWLEDGEMENTS

We would like to thank Joost Engelfriet for many helpfull comments on a first draft of this paper.

REFERENCES

[Aho] AHO, A.V. *Nested stack automata*, JACM 16, 3 (1969), 383-406

[BD] BILSTEIN, J. / DAMM, W. *Top-down tree-transducers for infinite trees* I, Proc. 6th CAAP, LNCS 112 (1981), 117-134

[Cou] COURCELLE, B. *A representation of trees by languages*, TCS 6, (1978), 255-279 and 7, (1978), 25-55

[Da 1] DAMM, W. *The IO- and OI-hierarchies*, TCS 20, (1982), to appear

[Da 2] DAMM, W. *An algebraic extension of the Chomsky-hierarchy*, Proc. MFCS'79, LNCS 74 (1979), 266-276

[DF] DAMM, W. / FEHR, E. *A schematalogical approach to the analysis of the procedure concept in ALGOL-languages*, Proc. 5th CAAP, Lille, (1980), 130-134

[DGu] DAMM, W. / GUESSARIAN, I. *Combining T and level-N*, Proc. MFCS'81, LNCS 118 (1981), 262-270

[ES] ENGELFRIET, J. / SCHMIDT, E.M. *IO and OI*, JCSS 15, 3 (1977), 328-353 and JCSS 16, 1 (1978), 67-99

[Fi] FISCHER, M.F. *Grammars with macro-like productions*, Proc. 9th SWAT, (1968), 131-142

[Gal] GALLIER, J.H. *Deterministic finite automata with recursive calls and DPDA's* technical report, University of Pennsylvania, (1981)

[Goe 1] GOERDT, A. *Eine automatentheoretische Charakterisierung der OI-Hierarchie*, to appear

[Goe 2] GOERDT, A. *Characterizing generalized indexed languages by n-pda's* Schriften zur Informatik und Angewandten Mathematik, RWTH Aachen, to appear

[Gre] GREIBACH, S.A. *Full AFL's and nested iterated substitution*, Information and Control 16, 1 (1970), 7-35

[Kle] KLEIN, H.-J. personal communication

[Kot] KOTT, L. *Sémantique algébrique d'un langage de programmation type ALGOL* RAIRO 11, 3 (1977), 237-263

[Mas] MASLOV, A.N. *Multilevel stack automata*, Problemy Peredachi Informatsii 12, 1 (1976), 55-62

[PDS] PARCHMANN, R. / DUSKE, J. / SPECHT, J. *On deterministic indexed languages*, Information and Control 45, 1 (1980), 48-67

[Wa] WAND, M. *An algebraic formulation of the Chomsky-hierarchy*, Category Theory Applied to Computation and Control, LNCS 25 (1975), 209-213

FAST DETECTION OF POLYHEDRAL INTERSECTIONS

David P. Dobkin+

Electrical Engineering and Computer Science Department
Princeton University
Princeton, NJ 08540

David G. Kirkpatrick

Department of Computer Science
University of British Columbia
Vancouver, British Columbia

ABSTRACT

Methods are given for unifying and extending previous work on detecting polyhedral intersections. The technique of dynamic (vs. static) description is introduced and used to extend previous results. New upper bounds of O(log n) and O($\log^2$n) are given on plane-polyhedron and polyhedron-polyhedron intersection problems.

1. Introduction

A fundamental problem in geometric computing is that of detecting polyhedral intersections. Versions of this problem lie at the core of such problems as linear programming[Da], hidden surface elimination[War,Wat] and computer vision[Wi]. In a previous paper [CD], the detection problem for polyhedra intersection problems was shown to be of lower complexity than the computation problem. Solutions of complexity $c \log^k n$ (for fixed constants c and k) were given for instances of the former problem (of input size n). And, linear lower bounds are known on the computation problems[SH,MP].

The results of [CD] are unified and extended here. This is done by extending the method of dynamically defining convex polyhedra from [K]. Using this method, convex polygons and polyhedra are defined through a hierarchy of descriptions each refining previous definitions. A coarse description of the object is given. Then, at each stage, more detail is given about a smaller part of the object. In moving from step to step of the detection algorithm (and level to level of the hierarchy), finer descriptions of smaller portions of the object are given. These portions are those which are shown to be relevant to possible intersections if the two objects intersect. Details of the hierarchical method used for dynamic description are given in Section 2.

The efficiency of our algorithms is achieved by balancing the complexity of the algorithm. These results are presented in Section 4.

Static-dynamic intersection methods are considered in Section 3. Applications to detecting intersections between polyhedra, which are dynamically described, and lines and planes

+This research supported in part by the National Science Foundation under Grant MCS81-14207.

are given. Since lines and planes lack structure, they are described in a static manner. O(log n) operation algorithms are given for these problems.

The conclusions include a presentation of some open problems involving higher dimensional extensions and some applications of the algorithms to relevant problems.

2. Hierarchical Representations of Convex Polyhedra

As stated above, the algorithms are based on hierarchical descriptions of objects. These descriptions give two representations - an inner one and an outer one. In the inner representation, the polyhedron is "grown" from descriptions of increasing detail. Each new description gives a more accurate description of a polyhedron interior to the original object. If at any stage in the computation an intersection with an inner representation is detected, this is guaranteed to also be an intersection with the object itself. The outer representation "shrinks" the polyhedron from a superset of its points by adding detail locally as necessary. If at any point in this description a non-intersection is detected, no intersection of the original objects can occur. Details of this method are given below for polygons and polyhedra. In the next section, these methods are used to detect static-dynamic intersections. A variant of this method is used in section 4 to detect dynamic-dynamic intersections. Further unification of the techniques of this paper will allow the results of section 4 to be presented in a hierarchical form.

2.1. The two dimensional case

Let P be a polygon with vertices V(P) and edges E(P). Inner and outer representations of P are defined by:

Definition: An ***inner polygonal representation*** of P is an ascending chain P_i i=1,...,k of polygons where P_{i+1} is derived from P_i as follows: Each edge (u,v) in E(P_i) which is not in E(P) is replaced by edges (u,w) and (w,v) and the vertex w is added to V(P_i) in forming V(P_{i+1}). P_k is P.

Definition: An ***outer polygonal representation*** of P is a descending chain P_i i=1,...,k of polygons where P_{i+1} is derived from P_i as follows: If (u,v) and (v,w) are adjacent edges of P_i and v is not a vertex of P, then k and l are chosen on (u,v) and (v,w) such that (k,l) is the extension of an edge of P and {(u,v),(v,w)} is replaced by {(u,k),(k,l),(l,w)}. k and l are selected to balance the number of unspecified edges in (u,k) and (l,w).

An inner representation is a "growing out" of a polygon by adding new vertices to extend its perimeter. And, an outer representation if a "growing in" by adding new edges to limit its area. For an inner representation, the vertices considered at each stage are a subset of those in V(P). For an outer representation, the halfplanes defining the polygon at each stage are a subset of those defining P. However, this may lead to edges of P_i which contain the corresponding edges of P. Examples of these representations are given in Figure 1. Representations requiring space O(n) and having height k = O(log n) are formed by applying the process mentioned in each definition. For inner representations, P_i can be formed from P_{i+1} by deleting every other vertex. For outer representations, P_i can be formed from P_{i+1} by deleting every second bounding half-plane.

lines determine the segment of the line which intersects the polygon (or polyhedron) and thus are easily adapted to algorithms for segment or point intersections. Plane-polyhedron algorithms are based on projection techniques and are of necessity detection algorithms.

3.1. The two dimensional case

In deriving line-polygon intersection algorithms, it is sufficient to find an intersection point at any level of the hierarchy of an inner representation or separation information at any level for an outer representation. Lemma 2.1 is applied to actually determine the intersection. Using an inner representation, the initial test for intersection with P_1 requires only a constant number of operations to determine the vertex of P_1 closest to the line. P_1 is now grown towards P_2 by including the neighbors of this nearest vertex. Next, the relevant sections of P_2 are tested against the line and the process is repeated. At each level, the polygon grows by only a constant number of vertices (the nearest neighbors of the previous closest vertex) and the iteration requires a constant number of operations yielding:

Theorem 3.1: Given a polygon P of n vertices and a line L, O(log n) operations suffice to compute the intersection of L and P.

Corollary: Given a polygon P of n vertices and a line segment S, O(log n) operations suffice to compute the intersection of S and P.

Corollary: Given a polygon P of n vertices and a point R, O(log n) operations suffice to compute the intersection of R and P.

A dual of the above argument could have been applied to an outer polygonal representation of P yielding the same result.

3.2. The three dimensional case

The line-polyhedron intersection problem may be solved by a technique similar to the line-polygon intersection algorithm. This method easily extends to both inner and outer polyhedral representations through the use of Lemma 2.1. An alternative approach is to consider the projections of the line and polyhedron onto a plane normal to the line. The resulting point lies in the resulting polygon if and only if the line and polyhedron intersect. Having detected an intersection, O(log n) operations suffice to determine the points on the boundary of the polyhedron which lie on the line. Lemma 2.2 shows that the hierarchical description of the polyhedron also gives a hierarchical description of the projection of the polyhedron onto a plane. These techniques yield:

Theorem 3.2: Given a polyhedron P of n vertices and a line L, O(log n) operations suffice to compute the intersection of L and P.

Corollary: Given a polyhedron P of n vertices and a line segment S, O(log n) operations suffice to compute the intersection of S and P.

Corollary: Given a polyhedron P of n vertices and a point R, O(log n) operations suffice to compute the intersection of R and P.

A variant of the last technique solves the plane-polyhedron intersection problem. Here, only an intersection detector is possible since the description of the intersection may require O(n) operations. Projecting the plane and polyhedron onto a plane normal to the plane yields a line and polyhedron which intersect if and only if the original plane and polyhedron intersect. Once again, Lemma 2.2 gives a method for finding the hierarchical description of the

2.2. The three dimensional case

In three dimensions, the intuition is the same as that presented above. Inner representations now involve growing faces out of each existing face and outer representations involve decreasing size by adding intermediate bounding halfspaces. Letting V(P) and F(P) represent the vertices and faces of polyhedron P, the details are as follows:

Definition: An ***inner polyhedral representation*** of P is an ascending chain P_i ,i=1,..,k of polyhedra where P_{i+1} is formed from P_i as follows: For each face (u,v,w) $\in F(P_i)$, either (u,v,w) $\in F(P_{i+1})$ or there is a vertex x $\in V(P_{i+1})-V(P_i)$ with (u,v,x), (v,w,x), and (w,u,x) all faces of P_{i+1}.

Definition: An ***outer polyhedral representation*** of P is a descending chain P_i i=1,...,k of polyhedra where P_{i+1} is formed from P_i as follows: If $P_i = \bigcap_{j=1}^{s_i} H_j$ then $P_{i+1} = \bigcap_{j=1}^{s_i} H'_j$ where either $H'_j = H_j$ or H'_j is all of three space. Further, if H_{j_1} and H_{j_2} are adjacent in P_i, then not both of H'_{j_1} and H'_{j_2} are all of three space. And, if H'_j is all of three space, then H_j is adjacent to at most some constant number of half-spaces in P_i.

To form P_i from P_{i+1} in an inner representation remove an independent set of low degree and form the convex hull of the remaining vertices. This computation requires linear time and gives a representation of linear space and O(log\ n) height. Dually, in an outer representation, form P_i from P_{i+1} by removing an independent set of bounding half-spaces of low degree. Again, a representation requiring space O(n) and having height k = O(log n) results after O(n) computation.

2.3. Basic properties of inner and outer representations

Inner and outer representations are useful to intersection problems because of their shallow (O(log n)) depth, ease of creation (linear time) and local nature. When the area of a potential intersection has been identified, it is possible to use either of the representations to grow the polygon or polyhedron locally within that region in a constant number of operations per iteration. This property are captured as follows:

Lemma 2.1: Let $p_i(d)$ be the maximal vertex of P_i in the direction d where P_i is the ith member of a hierarchy for an inner or outer representation for a polygon or polyhedron. Then, either $p_{i+1}(d) = p_i(d)$ or $p_{i+1}(d)$ is one of the new neighbors of $p_i(d)$ in P_{i+1}.

Proof: The result in all cases follows from the convexity of each P_i. In the case of an inner polygonal representation, observe that a tangent line in direction d passing through $p_i(d)$ divides the plane into two halfplanes with P_i lying strictly within one of the halfplanes. If added vertices lie within the other halfplane and are not adjacent to $p_i(d)$, the resulting polygon cannot be convex. similar contradictions yield the same result in all other cases. ▪

Lemma 2.2: If Q is any plane and if $P_1,\ldots,P_k$ is an inner (resp. outer) polyhedral representation of P, then $P_1 \cap Q,\ldots,P_k \cap Q$ is an inner (resp. outer) polygonal representation of $P \cap Q$.

Proof: The convexity of P and P_i for all i, shows that the $P_1 \cap Q,\ldots,P_k \cap Q$ and $P \cap Q$ are all convex. Convexity also guarantees that the $P_i \cap Q$ grow (or shrink) appropriately. ▪

3. Static-Dynamic Intersection Methods

Hierarchical representations are used to derive O(log n) algorithms for intersecting polyhedra with linear subspaces of various dimensions. The point-in-polygon and point-in-polyhedron results were previously known but all others improve previous results[CD].

Algorithms are given for the line-polygon intersection problem in the plane and the line-polyhedron and plane-polyhedron problems in 3 dimensions. Intersection problems involving projected polygon and Theorem 3.1 yields:

Theorem 3.3: Given a polyhedron P of n vertices and a plane R, O(log n) operations suffice to compute the intersection of R and P.

4. Dynamic-Dynamic Intersection Methods

4.1. The two dimensional case

Intersection problems involving two hierarchically described objects are solved by dynamic-dynamic methods. The presentation of the two dimensional case simplifies that of [CD] and sets idea for the 3 dimensional case. A *monotone polygonal chain* **(MPC)** is defined to be a sequence of vertices and edges of a convex polygon given in order of increasing y-coordinate. By convexity, an MPC will either be left-oriented or right-oriented. Semi-infinite rays called *endedges* are attached to the beginning and end of the MPC. These edges run parallel to the x-axis towards *+inf* if right-oriented or *−inf* if left-oriented. O(log n) operations suffice to decompose a convex polygon P into MPC P_L and P_R with the vertices of P_L (resp. P_R) given in clockwise (resp. counter-clockwise) order. This decomposition can be done in any coordinate system. and has the property that P = $P_L \cap P_R$ and $P \sqsubseteq P_L, P_R$. In higher dimensions, extensions of this decomposition method simplify algorithm presentations via the following:

Lemma 4.1: Convex polygons P and Q intersect if and only if P_L and Q_R intersect and P_R and Q_L intersect.

Proof: If P and Q intersect, then since $P \sqsubseteq P_L, P_R$ and $Q \sqsubseteq Q_L, Q_R$, it is obvious that P_L and Q_R intersect and P_R and Q_L intersect.

If P and Q do not intersect, then P_L must be strictly to the right of Q_R or P_R must be strictly to the left of Q_L. Since the finite parts of each of these polygonal chains do not intersect and the semi-infinite parts grow away from each other, no intersection can take place. ▪

Given this reduction, it remains to present an algorithm for intersecting chains. The algorithm involves a generalization of binary search. At each iteration, an edge of each chain is selected and extended infinitely in each direction. The intersection of these supporting lines gives information (based on the properties of MPC) which allows half of the edges of one (or both) polygons to be ignored without missing the detection of an intersection. Edges are not eliminated, but the structural information they provide is discarded and a new endedge is introduced preserving the MPC properties. A simple case analysis shows that the newly formed chains intersect if and only if the original chains did.

Let R (resp. L) be a right (resp left) MPC with edges $r_1, r_2, \ldots r_m$ (resp. $l_1, l_2, \ldots l_n$). The edges r_1, r_m, l_1 and l_n are now rays and all other edges are finite. Let i = m/2 and j = n/2, and consider the four regions formed by the intersection of the lines R_i and L_j supporting the edges r_i and l_j. R and L can each exist in only two of these regions. Further, L and R can only coexist in one of the four regions. Label the regions as the R-region, the L-region, the LR-region and the empty region as shown in Figure 2. New MPCs R' (resp. R'') are defined to be R with the edges above (resp. below) r_i replaced by the semi-infinite ray parallel to the x-axis and intersecting r_i at its vertex. L' and L'' are defined from L in an analogous manner. The algorithm relies on the following:

Lemma 4.2: If the lines R_i and L_j intersect and the segments r_i and l_j do not, then if the LR-region is above the empty region (i.e. seeks $+\infty$ in the y-direction)

i) If the upper endpoint of r_i does not lie in the LR-region, then R intersects L if and only if R'' intersects L.

ii) If the upper endpoint of l_j does not lie in the LR-region, then R intersects L if and only if R intersects L''.

iii) If both endpoints of r_i and l_j lie in the LR-region and the lower endpoint of r_i has smaller (resp. larger) y-coordinate than the lower endpoint of l_j, then R intersects L if and only if R'' intersects L.

Proof: (See Figure 2) In case i), since the upper endpoint of r_i does not lie in the LR region, all points of R above r_i lie in that region by convexity. A similar argument handles case ii).

In case iii), if the lower endpoint of r_i has smaller y-coordinate than the lower endpoint of l_j, then the lower part of R cannot intersect the upper part of L. The lower part of R can never intersect the lower part of L twice and the upper part of L can never intersect the upper part of R twice. Therefore, either the intersection is exactly a vertex or edge or the upper part of R must be involved. If the intersection is restricted to the boundary, it must involve the upper part of R, hence R'' must intersect L. ▪

The extension to the case where the LR-region lies below the empty region yields:

Theorem 4.3: Given two polygons, O(log n) operations suffice to generate either

a) A point common to both polygons
or

b) A line supporting an edge of one polygon which separates the two polygons

Proof: In a constant number of operations, half of one of the two chains, L or R can be eliminated without changing the intersection status of the reduced problem. To achieve this, the algorithm first considers the middle edges r_i and l_j and their supporting lines R_i and L_j. If R_i and L_j do not intersect, two cases arise depending on whether L_j is to the left or right of R_i. In the first case, there is no intersection and R_i and L_j are separating lines. In the second, replacing i by i+1 yields a situation in which R_i and L_j cannot be parallel, so the algorithm proceeds. If R_i and L_j intersect and r_i and l_j also intersect, then a point of intersection has been found. Finally, the two remaining cases handling different orientations of intersecting lines R_i and L_j are considered in Lemma 4.2.

The algorithm will eventually reduce one of the chains to a wedge of two edges. At this point, it is sufficient to apply an extension of the segment-polygon intersection detector given in [CD] to find a point of intersection or separating edge. The two intersection tests need not report the same point of intersection. If neither of the reported points belongs to both of the polygons, it must be the case that one belongs to each. In this case, a point belonging to both can be easily found. ▪

This theorem guarantees a separating line which is an extension of an edge of one of the polygons. While this is unnecessary here, it proves crucial in the three dimensional case.

4.2. The three dimensional case

4.2.1. Methods of preprocessing polyhedra

The discussion of 2-dimensional objects ignored representational issues since any representation of a convex polygon in any coordinate system was suitable. This was true because polygons are essentially 1-dimensional manifolds and chains can be represented as (piecewise) 1-dimensional objects. Similarly, 3 dimensional polyhedra can be represented as 2-dimensional manifolds as planar subdivisions. Unfortunately, no known techniques reduce this subdivision to a 1-dimensional manifold to which simple ordering properties might be applied. A 3-dimensional polyhedron will be viewed as a sequence of cross-sections each of which is a polygon. Appropriate choices of cross-sections allow convexity to play a key role in the algorithms given here. For any representation of a polyhedron in an xyz coordinate system, consider x,y cross-sections corresponding to the z-values of all its vertices. These cross sections together with the edges joining adjacent cross-sections then give a characterization of the complete polyhedron. A *drum* is defined as 2 adjacent cross-sections along with all of their connecting edges. In this representation, a polyhedron of n vertices, might be decomposed into as many as n-1 drums.

The drum representation of a polyhedron has some useful properties. Even though a drum represents a 3-dimensional piece of a 3-dimensional object, there is no freedom of motion in passing from the bottom to the top of a drum. This motions consist of travel along single edges on which no vertices lie. The simplicity of this motion allows the view of a drum as a continuous transformation from its bottom face to its top face along the connecting edges. Thus in a sense, drums are 2½ dimensional objects, lying between polygons and polyhedra. This representation allows algorithms which work for polygons to be modified to work on drums.

The space and time requirements of the drum representation are unfortunate. A polyhedron might be decomposed into O(n) drums each requiring O(n) space for its description. So, $O(n^2)$ space and time might be necessary for generating and storing this representation. These bounds are unsatisfying in light of other representations requiring only linear space from which intersections may be computed in O(n log n) time. Recent work has provided a first step towards circumventing this difficulty. In [DM], a method is given which requires O(n log n) preprocessing time and O(n log n) storage for representing the drum decomposition of a polyhedron. Since this method might represent as much as $O(n^2)$ information, it is not possible to store information in a random access fashion. Rather, $O(\log^2 n)$ operations are required to retrieve specific information about particular aspects (e.g. edges, vertices or faces) of particular drums. O(log n) operations at each iteration are sufficient to give the information necessary to the detection algorithms given here.

In the algorithms given below, preprocessing is assumed which makes available in a random-access fashion, all the necessary information about a polyhedron. Any time bounds which take advantage of this storage scheme must be multiplied by O(log n) if the O(n log n) space and time preprocessing of [DM] is used. When considering 2 polyhedra, it is *not* assumed that each has been preprocessed in the same xyz coordinate system. Thus, the representation is robust being invariant under the translation, rotation and scaling of objects.

4.2.2. Detecting drum-drum intersections

A drum-drum intersection detector forms the core of the polyhedron-polyhedron intersection detector. Separation information for 2 non-intersecting drums is used to remove half of one polyhedron from consideration in the polyhedron-polyhedron intersection algorithm. Thus, polyhedron-polyhedron intersection problems are reduced to O(log n) drum-drum intersection problems.

Drum-drum intersections are detected by generalizations of the techniques used to detect polygon-polygon intersections. The structure of a drum as the continuous transformation of its bottom into its top is crucial. However, the change to 3 dimensions adds complexity to the analysis which resolved the polygon-polygon intersection problem. To set ideas, consider first the problem of detecting polygon-drum intersections.

Let P be a polygon and Q a drum. If R is the intersection of the plane of P with Q, then P and Q intersect if and only if P and R intersect. Determining the vertices and edges of R explicitly requires a linear number of operations. Therefore, R is considered as an implicitly specified object. The polygon-polygon intersection algorithm is used to detect the intersection of P and R. Additional computation is done each time an edge of R is needed. R is described as a clockwise sequence of vertices consisting of 2 (or possibly 1 or 0) vertices from the intersection of the plane and the top of the drum, followed by vertices derived from intersections of the plane and consecutive edges connecting the top and bottom faces of the drum, followed by 2 (or 1 or 0) vertices from the intersection of the plane and the bottom of the drum and finally consisting of vertices derived from intersections of the plane and consecutive edges connecting the bottom and top faces of the drum. Since the representation is presented in no more than four components, the needed edges of R can be found in a constant number of operations. Thus, intersecting a drum and a polygon is as easy (after O(log n) operations) as intersecting two polygons leading to

Theorem 4.4: Given a drum and a polygon, O(log n) operations suffice to compute either

a) A point common to both
   or
b) A line supporting an edge of the polygon or a plane supporting a face (or top or bottom) of the drum (or both) which separates the two objects.

Proof: To begin, an implicit representation for R is found in O(log n) operations. From this representation, desired vertices of R can be found in a constant number of operations. Since, R and P are coplanar, by construction, the algorithm of Theorem 4.3 yields the result. ▪

For the problem of detecting drum-drum intersections 2½ dimensional analogs of polygon-polygon intersection detectors are used. Each drum is decomposed into left and right halves relative to the plane formed by the normals to the tops of the two *drums*[1]. Conceptually this division is done by shining a beam of light in the direction of the normal to this plane starting at $+\infty$ (resp. $-\infty$) to define the right (resp. left) half drum. All faces lit by this light (consisting of those having positive component of their normals in this direction) belong to the relevant half drum. These halfdrums are then made semi-infinite by adding endfaces perpendicular to the drum top and extending towards $+\infty$ *or* $-\infty$. For a drum D, this decomposition into left and right halfdrums D_L and D_R satisfies again the properties that $D = D_R \cap D_L$ and $D \sqsubseteq D_L, D_R$. Using these results, it is easy to verify that

Lemma 4.5: If D and E are drums which have been decomposed into left and right halves as described above, then $D \cap E$ iff $D_L \cap E_R$ and $D_R \cap E_L$.

Proof: If $D \cap E$, then since $D \sqsubseteq D_L$, D_R and $E \sqsubseteq E_L$, E_R, it is obvious that $D_L \cap E_R$ and $D_R \cap E_L$.
If D and E do not intersect, assume without loss of generality that there is a face of D which forms a separating plane between D and E. Assume that this face belongs to D_L (the case of D_R following in an obvious manner). Then, D must lie to the left of this face and E to its right (with left and right defined relative to the decomposition of the drums into halfdrums. So, any extension of E to the right cannot intersect this plane and hence cannot intersect D_L. Therefore, D_L and E_R cannot intersect. ▪

---

1 In the case where the two drum tops are parallel any plane including the normal to the drum tops will suffice. In this case, the problem is first reduced (in constant time) to one in which drum tops and bottoms are (pairwise) coplanar. This will have no effect on running times and will make the algorithms avoid unnecessary work.

Given this reduction, it remains to generalize the polygon algorithm to the case of halfdrums. The middle face of each halfdrum is selected and extended infinitely in all directions. The intersection of these supporting planes then gives information (based on the properties of halfdrums) which allows the identification of that half of the faces of one drum which can be ignored without missing the detection of an intersection. Faces are not eliminated, but the structural information they provide is discarded and an endface is created as a semi-infinite slab preserving the halfdrum properties. A simple case analysis shows that the newly formed halfdrums intersect if and only if the original drums did.

To set notation, consider a right halfdrum R and a left halfdrum L with faces $r_1, r_2, \ldots r_m$ and $l_1, l_2, \ldots l_n$ respectively. Recall that in these representations, the endfaces r_1, r_m, l_1 and l_n are semi-infinite and all other faces are finite. Let i = m/2 and j = n/2, and consider the four regions formed by the intersection of the planes R_i and L_j supporting the faces r_i and l_j. Again, R and L can each exist in only two of these regions. L and R can only coexist in one of the four regions. The regions are labeled as the R-region, the L-region, the LR-region analogous to the planar regions shown in Figure 2. The halfdrums R' (resp. R'') are defined as R with the faces beyond (resp. before) r_i replaced by the semi-infinite endface of extension of r_i. L' and L'' are defined from L in an analogous fashion.

Lemma 4.6: If the planes R_i and L_j intersect and the faces r_i and l_j do not and the LR-region is above the empty region (i.e. seeks $+\infty$) then

i) If the upper edge of r_i does not lie in the LR-region, then R intersects L if and only if R'' intersects L.

ii) If the upper edge of l_j does not lie in the LR-region, then R intersects L if and only if R intersects L''.

iii) If all edges of r_i and l_j lie in the LR-region and the lower edge of r_i has a smaller (resp. larger) normal than the lower edge of l_j, then R intersects L if and only if R'' intersects L.

Proof: (Shown in projection in Figure 2) In case i), since the upper edge of r_i does not lie in the LR region, all points of R above r_i lie in that region by convexity. A similar argument handles case ii).

In case iii), if the lower edge of r_i has smaller normal than the lower edge of l_j, then the lower part of R cannot intersect the upper part of L. As always, the lower part of R cannot intersect the lower part of L twice and the upper part of L cannot intersect the upper part of R twice. Since an intersection must involve two "punctures" or be restricted to the boundary (in which case it must involve R''), the problem reduces to detecting the intersection of R'' and L. ▪

This theorem suggests immediately an algorithm for detecting drum-drum intersections in O(log n) operations. r_i and l_j are considered and R_i and L_j are formed yielding the four regions L,R, LR and empty. If l_i and r_j intersect, the algorithm reports an intersection and halts. If L_i and R_j are parallel, one of two situations results. If there can be no intersection (i.e. L_i and R_j are separating planes), the algorithm reports so and halts. Otherwise, i is set to i+1 and the algorithm continues. If none of these cases result, it must be the case that the four regions exist in a configuration like those shown in projection in Figure 2 or a similar configuration with the empty region above the LR-region. In the former case, the results of Lemma 4.6 give us a method of removing half of one drum from consideration in O(log n) operations. In the latter case, an obvious analog of Lemma 4.6 gives the same result. This leads to:

Theorem 4.7: Given two preprocessed drums, O(log n) operations suffice to determine either

a) A point common to both
or

b) A plane supporting a face or edge of one of the drums which separates the two drums.

4.2.3. Detecting polyhedral intersections

Finally, there remains the extension to polyhedral-polyhedral intersection problems. The algorithm of the previous section could be easily extended to the problem of detecting drum-polyhedron intersections. In that case, the drum is first compared to the middle drum of the *polyhedron*[2]. If these drums intersect, it is reported and the algorithm halts. If not, the result of Theorem 4.7 gives a separating plane supporting one of the drums. If it supports the drum belonging to the polyhedron, then it also separates the polyhedron from the drum. If it supports the separate drum, then one of three cases results. If it does not intersect the polyhedron, it acts as a separating plane and there can be no intersection. If it intersects the polyhedron above its middle drum, then the bottom part (lower half of its drums) of the polyhedron can be eliminated from further consideration of intersections. Similarly, if it intersects the polyhedron below its middle drum, the upper half of the polyhedron is eliminated from further consideration. Convexity guarantees that a plane cannot intersect the polyhedron both above and below its middle drum without intersecting the middle drum. This fact forms the basis of the algorithm which follows.

In considering polyhedron-polyhedron intersection problems, it is worthwhile to set some notation. The *waist* of a polyhedron is its middle drum. The *cone* of a drum of a polyhedron is formed by extending all its faces infinitely in both directions and computing their intersection. The cone, which may or may not be closed, is the largest convex polyhedra for the given drum. It is the polyhedron formed as the intersection of the halfspaces defined by the infinite extensions of the faces of the drum. Therefore, any polyhedron having this drum as its waist must be contained in its cone. However, the waist of the cone is exactly the drum which generated the cone. Therefore, if two drums do not intersect, their cones cannot intersect both above and below the drums. This fact is used to eliminate half of a polyhedron from consideration in intersection detection problems. leading to the result:

Theorem 4.8: Given two preprocessed polyhedra P and Q of p and q vertices respectively, $O(\log^2(p+q))$ operations suffice to determine either

a) A point common to both
or

b) A plane supporting a face or edge of one of the polyhedra and separating them.

Proof: The proof follows from a method of dividing the number of drums of one of the polyhedra in half in O(log (p+q)) operations. The resultant problem is shown to have the same form. Let E be the waist of P, F be the waist of Q, A be the cone of E and B the cone of F as shown in Figure 3. The algorithm of Theorem 4.7 is used to detect whether E and F intersect. If they do, the algorithm exits in case a of this theorem. If not, a plane T is found which is an extension of a face or edge of E (without loss of generality) and hence P and separates E from F. Two cases now result. If T is an extension of a face or face-edge of E, T must also separate P

2 If the preprocessing direction of the polyhedron is parallel to the top of the drum some difficulties result. This is resolved by doing (in O(log n) operations) a binary search to eliminate all drums of the polyhedron except those which could possibly intersect the drum (i.e. occur in the range of values between the drum top and bottom).

from F. In this case, the ideas from the drum-polyhedron intersection detector eliminate half of F from further consideration. The case where T is an extension of the top or bottom of E (or of an edge defining the top or bottom) is more complex.

Assume without loss of generality that T is an extension of the top of E (all other cases being similar). Now, since T separates E from F, F must lie "above" E. A and F intersect because otherwise a separating plane which was an extension of a face or face-edge of E would have been found. Therefore, F must intersect A above E. Now since F and A intersect above E, A and B also intersect above E. Observe that faces of A and B cannot intersect below E by convexity. Therefore, the bottom of A (and hence the bottom of P) can be eliminated from further intersections. ▪

5 Conclusions and possible extensions

A methodology for studying polyhedral intersection detection algorithms has been presented. The benefits of the methodology are twofold, providing a cleaner presentation of intersection algorithms and improving known results for these problems. There remain many open problems.

The techniques used to state and prove these results in three dimensions differ very little from those used in two dimensions. This suggests the possibility of extending these algorithms to arbitrary dimensions and achieving $O((d \log n)^2)$ as a time bound for intersection detection in d dimensions. There also remains open the problem of determining whether three (or more) polyhedra have a point in common. Were it possible to achieve both of these extensions, it might be possible to produce a sub-exponential algorithm for linear programming having a form different. from the ellipsoid algorithm.

There also remain the practical issues of implementing the algorithms presented here with the goal of achieving improved methods for hidden surface elimination.

Acknowledgement

We would like to thank Dan Field whose comments helped make the final presentation of this paper more coherent. We also acknowledge his help in identifying a bug in the original presentation of Lemma 4.1

6. References

[CD] B. Chazelle and D. Dobkin, Detection is easier than computation, ACM Symposium on Theory of Computing, Los Angeles, Ca, May, 1980, 146-153.

[Da] G. B. Dantzig, *Linear Programming and its Extensions*, Princeton University Press, Princeton, NJ, 1963.

[DM] D. P. Dobkin and J. I. Munro, Efficient uses of the past, 21st Annual Symposium on Foundations of Computer Science, Syracuse, NY, October, 1980, 200-206.

[K] D. G. Kirkpatrick, Optimal search in planar subdivisions, detailed abstract, Univ. of British Columbia, Vancouver, B.C., Canada, 1980.

[MP] D. Muller and F. Preparata, Finding the intersection of 2 convex polyhedra, Technical Report, University of Illinois, Oct., 1977.

[Sh] M. Shamos, *Computational Geometry*, PhD Thesis, Yale U., May, 1978.

[War] J. E. Warnock, A hidden-surface algorithm for computer generated half-tone pictures, University of Utah Computer Science Department, TR 4-15, 1969.

[Wat] G. S. Watkins, A real-time visible surface algorithm, University of Utah Computer Science Department, UTEC-CSc-70-101, June, 1970.

[Wi] P. H. Winston, *The Psychology of Computer Vision*, McGraw Hill, New York, 1975.

Figure 1: The polygon P = ABCDEF has inner representation $\{P_1, P_2\}$ where $P_1 = ACE, P_2 = P$ and outer representation $\{Q_1, Q_2\}$ where $Q_1 = XYZ, Q_2 = P$

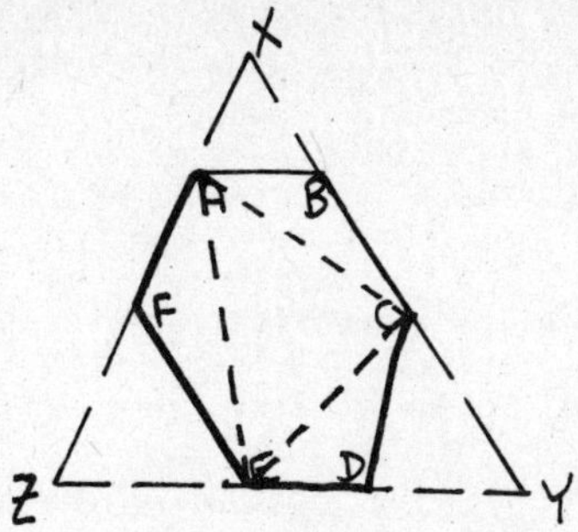

Figure 2: Regions involved in testing for polygonal intersections.

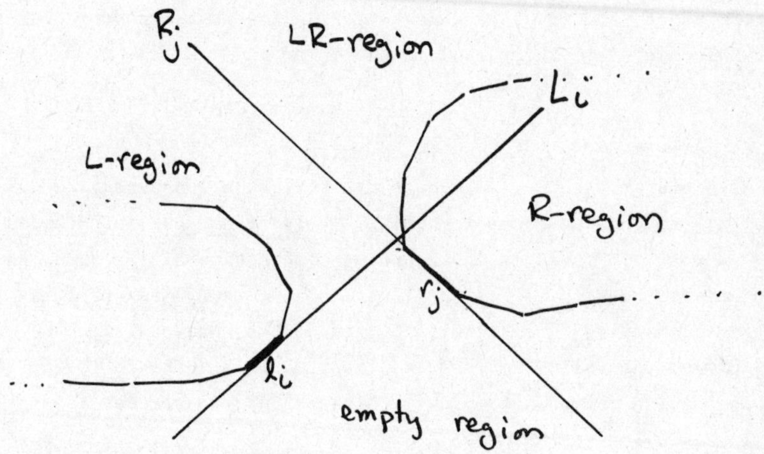

Figure 3: A polyhedron P with its waist and cone.

ON REVERSAL-BOUNDED COUNTER MACHINES AND ON PUSHDOWN AUTOMATA WITH A BOUND ON THE SIZE OF THE PUSHDOWN STORE

Pavol Ďuriš
Computer Center
Slovak Academy of Science
84235 Bratislava, Czechoslovakia

Zvi Galil
School of Mathematical Sciences
Tel-Aviv University
Tel-Aviv, Israel

Abstract

The two main results of the paper are: (1) a fine hierarchy of reversal-bounded counter machine languages; and (2) a tape is better than a pushdown store for two-way machines, in the case where their size is sublinear.

Introduction

If M is a two-way counter machine, we denote by $L(M)$ the language accepted by M. For a function $f(n)$, a two-way counter machine M is <u>f(n) reversal bounded</u> if for every string $w \in L(M)$, there is an accepting computation of M on w using at most $f(|w|)$ reversals, where $|w|$ is the length of w, and a reversal is a change from pushing to popping or vice versa by one of the counters.

In [1] Chan proved the following Theorem (Theorem 7.2): "The following bounds define strictly increasing reversal complexity classes for two-way deterministic counter machines: 0, 1, log n, and n."

Our first main result is refining Chan's hierarchy: We say that a function $f(n)$ is <u>reversal constructible</u> if there is a deterministic two-way counter machine which, on input of length n, can create a counter of length $f(n)$, with all counters making at most $O(f(n))$ reversals in the process.

<u>Theorem 1</u>. Let $f_1(n)$, $f_2(n)$ be two integer-valued functions such that $\liminf_{n\to\infty}(f_1(n)/f_2(n)) = 0$ and $f_2(n) \le (n-1)/2$ for all n. Moreover, if $f_2(n)$ is reversal-constructible, then the language

$$L = \left\{xy\#yx^R \,\middle|\, |xy\#yx^R| = n,\ n > 0,\ x \in \{0,1\}^*,\ |x| \le f_2(n),\ y \in \{2\}^*\right\}$$

is recognized by an $f_2(n)$ reversal-bounded two-way deterministic counter machine, but it cannot be recognized by any $f_1(n)$ reversal-bounded two-way deterministic counter machine.

<u>Corollary 1</u>. For every pair of integers $0 \le k_1 < k_2$, resp., for every pair of real numbers $0 \le r_1 < r_2 \le 1$, there is a language which is recognized by a

$(\log n)^{k_2}$ resp. n^{r_2} reversal-bounded two-way deterministic counter machine, but it cannot be recognized by any $(\log n)^{k_1}$ resp. n^{r_1} reversal-bounded two-way deterministic counter machine.

Corollary 2. For every function f with $1 \leq f(n)$ and $\liminf_{n\to\infty}(f(n)/n) = 0$, the $f(n)$ reversal-bounded two-way nondeterministic counter machines are better than the corresponding deterministic machines.

We define 2DPDA(f(n)) to be the class of languages accepted by two-way deterministic pushdown automata (2dpda's) whose pushdown stores are never longer than $f(n)$ on inputs of size n. We denote by DSPACE(f(n)) the class of languages accepted by $f(n)$ space-bounded Turing machines. It is well known that for every f, $\text{2DPDA}(f(n)) \subseteq \text{2DPDA}(n) = \text{2DPDA}$. (The latter is the class of languages accepted by unrestricted 2dpda's.) A well known open problem is whether $\text{2DPDA} \subsetneq \text{DPSACE}(n)$ (see [4]), or in our notation whether $\text{2DPDA}(n) \subsetneq \text{DSPACE}(n)$. Stated differently, this problem is actually whether a linear tape is better than a linear pushdown store for two-way machines. We still cannot solve the problem, but we can solve an easier version of it.

Theorem 2. For f that satisfies $f(n) = o(n)$ and $\limsup_{n\to\infty}(f(n)/\log\log n) > 0$, $\text{2DPDA}(f(n)) \subsetneq \text{DSPACE}(f(n))$.

Remark. 2DPDA(f(n)) = DSPACE(f(n)) = regular languages, for $f(n) = o(\log\log n)$. Theorem 2 follows as a corollary from Theorem 3.

Theorem 3. If a language L over a one-symbol alphabet is in 2DPDA(f(n)) and $f(n) = o(n)$, then L is regular.

The proof of Theorem 2 is immediate (given Theorem 3) using the known result that there exist nonregular languages over a one-symbol alphabet in DSPACE(log log n) [3]. Theorem 3 does not hold for languages over a two-symbol alphabet. We define a nonregular language L_1 and prove:

Theorem 4. L_1 is in 2DPDA(log log n).

The proofs

The proof of Theorem 1 is similar to the proof of our main result in [2]. Figures 1-5 in [2] can be used to understand the proof here. The y-axis in these figures should be understood as representing the contents of one of the counters. We define an internal computation of a counter machine A on a triple (x,y,z) as a computation on input xyz that starts at one of the end symbols of y, ends at a symbol out of y, during which A scans y and each counter is either always empty or always nonempty (Figure 2 in [2]). We define functions f_y (Figure 3 in [2]) that describe completely the internal computations on (x,y,z). This is possible because the length of internal computations is bounded. (Figure 4 in [2] shows the three possible contradictions one gets if one assumes that an internal computation can be longer than a certain bound.) Using a counting argument we derive two strings u and v with

$f_u = f_v$, and consequently show that A hardly distinguishes between u and v: For every x and z, there is an internal computation between two configurations of A on (x,u,z) if and only if there is an internal computation between the same configurations on (x,v,z). The latter fact follows from the fact that $f_u = f_v$ by the ability to "copy" the two computations implied by the definitions of f_u and f_v (Figure 5 in [2]). Finally, we will be able to fool the machine by replacing an occurrence of u by v.

Proof of Theorem 1. Let M be a two-way deterministic counter machine with k counters and let Q be the set of internal states of M. A configuration of M is a (k+2)-tuple $(q,h,s_1,\dots,s_k)$, where $q \in Q$, h is the position of the input head of M and s_i is the length of the i-th counter of M. (Note that there are (n+2) positions of the input head of M on input of size n, where position 0 resp. (n+1) is the position of the left resp. right endmarker.) If x is an input of M and C and C' are configurations of M on x, we denote by $C \vdash_x C'$ the fact that M goes in one step from C to C'. If $C = (q,h,s_1,\dots,s_k)$ is a configuration of M, we denote by $pr_o(C) = q$, $pr_1(C) = h$ and $pr_j(C) = s_{j-1}$ for $j = 2,3,\dots,k+1$. For a set S we denote by $|S|$ the size of S, and for a string x we denote by $|x|$ the length of x.

Definition 1. Let $C_o,C_1,\dots,C_r$ be a sequence of configurations of M; let x,y,z be strings, where $y \in \{0,1\}^*$ and $|y| \geq 1$. We say that the sequence $C_o,C_1,\dots,C_r$ is an internal computation of M from C_o to C_r on the triple (x,y,z) if (i), (ii), (iii) and (iv) hold.

(i) $C_o \vdash_{xyz} C_1 \vdash_{xyz} \cdots \vdash_{xyz} C_r$

(ii) $|x| + 1 \leq pr_1(C_i) \leq |xy|$ for $i = 0,1,\dots,r-1$

(iii) $pr_1(C_o) \in \{|x|+1, |xy|\}$ and $pr_1(C_r) \in \{|x|,|xy|+1\}$

(iv) for $j = 2,3,\dots,k+1$, either $pr_j(C_i) > 0$ for $i=0,1,\dots,r$ or $pr_j(C_i) = 0$ for $i=0,1,\dots,r$.

Let $C_o,C_1,\dots,C_r$ be a sequence of configurations of M. By $\min_j(C_o,C_1,\dots,C_r)$ resp. $\max_j(C_o,C_1,\dots,C_r)$ we denote the minimum resp. maximum number of the sequence

$$0,pr_j(C_1) - pr_j(C_o),pr_j(C_2) - pr_j(C_o),\dots,pr_j(C_r) - pr_j(C_o)$$

for $j = 2,3,\dots,k+1$.

We choose an integer m such that

$$[2|Q|(2|Q|m+2)^k(|Q|m+1)^k+1]^{2^{k+1}|Q|} < 2^m . \tag{1}$$

Definition 2. Let $\bar{x}$ and $\bar{z}$ be two arbitrary but fixed strings. Let $S_1 = C$ and $S_2 = C \times \underbrace{Z \times \dots \times Z}_{k \text{ times}}$, where C is the set of all configurations of M and Z is the set of all integers. For each string y in $\{0,1\}^m$ we define a partial function $f_y: S_1 \to S_2$ as follows. Let C_o be an arbitrary configuration of M. If the sequence $C_o,C_1,\dots,C_r$ of configurations of M is an internal computation of M from C_o to C_r on the triple $(\bar{x},y,\bar{z})$, and moreover, $pr_j(C_o) \in \{0,|Q|m+1\}$ for $j = 2,3,\ldots,k+1$, then $f_y(C_o) = (C_r, -min_2(C_o,\ldots,C_r), -min_3(C_o,\ldots,C_r),\ldots, -min_{k+1}(C_o,\ldots,C_r))$ and if there is no such computation, then $f_y(C_o)$ is undefined.

Note that since M is deterministic, f_y is indeed a partial function.

Lemma 1. Let x,x',y,z,z' be five strings, where y is in $\{0,1\}^m$. Let $C_o,C_1,\ldots,C_r$ be an internal computation of M from C_o to C_r on (x,y,z) and let C'_o be a configuration of M such that $pr_o(C'_o) = pr_o(C_o)$, $pr_1(C'_o) = pr_1(C_o) - |x| + |x'|$, and $pr_j(C'_o) = 0$ if $pr_j(C) = 0$ and $pr_j(C'_o) > -min_j(C_o,\ldots,C_r)$ if $pr_j(C_o) > 0$ for $j = 2,3,\ldots,k+1$. Then the sequence of configurations of M $C'_o,C'_1,\ldots,C'_r$, where $C'_o \vdash_{x'yz'} C'_1 \vdash_{x'yz'} \cdots \vdash_{x'yz'} C'_r$, is an internal computation of M from C'_o to C'_r on (x',y,z'), and moreover,

$$pr_o(C'_i) = pr_o(C_i),\quad pr_1(C'_i) = pr_1(C_i) - |x| + |x'| \quad \text{and}$$

$$pr_j(C'_i) = pr_j(C_i) - pr_j(C_o) + pr_j(C'_o) \quad \text{for } i=0,1,\ldots,r \text{ and for } j=2,3,\ldots,k+1.$$

The proof follows by induction from the fact that M moves the input head and decreases resp. increases the counters during the computation $C'_o,C'_1,\ldots,C_r$ exactly as it does during the computation $C_o,C_1,\ldots,C_r$, because the input head of M scans only the string y during the computation $C_o,C_1,\ldots,C_{r-1}$ (see (ii) of def. 1) and the inequality $pr_j(C'_o) > -min_j(C_o,\ldots,C_r)$ guarantees that the j-th counter is never empty during the computation $C'_o,\ldots,C'_r$.

Lemma 2. There are two different strings u,v in $\{0,1\}^m$ such that for every pair of strings x,z and every pair of configurations of M C_o,C_r, there is an internal computation of M from C_o to C_r on (x,u,z) if and only if there is an internal computation of M from C_o to C_r on (x,v,z).

Proof. Let $C_o,C_1,\ldots,C_r$ be an internal computation of M from C_o to C_r on (x,y,z), where y is a string in $\{0,1\}^m$. We first show that for every j, $2 \leq j \leq k+1$, if $pr_j(C_o) > 0$ then

$$(2)\qquad 0 \leq -min_j(C_o,\ldots,C_{r-1}) \leq |Q|m-1 \quad\text{and}\quad 0 \leq max_j(C_o,\ldots,C_{r-1}) \leq |Q|m-1\ .$$

We show only the first half of (2). The other half is similar. We assume to the contrary that for some j, $2 \leq j \leq k+1$, $pr_j(C_o) > 0$ and $-min_j(C_o,\ldots,C_{r-1}) \geq |Q|m$. We consider the sequence of pairs $(pr_o(C_o),pr_1(C_o))$, $(pr_o(C_1),pr_1(C_1)),\ldots,$ $(pr_o(C_{|Q|m}),pr_1(C_{|Q|m}))$. Note that $r-1 \geq |Q|m$, because the j-th counter of M must decrease from $pr_j(C_o)$ by at least $|Q|m$ during $(r-1)$ computation steps. The number of all different pairs of the form $(pr_o(C_\ell),pr_1(C_\ell))$ is at most $|Q|m$ (since $|y| = m$). Therefore, there are two indices s and t, $s < t$, such that

$$(3)\qquad pr_o(C_s) = pr_o(C_t) \quad\text{and}\quad pr_1(C_s) = pr_1(C_t).$$

By (iv) of def. 1, the sequence of pairs $(pr_o(C_i),pr_1(C_i))$, $i = 0,\ldots,r$ is periodic, and by (3) the size of the period is at most r. But this implies that $|x| + 1 \leq pr_1(C_r) \leq |xy|$ --a contradiction to (iii) of def. 1.

Since $pr_j(C_{r-1}) - 1 \leq pr_j(C_r) \leq pr_j(C_{r-1}) + 1$ for $j = 2,3,\dots,k+1$, then by (2) we have that for every j, $2 \leq j \leq k + 1$, if $pr_j(C_o) > 0$ then

(4) $$0 \leq - \min_j(C_o,\dots,C_r) \leq |Q|m \quad \text{and} \quad 0 \leq \max_j(C_o,\dots,C_r) \leq |Q|m .$$

If $C_o,C_1,\dots,C_r$ are the configurations from def. 2, then $pr_1(C_o) \in \{0, |Q|m+1\}$, and by (4) and by (iv) of def. 1,

(5) $$0 \leq pr_j(C_r) \leq 2|Q|m + 1 \quad \text{for } \underline{\text{every}} \ j = 2,3,\dots,k + 1 .$$

By definitions 1, 2, by (4) and (5), each f_y is a partial function from S_1' into S_2', where $S_1' = Q \times \{|\overline{x}| + 1, |\overline{x}| + m\} \times \{0, |Q|m + 1\}^k$ and
$S_2' = (Q \times \{|\overline{x}|, |\overline{x}| + m + 1\} \times \{0,1,\dots,2|Q|m + 1\}^k) \times \{0,1,\dots, |Q|m\}^k$.
The cardinality of the set of all partial functions from S_1' into S_2' is $[2|Q|(2|Q|m+2)^k (|Q|m+1)^k + 1]^{2^{k+1}|Q|}$. On the other hand, there are 2^m strings in $\{0,1\}^m$. By (1) there are two different strings u and v in $\{0,1\}^m$ with $f_u = f_v$.

Now, let $C_o,C_1,\dots,C_r$ be an internal computation of M from C_o to C_r on (x,u,z). By (iv) of def. 1, for $2 \leq j \leq k + 1$, if $pr_j(C_o) > 0$ then

(6) $$pr_j(C_o) > - \min_j(C_o,\dots,C_r) ,$$

because the j-th counter does not become empty during the computation $C_o,C_1,\dots,C_r$. We consider the sequence of configurations of M $\overline{C}_o,\overline{C}_1,\dots,\overline{C}_r$, where $\overline{C}_o \vdash_{\overline{x}u\overline{z}} \overline{C}_1 \vdash_{\overline{x}u\overline{z}} \dots \vdash_{\overline{x}u\overline{z}} \overline{C}_r$, ($\overline{x},\overline{z}$ are the strings from def. 2), and

(7) $$\begin{cases} pr_o(\overline{C}_o) = pr_o(C_o) , \quad pr_1(\overline{C}_o) = pr_1(C_o) - |x| + |\overline{x}|, \quad \text{and} \\ \text{for } j = 2,3,\dots,k + 1 \quad pr_j(\overline{C}_o) = \begin{cases} |Q|m+1 & \text{if } pr_j(C_o) > 0 \\ 0 & \text{if } pr_j(C_o) = 0 \end{cases} . \end{cases}$$

By (7) and (4), for $2 \leq j \leq k + 1$, if $pr_j(C_o) > 0$, then $pr_j(\overline{C}_o) = |Q|m+1 > - \min_j(C_o,\dots,C_r)$, and thus by (7) and by Lemma 1, the sequence $\overline{C}_o,\overline{C}_1,\dots,\overline{C}_r$ is an internal computation of M from $\overline{C}_o$ to $\overline{C}_r$ on $(\overline{x},u,\overline{z})$; and moreover,

(8) $$\begin{cases} pr_o(\overline{C}_i) = pr_o(C_i), \quad pr_1(\overline{C}_i) = pr_1(C_i) - |x| + |\overline{x}| \quad \text{and} \\ pr_j(\overline{C}_i) = pr_j(C_i) - pr_j(C_o) + pr_j(\overline{C}_o) \quad \text{for } i = 0,1,\dots,r \quad \text{and} \\ \text{for } j = 2,3,\dots,k + 1. \end{cases}$$

Since $f_u = f_v$, there is an internal computation $\tilde{C}_o,\tilde{C}_1,\dots,\tilde{C}_s$ of M from $\tilde{C}_o = \overline{C}_o$ to $\tilde{C}_s = \overline{C}_r$ on $(\overline{x},v,\overline{z})$; and moreover,

(9) $$\min_j(\tilde{C}_o,\dots,\tilde{C}_s) = \min_j(\overline{C}_o,\dots,\overline{C}_r) \quad \text{for } j = 2,3,\dots,k + 1 .$$

By (8),

(10) $$\min_j(C_o,\dots,C_r) = \min_j(\overline{C}_o,\dots,\overline{C}_r) \quad \text{for } j = 2,3,\dots,k + 1 .$$

We consider the configurations $C'_o = C_o, C'_1, \ldots, C'_s$, where $C'_o \vdash_{xvz} C'_1 \vdash_{xvz} \cdots \vdash_{xvz} C'_s$. Since $\tilde{C}_o = \overline{C}_o$, by (7), (6), (10), (9), we have

$$(11)\quad \begin{cases} pr_o(C_o) = pr_o(\tilde{C}_o),\ pr_1(C_o) = pr_1(\tilde{C}_o) - |\overline{x}| + |x| \text{ and} \\ pr_j(C_o) = 0 \text{ if } pr_j(\tilde{C}_o) = 0 \text{ and } pr_j(C_o) > -\min_j(\tilde{C}_o, \ldots, \tilde{C}_s) \text{ if} \\ pr_j(\tilde{C}_o) > 0 \text{ for } j = 2,3,\ldots,k+1. \end{cases}$$

Hence, by Lemma 1, the sequence $C'_o, C'_1, \ldots, C'_s$ is an internal computation of M from $C'_o = C_o$ to C'_s on (x,v,z); and moreover,

$$(12)\quad \begin{cases} pr_o(C'_i) = pr_o(\tilde{C}_i),\ pr_1(C'_i) = pr_1(\tilde{C}_i) - |\overline{x}| + |x| \text{ and} \\ pr_j(C'_i) = pr_j(\tilde{C}_i) - pr_j(\tilde{C}_o) + pr_j(C'_o) \text{ for } i = 0,1,\ldots,s \\ \text{and for } j = 2,3,\ldots,k+1\ . \end{cases}$$

But $\tilde{C}_s = \overline{C}_r$, $\tilde{C}_o = \overline{C}_o$ and $C'_o = C_o$, and by (8) and (12), we have $pr_j(C'_s) = pr_j(C_r)$ for $j = 0,1,\ldots,k+1$, i.e., $C'_s = C_r$, and therefore, $C_o = C'_o, C'_1, \ldots, C'_s = C_r$ is the internal computation of M from C_o to C_r on (x,v,z). □

We now complete the proof of Theorem 1. We assume to the contrary that M is $f_1(n)$ reversal bounded and accepts L. This implies that M accepts every string $w \in L$ using at most $d\, f_1(|w|)$ reversals for some constant $d > 0$. Let u,v be the strings from Lemma 2. Note that $|u| = |v| = m$. Since $\liminf_{n\to\infty}(f_1(n)/f_2(n)) = 0$, there is an integer n_o such that $m(df_1(n_o) + k + 1) \leq f_2(n_o)$. Let $g = df_1(n_o) + k + 1$ and let $C_o, C_1, \ldots, C_f$ be the accepting computation of M on the string $w = x_1x_2\ldots x_g y\#yx_g^R x_{g-1}^R \ldots x_1^R$ in L, where $|w| = n_o$, $y \in \{2\}^*$ and each $x_i \in \{u,v\}$. Without loss of generality we assume that M scans the left endmarker of the input tape at C_o and at C_f. For $j = 1,2,\ldots,k$, let p_j be the number of the configurations C_i, $0 \leq i \leq f$, at which the j-th counter of M is increased from zero or decreased to zero. Clearly, $\sum_{j=1}^{k} p_j \leq$ number of reversals $+ k \leq$ $df_1(n_o) + k$ and therefore, $\sum_{j=1}^{k} p_j < g$. This implies that there is an index h, $1 \leq h \leq g$, such that if x_h is scanned by M at step i, $0 \leq i \leq f - 1$, then no counter is increased from zero or decreased to zero at step $i + 1$. Let $C_{i_1}, C_{i_2}, \ldots C_{i_t}$ be all the configurations at which the input head of M leaves or enters the substring x_h. Consider the string $w' = x_1x_2\ldots x_{h-1}x'_h x_{h+1}\ldots x_g y\#yx_g^R \ldots x_h^R \ldots x_1^R$, where x'_h is u resp. v if x_h is v resp. u. We derive a contradiction by showing that M accepts also $w'(w' \notin L)$: Let $C_{i_o} = C_o$ and $C_{i_{t+1}} = C_f$. It suffices to show that there is a computation of M from C_{i_ℓ} to $C_{i_{\ell+1}}$ on w' for $i = 0,1,\ldots,t$. If

ℓ is even, then the computation from C_{i_ℓ} to $C_{i_{\ell+1}}$ on w' is identical to the computation from C_{i_ℓ} to $C_{i_{\ell+1}}$ on w, because the input head does not scan the substring x_h during the latter. If ℓ is odd, then there is an internal computation of M from C_{i_ℓ} to $C_{i_{\ell+1}}$ on $(x_1 \dots x_{h-1}, x_h, x_{h+1} \dots x_g y \# y x_g^R \dots x_1^R)$, by the choice of x_h. By Lemma 2, there is also a computation of M from C_{i_ℓ} to $C_{i_{\ell+1}}$ on w'. □

Proof of Corollary 1. Chan [1] showed that the functions $\lceil \log n \rceil^k$ and $\lceil n^{1/p} \rceil^q$ (for integers k, $p > q \geq 1$) are reversal constructible. □

Proof of Corollary 2. The language $L' = \{x\#x' \mid x' \neq x^R,\ x,x' \in \{0,1\}^*\}$ is recognized by a one reversal-bounded one-way nondeterministic counter machine. If there were an $f(n)$ reversal-bounded two-way deterministic counter machine M_1 recognizing L', then there would be such a machine M_2 recognizing $\{x\#x^R \mid x \in \{0,1\}^*\}$, because these deterministic machines (with reversal-constructible $f(n)$), are closed under complement. But M_2 cannot exist by Theorem 1. (In this case $f_1(n) = f(n)$ and $f_2(n) = (n-1)/2$.) □

Proof of Theorem 3. Let A be a 2dpda with a set Q of internal states and with a set Γ of stack symbols. By $\ell s(a^n)$ we denote the maximum length of stack used by A on the input a^n. We define two constants:

$$(13) \qquad p = |Q|\ |\Gamma|^{|Q||\Gamma|+2}, \quad k = 1/(3p),$$

and prove

Lemma 3. There is $n_o = n_o(p)$, such that for $n > n_o$, if A accepts a^n with $\ell s(a^n) < kn$, then A must accept $a^{n'}$ with $\ell s(a^{n'}) = \ell s(a^n)$, where $n' = n - p!$.

Now, assume $L \subseteq \{a\}^*$ is accepted by a 2dpda A whose pushdown store is never longer than $f(n) = o(n)$ on a^n. Choose $n_1 \geq n_o$ such that for all $n > n_1$ $f(n) < kn$. If $a^n \in L$ and $n > n_1$, then by Lemma 3 there is $n' < n$ such that $a^{n'} \in L$ and $\ell s(a^{n'}) = \ell s(a^n)$. Consequently, $\max_{a^n \in L} \ell s(a^n) = \max_{a^n \in L,\ n \leq n_1} \ell s(a^n) = \text{constant}$. Hence, L is regular because its pushdown store can be simulated by the finite state control. □

Proof of Lemma 3. A configuration of a 2dpda A is a triple (q,z,i), where $q \in Q$, $z \in \Gamma^*$ is the string in the stack and i is the position of the head on the input tape. If $C = (q,z,i)$ is a configuration of A, then we denote by $pr_o(C) = q$, $pr_1(C) = z$ and $pr_2(C) = i$. We denote by $|z|$ the length of z, and by $[z]_\ell$ the suffix of z of size ℓ. $[z]_1$ is the symbol at the top of the stack. Without loss of generality we assume that A accepts only when its input head scans the left endmarker. As before we use the notation $C \vdash_x C'$ if A goes in one step from C to C' on input x.

A computation segment of A on input x is a sequence of configurations $C_o,\dots,C_m$ such that $C_o \vdash_{\overline{x}} C_1 \vdash_{\overline{x}} \dots \vdash_{\overline{x}} C_m$ and A scans an endmarker in C_o and in C_m but not in C_i for $0 < i < m$. The proof follows from the claim by an induction on the number of computation segments in the computation of A on a^n:

Claim. Assume $C_o,\dots,C_m$ is a computation segment of A on a^n. Then there is a computation segment $C'_o,\dots,C'_m$ of A on $a^{n'}$ such that:

(i) $pr_o(C'_o) = pr_o(C_o)$, $pr_1(C'_o) = pr_1(C_o)$

(ii) $pr_o(C'_m) = pr_o(C_m)$, $pr_1(C'_m) = pr_1(C_m)$

(iii) in C_o and C'_o, A scans the same endmarker

(iv) in C_m and C'_m A scans the same endmarker

(v) $\max\limits_{0 \le i \le m'} \{|pr_1(C'_i)|\} = \max\limits_{0 \le i \le m} \{|pr_1(C_i)|\}$.

Proof. First, assume that there is no index h, $1 \le h \le m - 1$, such that $n/3 + p \le pr_2(C_h) \le 2n/3 - p$. For n large enough $n/3 + p < n'$, and $C'_i = C_i$ for $i = 0,\dots,m$ and $m' = m$ will do. So we can assume that there is such an index h and we choose a minimal such h. Note that $h \ge n/3 + p$. There must be an index t, $1 \le t \le h - p$, such that $pr_1(C_{t+r}) \ge pr_1(C_t)$ for every $r = 1,\dots,p$. Otherwise, for every p steps there must be a decrease in the size of the stack and the size of the stack decreases eventually by $h/p \ge n/(3p) = kn$ --a contradiction $(\ell s(a^n) < kn)$. We choose a minimal such t.

There are two cases left:

Case 1. $|pr_1(C_{t+r})| - |pr_1(C_t)| \le |Q||\Gamma|$ for every $r = 1,2,\dots,p$. Then there are two indices i,j, $t \le i < j \le t + p$, such that $pr_o(C_i) = pr_o(C_j)$ and $[pr_1(C_i)]_{\ell_i} = [pr_1(C_j)]_{\ell_j}$, where $\ell_s = 1 + |pr_1(C_s)| - |pr_1(C_t)|$, because $\ell_s \le \ell \equiv |Q||\Gamma| + 1$, the number of all strings over Γ with length at most ℓ is at most $|\Gamma|^{|Q||\Gamma|+2}$ and $p + 1 > |Q|.|\Gamma|^{|Q||\Gamma|+2}$. If $pr_2(C_i) > pr_2(C_j)$ (resp. $pr_2(C_i) < pr_2(C_j)$), then A periodically approaches the left endmarker ¢ (resp. right endmarker \$) with a period of size at most p and simultaneously the stack is in a loop; see Figure 1a (resp. 1b). Therefore, for sufficiently large n there are configurations $C'_o,\dots,C'_{m'}$, with the desired properties. If $pr_2(C_i) = pr_2(C_j)$, then A is in a loop; see Figure 1c. But then, it is impossible for A to scan an endmarker at C_m for the first time after C_o --a contradiction.

Case 2. There is an index r, $1 \le r \le p$, such that $|pr_1(C_{t+r})| - |pr_1(C_t)| \ge |Q||\Gamma| + 1$. Let r be such a minimal index. For $j = 0,1,\dots,|Q||\Gamma|$, let i_j, $t \le i_j \le t + r$ be the maximal index with $|pr_1(C_{i_j})| = |pr_1(C_t)| + j$. Obviously, there are two indices i_u and i_v, $t \le i_u \le i_v \le t + r$, such that $pr_o(C_{i_u}) = pr_o(C_{i_v})$ and $[pr_1(C_{i_u})]_1 = [pr_1(C_{i_v})]_1$, because the number of the configurations C_{i_j} is $|Q||\Gamma| + 1$. This means that if $pr_2(C_{i_u}) > pr_2(C_{i_v})$ (resp. $pr_2(C_{i_u}) <$

$< pr_2(C_{i_v})$, resp. $pr_2(C_{i_u}) = pr_2(C_{i_v})$), then the stack periodically increases and simultaneously the input tape head periodically approaches the left endmarker (resp. the right endmarker, resp. the input tape head is in a loop); see Figure 2a (resp. 2b, resp. 2c). So in all three cases the stack periodically increases (with a period of size at most $|Q||\Gamma| \leq p$) during at least $n/3$ steps (by the choice of h), and therefore A must use a stack of length at least $n/(3p) = kn$ --a contradiction.□

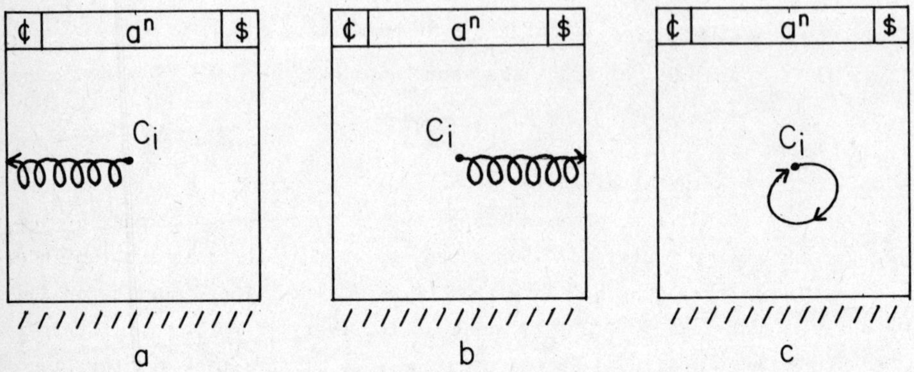

Figure 1. The three subcases of case 1.

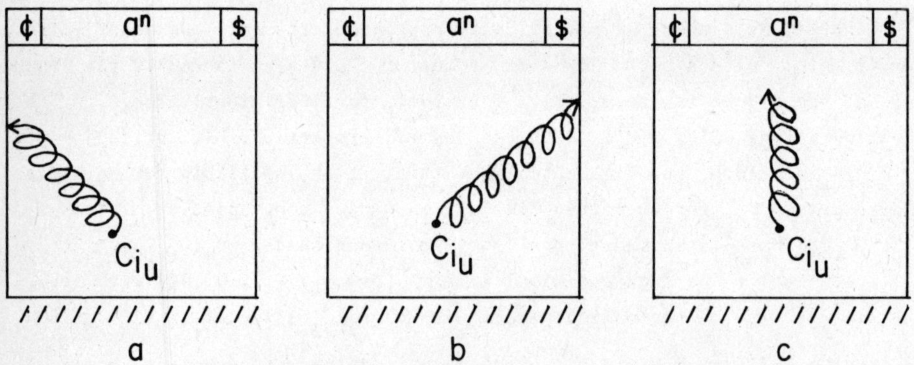

Figure 2. The three subcases of case 2.

We now define the language L_1 of Theorem 4. Let a, b, 0, 1 be four different symbols. We define a homomorphism h as follows: h(a) = 0, h(b) = 1, h(0) = h(1) = empty string. Then

$$L_1 = \left\{ w_1\#w_2\ldots\#w_{2^{2^n}} \;\middle|\; n \geq 0,\ w_i = x_1y_1x_2y_2\ldots x_{2^n}y_{2^n} \text{ for every } i = 1,2,\ldots,2^n, \right.$$

$$\left. \text{where } y_1 < \ldots < y_{2^n},\ \text{every } y_j \in \{0,1\}^n,\ \text{every } x_j \in \{a,b\}, \text{ and } h(w_1) < h(w_2) < \ldots < h(w_{2^{2^n}}) \right\}.$$ [1]

Note that $y_1 = \underbrace{00\ldots0}_{n}$, $y_2 = \underbrace{00\ldots01}_{n}$, ..., $y_{2^n} = \underbrace{11.111}_{n}$, and $w_1 = ay_1ay_2\ldots ay_{2^n}$, $w_2 = ay_1ay_2\ldots ay_{2^n-1}by_{2^n},\ldots,w_{2^{2^n}} = by_1by_2\ldots by_{2^n}$.

We leave the details of the proof of Theorem 4 to the reader. We only note that the 2dpda has to be constructed with some care so that its stack is never longer than loglog n also for strings not in L_1.

References

[1] T-h. Chan, "Reversal complexity of counter machines," Proc. 13th Annual STOC, Milwaukee, 1981, pp. 146-157.

[2] P. Ďuriš and Z. Galil, "Fooling a two-way automaton or one pushdown store is better than one counter for two-way machines," Proc. 13th Annual STOC, Milwaukee, 1981, pp. 177-188.

[3] A.R. Freedman and R.E. Ladner, "Space bounds for processing contentless inputs," JCSS 11 (1975), 118-128.

[4] Z. Galil, "Some open problems in the theory of computation as questions about two-way deterministic pushdown automaton languages," Math. Sys. Theory 10 (1977), 211-228.

---

[1] By $y_i < y_j$ we mean that the binary number represented by y_i is smaller than the one represented by y_j.

MULTIHEAD FINITE STATE AUTOMATA AND CONCATENATION

Pavol Ďuriš
Computing Centre
Slovak Academy of Sciences
842 35 Bratislava, Czechoslovakia

Juraj Hromkovič
Department of Theoretical Cybernetics
Komensky University
842 15 Bratislava, Czechoslovakia

Abstract. The following results are shown :

(1) The class of languages accepted by the one-way nondeterministic simple k-head finite automata $\mathcal{L}$(NSPk-HFA) is not closed under concatenation for any $k \geq 2$.

(2) The class $\bigcup_k \mathcal{L}$(NSPk-HFA) is closed under concatenation.

(3) The class of languages recognized by one-way k-head deterministic finite state automata $\mathcal{L}$(1DFA(k)) and the class of languages recognized by one-way k-head deterministic sensing finite state automata $\mathcal{L}$(1DSeFA(k)) are not closed under concatenation, Kleene star and reversal.

Introduction. This paper is divided in two parts, because it consists of two different works. The first part " $\mathcal{L}$(NSPk-HFA) and concatenation" is the common work of both authors and the second part " Closure properties of $\mathcal{L}$(1DFA(k)) and $\mathcal{L}$(1DSeFA(k)) " is the paper of the second author.

In [1, 4], many investigations about one-way simple resp. sensing simple multihead finite automata SMFA's resp.SNSMFA's have been made. The SMFA is the one-way multihead finite automaton whose only one head (called "reading" head) is capable of distinguishing the symbols in the input alphabet, and whose other heads (called "counting" heads) can only detect whether they are on the left endmarker " ¢ ", the right endmarker " \$ " or on a symbol in the input alphabet. (The reader is referred to [3] for formal definition of SMFA.) A SNSMFA is the SMFA whose heads are allowed to sense the presence of other head on the same input position. (The concept of "sensing" was introduced by Ibarra [2].)

By $\mathcal{L}$(NSPk-HFA) we denote the class of languages accepted by the one-way nondeterministic simple k-head finite automata. The following open problems are given in [1] :

(1) Are the one-way nondeterministic resp. deterministic sensing two-head finite automata more powerful than one-way nondeterministic resp. deterministic two-head finite automata ?

(2) For each $k \geq 2$, is $\mathcal{L}$(NSPk-HFA) closed under concatenation ?

(3) Is $\bigcup_k \mathcal{L}$(NSPk-HFA) closed under concatenation ?

We will show that the class $\mathcal{L}$(NSPk-HFA) is not closed under concatenation for any $k \geq 2$ and that the class $\bigcup_k \mathcal{L}$(NSPk-HFA) is closed under concatenation. Unfortunately we were not able to solve the first problem listed above.

We consider the family of languages recognized by one-way k-head deterministic [sensing] finite state automata $\mathcal{L}$(1DFA(k)) [$\mathcal{L}$(1DSeFA(k))] in the second part of the paper. Let us describe informally a one-way k-head deterministic finite state automaton 1DFA(k). It is a device, which consists of a finite-state control, a single read-only input tape with a right endmarker \$ and k one-way reading heads which move on the tape from left to right. The automaton 1DFA(k) starts its work on a word in the initial state q_0 with reading heads adjusted on the first symbol of the input word. It works in steps. In one step an automaton reads one symbol by one of its reading heads [in every state it is unambiguously determined which of the heads can read] and changes its state depending on the current state and the symbol read. At the same time the head,which is reading in this step, may move one symbol to the right or remain stationary. An automaton 1DFA(k) accepts an input word v in case it ends its work on the input word v in a final state with all reading heads adjusted on the endmarker \$.

The automaton 1DSeFA(k) is almost the same device as 1DFA(k) . The difference being the fact the automaton 1DSeFA(k) can detect coincidence of the heads.

The notion of multihead finite automaton was apparently first described by Piatkowski [5] and wos soon thereafter exetensively studied by Rosenberg [6,7]. In [2] Rosenberg presented the assertion that the class $\mathcal{L}$(1DFA(k)) in not closed under concatenation, Kleene star and reversal. The proof of this assertion wos insufficient as it is pointed out by Floyd [8] .

We show in the second part of this paper that the families of languages $\mathcal{L}$(1DFA(k)) and $\mathcal{L}$(1DSeFA(k)) are not closed under concatenation, Kleene star and reversal for $k \geq 2$. This solves the open problems mentioned by Sudborough [9] . These results are continuation of the paper [10] , where it is shown, that $\mathcal{L}$(1DFA(2)) is not closed under concatenation with regular sets, Kleene star and reversal, but the proof's technique is quite different.

1. $\mathcal{L}$(NSPk-HFA) and concatenation.

<u>Theorem 1.</u> The class $\bigcup_k \mathcal{L}$(NSPk-HFA) is closed under concatenation.

<u>Proof.</u> The proof is very similar to the proof of the Theorem 6.2.(2)in [1]. Let M_1 resp. M_2 be a NSPk_1-HFA resp. a NSPk_2-HFA. We consider the NSP(k_1+k_2-1)-HFA M which acts as follows. While the reading head of M reads the first part of the input word x, M simulates (by using the reading head and k_1-1 counting heads) the action of M_1 on the first part, and simultaneously M moves other k_2-1 counting heads by the same way as moves the reading head. Let $H_1, H_2, \ldots, H_{k_1}$ be the heads of M simulating the action of M_1. For each $i = 1, 2, \ldots, k_1$, M nondeterministically gusses the arrival of the head H_i at the right end of the first part of x, and after that, head H_i stop. If M finds out that M_1 accepts the first part in simulating the action of M_1 in this way, M next proceeds to read the latter part of x by simulating by using the reading head and other k_2-1 counting heads the action of M_2, and simultaneously M moves k_1-1 counting heads, which were used for simulation of M_1, by the same way as moves the reading head. M accepts x iff the latter part is also accepted by M_2, and if the reading head and all k_1-1 counting heads which were used for simulation of M_1 reach the right endmarker \$ at the same time.

To prove the following theorem, we will use a generalized technique of Ibarra et al. in [3] and the language $\{a^n b^n \mid n \geq 1\}^k$ suggested by the authors of [1] .

<u>Theorem 2.</u> The class $\mathcal{L}$(NSPk-HFA) is not closed under concatenation for any $k \geq 2$.

<u>Proof.</u> For each $k \geq 2$, let L_k be the language $\{a^n b^n \mid n \geq 1\}^k$. To

prove this theorem, it is sufficient to show that the language $L_{(k+1)k}$ cannot be recognized by any one-way nondeterministic simple k-head finite automaton because the language L_1 is recognized by an NSP2-HFA.

To the contrary we suppose that there is an NSPk-HFA A recognizing $L_{(k+1)k}$, and A has m states. (Without loss of generality we assume that input tape of A has no left endmarker.) To prove that $L_{(k+1)k}$ cannot be recognized by A, first we will show, by using a pumping technique for the sequence of configurations, that if A accepts w, then A accepts a word w' not in $L_{(k+1)k}$.

A <u>configuration</u> of the automaton A is a (k+1)-tuple $(q, h_1,\dots,h_k)$, where q is the state of the finite control and h_i is the position of the i-th head. An <u>increment</u> of the automaton A is a (k+1)-tuple $(q, h_1,\dots,h_k)$, where q is the state of the finite control a each h_i is either 0 or 1. (Informally, the increment describes moving the heads at one step of computation.) Let the sequence of the configurations $c_o, c_1,\dots c_t$ be a computation of A on an input word. We say that the sequence of the increments $d_o, d_1,\dots,d_{t-1}$, where $d_i=(q^i, h_1^{i+1}-h_1^i,\dots$ $\dots,h_k^{i+1}-h_k^i)$ if $c_i=(q^i, h_1^i,\dots,h_k^i)$ and $c_{i+1}=(q^{i+1}, h_1^{i+1},\dots,h_k^{i+1})$ for each $i=0, 1,\dots,t-1$, is the sequence of the increments of the computation $c_o, c_1,\dots,c_t$. A <u>segment</u> is the arbitrary finite sequence of the increments. The <u>length of the segment</u> is the number of the increments in it. Let $d_i=(q^i,h_1^i,\dots,h_k^i)$, $d_{i+1}=(q^{i+1}, h_1^{i+1},\dots,h_k^{i+1}),\dots$ $\dots,d_j=(q^j, h_1^j,\dots,h_k^j)$ be a segment. If $q^i=q^j$, then we say that the segment $d_i, d_{i+1},\dots,d_{j-1}$ is the <u>q^i- cycle</u>; we say that the k-tuple $(\sum_{l=i}^{j-1} h_1^l,\dots,\sum_{l=i}^{j-1} h_k^l)$ is the <u>parameter</u> of this cycle. A cycle is the q-cycle for some state q. If s_1 is the segment $d_h,\dots d_i$, and s_2 is the segment $d_j,\dots,d_l$, then by s_1, s_2 we denote the segment $d_h,\dots,d_i,d_j,\dots,d_e$.

For n large enough, we consider the word $w=y_1y_2\dots y_k$ in $L_{(k+1)k}$, where $y_i=y=x_1x_2\dots x_{k+1}$ for $i=1,2,\dots k$, and $x_i=x=a^nb^n$ for $i=1, 2,\dots,k+1$. Let the sequence of the configurations $c_o, c_1,\dots,c_t$

be an accepting computation of A on the word w with the sequence of the increments $d_o, d_1, \ldots, d_{t-1}$. Since A has only $k-1$ counting heads there is an index j_o, $1 \leq j_o \leq k$, such that no counting head reaches the right endmarker \$ while the reading head reads the subword y_{j_o} during the computation $c_o, c_1, \ldots, c_t$. Now we fix arbitrary number i_o, $1 \leq i_o \leq k+1$. Let $c_f, c_{f+1}, \ldots, c_g$, $0 \leq f < g \leq t$, be the subsequence of the configurations of the sequence $c_o, c_1, \ldots, c_t$ such that exactly at c_f resp. c_g the reading head enters resp. leaves the i_o-th subword a^n of the word y_{j_o}. Since during the computation $c_f, c_{f+1}, \ldots, c_g$, the reading head reads the symbol "a" only and no couting head reaches the right endmarker \$, we have

<u>Fact 1.</u> If the segment $d_f, \ldots, d_g$ can be written in the form s_1, p_1, s_2, p_2, s_3, where s_1, s_2, s_3 are the segments and p_1, p_2 are the q-cycles (for some internal state q), there is an accepting computation of A on w with the sequence of the increments $d_o, \ldots, d_{f-1}, s_1, p_1, p_2, s_2, s_3, d_{f+1}, \ldots, d_{t-1}$.

Since every segment with the length at least $m+1$ contains a cycle (because A has exactly m internal states), by Fact 1, we have

<u>Fact 2.</u> There is a permutation of the increments $d_f, \ldots, d_g$ which can be written in the form

$$(*) \qquad s_1, p_1, s_2, p_2, \ldots, s_r, p_r, s_{r+1},$$

where $r \leq m$, each s_i is a segment with the length at most m, each p_i can be written in the form $p_i = p_i^1, p_i^2, \ldots, p_i^{l_i}$, where each p_i^j is a q^i- cycle with the length at most m and there is an accepting computation of A on w with the sequence of the increments $d_o, \ldots, d_{f-1}, s_1, p_1, s_2, p_2, \ldots, s_r, p_r, s_{r+1}, d_{g+1}, \ldots, d_{t-1}$.

<u>Fact 3</u>. Let p_i^j's be the cycles from the Fact 2. For the segment $(*)$, there is a parameter $v = (v_1, \ldots, v_k)$ with $v_1 > 0$ and $0 \leq v_i \leq m$ for $i = 1, 2, \ldots, k$, such that the number of the cycles p_i^j with the parameter v is at least $(n-(m+1)m)/(m(m+1)^k)$.

<u>Proof.</u> Since the reading head crosses the i_o-th subword a^n of the word y_{j_o} during the part of the computation corresponding to the segment $(*)$, there is n increments (in the segment $(*)$) at which the reading head is moved to the right. Clearly, at least $n-(m+1)m$ increments from these n increments are contained in the cycles p_i^j, because $r \leq m$

and the length of each s_i is at most m, see Fact 2. This implies, that the number of the cycles p_i^j with parameters whose first component is greater than zero is at least $(n-(m+1)m)/m$. Since the number of all different parameters, for the cycles with the length at most m, is at most $(m+1)^k$, then there is a parameter v such that the number of the cycles p_i^j with the parameter v is at least $(n-(m+1)m)/(m(m+1)^k)$.

Since the number i_o, $1 \leq i_o \leq k+1$, was selected arbitrarly, by Fact 3, we have that there is an accepting computation of A on w with the sequence of the increments

$$(**) \qquad u_1,\ z_1,\ u_2,\ z_2,\ldots,u_{k+1},\ z_{k+1},\ u_{k+2} \ ,$$

where for $i = 1, 2,\ldots,k+1$, z_i is the segment corresponding to the part of this accepting computation at which the reading head reads the i-th subword a^n of the word y_{j_o} , and z_i is of the form as in $(*)$,and each u_i is a segment. Further, by Fact 3, there are the parameters $v^i = (v_1^i,\ldots,v_k^i)$ for $i = 1, 2,\ldots,k+1$, with $v_1^i > 0$ and $0 \leq v_j^i \leq m$ for $i = 1, 2,\ldots,k+1$ and $j = 1, 2,\ldots,k$, such that the number of the cycles with parameter v^i is at least $(n-(m+1)m)/(m(m+1)^k)$ in the segment z_i for $i = 1, 2,\ldots,k+1$. Clearly there are the rational numbers $r_1,\ldots$ $\ldots,r_{k+1}$ such that

$$(***) \qquad \sum_{i=1}^{k+1} r_i v^i = \bar{0} \ ,$$

where $\bar{0} = (\underbrace{0,\ldots,0}_{k\text{-times}})$ and $r_i \neq 0$ for some $1 \leq i \leq k+1$, because the vectors $v^i \neq \bar{0}$ are linearly dependet. Without loos of generality we can assume that r_i's in $(***)$are integers.

Let w be the word as above. Now we consider the word $w' = y_1\ldots$ $\ldots y_{j_o-1}\, y'_{j_o}\, y_{j_o+1}\ldots y_k$, where $w = y_1\ldots y_k$, $y'_{j_o} = a^{n_1}b^n a^{n_2}b^n\ldots a^{n_{k+1}}b^n$, and $n_i = n+r_i v_1^i$ for $i = 1, 2,\ldots,k+1$. (Note that all $n_i > 0$ for n large enough.) Since $r_i \neq 0$ for some i and $v_1^i > 0$ for all i, see above, then $n_i \neq n$ for some i an therefore $w' \notin L_{(k+1)k}$. To prove this theorem we show that the word w' will be accepted by A , too. By $|y|$ we denote the length of the word y. By $(**)$, $(***)$ and by

$$|y'_{j_o}| = 2(k+1)n + \sum_{i=1}^{k+1} r_i v_1^i = 2(k+1)n+0 = |y_{j_o}|$$

, we have that there is

an accepting computation of A on w' with the sequence of the increment $u_1, z'_1, u_2, z'_2, \ldots u_{k+1}, z'_{k+1}, u_{k+2}$, where the segment z'_i is obtained by inserting if ($r_i \geq 0$) or by deleting (if $r_i < 0$) r_i cycles with parameter v^i from the segment z_i for $i = 1, 2, \ldots, k+1$. (Note that it can be deleted r_i cycles with parameter v^i from the segment z_i, because this segment contains at least $(n-(m+1)m)/(m(m+1)^k)$ cycles with the parameter v^i, see above, and $(n-(m+1)m)/(m(m+1)^k) \geq r_i$ for n large enough.)

2. Closure properties of $\mathcal{L}$(1DFA(k)) and $\mathcal{L}$(1DSeFA(k)).

A configuration of the 1DFA(k) [1DSeFA(k)] working on the input word w is a (k+1)-tuple $(q, i_1, i_2, \ldots, i_k)$ where q is the state of the finite state control and i_j is the position of the j-th head on the input word w.

Let us consider the following languages for arbitrary natural f.

$C_f(n) = \{ucw_1cw_2c\ldots cw_fcw_fc\ldots cw_2cw_1 \mid |u| = |w_i| = n$ and $u, w_i \in \{a,b\}^*$ for $1 \leq i \leq f\}$;

$D_f(n) = \{v_1dv_1d \mid v_1 \in C_f(n)\}$;

$E_f(n) = \{ucw_1cw_2c\ldots cw_fcw_{f+1}c\ldots cw_{2f-1}cw_{2f} \mid |u| = |w_i| = n$ and $u, w_i \in \{a,b\}^*$ for $1 \leq i \leq 2f$ and $\exists\, j \in \{1,2,\ldots,f\}$ that $w_j \neq w_{2f-j+1}\}$

$F_f(n) = \{v_1cw_1cw_2c\ldots cw_fcw_fc\ldots cw_2cw_1dv_2cw_1cw_2c\ldots cw_fcw_fc\ldots cw_2cw_1d \mid |v_1| = |v_2| = |w_i| = n$; $v_1, v_2, w_i \in \{a,b\}^*$ for $1 \leq i \leq f$ and $v_1 \neq v_2\}$

Let $C_f = \bigcup_{n=1}^{\infty} C_f(n)$; $D_f = \bigcup_{n=1}^{\infty} D_f(n)$; $E_f = \bigcup_{n=1}^{\infty} E_f(n)$ and $F_f = \bigcup_{n=1}^{\infty} F_f(n)$ for arbitrary $f = 1,2,3\ldots$

Theorem 1 Let L be an arbitrary language fulfiling the following conditions :

(1) $L \supseteq C_f \cup D_f$

(2) $L \cap (E_f \cup F_f) = \emptyset$

Let $f = \binom{k}{2}$, where $k \geq 2$. Then L is not in $\mathcal{L}$(1DSeFA(k)).

Idea of the proof : The proof is done by contradiction.

We assume that there exists and 1DSeFA(k) automaton A which recognizes a language L satisfying (1) and (2). We will show, that if the automaton A accepts every word in $C_f \cup D_f$, where $f = \binom{k}{2}$, then A accepts a word y\` which belongs to $E_f \cup F_f$.

A <u>prominent configuration</u> is a configuration of the computation on the word y in $C_f \cup D_f$, from which the automaton A moves one of its heads on the symbol c, d or \$. The number of the prominent configuration is bounded by a polynomial in n, let us say p\`(n).

We call the subsequence of prominent configuration of the computation on the word x the <u>pattern</u> of x.

Let y be a word in $C_f(n) \cup D_f(n)$ for sufficienly large n. Each word $y \in C_f(n) \cup D_f(n)$ has initial subvord v_1 in $C_f(n)$. The number of all words in $C_f(n)$ is

$$2^{\left[\binom{k}{2}+1\right]n}$$

We shall consider the initial computation on the word y, which begins in the initial configuration and ends in the configuration in which one of the heads reads trough the whole word v_1. The number of patterns of initial computations of all $v_1 \in C_f(n)$ is bounded by a polynom p(n), because the length of the pattern is a constant. Then there exist

$$\frac{2^{\left[\binom{k}{2}+1\right]n}}{p(n)}$$

different words v_1 in $C_f(n)$ with the same pattern d of initial computation.

Now, we distinguish the following two cases accoding to the last prominent configuration $(q, i_1, i_2, \ldots i_k)$ of the pattern d.

(1) All $i_j > n$ for $j = 1,2,\ldots,k$.

(2) There exists $j \in \{1,2,\ldots,k\}$ such that $i_j \leq n$.

In case (1) we consider the input word y in $D_f(n)$. Let $x = w_1cw_2\ldots$ $\ldots cw_fcw_fc\ldots cw_2cw_1$. For sufficiently large n it can be shown, that there exist two different words $y_1 = u_1cxdu_1cxd$ and $y_2 = u_2cxdu_2cxd$ with the same pattern. Since in this pattern A cannot read the both words u_1 in y_1 (and both words u_2 in y_2) at the same time [i.e., with one of it heads on the first occurrence and another head on the second occurrence of this word], the automaton A accepts the word $y' = u_1cxdu_2cxd$, which belongs to $F_f(n)$.

In case (2) we consider the input word y in $C_f(n)$. It can be shown [for sufficiently large n] that there exist two different words

$$y_1 = ucw_2 \ldots cw_{i_o} c \ldots cw_f cw_f c \ldots cw_{i_o} c \ldots cw_1 \quad \text{and}$$

$$y_2 = ucw_1 \ldots cw'_{i_o} c \ldots cw_f cw_f c \ldots cw'_{i_o} c \ldots cw_1$$

with the same pattern in which the subwords w_{i_o} $[w'_{i_o}]$ are not read at the same time. The automaton A accepts (similarly as in Yao and Rivest [11]) the word $y' = ucw_1 c \ldots cw_{i_o} c \ldots cw_f cw_f c \ldots cw'_{i_o} c \ldots cw_1$, which belongs to $E_f(n)$.

<u>Corollary 1.</u> Let L be an arbitrary language fulfilling the following conditions :

(3) $\quad L \supseteq \{e\} \cdot C_f \cup \{e\} \cdot D_f$

(4) $\quad L \cap (\{e\} \cdot E_f \cup \{e\} \cdot F_f) = \emptyset$

Let $f = \binom{k}{2}$, where $k \geq 2$. Then the language L is not in $\mathfrak{L}(\text{1DSeFA}(k))$.

<u>Proof.</u> It is a matter of easy technical considerations to show that if there would exist a language L' satisfying the conditions of Corollary 1 such that $L' \in \mathfrak{L}(\text{1DSeFA}(k))$, then there would exist a language L'' fulfilling the conditions of Theorem 1 such that $L'' \in \mathfrak{L}(\text{1DSeFA}(k))$.

<u>Theorem 2.</u> For $k \geq 2$ the families $\mathfrak{L}(\text{1DSeFA}(k))$ and $\mathfrak{L}(\text{1DFA}(k))$ are not closed under concatenation.

<u>Proof.</u> Let us consider the following languages :

$L_1 = \{a,b\}^* c \cup \{\varepsilon\}$, $L_2 = \{udud \mid u \in \{a,b,c\}^*\} \cup \{\varepsilon\}$,

$G_f = \{w_1cw_2c \ldots cw_f cw_f c \ldots cw_2cw_1 \mid w_i \in \{a,b\}^* \text{ for } 1 \leq i \leq f\} \cup \{\varepsilon\}$

for $f = 1,2,3 \ldots$

Clearly $L_1 \in \mathfrak{L}(\text{1DFA}(1))$, $L_2 \in \mathfrak{L}(\text{1DFA}(2))$ and $G_f \in \mathfrak{L}(\text{1DFA}(k))$ for $f \leq \binom{k}{2}$. But the language $L_1L_2G_{\binom{k}{2}}$ is not in $\mathfrak{L}(\text{1DSeFA}(k))$, because it satisfies the conditions (1) and (2) of Theorem 1 .

<u>Theorem 3.</u> For $k \geq 2$ the families $\mathfrak{L}(1DSeFA(k))$ and $\mathfrak{L}(1DFA(k))$ are not closed under reversal.

<u>Proof.</u> The language $L_2 \cup \{a,b\}^* c\ G_{\binom{k}{2}}$ does not belong to $\mathfrak{L}(1DSeFA(k))$ but the language $L_2^R \cup G_{\binom{k}{2}}\ c\ \{a,b\}^*$ belongs to $\mathfrak{L}(1DFA(k))$.

<u>Theorem 4.</u> For $k \geq 2$ the families $\mathfrak{L}(1DFA(k))$ and $\mathfrak{L}(1DSeFA(k))$ are not closed under Kleene star.

<u>Proof.</u> Let us consider the language $L_5 = \{e\} \cdot L_2 \cup \{a,b\}^* c\ G_{\binom{k}{2}} \cup \{e\}$, which belongs to $\mathfrak{L}(1DFA(k))$. Since L_5^* satisfies the conditions (3) and (4) of Corollary 1, L_5^* is not in $\mathfrak{L}(1DSeFA(k))$.

Several known results follow as easy consequences of Theorem 1.

<u>Corollary 2.</u> For $k \geq 2$ the class $\mathfrak{L}(1DFA(k))$ $[\mathfrak{L}(1DSeFA(k))]$ is not closed under intersection and union.

<u>Proof.</u> Since the class $\mathfrak{L}(1DFA(k))$ $[\mathfrak{L}(1DSeFA(k))]$ is closed under complement it suffices to show that $\mathfrak{L}(1DFA(k))$ $[\mathfrak{L}(1DSeFA(k))]$ is not closed under union. The languages L_2 and $\{a,b\}^* \cdot c\ G_{\binom{k}{2}}$ belongs to $\mathfrak{L}(1DFA(k))$, but the language $L_2 \cup \{a,b\}^* c\ G_{\binom{k}{2}}$ is not in $\mathfrak{L}(1DSeFA(k))$.

<u>Corollary 3.</u> For $k \geq 2$ the classes $\mathfrak{L}(1DFA(k))$ and $\mathfrak{L}(1DSeFA(k))$ are not closed under substitution, homomorphism and nonerasing homomorphism.

<u>Proof.</u> To proove this corollary, it is sufficient to show that $\mathfrak{L}(1DFA(k))$ and $\mathfrak{L}(1DSeFA(k))$ are not closed under nonerasing homomorphism. Clearly the language $L_7 = \{e\}\ L_2 \cup \{g\}\ \{a,b\}^* \cdot \{c\} \cdot G_{\binom{k}{2}}$ belongs to $\mathfrak{L}(1DFA(k))$.
Let us define a nonerasing homomorphism h as follows :

$h(e) = h(g) = e$, $h(a) = a$, $h(b) = b$, $h(c) = c$, $h(d) = d$.

Then $h(L_7)$ satisfies the conditions (3) and (4) of Corollary 1.

Corollary 4. For $k \geq 2$:

$$\mathcal{L}(1DSeFA(k)) \subsetneq \mathcal{L}(1DSeFA(k+1))$$

$$\mathcal{L}(1DFA(k)) \subsetneq \mathcal{L}(1DFA(k+1)) \qquad [11]$$

Proof. The language $L_2 \cup \{a,b\}^* \cdot \{c\} \cdot G_{\binom{k}{2}}$ belongs to $\mathcal{L}(1DFA(k+1))$.

Acknowledgments

This work was supported in part by the grant SPZV I - 5 - 7/7 .

We would like to thank Branislav Rovan, Akira Nakamura and Katsushi Inoue for their comments concerning this work.

References

1. K. Inoue, I. Takanami, A. Nakamura and T. Ae, One-Way Simple Multihead Finite Automata, Theoret. Comput. Sci. 9 (1979), 311 - 328 .

2. O. H. Ibarra, A Note On Semilinear Sets And Bounded-Reversal Multihead Pushdown Automata, Information Processing Lett. 3 (1974), 25-28.

3. O. H. Ibarra, S.K. Sahni and C.E. Kim, Finite Automata with Multiplication, Theoret. Comput. Sci. 2 (1976), 271 - 294 .

4. O. H. Ibarra and C. E. Kim, A Useful Device For Showing The Solvability Of Some Decision Problems, J. Comput . System. Sci. 13 (1976), 153 - 160 .

5. T.F. Piatkowski, N - head finite state machines, Ph. D. Dissertation, University of Michigan 1963 .

6. A. L. Rosenberg, On multihead finite automata, IBM J. R. and D. 10 (1966), 388 - 394 .

7. A. L. Rosenberg, Nonwriting extensions of finite automata, Ph. D. Dissertation, Harward University (1965).

8. R. W. Floyd, Review 14, 353 of above paper by Rosenberg, Computing Review 9 (1968) , 280 .

9. I. H. Sudborough, One-way multihead writing finite automata, Information and Control 30 (1976), 1 - 20 .

10. J. Hromkovič, Closure properties of the family of languages recognized by one-way two-head deterministic finite state automata, in Proceedings of the 10th International Symposium MFCS`81, Lecture Notes in Computer Science 118, Springer Verlag 1981, 304 - 313 .

11. A. C. Yao and R. L. Rivest, K + 1 heads are better then K, Journal of ACM 25 (1978), 337 - 340 .

CONDITIONS ENFORCING REGULARITY
OF CONTEXT-FREE LANGUAGES

by

A. Ehrenfeucht
D. Haussler
Dept. of Computer Science
University of Colorado at Boulder
Boulder, Colorado 80309
U.S.A.

and

G. Rozenberg
Institute of Applied Mathematics
and Computer Science
University of Leiden
Wassenaarseweg 80
2333 AL Leiden
The Netherlands

The class of context-free languages (L_{CF}) and the class of regular languages (L_{REG}), where $L_{REG} \subsetneq L_{CF}$, are important classes of languages within formal language theory (see, e.g., [H] and [S]). In order to understand the relationship between "context-freeness" and "regularity" one can proceed in (at least) two different ways:
(1). Investigate conditions under which a context-free grammar will generate a regular language; several restrictions of this kind are known, the self-embedding property is a classical example of such a condition (see, e.g., [H] and [S]).
(2). Investigate conditions which imposed on (the interrelationship of words in) a context-free language will guarantee that the generated language is regular. Several conditions of this kind are known (see, e.g., [ABBL] and [ABBN]).

This paper presents several results concerning the second line of research discussed above.

1. STRONG ITERATIVE PAIRS.

A fundamental property of context-free languages is the celebrated pumping property (see, e.g., [H] and [S]). Based on it the notion of an iterative pair was introduced in [B] (see also [ABBL]). If K is a language, $K \subseteq \Sigma^*$ then $p = (x,y,z,u,t)$ with $x,y,z,u,t \in \Sigma^*$ is an iterative pair in K if, for every $n \geq 1$, $xy^nzu^nt \in K$ where yu is a nonempty word. Such a synchronized pumping of subwords (y and u) in a word (xyzut) of K gives one a possibility (using one iterative pair only) to generate context-free but not regular languages (e.g., $\{a^nb^n : n \geq 1\}$). However, if one desynchronizes such a pumping, that is one requires that for all $r,s \geq 0$, $xy^rru^st \in K$ then an iterative pair yields a regular language. This observation leads one to a conjecture that if each iterative pair $p = (x,y,z,u,t)$ of a context-free language K is very degenerate (that is, for all $r,s \geq 0$, $xy^rzu^st \in K$) then K must be regular. This conjecture was shown in [B] to be true. An iterative pair allows only "upward pumping" expressed by the fact that $n \geq 1$ and in this sense it does not fully formalize the idea from the pumping lemma for context-free languages. There, also the "downward pumping" (i.e. $n = 0$) is allowed; it is well-known that this downward pumping is a very essential part of the pumping property for context-free languages.

If in the definition of an iterative pair we require "$n \geq 0$" rather than "$n \geq 1$" then we get a strong iterative pair. Then the "full version" of the conjecture mentioned above is:

Conjecture 1. If each strong iterative pair of a context-free language K is very degenerate then K is regular. □

We prove the following result.

Theorem 1. Conjecture 1 holds. □

The above result solves a problem remaining open since [B] ([B1] and [ABBL]). Also, Theorem 1 generalizes the above mentioned result from [B] which can be obtained directly from our theorem.

2. COMMUTATIVE LINEAR LANGUAGES.

Let for a word w, c(w) denote the commutative image of w, i.e., the set of all words that can be obtained from w be permuting (occurrences of) letters in it. For a language K, its commutative image is defined by $c(K) = \bigcup_{w \in K} c(w)$. We say that a language K is commutative if $K = c(K)$. Commutative languages form a very active research topic within formal language theory (see, e.g., [ABBL], [L1], [L2] and [SS]). In the literature there are several conjectures known which relate regularity and commutativeness of a formal language (see, e.g., [ABBL] and [L1]).

Linear languages form perhaps a closest natural extension of regular languages; the only difference being that in generating the former one can insert substrings inside strings already generated (rather than one the edge of strings only as happens in right-linear grammars). It seems quite feasible that requiring a linear language being commutative removes (the consequences of) the difference mentioned above. Hence the following was conjectured ([L1] and [L3]).

Conjecture 2. If a language K is commutative and linear then it is regular. □

We prove that the above conjecture is true; as a matter of fact we prove a more general result.

Let $\Sigma = \{a_1,\ldots,a_d\}$, $d \geq 1$, be an arbitrary but fixed alphabet. Let $\rho = v_0, v_1, \ldots, v_d$ be a sequence of vectors each of which has d components where every component is a nonnegative integer. We say that ρ is a base if and only if $v_i(j) = 0$ for all $i,j \geq 1$ such that $i \neq j$. The ρ-set, denoted $\theta(\rho)$, is defined by $\theta(\rho) = \{v \in \psi(\Sigma^*) : v = v_0 + \ell_1 v_1 + \ell_2 v_2 + \ldots + \ell_d v_d$ for some nonnegative integers $\ell_1,\ldots,\ell_d\}$,
where for a language K, $\Psi(K)$ denotes the set of Parikh vectors of K.

Let $X \subseteq \Psi(\Sigma^*)$. We say that X is periodic if and only if there exists a base ρ

such that $X = \theta(\rho)$. A language $K \subseteq \Sigma^*$ is <u>periodic</u> if and only if K is commutative and $\Psi(K)$ is periodic; the base of $\Psi(K)$ is also called the base of K and denoted <u>base</u>(K).

Let K be a periodic language where <u>base</u>(K) $= v_0, v_1, \ldots, v_d$. The size of K, denoted <u>size</u>(K), is defined by <u>size</u>(K) $= \max_{1 \le i \le d} \{\max\{v_0(i) \pmod{v_i(i)}, v_i(i)\}\}$, where, for a vector z, z(i) denotes the i-th component of z.

We prove the following result.

<u>Theorem 2</u>. Let $K \subseteq \Sigma^*$. If there exists a positive integer q such that for each $w \in K$ there exists a periodic language $L_w \subseteq K$ where $w \in L_w$ and size $(L_w) \le q$ then K is a finite union of periodic languages. □

Using this result we prove

<u>Theorem 3</u>. A language K is a commutative linear language if and only if K is a finite union of periodic languages. □

Since it is easily seen that each periodic language is regular the above result yields.

<u>Theorem 4</u>. Conjecture 2 holds. □

3. INCLUDING SQUARES.

A very fundamental structure of a string (or a language) is a repetition of its substrings. For example, a string x is said to be a <u>pure-square</u> if x = yy where y is a nonempty string, x is a <u>square</u> if x contains a pure square as a subword and x is <u>square-free</u> if it is not a square. Such structures were for the first time systematically investigated by Thue ([T]) and later on in very many papers concerning various branches of mathematics (see, e.g., [Be], [BEM], [S] and references therein). These structures turned out to be of fundamental importance in formal language theory (see, e.g., [ABBL], [B2], [S]). It was proved recently (see [ER] and [RW]) that the set of all squares (over an alphabet containing at least three letters) is not a context-free language. This result (and its proofs) support the rahter old and very powerful conjecture (see, e.g., [ABBL]).

<u>Conjecture 3</u>. If a context-free language $K \subseteq \Delta$ contains all squares over Δ^* then K is regular. □

The intuition behind this conjecture is that if a context-free grammar generates all squares over Δ then it generates "almost all words" over Δ. We are not able to either prove or disprove this conjecture, however, we can prove that a somewhat weaker form of this conjecture is false.

<u>Theorem 5</u>. There exists a context-free language $K \subseteq \{a,b\}^*$ such that K contains all pure squares over {a,b} and K is not regular. □

4. INSERTION SYSTEMS.

Insertion systems formalize a very special type of semi-Thue systems. An insertion system is a triple $G = (\Delta, I, w)$ where Δ is a finite nonempty alphabet. I is a finite nonempty subset of Δ^+ and $w \in \Delta^*$; I is called the insertion set of G and w is called the axiom of G. If $w = \Lambda$ then we say that G is pure. For $u \in \Delta^*$, $v \in \Delta^+$ we say that u directly derives v (in G) if $u = u_1u_2$ for some $u_1, u_2 \in \Delta$ and $v = u_1zu_2$ where $z \in I$; we write then $u \underset{G}{\Rightarrow} v$. Then $\overset{*}{\underset{G}{\Rightarrow}}$ denotes the transitive and the reflexive closure of the $\underset{G}{\Rightarrow}$ relation; if $u \overset{*}{\underset{G}{\Rightarrow}} v$ then we say that u derives v (in G). The language of G, denoted L(G), is defined by $L(G) = \{v \in \Delta^* : w \overset{*}{\underset{G}{\Rightarrow}} v$; it is referred to as an insertion language or a pure insertion language if G is pure.

The insertion languages form a very natural generalization of restricted Dyck languages. Clearly the class of insertion languages strictly contains the class of restricted Dyck languages and it is strictly contained in the class of context-free languages.

In order to establish conditions under which an insertion language becomes regular we have to prove two results first. These results are of independent interest: the first of them generalizes the celebrated theorem by Higman (see [Hi]) on ordering of words by the sparse subword relationship, the second one provides a new algebraic characterization of regular languages. In order to state those results we need some additional terminology.

Let us recall (see, e.g., [Hi] and [N]) that a relation that is reflexive and transitive is called a quasi-order (qo). If $\leq$ is a quasi-order defined on a set S, then $\leq$ is called a well-quasi-order (wqo) if and only if any of the following holds.

(1). $\leq$ is well founded on S, i.e., there exist no infinite strictly descending sequences of elements in S and each set of pairwise incomparable elements is finite.

(2). For each infinite sequence $\{x_i\}$ of elements in S there exist $i < j$ such that $x_i \leq x_j$.

(3). Each infinite sequence of elements in S contains an ascending infinite subsequence.

Given a finite nonempty set of words $I \subset \Delta^+$ we say that I is subword complete if and only if there exists a positive integer m such that for each word z in Δ^* longer than m there exist $u, v \in \Delta^*$ and $w \in I$ such that $z = uwv$.

Let I be a finite nonempty subset of Δ^+. For $x, y \in \Delta^*$ we write $x \leq_I y$ if $x \overset{*}{\underset{G}{\Rightarrow}} y$ where G is the insertion system (Δ, I, x).

Theorem 6. Let I be a finite nonempty subset of Δ^+. Then $\leq_I$ is a well-quasi-order if and only if I is subword complete. □

A quasi-order $\leq$ on Δ^* is called monotone if and only if for all $x_1, x_2, y_1, y_2 \in \Delta^*$ the following holds: if $x_1 \leq y_1$ and $x_2 \leq y_2$ then $x_1x_2 \leq y_1y_2$. A set $S \subseteq \Delta^*$ is upwards closed under $\leq$ if and only if whenever $x \in S$ and $x \leq y$ then $y \in S$.

Theorem 7. Let $K \subseteq \Delta^*$. K is regular if and only if there exists a monotone wqo $\leq$

on Δ^* such that K is upwards closed under $\leq$. □

Using the above two results we can provide the following characterization of regular insertion languages.

Theorem 8. Let K be the insertion language generated by an insertion system $G = (\Delta, I, w)$. Then K is regular if and only if I is subword complete. □

ACKNOWLEDGEMENTS.

The authors gratefully acknowledge the support of NSF grant MSC 79-03838.

REFERENCES

[ABBL] J.M. Autebert, J. Beauquier, L. Boasson and M. Latteux, Very small families of algebraic nonrational languages, in R. Book (ed.), Formal language theory; perspectives and open problems, 1980, Academic Press, London, New York, 89-108.

[ABBN] J.M. Autebert, J. Beauquier, L. Boasson and M. Nivat, Quelques problèmes ouverts en théorie des languages algébriques, 1979, RAIRO Informatique Theorique, v. 13, 363-379.

[BEM] D.R. Bean, A. Ehrenfeucht and G.F. McNulty, Avoidable patterns in strings of symbols, 1979, Pacific Journal of Mathematics, v. 85, n.2, 261-293.

[Be] J. Berstel, Sur les mots sans carré definis par un morphisme, 1979, Springer Lecture Notes in Computer Science, v. 71, 16-25.

[B] L. Boasson, Un critère de rationnalité des languages algébriques, in M. Nivat (ed.), Automata, Languages and Programming, 1973, North-Holland, Amsterdam, 359-365.

[B1] L. Boasson, private communication.

[ER] A. Ehrenfeucht and G. Rozenberg, On the separating power of EOL systems, RAIRO Informatique Theorique, to appear.

[H] M. Harrison, Introduction to formal language theory, 1978, Addison-Wesley, Reading, Massachusetts.

[Hi] G.H. Higman, Ordering by divisibility in abstract algebras, 1952, Proc. London Math. Society, v.3, 326-336.

[L1] M. Latteux, Ph.D. thesis, 1979, University of Lille.

[L2] M. Latteux, Cônes rationnels commutatifs, 1979, Journal of Computer and Systems Science, v. 18, 307-333.

[L3] M. Latteux, private communication.

[NW] C.St.J.A. Nash-Williams, A survey of the theory of well-quasi-ordered sets, in Combinatorial Structures and Their Applications, 1970, Gordon and Breach, New York, London, 293-300.

[RW] R. Ross and K. Winklman, Repetitive strings are not context-free, RAIRO Informatique Theorique, to appear.

[S] A. Salomaa, Jewels of formal language theory, 1981, Computer Science Press, Rockville, Maryland.

[T] A. Thue, Über unendliche Zeichenreihen, 1906, Norske Vid. Selsk.Skr., I Mat. Nat. Kl., Christiania, v. 7, 1-22.

REPETITIONS IN HOMOMORPHISMS AND LANGUAGES

A. Ehrenfeucht
Department of Computer Science
University of Colorado at Boulder
Boulder, Colorado, 80309
U.S.A.

and

G. Rozenberg
Institute of Applied Mathematics
and Computer Science
University of Leiden
Leiden, The Netherlands

Repetitions of subwords in words form the very fundamental (combinatorial) structure of formal languages. A systematic investigation of such repetitions was initiated by Thue in [T]. Since then this problem area was a subject of an active investigation in numerous areas of mathematics and in formal language theory (see, e.g., [BEM], [C], [D], [MH], [P] and [S1]). As a matter of fact, recently one notices a revival of interest in "Thue problems" among formal language theorists (see, e.g., [B], [H], [K], [S2]). In particular it was discovered that the theory of nonrepetitive sequences of Thue [T] is strongly related to the theory of (iterative) homomorphisms on free monoïds. It was pointed out in [B] that most (if not all) examples of the so called square-free sequences constructed in the literature are either DOL sequences or their codings (see, e.g. [RS]). In this way a very significant connection was established between the theory of (non)repetitive sequences and the theory of DOL systems. It seems that the benefit is two-sided: the theory of nonrepetitive sequences originates a new and very interesting research area within the theory of homomorphisms on free monoids as conceived in the theory of DOL systems while the theory of DOL systems provides a better insight into the theory of (non)repetitive sequences (see, e.g., [B] and [S2]).

Since repetitions of subwords form such a basic structure in formal languages the research concerning the general area of Thue problems forms a very fundamental part of research in formal language theory.

In this paper we investigate "the repetitive properties" of homomorphisms and languages.

1. A CHARACTERIZATION OF SQUARE-FREE HOMOMORPHISMS

Let Σ be a finite nonempty alphabet. A word $x \in \Sigma^+$ is called a *pure square* if $x = yy$ for some $y \in \Sigma^+$; x is called a *square* if x contains a subword which is a pure square, otherwise x is called *square-free* . We use $SQ(\Sigma)$ and $SF(\Sigma)$ to denote the set of all squares over Σ and the set of all square-free words over Σ respectively. For a finite nonempty alphabet Δ we use $HOM(\Sigma,\Delta)$ to denote the set of all homomorphisms from Σ^*

into Δ^*. A homomorphism $h \in HOM(\Sigma,\beta)$ is called *square-free* if $(h(x) \in SF(\Delta)$ whenever $x \in SF(\Sigma)$. Hence square-free homomorphisms are homomorphisms preserving the square-free property; they form an important subject of investigation in the theory of (non) repetitive sequences and languages (see, e.g., [B],[S]).

Let $h \in HOM(\Sigma,\Delta)$. Then

$$T_h = \{w \in SF(\Sigma) : (\exists a,b)_\Sigma (\exists u)_{\Sigma^*} [w = aub \text{ and either } h(u) \sqsubseteq h(a) \text{ or } h(u) \sqsubseteq h(b)]\},$$

where for words x, y we write $x \sqsubseteq y$ if x is a subword of y. Also let

$$T_0 = \{w \in SF(\Sigma) : |w| \leq 3\}.$$

We have obtained the following structural characterization of square-free homomorphisms.

Theorem 1. Let $h \in HOM(\Sigma,\Delta)$. Then h is square-free if and only if $h(T_0 \cup T_h) \subseteq SF(\Delta)$. □

A well-known result by Thue (see [T] and also [BEM]) says that a sufficient condition for a homomorphism $h \in HOM(\Sigma,\Delta)$ to be square-free is as follows:

(1). $(\forall a,b)_\Sigma [h(a) \sqsubseteq h(b)$ implies $a = b]$ and

(2). $h(T_0) \sqsubseteq SF(\Delta)$.

It is easily seen that this theorem by Thue is a simple corollary of our Theorem 1.

Now, for a homomorphism $h \in HOM(\Sigma,\Delta)$ let $maxr(h) = \max\{|h(a)| : a \in \Sigma\}$ and $minr(h) = \min\{|h(a)| : a \in \Sigma\}$, where for a word x, $|x|$ denotes its length. In [B] Berstel proves the following result:

a homomorphism $h \in HOM(\Sigma,\Sigma)$ is square-free if and only if $h(x) \in SF(\Sigma)$ for each square-free word x such that $|x| \leq 2 + \left\lfloor 2 \frac{maxr(h)}{minr(h)} \right\rfloor$.

Based on our theorem 1 we can prove the following result.

Theorem 2. A homomorphism $h \in HOM(\Sigma,\Sigma)$ is square-free if and only if $h(x) \in SF(\Sigma)$ for each square-free word x such that $|x| \leq 2 + \left\lfloor \frac{maxr(h)}{minr(h)} \right\rfloor$. □

Since $\left\lfloor \frac{2maxr(h)}{minr(h)} \right\rfloor \geq \left\lfloor \frac{maxr(h)}{minr(h)} \right\rfloor + 1$ our bound is strictly better than this of the Berstel theorem mentioned above.

2. ON SQUARE-FREENESS TEST SETS

The characterization results discussed in the last section provide one with "test sets" for testing the square-freeness of a homomorphism. A homomorphism $h \in HOM(\Sigma,\Delta)$ is square-free if h(x) is square-free for all $x \in SF(\Sigma)$. Since $SF(\Sigma)$ is infinite for $\# \Sigma \geq 3$ (where for a finite set A, #A denotes its cardinality) such a definition is not effective. On the other hand the results from the last section allow one, given a homomorphism h, to construct effectively a finite set F_h (of square-free words), such that h is square-free if and only if h(x) is square-free for every $x \in F_h$. In this sense such a set F_h is called a *square-free test set*. We will look now more closely into square-freeness test sets referred in this paper simply as *test sets*.

Thus given a homomorphism $h \in HOM(\Sigma,\Delta)$ we say that a set $X \subseteq \Sigma^+$ *tests* h if and only if $(h(X) \subseteq SF(\Delta))$ implies $(h(SF(\Sigma)) \subseteq SF(\Delta))$. Consequently Theorem 2 can be restated as follows.

Theorem 2'. Let $h \in HOM(\Sigma,\Delta)$. Then $\{w \in SF(\Sigma) : |w| \leq 2 + \left\lfloor \frac{maxr(h)}{minr(h)} \right\rfloor \}$. □

In order to make the test set smaller one would like to replace the "≤" sign from the above result by the "=" sign. Indeed this can be done under an additional assumption (the reader should be warned that the construction is not trivial!). In what follows, for a finite set A, #A denotes the cardinality of A.

Theorem 3. Let $h \in HOM(\Sigma,\Delta)$, $\#\Sigma \geq 3$ and let $m \geq 2 + \left\lfloor \frac{maxr(h)}{minr(h)} \right\rfloor$.
Then $\{w \in SF(\Sigma) : |w| = m\}$ tests h. □

It is easily seen that the above theorem is false if $\#\Sigma < 3$.

The tests sets we have considered above were "adjusted to h" in the sense that very specific parameters concerning h were used to define these test sets (namely $maxr(h)$ and $minr(h)$). A natural next step is to consider test sets which will be universal for all homomorphisms in $HOM(\Sigma,\Delta)$ with fixed Σ and Δ. This can be done as follows.
Let $\Sigma_\omega = \{a_1,a_2,\ldots.\}$ be a fixed infinite alphabet and then let, for each $n \geq 1$, $\Sigma_n = \{a_1,\ldots,a_n\}$. Let $n,m \geq 1$. The family $T(n,m)$ of (n,m) *test sets* is defined as follows:

$X \in T(n,m)$ if and only if

$X \subseteq SF(\Sigma_n)$ and $(\forall h)_{HOM(\Sigma_n,\Sigma_m)} [h(X) \subseteq SF(\Sigma_m)$ if and only if h is square-free].

Clearly, we are interested in the existence of *finite* (n,m) test sets.
Here we have the following result.

Theorem 4. Let $n,m \geq 1$. Then $T(n,m)$ contains a finite nonempty set if and only if either $n \leq 3$ or $m \leq 2$. □

3. REPETITIVENESS AND STRONG REPETITIVENESS

An example of repetitions (of subwords in words) in formal languages is the effect of pumping in an infinite context-free language. Then we get a word, say w, such that all its powers (repetitions) appear in words of the given language. This idea can be formalized in two different (weaker and stronger) forms. (For a language K, $sub(K)$ denotes the set of its subwords).

A language $K \subseteq \Sigma^*$ is called *repetitive* if and only if
$(\forall n)_{\geq 1} (\exists w)_{\Sigma^+} [w^n \in sub(K)]$; K is called *strongly repetitive* if
$(\exists w)_{\Sigma^+} (\forall n)_{\geq 1} [w^n \in sub(K)]$.

Clearly, every strongly repetitive language is also repetitive, but the converse does not have to be true in general. As the direct consequence of the pumping lemma we get that every infinite context-free language is strongly repetitive, and so repetitiveness implies strong repetitiveness in a trivial way.

However the situation in DOL languages is much more involved. The pumping-like properties do not hold for DOL languages and "detecting" repetitiveness in a DOL language becomes a challenging problem. We have obtained the following result.

Theorem 5. It is decidable whether or not L(G) is repetitive for an arbitrary DOL system.

This result yields also the decidability of the strong repetitiveness property because we have the following.

Theorem 6. Let K be a DOL language. Then K is repetitive if and only if K is strongly repetitive.

4. COPYING SYSTEMS

From the existing literature concerning "Thue problems" one can certainly draw the conclusion that this problem area is mathematically quite challenging. On the other hand repetitions (in languages and homomorphisms) play an important role in formal language theory and so their nature should be well understood. Thus the topic of repetitions (in languages and homomorphisms) forms an interesting and well motivated research topic.

A way to understand repetitiveness in formal languages is to consider repetitions in their "pure grammatical form", that is introduce grammatical systems that explicitly use repetitions as the way of language generation.

A *copying system* is an ordered pair $G = (\Sigma, w)$ where Σ is a finite nonempty alphabet and $n \in \Sigma^*$. Then for words $u, w \in \Sigma^*$ we say that u *directly derives* w, written $u \underset{G}{\Rightarrow} w$, if $u = xyz$ and $w = xyyz$ for some $x, y, z \in \Sigma^*$. Then $\overset{*}{\underset{G}{\Rightarrow}}$ denotes the reflexive and the transitive closure of $\underset{G}{\Rightarrow}$. The *language of* G is defined by $L(G) = \{x \in \Sigma^* : w \overset{*}{\underset{G}{\Rightarrow}} x\}$; L(G) is referred to as a *copying language*. Analyzing copying languages turns out to be a difficult task. (The reader should consider the problem of proving or disproving whether the language of the copying system $G = (\{a,b,c\}, abc)$ is context-free).

We will provide now a result allowing one to prove that certain copying languages are not regular.

Given a copying system $G = (\Sigma, w)$, the relation $\overset{*}{\underset{G}{\Rightarrow}}$ is a partial order on Σ^*. Hence for a language $K \subseteq \Sigma^*$ we can distinguish the set of minimal elements of K, $min(K) = \{x \in K : (\forall y)_K[\text{if } y \overset{*}{\underset{G}{\Rightarrow}} x \text{ then } x = y]\}$. Also we say that K is *upward closed* under $\overset{*}{\underset{G}{\Rightarrow}}$ if $(\forall x,y)_{\Sigma^*}[\text{if } x \in K \text{ and } x \overset{*}{\underset{G}{\Rightarrow}} y \text{ then } y \in K]$. In what follows, for a word z, $alph(z)$ denotes the set of letters occurring in z.

Theorem 6. Let $G = (\Sigma, w)$ be a copying system and let $K \subseteq \Sigma^*$. If

(1). K is regular,

(2). K is upwards closed under $\overset{*}{\underset{G}{\Rightarrow}}$, and

(3). $(\exists x)_K[\#alph(x) \geq 3]$

then $min(K)$ is infinite.

As an application of this result we can show that

Corollary. Let G = ({a,b,c}, abc). Then L(G) is not regular. □

We don't know of any other way to prove the above corollary.

ACKNOWLEDGEMENTS

The authors gratefully acknowledge the support of NSF grant MSC 79-03838.

REFERENCES

[B] J. Berstel, Sur les mots sans carré définis par un morphisme, 1979, *Springer Lecture Notes in Computer Science*, v71, 16-25.

[BEM] D.R. Bean, A. Ehrenfeucht and G.F. Mc Nulty, Avoidable patterns in strings of symbols, 1979, *Pacific Journal of Mathematics*, v85, no.2, 261-293.

[C] A. Cobham, Uniform tag sequences, *Mathematical Systems Theory*, 1972, v.6, n.2, 164-191.

[D] F.M. Dekking, Combinatorial and statistical properties of sequences generated by substitutions, 1980, Ph.D. Thesis, University of Nijmegen, Holland.

[H] M. Harrison, *Introduction to formal language theory*, 1978, Addison-Wesley, Reading, Massachussetts.

[K] J. Karhumaki, On cubic-free ω-words generated by binary morphisms, 1981 to appear.

[MH] M. Morse and G. Hedlund, Unending chess, symbolic dynamics and a problem of semigroups, 1944, *Duke Math. Journal*, v.11, 1-7.

[P] P.A. Pleasants, Non-repetitive sequences, 1970, *Proc. Cambridge Phil. Society*, v.68, 267-274.

[RS] G. Rozenberg and A. Salomaa, *The mathematical theory of* L *systems*, 1980, Academic Press, London, New York.

[S1] A. Salomaa, Morphisms on free monoids and language theory, in R.V. Book, ed., *Formal language theory, perspectives and open problems*, 1980, Academic Press, London, New York, 141-166.

[S2] A. Salomaa, *Jewels of formal language theory*, Computer Science Press, 1981.

[T] A. Thue, Uber unendliche Zeichenreihen, 1906, Norske Vid. Selsk. Skr., I Mat. Nat. Kl., Christiania, v.7, 1-22.

PARAMETER PASSING COMMUTES WITH IMPLEMENTATION OF PARAMETERIZED DATA TYPES

H. Ehrig

H.-J. Kreowski

Technische Universität Berlin

Fachbereich Informatik

D -1000 Berlin 12

ABSTRACT

In this paper we introduce the notion of implementations of parameterized data types generalizing our algebraic implementation concept of actual types as studied in earlier papers.

A typical example is the implementation of binary trees bintree(data), by strings with brackets bracketstring(data), where data is the common formal parameter part of both parameterized specifications. Parameter passing means to replace the formal parameter data by an actual parameter like integers int leading to bintree(int) and bracketstring(int) respectively. The main result of this paper shows that parameter passing commutes with implementation. This means for our example that starting with a correct implementation of bintree(data) by bracketstring(data) correct parameter passing from data to int leads to a correct induced implementation of bintree(int) by bracketstring(int) where the induced implementation is an algebraic implementation of actual types as studied in our earlier papers. In other words the following diagram of parameter passing and implementations commutes:

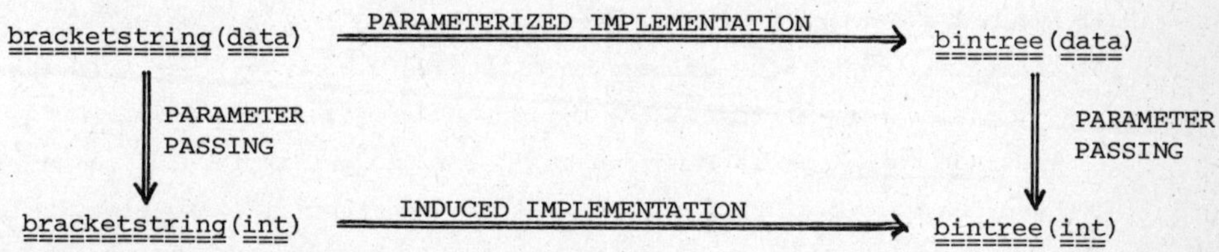

1. INTRODUCTION

In /EKP 80/ we introduced algebraic implementations of abstract data types which are not yet suitable for parameterized types. On the other hand the concept of parameterized data types was introduced in /ADJ 78/ and parameter passing was studied in /ADJ 80/. As shown in /Flo 81/, /EF 81/, /EKMP 80/ and /BG 79-80/ parameterization and implementation are key concepts in the development of software systems.

Hence it is necessary to study the compatibility of both concepts in detail. The general idea of such a compatibility is discussed already in /BG 79-80/ within the framework of 2-categrories. A system like CAT proposed in /BG 79-80/ seems to be most important for efficient development of software systems.

Consider the following example: Having shown that sets of natural numbers can be implemented by strings of natural numbers using hash-tables (see /EKMP 81/), we would also like to be sure to get a correct implementation when natural numbers are replaced by integers. Using our present concepts we cannot be sure. The obvious idea is to consider implementations of parameterized types like the implementation of sets of data by strings of data using hash-tables. Then the main result of this paper shows that the correctness of such a parameterized implementation implies the correctness of all induced actual implementations, especially that of sets of integers by strings of integers.

In Section 2 of this paper we review the concept of parameterized specifications and parameter passing as studied in /ADJ 81/. For the corresponding algebraic theory of parameterized specifications with requirements (like data constraints or initial restrictions in the sense of /BG 80/ and /Rei 80/) we refer to /Ehr 81/. In Section 3 we introduce the main concept of this paper, the implementation of parameterized data types including syntax, semantics and correctness. The main result in Section 4 ist the following: Given an implementation IMPL:SPEC1(SPEC) $\Longrightarrow$ SPEC0(SPEC) of parameterized types and a parameter passing morphism h:SPEC $\longrightarrow$ SPEC' then we have an induced implementation IMPL':SPEC1(SPEC') $\Longrightarrow$ SPEC0(SPEC'). In Theorems 4.3 and 4.4 we show how syntax and semantics of IMPL and IMPL' are related while Theorem 4.5 shows that corrrectness of IMPL implies correctness of IMPL'. These results can be summarized in the conclusion that correct parameter passing commutes with correct implementation. In this version we only give the proof ideas of the main results while all proofs will appear in the full version. In Section 5 we discuss how those results can be extended to parameterized parameter passing such that the induced implementation becomes a correct implementation of parameterized types. Furthermore we show how our results are related to those in /Hup 81/ and /Gan 81/. In these papers similar problems are discussed, however, without considering some of our main correctness criteria. Moreover the implementation concepts in /Hup 81/ and /Gan 81/ do not provide the concept of restriction which is an essential feature in our approach. After acception of this paper we have heard from D. Sanella and M. Wirsing that they also have a paper for the same conference on nearly the same subject (see /SW 82/). In contrast to our concept of implementation of parameterized specifications, their concept is based on loose theories and the nonfunctorial procedure concept in CLEAR (see /BG 80/).

2. PARAMETERIZED TYPES AND SPECIFICATIONS

We shall assume the algebraic background of /ADJ 76-78/ or /EKP 78/ which is based on universal algebra and category theory (see /HS 73/, /ML71/). But we will review the most important notions in connection with this paper. Moreover, we review the basic algebraic case of parameterized data types and specifications as given in /ADJ 81/. An <u>abstract data type</u> is regarded as (the isomorphism class of) a many-sorted (heterogeneous) algebra which is minimal, meaning that all data elements are "accessible" using constants and operations of the algebra. A many-sorted algebra consists of an indexed family of sets (called <u>carriers</u>) with an indexed family of operations between those carriers. The indexing system is called a <u>signature</u> and consists of a set S of <u>sorts</u> which indexes the carriers and a family $\langle \Sigma_{w,s} / w \in S^* \text{ and } s \in S \rangle$ of operation names (Σ is called the <u>operator domain</u>); a symbol $\sigma \in \Sigma_{w,s}$ with $w=s1\ldots sn$ names an operation $\sigma_A : A_{s1} x \ldots x A_{sn} \longrightarrow A_s$ in an algebra A with signature Σ. The pair $\langle S,\Sigma \rangle$ determines the category $\underline{Alg}_{S,\Sigma}$ of all S-sorted Σ-algebras with Σ-homomorphisms between them.

A <u>specification</u>, SPEC=$\langle S,\Sigma,E \rangle$, is a triple where $\langle S,\Sigma \rangle$ is a signature and E is a set of equations. $\underline{Alg}_{SPEC}$ is the category of all SPEC-algebras, i.e., all S-sorted Σ-algebras satisfiying the equations E. When we write the <u>combination</u> SPEC'=SPEC+$\langle S',\Sigma',E' \rangle$ we mean that S and S' are disjoint, that Σ' is an operator domain over S+S' which is disjoint from Σ, and that E' is a set of axioms over the signatur $\langle S+S',\Sigma+\Sigma' \rangle$.

We follow /ADJ 76-78/ in saying that the semantics of a specification SPEC is the (isomorphism class of the) algebra T_{SPEC} which is initial in $\underline{Alg}_{SPEC}$. T_{SPEC} can be constructed as a quotient $T_{SPEC}=T_{\langle S,\Sigma\rangle}/\equiv_E$ of the term algebra $T_{\langle S,\Sigma\rangle}$ (corresponding to the signature $\langle S,\Sigma\rangle$) by the congruence generated from the equations E.
Now let us consider parameterized data types and specifications:

2.1 DEFINITION

A parameterized data type PDAT=<SPEC,SPEC1,T> consists of the following data:

PARAMETER DECLARATION SPEC=$\langle S,\Sigma,E\rangle$

TARGET SPECIFICATION SPEC1=SPEC+$\langle S1,\Sigma 1,E1\rangle$

and a functor $T:\underline{Alg}_{SPEC} \longrightarrow \underline{Alg}_{SPEC1}$. PDAT is called persistent (strongly persistent) if T is, i.e. for every SPEC-algebera A, we have $V(T(A))\cong A$ (resp. $V(T(A))=A$) where V is the forgetful functor from SPEC1- to SPEC-algebras.

2.2 DEFINITION

1. A parameterized specification PSPEC=<SPEC,SPEC1> consists of the following data:

PARAMETER DECLARATION SPEC=$\langle S,\Sigma,E\rangle$

TARGET SPECIFICATION SPEC1=SPEC+$\langle S1,\Sigma 1,E1\rangle$.

The semantics of the specification is the free construction (see /ADJ 78/), $F:\underline{Alg}_{SPEC} \longrightarrow \underline{Alg}_{SPEC1}$, i.e., the (abstract) parameterized type PDAT=<SPEC,SPEC1,F>.
PSPEC is called (strongly) persistent if the free construction F is (strongly) persistent and the unit $\eta(A):A \longrightarrow VF(A)$ for $A\in\underline{Alg}_{SPEC}$ is a natural isomorphism (identity).

Remark:

For simplicity of presentation we only allow equations in the parameter declaration SPEC. For the case of parameterized specifications with requirements in the sense of /BG 80/ and /Rei 80/ we refer to our paper /Ehr 81/.

2.3 EXAMPLES

1. Binary trees bintree provide a typical example of a parameterized data type (see /ADJ 18/). They are generated as labelled LEAFs or labelled roots with a LEFT son or a RIGHT son or BOTH respectively. The actual labels are not specified, but the formal parameter data (consisting of one sort data only) requires some label alphabet. As a sample of retrieval operations we want to measure the HEIGHTs of the trees. For this computation we assume to have a specification int of integers (including constant 0,SUCCessor, PREDecessor, and MAXimum of two integers).

```
bintree(data+int)=
    data+int+
    sorts: bintree
    opns:  LEAF:data ⟶ bintree
           LEFT:bintree data ⟶ bintree
           RIGHT:data bintree ⟶ bintree
           BOTH:bintree data bintree ⟶ bintree
           HEIGHT:bintree ⟶ int
```

```
eqns:   HEIGHT(LEAF(x))=O
        HEIGHT(LEFT(B,x))=SUCC(HEIGHT(B))
        HEIGHT(RIGHT(x,B'))=SUCC(HEIGHT(B'))
        HEIGHT(BOTH(B,x,B'))=SUCC(MAX(HEIGHT(B),HEIGHT(B')))
```

The obvious specifications of int and data are omitted. Note that int is considered as formal parameter because the height can be computed by the given equations relative to an arbitrary int-algebra. Especially, this means that bintree is persistent.

A more elaborate specification of binary trees, which allows also to count the number of leafs, edges or nodes respectively, to test ballancedness or degeneratedness, to traverse binary trees in some orders, can be found in /EFK 80/.

2. The parameterized specification bracketstring has the same formal parameter as bintree. Bracketstrings are generated from the empty string INIT by Left-ADDition of data-elements, an OPENing or CLOSing bracket, or a COMMA. They can also be built up by Right-ADDition or CONCATenation. Moreover, the DEPTH of the bracket structure is specified. For each bracketstring, DEPTH returns a sequence of integers (intseq) representing the increasing and decreasing differences between opening and closing brackets while the string is traversed from left to right. We assume to have a specification intseq which provides all necessary operation (i.e. the EMPTY sequence, INSERTion of integers, access to the MAXIMUM entry, INCREASing and DECREASing of each entry of a sequence by one.)

```
bracketstring(data+int)=
    data+intseq+
    sorts:  alphabet, bracketstring
    opns:   INCL:   data ⟶ alphabet
            OPEN:        ⟶ alphabet
            CLOSE:       ⟶ alphabet
            COMMA:       ⟶ alphabet
            INIT:        ⟶ bracketstring
            LADD:   alphabet bracketstring ⟶ bracketstring
            RADD:   bracketstring alphabet ⟶ bracketstring
            CONCAT: bracketstring bracketstring ⟶ bracketstring
            DEPTH:  bracketstring ⟶ intseq
    eqns:   CONCAT(INIT,S)=S
            CONCAT(LADD(a,S),S')=LADD(a,CONCAT(S,S'))
            CONCAT(CONCAT(S,S'),S")=CONCAT(S,CONCAT(S',S"))
            RADD(S,a)=CONCAT(S,LADD(a,INIT))
            DEPTH(INIT)=EMPTY
            DEPTH(LADD(INCL(x),S))=DEPTH(S)
            DEPTH(LADD(OPEN,S))=INSERT(SUCC(O),INCREASE(DEPTH(S)))
            DEPTH(LADD(CLOSE,S))=INSERT(PRED(O),DECREASE(DEPTH(S)))
            DEPTH(LADD(COMMA,S))=DEPTH(S)
```

We come now to the problem of parameter passing. In the basic algebraic case parameter passing morphisms are just specification morphisms.

2.4 DEFINITION

1. A specification morphism $h:\langle S,\Sigma,E\rangle \longrightarrow \langle S',\Sigma',E'\rangle$ consists of a mapping $h_S:S \longrightarrow S'$ and a (S^*xS)-indexed family of mappings $h_\Sigma:\Sigma \longrightarrow \Sigma'$ (where $h_{\Sigma(w,s)}:\Sigma_{w,s} \longrightarrow \Sigma'_{h_S(w),h_S(s)}$). This is subject to the condition that every equation of E, when translated by h, belongs to E', in short $h(E) \subseteq E'$.

The morphism h is called simple if $\langle S,\Sigma,E\rangle \subseteq \langle S',\Sigma',E'\rangle$ and h_S, h_Σ are inclusions.

2. The category of all specifications and specification morphisms is called CATSPEC.

3. For each specification morphism $h:SPEC \longrightarrow SPEC'$ there is a functor $V_h:\underline{Alg}_{SPEC'} \longrightarrow \underline{Alg}_{SPEC}$ called forgetful functor with respect to h (see /ADJ 81/).

In the following we define standard parameter passing as in /ADJ 81/.

2.5 DEFINITION (Standard Parameter Passing)

Given a parameterized specification PSPEC=<SPEC,SPEC1>, a specification SPEC', called actual parameter, and a specification morphism $h:SPEC \longrightarrow SPEC'$, called parameter passing morphism, then the value specification SPEC1' is given as pushout object in the following parameter passing diagram

$$\begin{array}{ccc} SPEC & \xrightarrow{\ s\ } & SPEC1 \\ \downarrow{\scriptstyle h} & & \downarrow{\scriptstyle h'} \\ SPEC' & \xrightarrow[\ s'\ ]{} & SPEC1' \end{array}$$

where h is given as above, s and s' are simple specification morphisms and SPEC1', called value specification, is defined by

$$SPEC1'=SPEC'+\langle S1',\Sigma1',E'\rangle,$$

with $S1'=S1$, $\Sigma1'=h'(\Sigma1)$, and $E1'=h'(E1)$ where

$$h':SPEC1 \longrightarrow SPEC1'$$

is a specification morphism defined by

$$h'_S(x)=\text{if } x\in S1 \text{ then } x \text{ else } h_S(x) \text{ and}$$
$$h'_\Sigma(y)=\text{if } y\in\Sigma1 \text{ then } y \text{ else } h_\Sigma(y).$$

The mechanism of standard parameter passing is called correct if the following two conditions are satisfied:

1. actual parameter protection, i.e. $V_{s'}(T_{SPEC1'})=T_{SPEC'}$
2. passing compatibility, i.e. $F\cdot V_h(T_{SPEC'})=V_{h'}(T_{SPEC1'})$

where $T_{SPEC'}$ and $T_{SPEC1'}$ are initial algebras and F the semantics of PSPEC (see 2.2).

Interpretation: The value specification SPEC1', also written SPEC1(SPEC'), is the result of replacing the formal parameter SPEC in SPEC1, also written SPEC1(SPEC), by the actual parameter SPEC'.

Actual parameter protection means that the actual parameter SPEC' is protected in the value specification SPEC1'. Passing compatibility means that the semantics of parameter passing, especially the transformation from $T_{SPEC'}$ to $T_{SPEC1'}$ is compatible with the semantics F of PSPEC.

The main result for standard parameter passing is the following (see Theorem 5.2 in /ADJ81/):

2.6 THEOREM (Correctness of Standard Parameter Passing)

Standard parameter passing is correct (with respect to all actual parameters SPEC' and all parameter passing morphisms h:SPEC ⟶ SPEC') if and only if the given parameterized specification PSPEC=<SPEC,SPEC1> is (strongly) persistent.

2.7 EXAMPLE

To demonstrate the parameter passing mechanism, we intend to construct binary trees of integers (cf. 2.3.1). Hence the int-part of the formal parameter can be used as actual parameter, and the corresponding parameter passing morphism h:data+int ⟶ int assigns the sort int to the sort data while the int-part is mapped identically. According to 2.5 the value specification bintree(int) is obtained from the parameterized specification bintree(data+int) by erasing the two fragments of text 'data+' and by replacing all occurrences of the sort data by the sort int.

Note that the same parameter passing morphism defines also an actualization of our second example. This leads to bracketstring(int) where the elements of the strings are integers, opening and closing brackets, and commas.

3. IMPLEMENTATION OF PARAMETERIZED TYPES

Now we are going to define implementations of parameterized types given by parameterized specifications. This generalizes our implementation concept for "actual types" in /EKP80/ and /EKMP 80/.

3.1 GENERAL ASSUMPTION

We asume to have the following persistent parameterized specifications PSPEC0=<SPEC,SPEC0> and PSPEC1=<SPEC,SPEC1> with

SPEC=<S,Σ,E> (parameter declaration)

SPEC0=SPEC+<S0,Σ0,E0> (target specification 0)

SPEC1=SPEC+<S1,Σ1,E1> (target specification 1)

Remark: We assume persistency of PSPEC0 and SPEC1 because this is necessary and sufficient for correctness of standard parameter passing (see Thm. 2.6).

3.2 DEFINITION (Implementation)

An implementation of PSPEC0 by PSPEC1, written IMPL:PSPEC1⟹PSPEC0, is a pair

IMPL=(ΣSORT,EOP)

of operations ΣSORT, called sorts-implementing operations, and equations EOP, called operations-implementing equations, such that

SORTIMPL=SPEC1+<S0,ΣSORT,$\emptyset$> (sort implementation level)

OPIMPL=SORTIMPL+<$\emptyset$,Σ0,EOP> (operation implementation level)

and IDIMPL=OPIMPL+<$\emptyset$,$\emptyset$,E0> (identification level)

are combinations (see introduction of Section 2) and for all σ: ⟶ s, σ:s1...sn ⟶ s in ΣSORT the range s belongs to S0.

The semantics of IMPL is the following functor $SEM_{IMPL}:\underline{Alg}_{SPEC} \longrightarrow \underline{Alg}_{SPEC0}$ defined as the composition

$$SEM_{IMPL} = \underline{Alg}_{SPEC} \xrightarrow{FREE1} \underline{Alg}_{SPEC1} \xrightarrow{FREEIMPL} \underline{Alg}_{IDIMPL} \xrightarrow{RESTR} \underline{Alg}_{SPEC0}$$

where FREE1 and FREEIMPL are the free constructions corresponding to the forgetful functors $V1:\underline{Alg}_{SPEC1} \longrightarrow \underline{Alg}_{SPEC}$ and $VIMPL:\underline{Alg}_{IDIMPL} \longrightarrow \underline{Alg}_{SPEC1}$ respectively. The restriction functor RESTR is the composition

$$RESTR = \underline{Alg}_{IDIMPL} \xrightarrow{V} \underline{Alg}_{SPEC0} \xrightarrow{REACH} \underline{Alg}_{SPEC0}$$

of the forgetful functor $V:\underline{Alg}_{IDIMPL} \longrightarrow \underline{Alg}_{SPEC0}$ and the reachability functor REACH which is defined in 3.3 explicitly.

Remarks: The syntax of an implementation in the parameterized case is exactly the same as in the standard case of /EKMP 80/. For simplicity of presentation we have not introduced the general case including hidden components HID=(SHID,ΣHID,EHID) where hidden sorts, operations and equations can be used in the implementation (see 6.1 in /EKMP 80/). The semantics SEM_{IMPL} in the parameterized case corresponds to IR-semantics in the standard case (see 5.7 in /EKMP 80/). The construction SEM_{IMPL} is composed of the semantics FREE1 of the parameterized specification PSPEC1, followed by a SYNTHESIS step (free contruction from $\underline{Alg}_{SPEC1}$ to $\underline{Alg}_{OPIMPL}$), an INDENTIFICATION step (free construction from $\underline{Alg}_{OPIMPL}$ to $\underline{Alg}_{IDIMPL}$) and the RESTRICTION step RESTR.

Note that the free construction FREEIMPL is the composition of the free constructions SYNTHESIS and IDENTIFICATION. The semantics corresponds to IR-semantics because we first have the IDENTIFICATION and then the RESTRICATION step. This case is easier to handle in the parameterized case then the RI-semantics where RESTRICTION is followed by IDENTIFICATION (see 4.2 in /EKMP 80/). Formally we obtain the IR-semantics S_{IMPL} in the standard case if we apply SEM_{IMPL} to the initial SPEC-algebra T_{SPEC} because we have $FREE1(T_{SPEC})=T_{SPEC1}$.

3.3 LEMMA

1. Let $FREE0:\underline{Alg}_{SPEC} \longrightarrow \underline{Alg}_{SPEC0}$ be the free construction with respect to $V0:\underline{Alg}_{SPEC0} \longrightarrow \underline{Alg}_{SPEC}$ with counit ε. Then there is a functor $REACH:\underline{Alg}_{SPEC0} \longrightarrow \underline{Alg}_{SPEC0}$, called REACHABILITY, such that REACH(A) is the image of $\varepsilon(A):FREE0 \cdot V0(A) \longrightarrow A$.
2. If we have $A \in \underline{Alg}_{SPEC0}$ with $V0(A)=T_{SPEC}$ then REACH(A) ist the image of the evaluation $eval(A):T_{\Sigma+\Sigma 0} \longrightarrow A$.

Remark: Part 2 of the lemma shows that the REACHABILITIY construction in the standard case (see 4.2 in /EKMP 80/) is a special case of the parameterized construction.

Now we are going to define correctness of implementations where we use the notation Σ(SPEC) to denote the operations of SPEC.

Obviously we have to require that the semantics SEM_{IMPL} of the implementation yields the semantics FREE0 of the parameterized specification PSPEC0 to be implemented.

This property is called IR-correctness. Moreover the intention of correctness is that each operation call in SPEC0, i.e. a SPEC0-term t with variables, can be represented by a "synthezised" operation call in SPEC1, i.e. a term t^* with variables in SORTIMPL. Representation means that the term t in SPEC0 regarded as a term in OPIMPL is equivalent to the term t^* in SORTIMPL. This property will be referred as OP-completeness.

3.4 DEFINITION (Correctness)

An implementation IMPL:PSPEC1 $\Longrightarrow$ PSPEC0 as given in 3.2 is called

1. IR-correct, if we have $SEM_{IMPL} \cong FREE0$ where FREE0 is the semantics of PSPEC0.
2. OP-complete, if for each family of variables $X=(X_s)_{s\in S+S0}$ with $X_s=\emptyset$ for $s\in S0$ and for each term $t\in T_{\Sigma(SPEC0)}(X)$ there is a term $t^*\in T_{\Sigma(SORIMPL)}(X^*)$ such that t is OPIMPL-equivalent to t^*, i.e. $t \equiv_{OPIMPL} t^*$, where $X^*_s=X_s$ for $s\in S$ and $X^*_s=\emptyset$ otherwise.

Remarks:

1. IR-correctness implies $SEM_{IMPL}(T_{SPEC})=FREE0(T_{SPEC})=T_{SPEC0}$ which corresponds exactly to IR-correctness in the standard case (see 5.7 in /EKMP 80/).
2. For $X=\emptyset$ OP-completeness in the parameterized case corresponds exactly to OP-completeness in the standard case (see 4.6 in /EKMP 80/).

3.5 EXAMPLE

If one pushes trees over to the left, one obtains a well-known linear representation of a tree where the representations of the sons are separated by commas and enclosed by brackets and the root label is added to the left. This is the idea of the following implementation of the binary tree specification using bracketstrings (cf. 2.3).

```
bracketstring(data+int) impl bintree(data+int) by
    sorts impl opns: c:bracketstring ---> bintree
    opns impl eqns:  LEAF(x)=c(LADD(INCL(x),INIT))
      LEFT(c(S),x)=c(LADD(INCL(x),LADD(OPEN,RADD(RADD(S,COMMA),CLOSE)))))
      RIGHT(x,c(S))=c(LADD(INCL(x),LADD(OPEN,LADD(COMMA,RADD(S,CLOSE)))))
      BOTH(c(S),x,c(S'))=
         c(CONCAT(LADD(INCL(x),LADD(OPEN,S)),LADD(COMMA,RADD(S',CLOSE))))
      HEIGHT(c(S))=MAXIMUM(DEPTH(S))
```

Remark: In the framework of the general implementation concept with hidden components (see /EKMP 80/) we would introduce a hidden operation

EXPRESSION:bracketstring data bracketstring $\longrightarrow$ bracketstring with hidden equation

```
    EXPRESSION(S,x,S')=CONCAT(LADD(INCL(x),LADD(OPEN,S)),LADD(COMMA,RADD(S',CLOSE)))
```

such that the equations for LEFT, RIGHT and BOTH could be replaced by the following ones:

LEFT(c (S),x)=c(EXPRESSION(S,x,INIT))

RIGHT(x,c(S))=c(EXPRESSION(INIT,x,S))

BOTH(c(S),x,c(S'))=c(EXPRESSION(S,x,S'))

In the implementation above the sort bintree is a copy of the sort bracketstring, and the bintree-operations are derived from bracketstring-operations so that the implementation is OP-complete. Moreover, one can show that the representations which are accessible by bintree-operations are those bracketstrings with only positive entries in their depth sequence and with equally many opening and closing brackets. So the RESTRICTION step in the semantics is nontrivial in this case. In contrast to that the IDENTIFICATION step has no semantical effect because the bintree-equations are already satisfied on the operation implementation level in an appropriate way. Finally, IR-correctness can be shown using the correspondence between binary trees and their bracketstring representation as observed above.

4. THE MAIN RESULTS

In this section we give the main results concerning parameter passing for implementations of parameterized specifications. First we give an explicit construction for induced implementations.

4.1 DEFINITION (Induced Implementation)

Given an implementation IMPL=(ΣSORT,EOP) of PSPEC0 by PSPEC1 as defined in 3.2, a parameter passing morphism h:SPEC $\longrightarrow$ SPEC' and the corresponding value specifications SPEC0' and SPEC1' with h0:SPEC0 $\longrightarrow$ SPEC0' and h1:SPEC1 $\longrightarrow$ SPEC1' as defined in 2.4 and 2.5. Now let

$$\Sigma SORT' = \{h2(\sigma)/\sigma \in \Sigma SORT\} \text{ , and}$$

$$EOP' = \{h2(e)/e \in EOP\}$$

where h2(σ:s1...sn $\longrightarrow$ s)=σ:h1(s1)...h1(sn) $\longrightarrow$ h1(s) and h2(e) is obtained from e by replacing each σ by h2(σ) and each variable for a sort s$\in$S by a corresponding variable for the sort h(s)$\in$S'.

Then

$$IMPL' = (\Sigma SORT', EOP')$$

is called induced implementation IMPL' of SPEC0' by SPEC1', written IMPL':SPEC1' $\Longrightarrow$ SPEC0'.

Remark: It will be shown in Theorem 4.3 that the induced implementation IMPL' is in fact an implementation of SPEC0' by SPEC1' in the standard sense. The semantics of IMPL' is essentially determined by that of IMPL (Theorem 4.4). In Theorem 4.5 we will show that correctness of IMPL implies that of IMPL'.

4.2 EXAMPLE

The implementation of bintree(data+int) by bracketstring(data+int) in 3.5 induces an implementation of the corresponding value specification according to 2.7.

This induced implementation is obtained from the given one by replacing the parameterized specifications bintree and bracketstring by the value specifications and by interpreting the variable x as integer variable.

4.3 THEOREM (Syntax of Induced Implementations)

Given an implementation IMPL:PSPEC1 $\Longrightarrow$ PSPEC0 of parameterized specifications and a parameter passing morphism h:SPEC $\longrightarrow$ SPEC', then the induced implementation IMPL':SPEC1' $\Longrightarrow$ SPEC0' is an implementation in the standard sense where SORTIMPL', OPIMPL' and IDIMPL' can be characterized to be pushouts in CATSPEC (see 2.5) in the following diagrams, where the horizontal morphisms are inclusions and the vertical ones are induced by h:

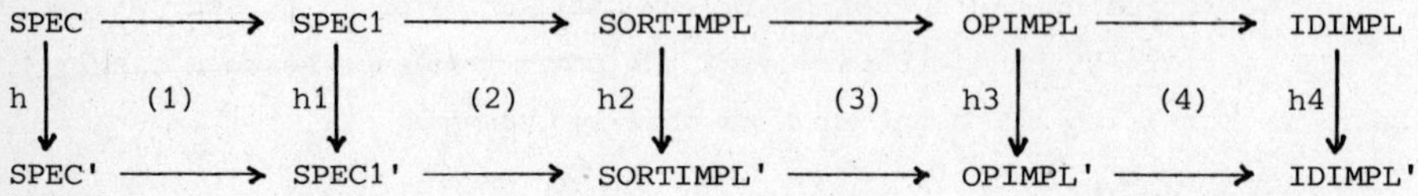

Remark: Note that SPEC0' and SPEC1' are the value specifications of SPEC0 and SPEC1 respectively (see 2.5), and we have by definition of standard implementations

SORTIMPL'=SPEC1'+$\langle$SO', ΣSORT', $\emptyset\rangle$

OPIMPL'=SORTIMPL'+$\langle\emptyset$, ΣO', EOP'$\rangle$

IDIMPL'=OPIMPL'+$\langle\emptyset$, $\emptyset$, EO'$\rangle$

Proofidea: Let SPEC1', SORTIMPL', OPIMPL' and IDIMPL' be pushouts in diagrams (1) - (4) respectively. Then the explicit constructions due to 2.5 coincide with that in 4.1. The remaining syntactical properties are easy to check.

4.4 THEOREM (Semantics of Induced Implementations)

Given an implementation IMPL:PSPEC1 $\Longrightarrow$ PSPEC0 with semantics $SEM_{IMPL}:\underline{Alg}_{SPEC} \longrightarrow \underline{Alg}_{SPEC0}$, a parameter passing morphism h:SPEC $\longrightarrow$ SPEC' and let IMPL':SPEC1' $\Longrightarrow$ SPEC0' be the induced implementation with semantics $S_{IMPL'}$. Furthermore assume that the semantics SEM_{IMPL} is persistent with respect to the forgetful functor $V0:\underline{Alg}_{SPEC0} \longrightarrow \underline{Alg}_{SPEC}$. Then the semantics $S_{IMPL'}$ is uniquely defined by the following properies:

1. $V0'(S_{IMPL'})=T_{SPEC'}$
2. $V_{h0}(S_{IMPL'})=SEM_{IMPL}\cdot V_h(T_{SPEC'})$

where $V0'$, V_{h0} and V_h are forgetful functors, $T_{SPEC'}$ the initial SPEC'-algebra and $S_{IMPL'}=SEM_{IMPL'}(T_{SPEC'})$.

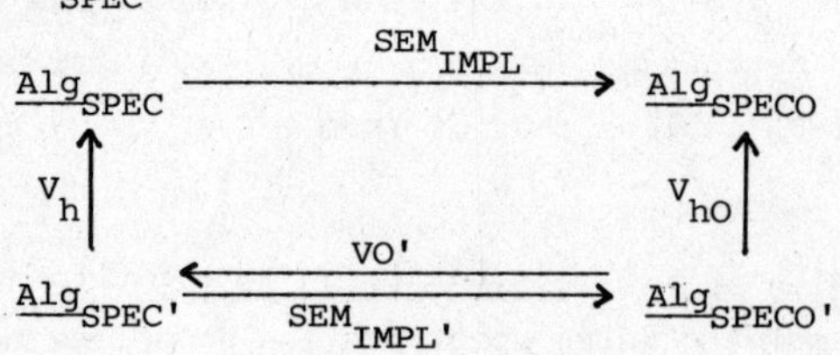

<u>Remark:</u> Similar to Theorem 2.6 the persistency of SEM_{IMPL} is necessary and sufficient if properties 1 and 2 are required for all actual parameters SPEC' and all parameter passing morphisms $h:SPEC \longrightarrow SPEC'$.

<u>Proofidea:</u> The proof is based on the EXTENSION LEMMA and three additional lemmas. Since SEM_{IMPL} is persistent the EXTENTION LEMMA implies that there is a unique persistent extension $F':\underline{Alg}_{SPEC'} \longrightarrow \underline{Alg}_{SPECO'}$ of SEM_{IMPL} such that properties 1 and 2 are satisfied with $S_{IMPL'}$ replaced by $F'(T_{SPEC'})$. The main part to show is

$$F'=SEM_{IMPL'}$$

where similar to 3.2 $SEM_{IMPL'}$ is given by $SEM_{IMPL'}$ =RESTR'·FREEIMPL'·FREE1'. Using again the EXTENTION LEMMA we have to show

3. $VO'\cdot SEM_{IMPL'}=id_{\underline{Alg}_{SPEC'}}$

4. $V_{hO}\cdot SEM_{IMPL'}=SEM_{IMPL}\cdot V_h$.

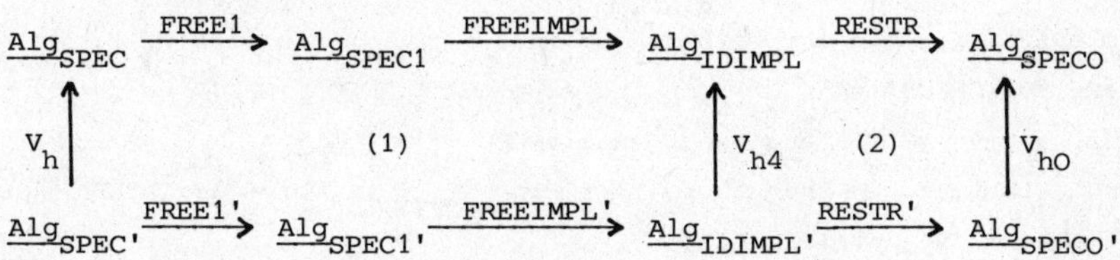

We need the following three lemmas:

<u>LEMMA1:</u> VO·RESTR=V4 where VO and V4 are forgetful functors corresponding to $SPEC \subseteq SPECO$ and $SPEC \subseteq IDIMPL$.
Analogously, VO'·RESTR'=V4'.

<u>LEMMA 2:</u> SEM_{IMPL} persistent iff FREEIMPL·FREE1 persistent.

<u>LEMMA 3:</u> $RESTR\cdot V_{h4}=V_{hO}\cdot RESTR'$.

LEMMA 2 implies by assumption that FREEIMPL·FREE1 is persistent. Now we are able to prove properties 3 and 4.

$$
\begin{aligned}
VO'\cdot SEM_{IMPL'} &= VO'\cdot RESTR'\cdot FREEIMPL'\cdot FREE1' \\
&= V4'\cdot FREEIMPL'\cdot FREE1' && \text{(LEMMA 1)} \\
&= id_{\underline{Alg}_{SPEC'}} && \text{(by EXTENSION LEMMA and persitency of FREEIMPL·FREE1)}
\end{aligned}
$$

$$
\begin{aligned}
V_{hO}\cdot SEM_{IMPL'} &= V_{hO}\cdot RESTR'\cdot FREEIMPL'\cdot FREE1' \\
&= RESTR\cdot V_{h4}\cdot FREEIMPL'\cdot FREE1' && \text{(LEMMA 3)} \\
&= REST\cdot FREEIMPL\cdot FREE1\cdot V_h && \text{(EXTENSION LEMMA)} \\
&= SEM_{IMPL}\cdot V_h \quad .
\end{aligned}
$$

4.5 THEOREM (Correctness of Semantics)

Given an implementation IMPL:PSPEC1 $\Longrightarrow$ PSPECO with induced implementation IMPL':SPEC1' $\Longrightarrow$ SPECO' as in 4.3 and 4.4, then we have

1. IMPL IR-correct implies IMPL' IR-correct ,
2. IMPL OP-complete implies IMPL' OP-complete .

Proof (sketch):

1. IMPL IR-correct means SEM_{IMPL}=FREEO. Since FREEO is persistent by general assumption 3.1 we have also persistency of SEM_{IMPL}. Hence we are able to use the proof of Theorem 4.4 with SEM_{IMPL}=FREEO showing that $SEM_{IMPL'}$ is the unique extension of FREEO. On the other hand the EXTENSION LEMMA implies that the unique extension of FREEO is the free construction FREEO':$\underline{Alg}_{SPEC'} \longrightarrow \underline{Alg}_{SPECO'}$ such that we have $SEM_{IMPL'}$=FREEO'. Moreover we have FREEO'($T_{SPEC'}$)=$T_{SPECO'}$. This implies $S_{IMPL'}=T_{SPECO'}$ which means IR-correctness of IMPL'.

2. We have to show that for each $\bar{t}\in T_{\Sigma(SPECO')}$ there is a $\bar{t}^*\in T_{\Sigma(SORT/IMPL)}$ which is OPIMPL'-equivalent to $\bar{t}$. This can be shown by induction on the size of $\bar{t}$. For size($\bar{t}$)=1 we have $\bar{t}\in\Sigma(SPECO')=\Sigma'+\Sigma O'$. In the case $\bar{t}\in\Sigma'\subseteq\Sigma(SORTIMPL')$ we can take $\bar{t}^*=\bar{t}$. Otherwise we have $\bar{t}\in\Sigma O'$ and hence also $t\in\Sigma O$ with $hO(t)=\bar{t}$.
OP-completeness of IMPL implies that there is $t^*\in T_{\Sigma(SORTIMPL)}$ which is OPIMPL-equivalent to t. Taking $\bar{t}^*=h2(t^*)$ we have:

$$\bar{t}=hO(t)=h3(t)\equiv_{OPIMPL'} h3(t^*)=h2(t^*)=\bar{t}^*\in T_{\Sigma(SORTIMPL')}$$

This completes the proof for size($\bar{t}$)=1.
For size($\bar{t}$)=N>1 we again consider two cases. If the root of $\bar{t}$ belongs to Σ' the corresponding term $\bar{t}^*$ can be obtained by applying the inducation hypothesis to the arguments of the root in $\bar{t}$. If the root $\bar{\sigma}$ of $\bar{t}$ belongs to $\Sigma O'$ we have $\sigma\in\Sigma O$ with $hO(\sigma)=\bar{\sigma}$. Now we consider all proper maximal subterms of $\bar{t}$ with sorts in S' (not in SO'), say $\bar{t}1,\dots,\bar{t}m\in T_{\Sigma(SPECO')}$ with sorts $s1,\dots,sm\in S'$.
Let x1,...,xm be pairwise different variables of sort s1,...,sm and $\bar{X}=\{x1,\dots xm\}$.
Then there is $\bar{t}O\in T_{\Sigma(SPECO')}(\bar{X})$ and an assignment ass : $\bar{X}\longrightarrow T_{\Sigma(SPECO')}$ defined by $ass(xi)=\bar{t}i$ for i=1,...,m with $ass^{\S}(\bar{t}O)=\bar{t}$. By choice of $\bar{t}1,\dots,\bar{t}m$ we have also $tO\in T_{\Sigma(SPECO)}(X)$ with $hO(tO)=\bar{t}O$ and $X_s=\bar{X}_{h(s)}$ for $s\in S+SO$. Now we use OP-completeness of IMPL to obtain $tO^*\in T_{\Sigma(SORTIMPL)}(X)$ which is OPIMPL-equivalent to tO. Hence also $\bar{t}O=hO(tO)$ is OPIMPL'-equivalent to $\bar{t}O=h2(tO^*)$.
Now we use induction hypothesis to find $\bar{t}1^*,\dots,\bar{t}m^*\in T_{\Sigma(SORTIMPL')}$ which are OPIMPL'-equivalent to $\bar{t}1,\dots,\bar{t}m\in T_{\Sigma(SPECO')}$ respectively. Define a new assignment $\overline{ass}$ by $\overline{ass}(xi)=\bar{t}i^*$ for i=1,...,m and let $\bar{t}^*=\overline{ass}^{\S}(\bar{t}O^*)\in T_{(SORTIMPL')}$. Then we have

$$\bar{t}=ass^{\S}(\bar{t}O)\equiv_{OPIMPL'}\overline{ass}^{\S}(\bar{t}O)\equiv_{OPIMPL'}\overline{ass}^{\S}(\bar{t}O^*)=\bar{t}^*$$

because of $ass(xi)=\bar{t}i\equiv_{OPIMPL'}\bar{t}i^*=\overline{ass}(x_i)$ for i=1,...,m and $\bar{t}O\equiv_{OPIMPL'}\bar{t}O^*$.
this completes the proof.

From theorem 4.3, 4.4 and 4.5 we conclude:

4.6 CONCLUSION (Commutativity of Parameter Passing with Implementation)

Correct parameter passing commutes with correct implementation, i.e. if IMPL:PSPEC1 ⟹ PSPEC0 is correct and h:SPEC ⟶ SPEC' a parameter passing morphism then we have the following commutative diagram of correct implementation and parameter passing steps:

```
SPEC1(SPEC)  ==PARAMETERIZED IMPLEMENTATION IMPL==>  SPEC0(SPEC)
    ||                                                    ||
    ||  PARAMETER PASSING              PARAMETER PASSING  ||
    \/                                                    \/
SPEC1(SPEC') ==========================================>  SPEC0(SPEC')
              INDUCED IMPLEMENTATION IMPL'
```

5. FURTHER DEVELOPMENT AND CONCLUSION

There are several ways to extend the constructions and results given in Section 3 and 4. This is easy to see for the case of implementations with hidden parts (see Remark in 3.2). Moreover we can use parameterized specifications with requirements in the sense of /Ehr 81/ instead of the basic algebraic case considered in Definition 2.2. This allows to add requirements like initial restrictions, e.g. initial(bool), and general logical formulas instead of equations. In this framework we can formulate parameterized specifications like set(data) and string(data), where initiality of the bool-part in data is essential, and also an implementation of set(data) by string(data). Parameter passing from data to int leads to the induced implementation of set(int) by string(int) which was studied independently in /EKMP 80/ before.

On the other hand we can also consider parameterized parameter passing instead of standard parameter passing. That means the actual parameter and hence also the value specification are parameterized specifications. Actually there are only slight changes in Theorems 4.3, 4.4 and 4.5 and the corresponding proofs for the case of parameterized parameter passing. Essentially we only need an additional lemma showing compatibility of different restriction constructions. If we take a "passing consistent" parameter passing morphism h:data ⟶ stack(par) to the parameterized specification stack(par) of stacks of parameters, the correct implementation IMPL:string(data) ⟹ set(data) induces a correct implementation IMPL':string * stack(par) ⟹ set * stack(par) of parameterized types, where * corresponds to the composition of parameterized types in the sense of /ADJ 81/.

All the generalizations discussed above seem tho be straight-forward. But if we change the semantics of implementations from IR-semantics to RI-semantics (first RESTRICTION and then IDENTIFICATION), which is studied in /EKMP 80/ in addition to IR-semantics, problems seem to be more difficult. But we are safe because IR-correctness implies RI-correctness (see /EKMP 80/).
Another problem is to induce a correct implementation like IMPL':stack * string(data) ⟹ stack * set(data) from IMPL:string(data) ⟹ set(data). This, for example, is intended in /Gan 81/ but instead of stack * string(data) the source of the induced implementation is something like stack * IDIMPL(data).

The approach in /Gan 81/ with respect to parameter passing corresponds to /ADJ 81/ with final algebra semantics. The implementation concept in /Gan 81/ lacks a counterpart of OP-completeness. The intention of Theorem 8 in /Gan 81/, however, is similar to that in Theorem 4.3 and part 1 of 4.5. As mentioned above all constructions in /Gan 81/ are done with respect to final algebra semantics.

We should also mention the approach in /Hup 81/ where also implementation of specifications in connection with parameter passing is studied. Specifications are considered to be pairs of canons which syntactically correspond to parameterized specifications with requirements in the sense of /Ehr 81/.

Unfortunately, the semantics of pairs of canons is nonfuctorial and there is no counterpart for correctness of parameter passing which is essential in our Theorems 4.4 and 4.5. As mentioned in the introduction an important feature in our implementation concept is the RESTRICTION construction which has no counterpart in /Gan 81/ and /Hup 81/.

Finally let us give some brief remarks to the twin paper /SW 82/ on implementation of parameterized specifications presented for this conference. Sanella's and Wirsing's approach is based on loose theories with hierarchy constraints in the sense of /BDPPW 79/ which is a variant of the data constraints in CLEAR. The implementation concept in /SW 82/ is similar to our concept in /EKP 80/ without the SYNTHESIS step but including RESTRICTION and INDENTIFICATION. Implementations of parameterized specifications are defined to be correct in /SW 82/ if for all actual parameters the induced implementations are correct. We think that this should be one of the main results (see Thm 4.5). On the other hand they seem to be able to get rid of some problems because they use loose theories instead of initial and free semantics.

6. REFERENCES

/ADJ 76-78/ (JAG,JWT,EGW) *): An initial algebra approach to the specification, correctness, and implementation of abstract data types, IBM Research Report RC-6487, Oct. 1976. Current Trends in Programming Methodology, IV: Data Structuring (R.T.Yeh, Ed.) Prentice Hall, New Jersey (1978), pp. 80-149

/ADJ 78/ (JWT, EGW, JBW) *): Data Type Specification: parameterization and the power of specification techniques, Proc. SIGACT 1oth Annual Symp. on Theory of Computing, Mai 1978, pp. 119-132

/ADJ 80/ (HE,HJK,JWT,EGW,JBW) *): Parameterized data types in algebraic specifications languages (short version), Proc. 7th ICALP Nordwijkerhout, July 1980: Lect. Not. in Comp. Sci.88 (1980), pp. 157-168

/ADJ 81/ (HE, HJK, JWT, EGW, JBW) *): Parameter Passing in Algebraic Specification Languages, Proc. Workshop on Program Specification, Aarhus, August 1981

/BDPPW 79/ Broy, M., Dosch, W., Partsch, H., Pepper, P. and Wirsing, M.: Existential quantifiers in abstract data Types, Proc. 6th ICALP, Graz, Lect. Not. in Comp. Sci. 71(1979), pp. 73-87

/BG 79-80/ Burstall, R.M., Goguen, J.A.: CAT, a System for the Structured Elaboration of Correct Programs from Structured Specifications, preliminary draft, 1979/1980

/BG 80/ --: The Semantics of CLEAR, a Specification Language, Proc. 1979 Copenhagen Winter School on Abstract Software Specifications (1980), Lect. Not. in Comp. Sci. (1980)

/Ehr 78/ Ehrich, H.-D.: On the theory of specification, implementation and parameterization of abstract data types, Research Report Dortmund 1978, Journal ACM 29,1 (1982), pp. 206-227

/Ehr 81/ Ehrig, H.: Algebraic Theory of Parameterized Specifications with Requirements, Proc. 6th CAAP, Genova 81, Lect. Not. in Comp. Sci. 112 (1981), pp. 1-24

/EF 81/ Ehrig, H., Fey, W.: Methodology for the specification of software systems: From requirement specifications to algebraic design specifications, Proc. GI 81, München, Informatik-Fachberichte 50, 1981, pp. 255-269

REFERENCES (cont'd)

/EFK 80/ Ehrig, H., Fey, W., Kreowski, H.-J.: Some Examples of Algebraic Specifications and Implementations: Part 1, Techn. University Berlin, Report No. 80-31, 1980

/EKP 78/ Ehrig, H., Kreowski, H.-J., Padawitz, P.: Stepwise specification and implementation of abstract data types: Techn. University Berlin, Report, Nov. 1977, Proc. 5th ICALP, Udine, July 1978: Lect. Not. in Comp. Sci. 62 (1978), pp. 205-226

/EKP 80/ --: Algebraic Implementation of Abstract Data Types: Concept Syntax, Semantics, Correctness: Proc. 7th ICALP, Nordwijkerhout, July 1980, Lect. Not. in Comp. Sci. 85 (1980), pp. 142-156

/EKMP 80/ Ehrig, H., Kreowski, H.-J., Mahr, B., Padawitz, P.: Algebraic Implementations of Abstract Data Types, to appear in Theoret. Comp. Science

/Flo 81/ Floyd, Ch., Kopetz, H. (eds.): Software Engineering - Entwurf und Spezifikation, Proc. 2nd German Chapter of the ACM-Meeting, Teubner-Verlag, Stuttgart 1981

/Gan 81/ Ganzinger, H.: Parameterized specifications: Parameter Passing and Optimizing Implementation, Techn. Report, TU München, August 1981

/Gut 76/ Guttag, J.V.: Abstract data types and development of data structures; supplement to Proc. Conf. on Data Abstraction, Definition, and Structure, SIGPLAN Notices 8, March 1976

/HS 73/ Herrlich, H., Strecker, G.: Category Theory, Allyn and Bacon, Rockleigh 1973

/Hup 81/ Hupbach, U.L.: Abstract Implementation and Parameter Substitution, submitted to 3rd Hungarian Comp. Sci. Conf., Budapest 1981

/ML 71/ MacLane, S.: Categories for the Working Mathematician; Springer Verlag, New York/Heidelberg/Berlin 1971

/Rei 80/ Reichel, H.: Initially Restricting Algebraic Theories, Proc. MFCS'80, Rydzyna, Sept. 1980, Lect. Not. in Comp. Sci. 88 (1980), pp. 504-514

/SW 82/ Sanella, D., Wirsing, M.: Implementation of Parameterized Specifications, 1982, this volume

---

*) ADJ-authors: J.A. Goguen (JAG), J.W. Thatcher (JWT), E.G. Wagner (EGW), J. B. Wright (JBW)
co-authors: H. Ehrig (HE), H.-J. Kreowski (HJK)

An Operational Semantics for Pure Dataflow

A.A.Faustini
Department of Computer Science
University of Warwick
Coventry CV4 7AL UK

Abstract

In this paper we prove the equivalence of an operational and a denotational semantics for pure dataflow. The term pure dataflow refers to dataflow nets in which the nodes are functional (i.e. the output history is a function of the input history only) and the arcs are unbounded fifo queues. Gilles Kahn gave a method for the representation of a pure dataflow net as a set of equations; one equation for each arc in the net. Kahn stated, and we prove, that the operational behaviour of a pure dataflow net is exactly described by the least fixed point solution to the net's associated set of equations.

In our model we do not require that nodes be sequential nor deterministic, not even the functional nodes. As a consequence our model has a claim of being completely general.

Our proof of the Kahn Principle makes use of two player infinite games of perfect information. Infinite games turn out to be an extremely useful tool for defining and proving results about operational semantics.

1. Introduction

Dataflow is a model of parallel computation in which a network of asynchronous computing stations compute using data that flows through the network.

A dataflow net is a directed graph the nodes of which are asynchronous computing stations and the arcs of which are unidirectional communiction lines along which units of data (datons) flow. In this paper we are interested in dataflow nets in which the nodes are continuously operating autonomous computing devices and the arcs are 'pipes' which allow unbounded fifo queueing. This model of dataflow has been extensively studied and is often refered to as pipeline or stream flow (Adams[0], Arnold[1], Karp & Miller[5] and Arvind & Gostelow[2]).

The following is an example of a dataflow net that computes the sequence 1,2,6,24,120,.... of factorials. The node labelled '*' repeatedly awaits the arrival of a daton on both its input arcs and as soon as both datons arrive they are consumed and a daton representing their product is output. The node labelled '+' processes in the same way except it outputs the sum of the incoming datons. The node labelled 'ONE' is a 'constant' node. It has no input and produces as output an endless stream of datons representing the natural number 1.

The remaining nodes are all nodes that manipulate datons. The one labelled 'NEXT' throws away the first daton that arrives but thereafter passes on the rest. The node labelled 'FBY' (followed by) awaits the arrival of the first daton on the input

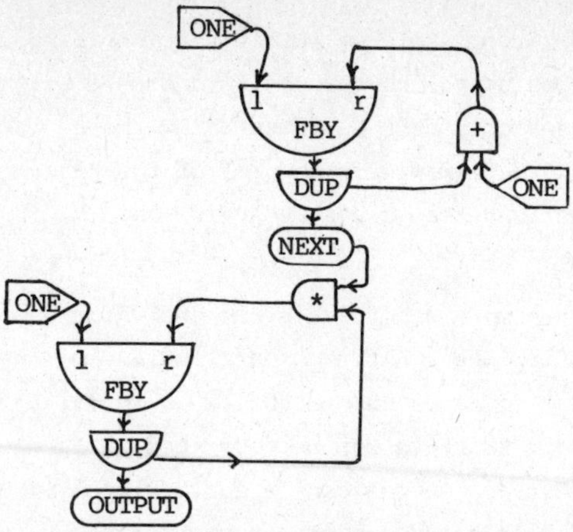

Figure A

A simple dataflow net and its corresponding set of equations

x = fby(l,y)
y = plus(x,l)
z = next(x)
w = times(z,v)
v = fby(l,v)

labelled 'l' passes this on as its first output but thereafter passes on whatever appears on the input labelled 'r'. Any future input on 'l' is thrown away. The node labelled 'DUP' (duplicator) simply sents a copy on both its output arcs of any daton input.

The Kahn Principle

All the nodes used in figure A have one property in common, namely they are all functional. A node is said to be functional iff the entire sequence of datons output is determined by the entire sequences of the datons input. This means that the node has no internal randomness and that the contents of the node's output sequence is not dependent upon the rate of arrival of inputs (though the input rate can effect the output rate). A classic example of a non-functional node is the 'merge' node that passes along its single output line whatever appears at either of the input arcs choosing at random if datons are waiting on both input arcs.

In this paper we are interested in a subset of pipeline dataflow, namely the subset in which all nodes are functional. We call this subset of pipeline dataflow *pure dataflow*. Gilles Kahn[4] was the first to study pure dataflow and he pointed out that a pure dataflow net can be represented by a set of equations (figure A). Rather than study parallel computation in terms of the complex behaviour of a network of machines Kahn wanted to study it in terms of the properties of the solution to a set of equations. It is a well known result that under certain conditions a system of equations such as those in figure A has a least fixed point solution (see Manna[6]). Kahn was the first to realise the principle (*the Kahn principle*) that the operational behaviour of a pure dataflow net can be described by the least fixed point solution to the set of equations associated with the net. Although Kahn was the first to realise this principle he never published a formal proof nor did he define precisely the concepts of node, net, etc.

2. A Formal Operational semantics

If we are to give a formal proof of the Kahn principle we must first formalise the operational semantics for pure dataflow. One approach would be to define a select set of primitive functional nodes and to consider only nets build up using these primitives. If the primitives are sequential and deterministic a proof of the Kahn principle is not very difficult and such a proof has been given by Arvind and Gostelow[2].

Our goal is to prove the Kahn principle in a more general system, one which has a claim to being able to formalise any pure dataflow net. Although dataflow is an informal concept one would expect that a general model of pure dataflow would be:

(i) Complete: in that any computable history function can be described.

(ii) Have the encapsulation property: in that any subnet can be encapsulated in a node. This form of modularization means that any subnet can be replaced by a node having the same input/output behaviour

To give directly a general operational semantics for pure dataflow is extremely difficult. The problems are

(i) to decide which formal objects corresponds to an asynchronous computing station

(ii) to ensure that these formal object describes only functional computing stations.

In this paper we shall look at these two issues separately. To begin with we give a formal operational semantics for pipeline dataflow in general. Thus our operational model is capable of describing any node which deserves to be called functional. Note our nodes need not be sequential. A formal operational semantics for pipeline dataflow in which the nodes are sequential is given by Arnold[1].

Nodes as non-deterministic automata

We think of our nodes as 'black boxes' with datons being fed in, one by one, through input arcs and datons being output, one by one, through output arcs. Although a simple node usually produces output at the same rate at which it consumes input, a more complex node may produce output at a different rate, perhaps faster or slower than the rate at which it consumes input. It may also consume and produce at different rates on different input or output arcs.

To reduce notational complexity we will assume for the rest of this paper that datons represent only the natural numbers.

With each node we associate an internal state which may change as the node moves from one stage in its computation to the next. (Some authors restrict themselves to a subset of pure dataflow in which nodes have no memory. Naturally this model is very 'incomplete'. It also lacks the encapsulation property - subnets have memory, in the form of daton queues, but nodes have none). When our nodes are first "activated", they moves automatically into a known initial state. Thereafter they may move to other internal states depending upon what a node is to compute. We can think, informally, of the internal state of a node as having two distinct roles.

One role of internal state is as a "marker", marking the current step in the algorithm specifying a node's behaviour.

The second use of internal state is as memory. To produce an output, our nodes may require access to all of their previous inputs and, therefore, a possibly unbounded amount of memory may be required.

Although we can, informally, think of internal memory as having two distinct functions this does not mean that nodes need separate internal states for each of these functions. On the contrary, our nodes may encode both of these functions within a single internal state.

With each of our node's input arcs we associate a one place input buffer. This buffer is empty if the input queue is empty, otherwise it holds the daton at the head of the input queue. Our node is able to remove a daton from an input arc by erasing the contents of the corresponding input buffer.

The contents of each input buffer together with the internal state give a snapshot description of our node. This snapshot is called the "cause" of computation. With every possible "cause" our nodes (are required) to associate some "effect". An "effect" may be to erase some or all of the nodes input buffer; it may be to change internal state or it may be to output a daton on some or all of the output arcs or a combination of these 3 activities.

For example, consider the node that computes the running total of its inputs. At some point in this node's computation a snapshot may reveal that it is in state q_{27} (meaning that the current total is presently 27). If a daton representing 3 is in the input buffer it will "cause" the following "effect": the 3 would be erased from the input buffer; the node would move to the new internal state q_{30} and a 30 would be output. We can see from this example how "causes" and "effects" are paired. We call such a pair a transition. The only property we require of transitions is that for every "cause" there is at least one possible "effect". Since a "cause" may have more than one "effect" associated with it, our nodes may be non-deterministic.

If one or more of the input buffers associated with a "cause" is empty, then it is still possible to associate an "effect" with that "cause". In some cases the "effect" may be to do nothing, which we call busy waiting. On the other hand the "effect" may be to cause some activity, and we call this computing on empty buffers. It is possible for sequential nodes to compute when some of their buffers are empty, but only if they completely ignore the contents of these buffers. Using Kahn's Wait primitive, for example, it is possible to wait for the appearance of a daton down the first arc and output it when it arrives even if the second buffer is empty. But when a Wait is invoked, the node must do just that and has no way of knowing whether or not anything has arrived in the other buffer.

The more general nodes which we allow, however, are capable of performing other activities (such as output) while waiting for input on certain arcs - in other words, they are essentially able to do more than one thing at the same time. A very simple example of such a node is the 'double identity' node. This node has two inputs and two outputs and echos the first input on the first output, and the second input on the second output. Such a node cannot be sequential because it cannot allow both outputs to 'run dry' when only one of the inputs does so. This ability to compute while waiting is essential if our model is to be in any sense general. In fact any model that is unable to compute in this way will be deprived of the encapsulation property.

The following formal definition of a node is based on the informal ideas presented above. A node is specified by: the number of input and output arcs; the initial internal state; the set of all possible internal states, and the collection of all possible cause-effect pairs.

(2A) Definition A node is a sequence $\langle Q,q,n,m,T\rangle$
where

Q is a countable set with nil $\notin Q$
(the set of all possible internal states)

$q \in Q$
(the initial internal state)

$n,m \in \omega$
(the number of input & output ports respectively)

$T \subseteq (B^n \times Q) \times (E^n \times Q' \times B^m)$
(the transition relation)
such that
$BW \subseteq T$
where
$BW = \{ \langle c, nil^{n+m+1}\rangle \mid c \in (B^n \times Q) \}$
$B = \omega \cup \{ nil \}$
$Q' = Q \cup \{ nil \}$
$E = \{ tt , nil \}$

<u>Some</u> <u>examples</u>

In the following examples we shall represent a node's transition relation using schemas in which the left column represents the "cause" component ($B^n \times Q$) and the right column the "effect" component ($E^n \times Q \times^m B$). For simplicity we also omit any busy wait transition (i.e. transitions in which the effect components are all nil).

1. The following is a formal definition of the 'merge' node:
$\langle Q,q,2,1,T\rangle$
where
$Q = \{ q \}$
T is all the transitions of the form

```
<nil,  y,q>   ->   <nil, tt,nil,  y>
<  x,nil,q>   ->   < tt,nil,nil,  x>
<  x,  y,q>   ->   < tt,nil,nil,  x>
               ↳   <nil, tt,nil,  y>
```

for any $x,y \in \omega$

2.The following is an example of a non-determinate node with deterministic input/output behaviour. The node we define is called 'parallel or' but first let's look at the 'simple or' whose formal definition is

$\langle \{ q \}, q, 2, 1, R \rangle$

where R is all the transitions of the form

$\langle x,y,q \rangle \rightarrow \langle tt, tt, nil, x \text{ or } y \rangle$

$\forall x,y \in \{ 1,\emptyset \}$

(1 and Ø denote True & False respectively)

The simple 'or' awaits for a daton to arrive on both input arcs and on arrival they are both consumed and their logical 'or' is output. The parallel version of this node takes advantage of the following equalities:

1 or y = 1

x or 1 = 1

$\forall x,y \in \{ 1,\emptyset \}$.

Our parallel version awaits the arrival of a daton in either buffer as soon as a 1 arrives on either input, it outputs a 1. For the sake of argument let us assume that a 1 arrives in the left buffer; the node erases the 1 and outputs a copy without waiting for the corresponding right input. Our node then records using internal memory that it is one ahead on the left input. If another 1 arrives in the left input and still nothing arrives in the right input then another 1 is output and the node records that it is two ahead on the left input. The node can carry on like this indefinitely or until a Ø arrives in the left input in which case it must allow right hand input to catch up. This is only half the explaination the other can be extracted from the following formal definition

$\langle \{ B_i \mid i \in \omega \}, B_\emptyset, 2, 1, R \rangle$

where R is

$\forall x,y \in \{ 1,\emptyset \}$

$$\begin{array}{lll}
\langle x, & y, B_\emptyset \rangle \rightarrow \langle tt, tt, & nil, x \text{ or } y \rangle \\
\langle 1, & nil, B_\emptyset \rangle \rightarrow \langle tt, nil, & B_1, 1 \rangle \\
\langle nil, & 1, B_{2i} \rangle \rightarrow \langle nil, tt, & B_{2i+2}, 1 \rangle \\
\langle 1, & nil, B_{2i+1} \rangle \rightarrow \langle tt, nil, & B_{2i+3}, 1 \rangle \\
\langle 1, & y, B_{2i+1} \rangle \rightarrow \langle tt, tt, & nil, 1 \rangle \\
\langle x, & 1, B_{2i+2} \rangle \rightarrow \langle tt, tt, & nil, 1 \rangle
\end{array}$$

$\langle\ x, nil, B_{2i+2}\rangle \to \langle\ tt, nil,\ B_{2i},\ nil\rangle$
$\langle\ x,\ \emptyset, B_{2i+2}\rangle\ \nearrow$
$\langle nil,\ y, B_{2i+3}\rangle \to \langle nil,\ tt, B_{2i+1},\ nil\rangle$
$\langle\ \emptyset,\ y, B_{2i+3}\rangle\ \nearrow$
$\langle nil,\ y,\ B_1\rangle \to \langle nil,\ tt,\ B_\emptyset,\ nil\rangle$
$\langle\ \emptyset,\ y,\ B_1\rangle\ \nearrow$

Note that the even states b_2, b_4,... code up the deficit of the left input whilst the odd states b_1, b_3,... code up the deficit of the right input.

In a similar way we could define other non-sequential nodes such as 'parallel and', and 'wise' if-then-else.

<u>Dataflow nets</u>

A closed net is a directed graph in which there are no "loose" ends, that is every arc has as its source the output port of some node and as its destination the input port of a node. Figure A is an example of a closed net. Obviously closed nets do not have input or output we shall deal with this later. It is not difficult to give a formal definition of closed net see [7].

The current state of a closed net is, roughly speaking, a vector of node states that records the current state of each node and a vector of sequences that records the current contents of each arc in the net. The initial net state is one in which vector of node states records each node as being in its initial state and the vector of sequences records each arc as being empty. A net computes by moving from one net state to another via net transitions. A net transition is a vector of node transitions such that the vector contains one transition for each node in the net. A net computation is a countable sequence of net transitions. Finite sequences defining a partial net computation and infinite sequences defining complete net computations. Formal definitions of all these terms are given in [7].

The problem with closed nets is that they do not allow the net to have input or output arcs. Open nets (subnets) on the other hand have input and output arcs. The input arcs having no source node and the output arcs having no destination node. Rather than define computation for subnets we close any subnet by attaching it to an environment node and use the definition of computation over closed nets. An environment node is a node that is able to simulate any 'real' environment that the subnet may be placed in. To connect an environment node to a subnet we attach the output arcs of the environment node to the input arcs of the subnet and the output arcs of the subnet to the input arcs of the environment node.

Theorem (the encapsulation property)

Any subnet can be replaced in any pipeline dataflow context by a node having the same input/output behaviour.

Proof Since our model pipeline dataflow is completely general we can easily construct a node that simulates the input/output behaviour of any subnet. A proof of this appears in [7]. Note that in models like Arnold's[1] the encapsulation property does not hold.

<u>Subnets and Functionality</u>

Suppose that an observer places himself on an arc. He witnesses its traffic a (possibly infinite) sequence of natural numbers called the <u>history</u> of the arc. Since a node has its own memory we can think of the node as computing a function from the histories of the input lines to the histories of its output lines (i.e. a history function). In this section we formally define what it means for a subnet to compute a history function.

One approach of defining what it means for a subnet to compute a history function f is to assume that when computation begins all the datons that the subnet is ever to receive are queued up on the subnets input arcs. If the entire input is α then we simply require that there exists an (infinite) net computation sequence which "accumulates" $f(\alpha)$ on the output arcs. If the the nodes in a model are sequential and deterministic then this definition is adequate. However in our model nodes may be non-deterministic and non-sequential and so we require a more general definition of functionality.

There are other reasons why the sequential definition of functionality is unrealistic. In practice a subnet may never have an infinite sequence of datons on its input arcs. On the contrary, the input arcs are usually empty to begin with and even at some intermediate stages in the computation. Since we allow atomic subnets (nodes) to compute and even produce output while waiting for input, it is not enough to require that the subnet function properly (i.e. compute f) only when it is provided datons at a faster rate than it consumes them. For example, we can define a node which copies its input buffer when it is full but outputs zeros when the buffer is empty. This node would, according to the sequential definition of functionality, compute the identity function - but in actual practice it could use its empty buffer transition with disastrous effect.

The second problem with the sequential approach is that it requires only that $f(\alpha)$ be <u>possible</u> as the output history, but not necessary. Since our subnets are non-deterministic, this distinction (between possible and necessary activity) is crucial. We can certainly define a node which outputs a random sequence of datons, and the node would, according to the above definition, compute every function!

Furthermore, we cannot repair this last problem by requiring that <u>every</u> sequence of transitions produces $f(\alpha)$ as output. This requirement is unfair (too strict) because it rules out any sort of control or direction of the activity of a subnet. Such control, however, is necessary because our subnets(including atomic subnets) are non-deterministic devices capable of doing more than one thing (e.g. input and output) at the same time. If computation proceeds at random one vital activity may be neglected even though the computation as a whole never stops. We call such a situation "livelock" (the term is due to E. A. Ashcroft).

For example, we could design a node which computes the identity function but whose transitions code up two different internal activities. One activity is to build up an internal memory (queue) of inputs, an the other is to output stockpiled datons. The node is non-deterministic because each cause is associated with (possibly) two effects, one stockpiling and the other outputing. A computation sequence for which all but finitely many operations are stockpiling operations would be in livelock and would fail to produce the required output.

The problem with the sequential approach is that it allows no "choice" in the sequence of transitions (our nodes may be non-deterministic). The dynamic version must allow a subnet to be used in conjunction with a "fair" strategy for avoiding livelock. Strategies would be used to repeatedly choose the next transition to be performed, the choice being based on the previous history of the computation.

If we want to think in anthropomorphic terms, we can imagine a strategy being used by the controller of the subnet who is attempting to ensure that the subnet produces the correct output. The controller's strategy must work no matter how the input arrives from the external environment, i.e. no matter at what rate the input datons arrive. The fact that a subnet computes a function does not mean that the controller succeeds no matter what choices he makes; it means only that he has some strategy which ensures success in his battle with a "hostile" environment. i.e. a totally correct strategy.

Our correct definition formalises this anthropomorphic view in terms of winning strategies for infinite games of perfect information (Davis[8]).

The idea that subnets require controlling strategies, in order to choose transitions, suggest the following infinite game.

Let O be a subnet

Let f be a history function

The infinite game G(f,O) is as follows

(i) The game begins with the subnet in its initial state and all the arcs empty.

(ii) The two players alternate in making moves, 'I' playing first.

(iii) On each of his moves 'I' places a daton on some or all input arcs (possibly none).

(iv) on each move 'II' chooses a compatible subnet transition.

(v) player 'II' wins iff he made an infinite sequence of moves producing $f(\alpha)$, α being the history produced by 'I' moves. We can think of player 'I' as the controller of an environment node that is able simulate all possible input activity of a subnet. Thus 'I' chooses an environment node transition, the output of the environment node being the input to the subnet.

In this game a strategy for player 'II' is a monotonic function τ that takes a sequence of moves for 'I' and produces a sequence of (responses) moves for 'II'.

A winning (totally correct) strategy for 'II' is then a strategy τ such that if A is an infinite sequence of moves of 'I' that produce α then $\tilde{\tau}(A)$ is an infinite sequence of moves for 'II' that produces $f(\alpha)$,

where $\tilde{\tau}(A) = \bigcup_{i \in \omega} \tau(A|i)$ (A|i is read A restricted to i)

The use of infinite games allows the following definition of subnet functionality:

(3A) Definition A subnet O is said to compute a history function f iff there exists a totally correct strategy for player 'II' for G(f,O) and any other strategy γ for 'II' is such that if A, an infinite sequence of moves for 'I', produces α then $\tilde{\gamma}(A)$ produces an initial segment of $f(\alpha)$ (i.e. a partially correct strategy).

(3B) Theorem Every history function computed by an subnet is continuous (in the sense of Kahn[4]).

Proof see [7]

(3C) Theorem (the universality property)

Every continuous history function is the function computed by some atomic subnet (i.e.node).

Proof see [7], hint to proof: It is possible to construct a node such that at the nth step in the computation the node node will have output $f(\alpha|n)|n$.

(3D) Corollary (the abstraction property)

Any pure dataflow subnet can be replaced in any pure dataflow context by any atomic subnet (node) that computes the same history function.

Proof Directly from 3B and 3C.

4. A Proof of the Kahn Principle

Before we give the main result we state the following lemmas:

(4A) Lemma Any pure dataflow net can be build using the following

i) Juxtaposition: the placing side by side of two subnets to form a subnet.

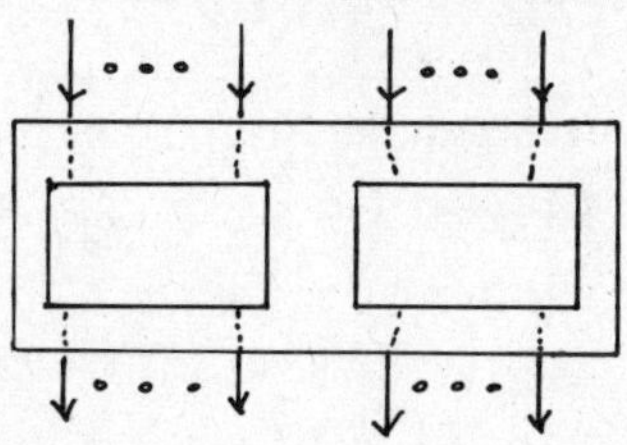

ii) Iteration: Bending back the output arc of a subnet to an input arc of the same subnet.

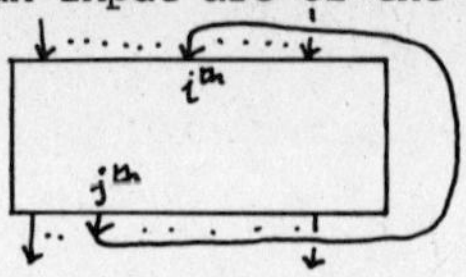

Proof Layout all the nodes in the net (composition) then apply iteration to make neccesary interconnections.

(4B) Definition A net is said to be Kahnian iff the activity of the net is that predicted by the least fixed point solution to the set of equations associated with the net.

(4C) Lemma The juxtaposition of two Kahnian nets gives a Kahnian net.

Proof Straight forward

(4D) Lemma Iterating a Kahnian subnet gives an Kahnian subnet.

Proof To illustrate the ideas behind the proof while avoiding notational complexity we consider the case of a Kahnian subnet ρ with 3 input arcs and one output arc. (the general case is treated in [7]).

let us assume that the following system of equations is associated with ρ:

$$A_\emptyset = E_\emptyset(\bar{A}, x_\emptyset, x_1, x_2)$$
$$\vdots \quad \vdots \quad \vdots \quad \vdots \quad \vdots$$
$$A_{p-1} = E_{p-1}(\bar{A}, x_\emptyset, x_1, x_2)$$

As ρ is Kahnian the equations have the following solution:

$$\lambda\, x_\emptyset, x_1, x_2\ \mu\, \bar{A}\ \langle E_\emptyset(\bar{A},\bar{x}), \ldots, E_{p-1}(\bar{A},\bar{x})\rangle$$

Let us assume that the output arc of ρ is associated with the ith component of the above vector then we associate the following function with ρ:

$$\lambda\, x_\emptyset, x_1, x_2\ \mu_i \bar{A} \langle E_\emptyset(\bar{A},\bar{x}), \ldots, E_{p-1}(\bar{A},\bar{x})\rangle \quad (= f)$$

We then iterate ρ by bending back the output of ρ to feed its second input arc (see diagram). Since ρ is Kahnian it computes f hence:

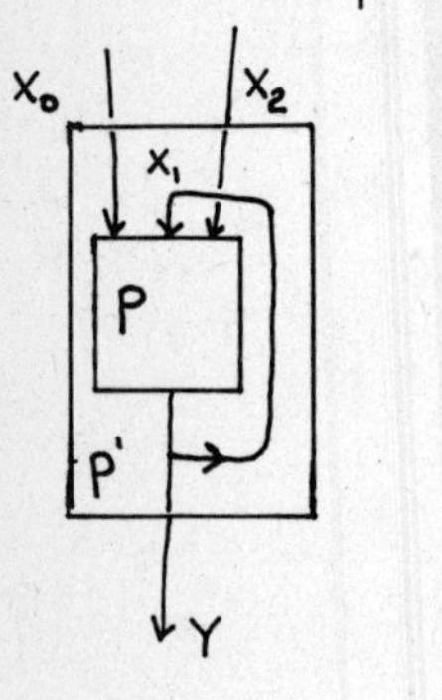

Let τ be a totally correct strategy for the game $G(f,\rho)$ then there exists a winning strategy τ' for $G(h',\rho')$ such that

$$h' = \lambda\, x_\emptyset, x_2\ \mu\, x_1\ f(x_\emptyset, x_1, x_2)$$

ρ' is the two input one output subnet formed by encapsulating ρ and the looping arc.

τ' is a totally correct strategy derived from τ using an auxiliary game in which τ is applied to $\langle x_\emptyset, x_2\rangle$ and its own output.

Since τ' is derived from τ, the first output of τ' will be $f(x_\emptyset, \Lambda, x_2)|1$ (since ρ has no input to the second input). The second output of ρ' will be $f(x_\emptyset, f(x_\emptyset, \Lambda, x_2)|1, x_2)|2$ (as τ is playing against itself). If we continue the process we get the following

$Y|1 = f(x_\emptyset, \Lambda, x_1)|1$ (ρ' first output)

$Y|2 = f(x_\emptyset, f(x_\emptyset, \Lambda, x_2)|1, x_2)|2$ (ρ' second output)

$\vdots \quad \vdots \quad \vdots \quad \vdots \quad \vdots$

$Y|i{+}1 = f(x_1, Y|i, x_2)|i{+}1$ (ρ' $i{+}1^{th}$ output)

hence ρ' does compute $\lambda x_\emptyset, x_2\ f(x_\emptyset, \mu x_1\ f(x_\emptyset, x_1, x_2), x_2)$

This means that

$h' = \lambda x_\emptyset, x_2\ \mu x_2\ \mu_i \bar{A}\ \langle E_\emptyset(\bar{A}, \bar{x}), \ldots, E_{p-1}(\bar{A}, \bar{x})\rangle$

As iterated least fixed points are equivalent to simultaneous least fixed points then we have that the subnet ρ' is output Kahnian (i.e. its output is that predicted by the least fixed point). It is not difficult to prove that all output Kahnian nets are Kahnian (such a proof is given in [7]).
Therefore ρ' is Kahnian

(4E) Theorem All pure dataflow nets are Kahnian

Proof By induction on the size of a net
(i.e. the number of nodes within a net)
base step (n = 1) all atomic subnets are Kahnian (easy)
assume all nets of size n-1 are Kahnian

(i) adding an extra node using juxtaposition is Kahnian (4C)

(ii) iterating any net arising from (i) is Kanhian (4D)

therefore all pure dataflow nets are Kahnian.

Possible Extensions

If result 4E (the Kahn principle) is seen as a result of descriptive semantics we would look for ways of extending the mathematical approach to handle a broader class of nodes and nets (i.e. not just pure dataflow). One such extension involves changing the basic domain of histories by introducing a special kind of daton called a "hiaton" (from "hiatus" meaning a pause; the term is due to W.Wadge and E. Ashcroft). A hiaton can be thought of as a unit of delay that (notionally) travels along with the ordinary datons and allows a node to produce something regularly even if it has no real output. Hiatonic streams code up timing information and it should be possible to use them to handle nodes and nets which are time sensitive.

On the other hand, if the operational semantics is seen as an implementation of a functional programming language (so that the Kahn principle states the correctness of the implementation) then we would look for ways to extend the language. The most obvious extension is to allow the user to include equations defining functions, including recursive equations. The implementation of such a language (which is similar to Structured Lucid[3]) involves either dynamically growing nets or (notionally) infinite nets (but still pure dataflow). The methods of this paper extend fairly easily to such nets and permit a proof of the correspondingly extended Kahn principle.

6. Acknowledgements

I would like to thank Bill Wadge for the time, effort and encouragement he has given to me. I would also like to thank the other members of the Warwick dataflow group who also helped in various ways in the preparation of this paper. In addition, the support of the SERC Distributed Computing Programme is gratefully acknowledged.

References

[Ø] Adams D.
A computation model with dataflow sequencing
Ph.D Thesis (Stanford University 1968)
Technical report No. CS 117

[1] Arnold Andre
Semantique des processus communicants
RAIRO Vol 15 No 2
1981

[2] Arvind and Gostelow, Kim P.
Some relationships between asynchronous interpreters of a dataflow language.
Formal Description of Programming Concepts
St. Andrews N.B., Canada 1977

[3] E.A. Ashcroft & W.Wadge
Structured Lucid
Theory of Computation, Report No33
University of Warwick, Coventry

[4] Kahn Gilles
The semantics of a simple language for parallel programming.
IFIPS 74

[5] R.M. Karp & R.E. Miller
Properties of a model for Parallel Computations:
Determinacy, Termination, Queueing
SIAM J. Applied Math XIV (Nov 1966) pp1390-411.

[6] Z. Manna
Mathematical Theory of Computation
(Mc Graw-Hill 1974)

[7] A.A.Faustini
The Equivalence Between an Operatational and a denotational semantics for pure dataflow
Ph.D Thesis (In preparation)
University of Warwick, Coventry

[8] M. Davis
Infinite games of perfect information
Advances in Game theory
Annals of Mathematical Studies
V. 52 Princeton University Press
Princeton N.J. pp85-1Ø1

Some Properties of D-Continuous Causal Nets

C. Fernândez and P.S. Thiagarajan
Gesellschaft für Mathematik
und Datenverarbeitung
5205 St. Augustin 1, W.Germany

0. Introduction

The aims of this paper are twofold. Our first aim is to formulate a model of non-sequential processes called D-continuous causal nets (CCN's). The second aim is to establish a number of properties of CCN's.

It seems reasonable to demand that the causality relation in a non-sequential process be a partial ordering relation. One is then naturally lead to consider posets as a basis for building up a model of non-sequential processes. The question then arises: Which class of posets should be chosen to serve this purpose? We feel that it is too early to give a firm answer to this question. The main reason being that at present not enough is known about concurrent systems and processes, especially from a practical standpoint. Thus at this stage, one can merely speculate about the properties that a 'meaningful' non-sequential process should have. In this paper, we speculate from the standpoint offered by one approach, namely, the net theory of systems and processes [1]. More specifically, C.A. Petri has carried out two related attempts [2 , 3] to formalize the notion of a non-sequential process. From these attempts, a number of properties of processes emerge which Petri offers as candidates to be studied in theory and evaluated in practice. Our main aim here is to use the CCN model as a medium for displaying a good many of these properties. In particular, we would like to expose D-continuity. To do so, we demand that our posets called causal nets be D-continuous. D-continuity is a generalization - to posets - of Dedekind's classic definition of the continuity (completeness) of the reals.

The paper is organized as follows. In the next section we introduce the notion of a causal net which is basically a set of partially ordered occurrences of events and conditions. In section 2 we define D-continuity for posets in general and establish a key property of D-continuous posets. Section 3 is the heart of the paper. We develop a number of properties of CCN's and indicate why these might be nice properties for a non-sequential process to have. In the concluding section we offer a more detailed review of related work.

1. Causal Nets

We first introduce the notion of a net and some related terminology.

Definition 1.1 A net is a triple $N = (S,T;F)$ with:

a) $S \cap T = \phi \ \wedge \ S \cup T \neq \phi$

b) $F \subseteq (S \times T) \cup (T \times S)$

c) $dom(F) \cup codom(F) = S \cup T$

S is the set of S-elements, T is the set of T-elements and $X = S \cup T$, the set of elements of N. F is the flow relation. In diagrams, S-elements are drawn as circles and T-elements as boxes. If $(x,y) \in F$ then this is indicated by a directed arc going from x to y. The following notation will be repeatedly used. Let $x \in X$, then:

$${}^{\circ}x = \{y \in X \mid (y,x) \in F\} \qquad \text{(The pre-set of x)}$$

$$x^{\circ} = \{y \in X \mid (x,y) \in F\} \qquad \text{(The post-set of x)}$$

Within net theory, the structure of a concurrent system is represented by a net. The distributed state of the system is denoted by a token distribution (marking) over the S-elements.

The dynamic behaviour of the system is modelled by the firing rules which specify how the marking is to be changed through the firing of the T-elements. A variety of net models, with very different interpretations and expressive power can be developed and studied using this general idea [4]. An example of a very elementary net model (in the jargon, a condition/event system) is shown in fig. 1.

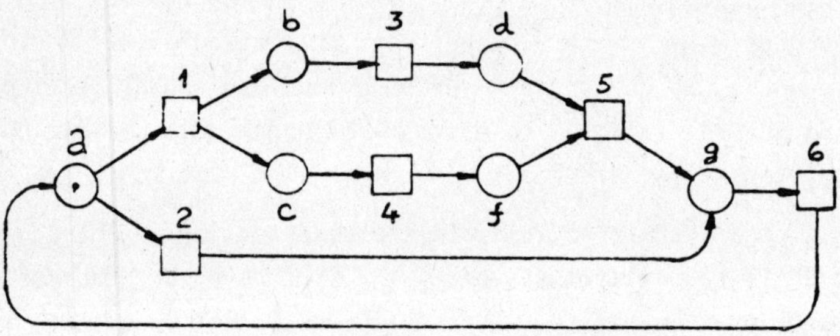

Fig. 1

The firing rule is: Whenever a T-element, say t, has exactly one token on each element of ${}^{\bullet}t$ and no tokens on any of the elements of $t^{\bullet}$, it may fire. When t fires, one token is removed from each element of ${}^{\bullet}t$ and one token is added to each element of $t^{\bullet}$. Suppose two T-elements, say t_1 and t_2, can both fire at a marking. If t_1 and t_2 share a S-element (${}^{\bullet}t_1 \cap {}^{\bullet}t_2 \neq \phi$ or $t_1^{\bullet} \cap t_2^{\bullet} \neq \phi$), then they are in conflict; only one of them may fire. If they are not in conflict, they can fire concurrently. This means that in general, a run of the system will consist of a set of partially ordered occurrences of S-elements and T-elements. For example, one run (which we shall call a process) of the system shown in fig. 1 is:

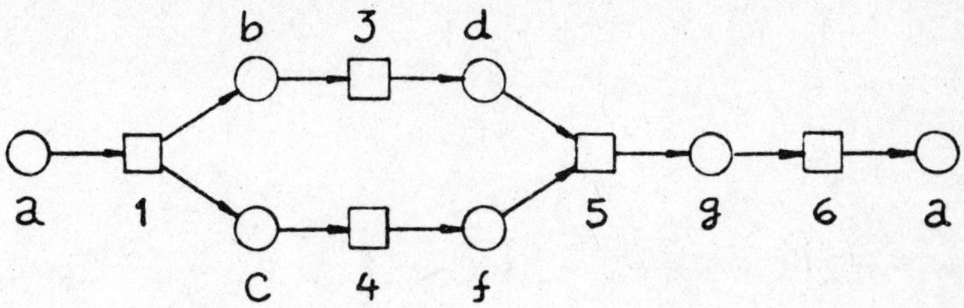

Fig. 2

Some notable features of the net shown in fig. 2 are: It is acyclic, i.e. F^+ is asymmetric. For every S-element x, $|{}^\bullet x|, |x^\bullet| \le 1$. Because of these two features, there is a "standard" way of marking the net and playing the token game on it. On fig. 2, we mark the left most S-element a with one token and systematically go from left to right.

The point is, nets of the type shown in fig.2 can be used for representing the non-sequential processes that are supported by a marked net, which in turn is the model of a concurrent system. Such a model of a non-sequential process can be studied in its own right without nailing down the related notion of a system. This is what we intend to do in this paper. Nets of the sort shown in fig.2 are called occurrence nets.

Definition 1.2 An occurrence net is a net $N = (B,E;F)$ where:

a) N is acyclic. [i.e. $(x,y) \in F^+ \Rightarrow (y,x) \notin F^+$]

b) $\forall\, b \in B$: $|{}^\bullet b|, |b^\bullet| \le 1$ (conflict-free for every marking)

B is the set of conditions and E, the set of events. The class of occurrence nets is rather large. We shall restrict the scope of our study by focusing on causal nets.

Definition 1.3 A causal net is an occurrence net $N = (B,E;F)$ with:

a) N is simple. [i.e. $\forall\, x,y \in X = B \cup E$: $({}^\bullet x = {}^\bullet y \wedge x^\bullet = y^\bullet) \Rightarrow x=y$]

b) $\forall\, e \in E$: $0 < |{}^\bullet e| < \infty \wedge 0 < |e^\bullet| < \infty$

c) $\forall\, b \in B$: $|{}^\bullet b| = |b^\bullet| = 1$

A causal net is to be understood as the most detailed description of a process. At this level of description, we should like an element to be completely characterized by its pre-set and post-set. Hence the demand that N be simple. An event e can occur when its pre conditions (${}^\bullet e$) hold. When e occurs, the pre conditions cease to hold and the post conditions ($e^\bullet$) begin to hold. We would like for each event, both the cause and effect of its occurrence to be finite and non-empty. This is expressed by b). The requirement c) states that, in this paper we will concentrate on processes that have neither a beginning nor an end. There is no deep explanation involved. Most of the results that we prove hold (with a few minor modifications) for the finite case. It is just that, not having to consider each time the finite case, make the proofs a bit tidier. A portion of a causal net is shown in fig.3.

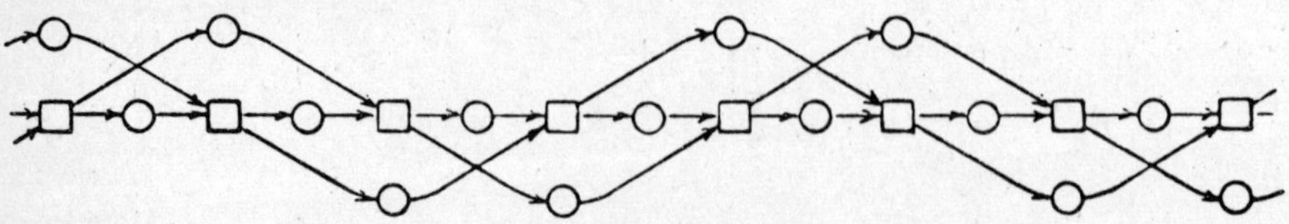

Fig. 3

A causal net (and indeed an occurrence net) may be viewed as a poset:

Proposition 1.1 Let $N = (B,E;F)$ be a causal net, $X = B \cup E$ and $\leq = F^*$. Then $(X;\leq)$ is a poset.

Given a causal net $N=(B,E;F)$ and the associated poset $(X;\leq)$ one can restrict $\leq$ to just the events of $N(\leq')$ and get $(E;\leq')$.

In [5] and [6], this structure is called an elementary event structure. Whether one works with $(X;\leq)$ or $(E;\leq')$ is often a matter of taste and convenience. For our purposes though, it is important to keep the conditions around. For a more detailed discussion of this issue the interested reader is referred to [4] and [7].

In what follows, we will abuse notations and not distinguish between a causal net $N=(B,E;F)$ and its associated poset $(X;\leq)$. Moreover, we will often employ the derived relations $\geq$, $<$, $>$, $\not\leq$, etc. in the standard fashion. We conclude this section with a simple but useful observation concerning causal nets (occurrence nets).

Proposition 1.2 Let $N = (B,E;F)$ be a causal net. Then:

(1) $\forall\, x,y \in X$: If $x < y$ then $\exists\; x_o, x_1, \ldots, x_k \in X$ such that: $x=x_o$, $x_k=y$ and for $0 \leq i < k$, $(x_i, x_{i+1}) \in F$.

(2) $\forall\, e \in E$, $\forall\, b_1, b_2 \in {}^{\bullet}e\ (e^{\bullet})$, b_1 co b_2 (i.e. $b_1 \not\leq b_2 \wedge b_2 \not\leq b_1$)

(3) Let $x,y \in X$ and $x < y$. Then $\exists\, y' \in {}^{\bullet}y$ and $x' \in x^{\bullet}$ such that $x' \leq y$ and $x \leq y'$

Proof Trivial. □

2. D-continuity

We will define D-continuity for posets in general. In what follows we assume that $X \neq \phi$. Let us start with:

Definition 2.1 Let $(X;\leq)$ be a poset, $l,s \subseteq X$ and $l,s \neq \phi$. Then:

a) l is a li-set (chain) iff $\forall\, x,y \in l$: $x \leq y \vee y \leq x$

b) l is a line (a maximal chain) iff l is a li-set and $\forall\, x \notin l$: $l \cup \{x\}$ is not a li-set

c) The set of lines of $(X;\leq)$ is denoted as L.

d) $li := < \cup > \cup\, id|X$

e) $co := \{(x,y) \in X\times X \mid x \not< y \wedge y \not< x\}$ [i.e. $co = (X\times X - li) \cup id|X$]

f) s is a co-set (anti-chain) iff $\forall\, x,y \in s$: $x \text{ co } y$

g) s is a slice (maximal anti-chain) iff s is a co-set and $\forall\, x \notin s$: $s \cup \{x\}$ is not a co-set.

h) The set of slices of $(X;\leq)$ is denoted by SL.

Using the axiom of choice - which we assume in this paper - it is easy to show that for every li-set (co-set) there exist a line (slice) in which the li-set (co-set) is contained.

In the axiomatization of net theory, the relation co plays a fundamental role. It is also very useful for dealing with our posets as we will see. A slice is used to represent the stage up to which a process has progressed at a certain "time". In fact, for non-sequential processes a slice is the counterpart to the normal notion of sequential time. A line, viewed as an ascending chain describes the life history of a sequential entity (state variable, object, signal, a particle) participating in a process. We can now say what a D-cut is.

Definition 2.2 Let $(X;\leq)$ be a poset, $A \subseteq X$ and $\overline{A} = X-A$. Then $(A,\overline{A})$ is a Dedekind-cut (D-cut) of X iff:

a) $\phi \neq A \neq X$

b) $\forall\, x \in A,\ \forall\, y \in \overline{A} : \neg(y \leq x)$

$(A,\overline{A})$ is a non-trivial partition of X which in the sense of b) "respects" the $\leq$ relation. We will almost always abuse notation and say A is a D-cut instead of $(A,\overline{A})$ is a D-cut. Through the remaining portions of this paper D denotes the set of D-cuts of X; Max(A), the set of maximal elements of A; Min($\overline{A}$) the set of minimal elements of $\overline{A}$. Finally, $M(A) := Max(A) \cup Min(\overline{A})$.

Let Z, Q and R be the set of integers, rationals and reals respectively with the usual ordering. For any D-cut A in Z, $|M(A)| = 2$ (a jump). For certain "bad" D-cuts A in Q, $|M(A)| = 0$ (a gap). For every D-cut A in R, $|M(A)| = 1$ (complete; no jumps, no gaps).

The completeness (continuity) of the reals expressed by $|M(A)| = 1$ is what we would like to transport to causal nets. For posets, however, the set M(A) will be in general too large. Hence we will have to first refine Max(A) (Min($\overline{A}$)) down to Obmax(A) (Obmin($\overline{A}$)). We choose from Max(A) those elements which have the Obmax property. To see what this property is:

Let (X;≤) be a poset, $A \in D$, $l \in L$ and $x \in A$. We say that l exits from A at x iff $x \in Max(A \cap l)$. Now, x is said to have the Obmax property iff $\forall A \in D$: if $x \in A$ then either every line l passing through x exits from A at x or no line l passing through x exits from A at x.

The formal definition we use however is the original one given by C.A.Petri because it is easier to work with:

Definition 2.3 Let (X;≤) be a poset and A a D-cut of X. Then:

a) $Obmax(A) := \{x \in Max(A) \mid \forall B \in D, \forall l \in L: x \in Max(B \cap l) \Rightarrow x \in Max(B)\}$

b) $Obmin(\overline{A}) := \{x \in Min(\overline{A}) \mid \forall B \in D, \forall l \in L: x \in Min(\overline{B} \cap l) \Rightarrow x \in Min(\overline{B})\}$

c) $c(A) := Obmax(A) \cup Obmin(\overline{A})$

Consider the finite poset shown in fig.4.

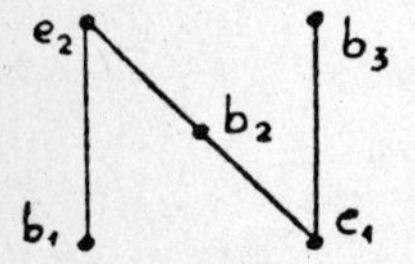

Fig. 4

$A = \{b_1, e_1\}$ is a D-cut and Max(A) = A. $e_1 \notin Obmax(A)$ because for the D-cut $B = \{b_1, e_1, b_3\}$ and the line $l = \{e_1, b_2, e_2\}$ we have: $e_1 \in Max(B \cap l)$ and $e_1 \notin Max(B)$. Similarly for the D-cut $A_1 = \{b_1, e_1, b_2\}$, $e_2 \notin Obmin(\overline{A_1})$.

We are now ready to state what D-continuity is:

Definition 2.4 Let (X;≤) be a poset. (X;≤) is Dedekind-continuous (D-continuous) iff $\forall A \in D, \forall l \in L : |c(A) \cap l| = 1$

It is important to keep in mind that this definition of continuity has been developed for posets which are candidates for modelling non-sequential processes. If (X;≤) is a poset and A is a D-cut then we interpret c(A) as follows: The associated process has reached a stage at which everything below c(A) has definitely occurred and everything above c(A) has definitely not occurred. Now continuity states that, at this stage, for every sequential component (modelled by a line) one should be able to say in an unambiguous fashion, what this sequential component is doing. Hence the demand $|c(A) \cap l| = 1$.

Below we show three examples of posets which are not D-continuous:

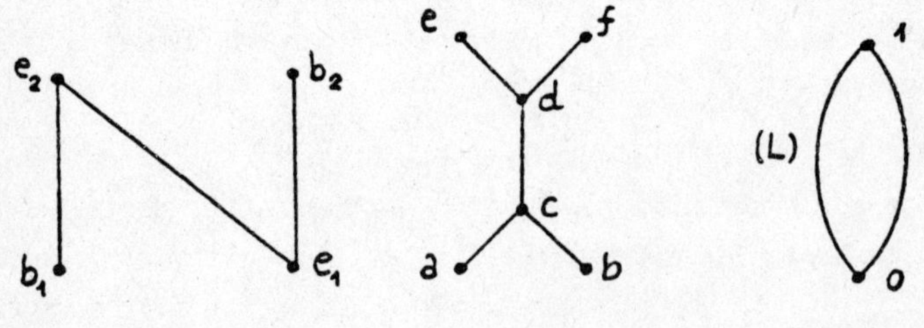

(a) (b) (c)

Fig.5

Case 1 $\downarrow s \neq X$

Set $A=\downarrow s$. Then $\overline{A}=s^+$. $A\neq\phi$ since $s\neq\phi$. Hence A is a D-cut. Consequently $|l\cap c(A)|=1$. Let $l\cap c(A)=\{z\}$. By the construction of A, we have Max(A)=s. Hence if $z\in \text{Obmax}(A)$ then $z\in s$ which implies $s\cap l\neq\phi$, a contradiction. This means that $z\in \text{Obmin}(\overline{A})$ which in turn means that $z\in s^+$. Let $t\in s$ such that $z>t$. $t\notin l$ because otherwise $l\cap s\neq\phi$. But then $t\notin l$ implies that $B=A-\{t\}\neq\phi$. Clearly B is a D-cut. Since $\overline{B}\cap l=\overline{A}\cap l$, we have $z\in \text{Min}(\overline{B}\cap l)$. On the other hand $z\notin \text{Min}(\overline{B})$ since $t\in\overline{B}$ and $t<z$. This implies that $z\notin \text{Obmin}(\overline{A})$, which is once again a contradiction.

Case 2 $\downarrow s = X$

Then we can consider $A=s^-\neq\phi$ since $s\neq X$, and the proof is identical to that for the previous case. □

K-density is strictly weaker than D-continuity because the posets shown in fig.5(b) and (c) are both K-dense but not D-continuous. Arguments in favor of K-density have been given by C.A.Petri [2] and E. Best [10]. G. Winskel [6] argues against K-density and hence against D-continuity claiming that it is too restrictive. Our position is: K-density and the stronger D-continuity are restrictives properties. However, the class of posets that possess D-continuity constitutes an interesting and non-trivial class, and we would like to thoroughly understand the properties, capabilities and limitations of D-continuous causal nets before considering larger classes of posets as models for non-sequential processes.

3. D-continuous causal nets

Returning to the study of causal nets, we shall start with:

Definition 3.1 A D-continuous causal net (CCN) is a causal net $N = (B,E;F)$ such that $(X;\leq)$ is a D-continuous poset where $X = B\cup E$ and $\leq = F^*$.

Proposition 3.1 Let $N = (B,E;F)$ be a CCN, A a D-cut of N, $x\in \text{Max}(A)$ and $y\in \text{Min}(\overline{A})$.

Then: (1) $x\in \text{Obmax}(A)$ iff $|x^\bullet| = 1$

(2) $y\in \text{Obmin}(\overline{A})$ iff $|{}^\bullet y| = 1$

Proof Follows from definitions and prop.1.2. See [8]. □

Proposition 3.2 Let $N = (B,E;F)$ be a CCN. Then: $\forall e\in E$: $|{}^\bullet e|, |e^\bullet| \geq 2$.

Proof If $e\in E$ and $|{}^\bullet e|$ $(|e^\bullet|)=1$, then it is easy to find a D-cut A and a line l such that $|c(A)\cap l| = 2$. □

This result expresses the important fact that an event constitutes the interaction of at least two entities. The "internal history" of a single object will not be represented in our model. Indeed, the very existence of an object can be verified only by (an observer) interacting with it. From prop.3.1 and 3.2 it follows easily that for any D-cut, $c(A)\subseteq B$.

The poset shown in (a) is not D-continuous because for the D-cut $A = \{b_1,e_1\}$ and the line $l = \{e_1,e_2\}$ we have $c(A) \cap l = \phi$. In (b), for the D-cut $A = \{a,b,c\}$ and any line l, we have $|c(A) \cap l| = 2$. The poset shown in (c) is dense. Two distinct copies of the closed interval [0,1] on the reals have been pasted together (synchronized) at 0 and 1.

Let $X = \{0,1\} \cup X^L \cup X^K$ where $L \neq K$ and $X^i = \{x^i | x \in (0,1),\ i \in \{L,K\}\}$. $\leq'$ is the least relation (in the sense of set inclusion) satisfying:

a) $\forall x^i \in X^L \cup X^K : 0 <' x^i <' 1$

b) $\forall x^i, y^j \in X^L \cup X^K : x^i \leq' y^j$ iff $i=j$ and $x \leq y$

($i,j \in \{L,K\}$ and $\leq$ is the usual ordering on the reals)

$(X;\leq')$ is not D-continuous because for the D-cut $A = \{0\} \cup X^K$ we have $Max(A) = \phi = Min(\overline{A})$. Hence for any line l (say, $\{0,1\} \cup X^L$) we have $c(A) \cap l = \phi$.

We will now establish a few key properties of D-continuous posets.

<u>Proposition 2.1</u> Let $(X;\leq)$ be a D-continuous poset and A a D-cut of $(X;\leq)$. Then c(A) is a slice.

<u>Proof</u> See [8]. □

Thus, in a D-continuous poset, for every D-cut A, c(A) indeed describes the "state" of the associated process.

This is an appropriate place to connect up the notion of a D-cut with a standard notion associated with posets. Following [9], we first state:

<u>Definition 2.5</u> Let $(X;\leq)$ be a poset and $A \subseteq X$. Then:

a) $\downarrow A = \{x \in X | \exists y \in A : x \leq y\}$

b) $\uparrow A = \{x \in X | \exists y \in A : x \geq y\}$

c) $\forall x \in X : \downarrow x = \downarrow\{x\},\ \uparrow x = \uparrow\{x\}$

d) A is a <u>lower</u> (<u>upper</u>) set iff $A = \downarrow A$ ($\uparrow A$)

e) $A^- = \downarrow A - A$. $A^+ = \uparrow A - A$.

<u>Proposition 2.2</u> Let $(X;\leq)$ be a poset and $A \subseteq X$ such that $\phi \neq A \neq X$. Then: A is a D-cut if and only if A ($\overline{A}$) is a lower (upper) set.

<u>Proof</u> Follows at once from the definitions. □

D-continuous posets possess an important property called K-density.

<u>Definition 2.6</u> A poset $(X;\leq)$ is <u>K-dense</u> iff $\forall\, l \in L,\ \forall\, s \in SL : |l \cap s| = 1$

The poset shown in fig.5(b) is K-dense but not the one shown in fig.5(a).

<u>Theorem 2.1</u> Let $(X;\leq)$ be a D-continuous poset. Then $(X;\leq)$ is K-dense.

<u>Proof</u> Let $s \in SL$ and $l \in L$. If $s = X$ then every line is a singleton and we at once have K-density. We can assume that $s \neq X$. By def. of l and s we know that $|l \cap s| \leq 1$. The proof is an indirect one. Suppose that $l \cap s = \phi$

Our next aim is to characterize the lines of a CCN.

Theorem 3.1 Let $N = (B,E;F)$ be a CCN and $\phi \neq l \subseteq X$ a li-set. l is a line if and only if $\forall x \in l : |{}^{\bullet}x \cap l| = 1 = |x^{\bullet} \cap l|$.

Proof (=>) Follows from prop.1.2 and from the fact that $|{}^{\bullet}x|, |x^{\bullet}| < \infty$. See [8].

(<=) (Indirect)

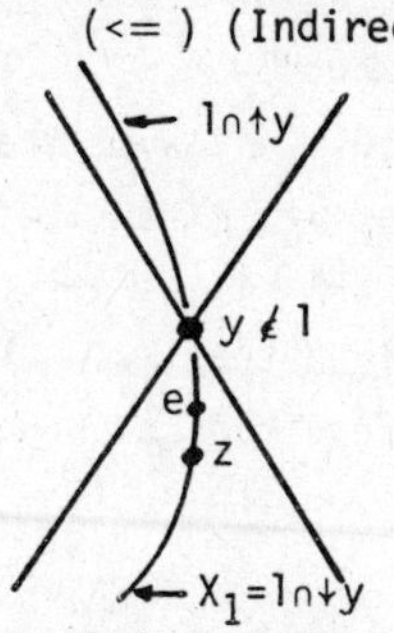

Let l be a li-set such that $\forall x \in l : |{}^{\bullet}x \cap l| = 1 = |x^{\bullet} \cap l|$. Suppose $y \notin l$ and $\forall x \in l : x$ li y (i.e. $l \subseteq {\downarrow}y \cup {\uparrow}y$). Then $l \cup \{y\}$ is also a li-set. Let $l' \in L$ such that $l \cup \{y\} \subseteq l'$. Since $l \neq \phi$, then we have $l \cap {\downarrow}y \neq \phi$ or $l \cap {\uparrow}y \neq \phi$. Without loss of generality assume that $l \cap {\downarrow}y \neq \phi$. Let $X_1 = l \cap {\downarrow}y$, $A = {\downarrow}X_1$ and $\overline{A} = X\text{-}A$.

$A \neq \phi$ since $X_1 \neq \phi$. $A \neq X$ since $y \notin A$. Thus $(A,\overline{A})$ is a D-cut. Let $\{z\} = l' \cap c(A)$. $z \in B$ since $c(A) \subseteq B$. Where could z lie?

Case 1 $z \in A$

Then $z \in X_1$ since $z \in \mathrm{Obmax}(A)$. This means that $z \in l$ and $z < y$. Let $\{e\} = z^{\bullet}$. $e \in l$ by hypothesis and $e \leq y$ by prop.1.2, i.e. $e \in l \cap {\downarrow}y = X_1 \subseteq A$. A contradiction since $e > z$ and $z \in \mathrm{Obmax}(A)$ together imply that $e \in \overline{A}$.

Case 2 $z \in \overline{A}$ (i.e. $z \notin X_1$)

Let $\{e\} = {}^{\bullet}z$. $e \in A = {\downarrow}X_1$ since $z \in \mathrm{Obmin}(\overline{A})$. $e \in {\downarrow}X_1$ implies that $\exists\ u \in X_1$ such that $e \leq u$. We shall show that $u=e$. To this end note that $u \in X_1 = l \cap {\downarrow}y$ implies $u \in l \subseteq l'$. Since $z \in l'$ too, we have z li u. $u \not\geq z$ since $u \in A$ and $z \in \overline{A}$. Thus $u < z$ and by prop.1.2 $u \leq e$. Consequently, $u=e$. This means that $e \in X_1$. Let $b \in e^{\bullet} \cap l \subseteq l'$. b exists by hypothesis. If $b \neq z$ then by prop.1.2 b co z, a contradiction since $b, z \in l'$. If $b = z$ then $z \in l$. Since $y \in \overline{A}$, $z \in \mathrm{Obmin}(\overline{A})$ and $z, y \in l'$, we must have $z \in {\downarrow}y$. Thus $z \in l \cap {\downarrow}y = X_1 \subseteq A$, which is a contradiction. This completes the proof. □

We have shown a detailed proof of this theorem for a number of reasons. It is a very useful characterization of lines; it enables one to construct a specific line having some desired properties. The proof which is not obvious, depends crucially on D-continuity and the fact that $|{}^{\bullet}x|, |x^{\bullet}| < \infty$ for a causal net.

To state and prove the next result we need some additional terminology.

Definition 3.2 Let $N = (B,E;F)$ be a causal net, $x,y \in X$ and $l \in L$. Then:

(1) $[x,y] := \{z \in X \mid x \leq z \leq y\}$

(2) The path between x and y along l is denoted as $\Pi[x,y;l]$ and is given by $\Pi[x,y;l] = l \cap [x,y]$

Theorem 3.2 Let $N = (B,E;F)$ be a CCN, $x,y \in X$ with $x < y$. Then $|[x,y]| < \infty$.

Proof (Indirect) We assume that $|[x,y]|=\infty$. Let $x=x_0$ and $x_0^{\bullet}=\{y_0^1, y_0^2, \ldots, y_0^{k_0}\}$. We know that $|x_0^{\bullet}|<\infty$ and also $[x,y]=\{x_0\}\cup\bigcup_{i=1}^{i=k_0}[y_0^i, y]$. We have $|\bigcup_{i=1}^{i=k_0}[y_0^i,y]|=\infty$ since $|[x,y]|=\infty$. This means that $\exists\, y_0^j\in x_0^{\bullet}$ such that $y_0^j<y$ and $|[y_0^j,y]|=\infty$. Let $y_0^j=x_1$. We can repeat this argument at x_1 to obtain an element $x_2\in x_1^{\bullet}$ such that $x_2<y$ and $|[x_2,y]|=\infty$. Indeed we can obtain a set of elements $U=\{x_0,x_1,x_2,\ldots\}$ such that, $\forall\, i\in\mathbb{N}$ $x_{i+1}\in x_i^{\bullet}$, $x_{i+1}<y$ and $|[x_{i+1},y]|=\infty$. Let $l\in L$ such that $x,y\in l$ and consider $l'=(l\cap{\downarrow}x)\cup U$. By the construction of l', if $z\in l'$ then $z<y$. Moreover, by theorem 3.1, l' is a line. Set $\bar{A}={\uparrow}y$ and $A=X-\bar{A}$. It is easy to see that $(A,\bar{A})$ is a D-cut. By the D-continuity of N, $\exists\, z\in B$ such that $\{z\}=c(A)\cap l'$. Let $z^{\bullet}=\{e\}$. By theorem 3.1, $e\in l'$. Hence $e<y$. This is a contradiction because $z\in c(A)$ which implies that $e\in\bar{A}$ which in turn means that $y\le e$. □

Corollary 3.1 Let $N=(B,E;F)$ be a CCN, $x,y\in X$ with $x<y$. Let $l\in L$ such that $x,y\in l$. Then $|\Pi[x,y;l]|<\infty$.

Corollary 3.2 Let $N=(B,E;F)$ be a CCN and $x,y\in X$ with $x<y$. Then:

$\exists\, n(x,y)\in\mathbb{N}$ such that $\forall\, l\in L$: If $x,y\in l$ then $|\Pi[x,y;l]|\le n(x,y)$.

A different proof of corollary 3.1 can be found in [10]. The property stated in corollary 3.2 will be called bounded-discreteness (b-discrete). This is a nice property which guarantees that if x is a cause of y ($x<y$) then "all" effects will be transported from x to y within a finite number of steps.

In fig. 6(a), we show a causal net which is not b-discrete. However the net in fig. 6(b) is b-discrete (it is also K-dense). Indeed, by throwing in additional S-elements, this second causal net can be completed to become a CCN.

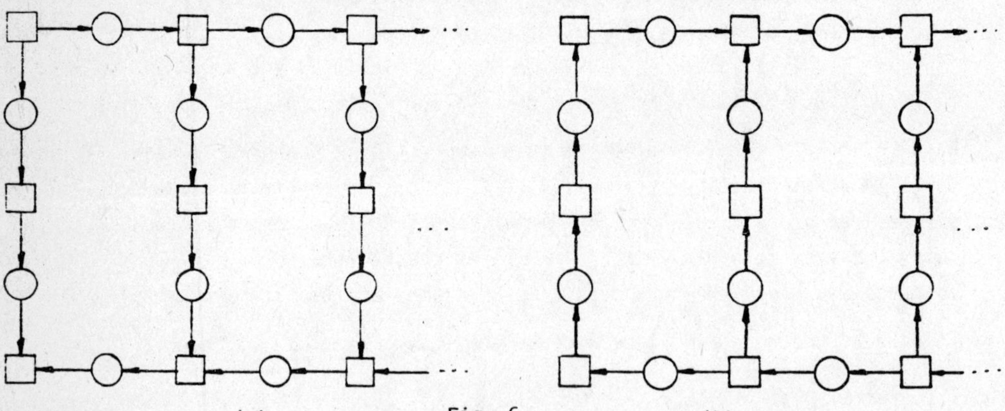

(a) Fig. 6 (b)

Next we claim that a CCN is connected with respect to both the ordering and the co relation.

Definition 3.3 Let $N = (B,E;F)$ be a causal net. Then:

a) N is li-coherent iff $li^* = X \times X$.

b) N is co-coherent iff $co^* = X \times X$.

c) N is coherent iff N is li-coherent and co-coherent

Theorem 3.3 Let $N = (B,E;F)$ be a CCN. Then N is coherent.

Proof See [8]. □

li-coherence ensures that we are not dealing with two unconnected non-sequential processes. (We should deal with them one at a time.) co-coherence arises out of the desire to treat the relations li and co on an equal basis.

The next property of a CCN that we wish to establish formalizes the intuitive demand that the relations li and co should uniquely determine the underlying partially ordering relation (up to "reverse").

Definition 3.4 A poset $(X;\leq)$ is called a natural order iff for every other poset $(X;\leq')$, $co = co'$ (or equivalently $li = li'$) implies that $\leq' = \leq$ or $\leq' = \geq$.

Paraphrasing C.A.Petri [3], in a natural order, direction is a 1-bit convention. To get a bit more feel for this property, consider the (finite) poset shown in fig.7(a). This is not a natural order because the poset shown in (b) has the same co structure, but it is neither identical to nor the "reverse" of the poset shown in (a).

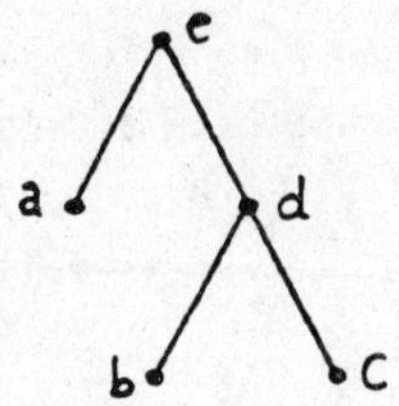

(a)

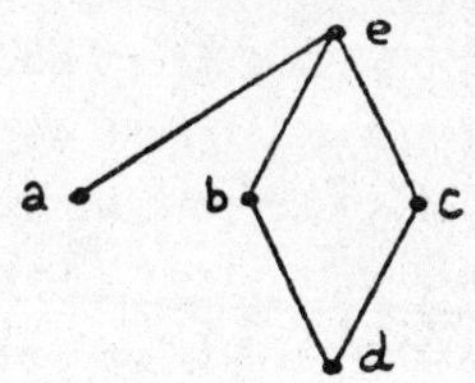

(b)

Fig. 7

To show that a CCN is a natural order it is useful to identify the notions of a E-predecessor and a E-successor.

Definition 3.5 Let $N = (B,E;F)$ be a CCN and $e,e' \in E$.

a) e' is a E-predecessor of e iff $e' < e$ and $\forall\, l \in L$: $e',e \in l \Rightarrow |\Pi[e',e;l]| = 3$

b) e' is a E-successor of e iff e is a E-predecessor of e'.

Due to lack of space, we will merely indicate the major steps of the proof that a CCN is a natural order.

Lemma 3.1 Let $N = (B,E;F)$ be a CCN and $(X;\leq')$ a poset such that $co = co'$. Let $e,e_1 \in E$ and $b_1 \in B$ such that e_1 is a E-predecessor of e and $b_1 \in e_1^{\bullet} \cap {}^{\bullet}e$. Then in $(X;\leq')$: Either $e_1 <' b_1 <' e$ or $e <' b_1 <' e_1$.

Lemma 3.2 Let $N = (B,E;F)$ be a CCN and $(X;\leq')$ a poset such that $co = co'$. Let $e \in E$. Then:
Either $(\forall\, b \in {}^{\bullet}e : b <' e$ and $\forall\, b' \in e^{\bullet} : e <' b')$
or $(\forall\, b \in {}^{\bullet}e : e <' b$ and $\forall\, b' \in e^{\bullet} : b' <' e)$

Theorem 3.4 Let $N = (B,E;F)$ be a CCN. Then N is a natural order.

Proof See [8]. □

As a consequence, if $N = (B,E;F)$ is a CCN then a good deal of the results concerning N can be transported to the CCN, $N' = (B,E;F^{-1})$. In some sense the major portions of the theory of CCN's will be invariant with respect to direction.

The last result we shall mention concerns the set of slices of a CCN. To do so, the set of slices will have to be augmented with two special elements. We also need to introduce an ordering relation between a pair of slices.

Definition 3.6 Let $N = (B,E;F)$ be a CCN and SL its set of slices. Then:

(1) $SL' = SL \cup \{\bot,\top\}$ where $\bot,\top \notin SL$.

(2) $\forall\, s,s' \in SL : s \sqsubseteq s'$ iff $\forall\, x \in s : \exists\, x' \in s'$ such that $x \leq x'$.

(3) $\forall\, s \in SL : \bot \sqsubseteq s \sqsubseteq \top$.

Theorem 3.5 Let $N = (B,E;F)$ be a CCN. Let SL' and $\sqsubseteq$ be defined as above. Then $(SL'; \sqsubseteq)$ is a complete lattice. In fact, $(SL'; \sqsubseteq)$ is an algebraic lattice.

Proof Following [6], we first observe that $(D_0; \subseteq)$ is an algebraic lattice, where $D_0 = \{A \subseteq X \mid A = {\downarrow}A\}$. Next we set up a scheme for going back and forth between D_0 and SL'. If $s \in SL$ then we associate the lower set ${\downarrow}s$ with s. By convention, we associate ϕ with $\bot$ and X with $\top$. We can go from D_0 to SL' as follows:
(If $X_1 \subseteq X$ then $X_1^{\bullet} = \{y \in x^{\bullet} \mid x \in X_1\}$
Let $A \in D_0$. Then:

$$\hat{s}(A) = \begin{cases} c(A) \cup (Max(A) \cap E) - (Max(A) \cap E)^{\bullet}, & \text{if } \phi \neq A \neq X \\ \bot, \text{ if } A = \phi \\ \top, \text{ if } A = X \end{cases}$$

It is easy to show that $\hat{s}(A) \in SL'$. After this, it is tiresome but straightforward to exploit the properties of $(D_0; \subseteq)$ to establish the theorem.
(For more details, see [8]). □

Collecting together the main results of this paper, we have:

Theorem 3.6 Let $N = (B,E;F)$ be a CCN. Then N is:

(1) K-dense.

(2) b-discrete.

(3) li-coherent and co-coherent and hence coherent.

(4) A natural order.

In addition:

(5) $\forall\, e \in E : |{}^{\bullet}e|, |e^{\bullet}| \geq 2$.

(6) $l \in L \iff l$ is a li-set $\wedge$ $\forall\, x \in l : |{}^{\bullet}x \cap l| = 1 = |x^{\bullet} \cap l|$.

(7) $(SL'; \sqsubseteq)$ is an algebraic lattice.

4. Conclusions

In this paper we have presented a model of non-sequential processes called D-continuous causal nets. We interpret a D-cut as representing the state of affairs of a process and a line as the life history of a sequential component taking part in the process. D-continuity then captures the entirely justifiable demand in every state of affairs, one should be able to nail down the status of every sequential component participating in the process. D-continuity is a succinct way of endowing a process with a variety of interesting properties. To bring this out we have shown that a CCN is K-dense, b-discrete, li-coherent, co-coherent and is a natural order. In addition we have pointed out that (SL'; $\sqsubseteq$) is an algebraic lattice. This gives rise to the hope that the theory of continuous lattices [9] can be brought to bear upon the study of CCN's.

The earliest attempt to study processes using nets is due to A.W.Holt et al. [11]. Latter, A.Mazurkiewicz [12] used the trace notion to elegantly characterize the processes of a basic system model based on nets. A trace is essentially a partially ordered occurrences of events. Conditions are suppressed. J.Winskowski [13] chooses conditions as the primary notion (event is a derived concept) and studies his process model from an algebraic point of view. We feel that having events as second class citizens leads to unnecessary complications without adequate returns. The event structures considered in [5] and [6] are, from our standpoint, a special kind of a system model rather than a process model. This is because an event structure represents a set of potential histories rather than <u>the</u> evolving history of a concurrent system.

Processes in their own right (without referring to a specific system model) was considered by C.A.Petri in [2] where K-density is proposed as a basic property of processes. Based on this work, E.Best [10] has carried out a detailed study of various kinds of density notions related to K-density and their consequences. Indeed, we are happy to acknowledge that it was E.Best who made the useful suggestion that a CCN might be b-discrete. More recently, our collegue H.Plünnecke has derived a number of results shown in this paper in a more general setting [14].

Acknowledgement

We thank Brigitte Hönig for kindly volunteering to type the manuscript and doing a good job of it.

References.

1. C.A.Petri: Introduction to General Net Theory. Lecture Notes in Computer Science, Ed. W.Brauer, Vol. 84, Springer Verlag (1980).

2. C.A.Petri: Non-Sequential Processes. Interner Bericht ISF-77-5, Gesellschaft für Mathematik und Datenverarbeitung, 5205 St. Augustin 1, W.Germany (1977).

3. C.A.Petri: Concurrency. Lecture Notes in Computer Science, Ed. W.Brauer, Vol. 84, Springer Verlag (1980).

4. H.J.Genrich, K.Lautenbach and P.S.Thiagarajan: Elements of General Net Theory. Lecture Notes in Computer Science, Ed. W.Brauer, Vol. 84, Springer Verlag (1980).

5. M.Nielson, G.Plotkin and G.Winskel: Petri Nets, Event Structures and Domains, Part I. Theoretical Computer Science, Vol. 13, No. 1 (1981). pp. 85 - 108.

6. G.Winskel: Events in Computation. CST-10-80. Ph.D.Dissertation, Department of Computer Science, University of Edinburgh, G.B. (1980).

7. C.A.Petri: State-Transition Structures in Physics and Computation. To Appear in International Journal of Theoretical Physics, Vol. 21, No. 10/11 (1982).

8. C.Fernândez and P.S.Thiagarajan: Some Properties of D-continuous Causal Nets. ISF-Report 81.02, Gesellschaft für Mathematik und Datenverarbeitung, 5205 St.Augustin, W.Germany (1981).

9. G.Gierz, K.H.Hoffman, K.Keimal, J.D.Lawson, M.Mislove and D.Scott: A Compendium of Continuous Lattices, Springer Verlag, Berlin, Heidelberg, New York (1980).

10. E.Best: A Theorem on the Characteristics of Non-Sequential Processes. Fundamenta Informaticae, Vol. 3, No. 1 (1980). pp. 77 - 94.

11. A.W.Holt et al.: Information System Theory Project. Final Report, RADC-TR-G8-305, Applied Data Research Inc., Princeton New Jersey, U.S.A. (1968).

12. A.Mazurkiewicz: Concurrent Program Schemes and their Interpretation. Report DAIMI PB-78, Computer Science Department, Aarhus University, Aarhus, Denmark (1977).

13. J.Winkowski: Behaviours of Concurrent Systems. Theoretical Computer Science, Vol. 12, No. 1 (1980). pp 39 - 60.

14. H.Plünnecke: Schnitte in Halbordnungen. ISF-Report 81.09, Gesellschaft für Mathematik und Datenverarbeitung, 5205 St. Augustin, West Germany (1981).

A BRANCHING PROCESS ARISING IN DYNAMIC HASHING, TRIE SEARCHING AND POLYNOMIAL FACTORIZATION

Philippe FLAJOLET
INRIA
78150 - Rocquencourt
(France)

Jean-Marc STEYAERT
Ecole Polytechnique
91128 - Palaiseau
(France)

ABSTRACT :

We obtain average value and distribution estimates for the height of a class of trees that occurs in various contexts in computer algorithms : in trie searching, as index in several dynamic schemes and as an underlying partition structure in polynomial factorization algorithms. In particular, results given here completely solve the problem of analyzing Extendible Hashing for which practical conclusions are given. The treatment relies on the saddle point method of complex analysis which is used here for extracting coefficients of a probability generating function, and on a particular technique that reveals periodic fluctuations in the behaviour of algorithms which are precisely quantified.

1 - INTRODUCTION

Large files on secondary storage can be kept using a hashing table which, for each record, gives the address of a *page* (bucket) containing that record. However, when the file grows, buckets overflow and a collision resolution method has to be adopted. The simplest strategy consists in chaining overflow buckets but this has the disadvantage of eventually degenerating into a sequential search (with a high number of disk accesses to locate a record).

Several schemes, referred to here as *dynamic hashing schemes*, have been proposed around 1977 : they are *Dynamic Hashing* [La 78], *Extendible Hashing* [FNPS 79] and *Virtual Hashing* [Li 78]. The idea is essentially to refine locally the hashing function and accordingly split buckets that would otherwise overflow. *Direct access to records* is preserved provided one maintains an *index (directory)* which keeps track of the successive splittings. The index is therefore a binary tree with leaves containing page pointers. The above description applies especially to Dynamic Hashing ; Extendible Hashing relies on the further idea of paging the directory using a perfect tree

embedding. We propose here to analyse the *expected height* and *size* of the index in Dynamic Hashing and Extendible Hashing.
In an other perspective, index trees for dynamic hashing algorithms can be considered as *tries* [Kn 73,6.3] over binary sequences. Therefore many analytical results translate from trie-searching to dynamic hashing [La 78], [FNPS 79]. Vice-versa, our estimations formulated here in terms of dynamic hashing algorithms also apply to the average (over binary sequences) lenght of the longest branch in trie searching.
Lastly, recent developments of *polynomial factorization algorithms* [CZ 81] [La 81] use a recursive refinement of a partition structure and the underlying branching process can be shown equivalent to a biased generation of tries. The performance of these algorithms depends essentially on the height of the associated tree and here again our methods can be applied.
We propose to prove in this paper :

<u>THEOREM 1</u> : *The average height of the index in Dynamic/Extendible Hashing corresponding to a file of* n *records where page capacity is equal to* $b \geq 1$ *satisfies*

$$\overline{H}_n = (1 + \frac{1}{b}) \log_2 n + P((1 + \frac{1}{b}) \log_2 n) + o(1),$$

where P *is a periodic function given by*

$$P(u) = \Sigma\, p_k\, e^{-2ik\pi u} \quad \text{with}$$

$$\begin{cases} p_o = \dfrac{1}{b\log 2}\,[\gamma - \log\beta] \\ p_k = \dfrac{1}{b\log 2}\,\beta^{-\chi_k}\,\Gamma(\chi_k)^{\dagger} \quad \textit{where} \quad \chi_k = \dfrac{2ik\pi}{b\log 2} \quad \textit{and} \quad \beta = \dfrac{1}{(b+1)!} \end{cases}$$

This quantity $\overline{H}_n$ is also the average height of a trie in which subfiles of size $\leq b$ are stored sequentially [Kn 73,6.3.20].

<u>THEOREM 2</u> : *The average size of the index in Extendible Hashing for a file of* n *records where page capacity is* $b \leq 2$ *satisfies*

$$\overline{S}_n = Q((1 + \frac{1}{b}) \log_2 n) n^{1+1/b} . (1 + o(1)),$$

where Q *is a periodic function given by*

$$Q(u) = \quad q_k\, e^{-2ik\pi u} \quad \textit{with}$$

$$\begin{cases} q_o = \dfrac{-1}{b\log 2}\,\beta^{1/b}\,\Gamma(-\dfrac{1}{b}) \\ q_k = \dfrac{-1}{b\log 2}\,\beta^{-\chi_k+1/b}\,\Gamma(\chi_k - \dfrac{1}{b}) \quad \textit{where} \quad \chi_k = \dfrac{2ik\pi}{b\log 2} \end{cases}$$

---

† Here $\Gamma(s)$ is the classical gamma function and γ is the Euler constant.

Coarser results under an approximate probabilistic model (the Poisson model) have been derived by [Ya 80] [Re 81] and are based on explicit expressions for probabilities which are available in that particular model. The difficulty in our case largely comes from the fact that no "closed-form" formulae are available for the probabilities involved in the analysis. We therefore need a recourse to complex analysis. We use here the *saddle point method* in order to extract asymptotic values of probabilities from their generating functions.

Theorem 2 therefore solves the analytic problems left open in [FNPS 79] regarding the performances of Extendible Hashing which are summarized in Figure 1 (the first column is an oversimplified version of our Theorem 2). The dominating fact is the *non-linearity* of the growth of the index to be discussed briefly in section 3.

Directory size (# pointers)	$\approx \frac{e}{b\log 2} \; n^{1+1/b}$ + fluctu.
File size (# pages)	$\approx \frac{n}{b\log 2}$ + fluctu.
Access time (# disk accesses)	Insert/Delete $3+\varepsilon(b)$ Querry $2+\varepsilon(b)$

Figure 1 : The performance of Extendible Hashing

Finally, in Section 4, we indicate how to extend our methods to cope with the case of a biased distribution on bits of keys of hashed values. Consideration of this situation is motivated by some recent improvements on Berlekamp's factorization algorithm [Kn69], [CZ81], [La81] and we prove :

THEOREM 3 : *The expected height of a simple trie* (b=1) *of* n *leaves when bits in keys have a biased probability of* p *for zeros and* q *for ones satisfies*

$$\overline{H}_n = \frac{2\log_2 n}{\log_2 (p^2+q^2)^{-1}} + O(1)$$

This theorem solves a problem left open in [La81] whose algorithm appears to factorize a plynomial with r factors in approximately $(2+\varepsilon)\log_2 r$ "main" steps.

Let us last mention that other estimates of average "height" in combinatorial structures are usually non-elementary. Known cases include general trees [dBKR 72], binary trees [FO 80 , hash tables Go81 and search trees [Ro 79]. Periodicities described by Fourier series of a similar form classically arise in the analysis of algorithms but they are usually derived in a different way (Mellin transform or triangular function techniques) ; examples are : register allocation, sorting networks, Patricia trees, radix-exchange sort, carry propagation...

2 - DEVELOPMENTS

Let us call a trie formed with binary keys with subfiles of size $\leq b$ stored sequentially a *b-trie* . The analysis is performed under the statistical assumption that bits in keys (or in hashed values) are uniformly and identically distributed. We let π_n^h denote the *probability* that a b-trie formed with n keys has height $\leq h$. We thus have for the quantities of Theorems 1-2 :

$$\overline{H}_n = \sum_h h(\pi_n^h - \pi_n^{h-1}) = \sum_h (1 - \pi_n^h) \qquad (1)$$

$$\overline{S}_n = \sum_h 2^h(\pi_n^h - \pi_n^{h-1}) = 1 + \sum_h 2^h(1 - \pi_n^h). \qquad (2)$$

These theorems are proved through the following chain of lemmas :

<u>*LEMMA 1*</u> *: [Combinatorial Counting Lemma] The probabilities* π_n^h *are given by*

$$\pi_n^h = \frac{n!}{2^{nh}} [x^n] \left(1 + \frac{x}{1!} + \frac{x^2}{2!} + \dots + \frac{x^b}{b!}\right)^{2^h} . \qquad (3)$$

There the notation $[x^n]\, f(x)$ represents the n-th Taylor coefficients of of f : if $f(x) = \Sigma f_n x^n$, then $[x^n]f(x) = f_n$. Lemma 1 is obtained by reducing the continuous problem to a counting problem of permutations with limited repetitions [DB 62]. For what follows, it is convenient to introduce a notation for the truncated exponential

$$e_b(x) = \sum_{0 \leq j \leq b} \frac{x^j}{j!}, \qquad (4)$$

and Lemma 1 becomes :

$$\pi_n^h = n![x^n]e_b\left(\frac{x}{2^h}\right)^{2^h} . \qquad (5)$$

To evaluate π_n^h, we appeal to Cauchy's residue theorem :

$$[x^n]f(x) = \frac{1}{2i\pi} \int_\Gamma f(z) \frac{dz}{z^{n+1}} \qquad (6)$$

where Γ is inside the domain in which f is analytic, and simply encircles the origin. Hence, using (6) in (5) :

$$\pi_{n-1}^h = \frac{(n-1)!}{2i\pi} \int_\Gamma e^{g(z)}\, dz \qquad (7)$$

where $g(z) = 2^h \log e_b(\frac{z}{2^h}) - n \log z$. Let s be a zero of $g'(z)$; such a point is a *saddle point* of $g(z)$ (and of $e^{g(z)}$) since in a vicinity of s, there is a direction along which g increases and a direction along which g decreases (see Figure 2).

We propose to take for contour Γ a contour that crosses the saddle point closest to the origin along the direction of decrease and hope for localization properties of the resulting integral (7).

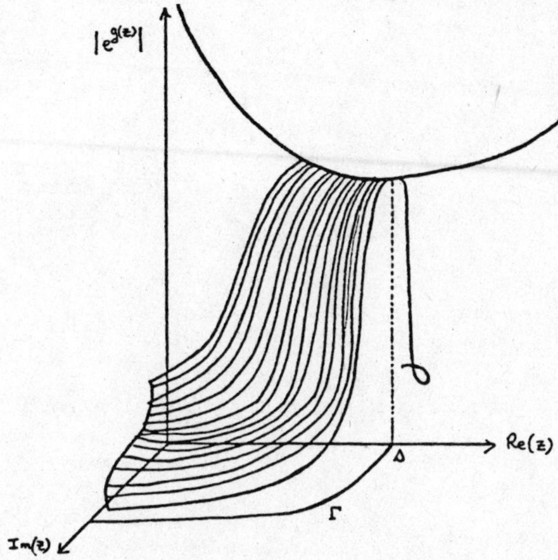

Figure 2 : The Topography of $|e^{g(z)}|$

LEMMA 2 : [Closest saddle point] For n *large enough and* $h > (1 + \frac{1}{b})\log_2 n - \log_2 \log n$, *the zero of smallest modulus of* $g'(s)$, s *is real and satisfies :*

$$s = s(h,n) = n + \beta \lambda^{-b} - \beta \lambda^{-(b+1)} n^{-1/b} + \ldots \qquad (8)$$

where $\beta = \frac{1}{(b+1)!}$ *and* $\log_2 \lambda = h - (1 + \frac{1}{b}) \log_2 n$.

Consideration of a domain centered aroud $(1 + \frac{1}{b}) \log_2 n$ was first heuristically suggested by previous results on the Poisson model [Re 81].
We now take for contour Γ the *circle* of radius $s = s(h,n)$. We split this contour into :

$$\Gamma = \Gamma_0 + \Gamma_1 \text{ with } \Gamma_0 = \left\{ z/|z| = s \; ; \; |\mathrm{Argt}(z)| < n^{-1/2} \log n \right\}$$

and prove the main contribution in the integral (7) to come from Γ_0.

LEMMA 3 : [Localization property]

$$\int_{\Gamma_1} e^{g(z)} dz = O\left(\frac{n^{1/2}}{(n-1)!} \, e^{-\frac{1}{2}\log^2 n} \right). \qquad (9)$$

Next we need to prove that Γ_0 is "small enough", so that local expansions around s can be applied.

LEMMA 4 : [Local approximation property]

$$\int_{\Gamma_0} e^{g(z)} dz - \int_{\Gamma_0} e^{g(s) + \frac{1}{2} g''(s) (z-s)^2} dz = O\left(\frac{e^{h(s)}}{\sqrt{h''(s)}} n^{-1/2}\right). \quad (10)$$

Summarizing Lemmas 3-4, the main contribution for π_n^h comes from a "small" zone around s, and there the first two terms in the expansion of g(z) suffice to give the main contribution of the integral. Now, it is easy to prove that

$$\int_{\Gamma_0} e^{g(z) + \frac{1}{2} g''(s) (z-s)^2} dz \sim \int_{s-i\infty}^{s+i\infty} e^{g(s) + \frac{1}{2} g''(s) (z-s)^2} dz$$

$$= i e^{g(z)} \sqrt{\frac{2\pi}{g''(s)}} . \quad (11)$$

We can state

PROPOSITION 1 : The probability distribution of height satisfies :

$$\pi_{n-1}^h = \frac{(n-1)! e^{g(s)}}{\sqrt{2\pi g''(s)}} (1 + O(n^{-1/2})) + \textit{exp. small terms},$$

where s *is the smallest positive real number satisfying the equation :*

$$\frac{e_{b-1}\left(\frac{s}{2^h}\right)}{e_b\left(\frac{s}{2^h}\right)} - \frac{n}{s} = 0.$$

At this stage, we can use Lemma 2 to estimate g(s), g"(s)... asymptotically ; the main terms of $e^{g(s)}$ cancel with (n-1)!. Using the fact that h assumes only integer values and centering h around $\lfloor (1 + \frac{1}{b}) \log_2 n \rfloor$ we get

PROPOSITION 2 : The probability distribution of height satisfies

$$\pi_n^h = e^{-\beta(n)} 2^{-b\delta} (1 + O(n^{-1/b})).$$

where

$$\delta = h - \lfloor (1 + \frac{1}{b}) \log_2 n \rfloor \; ; \; \beta(n) = \frac{1}{(b+1)!} 2^{b\{(1 + \frac{1}{b}) \log_2 n\}}$$

and

$\{u\} = u - \lfloor u \rfloor$ *is the fractional part of* u.

A few observations can now be made concerning this result :

a) The estimate is valid for $\delta > -\log_2 \log n$ (see Lemma 2). However due to the monotonicity of the $\{\pi_n^h\}_{h \geq 0}$, we have that for $h < (1 + \frac{1}{b}) \log_2 n - \log_2 \log n$, the probability π_n^h is exponentially small.

b) The expression has been put under a form that shows the π_n^h for h "around" $\lfloor (1 + \frac{1}{b}) \log_2 n \rfloor$ to exhibit *asymptotic periodicities* : if $n' = n \, 2^{b/(b+1)}$ the distribution of $\pi_{n'}^h$ is asymptotically equivalent to that of π_n^h shifted.

c) Proposition 2 is insufficient to conclude on the average height : the error terms are relative to π_n^h ; as $h \to \infty$, $\pi_h^n \to 1$ and at one stage these error terms obscure the behaviour of the *tail* of the distribution. We thus need :

LEMMA 5 : [Exponential tail of the distribution]
If $h = (1 + \frac{1}{b}) \log_2 n + \log_2 \log n + \delta$ *then*

$$\pi_n^h = O\left(\frac{2^{-\delta b}}{(\log n)^b}\right) .$$

PROOF : We now need to estimate $1 - \pi_n^h$ in the given range. To do so we express this quantity as

$$n! [x^n] \; e^x - e_b(\frac{x}{2^h})^{2h}$$

and again estimate it by Cauchy's theorem. We choose now as contour of integration an approximate saddle-point circle of radius n and use majorizations on the functions there. □

We thus see that the distribution of height is strongly peaked around $(1 + \frac{1}{b}) \log_2 n$. We obtain more precise results with Proposition 2 and a few manipulations show :

LEMMA 6 : The average height satisfies :

$$\overline{H}_n = (1 + \frac{1}{b}) \log_2 n + P((1 + \frac{1}{b}) \log_2 n) + O\left(\frac{1}{(\log n)^b}\right) ,$$

where

$$P(x) = -\{x\} + \sum_{j \in Z} \left[\sigma(j) - e^{-\beta 2^{-jb} 2^{b\{x\}}}\right]$$

with $\sigma(j)$ *the step function :* $\sigma(j) = 1$ *if* $j > 0$; $\sigma(j) = 0$ *otherwise.*

A similar result holds for $\overline{S}_n$. To obtain information on the amplitudes and mean values of P and Q, one can compute Fourier coefficients ; adequate change of variables and a pinch of analytic continuation lead to the Eulerian integrals for the gamma function which ultimately establishes Theorems 1-2.

3 - SOME CONCLUSIONS ON EXTENSIBLE HASHING

The vality of the estimates of Propositions 1-2 and Theorems 1-2 has been tested both by computing the exact values of expected directory (index) size and by running fairly extensive simulations in a wide range of values of b (b = 2..500). The domain of values of n which we have considered ($n = 1..10^4$) has no claim of being representative of practical file sizes but it is sufficient to demonstrate, already in this low range, excellent agreement between our approximations and the actual behavior of extendible hashing tables.

The dominating conclusion is that values of probabilities and directory size estimated by the saddle point integral, i.e., obtained by retaining the main term in Proposition 1, are hardly distinguishable from the exact values. Predictions based on them only lead to slightly overestimating the expected directory size by at most a few percent.

The asymptotic values predicted by the main terms in Theorem 2 are coarser. They overestimate the height of the tree by an amount of about 1-2 for these small values of n ; this corresponds to overestimating the directory size by a factor of 2-4. As n increases, the agreement becomes better and better but the speed of convergence is inversely related to b (a fact also consistent with our error terms of order $n^{-1/b}$ for probabilities).

Figure 3 displays the exact values of expected directory size for b = 10, compared to each of the two approximations we have discussed.

Figure 4 shows the values of directory size as estimated from a sample of 50 simulations for each value of n, when b = 50.

To simplify the discussion of the trade-offs between expected directory size and page capacity for a given file size, we can retain only the main term in the expression provided by Theorem 1, further reducing the periodic function to its mean value. The rough expression for directory size obtained in this way is thus

$$q_0 n^{1+1/b} = \frac{1}{\log 2}\,[(b+1)!]^{-1/b}\,\Gamma(1-\frac{1}{b})\,n^{1+1/b}$$

which is numerically close to

$$\frac{e}{b\log 2}\,n^{1+1/b} = \frac{3.92}{b}\,n^{1+1/b}.$$

This formula exhibits a *nonlinear growth*. For a practical range of values of n, for instance $n \leq 10^{10}$, the nonlinearity is very perceptible when b is small but becomes hardly detectable when b exceeds say 30-50. The analysis shows for instance that b = 10 and $n = 10^5$ lead to an index of an expected size larger than the file itself.

The above formulae can therefore be used to decide when a secondary index is necessary of whether compromise chaining solutions have to be adopted.

As a final conclusion, the results provided by Proposition 1 when b is large, and the estimates of Theorems 1-2 when b is small can be used to reserve the necessary storage for the directory of extendible hashing

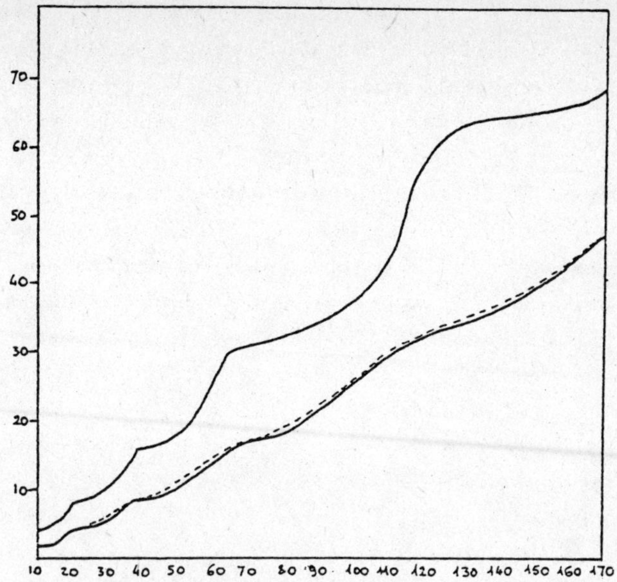

Figure 3 : Directory size versus file size when b = 10
The lower line represents the exact values ; the dotted line shows values computed from the main term in Proposition 1 and the upper line is the main term of theorem 2.

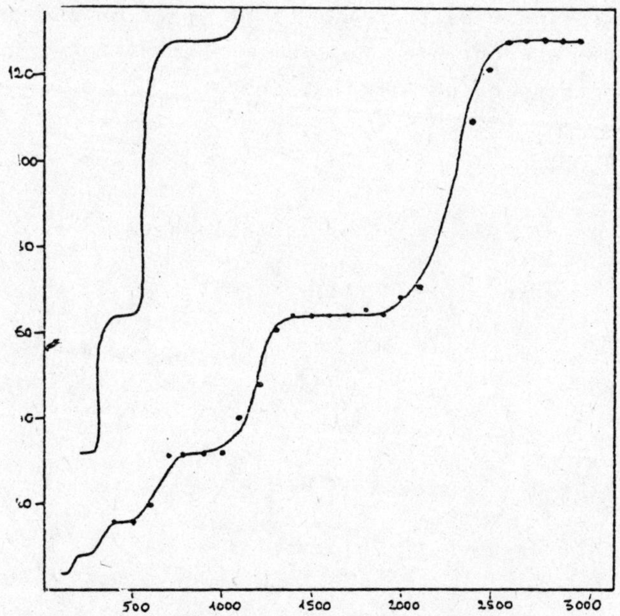

Figure 5 : Directory size versus file size.
The lower line represents the values predicted by retaining the main term in Proposition 1. Each spot is an average over 50 simulations and the upper line displays the asymptotic values corresponding to theorem 2

tables with extremely small probabilities of failure. Programs for them could, for instance, be easily built into implementations of the algorithm to attain optimal storage occupation in all cases.

4 - TRIES WITH A BIASED DISTRIBUTION AND POLYNOMIAL FACTORIZATION

Let us consider simple tries in which binary keys satisfy the following distribution : zeros occur with probability α and ones with probability $\beta=1-\alpha$; a key with k 0's and m-k 1's has therefore probability $\alpha^k\beta^{m-k}$. Let π_n^m denote the probability that a trie with n keys has height $\leq m$.
We first have :

LEMMA 7 : [*Combinatorial counting lemma*]
In the biased case, the probabilities π_n^m *are given by :*

$$\pi_n^m = n!\,[x^n] \prod_{k=0}^{m} (1+\alpha^k\beta^{m-k}x)^{\binom{m}{k}} .$$

The rather surprising form of this generating function excludes the possibility of a closed form for coefficients. Notice however that in the case $\alpha=\beta=\frac{1}{2}$ it coincides with the expression given in Lemma 1 when b=1. We again have to ressort to complex analysis in order to obtain asymptotic information on the probabilities. Since no information from approximate Poisson models is available, part of the difficulty also lies in guessing the appropriate range of values of m in relation to n and α,β, and the corresponding saddle-point. Let

$$\theta = (\alpha^2+\beta^2)^{-1} ;$$

we can show that :

(i) For m close to $\ell(n) = 2\,\dfrac{\log_2 n}{\log\theta}$, the main saddle point is

$$s = n + \frac{1}{n^2\theta^m} + \cdots$$

(ii) For $m=\ell(n)+\delta$ with small δ, the distribution of height satisfies asymptotically :

$$\pi_n^m \sim e^{-\frac{1}{2}\theta^\delta}$$

(iii) The tail of the distribution is again exponentaial.

This permits to conclude with the proof of Theorem 3.
We cannot devote too much space here to a formal justification of Lazard's Algorithm L which is given in Figure 6. Let us only mention that is starts like Berlekamp's Algorithm A but has the strong advantage of avoiding a scan over all the values of the field of coefficients GF_p.

A : Construct a basis $(w_1(x),\ldots,w_r(x))$ of the vector space V of polynomials $v(x)$, $d^\circ(v) < n$, such that

$$v^p(x) \equiv v(x) \bmod f(x) \; ;$$

(r is the number of irreductible factors of f).

B : Set $S \in F_p(x)$ to $\{1\}$

<u>While</u> card(S) < r <u>do</u>

C : Let $v(x) = \Sigma\; c_i\; w_i(x)$ be a random polynomial in V ;

Let $u(x) = \frac{1}{2}\,(v^{p-1} + v^{(p-1)/2})$;

<u>For all</u> $s(x) \in S$ <u>do</u>

let $t(x) = u(x) \times s(x) \bmod f(x)$

<u>if</u> $t(x) \neq 0$ and $t(x) \neq s(x)$ <u>then</u>

remove s(x) from S and add t(x) and s(x)−t(x) to S

<u>fi</u>

<u>od</u>

<u>od</u>

D : The irreductible factors of f(x) are the gcd $(s(x)-1, f(x))$ for $s \in S$.

Figure 6 : The factorization algorithm L for polynomials over $GF_q(x)$

The dominant factor in the cost of algorithm L is the number of main iterations, i-e the number of executions of block C inside the while-loop, where a few products and one exponentiation are performed. It can be shown formally that for a polynomial with r irreducible factors, this number is, on the average, equivalent to the expected height of a trie formed of r binary sequences with biased probabilities

$$\alpha = \frac{1}{2} + \frac{1}{2p} \qquad \beta = \frac{1}{2} - \frac{1}{2p} \quad .$$

Corollary : Algorithm L *factories a polynomial with* r ***irreducible*** *factors over* GF_p *in :*

- $O(n^3)$ *elementary steps for phase A ;*
- $\dfrac{2 \log_2 r}{\log_2(\alpha^2+\beta^2)^{-1}} + O(1)$ C-*steps on the average in phase* B ;
- r gcd's *for phase* D.

Figure 7 compares the main **term** **of** Theorem 3 with the values observed in [La81]. The agreement is excellent even for the very small values of r tabulated there. Finally a similar algorithm of [La81] avoiding phase (A) also lends itself to a complete analysis when using Theorem 3.

k / q	2	3	4	5	6	7	8	c(p)
3	2,25	2,3660	2,3772	2,3887	2,3921	2,3954		2,3584
5	2,0833	2,1907	2,1897	2,1965	2,1942	2,1941		2,1199
7	2,0417	2,1469	2,1425	2,1483	2,1444	2,1435		2,0600
41	2,0012	2,1043	2,0966	2,1014	2,0958	2,0941		2,0017
∞	2	2,1031	2,0952	2,1001	2,0944	2,0927	2,0898	2,0000

Figure 7 : The number of main iterations performed by Algorithm L (normalized through division by $\log_2 r$) compared with

$$c(p) = \frac{2}{\log_2 \theta} \quad \text{with } \theta = 2(1+p^2)^{-1}.$$

5 - REFERENCES

[CZ81] Cantor D.G. and Zassenhaus H. : "On Algorithms for Factoring Polynomials over Finite Fields", Math. of Comp. 36 (1981) pp 587-592

[DB61] De Bruijn N.G. : Asymptotic Methods in Analysis , North-Holland P.C., Amsterdam (1961)

[DB62] David F.N. and Barton D.E., Combinatorial Chance , Charles Griffin, London (1962).

[FNPS] Fagin R., Nievergelt J. Pippenger N. and Strong H.R., "Extendible Hashing - A Fast Access Method for Dynamic Files", ACM Trans. on Database System, 4 (1979) pp. 315-344.

[FO81] Flajolet P. and Odlyzko A. : "The Average Height of Binary Trees and Other Simple Trees", JCSS to appear

[Go80] Gonnet G., "Expected Length of the Longest Probe Sequence in Hashing", JACM 28 (1980) pp. 289-304

[He78] Henrici P., Applied and Computational Complex Analysis, Vol. 2, J. Wiley, New York (1978)

[Kn69] Knuth D.E. : The Art of Computer Programming, Vol. 2, Addison-Wesley, Reading (1969)

[Kn73] Knuth D.E., The Art of Computer Programming, Vol. 3, Addison-Wesley, Reading (1973).

[La78] Larson P.A., "Dynamic Hashing", BIT 18 (1978) pp. 184-201.

[La81] Lazard D, "Factorisation des Polynômes", in 4° Journées Algorithmiques, Poitiers (1981), also sumbitted for publication.

[Li78] Litwin W., "Virtual Hashing : A Dynamically Changing Hashing", in Proc. Very Large Data Bases Conf., Berlin (1978) pp. 517-523.

[Me80] Mendelson H., "Extendible Hashing : Analysis for Design", Rochester University Report n° 8019 (1980).

[Re81] Regnier M., "On the Average Height of Trees in Digital Searching and Dynamic Hashing", IPL (to appear).

[Ro79] Robson J.M. : "The Height of Binary Search Trees", Austral. Comp. J. 11 (1979) pp 151-153.

[Ya80] Yao A., "A Note On the Analysis of Extendible Hashing", IPL 11 (1980) pp. 84-86.

A SOUND AND COMPLETE HOARE AXIOMATIZATION OF THE ADA-RENDEZVOUS

(extended abstract)

Rob Gerth[1]
Department of Computer Science, University of Utrecht
P.O. Box 80.002, 3508 TA Utrecht, the Netherlands.

0. ABSTRACT.

A HOARE-axiomatization is constructed for the ADA rendezvous, embedded in a subset of the ADA concurrency section. The well-known CSP proof system of Apt, Francez and de Roever is taken as a starting point. We prove the axiomatization to be sound and relatively complete.

1. INTRODUCTION.

We study the basic synchronization primitive - the *rendezvous* - of the programming language ADA [ARM81]. A proof system is constructed for partial correctness properties for a subset, ADA-CS, of its concurrency section. The proof system is then proven to be sound and relatively complete.

As CSP [Hoa78] is one of the languages which influenced the design of ADA, it should come as no surprise that the resulting proof system is similar to proof systems for CSP; especially to the one in [AFR80].

Within the latter system, CSP-synchronization is captured by a *general invariant* and a *cooperation test.* A rendezvous can be characterized as something akin to a procedure-call. We will show how the notion of cooperation can be combined with a procedure-call-rule, as expressed in our formation-rule. Notably, we will retain the idea of one proof per procedure-body which suffices for each call. This rule is inspired by [Ron81] and [Ger82a].

In this abstract, we first describe the subset ADA-CS. Next, in section 3, a proof system for ADA-CS is constructed that closely follows the example of the CSP proof system in [AFR80]. In section 4, the soundness and completeness proof are sketched. Space limitations prevents us from including full proofs. For these and an example-proof of an ADA-CS program, the reader is referred to [Ger82b]. We conclude, in section 5, with a discussion of our work.
The reader is assumed to be familiar with the CSP-system in [AFR80].

2. THE SUBSET, ADA-CS.

The syntax of the subset of ADA is described by the following augmented BNF-grammar. The conventions used are similar to those in [ARM81]: *Italicized* prefixes in the nonterminals are irrelevant; "[...]" denotes an optional part, "{...}" denotes repetition, zero or more times. We have taken some liberties with the ADA-syntax, which is somewhat verbose.

---

[1] The author is supported by the Dutch Organization for the Advancement of Pure Research (ZWO).

```
program ::= begin task {task} end
task ::= task task_id decl begin stats end
decl ::= {entry_decl}{var_decl}
entry_decl ::= entry entry_id (formal_part)
var_decl ::= var_id_list:int | var_id_list:bool
var_id_list ::= var_id{,var_id}
formal_part ::= [var_id_list][# var_id_list]
stats ::= stat{;stat}
stat ::= null | ass_st | if_st | while_st | call_st | acc_st | sel_st
ass_st ::= var_id := expr
if_st ::= if bool_expr then stats else stats end if
while_st ::= while bool_expr do stats end while
call_st ::= call task_id.entry_id (actual_part)
actual_part ::= {expr}[# var_id_list]
acc_st ::= accept entry_id (formal_part) do stats end accept
sel_st ::= select sel_br {or sel_br} end select
sel_br ::= bool_expr : acc_st [;stats]
expr ::= "expression"
bool_expr ::= "boolean expression"
id ::= "identifier"
```

Thus, an ADA-CS program consists of a fixed set of tasks. These tasks are all activated simultaneously and excuted in parallel. When execution reaches the end of the task-body, the task terminates. Each task can have declarations for entries, which may be called by other tasks. The actions to be performed, when such an entry is called, are specified by corresponding accept-statements. Execution of an accept is synchronized with the excution of a corresponding entry-call. Consequently, a task executing an accept or entry-call, will be suspended until another process reaches a corresponding entry-call or accept,after which the statements of the accept-body are executed by the called task, while the calling task remains suspended. This action is called a *rendezvous* and is the primary means of communication between and synchronization of tasks; in particular, there are no global variables. After a rendezvous, the two tasks continue their execution in parallel.

Apart from the synchronization, an entry-call is executed as an ordinary procedure-call. An entry-declaration may specify a formal_part. Only parameters of type int are allowed. The first set of parameters, closed off by the '#'-sign, is of mode in; the second set is of mode in out. Hence, in the actual_part of a corresponding call, the first set of actual parameters may be expressions, the second set must be variables.

The formal_part of an accept-statement must match the one of the corresponding entry-declaration. A task may only contain accept-statements for one of its own entries, but it may contain more than one accept-statement for the same entry.

The select-statement allows a task to wait for synchronization with one of a set of alternatives. First, all boolean expressions are evaluated to determine which branches of the select-statement are open. If all are closed, the statement aborts. Otherwise, the task, if necessary, waits until a rendezvous corresponding with one of the open branches is possible. (Notice that each branch starts with an accept-statement.) If more than one rendezvous is possible, one is selected arbitrarily.

Two more or less implicit changes w.r.t. the ADA semantics are the following:

(1) the removal of entry-queues[1], and

(2) deadlock instead of abortion in case an entry is called of an already terminated task.

3. THE PROOF SYSTEM.

A characteristic tendency in proof systems for concurrent languages is the reduction to sequential reasoning. Of course there is a price to pay: In [OwG76] an *interference freedom test* has to be introduced and in [AFR80] a *cooperation test*.

In the CSP-system, this reduction is brought about by introducing two axioms for local reasoning about processes in isolation:

(1) $\{p\}\ P_i!a\ \{q\}$ and (2) $\{p\}\ P_j?x\ \{q\}$.

The actual test whether these pre- and post-assertions are compatible with the communication action, is deferred to a second global stage: that of the cooperation test. To express this test, a *general invariant*, GI, is introduced to tie the local reasonings, within each of the processes, globally together. In particular, GI is used to distinguish among all communication possibilities, i.e., the *syntactically* matching ones, the ones which may actually occur, i.e., the *semantically* matching ones. Also, auxiliary variables have to be introduced to express the necessary assertions and invariants. As the variables appearing free in GI have to be updated when communication occurs to model synchronization, GI cannot hold throughout the whole program. Hence the introduction of *bracketed sections* (each associated with a unique communication-action) to which the updating of GI-variables is confined and inside of which GI need not hold.

The reader will find these concepts reappearing (for the same reasons) in the ADA-CS proof system to be developed now.

A rendezvous may be viewed as a double CSP-communication, as the translation shows:

	ADA-CS:	CSP:
T_1:	call T_2.entry(e#x)	$T_2!(e,x);\ T_2?x$
T_2:	accept entry(u#v) do S end accept	$T_1?(u,v);\ S;\ T_1!v$

Correspondingly, in the proof system the following axiom and proof rules are adopted:

A1. *call* $\{p\}$ call T.entry($\vec{e}\#\vec{x}$) $\{q\}$

R1. *accept*
$$\frac{\{p_1\}\ S\ \{q_1\}}{\{p\}\ \underline{\text{accept}}\ \text{entry}(\vec{u}\#\vec{v})\ \underline{\text{do}}\ S\ \underline{\text{end}}\ \underline{\text{accept}}\ \{q\}}$$

The reason to use an accept-*rule* rather than an *axiom*, is to force proofs of the accept-bodies to be given.

R2. *select*
$$\frac{\{p\wedge b_1\}\ S_1\ \{q\},\ \ldots\ ,\ \{p\wedge b_n\}\ S_n\ \{q\}}{\{p\}\ \underline{\text{select}}\ b_1{:}S_1\ \underline{\text{or}}\ \ldots\ \underline{\text{or}}\ b_n{:}S_n\ \underline{\text{end}}\ \underline{\text{select}}\ \{q\}}$$

Remember that waiting, in case no rendezvous is immediately possible, is not a partial correctness notion.

---

[1] This is not serious, as in ADA-CS entry-queues cannot be used explicitely within programs. Hence, entry-queues only define an implementation of a fair scheduler, see [PR82]. As such, they are not relevant for partial correctness properties.

These are augmented by the usual *assignment*-axiom (A2), the *null*-axiom (A3 {p}<u>null</u>{p}) and the *if*-, *while*-, *composition*-, *consequence*- and *conjunction*-rules (R3...R7). We also need a substitution rule to remove auxiliary variables from assertions (see below)

R8. *substitution* $\dfrac{\{p\}\ S\ \{q\}}{\{p[t/z]\}\ S\ \{q\}}$, provided $z \notin FV(S,q)$

Next, a *general invariant* GI is introduced and the concept of *bracketed sections*. Here we must be careful:

Definition. A task is *bracketed* if the brackets "<" and ">" are interspersed in its text, so that for each program-section <S> (to be called a *bracketed section*), S is of the form (1) S_1; <u>call</u> entry($\vec{e}\#\vec{x}$); S_2 , or

(2) <u>accept</u> entry($\vec{u}\#\vec{v}$) <u>do</u> T_1 , or

(3) T_2 <u>end</u> <u>accept</u>

where S_1, S_2, T_1 and T_2 do not contain calls or accepts and may be <u>null</u>-statements.

It would have been wrong to replace (2) and (3) together by the single clause

(2') <u>accept</u> entry($\vec{u}\#\vec{v}$) <u>do</u> T_1; T; T_2 <u>end</u> <u>accept</u>.

The idea is that GI must hold when a communication-action is executed; that is, upon entrance of and exit from the associated bracketed section. But as the "body", T, of an accept may contain other calls or accepts, the validity of GI would not have been assured at these points, since GI would not have been required to hold within S.

Auxiliary variables are introduced to express assertions and invariants. These variables do not affect program-control during execution. Correspondingly, a proof rule is needed to remove assignments to auxiliary variables.

R9. *AV* Let AV be a set of variables such that $x \in AV \Rightarrow x$ appears in S' only in assignments of the form y:=x, where $y \in AV$. Then

$$\frac{\{p\}\ S'\ \{q\}}{\{p\}\ S\ \{q\}},$$

provided S is obtained from S' by deleting assignments to variables in AV and $FV(q) \cap AV = \emptyset$.

Although a rendezvous is modelled by two CSP-communications, it makes sense not to separate them entirely, because, disregarding the synchronization, a rendezvous is no more than an ordinary procedure-call, which we want to treat as a meaningful whole. This will influence the formulation of our cooperation test.

Definition. Let <S_1> and <S_2> be a *communication pair*:

$S_1 \equiv S_1'$; <u>call</u> T.entry_1(e#x); S_1''

$S_2 \equiv$ <u>accept</u> entry_2($\vec{u}\#\vec{v}$) <u>do</u> S_2';> S <;S_2'' <u>end</u> <u>accept</u>

(S_1 and S_2 contained in different tasks)

We say that <S_1> and <S_2> (syntactically) *match*, if 'entry_1' and 'entry_2' are the same name, and S_2 is part of the body of task T.

The wary reader will have noticed that the formal parameters of the entries are *local* w.r.t. the corresponding accepts. However, to facilitate the proofs in section 4, we do not introduce a *block rule*. Instead we will restrict, without loss of generality, the set of ADA-CS programs: *ADA-CS tasks may not have name-clashes between the formal parameters of its entries and its 'normal' variables*. This allows us to restrict the variables appearing free in assertions, thus obliterating the need of a block rule. The following definition reflects this.

Definition. Consider (a proof of) an ADA-CS program <u>begin</u> <u>task</u> T_1 ... <u>task</u> T_n <u>end</u>. The proofs of $\{p_i\}\ T_i\ \{q_i\}$ (i=1..n) *cooperate w.r.t. GI* if

(1) the assertions used in the proof of $\{p_i\}\ T_i\ \{q_i\}$ have no free variables subject to change in T_j ($i \neq j$) and contain formal parameters of an entry only if they appear in the proof of the body for an accept for this entry.

(2) $\{pre(S_1) \wedge pre(S_2) \wedge GI\}\ S_1 \parallel S_2\ \{post(S_1) \wedge post(S_2) \wedge GI\}$
holds for all matching communication pairs $<S_1>$ and $<S_2>$ within the program.

As in the CSP proof system, we need an additional rule to establish cooperation. This rule basically expresses the value transfer during a communication. In CSP this is simple, as the execution of two matching io-commands, $P_i!a$ and $P_j?x$, is equivalent with executing the assignment x:=a. In ADA however, a rendezvous results in a procedure-call. In order to render the semantics of such a call simple, a few restrictions are placed on the actual parameters of a call. (After all, we are not interested in the purely sequential aspects of ADA.) Hence:

For any entry-call <u>call</u> entry$(e_1,e_2,\ldots,e_m\#x_1,x_2,\ldots,x_n)$
to an entry declared as <u>entry</u> entry$(u_1,u_2,\ldots,u_m\#v_1,v_2,\ldots,v_n)$
the following assumptions are made about the parameter lists $\vec{e}$, $\vec{x}$ and $\vec{u}$:

(1) $FV(\vec{e}) \cap \vec{x} = \emptyset$ and no u_i appears on the left-hand side of any assignment or as value-result actual parameter of any call within the "bodies of entry",

(2) the x_i are all distinct, and

(3) $(s \in (FV(\vec{e}) \cup \vec{x}) \wedge s \notin \vec{u} \cup \vec{v})) \Rightarrow s \notin FV(\text{"bodies of entry"})$
where "bodies of entry" denote the bodies of the accepts for entry.

A remark should be made now. According to the ADA-standard [ARM81, 6.2], programs should not depend on specific mechanisms for parameter-passing and should not use aliasing. This justifies our using call-by-value-result (call-by-copy for the purist) in the ADA-CS subset and the introduction of the above restrictions; only (1) appears to be a real restriction. In fact, instead of (3) the following even stronger assumption will be made: *An ADA-CS program may not have tasks which contain variables with the same name as in other tasks of the program*. Proofs of such tasks simply cannot be combined because of the resulting name-clashes.

Under the above restrictions the parameter-transfer during the execution of an entry-call may be simulated by a substitution ([Apt81b]):

<u>begin</u> <u>new</u> $\vec{u},\vec{v}$; $\vec{u}:=\vec{e}$; $\vec{v}:=\vec{x}$; S ;$\vec{x}:=\vec{v}$ <u>end</u> $\equiv S[\vec{e}/\vec{u}, \vec{x}/\vec{v}]$. ($1)

Moreover, if {p} S {q} then {p[·]} S[·] {q[·]} (where $[\cdot] \equiv [\vec{e}/\vec{u}, \vec{x}/\vec{v}]$). Hence, the input-output behaviour of a call is obtained by substituting in the canonical (!) proof, {p} S {q}, of the procedure-body S.

The well-known call-rules, associated with the above result on substitution (cf. [Apt81b]), are too simple because we have bracketed sections to consider too. Hence the following rule:

R10. *formation*

$$\frac{\begin{array}{l}\{p_1 \wedge p_2 \wedge GI\}\ S_1';\ S_1''[\cdot]\ \{\overline{p}_1 \wedge \overline{p}_2[\cdot] \wedge GI\} \\ \{\overline{p}_2\}\ S\ \{\overline{q}_2\} \\ \{\overline{p}_1 \wedge \overline{q}_2[\cdot] \wedge GI\}\ S_2'[\cdot];\ S_2''\ \{q_1 \wedge q_2 \wedge GI\}\end{array}}{\{p_1 \wedge p_2 \wedge GI\}\ S_1';\ \underline{\text{call}}\ T_j.a(\vec{e}\#\vec{x});S_1''\ \|\ \underline{\text{accept}}\ a(\vec{u}\#\vec{v})\ \underline{\text{do}}\ S_2';{>}S{<};S_2''\ \underline{\text{end}}\ \underline{\text{accept}}\ \{q_1 \wedge q_2 \wedge GI\}}$$

where (1) the call is contained in task T_i and the accept in task T_j ($i \neq j$),

(2) $[\cdot] = [\vec{e}/\vec{u}, \vec{x}/\vec{v}]$,

(3) p_1, $\overline{p}_1$ and q_1 belong to the proof of T_i and $FV(\overline{p}_1) \cap \vec{x} = \emptyset$, and

(4) p_2, $\overline{p}_2$, q_2 and $\overline{q}_2$ belong to the proof of T_j.

In this rule, the first and third premiss (above the line) express the invariance checks of GI over the bracketed sections. The second premiss does not refer to actual parameters. This means that a proof of the body, S, of an accept *need only be given once* and that this *canonical* proof suffices for the cooperation test for matching communication pairs containing this accept. In the first premiss, we must show that the input is legal by deriving $\overline{p}_2[\cdot]$. If the input is legal, $\overline{q}_2[\cdot]$ specifies the output of the body S. The intermediate assertion $\overline{p}_1$ is used to retain information about the variables of T_i which do not appear in the actual result-parameter list of the call. This information cannot be placed in $\overline{p}_2$, because $\overline{p}_2$ is an assertion belonging to the proof of T_j and hence may not contain variables subject to change in T_i.

Now, the (usual) parallel composition (meta-) rule can be stated :

R11. *parallel composition*

$$\frac{\text{proofs of } \{p_i\}\ T_i\ \{q_i\},\ i=1..n \text{ cooperate w.r.t. GI}}{\{p_1 \wedge \ldots \wedge p_n \wedge GI\}\ \underline{\text{begin}}\ \underline{\text{task}}\ T_1\ \ldots\ \underline{\text{task}}\ T_n\ \underline{\text{end}}\ \{q_1 \wedge \ldots \wedge q_n \wedge GI\}},$$

provided no variable free in GI is subject to change outside a bracketed section.

4. SOUNDNESS AND COMPLETENESS.

In this section, soundness and completeness proofs for the ADA-CS proof system are sketched. For full proofs, the reader is referred to the full version of the paper [Ger 82b]. The proof is based on the translation of ADA-CS into CSP. However, to circumvent some purely technical details, a slight generalization of CSP, CSP^+, will be used as target language.

CSP^+ is CSP augmented with some additional communication primitives, but without the distributed termination convention. The new primitives are characterized by generalization of syntactical matching:

(1) P_i.a?x and P_j.b!e, where 'a' and 'b' are arbitrary identifiers.
These only match if, besides the usual constraints, a≡b holds. Execution of a matching pair results, as usual, in assignment of expression e to variable x.

(2) ?x and !e.
A command ?x (within P_i) matches with P_i!e (or !e) in *any other* process. Execution is as usual.

(3) $P_i?(x_1,\ldots,x_m)$ and $P_j!(e_1,\ldots,e_m)$.
These match as usual. Execution results in the simultaneous assignment of e_i to x_i. All variables x_i should be different and the number of variables and values in each *syntactically* matching pair should be equal.

Of course, these new primitives may be combined so as to allow constructs like !(e,t), P_i.a?(x,y) and .c?(u,v,w), with obvious semantics.

The translation T: ADA-CS → CSP^+ is now defined as follows (induction on complexity):

T(<u>begin</u> <u>task</u> T_1 ... <u>task</u> T_n <u>end</u>) = $[P_1 \| \ldots \| P_n]$ ($P_i \equiv T(T_i)$)

T(<u>call</u> $T_i.a(\vec{e}\#\vec{x})$) = $P_i.a!(\vec{e},\vec{x})$; $P_j.a?\vec{x}$

T(<u>select</u> b_1:S_1 <u>or</u> ... <u>or</u> b_n:S_n <u>end</u> <u>select</u>) , where S_i≡<u>accept</u> $a_i(\vec{u}_i\#\vec{v}_i)$ <u>do</u> S_{i1} <u>end</u> <u>accept</u>; S_{i2}

$$= [\mathop{\square}_{i}^{n} b_i; a_i?(\vec{u}_i\ \vec{v}_i) \rightarrow T(S_{i1}); a_i!\vec{v}_i; T(S_{i2})]$$

In all remaining occurrences of accept-statements

T(<u>accept</u> $a(\vec{u}\#\vec{v})$ <u>do</u> S <u>end</u> <u>accept</u>) = $[a?(\vec{u},\vec{v}) \rightarrow T(S); a!\vec{v}]$

In the other cases, the translation is the identity mapping.

Correctness of this translation is stated by

Theorem 1. For each program T∈ADA-CS and assertions p and q

$$\models \{p\}\ T\ \{q\} \Leftrightarrow\ \models \{p\}\ T(T)\ \{q\},$$

where validity is defined relative to some semantics, not further specified in this abstract.

A proof system for CSP^+ is obtained by an obvious redefinition of syntactical matching in the CSP system, besides some trivial changes which are connected with the different communication primitives. Soundness and completeness of the CSP system (see [Apt81a]) carry over to the CSP^+ system. This is intuitively clear, as the differences between CSP^+ and CSP are (1) a refinement of *syntactical* matching and (2) the ability to transfer a *syntactically* determined sequence of values between processes. For proofs we refer to [Ger82b] or [Fra82]. As we shall see, having a sound and complete proof system allows us to answer semantic questions by the construction of formal proofs.

We need some notation: A denotes the ADA-CS proof system and C the CSP^+ proof system. L denotes the language of Peano arithmetic (or some first order countable extension) and is the assertion language; J is some model of L. $Tr_J \stackrel{D}{=} \{\varphi \in L \mid J \models \varphi\}$ and we write $B \vdash_{\mathcal{D}} \Phi$ if the formula Φ can be proven in the proof system $\mathcal{D}$, using the assertions in B in the consequence-rule. When this is clear from the context, references to B and/or $\mathcal{D}$ will be omitted.

Soundness theorem. For any program S∈ADA-CS and p,q∈L

$$Tr_J \vdash_A \{p\}\ S\ \{q\} \Rightarrow J \models \{p\}\ S\ \{q\}$$

As in the case of the soundness proof of the CSP proof system, we too, run into some difficulties. Firstly, the parallel composition rule is not a Hoare-style proof rule because of its reference to cooperating proofs. Secondly, it is not clear how to assign meaning to an isolated call or accept, which makes it difficult to prove soundness of the corresponding rules and axioms. Therefore, the proof system A is changed into an equivalent proof system A' which does use the ordinary notion of proof, by explicitly listing all conditions required in establishing cooperation.

To this end, *proof outlines* are introduced. If S is some ADA-CS task-body, a proof outline for S associates with each sub-statement R of S, a pre-assertion, pre(R), and a post-assertion, post(R). The following lemma connects the existence of a formal proof with 'validity' of a proof outline (see also [Apt81a])

Lemma 1. Let S be an ADA-CS task (or part of one) and p,q∈L. Then

$Tr_J \vdash_A \{p\}\ S\ \{q\}$ iff there is a proof outline of S such that for each sub-statement R of S, the following *verification conditions* are true in J:

1. $p \supset pre(S)$, $post(S) \supset q$
2. $pre(\underline{null}) \supset post(\underline{null})$
3. $pre(R) \supset post(R)[e/x]$, if R≡x:=e
4. $pre(R) \wedge b \supset pre(R_1)$, $pre(R) \wedge \neg b \supset pre(R_2)$, $post(R_i) \supset post(R)$ (i=1..2)
   if R≡<u>if</u> b <u>then</u> R_1 <u>else</u> R_2 <u>end</u> <u>if</u>
5. $pre(R) \wedge b \supset pre(R_1)$, $post(R_1) \supset pre(R)$, $pre(R) \wedge \neg b \supset post(R)$
   if R≡<u>while</u> b <u>do</u> R_1 <u>end</u> <u>while</u>
6. $pre(R) \wedge b_i \supset pre(R_i)$, $post(R_i) \supset post(R)$ (i=1..n)
   if R≡<u>select</u> b_1:R_1 <u>or</u> ... <u>or</u> b_n:R_n <u>end</u> <u>select</u>
7. $pre(R) \supset pre(R_1)$, $post(R_1) \supset pre(R_2)$, $post(R_2) \supset post(R)$
   if R≡R_1;R_2

and such that $FV(pre(R)) \cap \vec{x} = \emptyset$ if R≡<u>call</u> T.a($\vec{e}\#\vec{x}$)

Such a proof outline is called *valid* (w.r.t. J) for {p}S{q}, and VC({p}S{q}) denotes the set of verification conditions.

In order to combine the isolated, sequential proofs (or proof outlines), A imposes a second global set of constraints on the assertions of the proof outlines, the *cooperation conditions*, as embodied in the cooperation test:

For any matching communication pair,

S_1';<u>call</u> T.a($\vec{e}\#\vec{x}$);S_1'' and <u>accept</u> a($\vec{u}\#\vec{v}$)<u>do</u> S_2';>S<;S_2'' <u>end</u> <u>accept</u>,

the following two formulae should be valid in J

$$\{pre(S_1') \wedge pre(S_2') \wedge GI\}\ S_1';S_2'[\cdot]\ \{pre('call') \wedge post(S_2'[\cdot]) \wedge GI\}$$

$$\{pre('call') \wedge pre(S_2'')[\cdot] \wedge GI\}\ S_2''[\cdot];S_1''\ \{post(S_1'') \wedge post(S_2'') \wedge GI\}.[1]$$

The set of these conditions for valid proof outlines for $\{p_i\}T_i\{q_i\}$ (i=1..n) w.r.t. GI, is denoted by CC($\{p_i\}T_i\{q_i\}$ i=1..n, GI).

Basing out argument on lemma 1, we replace the axiom A1 and the proof rules R1, R2,

---

[1] Defining cooperation directly in terms of the formulae to be proven, instead of relying on the formation-rule, was suggested by W.P. de Roever. Thus, some problems are circumvented in defining validity of the formation-rule.

R10 and R11 of A by the single rule

R11'. *combined rule* $\dfrac{VC(\{p_i\}T_i\{q_i\})\ ,\ CC(\{p_i\}T_i\{q_i\}\ i=1..n,\ GI)}{\{p_1\wedge\ldots\wedge p_n\wedge GI\}\ \underline{begin}\ \underline{task}\ T_1\ \ldots\ \underline{task}\ T_n\ \underline{end}\ \{q_1\wedge\ldots\wedge q_n\wedge GI\}}$

provided (1) no assertion in the proof outline of T_i contains variables subject to change in T_j ($i\neq j$) and formal parameters only appear in assertions belonging to the outlines of corresponding accept-bodies,
(2) GI does not have free variables subject to change outside bracketed sections.

The resulting proof system A' consists of the axioms A2..3 and the rules R3..9 and R11'. Because of lemma 1, equivalence of A and A' is not difficult to show, hence it suffices to prove A' sound. Similar changes can be made to the CSP^+ proof system C. In particular, a lemma analogous to lemma 1 holds (see [Apt81a]). The resulting proof system is called C' and is equivalent with C. (In order to stay in the spirit of [Apt 81a], C' retains the C formation rule.)

As A' uses the ordinary notion of proof, it suffices to prove soundness of the axioms and proof rules. For these proofs, an important observation is the following one: *Because of theorem 1 and soundness and completeness of* C'

$$J\models\{p\}\ S\ \{q\}\ \Leftrightarrow\ J\models\{p\}\ T(S)\ \{q\}\ \Leftrightarrow\ Tr_J\vdash_{C'}\{p\}\ T(S)\ \{q\}.$$

This concludes the preliminaries and we continue with proving

Soundness of the combined rule.

By the above observation, it suffices to prove

$$Tr_J\vdash_{C'}\{p_1\wedge..\wedge p_n\wedge GI\}\ [P_1\|\ldots\|P_n]\ \{q_1\wedge\ldots\wedge q_n\wedge GI\}\qquad (P_i\equiv T(T_i)),\qquad (\$2)$$

assuming the conditions in $VC(\{p_i\}T_i\{q_i\})$, $i=1..n$, to hold and proofs of the translations of the formulae in $CC(\{p_i\}T_i\{q_i\}\ i=1..n,\ GI)$ to be given.

We will establish the premisses of the C' combined rule.
Using the ADA-CS proof outlines, it is straightforward to construct (valid) CSP^+ proof outlines for the translations and hence to obtain validity of $VC(\{p_i\}P_i\{q_i\})$ $i=1..n$, the first premiss of the C' combined rule.

Next, we must show that ADA-CS cooperation implies CSP^+ cooperation. Consider the following proof outlines of a matching communication pair in the ADA-CS program:

$\{p_1'\}<S_1'\{p\}\underline{call}\ T_j.a(\vec{e}\#\vec{x})\{q\}S_1''>\{q_1''\}$

$\{\bar{p}\}<\underline{accept}\ a(\vec{u}\#\vec{v})\ \underline{do}\{p_2'\}S_2'>\{q_2'\}S\{p_2''\}<S_2''\{q_2''\}\underline{end}\ \underline{accept}>\{\bar{q}\}$

The proof outlines of the translation, are as follows $(R_i\equiv T(S_i))$:

$\{p_1'\}<R_1'\{p\}P_j.a!(\vec{e},\vec{x})>\{p\}<P_j.a?\vec{x}\{q\}R_1''>\{q_1''\}$

$\{\bar{p}\}<a?(\vec{u},\vec{v})\rightarrow\{p_2'\}R_2'>\{q_2'\}R\{p_2''\}<R_2''\{q_2''\}a!\vec{v}>\{\bar{q}\}$

By way of example, we prove CSP^+ cooperation of the first matching pair of bracketed sections: $\{p_1'\wedge\bar{p}\wedge GI\}\ R_1';P_j.a!(\vec{e},\vec{x})\ \|\ a?(\vec{u},\vec{v})\rightarrow R_2'\ \{p\wedge q_2'\wedge GI\}$.
Using the arrow rule, we may replace '→' by ';' in the statement on the right. We intend to use the C' formation rule, hence we must prove its premisses:

$$\vdash\{p_1'\wedge\bar{p}\wedge GI\}R_1'\{r\}\ ,\ \vdash\{r\}P_j.a!(\vec{e},\vec{x})\|a?(\vec{u},\vec{v})\{s\}\ ,\ \vdash\{s\}R_2'\{p\wedge q_2'\wedge GI\},\qquad (\$3)$$

where r and s are yet to be determined.

We may assume to have proofs of the translations of the A' cooperation conditions; in particular, we may assume $\vdash\{p_1'\wedge\bar{p}\wedge GI\}R_1';R_2'[\cdot]\{p\wedge q_2'[\cdot]\wedge GI\}$ to hold. Hence, defining r to be the intermediate assertion between R_1' and $R_2'[\cdot]$, takes care of the first premiss in ($3) (this assertion exists because we have a formal proof). As $FV(r)\cap(\vec{u}\cup\vec{v})=\emptyset$, we can take $s\equiv r\wedge\vec{u}=\vec{e}\wedge\vec{v}=\vec{x}$ in the second premiss (apply the *C'* preservation and communication axioms).

When introducing the formation rule, we argued the equivalence between assignment and substitution in parameter-passing (cf. ($1)). This implies that

$$\models \{r\}\ R_2'[\cdot]\ \{p\wedge q_2'[\cdot]\wedge GI\} \ \Leftrightarrow\ \models \{r\}\ \vec{u}:=\vec{e};\ \vec{v}:=\vec{x};\ R_2';\ \vec{x}:=\vec{v}\ \{p\wedge q_2'[\cdot]\wedge GI\},$$

since $FV(r,p,q_2'[\cdot],GI)\cap(\vec{u}\cup\vec{v}) = \emptyset$. And hence $\models \{r\wedge\vec{u}=\vec{e}\wedge\vec{v}=\vec{x}\}\ R_2'\ \{p\wedge q_2'[\vec{e}/\vec{u}]\wedge GI\}$.
Finally, using completeness of *C'*, applying the preservation axiom to $\{\vec{u}=\vec{e}\}$ and noticing that $\models q_2'[\vec{e}/\vec{u}]\wedge\vec{u}=\vec{e}\supset q_2'$, we get $\vdash \{s\}\ R_2'\ \{p\wedge q_2'\wedge GI\}$, the third premiss of the *C'* formatio rule. Hence, this rule may be applied, thus establishing cooperation of the above matching pair.

When trying to prove cooperation of the second matching pair

$$\{p\wedge p_2''\wedge GI\}\ P_j.a?\vec{x};R_1''\ \|\ R_2'';a!\vec{v}\ \{q_1''\wedge\bar{q}\wedge GI\},$$

we run into a difficulty, because we need invariance of the value parameters, $\vec{u}$, over the translation of the accept-body. For this, the translations of the ADA-CS outlines are too weak (in ADA-CS, invariance is a direct consequence of the semantics). Hence, the CSP^+ proof outlines and GI have to be slightly strenghtened, implying that the above cooperation proof changes too. None of this, however, introduces essential difficulties and the method of proof stays the same; cf. [Ger82b].

Thus, CSP^+ cooperation is shown, and this establishes the second premiss of the *C'* combined rule, $CC(\{p_i\}P_i\{q_i\}\ i=1..n,\ GI)$. Hence the rule may be applied, thus proving ($3) and soundness of the A' combined rule.

Because of the close correspondence between A' and *C'*, soundness of the other rules and axioms is trivial.

Completeness theorem. For any S∈ADA-CS and $p,q\in L$

$$J\models\{p\}\ S\ \{q\}\ \Rightarrow\ Tr_J\vdash_A\{p\}\ S\ \{q\}.$$

Because of theorem 1 and soundness of *C*, this takes the following simpler form

$$Tr_J\vdash_C\{p\}\ T(S)\ \{q\}\ \Rightarrow\ Tr_J\vdash_A\ \{p\}\ S\ \{q\}.$$

Let $S\equiv$ <u>begin</u> <u>task</u> T_1 ... <u>task</u> T_n <u>end</u> and assume we have $\vdash\{p\}T(S)\{q\}$. In this proof, go back to the (only) application of the *C* parallel composition rule, yielding

$$\vdash\{p_1\wedge\ldots\wedge p_n\wedge GI\}\ [T(T_1)'\|\ldots\|T(T_n)']\ \{q_1\wedge\ldots\wedge q_n\wedge GI\},$$

where $T(T_i)'$ denotes $T(T_i)$ augmented with auxiliary variables (notice that $T(T_i)'=T(T_i'))$. This implies that we have proofs for $\{p_i\}T(T_i')\{q_i\}$ and CSP^+ cooperation w.r.t. GI. From these, ADA-CS proofs are constructed for $\{p_i\}T_i'\{q_i\}$, simply by defining for each component statement S of T_i', $pre(S)\equiv pre(T(S))$ and $post(S)\equiv post(T(S))$. Validity of these proofs is obvious; ADA-CS cooperation remains to be shown. I.e., for each communication pair $S_1';\underline{\text{call}}\ T_j.a(\vec{e},\vec{x});S_1''$, $\underline{\text{accept}}\ a(\vec{u}\#\vec{v})\ \underline{\text{do}}\ S_2';>S<;S_2''\ \underline{\text{end}}\ \underline{\text{accept}}$ the premisses of the A formation rule must be shown to hold. This is in fact straightforward, using the following lemma which states some general conditions under which variable- substitution preserves provability.

Lemma 2. Let $S\in$ADA-CS, $p,q\in L$, $\vec{u}$, $\vec{v}$ and $\vec{x}$ sequences of distinct variables and $\vec{e}$ a sequence of expressions, such that

(i) $FV(\vec{e},q)\cap\vec{x}=\emptyset$, $\vec{u}\cap\vec{v}=\emptyset$ and $FV(S,\vec{u},\vec{v})\cap(FV(\vec{e})\cup\vec{x})=\emptyset$

(ii) the variables in $\vec{u}$ do not appear on the left-hand side of any assignment in S or as value-result parameter of any call in S.

Then (1) $Tr_J \vdash_A \{p\}\ S\ \{q\} \qquad Tr_J \vdash_A \{p[\cdot]\}\ S[\cdot]\ \{q[\cdot]\} \qquad ([\cdot]\equiv[\vec{e}/\vec{u}, \vec{x}/\vec{v}])$

(2) $Tr_J \vdash_C \{p\}\ T(S)\ \{q\} \qquad Tr_J \vdash_C \{p[\cdot]\}\ T(S[\cdot])\ \{q[\cdot]\}$

CSP^+ cooperation of the first pair of bracketed sections in the translations of the above communication pair, yields $(T(S_i)=R_i)$:

$$\vdash \{p_1\wedge p_2\wedge GI\}\ R_1'\ \{p\}\ ,\ \vdash \{p\}\ P_j.a\ (\vec{e},\vec{x})\| a?(\vec{u},\vec{v})\ \{q\}\ ,\ \vdash \{q\}\ R_2'\ \{p_1'\wedge p_2'\wedge GI\},$$

where $q\equiv p\wedge\vec{u}=\vec{e}\wedge\vec{v}=\vec{x}$, and the other assertions are taken from the appropriate outlines. Furthermore, we may assume $FV(p_1')\cap\vec{x}=\emptyset$. This is a consequence of the fact that only formulae of the form $\{r\}a!\vec{v}\|P_j.a?\vec{x}\{r\wedge\vec{x}=\vec{v}\}$ in which $FV(r)\cap\vec{x}=\emptyset$ can be proven in C (see the communication axiom). As R_1' and R_2' are *sequential* statements, we obtain by translating the CSP^+ proof outlines and using lemma 1 and 2 that:

$$\vdash_{A'} \{p_1\wedge p_2\wedge GI\}\ S_1';S_2'[\cdot]\ \{p_1'\wedge p_2'[\cdot]\wedge GI\},$$

the first premiss of the A' formation rule.

The second premiss, $\vdash_{A'}\{p_2'\}S\{q_2'\}$ $(q_2'\equiv pre(R_2''))$, is clear, as S is a sequential statement. Finally, CSP^+ cooperation of the second pair of bracketed sections yields

$$\vdash \{p_1'\wedge q_2'\wedge GI\}\ R_2''\ \{\bar{p}\}\ ,\ \vdash \{\bar{p}\wedge\vec{x}=\vec{v}\}\ R_1''\ \{q_1\wedge q_2\wedge GI\},$$

whence, using lemma 2 again (and translating the proofs)

$$\vdash_A\ \{p_1'\wedge q_2'[\cdot]\wedge GI\}\ R_2''[\cdot]\ \{\bar{p}[\cdot]\}\quad ,\ \vdash_A\ \{\bar{p}[\vec{e}/\vec{u}]\wedge\vec{x}=\vec{v}\}\ S_1''\ \{q_1\wedge q_2\wedge GI\}.$$

Because $\models \bar{p}[\vec{e}/\vec{u}]\wedge\vec{x}=\vec{v}\leftrightarrow\bar{p}[\cdot]\wedge\vec{x}=\vec{v}$ and $FV(\bar{p}[\cdot],S_1'',q_1,q_2,GI)\cap\vec{v}=\emptyset$, this implies

$$\vdash \{p_1'\wedge q_2'[\cdot]\wedge GI\}\ R_2''[\cdot];R_1''\ \{q_1\wedge q_2\wedge GI\},$$

which is the third premiss of the A formation rule.

Thus, ADA-CS cooperation of the proofs has been shown. Application of the A parallel composition rule yields

$$\vdash_A\ \{p_1\wedge\ldots\wedge p_n\wedge GI\}\ \underline{\text{begin}}\ \underline{\text{task}}\ T_1\ \ldots\ \underline{\text{task}}\ T_n\ \underline{\text{end}}\ \{q_1\wedge\ldots\wedge q_n\wedge GI\}.$$

Finally, application of the A consequence, substitution and AV rule allows the conclusion $\vdash_A\{p\}S\{q\}$, thus establishing completeness of the ADA-CS proof system.

5. DISCUSSION.

In this paper we have studied the ADA rendezvous in a subset of the ADA concurrency section, ADA-CS. Using the basic ideas of the CSP proof system in [AFR80], we have constructed a partial correctness proof system and have proven that this completely axiomatizes ADA-CS (disregarding failure, termination and deadlock).

ADA-CS communication is basically captured by our formation rule, which combines a simple procedure-call rule with a cooperation test. The idea of canonical proofs for the accept-bodies is retained, by observing that an ADA-CS communication action splits into two CSP-like communications, so that the cooperation test can be restricted to a small prelude and postlude of each accept-body. Along the way, some restrictions on the actual parameters were introduced. Although these restrictions do not reduce the 'power' of the subset, the reader may wonder whether it is really necessary to introduce them. We believe not. The restrictions were introduced so as to allow a very simple call rule to be used and we expect the same techniques to apply to more general rules such as in [GL80].

Canonicity (or rather the absence of it) subtly affects the cooperation test: Accept-bodies may contain other calls or accepts. So, if two different proofs of an accept-body are used in a program-proof, two different cooperation tests must be checked for each matching communication pair which references a call or accept in the accept-body, because the pre- and post-assertions of the call or accept will in general be different in the different proofs of the accept-body. Hence, more than for sequential languages, canonicity is something to be desired in proof systems for concurrent languages (a similar remark applies to interference freedom tests).

This paper does not discuss total correctness, absence of deadlock and the proof of safety properties. Using the CSP proof system, it is straightforward to strengthen the current system to prove total correctness and absence of deadlock. Extension to a safety proof system is more difficult and we refer the reader to [Ger82a] in which a safety proof system is constructed (for a more general language than ADA-CS).

After constructing the ADA-CS proof system, we learned of independent work on ADA by Barringer & Mearns, [BM81]. They attempt to construct a proof system for a larger subset of the ADA concurrency section than ADA-CS, containing, f.i., real-time constructs and the terminate-statement; they also address the problems of deadlock and termination. Their starting point, too, is [AFR80]; there are however some problems with their application of cooperation.

ACKNOWLEDGEMENTS.

I would like to thank Adrie van Bloois, Marly Roncken and Job Zwiers for some fruitful discussions and especially Willem P. de Roever for his stimulating guidance.

REFERENCES.

Reference [Ger81] is not cited in the paper.

[Apt81a] Apt, K.: Formal Justification of a Proof System for Communicating Sequential Processes. to appear

[Apt81b] Apt, K.: Ten Years of Hoare's Logic: A Survey - Part 1. TOPLAS 3-4 p.431-484, 1981.

[AFR80] Apt, K., N.Francez, W.P.de Roever: A Proof System for Communicating Sequential Processes. TOPLAS 2-3 p.359-385, 1980.

[ARM81] The Programming Language ADA. Reference manual. LNCS 106, Springer Verlag, New York, 1981.

[BM81] Barringer, H., I.Mearns: Axioms and Proof Rules for ADA Tasks. Technical report, Dept. of Computer Science, University of Manchester, 1981.

[Fra82] Francez, N., E.M.Clarke, C.Nikolaou: Extended Naming Conventions for Communicating Processes and their Proof Rules. Proc. 9th Symp. on POPL, 1982.

[Ger81] Gerth, R.: A Proof System for a Subset of the Concurrency Section of ADA. Technical report RUU-CS-81-17, Dept. of Computer Science, University of Utrecht, 1981.

[Ger82a] Gerth, R., W.P. de Roever, M. Roncken: Procedures and Concurrency: A Study in Proof. Proc. Vth International Symposium on Programming, Turijn, 1982.

[Ger82b] Gerth, R.: A Sound and Complete Hoare Axiomatization of the ADA Rendezvous. Technical report, Dept. of Computer Science, University of Utrecht, 1982.

[GL80] Gries, D., G.Levin: Assignment and Procedure Call Proof Rules. TOPLAS 2-4 p.564-580, 1980.

[OwG76] Owicki, S., D.Gries: An Axiomatic Proof Technique for Parallel Programs 1. Acta Inf. 6 p.319-340, 1976.

[PR82] Pnueli, A., W.P. de Roever: Fairness in the programming language ADA. Technical report, Dept. of Computer Science, Weizmann Instute, Israel, 1982.

[Ron81] Roncken, M., R.Gerth, W.P. de Roever: A Proof System for Brinch Hansen's Distributed Processes. Proc. GI81 München, 1981.

Universal Realization, Persistent Interconnection and Implementation of Abstract Modules[1]

by J. Goguen and J. Meseguer
Computer Science Laboratory
SRI International, 333 Ravenswood Ave, Menlo Park CA

1 Introduction

Abstract modules are now widely used as models for software system components [25, 27, 5]. Such modules have a visible interface consisting of procedures that can produce externally visible values and may also alter hidden internal states. This paper contributes to the foundations of software engineering with four main results. The first is a minimal realization theorem for abstract modules. Using the framework of conditional equational theories, we generalize an abstract form (called "universal realization") of the classical minimal state realization theorem for automata to abstract modules. Our second main result is a basic theorem about consistent (more precisely "persistent") interconnections of theories; it has applications to the consistency of interconnections and implementations of parameterized abstract modules. The third result gives simple equivalent syntactic and semantic characterizations of when it is possible to implement one abstract module with another. Our fourth main contribution extends this notion of implementation to parameters, with suitable definitions for "vertical" and "horizontal" composition of parameterized implementations (in the sense of [12]), and proves some fundamental properties of these compositions, including associativity and the "double law" of [12]. This paper emphasizes fundamentals, particularly basic mathematical results; there is not enough space here for detailed motivation or examples. This work is related to a great deal of recent literature, particularly Ganzinger [10] which we often cite below. We assume familiarity with software engineering issues, the literature on abstract data types (hereafter, "ADTs"), equational logic, and with some notions from category theory (including category, functor, full subcategory, and adjoint functor). Some other notions are explained as used (such as pushout), but the proofs have been condensed due to space limitations.

We wish to point out some distinctions that may help the reader avoid certain common pitfalls. The first is between specification and theory: a **specification** is a (usually finite) description of what a module is supposed to do, while the corresponding **theory** contains **all** consequences of that description, and may be an infinite object. Specifications are needed for practical purposes, while theories are useful for theoretical purposes. The situation is analoguous to that of the real numbers: in practice we must deal with finite descriptions, but for theoretical work it is convenient to have the complete structure available. Our second distinction is between **ADTs** and **modules**. Quite simply, a module can have hidden sorts while an ADT cannot. This suggests a resolution of the apparent conflict between "initial" and "final" algebra semantics: initial semantics is appropriate for ADTs, while final semantics is an option (not always optimal) for modules. The third distinction is between the **syntactic** level of theories and specifications, and the **semantic** level of actual software (and/or hardware) modules. To understand what some system does, we must use descriptions, e.g., axioms about its visible behavior. Conversely, software to realize such a description must give a model whose behavior satisfies the axioms; we will use the phrase "abstract module" to refer to a collection of models having the same behavior. (Note also that we use the word "machine" informally for an interconnection of abstract modules or other machines, much as in [25].) It should not be supposed that because we use such abstract concepts as theories and pushouts that our results do not have practical application; indeed, we believe that a conceptually simple foundation for software engineering is possible only through using such idealizations. We wish to thank R. M. Burstall for his suggestions on this paper.

---

[1] Supported in part by Office of Naval Research Contract N00014-80-0296.

1.1 Universal Realization

Our first main result says that a given behavior has a unique "minimal" realization as a module without redundant internal states. This intuition is often captured by asserting a "final" algebra in the category of algebras with the same behavior. Our universal formulation is more sweeping in that it applies to a larger category of algebras, and it is also more general mathematicaly. As an example, let us consider a list processing module M like that of [29]: it has sorts atom, sexpr, bool, and [storage], the latter being hidden; it has operations

nil: → sexpr

cons: sexpr, sexpr → sexpr

quote: atom → sexpr

which not only produce the indicated values, but also (as a "side effect") change the [storage] value, i.e., they are really functions

nil: [storage] → [storage], sexpr

cons: [storage], sexpr, sexpr → [storage], sexpr

quote: [storage], atom → [storage], sexpr

Let us assume that this module also has the following functions without side effect

car, cons: [storage], sexpr → sexpr

cellp: [storage], sexpr → bool

These too could be written without the [storage] argument. The purpose of the cellp function is to interrogate whether or not a given sexpr already has storage allocated for it in M; the other functions are as in LISP. As a sample computation on M, assuming that atoms are letters and abbreviating quote(a) to 'a, the input car(car(cons('a,cons('b,nil)))) would produce the output 'b. Now, it may be that in response to the input cons(cdr(cons('a,cons('b,nil))),cons('b,nil)), M allocates storage for cons('b,nil) twice, or it may be that it recognizes that it has already allocated it once, thus requiring a smaller [storage]. This property is sometimes desirable, and M is called a "ULIST machine" in [29] if it has that property; "hash cons" is also used to describe the corresponding cons operation. The ULIST property is actually a minimal realization property, and thus can be expressed elegantly by a universal[2] condition.

The universal realization theorem for automata [16] asserts that, for behavior and machine homomorphisms that are surjective on the input sort, every behavior has a minimal realization that is (co)universal among all reachable realizations. The same result is proved here for any conditional equational theory **T**, using a notion of behavior relative to a subset of "visible" sorts. We also construct an initial realization that plays a dual role, and show that the couniversal realization is final among all the realizations of a behavior. The couniversal realization is obtained as a generalized "Nerode" quotient of the initial realization. These results answer questions raised by [19, 18, 31, 28, 10] and others. Note that our use of conditional theories generalizes most previous work in this area.

1.2 Persistent Interconnection of Modules and Implementations

With their language Clear, Burstall and Goguen [2, 3] introduced the basic ideas that a large specification can be composed by putting together theories (of system components), and that this interconnection is accomplished by taking a colimit of the theories involved (this builds on the earlier use of colimits for interconnections of general systems [15]). In particular, the application of a parameterized specification (such as **List[X]**) to an actual parameter

---

[2] This is a convenient pun on the letter U, which meant "unique" in [29].

(such as **Int**) is accomplished with a pushout. However, this work did not address two important issues: (1) "hidden" internal states of modules; and (2) "protection" of the actual parameter from (a) the addition of new elements, and (b) the identification of old elements. Distinguishing between visible and hidden sorts permits us to apply methods developed for ADTs to abstract modules and thus to handle issue (1). Conditions (2a) and (2b) correspond to what Guttag [19] calls "sufficient completeness" and "consistency" respectively, and the combination of the two is called "persistence" [10], corresponding to the equivalent semantic condition of [30]. This notion can also be applied to any extension of one theory to another; in particular, we may require that a parameterized specification be a persistent extension of its parameter theory. Moreover, these two issues can be combined, leading to parameterized abstract modules. Our second main result says that any pushout of persistent theory extensions, along arbitrary theory morphisms, is again persistent. This implies that any interconnection of persistent parameterized specifications is persistent, and in particular gives "correctness of parameter passing" results like those of [10, 7], including the associativity of composition by parameter instantiation. The notion of persistence also has applications to the important problem of implementing one abstract module with another. Our third main contribution is give simple equivalent syntactic and semantic characterizations of what appears to be the most natural and general version of the implementation notion. Finally, we extend it to handle parameters, define both vertical and horizontal composition of implementations, and prove basic properties such as associativity of each composition, and the commutativity of vertical with horizontal composition. This is the so-called "double law" of [12] which expresses a basic requirement for software engineering, that the order in which parts of a machine are implemented should not effect the correctness of the implementation.

2 Conditional Theories

Let S be a set with elements called **sorts**. We assume familiarity with the concepts of an **S-sorted set** $A = \{A_s\}$, an **S-sorted function** $f = \{f_s\}$, an **S-sorted signature**[3] $\Sigma = \{\Sigma_{w,s} \mid w \text{ in } S^*, s \text{ in } S\}$ and with the concepts of **Σ-algebra** and **Σ-homomorphism**. For $X = \{X_s\}$ an S-sorted set, let $T_\Sigma X$ denote the free Σ-algebra on X, which can be constructed as the (S-sorted) set of all well-formed Σ-terms using "variables" from X. The universal property of the S-sorted inclusion $\eta: X \rightarrow T_\Sigma X$ is: for any Σ-algebra A, any S-sorted function $f: X \rightarrow A$ extends to a unique Σ-homomorphism $f^\#: T_\Sigma X \rightarrow A$ such that $\eta \circ f^\# = f$. This property characterizes T_Σ uniquely up to Σ-isomorphism. For each word $w = s1...sn$ in S^*, let X(w) denote the S-sorted set with $X(w)_s = \{xi \mid si = s\}$. We write "$\lambda(w)s.\ t$" to indicate that t is in $T_\Sigma X(w)_s$, and we may say that t has **rank** (w,s). If A is a Σ-algebra, then a term $\lambda(w)s.\ t$ has a denotation as a function $A(t): A^w \rightarrow A_s$ in the standard way, where $A^w = A_{s1} \times ... \times A_{sn}$. We say that A **satisfies** the equation $\lambda(w)s.\ t = t'$ iff $A(t) = A(t')$. A **conditional equation** has the form

(★) $\lambda(w)s.\ t1 = t'1\ \&...\&\ tn = t'n \Rightarrow t = t'$,

where ti and t'i, for $1 \leq i \leq n$, belong to $T_\Sigma X(w)_{si}$ for some si, and t,t' to $T_\Sigma X(w)_s$. A Σ-algebra A **satisfies** (★) iff whenever $\underline{a}$ in A^w satisfies $A(ti)(\underline{a}) = A(t'i)(\underline{a})$ for $1 \leq i \leq n$, then $A(t)(\underline{a}) = A(t')(\underline{a})$. Given $w = s1...sn$ in S^*, given a term $\lambda(w)s.\ t$, and given terms $\lambda(v)si.\ ti$ for $1 \leq i \leq k$, let $\lambda(v)s.\ t(t1,...,tk)$ denote the substitution $t(x1 \leftarrow t1,...,xk \leftarrow tk)$.

Definition 1: A conditional **presentation** is a triple $T = (\Sigma,E,C)$, with Σ an S-sorted signature, $E = \{E_{w,s}\}$ an $S \times S^*$-sorted family with $E_{w,s}$ a set of Σ-equations of rank (w,s), and $C = \{C_{w,s}\}$ a corresponding family of sets of conditional Σ-equations; we may also write T as a quadruple (S,Σ,E,C). A Σ-algebra A is a **T-algebra** iff it satisfies all equations in E and C. Let $\mathbf{Alg}_T$ denote the category of T-algebras with Σ-homomorphisms (also called **T-homomorphisms**) among them. The **quasi-closure** $T^\bullet$ of a conditional presentation $T = (\Sigma,E,C)$ is the smallest presentation $(\Sigma,E^\bullet,C^\bullet)$ containing T and closed under the following rules of deduction, extending those in [13]:

[3]For technical convenience we assume that $\Sigma_{w,s} \cap \Sigma_{w',s'} = \emptyset$ if $(w,s) \neq (w',s')$.

1. $E^\bullet_{w,s}$ is an equivalence relation for each w in S* and s in S.
2. If w=s1...sk and w′ are in S*, and if λ(w)s. t=t′ and λ(w′)si. ti=t′i are in $E^\bullet$ for 1≤i≤k, then λ(w′)s. t(ti,...,tk)=t′(t′1,...,t′k) is in $E^\bullet$.
3. If w is in S* and (for λ the empty string) if λ(λ)s. t=t′ is in $E^\bullet$, then λ(w)s. t=t′ is in $E^\bullet$.
4. If λ(w)s. t1=t′1 &...& tn=t′n ⇒ t=t′ is in $C^\bullet$, then:

   a. Given w′=s′1...s′k with s′j=s, and given a term λ(w′)s′. t0, then λ(w.(w′/j))s′. t1=t′1 &...& tn=t′n ⇒ t0(xj←t)=t0(xj←t′) is in $C^\bullet$, where w′/j denotes w′ with s′j deleted; and

   b. If w=s1...sk, and given terms λ(w′)si. t″i for 1≤i≤k, then λ(w′)s. t1(t″1,...,t″k)=t′1(t″1,...,t″k) &...& tn(t″1,...,t″k)=t′n(t″1,...,t″k) ⇒ t(t″1,...,t″k)=t′(t″1,...,t″k) is in $C^\bullet$.

5. If λ(w)s′i. ti=t′i are in $E^\bullet$ for 1≤i≤n and if λ(w)s. t1=t′1 &...& tn=t′n ⇒ t=t′ is in $C^\bullet$, then λ(w)s. t=t′ is in $E^\bullet$.

Let us call a conditional presentation **quasi-closed**, or a **conditional theory**, iff it is closed under these rules. A conditional specification T is **equational** iff it is of the form (Σ,E,∅), and let us call a conditional theory **equational** iff it has a presentation of that form. Note that if T is equational, only the rules (1) - (3) apply; indeed, they are deductively complete [13]. The **equational part** of a conditional theory T = (Σ,E,C) is the equational theory EqT = (Σ,E). ∎

Proposition 2: The above rules are **equationally complete**, in the sense that given a conditional presentation T = (Σ,E,C), an equation is in $E^\bullet$ iff it is satisfied by every algebra in $\mathbf{Alg}_T$.

Proof: "Only if" follows from soundness of the rules. Conversely, $E^\bullet$ is closed under rules (1) - (3), so by [13] the algebra $F_{X(w)} = \{T_\Sigma X(w)_s/E^\bullet_{w,s}\}$ is the free EqT-algebra on X(w). Rules (4b) and (5) can be used to show that each $F_{X(w)}$ actually satisfies T. Then $F_{X(w)}$ is the free T-algebra on X(w), because $\mathbf{Alg}_{EqT}$ is a full subcategory of $\mathbf{Alg}_T$. Now if some equation λ(w)s. t=t′ is satisfied by $\mathbf{Alg}_T$, then it is satisfied by $F_{X(w)}$ and therefore is in $E^\bullet_{w,s}$. ∎

The rules above are not complete for conditional equational deduction; but the conditional theories that they generate are more convenient to work with, and are sufficiently rich for the purposes of this paper.

3 Modules, Behaviors and Realizations

Modern theoretical work on ADTs has not, in general, exploited the analogy with automaton theory, but instead has concentrated on such algebraic and logical issues as initiality, consistency, and completeness [14, 19, 18]; two notable early exceptions are [31] and [11]. The difference between an ADT and a module is that some sorts of the latter may be "hidden;" i.e., a module can have internal states. This section discusses the minimal realization of modules, first for the equational case, and later for the conditional case. More precisely, we show that given a specification with hidden sorts and given a behavior (i.e., a model of the visible part of the specification) there are, in various senses, simplest modules realizing that behavior: initial, final, and couniversal. Each of these properties characterizes a module uniquely up to isomorphism, and the latter two characterize the same module, which is also obtained as a generalized "Nerode" quotient of the initial realization.

Definition 3: A conditional **specification** M is a conditional presentation T = (S,Σ,E,C) together with a subset H ⊆ S of "hidden" or "invisible" sorts; such an M is therefore conveniently given as a tuple M = (S,H,Σ,E,C). Let us call T = (Σ,E,C) the underlying **presentation** of M; we say that M is **equational** iff T is equational, and that M is a **specification theory** iff T is a theory. Let V=S-H, the set of **visible** (or "observable") sorts. An **M-module** is a T-algebra. ∎

A theory of behaviors for a specification M is obtained by restricting its presentation T to the subset of visible sorts, denoted $T|_V$. Because this is the theory of what is visible, its equations should use only "external terms" of T, i.e., terms of the form $\lambda(w)v.\ t$ with w in V* and v in V. However, there is a difficulty: the sort set of $T|_V$ should be V, but the external terms may involve derived operations with hidden sorts. Our solution[4] is to construct a new V-sorted signature Σ^R containing all the external terms; these derived operators represent the capabilities which a user may invoke at the visible interface to a module. We will use the following notation in this definition: given an S-sorted signature S, its **derived signature** $\mathbf{Der}\Sigma$ has $\mathbf{Der}\Sigma_{w,s} = T_\Sigma X(w)_s$, all the s-sorted derived operators with variables in X(w). The universal property of the inclusion of $T_\Sigma X(w)$ into $T_{\mathbf{Der}\Sigma}(T_\Sigma X(w))$ applied to the identity on the $\mathbf{Der}\Sigma$-algebra $T_\Sigma X(w)$ gives a $\mathbf{Der}\Sigma$-homomorphism $\{\varepsilon_{w,s}: T_{\mathbf{Der}\Sigma}(T_\Sigma X(w))_s \rightarrow T_\Sigma X(w)_s\}$. It can be seen as reducing an expression composed of derived operators into a single derived operator.

Definition 4: Given a specification M = (S,H,Σ,E,C), its **behavior specification** is the **restriction** of M to V=S-H, a V-sorted conditional presentation $M|_V = (\Sigma^R, E^R, C^R)$, also written M^R, defined as follows:

1. $\Sigma^R_{w,v} = \mathbf{Der}\Sigma_{w,v}$ for w in V* and v in V.
2. $E^R_{w,v} = \{\lambda(w)v.\ t(x1,...,xk) = t'(x1,...,xk) \mid \lambda(w)v.\ t=t' \text{ in } E^\bullet_{w,v}\} \cup \{\lambda(w)v.\ \alpha = \varepsilon_{w,v}(\alpha)(x1,...,xk) \mid \alpha \text{ in } T_{\Sigma^R}(X(w))_v\}$ for w=v1...vk in V* and v in V.
3. $C^R_{w,v} = \{\lambda(w)v.\ t1(x1,...,xk) = t'1(x1,...,xk)\ \&...\&\ tn(x1,...,xk) = t'n(x1,...,xk) \Rightarrow t(x1,...,xk) = t'(x1,...,xk) \mid \lambda(w)v.\ t1=t'1\ \&...\&\ tn=t'n \Rightarrow t=t' \text{ is in } C^\bullet_{w,v}\}$ for w=v1...vk in V* and v in V.

The category $\mathbf{Alg}_{T|_V}$ will be denoted $\mathbf{Beh}_M$ and a $\mathbf{Beh}_M$-algebra will be called an **M-behavior** or a **V-behavior**. We now introduce the **behavior functor** B: $\mathbf{Alg}_T \rightarrow \mathbf{Beh}_M$ which sends each T-algebra M (i.e., each M-module) to its **behavior,** the Σ^R-algebra B(M) with $B(M)_v = M_v$ for each v in V, and B(M)(t(x1,...,xk)) = M(t) for each Σ-term $\lambda(w)v.\ t$, with w=s1...sk in V* and v in V. Moreover, $B(f) = \{f_v\}_{v\in V}$ for f a Σ-homomorphism. A Σ^R-homomorphism between two behaviors is called a **behavior map.** A T-module M **realizes** a behavior A iff B(M)=A. ∎

3.1 The Equational Case

Throughout this section M = (S,H,Σ,E) is an equational specification, T = (S,Σ,E) is its presentation, and V=S-H. In this setting we may assume without loss of generality that each nonempty $\Sigma_{w,s}$ has w of the form $w = \underline{h}\ \underline{v}$ with $\underline{h}$=h1...hm for hj in H and $\underline{v}$=v1...vk for vj in V. By convention, w, $\underline{h}$, and $\underline{v}$ often have this meaning below.

Theorem 5: Initial Realization. For each M-behavior A there is a realization IA of A such that for each M-module M and each behavior map f: A → B(M), there is a unique T-homomorphism $f^\#$: IA → M such that $B(f^\#) = f$.

Proof: Define IA = $\{IA_s\}$ as follows: $IA_v = A_v$ for each visible sort v. For a hidden sort h, IA_h is the quotient under the least equivalence relation Q* containing the following relation Q on the set of all pairs $(t,\underline{a})$ such that $\lambda(\underline{v})h.\ t$ is a Σ-term with $\underline{v}$ in V* and $\underline{a}$ in $A^{\underline{v}}$: $(\lambda(\underline{v})h.\ t,\underline{a})\ Q\ (\lambda(\underline{v}')h.\ t', \underline{a}')$, for $\underline{v}'$=v1...vk in V*, iff there are Σ-terms $\lambda(\underline{v})vj.\ tj$, $1 \le j \le k$ such that $\lambda(\underline{v})h.\ t = t'(t1,...,tk)$ is in $E^\bullet$ and $\underline{a}' = (A(t1)\underline{a},...,A(tk)\underline{a})$. The Q*-equivalence class of $(t,\underline{a})$ will be denoted $[(t,\underline{a})]$. We now define a Σ-structure on IA. Assuming σ in $\Sigma_{w,v}$ (with $w = \underline{h}\ \underline{v}$, $\underline{h}$=h1...hm in H*, $\underline{v}$ in V*, and v in V), $[(\lambda(uj)hj.\ tj,\underline{a}j)]$ in IA_{hj} for $1 \le j \le m$, and $\underline{a}$ in $A^{\underline{v}}$, let n_k be the length #(u1...uk) of the string u1...uk, let

$\underline{t} = (t1(x1,...,xn_1),...,tk(xn_{k-1}+1,...,xn_k),...,tm(xn_{m-1}+1,...,xn_m))$,

and let $\underline{x}_{\underline{v}} = (xn_m+1,...,xn_m+\#\underline{v})$. Then the operation IA(σ) is defined by

(1) $IA(\sigma)([(t1,\underline{a}1)],...,[(tm,\underline{a}m)],\underline{a}) = A(\sigma(\underline{t},\underline{x}_{\underline{v}}))(\underline{a}1,...,\underline{a}m,\underline{a})$.

Note that when $\underline{h} = \lambda$, then IA(σ) is A(σ). Therefore B(IA)=A, and IA is indeed a realization of A. Next, for σ in $\Sigma_{w,h}$ with h in H, we define

(2) $IA(\sigma)([(t1,\underline{a}1)],...,[(tm,\underline{a}m)],\underline{a}) = [(\sigma(\underline{t},\underline{x}_{\underline{v}}),\underline{a}1...\underline{a}m\ \underline{a})]$.

---

[4] A conceptually simpler approach is to use Lawvere theories [24], where $T|_V$ is just a subtheory of T; however, this requires more in the way of preliminary definitions.

One then checks that the definition of IA(σ) does not depend on the representatives chosen in Q*-equivalence classes. By extending definitions (1) and (2) to Σ-terms, and using the definition of Q* and the fact that A is a $T|_V$-algebra, it can be shown that IA satisfies the equations of T. To conclude, for M in Alg_T and f: A→ BM a behavior map, note that a T-homomorphism $f^{\#}$: IA→M with B($f^{\#}$)=f must satisfy (i) $f^{\#}_v = f_v$ for v in V, and (ii) $f^{\#}[(\lambda(\underline{v})h.\ t,\underline{a})]$ = M(t)($f^{\underline{v}}(\underline{a})$) for h in H, because $f^{\#}$ is a homomorphism and, by definition, IA(t)($\underline{a}$)=[(t, $\underline{a}$)]. Conditions (i) and (ii) are a well-defined specification of $f^{\#}$ as a T-homomomorphism; therefore $f^{\#}$ exists and is unique. ∎

For M in $\mathbf{Alg_T}$ let εM: IB(M) → M be the unique T-homomorphism induced by the identity map on B(M); i.e., $\varepsilon M = (id_{B(M)})^{\#}$. We will say that M is a **reachable** realization of its behavior B(M) iff εM is surjective.

Theorem 6: Final Realization. For every behavior A in $\mathbf{Beh_M}$, there is a reachable realization NA of A such that for any other reachable realization M of A there exists a unique T-homomorphism f: M → NA such that B(f)=id_A.

Proof: f is unique because the universal property of IA implies that εNA = f∘εM and ε(M) is surjective. Any reachable réalization M of A is isomorphic to the quotient IA/Q(εM), where Q(εM) is the congruence induced by εM. Conversely, any congruence $Q' = \{Q'_s\}$ on IA with Q'_v the identity relation on A_v for each v in V, defines a reachable realization. We will be finished if we show there is a maximum congruence of this kind. It is known in universal algebra, e.g., Lemma 10.2 of [17], that the smallest congruence containing a family of congruences on an algebra is the transitive closure of their set-theoretic union. Clearly, the transitive closure Q* of the union of all congruences Q′ on IA with Q'_v the identity relation for v in V, also has Q^*_v the identity relation. Thus Q* defines the desired NA. ∎

As for automata, the final or minimal realization of a behavior A can be characterized explicitly by a "Nerode" congruence on IA that identifies two elements of a hidden ("state") sort iff they behave the same with respect to the visible sorts. This congruence, denoted **ner**, is defined as follows: for e,e′ in IA_s, e $\mathbf{ner}_s$ e′ iff for every Σ-term λ(w)v. t with v in V such that s=sk in w=s1...sn, and every choice of elements ej in IA_{sj} for j≠k, the equality

(†) IA(t)(e1,...,ek-1,e,ek+1,...,en)=IA(t)(e1,...,ek-1,e′,ek+1,..en)

holds. One then checks that **ner** is a Σ-congruence and that IA/**ner** is a realization of A.

Lemma 7: Nerode. IA/**ner** is a final realization of A.

Proof: Let Q* be the final realization congruence for NA, and suppose that there is a pair (e,e′) in Q^*_h that does not belong to ner_h for some h in H. This means that there is a Σ-term λ(w)v. t with w=$\underline{h}$ $\underline{v}$, $\underline{h}$=h1...hm, h=hk, v in V, and there are elements $\underline{a}$ in $A^{\underline{v}}$ and ej=[(tj,$\underline{a}$j)] in IA_{hj} for j≠k, such that if e=[(tk,$\underline{a}$k)] and e′=[(t′k,$\underline{a}$′k)] then IA(t)(e1,...,e,...,em,$\underline{a}$)≠IA(t)(e1,...,e′,...,em,$\underline{a}$) and NA(t)(e1,...,e,...,em,$\underline{a}$)=NA(t)(e1,...,e′,...,em,$\underline{a}$). But this is impossible, because NA a quotient algebra of IA with Q^*_v the identity implies that NA(t)(e1,...,e,...,em,$\underline{a}$) = A(t($\underline{t}$,$\underline{x}_v$))($\underline{a}$1,...,$\underline{a}$k,...,$\underline{a}$m,$\underline{a}$) = IA(t)(e1,...,e,...,em,$\underline{a}$), by definition of IA(t), and similarly for NA(t)(e1,...,e′,...,em,$\underline{a}$). ∎

Before generalizing Goguen's universal realization theorem for automata [16], we must generalize the concept of input to an arbitrary theory T and given set H of hidden sorts. For the theory of automata, S = {input,[state],output}, H = {[state]}, and input is an input sort. Similarly, for the theory of module that is a cell containing a set of integers, S = {int,[set],bool}, H = {[set]}, and int is an input sort.

Definition 8: A Σ-term λ($\underline{h}$ $\underline{v}$)s. t is called **external** if s is in V and there is a Σ-term λ($\underline{v}$)s. t′ such that λ($\underline{h}$ $\underline{v}$)s. t=t′ is in E•. If s is a hidden sort, or if such a t′ does not exist, then t is called **nonexternal.** A visible sort v is called an **input sort** if there is a nonexternal term λ($\underline{h}$ $\underline{v}$)s. t with v occurring in $\underline{v}$ such that whenever an equation λ($\underline{h}$ $\underline{v}$)s. t=t′(x1,...,xm,t1,...,tn) is in E• for some Σ-term λ($\underline{h}\underline{v}'$)s. t′ with $\underline{v}'$=v1...vn, then v occurs in $\underline{v}'$. A nonexternal Σ-term λ($\underline{h}$ $\underline{v}$)s. t is called **reduced** if all the sorts in $\underline{v}$ are input sorts; otherwise t is called **nonreduced.**

Proposition 9: For each nonexternal Σ-term λ($\underline{h}$ $\underline{v}$)s. t, there is an equation λ($\underline{h}$ $\underline{v}$)s. t=t′(x1,...,xm,t1,...,tn) in E•with λ($\underline{h}$ $\underline{v}'$)s. t′ reduced, with $\underline{v}'$=v1...vn in V*, and with tj of rank ($\underline{v}$,vj) for 1≤j≤n.

Proof: Each $E^\bullet$-equivalence class [t] of Σ-terms can be assigned an integer **depth**, $d[t]=\min\{dt' \mid t' \text{ in } [t]\}$, where for t a Σ-term we define dt=0 if t=xk for some k, and $d(\sigma(t1,...,tn))=1+\max\{dti \mid 1\leq i\leq n\}$, for σ in Σ and $n\geq 0$. Then, for any Σ-terms λ(s1...sn)s. t and λ(v)sj. tj for $1\leq j\leq n$, we have $d[t(t1,...,tn)]\leq d[t]+\max\{d[tj] \mid 1\leq j\leq n\}$. Let $\lambda(\underline{h}\ \underline{v})$s. t be a nonreduced term. If $\lambda(\underline{h}\ \underline{v})$s. t=t′ is in $E^\bullet$ for some Σ-term $\lambda(\underline{h})$s. t′, then there is nothing to prove. So we may assume $\underline{v}'$ is nonempty for any $\lambda(\underline{h}\ \underline{v})$s. t=t′(x1,...,xm,t1,...,tn) in $E^\bullet$ with t′ of rank $(\underline{h}\ \underline{v}',s)$. Let [t′] be an equivalence class that satisfies an equation of this form for t, and has d[t′] minimal among those classes [t″] satisfying equations of this form for t. Let $\underline{v}'$=v′1...v′n. If $\lambda(\underline{h}\ \underline{v}')$s. t′ is nonreduced, there are by definition Σ-terms $\lambda(\underline{h}\ \underline{v}'')$s. t″ and $\lambda(\underline{v}')$v″j. tj for $1\leq j\leq q$ with $q\geq 1$ and $\underline{v}''$=v″1...v″q such that the equation $\lambda(\underline{h}\ \underline{v}')$s. t=t″(x1,...,xm,t1,...,tq) is in $E^\bullet$ and at least one of the v′k is not among the v″j. Since d[t′] is minimal, each tj has to satisfy $\lambda(\underline{v}')$v″j. tj=xi in $E^\bullet$ for some integer i. This shows that {v″1,...,v″q} is properly contained in {v′1,...,v′n}. After a finite number of such steps, we get a reduced Σ-term $\lambda(\underline{h}\ \underline{v}^k)$s. t^k such that there is a $E^\bullet$-equation $\lambda(\underline{h}\ \underline{v})$s. t=$t^k$(x1,...,xm,t1,...,tk) with $\lambda(\underline{v})vj^k$. tj for $1\leq j\leq k$ and $\underline{v}^k=v1^k...vk^k$ in V*. Moreover, $[t]^k$ is nonexternal; otherwise, t would be external. ∎ From this we get

Proposition 10: In defining the Nerode congruence, it suffices to require the equality (†) for each reduced nonexternal Σ-term λ(w)v. t. ∎

Let $\mathbf{ReachAlg}_T$ be the category with objects reachable T-algebras and with T-homomorphisms surjective on input sorts, and let $\mathbf{InputBeh}_T$ be the category with objects behaviors and with behavior mappings surjective on input sorts. The behavior functor B restricts to a functor B: $\mathbf{ReachAlg}_T \to \mathbf{InputBeh}_T$. Similarly, the initial realization functor I restricts to a functor I: $\mathbf{InputBeh}_T \to \mathbf{ReachAlg}_T$ left adjoint right inverse to the above functor B. We now prove the universal realization theorem, which asserts that N is right adjoint right inverse to B.

Theorem 11: Universal Realization. For each behavior A in $\mathbf{Beh}_T$, reachable T-module M, and behavior map f: B(M) → A surjective on input sorts, there exists a unique T-homomorphism $f^\$$: M → NA such that $B(f^\$)=f$.

Proof: Consider the diagram

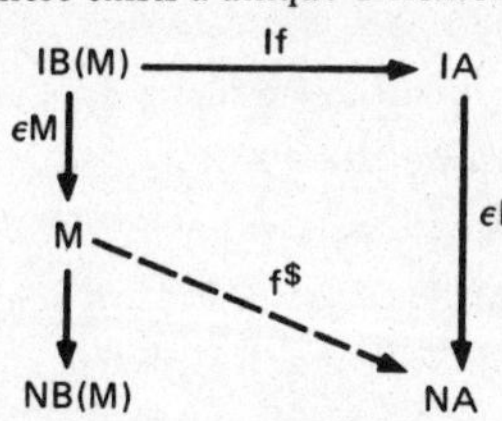

By the universal property of IB(M), such an f must satisfy f∘εM=εNA∘If. As εM is surjective, f is unique. To prove its existence, it is enough to show it for the case M=NBM. By condition (ii) of Theorem 5, $(If)_h[(t,\underline{a})] = IA(t)f^u(\underline{a}) = [(t,f^u\underline{a})]$ for h in H. As NBM and NA are defined by their Nerode congruences, all we have to show is that for each h in H, $[(t,\underline{a})]\ \mathbf{ner}_h\ [(t,\underline{b})]$ implies $[(t,f^u(\underline{a}))]\ \mathbf{ner}_h\ [(t,f^v(\underline{b}))]$. We will use the characterization of **ner** in Proposition 10. Let $\lambda(\underline{h}\ \underline{v})$v. t″ be reduced Σ-term with h = hk in $\underline{h}$=h1...hm, and let $\underline{d}$ in $IA^{\underline{v}}$, ej = [(tj,dj)] in IA_{hj}, for $1\leq j\leq m$, $j\neq k$. By Proposition 9 and the definition of IA, we may assume that the tj are all reduced. As f is surjective on input sorts, we then have $\underline{d}=f^{\underline{v}}(\underline{c})$, $dj=f^{uj}(cj)$, for some $\underline{c}$ in $B(M)^{\underline{v}}$, cj in $B(M)^{uj}$, $1\leq j\leq m$, $j\neq k$. If $[(t,\underline{a})]\ \mathbf{ner}_h\ [(t',\underline{b})]$, we have

$IA(t'')(e1,...,[(t,f^u(\underline{a})],...,em,\underline{d}) = IA(t'')\circ Ff^{\underline{h}\ \underline{v}}([(t1,c1)],...,[(t,\underline{a})],...,[(tm,cm)],\underline{c})$ (because If is a T-homomorphism)

$= Ff_h\circ FB(M)(t'')([(t1,c1)],...,[(t,\underline{a})],...,[(tm,cm)],\underline{c}) = Ff_h\circ FB(M)(t'')([(t1,c1)],...,[(t,\underline{b})],...,[(tm,cm)],\underline{c})$

$= IA(t'')(e1,...,[(t',f^v(\underline{b}),...,em,\underline{d})$, showing that $[(t,f^u(\underline{a}))]\ \mathbf{ner}_h\ [(t',f^v(\underline{b}))]$, as desired. ∎

Similar results have also been obtained by Ganzinger [10] for unconditional equations; actually, our universal realization result is also somewhat more general because of our use of input sorts, which permit an exact generalization of [16]. The results of this section motivate the following

Definition 12: A **module specification MS** is a specification **M** together with an **M**-behavior A; in the equational case, this gives a tuple (S,H,Σ,E,A), and in the conditional case (S,H,Σ,E,C,A), both with A in $\mathbf{Beh}_M$. Let $\mathbf{Mod}_{MS}$ denote the subcategory of $\mathbf{Alg}_T$ with objects all **M**-modules M such that B(M)=A, and with morphisms T-homomorphisms f such that $B(f)=id_A$, where T is the presentation of **M**. We now define an **abstract M-module** to be a category of the form $\mathbf{Mod}_{MS}$; its objects are all M-modules with the same behavior A. (A refinement uses instead all modules with behavior **isomorphic** to A; this captures the concept of "abstractness" more fully.) ∎

In practice, one will often define A as the initial algebra of some presentation; then one may take the final **M**-module realizing A, or any other representative of the same abstract module. ADTs are just modules with all sorts visible; this is the special case where initial algebra semantics is appropriate, and since behaviors have no hidden sorts, it is natural that initial semantics should be used for them. Notice that in practical applications, one is often not interested in the final realization of a given machine. For example, the familiar pointer-array realization of **Stack** is not final (it is not even reachable); inter-module communication schemes and fault-tolerance may also introduce state redundancy. Thus, there is little motivation to develop a "final algebra semantics" parallel to the initial algebra semantics of **[14]**.

3.2 The Conditional Case

Let **M** = (S,H,Σ,E,C) be a conditional specification with V = S-H nonempty, and let T = (S,Σ,E,C) be its presentation. We shall say T (or **M**) has **visible conditions** iff whenever λ(w)s. t1 = t′1 &...& tn = t′n ⇒ t = t′ is in C, the terms t1,t′1,...,tn,t′n all have visible sorts. Let EqM = (S,H,Σ,$E^\bullet$) where $E^\bullet$ is the equational part of the quasi-closure of T.

Theorem 13: <u>Initial</u> <u>Realization</u>. For each M-behavior A there is a realization of A, $I^{©}A$ in $\mathbf{Alg}_T$ such that for each M-module M and behavior map f: A→B(M), there is a unique T-homomorphism $f^\dagger$: $I^{©}A \to M$ with $B(f^\dagger)=f$.

Proof: By remarks in Section 2, the left adjoint I (resp. $I^{©}$) to the behavior functor B: $\mathbf{Alg}_{EqT} \to \mathbf{Beh}_{EqM}$ (resp. B: $\mathbf{Alg}_T \to \mathbf{Beh}_M$ sends A to the initial algebra of the equational (resp. conditional) theory obtained by enriching $\Sigma_{w,s}$ in EqT (resp. in T) with constants from A_s and enriching $E_{w,s}$ with equations $\varepsilon''(t)=\varepsilon'(t)$ for each t in $T_\Sigma R(A)$ where ε': $T_\Sigma R(A) \to A$ is the unique Σ^R-homomorphism induced by the identity on A, and ε'': $T_{\mathbf{Der}\Sigma}(A) \to T_\Sigma A$ is the unique **Der**Σ-homomorphism induced by the identity on $T_\Sigma A$ with the natural structure of a **Der**Σ-algebra (recall $\mathbf{Der}\Sigma = \{T_\Sigma X(w)_s\}_{w\in S^*, s\in S}$ and note that $\Sigma^R \subseteq \mathbf{Der}\Sigma$, so $T_\Sigma R(A) \subseteq T_{\mathbf{Der}\Sigma}(A)$). Thus, there is a natural surjective T-homomorphism r: IA → $I^{©}A$ mapping equivalence classes to equivalence classes. Theorem 5 shows that B(IA) = A. We have only to show that $B(I^{©}A)=A$, i.e., that $I^{©}A$ realizes A. For this, it suffices to prove that the final realization NA of IA is an M-module, because then we will have a unique T-surjection

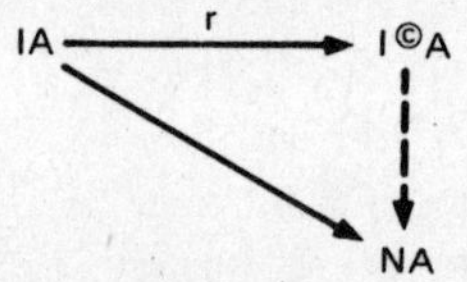

such that the diagram commutes. Let $\lambda(\underline{h}\ \underline{v})s.\ t1=t' \&...\& tn=t'n \Rightarrow t=t'$ in C, let $\underline{h}$ = h1...hn, let $\underline{v}$ = v1...vk, let $\underline{a}$ in $A^{\underline{v}}$, and $[(t''j,\underline{a}j)]$ in NA_{hj} for $1 \leq j \leq n$, be such that for $1 \leq i \leq n$,

(i) $NA(ti)([(t''1,\underline{a}1)],...,[(t''m,\underline{a}m)],\underline{a}) = NA(t'i)([(t''1,\underline{a}1)],...,[(t''m,\underline{a}m)],\underline{a})$, but

(ii) $NA(t)([(t''1,\underline{a}1)],...,[(t''m,\underline{a}m)],\underline{a}) \neq NA(t')([(t''1,\underline{a}1)],...,[(t''m,\underline{a}m)],\underline{a})$.

By definition of NA, (i) becomes for each $1 \leq i \leq n$

(iii) $A(ti(\underline{t}'',\underline{x}_v))(\underline{a},...,\underline{a}m,\underline{a}) = A(t'i(\underline{t}'',\underline{x}_v))(\underline{a}1,...,\underline{a}m,\underline{a})$.

For the sort v of the terms t,t′ to be visible gives a contradiction, because (ii) evaluates as in (iii) to an inequality that contradicts the conditional equation

(iv) $\lambda(u1...um\ \underline{v})v.\ t1(\underline{t}'',\underline{x}_v)=t'1(\underline{t}'',\underline{x}_v) \&...\& tn(\underline{t}'',\underline{x}_v)=t'n(\underline{t}'',\underline{x}_v) \Rightarrow t(\underline{t}'',\underline{x}_v)=t'(\underline{t}'',\underline{x}_v)$,

which is in $T|_V$ by rule (4b) of Definition 1, and thus is satisfied by A. If the sort h of t,t′ is hidden, then by Lemma 7, (ii) means that there is a Σ-term $\lambda(\underline{h}'\ \underline{v}')v.\ t0$ for $\underline{h}'$ = j1...jq in H*,$\underline{v}'$ in V* and v in V such that h = jp and there are elements $ek=[(\lambda(\underline{v}'k)jk.\ t'''k,\underline{a}'k)]$ in NA_{jk} for $1 \leq k \leq q$ with k≠q, and $\underline{a}'$ in $A^{\underline{v}'}$ such that

(v) $NA(t0)(e1,...,[t(\underline{t}'',\underline{x}_v),\underline{a}1...\underline{a}m\underline{a}],...,eq,\underline{a}') \neq NA(t'0)(e1,...,[t(\underline{t}'',\underline{x}_v),\underline{a}1...\underline{a}m\ \underline{a}],...,eq,\underline{a}')$.

Evaluating (v) as in (iii), we obtain an inequality that contradicts the conditional equation

(vi) $\lambda(u1...um\ \underline{v})v.\ t1(\underline{t}'',\underline{x}_{\underline{v}})=t'1(\underline{t}'',\underline{x}_{\underline{v}})\ \&...\&\ tn(\underline{t}'',\underline{x}_{\underline{v}})=t'n(\underline{t}'',\underline{x}_{\underline{v}}) \Rightarrow t'0(xr\leftarrow t(\underline{t}'',\underline{x}_{\underline{v}}))=t'0(xr\leftarrow t(\underline{t}'',\underline{x}_{\underline{v}}))$

in $T|_V$ where $r=n_1+...+n_{p-1}+1$ with $n_k=\#(\underline{v}'k)$, and $t'0=t0(t'''1(x1,...,xn_1),xr,...,t'''q(xn_1+...+n_{q-1}+2, ...,xn_1+...+n_{q+1}),\underline{x}_{\underline{v}'})$. This shows that NA is an M-module. ▮

As in Section 3, we shall call an **M**-module M **reachable** iff the natural homomorphism $\varepsilon^{©}: I^{©}B(M) \rightarrow M$ is surjective. As a corollary of the above proof we get

Theorem 14: Universal Realization. Let **M** be a conditional specification with visible conditions. For each **M**-behavior A, the final Eq**M**-realization NA of A is an **M**-module, and for each reachable **M**-module M and behavior map surjective on input sorts f: $B(M) \rightarrow A$, there is a unique **M**-homomorphism $f^{\ddagger}: M \rightarrow NA$ such that $B(f^{\ddagger})=f$. ▮

Example: We give a conditional specification **M** and an **M**-behavior A whose final Eq**M**-realization NA is **not** an **M**-realization of A; this shows why conditional specifications should have visible conditions. We first give a specification **Aut** for automata: $S=\{\underline{input},\underline{[state]},\underline{output}\}$ with $\underline{[state]}$ hidden; $\Sigma=\{\underline{nil},*,s0,\underline{next},\underline{out}\}$; and E makes $(\underline{input},\underline{nil},*)$ the theory of monoids and $\underline{next}$ in $\Sigma_{\underline{input}\ \underline{[state]},\ \underline{[state]}}$ a monoid action, with no equations for $\underline{out}$ in $\Sigma_{\underline{[state]},\ \underline{output}}$ or s0 in $\Sigma_{\lambda \underline{[state]}}$. **M**′ is obtained by enriching **Aut** with operations $\{\star,e\}$ and with equations making $(\underline{[state]},\star,e)$ the theory of monoids, plus the extra equation $e=s0$. **M** is obtained by enriching **M**′ with the conditional equation $\lambda(\underline{[state]}\underline{[state]})\underline{[state]}.\ x\star x=y\star y \Rightarrow x=y$. One can now check that Eq**M**=**M**′ and that $\mathbf{M}|_{\{\underline{input},\underline{output}\}} = \mathbf{M}'|_{\{\underline{input},\underline{output}\}}$. Let M be the following "flip-flop" module: its monoid of inputs is (Z,0,+), the additive monoid of integers; its monoid of states is $(Z_2,0,1)$, where Z_2 is the additive monoid of integers modulo 2; its transition function is $\underline{next}(n,[m])=[n+m]$, where [n] denotes the residue of n modulo 2; its output set is {0,1}, and $\underline{out}$ is the identity map. Then M is the final **M**′-realization of its behavior A=B(M), but M is **not** an **M**-module, because $0+0=1+1$ in Z_2 yet $0\neq 1$. ▮

4 Persistent Interconnection and Implementation

We consider only the equational case but conjecture that the main results generalize in an appropriate form to the conditional case. We will need the notion of a theory morphism. A **theory morphism presentation** from one equational theory $T=(S,\Sigma,E^{\bullet})$ to another $T'=(S',\Sigma',E'^{\bullet})$ is a pair G=(g,G) with g: $S\rightarrow S'$ a function and G a $S^*\times S$-indexed family of functions $G_{w,s}: \Sigma_{w,s} \rightarrow \mathbf{Der}\Sigma'_{g^*(w),g(s)}$ (where g* is the extension of g to strings) such that if $\lambda(w)s.\ t=t'$ is in E, then the equation $\lambda(g^*(w))g(s).\ G^*(t)=G^*(t')$ is in $E'^{\bullet}$ (where G* is the extension of G to terms, e.g., $G^*(\sigma(t1,...,tn))=G(\sigma)(G^*(t1),....G^*(tn)))$. Two theory morphism presentations (G1,g1),(G2,g2): $T\rightarrow T'$ are **equivalent** iff $G1(\sigma)=G2(\sigma)$ is in $E'^{\bullet}$ for each σ in Σ. A **theory morphism** from T to T′ is an equivalence class of theory morphism presentations. By convention, we denote theory morphisms by their presentations (G,g). A theory morphism G=(g,G): $T\rightarrow T'$ is **injective** iff g is injective and $\lambda(g^*(w))g(s).\ G^*(t)=G^*(t')$ is in $E'^{\bullet}$ iff $\lambda(w)s.\ t=t'$ is in $E^{\bullet}$. G is an **isomorphism** iff it is injective, g is bijective, and for any Σ'-term t′ there is a Σ-term t such that $t'=G^*(t)$ is in $E'^{\bullet}$. The **composition** of theory morphisms (g,G): $T\rightarrow T'$ and (g′,G′): $T'\rightarrow T''$ is the theory morphism $(g'\circ g, G'\circ^* G)$. This gives a category with objects theories and morphisms theory morphisms. Let j denote the inclusion of V into S, and let J denote the inclusion of Σ^R into **Der**Σ; then J=(j,J): $T|_V \rightarrow T$ is an injective theory morphism, called the **canonical inclusion** of $T|_V$ into T. Then one can check that any theory morphism G=(g,G): $T\rightarrow T'$ factors through the canonical inclusion for $T'|_{g(S)}$ as $T \overset{G}{\rightarrow} T'|_{g(S)} \overset{J}{\rightarrow} T'$.

Definition 15: A theory morphism G: $T \rightarrow T'$ is **persistent** iff the above G: $T\rightarrow T'|_{g(S)}$ is an isomorphism. ▮

Intuitively, this means that T1 is (up to isomorphism) a restriction of T2 to a subset of its sorts. Persistence can also be characterized model-theoretically. Given a theory morphism G: $T\rightarrow T'$, then a T-algebra U_GM can be associated to any T′-algebra M by translating the operations of M through G: the carrier is $U_GM_s=M_{g(s)}$ and the operations are given by $U_G M(\sigma) = M(G(\sigma))$ This gives a "forgetful" functor U_G: $Alg_{T'} \rightarrow Alg_T$; U_G always has a left adjoint, denoted T_G. When G is the canonical inclusion of a restriction to visible sorts, then U_G is the behavior functor, and we know (by the construction of Theorem 5) that T_G is the initial realization functor I and that the unit maps ηA: $A \rightarrow U_G T_G A$ are identities. It is also known [24, 1] that U_G is an isomorphism iff G is. Hence if G is persistent, then ηA is an isomorphism. Conversely if ηA is an isomorphism, then for each w there are isomorphisms $T_T X(w) \simeq U_G T_G T_T X(w)$ induced on equivalence classes by G*. This shows that G is persistent, and therefore we have

Theorem 16: [10] A theory morphism G is persistent iff the unit of the adjunction $T_G \dashv U_G$ is an isomorphism. ∎

It is now well-known that theories can be put together along shared parts using the pushout construction [2]. If G1: T → T1 and G2: T → T2 are theory morphisms, then T3 together with G1′ and G2′ is their **pushout** iff the inner square below commutes, and for any other such commutative square, such as the outer one below, there is a unique theory morphism G: T3 → T4 such that the diagram commutes.

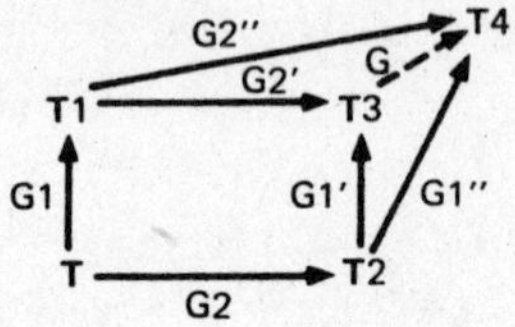

G1′, also denoted $G1 \star_{G2} T2$, is called the **pushout of G1 along G2**, and T3 may be denoted $T1 \star_{G2} T2$ or $T1 \star_{G1} T2$. A result similar to the following (but more complicated to state) has also been proved by Ganzinger [10].

Theorem 17: Persistence is stable under pushouts. In the pushout diagram above, if G1 is persistent, then so is G1′.

Sketch of proof: We may assume that $T = T1|_S$ for S the set of sorts of T and we may replace the original signature Σ1 of T1 by DerΣ1. The new equations are as in Definition 4, but now for all the sorts of T1. In this way, we may reduce to the case where the presentations (Σ,E),(Σ1,E1) of T,T1 satisfy $\Sigma \subseteq \Sigma1$ and $E \subseteq E1$. The morphism G2 is arbitrary, but one can show that there is a presentation (Σ2,E2) of T2 such that (as sets) $\Sigma \subseteq \Sigma2$, and $E \subseteq E2$. The pushout T3 has then a presentation (Σ3,E3) with $\Sigma3 = \Sigma1 \cup \Sigma2$ and $E3 = E1 \cup E2$. By the definition of persistence above, we have to prove that if t2,t′2,t3 are Σ3-terms of rank (w,s2) with w in S2* and s2 in S2 (the sort set of T2) and if t2,t′2 are Σ2-terms, then: (i) there is a Σ2-term t such that λ(w)s2. t3 = t is in E3•; and (ii) if λ(w)s2. t2 = t′2 is in E3• then it is also in E2•. To prove (i), one shows that for any occurrence in t3 of an operator σ1 not in Σ2 there is a maximal occurrence in t3 of a Σ1-term t1 that "covers" σ1 and such that ε(t1) is a Σ-term (as in Definition 4 we have an equation t1 = ε(t1) in E1). One then gets, by applying such equations to all maximal occurrences of Σ1-terms covering operators not in Σ2 occurring in t3, a Σ2-term fl(t3), called the **folding** of t3, that satisfies (i). To prove (ii), one reasons on a given sequence of elementary E3-steps of replacing equals by equals, with t2 the first element of the sequence and t′2 the last. Using rules (2) and (3) of Definition 1 (or equivalently, the abstraction and concretion rules of [13]) one reduces to the case where all the intermedite terms of the chain are of the form λ(w)s2. tk; by (i) we then get foldings fl(tk). Obviously fl(t2) = t2 and fl(t′2) = t′2. By a case analysis of whether each intermediate step was induced by an equation in E1 or in E2, one then shows that there are sequences of elementary E2-steps joining each fl(tk) with fl(tk+1), and this shows (ii). ∎

For future reference we state the following easy fact:

Lemma 18: The composition of two persistent morphisms is persistent. ∎

4.1 Parameterized Modules and Interconnections

We now apply the above to interconnecting specifications, and in particular to the instantiation of parameterized specifications. This is a topic that has received much attention in the literature, but is, we believe, simpler than has generally been realized. First, for M1 and M2 specification theories, we define a **specification morphism** G: **M**→**M′** to be a morphism of the underlying theories such that the sort function preserves hidden sorts; we will also say that G is a **view** of **M′** as **M**. Next, we define a **parameterized specification** to be a pair (**B**,**P**) of specifications together with a inclusion specification morphism **P**→**B**; we call **P** the **parameter specification** (a "meta-sort" in [2] or a "requirement" in [12]), **B** the **body** of the specification, and **P**→**B** the **parameter inclusion** morphism; we may also write **B[P]** for (**B**,**P**). Call **B[P]** persistent iff its parameter inclusion morphism is. Given a parameterized specification (**B**,**P**) and a view G of a specification **B′** as **P**, we define the **application** (or **instantiation**) of **B[P]** to **B′** **along** G to be the pushout $\mathbf{B}\star_G\mathbf{B}'$, also written $\mathbf{B}_G[\mathbf{B}']$ or even **B[B′]** for short. Let us call the application **persistent** iff the morphism **B′** → **B[B′]** is persistent (called "correct parameter passing" in [7]). Theorem 17 shows that a sufficient condition for an application to be persistent is that the parameterized specification is persistent. However, not all interesting parameterized specifications actually have persistent inclusions: consider (**Gp**,**Mon**) with J: **Mon**→**Gp** the inclusion of the theory of monoids into the theory of groups. Although J is injective, the unit map ηM: $M \to U_J T_J M$ is not necessarily injective. For example, if $M = \{e,a\}$ with $a^2 = a$, then $T_J M = \{e\}$.

We can also apply one parameterized specification to another: given (**B**,**P**),(**B′**,**P′**), and a view G of **B′** as **P**, we form $\mathbf{B}_G[\mathbf{B}']$ as before, and define the parameterized specification resulting from the application to be ($\mathbf{B}_G[\mathbf{B}']$,**P′**), using the composition **P′**→**B′**→**B[B′]**. We can now define the composition of instantiations, as shown in

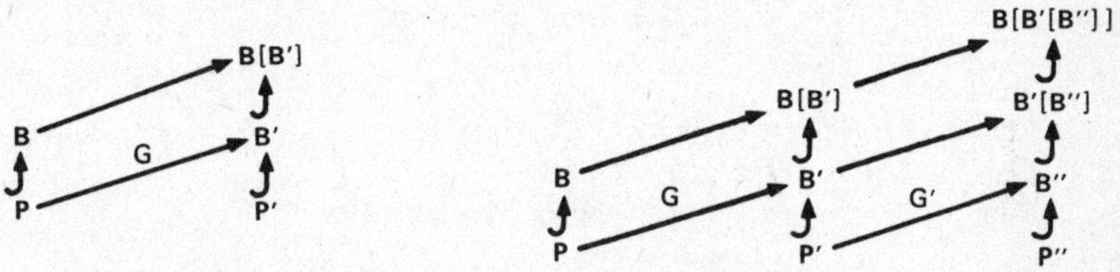

This composition is associative by straightforward diagram chasing, and is persistent if both parameterized specifications are, by Theorem 17 and Lemma 18. An **extension** (or **enrichment**) of a parameterized specification (**B**,**P**) is a theory inclusion **B**→**B′**; or (equivalently) is another parameterized specification (**B′**,**P**) together with **B**→**B′** that commutes with the parameter inclusions. (**B′**,**P**) is persistent if **B**→**B′** and (**B**,**P**) are. For example, we might enrich a basic list processing module (parameterized by atoms) with operations caar(L)=car(car(L)) and cadr(L)=car(cdr(L)).

It can be shown (for example using the "comma category" construction) that the category with specification theories as objects and with specification morphisms has colimits. This can be used to show that the constructions of Clear [2] are "consistent" in the sense that if all theory extensions (including parameter inclusions and theory enrichments) are persistent, then so is the resulting theory denoted by some Clear text.

We can use a parameterized specification (**B**,**P**) to define a **parameterized module specification**, provided that all the parameter sorts are visible, as follows: First note that there is a functor I: $\mathbf{Alg}_\mathbf{P} \to \mathbf{Beh}_\mathbf{B}$ left adjoint to the forgetful functor induced by the inclusion of **P** in **B**; given a **P**-algebra A, IA is its associated initial $\mathbf{Beh}_\mathbf{B}$-algebra, which we think of as an ADT of behaviors. We can then form the abstract module of the module specification formed from **B** by adding the behavior IA. This approach seems very natural for the familiar examples: Consider the parameterized specification **List[Triv]**, where **Triv** is the theory with one sort <u>elt</u> and no equations, and **List** contains the usual equations for [<u>list</u>]s of <u>elt</u>s, with [<u>list</u>] hidden. Then a **Triv**-algebra A is just a set, and the functor I takes A to the visible behavior of lists of elements from A. The abstract module that results is just the category of all modules that realize this behavior. Notice that if we include a sort <u>bool</u> among the visible sorts, along with some boolean valued tests in **B**, and also give **B** the usual equations for Boolean algebra, leaving **P**=**Triv**, then IA will have the expected visible behavior for lists of elements from set M, including Boolean tests and the usual model for bool with exactly two distinct constants (true and false). Of course, this may not be the most elegant way to include an environment of basic sorts; later work will investigate the relationship to, and possible uses of, such ideas as based theories and data constraints [3, 22, 8, 28].

4.2 Behavioral Equivalence

The forgetful functor U_G: $\mathbf{Alg}_{T'} \rightarrow \mathbf{Alg}_T$ associated to a theory morphism G: T → T′ can be thought of as a generalized behavior functor. G provides a "view" of T′ from T, which may hide not only sorts, but also certain operations and equations on the sorts visible via G.

Definition 19: Two T′-modules M and M′ are G-**behaviorally equivalent** iff (i) $U_GM = U_GM'$ and (ii) there is a T′-module M″ and surjective T′-homomorphisms f: M→M″ and f′: M′→M″ such that $U_Gf = U_Gf' = id_{U_GM}$. V-**behavioral equivalence** is G-behavioral equivalence for G the canonical inclusion $T'|_V \rightarrow T'$. ∎

Condition (ii) is non-vacuous: a reachable and a nonreachable realization of the same behavior may not be behaviorally equivalent, but two reachable realizations are equivalent iff (i) holds. We leave the reader to check the following

Lemma 20: Let T be an S-sorted theory, and let G=(g,G): T→T′ be a theory morphism. Then T′-algebras M and M′ are G-behaviorally equivalent iff they are g(S)-behaviorally equivalent. ∎

The following is a straightforward generalization of the Final Realization Theorem and Nerode Lemma of Section 3.1.

Theorem 21: Final Algebra Theorem for Behavioral Equivalence.

(i) Behavioral equivalence is an equivalence relation.

(ii) Each equivalence class [M] contains a representative NM such that for any other M′ in the class there is a unique surjective homomorphism f: M′→NM such that $U_Gf = id_{U_GM}$.

(iii) NM can be constructed from any representative M by imposing the following equivalence relation: e **ner** e′ iff for any term λ(w)g(s). t′ in T′ with w=s′1...s′n and e,e′ of sort s′k, and for any elements ej in $M_{s'j}$ with j≠k, one has M(t′)(e1,...,ek-1,e,...,en)=M(t′)(e1,...,ek-1,e′,...,en).

(iv) N defines a functor on the subcategory of $\mathbf{Alg}_{T'}$ with homomorphism surjective on input and hidden sorts. ∎

Theories themselves can be considered as modules, so that the above concepts apply to them. For each theory T and set V of visible sorts there is a behaviorally equivalent theory NT with same behavior theory $T|_V$ which is final among all theories behaviorally equivalent to T. More precisely, the category of S-sorted equational theories with theory morphisms leaving the sorts fixed is a category of S*×S-sorted algebras defined by an equational theory $\mathbf{Th}_S$ [1, 13]. If V⊆S is a set of visible sorts, there is a natural (and persistent!) theory inclusion J: $\mathbf{Th}_V \rightarrow \mathbf{Th}_S$ such that U_J is precisely theory restriction, i.e., $U_JT = T|_V$. Two theories are then (V-)**behaviorally equivalent** iff they are J-behaviorally equivalent for this J. As a consequence, the following construction can be given for the final theory NT of theory T=(Σ,E): add to E an equation λ(u)s. t=t′ for u=r1...rm whenever for any Σ-term λ(w)v. t0 (with w=s1...sn, s=sk, and v in V) and Σ-terms λ(w′)sj. tj (for 1≤j≤n with j≠k) and λ(w′)rp. t′p (for 1≤p≤m) with w′ in V*, the equation t0(t1,...,tk-1,t(t′1,...,t′m),...,tn) = t0(t1,...,tk-1,t′(t′1,...,t′m),...,tn) is in E.

Lemma 22: If the theories T1 and T2 are V-behaviorally equivalent with $T1|_V = T$, for G: T→T′ a theory morphism and T′ V′-sorted, then $T1 \star_G T'$ and $T2 \star_G T'$ are V′-behaviorally equivalent, with $(T1 \star_G T')|_{V'} = T'$.

Proof: Stability of persistence under pushouts implies the pushouts of T1 and T2 along G can be chosen with V′-restriction T′. The surjections to a T3 with same V-restriction are coequalizers, and thus preserved by pushouts. ∎

Lemma 23: Let T = (Σ,E) be an S-sorted theory, let V⊆S, and let A be a V-behavior. Then the final T-realization NA of A is an NT-algebra.

Proof: Let t=t′ of rank (h1...hm $\underline{v}$,s) be one of the equations added to E as above to form NT. Let bi be in IA_{hi} for $1 \leq i \leq m$, $\underline{a}$ in $A^{\underline{v}}$, and t0 a Σ-term of rank (w,v) with s occurring in w and v in V. We then have for any e1,...,en that IA(t0)(e1,...,IA(t)(b1,...,bm,$\underline{a}$),...,en) = IA(t0)(e1,...,IA(t′)(b1,...,bm,$\underline{a}$),...,en), because picking representatives for the bi and the ej and applying the definition of IA the equation becomes A(t′0)($\underline{a}'$)=A(t″0)($\underline{a}'$), with t embedded in t′0 and t″0 the replacement of t by t′ in t′0, which holds since t′0=t″0 is in E by hypothesis. ∎

Given that NT is the final theory associated to T, one might expect that the initial NT-algebra and its minimal realization coincide. However, this is not the case, as the following shows.

Example: Let **Mod** be the theory of modules, with sorts {$\underline{ring}$,$\underline{module}$} and operations and equations making ($\underline{ring}$, +, -, ., 0, 1) the theory **Ring** of commutative rings, ($\underline{module}$, +, -, 0) the theory of abelian groups, and a multiplication by scalars *: $\underline{ring}$ $\underline{module}$→$\underline{module}$ with the usual vector space like axioms. **Ring** is a subtheory of **Mod**, hence we can glue two disjoint copies of **Mod** along the common subtheory **Ring** (i. e., take the pushout of the inclusion **Ring→Mod** along itself) to obtain a theory **T0** with sorts {$\underline{ring}$,$\underline{module1}$,$\underline{module2}$}; **T0**-algebras are pairs of modules over the same ring. Now define T by adding to **T0**: a constant q of sort $\underline{module1}$; an operation σ: $\underline{module1}$→$\underline{module2}$ satisfying the equations σ(n*q)=n*σ(q) for each n in Z the ring of integers, and σ(5*q)=0; let the visible sorts be $\underline{ring}$ and $\underline{module2}$. The initial T-algebra has carriers Z,Z,Z_5 for the sorts $\underline{ring}$, $\underline{module1}$, $\underline{module2}$, where Z_5 is the integers modulo 5. Its final realization has carriers Z,Z_5,Z_5, but is not the initial algebra of NT because the equation σ(x*(5*q))=σ(x*0) does not hold in T. To prove this we exhibit one T-algebra where this equation fails. Let the ring be Z[x], polynomials with integer coefficients; for $\underline{module1}$ take the group Z×Z with q=(0,1) and Z[x]-module structure given by x*(n,m)=(n+m,m); for $\underline{module2}$ take the group Z×Z_5, with x*(n,[m])=(n,[m]); finally, define σ by σ(n,m) = $\underline{if}$ n=0 $\underline{then}$ (0,[m]) $\underline{else}$ (n+m,[0]). In this algebra, σ(x*(5*q))=σ(5,5)=(10,[0])≠(0,[0]). ∎

4.3 Implementations

Let us assume that **Mi**=(Si,Hi,Σi,Ei) are specification theories with Si-Hi=V for some fixed set V of visible sorts; that Ti=(Si,Σi,Ei) is the underlying theory of **Mi**; and that Ki: T=(V,Σ,E)→Ti is a persistent canonical extension, i.e., $Ti|_V$=T. Because the Hi are known, we can write Ti for **Mi** if convenient. Let **M**=(V,∅,Σ,E), let Ki also denote the specification morphism **M→Mi**, and let Bi, Ii, Ni, etc. denote the behavior, initial, final, etc. functors associated with Ki. (Notice that we may assume any persistent extension K: T→T′ is of the form T=$T'|_V$ with K the canonical inclusion, by renaming Σ′ as needed.) A theory morphism G: Ti→Tj is a **theory morphism over** T iff G∘Ki=Kj. $T_{\Sigma i}$ will denote the theory presented by (Si,Σi,∅), and Pi: $T_{\Sigma i}$→Ti the theory morphism leaving the sorts fixed and mapping each σ in Σi to σ(x1,...,xn). Note that if G=(g,G): $T_{\Sigma i}$→Tj is a theory morphism, then the pair (g,G) defines a theory morphism $T_{\Sigma i}$→$T_{\Sigma j}$ also denoted G, and satisfying Pi∘G=G. The following gives the basic notions of implementation and vertical composition; these are somewhat like an Ada package, and a use of one Ada package within another.

Definition 24: For M1 and M2 persistent over T, a theory morphism G: $T_{\Sigma 1}$→T2 is an **implementation of M1 by M2 over** T iff the left hand diagram below commutes.

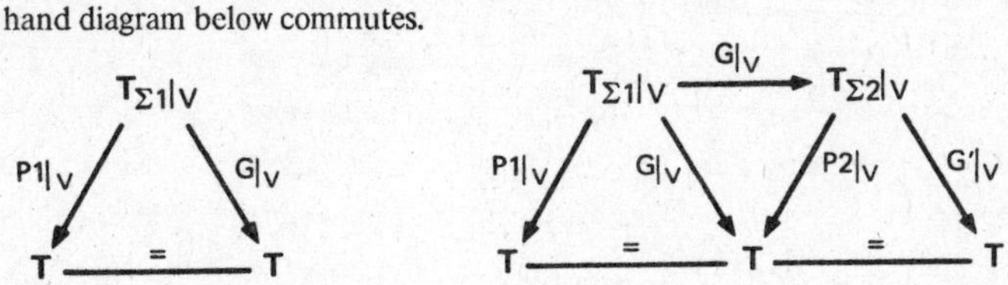

(Note that this is equivalent to requiring that t=G(t) is in $E1^R$ for each Σ1-term λ($\underline{v}$)v. t with $\underline{v}$ in V* and v in V.) If

G: $T_{\Sigma 1} \to T1$ and G′: $T_{\Sigma 2} \to T3$ are implementations over T, then their **vertical composition** G′∘G is the map $T_{\Sigma 1} \xrightarrow{G} T_{\Sigma 2} \xrightarrow{G'} T3$. By the right hand diagram, this is an implementation of **M1** by **M3** over T. Moreover, vertical composition is **associative**: (G″∘G′)∘G = G″∘(G′∘G). ∎

Theorem 25: G: $T_{\Sigma 1} \to T2$ is an implementation of **M1** by **M2** over T iff G factors as $T_{\Sigma 1} \xrightarrow{P1'} T1' \xrightarrow{G^{\#}} T2$ with T1 and T1′=(S1,Σ1,E1′) behaviorally equivalent over T via the maps $P1 \star_{P1'} T1'$, $P'1 \star_{P1} T1$, and $G^{\#}$ over T.

Proof: The "if" part follows from the definition of behavioral equivalence and $G^{\#} = id_T$ because $G^{\#}$ is over T. For the "only if" part, for t,t′ Σ1-terms of rank (w,s) define $E1'_{w,s}$ by t=t′ iff G(t)=G(t′) in E2; and T′=(S1,Σ1,E1′). G clearly factors as $G = G^{\#} \circ P'1$. By definition of E1′ and G an implementation, $G^{\#}|_V = id_T$. Hence $G^{\#}$ is over T, and T′ is a persistent T-extension. We have left to show behavioral equivalence via the pushout of P1 and P1′. As S1*×S1-sorted algebras, T1 and T1′ are quotients of $T_{\Sigma 1}$ by congruences E1 and E1′. The pushout T1″ of P1 and P1′ is then the quotient associated to the congruence E1″ generated by the union of E1 and E1′. By definition of E1′ and G an implementation, for each $\underline{v}$ in V* and v in V, we have $E1_{\underline{v},v} = E1'_{\underline{v},v}$. by Lemma 10.2 in [17] again, $E1''_{\underline{v},v} = E1_{\underline{v},v}$. Hence T1,T1′, and T1″ are V-behaviorally equivalent. ∎

Definition 26: Viewing E1 and E1′ above as congruences, their intersection defines a theory $T1^{\dagger}$=(S1,Σ1,E1∩E1′) that is V-behaviorally equivalent to T1. P1 and P1′ factor through $P1^{\dagger}$ as $P1 = P1^{\#} \circ P1^{\dagger}$, $P1' = P1'^{\#} \circ P1^{\dagger}$; and T1″ in the theorem is also the pushout of $P1^{\#}$ and $P'1^{\#}$. Let $T_{\Sigma 1} \to T2$ be an implementation of **M1** by **M2** over T, and let L: T→T′ be a theory morphism. Let $T1^{\dagger} \star_L T' = (S1^{\$}, \Sigma 1^{\$}, E1^{\$}) = T1^{\$}$. We define the **pushout along** L of the implementation G to be the theory morphism $T_{\Sigma 1}\$ \to T2 \star_L T'$ obtained by composing $P1^{\$}$: $T1_{\Sigma}\$ \to T1^{\$}$ with $(G^{\#} \circ P1'^{\#}) \star_L T'$. ∎

Theorem 27: <u>Pushouts of Implementations are Implementations</u>. The pushout of an implementation G of **M1** by **M2** over T along a theory morphism L: T→T′ is an implementation of $T1 \star_L T'$ by $T2 \star_L T'$ over T′.

Proof: Using the above notation, first note that the pushout along L of the pushout square formed by $T1^{\dagger}$, T1, T1′ and T1″ is a pushout square of behaviorally equivalent theories over T′ by Lemma 22 and the fact that a pushout of a pushout a pushout. Composing that square with $P1^{\$}$ gives another pushout square, since $P1^{\$}$ is epi. This shows that the pushout of the implementation G along L factors as required. ∎

In many applications the above L: T→T′ is the map T→**B[T]** obtained by applying a parameterized specification **B[P]** to T. The pushout of Ti along L is then **B[Ti]**, and if G was an implementation of **M1** by **M2** over T, we have proved that the pushout of the implementation G, denoted **B[G]**, is an implementation of **B[M1]** by **B[M2]** over **B[T]**. By looking at the details of the pushout construction, and chasing the appropiate diagrams one can prove

Theorem 28: <u>Parameterization Commutes with Vertical Composition of Implementations</u>. If G is implementation of M1 by M2 and G′ of M2 by M3, then **B[G′]∘B[G]=B[G′∘G]**. ∎

An implementation G of **M1** by **M2** allows one to implement an **M1**-realization of a behavior A by means of an arbitrary **M2**-realization of the same behavior. This is possible because the pair of maps $T1 \xleftarrow{P1} T_{\Sigma 1} \xrightarrow{G} T2$ provides a "common view" of T1 and T2 relative to T. Before stating the next theorem, characterizing the semantics of implementations, we define the universal representation map associated to a theory morphism G: $T_{\Sigma 1} \to T2$ which is the identity on the sorts V, for T1 and T2 as above; it is similar to a concept introduced by Hoare [20]. We first define the **Σ1-reachable part** of a T2-algebra M, denoted $R_{\Sigma 1}M$, to be the smallest Σ1-subalgebra of $U_G M$ generated by the behavior of M, i.e., by the sets M_v with v in V. The **universal representation map repM**: $R_{\Sigma 1}M \to R1(M)$ is by definition the unit map $\eta R_{\Sigma 1}M$ of the adjunction $T_{P1} \dashv U_{P1}$; hence it is the surjection obtained by imposing the equations E1 on $R_{\Sigma 1}M$. Intuitively, we shall be able to use G and M to "implement" a T1-realization of the behavior A of M if the V-sorted function $\{\mathbf{repM}_v: A_v \to R1(M)_v\}_{v \in V}$ is a T-isomorphism from A to B1(R1(M)). Theorem 29 below shows that this semantic condition is equivalent to the above syntactic definition of implementation. This seems to support the conclusion that our notion of implementation is fully general and natural.

Theorem 29: Semantic Characterization of Implementations. A theory morphism $G: T_{\Sigma 1} \rightarrow T2$ which is the identity on the sorts V is an implementation of T1 by T2 over T iff for each M in Alg_{T2} with behavior A, the V-sorted function $\{\mathbf{repM}_v: A_v \rightarrow R1(M)_v\}_{v \in V}$ is a T-isomorphism from A to B1(R1(M)).

Proof: For "only if," let M be a T2-realization of a behavior A. With the above notation, G factors through $\mathbf{T1}^\dagger$; hence $U_G M$ is a $\mathbf{T1}^\dagger$-algebra, and $B1^\dagger(R_{\Sigma 1}M) = A$. By Lemma 23 and the definition of NA, one can check that $N1^\dagger A = N1A$. Hence $N1^\dagger A$ is a T1-algebra, and there is a unique surjection f: $R1(M) \rightarrow N1^\dagger A$ with $f \circ \mathbf{repM}$ the canonical quotient $R_{\Sigma 1}M \rightarrow N1^\dagger A$. This shows that $\{\mathbf{repM}_v\}$ is a T-isomorphism from A to B1R1(M). For the "if" part, assume that G is not an implementation, and let t of rank ($\underline{v}$,v) be a $\Sigma 1$-term such that t(x1,...,xn) = G(t)(x1,...,xn) is not in $E1^R$. Take $M = T_{T2}X(\underline{v})$. By definition of U_G we have $R_{\Sigma 1}M(t)(x1,...,xn) = G(t)(x1,...,xn)$. Hence B1(R1(M))(t)([x1],...,[xn]) = [G(t)(x1,...,xn)]. If $\{\mathbf{repM}_v\}$ were T-homomorphism it would have to map t and G(t) to [G(t)],and hence would not be injective, because by hypothesis $t \neq G(t)$ in $T_{T2}X(\underline{v})$. ∎

The notions of vertical and horizontal composition were introduced intuitively in [12]: vertical composition of implementations permits one to pass from high level specifications to lower level implementations; horizontal composition permits one to combine two implementations at the same level into a single implementation by "instantiation." By iterating steps of vertical and horizontal composition, one can put together many implementation steps of a software design into a single total implementation. For such a methodology of putting implementations together to be sound, the order in which the steps of vertical an horizontal composition are taken should not effect the final overall result. This is guaranteed by the "double law" theorem below.

Definition 30: Let **M1 = B1[T]** and **M2B2[T]** be persistent T-extensions, and let $G: T_{\Sigma 1} \rightarrow$ **B2** an implementation of **B1[T]** by **B2[T]** over T; similarly, let $G': T_{\Lambda 1} \rightarrow$ **C2** be an implementation of **C1[T']** by **C2[T']** over T'. Let F: T $\rightarrow$ $T_{\Lambda 1}$ be a **"fitting"** morphism (notation as in definition 26). Then the **horizontal composition** of G and G', denoted $G \star_{F\#} G'$, is the implementation of **B1[C1]** by **B2[C2]** associated to the theory morphisms (i) $\mathbf{B1}^\dagger[\mathbf{C1}^\dagger] \xrightarrow{B1^\dagger[Q1^\#]} \mathbf{B1}^\dagger[\mathbf{C1}] \xrightarrow{P1^\#[C1]} \mathbf{B1[C1]}$ (which makes $\mathbf{B1}^\dagger[\mathbf{C1}^\dagger]$ and **B1[C1]** behaviorally equivalent over T'; and where the Q1: $T_{\Lambda 1} \rightarrow$ **C1**, etc. denote the canonical projections,) and (ii) $\mathbf{B1}^\dagger[\mathbf{C1}^\dagger] \xrightarrow{[G^\# \circ P1'^\#][C1^\dagger]} \mathbf{B2}[\mathbf{C1}^\dagger] \xrightarrow{B2[G'^\# \circ Q1'^\#]} \mathbf{B2[C2]}$. One can check that this is an implementation over T' by using Theorem 27, and chasing the diagram below. Also by using associativity of pushouts, one can prove that horizontal composition is **associative**: $(G \star_F G') \star_{F'} G'' = G \star_{F^*} (G' \star_{F'} G'')$, where F* denotes the composition of F with the pushout of F' along the extension $\mathbf{C1}^\dagger[\mathbf{T'}]$. ∎

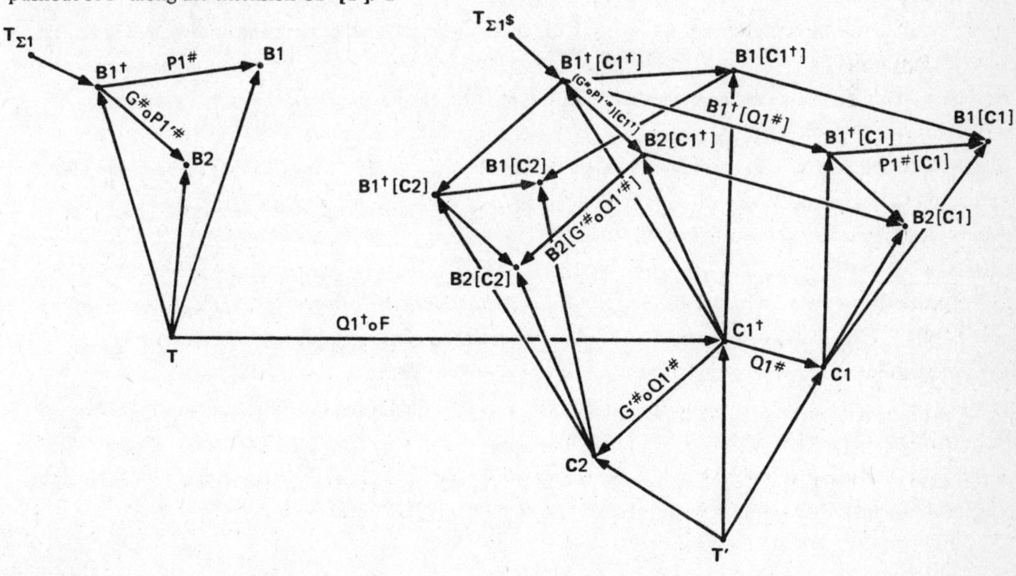

The following can be proved by chasing the appropiate (rather large!) diagram using the results in this section.

Theorem 31: Double Law. Let G and G′ be implementations of **B1** by **B2**, and **B2** by **B3**, over T; similarly, let H and H′ be implementations of **C1** by **C2**, and **C2** by **C3**, over T′. Let F and F′ be fitting morphisms from G to H, G′ to H′ such that $H \circ F = F' \circ G$. Then $(G' \circ G) \star_F (H' \circ H) = (G' \star_{F'} H') \circ (G \star_F H)$. ∎

Remark: To avoid cumbersome notation we have assumed that all persistent extensions are canonical. But in practice, one wants to be able to rename sorts and operations. A variant definition of implementation allowing this and still satisfying all the above results is: if Li: $Ti|_V \simeq T$ is the theory isomorphism associated to the persistent T-extension Ki, then G: $T_{\Sigma 1} \rightarrow T2$ is an **implementation of T1 by T2 over** T iff the following diagram commutes:

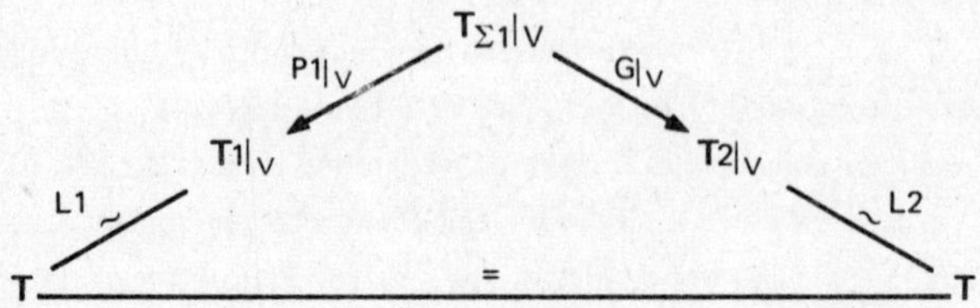

5 Bibliography

1. Benabou, J. "Structures Algebriques dans les Categories." *Cahiers de Topologie et Geometrie Differentiel 10* (1968), 1-126.

2. Burstall, R. M. and Goguen, J. A. "Putting Theories together to Make Specifications." *Proceedings, Fifth International Joint Conference on Artificial Intelligence 5* (1977), 1045-1058.

3. Burstall, R. M., and Goguen, J. A. The Semantics of CLEAR, a Specification Language. In *Proceedings of the 1979 Copenhagen Winter School on Abstract Software Specification*, Springer-Verlag, 1980, pp. 292-332.

4. Burstall, R. M. and Goguen, J. A. An Informal Introduction to Specifications using CLEAR. In *The Correctness Problem in Computer Science*, Boyer, R. and Moore, J, Ed.,Academic Press, 1981, pp. 185-213.

5. Dijkstra, E. W. Notes on Structured Programming. In *Structured Programming*, Hoare, C. A. R., Ed.,Academic Press, 1972.

6. Ehrich, H. On Realization and Implementation. In *Proceedings, 1981 Conference on Mathematical Foundations of Computer Science*, Springer-Verlag, 1981.

7. Ehrig, H., Kreowski, H.-J., Thatcher, J., Wagner, E.G., and Wright, J. Parameter Passing in Algebraic Specification Languages. In *Proceedings, 1980 ICALP*, Springer-Verlag, 1980.

8. Ehrig, H. Algebraic Theory of Parameterized Specifications with Requirements. In *Trees in Algebra and Programming*, Springer-Verlag, 1981.

9. Eilenberg, S. and Wright, J. B. "Automata in General Algebras." *Information and Control 11* (1967), 452-470.

10. Ganzinger, H. Parameteric Specifications, Parameter Passing and Optimizing Implementations. Tech. Rept. TUM-18110, Technical University of Munich, 1981.

11. Giarrantana, V., Gimona, F. and Montanari, U. Observability Concepts in Abstract Data Specifications. In *Proceedings, Conference on Mathematical Foundations of Computer Science*, Springer-Verlag, 1976.

12. Goguen, J. A., and Burstall, R. M. CAT, a System for the Structured Elaboration of Correct Programs from Structured Specifications. SRI, International; Computer Science Lab, 1980.

13. Goguen, J. A. and Meseguer, J. "Completeness of Many-sorted Equational Logic." *SIGPLAN Notices 17*, 1 (1982), 9-17. Extended version to appear as SRI Technical Report.

14. Goguen, J. A., Thatcher, J. W. and Wagner, E. An Initial Algebra Approach to the Specification, Correctness and Implementation of Abstract Data Types. In *Current Trends in Programming Methodology*, R. Yeh, Ed.,Prentice-Hall, 1978.

15. Goguen, J. Mathematical Foundations of Hierarchically Organized Systems. In E. Attinger, Ed., *Global Systems Dynamics*, S. Karger, 1971, pp. 112-128.

16. Goguen, J. A. "Realization is Universal." *Mathematical System Theory 6* (1973), 359-374.

17. Gratzer, G.. *Universal Algebra.* Springer-Verlag, 1979.

18. Guttag, J. V., Horning, J. J. "The Algebraic Specification of Abstract Data Types." *Acta Informatica 10* (1978), 27-52.

19. Guttag, J. V. *The Specification and Application to Programming of Abstract Data Types.* Ph.D. Th., University of Toronto, 1975. Computer Science Department, Report CSRG-59.

20. Hoare, C. A. R. "Proof of Correctness of Data Representation." *Acta Informatica 1* (1972), 271-281.

21. Hornung, G. and Raulefs, P. Initial and Terminal Algebra Semantics of Parameterized Abstract Data Type Specificatons with Inequalities. In *Trees in Algebra and Programming*, Springer-Verlag, 1981.

22. Hupbach, U. L. Abstract Implementation of Abstract Data Types. In *MFCS '80*, Springer-Verlag, 1980, pp. 291-304.

23. Kamin, S. Final Data Type Specifications: A New Data Type Specification Mehtod. In *Proceedings, 7th POPL*, ACM, 1980, pp. 131-138.

24. Lawvere, F. W. "Functorial Semantics of Algebraic Theories." *Proceedings, National Academy of Sciences 50* (1963). Summary of Ph.D. Thesis, Columbia University.

25. Levitt, K., Robinson, L. and Silverberg, B. The HDM Handbook. SRI, International, Computer Science Lab, 1979. Volumes I, II, III.

26. Milner, R. An Algebraic Definition of Simulation between Programs. Tech. Rept. CS-205, Stanford University, Computer Science Department, 1972.

27. Parnas, D. L. "On the Criteria to be Used in Decomposing Systems into Modules." *Communications of the Association for Computing Machinery 15* (1972).

28. Reichel, H. Behavioral Equivalence -- A Unifying Concept for Initial and Final Specifications. In *Proceedings, Third Hungarian Computer Science Conference*, Springer-Verlag, 1981.

29. Spitzen, J., Levitt, K., and Robinson, L. "An Example of Hierarchical Design and Proof." *Communications of the ACM 21*, 12 (1978), 1064-1075.

30. Thatcher, J. W., Wagner, E. G. and Wright, J. B. Data Type Specification: Paramerization and the Power of Specification Techniques. In *Proceedings of 1979 POPL*, ACM, 1979.

31. Wand, M. "Final Algebra Semantics and Data Type Extension." *J. Comp. Sys. Sciences 19* (1979), 27-44.

Heaps on Heaps

Gaston H. Gonnet

J. Ian Munro

Department of Computer Science
University of Waterloo
Waterloo, Ontario, N2L 3G1
Canada

ABSTRACT

As part of a study of the general issue of complexity of comparison based problems, as well as interest in the specific problem, we consider the task of performing the basic priority queue operations on a heap. We show that in the worst case:

(i) log log n comparisons are necessary and sufficient to insert an element into a heap. (This improves the previous upper and lower bounds of log n and $O(1)$.)

(ii) log n + g(n) - $\varepsilon(n)$ comparisons are necessary and sufficient to replace the maximum in a heap. ($\varepsilon(n)$ denotes a function in the range [0,1]. This improves the previous upper and lower bounds of 2 log n and log n.)

(iii) 1.625 n + $O(\log n * g(n))$ comparisons are sufficient to create a heap. 1.37 ... n comparisons are necessary not only in the worst case but also on the average.

1. Introduction

One of the most elegant of storage structures is the representation of a priority queue as a heap. A heap ([Williams], [Knuth]) is defined as a structure on the first n locations of an array with the property that the element in location i is smaller than that in location $\lceil i/2 \rceil$, thus inducing a complete binary tree with the property that the value of the father is greater than that of the son. It is well known that a heap enables us to perform the basic priority queue operations, insert an element and rebalance after extracting the maximum in $O(\log n)$ basic operations. Furthermore, a heap can be created in about 2n comparisons ([Floyd], [Knuth], [Williams]). These results are very old by the standards of our field, dating back to the decade before the last. Our aim, in this paper, is to re-examine the algorithms for performing these basic operations on a heap. We are able to establish new upper and lower bounds on the number of comparisons necessary in the worst case to perform these tasks. While our algorithms may be of some interest in implementing heaps, we are using this structure primarily as a paradigm for the study of computational complexity of comparison based problems.

2. Insertion and Promotion

Observe that the elements on the path from any node to the root must be in sorted order. Our idea is simply to insert the new element by performing a binary search on the path from location $n+1$ to 1. As this path contains $\lceil \log(n+1) \rceil$ old elements the algorithm will require $\lceil \log([1+\log(n+1)\rceil = \lceil \log \log(2n+1) \rceil$ comparisons in the worst case. We note that the number of moves will be the same as those required in a carefully coded standard algorithm.

It was this simple observation which sparked our interest in heap manipulation algorithms. Indeed, it is very useful as a basis for the extraction algorithm presented in the next section. However, the reader may find the fact that this bound is tight more interesting.

Theorem 1:

$\lceil \log \log(2n+1) \rceil$ comparisons are necessary and sufficient to insert an element into a heap.

Essence of Proof:

The upper bound is given above. The lower bound is based on the fact that the new element, when inserted, will lie on an ordered path of length $\log n$ from the root to some leaf. At this point care must be taken as this path may differ substantially from any such path in the original heap, i.e., it may be a path involving reshuffled elements. In particular, several (previously incomparable) elements from the same "level" of the original heap (same distance from the root) may be on this path.

If there are elements on the path from r different levels of the original heap, then we can show $\lceil \log(r+1) \rceil$ comparisons involving the new element are required. The proof is completed by taking into account necessary comparisons between elements from the same original level which are on the path.

3. Extraction and Demotion

Based on the insertion algorithm of the previous section, we can easily extract the minimum and reorder the heap in $\log n + \log\log n$ comparisons. Simply let the "empty location" filter down to the bottom level ($\lceil \log(n+1) \rceil - 1$ comparisons) and then perform an insertion of the element previously in location n (or a new element if one is to be added) along the path from the empty spot to the root. This bound can, however, be improved as follows. For simplicity assume we are removing the maximum and simultaneously inserting a new element.

> Remove the maximum, creating a "hole" at the top of the heap.
>
> Find the path of maximum sons down r levels to some location, say $A(i)$
>
> IF New element > $A(i)$
>
> Then Perform a binary search with the new element along the path of length r
>
> Else Promote each element on the path to the location of its father and recursively apply the method starting at location $A(i)$.

The number of comparisons required is, then,

$$C(n) = r + 1 + \text{Max} \begin{cases} \lceil \log(r+1) \rceil \\ C(\lceil n/2^r \rceil) \end{cases}$$

Choosing $r = \lceil \log n - \log\log n \rceil$, we see that $C(n)$ can be reduced to $\lceil \log n \rceil + g(n)$ where $g(x) = 0$ for $x \leq 1$ and $g(n) = g(\lceil \log n \rceil) + 1$. Indeed the optimal choice of r may differ by 1 from the bound suggested and the bound on $C(n)$ may also be reduced by 1 for certain values of n. However, for this informal presentation we omit these awkward details.

As it happens, this algorithm, with judicious choice of r, minimizes the number of comparisons necessary to perform the update. The key idea of our proof is to use an adversary argument to force an optimal algorithm into the mould of repeatedly finding the path of maximum sons for a number of steps and asking whether the search has proceeded too far. In other words the optimal algorithm must follow the scheme of the one presented and so the bound follows from the optimal choice r. (The adversary argument is presented in the appendix.)

Theorem 2:

There is a function $\varepsilon(n)$ of modulus at most 1 such that $\log n + g(n) + \varepsilon(n)$ comparisons are necessary and sufficient to perform the operation replace maximum on a heap.

4. Creating a Heap

The usual algorithm for creating a heap [Floyd] requires $2n - O(\log n)$ comparisons. It is most easily described by a call to Create(A,1,n) which creates a heap in place on elements in locations 1 to n of the array A .

```
Create(A,i,n)
  Do case 2*i : n
    = if A(i) < A(n)  then Swap (A(i), A(n))
    > do nothing
    < Begin     Create(A,2*i,n)
                Create(A,2*i+1,n) ;
                Perform replace maximum operation as if
                a large element in  A(i)  had been replaced
                by the actual value of  A(i)
      End
```

Using the "standard" replace maximum technique this leads to the recurrence

$$T(n) = 2T(n/2) + 2 \log n$$
$$T(2^k - 1) = 2(2^k - k - 1)$$

and hence the stated bound on the number of element to element comparisons. Clearly the method of the previous section can be employed to reduce this bound. This is an improvement, but disappointing, as about $1.77 \ldots n$ comparisons are required. By way of contrast the following lower bound is easily derived.

Theorem 3:

$1.3644 \ldots n + O(\log n)$ comparisons are necessary, not only in the worst case, but also on the average to create a heap on n elements.

Proof:

A reasonably straight forward enumeration shows that there are $H(n) = \frac{n!}{\Pi t_i}$ valid heaps on a set on n numbers where t_i is the size of the heap rooted at node i . A lower bound on the average number of comparisons required to permit one of $n!$ possible input sequences to one of these orders is

$$\log(n!/H(n)) = \sum \log t_i$$

We are unable to give an algorithm which achieves this bound. Indeed we conjecture that it is not achievable and that the algorithm below minimizes the number of comparisons to create a heap on n elements in the worst case.

Theorem 4:

$\frac{13}{8} n + O(g(n) \log n)$ comparisons are sufficient to construct a heap on n elements.

Corollary:

$\log n + g(n) + \varepsilon(n)$ comparisons are sufficient to remove the maximum element from a heap are reconstitute the heap structure. This bound is within one comparison of optimal.

Outline of Proof:

We will outline a method of constructing a heap on 2^k elements using $\frac{13}{8}2^k - k - 2$ comparisons $(k \geq 3)$. A heap on n nodes can be viewed as a maximum element, a heap on $2^k - 1$ elements $(k = \lceil \log(n-1) - 1 \rceil$ or $\lceil \log(n-1) - 1 \rceil)$ and a heap on the remaining nodes. Using the technique below to form structures of size $2^k - 1$ for appropriate values of $k < \log n$, a set of at most $\log n$ such heaps are grafted in about $1/2 \log n(\log n + g(n))$ comparisons using the technique of the preceding section. The first term in this expression balances the "$-k$" term in the following construction for $n = 2^k$.

As seen in the discussion above, what we require is a method of constructing heaps of size $2^k - 1$. We find it easier to express our method for size 2^k. Since these structures are created and used serially the task is easily completed by "throwing away" the single element on the "bottom level". The basis of the method is the formation of binomial trees of size 2^k (see [Vuillemin]). As illustrated in figure 1 this is simply a tree structure on 2^i elements such that

(i) a single element is binomial tree of order 2^0

(ii) a binomial tree of order 2^i is constructed from two of order 2^{i-1} by making the smaller of the maximum values in these trees a son of the larger.

Our method proceeds as follows as the procedure CONVERT (see also figure 2) converts a binomial tree to a heap.

```
Procedure Convert (T, 2^r)
  Begin Convert (subtree of root of order 2^(r-1) , 2^(r-1)) ;
  This leaves an "extra element" on the bottom level of
  this heap, remove it;
  We now have 1 binomial tree of order 2^r
    (i = 1, ..., r - 2) and 2 singleton nodes
    all hanging from the root.
  Construct a binomial tree of order 2^(r-1) from there;
  Convert (this tree, 2^(r-1))
end
```

The number of comparisons required by this method can be shown to be

$$T(2^k) = 2T(2^{k-1}) + k$$

and yields the solution

$$T(2) = 1 \ ; \quad T(4) = 3 \ ; \quad T(8) = 8 \quad \text{and}$$

$$T(2^k) = \frac{13}{8} 2^k - k - 2 \quad (\text{for } k \geq 3)$$

We are inclined to believe our technique is optimal in the worst case when n is of the form 2^k or $2^k - 1$ and within a lower order term otherwise. By a careful examination of structures on 3 and 4 elements that we can show the method is optimal for 7-heaps.

Theorem 5:

8 comparisons are necessary and sufficient, in the worst case, to form a 7-heap. However, a 7-heap can be constructed using $7\frac{2}{7}$ comparisons on the average based on the binomial tree "building blocks". This yields an improvement in the average behaviour of our algorithm:

Theorem 6:

$T(2^k) \leq 1\frac{15}{28} n = 1.5357 \ldots n$ comparisons are sufficient, on the average, to construct a heap on n nodes.

5. References

[Floyd] R.W. Floyd, Algorithm 245, Treesort 3, CACM 7, 12 (Dec. 1964), 701.

[Knuth] D.E. Knuth, The Art of Computer Programming, Vol. 3 : Sorting and Searching, Addison-Wesley, 1973.

[Vuillemin] J. Vuillemin, A Data Structure for Manipulating Priority Queues, CACM 21, 4 (April 1978), 309-314.

[Williams] J.W.J. Williams, Algorithm 232, Heapsort, CACM 7, 6 (June 1964), 347-348.

APPENDIX

Sketch of Lower Bound Proof for Replacing Maximum Element in a Heap

Suppose that the heap upon which the extraction is to be performed is of the form indicated in figure 3.

(i) The largest j ($\le \log n$) elements are arranged along a path from the root. Call this path of length j the shaft.

(ii) The smallest elements in the structure are the ($n/2^j$ or so) descendants of the bottom element of the shaft.

(iii) The other elements lie between these, satisfying the heap property, and furthermore, tend to be arranged so that the higher their closest shaft ancestor is located, the larger the element.

(iv) The new element is smaller than all shaft elements but larger than all others.

The crucial property is that the last element of the shaft must be determined in order to perform the update. This follows since on removal of the maximum, the shaft element of level i is the ith largest element in the heap and so must be moved to a higher level. On the other hand, the largest of the small elements has the property that it cannot be raised to a higher level as there are not enough smaller elements to support it.

The adversary strategy is based on viewing the information which has been gathered as finding the path of maximum sons to some level (see figure 4). Call this path the chain. The chain partitions the remaining elements into those which are descendants of the last chain element (the inside) and those which are not (the outside). Notice that the chain (what we have learned) and the shaft (what we are to discover) coincide for the length of the shorter. The general approach of the adversary is to respond to queries so that the algorithm learns (almost) nothing about the relation of the inside elements to any but their ancestors. The chain is, of course, permitted to be extended one level per comparison, and the algorithm can always check to see whether the shaft is shorter than the chain.

The outcome of comparisons is given below:

Chain Element - New Element

- Answer according to the worst case as implied by the algorithm

Chain Element - Outside Element

- Answer as Chain element - New element

Inside - Outside

- Outside element is larger, supply the additional information that the chain is is extended by the one element which is not an ancestor of the (previously) inside element considered.

Inside - New

- As inside - outside

Inside - Inside

- This may be a compound step.
- If both inside elements are descendants of the same son of the last chain element, give an arbitrary outcome and extend the chain 1 step to avoid both.
- If both are sons of the last chain member, extend the chain arbitrarily.

Otherwise

- The higher inside element is declared to be larger but the chain is <u>not yet</u> extended -

  All this step to occur 3 times, then observe there are 6 inside elements which have been compared pairwise. Extend the chain 3 steps to one of the 8 subtrees which avoids all 6 elements.

We have omitted a number of details in this outline. In particular a full proof must include a strategy to follow when an inside - outside comparison is performed among a sequence of inside - inside comparisons of elements within 2 levels of the bottom of the chain. These details are tedious but not difficult. Hopefully the sketch presented above will convince the reader that any algorithm for replacing the maximum element of a heap can be forced to take at least as many comparisons as one which simply extends the chain and checks to see whether it is "long enough".

Figure 1 - A Bionomial Tree of Order 16

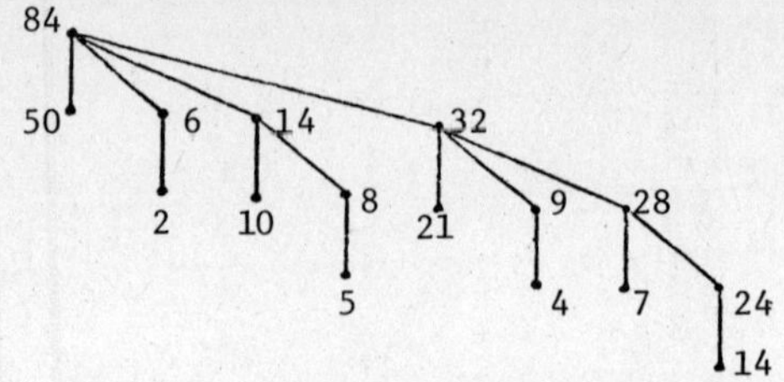

Figure 2 - Illustration of Heap Construction Algorithm

Construct a binomial tree of 2^r nodes and Convert it to a heap
Procedure Convert (T, 2^r)
Begin Convert (subtree of root of order 2^{r-1}, 2^{r-1});
This leaves an "extra element" on the bottom level of this heap, remove it;

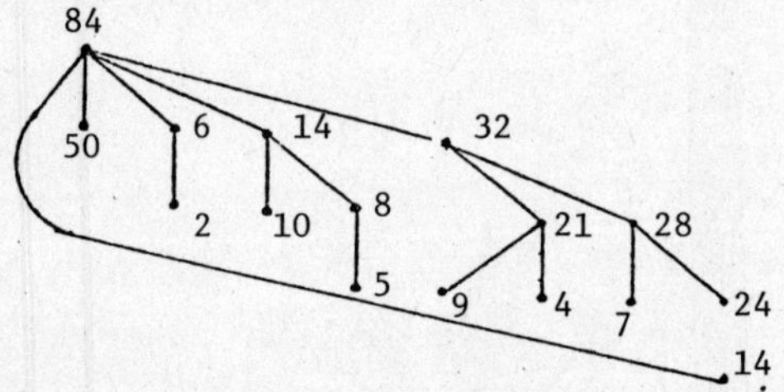

We now have 1 binomial tree of order 2^i ($i = 1, \ldots, r - 2$) and 2 singleton nodes all hanging from the root.

Construct a binomial tree of order 2^{r-1} from these;

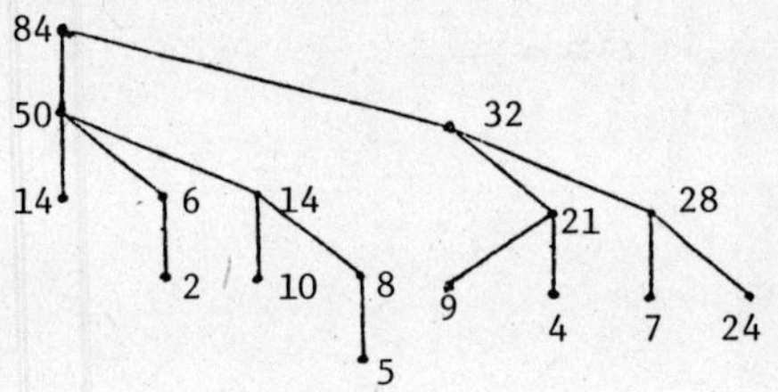

Convert (this tree, 2^{r-1})

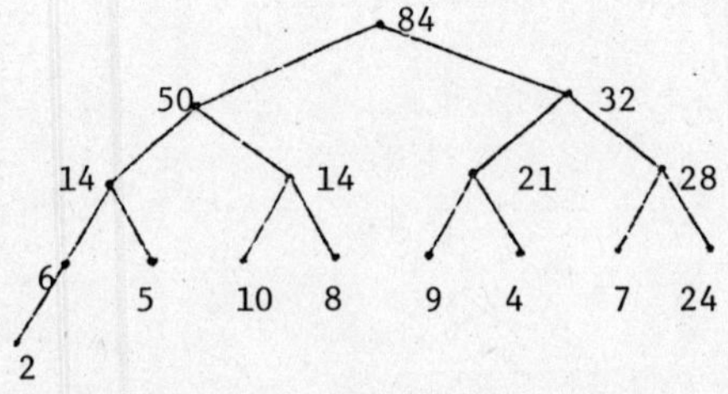

End

Figure 3: A hard case for heap update
"The way it is"

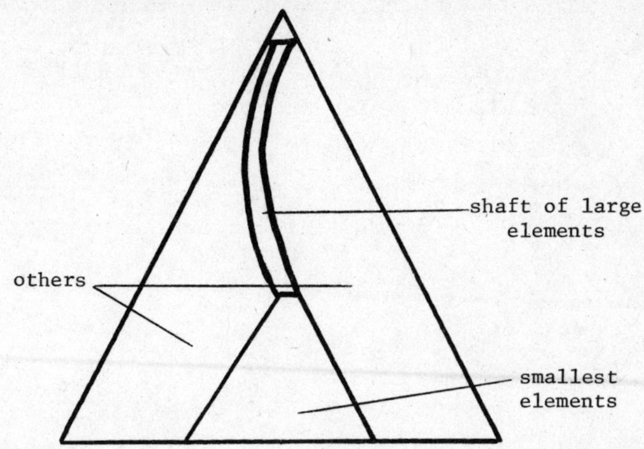

Figure 4: Information yielded by adversary
"What we know"

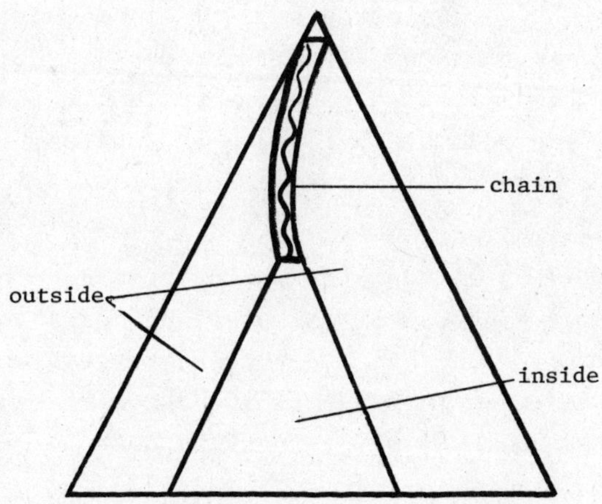

A BOUNDARY OF ISOMORPHISM COMPLETENESS IN THE LATTICE OF SEMIGROUP PSEUDOVARIETIES

A. Goralčíková, P. Goralčík, V. Koubek
Charles University
Faculty of Mathematics and Physics
Malostranské nám. 25, 118 00 Praha 1, ČSSR

0. Introduction

Part of the research concerning the graph isomorphism testing is devoted to polynomial reductions to isomorphism testing of other combinatorial structures. Such reductions have produced a variety of polynomially equivalent problems in the form of isomorphism complete classes [3]. Although equivalent, some are more interesting than others. If an isomorphism complete class $\underset{\sim}{A}$ is properly contained in $\underset{\sim}{B}$ the reduction to $\underset{\sim}{A}$ seems to be better than to $\underset{\sim}{B}$, in capturing the problem. For example, Booth [2] reduced the problem to semigroups, but the much more restricted class of semilattices is also isomorphism complete [3] so the task can be done with much simpler structure.

In algebra naturally arise classes of finite algebras closed under the basic algebraic constructions - finite products, subalgebras and homomorphic images - the so called pseudovarieties. Ordered by inclusion, the pseudovarieties form a complete lattice and one can try to find out how much down in this hierarchy one can go without loosing isomorphism completeness.

Let us call a present boundary of isomorphism completeness in a lattice of pseudovarieties a set of pairwise incomparable isomorphism complete pseudovarieties such that every pseudovariety which does not contain a pseudovariety from this set can be shown to have lower time complexity of the isomorphism testing than the best now known estimates for graphs.

This is clearly a notion depending on the present state of our knowledge, and as such is not a mathematical notion at all. However, properly understood, it may throw some light on the present situation.

In this note we describe a boundary in the lattice of semigroup pseudovarieties. The pseudovarieties which are not above some member of this boundary are closely related to groups and the isomorphism testing for them consumes $n^{\log n + o(1)}$ time. We cannot say with certainty that the members of the boundary are the minimal isomorphism complete pseudovarieties but they are very likely so, since we show that in every pseudovariety properly contained in some boundary pseudovariety the isomorphism testing is polynomial.

1. Semigroup pseudovarieties

In this paper only finite semigroups are considered throughout. For basic notions about semigroups see [5]. As for notation, $|X|$ denotes the number of elements of X, $\langle a,b,\dots \rangle$ denotes the semigroup generated by $a,b,\dots$ For a semigroup S, the set $S^2 = \{xy ; x,y \in S\}$ is not to be confounded with $S \times S$. For a non-void ideal $I \neq \emptyset$ of S, i. e. a subset $I \subseteq S$ such that both $SI \subseteq I$ and $IS \subseteq I$, the Rees quotient S/I is obtained by adjoining zero 0 to S and identifying all elements of I with 0. The intersection of all non-void ideals of S, known as the kernel of S, will be denoted by $K(S)$.

For a class $\underset{\sim}{M}$ of semigroups, $[\underset{\sim}{M}]$ denotes the pseudovariety generated by $\underset{\sim}{M}$; we have $S \in [\underset{\sim}{M}]$ iff S is a homomorphic image of a subsemigroup of a finite product $S_1 \times \dots \times S_k$ for some $S_1,\dots,S_k \in \underset{\sim}{M}$. In case $\underset{\sim}{M}$ consists of a single semigroup, $\underset{\sim}{M} = \{S\}$, we write $[S]$ for $[\underset{\sim}{M}]$.

Semigroup pseudovarieties under inclusion form a complete lattice with the least element $\underset{\sim}{T}$, the trivial pseudovariety containing only the trivial (= one-point) semigroups. A pseudovariety $\underset{\sim}{R}$ is said to cover a pseudovariety $\underset{\sim}{P}$ if for any pseudovariety $\underset{\sim}{Q}$ the inclusions $\underset{\sim}{P} \subseteq \underset{\sim}{Q} \subseteq \underset{\sim}{R}$ imply $\underset{\sim}{Q} = \underset{\sim}{P}$ or $\underset{\sim}{Q} = \underset{\sim}{R}$. Let us list the atomic pseudovarieties of semigroups, i. e. the minimal pseudovarieties containing non-trivial semigroups. They are:

- $\underset{\sim}{S}$ - the semilattices, generated by a two-point semilattice $\langle a,b ; a^2=a , b^2=b , ab=ba=a \rangle$
- $\underset{\sim}{Z}$ - the zero semigroups, generated by $\langle c,d ; c^2=d^2=cd=dc=c \rangle$
- $\underset{\sim}{L}$ - the left-zero semigroups, by $\langle u,v ; u^2=uv=u , v^2=vu=v \rangle$
- $\underset{\sim}{R}$ - the right-zero semigroups, by $\langle x,y ; x^2=yx=x , y^2=xy=y \rangle$
- $\underset{\sim}{G}_p$ - the elementary abelian p-groups, for p prime, generated by a cyclic group of order p.

Important non-atomic pseudovarieties are the <u>groups</u> $\underset{\sim}{G}$ and the <u>simple semigroups</u> $\underset{\sim}{K} = \{S ; \forall s \in S \ (SsS = S)\}$. We have $\underset{\sim}{G} \subseteq \underset{\sim}{K}$ and $K(S) \in \underset{\sim}{K}$ for every semigroup S.

The join $\underset{\sim}{A} \vee \underset{\sim}{B}$ of two pseudovarieties $\underset{\sim}{A}$, $\underset{\sim}{B}$ can be described as the pseudovariety formed by homomorphic images of subsemigroups of products $A \times B$ for $A \in \underset{\sim}{A}$ and $B \in \underset{\sim}{B}$. Every pseudovariety $\underset{\sim}{A}$ is covered by $\underset{\sim}{A} \vee \underset{\sim}{Z}$ - the pseudovariety of <u>inflations</u> of semigroups from $\underset{\sim}{A}$. We have $S \in \underset{\sim}{A} \vee \underset{\sim}{Z}$ iff S has an endomorphism f such that $S^2 \subseteq f(S) \in A$, $f^2 = f$. An inflation S is described up to isomorphism by the image $f(S)$ of S by the inflation endomorphism f together with the inflation <u>valuation</u> $i(s) = |f^{-1}(s)|$ for $s \in f(S)$. If $\underset{\sim}{A}$ is a pseudovariety of <u>bands</u> (= semigroups of idempotents) then the inflation endomorphism is uniquely determined by $f(x) = x^2$. $\underset{\sim}{Z}$ may be considered as inflations of trivial semigroups.

Members of $\underset{\sim}{L} \vee \underset{\sim}{R}$ are called <u>rectangular bands</u>, of $\underset{\sim}{L} \vee \underset{\sim}{G}$ <u>left groups</u>, of $\underset{\sim}{R} \vee \underset{\sim}{G}$ <u>right groups</u>, of $\underset{\sim}{R} \vee \underset{\sim}{L} \vee \underset{\sim}{G}$ <u>rectangular groups</u>; all are contained in $\underset{\sim}{K}$.

Let be given a group G, a left-zero semigroup X, a right-zero semigroup Y, and a mapping $P : Y \times X \longrightarrow G : (y,x) \mapsto p_{y,x}$. Defining multiplication on $G \times X \times Y$ by $(a,x,y)(b,u,v) = (ap_{y,u}b, x, v)$, we get the <u>Rees matrix semigroup</u> $S = \mathcal{M}(G,X,Y,P)$ of type $(|X|, |Y|)$ with the <u>structure group</u> G and the <u>sandwich matrix</u> P. We can factor G out of S by the homomorphism $(a,x,y) \longmapsto (x,y)$ of S onto the rectangular band $X \times Y$. Every simple semigroup K is isomorphic to some Rees matrix semigroup. Two Rees matrix semigroups $\mathcal{M}(G,X,Y,P)$ and $\mathcal{M}(G,X,Y,P')$, differing at most by their sandwich matrices, are isomorphic iff there exist bijections $f : X \longrightarrow X$, $g : Y \longrightarrow Y$, mappings $c : X \longrightarrow G$ and $r : Y \longrightarrow G$, and an automorphism $h : G \longrightarrow G$ such that $p'_{g(y),f(x)} = r(y)h(p_{y,x})c(x)$. We then say that the sandwich matrices P and P' are <u>equivalent.</u>

Let U, V be semigroups given by the following tables

U	a	b	c	0
a	0	c	0	0
b	0	0	0	0
c	0	0	0	0
0	0	0	0	0

V	a	b	c	0
a	0	c	0	0
b	c	0	0	0
c	0	0	0	0
0	0	0	0	0

<u>STATEMENT 1</u>. <u>Let</u> S <u>be a semigroup such that</u> $S^2 \neq K(S)$. <u>Then either</u> $\underset{\sim}{S} \subseteq [S]$ <u>or</u> $U \in [S]$ <u>or</u> $V \in [S]$.

Proof. If $K(S) \neq 0$ we factor it out by passing to $S/K(S)$, so let $K(S) = 0$. Assume first that there exists $c \in S$ with $c^2 \neq 0$. Let e denote the idempotent in $\langle c \rangle$. If $e \neq 0$ then $\{e,0\}$ is a two-point semilattice, thus $\underset{\sim}{S} \subseteq [S]$. If $e=0$ then $\langle c \rangle$ has a quotient $P = \{c,c^2,0\}$ obtained by identifying c^k with 0 for all $k \geqslant 3$. Let R be the subsemigroup of $P \times P \times P$ generated by $a=(c^2,c,c)$, $b=(c,c^2,c)$. Then $R = \{a,b,ab,a^2,b^2,0\}$, $J = \{a^2,b^2,0\}$ is an ideal with $R/J = V$.

Assume next that $c^2 = 0$ for all $c \in S$. Since $S^2 \neq 0$ there must exist $a,b \in S$, $a \neq b$, with $ab \neq 0$. We have $ab \notin \{a,b\}$, for if, say, $a=ab$ then $ab = ab^2 = 0$. We obtain U or V as a quotient of $\langle a,b \rangle$ by identifying all elements in $\langle a,b \rangle - \{a,b,ab\}$ with 0 .

Let W be a semigroup given by the following table

W	a	b	c	d
a	b	b	b	c
b	b	b	b	b
c	c	c	c	c
d	d	d	d	d

and let W^{op} be the opposite semigroup to W .

<u>STATEMENT 2.</u> <u>Let</u> S <u>be a semigroup such that</u> $S^2 = K(S) \neq S$. <u>If</u> S <u>is not an inflation of</u> $K(S)$ <u>then either</u> $\underset{\sim}{Z} \vee \underset{\sim}{L} \vee \underset{\sim}{R} \subseteq [S]$ <u>or</u> $W \in [S]$ <u>or</u> $W^{op} \in [S]$.

Proof. Assume $\underset{\sim}{Z} \vee \underset{\sim}{L} \vee \underset{\sim}{R} \nsubseteq [S]$. Then $K(S)$ is either a left group or a right group. Assume that $K(S)$ is a left group. Factoring groups out from $K(S)$ we get a semigroup T , with $K(T)$ a left-zero semigroup, which is not an inflation of $K(T)$, hence there exist $a,u \in T$ such that $au \neq a^2u^2$. Setting $a^2=b$, $au=c$, $u^2=d$, we get W . If $K(S)$ is a right group we obtain W^{op} in a similar way.

For p prime let $K_p = \mathcal{M}(C_p,2,2,\begin{pmatrix} a & 1 \\ 1 & 1 \end{pmatrix})$, where C_p is a cyclic group of order p , $2 = \{0,1\}$, $a \in C_p$, $a \neq 1$.

<u>STATEMENT 3.</u> <u>Let</u> S <u>be a simple semigroup</u>, <u>i. e.</u>, $S = K(S)$. <u>Then either</u> $S \in \underset{\sim}{L} \vee \underset{\sim}{R} \vee \underset{\sim}{G}$ <u>or</u> $K_p \in [S]$ <u>for some prime</u> p .

Proof. If $S \notin \underset{\sim}{L} \vee \underset{\sim}{R} \vee \underset{\sim}{G}$ then S contains some subdirectly irreducible Rees matrix semigroup $\mathcal{M}(G,X,Y,P)$. The latter must contain a subsemigroup isomorphic to $\mathcal{M}(G,2,2,\begin{pmatrix} b & 1 \\ 1 & 1 \end{pmatrix})$, $b \neq 1$, and this in turn a subsemigroup $\mathcal{M}(\langle b \rangle,2,2,\begin{pmatrix} b & 1 \\ 1 & 1 \end{pmatrix})$ which can be factorized onto K_p for a prime p dividing the order of b .

2. Reductions

Let $\underset{\sim}{I}$ be an isomorphism complete class of graphs, $\underset{\sim}{A}$ a pseudovariety of semigroups. A function $(X,R) \mapsto S(X,R)$ assigning to every graph from $\underset{\sim}{I}$ a semigroup from $\underset{\sim}{A}$ in such a way that any two graphs (X,R), $(X',R') \in \underset{\sim}{I}$ are isomorphic iff $S(X,R)$ and $S(X',R')$ are so, is a *reduction to* $\underset{\sim}{A}$ (of the graph isomorphism problem). As soon as a reduction to $\underset{\sim}{A}$ is produced $\underset{\sim}{A}$ is proved to be isomorphism complete.

STATEMENT 4. *Pseudovariety* $[U]$ *is isomorphism complete.*

Proof. For a directed graph (X,R) without loops and without isolated points define a mapping $\varphi : X \to U^R$ by

$$[\varphi(x)](r) = \begin{cases} a & \text{if } r=(x,y) \\ b & \text{if } r=(t,x) \\ 0 & \text{otherwise} \end{cases}$$

where $a,b \in U$. The image $\operatorname{Im}\varphi$ generates a subsemigroup of U^R isomorphic to the semigroup $S(X,R) = (X \cup R \cup 0\ ,\ .\ )$ with $x.y = (x,y)$ if $(x,y) \in R$ and $x.y = 0$ otherwise. Clearly, $(X,R) \to S(X,R)$ is a reduction to $[U]$.

STATEMENT 5. *Pseudovariety* $[V]$ *is isomorphism complete.*

Proof. For an undirected graph (X,E) without loops and without isolated points define a mapping $\psi : X \to V^E$ as follows: for every $e = \{x,y\} \in E$ choose a bijection $\alpha_e : \{x,y\} \to \{a,b\}$ and set

$$[\psi(x)](e) = \begin{cases} \alpha_e(x) & \text{if } x \in e \\ 0 & \text{if } x \notin e \end{cases}$$

Then $\operatorname{Im}\psi$ generates a subsemigroup of V^E isomorphic to the semigroup $S(X,E) = (X \cup E \cup 0\ ,\ .\ )$ with $x.y = \{x,y\}$ if $\{x,y\} \in E$, $x.y = 0$ otherwise. Clearly, $(X,E) \to S(X,E)$ is a reduction to $[V]$.

STATEMENT 6. *The pseudovariety of inflations of rectangular bands is isomorphism complete.*

Proof. For a directed graph (X,R) without loops take the left-zero semigroup $L = (X, \circ)$ and the right-zero semigroup $R = (X, *)$ and inflate $L \times R$ by $i(x,y) = 3$ for $x=y$, 2 for $(x,y) \in R$, 1 for $(x,y) \notin R$, to get $S(X,R)$ for a reduction to $\underset{\sim}{L} \vee \underset{\sim}{R} \vee \underset{\sim}{Z}$.

<u>STATEMENT 7. Pseudovariety W is isomorphism complete.</u>

Proof. Let $\underset{\sim}{B}$ denote the pseudovariety of unary algebras (X,f,g) with two operations, f and g, satisfying the equations $f(f(x)) = g(f(x)) = f(x)$ and $g(g(x)) = f(g(x)) = g(x)$. Using the fact that $\underset{\sim}{B}$ is isomorphism complete [6], we assign to $(X,f,g) \in \underset{\sim}{B}$ a semigroup $S \in [W]$ defined on a disjoint union $X \cup \{s,t,u,v,w\}$ as follows: denoting $Y = f(X) = g(X)$, $Z = X-Y$, we require that $X \cup \{u,w\}$ be left zeros of S, $s^2=st=sv=t^2=ts=tv=u$, $vs=vt=v^2=w$, $sx=x$ for all $x \in X$,

$$tx = \begin{cases} f(x) & \text{for } x \in Z \\ u & \text{for } x \in Y \end{cases}, \quad vx = \begin{cases} g(x) & \text{for } x \in Z \\ w & \text{for } x \in Y \end{cases}$$

This reduces the isomorphism problem for $\underset{\sim}{B}$ to that for $[W]$.

<u>STATEMENT 8. Pseudovariety K_p is isomorphism complete.</u>

Proof. Let (X,R) be a directed graph. For every $(x,y) \in X^2$ define a 2×2-matrix $P(x,y) = (p_{i,j}^{(x,y)})$, by $P(x,y) = \begin{pmatrix} a & 1 \\ 1 & 1 \end{pmatrix}$ if $x=y$ or $(x,y) \in R$, $P(x,y) = \begin{pmatrix} 1 & 1 \\ 1 & 1 \end{pmatrix}$ otherwise, and form the product

$$\prod_{(x,y)\in X^2} \mathcal{M}(C_p,2,2,P(x,y)) = \mathcal{M}(C_p^{X^2},2^{X^2},2^{X^2},P)$$

where P is a matrix with entries $p_{f,g} = \{p_{f(x,y),g(x,y)}^{(x,y)} ; (x,y)\in X^2\}$ for $f,g:X^2 \to 2$. Factorize this product by the homomorphism

$$h: C_p^{X^2} \to C_p: \quad c \longmapsto \prod\{c(x,y);(x,y)\in X^2\} \qquad \text{onto } \mathcal{M}(C_p,2^{X^2},2^{X^2},h(P))$$

and select a subsemigroup $\mathcal{M}(C_p,X,X,P(X,R))$ where $P(X,R)$ is a submatrix of $h(P) = (h(p_{f,g}))$ with entries $p_{u,v}^{(X,R)} = h(p_{f_u,g_v})$, where

$f_u(x,y) = \begin{cases} 0 & \text{for } u=x \\ 1 & \text{for } u\neq x \end{cases}$, $g_v(x,y) = \begin{cases} 0 & \text{for } v=y \\ 1 & \text{for } v\neq y \end{cases}$. Clearly, the semigroup thus obtained is in K_p and we have

$$p_{u,v}^{(X,R)} = \begin{cases} a & \text{if } u=v \text{ or } (u,v) \in R \\ 1 & \text{otherwise} \end{cases}$$

Next we show that the assignment $(X,R) \to \mathcal{M}(C_p,X,X,P(X,R))$ is an isomorphism problem reduction for the isomorphism complete class of bipartite directed graphs (X,R) with X partitioned into two parts, X_1 and X_2, in such a way that $R \subseteq X_1 \times X_2$, and which in addition are d-regular (outdegrees of points in X_1 = indegrees of points in $X_2 = d$) with $5 < d < |X|/3$, and such that to each $x \in X_i$ there exists $y \in X_i$ with at most four neighbours in common, $i=1,2$.

Let be given two such graphs (X,R), (X',R'). If $f:X \to X'$ is an isomorphism of (X,R) onto (X',R') then for $P(X,R) = P = (p_{x,y})$ and $P(X',R') = P' = (p'_{x,y})$ we have $p'_{f(x),f(y)} = p_{x,y}$, hence the sandwich matrices are equivalent.

Assume conversely that $p'_{f(x),g(y)} = r(x)h(p_{x,y})c(y)$ for some bijections $f,g:X \to X'$, functions $r,c:X \to C_p$, and $h \in \mathrm{Aut}(C_p)$.

First, it is easy to identify X_1 and X_2 from P. Indeed, $x \in X_1$ if there is more than one occurrence of a in the i-th row of P; $x \in X_2$ if there is only one. We show that $f(X_2) \subseteq X_2'$. Assume to the contrary that $f(x) \in X_1'$ for some $x \in X_2$. Then the $f(x)$-th row in P' has $d+1$ entries a and $n-d-1$ entries 1. Denote

$$A = \{y \in X-\{x\} \;;\; p'_{f(x),g(y)} = a\}, \quad B = \{y \in X-\{x\} \;;\; p'_{f(x),g(y)} = 1\}$$

The function $c:X \to C_p$ must be constant on both A and B. Further, $|A| \geq d$, $|B| \geq n-d-2$. For an arbitrary $z \in X_2$, $z \neq x$, there must be distinct $b_1,b_2 \in C_p$ such that

$$p'_{f(z),g(y)} = \begin{cases} b_1 & \text{for } y \quad A-\{z\} \\ b_2 & \text{for } y \quad B-\{z\} \end{cases}$$

It follows that $b_1=a$, $b_2=1$, and $f(z) \in X_1'$, thus $f(X_2) = X_1'$. But then for any two rows in P' indexed by two distinct elements of X_1' there are at least five a's in the same places, a contradiction with the properties of (X,R). We have proved so far that $f(X_i) = X_i'$, for $i=1,2$, and that $c(x)$ is constant on X, $c(x) = c$ for all $x \in X$. In a similar way we prove that $g(X_i) = X_i'$, $i=1,2$, and $r(y) = r$ for all $y \in X$.

We conclude the proof by showing that $f=g$. For $x \in X_2$, $y \in X$

$$p'_{f(x),g(y)} = \begin{cases} rc & \text{for } y \neq x \\ rh(a)c & \text{for } y=x \end{cases}$$

whence $f(x) = g(x)$. Similarly for $x \in X_1$. Moreover, $rc=1$, $rh(a)c = = a$, thus $h(a)=a$, $p'_{f(x),f(y)} = p_{x,y}$, hence f is an isomorphism of the graphs.

THEOREM. The pseudovarieties $[U],[V],[W],[W^{op}],[K_p]$ for p prime, and $\underset{\sim}{L} \vee \underset{\sim}{R} \vee \underset{\sim}{Z}$ form a boundary of isomorphism completeness. More explicitly, (1) each of them is isomorphism complete, (2) every pseudovariety properly contained in any one of them has a polynomial time isomorphism test, (3) if a pseudovariety does not contain any member of the list then S is contained in $(\underset{\sim}{Z} \vee \underset{\sim}{L} \vee \underset{\sim}{G}) \cup (\underset{\sim}{Z} \vee \underset{\sim}{R} \vee \underset{\sim}{G}) \cup (\underset{\sim}{L} \vee \underset{\sim}{R} \vee \underset{\sim}{G})$, (4) the pseudovarieties $(\underset{\sim}{Z} \vee \underset{\sim}{L} \vee \underset{\sim}{G})$, $(\underset{\sim}{Z} \vee \underset{\sim}{R} \vee \underset{\sim}{G})$, $(\underset{\sim}{L} \vee \underset{\sim}{R} \vee \underset{\sim}{G})$ admit an $n^{\log n + o(1)}$ time isomorphism test.

Proof. (1) has been established in Section 2, (2) is straightforward, (3) follows from Statements 1,2 and 3, (4) is due to the existence of log n generators for any group of size n ; in case of inflations of left groups a polynomial time extraction of an injection from a correspondence (cf. [4]) must be used.

REFERENCES

[1] L. Babai: Moderately exponential bound for graph isomorphism, FCT 81, Lecture Notes in Comp. Sci. 117, Springer 1981, 34-50.

[2] K. S. Booth: Isomorphism testing for graphs, semigroups and finite automata are polynomially equivalent problems, SIAM J. Comput. 7(1978), 273-279.

[3] K. S. Booth, Ch. J. Colbourn: Problems polynomially equivalent to graph isomorphism, Tech. Rep. CS-77-04, Univ. of Waterloo, 1979.

[4] N. Christofides: Graph theory, an algorithmic approach, Acad. Press, New York, London, San Francisco, 1975.

[5] A. H. Clifford, G. B. Preston: The algebraic theory of semigroups, AMS, Providence, Rhode Island, 1967.

[6] L. Kučera, V. Trnková: Isomorphism completeness for some algebraic structures, FCT 81, Lecture Notes in Comp. Sci. 117, Springer 1981, 218-225.

Derived Pairs, Overlap Closures, and Rewrite Dominoes:
New Tools for Analyzing Term Rewriting Systems

John V. Guttag[1]
MIT Laboratory for Computer Science

Deepak Kapur
David R. Musser
General Electric Research and Development Center

Abstract

Starting from the seminal work of Knuth and Bendix, we develop several notions useful in the study of term rewriting systems. In particular we introduce the notions of "derived pairs" and "overlap closure" and show that they are useful in analyzing sets of rewrite rules for various properties related to termination. We also introduce a new representation, based on rewrite dominoes, for rewrite rules and sequences of rewrites.

1. Introduction

We introduce three new tools for the study of term rewriting systems. Derived pairs of a rewrite rule generalize the well-known idea of "critical pairs" introduced by Knuth and Bendix (1970) in their development of a method of proving the confluence property. The overlap closure of a set of rules is a set of rules that corresponds to a subset of the transitive closure of the rewriting relation. Its construction is based on the use of derived pairs obtained from superpositions of the right hand side of one rule with the left hand side of another. This process is closely related to the Knuth-Bendix process, which uses critical pairs for generating new rules in an attempt to achieve confluence. We use the overlap closure in proving - or disproving - that a rewriting relation is uniformly terminating (more commonly called finitely terminating or noetherian.) It thus provides an interesting dual method to the Knuth-Bendix process, in which the validity of the critical pair test for confluence depends upon uniform termination. The combination of uniform termination and confluence provides a decision procedure for the theory of the equations corresponding to the original rules.

In the study of derived pairs and overlap closures we found it useful to devise a new way of representing rewrite rules and sequences of rewrites using what we call rewrite dominoes and "rewrite domino layouts." We will introduce this representation and use it in presenting the proofs of our main results about the overlap closure. We believe that this representation also will be useful in the study of other areas of rewrite rule theory.

Like the Knuth-Bendix process, the overlap closure process may fail to terminate (that is, it may continue to generate new rules indefinitely). In fact, when the original rules are uniformly terminating, it will usually happen that overlap closure generation is nonterminating. In this case, the overlap closure process does not by itself yield a proof of uniform termination, but it may be useful as an aid in applying other known methods of proving uniform termination [see Huet and Oppen, 1980]. It can also be used in proving what we call "restricted termination," i.e.,

---

[1] Work partially supported by the National Science Foundation under grant MCS78-01798 and by an Office of Naval Research Contract with DARPA funding #N00014-75-C-0661.

termination for all terms up to a given size. Some applications of restricted termination are discussed in Guttag, Kapur and Musser (1981).

Perhaps more important is the case where the original rules are not uniformly terminating. One would often like to be able to detect this situation quickly, e.g., in order to avoid wasting time attempting to construct a proof of uniform termination. We show that under some reasonable restrictions on the form of rewrite rules, the overlap closure construction provides such a test. I.e., we show that if the rules are globally finite (that is to say, the number of different terms to which any term can be rewritten is finite) and every rule is right-linear or every rule is left-linear, the overlap closure construction can be used to effectively search for cycles in the rewriting relation. That it does so "quickly" enough to be useful is a claim for which we have limited empirical evidence, as discussed in the Conclusion section. Although undecidable in general, global finiteness can be shown in many cases by methods discussed in Guttag, Kapur, and Musser (1981).

2. Definition of Overlap Closure

For the most part we use standard definitions and terminology for term rewriting systems from Huet (1980) and Huet and Oppen (1980). There are a few exceptions, such as "uniform termination" for "finite termination," and "terminal form" for "normal form." In Guttag, Kapur, and Musser (1981), the reader will find a thorough discussion of this background material. Here we confine ourselves mainly to the definitions of "derived pairs," a generalization of the Knuth and Bendix's notion of "critical pairs," and of "overlap closure."

Two terms are said to overlap if one is unifiable with a nonvariable subterm of the other. If s and t overlap, we define their superposition: either

a) s unifies with a nonvariable subterm t' of t, by the most general unifier (m.g.u.) Θ, in which case $\Theta(t)$ is called a superposition of s and t; or

b) a nonvariable subterm s' of s unifies with t, by m.g.u. Θ, in which case $\Theta(s)$ is called a superposition of s and t.

The notation [t with u at i] stands for the term obtained from t by replacing the subterm at position i by u. A "subterm position" and "corresponding subterm" within a term is a finite sequence of nonnegative integers separated by "." and a related term determined as follows: to the null sequence (denoted $\langle\rangle$) corresponds the entire term. If $f(t_1,...,t_n)$ is the subterm at position i, the subterm at position i.j is t_j. We write t/i for the subterm at position i within term t.

Now consider ordered pairs of terms (r,s) and (t,u) such that s and t overlap, as above. (If the variables of t must be renamed, the same renaming must be applied to u.) Then along with the superposition $\Theta(t)$ or $\Theta(s)$ we obtain the derived pair of terms, $\langle p,q\rangle$, where

a) if s unifies with a nonvariable subterm t/i by m.g.u. Θ,

$p = [\Theta(t) \text{ with } \Theta(r) \text{ at } i]$
$q = \Theta(u)$;

b) if a nonvariable subterm s/i unifies with t by m.g.u. Θ,

$p = \Theta(r)$
$q = [\Theta(s) \text{ with } \Theta(u) \text{ at } i]$.

In the case of a rewriting system R = $\{(l_i \rightarrow r_i)\}$, the derived pairs obtained from the pairs (r_i, l_i) and (l_j, r_j) are called critical pairs.

Consider, for example, obtaining a critical pair from the rewrite rules:

$$x^{-1} \bullet x \rightarrow e$$
$$(x' \bullet y') \bullet z' \rightarrow x' \bullet (y' \bullet z')$$

We begin by constructing the ordered pairs $(e, x^{-1} \bullet x)$ and $((x' \bullet y') \bullet z', x' \bullet (y' \bullet z'))$. Now $x^{-1} \bullet x$ can be unified with $x' \bullet y'$ using the substitution $\Theta = [x^{-1}/x', x/y']$. This leads to the derived pair $\langle e \bullet z', x^{-1} \bullet (x \bullet z')\rangle$ which is a critical pair of the rules.

Using derived pairs, the overlap closure of R, written **OC(R)**, is defined inductively as follows:

a. Every rule $r \rightarrow s$ in R is also in **OC(R)**.

b. Whenever $r \rightarrow s$ and $t \rightarrow u$ are in **OC(R)**, every derived pair $\langle p,q \rangle$ of (r,s) and (t,u) is in **OC(R)** (as $p \rightarrow q$).

c. No other rules are in **OC(R)**.

Examples of overlap closures:

i. Let R = $\{f(x) \rightarrow g(x)\}$, then **OC(R)** = **R**.

ii. Let R = $\{f(x) \rightarrow g(h(x)), h(x) \rightarrow k(x)\}$, then **OC(R)** = **R** $\cup \{f(x) \rightarrow g(k(x))\}$.

iii. Let R = $\{x \bullet (y \bullet z) \rightarrow (x \bullet y) \bullet z\}$, then from the superposition $(x \bullet (x' \bullet y')) \bullet z'$ we obtain the rule

$$x \bullet ((x' \bullet y') \bullet z') \rightarrow ((x \bullet x') \bullet y') \bullet z'$$

and from the superposition $(x \bullet ((x' \bullet y') \bullet z')$ we obtain

$$x \bullet (x' \bullet (y' \bullet z')) \rightarrow (x \bullet (x' \bullet y')) \bullet z'.$$

These rules then lead to further rules, and **OC(R)** is infinite.

vi. Let R = $\{f(x) \rightarrow g(x), g(h(x)) \rightarrow f(h(x))\}$. Then **OC(R)** consists of **R** and the reflexive rules $f(h(x)) \rightarrow f(h(x))$ and $g(h(x)) \rightarrow g(h(x))$.

The overlap closure **OC(R)** has a rich structure since the overlap closure construction preserves some properties of a rewriting system R. The following lemma shows that every derived pair of two rewrite rules is also a rewrite rule, implying that the overlap closure **OC(R)** is a rewriting system.

Lemma 2.1: If r,s,t,u are terms such that (r,s) and (t,u) are rewrite rules, then every derived pair <p,q> of (r,s) and (t,u) is also a rewrite rule.

Proof: One has to verify that for each case in the definition of derived pair that every variable that occurs in q occurs also in p. □

Let us consider some other properties, based on the properties of its rules, of a rewriting system **R**

A term is said to be linear if no variable occurs in it more than once. A rewrite rule is left-linear if its left term is linear, right-linear if its right term is linear, and linear if its left and right terms are linear.

A rewriting system is called left-linear, right-linear, or linear, based on whether each of its rules is left-linear, right-linear, or linear, respectively. The following lemma implies that the overlap closure **OC(R)** of a right-linear (left-linear, linear) **R** is also right-linear (left-linear, linear).

Lemma 2.2: If r → s and t → u are two right linear rules with disjoint variable sets, then each of their derived pairs, <p, q> is also right linear.

Proof: See C.1 in Guttag, Kapur and Musser (1981).

The name "overlap closure" comes from the fact that the rules of **OC(R)** are a subset of the transitive closure of the rewriting relation of **R**:

Lemma 2.3: If p → q is in **OC(R)** then p $\rightarrow^{+}$ q (using **(R)**.

Proof: By induction on the construction of p → q in **OC(R)**.

Corollary 2.4: If **OC(R)** contains a reflexive rule, t → t, then the rewriting relation of **R** has a cycle.

Proof: Immediate from the above lemma. □

We would like to have the converse of this corollary, that if the rewriting relation of **R** has a cycle, then **OC(R)** contains a reflexive rule. This would permit searching for cycles by incrementally computing **OC(R)**, looking for a reflexive rule. While we have not been able to prove this in full generality, we will present in the next section a restricted version and its proof. The proof is not easy, because the overlap closure of **R** is in general much smaller than the full transitive closure of **R**. It is this small size, relative to the transitive closure, however, that makes it feasible to use the overlap closure as the basis of an approach to proving uniform termination or, at least, a useful notion of "restricted termination," as discussed in [Guttag, Kapur, and Musser, 1981].

3. Rewrite Dominoes and the Main Overlap Closure Theorem

In order to be able to prove the major result about the overlap closure, we need to be able to deal precisely with the various cases of overlap between successive applications of rewrite rules in a rewrite sequence. We have found it useful to introduce a new representation of rewriting that helps to make such cases clear.

The domino representation (or rewrite domino) of a rewrite rule is a rectangle divided into left and right halves in which are inscribed tree representations of the left and right terms of the rule. Function symbols in the terms are represented by labelled circles in the trees. Variable symbols are represented by labeled rectangles, called "variable boxes." For examples of some rules and their corresponding rewrite dominoes, see Figure 1.

For each kind of domino (that is, each domino corresponding to a specific rule), we assume there is an infinite stock of dominoes of that kind with their variable rectangles filled in with all possible terms. For each such domino, we also assume an infinite number of copies are available in the stock.

A sequence of rewrites can be represented by a domino layout, which is a two-dimensional arrangement of dominoes that obeys the rules of matching corresponding to those of term rewriting. Before giving the formal definition of a layout, we refer the reader to an example of a rewrite sequence using the rules given in Figure 1 and its corresponding domino layout as shown in Figure 2. Another example is in Figure 3, and the two layouts in Figures 2 and 3 could be concatenated to give a single longer layout.

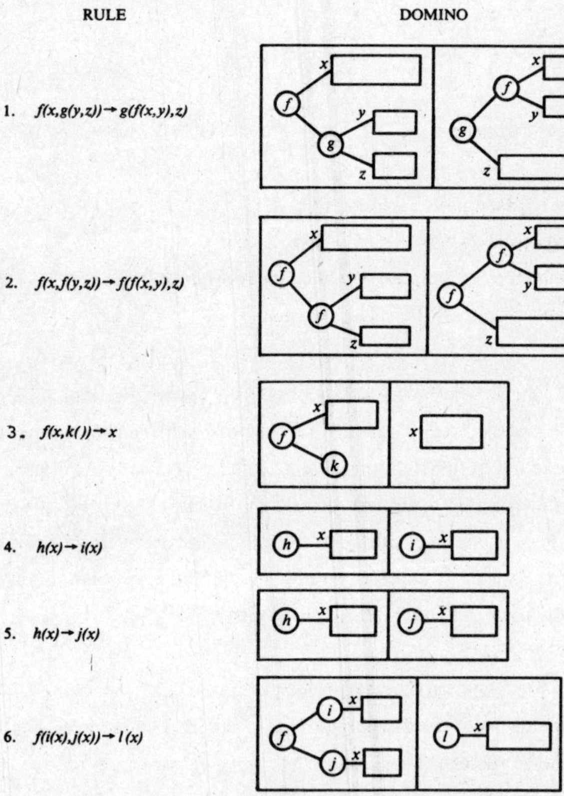

Figure 1. A set of rewrite rules and their corresponding rewrite dominoes.

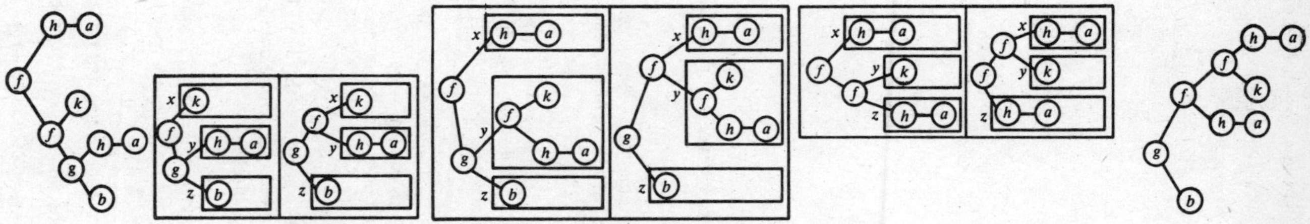

$$f(h(a),f(k,g(h(a),b))) \xrightarrow{1} f(h(a),g(f(k),h(a),b)) \xrightarrow{1} g(f(h(a),f(k,h(a))),b) \xrightarrow{2} g(f(f(h(a),k),h(a)),b)$$

Figure 2. A rewrite domino layout and the corresponding rewriting sequence (using dominoes of Figure 1).

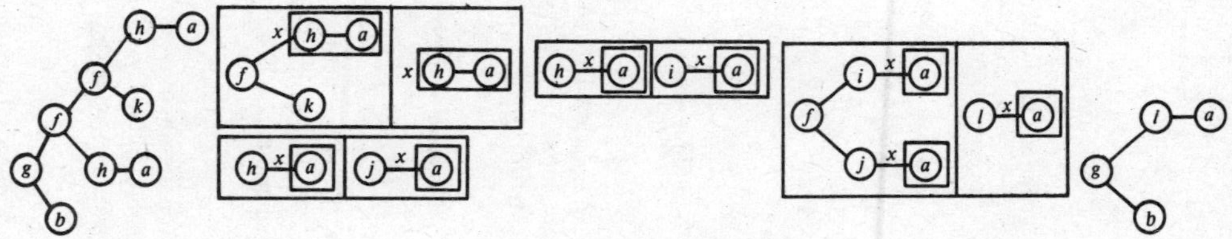

$$g(f(f(h(a),k),h(a)),b) \xrightarrow{3,5} g(f(h(a),j(a)),b) \xrightarrow{4} g(f(i(a),j(a)),b) \xrightarrow{6} g(l(a),b)$$

Figure 3. Another layout (a continuation of the layout in Figure 2).

We draw trees oriented sideways with the root at the left, and we will use nested triangles to represent trees schematically. We define a unit layout from t to w to be a horizontal arrangement of a tree t, a domino with trees u and v, and another tree w,

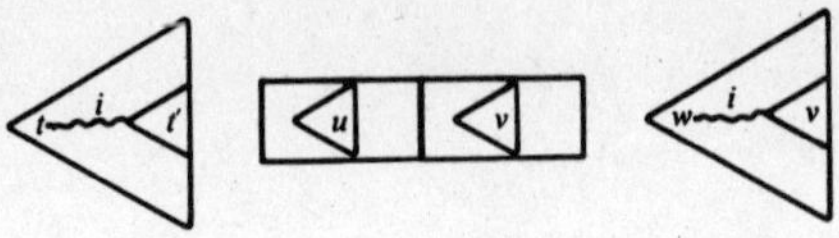

in which

1. at some position,i, in t there is a subtree t'that is identical to u, ignoring the variable boxes that appear in u;

2. the roots of t' and u are horizontally aligned;

3. w is the tree [t with v at i] and the roots of t and w are horizontally aligned.

A layout from t to v is defined as

1. a unit layout from t to v; or

2. the concatenation of a layout from t to u with a layout from u to v, with both copies of u dropped from the arrangement; or

3. any arrangement obtained from a layout by translating horizontally any domino, as long as no other domino or end tree is overlaid or crossed (this allows compaction of a layout by placing one domino above another when they match disjoint subterms).

The examples in Figures 2 and 3 illustrate a number of observations we can make about this representation of rewriting:

1. In a domino layout there is no distinction between different orders of rewriting when the rules are being applied to disjoint subterms. One can think of these rules being applied in parallel, since the order of application is always immaterial in this case. The layout representation just makes this property especially evident.

2. To the property that "the rightmost term of a rewrite sequence is terminal" corresponds the property that "there is no way to play a domino on the layout" (formally, there is no way to concatenate a unit layout onto the layout). The layout is said to be blocked. (The layout in Figure 3 is blocked.)

3. Thus the rules have the uniform termination property if and only if every possible layout eventually is blocked. Equivalently, there are no infinite layouts.

Our purpose with this representation of rewriting is to provide a conceptual tool for finding and presenting proofs of new results about term rewriting systems. The first result we will prove with the aid of rewrite dominoes is one that will allow us to speed up the search for cycles by considering only those sequences of rewrites in which a "major rewrite" occurs.

A rewrite $t_0 \rightarrow t_1$ is called a major rewrite if it is by application of a rule, $t \rightarrow u$, to the entire term t_0; i.e., for some substitution Θ, $\Theta(t) = t_0$ and $\Theta(u) = t_1$. When only a proper subterm of t_0 is matched, $t_0 \rightarrow t_1$ is called a minor rewrite.

In a layout, a domino is called a major domino (of the layout) if it represents a major rewrite, and a minor domino otherwise. Pictorially, major dominoes are those that span the width of the layout. A major cycle is a cycle in which at least one of the rewrites is major.

Theorem 3.1: If a rewriting relation has a cycle, it has a major cycle.
Proof: Let us define the corridor of a domino in a layout to be the horizontal strip across the layout determined by the position and width of the domino:

Any two corridors in a layout are either disjoint or one is contained in the other. Therefore, we can find a corridor that is spanned by a domino and which contains a layout as follows: start with any leftmost domino and follow its corridor to the right; whenever a domino is encountered that doesn't lie in the corridor, adopt its corridor. When we reach the right end, we have a corridor containing a layout including a domino that is major with respect to it. If the whole layout is cyclic, the identified layout will be also, and will represent a major cycle. □

We now want to define some terminology and some manipulations of layouts that will be useful in proving theorems about the overlap closure of a set of rules. Consider an adjacent pair of dominoes in a layout. Let t and u be the trees on the adjacent halves, where a subtree t' of t is identical to u (possibly t' = t):

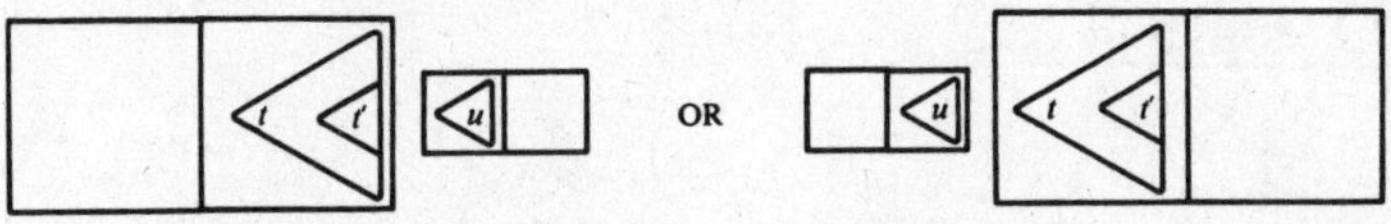

If either of t' or u is contained entirely within a variable box, i.e., the match is not between two nonvariable subterms, we say that the pair of dominoes is weakly matched, and otherwise that it is strongly matched. In Figure 3, the domino pair

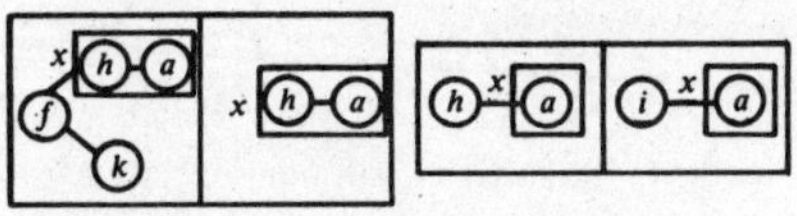

is weakly matched. Similarly the pair

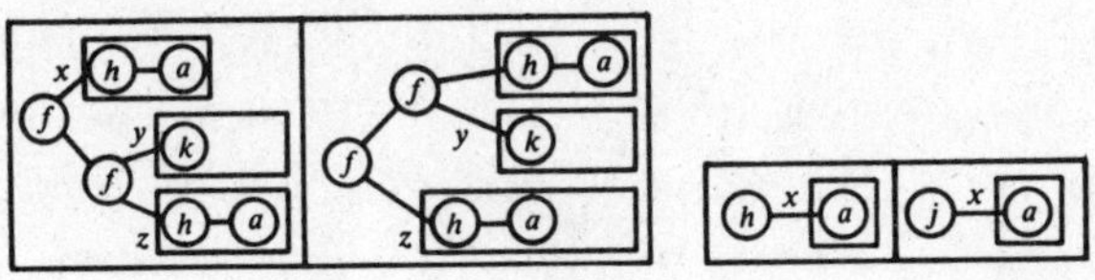

that appears in the concatenation of the layouts of Figures 2 and 3 is weakly matched, while all the other adjacent pairs are strongly matched.

Now suppose we have two weakly matched dominoes, as in Figure 4a, where t' is contained in the x variable box. If the (s,t) domino is right-linear (i.e., t is linear), then the pair of dominoes can be transposed as follows: remove the (u,v) domino from the layout and move the (s,t) domino to the right, so that copies of the (u,v) domino can be inserted to the left of the (s,t) domino, one adjacent to each x box in s (see Figure 4b). Then the resulting configuration is still a layout, (the dominoes all match, using the same set of rules) with the same end trees. This is the case also when a symmetric kind of transposition is performed on the layout in Figure 5a, producing the layout in Figure 5b, where we assume that the (u,v) domino is left-linear.

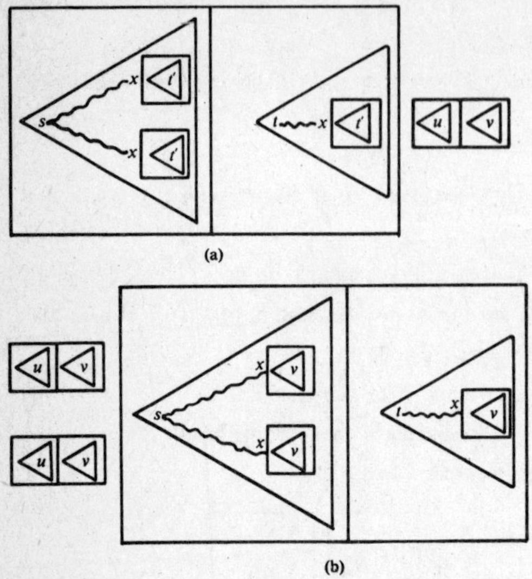

Figure 4. Transposition of weakly matched dominoes, where left domino is right-linear.

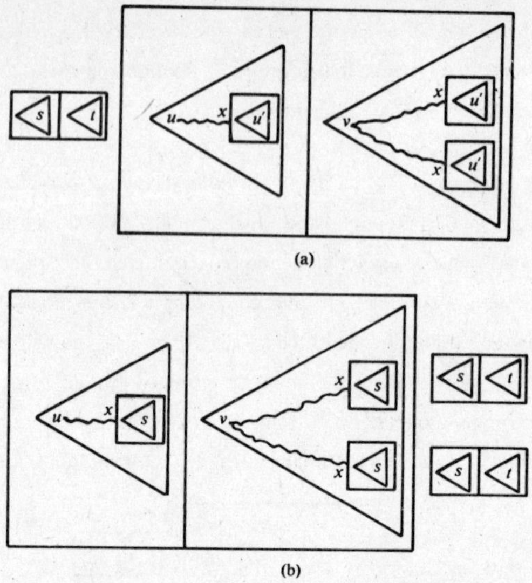

Figure 5. Transposition of weakly matched dominoes, where right domino is left-linear.

Such transpositions cannot necessarily be performed on strongly matched dominoes, but we will define a different kind of manipulation for this case. Strong matching corresponds to the concept of overlapping in the definition of derived pairs: if (r,s) and (t,u) are rules that have a derived pair ⟨p,q⟩, then the dominoes corresponding to (r,s) and (t,u) can be placed in a layout so that they are strongly matched. The layout configuration shows just where the strong match occurs and identifies a potential derived pair.

Suppose now that instead of our stock of dominoes corresponding to a given rule set <u>**R**</u>, we have a stock corresponding to **OC(<u>R</u>)**, the overlap closure of <u>**R**</u>. Then for any strongly matched pair of dominoes in a layout there is a domino in our stock which corresponds to a derived pair generated by the matching pair. By Lemma B.1 in Guttag, Kapur and Musser (1981), we can replace the strongly matched pair in the layout by the "derived pair domino" thus identified, and the result will still be a layout with the same end trees.

We are now in a position to prove:

Theorem 3.2: Suppose the rewriting relation of <u>**R**</u> is globally finite and every rule in <u>**R**</u> is right-linear. If the rewriting relation of <u>**R**</u> has a cycle, **OC(<u>R</u>)** contains a reflexive rule.

Proof: (By construction.) Let (*) $t_0 \rightarrow t_1 \rightarrow \cdots \rightarrow t_n \rightarrow t_0$ be a given cycle.

Corresponding to (*) is a cyclic domino layout

(**) 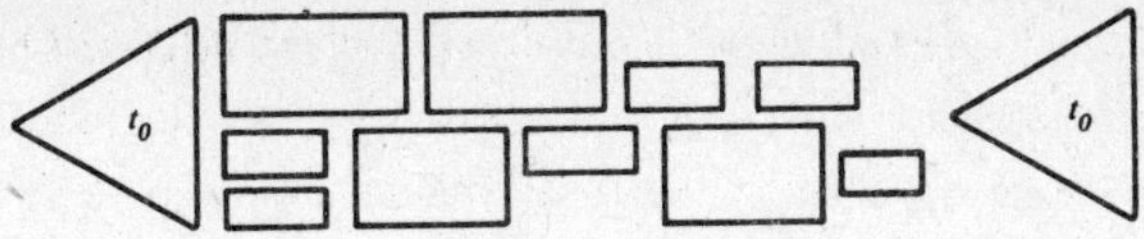

where the dominoes correspond to rules of $\underline{R}$. In fact since each of these rules is also in OC($\underline{R}$), we may take this layout as a layout of dominoes corresponding to rules of OC($\underline{R}$). We will show how to manipulate this layout to a form that shows there is a reflexive rule t $\dashrightarrow$ t in OC($\underline{R}$).
We describe the manipulations as an algorithm operating on the cyclic layout (**).

Step 1. [Extract major cycle.] As in the proof of Theorem 3.1, extract from (**) a sublayout representing a major cycle, making it the layout subject to the following steps. Also replace t_0 with its subterm matched by the layout.

Step 2. [Push major dominos to right end.] Manipulate the layout to a form in which all of the major dominoes are together at the right end, by means of transpositions or replacements by derived pair dominoes: whenever $\underline{D}$ is a major domino and $\underline{E}$ is a minor domino adjacent to $\underline{D}$ on the right, either $\underline{D}$ and $\underline{E}$ are weakly matched, in which case they can be transposed, or they are strongly matched, in which case they can be replaced by the derived pair domino they define which is a major domino. This derived pair domino is also right linear, as Lemma C.2 in Guttag, Kapur, and Musser (1981) shows.

Step 3. [Look for cycle among major dominoes.] There is now a nonempty sequence of major dominoes $D_1, \ldots, D_m$ at the right end of the layout: 

These dominoes can only be strongly matched - except for the case where the right-hand side of D_i is just a variable, but shortly we will show that such a possibility can be ruled out. If there is some contiguous subsequence $D_i, \ldots D_j$ that forms a cyclic layout

then, since there can only be strong matches, these dominoes can be combined by j - i + 1 replacements into a single domino $\underline{D}$ that forms a cyclic layout:

Let $\underline{D}$ represent (p,q). Then there is a substitution Θ such that $u_0 = \Theta(p)$ and $\Theta(q) = u_0$, i.e., Θ unifies p and q. Furthermore, a derived pair of (p,q) and (p,q) is the reflexive rule $(\Theta(p), \Theta(q))$. Since this is in OC($\underline{R}$), we terminate the algorithm.

Step 4. [Duplicate.] If no such subsequence exists, construct a copy of the layout adjacent to it and return to Step 2 with the resulting layout: 

That concludes the statement of the algorithm. Before considering the question of termination of the algorithm, we dispense with the detail mentioned in Step 3: the case of adjacent major dominoes $\underline{D}$ and $\underline{E}$ where the right term u of $\underline{D}$ is a variable. We can assume the left term t of $\underline{D}$ is not a variable (if it were then it would have to be the same variable as u and we would already have a reflexive rule). Since the layout is cyclic, if we drop $\underline{D}$ from the layout, we obtain a layout that has as its right end term a proper subterm identical to the left end term. From this we conclude that the term rewriting relation is not globally finite, contrary to assumption. This contradiction rules out the case under discussion.

Each step of this algorithm is effective and terminating. Overall termination is guaranteed by the following facts:

a. At the k th execution of Step 2, the number of major dominoes, m, at the right end is at least 2^k.

b. Let $t_0'[k]$ denote the term to the left of D_1 in the layout at the k th execution of Step 3. Since each $t_0'[k]$ is derived from t_0 and the rewriting relation is globally finite, there are only finitely many distinct possibilities for $t_0'[k]$. By a), then, there is one such term for which arbitrarily long layouts of major dominoes exist. Again by global finiteness, these layouts cannot all continue without producing a term, u_0, that is a duplicate of some term previously obtained in the layout.

Since the algorithm always terminates, and does so with a reflexive rule in **OC($\underline{R}$)**, this proves the theorem. □

The corresponding theorem obtained by replacing "right-linear" by "left-linear" can also be proved in a similar manner. Combining these theorems with Corollary 2.4 we have:

Theorem 3.3: Suppose the rewriting relation of $\underline{R}$ is globally finite and every rule in $\underline{R}$ is right-linear or every rule in $\underline{R}$ is left-linear. Then the rewriting relation of $\underline{R}$ is uniformly terminating if and only if **OC($\underline{R}$)** contains no reflexive rule.

Some applications of this theorem are explored in Guttag, Kapur, and Musser, 1981

Dershowitz (1981) and Pettorossi (1981) have explored the idea of matching left hand sides of rewrite rules with right hand sides in studying termination. Dershowitz proposed a "forward chain" construction for rewriting systems and proved that a right-linear rewriting system is uniformly terminating if and only if it has no infinite forward chains. However, for left-linear systems the analogous result requires that the left-hand sides of the rules be nonoverlapping, a problem that we had independently encountered when considering the forward chain construction and a similar backward chain construction. We were thus led to invent the overlap closure construction. The following example from Dershowitz (1981) illustrates the advantage of the overlap closure construction over forward chains. Using the forward chain construction, it is not possible to determine the nontermination of this left-linear rewrite system, as pointed out by Dershowitz. The rewriting system is

$$f(a(), b(), x) \rightarrow f(x, x, b()) \quad \text{and} \quad b() \rightarrow a().$$

These rules have only two forward chains, both finite:

$$f(a(), b(), x) \Rightarrow f(x, x, b()) \Rightarrow f(x, x, b()) \quad \text{and} \quad b() \Rightarrow a(),$$

but we cannot conclude anything about the termination of the rules because they are not right-linear and, although they are left-linear, the left-hand sides are overlapping. But in the overlap closure construction, the rules have a derived pair rule

$$f(b(\,),\ b(\,), x) \rightarrow f(x, x, b(\,)),$$

which, when overlapped with itself, gives the reflexive rule

$$f(b(\,), b(\,), b(\,)) \rightarrow f(b(\,), b(\,), b(\,)),$$

as a derived pair; proving that the rules are nonterminating.

4. Conclusion

We have discussed two ways to make use of finite subsets of the overlap closure: proving restricted termination and disproving uniform termination. We have explored, without much success, using such finite subsets as parts of proofs of uniform termination. We conjecture that for certain classes of term rewriting systems it should be possible to compute a bound, n, such that if a cycle exists, there exists a cycle in which every term is of size n or less. For such classes, the overlap closure would provide a decision procedure for uniform termination.

Another open question about the generality of the overlap closure construction is whether the assumption of left-linearity or right-linearity is necessary. Although we have not been able to find proofs of our results without this assumption, we have also been unable to construct a counterexample. In any case, as discussed above, the overlap closure construction is more general than either forward or backward chain constructions.

For the class of term rewriting systems to which it may be applied, constructing the overlap closure is as useful as constructing the complete transitive closure. Furthermore, using the overlap closure to show restricted termination or the absence of uniform termination will always involve computing fewer terms than would using the transitive closure. We do not yet have much empirical or analytical evidence as to the absolute efficiency of using the overlap closure for these purposes. The key question is how many terms must be examined in order to demonstrate that no cycle is possible for terms of up to size n. The few examples we have tried, using a preliminary implementation, we have found encouraging.

Acknowledgments

The basic idea of conducting a search for repeated terms (cycles) or subterms sprang from discussions in 1977 between one of the authors (Musser) and Dallas Lankford. We thank P. Gloess, G. Huet, and J. Levy for their interest and assistance in refuting some of our earlier conjectures, thus helping us arrive at the notion of the overlap closure and the theorems of Section 3. We also thank P. Narendran for assistance in constructing the proof of the theorems in the Appendix and J. Goguen for discussions of the approach to term rewriting used in OBJ.

References

N. Dershowitz, "Termination of Linear Rewriting Systems - Preliminary Version," in Automata, Languages, and Programming, Eighth Colloquium, Israel (Eds: S. Even and O. Kariv), LNCS 115, Springer Verlag, New York, 1981.

J.A. Goguen and J. Tardo, "An Introduction to OBJ-T,"Proc. of Conf. on Specification of Reliable Software (1979).

J.V. Guttag, E. Horowitz, and D.R. Musser, "Abstract Data Types and Software Validation," Comm. A.C.M. 21 (1978), 1048-1064.

J.V. Guttag, D. Kapur, and D.R. Musser,On Proving Uniform Termination and Restricted Termination of Rewriting Systems, Report No. 81CRD272, G.E. C. Research and Development, Schenectady, New York, Nov. 1981.

G. Huet, "Confluent Reductions: Abstract Properties and Applications to Term Rewriting Systems," J. ACM 27 (1980), 797-821.

G. Huet, D.S. Lankford, "On the Uniform Halting Problem for Term Rewriting Systems," Rapport Laboria 283, IRIA, March, 1978.

G. Huet, D.C. Oppen, "Equations and Rewrite Rules: a Survey," Formal Languages Perspectives and Open Problems (R. Book, ed.), Academic Press (1980).

D.E. Knuth, P. Bendix, "Simple Word Problems in Universal Algebra." Computational Problems in Abstract Algebra (J. Leech, ed.), Pergamon Press (1970), 263-297.

D. Musser, "Abstract Data Type Specification in the AFFIRM system." IEEE Transactions on Software Engineering 6 (1980), 24-31.

G.E. Peterson and M.E. Stickel, Complete Sets of Reductions for Equational Theories With Complete Unification Algorithms, Tech. Report, Dept. of Computer Science, U. of Arizona, Tucson, Sept. 1977.

A. Pettorossi, "Comparing and Putting Together Recursive Path Ordering, Simplification Orderings, And Non-Ascending Property for Termination Proofs of Term Rewriting Systems," in Automata, Language, and Programming, Eighth Coll., Israel (Eds: S. Even and O. Kariv), LNCS115, Springer Verlag, New York, 1981.

A PROGRAMMING LANGUAGE FOR THE INDUCTIVE SETS, AND APPLICATIONS

David Harel[1,2]
The Weizmann Institute
Rehovot, Israel

Dexter Kozen[2,3]
Aarhus University
Aarhus, Denmark

Abstract

We introduce a programming language IND that generalizes alternating Turing machines to arbitrary first-order structures. We show that IND programs (respectively, everywhere-halting IND programs, loop-free IND programs) accept precisely the inductively definable (respectively, hyperelementary, elementary) relations. We give several examples showing how the language provides a robust and computational approach to the theory of first-order inductive definability. We then show: (1) on all acceptable structures (in the sense of Moschovakis [Mo]), r.e. Dynamic Logic is more expressive than finite-test Dynamic Logic. This refines a separation result of Meyer and Parikh [MP]; (2) IND provides a natural query language for the set of fixpoint queries over a relational data-base, answering a question of Chandra and Harel [CH2].

1. Introduction

In this paper we introduce a programming language IND. In its most basic form, the language consists of only 3 types of statements:

ℓ_1: $y \leftarrow \exists$ (or $y \leftarrow \forall$)

ℓ_2: <u>accept</u> (or <u>reject</u>)

ℓ_3: <u>if</u> $R(\bar{x})$ <u>then</u> <u>goto</u> ℓ_4

where $R(\bar{x})$ is an atomic first-order formula.

An IND program P can run in any first-order structure of the same similarity type. The input is an initial assignment to variables $\bar{x}=x_1,\dots,x_n$, where $\bar{x}$ contains (at least) all the free variables of the program, and execution starts at the first statement. Statements of the form ℓ_1 assign an arbitrary element of the domain existentially (universally) to variable y, just as in alternating Turing machines [CKS]. A statement of the form ℓ_2 causes immediate acceptance or rejection, and ℓ_3 is an ordinary conditional branch. The definition of acceptance of the input $\bar{x}$ is the same as in alternating Turing machines [CKS] in-

---

1) Research supported in part by a Bath-Sheva fellowship.
2) Work done in part at IBM Thomas J. Watson Research Center, Yorktown Heights, New York 10598, USA.
3) On leave from IBM Thomas J. Watson Research Center, Yorktown Heights, New York 10598, USA.

volving an inductively-defined labeling of the computation tree with either 0 (reject), 1 (accept), or ⊥ (undefined); see Section 3.

In Section 5 we show:

(1) IND programs accept precisely the relations definable by elementary (first-order) induction.

(2) IND programs which halt on all inputs (i.e., either accept or reject) accept precisely the hyperelementary (or inductive, co-inductive) relations.

(3) Loop-free IND programs accept precisely the elementary (first-order definable) relations.

In countable acceptable structures (see [Mo]) such as the natural numbers N, (1) and (2) become

(1) IND programs accept precisely the Π_1^1 relations.

(2) IND programs which halt on all inputs accept precisely the Δ_1^1 relations.

IND provides a computational intuition for the theory of inductive definability [Mo] which seems to be missing from the literature. For example, our proof of (2) involves showing that if both a relation and its complement are accepted by IND programs P_1 and P_2, then the two programs can be simulated by a third program that always halts, P_3. P_3 simulates steps of P_1 and P_2 alternately, halting whenever one or the other halts, just as in the usual Turing machine proof that an r.e., co-r.e. set is recursive. Many other elementary results, such as the Stage Comparison Theorem, Closure Theorem, and Separation Theorem [Mo], have machine-based proofs using IND that recall analogous proofs in recursion theory that use Turing machines. The availability of such a tool is especially important now that concepts central to inductive definability theory have resurfaced in computer science in recent work on program logics [MP, T], and program verification in the presence of fairness or unbounded nondeterminism [AP, LPS, GFMR].

In Section 6 we use IND to characterize the expressive power of Dynamic Logic. Meyer and Parikh [MP] have shown that Dynamic Logic with unrestricted recursively enumerable programs (DL_{re}) is strictly more expressive that many limited versions, such as DL with finite tests (DL_{ft}). The result is proved by transferring the problem to the problem of distinguishing ω^ω and $\omega^\omega \cdot 2$ in fragments of infinitary logic, and does not provide any insight into the inherent computational power of DL. In Section 6 we show that on any acceptable structure, DL_{re} is more expressive than DL_{ft}. Specifically, we show that in any acceptable structure, DL_{re} and DL_{ft} define exactly the IND complexity classes $\tau(\omega_1^{CK})$ and $\tau(\omega)$, respectively, where ω_1^{CK} is the first non-recursive ordinal. In any structure, $\tau(\omega)$={relations definable by first-order logic}, and on recursive acceptable structures (such as N), $\tau(\omega_1^{CK}) = \Delta_1^1$. The classes $\tau(\omega)$ and $\tau(\omega_1^{CK})$ can be separated on any acceptable structure by a simple diagonalization argument.

It should be emphasized that the expressiveness results of [MP] are <u>schematic</u>, in the sense that they consider $L_1 \leq L_2$ if there is an interpretation of L_1 in L_2 which holds uniformly over all structures, whereas we will write $L_1 \leq L_2$ if <u>for each structure</u> there is an interpretation of L_1 in L_2. The former gives stronger positive expressibility results, and the latter gives stronger negative expressibility results (such as $DL_{ft} \neq DL_{re}$). Our positive expressibility results (such as $DL_{re} \equiv \tau(\omega_1^{CK})$) are not to be interpreted schematically.

In Section 7 we show the connection between inductive definability and the fixpoint queries of [AU, CH] for relational data bases. Coupled with a recent result of Immerman [I], this easy observation shows that IND defines exactly the class of fixpoint queries FP, thus answering a question of Chandra and Harel [CH].

2. Programming examples

The language IND in its above form is very simple, and this makes formal semantics and formal proofs easier. However, the language is also quite robust, in the sense that more powerful programming constructs can be added without changing expressive power. For example, an unconditional jump can be obtained by using the test y=y in the conditional. Certain more complicated conditional forms, such as

<u>if</u> $R(\bar{x})$ <u>then</u> <u>goto</u> ℓ_1 <u>else</u> <u>goto</u> ℓ_2
<u>if</u> $R(\bar{x})$ <u>then</u> <u>accept</u> <u>else</u> <u>reject</u>
<u>if</u> $\neg R(\bar{x}) \vee S(\bar{x})$ <u>then</u> <u>goto</u> ℓ

are obtained by manipulation of control flow. The assignment statement $y \leftarrow t$ is obtained by

$y \leftarrow \exists$
<u>if</u> $y \neq t$ <u>then</u> <u>reject</u>

or

$x \leftarrow \exists$
<u>if</u> $x \neq t$ <u>then</u> <u>reject</u>
$y \leftarrow \exists$
<u>if</u> $y \neq x$ <u>then</u> <u>reject</u>

where x is a new variable, if y occurs in t.

There is a loop-free program to compute any first-order formula. For example, an element x of a Boolean algebra is <u>atomless</u> if it satisfies the formula

$$\forall y \leq x \quad (y \neq 0 \supset \exists z \leq y \quad (0 \neq z \wedge z \neq y))$$

The set of such elements is accepted by the program

```
y←∀
if ¬ y≤x ∨ y=0 then accept
z←∃
if ¬ z≤y ∨ 0=z ∨ z=y then reject
accept.
```

It is clear, however, that IND programs can accept sets that are not first-order definable. For example, ℓ_1 below accepts all pairs (x,y) in the reflexive transitive closure of R, and ℓ_2 accepts y iff R is well-founded below y:

```
ℓ1: if x=y then accept            ℓ2: x←∀
    z←∃                               if ¬R(x,y) then accept
    if ¬R(x,z) then reject            y←x
    x←z                               goto ℓ2
    goto ℓ1
```

The statement $\ell_5 \vee \ell_6$ which accepts if either the program starting at ℓ_5 or that starting at ℓ_6 accepts is encoded by

```
y←∃
if y=z then goto ℓ5 else goto ℓ6
```

where y is a new variable and z is any other variable. The statement $\ell_5 \wedge \ell_6$ is defined similarly, using ∀ instead of ∃. One can also encode the statement $\neg \ell_5$ which accepts (rejects) iff the computation starting at ℓ_5 rejects (accepts). This is done by taking the whole program P and constructing its dual $\bar{P}$ by interchanging ∀/∃ and <u>accept</u>/<u>reject</u> statements. The program $\bar{P}$ then accepts (rejects) exactly when program P rejects (accepts), starting at any point.

The statement $\neg \ell_5$ is then given by <u>goto</u> $\bar{\ell}_5$ where $\bar{\ell}_5$ is the statement corresponding to ℓ_5 in the dual program. Of course, the statement $\neg \bar{\ell}_5$ in the dual program is replaced by <u>goto</u> ℓ_5.

These constructs allow us to encode the statement

<u>if</u> $\varphi(\bar{x})$ <u>then</u> <u>goto</u> ℓ_1 <u>else</u> <u>goto</u> ℓ_2,

where $\varphi(\bar{x})$ is any first-order formula, or for that matter any relation computed by a program that always halts:

$$(m_1 \wedge \ell_1) \vee (\neg m_1 \wedge \ell_2)$$

where m_1 is the first statement of a program computing $\varphi(\bar{x})$.

One of our main results is that there is an IND program that accepts any relation definable by first-order induction. For example, the subgroup H of G generated by a,b is the least subset of G such that

$$x \in H \leftrightarrow x=a \vee x=b \vee \exists y \in H \ \ \exists z \in H \ \ x=y \cdot z \vee x=y^{-1}$$

Membership in H is computed by the program

ℓ_1: <u>if</u> $x=a \vee x=b$ <u>then</u> <u>accept</u>
$\quad y \leftarrow \exists$
$\quad$ <u>if</u> $x=y^{-1}$ <u>then</u> <u>goto</u> ℓ_3
$\quad z \leftarrow \exists$
$\quad$ <u>if</u> $x \neq y \cdot z$ <u>then</u> <u>reject</u>
$\quad \ell_2 \wedge \ell_3$
ℓ_2: $x \leftarrow z$
$\quad$ <u>goto</u> ℓ_1
ℓ_3: $x \leftarrow y$
$\quad$ <u>goto</u> ℓ_1

To give an example involving an unbounded alternation of quantifiers, consider a two-person game like chess or go. The set of board positions from which a given player has a forced win is defined inductively from the legal-move and (immediate) win predicates by

$$\text{force}(x) \leftrightarrow \text{win}(x) \vee \exists y(\text{legal-move}(x,y) \wedge \neg\text{win}(y) \wedge \forall z(\text{legal-move}(y,z) \rightarrow \text{force}(z)))$$

and is accepted by the program

ℓ_1: <u>if</u> win(x) <u>then</u> <u>accept</u>
$\quad y \leftarrow \exists$
$\quad$ <u>if</u> $\neg$legal-move(x,y) $\vee$ win(y) <u>then</u> <u>reject</u>
$\quad x \leftarrow \forall$
$\quad$ <u>if</u> $\neg$legal-move(y,x) <u>then</u> <u>accept</u>
$\quad$ <u>goto</u> ℓ_1

IND programs can run for more than a finite amount of time and still halt. An example of a program that runs in N for time $\omega+1$ is

$\quad y \leftarrow \forall$
ℓ_1: <u>if</u> $y=0$ <u>then</u> <u>accept</u>
$\quad y \leftarrow y-1$
$\quad$ <u>goto</u> ℓ_1

In N, the running times of IND programs are exactly the recursive ordinals. In fact, we can take the set of computation trees of IND programs as a set of notations for recursive ordinals.

3. Semantics of acceptance

The semantics of acceptance is formally almost identical to that of alternating Turing machines [CKS]. Intuitively, it consists of two stages: (1) generation of the computation tree downwards from the root, and (2) evaluation of the acceptance function upwards from the leaves to the root. Associated with each node of the computation tree is a unique configuration (ℓ,v) where ℓ is the label of one of the statements in the program and v is a valuation of program variables over the domain of computation A. If a node of the computation tree is labeled c, then its immediate descendants are labeled with all elements of N(c), the next configurations of c, which are defined by cases, depending on the statement stmt(c) labeled by c's first component:

$$N(\ell,v)=\begin{cases}\{(\ell',v[y\leftarrow a])\mid a\in A\} & \text{if } stmt(\ell,v) \text{ is } y\leftarrow\exists \text{ or } y\leftarrow\forall\\ \emptyset & \text{if } stmt(\ell,v) \text{ is } \underline{accept} \text{ or } \underline{reject}\\ \{(m,v)\} & \text{if } stmt(\ell,v) \text{ is } \underline{if}\ R(\bar{x})\ \underline{then}\ \underline{goto}\ m \text{ and}\\ & \quad A,v\models R(\bar{x})\\ \{(\ell',v)\} & \text{if } stmt(\ell,v) \text{ is } \underline{if}\ R(\bar{x})\ \underline{then}\ \underline{goto}\ m \text{ and}\\ & \quad A,v\models \neg R(\bar{x})\end{cases}$$

where ℓ' denotes the next statement after ℓ in the program (or the first statement, if ℓ was the last). The root of the tree is the start configuration. The acceptance function e* can be regarded as a labeling of nodes of the computation tree with either 0 (reject), 1 (accept), or $\bot$ (undefined), but formally its domain is the set C of configurations. It is defined as the supremum of a chain of approximating labelings e^α. Intuitively, $e^\alpha(c)=1$ (respectively, 0) if c has been determined to be an accept (respectively, reject) configuration by time α; $e^\alpha(c)=\bot$ if neither has been determined by time α. At time 0, nothing is determined, thus $e^0(c)=\bot$ for all c. At time 1, the leaves of the tree, corresponding to accept and reject statements, are labeled 1 and 0, respectively, and everything else is labeled $\bot$. If $stmt(c)=y\leftarrow\exists$ and $e^\alpha(d)=1$ for some $d\in N(c)$, then $e^{\alpha+1}(d)=1$. If $stmt(c)=y\leftarrow\forall$ and all $d\in N(c)$ are eventually labeled 1, then c becomes labeled 1 upon completion of the labeling of N(c). Note that, because of unbounded nondeterminism, it may take more than a finite amount of time for a configuration to become labeled 0 or 1.

Formally, let C be the set of configurations, let Ord be the class of ordinals, and let $*\notin Ord$ with $\alpha<*$ for all $\alpha\in Ord$. Define the sequence $e^\alpha:C\to\{0,1,\bot\}$ inductively by $e^\alpha=\bigsqcup_{\beta<\alpha}\tau(e^\beta)$, where τ is the $\sqsubseteq$-monotone map defined by

$$\tau(e)(c) = \begin{cases} 1 & \text{if stmt}(c) = \underline{\text{accept}} \\ 0 & \text{if stmt}(c) = \underline{\text{reject}} \\ \bigvee_{d\in N(c)} e(d) & \text{if stmt}(c) = y\leftarrow\exists \\ \bigwedge_{d\in N(c)} e(d) & \text{if stmt}(c) = y\leftarrow\forall \\ e(d) & \text{if stmt}(c) = \underline{\text{if}}\ R\ \underline{\text{then}}\ \underline{\text{goto}}\ m \text{ and } N(c)=\{d\}. \end{cases}$$

The meet $\bigwedge$ and join $\bigvee$ are with respect to the ordering $0<\bot<1$, and should not be confused with the approximation ordering $\sqsubseteq$ with join $\sqcup$, defined by $\bot\sqsubseteq 0$, $\bot\sqsubseteq 1$ and extended pointwise to labelings. e^* is the $\sqsubseteq$-least fixpoint of τ.

We say <u>c becomes properly labeled at time α</u> if α is the least ordinal such that $e^\alpha(c)\neq\bot$, and write $o(c)=\alpha$. If no such α exists, we write $o(c)=*$. Thus $e^*(c)=e^{o(c)}(c)$. The <u>running time of P on input $\bar{x}$</u> is defined to be $o(c)$, where c is the start configuration $(\ell_1,\bar{x})$. We denote this by $\text{TIME}(P,\bar{x})$. The program P is said to <u>accept</u> $\bar{x}$ if $e^*(c)=1$ and <u>reject</u> $\bar{x}$ if $e^*(c)=0$, where c is the start configuration of P on $\bar{x}$; in either case $\text{TIME}(P,\bar{x})<*$ and P is said to <u>halt</u> on $\bar{x}$. If $\text{TIME}(P\bar{x})=*$, then $e^*(c)=\bot$ and P does not halt on $\bar{x}$. Call a program P <u>β-time bounded</u> if $\text{TIME}(P,\bar{x})\leq\beta$ for all inputs $\bar{x}$ accepted by P (P need not halt on other inputs). Define the complexity class

$$\tau(\alpha) \;=\; \bigcup_{\beta<\alpha}\{\text{relations accepted by } \beta\text{-time bounded IND programs}\}.$$

4. The shuffle construction

If A and $\bar{A}$ are both r.e, then A can be proved recursive by constructing a Turing machine T_3 which simulates steps of T_1 and T_2 alternately, where T_1 accepts A and T_2 accepts $\bar{A}$. In this section we give a similar construction for IND programs.

Suppose P and Q are programs with <u>disjoint</u> sets of variables $\bar{x}$ and $\bar{y}$, respectively, and statement labels $\ell_1,\dots,\ell_p$ and $m_1,\dots,m_q$, respectively. By adding dummy statements, we can assume without loss of generality that p and q are relatively prime. Now we shuffle the statements of P and Q to get the program PQ with 2pq statements labeled by all pairs of the form $(\ell_{\underline{i}},m_j)$ and $(\ell_i,m_{\underline{j}})$, $1\leq i\leq p$, $1\leq j\leq q$, arranged in the order

$(\ell_{\underline{1}},m_1),(\ell_2,m_{\underline{1}}),(\ell_{\underline{2}},m_2),(\ell_3,m_{\underline{2}}),\dots,(\ell_{\underline{p}},m_i),(\ell_1,m_{\underline{i}}),\dots,(\ell_{\underline{p}},m_q),(\ell_1,m_{\underline{q}})$.

The underline tells which statement of P or Q is the next to be simulated. The statement of PQ labeled by $(\ell_{\underline{i}},m_j)$ is the same as the statement of P labeled by ℓ_i, unless it is a conditional jump

$$\ell_i\colon\ \underline{\text{if}}\ R(\bar{x})\ \underline{\text{then}}\ \underline{\text{goto}}\ \ell_k$$

in which case we take

$$(\underline{\ell_i}, m_j): \underline{\text{if}}\ R(\bar{x})\ \underline{\text{then}}\ \underline{\text{goto}}\ (\ell_k, \underline{m_j}).$$

A symmetric remark holds for statements labeled $(\ell_i, \underline{m_j})$. Thus PQ simulates steps of P and Q alternately. Since the variables of P and Q are disjoint, these simulations do not interfere with each other. The formal statement of this property involves the relationship between the successor configuration maps N_{PQ} and N_P, N_Q. Observe that there is a natural one-to-one correspondence between the configurations C_{PQ} of PQ and pairs $(c,d) \in C_P \times C_Q \cup C_Q \times C_P$:

$$((\underline{\ell_i}, m_j), \bar{a}, \bar{b}) \longmapsto ((\ell_i, \bar{a}), (m_j, \bar{b}))$$

$$((\ell_i, \underline{m_j}), \bar{a}, \bar{b}) \longmapsto ((m_j, \bar{b}), (\ell_i, \bar{a})).$$

The order of the components in $(c,d) \in C_P \times C_Q \cup C_Q \times C_P$ tells which of P,Q is next to be simulated. Hence we will identify elements of C_{PQ} with the corresponding elements of $C_P \times C_Q \cup C_Q \times C_P$. Then by construction of PQ,

$$N_{PQ}(c,d) = \{(d,c') \mid c' \in N(c)\}$$

where $N(c) = N_P(c)$ if $c \in C_P$, $N_Q(c)$ if $c \in C_Q$.

The following theorem says that the label assigned by e* to a particular configuration $(c,d) \in C_P \times C_Q$ of PQ is either the one assigned to c by P or the one assigned to d by Q, depending on which is labeled sooner. Moreover (c,d) is labeled in PQ within at most double the time it takes to label either c or d in P or Q, respectively.

<u>Theorem 1</u> Let $(c,d) \in C_P \times C_Q \cup C_Q \times C_P$.

(i) $$e^*(c,d) = \begin{cases} e^*(c) & \text{if } o(c) \le o(d) \\ e^*(d) & \text{if } o(c) > o(d) \end{cases}$$

(ii) $$o(c,d) = \min(2 \cdot o(c),\ 2 \cdot o(d)+1).$$

<u>Proof</u> Let $e: C_P \times C_Q \cup C_Q \times C_P \to \{0,1,\bot\}$ be the map

$$e(c,d) = \begin{cases} e^*(c) & \text{if } o(c) \le o(d) \\ e^*(d) & \text{if } o(c) > o(d). \end{cases}$$

It is easily shown by cases that e is a fixpoint of τ, therefore $e^* \sqsubseteq e$. That e is no more defined than e* follows from (ii), which can now be proved by transfinite induction on $\min(2 \cdot o(c), 2 \cdot o(d)+1)$. Curiously, the proof of (ii) depends on the fact that $e^* \sqsubseteq e$; this is because for statements $y \leftarrow \exists$ and $y \leftarrow \forall$, the time that the configuration becomes labeled depends on what the label is. □

If the variables of P and Q are not disjoint, define the shuffle PQ as follows: rename the variables of P to get a program P' having no variables in common with Q. Let $x_1,\ldots,x_k$ be the variables common to P and Q and let $y_1,\ldots,y_k$ be their replacements in P'. Define PQ to be the program which assigns $y_i \leftarrow x_i$, $1 \leq i \leq k$, then runs P'Q.

Corollary 1 Let P, Q be two programs with a common set $\bar{x}$ of input variables. Then PQ accepts (rejects) $\bar{x}$ iff either

(i) $\mathrm{TIME}(P,\bar{x}) \leq \mathrm{TIME}(Q,\bar{x})$ and P accepts (rejects) $\bar{x}$; or

(ii) $\mathrm{TIME}(P,\bar{x}) > \mathrm{TIME}(Q,\bar{x})$ and Q accepts (rejects) $\bar{x}$. □

5. Main results

Theorem 2 (i) IND programs accept precisely the relations definable by first-order induction;

(ii) IND programs which halt on all inputs accept precisely the hyper-elementary (or inductive, coinductive) relations;

(iii) loop-free IND programs accept precisely the first-order definable relations.

Proof (i) Every IND program accepts only inductively definable relations, because the definition of the acceptance function e* is a classical first-order inductive definition over the domain of computation (see [Mo]). Conversely, every inductively definable relation is given by a first-order formula $\varphi(S,\bar{x})$ with free variables $\bar{x}=x_1,\ldots,x_n$, an n-ary predicate symbol S occurring only positively in φ, and some constants $\bar{a}=a_1,\ldots,a_m$, $m<n$. The fixpoint defined by φ is the least S* such that $S^*=\varphi(S^*,\bar{x})$. The inductive relation defined by $\varphi,\bar{a}$ is the (n-m)-ary relation $S^*(a_1,\ldots,a_m,x_{m+1},\ldots,x_n)$. A program to accept all $(x_{m+1},\ldots,x_n)$ satisfying $S^*(a_1,\ldots,a_m,x_{m+1},\ldots,x_n)$ first assigns a_i to x_i, $1 \leq i \leq m$, and then enters a loop labeled ℓ_1 which determines whether $S^*(\bar{x})$. Within the loop it decomposes $\varphi(S,\bar{x})$, using $y \leftarrow \forall$ and $y \leftarrow \exists$ to eliminate quantifiers, $\ell_1 \wedge \ell_2$, $\ell_1 \vee \ell_2$, $\neg \ell_1$ to eliminate logical connectives, and conditionals for atomic formulas; this leaves only occurrences of $S(\bar{y})$, which are handled by assigning $\bar{y}$ to $\bar{x}$ followed by an unconditional jump back to ℓ_1.

(ii) Any program P accepting S which halts on all inputs has a dual $\bar{P}$ which also halts on all inputs, and accepts the complement of S. Thus by (i), S is both inductive and coinductive. Conversely, suppose the set S is both inductive and coinductive. By (i), there are programs P and Q accepting S and $\bar{S}$, respectively. Modify P and Q so that they never reject, by replacing all statements ℓ: reject with ℓ: goto ℓ. By Corollary 1, the shuffle $P\bar{Q}$ accepts S and rejects $\bar{S}$.

(iii) It has already been argued in Section 2 that every first-order definable relation is computed by a loop-free program. The converse is obtained by observing that every loop-free program is equivalent to one with only forward jumps; a formula is now easy to construct. □

Observe from the proof of Theorem 2(i) that there is a strong connection between the running times of IND programs and the ordinals at which inductive definitions close (see [Mo]). The closure ordinal κ^A of a structure A is defined in [Mo] as the supremum of closure ordinals of all possible inductive definitions. By the proof of Theorem 2(i) we see that (for infinite structures) this is just the supremum of running times of IND programs in A. The following theorem relates these concepts to the complexity classes $\tau(\alpha)$ defined in Section 3.

Theorem 3

(i) $\tau(\omega)$ = {first-order definable relations}

(ii) $\tau(\kappa^A)$ = {hyperelementary relations}

Remark Part (ii) is exactly the closure theorem of Moschovakis [Mo, p. 33].

Proof (i) Clearly, any loop-free program can run for only finitely many steps, independent of the input. Conversely, any c-time bounded program, $c<\omega$, can be made to halt on all inputs by shuffling it with a "clock", i.e. a program that on all inputs runs for c+1 steps, then rejects. The resulting program now has a finite, uniform time bound d, independent of the input. But any such program is equivalent to a loop-free program obtained by unwinding the loops d+1 times. The result follows from Theorem 2(iii).

(ii) ($\supseteq$) Let P be a program that halts on all inputs. Let P_1 be P modified so as never to reject, as in the proof of Theorem 2(ii), and let P_2 be $\bar{P}$ modified so as never to reject, where $\bar{P}$ is the dual of P. Then P_1P_2 accepts all inputs and $\forall\bar{x}$, $\mathrm{TIME}(P,\bar{x}) \leq \mathrm{TIME}(P_1P_2,\bar{x})$. Let P_3 be the program which chooses the input universally by executing $y \leftarrow \forall$ for all input variables, then executes P_1P_2. Then $\mathrm{TIME}(P_3,\bar{x})$ is a constant β independent of the input, and $\forall\bar{x}$ $\mathrm{TIME}(P,\bar{x}) \leq \beta < \kappa^A$.

($\subseteq$) Let P be β-time bounded, $\beta<\kappa^A$. If we can construct an α-clock, $\beta<\alpha$, then it can be shuffled with P to give a program accepting the same set as P, but always halting. The result then follows from Theorem 2(ii). Since $\beta<\kappa^A$, there exists a program Q which runs for time $\alpha>\beta$ on some input $\bar{x}$. Let Q_1 assign $\bar{x}$ to all input variables, then run Q. Q_1 halts on all inputs in time exactly $\alpha+c$ and either accepts all inputs or rejects all inputs, so either Q_1 or $\bar{Q}_1$ gives an appropriate clock. □

6. An application to Dynamic Logic

The programming language IND originally arose in our attempt to clarify a result of Meyer & Parikh [MP] on the relative expressibility of four variants of first-order Dynamic Logic (DL), namely DL_{reg}, DL_{cf}, DL_{ft}, and DL_{re}. Programs of DL_{re} are all r.e. sets of sequences of assignments x:=t and tests $\varphi(\bar{x})$?, called seqs, where t is a term and φ a formula of DL_{re}. One obtains DL_{reg}, DL_{cf}, and DL_{ft} by allowing, respectively, only regular expressions or flowchart programs (so that the set of seqs is regular), recursion schemes (so that the set of seqs is context free), or r.e. sets of seqs, but each with at most finitely many distinct tests.

Meyer & Parikh prove that DL_{reg} is strictly less expressive than DL_{re} (in symbols, $DL_{reg}<DL_{re}$) by the following sequence:

$$(*) \qquad DL_{reg} \underset{ⓐ}{\leq} DL_{cf} \underset{ⓑ}{\leq} DL_{ft} \underset{ⓒ}{\leq} L_{ba} \underset{ⓓ}{<} L^{CK}_{\omega_1\omega} \underset{ⓔ}{\equiv} DL_{re}$$

where $L^{CK}_{\omega_1\omega}$ is infinitary first-order logic with r.e. disjunctions, and L_{ba} is the same language restricted to bounded quantifier alternation. The bulk of the proof is devoted to ⓓ, which uses an Ehrenfeucht-Frassé argument to show that L_{ba} cannot distinguish between the ordinals ω^{ω} and $\omega^{\omega}\cdot 2$, while $L^{CK}_{\omega_1\omega}$ can define any recursive ordinal up to isomorphism.

In this part of their paper, all resemblance to Dynamic Logic has been lost. This was taken as evidence in support of the stand that there is really nothing dynamic about Dynamic Logic, and one should do all one's work in infinitary logic [MT]. We disagree, and in fact find the main result of [MP] a bit misleading, for the simple reason that $L^{CK}_{\omega_1\omega}\equiv L_{ba}$ in virtually every structure arising in computer science (for example, the natural numbers, N, any recursively defined data type, or any structure whose elements are all named by closed terms). This is because every $L^{CK}_{\omega_1\omega}$ formula is equivalent to a quantifier-free formula, by replacing $\exists x\ \varphi(x)$ with $\bigvee_t \varphi(t)$, where the join is over the set of closed terms. One's intuition is still that $DL_{reg}<DL_{re}$, even restricted to such structures. Our results of this section show that $DL_{ft}<DL_{re}$ on any acceptable structure [Mo] (or arithmetic universe [H]). These structures contain a

first-order definable copy of the natural numbers and first-order predicates for coding and decoding sequences of elements into single elements. This allows assigning codes or Gödel numbers to programs and formulas so that they can be decoded and manipulated by other programs and formulas. The proof reveals the computational power of the various versions of DL in terms of the complexity classes $\tau(\alpha)$.

<u>Theorem 4</u> On any acceptable structure,

(i) $DL_{reg} \equiv DL_{cf} \equiv DL_{ft} \equiv \tau(\omega)$

(ii) $DL_{re} \equiv \tau(\omega_1^{CK})$

(iii) $\tau(\omega_1^{CK}) - \tau(\omega) \neq \emptyset$

where ω_1^{CK} is the first nonrecursive ordinal.

For example, on $\mathbb{N}$, whose closure ordinal is ω_1^{CK}, $DL_{re} \equiv \Delta_1^1$ and $DL_{ft} \equiv$ {first-order definable relations}. This follows from Theorems 3, 4 and Kleene's Theorem (Δ_1^1 = hyperelementary on $\mathbb{N}$).

<u>Proof</u> (i), (ii), ($\supseteq$) This direction does not need the assumption of acceptability. The case (i) follows from Theorem 3(i) and the fact that DL contains first-order logic. Similarly, on any structure A, $\tau(\omega_1^{CK}) < DL_{re}$, since if P is any IND program and α any recursive ordinal, there is a DL_{re}-formula φ_α such that

$$A \models \varphi_\alpha(c) \text{ iff } e^\alpha(c) = 1$$

for any configuration c, defined recursively by

$$\begin{aligned}
\varphi_0 &\leftrightarrow \underline{\text{false}} \\
\varphi_{\alpha+1}(c) &\leftrightarrow \text{stmt}(c) = \underline{\text{accept}} \\
&\quad \vee\ \text{stmt}(c) = y{\leftarrow}\exists \wedge \exists d{\in}N(c)\ \varphi_\alpha(d) \\
&\quad \vee\ \text{stmt}(c) = y{\leftarrow}\forall \wedge \forall d{\in}N(c)\ \varphi_\alpha(d) \\
&\quad \vee\ \text{stmt}(c) = \underline{\text{if}} \ldots \underline{\text{then}} \ldots \wedge \exists d{\in}N(c)\ \varphi_\alpha(d) \\
\varphi_\lambda &\leftrightarrow \langle\{\varphi_\alpha? \mid \alpha<\lambda\}\rangle\ \underline{\text{true}},\ \lambda \text{ a limit ordinal.}
\end{aligned}$$

The crucial point of this definition is that it is <u>effective</u>, in the sense that there is a recursive function r such that r('α')='φ_α', where 'α' and 'φ' denote codes for recursive ordinals and DL_{re} formulas. This fact is needed in the definition of φ to insure that the set $\{\varphi_\alpha? \mid \alpha<\lambda\}$ is r.e., so that φ_λ will be a DL_{re} formula. Now, if $A \in \tau(\omega_1^{CK})$, then A is accepted by an IND program P which is α-time bounded for some recursive ordinal α; thus for any input $\bar{a} \in A^k$,

$$P \text{ accepts } \bar{a} \leftrightarrow e^{\alpha}(\ell_1,\bar{a}) = 1 \leftrightarrow A\models\varphi_{\alpha}(\ell_1,\bar{a}).$$

Then $\varphi_\alpha(\ell_1,\bar{x})$ is a DL_{re} formula defining A.

(i), (ii), ($\subseteq$) We describe first an IND program to decide the satisfiability of DL_{re} formulas in A, consisting of a main program SATIS(p,x) and subroutine COMPUTE(q,x,y). SATIS('φ','$\bar{a}$') will determine if $A,\bar{a}\models\varphi$ and COMPUTE('π','$\bar{a}$','$\bar{b}$') will determine if state $\bar{a}$ goes to state $\bar{b}$ under program π, where '$\bar{a}$','$\bar{b}$' are codes of sequences $\bar{a},\bar{b}$ of elements of A, and 'φ' and 'π' are codes of a DL_{re} formula φ and a DL_{re} program π.

Initially, SATIS('φ','$\bar{a}$') assigns a code for the list of free variables of φ (available from 'φ') to a variable v, and assigns '$\bar{a}$' to w. This models the assignment of the values $\bar{a}$ to the list of variables in v, in the same order. It now proceeds by cases, depending on the form of φ. If $\varphi=\psi\wedge\sigma$, it uses the program construct $\wedge$ defined in Section 2 to check both ψ and σ, and similarly for $\vee,\neg$. If $\varphi=\exists y\psi$, it executes $z\leftarrow\exists$; then, if the DL_{re} variable y is in the list v, it modifies the corresponding value in the list w to the value of z; otherwise, it appends the name of y to the list v and the value of z to the list w. If $\varphi=\forall y\psi$ it does the same, using $z\leftarrow\forall$ instead of $z\leftarrow\exists$. If $\varphi=\langle\pi\rangle\psi$, since

$$A,\bar{a}\models\langle\pi\rangle\psi \text{ iff } \exists\bar{b}\ \bar{a} \text{ goes to } \bar{b} \text{ under } \pi \text{ and } A,\bar{b}\models\psi,$$

SATIS executes $z\leftarrow\exists$ and interprets the result as a code '$\bar{b}$'. It then calls SATIS('ψ','$\bar{b}$') and COMPUTE('π','$\bar{a}$','$\bar{b}$') in parallel, using $\wedge$.

Finally, if $\varphi=R(\bar{x})$ where $R(\bar{x})$ is atomic, it picks out the current values in the list w corresponding to DL_{re} variables $\bar{x}$ and assigns them to IND variables $\bar{y}$, then executes

<u>if</u> R($\bar{y}$) <u>then</u> <u>accept</u> <u>else</u> <u>reject</u>.

COMPUTE('π','$\bar{a}$','$\bar{b}$') determines whether state $\bar{a}$ goes to state $\bar{b}$ under DL_{re} program π. Recall that a program π consists of an r.e. set of seqs; each seq is a finite sequence $s_0;\ldots;s_{k-1}$ for some k; and each s_i is either an assignment y:=t or a test φ?. The code 'π' gives a Gödel number for the set of seqs, and $\bar{a}$ goes to $\bar{b}$ under π iff $\bar{a}$ goes to $\bar{b}$ under some seq of π. COMPUTE chooses a seq existentially using $i\leftarrow\exists$, and then tries to determine if the i'th seq of π, say $seq_i=s_0;\ldots;s_{k-1}$, takes $\bar{a}$ to $\bar{b}$. It could do this by starting from $\bar{a}_0=\bar{a}$, deterministically applying $s_0,s_1,\ldots,s_{k-1}$ in succession to get a sequence $\bar{a}_1,\ldots,\bar{a}_k$ of intermediate states, and accepting if $\bar{a}_k=\bar{b}$. However, for a later application, it will be better to keep COMPUTE loop-free. Thus, the program instead guesses a code for the entire sequence $\bar{a}_0,\bar{a}_1,\ldots,\bar{a}_k$ with a single $z\leftarrow\exists$, and then determines whether s_j takes $\bar{a}_j$ to $\bar{a}_{j+1}$, $0\leq j<k$, by executing

$j \leftarrow \forall$; if j is not the code for a natural number < k then accept; check if s_j takes $\bar{a}_j$ to $\bar{a}_{j+1}$. For s_j of the form y:=t, the check is straightforward. For s_j of the form $\psi?$, the program checks whether $\bar{a}_j = \bar{a}_{j+1}$, then whether $A, \bar{a}_j \models \psi$ by a recursive call to SATIS.

Holding 'φ' fixed, SATIS('φ','ā') accepts (the codes of) the set defined by φ. The theorem is now proved by analyzing the time complexity of SATIS and COMPUTE on fixed φ. All encoding and decoding operations can be done without loops, since they are first-order definable. The choice of seq_i in COMPUTE can be done without a loop since π is r.e. and thus first-order definable. We were careful to avoid loops in the processing of a seq in COMPUTE. Thus each iteration of SATIS and COMPUTE takes constant time before it recurs on a subformula; therefore there is a constant c such that

$$\forall \bar{a}\ \mathrm{TIME}(\mathrm{SATIS}('\varphi','\bar{a}')) \leq c \cdot h(\varphi)$$

where h(φ) is the <u>height</u> of φ, defined by:

$$\begin{aligned}
h(\varphi) &= 1,\ \varphi \text{ atomic},\\
h(\varphi \vee \psi) &= h(\varphi \wedge \psi) = \max\{h(\varphi), h(\psi)\} + 1,\\
h(\forall x \varphi) &= h(\exists x \varphi) = h(\neg\varphi) = h(\varphi) + 1,\\
h(\langle\pi\rangle\varphi) &= \max\{h(\pi), h(\varphi)\} + 1,\\
h(\pi) &= \sup\{h(\sigma) \mid \sigma \text{ a seq of } \pi\} + 1,\\
h(\sigma) &= \sup\{h(\varphi) \mid \varphi? \text{ a test of } \sigma\} + 1,\ \sigma \text{ a seq.}
\end{aligned}$$

Thus it remains to show that

$$\begin{aligned}
h(\varphi) &< \omega_1^{CK}, \quad \varphi \text{ in } DL_{re},\\
h(\varphi) &< \omega \quad\ \ , \quad \varphi \text{ in } DL_{ft}.
\end{aligned}$$

The former follows from the fact that there is a recursive code 'φ' for each φ in DL_{re}, and h is effective with respect to this code. The latter follows from the fact that the suprema in the definition of h(π) and h(σ) are finite, since there are only finitely many tests.

(iii) This is a straightforward diagonalization. Construct an IND program P which, on input 'φ(x)', φ(x) a first-order formula with one free variable x, accepts iff ¬φ('φ'). P runs for time $c \cdot h(\varphi) < \omega$, so the set it accepts is in $\tau(\omega+1) \subseteq \tau(\omega_1^{CK})$, and not in $\tau(\omega)$ = {first-order-definable sets} for obvious reasons. □

7. IND as a Data Base Query Language

There has been much recent work in the theory of relational data bases. In the relational model, a data base is a collection of finite tables [C1] and can be viewed simply as a finite first-order structure $B=(D,R_1,\ldots,R_k)$. Queries are (partial) functions from data bases to relations, and a query language is a set of formal expressions defining such functions; see [CH1].

In [C2] Codd introduced the languages of the relational algebra and calculus, which are equivalent in expressive power. The latter is essentially the first order language of similarity type $(=, R_1,\ldots,R_k)$. In [AU] it was pointed out that many useful queries definable naturally by least fixpoints of first-order formulas, such as the transitive closure of a binary relation, are not first-order-definable, and it was suggested therein that the first-order language of [C2] be augmented with an appropriate least fixpoint operator. In such a language the transitive closure of R would be the least fixpoint S of $S=R\cup R\circ S$, where $\circ$ is relational composition. A formal version of such an extension was subsequently supplied in [CH2], where fixpoint operators were allowed to alternate with any number of first-order constructs. A hierarchy of height ω^2 of sets of queries is defined in [CH2], in which those queries at level $\omega\cdot i$ are obtained by applying a least fixpoint operator to queries at lower levels. The set of queries constituting the entire hierarchy is termed FP, for <u>fixpoint queries</u>.

It is shown in [CH2] that FP is a very restricted subset of the set of all computable queries [CH1]; in particular, all queries in FP are polynomial-time computable. There is also a close correspondence with the queries definable by Kowalski's logic programs; see [K, GM, CH3]. However, it was left as an open problem in [CH2] whether there is a natural computational query language for defining the fixpoint queries.

At this point, one observes that the least fixpoint operator as defined in [AU, CH2] corresponds exactly to an inductive definition as defined in [Mo], so that a single fixpoint operator applied to a first-order formula corresponds to a first-order inductive definition. Recently, however, Immerman [I] has shown that the hierarchy of fixpoint queries in fact collapses down to level ω. In other words, all queries in FP are definable by a single application of a fixpoint operator to a first-order formula. Hence, we obtain:

<u>Lemma</u> A relational function on finite structures is in FP iff it is uniformly first-order inductively definable (i.e., there is a single first-order inductive definition which, given the input structure, defines the output relation).

Theorem IND defines precisely the fixpoint queries on relational data bases.

We might remark that the $x \leftarrow \forall$ statement of IND and the parallel method of execution implied by its semantics reminds one of the "for all tuples t in relation R" construct used in some real query language with parallel execution semantics; see [AU, section 7]. It remains to be seen whether a rigorous definition of the semantics of such a language, together with the dual "for some tuple t in R", yields a language equivalent to IND.

References

[AU] Aho, A.V. and J.D. Ullman, Universality of data retrieval languages. *Proc. 6th ACM Symp. on Principles of Programming Languages*, Jan. 1979, 110-117.

[AP] Apt, K. and G. Plotkin, A Cook's Tour of Countable Nondeterminism, ICALP '81.

[B] Barwise, J. *Admissible Sets & Structures*. Springer-Verlag 1975.

[CH1] Chandra, A.K. and D. Harel, Computable queries for relational data bases. *JCSS 21*; 2, Oct. 1980.

[CH2] Chandra, A.K. and D. Harel, Structure and Complexity of Relational Queries, *Proc. 21st IEEE Symp. on Foundations of Computer Science*, Oct. 1980, 333-347.

[CH3] Chandra, A.K. and D. Harel, Horn clauses and the fixpoint query hierarchy. *SIGACT-SIGMOD Symp. on Principles of Data Base Systems*, March, 1982.

[CKS] Chandra, A.K., D. Kozen and L. Stockmeyer, Alternation, *J. ACM*, Jan. 1981.

[C1] Codd, E.F., A relational model for large shared data bases. *CACM 13*; 6, June 1970.

[C2] Codd, E.F., Relational completeness of data base sublanguages. In *Data Base Systems* (Rustin, ed.), Prentice Hall, 1972.

[C] Cook, S.A. Soundness and Completeness of an Axiom System for Program Verification, *SIAM J. on Computing 7*; 1, (1978).

[GM] Gallaire, H. and J. Minker (eds.), *Logic and Data Bases*, Plenum, New York (1978).

[GFMR] Grumberg, Francez, Makowsky and de Roever, A Proof Rule for fair Termination of Guarded Commands, Technion Tech. Report #197, Feb. 1981.

[H] Harel, D. *First-Order Dynamic Logic*. Lecture Notes in Computer Science 68, Springer-Verlag 1979.

[I] Immerman, N. Relational queries computable in polynomial ti,e. *14th ACM Symp. on Theory of Computing*, May 1982.

[K] Kowalski, R.A. Predicate logic as a programming language. *Proc. IFIP74*, North-Holland 1974, 556-574.

[LPS] Lehman, D., A. Pnueli and J. Stavi, Impartiality, Justice and Fairness: The Ethics of Concurrent Termination, ICALP '81.

[MT] Meyer, A.R. and J. Tiuryn, A Note of Equivalences Among Logics of Programs. *Proc. Workshop on Logics of Programs 1981*, Lecture Notes in Computer Science 131, Springer-Verlag, 282-299.

[MP] Meyer, A.R. and R. Parikh, Definability in Dynamic Logic, *Proc. 12th ACM Symp. on Theory of Computing* (1980), 1-8.

[MW] Meyer, A.R. and K. Winkelmann, On the Expressive Power of Dynamic Logic, *Proc. 12th ACM Symp. on Theory of Computing* (1979), 167-175.

[Mi] Mirkowska, G. On Formalized Systems of Algorithmic Logic, Bull. Acad. Pol. Sci., Ser. Math. Astr. Phys. *22* (1974), 421-428.

[Mo] Moschovakis, Y.N. *Elementary Induction on Abstract Structures*, North-Holland, 1974.

[Pr] Pratt, V. Semantical Considerations on Floyd-Hoare Logic. *Proc. 17th IEEE Symp. on Found. of Comp. Science* (1976), 109-121.

[T] Tiuryn, J. Unbounded Program Memory adds to the Expressive Power of First-Order Dynamic Logic, *Proc. 22nd IEEE Symp. on Found. of Comp. Science* (1981).

A Lower Bound for the Formula Size of Rational Functions

K.A. Kalorkoti
Department of Computer Science
Edinburgh University
Edinburgh, EH9 3JZ.

1. Introduction

In this paper we provide a method for bounding from below the formula size of rational functions over arbitrary fields. The basic operations allowed are addition, subtraction, multiplication and division. The method is based on Nečiporuk [4] (also followed in Savage [5]). It is quite easy to adapt his argument if the field is finite. Also if attention is restricted to polynomials over infinite fields and division is not allowed then there is again a fairly easy adaptation. As one would expect the general case presents some difficulties in connection with division. These are overcome by the use of formal power series.

The results are used to show that the $n \times n$ determinant has formula size at least $\Omega(n^3)$. We thus have an algebraic analogue to the $\Omega(n^3)$ lower bound for the Boolean determinant due to Kloss [3].

II. Preliminaries

Throughout k will be a field and, unless otherwise stated, X,Y,Z will be finite sets of indeterminates over k with $X \cap Y = X \cap Z = \emptyset$.

Definition. A formula of $k(X)$ is any expression obtained by using the following rules a finite number of times:

(a) w is a formula where $w \in k \cup X$.

(b) $(f_1 \circ f_2)$ is a formula where f_1, f_2 are formulae and $\circ \in \{+,-,\times,/\}$.

The size of a formula f, denoted by $L(f)$, is the number of times rule (b) is used in its construction. The formula f can be reduced to give a numerator and a denominator, both of these being polynomials. If the denominator is non-zero then f corresponds to a rational expression, i.e. an element of $k(X)$. Given $r \in k(X)$ the formula size of r, denoted by $L(r)$, is the size of a minimal formula for r.

Remark We often want to regard an element r of $k(X)$ as a rational function from $k^{|X|}$ into k. In this case a formula f is also regarded as a (partial) function and we say that f is a formula for r if and only if it is equal to r as a partial function. The formula size of the rational function r is denoted by $L^*(r)$. For infinite fields we have $L^*(r) \geq L(r)$ since two rational expressions are equal as elements of $k(X)$ whenever they are equal as rational functions. The situation is different for finite fields; for example $x^2 + x$ and 0 are distinct in $GF(2)(x)$ but are equal as functions over $GF(2)$. Thus $L(x^2 + x) > 0$ while $L^*(x^2 + x) = 0$. The first theorem we prove gives a lower bound for L over all fields k and hence for L^* when k is infinite. The second theorem provides a lower bound for L^* when k is finite. From now on elements of $k(X)$ will be thought of as formal rational expressions and not as functions, unless otherwise stated.

A computation tree T is a rooted directed tree with its edges directed away from the leaves and towards the root. The leaves are labelled with indeterminites or elements of k. If v is any other vertex of indegree d then v is labelled with a function form $k(X)^d$ to $k(X)$. Such vertices are called computation vertices and the number of them is denoted by $C(T)$. Given a formula f we can associate a computation tree T with f in the usual way. T has indegree 2 and each computation vertex is labelled with $+,-,\times$ or $/$. Moreover $C(T) = L(f)$. The following is well known and easy to prove:

1. Lemma Suppose T has l leaves and indegree d. Then $C(T) \geq (l-1)/(d-1)$.//

Let $k[[X]]$ be the ring of formal power series in X over k. The elements of $k[[X]]$ are expressions of the type

$$f = \sum_{i=0}^{\infty} f_i$$

where f_i is either 0 or a form in X of degree i. Addition and multiplication in $k[[X]]$ are carried out in the obvious manner. The order of f, denoted by $\mathrm{ord}(f)$, is the least i such that $f_i \neq 0$ if $f \neq 0$, and ∞ otherwise. Clearly, the polynomial ring $k[X]$ is embedded in $k[[X]]$.

Suppose $r \in k(X)$ and we want a lower bound to its formula size. It will be convenient for us to expand r as a formal power series. This, however, is not always possible. Fortunately, for our purposes, there is little loss in restricting attention to those elements of $k(X)$ which can be so expanded. We proceed to describe the set of all such elements more formally.

It is easy to show that f is a unit in $k[[X]]$ (i.e. there is a g such that $fg = 1$) if and only if $\mathrm{ord}(f) = 0$. (All results which are used here without proof will be found in Zariski-Samuel [6, Vol.II].) Let

$$k^u(X) = \{r \in k(X) \mid \exists p,q \in k[X] \text{ s.t. } r = p/q \text{ and } q \text{ is a unit in } k[[X]]\}.$$

Clearly $k^u(X)$ is a subring of $k(X)$. Define

$$P_X : k^u(X) \longrightarrow k[[X]]$$

as follows: given $r \in k^u(X)$ let $r = p/q$ where q is a unit in $k[[X]]$ with inverse q^{-1}. Then $P_X(r) = pq^{-1}$. Easily, P_X is well defined and is in fact an 1 - 1 homomorphism, i.e. an embedding.

Definition A substitution of $k[[Y]]$ into $k[[Z]]$ consists of:

(a) a function $\sigma : Y \longrightarrow k[Z]$ such that $\mathrm{ord}(\sigma(y)) > 0$ for all $y \in Y$.

(b) The unique extension of σ to a homomorphism $k[[Y]] \longrightarrow k[[Z]]$ given by

$$f^{\sigma}(y_1,\ldots,y_n) = f(\sigma(y_1),\ldots,\sigma(y_n)).$$

(See Zariski-Samuel [6, Vol II, p135] where a wider class of substitutions is allowed.)

Let $W \subseteq Y \cap Z$. Then σ is said to respect W if $\sigma(w) = w$ for all $w \in W$. Given $f \in k[[X,Y]]$ and $g \in k[[X,Z]]$ we say that f represents g with respect to X if there exists a substitution σ which respects X such that $f^{\sigma} = g$. If $r = p/q \in k^u(X,Y)$ and q is a unit in $k[[X,Y]]$ then we put $r^{\sigma} = p^{\sigma}/q^{\sigma}$. Note that q a unit implies $\mathrm{ord}(q) = 0$ which implies $q^{\sigma} \neq 0$. Moreover r is well defined.

2. Lemma Let $r \in k^u(Y)$ and σ a substitution of $k[[Y]]$ into $k[[Z]]$. Then $P_Y(r)^{\sigma} = P_Z(r^{\sigma})$.

Proof Let $r = p/q$ where q is a unit in $k[[Y]]$. Then, recalling that σ is a homomorphism, we have:

$$\begin{aligned} 1^{\sigma} = 1 &\iff (q^{-1}q)^{\sigma} = 1 \\ &\iff (q^{-1})^{\sigma}q^{\sigma} = 1 \\ &\iff (q^{-1})^{\sigma} = (q^{\sigma})^{-1} \\ &\iff p^{\sigma}(q^{-1})^{\sigma} = p^{\sigma}(q^{\sigma})^{-1} \\ &\iff P_Y(r)^{\sigma} = P_Z(r^{\sigma}). // \end{aligned}$$

Suppose f and g are as above and f represents g with respect to X. We would like to have a lower bound for $|Y|$ in terms of g; the reason for this will become clear in §III. If f and g were both polynomials they could be regarded as polynomials in X with coefficients in $k[Y]$ and $k[Z]$ respectively. Furthermore they could be written uniquely as

$$f = \sum_{i=0}^{a} f_i(Y)\, M_i(X),$$

$$g = \sum_{i=0}^{b} g_i(Z)\, M_i(X),$$

where $a = \deg(f)$, $b = \deg(g)$ (these being with respect to X) and the $M_i(X)$ are distinct monomials in X.

(Elements $s_1,\ldots,s_n$ of $k(Y)$ are said to be algebraically independent over k if the only polynomial P with coefficients in k such that $P(s_1,\ldots,s_n) = 0$ is the zero polynomial. The transcendence degree over k of a subset S of $k(Y)$ is the maximum number of algebraically independent elements (over k) of S. This number is at most $|Y|$. (In this paper transcendence degrees will always be over k. In view of this we shall henceforth omit the phrase "over k" and use the abbreviation tr.d.S.) The concept is analogous to dimension in vector spaces. Further material will be found in Zariski-Samuel [6, Vol.II].)

Define $td_X(g)$ to be $\text{tr.d.}\{g_0,\dots,g_b\}$. Now $f^\sigma = g$ if and only if $f_i^\sigma = g_i$ for $0 \le u \le b$ and $f_i^\sigma = 0$ for $b < i \le a$. It follows from this that

$$\text{tr.d.}\{f_0,\dots,f_a\} \ge \text{tr.d.}\{g_0,\dots,g_b\}.$$

But

$$|Y| \ge \text{tr.d. } k[Y] \qquad (*)$$
$$\ge \text{tr.d.}\{f_0,\dots,f_a\}$$

Thus $|Y| \ge td_X(g)$.

Unfortunately the inequality (*) is false if $k[Y]$ is replaced by $k[[Y]]$ (indeed if $|Y| > 1$ then $k[[Y]]$ contains infinitely many algebraically independent elements). The next two definitions and lemmas translate the above idea to formal power series in such a way as to avoid the stated difficulty.

Definition Let $f_i \in k[[Y]],\ i \in I$, where $f_i = \sum_{j=0}^{\infty} f_{ij}$. Let $m_f = \min_{i \in I} \text{ord}(f_i)$ if some $f_i \neq 0$ and 0 otherwise. Then we define

$$td\{f_i \mid i \in I\} = \text{tr.d.}\{f_{im_f} \mid i \in I\}.$$

Note that this is always at most $|Y|$.

If $r_i \in k^u(Y),\ i \in I$, then put

$$td\{r_i \mid i \in I\} = td\{P_Y(r_i) \mid i \in I\}.$$

3. Lemma Let $f_i \in k[[Y]],\ i \in I$, and $g_i \in k[[Z]],\ i \in I$. Suppose there exists a substitution σ such that $f_i^\sigma = g_i$ for all $i \in I$. Then $|Y| \ge td\{g_i \mid i \in I\}$.

Proof Let $Y = \{y_1,\dots,y_s\}$ and $Z = \{z_1,\dots,z_t\}$. Put

$$f_i' = \sum_{j=0}^{m} f_{ij}$$

where $m = m_g$. Then, for all $i \in I$,

$$f_i'(\sigma(y_1),\dots,\sigma(y_s)) = g_{im}(z_1,\dots,z_t) + h_i(z_1,\dots,z_t)$$

where $\text{ord}(h_i) > m$. We claim that:

$$\text{tr.d.}\{f_i' \mid i \in I\} \ge \text{tr.d.}\{g_{im} \mid i \in I\}.$$

For suppose P is a non-zero polynomial such that

$$P(f_{i_1}',\dots,f_{i_r}') = 0,\ i_1,\dots,i_r \in I.$$

Let $P = H + G$ where H is the homogeneous part of P of lowest degree. It easily follows that

$$H(g_{i_1m} + h_{i_1},\dots,g_{i_rm} + h_{i_r}) = 0.$$

Now the left-hand side can be written as $H(g_{i_1m},\ldots,g_{i_rm}) + Q$ where each term in Q is of degree greater than any non-zero term in $H(g_{i_1m},\ldots,g_{i_rm})$, the degree being with respect to Z. Thus $H(g_{i_1m},\ldots,g_{i_rm}) = 0$ and the claim follows.

The result is now proved since $|Y| \geq \text{tr.d.}\{f_i' \mid i \in I\}$.//

Let $f \in k[[X,Y]]$ and $g \in k[[X,Z]]$ and suppose there exists a substitution σ which respects X such that $f^\sigma = g$. We can regard f and g as elements of $k[[Y]][[X]]$ and $k[[Z]][[X]]$ respectively. Thus f can be written uniquely as

$$f = \sum_{i=0}^{\infty} f_i(X)$$

where $f_i(X) \in k[[Y]][X]$ and is either 0 or a form of degree i (with respect to X). Let $\{M_{ij}(X) \mid 0 \leq j \leq s_i\}$ be the set of all monomials in X of degree i. Then $f_i(X)$ can be written uniquely as

$$f_i(X) = \sum_{j=0}^{s_i} f_{ij}(Y)M_{ij}(X)$$

where $f_{ij}(Y) \in k[[Y]]$. Similarly for g.

Note that $f^\sigma = g$ if and only if $f_{ij}^{\sigma} = g_{ij}$ for $i \geq 0$ and $0 \leq j \leq s_i$.

<u>Definition</u> $td_X(g) = \max\{td\ S \mid S \subseteq \{g_{ij} \mid i \geq 0,\ 0 \leq j \leq s_i\}\}$

From the above remarks and (3) we have

4. <u>Lemma</u> Let f and g be as above. If f represents g with respect to X then $|Y| \geq td_X(g)$.//

We now look at the effect of restricting attention from $k(X)$ to $k^u(X)$.

<u>Definition</u> Let $r(x_1,\ldots,x_n) \in k(X)$ and $\alpha_1,\ldots,\alpha_n \in k$. Then we call $r(x_1 - \alpha_1,\ldots,x_n - \alpha_n)$ the <u>translate</u> of g by $\alpha_1,\ldots,\alpha_n$.

It is easily seen that if k is infinite then each $r \in k(X)$ has a translate $s \in k^u(X)$. The following is easy to prove:

5. <u>Lemma</u> Let $r,s \in k(X)$ with s a translate of r. Then $L(r) \geq \frac{1}{2}(L(s)-1)$.//

III <u>The Results</u>

6. <u>Theorem</u> Let $f \in k(X)$ and $X_1,\ldots,X_t$ be a partition of X. Suppose f has a translate $g \in k^u(X)$. Then

$$L(f) \geq \frac{1}{46} \sum_{i=1}^{t} td_{X_i}(g).$$

Proof Let T be the tree of a minimal formula for g, l_i the number of leaves of T with a label from X_i and $l = \sum_{i=1}^{t} l_i$. Then by (1),

$$C(T) \geq l-1 \qquad (*).$$

Fix i and call an indeterminate in X_i fixed and one which is not in X_i free. For this proof a subtree of T is any vertex of T together with all of its predecessor vertices and edges.

Note that if a subtree has no fixed indeterminates then it computes a rational expression of form $(p+a)/(q+b)$ where p,q are polynomials in free indeterminates of order greater than 0 and $a,b \in k$. If a subtree has exactly one leaf labelled with a fixed indeterminate then it computes an expression of form $(px + cx + p' + c')/(qx + dx + q' + d')$ where p,p',q,q' are polynomials in free indeterminates of order greater than 0 and $c,c',d,d' \in k$. We shall call a,b and c,c',d,d' the constants of the two subtrees.

Starting with T, apply the following transformations as many times as possible.

(a) If a subtree has no fixed indeterminates contract it to a single computation vertex attached to four new leaves. The leaves are labelled with two new free indeterminates z_1, z_2 and the constants a,b of the original subtree. The computation vertex is labelled with $(z_1 + a)/(z_2 + b)$.

(b) If a subtree has exactly one leaf labelled with a fixed indeterminate x contract it to a single computation vertex attached to nine new leaves. The leaves are labelled with x, four new free indeterminates z_1,z_2,z_3,z_4 and the constants a,b,c,d of the original subtree. The computation vertex is labelled with $(z_1x + ax + z_2 + b)/(z_3x + cx + z_4 + d)$.

Let T_i be the tree thus obtained and Z_i the set of free indeterminates in T_i. The tree T_i computes an expression $g_i \in k(X_i,Z_i)$. By induction on the number of steps (a) and (b) used it is easily seen that g_i represents g with respect to X_i and in fact $g_i \in k^u(X_i,Z_i)$. Thus, by (4),

$$|Z_i| \geq td_{X_i}(g) \qquad (**).$$

Let c_0,c_1,c_2 be the number of computation vertices that are roots of full subtrees of T_i with zero, one and more than one fixed indeterminates respectively. Note that any computation vertex with at least two fixed indeterminates is unaffected by the transformations and so it still has indegree 2. Now because of transformations (a) and (b) we have $c_0 \leq c_2 + 1$ and $c_1 \leq l_i$. Also $c_2 \leq l_i - 1$ by induction on c_2. Thus

$$C(T_i) = c_0 + c_1 + c_2 \leq 3l_i - 1.$$

But, by (1),

$$C(T_i) \geq \frac{l_i + |Z_i| - 1}{8}$$

and so

$$l_i \geq \frac{|Z_i| + 7}{23}$$

$$> \frac{1}{23} td_{X_i}(g) \quad , \text{ by } (**).$$

This with (*) gives

$$L(g) = C(T) > \frac{1}{23} \sum_{i=1}^{t} td_{X_i}(g) - 1$$

and the result follows from (5).//

Remark If $f \in k^u(X)$ then the above proof shows that $L(f) \geq \frac{1}{23} \sum_{i=1}^{t} td_{X_i}(f)$.

We now deal with functions over finite fields. Let $X = \{x_1,\ldots,x_n\}$ be a set of variables over k and $W \subseteq X$.

Definition A substitution of X parallel to $X - W$ is a function $\sigma: X \longrightarrow k \cup X$ such that $\sigma(x) = x$ for all $x \notin W$ and $\sigma(x) \in k$ for all $x \in W$.

If $f(x_1,\ldots,x_n) : k^n \longrightarrow k$ we put

$$f^\sigma(x_1,\ldots,x_n) = f(\sigma(x_1),\ldots,\sigma(x_n))$$

and call f^σ a W-specialization of f. Put

$$sp_{X-W}(f) = \#(\text{distinct W-specializations of } f).$$

A few simple changes to the proof (6) now yield.

7. Theorem Let $f(x_1,\ldots,x_n) : k^n \longrightarrow k$ and $X_1,\ldots,X_t$ be a partition of X. Then

$$L^*(f) \geq \frac{1}{7} \sum_{i=1}^{t} \log_d sp_{X_i}(f)$$

where $d = |k|$.//

Remark Neither of the bounds of (6) and (7) can grow faster than $|X|^2$. This is an inherent limitation of Nečiporuk's method. An expression which achieves this order of growth for (6) is

$$u = \sum_{i=1}^{n} \sum_{j=i+1}^{n} x_j \, x_i^{j-1}.$$

To see this take $X_i = \{x_i\}$ and note that

$$td_{X_i}(u) \geq \text{tr.d. } \{x_{i+1}, \ldots, x_n\} = n-i.$$

Thus

$$L(u) \geq \frac{1}{23} \sum_{i=1}^{n} (n-i) = \Omega(n^2).$$

It follows that for infinite fields we have $L^*(u) \geq \Omega(n^2)$.

IV. An Application

Let $M = (x_{ij})_{n \times n}$ where the x_{ij} are indeterminates over k. Define $\det M \in k^u(x_{11}, x_{12}, \ldots, x_{nn})$ by

$$\det M = \sum_{\sigma \in S_n} (-1)^{s(\sigma)} \prod_{i=1}^{n} x_{i,i\sigma}$$

where $s(\sigma)$ is 0 or 1 according as σ is even or odd.

8. Proposition $L(\det M) \geq \Omega(n^3)$

Proof Apply (6) by putting $X_i = \{x_{1i}, x_{2i+1}, \ldots, x_{n\ i+n-1}\}$ all indices being taken modulo n. We claim that $td_{X_i}(\det M) \geq \frac{1}{2}n(n-1)$. By symmetry it suffices to show this for $i = 1$.

Let $d_{ij} = x_{11} \ldots \hat{x}_{ii} \ldots \hat{x}_{jj} \ldots x_{nn}$ for $1 \leq i < j \leq n$, where ^ denotes a missing term. In det M there are $\frac{1}{2}n(n-1)$ distinct terms d_{ij}. Moreover the coefficient of d_{ij} is $x_{ij}x_{ji}$. The claim now follows. Thus

$$L(\det M) \geq \frac{1}{23} \sum_{1}^{n} \tfrac{1}{2}n(n-1) = \Omega(n^3). //$$

10. Proposition Let k be a finite field and $\det : k^{n^2} \to k$ the determinant function. Then

$$L^*(\det) \geq \Omega(n^3).$$

Proof Partition the variables as in (8). By a trivial adaptation of the lemma in Kloss [3] (also followed in Savage [5, p. 105]) we have $sp_{X_i}(\det) \geq |k|^{\frac{1}{2}n(n-1)}$ for each i. The result now follows from (7).//

Putting (8) and (9) together we have:

10. Theorem Let k be any field and $\det : k^{n^2} \to k$ the determinant function. Then

$$L^*(\det) \geq \Omega(n^3). //$$

We finish by remarking that the best known upper bound for L*(det) is $O(n^{\log n})$ obtained by Csanky [1] and Hyafil [2].

Acknowledgement

I should like to thank Dr. L.G. Valiant for suggesting the above area of research to me and Dr. S. Skyum for his helpful comments on a preliminary draft of this paper.

References

[1] L. CSANKY. Fast parallel inversion algorithms. SIAM J. on Computing, Vol. 5, No. 4 (1976), 618-623.

[2] L. HYAFIL. On the parallel evaluation of multivariate polynomials. Proc. Tenth ACM Symp. on Theory of Computing (1978), 193-195.

[3] B.M. KLOSS. Estimates of the complexity of solutions of systems of linear equations. Dokl. Akad. Nauk. SSSR, Vol. 171, No. 4 (1966), pp. 781-783. Sov. Math. Dokl., Vol. 7, No. 6 (1966), pp. 1537-1540.

[4] È.I. NEČIPORUK. A Boolean function. Dokl. Akad. Nauk. SSSR, Vol. 169, No. 4 (1966), pp. 765-766. Sov. Math. Dokl., Vol. 7, No. 4 (1966), pp. 999-1000.

[5] J.E. SAVAGE. The complexity of computing. Wiley, New York (1976).

[6] O. ZARISKI and P. SAMUEL. Commutative Algebra. Van Nostrand, Princeton, N.J. (1958) (2 volumes).

ON THE EQUIVALENCE PROBLEM FOR BINARY DOL SYSTEMS

Juhani Karhumäki
Department of Mathematics
University of Turku
Turku, Finland

ABSTRACT

It is shown that to test whether two DOL sequences in the binary case coincide it is enough to test whether four first words of these sequences are the same. The result is optimal.

1. INTRODUCTION

During several years the DOL equivalence problem was one of the most interesting open problems within the theory of formal languages. The problem is as follows. Given two morphisms h and g of a finitely generated free monoid Σ^* and an element ω of Σ^*. Does there exist an algorithm to decide whether or not the equation $h^n(\omega) = g^n(\omega)$ holds true for all $n \geq 0$?

The problem was solved positively by Culik and Fris (1977). Later a shorter proof was given by Ehrenfeucht and Rozenberg (1978).Moreover, from the arguments of Ehrenfeucht and Rozenberg (1978) it was deduced in Ehrenfeucht and Rozenberg (1980) an explicit bound n_0 depending on the two systems such that if the two sequences coincide up to the level n_0 then they will coincide for ever.

There are no known examples of two nonequivalent DOL systems such that their sequences would differ from each other for first time "far" from the beginning. This situation has led to the following <u>2n-conjecture</u>, see Salomaa (1978b): For two DOL systems over an n-letter alphabet, to test the equivalence of these systems it is enough to test whether 2n first words of the sequences are the same.

It is known that 2n would be close to optimal. Indeed, there are examples showing that $[3/2\ n]$ is not enough. The gap between the n_0 given in Ehrenfeucht and Rozenberg (1980) and 2n is huge.

Our purpose here is to fill this gap in the case of binary DOL systems. We shall prove the 2n-conjecture in this case. It follows from the known example, see Nielsen (1974), that our bound is optimal. Our proof is based on a characterization of equality languages of binary morphisms given in Ehrenfeucht et.al. (1981).

Our approach gives also solutions to some related problems concerning DOL and DTOL systems. For instance, we show that the 2n-conjecture, interpreted in a natural way, holds true for DTOL systems over the binary alphabet, too.

2. PRELIMINARIES

In this note we need only very basic terminology of the theory of formal languages and the theory of free monoids. For few unexplained notions we refer to Harrison (1978). More background material concerning DOL systems can be found in Rozenberg and Salomaa (1980).

A free monoid generated by a finite alphabet Σ is denoted by Σ^* and its identity, so-called empty word, by λ. Elements of Σ^* are words. For a word x the notation $|x|$ denotes its length and the notation $\mathrm{pref}_k(x)$, for $k \geq 1$, its prefix of the length k. If $|x| < k$ we set $\mathrm{pref}_k(x) = x$. For a word x in Σ^* and a letter c in Σ, $\#_c(x)$ denotes the number of c's in x. In the case of the binary alphabet $\{0,1\}$ the <u>ratio</u> $r(x)$ of a nonempty word x is defined as $\#_0(x) : \#_1(x)$. We call such a word <u>ratio-primitive</u> if none of its prefixes has the same ratio as the whole word. By a <u>primitive</u> word we mean, as usual, a nonempty word x which is not a proper power of any word, i.e. the relation $x = z^n$ implies that $x = z$ and $n = 1$. Finally, for two words x and y the notation $x^{-1}y$ (resp. yx^{-1}) is used to denote the left (resp. right) quotient of y by x.

A <u>DOL system</u> is a triple (Σ,h,ω) where Σ is a finite alphabet, h is a morphism from Σ^* into itself and ω is a nonempty word of Σ^*. A DOL system $G = (\Sigma,h,\omega)$ defines the sequence

$$\omega, h(\omega), h^2(\omega), \ldots$$

Such a sequence (resp. set of words) is called a <u>DOL sequence</u> (resp. <u>DOL language</u>) or a <u>DOL sequence</u> (resp. <u>DOL language</u>) <u>generated by G</u>. We call two DOL systems <u>equivalent</u> if they generate the same DOL sequence. The <u>DOL sequence equivalence problem</u> is the problem of whether there exists or not an algorithm to decide the equivalence of two given DOL systems.

In this paper we consider only the case when Σ is binary, say $\{0,1\}$. We call a morphism h <u>periodic</u> if there exists a word p such that $h(\Sigma) \subseteq p^*$. The set $\{\alpha,\beta\}$ of two words is called <u>marked</u> if $\mathrm{pref}_1(\alpha) \neq \mathrm{pref}_1(\beta)$. Let h be a nonperiodic morphism on $\{0,1\}^*$. It is well known that $h(01) \neq h(10)$. Let z_h be the maximal common prefix of

$h(01)$ and $h(10)$. Consequently, $|z_h| < |h(01)|$. Now the following result is easy to see.

LEMMA 1. For any word $x \in \Sigma^* 0 \Sigma^* \cap \Sigma^* 1 \Sigma^*$, $h(x)$ has the prefix z_h. For any two words x and y such that $x,y \in \Sigma^* 0 \Sigma^* \cap \Sigma^* 1 \Sigma^*$ and $pref_1(x) \neq pref_1(y)$, $pref_{|z_h|+1}(h(x)) \neq pref_{|z_h|+1}(h(y))$.

Let h and g be two morphisms on Σ^*. Following Salomaa (1978a) we define the equality set of the pair (h,g), in symbols $E(h,g)$, by

$$E(h,g) = \{x \in \Sigma^* \mid h(x) = g(x)\} .$$

A basic property of binary equality sets is as follows.

LEMMA 2. For a given equality set over a binary alphabet, all of its nonempty words have the same ratio.

From the arguments in Ehrenfeucht et.al. (1981) the following characterization for the equality sets over a binary alphabet can be derived.

THEOREM 1. For a pair (h,g) of binary morphisms such that at least one of them is injective the equality set $E(h,g)$ is one of the following forms:

(i) $\{u,v\}^*$ for some (possibly empty) words u and v,
(ii) $\{uw^*v\}^*$ for some nonempty words u, w and v satisfying:
w, uw^iv, for $i \geq 0$, and vu are ratio-primitive, $pref_1(w) \neq pref_1(v)$ and $w \in \Sigma^* 0 \Sigma^* \cap \Sigma^* 1 \Sigma^*$.

Finally, we say that two morphisms h and g agree on a word x if $h(x) = g(x)$ and that they agree on a language L if they agree on each word of L, i.e. $L \subseteq E(h,g)$.

3. MAIN RESULT

Here we prove our main result.

THEOREM 2. Let $H = (\{0,1\},h,\omega)$ and $G = (\{0,1\},g,\omega)$ be two DOL systems. The following conditions are equivalent:

(i) H and G are equivalent,
(ii) $h^i(\omega) = g^i(\omega)$ for $i = 0,1,2,3$.

Proof. Clearly, (i) implies (ii). So we assume that (ii) holds true, and we shall prove (i).

If both h and g are periodic, then the result is easily seen to hold. So let e.g. h be nonperiodic, in other words injective. By Theorem 1, we have two cases.

I $E(h,g) = \{u,v\}^*$ for some (possibly empty) words u and v. Now, our assumption implies

(1) $$\omega, h(\omega), h^2(\omega) \in \{u,v\}^* .$$

From this and Lemma 1 it follows that $r(\omega) = r(h(\omega))$. Consequently, for any word x such that $r(x) = r(\omega)$, we have $r(x) = r(h(x))$, i.e. h preserves the "correct ratio". Since $\omega \in \{u,v\}^*$ we have e.g. $\omega = uz$ for some word z. Hence, $h(\omega) = h(u)h(z)$ where $r(h(u)) = r(\omega)$, and so, by the fact $h(\omega) \in E(h,g)$, we obtain that $h(u) \in \{u,v\}^*$.

If both ω and $h(\omega)$ are in u^* we are done. Indeed, in this case $h^n(\omega) \in u^* \subseteq E(h,g)$ for all $n \geq 0$. So assume that $\omega \in \{u,v\}^* v \{u,v\}^*$ or $h(\omega) \in \{u,v\}^* v \{u,v\}^*$. In the first case we obtain, as above, that $h(v) \in \{u,v\}^*$. The same conclusion can be drawn also in the second case when only the fact $h^2(\omega) \in \{u,v\}^*$ is used. Consequently, we have also now that $h^n(\omega) \in \{u,v\}^*$ for all $n \geq 0$. This completes the proof of case I.

II $E(h,g) = \{uw^*v\}^*$ for some nonempty words u, w and v. Moreover, u, w and v satisfy the conditions: w, uw^iv, for $i \geq 0$, and vu are ratio-primitive, $pref_1(w) \neq pref_1(v)$ and w contains both 0 and 1 as a subword. Since h is nonperiodic we set, as earlier, z_h to be the maximal common prefix of $h(01)$ and $h(10)$. We define

(2) $$\alpha = \begin{cases} z_h & \text{if } |z_h| < |h(v)| \\ h(v) & \text{if } |z_h| \geq |h(v)| . \end{cases}$$

Now, by Lemma 1, α is a prefix of both $h(w)$ and $h(v)$, and moreover $pref_{|\alpha|+1}(h(w)) \neq pref_{|\alpha|+1}(h(v))$.

Let us recall our assumption

(3) $$\omega, h(\omega), h^2(\omega) \in \{uw^*v\}^* .$$

If ω and $h(\omega)$ are both in $\{uw^iv\}^*$, for some i, we are done, the reasoning being as in case I. In the other case there exist integers i and j, with $i > j$, such that $\{\omega, h(\omega)\}$ contains a word both from $\{uw^*v\}^* uw^iv \{uw^*v\}^*$ and from $\{uw^*v\}^* uw^jv \{uw^*v\}^*$.

By our assumption, $h(uw^iv)$ and $h(uw^jv)$ are in $\{uw^*v\}^*$. Let $C = \{w, vu\}$. Then C is marked and therefore there exists a unique word γ in C^* such that

$$u\gamma = h(uw^j)\alpha y$$

for some word y not containing either w or vu as a suffix. We claim that $y=\lambda$ or $y=u$. This follows since $h(uw^iv)$ and $h(uw^jv)$ are both in uC^*v, C is marked and $\mathrm{pref}_{|\alpha|+1}(h(w)) \neq \mathrm{pref}_{|\alpha|+1}(h(v))$. Indeed, if in (2) $|h(v)| > |\alpha|$, then $y=\lambda$, and if $|h(v)| = |\alpha|$, then $y=u$. Consequently, we have either

$$(4) \qquad \begin{cases} h(uw^j)\alpha & \in uC^* \\ \alpha^{-1}h(v) & \in C^*v \\ \alpha^{-1}h(w^{i-j})\alpha & \in C^* \end{cases}$$

or

$$(4') \qquad \begin{cases} h(uw^j)\alpha & \in uC^*v \\ \alpha^{-1}h(v) & = \lambda \\ \alpha^{-1}h(w^{i-j})\alpha & \in uC^*v. \end{cases}$$

Now, we look at the third relation of (4) in detail. By Lemma 2 and the form of $E(h,g)$, we have $r(w) = r(vu) = r(\omega)$. Further, as shown in case I, h preserves the "correct ratio". Therefore $r(\alpha^{-1}h(w)\alpha) = r(\omega)$. So it follows from the ratio-primitivinesses of w and vu and from the third relation of (4) that

$$(5) \qquad \alpha^{-1}h(w)\alpha \in C^*.$$

This, in turn, applied to the first relation of (4) yields

$$(6) \qquad h(u)\alpha \in uC^*.$$

Here the fact that C is a code is needed.

In the case (4´) the similar arguments can be used. Now the facts that the words uw^iv, for $i \geq 0$, are ratio-primitive and that also the set $\{uw^iv \mid i \geq 0\}$ is a code yield

$$(5') \qquad \alpha^{-1}h(w)\alpha \in uC^*v$$

and

$$(6') \qquad h(u)\alpha \in uC^*v.$$

Finally, we are ready to finish this proof. Indeed, by (4), (5) and (6) or alternatively (4´), (5´) and (6´), we obtain

$$h(uw^*v) \subseteq uC^*v = \{uw^*v\}^* = E(h,g),$$

which together with $\omega \in E(h,g)$ implies (i).

Next we recall an example, due to Nielsen (1974), which shows that our Theorem 2 is optimal. Let H and G be DOL systems with the starting word ab and the morphisms h and g defined by

$$h(a) = abb \quad , \quad g(a) = abbaabb$$
$$h(b) = aabba \quad , \quad g(b) = a \quad .$$

Then,

$$h^0(ab) = ab = g^0(ab)$$
$$h(ab) = abbaabba = g(ab)$$
$$h^2(ab) = (abbaabbaaabbaabb)^2 = g^2(ab)$$

and

$$suff_2(h^3(ab)) = ba \neq aa = suff_2(g^3(ab)),$$

where the notation $suff_2$ denotes the suffix of length 2.

It is instructive to consider the above example in the light of equality sets. Clearly, $E(h,g) = \{ab,ba\}^*$. Since the starting word ab belongs to $E(h,g)$ we must have $h(ab) = g(ab)$. Moreover, we have $h(ab) \in E(h,g)$. So it follows that $h(h(ab)) = g(h(ab)) = g(g(ab))$. But now this word is not any more in $E(h,g)$ since $suff_2(h^2(ab)) = bb$ and so we can at once conclude that $h^3(ab) \neq g^3(ab)$.

4. GENERALIZATIONS

In this section we discuss about the generalizations of Theorem 2. The equivalence of two DOL systems, with morphisms h and g, can be interpreted as "morphisms h and g agree on the DOL language generated by one of the systems". So an obvious generalization is to allow that the morphism of the DOL system is different from h and g. We have the result.

THEOREM 3. Let h and g be morphisms $\{0,1\}^* \to \{0,1\}^*$ and $G = (\{0,1\},f,\omega)$ a DOL system. Then the following conditions are equivalent:

(i) h and g agree on the language generated by G,

(ii) $h(f^i(\omega)) = g(f^i(\omega))$ for $i = 0,1,2,3$.

Proof. The proof of Theorem 2 is valid also now after one observation: In that proof it is unnecessary to require that the morphism h in (1) and (3) is one of those used in the considered equality sets.

Another way of generalizing Theorem 2 is to consider so-called DTOL systems, cf. Rozenberg and Salomaa (1980). A DTOL system is a $(k+2)$-tuple $(\Sigma, h_1, \ldots, h_k, \omega)$, where $k \geq 1$ and each of the triples (Σ, h_j, ω) is a DOL system. A DTOL system $(\Sigma, h_1, \ldots, h_k, \omega)$ generates a tree of words as follows:

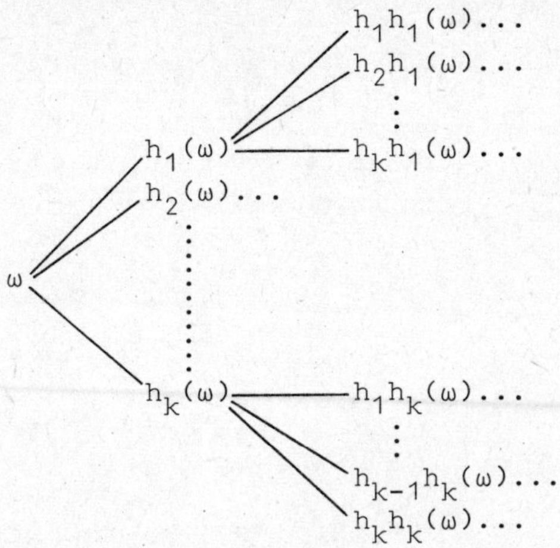

The set of all words in this tree is called the DTOL language generated by G. As in the case of DOL systems we call two DTOL systems $(\Sigma, h_1, \ldots, h_k, \omega)$ and $(\Sigma, g_1, \ldots, g_k, \omega)$ equivalent if they generate the same tree of words, i.e. if $h_{i_1} \ldots h_{i_s}(\omega) = g_{i_1} \ldots g_{i_s}(\omega)$ holds true for all $s \geq 0$ and $i_j \in \{1, \ldots, k\}$.

Theorem 2 can be generalized to

THEOREM 4. Let $H = (\{0,1\}, h_1, \ldots, h_k, \omega)$ and $G = (\{0,1\}, g_1, \ldots, g_k, \omega)$ be two DTOL systems. Then the following conditions are equivalent:

(i) H and G are equivalent,

(ii) $h_{i_1} \ldots h_{i_s}(\omega) = g_{i_1} \ldots g_{i_s}(\omega)$ for $s \leq 3$ and $i_j \in \{1, \ldots, k\}$.

Proof. Again the proof is basically that of Theorem 2. Indeed, as there, we can derive from the assumption (ii) that either all words of the language generated by H are in u^* for some word u or for each i and j in $\{1, \ldots, k\}$

$$h_j(E(h_i, g_i)) \subseteq E(h_i, g_i),$$

which together with the assumption $\omega \in \bigcap_{i=1}^{k} E(h_i, g_i)$ implies the result.

Theorem 4 shows that the equivalence problem for binary DTOL trees (sequences) is decidable - a result which, as far as I know, is not explicitly mentioned anywhere, but which can be easily derived from the main theorem of Culik and Richier (1979). Although our algorithm for deciding the equivalence of two DTOL trees is very simple, the problem is, in general, and even in a three-letter case, still open. On the other hand, the problem of whether two DTOL systems generate the same language is shown to be undecidable in Rozenberg (1972).

We also have the following generalization of Theorem 3.

THEOREM 5. Let h and g be morphisms of $\{0,1\}^*$ and $G = (\{0,1\}, f_1, \ldots, f_k, \omega)$ a DTOL system. Then the following conditions are equivalent:

(i) h and g agree on the language generated by G,

(ii) $h(f_{i_1} \ldots f_{i_s}(\omega)) = g(f_{i_1} \ldots f_{i_s}(\omega))$ for all $s \leq 3$ and $i_j \in \{1, \ldots, k\}$.

<u>Proof.</u> Now again the observation of the proof of Theorem 3 is valid. Indeed, we obtain along the lines of the proof of Theorem 2 that (ii) implies that either all words of the language generated by G are in u^* for some word u or

$$f_j(E(h,g)) \subseteq E(h,g) \quad \text{for} \quad j = 1, \ldots, k,$$

which together with the fact $\omega \in E(h,g)$ yields (i).

Theorems 3 and 5 give simple solutions to the problems which are referred to as morphism equivalence problems for binary DOL and DTOL languages. To be precise, such problems are as follows, cf. Culik and Salomaa (1979): The <u>morphism equivalence problem</u> for the family $\mathcal{L}$ of languages is to decide whether for a given language L in $\mathcal{L}$ and for two morphisms h and g, h and g agree on L. Culik and Richier showed that this problem is decidable for ETOL languages, cf. Rozenberg and Salomaa (1980), over a binary alphabet. Our Theorems 3 and 5 give considerably simpler algorithms for some subfamilies of this family, namely, for DOL and DTOL languages over a binary alphabet.

ACKNOWLEDGEMENT. The author is grateful to Dr. M. Linna for useful comments and to the Academy of Finland for the excellent working conditions under which this research was carried out.

REFERENCES

Culik, K. II and Fris, I. (1977), The decidability of the equivalence problem for DOL-systems, Inform. Contr. 35, 20-39.

Culik, K. II and Richier, J.L. (1979), Homomorphism equivalence on ETOL languages, Intern. J. Computer Math. 7, 43-51.

Culik, K. II and Salomaa, A. (1979), On the decidability of homomorphism equivalence for languages, JCSS 17, 163-175.

Ehrenfeucht, A., Karhumäki, J. and Rozenberg, G. (1981), On binary equality sets and a solution to the Ehrenfeucht Conjecture in the binary case, manuscript.

Ehrenfeucht, A. and Rozenberg, G. (1978), Elementary homomorphisms and a solution to the DOL sequence equivalence problem, Theoret. Comput. Sci. 17, 169-183.

Ehrenfeucht, A. and Rozenberg, G. (1980), On a bound for the DOL sequence equivalence problem, Theoret. Comput. Sci. 12, 339-342.

Harrison, M. (1978), "Introduction to Formal Language Theory", Addison-Wesley, Reading.

Nielsen, M. (1974), On the decidability of some equivalence problems for DOL systems, Inform. Contr. 25, 166-193.

Rozenberg, G. (1972), The equivalence problem for deterministic TOL systems is undecidable, Inform. Process. Lett. 1, 201-204.

Rozenberg, G. and Salomaa, A. (1980), "The Mathematical Theory of L Systems", Academic Press, New York.

Salomaa, A. (1978a), Equality sets for homomorphisms of free monoids, Acta Cybernetica 4, 127-139.

Salomaa, A. (1978b), DOL equivalence: The problem of iterated morphisms, E.A.T.C.S. Bulletin 4, 5-12.

RESULTS ON THE PROPOSITIONAL μ-CALCULUS

Dexter Kozen[1]
Aarhus University
Aarhus, Denmark

Abstract

We define a propositional version of the μ-calculus, and give an exponential-time decision procedure, small model property, and complete deductive system. We also show that it is strictly more expressive than PDL. Finally, we give an algebraic semantics and prove a representation theorem.

1. Introduction

The propositional μ-calculus refers to a class of programming logics consisting of propositional model logic with a μ (least fixpoint) operator. The μ-calculus originated with Scott and deBakker [SdB] and was developed further by Hitchcock and Park [HP], Park [Pa], deBakker and deRoever [dBR], deRoever [dR], and others. The system we consider here is very similar to one appearing in [dB, chp.8]. Our results however are more inspired by the work of Pratt [Pr], who considers a version $P\mu$. He shows that $P\mu$ encodes PDL, and extends his exponential-time decision procedure for PDL to $P\mu$. He leaves open the problem of strict containment of PDL and does not give a deductive system. The usual proof rules do not readily apply to $P\mu$ due to its formulation as a least root calculus rather than a least fixpoint calculus; this was done in order to capture the reverse operator of PDL. Also, Pratt imposes a rather strong version of syntactic continuity on $P\mu$ which we would like to weaken, since it renders illegal by fiat such useful formulas as $\mu Q.[a]Q$ (this is the negation of the infinite-looping operator Δa of Streett [S]). The restriction allows Pratt's filtration-based decision procedure to extend to $P\mu$, whereas no filtration-based decision procedure can work in the presence of $\mu Q.[a]Q$, since the operator $[a]Q$ is not continuous.

Here we propose weakening the syntactic continuity requirement and returning to the original least-fixpoint formulation to get a system $L\mu$. We lose the ability to encode the reverse operator, however we can show

(1) $L\mu$ encodes PDL with tests and looping (Δ) but without reverse;

1) On leave from IBM Thomas J. Watson Research Center, Yorktown Heights, New York 10598, USA.

thus by a result of Streett, $L\mu$ is strictly more expressive than PDL.

(2) We give an exponential-time decision procedure. This improves Streett's upper bound for PDL with Δ.

(3) We give a deductive system for $L\mu$, including the fixed point induction rule of Park [Pa], and prove completeness.

(4) We describe briefly an algebraic semantics and prove a representation theorem.

Familiarity with the μ-calculus and PDL is assumed; see [dB,dR,FL].

2. Syntax and Semantics

$L\mu$ has primitive propositions $P,Q,\ldots$ and programs $a,b,\ldots$, and formulas P, $X\vee Y$, $\neg X$, $\langle a\rangle X$, and $\mu Q.X$, the last allowed only if certain syntactic restrictions are met. We at least require syntactic monotonicity: each occurrence of Q in X is under an even number of negations. We will indicate this by writing such formulas $\mu Q.pQ$. Boolean operators $\wedge,\rightarrow,\equiv,0,1$ are defined as usual; $[a]X = \neg\langle a\rangle\neg X$ and $\nu Q.pQ = \neg\mu Q.\neg p\neg Q$. ν is the greatest fixpoint operator. σ represents either μ or ν. In practice we will distinguish between variables (those Q bound by some σQ) and other primitive propositions, although formally there is no distinction. We will often think of $\vee,\wedge,[\,],\bar{P}(=\neg P)$ as primitive, eliminating occurrences of $\neg$ by deMorgan's laws. A formula in such form is called positive.

In section 5 we will also impose the following syntactic restriction, which is somewhat weaker than Pratt's restriction:

(2.1) If $\sigma R.qR$ and $\sigma S.rS$ are subformulas of $\mu Q.pQ$ (possibly $\mu Q.pQ$ itself) each containing an occurrence of Q, then no two occurrences of variables R and S are conjunctively related. (Two formulas are conjunctively related in a positive formula X if $\wedge$ is at the root of the smallest subformula of X containing them). This is explained in section 5.

A standard model is a tuple $M = (S^M,\rho^M,\pi^M)$ where S^M is a set of states, $\rho^M\colon a\mapsto a^M \subseteq S^M\times S^M$, and $\pi^M\colon P\mapsto P^M \subseteq S^M$. Each formula defines both a set in S^M and an operator on subsets of S^M. If $X=X(\bar{Q})$ has free variables all among $\bar{Q} = Q_1,\ldots,Q_k$, then X defines a k-ary set operator $X^M\colon (S^M)^k\rightarrow S^M$ as follows:

$$p^M(\bar{A}) \quad = P^M \text{ , P a primitive proposition,}$$

$$Q_i^M(\bar{A}) \quad = A_i \text{ , } Q_i \text{ a variable,}$$

$$X \vee Y^M(\bar{A}) \quad = X^M(\bar{A}) \cup Y^M(\bar{A}),$$

$$\neg X^M(\bar{A}) \quad = S^M - X^M(\bar{A}),$$

$$\langle a\rangle X^M(\bar{A}) \quad = \{s \mid \exists t \in X^M(\bar{A}) \ (s,t) \in a^M\},$$

$$\mu Q.pQ^M(\bar{A}) = \cap\{B \mid p^M(B,\bar{A}) \subseteq B\}.$$

$\mu Q.pQ^M$ can also be defined equivalently as

$$\mu Q.pQ^M(\bar{A}) = \cup_\alpha p^\alpha 0^M(\bar{A}),$$

where

$$p^0 X^M(\bar{A}) \quad = X^M(\bar{A})$$

$$p^{\alpha+1} X^M(\bar{A}) = p^M(p^\alpha X^M(\bar{A}),\bar{A})$$

$$p^\lambda X^M(\bar{A}) \quad = \cup_{\beta<\lambda} p^\beta X^M(\bar{A}) \text{ , } \lambda \text{ a limit ordinal.}$$

The equivalence of these two definitions is the Knaster-Tarski theorem. $X^M(\bar{Q})$ can also be interpreted as a subset of S^M by taking

$$X^M = X^M(Q_1^M,\dots,Q_k^M).$$

We write $s \models X$ and say s satisfies X if $s \in X^M$. The infinitary formulas $p^\alpha X$ can be represented physically, modulo the representation of ordinals, by associating the ordinal α with the root of pX, along with a two-way pointer to each occurrence of X. There is no ambiguity, provided X is free for Q in pQ. We will use these formulas and this representation in the algorithm.

3. Expressiveness Results

Lμ subsumes PDL (without reverse), as shown by Pratt [Pr]. For example, the PDL formula <a*>X is given by $\mu Q.X \vee \langle a\rangle Q$. However, unlike PDL, there are monotone operators that are not continuous: [a]Q is one. If pQ is continuous in Q in the model M, then $\mu Q.pQ^M \equiv p^\omega 0^M$, but in any model, $\mu Q.[a]Q = \{s \mid$ there are no infinite a-paths out of s$\}$. (This is $\neg\Delta a$ in the notation of Streett [S]). For example, in the model pictured, $\mu Q.[a]Q \equiv p^{\omega+1}0$ but the top state s satisfies $\mu Q.[a]Q - p^\omega 0$. The question raised by Pratt about the strict expressiveness of Pμ over PDL is still open, but the following result of Street shows that Lμ is strictly more expressive, and in a way which shows why filtration techniques fail for Lμ:

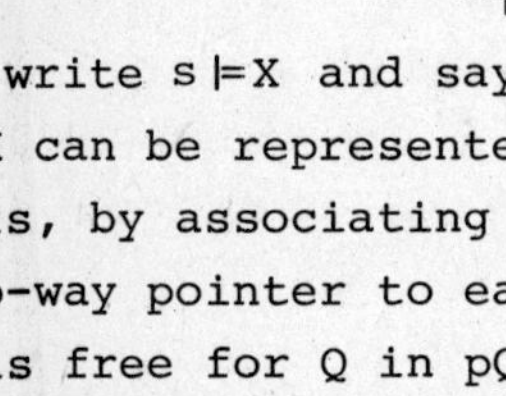

Proposition (Streett [S]). $\mu Q.[a]Q$ is not equivalent to any PDL formula.

Proof Suppose $\mu Q.[a]Q \equiv X \in$ PDL. Consider the model pictured above. Then $s \models \mu Q.[a]Q$ and $s \models X$. However, in any finite filtrate over a set containing X, the equivalence class [s] of s still satisfies X, but cannot satisfy $\mu Q.[a]Q$ since there is an infinite a-path out of it. □

The above proof assumes $\mu Q.[a]Q \equiv X$ in all models and derives a contradiction. However we can show that $L\mu$ is strictly more expressive than PDL in the stronger sense that there is a model M and a formula X of $L\mu$ such that no PDL formula Y is equivalent to X on M.

Proposition In the model

the formula $\mu Q.[a]\langle a\rangle Q$ defines the even states, whereas all PDL formulas, even with test and reverse, define only finite and cofinite sets. □

The proof is omitted. Intuitively, PDL cannot simulate an unbounded alternation of [a] and <a>.

4. A Deductive System

The deductive system is equational, as in [KP]. All formulas in a deduction are of the form $X \equiv Y$ or $X \leq Y$, the latter abbreviating $X \vee Y \equiv Y$. The logical axioms and rules are those for equational logic, including substitution of equals for equals, provided the syntactic restrictions on μ formulas are not violated. The nonlogical axioms and rules are:

(4.1) axioms for Boolean algebra

(4.2) $\langle a\rangle X \vee \langle a\rangle Y \equiv \langle a\rangle(X \vee Y)$

(4.3) $\langle a\rangle X \wedge [a]Y \leq \langle a\rangle(X \wedge Y)$

(4.4) $\langle a\rangle 0 \equiv 0$

(4.5) $p(\mu Q.pQ) \leq \mu Q.pQ$

(4.6) $\dfrac{pX \leq X}{\mu Q.pQ \leq X}$, X free for Q in pQ

(4.1)-4.4) are axioms of propositional modal logic. (4.5) and (4.6) say that $\mu Q.pQ$ is the $\leq$-least object X such that $pX \leq X$. (4.6) is the fixpoint induction rule of Park [Pa].

The following are some basic theorems and derived rules of this system. We refer the reader to [dB,dR] for omitted proofs.

Proposition 4.7. The following are provable:

(i) (change of bound variable) $\mu Q.pQ \equiv \mu P.pP$, provided neither Q nor P occurs in pR.

(ii) (monotonicity) $\dfrac{X \leq Y}{pX \leq pY}$, X,Y free for Q in pQ

(iii) $\mu Q.X \equiv X$, Q not free in X

(iv) $p(\sigma Q.pQ) \equiv \sigma Q.pQ$

(v) $\dfrac{pQ \leq qQ}{\sigma Q.pQ \leq \sigma Q.qQ}$

(vi) $\dfrac{p(\mu Q.X \wedge pQ) \leq X,}{\mu Q.pQ \leq X}$ Q not free in X, X free for Q

(vii) $\dfrac{p(X \wedge \mu Q.pQ) \leq X,}{\mu Q.pQ \leq X}$ X free for Q

Proof (vi).

(a)	$p(\mu Q.X\wedge pQ) \leq X$	(assumption)
(b)	$X \wedge p(\mu Q.X\wedge pQ) \leq X$	(a),(4.1)
(c)	$p(X \wedge \mu Q.X\wedge pQ) \leq X$	(a),(4.1),(ii)
(d)	$p(X \wedge \mu Q.(X\wedge p(X\wedge Q))) \leq X$	(c),(ii),(v)
(e)	$p(X \wedge \mu Q.(X\wedge p(X\wedge Q))) \leq X \wedge p(X \wedge 0\,Q.(X\wedge p(X\wedge Q)))$	(d),(4.1)
(f)	$p(X \wedge \mu Q.(X\wedge p(X\wedge Q))) \leq \mu Q.(X\wedge p(X\wedge Q)))$	(e),(4.5)
(g)	$p(X \wedge \mu Q.(X\wedge p(X\ Q))) \leq X \wedge \mu Q.(X\wedge p(X\wedge Q))$	(d),(f)
(h)	$\mu Q.pQ \leq X \wedge \mu Q.(X\wedge p(X\wedge Q))$	(g),(4.6)
(i)	$\mu Q.pQ \leq X$	(h),(4.1). □

4.7(vi) says that if $X \wedge \mu Q.pQ$ is consistent, then $X \wedge p(\mu Q.\neg X\wedge pQ)$ is; intuitively, the iteration $p^{\alpha}0$ has to capture a state of X for the first time.

5. Main Results

In this section we show completeness of the axioms and give an exponential time decision procedure and small model property. These results are based on a common construction which can be described as a tableau or semantic tree method. Similar methods have been used in program logics by Pratt [Pr1] and Emerson and Clarke [EC].

Let W be a positive formula of Lμ. Assume by 4.7(i) that no variable is bound twice and no primitive proposition occurs both bound and free. The closure cl(W) is the smallest set containing W and closed under subformula and the rule $\sigma Q.pQ \in cl(W) \rightarrow p(\sigma Q.pQ) \in cl(W)$. cl(W) is no larger than $|W|$, because each element is e(X) for some subformula X of W, where e(X) is obtained from X by repeatedly replacing the variables Q by the unique subformula $\sigma Q.pQ$ of W. The order of replacement does not matter, the process must halt since the only new variables introduced with $\sigma Q.pQ$ are quantified in a subformula of W containing $\sigma Q.pQ$ properly. We distinguish two kinds of σ-subformulas of $e(X) \in cl(W)$: those that have been regenerated and those that have not. The former are those that replaced a variable in the above construction of $e(X)$.

To construct a tableau T for W, start with the root r_T labeled $\Phi_{r_T} = \{W\}$, and apply the following extension rules:

$\wedge$-rule : if $X \wedge Y \in \Phi_s$ then add node t labeled $\Phi_t = \Phi_s \cup \{X,Y\}$ and unlabeled edge $s \to t$.

$\vee$-rule : if $X \vee Y \in \Phi_s$ then add nodes t,u with $\Phi_t = \Phi_s \cup \{X\}$, $\Phi_u = \Phi_s \cup \{Y\}$, and unlabeled edges $s \to u$, $s \to t$.

σ-rule : if $\sigma Q.pQ \in \Phi_s$, add t with $\Phi_t = \Phi_s \cup \{p(\sigma Q.pQ)\}$ and unlabeled edge $s \to t$.

$\diamond$-rule: for each $\langle a \rangle X \in \Phi_s$, add node t with $\Phi_t = \{X\} \cup \{Y \mid [a]Y \in \Phi_s\}$ and edge $s \to t$ labeled a.

The $\wedge$-, $\vee$-, σ-rules are applied until Φ_s does not grow, then the $\diamond$-rule is applied. This must occur eventually since each $\Phi_s \subseteq cl(W)$. Thus there are at most $2^{|W|}$ distinct labels. Call s a strong node if either no rule applies to s or the $\diamond$- rule was applied; a weak node otherwise. The weak interval of s consists of s and all weak ancestors on the path back up to, but not including, the next strong node. A regeneration of a σ-formula is an application of the σ-rule to it. For every occurrence of a subformula X of a formula in Φ_s, its trace is the sequence of occurrences of X stemming from that occurrence of X in Φ_s. For example, if Z is an occurrence of a subformula of X in $X \wedge Y \in \Phi_s$, and the $\wedge$-rule is applied to $X \wedge Y$, the corresponding occurrence of Z in X in the successor of s is on the same trace. A trace can be duplicated at applications of the σ-rule, since there can be several occurrences of the same formula stemming from one occurrence. If the same formula from two different sources appears in Φ_s, then one copy is discarded and the traces of corresponding subformulas merged.

The syntactic condition (2.1) implies that no element of $cl(W)$ contains two conjunctively related occurrences of the same μ-formula. This is proved by induction on the generation of $cl(W)$. Let $\mu Q.pQ$ be an occurrence of a μ-formula in T. Follow its trace until it is exposed and regenerated. There is now one copy of $\mu Q.pQ$ in $p(\mu Q.pQ)$ for each Q in pQ.

Follow the trace of each one of these; by the syntactic requirement (2.1), they must split apart and go down different branches of the tree before one is regenerated. In fact, any two occurrences of $\mu Q.pQ$ in different formulas of Φ_s must have disjoint traces back up to their first regenerations.

We now give an alternating Turing machine algorithm to refute W by constructing the tableau and rejecting if certain conditions are met. The algorithm starts with one process at the root r_T with input $\Phi_{r_T} = \{W\}$. It then constructs the tableau by applying the $\vee$-, $\wedge$-, and σ-rules in a regular fashion; at the application of $\vee$-rules, it makes an existential branch, spawning two processes, each of which takes one of the successors. At the application of $\diamond$-rules it makes a universal branch, spawning a process for each successor. If a process at a strong node s finds both $P, \bar{P} \in \Phi_s$, it rejects. If not, and if no rules apply (for example if Φ_s contains only formulas P and [a]X) then it accepts.

Besides this action, each occurrence of a μ-formula in Φ_s has a <u>priority</u> (position in a priority queue) and a <u>count</u>. The μ-formula goes onto the back of the queue when it is first regenerated, and its count is set to 0. Whenever it is regenerated, its count is incremented and all counts of formulas of lower priority are reset to 0. When two occurrences X,X' of a formula appear in Φ_s, they must be merged. This is done as follows: Let $\mu Q_1.p_1Q_1, \ldots, \mu Q_n.p_nQ_n$ be the regenerated μ-formulas of X in order of decreasing height of $e^{-1}(\mu Q_i.p_iQ_i)$ in W. Note that the $e^{-1}(\mu Q_i.p_iQ_i)$ are linearly ordered by the subformula relation. Also note that all occurrences of $\mu Q_i.p_iQ_i$ have the same count, and that they will have gone down two different branches of the tree by the time they become exposed again; thus there is only need to represent each $\mu Q_i.p_iQ_i$ once in the priority queue. Thus each $\mu Q_i.p_iQ_i$ appears once on the queue and in the order $\mu Q_1.p_1Q_1, \ldots, \mu Q_n.p_nQ_n$, since $\mu Q_1.p_1Q_1$ must have been regenerated first. Let $\mu Q_1.p_1Q_1', \ldots, \mu Q_n.p_nQ_n'$ be the corresponding occurrences in X'. To merge, keep the sequence of lexicographically higher priority (say $\mu Q_1.p_1Q_1, \ldots$) and delete the other one. Think of the sequence $\mu Q_1.p_1Q_1', \ldots$ as merging <u>into</u> $\mu Q_1.p_1Q_1, \ldots$ If any count ever exceeds $2^{|W|}$, the process rejects. We claim

(5.1) there can be no trace of $\mu Q.pQ$ with more than $|W|^2 \cdot 2^{|W|^3}$ regenerations before rejecting.

An element of the queue can only change priority, by merging with something of lexicographically higher priority or something being deleted in front of it, at most $|W|^2$ times, the maximum length of the queue. Every time its count is set back, either it was because something of higher priority was regenerated, or its priority changed, thus either its lexicographic priority increased or something with a higher priority had its count increased. Thus some counter must run out after $|W|^2 \cdot 2^{|W|^3}$ steps. The condition (2.1) was used to insure that new copies of a μ-formula come into the back of the queue; this is exactly what fails in the general case.

The set Φ_s can be represented by a set of pebbles on subterms of W, a pebble on X denoting $e(X) \in \Phi_s$. We also need to maintain the priority queue with $|W|^2$ counters, each holding an integer value $\leq 2^{|W|}$. Thus the algorithm uses alternating $O(|W|^3)$ space, which, despite the possibility of infinite computations, can be simulated in deterministic exponential time [CKS].

Theorem 5.2. The following are equivalent:

(i) W is consistent ;

(ii) the algorithm does not reject ;

(iii) W has a finite tree-like model of depth $d = |W|^2 \cdot 2^{|W|^3}$ and 2^d states.

Proof. (i)→(ii) Suppose W is consistent. In the tableau T, replace each occurrence $\mu Q.pQ$ in Φ_s by a formula $\mu Q.R \wedge pQ$ inductively down the tree, to get Φ'_s. R is a conjunction of k formulas, where k is the count of $\mu Q.pQ$ at s. If k=0, R=1; otherwise, let t_0 be the most recent time in $\mu Q.pQ$'s history that its counter was 0, and let $t_0, t_1 \ldots, t_{k-1}$ be all the nodes along its trace up to s at which $\mu Q.pQ$ was regenerated; let $R = \bigwedge_{i=0}^{k-1} \neg \Phi''_{t_i}$, where Φ''_t is obtained from Φ'_t by deleting all R's from the lower priority μ-formulas.

We construct a set C of nodes containing r_T such that

(a) if $s \in C$ and s is an $\vee$-node, then some successor of s is in C;

(b) for all other nodes $s \in C$, all successors of s are in C ;

(c) every Φ'_s, $s \in C$, is consistent.

We start by setting $C = \{r_T\}$; W is consistent by assumption. If Φ'_s is consistent and the $\vee$-rule is applied at s to $X \vee Y$, then one of the successors Φ'_t, Φ'_u must be consistent by (4.1) since Φ'_t is $\Phi'_s \cup \{X\}$ with perhaps some formulas deleted due to merging; no counts change. Thus one of t,u can be added to C. Similarly, at applications of the $\wedge$-, $\diamond$-, and ν-rule, C can be extended with all successors (there is no duplication of traces in the ν-rule, due to 2.1), since if Φ_s is consistent then all its successors are, by (4.1)-(4.4) and 4.7(iv). At applications of the μ-rule to $\mu Q.R\wedge pQ$, we need to show that if $\mu Q.R\wedge pQ \in \Phi'_s$ and Φ'_s is consistent, then $p(\mu Q.(R\wedge\neg\Phi''_s\wedge pQ)) \wedge \Phi''_s$ is consistent, where Φ''_s is obtained from Φ'_s by deleting the R's in all lower priority subterms, whose counts were reset to 0. But $\Phi'_s \leq \Phi''_s$ by monotonicity, thus if $\mu Q\wedge(R\wedge pQ) \wedge \Phi'_s$ is consistent, then $\mu Q.(R\wedge pQ) \wedge \Phi''_s$ is, and thus $p(\mu Q.(R\wedge\neg\Phi''_s\wedge pQ)) \wedge \Phi''_s$ is by 4.7(vi). Thus the set C exists. Moreover, C does not contain any node rejected because of $P,\bar{P}\in\Phi_s$, since all nodes of C are consistent; and any nodes rejected because a counter ran out must have an occurrence of $\mu Q.pQ$ regenerated at two ancestors s an t with $\Phi_s=\Phi_t$, the priority of $\mu Q.pQ$ unchanged and its count nonzero on the path from s down to t. Then $\mu Q.R\wedge pQ\in\Phi'_t$ and R contains $\neg\Phi''_s$, thus $\Phi'_t \leq \neg\Phi''_s$; and $\Phi'_t \leq \Phi''_t \leq \Phi''_s$, since $\Phi_t=\Phi_s$, and all μ-formulas with lower priority have R=1 in both Φ''_t and Φ''_s , and all higher priority μ-formulas were not changed between s and t (otherwise $\mu Q.pQ$'s count would have been reset). Thus Φ'_t is inconsistent and cannot be in C, and neither can any descendant.

Thus the algorithm cannot reject, because the computation tree is isomorphic to the tableau, and the set C forms a barrier to the computation of 0's back up the tree, so 0 cannot be assigned to the root.

(ii)→(iii) If the algorithm does not reject, prune all nodes in the tableau corresponding to nodes in the computation tree labeled 0; the set so obtained satisfies (a) and (b) above, and contains the root. Moreover no trace in T regenerates $\mu Q.pQ$ more than $|W|^2\cdot 2^{|W|^3}$ times, by (5.1).

Let Φ'_s be Φ_s with all μ-formulas $\mu Q.pQ$ replaced by $p^{d-c}0$, where $d = |W|^2\cdot 2^{|W|^3}$, and c is the maximum number of times $\mu Q.pQ$ is regenerated on any path out of s. Define the model $T = (S^T,\rho^T,\pi^T)$ where S^T = {strong nodes in C}, ρ^T: $a\mapsto a^T = \{(s,t)\,|\,s\to u$ in T on some edge labeled a, and u is in the weak interval of t$\}$; and π^T: $P\mapsto P^T = \{s\,|\,P\in\Phi_s\}$. Let $X^L = \{s\in S^T\,|\,X\in\Phi'_s\}$. We show by induction on formula structure that

(5.3) $$p(\bar{X})^L \subseteq p^T(\bar{X}^L),$$

where $\bar{X}^L = X_1^L,\ldots,X_n^L$.

Then $r_T \models W$ follows by specializing $\bar{X}$ to the null sequence and p=W. The basis is given by

$$P(\bar{X})^L = P^L = P^T$$
$$\bar{P}(\bar{X})^L = \bar{P}^L \subset \bar{P}^T$$
$$Q_i(\bar{X})^L = X_i^L = Q_i^T(\bar{X}^L),$$

the first two by definition of π^T. The induction cases $\wedge$ and $\vee$ are straightforward; for <a>, if $s \in \langle a\rangle p(\bar{X})^L$ then $(s,t)\in a^T$ for some $t \in p(\bar{X})^L$ by definition of the tableau; Then $t \in p^T(\bar{X}^L)$ by induction hypothesis, so $s \in \langle a^T\rangle p^T(\bar{X}^L) = \langle a\rangle p^T(\bar{X}^t)$. If $s \in [a]p(\bar{X})^L$ then all $(s,t)\in a^T$ have $t \in p^T(\bar{X}^L)$, so $s \in [a]p^T(\bar{X}^L)$. Occurrences of $\mu Q.pQ$ were replaced by p^n0; for this case,

$$\begin{aligned} p^n0(\bar{X})^L &\subseteq \cup_{m<n}\ p(p^m0(\bar{X}),\bar{X})^L \\ &\subseteq \cup_{m<n}\ p^T(p^m0(\bar{X})^L,\bar{X}^L) \\ &\subseteq \cup_{m<n}\ p^T(p^m0^T(\bar{X}^L),\bar{X}^L) \\ &\subseteq \quad p^n0^T(\bar{X}^L) \end{aligned}$$

The first step is by the μ-rule in the generation of the tableau, and the other steps are by induction hypothesis. Finally,

$$\begin{aligned} \nu Q.pQ(\bar{X})^L &\subseteq p(\nu Q.pQ(\bar{X}),\bar{X})^L \\ &\subseteq p^T(\nu Q.pQ(\bar{X})^L,\bar{X}^L) \end{aligned}$$

by induction hypothesis; since $\nu Q.pQ^T(\bar{X}^L)$ is the greatest fixpoint,

$$\nu Q.pQ(\bar{X})^L \subseteq \nu Q.pQ^T(\bar{X}^L).$$

A small model is obtained from T by observing that the tree T is regular, because the tableau rules were applied in a regular fashion, thus there are at most d distinct subtrees up to isomorphism, and hence d distinct theories, since the theory of a node depends only on its subtree (this is false in the presence of the reverse operator). Thus a finite model can be formed by creating loops.

(iii)→(i) This asserts the soundness of the deductive system and is left to the reader. □

6. Algebraic Semantics and a Representation Theorem

One can give an algebraic semantics whose models are Boolean algebras with operators <a>,μ satisfying the axioms (4.1)-(4.6). This is the approach taken in [Pr]. Over this semantics, completeness is obtained easily by constructing a Lindenbaum algebra from formulas. In this case the completeness theorem of Section 5 can be considered a proof of equivalence between the two semantics. Moreover, every algebraic model is algebraically isomorphic to a <u>nonstandard</u> state model, by the Stone construction (see [K1]); that is,

$$\begin{aligned} \text{states} &= \{\text{ultrafilters}\}, \quad P^M = \{u \mid P\in u\}, \\ a^M &= \{(u,v) \mid \forall X\ X\in v \rightarrow \langle a\rangle X\in u\} \\ &= \{(u,v) \mid \forall X\ [a]X\in u \rightarrow X\in v\}. \end{aligned}$$

The construction insures that $\mu Q.pQ^M$ is the least element of the algebra closed under p^M and that $\cup_\alpha p^\alpha 0^M \subseteq \mu Q.pQ^M$, but equality does not hold in general. Define an algebra to be <u>μ-complete</u> if the ≤-supremum $\bigvee_\alpha p^\alpha 0^M$ exists and is equal to $\mu Q.pQ^M$. This property corresponds to *-continuity in dynamic algebras [K3]. Then the set $\mu Q.pQ^M - \cup_\alpha p^\alpha 0^M$ is nowhere dense in the nonstandard representation of the algebra constructed above, thus in countable algebras, the union of all such sets is meager and can be deleted without changing the algebra (see [K2]). In this way we have shown

<u>Theorem</u>. Every countable μ-complete algebra is isomorphic to a standard model.

Moreover, all standard models are μ-complete. Thus μ-completeness characterizes the countable standard models up to isomorphism.

<u>References</u>

[HP] P. Hitchcock and D.M.R. Park, Induction Rules and Termination Proofs, *Proc. 1st ICALP*, 1973, 225-251.

[KP] D. Kozen and R. Parikh, An Elementary Proof of the Completeness of PDL, *TCS 14* (1981), 113-118.

[K1] D. Kozen, A Representation Theorem for Models of *-free PDL, *Proc. 7th ICALP*, Springer LNCS 85 (1980), 352-362.

[K2] D. Kozen, On the Duality of Dynamic Algebras and Kripke Models, *Proc. Workshop on Logic of Programs*, Springer LNCS 125, 1-11.

[K3] D. Kozen, On Induction vs. *-continuity, *Proc. Workshop on Logics of Programs*, Springer LNCS 131 (1982), 167-176.

[Pa] D.M.R. Park, Fixpoint Induction and proof of program semantics, *Mach. Int.* 5, ed. Meltzer and Michie, Edinburgh Univ. Press, 1970, 59-78.

[Pr] V.R. Pratt, A Decidable μ-calculus (Preliminary Report), *Proc. 22nd FOCS*, Oct. 1981, 421-427.

[Pr1] V.R. Pratt, A near optimal method for reasoning about action, *JCSS 20* (1980), 231-254.

[SdB] D. Scott and J. deBakker, *A Theory of Programs*, unpublished, IBM, Vienna, 1969.

[S] R. Streett, Propositional Dynamic Logic of Looping and Converse, *Proc. 13th STOC*, May 1981, 375-383.

[CKS] A. Chandra, D. Kozen, L. Stockmeyer, *Alternation*, JACM, Jan. 1981.

[dB] J. deBakker, *Mathematical Theory of Program Correctness*, Prentice-Hall, 1980.

[dBR] J. deBakker and W. deRoever, A Calculus for Recursive Program Schemes, *Proc. 1st ICALP*, 1973, 167-196.

[dR] W.P. deRoever, *Recursive Program Schemes: Semantics and Proof Theory*, Ph.D. Thesis, Free University, Amsterdam, 1974.

[EC] E.A. Emerson and E.M. Clarke, Design and Synthesis of Synchronization Skeletons using Branching-Time Temporal Logic, *Proc. Workshop on Logics of Programs*, Springer LNCS 131 (1982), 52-71.

[FL] M. Fischer and R. Ladner, Propositional Dynamic Logic of Regular Programs, *JCSS 18:2* (79).

[HR] J. Halpern and J. Reif, The Propositional Dynamic Logic of Deterministic, Well-Structured Programs, (extended abstract), *Proc. 22nd FOCS*, Oct. 1981, 322-334.

AN ITERATION THEOREM FOR SIMPLE PRECEDENCE LANGUAGES

(Extended Abstract)

Yael Krevner and Amiram Yehudai

Tel-Aviv University

1. Introduction

Iteration theorems are among the most powerful tools for proving that languages are not in a certain family. Such theorems exist for context-free languages (the classical pumping lemma [BPS] and Ogden's lemma [O2]), deterministic languages [O1,HH] and one-counter languages [Bo]. More recently iteration theorems for simple languages and strict deterministic languages of degree n [K] and for LL languages [Be] were obtained.

The main result of this paper is such an iteration theorem for simple precedence languages. We also present a family of languages and provide a precise characterization of languages in the family which are simple precedence.

This extended abstract is organized as follows. In Section 2 we recall the definitions and basic properties of simple precedence languages. Then we present in Section 3 our iteration theorem. We also show how the iteration theorem is used to prove that a given language is not simple precedence. These simple proofs are contrasted with traditional arguments found in the literature. Section 4 presents a certain family of languages and a necessary and sufficient condition for a language in the family to be simple precedence. Next we prove in Section 5 our iteration theorem. Finally, Section 6 contains some conclusions.

2. Simple Precedence Grammars

Precedence-oriented parsing techniques were among the first techniques to be used in parsers for programming languages. This notion was incorporated into the theory of context-free grammars by Floyd [Fl] and Wirth and Weber [WW]. Precedence techniques allow very small parsers to be constructed, but require very restricted grammars. Moreover, not every deterministic language is generated by a simple precedence grammar [Fi].

We give the definition of a simple precedence grammar and some relevant properties. More details can be found in [AU1]. We use standard notation for context-free grammars.

Definition 1 [WW]. Let $G = (V,\Sigma,P,S)$ be a context-free grammar, where $V = N \cup \Sigma$, and let $X,Y \in V$; $A,B \in N$; $\alpha,\beta,\gamma \in V^*$; $a \in \Sigma$. The Wirth-Weber precedence relations $<\cdot$, $\doteq$ and $\cdot>$ are defined on $V \times V$ as follows:

1. We say that $X <\cdot Y$ if there exists $A \rightarrow \alpha XB\beta$ in P such that $B \overset{+}{\Rightarrow} Y\gamma$.

2. We say that $X \doteq Y$ if there exists $A \rightarrow \alpha XY\beta$ in P.

3. $\cdot>$ is defined on $V \times \Sigma$. We say that $X \cdot> a$ if $A \rightarrow \alpha BY\beta$ in P, $B \overset{+}{\Rightarrow} \gamma X$, and $Y \overset{*}{\Rightarrow} a\delta$. (Notice that Y will be a in the case $Y \overset{0}{\Rightarrow} a\delta$.)

Throughout this paper we use $\$$ (a new symbol) as an endmarker which is added to the left and right of a right sentential form, and we assume that $\$ <\cdot X$ for all X such that $S \overset{+}{\Rightarrow} X\alpha$, and $Y \cdot> \$$ for all Y such that $S \overset{+}{\Rightarrow} \alpha Y$.

It is easy to verify the following properties:

a. If $X <\cdot A$ or $X \doteq A$ and $A \rightarrow Y\alpha$ is in P, then $X <\cdot Y$.

b. If $A <\cdot a$, $A \doteq a$ or $A \cdot> a$ and $A \rightarrow \alpha Y$ is in P, then $Y \cdot> a$. (Appears as lemma 5.3 in [AU1]).

Definition 2 [WW,Y]. A reduced, Λ-free context-free grammar $G = (V,\Sigma,P,S)$ for which $S \overset{+}{\not\Rightarrow} S$ is said to be a simple precedence grammar (SPG) if (i) it is uniquely invertible (i.e., $A \rightarrow \beta$, $B \rightarrow \beta$ in P implies $A = B$), and (ii) the Wirth-Weber precedence relations are pairwise disjoint.

A language which is generated by an SPG is said to be a simple precedence language (SPL).

Note that every context-free language may be generated by a uniquely invertible grammar, and also by a grammar with pairwise disjoint Wirth-Weber relations. But both properties may be satisfied together only for a proper subfamily of the (deterministic) context-free languages.

The following notation will be needed in the sequel.

1. For a string α, $\underline{^{(k)}\alpha}$ are the k leftmost symbols of α (assuming $k \leq |\alpha|$). Similarly for $\underline{\alpha^{(k)}}$.

2. Let $\$\alpha\beta\$$ be a right sentential form with endmarkers. The notation $\alpha <\cdot \beta$ in this context says that $(\$\alpha)^{(1)} <\cdot {}^{(1)}(\beta\$)$. Also for $\doteq$ and $\cdot>$.

3. We say that α has only $<\cdot$ and $\doteq$ if every two adjacent symbols in α are related by exactly one of $<\cdot$ and $\doteq$.

4. We say that α has only $\doteq$ if every two adjacent symbols in α are related only by $\doteq$.

5. A derivation like $\$S\$ \overset{*}{\underset{R}{\Rightarrow}} \$\alpha\delta w\$ \overset{n}{\underset{R}{\Rightarrow}} \$\alpha\beta w\$$ always means (in this paper) that $\delta \overset{*}{\underset{R}{\Rightarrow}} \beta$ and that α and w are not involved in the derivation.

The following theorem is a restatement of Corollary 1 of Theorem 5.14 in [AU1], using our notation.

Theorem 1 [AU1]. Let G be an SPG, $n \geq 0$, $\alpha,\beta \in V^*$, $A \in N$ and $w \in \Sigma^*$. If $\$S\$ \overset{n}{\underset{R}{\Rightarrow}} \$\alpha Aw\$ \underset{R}{\Rightarrow} \$\alpha\beta w\$$ then (1) α has only $<\cdot$ and $\doteq$; (2) $\alpha <\cdot \beta$; (3) β has only $\doteq$; (4) $\beta \cdot> w$.

Theorem 1 enables us to uniquely identify the handle β in a right sentential form $\$\alpha\beta w\$$. (Recall that β is the handle of $\$\alpha\beta w\$$ if $\$S\$ \overset{*}{\underset{R}{\Rightarrow}} \$\alpha A w\$ \underset{R}{\Rightarrow} \$\alpha\beta w\$$). The production $A \to \beta$ used here is also determined uniquely. This forms the basis for a shift reduce parsing algorithm for SPGs. For details refer to [AU1].

Our results and proofs may be motivated by parser-related intuition. Such comments may be found in [KY]. To make the presentation more rigorous, we state the results and the proofs only in terms of the grammars.

3. An Iteration Theorem for SPLs

Our iteration theorem for SPLs will use the pumping lemma for context-free languages [BPS]. We now present a slightly modified statement of this well known result. Refer to [H] for more details.

Pumping Lemma. Let $L = L(G)$ be a context-free language, where $G = (V,\Sigma,P,S)$. There exists an integer $p = p(G)$ such that for every $v \in L$ if $|v| \geq p$ then there exists a factorization $v = v_1v_2v_3v_4v_5$ of v such that:

1. There exist $A \in N$, $\alpha_1,\alpha_2 \in V^*$, such that $S \overset{*}{\underset{R}{\Rightarrow}} \alpha_1 A v_5$; $A \overset{*}{\underset{R}{\Rightarrow}} \alpha_2 A v_4$; $A \overset{*}{\underset{R}{\Rightarrow}} v_3$; $\alpha_2 \overset{*}{\underset{R}{\Rightarrow}} v_2$; $\alpha_1 \overset{*}{\underset{R}{\Rightarrow}} v_1$.
2. For every $i \geq 0$, $v_1v_2^iv_3v_4^iv_5 \in L$.
3. $|v_2v_3v_4| \leq p$ and $|v_2v_4| > 0$.

Hereafter a G-factorization of $v \in L$ means a factorization which satisfies conditions (1) - (3) of the pumping lemma, with respect to a fixed grammar G.

We are now ready to present our main result.

Theorem 2--The iteration theorem for SPLs. Let $L = L(G)$ be an SPL, $G = (V,\Sigma,P,S)$ an SPG, and suppose there exist $v,v' \in L$ with G-factorizations $v = v_1v_2v_3v_4v_5$, $v' = v_1'v_2'v_3'v_4'v_5'$, respectively, satisfying the following two conditions:
(i) $v_2,v_2' \in x^+$ for some $x \in \Sigma^+$, and (ii) there exist $r \geq 0$ and $z \in \Sigma^+$ with ${}^{(1)}z = {}^{(1)}v_4'v_5'$ such that $v_1v_2^r\, v_2'^2v_3'v_4'\, z \in L$. Then for each $m \geq 0$, $v_1v_2^r\, v_2'^{m+1}v_3'v_4'^m\, z \in L$. □

When v,v' and the factorizations are fixed, we will denote $w(r,m,z) = v_1v_2^rv_2'^{m+1}v_3'v_4'^m\, z$. In these terms the theorem states that $w(r,1,z)$ in L implies $w(r,m,z)$ in L for each $m \geq 0$.

The proof of Theorem 2 will be given in Section 5. We now show how Theorem 2 can be used in conjunction with the classical pumping lemma to prove that a given language is not an SPL. Note that instead of the classical pumping lemma we could use the more powerful Ogden's lemma [O2], but this does not seem to yield better results in our case.

Example. Let $L_1 = \left\{a0^n1^n,\ b0^n1^{2n}\ |n \geq 1\right\}$.

To show that L_1 is not an SPL, assume for the sake of contradiction that $L_1 = L(G)$, where G is an SPG. Let p be the constant from the pumping lemma and consider $v = a0^p1^p$, $v' = b0^p1^{2p}$. In each G-factorization we must have $v_2 = 0^i$, $v_4 = 1^i$, $v_2' = 0^j$, $v_4' = 1^{2j}$ for some $i,j \geq 1$. Hence, $w(r,1,z) = v_1v_2^r\ v_2'^2v_3'v_4'\ z = a0^{c+ri+2j}\ 1^{d+2j}\ z$, where $c,d \geq 0$ are constants. No matter what c,d,i,j are, we can always choose $r \geq 0$ large enough so that there exists $t > 0$ for which $w(r,1,1^t) = a0^\ell 1^\ell \in L_1$. (Simply let $ri > d-c$ and $t = ri - (d-c) > 0$.) It follows from Theorem 2 that for each $m \geq 0$, $w(r,m,1^t) \in L_1$. But $w(r,2,1^t) = a0^{\ell+j}\ 1^{\ell+2j}$ which is not in L_1. Hence L_1 is not an SPL. □

Note how Theorem 2 is used as a splicing device.

L_1 from the example, together with $L_2 = \left\{a0^n1^m2^n,\ b0^n1^n2^m|m,n \geq 1\right\}$, are the deterministic languages given in the literature as non-SPLs. Arguments showing that L_1 is not an SPL can be found in [RSL,AU2], and similar arguments for L_2 appear in [Fi]. These arguments follow the intuition that the parser is "forgetful." In particular, for L_1, the parser must remember the first symbol it sees (a or b) and then count the number of 0's. Having no states, and being allowed only a limited form of stack manipulation, it cannot do both since the information about the first symbol is buried deep in the stack. These arguments are therefore rather ad-hoc and difficult to formalize. Note that the proof that L_2 is not an SPL using our iteration theorem is identical to the proof for L_1, taking $v = a0^p12^p$ and $v' = b0^p1^p2$.

4. A Strong Characterization of SPLs

As was explained above, a simple precedence parser cannot use an input marker to direct its action if the marker is followed by input symbols that must be counted. The language $\left\{0^na1^n,\ 0^nb1^{2n}|n \geq 1\right\}$ uses a "middle" marker (or, more precisely, two different markers a and b) to distinguish between the two ways the 1's need to be counted. A simple precedence parser can use such middle markers to direct its action, and it is possible to prove that this language is indeed an SPL [AU2]. If we consider $L_3 = \left\{a0^{2n}1^n,\ b0^{2n}1^{2n}|n \geq 1\right\}$, we can also identify two different middle markers for the two counting schemes. To do this note that $L_3 = \left\{a(00)^n0011^n,\ b0(00)^n0111^{2n}|n \geq 0\right\}$, and we can use 001 and 011 as the markers. It is possible to write an SPG for L_3. In general, we would like to show that a language with $m \geq 1$ different counting schemes of the same symbol (or string) is an SPL if and only if it is possible to identify at least m different middle markers, one for each counting scheme.

We now make this concept more precise, at the expense of limiting its application to a specific family of languages.

Definition 3. For each $m \geq 1$ let $\Sigma_m = \{a_1, a_2, \ldots, a_m, c\}$. Choose any alphabet Σ such that $\Sigma_m \subsetneq \Sigma$. For each $x \in (\Sigma-\Sigma_m)^+$ define $L_{x,m} = \{a_j x^n c^{jn} \mid 1 \leq j \leq m, n \geq 1\}$.

It should be evident that for $L_{x,m}$ to be an SPL, we need at least m middle markers. $L_{x,m}$ has at most $|x|$ such markers. The following will formalize this idea.

Theorem 3. For each $m \geq 1$ and $x \in (\Sigma-\Sigma_m)^+$, $L_{x,m}$ is an SPL if and only if $|x| \geq m$.

Proof. Let $k = |x|$, $m > k \geq 1$, and suppose for the sake of contradiction that G is an SPG, $L(G) = L_{x,m}$. Let p be the constant (for G) from the pumping lemma, and consider $L' = \{a_i x^p c^{ip} \mid 1 \leq i \leq m\}$. Each $v \in L'$ must have at least one G-factorization, and each such factorization must satisfy $v_2 \in \hat{x}_j^+$, for some j, $1 \leq j \leq k$, where $x_j = x^{(k-j+1)(j-1)}x$. Since $|L'| = m > k$, there must exist distinct $v, v' \in L'$ with factorizations $v = v_1v_2v_3v_4v_5$ and $v' = v_1'v_2'v_3'v_4'v_5'$ where $v_2, v_2' \in \hat{x}_j^+$ for some j, $1 \leq j \leq k$. Thus condition (i) of Theorem 2 is satisfied. For simplicity let $y = x^{(k-j+1)}$, $u = {}^{(j-1)}x$ so that $\hat{x}_j = yu$ and $uy = x$. Then $v_2 = (yu)^{\ell}$, $v_2' = (yu)^{\ell'}$, $\ell, \ell' \geq 1$. Furthermore, $v_1 \in a_i x^* u$, $v_3' \in yx^*c^*$, $v_4' = c^{\ell' i'}$ (assuming v, v' start with a_i, a_i', respectively, where $i \neq i'$). Then we can see that for sufficiently large r, there exists $z \in c^+$ so that $w(r,1,z) = v_1 v_2^r v_2'^2 v_3' v_4' z = a_i x^s c^{is} \in L_{x,m}$. By Theorem 2 it follows that $w(r,2,z) \in L_{x,m}$ but $w(r,2,z) = a_i x^{s+\ell'} c^{is+\ell' i'} \notin L_{x,m}$ since $i \neq i'$. Hence $L_{x,m}$ is a non-SPL.

Conversely, let $k = |x|$, $k \geq m$. We prove that $L_{x,m}$ is an SPL by constructing a simple precedence grammar for it.

For each $1 \leq j \leq m$, let $v_{j,1} = a_j^{(j-1)}x$, $v_{j,2} = x^{(k-j+1)(j-1)}x$, $v_{j,3} = x^{(k-j+1)}c^j$, $v_{j,4} = v_{j,4}'c = c^{j-1}c$ and $v_{j,5} = \Lambda$. Clearly then $L_{x,m} = \{v_{j,1}v_{j,2}^n v_{j,3} v_{j,4}^n v_{j,5} \mid 1 \leq j \leq m, n \geq 0\}$. Let $U = \{v_{j,1}, v_{j,2}, v_{j,3}, v_{j,4}' \mid 1 \leq j \leq m\}$ and let $\hat{U}$ denote the set of nonempty prefixes of U. We introduce the following nonterminal symbols $N = \{S\} \cup \{[u] \mid u \in \hat{U}\}$. By convention let $[\Lambda] = \Lambda$. Now let $G = (V, \Sigma, P, S)$ with $V = \Sigma \cup N$, $P = P_1 \cup P_2 \cup P_3 \cup P_4$ and where

$P_1 = \{S \to [v_{j,1}][v_{j,3}] \mid 1 \leq j \leq m\}$

$P_2 = \{[v_{j,3}] \to [v_{j,2}][v_{j,3}][v_{j,4}']\, c \mid 1 \leq j \leq m\}$

$P_3 = \{[ua] \to [u]\, a \mid u, ua \in \hat{U}, |a| = 1\}$ and

$P_4 = \{[a] \to a \mid a \in \hat{U}, |a| = 1\}$.

Figure 1 illustrates a typical derivation in the grammar. A proof that this is an SPG may be found in the full paper [KY]. □

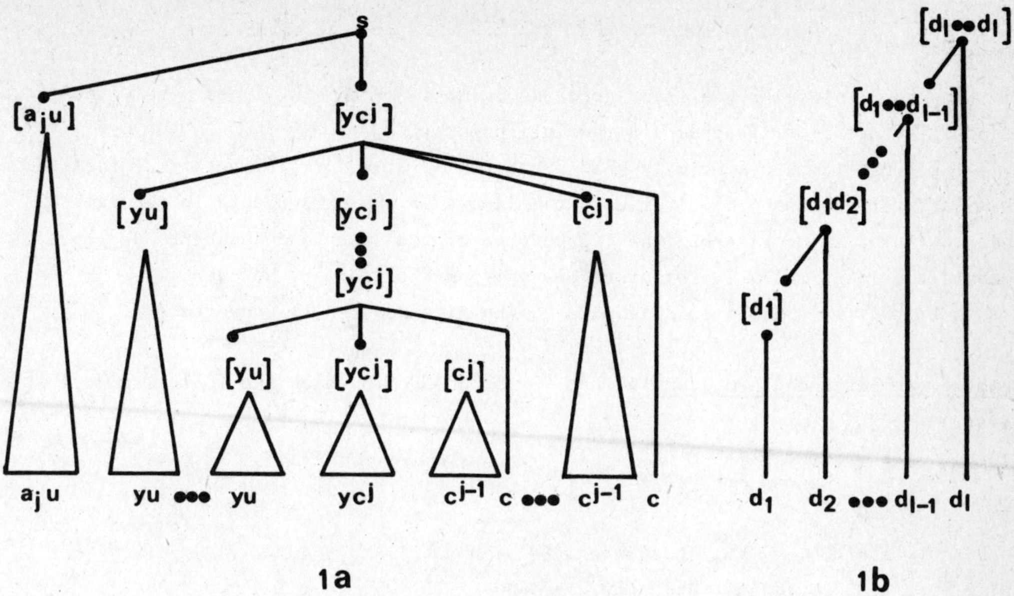

Figure 1. A typical derivation tree of the grammar in the proof of Theorem 3. Here $1 \leq j \leq m$, $u = {}^{(j-1)}x$, $y = x^{(k-j+1)}$ so that $x = uy$. Each triangle in Figure 1a represents a subtree of the form shown in Figure 1b.

Note that the fact that L_1 is not an SPL follows from Theorem 3 since it is isomorphic to $L_{0,2}$. More corollaries now follow.

Corollary 1. Let $L_3 = \left\{a0^{2n}1^n,\ b0^{2n}1^{2n} \mid n \geq 1\right\}$, $L_3' = L_3 \cup \left\{c0^{2n}1^{3n} \mid n \geq 1\right\}$, $L_4 = \left\{a0^{4n}1^n,\ b0^{4n}1^{2n},\ c0^{4n}1^{3n},\ d0^{4n}1^{4n} \mid n \geq 1\right\}$ and $L_4' = L_4 \cup \left\{e0^{4n}1^{5n} \mid n \geq 1\right\}$. L_3 and L_4 are SPLs; L_3' and L_4' are not SPLs.

Proof. L_3, L_3', L_4' and L_4' are isomorphic to $L_{x,2}$, $L_{x,3}$, $L_{y,4}$, $L_{y,5}$, respectively, where $x = 00$ and $y = 0000$. □

Note that L_3 is a homomorphic image of the non-SPL language $L_1 \cdot L_3 = \varphi(L_1)$ where $\varphi(0) = 00$ and $\varphi(d) = d$ for $d \in \{a,b,1\}$.

5. Proof of the Iteration Theorem for SPLs

To prove Theorem 2, we first need two results. Both are listed here without proof. The proofs will appear in the full paper [KY].

The first lemma essentially shows that two "similar" right sentential forms have "similar" derivations. This reflects the fact that the parser acts in the same way when the information it sees (the top portion of the stack and the next few input symbols) is identical. The proof relies only on the grammar, however.

Note that this lemma is analogous to the extended LR(k) theorem (cf. [H]).

Lemma 1 (the extended SPG lemma). Let G be an SPG in which the following derivations exist:

(1) $\$S\$ \overset{*}{\underset{R}{\Rightarrow}} \$\alpha\delta w\$ \overset{n}{\underset{R}{\Rightarrow}} \$\alpha\beta w\$$

(2) $\$S\$ \overset{*}{\underset{R}{\Rightarrow}} \$\alpha'\beta w'\$$

such that $w,w' \in \Sigma^*$; $\beta \in V^+$; $\alpha,\alpha' \in V^*$; $\delta \in V^+$; $n \geq 0$. And assume: (a) ${}^{(1)}w = {}^{(1)}w'$, (b) $\alpha^{(1)} = \alpha'^{(1)}$, (c) α' has only $<\cdot$ and $\doteq$.

Then derivation (2) is of the form: $\$S\$ \overset{*}{\underset{R}{\Rightarrow}} \$\alpha'\delta w'\$ \overset{n}{\underset{R}{\Rightarrow}} \$\alpha'\beta w'\$$. □

The next lemma shows how two derivations may be interleaved. Using it we will be able to splice words in an SPL.

Lemma 2. Let G be an SPG and let $\alpha_1,\alpha_2,\alpha_1',\alpha_2' \in V^*$, $A,A' \in N$, $v_1,v_2,v_3,v_4,v_5,v_1',v_2',v_3',v_4',v_5' \in \Sigma^*$. Suppose $v_2,v_2' \in x^+$ for some $x \in \Sigma^+$ and the following derivations exist in G: $\$S\$ \overset{*}{\underset{R}{\Rightarrow}} \$\alpha_1 A v_5\$$, $A \overset{*}{\underset{R}{\Rightarrow}} \alpha_2 A v_4$, $A \overset{*}{\underset{R}{\Rightarrow}} v_3$, $\alpha_1 \overset{*}{\underset{R}{\Rightarrow}} v_1$, $\alpha_2 \overset{*}{\underset{R}{\Rightarrow}} v_2$;

$\$S\$ \overset{*}{\underset{R}{\Rightarrow}} \$\alpha_1' A' v_5'\$$, $A' \overset{*}{\underset{R}{\Rightarrow}} \alpha_2' A' v_4'$, $A' \overset{*}{\underset{R}{\Rightarrow}} v_3'$, $\alpha_1' \overset{*}{\underset{R}{\Rightarrow}} v_1'$, $\alpha_2' \overset{*}{\underset{R}{\Rightarrow}} v_2'$.

Then, for every $k \geq 0$ there exists $z \in \Sigma^+$, where ${}^{(1)}z = {}^{(1)}x$, such that $\$S\$ \overset{*}{\underset{R}{\Rightarrow}} \$\alpha_1\alpha_2^k\alpha_2' z\$ \overset{*}{\underset{R}{\Rightarrow}} \$\alpha_1\alpha_2^k v_2' z\$$.

We are now ready to present the proof of the main result.

Proof of Theorem 2. Assume the G-factorizations for v and v' induce the following derivations:

(1) $\$S\$ \overset{*}{\underset{R}{\Rightarrow}} \$\alpha_1 A v_5\$$; $A \overset{*}{\underset{R}{\Rightarrow}} \alpha_2 A v_4$; $A \overset{*}{\underset{R}{\Rightarrow}} v_3$; $\alpha_1 \overset{*}{\underset{R}{\Rightarrow}} v_1$; $\alpha_2 \overset{*}{\underset{R}{\Rightarrow}} v_2$.

(2) $\$S\$ \overset{*}{\underset{R}{\Rightarrow}} \$\alpha_1' A' v_5'\$$; $A' \overset{*}{\underset{R}{\Rightarrow}} \alpha_2' A' v_4'$; $A' \overset{*}{\underset{R}{\Rightarrow}} v_3'$; $\alpha_1' \overset{*}{\underset{R}{\Rightarrow}} v_1'$; $\alpha_2' \overset{*}{\underset{R}{\Rightarrow}} v_2'$.

Consider the following two derivations:

(3) $\$S\$ \overset{*}{\underset{R}{\Rightarrow}} \$\alpha_1\alpha_2^r v_2 v_3 v_4^{r+1} v_5\$ \overset{*}{\underset{R}{\Rightarrow}} \$v_1 v_2^r v_2 v_3 v_4^{r+1} v_5\$$ (follows from derivation (1)).

(4) $\$S\$ \overset{*}{\underset{R}{\Rightarrow}} \$v_1 v_2^r v_2'^2 v_3' v_4' z\$$ (follows from assumption (ii)).

We apply Lemma 1 to derivations (3) and (4) with $\alpha = \alpha' = \Lambda$, $\beta = v_1 v_2^r$, $\delta = \alpha_1\alpha_2^r$, $w = v_2 v_3 v_4^{r+1} v_5$, $w' = v_2'^2 v_3' v_4' z$ and conclude that derivation (4) is of the form:

(4') $\$S\$ \overset{*}{\underset{R}{\Rightarrow}} \$\alpha_1\alpha_2^r v_2'^2 v_3' v_4' z\$ \overset{*}{\underset{R}{\Rightarrow}} \$v_1 v_2^r v_2'^2 v_3' v_4' z\$$.

On the other hand we can apply Lemma 2 to (1) and (2) and obtain the derivation

(5) $\$S\$ \overset{*}{\underset{R}{\Rightarrow}} \$\alpha_1\alpha_2^r\alpha_2' z_1\$ \overset{*}{\underset{R}{\Rightarrow}} \$\alpha_1\alpha_2^r v_2' z_1\$$

for some $z_1 \in \Sigma^+$, ${}^{(1)}z_1 = {}^{(1)}x$. Now we can apply Lemma 1 to derivations (5) and (4') choosing β to be v_2', $\delta = \alpha_2'$, $w = z_1$, $w' = v_2'v_3'v_4'z$ and $\alpha = \alpha' = \alpha_1\alpha_2^r$. Thus, derivation (4') can be written:

(4'') $\$S\$ \overset{*}{\underset{R}{\Rightarrow}} \$\alpha_1\alpha_2^r\alpha_2'v_2'v_3'v_4'z\$ \overset{*}{\underset{R}{\Rightarrow}} \$\alpha_1\alpha_2^r v_2'v_2'v_3'v_4'z\$$.

Next consider the following derivation:

(6) $\$S\$ \overset{*}{\underset{R}{\Rightarrow}} \$\alpha_1'\alpha_2'A'v_4'v_5'\$ \overset{*}{\underset{R}{\Rightarrow}} \$\alpha_1'\alpha_2'v_2'v_3'v_4'v_4'v_5'\$$ (follows from derivation (2)).

Appealing to Lemma 1 again, with derivations (6) and (4''), we can choose β to be $v_2'v_3'v_4'$, $\delta = A'$, $\alpha = \alpha_1'\alpha_2'$, $\alpha' = \alpha_1\alpha_2^r\alpha_2'$, $w = v_4'v_5'$ and $w' = z$. It follows that derivation (4'') is of the form:

$$\$S\$ \overset{*}{\underset{R}{\Rightarrow}} \$\alpha_1\alpha_2^r\alpha_2'A'z\$ \overset{*}{\underset{R}{\Rightarrow}} \$\alpha_1\alpha_2^r\alpha_2'v_2'v_3'v_4'z\$.$$

But $A' \Rightarrow v_2'A'v_4'$ (from the derivations in (2)). It follows that for every $m \geq 0$

$$\$S\$ \overset{*}{\underset{R}{\Rightarrow}} \$\alpha_1\alpha_2^r\alpha_2'A'z\$ \overset{*}{\underset{R}{\Rightarrow}} \$v_1v_2^r v_2'v_2'^m v_3'v_4'^m z\$;$$

Hence, for every $m \geq 0$, $v_1v_2^r v_2'^{m+1}v_3'v_4'^m z \in L$. □

6. Conclusions

We have obtained powerful and reasonably general tools for proving that languages are not simple precedence when that is the case. We have also been able to give a systematic way of producing simple precedence grammars in certain situations.

An extension of the precedence relations between two symbols is obtained by defining precedence relations between strings of length m and n (cf [AU1]). Thus the family of uniquely invertible (m,n) precedence languages is obtained. Our iteration theorem may be generalized to deal with uniquely invertible (1,k) precedence languages, and using it we determine that all the languages proved in the literature to be non-SPL are not uniquely invertible (1,k) precedence for any $k \geq 1$. This is particularly interesting since it is not known if the families of uniquely invertible (1,k) precedence languages form a hierarchy [AU2,S]. (Note that uniquely invertible (2,1) precedence languages coincide with the deterministic languages [G].) Details of this generalization, as well as additional comments, may be found in the full text [KY].

References

[AU1] A.V. Aho and J.D. Ullman, The theory of parsing, translation and compiling, Prentice-Hall, Vol. I, 1972.

[AU2] A.V. Aho and J.D. Ullman, The theory of parsing, translation and compiling, Prentice-Hall, Vol. II, 1973.

[Be] J.C. Beatty, Two iteration theorems for the LL(k) languages, TCS 12 (1980), 193-228.

[Bo] L. Boasson, Two iteration theorems for some families of languages, JCSS 7 (1973), 583-596.

[BPS] Y. Bar-Hillel, M. Perles and E. Shamir, On formal properties of simple phrase structure grammars, Z. Phonetik Sprachwiss. Kommunikat. 14 (1961), 143-172.

[Fi] M.J. Fischer, Some properties of precedence languages, proceedings of 1st STOC, 1969, 181-190.

[Fl] R.W. Floyd, Syntactic analysis and operator precedence, JACM 10 (1963), 316-333.

[G] S.L. Graham, Extended precedence languages, bounded right context languages and deterministic languages, IEEE Conf. record of the 11th Annual Symposium on Switching and Automata Theory (1970), 175-180.

[H] M.A. Harrison, Introduction to formal language theory, Addison-Wesley, 1978.

[HH] M.A. Harrison and I.M. Havel, On the parsing of deterministic languages, JACM 21 (1974), 525-548.

[K] K.N. King, Iteration theorems for families of strict deterministic languages, TCS 10 (1980), 317-333.

[KY] Y. Krevner and A. Yehudai, An iteration theorem for simple precedence languages, submitted for publication.

[O1] W.F. Ogden, Intercalation theorems for pushdown store and stack languages, Ph.D. Thesis, Stanford University, 1968.

[O2] W.F. Ogden, A helpful result for proving inherent ambiguity, Math. Systems Theory 2 (1968), 191-194.

[RSL] D.J. Rosenkrantz, P.M. Lewis III and R.E. Stearns, A simple language which is not a precedence language, unpublished manuscript (1968).

[S] I.H. Sudborough, private communication, 1979.

[WW] N. Wirth and H. Weber, Euler-a generalization of ALGOL and its formal definition, part I, CACM 9 (1966), 13-23.

[Y] A. Yehudai, A new definition for simple precedence grammars, BIT 19 (1979), 282-284.

The Power of Non-Rectilinear Holes*

Andrzej Lingas
Laboratory for Computer Science, MIT

Abstract: Four multiconnected-polygon partition problems are shown to be NP-hard.

Introduction

One of the main topics of computational geometry is the problem of optimally partitioning figures into simpler ones. Pioneers in this field mention at least two reasons for the interest :

(1) such a partition may give us an efficient description of the original figure, and
(2) many efficient algorithms may be applied only to simpler figures .

Besides inherent applications to computational geometry [C1], the partition problems have a variety of applications in such domains as database systems [LLMPL], VLSI and architecture design [LPRS] . Among others, the three following partition problems have been investigated :

MNRP (Minimum Number Rectangular Partition) . Given a rectilinear polygon with rectilinear polygon holes, partition the figure into a minimum number of rectangles.

MNCP1 (Minimum Number Convex Partition 1) . Given a polygon, partition it into a minimum number of convex parts .

MNDT1 (Minimum Number Diagonal Triangulation 1) . Given a polygon, partition it into a minimum number of triangles, by drawing not-intersecting diagonals .

In the above definitions, as in the course of the entire paper, we assume the following conventions . A *polygon* means a simple polygon (see [SH]), given by a sequence of pairs of integer-coordinate points in the plane, representing its edges. A *rectilinear polygon* is a polygon, all of whose edges are either horizontal or vertical . A *polygon with polygon holes* is a figure consisting of a polygon and a collection of not-overlapping, not-degenerate polygons lying inside it . The perimeter of the outer polygon and the contours of the inner polygons form *boundaries* of the figure, enclosing its *inside* equal to the inside of the outer polygon minus the boundaries and insides of the inner polygons . A *diagonal* of a planar figure is a line segment lying inside it and joining two of its non-adjacent vertices.

At first sight, MNRP and MNCP1 seem to be NP-hard. Surprisingly, both are solvable in time $O(n^3)$, where n is the number of corners of the input figure (see [LLMPL] and [C, CD]). The $O(n^3)$ time algorithm for MNRP uses a matching technique, that for MNCP1 is an example of a sophisticated dynamic programming approach. MNDT1 is also solvable in time $O(n^3)$, by a straightforward, dynamic programming procedure * *. In contrast to these results, we show the following problems to be NP-hard :

* This research was supported by NSF grants MCS-8006938 and MCS-7805849 .
** The known triangulation algorithm of time complexity O(nlogn) [GJPT] divides the input into n-2 triangles which is not always optimal [P].

PMNRP (Minimum Number Rectangular Partition for rectangles with *point* holes) . Given a rectangle with degenerate holes, i.e. isolated internal points, and a natural number k, decide whether the rectangle can be partitioned into k or fewer rectangles such that the points are not interior to any of the rectangles in the partition.

MNCP (Minimum Number Convex Partition) . Given a polygon with polygon holes, and a natural number k, decide whether the figure can be partitioned into k or fewer convex parts.

3MNCP1 (Three Dimensional Minimum Number Convex Partition 1) . Given a one-connected polyhedron and natural number k, decide whether the polyhedron can be partitioned into k or fewer convex parts.

MNDT (Minimum Number Diagonal Triangulation) . Given a polygon with polygon holes, and a natural number k, decide whether the polygon can be partitioned into k or fewer triangles, by drawing not-intersecting diagonals.

MNT (Minimum Number Triangulation) . Given a polygon with polygon holes, and a natural number k, decide whether the figure can be partitioned into k or fewer triangles.

The NP-hardness of 3MNCP1 explains why Chazelle was able to develop only approximation polynomial-time algorithms for this problem [C1].

The PMNRP problem allows point holes , i.e. degenerate polygon holes. The idea of point holes is not quite abstract . For instance, if we divide some area full of holes into rooms without holes, drawing lines of standard thickness δ, then holes of dimensions not exceeding δ may be viewed as point holes.

PMNRP and MNDT can easily be shown to be in NP. The membership of the three remaining NP-hard problems in NP is an open question .

The NP-completeness of PMNRP suggests that point holes are harder than rectilinear polygon holes . Similarly, the second and the fourth NP-hard result suggest that multiconnected polygons are much more difficult to decompose than one connected ones. In the proof of NP-hardness of MNCP, MDNT,and MNT strongly non-rectilinear holes play an important role. This, and the fact that point holes may also be viewed as non-rectilinear holes, explains the title .

It is interesting that if we look for a minimum edge length rectangular partition then rectilinear polygon holes are sufficient to obtain NP-completeness. The minimum edge length problems corresponding to the NP-hard minimum number partition problems are the more NP-hard (see [LPRS]).

This paper is an improved version of an original draft with the same title. The first reason for this improvement has been a recent paper of O'Rourke and Supowit [OS]. They obtained three NP-hardness results for minimum number decomposition problems, allowing overlapping of decomposing figures. Their proofs are by transformation from 3SAT, whereas we use a planar version of 3SAT which has been recently shown to be NP-complete by Lichtenstein [L] . If O'Rourke and Supowit knew about Lichtenstein's result, they could eliminate overlapping, which they used only in the design of crossovers. Taking this into consideration, their results coincide with ours in the case of the NP-hardness of MNCP. The optimal partitions of the multiconnected polygon, constructed by O'Rourke and Supowit in their proof of the NP-hardness of the minimum number convex decomposition problem, can be obtained by drawing not-intersecting diagonals. *Hence their proof technique (contrary to ours) also yields the NP-completeness of the minimum number diagonal convex partition problem.* In our original draft, truth setting components are unneccessarily complicated. Here they are reduced to simple variable loops, following the idea of O'Rourke and Supowit. The second reason has been the achievement of new results, i.e. the NP-hardness of MNDT, and MNT. In their proof, we again use ideas from [OS].

NP-hardness of PMNRP and MNCP

We shall assume a slightly less restricted version of planar 3SAT, PL3SAT, with the following instances :

3CNF formula F with variables x_i, $1 \leq i \leq n$, and clauses c_j, $1 \leq j \leq m$, and a planar bipartite graph $G=(\{x_i \mid 1 \leq i \leq n\} \cup \{c_j \mid 1 \leq j \leq m\}, E)$ such that $(x_i, c_j) \in E$ if and only if x_i or $\overline{x}_i$ is a literal of c_j.

To prove the NP-completeness of PMNRP we shall reduce a slight modification of PL3SAT to a generalization of PMNRP.

In comparison to PL3SAT, the modified PL3SAT (MPLSAT) allows arbitrary clauses consisting of two literals, but on the other hand, each clause with three literals has to contain at least one negated, and one positive literal. By adding new variables we can easily reduce PL to MPLSAT. Thus MPLSAT is NP-complete.

By a *rectilinear figure* we shall mean a polygon with holes in the form of *rectilinear polygons with rectlinear polygon holes, vertical or horizontal line segments, and isolated points*, where the inside polygons and line segments do not intersect but may touch one another. Clearly, the inside of a hole in a hole of a rectilinear figure is a part of the inside of the figure.We consider the following generalization of PMNRP :

GMNRP . Given a rectilinear figure, and a natural number k, decide whether the figure can be partitioned into k or fewer rectangles.

By *concave points* of a planar figure we shall mean not only the corners of its interior, reflex angles, but also its point holes, and the endpoints of its line segment holes. Depending on the context, we shall understand a *partition* of a figure into simpler ones either as the collection of the partitioning line segments or as the set of the simpler figures. The following lemma is an obvious generalization of Theorem 1 from [LLMPL].

Lemma 1 . In any minimum number partition of a rectilinear figure into rectangles, each line segment is colinear with a concave vertex of the figure.

We can simulate the boundaries of internal rectilinear polygons and segments by appropriate dense points. This, Lemma 1 , and the fact that we can find an optimal partition for each of the polygon holes of a rectilinear figure in polynomial time (see Introduction) yields :

Theorem 1 . GMNRD is many-one polynomial-time reducible to PMNRP.
Proof. Let F be a rectilinear figure. We may assume w.l.o.g. that the outer boundary of F is a rectangle. Otherwise we can easily construct a rectangle with a rectangular hole such that F can be embedded in the hole. The area between the rectangular boundary of the hole and the outer boundary of F forms a multiconnected hole in the resulting figure. Clearly, F can be partitioned into k rectangles if and only if the resulting figure can be partitioned into $k+4$ rectangles.

The lines colinear with boundary segments of F induce a rectilinear grid with at most n^2 grid points inside

F or on boundaries of F. Hence, we can partition F into n^2 or fewer rectangles. Between each pair of neighboring horizontal or vertical lines of the grid, let us respectively draw n^2 horizontal or vertical new lines . In other words, we embed the original grid in a new grid, n^2+1 times thinner. Let F' be the figure of the same external boundary as F, containing as point holes all the points of the new grid that lie on internal boundaries of F.

We shall show that there exists an optimal partition of F' into rectangles, containing all line segments lying on internal boundaries of F. This will prove that F can be partitioned into k or fewer rectangles if and only if F' can be partitioned into k+m or fewer rectangles, where m is the number of rectangles in a minimum number rectangular partition of the *polygons with polygon holes* that are holes in F. By applying the mentioned algorithm for MNRP, we can determine m in polynomial time. Hence, we shall obtain polynomial-time reducibility of GMNP to PMNRP .

Assume inductively that there is a minimum number rectangular partition of F', M, including all internal boundary segments of F lying on the first i-th bottom, horizontal grid lines plus k internal boundary segments lying on the i+1 line from the bottom . Notice that by Lemma 1 M lies on the new grid . It is sufficient to show how to construct a new optimal partition of F, additionally including one more of such horizontal segments on the i+1 line . When we have an optimal partition of F', including all horizontal boundary segments, we can repeat this inductive procedure for vertical segments.

Let s be such a horizontal segment not included in M , and let C be the collection of all new grid points that lie inside s, but not inside any horizontal segment of M. If C is empty then we are done . The number of rectangles in M is not greater than the number of new grid points inside s. For this reason, there are p, q ∈ C, such that p, q are neighbors in the new grid and p is an endpoint of a horizontal segment in M, disjoint from q (see Fig.1).

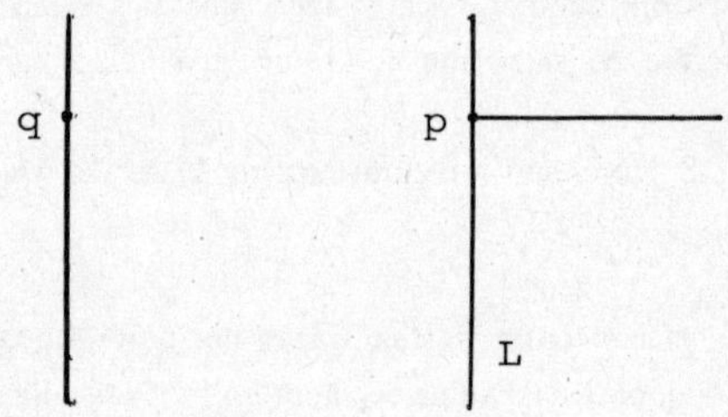

Fig.1.

Let L be the vertical line segment containing p. If L is colinear with a concave point of F, then we mark the pair (p,q) and look for another such a pair, unmarked as yet. Otherwise, we find the closest to p, horizontal segment of M or of the perimeter of F, that lies below p and touches L from both sides. Let u be the piece of L lying between p and the above segment . We move u towards the vertical line of q, pulling all horizontal segments touching u from the other side, and compressing the horizontal segments between u and the vertical line of q. Since p and q are neighbors in the new grid, we can not meet any vertical segment during this movement (see Lemma 1), before reaching the line of q. As a result, we obtain a new optimal partition of F', still including the same horizontal segments, with the set C decreased by p. Iterating this process we come to the situation where only marked pairs (p,q) may exist . If C is empty then we are done . Otherwise, there are two points of the original grid, lying on s, such that at least n^2 vertical segments lie between them in the partition of F', recently constructed. This contradicts the minimality of this partition ∎

In the proof of Theorem 1 , the density of the simulating points is essential . For instance, if we cover a tall tower of rectangular holes with too scattered colinear points then it might be more efficient to draw only a series of vertical lines passing through these points instead of drawing the boundaries of the rectangles .

Now it is clear that a reduction of MPLSAT to GMNRP implies the NP-completeness of MNRP.

Let (F, G) be an instance of MPLSAT, where F is a formula and G is the corresponding planar graph . To reduce MPLSAT to GMNRD we construct a rectilinear figure , and a natural number k such that F is satisfiable if and only if the figure, denoted by H, can be decomposed into k or fewer rectangles.

The basic component of H is a cranked wire (see Fig.2 (A)) .The dimensions of the cranks are not essential . Only the colinearity of segments is important. Each wire is several times bent 90° to form a closed loop. A straight section of wire needs to contain one or two cranks (See Fig. 2 (A)) . By applying isolated points we could even have a simpler form of wires . However this would decresase the uniformity of our proofs. We have the following, obvious lemma :

Lemma 2 . A separated wire loop is most efficiently partitioned into rectangles either horizontally or vertically but not both (see Fig. 2 (B,C)). Any other partition yields at least one rectangle more.

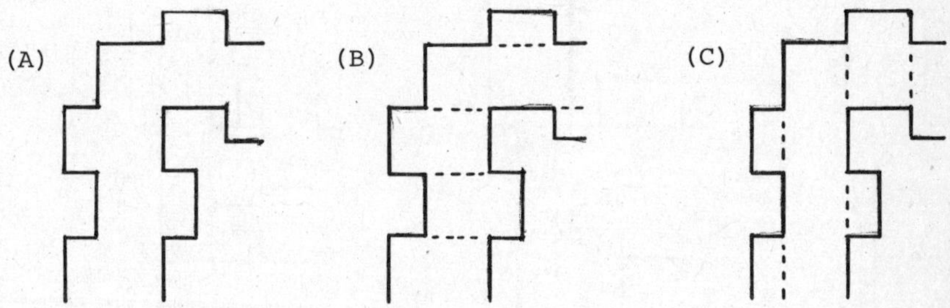

Fig.2. A section of a wire with two bends (A), and the vertical and horizontal partition of the sectiion (B,C) .

Each variable x corresponds in a one-to-one manner to a wire loop. We interprete the (absolute) vertical decomposition of the loop as setting x to 1, and the horizontal decomposition as setting x to 0 .

Each clause c corresponds in a one-to-one manner to a junction. Three and two argument clause junctions may occur in H . A three argument junction is shown in Fig. 3 (A) . Two argument junctions can be obtained by blocking one of the arms of the triple junction . The c-junction touches a loop bend (see Fig.3 (A)) if and only if the variable x corresponding to the loop appears in c . Loop bends touched by c junction correspond in a one-to-one manner to literals of c . The arm of such a bend that lengthens the junction , is vertical if x is a literal in c, and is horizontal if $\bar{x}$ occurs in c. If the c-junction is three argument, the above requirement can always be realized due to the fact that c contains at least one positive , and one negative literal. Owing the planarity of G, junctions and loops are arranged in such a way that they do not overlap.

Note that if the arm of a loop bend which lengthens a junction is partitioned by segments parallel to its direction, then the long rectangle inside it can be expanded inside the junction. For instance, see

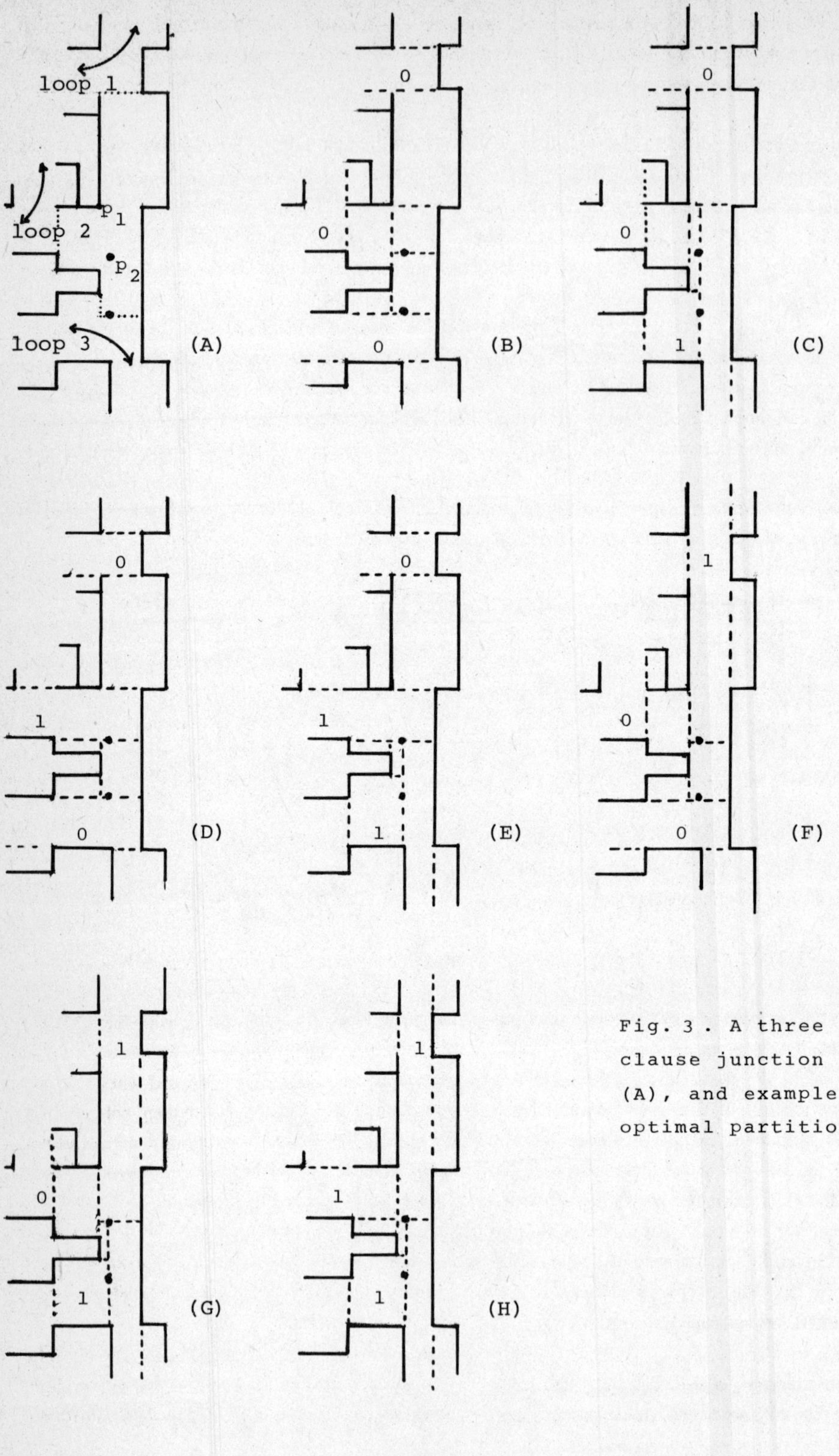

Fig. 3 . A three argument clause junction for GMNRP (A), and examples of its optimal partitions (B-H).

Fig. 3 (C, D) . By the orientation of the junction and Lemma 1, such a partition of the wire section means that the literal corresponding to the loop bend has the value 1 under the variable setting given by loops . This all enables us to prove :

Lemma 3 . If at least one loop adjacent to a clause junction brings 1 for the corresponding literal, then we can lengthen some rectangles occurring in the adjacent loops such that only 3 new rectangles are needed to partition the junction. Otherwise, at least 4 new rectangles are necessary .

The points p_1 , p_2 in Fig. 3 (A) are not horizontally colinear. Two rectangles coming from the bottom and top wire respectively are thus prevented from merging. Therefore, we can also prove :

Lemma 4 . In any partition of H, at least 3 rectangles lie wholly inside a clause junction.

Let k be the total minimum number of rectangles partitioning loops plus 3 times the number of clauses of F. It follows from Lemmas 2 through 4 that any partition of H can have no more than k rectangles only if F is satisfiable . On the other hand, if F is satisfiable then by Lemmas 2 and 3, we can cover H with k not overlapping rectangles. It suffices to partition the loops according to a 0, 1 assignment that satisfies F and to partition each clause junction using only three inside rectangles .

Lemma 5 . H can be partitioned into k or fewer rectangles if and only if F is satisfiable.

The construction of H can be performed in logarithmic-space. By Lemma 1 we may consider only these rectangular partitions of H , in which each edge is colinear with a concave vertex of F . Finally, the dimensions of H and the number k are polynomially related to the size of G. Summarizing :

Theorem 2 . GMNRP is strongly NP-complete .

By Theorem 1 we obtain :

Corollary 1 . PMNRP is strongly NP-complete .

In the case of MNCP, point holes are not allowed . Therefore, to prove the NP-hardness of MNCP we have to modify H . A new three argument junction is shown in Fig. 4 (A) . The sharp "sprouts" replace the isolated points and penisular segments of the old junction. Fig.4 (B) through (H) shows optimal partitions of the junction . The absence of point holes does not mean that the constructed figure does not have holes at all. First of all, any loop creates an island . We could even get rid of the islands surrounded by loops, using unclosed wires with odd number of bends, instead of the wire loops. However, if the planar G contains cycles then polygon one-connected islands surrounded by wires and junctions will still appear in the figure. Analogously we can prove:

Theorem 3 . MNCP is strongly NP-hard .

The details of the proof of Theorem 3 are left to the reader .

Corollary 2 . 3MNCP1 is strongly NP-hard .
Proof. The proof is by a reduction of MNCP to 3MNCP1. We transform the input polygon with polygon holes into a polyhedron consisting of two horizontal layers. The cross-sections of the first layer are equal to the input, multiconnected polygon. The cross-sections of the second layer are equal to a fixed rectangle whose horizontal

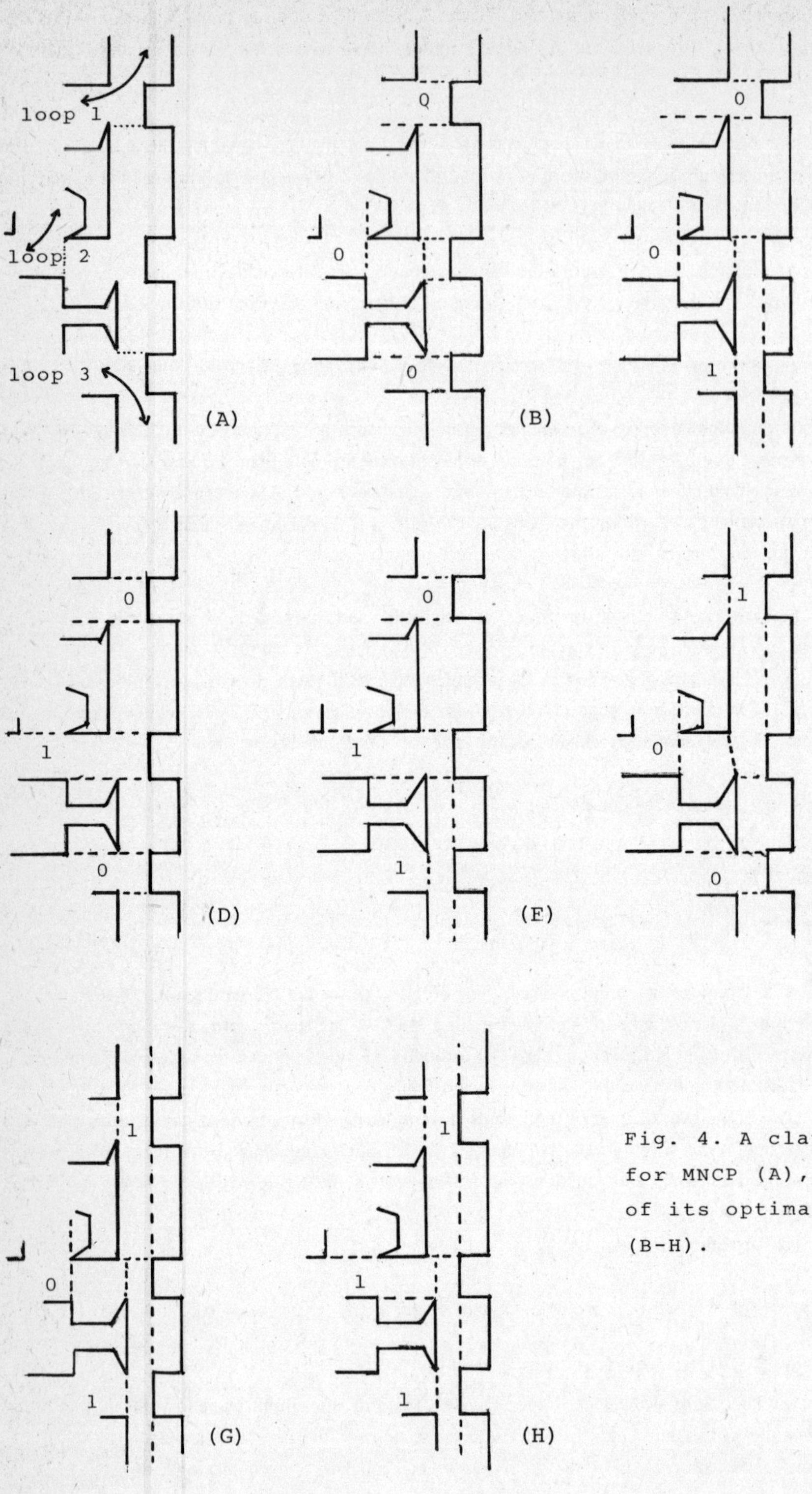

Fig. 4. A clause junction for MNCP (A), and examples of its optimal partitions (B-H).

projection includes the horizontal projection of the first layer. We may assume w.l.o.g. that the input polygon contains at least one hole. Therefore, it can be partitioned into k convex polygons if and only if the polyhedron can be partitioned into k+1 convex parts ∎

As in the rectilinear case, we could simulate the boundaries of polygon islands by dense points, obtaining as a corollary the NP-hardness of the problem of partitioning polygons with point holes into convex polygons . However the proof of this fact is much longer than that in the rectilinear case, and therefore we shall skip it .

NP-hardness of MNDT and MNT

The proof of NP-hardness for MNDT and MNT is by a direct reduction from PL3SAT. Let F be a 3CNF formula, where the bipartite graph G associated with F is planar. We shall construct the polygon with polygon holes, H, and the natural number k such that :

(i) H can be partitioned into k or fewer triangles if and only if F is satisfiable, and
(ii) there is a minimum number partition of H into triangles, where all edges of the triangles are diagonals of H .

Since the construction of H can be performed in log-space, the two above properties of H will imply NP-hardness of MNDT and MNT.

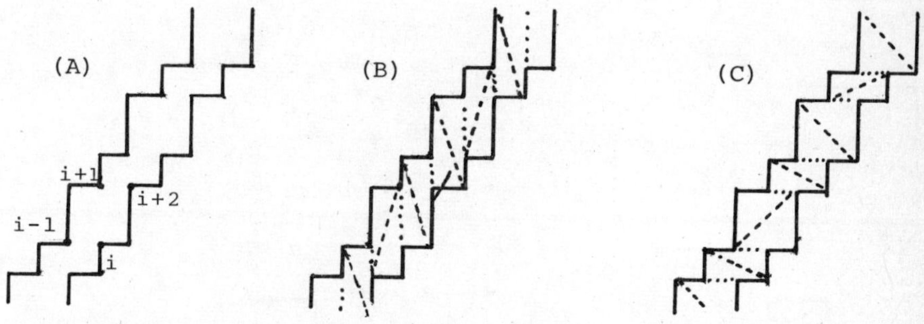

Fig.5. A straight section of a loop for MNDT and MNT (A), and its optimal partitions into triangles (B,C).

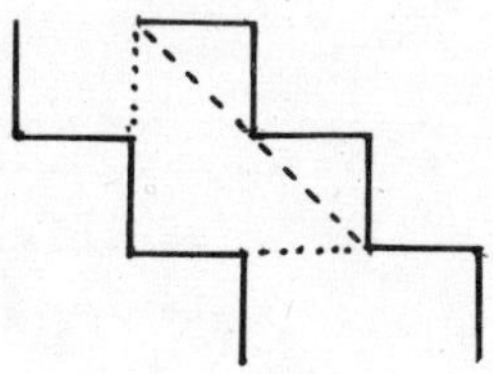

Fig.6. A triangulation of a piece of Masek's wire.

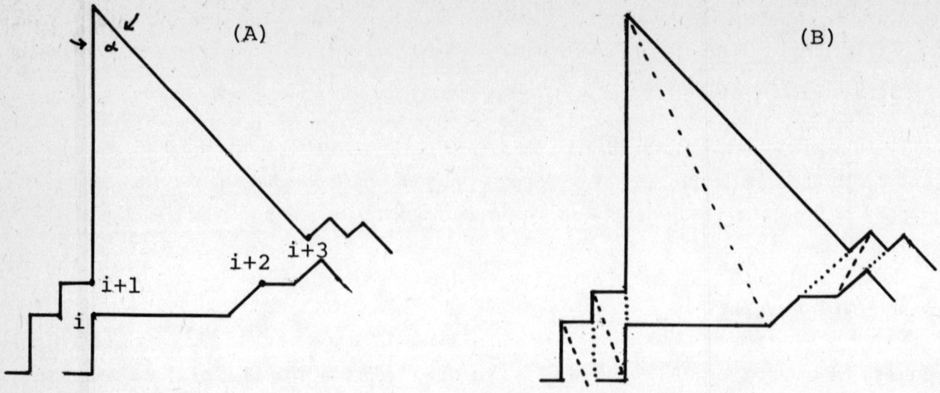

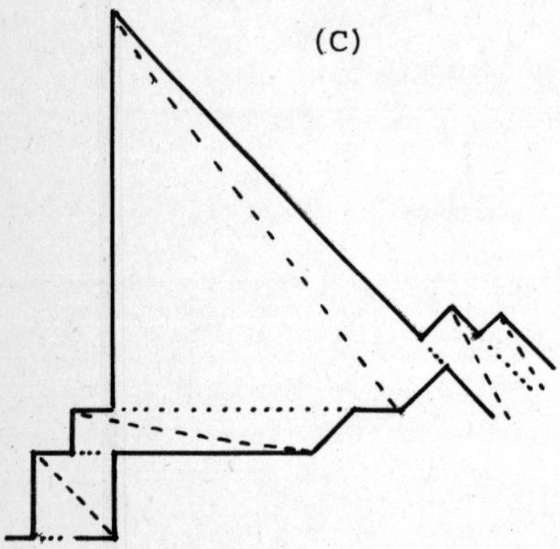

Fig. 7. A 90 - α° bend, where $0 < \alpha < 90$ (A), and two examples of its optimal triangulation (B,C).

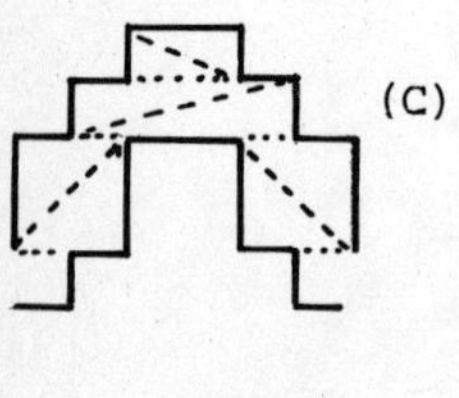

Fig.8. A 90° bend (A), and two examples of its optimal triangulation (B-C).

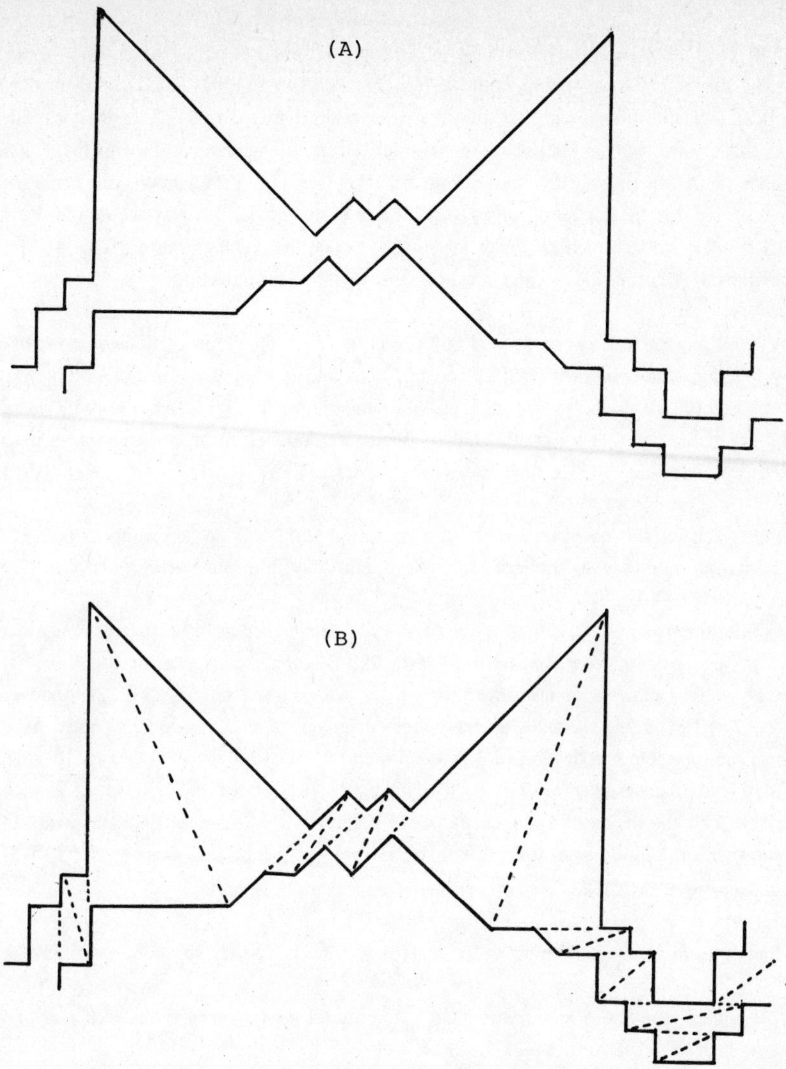

Fig.9. A signal invertor (A), and an example of an optimal triangulation of the invertor (B).

The design of H is similar to that from the previous NP-hardness proof . H again consists of variable loops and clause junctions . A straight section of a variable loop (see Fig. 5(A)) is similar to the wire orginally applied by Masek [M] , and then by O'Rourke and Supowit (see Fig. 6). Our modification consists in alternating the length of the vertical segments bounding such a section (assuming that it forms 45° angle with the horizontal direction). Due to this change, we can eliminate the possibility of the triangulation shown in Fig. 6. There remain two optimal methods of partitioning such a section into triangles (see Fig. 5(B,C)). We can connect pairs of its interior concave vertices either by horizontal or by vertical line segments. In this way we divide the section into rectangles. Then, it is not essential which diagonals are used to divide the rectangles into triangles . The horizontal method is interpreted as transmitting 1 and the vertical method as transmitting 0.

Loops may bend any angle between 0° and 90° (see Fig. 7) . This kind of bend is a modification of a bend invented by O'Rourke and Supowit [OS] . See Fig. 7 (B) and (C) for two ways of optimally partitioning such a bend into triangles . We shall also use another, 90° bend shown in Fig. 8 (A). Two 45° bends combined with this 90° bend invert the signal (see Fig. 9). The 90° bends are optional in the construction of invertors. They can be eliminated by deforming the square sides of loops.

Let us number the interior concave corners of a separated variable loop according to Fig. 5 through 8 , using consecutive natural numbers 1 through 2n. We obtain the following lemma :

Lemma 6 . In any minimum number partition of the loop into triangles, either each pair of concave vertices 2k, 2k+1 mod 2n, or each pair of concave vertices 2k-1, 2k, is connected by a diagonal.

Proof. Simultaneously, let us draw diagonals between each pair of concave vertices 2k-1, 2k , and each pair of concave vertices 2k, 2k+1 mod 2n. Next, let us erase these diagonals that lie inside 90° bends. As a result, we obtain a partition of the loop into a collection of quadrangles and 90° bends, say D (see Fig. 10). Consider any partition of the loop into triangles, say T. For each triangle $t \in T$, let $n(t)$ be the number of elements from D whose inside overlaps with the inside of t. Given $d \in D$, we define $T(d)$ as the sum of $n(t)^{-1}$ over all triangles t whose inside overlaps with the inside of d. It is clear that T partitions the loop into exactly $\Sigma_{d \in D} T(d)$ triangles. Lemma 6 results from the two following observations :

(i) for each quadrangle from D, the minimum value of T(d) is 1, and for each 90° bend the minimum value of T(d) is 4, and

(ii) the only way to achieve the above minimum values is to connect by diagonals either each pair of vertices 2k, 2k+1 mod 2n, or each pair of vertices 2k-1, 2k ∎

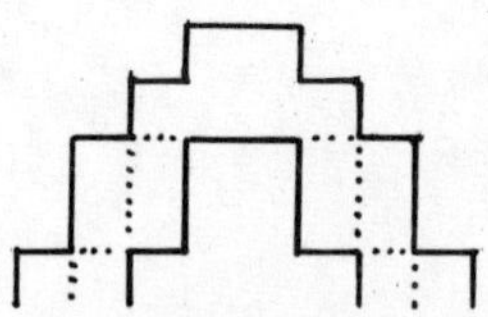

Fig.10. A partition of a loop section into quadrangles and 90° bends.

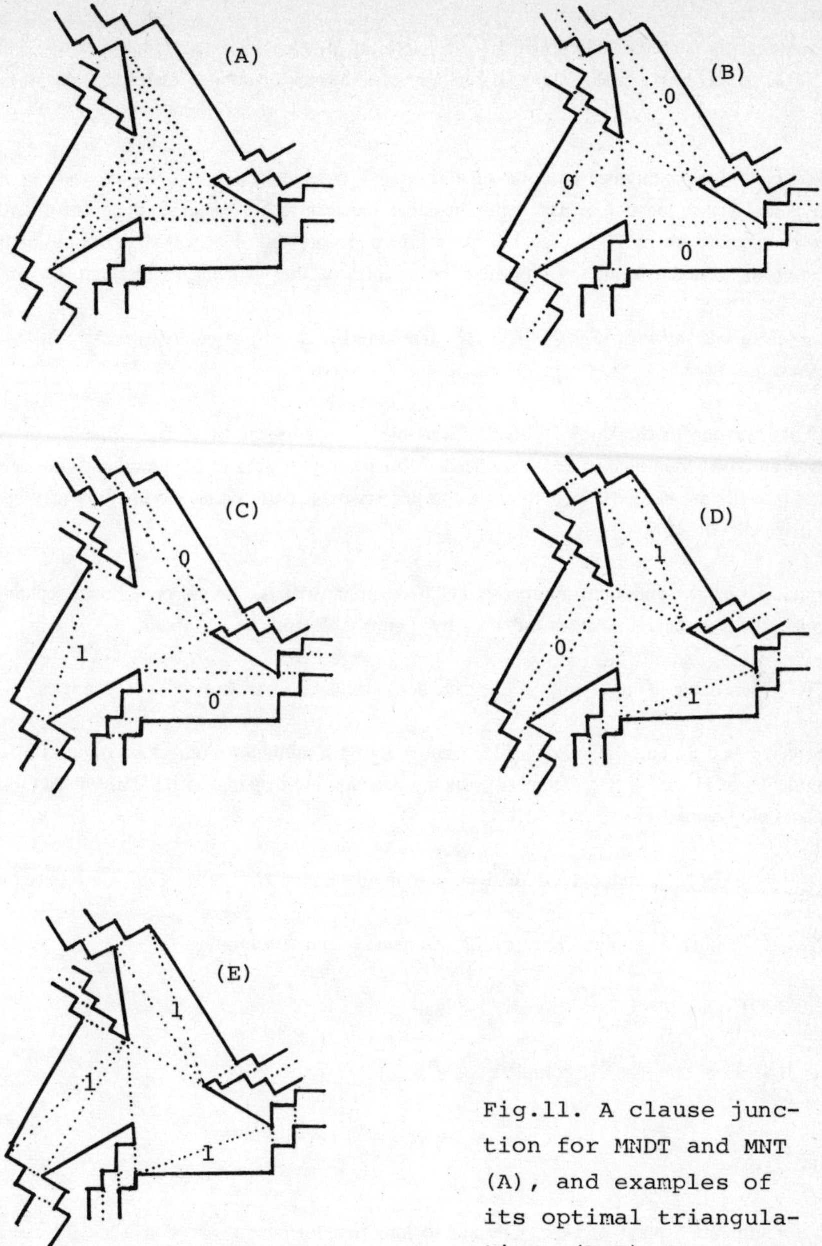

Fig.11. A clause junction for MNDT and MNT (A), and examples of its optimal triangulations (B-E).

Each straight section of a variable loop that is adjacent to a clause junction, corresponds to a negative or positive occurrence of the variable represented by the loop , in the clause represented by the junction . Signal invertors are installed in each variable loop in such a way that by Lemma 6 each loop has the following property :

Lemma 7 . In any minimum number partition of a separated variable loop into triangles, each of its straight sections adjacent to a clause junction is partitioned in either the relative horizontal or the relative vertical way . Any of two such sections are partitioned in the same horizontal or vertical way if and only if both of them correspond either to a negative or to a positive occurrence of the variable represented by the loop .

A clause junction is shown in Fig. 11 (A) . By examining Fig. 11 (B) through (E) we obtain the following lemma on clause junctions :

Lemma 8 . If at least one of the three sections of variable loops adjacent to a clause junction is partitioned horizontally then only two additional triangles are needed to partition the area of the junction . Otherwise, exactly three additional triangles are needed . In both cases, the line segments partitioning the junction may be restricted only to the diagonals of H.

Let us define k as the minimum number of not overlapping triangles necessary to cover separate variable loops plus twice the number of clauses of F . By Lemmas 7 and 8 we obtain :

Lemma 9 . F is satisfiable if and only if H can be partitioned into k or fewer triangles.

By Lemmas 6 and 8 , and the design of H, there is always a minimum number partition of H which is a diagonal triangulation of H, i.e. all line segments in such a partition are diagonals of H. This yields the following, modified version of Lemma 11.

Lemma 10 . F is satisfiable if and only if there is a triangulation of H consisting of k or fewer triangles .

Similarly, as Lemma 5 implies Theorem 2, Lemma 9 and 10 imply :

Theorem 4 . MNDT and MNT are strongly NP-hard .

Corollary 2 . MNDT is strongly NP-complete .

Final Remarks

From the application point of view, it is not so important to have a partition achieving the minimum number of parts. A nearly optimal partition is quite sufficient. The author believes that there are good approximation heuristics for the minimum number problems corresponding to the decision problems shown to be NP-hard in this paper.

In the proof of the NP-completeness of PMNRP is essential to allow point holes to be *corectilinear*, i.e. two or more point holes may occur on the same horizontal or vertical line. Open is the restricted version of PMNRP where the only holes allowed are non-corectilinear points [P].

Acknowledgements

I would like to express my appreciation to Ron Pinter, Ronald Rivest and Adi Shamir for their encouragment, to Tom Leighton for telling me about the NP-completeness of planar satisfiability, and to David Johnson for his critical remarks.

REFERENCES

[C] Chazelle,B., Computational Geometry and Convexity, PhD thesis, Yale University, 1980.

[C1] Chazelle,B., Convex Decompositions of Polyhedra, Proceedings of the 13th ACM SIGACT Symposium, Milwaukee, Wisconsin, May, 1981.

[CD] Chazelle,B. and D. Dobkin, Decomposing polygon into its convex parts, Proceedings of the 11th ACM SIGACT Symposium, New York, 1979.

[GJPT] Garey M.R., Johnson D.S., Preparata F.P., Tarjan R.E., Triangulating a simple polygon, Information Processing Letters, Vol. 7, No. 4, 1978.

[L] Lichtenstein,D., Planar Formulae and their Uses, to appear.

[LPRS] Lingas A., R.Pinter, R.Rivest and A.Shamir, Minimum Edge Length Decompositions of Rectilinear Figures, unpublished manuscript, MIT, 1981.

[M] Masek W., Some NP-complete set covering problems, unpublished manuscript, MIT, 1979.

[OS] O'Rourke J., K.Supowit, Some NP-hard polygon decomposition problems, submitted for publication.

[PLLML] Pagli,L., E.Lodi, F.Luccio, C.Mugnai and W.Lipski, On two dimensional data organization 2, Fundamenta Informaticae, Vol. 2, No.3, 1979.

[P] Pinter R., private communication, 1981.

[SH] Shamos, I. and D. Hoey, Geometric intersection problems, Proceedings of the 17th IEEE FOCS Symposium, 1976.

FIXED-POINT SEMANTICS FOR ALGEBRAIC (TREE) GRAMMARS

extended abstract

Damian Niwiński
Institute of Mathematics, Warsaw University
PL-00 901 Warsaw, PKiN IX p.

It follows from the series of papers of Arnold and Nivat (/AN 78/,/AN 77/,/N 79/), that the methods of algebraic semantics work still well when applied to non-deterministic recursive program schemas (ndrps) with cpo as a computation domain. A function computed by such a program is thought to produce, for a given input, a set of values resulting from finite terminating or infinite successful computation sequence for this input. Here the result of an infinite computation sequence is to be obtained as a least upper bound (lub) of an ascending chain of values and an infinite computation sequence is successful provided such a lub exists .

The Herbrand interpretation is known to be initial in the class of interpretations in cpo's. This means that a multivalued function computed by a ndrps in any interpretation can be viewed as a morphic image of the set of finite or infinite trees computed by this ndrps when freely interpreted in complete free ordered magma. A similar result is obtained for metric interpretations when a free magma is considered as a complete metric space.

Then, following algebraic semantics method, one would like to expect the set of trees computed by a program in Herbrand interpretation to be a solution of some system of equations associated to the program schema. However such a fixed-point semantics for ndrps was given only for those in the Greibach form and, exept of some separate examples (/P 80/), the class of all ndrps has been not treated in this way yet. The aim of our paper is to fill this gap and give an argument for equivalence between operational and denotational semantics for ndrps .

It turns out that the greatest fixed points combined with the least ones make a good tool for that matter. This idea was suggested to me by J.Tiuryn, it appears also in /P 80/ . Intuitively it corresponds to the fact, that both positive and negative information may increase during the run of infinite computation.

We consider ndrps's represented as algebraic tree grammars. In the first section we show, that a vector of languages, $T^{\infty}(S)$, of finite/infinite trees generated by a grammar S, can be obtained as a greatest fixed point of substitution to a vector of languages, say S', with S'_i being the language of the first contracting trees which occur in outermost derivations in S . S' in turn is proved to be a least fixed point of some polynomial vector function or, equivalently, to be generated by an alrebgaic tree grammar. Thus fixed point semantics for algebraic tree grammars is given in two steps: given a grammar S, we first find S' using least fixed points, and next we find $T^{\infty}(S)$ as a greatest fixed point of substitution to S'.

The second section is devoted to the grammars of words. The main result is a characterisation of the languages generated by algebraic grammars by means of finite terminating or infinite successful derivations, so called ∞-algebraic languages. We prove that L is ∞-algebraic iff L is equal to a component of a greatest fixed point of substitution into a vector of regular languages.

We leave as an open problem the question whether a similar characterisation is possible for ∞-algebraic polyadic languages.

I . TREE LANGUAGES AS FIXED POINTS

The basic definitions and notations are repetitions or slight variations of those in /AN 77/, /AN 78/, /N 79/ .

Let F be a finite set of function symbols, each f in F is given with arity ar(f) . Let V be a finite set of variables disjoint from F . For any such F and V, M(F,V) is the free F-magma generated by V. Its elements may be regarded as terms as well as finite trees.

Let Ω be a symbol not in $F \cup V$, let $ar(\Omega)=0$. $M(F\cup\{\Omega\},V)$, also written $M_{\Omega}(F,V)$ is ordered by syntactic order: $t \leqslant t'$ iff t' is obtained from t by replacing some Ω's in t by elements of $M_{\Omega}(F,V)$. By adding infinite trees as the least upper bounds of ideals, $M_{\Omega}(F,V)$ can be made into a complete free ordered magma $M^{\infty}_{\Omega}(F,V)$. The set of finite/infinite F-trees with variables among V, denoted by $M^{\infty}(F,V)$, can be now viewed as the set of maximal elements in $M^{\infty}_{\Omega}(F,V)$.

For $t,t_1,\ldots,t_m$ in $M_{\Omega}(F,V)$, $v_1,\ldots,v_m$ in V, $t[t_1/v_1,\ldots,t_m/v_m]$ is defined as usual for terms. Generally, for $t,t_1,\ldots,t_m$ in $M^{\infty}_{\Omega}(F,V)$,

$$t[t_1/v_1,\ldots,t_m/v_m]=\sup\left\{ t'[t'_1/v_1,\ldots,t'_m/v_m] : t',t'_1,\ldots,t'_m \in M_{\Omega}(F,V) \text{ and } t'\leqslant t,\ t'_1\leqslant t_1,\ldots,t'_m\leqslant t_m \right\} .$$

Now assume $V=\{v_1,\ldots,v_k\}$ and let $V_i=\{v_1,\ldots,v_i\}$ for $i\in[k]=\{1,\ldots,k\}$. Let $\varphi=\{\varphi_1,\ldots,\varphi_n\}$ be a set of function variables, disjoint from $F\cup V\cup\{\Omega\}$, each φ_i is given with arity m_i, $m_i\leq \mathrm{card}(V)$. For a set A let PA denote the power set of A. The product $PM^{\infty}(F,V_{m_1})\times\ldots\times PM^{\infty}(F,V_{m_n})$ will be denoted by $\vec{P}M^{\infty}(F,V)$; $\vec{P}M(F,V)$, $PM(F\cup\varphi,V)$ etc. have analogous meaning. $\vec{P}M^{\infty}(F,V)$ is completely ordered by $X\sqsubseteq Y$ iff $X_1\subseteq Y_1$ & ... & $X_n\subseteq Y_n$.

The OI-substitution operator is defined inductively as follows, for any W in $\vec{P}M^{\infty}(F\cup\varphi,V)$:

$$v_j\leftarrow W = v_j\ ,$$

$$f(t_1,\ldots,t_{ar(f)})\leftarrow W = \{f(t_1',\ldots,t_{ar(f)}') : t_i'\in t_i\leftarrow W\}\ ,$$

$$\varphi_j(t_1,\ldots,t_{m_j})\leftarrow W = \bigcup_{t\in W_j} t\left[(t_1\leftarrow W)/v_1,\ldots,(t_{m_j}\leftarrow W)/v_{m_j}\right]\ ,$$

$$A\leftarrow W = \bigcup_{s\in A} s\leftarrow W \qquad \text{for } A\subseteq M(F\cup\varphi,V),$$

$$S\leftarrow W = (S_1\leftarrow W,\ldots,S_n\leftarrow W) \qquad \text{for } S \text{ in } \vec{P}M(F\cup\varphi,V)\ .$$

The reader familiar with power set algebra of finite/infinite trees presented in /T 79/ may notice that for a finite set A the function $\lambda.y_1\ldots y_n.\ A\leftarrow(y_1,\ldots,y_n)$ is polynomial in that algebra.

With each S in $\vec{P}M(F\cup\varphi,V)$ we associate a mapping :
$\vec{P}M^{\infty}(F,V)\ni X\longmapsto S\leftarrow X\in\vec{P}M^{\infty}(F,V)$.
Clearly it is $\sqsubseteq$-monotonic and by Tarski's theorem it has a greatest fixed point, which we shall denote by $\nu.S$.

On the other hand, with any S in $\vec{P}M(F\cup\varphi,V)$ with S_i's finite, we can associate an algebraic tree grammar with terminal symbols in $F\cup V$ and non-terminal in φ. It can be written as a system of equations:

$$S\left\{\ \varphi_i(v_1,\ldots,v_{m_i}) = S_i\ , \quad \text{for } i\in[n]\ .\right.$$

The relation $\underset{S}{\rightarrow}$ on $M(F\cup\varphi,V)$ is now defined by :

$$t\underset{S}{\rightarrow}t' \text{ iff } t=\alpha\varphi_i(t_1,\ldots,t_{m_i})\beta \quad \text{(regarded as term) and}$$

$$t'=\alpha s\left[t_1/v_1,\ldots,t_{m_i}/v_{m_i}\right]\beta \text{ for some } s \text{ in } S_i\ .$$

A production $\varphi_i(v_1,\ldots,v_{m_i})\underset{S}{\rightarrow}s$, with s in S_i, is called sometimes a derivation rule.

The relation $\underset{S}{\overset{*}{\rightarrow}}$ is the reflexive-transitive closure of $\underset{S}{\rightarrow}$.

A finite or infinite sequence $t_0, t_1, \dots, t_m, \dots$ is called a derivation in S from t_0 if $t_m \underset{S}{\rightarrow} t_{m+1}$ provided t_{m+1} exists. A finite derivation is called terminating if the last element belongs to $M(F,V)$.

Let $T(S,t) = \{ t' \in M(F,V) : t \overset{*}{\underset{S}{\rightarrow}} t' \}$,

$T(S) = (T(S, \varphi_1(v_1,\dots,v_{m_1})),\dots,T(S, \varphi_n(v_1,\dots,v_{m_n})))$.

An infinite successful derivation will be defined as in /AN 77/, using the function $o : M(F\cup\varphi,V) \longrightarrow M_{\Omega}(F,V)$ which extracts the "outermost terminal factor" of a tree, o is defined inductively by

$$o(v_i) = v_i ,$$
$$o(f(t_1,\dots,t_{ar(f)})) = f(o(t_1),\dots,o(t_{ar(f)})) ,$$
$$o(\varphi_i(t_1,\dots,t_{m_i})) = \Omega .$$

Note that $t \underset{S}{\rightarrow} t'$ implies $o(t) \leqslant o(t')$ hence for every infinite derivation $t_0, t_1, \dots$, $\sup_{m<\omega} o(t_m)$ always exists. We call an infinite derivation successful with result t if $\sup_{m<\omega} o(t_m)$ belongs to $M^{\omega}(F,V)$ and is equal to t . We write $t \overset{\omega}{\underset{S}{\rightarrow}} t'$ if t' may be obtained from t as a result of an infinite successful derivation in S .

Let $T^{\omega}(S,t) = \{ t' \in M^{\infty}(F,V) : t \overset{\omega}{\underset{S}{\rightarrow}} t' \}$,$T^{\infty}(S,t) = T(S,t) \cup T^{\omega}(S,t)$,

$T^{\infty}(S) = (T^{\infty}(S, \varphi_1(v_1,\dots,v_{m_1})),\dots,T^{\infty}(S, \varphi_n(v_1,\dots,v_{m_n})))$.

A tree language $X \subseteq M^{\infty}(F,V)$ is called algebraic (∞-algebraic) if $X = T(S, \varphi_i(v_1,\dots,v_{m_i}))$ ($X = T^{\infty}(S, \varphi_i(v_1,\dots,v_{m_i}))$) for some S.

A derivation will be called outermost if every application of derivation rule is applied to an outermost occurence of φ_i. One checks that any finite terminating or infinite successful derivation may be replaced by an outermost one with the same result.

A tree $t \in M^{\infty}(F\cup\varphi,V)$ will be called contracting if its root is labelled by a symbol from $F \cup V$.

For a grammar $S\{\varphi_i(v_1,\dots,v_{m_i}) = s_i, \quad i\in[n]$, let

$S'_i = \{ t : \varphi_i(v_1,\dots,v_{m_i}) \underset{S}{\rightarrow} t_1 \underset{S}{\rightarrow} \dots \underset{S}{\rightarrow} t_{m-1} \underset{S}{\rightarrow} t$ for some $t_1,\dots,t_{m-1}$ and t is contracting while $t_1,\dots,t_m$ are not $\}$,

for $i \in [n]$.

Proposition 1 . $S' = (S'_1,\dots,S'_n)$ is a vector of algebraic tree languages .

Sketch of proof .

Assume first $s_i \cap V = \emptyset$ for all $i \in [n]$. In this case in order to generate S' we take a grammar S'' with terminal symbols in $F \cup \Psi \cup V$ and non-terminal alphabet $\{\Psi_1, \ldots, \Psi_n\}$:

$$S''\left\{ \Psi_i(v_1,\ldots,v_{m_i}) = \{t \in S_i : t \text{ is contracting}\} \cup \cup \left\{ \Psi_j(t_1,\ldots,t_{m_j}) : \varphi_j(t_1,\ldots,t_{m_j}) \in S_i \right\} , \; i\in[n] \right.$$

It is not very hard to see that any initial segment of an outermost derivation in S up to the first contracting step can be transformed into a terminating derivation in S'' by replacing φ_i's by Ψ_i's. On the other hand, a derivation in S'' becomes such a segment by converse replacing Ψ_i's by φ_i's . Hence $S' = T(S'')$.

The construction of a suitable S'' for general case is analogous to that presented in the proof of the "only if" part of Theorem II. □

One observe that if the grammar associated to S is in the Greibach normal form(i.e.all the trees in S_i's are contracting) then $S' = S$. In that case, by /AN 77/ $T^{\infty}(S) = \nu.S$. We prove in general

<u>Theorem</u> I . For any grammar S, $T^{\infty}(S) = \nu.S'$.

<u>Sketch of proof</u> .

Since by Tarski's theorem $\nu.S' = \bigcup\{X : X \subseteq S'_{\leftarrow}X\}$, it is enough to prove: (i) $X \subseteq S'_{\leftarrow}X$ implies $X \subseteq T^{\infty}(S)$,

(ii) $T^{\infty}(S) \subseteq S'_{\leftarrow}T^{\infty}(S)$.

To prove (i) we first establish two auxiliary results .

<u>Proposition</u> 2 . Assume for some X, $X \subseteq S'_{\leftarrow}X$. Then for any t in $M(F \cup \varphi, V_{m_i})$ and u in $M^{\infty}(F,V)$ such that $u \in t_{\leftarrow}X$, there exists t' in $M(F \cup \varphi, V_{m_i})$ such that $u \in t'_{\leftarrow}X$ and $t' \in t_{\leftarrow}S'$.

If $t \in M(F,V)$ we set $t' = t$ else the proof of Proposition 2 is by structural induction on t .

<u>Proposition</u> 3 . $t' \in t_{\leftarrow}S'$ implies $t \overset{*}{\underset{S}{\rightarrow}} t'$.

It follows immediately from Proposition 1 .

Now assume $X \subseteq S'_{\leftarrow}X$ and let $u \in X_i$ for some $i \in [n]$. We define inductively a sequence t_m, $m < \omega$, satisfying for each m

(a) $u \in t_{m\leftarrow}X$,

(b) $t_{m+1} \in t_{m\leftarrow}S'$,

by setting $t_0 = \varphi_i(v_1,\ldots,v_{m_i})$ and applying Proposition 2 in induction step. We have $o(t_m) \leqslant o(t_{m+1})$ for all m and since all the trees in S'_j's are contracting $o(t_m) = o(t_{m+1})$ only if $o(t_{m+1}) \in M(F,V)$. In that case we have $t_k = u$ for all $k > m$. Next, by Proposition 3, $t_0 \overset{*}{\underset{S}{\rightarrow}} t_1 \overset{*}{\underset{S}{\rightarrow}} \ldots$. Hence we observe that either $t_0 \overset{*}{\underset{S}{\rightarrow}} t_m = u$ for some m or the sequence may be completed to an infinite successful derivation, clearly with result u. In both cases $u \in T^{\infty}(S,x_i)$ and (i) is proved .

To prove (ii) assume $u \in T^{\infty}(S,x_i)$ and let $t_0 = \varphi_i(v_1,\dots,v_{m_i})$, $t_1,\dots,t_m,\dots$ be a finite terminating or infinite successful outermost derivation with result u . It is established in /AN 77/ that in this case $u \in t_1 \leftarrow T^{\infty}(S)$. However in the same way one proves $u \in t_m \leftarrow T^{\infty}(S)$ for any m .Let t_{m_0} be the first contracting tree in the derivation. By Proposition 1 $t_{m_0} \in S_i'$, hence $u \in t_{m_0} \leftarrow T^{\infty}(S) \subseteq S' \leftarrow T^{\infty}(S)$ as desired. □

A FIXED-POINT CHARACTERISATION OF ∞-ALGEBRAIC LANGUAGES

We follow /N 79/ in basic definitions and notations. For any finite set of symbols V , V^* denotes the set of all finite words over V , including the empty word e , V^{ω} denotes the set of all infinite words (of lenght ω) . The union $V^* \cup V^{\omega}$ is denoted by V^{∞} . It is ordered by the usual syntactic order $\leqslant$. The concatenation of words and of sets is defined in a standard way and written by juxtaposition. A singleton $\{x\}$ will be usually denoted by x .

Let A be a finite alphabet and let $\mathcal{X}$ be an infinite set of variables disjoint from A, $\mathcal{X} = \bigcup_{m<\omega} \mathcal{X}_m$, where $\mathcal{X}_m = \{x_1,\dots,x_m\}$.

The OI-substitution operator is defined inductively as follows, for any $X = (X_1,\dots,X_n)$ in $(P(A \cup \mathcal{X}_n)^{\infty})^n$:

$$x_i \leftarrow X = X_i \ ,$$

$$a \leftarrow X = a \qquad \text{for } a \text{ in } A \ ,$$

$$us \leftarrow X = (u \leftarrow X)(s \leftarrow X) \quad \text{for } u \text{ in } (A \cup \mathcal{X}_n)^*, \quad s \text{ in } A \cup \mathcal{X}_n \ ,$$

$$V \leftarrow X = \bigcup_{u \in V} u \leftarrow X \qquad \text{for } V \subseteq (A \cup \mathcal{X}_n)^* \ ,$$

$$G \leftarrow X = (G_1 \leftarrow X,\dots,G_n \leftarrow X) \quad \text{for } G \text{ in } (P(A \cup \mathcal{X}_n)^*)^n \ .$$

Note that the functions $\lambda . x_1 \dots x_n . V \leftarrow (x_1,\dots,x_n)$ for finite V's are just the polynomial functions in the algebra PA^{∞} with operations of set union, concatenation and singleton of the elements of A as constants .

The above definition of substitution may be thought as "algebraically motivated". Notice that it differs a little from the definition in /N 79/ which is borrowed from tree case and so may be thought as "computation theory motivated". For example $x_1 x_2 \leftarrow (\{aaa\dots\}, \emptyset)$ is equal to $\emptyset$ in the sense of the former and is equal to $\{aaa\dots\}$ in the sense of the latter one. However the substitution of the empty set in the context of an infinite word is in fact the only situation where these definitions differ.

With each G in $(P(A\cup\mathcal{X}_n)^*)^n$ we associate a mapping

$$(PA^\infty)^n \ni X \longmapsto G\leftarrow X \in (PA^\infty)^n ,$$

which we shall denote by $\widehat{G}$. Clearly it is monotonic whenever $(PA^\infty)^n$ ordered by component-wise set inclusion. Hence by Tarski's theorem $\widehat{G}$ has the greatest fixed point. Let us denote it by $\nu.G$.

Any G in $(P(A\cup\mathcal{X}_n)^*)^n$ with G_i's finite can be treated as an <u>algebraic grammar</u> G with terminal and non-terminal alphabets $\mathbf{A}$ and $\mathcal{X}_n$ respectively. G is just a system of equations

$$G\left\{ x_i = G_i , \quad i\in[n] .\right.$$

The relation $\underset{G}{\rightarrow}$ on $(A\cup\mathcal{X}_n)^*$ is defined by

$f \underset{G}{\rightarrow} f'$ iff for some g, h in $(A\cup\mathcal{X}_n)^*$, i in $[n]$, w in G_i :
$f = gx_ih$ and $f' = gwh$.

The relation $\overset{*}{\underset{G}{\rightarrow}}$ is the reflexive and transitive closure of $\underset{G}{\rightarrow}$. A finite or infinite sequence $f_0, f_1, \dots, f_m, \dots$ is called a <u>derivation</u> from f_0 if $f_m \underset{G}{\rightarrow} f_{m+1}$ provided f_{m+1} exists. A finite derivation is called <u>terminating</u> with <u>result</u> f if the last word of the derivation belongs to $\mathbf{A}^*$ and is equal to f.

Let $L(G,f) = \{f'\in A^* : f \overset{*}{\underset{G}{\rightarrow}} f'\}$,

$$L(G) = (L(G,x_1),\dots,L(G,x_n)) .$$

Let a(f) denote the maximal left factor of f contained in A^*. An infinite derivation $f_0, f_1, \dots$ is called <u>successful</u> with <u>result</u> u if $\sup_{m<\omega} a(f_m)$ belongs to A^ω and is equal to u. We write $f \overset{\omega}{\underset{G}{\rightarrow}} u$ if u may be obtained from f as a result of an infinite successful derivation in G.

A language L is called <u>algebraic</u> (<u>∞-algebraic</u>) if $L = L(G,x_1)$ ($L = L^\infty(G,x_1)$) for some algebraic grammar G. L is called <u>regular</u> if $L = L(G,x_1)$ for some regular grammar, i.e. an algebraic grammar satisfying either $G_i \subseteq \mathbf{A}^*\mathcal{X}_n$ for all i's or $G_i \subseteq \mathcal{X}_n\mathbf{A}^*$ for all i's.

The main result of this section is the following

<u>Theorem</u> II. A language $L\subseteq \mathbf{A}^\infty$ is ∞-algebraic iff for some G in $(P(A\cup\mathcal{X}_n)^*)^n$ with G_i's regular, $L = (\nu.G)_1$.

<u>Sketch of proof</u> of "only if".
The proof can be essentially derived from that of Theorem I.
Let, for $i\in[n]$, $G_i = \{u : x_1 \underset{G}{\rightarrow} f_1 \underset{G}{\rightarrow} \cdots \underset{G}{\rightarrow} f_{m-1} \underset{G}{\rightarrow} u$ for some $f_1, \dots, f_{m-1}$ and $u\in A(A\cup\mathcal{X}_n)^*\cup\{e\}$ while

$f_i \in \mathfrak{X}_n(A \cup \mathfrak{X}_n)^*\}$ for $i < m$.

First we establish that G_i' is regular for $i \in [n]$. In the case $e \notin G_i$ for $i \in [n]$, G_i''s are generated by a grammar analogous to that presented in the proof of Proposition 1 :

$$G'' \left\{ y_i = (G_i \cap A(A \cup \mathfrak{X}_n)^*) \cup \{ y_j w : x_j w \in G_i \} \right. , \text{ for } i \in [n],$$

in this case $G_i' = L(G'', y_i)$.

In general we take G'' over non-terminal alphabet $\{y_1, \ldots, y_n, z_1, \ldots, z_n, z_1', \ldots, z_n'\}$:

$$G'' \begin{cases} y_i = \{z_i, z_i'\} \quad \text{for } i \in [n] , \\ z_i' = \text{if } x_i \overset{*}{\underset{G}{\to}} e \text{ then } \{e\} \text{ else } \emptyset , \\ z_i = \{ w \in A(A \cup \mathfrak{X}_n)^* : \text{for some } k \geqslant 0 \ \ x_{i_1} x_{i_2} \ldots x_{i_k} w \in G_i \text{ and} \\ \qquad x_{i_l} \overset{*}{\underset{G}{\to}} e \text{ for } l \leqslant k \} \cup \{ z_j w : \text{for some } k \geqslant 0 \\ \qquad x_{i_1} x_{i_2} \ldots x_{i_k} x_j w \in G_i \text{ and } x_{i_l} \overset{*}{\underset{G}{\to}} e \text{ for } l \leqslant k \} . \end{cases}$$

Next we prove that $G_i = L(G'', y_i)$ for $i \in [n]$. Clearly G'' is regular.

Then we prove :

(i) $X \subseteq \hat{G}'(X)$ implies $X \subseteq L^{\infty}(G)$,

(ii) $L^{\infty}(G) \subseteq \hat{G}'(L^{\infty}(G))$.

This is done in a way similar to the proof of Theorem I . However, due to our definition of substitution, we have to exclude the situation where $L^{\infty}(G, x_j) = \emptyset$ for some j . The next result shows that this is always possible .

<u>Proposition</u> 4 . Let $\emptyset \neq L = L^{\infty}(G, x_i)$. Then L is also generated by some $\tilde{G}$ satisfying $L^{\infty}(\tilde{G}, x_j) \neq \emptyset$ for each j's .

This remark complets the proof of the "only if " part of Theorem II .

<u>Example</u>

Let $L \subseteq \{0,1\}^{\infty}$ be the "fair merge" of the sequences 0^{ω} and 1^{ω} , i.e. $L = (0^*11^*0)^{\omega}$. It can be generated by

$$G \begin{cases} x_1 = \{x_2 01 x_1\}, \\ x_2 = \{x_2 1, x_2 0, 1, 0\} . \end{cases}$$

Then G'' as above is

$$G'' \begin{cases} y_1 = \{y_2 01 x_1\}, \\ y_2 = \{y_2 1, y_2 0, 1, 0\} \end{cases}$$

hence

$$G_1' = L(G'', y_1) = \{0,1\}^* 01 x_1, \quad G_2' = L(G'', y_2) = \{0,1\}^* .$$

Finally

$$(\mathcal{V} . G')_1 = \mathcal{V}.(\{0,1\}^* 01 x_1, \{0,1\}^*) = (\{0,1\}^* 01)^\omega = L \quad . \square$$

In order to prove the "if" part of Theorem II we have to study greatest fixed points of $\hat{G}$ for various G's in more detailed way. It may happen that ω-iteration is not sufficient to obtain such a fixed point (see /P 80/ for an example) . Fortunately we may always represent it as a union of ω-iterations due to the notion of expansion we are to introduce .

<u>Definition</u> . Let $G \in (P(A \cup \mathcal{X}_n)^*)^n$. An <u>expansion</u> of f in G is any infinite sequence of words $F = (f_m)_{m<\omega}$ with $f_0 = f$, such that $f_{m+1} \in f_m \leftarrow G$.

Note that for an expansion F, $a(f_m) \leqslant a(f_{m+1})$ for any m, hence $\sup_{m<\omega} a(f_m)$ always exists . We say that an expansion F is <u>creative</u> if either $f_{m_0} \in A^*$ for some m_0 (and hence $f_{m_0+k} = f_{m_0}$ for $k<\omega$) or $\sup_{m<\omega} a(f_m) \in A^\omega$. We call an expansion F <u>flat</u> if $f_m \in \mathcal{X}_n \mathcal{X}_n^*$ for $m<\omega$,

<u>semi-flat</u> if $f_m \in \mathcal{X}_n (A \cup \mathcal{X}_n)^*$ for $m < \omega$,

<u>vain</u> if $f_{m_0} = e$ for some m_0 .

Let us denote by $E(G,x_i)$ the set of all expansions of x_i in G . We say that the expansions $F_1 \in E(G,x_{i_1}),\dots, F_k \in E(G,x_{i_k})$ $(F_i=(f_{i,m})_m)$ are <u>subexpansions</u> of an expansion $F \in E(G,x_i)$ indicated by f_m , provided $f_m = c_0 x_{i_1} c_1 x_{i_2} \dots c_{k-1} x_{i_k} c_k$ for some $c_0,\dots,c_k \in A^*$ and $f_{m+h} = c_0 f_{1,h} c_1 \dots c_{k-1} f_{k,h} c_k$ for $h < \omega$.

<u>Proposition</u> 5 . Let $F \in E(G,x_i)$. There exist subexpansions of F indicated by f_m for each $m < \omega$. $\square$

The following lemma is crucial for our understanding of greatest fixed points of substitutions .

<u>Lemma</u> I . For any G in $(P(A \cup \mathcal{X}_n)^*)^n$,

$$(\mathcal{V} . G)_i = \bigcup_{F \in E(G,x_i)} \bigcap_{m<\omega} f_m \leftarrow (A^\infty,\dots,A^\infty)$$

for $i \in [n]$.

<u>Outline of proof</u> .

Let us denote the right side of the equation above by X_i and

$\underbrace{(A^\infty,\dots,A^\infty)}_{n \text{ times}}$ by A^∞.

As usual we show :

(i) $Y \subseteq \hat{G}(Y)$ implies $Y \subseteq X$, for any Y in $(PA^\infty)^n$,

(ii) $X \subseteq \hat{G}(X)$.

To prove (i) assume $Y \subseteq \hat{G}(Y)$ and $u \in Y_i$. In a natural way we construct inductively an expansion F of x_i in G satisfying $u \in f_m \leftarrow Y$ for each m . Therefore $u \in \bigcap_{m<\omega} f_m \leftarrow Y \subseteq$
$\subseteq \bigcap_{m<\omega} f_m \leftarrow \bar{A}^\infty \subseteq X_i$.

The proof of (ii) follows from a careful analysis of various kinds of expansions mentioned above and is rather involved technically. □

Let us now consider the following problem: for what G, $(\mathcal{N}.G)_1$ is an ∞-algebraic language ?

The first approach is due to Arnold&Nivat'result : if all G_i's are finite and $\hat{G}$ is <u>contraction</u> (i.e. $G_i \subseteq (A \cup \mathcal{X}_n)^* \setminus \mathcal{X}_n(A \cup \mathcal{X}_n)^*$) then $(\mathcal{N}.G)_1$ is generated by a grammar associated to G, $G\ \{\ x_i = G_i\ ,\ i \in [n]$. Such a grammar is in the Greibach normal form. However, not all ∞-algebraic languages can be obtained in this way. First of all, finitness of G_i's is too strong requirement in general. Indeed, it turns out that if all G_i's are finite then $\hat{G}$ is a closed mapping (in the sense of the standard Cantor-like topology in A^∞) and hence $(\mathcal{N}.G)_1$ is a closed set. Therefore none non-closed ∞-algebraic language (like that in our Example) can be obtained as $(\mathcal{N}.G)_1$ for G with finite components.

Nevertheless, by the proof of the "only if" part of Theorem II, any ∞-algebraic language can be obtained as $(\mathcal{N}.G)_1$ for some contraction $\hat{G}$ with regular components. Now it seems to be rather suprising that in the "if" part of Theorem II the assumption of $\hat{G}$ being contraction is not necessary. This phenomenon however becomes comprehensible in light of the following definition and lemma.

Let $G \in (P(A \cup \mathcal{X}_n)^*)^n$. We say that $u \in A^\infty$ is <u>generated by a creative expansion</u> F of x_i in G if $\{u\} = \bigcap_{m<\infty} f_m \leftarrow \bar{A}^\infty$.

<u>Lemma</u> II . For any G in $(P(A \cup \mathcal{X}_n)^*)^n$ there exists G' in $(P(A \cup \mathcal{X}_{n+1})^*)^{n+1}$ such that :

(i) $(\mathcal{N}.G')_i = (\mathcal{N}.G)_i$ for $i \in [n]$,

(ii) every $u \in (\mathcal{N}.G')_i$ is generated by some creative expansion of x_i in G' , for $i \in [n+1]$.

<u>Outline of proof</u> .

Let $I = \{ i \in [n] : \text{there is some flat expansion of } x_i \text{ in } G \}$,
$J = \{ i \in [n] \setminus I: \text{there is some semi-flat expansion of } x_i \text{ in } G \}$.

Let $\mathcal{X}_I = \{x_i : i \in I\}$,
$\mathcal{X}_J = \{x_i : i \in J\}$.

Define

$$G_i' = \begin{cases} G_i & \text{for } i \in [n] \setminus (I \cup J) , \\ G_i \cup A \cup A\{x_i\} & \text{for } i \in I , \\ G_i \cup \{x_{n+1}\} & \text{for } i \in J , \\ A\{x_{n+1}\} & \text{for } i = n+1 . \end{cases}$$

Notice that for a flat expansion, say F, $f_{m \leftarrow} \overleftarrow{A}^{\infty} = A^{\infty}$ for each $m<\omega$. Hence, by Lemma I, $(\mathcal{N}.G)_i = A^{\infty}$ for $i \in I$. Similarly $(\mathcal{N}.G)_i \supseteq A^{\omega}$ for $j \in J$. It is a routine matter to show that G' satisfies (i) .

To prove that G' satisfies (ii) we use Lemma I and the fact that an expansion is not creative only if it has a flat or semi-flat subexpansion . □

For technical reason we also prove

<u>Proposition</u> 6 . Let $\emptyset \neq L = (\mathcal{N}.G)_1$ for some G in $(P(A \cup \mathcal{X}_n)^*)^n$. Then there exists a $G' \in (P(A \cup \mathcal{X}_m)^*)^m$ for some m , such that $(\mathcal{N}.G')_1 = L$ and $(\mathcal{N}.G')_i \neq \emptyset$ for each $i \in [m]$.

<u>Sketch of proof of the implication "if" of Theorem II</u> .

Let $\emptyset \neq L = (\mathcal{N}.G)_1$ for some G in $(P(A \cup \mathcal{X}_n)^*)^n$ with G_i's regular. By Lemma II and Proposition 6 we may assume $(\mathcal{N}.G)_i \neq \emptyset$ for $i \in [n]$ and

(7) any $u \in (\mathcal{N}.G)_i$ can be generated by a creative expansion .

For $i=1,\dots,n$ let H_i be a regular grammar which generates G_i, i.e. $G_i = L(H_i, y_{i,1})$. Let H_i be in the form $H_i \{ y_{i,j} = H_{i,j},\ j \in [k_i]$. The major observation is that we may assume that all H_i's satisfy

(8) $H_{i,j} \subseteq \{y_{i,1}, \dots, y_{i,k_i}\} (A \cup \mathcal{X}_n)^*$

and hence do not generate infinite words . We may also assume $L(H_i, y_{i,j}) \neq \emptyset$ (since $G_i \neq \emptyset$) .

We combine the grammars H_i into a one "large" grammar $\tilde{G}$:

$$\tilde{G} \begin{cases} y_{1,j} = H_{1,j} & , j \in [k_1] , \\ \dots\dots\dots\dots & \\ y_{n,j} = H_{n,j} & , j \in [k_n] , \\ x_1 = y_{1,1} & , \\ \dots\dots\dots\dots & \\ \dots\dots\dots\dots & \\ x_n = y_{n,1} & . \end{cases}$$

Note that x_i's , which occure in H_j's as terminal symbols, appear in $\tilde{G}$ among non-terminal ones .

Then we prove $(\mathcal{V}.G)_i = L^{\infty}(\tilde{G},x_i)$ for $i \in [n]$ (in particular L is ∞-algebraic) in standard way by showing

(i) $(\mathcal{V}.G)_i \subseteq L^{\infty}(\tilde{G},x_i)$ for $i \in [n]$,

(ii) $L^{\infty}(\tilde{G},x_i) \subseteq (\hat{G}(L^{\infty}(\tilde{G},x_1),\dots,L^{\infty}(\tilde{G},x_n))$.

The proof of (i) follows from Lemma I and (7) .

To prove (ii) assume $u \in L^{\infty}(\tilde{G},x_i)$. Clearly $u \in L^{\infty}(\tilde{G},y_{i,1})$ and let $y_{i,1} \xrightarrow[\tilde{G}]{} f_1 \xrightarrow[\tilde{G}]{} \dots$ be a derivation with result u . Then we can extract from it a derivation in H_i by "forbiding" all rules of the form $x_j \xrightarrow[\tilde{G}]{} y_{j,1}$. Since the former derivation was either finite and terminating or infinite and successful, and since H_i satisfies (8), the latter one turns out to be finite and terminating. Let f be the result of it, $f \in L(H_i, y_{i,1}) = G_i$. We prove $u \in f_{\leftarrow} L^{\infty}(\tilde{G},x_i)$. This remark completes the sketch of the proof of Theorem II .

As a corollary of Theorem II we derive the following result.

<u>Corollary</u> . Let $\emptyset \neq L \subseteq A^{\infty}$. Then L is generated by an algebraic grammar in the Greibach normal form iff $L = (\mathcal{V}.G)_1$ for some G in $(P(A \cup \mathcal{X}_n)^*)^n$ with G_i's finite and non-empty .

<u>Proof</u>.

The "only if" part was proved in /N 79/ (it also follows from the proof of Theorem II).

To prove the "if" part assume $L = (\mathcal{V}.G)_1$ for some G with finite components. Since finite languages are regular, L is ∞-algebraic. By the remark preceding Lemma II, L is a closed set. Then we apply the result of /N 79/ which states that any ∞-algebraic language closed in Cantor-like topology can be generated by an algebraic grammar in the Greibach normal form.

REFERENCES

/AN 77/ - A.Arnold, M.Nivat, Non-deterministic recursive program schemes, FCT 77, LNCS 56,Springer Verlag (1977), 12-21.

/AN 78/ - A.Arnold, M.Nivat, Metric interpretation of infinite trees and semantics of non deterministic recursive programs, Rapport no. IT-3-78,Universite de Lille.

/N 79/ - M.Nivat, Infinite words, infinite trees, infinite computation, Mathematical Centre Tracts 109 (1979),1-52.

/P 80/ - D.Park, On the semantics of fair parallelism, Abstract Software Specifications, LNCS 86, Springer Verlag(1980), 504-526.

/T 79/ - J.Tiuryn, Fixed points in the power set algebra of infinite trees, Schriften zur Informatik und angewandten Mathematik, RWTH Aachen, (1979).

COMPLETING BIPREFIX CODES

D. PERRIN
Université de Rouen, Laboratoire d'Informatique LITP
BP 67
76130 Mont-Saint-Aignan, France.

1. INTRODUCTION :

Several problems in automata theory are of the following kind : given an uncompletely specified automaton belonging to some family of automata, is it possible to complete it within this family ? (see for instance [7]).

The purpose of this paper is to present a result of this type : any finite biprefix code is included in a maximal recognizable biprefix code.

The difficulty of the problem is linked to the two-sided condition (prefix and suffix) defining biprefix codes. The corresponding problem for prefix codes would be of course trivial. But the same problem for general codes : "is any finite code included in a recognizable maximal code ?" is open ; a positive answer has been conjectured by A. Restivo [5].

The proof of this result heavily rests on the conjunction of two facts : First Y. Cesari has deeply investigated the structure of finite maximal biprefix codes [2], extending the results of M.P Schützenberger [8] who first studied these objects, and of myself [4] ; it happens that his results extend to the recognizable case and lead very close to the solution of our problem. Second, the systematic use of formal series in this matter proved to be a very powerful tool. This appeared to J. Berstel and myself during the elaboration of the chapter on biprefix codes of the book on codes that we are preparing [1]. Several results of this paper where obtained jointly with him.

2. BIPREFIX CODES :

Let A be an alphabet, A^* the free monoid over A. We use the notation $A^+ = A^* - 1$, where 1 denotes the empty word.

We denote by $\mathbb{Z} \ll A \gg$ the ring of series with coefficients in $\mathbb{Z}$ and non commuting variables in A. For a series S and a word $w \in A^*$, we denote by (S, w) the coefficient of w in S. For a subset X of A^*, we note $\underline{X}$ its characteristic series. It is the element of $\mathbb{Z} \ll A \gg$ defined by $(\underline{X}, x) = 1$ if $x \in X$ and 0 otherwise (for an introduction to series see [3] or [6]).

A subset X of A^+ is a prefix code if $XA^+ \cap X = \emptyset$. It is a suffix code if $A^+X \cap X = \emptyset$. It is a biprefix code if it is both a prefix code and a suffix code.

Let $X \subset A^+$ be a biprefix code. We define the indicator I_X of X as the series

$$I_X = \underline{A^*}\,(1 - \underline{X})\,\underline{A^*} \,. \qquad (2.1)$$

Let

$$V_X = A^* - A^* X, \quad U_X = A^* - X A^* \qquad (2.2)$$

A X-interpretation of a word $w \in A^*$ is a triple (v,x,u) such that $w = vxu$ with $v \in V_X$, $x \in X^*$, $u \in U_X$.

The following result shows that the indicator of a biprefix code has non-negative coefficients.

PROPOSITION 2.1. Let $X \subset A^+$ be a biprefix code. The coefficient (I_X, w) of a word $w \in A^*$ in the indicator of X is equal to the number of interpretations of w.

Proof : Since X is a prefix code, we have $\underline{XA^*} = \underline{X}\underline{A}^*$. Hence $\underline{U}_X = (1-\underline{X})\underline{A}^*$. And symmetrically, since X is a suffix code $\underline{V}_X = \underline{A}^*(1-\underline{X})$. We have therefore

$$I_X = \underline{V}_X\underline{A}^* \qquad (2.3)$$

$$I_X = \underline{A}^* \underline{U}_X \qquad (2.4)$$

Now from $\underline{U}_X = (1-\underline{X})\underline{A}^*$, we deduce that $\underline{A}^* = \underline{X}^* \underline{U}_X$. Substituting in Eq. (2.3), we obtain

$$I_X = \underline{V}_X \underline{X}^* \underline{U}_X. \qquad (2.5)$$

The coefficient of $w \in A^*$ in the product $\underline{V}_X \underline{X}^* \underline{U}_X$ is precisely equal to the number of interpretations of w and the result is proved.

□

Note that we have for $u, v, w \in A^*$, the inequality

$$(I_X, uvw) \geq (I_X, v) \qquad (2.6)$$

since, by Eq. (2.3), $(I_X, uvw) \geq (I_X, uv)$ and, by Eq. (2.4), $(I_X, uv) \geq (I_X, v)$.

For of subset X of A^* we define

$$H_X = \{v \in A^* \mid A^+ v A^+ \cap X \neq \emptyset\}. \qquad (2.7)$$

The set X is said to be thin if $H_X \neq A^*$. Any finite set is obviously thin and it can be shown that any recognizable code is thin (cf. [1]).

THEOREM 2.2. : For any biprefix code $X \subset A^+$, the following conditions are equivalent

(i) X is a thin maximal biprefix code.

(ii) The coefficients of I_X are bounded.

Moreover, if $d_X = \max\{(l_X, w) \mid w \in A^*\}$ we have

$$H_X = \{v \in A^* \mid (l_X, v) \leq d_X - 1\} \qquad (2.8)$$

Proof : (i) ⇒ (ii) let w be such that $X \cap A^+ w A^+ = \emptyset$. Suppose that the coefficients of l_X are not bounded ; let $u \in A^*$ be such that $(l_X, u) \geq |w| + 2$. Then, by Eq. (2.6),

$$(L_X, wu) \geq |w| + 2.$$

Since (L_X, wu) is equal to the number of left factors of wu in $V_X = A^* - A^*X$, there is at least one left factor u' of u such that $wu' \in V_X$. Then the word z= wu' has no right factor in X and since $w \notin H_X$, z is not a right factor of any element of X. One can show symmetrically that there exists a word $t \in A^*$ which has no left factor in X and is not a left factor of any element of X. Then it is easy to see that $X \cup tz$ is a biprefix code, contradicting the hypothesis that X is a maximal biprefix code.

(ii) ⇒ (i) Let $d_X = \max\{(l_X, w) \mid w \in A^*\}$. Let $v \in A^*$ be such that $(l_X, v) = d_X$. Then, since $\underline{X}\underline{A}^* = \underline{A}^* + (\underline{A} - 1) l_X$ we have for all $a \in A$ and $u \in A^*$,

$$(\underline{X}\,\underline{A}^*, auv) = 1 + (l_X, uv) - (l_X, auv). \qquad (2.9)$$

By Eq. (2.6), (l_X, uv) and (l_X, auv) are at least equal to (l_X, v). Hence $(l_X, uv) = (l_X, auv) = d_X$. Subtituting in Eq. (2.9) we obtain $(\underline{X}\underline{A}^*, auv) = 1$ or equivalently $auv \in XA^*$. We have therefore proved that for any $u \in A^+$, $uv \in XA^*$. This implies that $v \notin H_X$ and therefore that X is thin. It also implies that X is a maximal prefix code since for any $u \in A^+$, we have $uv \in XA^*$, showing that $X \cup u$ is not a prefix code. Therefore X is a thin maximal biprefix code.

Let us finally prove Eq. (2.8). If $v \in H_X$, there exists $u, w \in A^+$ such that $uvw \in X$. Then uv has one more right factor in U_X than v, namely uv itself. Therefore $(l_X, v) \leq (l_X, uv) - 1 \leq d_X - 1$. Conversely, if $(l_X, v) \leq d_X - 1$, let u be such that $(l_X, u) = d_X$. Then $(l_X, uv) = d_X$ and thus there exists a right factor $u' \in A^+$ of u such that $u'v \in U_X$. Since X is a maximal prefix code, there exists $w' \in A^+$ such that $u'vw' \in X$. Hence $v \in H_X$.

□

Let X be a thin maximal biprefix code. The integer

$$d_X = \max\{(\underline{I}_X, w) \mid w \in A^*\} \qquad (2.10)$$

is called the degree of X.

The set

$$K_X = X \cap H_X \qquad (2.11)$$

is called the kernel of X.

Example 2.1 Let $A = \{a, b\}$ and $X = a \cup ba^*b$. Then X is a recognizable maximal biprefix code. We have $V_X = 1 \cup a^* b$ and therefore $\underline{I}_X = \underline{A}^* + a^*b\underline{A}^*$, that is

$$\underline{I}_X = a^* + 2\, a^*b\underline{A}^*, \quad d_X = 2, \quad K_X = a. \qquad (2.12)$$

PROPOSITION 2.3. Let X be a thin maximal biprefix code, $d = d_X$ its degree and $K = K_X$ its kernel. Then

$$\underline{I}_X = \inf(d\underline{A}^*, \underline{I}_K). \qquad (2.13)$$

Proof : by definition

$$\underline{I}_X = \underline{A}^*(1-\underline{X})\underline{A}^*, \quad \underline{I}_K = \underline{A}^*(1-\underline{K})\underline{A}^*.$$

Let $w \in H_X$. Then any factor of w which belongs to X also belongs to K. Therefore $(\underline{A}^*\underline{X}\underline{A}^*, w) = (\underline{A}^*\underline{K}\underline{A}^*, w)$. This implies that $(\underline{I}_X, w) = (\underline{I}_K, w)$. Moreover we have $(\underline{I}_X, w) \le d-1$ by Eq. (2.8). Therefore $(\underline{I}_X, w) = \inf(d, (\underline{I}_K, w))$.

Now, if $w \notin H_X$, then $(\underline{I}_X, w) = d$ again by Eq. (2.8). But since $K \subset X$, we have $(\underline{A}^*\underline{K}\underline{A}^*, w) \le (\underline{A}^*\underline{X}\underline{A}^*, w)$ whence $(\underline{I}_X, w) \le (\underline{I}_K, w)$. We have again $(\underline{I}_X, w) = \inf(d, (\underline{I}_K, w))$.

□

As a corollary of Proposition 2.3, we deduce the following result whose first part was proved by Y. Césari for finite maximal biprefix codes [2].

THEOREM 2.4. A thin maximal biprefix code X is uniquely specified by its degree d_X and its kernel K_X.

Moreover, X is recognizable iff K_X is recognizable.

Proof : By proposition 2.3, given $d = d_X$ and $K = K_X$ we can compute I_X and therefore X since Eq. (2.1) is equivalent to

$$1 - \underline{X} = (1 - \underline{A})\, I_X\, (1 - \underline{A}). \qquad (2.14)$$

If X is recognizable, then H_X ie recognizable and therefore also $K = X \cap H_X$. Conversely, if K is recognizable, then by Eq. (2.5)

$$I_K = \underline{V}_K\, \underline{K}^*\, \underline{U}_K .$$

Since K is a recognizable subset of A^*, so are $U_K = A^* - KA^*$, K^* and $V_K = A^* - A^*K$. Therefore $\underline{V}_K$, $\underline{K}^*$ and $\underline{U}_K$ are $\mathbb{N}$-recognizable series, so that their product I_K. Now I_X as given by Eq. (2.13) is again an $\mathbb{N}$-recognizable series (see [3] p. 154). Then $\underline{V}_X = I_X(1-\underline{A})$ is the difference of two bounded $\mathbb{N}$-recognizable series. It is therefore $\mathbb{N}$-recognizable (see [3] p. 154) . Therefore the set V_X is recognizable and so is X since $X = AV_X - V_X$.

□

EXAMPLE 2.1. (Continued). Since $K_X = a$, we have

$$I_K = \underline{A}^* (1-a)\, \underline{A}^*$$

Thefore, for each word $w \in A^*$

$$(I_K, w) = 1 + |w|_b.$$

This gives $I_X = \inf (2\underline{A}^*, I_X) = a^* + 2a^*bA^*$.

3. COMPLETION OF BIPREFIX CODES :

For a biprefix code X, we define

$$m_X = \max \{(I_X, x) \mid x \in X\} \qquad (3.1)$$

which is an integer or ∞.

The following theorem characterizes the kernels of thin maximal biprefix codes.

THEOREM 3.1. Let $d \geq 1$ be an integer. A set $K \subset A^+$ is the kernel of a thin maximal biprefix code of degree d iff it satifies the two following conditions :

(i) K <u>is a biprefix code which is not maximal.</u>

(ii) $m_K \leq d-1$.

Proof : these conditions are necessary : let X be a thin maximal biprefix code. Let $x \in X$ be such that $(l_X, x) = m_X$. If, for $u, v \in A^+$ we have $uxv \in X$, then ux has one more right factor in U_X than x, namely ux itself. Therefore

$$(l_X, uxv) \geq (l_X, ux) \geq m_X + 1$$

a contradiction. This shows that $x \notin H_X$. The set $K = K_X$ is thus strictly contained in X and K is not a maximal biprefix code. Now, for any $x \in K$, we have by Eq. (2. 8), $(l_X, x) \leq d_X - 1$. And by Eq. (2. 13), $(l_X, x) = (l_K, x)$. Therefore $(l_K, x) \leq d_X - 1$. We have thus proved that K satisfies conditions (i) and (ii).

We now prove that the conditions (i) and (ii) are sufficient. Let $l \in \mathbb{Z} \langle\langle A \rangle\rangle$ be the series

$$l = \inf (d\underline{A}^*, l_K) \qquad (3.2)$$

For any $a \in A$, $w \in A^*$ we have $0 \leq (l_K, aw) - (l_X, w) \leq 1$ since aw has at most one more right factor in U_K than w. We then also have $0 \leq (l, aw) - (l, w) \leq 1$. This shows that the series $(1-\underline{A})l$ is the characteristic series of a set $U \subset A^*$:

$$\underline{U} = (1-\underline{A})\, l. \qquad (3.3)$$

Let $a, b \in A$ and $w \in A^*$. We show that

$$(\underline{U}, aw) = 0 \Rightarrow (\underline{U}, awb) = 0 . \qquad (3.4)$$

Suppose first that $(l, wb) \geq d$. Then $(l_K, wb) \geq d$ and also $(l_K, awb) \geq d$. Therefore $(l, wb) = (l, awb) = d$ and $(\underline{U}, awb) = 0$.

Suppose now that $(l, wb) \leq d-1$ or, equivalently that $(l_K, wb) \leq d-1$. Then we also have $(l_K, w) \leq d-1$. By the hypothesis $(l, aw)-(l, w) = (\underline{U}, aw) = 0$. But since $(l_K, w) \leq d-1$, we have $(l_K, aw) \leq d$. Therefore $(l, w) = (l_K, w)$ and $(l, aw) = (l_K, aw)$. We obtain $(l_K, aw) = (l_K, w)$. This means that aw has no more right factors in U_K than w. Therefore $aw \notin U_K$ or equivalently $aw \in KA^*$. This implies that

$(I_K, awb) = (I_K, wb)$ and, since $(I_K, wb) \leq d-1$, we obtain $(I, awb) = (I, wb)$ and $(\underline{U}, awb) = 0$. This proves (3.4).

We deduce from (3.4) that the set U contains all the left factors of its elements. In fact $1 \in U$ since $(\underline{U}, 1) = (I, 1) = (I_K, 1) = 1$. If $uv \in U$ with $u, v \in A^+$, let $uv = awb$ with $a, b \in A$, $w \in A^+$. Then by (3.4) we have $aw \in U$. An easy induction on $|v|$ proves that $u \in U$.

Let X be the set

$$X = UA - U \tag{3.5}$$

Then X is a prefix code : if $x \in X$, let $x = ua$ with $u \in U$, $a \in A$. All the proper left factors of x are left factors of u. They belong to U and are therefore not in X.

We can turn (3.5) into an equality between series, writing : $\underline{UA} + 1 = \underline{X} + \underline{U}$, or

$$1 - \underline{X} = \underline{U}(1-A) \tag{3.6}$$

By the definition of U in Eq. (3.3) this leads to

$$1 - \underline{X} = (1 - \underline{A})\, I\, (1 - \underline{A}). \tag{3.7}$$

The proof that the series $(1-A)\,I$ is the characteristic series of a set V containing all the right factors of its elements is symmetrical to the corresponding above proof for U. Then $1 - \underline{X} = (1-\underline{A})\,\underline{V}$ shows that X is a suffix code. Therefore X is a biprefix code. By Eq. (3.7), the indicator I_X of X is equal to I. Since I is, by definition, bounded, we obtain that X is a thin maximal biprefix code by Theorem 2.2. Since K is not maximal, its indicator I_K is not bounded (by Theorem 2.2). Therefore there exists a word $w \in A^*$ such that $(I_K, w) \geq d$. Then $(I, w) = d$. Hence $\max\{(I, w) \mid w \in A^*\} = d$ and the degree of X is equal to d.

Let us finally show that K is the kernel of X. We obviously have $K \subset H_X$ since for any $k \in K$, $(I, k) \leq (I_K, k) \leq m_K \leq d-1$. It is therefore enough to prove that $X \cap H_X = K \cap H_X$ or equivalently that for any $w \in H_X$,

$$(\underline{X}, w) = (\underline{K}, w). \tag{3.8}$$

We prove Eq. (3.8) by recurrence on $|w|$. If $|w| = 0$, both sides of (3.8) are zero. Let now $w \in H_X - 1$.

Since $(I, w) \leq d-1$, we have $(I, w) = (I_K, w)$ Hence $(\underline{A}^* \underline{K}\underline{A}^*, w) = (\underline{A}^* \underline{X}\underline{A}^*, w)$. Since all the factors of w are in H_X, we have by induction hypothesis $(\underline{X}, s) = (\underline{K}, s)$ for every proper factor of w. Therefore $(\underline{X}, w) = (\underline{K}, w)$. This concludes the proof of the theorem.

□

We now derive the main result of this paper :

THEOREM 3.2. Let $Y \subset A^+$ be a finite biprefix code and $d = m_Y + 1$. There exists a unique recognizable maximal biprefix code with degree d and kernel Y.

Proof : First, since Y is finite, $m_Y = \max \{(I_Y, y) \mid y \in Y\}$ is finite. By Theorem 3.1 there exists a thin maximal biprefix code of degree $d = m_Y+1$ whose kernel is Y. By Theorem 2.4 , X is unique and it is recognizable.

□

EXAMPLE 3.1. Let $A = \{a, b\}$ and $Y = \{a, bb\}$. We have

$$(I_Y, a) = 1, \ (I_Y, bb) = 2.$$

Therefore $m_Y = 2$. The unique recognizable maximal biprefix code with degree 3 and kernel Y is

$$X = a \cup bb \cup ba^+ b^+ a^+ b.$$

The indicator of X is

$$I_X = a^* + 2\, a^* b^* a^* + 3\, a^* b^+ a^+ bA^*.$$

The set Y is also included in the maximal biprefix code of degree 2 of Example 2.1 :

$$X' = a \cup ba^* b.$$

One may observe that $X \cap X' = Y$. This is a general fact : X' is the so-called *derivative* of X, whose indicator is obtained by decreasing by 1 the value of the coefficients of I_X equal to d_X. The intersection of X with its derivative is the kernel of X (see [2], [1]). We obtain in our example :

$$l_{X'} = a^* + 2a^* b^+ a^* + 2a^* b^+ a^+ bA^*$$
$$= a^* + 2a^* bA^*$$

as in Eq. (2.12).

We conjecture a result which is more general than Theorem 3.2. : any recognizable biprefix code is included in a maximal recognizable biprefix code. Theorem 3.1 cannot be used to prove this conjecture. In fact, for such a set as

$$Y = ba^* b$$

the coefficients of l_Y are not bounded on Y. This means that Y is not the kernel of any recognizable maximal biprefix code. However this set may obviously be completed by adding the singleton $\{a\}$. This suggests the possibility of solving the above conjecture by adding first a kernel to Y and then turning the resulting set into the kernel of a maximal recognizable code.

Finally, it is worth mentionning that not any thin biprefix code can be completed to a thin maximal biprefix code. In fact the algebraic language

$$Y = \{a^n b^n \mid n \geq 1\}$$

is a thin biprefix code. It is not included in any thin maximal biprefix code because the degree of this code could not be finite. As a matter of fact, Y is included in the restricted Dyck set D_2, defined by

$$D_2^* = \{w \in \{a,b\}^* \mid |w|_a = |w|_b\},$$

which is a maximal biprefix code which is not thin.

REFERENCES :

[1] J. Berstel, D. Perrin, M.P. Schützenberger, The Theory of Codes, to appear.

[2] Y. Césari, Propriétés combinatoires des codes biprefixes, in Théorie des codes (D. Perrin ed.) LITP, 1979 , 20-46.

[3] S. Eilenberg, Automata, Languages and Machines, Vol, A, Academic Press, 1974.

[4] D. Perrin, Codes asynchrones, Bull. Soc. Math. de France, 105, 1977, 325-404.

[5] A. Restivo, On codes having no finite completions, in Automata Languages and Programming (S. Michaelson ed.) Edinburgh University Press 1976, 38-44 .

[6] A. Salomaa, M. Soittola, Automata Theoretic Aspects of Formal Power Series, Springer-Verlag, 1978.

[7] M.P. Schützenberger, A remark on incompletely specified automata, Information and Control, 8, 1965, 373-376.

[8] M.P. Schützenberger, On a special class of recurrent events, Ann. Math. Stat. 32, 1961, 1201-1213.

ADVANCES IN PEBBLING

(Preliminary Version)

Nicholas Pippenger
IBM Research Laboratory
San Jose, CA 95193 USA

1. Pebbling

The purpose of this paper is threefold: to survey some known results on pebbling, to sketch the proofs of some new results, and to present some open problems. All of this will be done in the context of a new setting for pebbling problems, but first we shall give an informal description of the pebble game and some of its variations.

The pebble game is played on the vertices of an acyclic directed graph. A play of the game is a sequence of moves according to the following two rules.

Rule 1. If the immediate predecessors of a vertex all have pebbles on them, a pebble may be put on that vertex.

Rule 2. A pebble may be taken off a vertex.

The game begins with no pebbles on the graph. A *simple* play is one in which Rule 1 is applied to each vertex at most once. A *complete* play is one in which Rule 1 is applied to each vertex at least once. The game abstracts certain properties of computations, especially those dealing with *time* (reckoned as the number of moves in a play) and *space* (reckoned as the maximum number of pebbles on the graph at any move of the play).

We shall deal frequently in this paper with a variant of the pebble game in which there are available one or more pushdown stacks capable of holding names of vertices in the graph. The pushdown stacks are manipulated according to the following two rules.

Rule 3. If there is a pebble on a vertex, the name of that vertex may be pushed onto a stack.

Rule 4. If the name of a vertex is at the top of a stack, it may be popped off that stack and a pebble may be placed on that vertex.

The game now begins with no pebbles on the graph and no names on the stacks. This variant allows us to consider trade-offs among not only time and space but an additional computational resource, which might be called pushdowns (reckoned as the number of different stacks manipulated during a play).

The pebble game was introduced by Paterson and Hewitt [13], who raised the question of the minimum space required by complete plays for a given graph. Sethi [21] raised the question of the minimum space required by complete simple plays for a given graph. The pebble game with auxiliary pushdowns was introduced by Pippenger [18,20]. Another variant of the pebble game (with which we shall not deal in this paper) is the black-and-white pebble game, introduced by Cook and Sethi [3]. For a general survey of results on the pebble game and its variants, see Pippenger [19].

2. Lifting

In this section we shall introduce a new setting for the study of pebbling problems. This setting accomodates most known results on pebbling in a natural way; it also suggests new problems and conjectures.

It will be convenient in this paper to employ a special notion of graph, in which the vertices are presented in a specific total order, compatible with the partial order induced by the direction of the edges. Let an N-graph be an acyclic directed graph with vertices {1, ..., N} in which every vertex has at most two immediate predecessors (the number of immediate successors is not restricted) and in which every edge is directed out of a lower-numbered and into a higher-numbered vertex.

An N-graph will be called a pebble graph if, for every $1 \leq M \leq N$, there is at most one vertex $K \leq M$ out of which is directed an edge to some vertex $L > M$. Let a B-pebble N-graph be an N-graph that is the union of at most B pebble graphs.

An N-graph will be called a pushdown graph if there is at most one edge directed into or out of each vertex and if, for every pair of edges (K, L) and (K', L'), either the intervals {K, ..., L} and {K', ..., L'} are disjoint, or one is included in the other. Let an A-pushdown B-pebble N-graph be an N-graph that is the union of at most A pushdown graphs and at most B pebble graphs.

An important notion for our setting is that of lifting. A lift from an N-graph G to and N'-graph G' is a map p from the vertices of G onto the vertices of G' such that, whenever p(L)=L' and K' is an immediate predecessor of L', there exists an immediate predecessor K of L such that p(K)=K' or p(K)=L'. If there is a lift from G to G', we shall say that G is a lift of G'. The relation of lifting is reflexive and transitive.

Another important notion for our setting is that of simple lifting. We shall say that a lift p from G to G' is simple if, for any vertex L' in G', the inverse image $p^{-1}(L')$ is connected (so that there is a directed path from the lowest-numbered vertex to any other vertex). If there is a simple lift from G to G', we shall say that G is a simple lift of G'. The relation of simple lifting is also reflexive and transitive.

It is not hard to see that if the N'-graph G' has a complete play of the pebble game with R pushdowns in space S and time T, then there exists a lift G of G' that is an R-pushdown B-pebble N-graph with B=O(S) and N=O(T). Conversely, if an N'-graph G' has a lift G that is an A-pushdown B-pebble N-graph, then it has a complete play of the pebble game with A pushdowns in space O(B) and time O(N). In particular, an A-pushdown B-pebble N-graph itself has a complete play of the pebble game with A pushdowns in space O(B) and time O(N).

It is also not hard to see that if the N'-graph G' has a complete simple play of the pebble game with R pushdowns in space S and time T, then there exists a simple lift G of G' that is an R-pushdown B-pebble N-graph with B=O(S) and N=O(T). Conversely, if an N'-graph G' has a simple lift G that is an A-pushdown B-pebble N-graph, then it has a complete simple play of the pebble game with A pushdowns in space O(B) and time O(N). In particular, an A-pushdown B-pebble N-graph itself has a complete simple play of the pebble game with A pushdowns in space O(B) and time O(N).

Thus, to within constant factors in time and space, questions about pebbling with auxiliary pushdowns can be reduced to relationships of lifting and simple lifting among graphs. These relationships concern only the embeddability of graphs in other graphs. In particular, we can discuss pebbling with auxiliary pushdowns without mentioning either pebbles or pushdowns!

A basic property of lifts (and *a fortiori* of simple lifts) is the following. Let p be a lift from G to G', let $B_1, \ldots, B_L$ be vertices of G with $p(B_1)=B_1', \ldots, p(B_L)=B_L'$ and let $P_1', \ldots, P_L'$ be vertex-disjoint paths in G' from vertices $A_1', \ldots, A_L'$ to $B_1', \ldots, B_L'$ (in the order indicated). Then there exist vertices $A_1, \ldots, A_L$ in G with $p(A_1)=A_1', \ldots, p(A_L)=A_L'$ and vertex-disjoint paths $P_1, \ldots, P_L$ in G from $A_1, \ldots, A_L$ to $B_1, \ldots, B_L$ (in the order indicated). Roughly speaking, vertex-disjoint paths can be lifted from G' to G.

The notion of A-pushdown B-pebble N-graphs defined above is closely related to some notions of "computation graphs" that have appeared in the literature, specifically, to the "m-tape Turing machine graphs" of Paul, Tarjan and Celoni [14] and the "m*-head graphs" of Paul and Reischuk [15]. This relationship can be expressed formally by observing that a m-tape Turing machine graph or m*-head graph with n vertices has a simple lift that is an A-pushdown B-pebble N-graph with A=2m, B=O(m) and N=O(mn). Conversely, an A-pushdown B-pebble N-graph has simple lifts that are m-tape Turing machine and m*-head graph with n vertices, where m=O(A+B) and n=O(N). These relationships of mutual simple lifting between classes of graphs clearly show the equivalence of these classes as regards pebbling, and we shall see later that it implies a similar equivalence as regards separability.

3. Pebbling with Auxiliary Pushdowns

In this section we shall survey the known results on pebbling of general graphs, with and without auxiliary pushdowns, and sketch the proofs of the results concerning two or more pushdowns, which have not yet appeared in the literature.

First, let us consider space requirements. In the case of no auxiliary pushdowns, Hopcroft, Paul and Valiant [6] showed that every N-graph has a complete play of the pebble game in space O(N/log N), and Paul, Tarjan and Celoni [14] showed that there exist N-graphs that require space $\Omega(N/\log N)$. In the case of one or more auxiliary pushdowns, every N-graph has a complete play of the pebble game in space 3, and it is clear that there exist N-graphs that require space 3.

Next, for space in the range from N down to the lower bounds just indicated, let us consider time requirements. For the case of no auxiliary pushdowns, Lengauer and Tarjan [7] showed that every N-graph has a complete play of the pebble game in space S and time at most S exp exp O(N/S), and that there exist N-graphs that require time S exp exp $\Omega(N/S)$. This time-space trade-off can be written

$$T/N = \exp\exp\Theta(N/S),$$

since a factor of N/S can be absorbed into the factor exp exp $\Theta(N/S)$.

For the case of one auxiliary pushdown, Pippenger [18,20] showed that

$$T/N = \exp\Theta(N/S).$$

We shall see below that for two auxiliary pushdowns,

$$T/N = \Theta(N/S),$$

and that for R≥3 auxiliary pushdowns,

$$T/N = \Theta(\log_R(N/S)).$$

In the case of two pushdowns, the upper bound

$$T/N = O(N/S)$$

is easy. Letting $K=\lfloor S/3\rfloor$, we can deal with each successive interval of K vertices in time O(N), keeping the names of all previously pebbled vertices on the stacks.

For the lower bound

$$T/N = \Omega(N/S),$$

we shall use superconcentrators. An M-superconcentrator is a graph G with the following property. There are M distinguished vertices called inputs and M other distinguished vertices called outputs such that if $A_1, \ldots, A_L$ are distinct inputs and $B_1, \ldots, B_L$ are distinct outputs, then there exist vertex-disjoint paths $P_1, \ldots, P_L$ from $A_1, \ldots, A_L$ to $B_1, \ldots, B_L$ (not necessarily in the order indicated). Let the N-graph G on which the game is to be played be obtained from a series of superconcentrators of geometrically increasing sizes: the output of a 1-superconcentrator is identified with one of the inputs of a 2-superconcentrator, and so forth until the outputs of an (M/2)-superconcentrator are identified with half of the inputs of an M-superconcentrator. We may take $M=\Omega(N)$, since there exist N'-graphs that are M'-superconcentrators for $M'=\Omega(N')$ (see Valiant [22] or Pippenger [16]).

If there is a play of the pebble game on G with two pushdowns in space S and time T, then there is a lift F of G that is a 2-pushdown B-pebble C-graph, where $B=O(S)$ and $C=O(T)$. It is not hard to see that such a graph can be immersed in the plane with $U=O(BC)=O(ST)$ "nodes" (where a node is either a vertex of F or a crossing of two edges of F). It will thus suffice to show that $U=\Omega(N^2)$.

We claim that if a subgraph F' of F contains at least L/2 inverse images of distinct outputs of the L-superconcentrator in G, and if F' has fewer than L/64 edges directed into it from outside of it, then F' contains $U' \geq cL^2$ nodes (for some suitable constant $c>0$). The proof is by induction on L. For $L=2$, the claim is trivial. For $L\geq 4$, by the Planar Separator Theorem (see Lipton and Tarjan [9]), F' can be partitioned by the removal of $O(U'^{1/2})$ nodes into 16 parts, each containing at most L/32 of the given inverse images of outputs. Unless $U' \geq cL^2$, at least 8 of these parts must each contain at least L/64 of the given inverse images of outputs, and at least 4 of these parts must each have at most L/128 edges directed into them from outside of them. By the basic properties of superconcentrators and lifts, each of these four parts must contain at least L/4 inverse images of distinct inputs of the L-superconcentrator in G, which are inverse images of distinct outputs of the (L/2)-superconcentrator in G. Thus, by applying the inductive hypothesis to these 4 parts, $U' \geq 4c(L/2)^2 = cL^2$, which completes the proof of the claim. Taking $L=M$ yields $U \geq cM^2 = \Omega(N^2)$, which completes the proof of the lower bound.

In the case of $R\geq 3$ auxiliary pushdowns, the upper bound

$$T/N = O(\log_R(N/S))$$

is obtained as a generalization of the Postman Algorithm of M. J. Fischer and M. S. Paterson (see Pippenger [17]). The Postman Algorithm is in fact the special case $R=3$, $S=3$ of the result we need. To obtain the required generalization, we modify the Postman Algorithm in two ways.

First, we terminate non-recursively whenever the interval with which we have to deal has length at most $K=\lfloor S/3 \rfloor$ (rather than length one). We then have enough pebbles for the at most 2K immediate predecessors of the vertices in the interval, as well as for these vertices themselves. Second, when we proceed recursively, we partition the interval with which we have to deal into R-1 subintervals (rather than two subintervals). The depth of the tree of recursive invocations is then $\log_{(R-1)}(N/K)=O(\log_R(N/S))$ and the upper bound follows as in the special case.

For the lower bound, we use a counting argument based on a special class of graphs called permutaion graphs, which were introduced by Lengauer and Tarjan [7]. An <u>M-permutation graph</u> is graph with vertices $\{1, \ldots, N\}$, where $N=2M$, having edges $(L, L+1)$ for $1 \le L < M$ and $M+1 \le L < 2M$ and edges $(p(L), M+L)$ for $1 \le L \le M$ and some permutation p of $\{1, \ldots, M\}$ There are M! permutation graphs G_p, so that $\Omega(M \log M)=\Omega(N \log N)$ bits are required to uniquely identify a permutation graph. It is not hard to show that the plays of the pebble game on these graphs with R pushdowns in space S and time T can be encoded using $O(T \log (RS))$ bits in such a way that the encoding of the play uniquely identifies the graph on which the play takes place. This yields the lower bound

$$T/N = \Omega(\log_{(RS)} N).$$

This lower bound is weaker than one we have claimed, in that the number R of pushdowns and the number S of pebbles enter symmetrically. It is intuitively clear that additional pushdowns are more powerful than additional pebbles, and this intuition is confirmed by the following argument.

Suppose for convenience that S divides M. Let us say that two permutation graphs G_p and G_q are <u>S-equivalent</u> if pq^{-1} stabilizes each of the successive blocks $\{1, \ldots, S\}$, $\ldots$, $\{M-S+1, \ldots, M\}$ of length S. There are $M!/S!^{M/S}$ equivalence classes of permutation graphs, so that $\Omega(M \log (M/S))=\Omega(N \log (N/S))$ bits are required to uniquely identify an equivalence class. It is not hard to show that plays of the pebble game on these graphs with R pushdowns in space S and time T can be encoded using $O(T \log R)$ bits in such a way that the encoding of the play uniquely identifies the equivalence class of the graph on which the play takes place. This yields the claimed lower bound

$$T/N = \Omega(\log_R (N/S)).$$

It should be noted that this lower bound differs from the other lower bounds described in this section in that it does not give an explicit construction for a graph that is hard to pebble. The other lower bounds are all based on expanders and superconcentrators, for which explicit constructions are available in the work of Margulis [11] and Gabber and Galil [4].

We should also mention the situation for simple plays of the pebble game, although this situation is indeed too simple to be very interesting. For no auxiliary pushdowns or one auxiliary pushdown, there exist N-graphs that require space $\Omega(N)$ for any complete simple play of the pebble game. Since no significant saving of space is possible in these cases, no significant time-space trade-offs exist. For two or more auxiliary pushdowns, the upper bounds described above in fact apply to complete simple plays of the pebble game. Thus, the time-space trade-offs are the same in these cases, whether or not the plays are required to be simple.

The pebble game as we have discussed it thus far models computations using certain data structures: registers (pebbles) and pushdown stacks. Let us conclude this section by mentioning the possibility of incorporating other data structures (such as queues, deques and tapes) into our setting. The case of $C\geq 1$ tapes is easily dealt with by the methods used for pushdown stacks: for $C=1$ tapes we have

$$T/N = \Theta(N/S)$$

and for $C\geq 2$ tapes we have

$$T/N = \Theta(\log_C(N/S))$$

The case of $D\geq 1$ deques exhibits exactly the same time-space trade-off as $C=D$ tapes. (For the upper bounds, observe that each deque can simulate two pushdowns. For the lower bounds, observe that 1-deque graphs enjoy the same immersions in the plane as 2-pushdown graphs, and that each deque can be simulated by two heads on one tape, which can be simulated by two heads on two tapes (see Hartmanis and Stearns [5]), which can be simulated by four pushdowns.) The case of $Q\geq 1$ queues, however, seems more difficult. It is not hard to show that

$$T/N = O(Q(N/S)^{1/Q}),$$

and we conjecture that

$$T/N = \Omega(Q(N/S)^{1/Q}),$$

at least for simple plays of the pebble game.

4. Pebbling Pushdown Graphs

In the preceding section, we considered A-pushdown B-pebble N-graphs as lifts of other graphs. In this section, we shall consider the question of what graphs are lifts of A-pushdown B-pebble N-graphs. In its full generality, this question appears to be very difficult, so we shall restrict our attention to a special class of A-pushdown 1-pebble N-graphs. Let an <u>A-pushdown N-graph</u> be an N-graph that is the union of at most A pushdown graphs together with the pebble graph that has edges $(M, M+1)$ for $1\leq M<N$.

The study of the pebble game on 1-pushdown N-graphs was begun implicitly by Cook [2] (in his work on the time and space requirements for recognizing deterministic context-free languages) and was continued explicitly by Mehlhorn [12] (who called these graphs "mountain ranges"). They showed that every 1-pushdown N-graph has a complete play of the pebble game (without auxiliary pushdowns) in space $O(\log N)$, and that there exist 1-pushdown N-graphs that require space $\Omega(\log N)$. For space S in the range from N down to the lower bound just indicated, von Braunmuehl and Verbeek [1] showed that every 1-pushdown N-graph has a complete play of the pebble game in space S and time

$$T = N \exp O((\log N)/\log (S/\log N)),$$

and Verbeek [23] showed that there exist 1-pushdown N-graphs that require time

$$T = N \exp \Omega((\log N)/\log (S/\log N)).$$

(The bounds that they actually prove are somewhat sharper than these, but they fall short of establishing the time-space trade-off to within constant factors in time and space.)

The study of 2-pushdown N-graphs begins with the observation that they can be embedded in the plane (a property they share with "1-tape N-graphs" and "1-deque N-graphs", if these are defined in the obvious way). Lipton and Tarjan [10], using their Planar Separator Theorem (see Lipton and Tarjan [9]), have shown that every planar N-graph has a complete play of the pebble game (without auxiliary pushdowns) in space $O(N^{1/2})$, and it is not hard to see that there exist 2-pushdown N-graphs (or 1-tape N-graphs or 1-deque N-graphs) that require space $\Omega(N^{1/2})$. In this case the time-space trade-off remains to be determined.

The study of A-pushdown N-graphs for $A \geq 3$ has barely begun. Of course, every A-pushdown N-graph has a complete play of the pebble game (without auxiliary pushdowns) in space $O(N/\log N)$ (since every N-graph has, by the result of Hopcroft, Paul and Valiant [6]) and it is not hard to see that there exist A-pushdown N-graphs for which space $\Omega((N \log A)/(\log N)^2)$ is required (following a similar observation by Paul, Tarjan and Celoni [14] for m-tape Turing machine graphs). Thus in this case even the space requirements remain to be precisely determined.

Let us conclude this paper with some comments on the role that separator theorems seem to play in pebbling and with a separator conjecture that has some interesting consequences.

We shall say that an N-graph has an <u>M-separator</u> if there exists a set of at most M vertices whose removal allows the remainder of the graph to be partitioned into two parts, each containing at most 2N/3 vertices, with no edge directed out of one part into the other. We shall say that a graph with non-negative weights summing to 1 assigned to its vertices has a <u>strong weighted M-separator</u> if there exists a set of at most M vertices whose removal allows the remainder of the graph to be partitioned into two parts, each having weights summing to at most 1/2, with no edge directed out of one part into the other.

Let q be a non-negative non-decreasing function. We shall say that a class of graphs closed under taking subgraphs has q(N) separators if every N-graph in the class has an M-separator for some $M \leq q(N)$, and that it has strong weighted q(N) separators if every N-graph in the class has a strong weighted M-separator for some $M \leq q(N)$. Lipton and Tarjan have shown that if a class of graphs has q(N) separators, then it has strong weighted $q(N)+q(2N/3)+q(4N/9)+\ldots$ separators (see the proof of Corollary 3 in [9]).

Trees have O(1) separators (see Lewis, Stearns and Hartmanis [8]), and therefore have strong weighted O(log N) separators. This can be used to prove that 1-pushdown N-graphs can be pebbled in space O(log N), since these graphs are trees with some inessential extra edges.

Planar graphs have $O(N^{1/2})$ separators (see Lipton and Tarjan [9]), and therefore have strong weighted $O(N^{1/2})$ separators. This was used to prove that 2-pushdown N-graphs can be pebbled in space $O(N^{1/2})$, since these graphs are planar.

It is natural to conjecture that A-pushdown N-graphs have separation properties that would facilitate the determination of their space requirements and time-space trade-offs. We indeed conjecture that A-pushdown N-graphs have $O(N/\log_A N)$ separators, and therefore strong weighted $O(N/\log_A N)$ separators. It is not hard to see that no stronger conjecture is possible, since there exist A-pushdown N-graphs with only $\Omega(N/\log_A N)$ separators.

Aside from its possible consequences for pebbling, this conjecture has other computational consequences. First observe that if A-pushdown N-graphs have $O(N/\log_A N)$ separators, then A-pushdown B-pebble N-graphs have $O(BN/\log_A N)$ separators. Next observe that if G is a simple lift of G' and G has an M-separator, then G' has an M-separator.

Thus, by virtue of equivalence by mutual simple lifting, the multi-pushdown separator conjecture implies similar multi-tape and multi-head separator conjectures (and conversely, of course). These latter conjectures have several consequences for computations by multi-tape and multi-head machines. First, one could show that non-deterministic time T can be simulated by deterministic space O(T/log T) (strengthening the analogous result of Hopcroft, Paul and Valiant [6] for deterministic time T). Second, one could show that for some language, non-deterministic time T is more powerful than deterministic time T (using the technique of Paul and Reischuk [15], Theorem 2). Finally, one could show that for some language, non-oblivious time T is more powerful than oblivious time T (using the technique of Paul and Reischuk [15], Theorem 4).

5. References

[1] B. von Braunmuehl and R. Verbeek, "A Recognition Algorithm for DCFLs Optimal in Time and Space", IEEE Symp. on Foundations of Computer Science, 21 (1980) 411-420.

[2] S. A. Cook, "Deterministic CFL's Are Accepted Simultaneously in Polynomial Time and Log Squared Space", ACM Symp. on Theory of Computing, 11 (1979) 338-345.

[3] S. A. Cook and R. Sethi, "Storage Requirements for Deterministic Polynomial Time Recognizable Languages", J. Comp. and Sys. Sci., 13 (1976) 25-37.

[4] O. Gabber and Z. Galil, "Explicit Construction of Linear Size Superconcentrators", J. Comp. and Sys. Sci., 22 (1981) 407-420.

[5] J. Hartmanis and R. E. Stearns, "On the Computational Complexity of Algorithms", Trans. AMS, 117 (1965) 285-306.

[6] J. E. Hopcroft, W. J. Paul and L. G. Valiant, "On Time versus Space", J. ACM, 24 (1977) 332-337.

[7] T. Lengauer and R. E. Tarjan, "Upper and Lower Bounds on Time-Space Tradeoffs", ACM Symp. on Theory of Computing, 11 (1979) 262-277.

[8] P. M. Lewis, R. E. Stearns and J. Hartmanis, "Memory Bounds for the Recognition of Context-Free and Context-Sensitive Languages", IEEE Symp. on Switching Theory and Logical Design, 6 (1965) 191-202.

[9] R. J. Lipton and R. E. Tarjan, "A Separator Theorem for Planar Graphs", SIAM J. Appl. Math., 36 (1979) 177-189.

[10] R. J. Lipton and R. E. Tarjan, "Applications of a Planar Separator Theorem", SIAM J. Comp., 9 (1980) 615-627.

[11] G. A. Margulis, "Explicit Construction of Concentrators", Prob. Info. Trans., 9 (1973) 325-332.

[12] K. Mehlhorn, "Pebbling Mountain Ranges and Its Application to DCFL-Recognition", Internat. Coll. on Automata, Languages, and Programming, 7 (1980) 422-434.

[13] M. S. Paterson and C. E. Hewitt, "Comparative Schematology", Proj. MAC Conf. on Concurrent Systems and Parallel Computation, (1970) 119-127.

[14] W. J. Paul, R. E. Tarjan and J. R. Celoni, "Space Bounds for a Game on Graphs", Math. Sys. Theory, 10 (1977) 239-251.

[15] W. J. Paul and R. Reischuk, "On Alternation II", Acta Inf., 14 (1980) 391-403.

[16] N. Pippenger, "Superconcentrators", SIAM J. Comp., 6 (1977) 298-304.

[17] N. Pippenger, "Fast Simulation of Combinational Logic Networks by Machines without Random-Access Storage", Allerton Conf. on Communication, Control, and Computing, 15 (1977).

[18] N. Pippenger, "Comparative Schematology and Pebbling with Auxiliary Pushdowns", ACM Symp. on Theory of Computing, 12 (1980) 351-356.

[19] N. Pippenger, "Pebbling", IBM Japan Symp. on Mathematical Foundations of Computer Science, 5 (1980).

[20] N. Pippenger, "Pebbling with an Auxiliary Pushdown", J. Comp. and Sys. Sci., 23 (1981) 151-165.

[21] R. Sethi, "Complete Register Allocation Problems", SIAM J. Comp., 4 (1975) 226-248.

[22] L. G. Valiant, "Graph-Theoretic Properties in Computational Complexity", J. Comp. and Sys. Sci., 13 (1976) 278-285.

[23] R. Verbeek, "Time-Space Trade-Offs for General Recursion", IEEE Symp. on Foundations of Computer Science, 22 (1981) 228-234.

A POWERDOMAIN FOR COUNTABLE NON-DETERMINISM

(Extended Abstract)

G.D. Plotkin
Dept. of Computer Science
University of Edinburgh

1. Introduction

This paper proposes a general powerdomain for countable nondeterminism and uses it to give the denotational semantics of a simple imperative programming language with a fair parallel construct. As already known from the simple case of a discrete cpo [AP] countable nondeterminism seems to force the consideration of non-continuous functions. In the classical Scott-Strachey approach only continuous functions are allowed and it is necessary to extend the mathematics to a weaker kind of continuity and show how it is still possible to specify and work with least solutions to recursive equations for elements of domains and initial solutions to recursive domain equations.

Fairness or the finite delay property is a natural assumption that has been studied in many settings by many authors. The general idea is that no subprocess is to be delayed indefinitely. More exactly there are two main ways to define a fair computation sequence:

Weak Fairness No event is almost always possible (unless the sequence is finite).

Strong Fairness No event is infinitely often possible.

These statements are deliberately informal: all depends on what counts as an event (see also [AO,Kwo,LPS,Man,Par]). In the present paper only weak fairness is studied as there are no possible strong fairness phenomena in the simple language at hand.

Section 2 begins by defining an operational semantics for our language. This provides a concrete model against which it proves possible to test any denotational semantics. The definition is of the well-known restrictive or negative kind implied by the above formulations of fairness: first specify all execution sequences and then restrict attention to the fair ones (= rule out the unfair ones). Since our language is richer than the usual case of n sequential processes with shared memory the techniques used may be of interest. They comprise a structural operational semantics [Plo2] to specify transitions, redexes (here called actions) to specify potential occurrences (in our case these are also all possible) and residuals to trace potential occurrences through transitions [Bar]. Now it is well-known that fairness (in either form) implies countable nondeterminism. Section 2 concludes by using this idea on the meta-level to provide a generative or positive operational semantics in which all computation sequences are fair (and which gives all the fair sequences that the restrictive semantics does); this is proved in Theorem 1.

Section 3 begins with a review of the discrete case which suggests a suitable form of weak continuity (= ω_1-continuity $\overset{\text{def}}{=}$ preservation of lubs of increasing ω_1-sequences) and a suitable form of cpo (having a $\perp$ and lubs of ω_0- and ω_1-sequences). These assumptions permit least fixed-points to exist and give rise to a form of Scott induction (called ω_1-induction) that is used extensively in Section 4. The essential feature for handling countable nondeterminism seems to be the ability to take arbitrary countable unions. Now in the case of bounded (= finite) nondeterminism one needed only to take finite unions; the abstract view is that semilattices were needed and in [HP] all the various powerdomains previously considered were characterised as suitable free continuous semilattices. Here σ-semilattices seem indicated (as noted independently by Axel Poigné) and several candidates for the free weakly-continuous σ-semilattice are shown to exist (Theorem 2). Now the lack of continuity extends also to the powerdomain construction itself and that makes it impossible to solve recursive domain equations by the usual categorical analogue of the formula for the least fixed-point of a continuous function. In Theorems 5 and 6 and Corollary 1 an extension of the work in [SP] is presented that allows such equations to be solved in the presence of weak continuity (and Theorem 5 appears already in [AK]).

Section 4 begins with an attempt to use the preferred candidate for the powerdomain construct to give a denotational semantics to the example language. The idea is to use a recursively-specified domain of *resumptions* (as in [Plo1]). To the author's surprise, however, this does not work as it does not seem possible to define the semantics of the parallel construct; the problem is that with the preferred candidate there remains some continuity requirements and these are violated. However these difficulties do not arise with the alternate candidate. Finally various relationships between the operational and denotational semantics are established. Theorem 7 shows that the operational semantics determines the denotational semantics, and Theorem 8 shows the converse for some simple notions of behaviour derived from the operational semantics.

Clearly there remains much to do. The proposed powerdomains are shown to exist by highly nonconstructive methods of category theory. Direct existence along the lines of [Plo1,Smy] should be established and an investigation made of the effectiveness of the constructions and functions involved. This is extremely important as the loss of continuity seems to violate Scott's most reasonable thesis that all computable functions are continuous. Next the relation between the various semantics needs further investigation (see [HP] for some discussion of the so-called full-abstraction issue). The successful employment of ω_1-induction encourages an attempt to use it as a means of proving correct the many classical algorithms based on underlying fairness assumptions. It also seems feasible to extend the work to extensions of the current language where, in particular, both weak and strong fairness can be considered. Finally it is not at all clear what can be done in other settings where fairness considerations arise such as languages for message-passing or communication or dataflow languages where there is the difficult "fair merge" problem.

2. Operational Semantics

By adding a parallel construct to a simple imperative language we obtain a first setting for studying fairness. The language has three syntactic categories.

1. *ACom* A given set of *atomic commands*, ranged over by ac.
2. *BExp* A given set of *Boolean expressions* ranged over by b.
3. *Com* A set of *commands* ranged over by c and with abstract syntax given by:
   $c ::= ac \mid \underline{skip} \mid c_1;c_2 \mid \underline{if}\ b\ \underline{then}\ c_1\ \underline{else}\ c_2 \mid \underline{while}\ b\ \underline{do}\ c \mid c_1 \| c_2.$

Operational semantics is provided via a *labelled transition relation* [Kel,Mil] on a set, Γ, of *configurations* (ranged over by γ); To define Γ assume a given denumerable set S of *states* (ranged over by σ). Then $\Gamma =_{def} \{\langle c,\sigma\rangle\} \cup \{\sigma\}$. We will specify a transition relation $\rightarrow\ \subseteq \Gamma \times A \times \Gamma$ where $A =_{def} \{1,2\}^*$ is the set of *actions* (ranged over by a and b). The idea is that in a relation $\gamma \overset{a}{\rightarrow} \gamma'$ the action indicates which of the possible transitions is taken. We assume that the semantics of atomic commands and Boolean expressions are given by functions $\mathcal{A}$: ACom -> (S -> S) and $\mathcal{B}$: BExp -> (S -> T) (where T = {tt,ff} is the set of truth-values). Now the following rules specify the transition relation by structural induction on commands [Plo2].

Atomic Commands $\langle ac,\sigma\rangle \overset{\varepsilon}{\rightarrow} \mathcal{A}[\![ac]\!](\sigma)$ *Skip* $\langle \underline{skip},\sigma\rangle \overset{\varepsilon}{\rightarrow} \sigma$

Composition

$$\frac{\langle c_1,\sigma\rangle \overset{a}{\rightarrow} \langle c_1',\sigma'\rangle \mid \sigma'}{\langle c_1;c_2,\sigma\rangle \overset{a}{\rightarrow} \langle c_1';c_2,\sigma'\rangle \mid \langle c_2,\sigma'\rangle}$$

Conditional

1. $\langle \underline{if}\ b\ \underline{then}\ c_1\ \underline{else}\ c_2,\sigma\rangle \overset{\varepsilon}{\rightarrow} \langle c_1,\sigma\rangle$ (if $\mathcal{B}[\![b]\!](\sigma) = tt$)
2. $\langle \underline{if}\ b\ \underline{then}\ c_1\ \underline{else}\ c_2,\sigma\rangle \overset{\varepsilon}{\rightarrow} \langle c_2,\sigma\rangle$ (if $\mathcal{B}[\![b]\!](\sigma) = ff$)

Repetition

1. $\langle \underline{while}\ b\ \underline{do}\ c,\sigma\rangle \overset{\varepsilon}{\rightarrow} \langle c;\underline{while}\ b\ \underline{do}\ c,\sigma\rangle$ (if $\mathcal{B}[\![b]\!](\sigma) = tt$)
2. $\langle \underline{while}\ b\ \underline{do}\ c,\sigma\rangle \overset{\varepsilon}{\rightarrow} \sigma$ (if $\mathcal{B}[\![b]\!](\sigma) = ff$)

Parallel

1. $$\frac{\langle c_1,\sigma\rangle \overset{a}{\rightarrow} \langle c_1',\sigma'\rangle \mid \sigma'}{\langle c_1 \| c_2,\sigma\rangle \overset{1a}{\rightarrow} \langle c_1' \| c_2,\sigma'\rangle \mid \langle c_2,\sigma'\rangle}$$

$$2.\quad \frac{\langle c_2,\sigma\rangle \xrightarrow{a} \langle c_2',\sigma'\rangle \mid \sigma'}{\langle c_1 \| c_2,\sigma\rangle \xrightarrow{2a} \langle c_1 \| c_2',\sigma'\rangle \mid \langle c_1,\sigma'\rangle}$$

To see how the actions are working define a function, Act, sending commands to non-empty finite subsets of A by: $\mathrm{Act}(ac) = \mathrm{Act}(\underline{\text{skip}}) = \mathrm{Act}(\underline{\text{if}}\ b\ \underline{\text{then}}\ c_1\ \underline{\text{else}}\ c_2) = \mathrm{Act}(\underline{\text{while}}\ b\ \underline{\text{do}}\ c) = \{\varepsilon\}$; $\mathrm{Act}(c_1;c_2) = \mathrm{Act}(c_1)$; $\mathrm{Act}(c_1 \| c_2) = 1\,\mathrm{Act}(c_1) \cup 2\,\mathrm{Act}(c_2)$ and extend it to configurations by putting $\mathrm{Act}(\langle c,\sigma\rangle) = \mathrm{Act}(c)$; $\mathrm{Act}(\sigma) = \emptyset$. One can think of $\mathrm{Act}(\gamma)$ as the set of <u>potential</u> events of γ.

<u>Lemma 1</u> 1. $\forall\gamma\forall a\forall\gamma'.\gamma \xrightarrow{a} \gamma' \supset a \in \mathrm{Act}(\gamma)$

2. $\forall\gamma\forall a \in \mathrm{Act}(\gamma)\exists!\gamma'.\gamma \xrightarrow{a} \gamma'$

3. $\forall\gamma\forall a(\exists\sigma'\ \gamma \xrightarrow{a} \sigma') \equiv \{a\} = \{\varepsilon\} = \mathrm{Act}(\gamma)$

Intuitively parts 1 and 2 of Lemma 1 say there is a 1-1 correspondence between <u>potential</u> and <u>possible</u> events. To be able to express fairness we now need to see how possible actions change from one transition to another. For any a,b in $\mathrm{Act}(\gamma)$ we define the <u>residual actions</u> $\underline{\mathrm{Res}(b,\gamma,a)} \subseteq$ <u>A of b after the a transition from γ</u> by induction on the command in γ.

$\mathrm{Res}(b,\langle c,\sigma\rangle,a) = \emptyset$ (if c is atomic, <u>skip</u>, a conditional or a repetition)

$\mathrm{Res}(b,\langle c_1;c_2,\sigma\rangle,a) = \mathrm{Res}(b,\langle c_1,\sigma\rangle,a)$

$$\mathrm{Res}(1b_1,\langle c_1 \| c_2,\sigma\rangle,a) = \begin{cases} 1\,\mathrm{Res}(b_1,\langle c_1,\sigma\rangle,a_1) & (\text{if } a=1a_1 \text{ and } \langle c_1,\sigma\rangle \xrightarrow{a_1} \langle c_1',\sigma'\rangle) \\ \emptyset & (\text{if } a=1a_1 \text{ and } \langle c_1,\sigma\rangle \xrightarrow{a_1} \sigma') \\ \{1b_1\} & (\text{if } a=2a_2 \text{ and } \langle c_2,\sigma\rangle \xrightarrow{a_2} \langle c_2',\sigma'\rangle) \\ \{b_1\} & (\text{if } a=2a_2 \text{ and } \langle c_2,\sigma\rangle \xrightarrow{a_2} \sigma') \end{cases}$$

$\mathrm{Res}(2b_2,\langle c_1 \| c_2,\sigma\rangle,a)$ is defined symmetrically

<u>Lemma 2</u> 1. Either $\mathrm{Res}(b,\gamma,a)$ is empty and $b = a$ or else it is a singleton $\{b_1b_2\}$ (where $b = b_1ib_2$ for some i in $\{1,2,\varepsilon\}$) and $b \neq a$.

2. If $\gamma \xrightarrow{a} \gamma'$ and $b' \in \mathrm{Res}(b,\gamma,a)$ then $b' \in \mathrm{Act}(\gamma')$.

<u>Definition 1</u> An execution sequence $\gamma = \gamma_0 \xrightarrow{a_0} \gamma_1 \xrightarrow{a_1} \ldots \to \gamma_n \xrightarrow{a_n} \ldots$ of γ is <u>unfair</u> if it is infinite and there is an infinite sequence $b_m, b_{m+1}, \ldots$ where for every $k \geq m$ $b_k \in \mathrm{Act}(\gamma_k)$ and $b_{k+1} \in \mathrm{Res}(b_k,\gamma_k,a_k)$.

Pictorially an unfair sequence looks like this

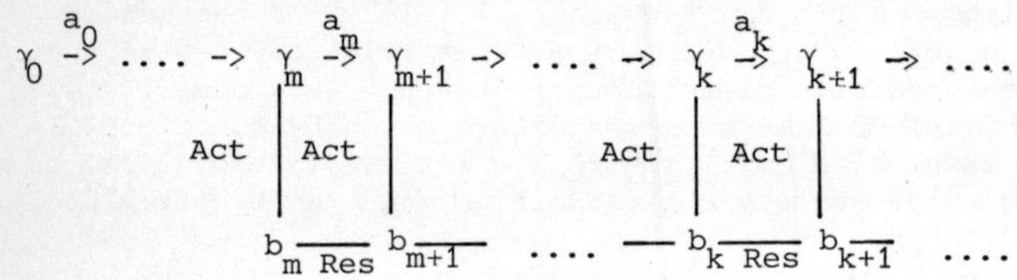

Intuitively the b_k correspond to an event which is almost always possible but never actual.

<u>Definition 2</u> A configuration <u>diverges</u> if it has an infinite fair execution sequence.

When commands are run for their final state a suitable measure of their behaviour is given by the relational approach modified to deal with termination. For any command c we define its relation and its termination domain by

$R[\![c]\!] = \{\langle\sigma,\sigma'\rangle \mid \langle c,\sigma\rangle \to^* \sigma'\}$ (where $\to\ = \bigcup\{\xrightarrow{a} \mid a \in A\}$) and $T[\![c]\!] = \{\sigma \mid \langle c,\sigma\rangle$ converges$\}$ respectively.

<u>Generative Semantics</u>

The operational semantics presented above can be considered <u>negative</u> or <u>restrictive</u> in that first a set of execution sequences is considered and then certain ones are ruled out as unfair. Now a <u>positive</u> or <u>generative</u> operational semantics is proposed in which only (and all) fair sequences can be generated in the first place. The idea is that at any point in a fair execution of $c_1||c_2$ there is an upper bound on the number of transitions that c_1 makes before c_2 makes one, since otherwise there is an action of c_2 almost always possible but never taken (and similarly for c_2).

To formalise the idea we add constructs $c_1||^m c_2$ and $c_1||_m c_2$ (for $m\geq 0$) to the language giving a new set gCom of commands. To execute $c_1||^m c_2$ one executes m+1 steps of c_1 (unless prevented by the termination of c_1); and then executes $c_1||_n c_2$ for an arbitrary $n\geq 0$; the execution $c_1||_m c_2$ proceeds symmetrically. As before, the generative semantics is given by a transition relation $\to_g \subseteq \Gamma_g \times A \times \Gamma_g$ where (evidently) $\Gamma_g = (\text{gCom} \times S) \cup S$; the rules are the same as before except for the parallel construct and ones for the new constructs.

<u>Parallel</u> 1.
$$\frac{\langle c_1||^m c_2,\sigma\rangle \overset{a}{\to}_g \gamma}{\langle c_1||c_2,\sigma\rangle \overset{a}{\to}_g \gamma}\ (m\geq 0) \qquad 2.\ \frac{\langle c_1||_m c_2,\sigma\rangle \overset{a}{\to}_g \gamma}{\langle c_1||c_2,\sigma\rangle \overset{a}{\to}_g \gamma}\ (m\geq 0)$$

<u>Left-Parallel</u> 1.
$$\frac{\langle c_1,\sigma\rangle \overset{a}{\to}_g \langle c_1',\sigma'\rangle|\sigma'}{\langle c_1||^0 c_2,\sigma\rangle \overset{1a}{\to}_g \langle c_1'||_n c_2,\sigma'\rangle|\langle c_2,\sigma'\rangle}\ (n\geq 0)$$

2.
$$\frac{\langle c_1,\sigma\rangle \overset{a}{\to}_g \langle c_1',\sigma'\rangle|\sigma'}{\langle c_1||^{m+1} c_2,\sigma\rangle \overset{1a}{\to}_g \langle c_1'||^m c_2,\sigma'\rangle|\langle c_2,\sigma'\rangle}\ (m\geq 0)$$

<u>Right-Parallel</u> (Symmetric to Left-Parallel)

To connect up the two approaches let $w: \Gamma_g \to \Gamma$ be the function which removes the labels of constituent parallel commands

<u>Lemma 3</u> If $\gamma \overset{a}{\to}_g \gamma'$ then $w(\gamma) \overset{a}{\to} w(\gamma')$

Now we can state a theorem that insofar as execution sequences are concerned the generative semantics captures the restrictive semantics.

<u>Theorem 1</u> For any execution sequence $\gamma_1 \overset{a_1}{\to}_g \gamma_2 \overset{a_2}{\to} \ldots$ the execution sequence $w(\gamma_1) \overset{a_1}{\to} w(\gamma_2) \overset{a_2}{\to} \ldots$ is fair and every fair execution sequence can be found thus.

3. <u>Powerdomains</u>

If we are to give denotational semantics to our language with its fair parallel construct then we need to be able to solve recursive domain equations involving a powerdomain for countable nondeterminism; for this purpose we want a powerdomain functor over a suitable category of partial orders. We start with a review of the discrete case.

<u>Definition 3</u> For any countable set X the powerdomain $\mathcal{E}(X_\perp)$ is the set of non-empty subsets of $X_\perp$ under the Egli-Milner partial order

$$X \sqsubseteq Y \text{ iff } (\forall x \in X \exists y \in Y.\, x \sqsubseteq y) \wedge (\forall y \in Y \exists x \in X.\, x \sqsubseteq y)$$

The <u>singleton function</u> $\{\cdot\}: X_\perp \to \mathcal{E}(X_\perp)$ and the <u>subset relation</u>, $\subseteq$, on $\mathcal{E}(X_\perp)$ have the usual set-theoretic definitions.

<u>Fact 1</u> 1. The powerdomain $\mathcal{E}(X_\perp)$ has a least element $\{\perp\}$, lubs of increasing ω_0-chains and increasing ω_1-chains (the latter being eventually constant).

2. Binary union $\cup: \mathcal{E}(X_\perp)^2 \to \mathcal{E}(X_\perp)$ is ω_0-and and ω_1-continuous and countable union $\bigcup: \mathcal{E}(X_\perp)^\omega \to \mathcal{E}(X_\perp)$ is ω_1-continuous but <u>not</u> in general ω_0-continuous.

3. For every monotonic $f: X_\perp \to \mathcal{E}(Y_\perp)$ (where Y is also any countable set) there is a unique function $f^\dagger: \mathcal{E}(X_\perp) \to \mathcal{E}(Y_\perp)$ such that the following diagram commutes

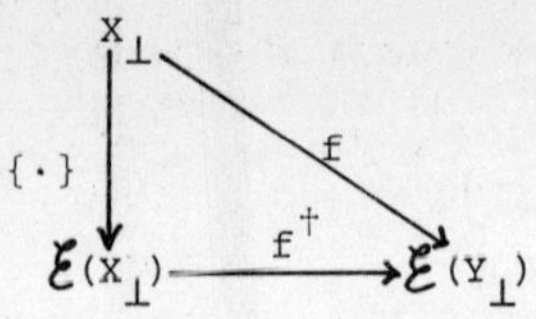

and such that $f^\dagger$ is ω_0-and ω_1-continuous (wrt $\sqsubseteq$) and preserves countable unions. Also if f is strict so is $f^\dagger$.

4. As a function, $(\cdot)^\dagger$ is monotonic, ω_1-continuous but not in general ω_0-continuous.

The non-continuity of extension leads to the non-continuity of important functionals for which a guaranteed fixed-point is required. Luckily we are saved by the completeness of the spaces involved.

<u>Fact 2</u> Let D be a po with a $\perp$ and lubs of increasing ω_0-and ω_1-sequences. Then any ω_1-continuous function f: D -> D has a least fixed-point $\mathrm{Fix}_f \overset{\mathrm{def}}{=} f^{\omega_1}$ where for $\kappa \leq \omega_1$ the κth iterate f^κ is defined by

$$f^0 = \perp,\ f^{\kappa+1} = f(f^\kappa),\ f^\lambda = \bigsqcup_{\kappa<\lambda} f^\kappa \ (\lambda \text{ a limit ordinal}).$$

How are we to react in the light of the above (carefully selected!) experience? In general it seems that we want a countable union function and that will involve us in non-ω_0-continuous (but ω_1-continuous) functions. On the other hand the partial orders we will use can be expected to be not too bad having lubs of increasing ω_0-and ω_1-sequences.

<u>Definition 4</u> Let $\underline{\underline{\mathrm{Pos}}}$ $(\kappa,\ldots;\lambda,\ldots)$ be the category whose objects are partial orders with lubs of increasing κ-chains and ... and whose morphisms are those monotonic functions preserving lubs of increasing λ-chains and ... . In particular set

$$\underline{\underline{A}} = \underline{\underline{\mathrm{Pos}}}\ (\omega_0,\omega_1;\omega_0,\omega_1) \quad \underline{\underline{A}}_1 = \underline{\underline{\mathrm{Pos}}}\ (\omega_0,\omega_1;\omega_1)$$

Here $\underline{\underline{A}}$ is the nicest category of partial orders we could hope to work in, but $\underline{\underline{A}}_1$ is the expected one. Both are Cartesian closed with the usual Cartesian product and pointwise-ordered function spaces (written D -> E and D $->_1$ E in $\underline{\underline{A}}$, $\underline{\underline{A}}_1$ respectively). In $\underline{\underline{A}}_1$ the least fixed-point operator Fix: (D $->_1$ D) $->_1$ D is ω_1-continuous but not, in general, ω_0-continuous.

In [HP] the available powerdomains for bounded nondeterminism [Plo1,Smy] were characterised as free semilattices over a category of partial orders. It now seems appropriate to try free σ-semilattices.

<u>Definition 5</u> A <u>semilattice</u> is a partial order <P,$\subseteq$> with binary lubs x $\cup$ y ($\subseteq$ is called <u>subset</u> and $\cup$ is called <u>binary union</u>). A <u>σ-semilattice</u> is a semilattice with countably infinite lubs $\bigcup x_i$.

<u>Definition 6</u> Let $\underline{\underline{\sigma\mathrm{SLPos}}}$ $(\kappa,\ldots;\lambda,\ldots;\mu,\ldots;\upsilon,\ldots)$ be the category whose objects are structures <D,$\sqsubseteq$,$\subseteq$> where <D,$\sqsubseteq$> is a $\underline{\underline{\mathrm{Pos}}}$ $(\kappa,\ldots;\lambda,\ldots)$ object and <D,$\subseteq$> is a σ-semilattice such that binary union is μ-continuous and ... (wrt $\sqsubseteq$) and countable union is υ-continuous and ... (wrt $\sqsubseteq$) and whose morphisms are those $\underline{\underline{\mathrm{Pos}}}$ $(\kappa,\ldots;\lambda,\ldots)$ morphisms preserving countable union. In particular set

$$\underline{\underline{B}}_0 = \underline{\underline{\sigma\mathrm{SLPos}}}(\omega_0,\omega_1;\omega_0,\omega_1;\omega_0,\omega_1;\omega_0,\omega_1)$$

$$\underline{\underline{B}} = \underline{\underline{\sigma\mathrm{SLPos}}}(\omega_0,\omega_1;\omega_0,\omega_1;\omega_0,\omega_1;\omega_1) \quad \underline{\underline{B}}_1 = \underline{\underline{\sigma\mathrm{SLPos}}}(\omega_0,\omega_1;\omega_1;\omega_0,\omega_1;\omega_1)$$

Here $\underline{\underline{B}}_0$ is the nicest category of σ-semilattices we could hope for where even countable union is ω_0-continuous; $\underline{\underline{B}}$ and $\underline{\underline{B}}_1$ are the categories corresponding to $\underline{\underline{A}}$ and $\underline{\underline{A}}_1$ where countable union is ω_1-continuous, but need not be ω_0-continuous (but we do assume binary union ω_0-continuous). Although the morphisms in $\underline{\underline{B}}_1$ are not ω_0-continuous in general, we do have

<u>Lemma 4</u> <u>Quasi-continuity</u> Let f: D $->_1$ E be a $\underline{\underline{B}}_1$-morphism. For any increasing ω_0-chain $a_0 \sqsubseteq a_1 \sqsubseteq \ldots$ we have $f(\bigsqcup a_n) \subseteq \bigsqcup f(a_n)$.

All these categories are related by various forgetful functors:

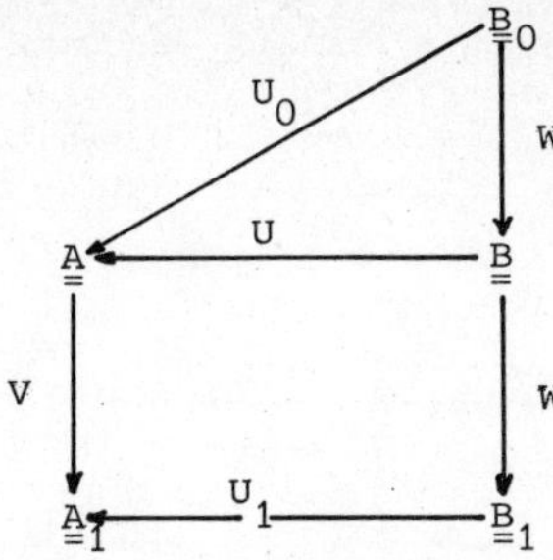

And we expect that the desired powerdomain will be a left-adjoint to U_1 or U or maybe even U_0 or $V \bullet U$.

Theorem 2 The functors U, U_0, V, W have left adjoints, called F, F_0, G, H. However U_1 has no left adjoint.

Proof The positive assertion uses Freyd's Adjoint Functor Theorem [Mac]. The negative one depends on the quasi-continuity lemma. ⊠

So possible powerdomains are $\mathcal{P} \stackrel{def}{=} U \bullet F, F_0$ and $\mathcal{P}_1 \stackrel{def}{=>} V \bullet U \bullet F \bullet G = V \bullet \mathcal{P} \bullet G$.

Not surprisingly the second is unacceptable because of:

Fact 3 Let D be an $\underline{\underline{A}}$ object and let x and y be two elements of $F_0U_0(D)$. Then if $x \sqsubseteq y$ we have $x \subseteq y$. Further if D has a least element then the converse also holds.

Now we examine the properties of our two candidate powerdomains. In $\underline{\underline{A}}$ we have a morphism $\{\cdot\}$: D -> $\mathcal{P}$D (called singleton) which is universal in the sense that to any f: D -> UA there is a unique $\underline{\underline{B}}$-morphism $f^\dagger$: FD -> A (the extension = left-adjunct of f) such that the following diagram commutes.

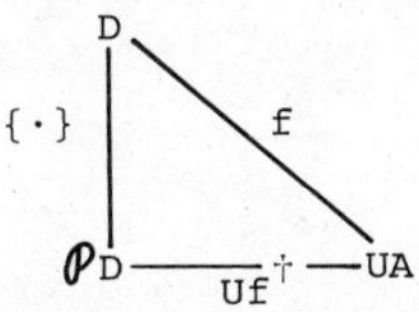

In $\underline{\underline{A}}_1$ analogous remarks hold with $\mathcal{P}_1, \{\cdot\}_1, f^{\dagger 1}, V \bullet U$ and $F \bullet G$ replacing $\mathcal{P}, \{\cdot\}, f^\dagger$, U and F. As an example one can check that $\mathcal{E}(X_\perp) = \mathcal{P}(X_\perp) = \mathcal{P}_1(X_\perp)$. We now try to generalise Fact 1.3.

Definition 7 A $\underline{\underline{\text{Pos}}}$-category is a category whose hom-sets are equipped with partial orders so that composition is monotonic. A functor of $\underline{\underline{\text{Pos}}}$-categories is locally-monotonic (= a $\underline{\underline{\text{Pos}}}$-functor) iff it is monotonic on morphisms; it is locally κ-continuous if it preserves lubs of κ-chains of morphisms.

Definition 8 Let G: $\underline{\underline{L}}$ -> $\underline{\underline{K}}$ be a $\underline{\underline{\text{Pos}}}$-functor. Then f: D -> GA is a G-orderepi iff whenever g,g': A -> A' are such that $(Gg) \bullet f \sqsubseteq (Gg') \bullet f$ then $g \sqsubseteq g'$.

Lemma 5 Let G: $\underline{\underline{L}}$ -> $\underline{\underline{K}}$ be a $\underline{\underline{\text{Pos}}}$-functor with left-adjoint F such that every f: D -> GA factorises as D $\stackrel{f'}{->}$ GA' $\stackrel{Gg}{->}$ GA where f' is a G-orderepi. Then the unit ε_D: D -> GFD is a G-orderepi and extension is an isomorphism of partial orders.

Theorem 3 In both $\underline{\underline{A}}$ and $\underline{\underline{A}}_1$ extension is monotonic and preserves lubs of increasing ω_0-and ω_1-chains. Further F and $F \bullet G$ are locally ω_0-and ω_1-continuous $\underline{\underline{\text{Pos}}}$ functors. Finally $\mathcal{P}$ and $\mathcal{P}_1$ are locally ω_1-continuous $\underline{\underline{\text{Pos}}}$ functors which are not in general ω_0-continuous.

There is no contradiction here with Fact 1.3 as in the first case extension has range in $\underline{\underline{B}}$ and in the second in $\underline{\underline{A}}$. Now we turn to issues involved with the bottom element, $\underline{\underline{1}}$.

Definition 9 $\underline{\underline{A}}^{\perp}$ (respectively $\underline{\underline{A}}_1^{\perp}, \underline{\underline{B}}^{\perp}$) is the full subcategory of $\underline{\underline{A}}$ (respectively $\underline{\underline{A}}_1, \underline{\underline{B}}$) with those objects D containing a least element, $\perp_D$; further $\underline{\underline{A}}_{\perp}$ (respectively $\underline{\underline{A}}_{1\perp}, \underline{\underline{B}}_{\perp}$) is the subcategory of $\underline{\underline{A}}^{\perp}$ (respectively $\underline{\underline{A}}_1^{\perp}, \underline{\underline{B}}^{\perp}$) with the same objects but only those morphisms preserving the least element, the strict ones.

These new categories can be pictured together in terms of a commuting diagram of natural forgetful functors (of which we name six).

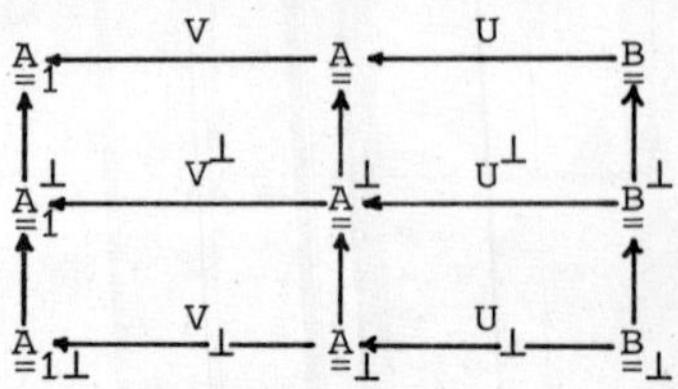

The next theorem says that our powerdomain construction also works when these variations are considered.

Theorem 4 If D is an $\underline{\underline{A}}$-object with a least element then FD has a least element too and the singleton function is strict; further extension preserves strictness. Consequently F cuts down to left adjoints $F^{\perp}$ and $F_{\perp}$ of $U^{\perp}$ and $U_{\perp}$ respectively. The corresponding assertions for $\underline{\underline{A}}_1$ also hold.

Solving Domain Equations

To solve recursive domain equations $D \cong F(D)$ one normally proceeds by analogy with fixed-point equations $x = f(x)$ where the solution is given as $\mathrm{Fix}_f = \bigsqcup_{n\geq 0} f^n(\perp)$ and this is justified by the ω_0-continuity of f. What one does is construct the solution as $\mathrm{Fix}_F = \underrightarrow{\lim}\, \Delta$ where $\Delta = \langle F^n(\perp), F^n(\perp_{F(\perp)})\rangle$ and justify that by the ω_0-continuity of F. Unfortunately neither $\mathcal{P}$ nor $\mathcal{P}$ have the needed continuity property and so we turn to a categorical generalisation of Fact 2, due to Adamek and Koubek [AK]. Below κ is always a limit ordinal.

Definition 10 Let $\underline{\underline{K}}$ be a category. It is a κ-category if it has an initial element, $\perp_K$, and it has direct limits of all $\underline{\underline{\lambda}}$-chains for $\lambda \leq \kappa$; for any D we write $\perp_D$ for the unique morphism from $\perp_K$ to D. Let $F\colon \underline{\underline{K}} \to \underline{\underline{L}}$ be a functor between κ-categories. It is κ-continuous if whenever Δ is an $\underline{\underline{\kappa}}$-chain and $\rho\colon \Delta \to D$ is a limiting cone then $F\rho\colon F\Delta \to FD$ is a limiting cone. Clearly the composition of κ-continuous functors is κ-continuous as are the constant and identity functors.

Definition 11 Let $F\colon \underline{\underline{K}} \to \underline{\underline{K}}$ be a functor. An F-algebra is a pair $\langle D,\alpha\rangle$ with $\alpha\colon FD \to D$. A morphism of F-algebras, $f\colon \langle D,\alpha\rangle \to \langle E,\beta\rangle$ is any morphism $f\colon D \to E$ such that the following diagram commutes

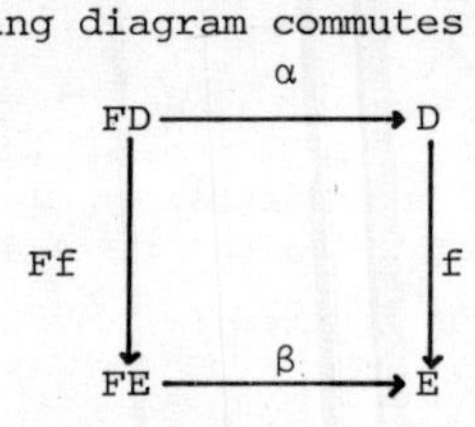

This clearly gives a category of F-algebras.

Theorem 5 Let $\underline{\underline{K}}$ be a κ-category and suppose $F\colon \underline{\underline{K}} \to \underline{\underline{K}}$ is κ-continuous. Then the initial F-algebra exists and can be constructed by the following Initial Algebra Construction

1. $D_0 = \perp_{\underline{\underline{K}}}$ and $D_{\lambda+1} = F(D_\lambda)$
2. $f_{01} = \perp_{D_1}$ and $f_{\lambda+1,\lambda+2} = F(f_{\lambda,\lambda+1})$
3. For limit λ'', $\langle f_{\lambda,\lambda''}\rangle_{\lambda<\lambda''}\colon \langle D_{\lambda'}, f_{\lambda,\lambda'}\rangle_{\lambda\leq\lambda'<\lambda''} \to D_{\lambda''}$ is a colimiting cone

4. For limit λ'', $f_{\lambda'',\lambda''+1}$ is the mediating morphism between the universal cone $\langle f_{\lambda+1,\lambda''}\rangle: \langle D_{\lambda+1}, f_{\lambda+1,\lambda'+1}\rangle_{\lambda\leq\lambda'<\lambda''} \to D_{\lambda''}$ and
$\langle Ff_{\lambda,\lambda''}\rangle_{\lambda<\lambda''}: \langle D_{\lambda+1}, f_{\lambda+1,\lambda'+1}\rangle_{\lambda\leq\lambda'<\lambda''} \to F(D_{\lambda''})$

Then $f_{\kappa,\kappa+1}: D_\kappa \to F(D_\kappa)$ is an isomorphism whose inverse gives the initial F-algebra, $\langle D_\kappa, f^{-1}_{\kappa,\kappa+1}\rangle$.

To apply these ideas we generalise [SP] and work in a $\underline{\underline{\mathrm{Pos}}}$-category setting.

Definition 12 Let $\underline{\underline{K}}$ be a $\underline{\underline{\mathrm{Pos}}}$-category. A pair $D \xrightarrow{f} E \xrightarrow{g} D$ is a projection pair (and f is an embedding and g is a projection) if $g \circ f = id_D$ and $f \circ g \sqsubseteq id_E$.

The elementary facts about embeddings and projections are shown in [SP]. In particular every projection g is determined by its corresponding embedding f and we write $g = f^R_E$. Also the embeddings form a category under $\underline{\underline{K}}$-composition which we denote by $\underline{\underline{K}}^E$. Finally both embeddings and projections are strict and so $\underline{\underline{A}}^{E}_{\perp} = \underline{\underline{A}}_{\perp}^{E}$ and and $\underline{\underline{A}}_{1}^{E} = \underline{\underline{A}}_{1\perp}^{E}$. Note that both have an initial object namely the one-point poset. To see they are both $\underline{\underline{\omega}}_1$-categories one checks both $\underline{\underline{A}}_\perp$ and $\underline{\underline{A}}_{1\perp}$ have both $\underline{\underline{\omega}}_0$-and $\underline{\underline{\omega}}_1$-limits and uses Theorem 6 below.

Definition 13 A $\underline{\underline{\mathrm{Pos}}}(\kappa)$ category is a $\underline{\underline{\mathrm{Pos}}}$-category in which the morphism partial orders have lubs of all increasing κ-chains and where composition is κ-continuous.

Theorem 6 Suppose $\underline{\underline{K}}$ is a $\underline{\underline{\mathrm{Pos}}}(\kappa)$ category with $\underline{\underline{\kappa}}$-limits. Then $\underline{\underline{K}}^E$ has $\underline{\underline{\kappa}}$-colimits and indeed for any $\underline{\underline{\kappa}}$-chain Δ in $\underline{\underline{K}}^E$ we have that $\mu: \Delta \to D$ is colimiting iff $id_D = \bigsqcup_{\lambda<\kappa} \mu_\lambda \circ \mu^R_\lambda$.

Turning to functors we note that if $T: \underline{\underline{K}}^{op} \times \underline{\underline{L}} \to \underline{\underline{M}}$ is a $\underline{\underline{\mathrm{Pos}}}$-functor then as in [SP] we can define a covariant $T^E: \underline{\underline{K}}^E \times \underline{\underline{L}}^E \to \underline{\underline{M}}^E$ with the same action as T on objects and with $T^E(f,g) \overset{\mathrm{def}}{=\!>} T(f^R,g)$ on morphisms.

Corollary 1 Let $\underline{\underline{K}},\underline{\underline{L}},\underline{\underline{M}}$ be $\underline{\underline{\mathrm{Pos}}}(\kappa)$ categories with all limits of $\underline{\underline{\kappa}}$-chains; let $T: \underline{\underline{K}}^E \times \underline{\underline{L}} \to \underline{\underline{M}}$ be a locally κ-continuous functor. Then T^E is κ-continuous.

Now we see that both $\mathcal{P}$ and $\mathcal{P}_1$ and the product and function-space functors all give ω_1-continuous functors. In addition both $\underline{\underline{A}}_\perp$ and $\underline{\underline{A}}_{1\perp}$ have categorical sums which are just the usual smash sums (e.g. see [SP]) these are also locally ω_1-continuous and so give ω_1-continuous functors.

We can therefore follow [HP], say, and obtain a domain of resumptions

$$R \cong S_\perp \to \mathcal{P}(S_\perp + (S_\perp \times R))$$

in $\underline{\underline{A}}$ (to be ranged over by r) and another one (also ranged over by r)

$$R_1 \cong S_\perp \to_1 \mathcal{P}_1(S_\perp + (S_\perp \times R_1))$$

in $\underline{\underline{A}}_1$. Below the isomorphism will be treated as an actual equality for simplicity's sake; similarly we will omit injection functions when dealing with sums. Again we should have used more accurate domain equations to model strictness phenomena, but the extra complications did not seem worthwhile here, and do not affect the theorems in the next section.

4. Denotational Semantics

By using resumptions we attempt to give a denotational semantics to our programming language; the idea will be to model the generative operational semantics. At first we try R; this will fail but R_1 will succeed.

An attempt to use $\underline{\underline{A}}$ To begin we develop a little "categorical programming". Let e_1 be an expression of type $\mathcal{P}(S_\perp + (S_\perp \times R))$ and let e_2 and e_3 be expressions of type $\mathcal{P}(D)$ monotonic in σ and where e_3 is ω_0-and ω_1-continuous in r. Then e = cases e_1 first σ'. e_2 second σ', r'. e_3 is of type $\mathcal{P}(D)$ and abbreviates $[\lambda\sigma' \in S_\perp. e_2, \lambda\sigma' \in S_\perp, r' \in R. e_3]^\dagger(e_1)$. If e_1,e_2 and e_3 are ω_1-continuous in a variable then so is e (and because of the extension we do not expect ω_0-continuity in general). Again, if e is an expression of type $\mathcal{P}(D)$ monotonic in n (ranging over

$N_\perp$) then the countable choice expression $\bigcup_n e$ abbreviates $(\lambda n \in N_\perp.e)^\dagger N$; this is ω_1-continuous in any variable that e is.

Now we try to define various useful combinators. The definitions are recursive and justified by an appeal to Fact 2.

Flattening The combinator (= operation) $|\cdot|: R \to (S_\perp \to S_\perp)$ is defined recursively by: $|r|\sigma = \underline{\text{cases}}\ r(\sigma)\ \underline{\text{first}}\ \sigma'.\ \{\sigma'\}\ \underline{\text{second}}\ \sigma',r'.|r'|^\dagger(\sigma')$

Composition To model the composition of commands we recursively define a composition combinator ; : $R \to (R \to_1 R)$ by:

$$r_1;r_2(\sigma) = \underline{\text{cases}}\ r_1(\sigma)\ \underline{\text{first}}\ \sigma'.\ \{\langle\sigma',r_2\rangle\}\ \underline{\text{second}}\ \sigma',r'.\{\langle\sigma',r';r_2\rangle\}$$

Parallelism We need three combinators corresponding to the three syntactic operators of the generative operational semantics. They are $||_L,||_R: N_\perp \to R \to_? R \to_? R$ and $||: R \to_? R \to_? R$ where we do not yet know which function spaces are intended. We will see there are no possible choices which make our attempted definitions work.

Try to define $||_L$ and $||_R$ by mutual recursion:

$$\begin{aligned} r_1||^m_L r_2(\sigma) = \underline{\text{cases}}\ & r_1(\sigma)\ \underline{\text{first}}\ \sigma'.\{\langle\sigma',r_2\rangle\} \\ & \underline{\text{second}}\ \sigma',r'.\ \underline{\text{if}}\ m=0\ \underline{\text{then}}\ \textstyle\bigcup_n\{\langle\sigma',r'||^n_R r_2\rangle\} \\ & \qquad \underline{\text{else}}\ \{\langle\sigma',r'||^{m-1}_L r_2\rangle\} \end{aligned}$$

($||_R$ is defined symmetrically).

If these definitions were legitimate we would then go on to define the parallel combinator by

$$r_1||r_2(\sigma) = \bigcup_n r_1||^n_L\ r_2(\sigma) \cup \bigcup_n r_1||^n_R\ r_2(\sigma)$$

However the definitions cannot be acceptable. For example in the definition of $||_L$ in order that the conditional expression be ω_0-continuous in r' it is necessary that $r_1||^m_R\ r_2$ be ω_0-continuous in r_1; but r_1 occurs in both the "first" and "second" branches of the definition of $||_R$ and so such continuity cannot be guaranteed. Despite some effort it was not found possible to produce any acceptable definitions and for that reason the attempt to use $\underline{\underline{A}}$ seems doomed to failure.

Using $\underline{\underline{A}}_1$ Here one tries the domain R_1. The cases construction $\underline{\text{cases}}\ e_1\ \underline{\text{first}}\ \sigma'.\ e_2\ \underline{\text{second}}\ \sigma',\ r'.\ e_3$ is introduced as above but now only ω_1-continuity of e_3 in r' is required; it abbreviates $[\lambda\sigma' \in S_\perp.\ e_2,\lambda\sigma' \in S_\perp,\ r' \in R_1.e_3]^{\dagger 1}\ (e_1)$. The countable union construction $\bigcup_n e$ is introduced as above and abbreviates $(\lambda n \in N_\perp\ e)^{\dagger 1}(N)$.

The flattening combinator $|\cdot|: R_1 \to_1 (S_\perp \to_1 S_\perp)$ and the composition combinator ; : $R_1 \to_1 R_1 \to_1 R_1$ are defined analogously to before and now the analogous definitions for the parallel combinators $||_L,||_R: N_\perp \to_1 R_1 \to_1 R_1 \to_1 R$ and $||: R_1 \to_1 R_1 \to_1 R_1$ are legitimate.

We are at last in a position to give the denotational semantics of our programming language. The denotational function $\mathcal{C}$: gCom $\to R_1$ is defined by structural induction on commands:

$$\mathcal{C}[\![ac]\!] = \lambda\sigma \in S_\perp.\quad \{\mathcal{A}[\![ac]\!](\sigma)\}_1$$

$$\mathcal{C}[\![\underline{\text{skip}}]\!] = id_{S_\perp}$$

$$\mathcal{C}[\![c_1;c_2]\!] = \mathcal{C}[\![c_1]\!];\ \mathcal{C}[\![c_1]\!]$$

$$\begin{aligned} \mathcal{C}[\![\underline{\text{if}}\ b\ \underline{\text{then}}\ c_1\ \underline{\text{else}}\ c_2]\!] = \lambda\sigma \in S_\perp.\ & \underline{\text{if}}\ \mathcal{B}[\![b]\!](\sigma)\ \underline{\text{then}}\ \{\langle\sigma, \mathcal{C}[\![c_1]\!]\rangle\}_1 \\ & \underline{\text{else}}\ \{\langle\sigma, \mathcal{C}[\![c_2]\!]\rangle\}_1 \end{aligned}$$

$$\begin{aligned} \mathcal{C}[\![\underline{\text{while}}\ b\ \underline{\text{do}}\ c]\!] = \mu r \in R_1.\lambda\sigma \in S_\perp.\ & \underline{\text{if}}\ \mathcal{B}[\![b]\!](\sigma) \\ & \underline{\text{then}}\ \{\langle\sigma, \mathcal{C}[\![c]\!];m\rangle\}_1\ \underline{\text{else}}\ \{\sigma\}_1 \end{aligned}$$

$$\mathcal{C}[\![c_1||^m\ c_2]\!] = \mathcal{C}[\![c_1]\!]\ ||^m_L\ \mathcal{C}[\![c_2]\!]$$

$$\mathcal{C}[\![c_1 ||_m c_2]\!] = \mathcal{C}[\![c_1]\!] ||_R^m \mathcal{C}[\![c_2]\!]$$
$$\mathcal{C}[\![c_1 || c_2]\!] = \mathcal{C}[\![c_1]\!] || \mathcal{C}[\![c_2]\!]$$

Here if e is an expression of type D that is ω_1-continuous in a variable x of type D then $\mu x \in D.e$ is the least x=e; it is ω_1-continuous in any variable that e is.

Relation with the operational semantics

The resumption semantics was introduced as an abstract version of the operational semantics. To formalise this we define Op; gCom -> R_1 by

$$\mathrm{Op}[\![c]\!](\sigma) = \bigcup\{\{<\sigma',\mathrm{Op}[\![c']\!]>\}_1 | \exists a <c,\sigma> \overset{a}{\rightarrow}_g <c',\sigma'>\} \cup \bigcup\{\{\sigma'\}_1 | \exists a <c,\sigma> \overset{a}{\rightarrow}_g \sigma'\}$$

This definition is easily justified. Now we see that the operational semantics determines the denotational semantics.

Theorem 7 $\mathcal{C}$ = Op.

The proof of this theorem makes heavy use of a form of Scott Induction which we call ω_1-induction (and contrast that with the usual ω_0-induction). A property $P \subseteq D$ is ω_0-(ω_1-) inductive if it has lubs of increasing ω_0-(respectively ω_1-) chains. The ω_1-induction rule is:

$$\frac{P(\bot) \quad \forall x\ P(x) \supset P(e)}{P(\mu x.e)}$$

provided P is both ω_0-and ω_1-inductive and $\lambda x.e$ is ω_1-continuous. What we hope is that ω_1-induction will prove as useful a tool for handling countable non-determinism as ω_0-induction has proved for sequential programming.

Finally we see that the operational semantics of section 2 can be obtained from the denotational semantics.

Theorem 8 1. For any c in Com and states σ, σ', $\sigma R[\![c]\!] \sigma'$ iff $\sigma' \in |\mathcal{C}[\![c]\!]|(\sigma)$

2. For any c in Com and state $\sigma, \sigma \in T[\![c]\!]$ iff $\bot \in |\mathcal{C}[\![c]\!]|(\sigma)$

Acknowledgements

I would like to thank Axel Poigné, Matthew Hennessy and Robin Milner for useful discussions, and Eleanor Kerse for the typing. The work was supported with the aid of an SERC grant.

References

[AK] Adamek, J. and Koubek, V. Least fixed points of a functor. JCSS, Vol. 19, No. 2, pp. 163-178, (1979).

[AO] Apt, K.R. and Olderog, E.-R. Proof rules dealing with fairness. Bericht Nr. 8104, Institut für Informatik und Praktische Mathematik, Kat. Christian-Albrechts Universität, (1981).

[AP] Apt, K.R. and Plotkin, G.D. A Cook's tour of countable non-determinism. Proc. ICALP 1981. LNCS Vol. 115 (eds. S. Even and O. Kariv). Berlin: Springer-Verlag, pp. 479-494, (1981).

[Bar] Barendregt, H.P. The lambda calculus, its syntax and semantics. Studies in Logic, Vol. 103, (1981). Amsterdam: North-Holland.

[HP] Hennessy, M.C.B. and Plotkin, G.D. Full abstraction for a simple parallel programming language. Proc. MFCS, LNCS Vol. 74, pp. 108-120 (ed. Becvar,J.) (1979), Berlin: Springer-Verlag.

[Kel] Keller, R. A fundamental theorem of asynchronous parallel computation in parallel processing, LNCS Vol. 24 (ed. T. Feng) Berlin: Springer-Verlag.

[Kwo] Kwong, Y.S. On the absence of livelock in parallel programs. Semantics of concurrent computation, LNCS Vol. 70, pp. 172-190 (ed. G. Kahn) Berlin: Springer-Verlag, (1979).

[LPS] Lehmann, D., Pnueli, A. and Stavi, J. Impartiality, justice and fairness: the ethics of concurrent termination. Proc. ICALP 1981, LNCS Vol. 115 (eds. S. Even and O. Kariv) Berlin: Springer-Verlag, pp. 264-277, (1981).

[Mac] MacLane, S. Categories for the Working Mathematician. Berlin: Springer-Verlag, (1971).

[Man] Manna, Z. Logics of programs. Proc. IFIP Congress 1980.

[Mil] Milner, R. A calculus of communicating systems. LNCS Vol. 92,(1980) Berlin: Springer-Verlag.

[Par] Park, D. A predicate transformer for weak fair iteration. Proc. 6th IBM Symposium on Mathematical Foundations of Computer Science, Hakone, Japan, (1981).

[Plo1] Plotkin, G.D. A powerdomain construction. SIAM Journal on Computation, Vol. 5, No. 3, pp. 452-487, (1976).

[Plo2] Plotkin, G.D. A structural approach to operational semantics. DAIMI FN-19. Computer Science Department, Aarhus University, (1981).

[Smy] Smyth, M.B. Powerdomains. JCSS, Vol. 16, No. 1, (1978).

[SP] Smyth, M. and Plotkin, G.D. The categorical solution of recursive domain equations. SIAM Journal on Computation. To appear. (1981).

Properties of a notation for combining functions

Jean-Claude Raoult

LRI, Bâtiment 490
Université Paris XI, Orsay
91405 ORSAY CEDEX

Ravi Sethi

Bell Laboratories
Murray Hill, New Jersey 07974

Abstract

A notation based on pipes in the UNIX™ operating system is proposed for combining functions in a linear order. Examples suggest that semantic rules using pipes (i.e. the notation) are easy to read and understand, even for readers with little knowledge of semantics. The readability is a consequence of the operational intuition associated with pipes. The operational view is that each function is handed a sequence of values. Generally the sequence is treated as a stack; a function pops zero or more arguments off the stack, pushes zero or more results onto the stack, and passes the stack to the next function. The new idea is that a function may skip over some number of values before picking up its arguments. This approach is suited to expressing the composition of operations on machine states in a programming language. Pipes mesh smoothly with other metalanguage concepts, e.g., lambda abstraction.

The bulk of the paper explores mathematical properties of pipes. In order for pipes to fit into lambda expressions, the arguments of the constructed function has to be well defined. Operationally speaking, we have to keep track of the elements in the stack.

Pipes allow continuation semantics to be written with direct operators: instead of the operator having to worry about its continuation, the second function in a pipe is essentially a continuation of the first. A connection is established between functions connected by pipes and more traditional continuation semantics. This connection is made possible by a combinator ***do*** that constructs continuation versions of direct operators, e.g., continuation style operators from the literature for arithmetic, assigning to an identifier, and determining the value of an identifier, can be constructed from their direct counterparts using ***do***. An example of the translation of a pipe based semantic rule for **let** expressions into a continuation based semantic rule is given.

1. Introduction

1.1. *Overview.* A new notation generalizing function composition is studied in this paper. The notation is suited to expressing the semantics of control flow in sequential languages. Extensive examples of its use in describing a language containing break and goto statements are given in [set81b], where it plays a central role in quickly constructing efficient compilers for the control flow aspects of a language.

The notation is motivated by *pipes* in the UNIX operating system, which pass the output of one program as input to another, thereby composing programs. For example, the command

wordlist | ***sort*** | ***removedupl*** | ***common*** *dictionary*

might check for spelling errors by taking a list of words, sorting, removing duplicates, looking up the words in the dictionary, and printing the words that are not found.[1]

Adapting this notation, the direct semantics of the assignment $a:=b$ can be written as

fetch b | ***assign*** a

where ***fetch*** b maps a state to a value-state pair, which is then mapped by ***assign*** a to an appropriately updated state. If continuation semantics is desired, then all we have to write is

[1] Ritchie [rit80] notes that, "Pipes appeared in Unix in 1972 ... at the suggestion (or perhaps insistence) of M. D. McIlroy."

fetch b | *assign* a | c

where c is the continuation for the statements following $a{:=}b$.

The formalization of | is a generalization of function composition because, in $f \mid g$, the number of arguments of g may be more or less than the number of results produced by f. The sources and targets of the combined function $f \mid g$ are adjusted depending on the sources and targets of g.

Simple examples in Section 2 suggest the use of the pipe notation. Section 3 contains formal definitions and statements of some basic properties. A symmetric notation is considered in Section 4 as a prelude to relating pipes with continuation style semantics in Section 5.

1.2. *Background.* Denotational semantic descriptions associate mathematical functions with constructs in a programming language, using a second language to specify the functions. This second language will be referred to here as a *metalanguage*. A metalanguage is needed to combine operations in other styles of semantic descriptions as well, e.g., with abstract data types.

Early metalanguages [bjo78, mos79] were simple extensions of the lambda notation of Church [chu41]: all lambda notation does is to allow functions to be defined and applied. Special notation for frequently occurring operations – like function composition – allows new functions to be built up from old ones without using lambda notation. For example, $g \circ f$ is a readable alternative to $\lambda x.g(f(x))$. Similarly, special notation is usually introduced for function updating: starting with a function f, $f[a/z]$ is often written for a function that agrees with f everywhere except at z, which it maps to a. It is well known from the work of Schönfinkel [sch24] and Curry [cur58] that bound variables and lambdas can systematically be eliminated using *combinators*, which are essentially lambda terms without free variables.

1.3. *Related work.* A number of combinators generalizing function composition have been proposed by Mosses [mos80, mos81] and Wand [wan80a, wan80b, wan82].

For some time Mosses [mos80, mos81] has argued that an algebraic approach would make denotational semantics easier to understand and use. He considers algebras of "actions" whose operations correspond to fundamental concepts of programming. Actions behave like functions, consuming and producing values. There are also combinators for composing actions. The operator >– [mos80] is closest to | but >– and | are quite different.[2]

Using generalizations of the standard ***B*** and ***S*** combinators [cur58], Wand [wan80a, wan80b, wan82] constructs clever representations of continuation semantics that look very much like code for a stack machine. The stack is implicit, since lists of arguments are viewed as stacks. In fact, the pipe mechanism of this paper was designed to allow an underlying stack to be used with direct operators. It is possible to use the direct operators to construct either direct or continuation semantics.

The connection between semantic rules using pipes and continuation style rules in [wan80a, wan80b, wan82] is made in Section 5 using the ***do*** family of combinators. The simplicity with which continuation style operators can be constructed from direct ones is suggested by the equality:

$$\textbf{\textit{do}} + \kappa\ u\ v \;=\; \kappa(u+v)$$

The continuation counterpart of + is ***do*** +. Note that ***do*** is essentially the same as the ***mkconfun*** combinator of Gordon [gor79, p.70].

1.4. *Preliminaries.* Some examples will be based on the following construct:

let id = exp_1 **in** exp_2

The meaning of this construct is suggested by the equivalence of the following two expressions.

let $x = a+b+c$ **in** $x{*}x{*}x$
$(a+b+c){*}(a+b+c){*}(a+b+c)$

Let expressions introduce a limited form of block structure: the following expression is equivalent to 10+5=15, since the inner let evaluates to 10.

let x=5 **in** ((**let** x=10 **in** x) + x)

There is enough subtlety to **let** expressions to make them a good vehicle for testing readability of a notation; this may explain why they have been considered in [mor73, mos80, tha81, wan80b].

Function application. The basic notation for representing the application of expression E_1 to E_2 is to

[2] In $a >\!-_n b$, the targets are determined by concatenating the targets of b to whatever is left over from the targets of a after b consumes n values. If b consumes more than n values, the remaining values are not taken from the targets of a, but from the sources i.e. from the input stream. Therefore with >– there is a separation of sources and targets, except as explicitly specified by the subscript of >–. With | on the other hand there is no such separation.

write E_1 followed by E_2 as in E_1E_2. Proliferation of parentheses will be avoided by consistently associating function application to the left; both $f\,a\,b$ and $f(a)b$ are equivalent to $(f(a))(b)$.

2. Informal description of pipes

Some of the properties of pipes will be introduced informally in this section by considering the meaning of simple program fragments.

2.1. *Basic semantic functions.* The meaning of a language construct will be built up from a small collection of basic semantic functions. For example, corresponding to the operator + is a function ***plus*** that adds its two arguments; ***times*** multiplies its two arguments.

Suppose that a *state* s maps an identifier a to a value $s(a)$. The semantics of an assignment to a will be specified using the function ***assign*** applied to a. In the following definition of ***assign*** a, s is some state, v is some value, and $s' = s[v/a]$ is the resulting state, i.e. $s'(a)=v$ and $s'(x)=s(x)$ for $x \neq a$.

$$(\textbf{\textit{assign}}\ a)(v,s) \quad = \quad s[v/a]$$

The basic function ***fetch*** is given by:

$$(\textbf{\textit{fetch}}\ b)(s) \quad = \quad (s(b),s)$$

2.2. *Properties of pipes.* The symbol | will be called a *pipe*.

2.2.1. Function composition is a special case of the pipe mechanism. If it makes sense to write $g \circ f = \lambda x.\ g(f(x))$, then

$$f \mid g \quad = \quad g \circ f$$

The meaning of $a{:=}b$ is therefore given by ***fetch*** b | ***assign*** a. A state s is mapped by ***fetch*** b to the pair $s(b),s$; the pair is then mapped by ***assign*** a to the new state $s[s(b)/a]$.

2.2.2. The number of arguments of g in $f \mid g$ need not agree with the the number of results of f. The operational view is that each function connected by a pipe is handed a finite sequence of values. Generally, the sequence is treated like a stack (the top is to the right); the function pops zero or more arguments off the sequence, pushes zero or more results onto the sequence, and passes the sequence to the next function. In the case where all the results of one function are arguments of the next, pipes merely compose functions.

For example, as above, a state s is mapped by ***fetch*** b to $s(b),s$. Similarly, ***fetch*** c maps s to $s(c),s$. Therefore, the term

$$\textbf{\textit{fetch}}\ b \mid \textbf{\textit{fetch}}\ c$$

maps s to $s(b),s(c),s$.

2.2.3. It is useful to allow a function to pass the rightmost j values in a sequence unchanged, treating the rest of the sequence as a stack – denoted using $|_j$ instead of $|$. Then $|$ is just $|_0$. For example, the meaning of $b+c$ is given by

$$(\,\textbf{\textit{fetch}}\ b \mid \textbf{\textit{fetch}}\ c\,) \ |_1\ \textbf{\textit{plus}}$$

As above, ***fetch*** b | ***fetch*** c maps state s to the sequence $s(b),s(c),s$. Here $|_1$ is needed to skip over the rightmost element s and add the two values. The result is the pair $s(b)+s(c),\ s$.

2.2.4. We assume that pipes associate to the left:

$$f \ |_i\ g \ |_j\ h \quad = \quad (\,f \ |_i\ g\,) \ |_j\ h$$

The parentheses in (***fetch*** b | ***fetch*** c) $|_1$ ***plus*** can therefore be dropped.

2.2.5. Expressions containing pipes will be linearized by associating to the left. The associativity rule is:

$$f \ |_i\ (\,g \ |_j\ h\,) \quad = \quad (\,f \ |_i\ g\,) \ |_{i+j}\ h$$

For example, consider the expression $b \times c + d \times e$. Based on the example in 2.2.3, the meanings of $b \times c$ and $d \times e$ are given by

$$\textbf{\textit{fetch}}\ b \mid \textbf{\textit{fetch}}\ c \ |_1\ \textbf{\textit{times}}$$

$$\textbf{\textit{fetch}}\ d \mid \textbf{\textit{fetch}}\ e \ |_1\ \textbf{\textit{times}}$$

Therefore the meaning of $b \times c + d \times e$ is given by

$$(\,\textbf{\textit{fetch}}\ b \mid \textbf{\textit{fetch}}\ c \ |_1\ \textbf{\textit{times}}\,) \mid (\,\textbf{\textit{fetch}}\ d \mid \textbf{\textit{fetch}}\ e \ |_1\ \textbf{\textit{times}}\,) \ |_1\ \textbf{\textit{plus}}$$

The subexpression at which the associative rule is applicable shows up more clearly in:

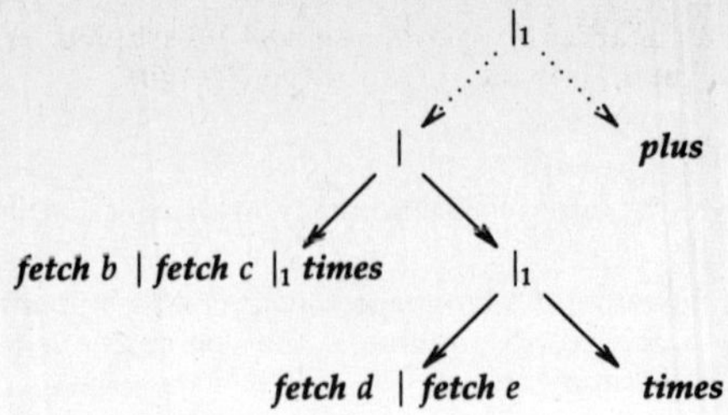

The first application of the associative rule linearizes $|_1$ ***times***; the next application linearizes $|$ ***fetch*** *e*, leading to the linearized form

$$\textbf{\textit{fetch}}\ b \ \mid\ \textbf{\textit{fetch}}\ c\ \ |_1\ \textbf{\textit{times}}\ \mid\ \textbf{\textit{fetch}}\ d\ \mid\ \textbf{\textit{fetch}}\ e\ \ |_1\ \textbf{\textit{times}}\ \ |_1\ \textbf{\textit{plus}} \tag{2.1}$$

2.2.6. In order for pipes to mesh cleanly with other metalanguage constructs, like lambda expressions, the arguments and results of a constructed function have to be well defined. The formalization of pipes in Section 3 takes care of such details. Fixing the number of arguments and results and allowing values to be skipped makes pipes different from the stack in POP-2 [bur77].

2.3. let *expressions.* The examples so far have illustrated particular properties of pipes. We now consider **let** $id = exp_1$ **in** exp_2, to allow a semantic rule using pipes to be compared with the semantic rules for **let** expressions in [mor73, mos80, tha81, wan80b].

The meaning of expression *exp*, written $[\![exp]\!]$ is a function from states to (value-state)[3] pairs; $[\![id]\!]$ is the identifier itself. The operation ***swap*** interchanges its two arguments:

$$\textbf{\textit{swap}}(x,y) \quad = \quad (y,x)$$

Using ***swap*** the meaning of the **let** expression is:

$$\textbf{\textit{fetch}}\ [\![id]\!]\ \mid\ [\![exp_1]\!]\ \mid\ \textbf{\textit{assign}}\ [\![id]\!]\ \mid\ [\![exp_2]\!]\ \ |_1\ \textbf{\textit{swap}}\ \mid\ \textbf{\textit{assign}}\ [\![id]\!] \tag{2.2}$$

The sequences of values that are passed by functions are shown below. For simplicity we assume that expressions have no side effects: only the snapshots of the stack would change if side effects did indeed occur. Let $v_1, s = [\![exp_1]\!]s$, $s' = s[v_1/[\![id]\!]]$, and $v_2, s' = [\![exp_2]\!]s'$.

	s
fetch $[\![id]\!]$	$s[\![id]\!], s$
$\mid [\![exp_1]\!]$	$s[\![id]\!], v_1, s$
$\mid$ ***assign*** $[\![id]\!]$	$s[\![id]\!], s'$
$\mid [\![exp_2]\!]$	$s[\![id]\!], v_2, s'$
$\|_1$ ***swap***	$v_2, s[\![id]\!], s'$
$\mid$ ***assign*** $[\![id]\!]$	v_2, s

The choice of left associativity for pipes can be motivated by the term (2.2). If pipes associated to the right then:

$$\cdots\ \ |_1\ \textbf{\textit{swap}}\ \mid\ \textbf{\textit{assign}}\ [\![id]\!] \quad \text{would equal} \quad \cdots\ \ |_1\ (\ \textbf{\textit{swap}}\ \mid\ \textbf{\textit{assign}}\ [\![id]\!]\ )$$

But then both ***swap*** and ***assign***$[\![id]\!]$ pass over the state s', which is not the intention.

2.4. *Application to compiler generation.* Here we briefly sketch the use of pipes in a compiler generator; details may be found in [set81b]. As in Section 2.2.5, linearized sequences of functions connected by pipes are constructed for assignment statements. In analogy with the use of the term "basic block" in [bac57] for straight line sequences of code, let a linearized sequence of functions in a pipe be called a *basic block.*

In a graph representation, edges between basic blocks are constructed for constructs like conditionals and while statements. In the rule for conditionals in Figure 1, both the true and false exits use the same continuation; in a graph representation there will be edges to the same vertex from the true and false parts. Environments in the semantic rules are eliminated as in [set81a].

Consider for example the statement

while ($r > n$) $r := r - n$;

Assuming that c is the continuation for the exit of this while statement, a straightforward translation yields

---

[3] The state field allows for side effects.

$$rec\ c_0 =$$

$$fetch\ r \mid fetch\ n \mid_1 gt \mid$$

$$cond(\ fetch\ r \mid fetch\ n \mid_1 minus \mid assign\ r \mid c_0\ ,\ c\ )$$

A graph representation of this term is suggested by:

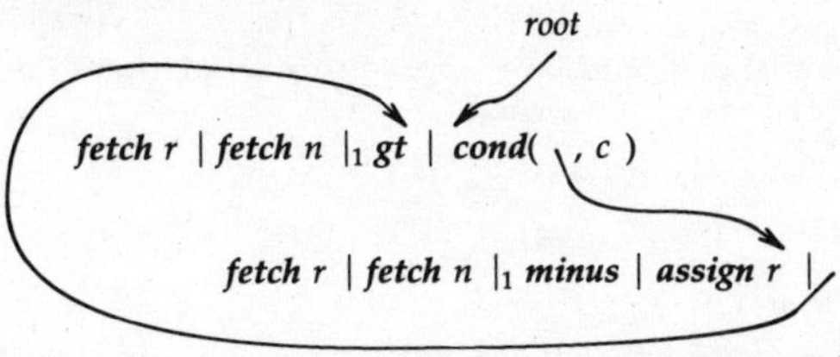

There are two basic blocks in the above diagram. Code can be generated from the above diagram in a number of ways. A simple code generator might simply print the graph in a suitable linearized form. In [set81b] the following stack machine like code is produced:

```
50:     fetch r
        fetch n
        gt
        onfalse goto 23
        fetch r
        fetch n
        minus
        assign r
        goto 50
23:     ...
```

```
stm     : ID ':' '=' exp ';'
                { $$ e c = $exp ¦ assign $ID ¦ c }
        ¦ IF '(' exp ')' stm
                { $$ e c = $exp ¦ cond( $stm e c , c ) }
        ¦ BREAK ';'
                { $$ e c = e(hbrk) }
        ¦ WHILE '(' exp ')' stm
                { $$ e c =
                        rec c0 =
                                let     e' = e[hbrk:=c];
                                in      $exp ¦ cond( $stm e' c0 , c )
                }
        ¦ '{' stm_s '}'
                { $stm_s }
        ;
stm_s   : ! empty
                { $$ e c = c }
        ¦ stm_s stm
                { $$ e c = $stm_s e ( $stm e c ) }
        ;
exp     : ID
                { fetch $ID }
        ¦ exp '+' exp
                { $exp.1 ¦ $exp.2 ¦1 plus }
        ;
```

Figure 1. The above semantic rules for statements in a simple language are in the input format of the compiler generator described in [set81b]. Instead of writing ⟦*exp*⟧ and ⟦*stm*⟧, **$exp** and **$stm** are written. **$$** refers to the meaning of the left hand side of a syntactic rule. The cond basic function is first supplied with a true and a false continuation; then a value and a state are supplied. Depending on the value, either the true or the false continuation is applied to the state.

3. Formalization of pipes

Functions $f_1, f_2 \cdots$, will be combined by pipes, where for $i=1,2, \cdots$, f_i takes $m_i \geq 0$ arguments and returns $n_i \geq 0$ results. When used without subscripts, f takes m arguments and has n results. The identity combinator I_d takes d arguments and returns them. I is an abbreviation of I_1.

The definition of $f \; |_j \; g$ is done in two stages: in Section 3.1 we define $I_d \; |_j \; f$ and then use it in Section 3.4 to define $f \; |_j \; g$.

3.1. The basic concept is that of a function f applied to a list of $d \geq m+j$ arguments: it passes over the top j and also leaves the bottom $d-m-j$ untouched.[4]

$$(I_d \; |_j \; f)(u_1, \ldots, u_{d-m-j}, v_1, \ldots, v_m, w_1, \ldots, w_j) =$$
$$\textbf{\textit{let}} \quad (x_1, \ldots, x_n) = f(v_1, \ldots, v_m)$$
$$\textbf{\textit{in}} \quad (u_1, \ldots, u_{d-m-j}, x_1, \ldots, x_n, w_1, \ldots, w_j)$$

Equivalently, the starting and ending configurations are:

$$u_1, \ldots, u_{d-m-j}, v_1, \ldots, v_m, w_1, \ldots, w_j$$
$$u_1, \ldots, u_{d-m-j}, x_1, \ldots, x_n, w_1, \ldots, w_j$$

3.2. Configurations help visualize some simple facts about pipes. As an exercise, given $d \geq m_1+j$ and $n_1=m_2$, let us show[5]

$$I_d \; |_j \; (f_2 \circ f_1) = (I_{d-m_1+n_1} \; |_j \; f_2) \circ (I_d \; |_j \; f_1)$$

Let $(x_1, \ldots, x_{n_1}) = f_1(v_1, \ldots, v_{m_1})$ and $(y_1, \ldots, y_{n_2}) = f_2(x_1, \ldots, x_{n_1})$. Then both sides lead to the following configurations:

$$u_1, \ldots, u_{d-m_1-j}, v_1, \ldots, v_{m_1}, w_1, \ldots, w_j$$
$$u_1, \ldots, u_{d-m_1-j}, x_1, \ldots, x_{n_1}, w_1, \ldots, w_j$$
$$u_1, \ldots, u_{d-m_1-j}, y_1, \ldots, y_{n_2}, w_1, \ldots, w_j$$

3.3. Provided $d' \geq m+j$ and $d \geq d'+i$, another simple fact is:

$$I_d \; |_i \; (I_{d'} \; |_j \; f) = I_d \; |_{i+j} \; f$$

Letting $(z_1, \ldots, z_n) = f(w_1, \ldots, w_m)$ we get

$$u_1, \ldots, u_{d-d'-i}, v_1, \ldots, v_{d'-m-j}, w_1, \ldots, w_m, x_1, \ldots, x_j, y_1, \ldots, y_i$$
$$u_1, \ldots, u_{d-d'-i}, v_1, \ldots, v_{d'-m-j}, z_1, \ldots, z_n, x_1, \ldots, x_j, y_1, \ldots, y_i$$

3.4. Based on the operational intuition in Section 2, $\times|+$ must be applied to a stack of at least three elements, and $\times|_1+$ to a stack of at least four elements. Suppose $f_1 \; |_j \; f_2$ is applied to a stack with m elements. Clearly $m \geq m_1$ or there will not be enough arguments for f_1. After f_1 is applied there will be $m-m_1+n_1$ elements in the stack. Then j elements are passed over and f_2 is applied to m_2 arguments, so we must have $m-m_1+n_1 \geq j+m_2$ i.e. $m \geq m_1+m_2-n_1+j$.

We want $f_1 \; |_j \; f_2$ to be a function with a definite number of arguments; it will take $m=\max(m_1, m_1+m_2-n_1+j)$ arguments from which it follows that it has $m-m_1-m_2+n_1+n_2$ results.

The definition is:

$$f_1 \; |_j \; f_2 = (I_{m-m_1+n_1} \; |_j \; f_2) \circ (I_m \; | \; f_1)$$

3.5. As stated in Section 2.2.4, $|_j$ is assumed to be left associative and to have lower precedence than juxtaposition.

---

[4] In the definition of $I_d \; |_j \; f$, ***let*** is used as a metalanguage construct. The use of ***let*** can be avoided by using lambda notation. In the following definition, x is a list of results and $x.i$ represents the i-th element of the list.

$$I_d \; |_j \; f =$$
$$\lambda u_1, \ldots, u_{d-m-j}, v_1, \ldots, v_m, w_1, \ldots, w_j.$$
$$(\lambda x. \; (u_1, \ldots, u_{d-m-j}, x.1, \ldots, x.n, w_1, \ldots, w_j)) \; (f(v_1, \ldots, v_m))$$

[5] The function composition combinator $\circ$ here is a generalization of the combinator $\circ$ in Sections 1-2. In Sections 1-2, $\circ$ composed functions of a single argument and result. Here, $f_2 \circ f_1$ will be written only when the number of arguments m_2 of f_2 equals the number of results n_1 of f_1. $f_2 \circ f_1$ is a function of m_1 arguments and n_2 results, which applies f_1 to its m_1 arguments and then applies f_2 to the n_1 results.

3.6. The next proposition connects the number of arguments of a function built up using pipes with the number of elements in a stack. Starting with a stack containing d_0 elements, let d_i be the number of elements in the stack after function f_i is applied. Since f_i pops m_i arguments and pushes n_i results, $d_i=d_{i-1}-m_i+n_i$. Moreover, f_i passes over j_i elements and expects m_i arguments, so $d_{i-1} \geqslant m_i+j_i$.

PROPOSITION 1. *Consider the function* $f = f_1 |_{j_2} \cdots |_{j_k} f_k$. *Given any* d_0, *define* $d_i=d_{i-1}-m_i+n_i$, $1 \leqslant i \leqslant k$, *and let* $j_1=0$. *Then*

(i) $d_0 - m = d_k - n$, *and*

(ii) $d_0 \geqslant m$ *if and only if* $d_{i-1} \geqslant m_i + j_i$, *for all* i, $1 \leqslant i \leqslant k$. *Moreover*, $d_0 = m$ *if and only if* $d_{i-1} \geqslant m_i + j_i$, *for all* i, $1 \leqslant i \leqslant k$, *and for some* i', $1 \leqslant i' \leqslant k$, $d_{i'-1} = m_{i'} + j_{i'}$.

3.7. Trees of pipes will be linearized using an associativity rule. Just as function composition is associative, the operator $|_0$ is associative. However, the associativity does not carry over to $|_j$, since h passes over the top j values in $g|_j h$, but h must pass over the top $i+j$ values in $f|_i(g|_j h)$. We therefore have to settle for the following limited associativity result.

PROPOSITION 2. $f \;|_i\; (g \;|_j\; h) = (f \;|_i\; g) \;|_{i+j}\; h$.

3.8. The operational intuition of elements being popped and pushed onto a stack is reinforced by the next proposition. Since pipes associate to the left, $f|g|h$ is defined in terms of $f|g$ and h. Operationally speaking though f will be applied first.

PROPOSITION 3. *Consider function* $f = f_1 |_{j_2} \cdots |_{j_k} f_k$. *Define* $d_0=m$ *and* $d_i = d_{i-1}-m_i+n_i$, $1 \leqslant i \leqslant k$. *Let* $j_1=0$. *Then,*

$$f_1 |_{j_2} \cdots |_{j_k} f_k = (I_{d_{k-1}} |_{j_k} f_k) \circ \cdots \circ (I_{d_0} |_{j_1} f_1)$$

3.9. So far the discussion has been in terms of values on a stack since associating types with values would have complicated the presentation. We expect a compiler generator to check types however. Given a term $f_1|_{j_2} \cdots |_{j_k} f_k$, in a forward scan we can simulate the popping and pushing of types to determine the types of the results. Proposition 1 can be used to check that the number of arguments expected by the term being checked and its number of results matches the surrounding context. Actually Proposition 1 applies even if a backward scan is made to check types since d_0 equals the number of arguments if and only if d_k equals the number of results.

4. A variant of pipes

A development analogous to that of Section 3 occurs if a list of elements is viewed as a stack with the top of the stack being to the *left*, instead of to the right. In this section, x is the top element in x,y,z.

The connective † will be used here to avoid confusion with the pipe connective | of Section 3. The distinction between | and † will become clear when we contrast the semantics of $b \times c + d \times e$ using the two connectives in Section 4.1.3. Informally, the depth of the stack is made explicit by the subscripts on †, thereby making it easier to generate code for a register machine.[6]

The discussion of † also provides a smooth transition between pipes in Section 3 and continuations in Section 5. Later in this section we formalize the connection between | and †. The connection between † and continuations will be established in Section 5.

4.1. *Examples.* The operators ***fetch***, ***assign***, and ***swap*** are as in Section 2.

4.1.1. Consider the expression $b+c$. Starting with the sequence s, the following snapshots show how the sequence $s(b)+s(c),s$ is reached.

	s
fetch b	$s(b)$, s
$\dagger_1$ ***fetch*** c	$s(b)$, $s(c)$, s
† ***plus***	$s(b)+s(c)$, s

After ***fetch*** b, the value of b is at the left end of the sequence, so ***fetch*** c has to pass over one element. However, when ***plus*** is applied, both its arguments are at the left end, so no elements are passed over.

4.1.2. Now consider **let** $id=exp_1$ **in** exp_2. The only difference between the term (4.1) below, and the

[6] The need for the † connective became evident while implementing a type checker for |. The examples in Section 2 suggested that the conceptual top of the stack be to the right. However, in the implementation, the leftmost element was at the head of the list. So typechecking was done by taking a term involving |, translating it into term involving † as discussed below in Section 4.2, and then doing the checking. Clearly, a new connective † can be avoided if the functionality of the basic operations is changed, e.g. let ***fetch'*** map states to state-value pairs instead of value-state pairs. However, our purpose is to study notations for combining given operations so we rule out the possibility of changing the given operations.

corresponding term (2.2) using pipes is that the number of elements passed over is different.

$$\textit{\textbf{fetch}}\ [\![id]\!]\ \dagger_1\ [\![exp_1]\!]\ \dagger_1\ \textit{\textbf{assign}}\ [\![id]\!]\ \dagger_1\ [\![exp_2]\!]\ \dagger\ \textit{\textbf{swap}}\ \dagger_1\ \textit{\textbf{assign}}\ [\![id]\!] \tag{4.1}$$

Once again, let $s' = s[[\![exp_1]\!]s/id]$.

	s
fetch $[\![id]\!]$	$s[\![id]\!],\ s$
$\dagger_1\ [\![exp_1]\!]$	$s[\![id]\!],\ [\![exp_1]\!]s,\ s$
$\dagger_1$ ***assign*** $[\![id]\!]$	$s[\![id]\!],\ s'$
$\dagger_1\ [\![exp_2]\!]$	$s[\![id]\!],\ [\![exp_2]\!]s',\ s'$
$\dagger$ ***swap***	$[\![exp_2]\!]s',\ s[\![id]\!],\ s'$
$\dagger_1$ ***assign*** $[\![id]\!]$	$[\![exp_2]\!]s',\ s$

4.1.3. The interesting example is the expression $b\times c+d\times e$. As in Section 4.1.1, the meanings of $b\times c$ and $d\times e$ are given by

$$\textit{\textbf{fetch}}\ b\ \dagger_1\ \textit{\textbf{fetch}}\ c\ \dagger\ \textit{\textbf{times}}$$

$$\textit{\textbf{fetch}}\ d\ \dagger_1\ \textit{\textbf{fetch}}\ e\ \dagger\ \textit{\textbf{times}}$$

Therefore the meaning of $b\times c+d\times e$ is given by

$$(\ \textit{\textbf{fetch}}\ b\ \dagger_1\ \textit{\textbf{fetch}}\ c\ \dagger\ \textit{\textbf{times}}\ )\ \dagger_1\ (\ \textit{\textbf{fetch}}\ d\ \dagger_1\ \textit{\textbf{fetch}}\ e\ \dagger\ \textit{\textbf{times}}\ )\ \dagger\ \textit{\textbf{plus}}$$

The associativity rule for $\dagger$ is just like that for pipes: $f\ \dagger_i\ (\ g\ \dagger_l\ h\ )$ equals $f\ \dagger_i\ g\ \dagger_{i+l}\ h$. Applying this rule to the above term we get the linearized form (contrast with the term (2.1)):

$$\textit{\textbf{fetch}}\ b\ \dagger_1\ \textit{\textbf{fetch}}\ c\ \dagger\ \textit{\textbf{times}}\ \dagger_1\ \textit{\textbf{fetch}}\ d\ \dagger_2\ \textit{\textbf{fetch}}\ e\ \dagger_1\ \textit{\textbf{times}}\ \dagger\ \textit{\textbf{plus}}$$

Note that the subscripts on $\dagger$ can be used to generate code for a register machine; the subscript identifies the registers that are affected by each operation. The subscripts in the term (2.1) on the other hand depend only on the operation and not on the number of values in the stack.

4.2. *Formalization.* The formalization of $\dagger$ is very similar to that of $|$.

4.2.1. For $d \geqslant m+l$,

$$\begin{aligned}(\ \boldsymbol{I}_d\ \dagger_l\ f)\ (u_1, \ldots, u_l, v_1, \ldots, v_m, w_1, \ldots, w_{d-m-l}) &= \\ \textit{\textbf{let}}\quad (x_1, \ldots, x_n) = f(v_1, \ldots, v_m)& \\ \textit{\textbf{in}}\quad (u_1, \ldots, u_l, x_1, \ldots, x_n, w_1, \ldots, w_{d-m-l})&\end{aligned}$$

4.2.2. *Definition.* For $m = \max(m_1, m_1+m_2-n_1+l)$,

$$f_1\ \dagger_l\ f_2 \ = \ (\ \boldsymbol{I}_{m-m_1+n_1}\ \dagger_l\ f_2\ )\circ(\ \boldsymbol{I}_m\ \dagger\ f_1\ )$$

In fact, $\dagger$ and $|$ are so similar that the proofs in Appendix A are based on axioms that apply to both. The following facts establish that the axioms do indeed apply to $\dagger$. As in Sections 3.2-3, configurations help visualize the proofs.

4.2.3. For $d \geqslant m_1+l$ and $n_1 = m_2$,

$$\boldsymbol{I}_d\ \dagger_l\ (\ f_2\circ f_1\ ) \ = \ (\ \boldsymbol{I}_{d-m_1+n_1}\ \dagger_l\ f_2\ )\circ(\ \boldsymbol{I}_d\ \dagger_l\ f_1\ )$$

4.2.4. For $d' \geqslant m+l$ and $d \geqslant d'+i$,

$$\boldsymbol{I}_d\ \dagger_i\ (\ \boldsymbol{I}_{d'}\ \dagger_l\ f\ ) \ = \ \boldsymbol{I}_d\ \dagger_{i+l}\ f$$

4.2.5. Let $\dagger_l$ be left associative and have lower precedence than juxtaposition.

4.2.6. The next proposition connects $\dagger$ and $|$.

PROPOSITION 4. *For* $d = m+j+l$,

$$\boldsymbol{I}_d\ |_j\ f \ = \ \boldsymbol{I}_d\ \dagger_l\ f$$

The relationship expressed by Proposition 4 carries over to larger terms.

PROPOSITION 5. *Define* $d_i = d_{i-1}-m_i+n_i$, $1 \leqslant i \leqslant k$. *Let* $j_i + l_i = d_{i-1}-m_i$ *for all* i, $1 \leqslant i \leqslant k$. *Then,*

$$\boldsymbol{I}_{d_0}\ |_{j_1}\ f_1 \cdots |_{j_k}\ f_k \ = \ \boldsymbol{I}_{d_0}\ \dagger_{l_1}\ f_1 \cdots \dagger_{l_k}\ f_k$$

5. Continuation counterparts of direct operators

5.1. *Streams of arguments.* One criticism of the formulation of pipes in Section 3 is that it is all too discrete: a function pops m arguments and pushes n results back onto the sequence. An incremental view is facilitated by "currying" functions so that they take their arguments one at a time rather than all at once.

5.1.1. *Currying* is a well known technique for converting a function that takes a list of arguments into a higher order function that takes arguments one at a time. For example, corresponding to + is a function +' that takes an argument, like 1, and produces a function, (+'1) that increments its argument e.g. (+'1)2=3, (+'1)3=4. Schönfinkel [sch24] introduced this concept, but it is named after Curry who made extensive use of it.

5.1.2. The correspondence between a function and its curried counterpart is so obvious that the same notation is generally used for both. So here are curried versions of the direct operators in Section 2.

$$\begin{aligned}\textbf{assign}\ a\ v\ s &= s[v/a]\\ \textbf{plus}\ u\ v &= u+v\\ \textbf{fetch}\ a\ s &= (s(a),s)\\ \textbf{swap}\ x\ y &= (y,x)\end{aligned}$$

5.2. *Continuation style operators.* ***fetch*** of course was already curried, so it still produces two things – a value and a state. The arguments of ***swap*** are now curried, but it produces all its results at once. In order to be truly incremental, the results of ***fetch*** and ***swap*** must be consumed one at a time as they are produced. Continuations will be used for this purpose.

5.2.1. Given a direct operator f that produces a single result, the corresponding continuation operator can be constructed using a combinator $\boldsymbol{do}_{m,1}$ [gor79, p.70]. Since the subscripts on ***do*** are determined solely by f, they will be suppressed.

$$\textbf{do}\ f\ \kappa\ u_1 \cdots u_m = \kappa(f\ u_1 \cdots u_m)$$

Functions like κ are called *continuations.*

5.2.2. The link between a producer and consumer is established by generalizing the ***do*** combinator:

$$\begin{aligned}&\textbf{do}_{m,n}\ f\ \kappa\ u_1 \cdots u_m =\\ &\qquad \textbf{let}\ \ (v_1, \cdots ,v_n) = f\ u_1 \cdots u_m\\ &\qquad \textbf{in}\ \ \kappa\ v_1 \cdots v_n\end{aligned}$$

Once again, the subscripts m,n depend only on f and can be suppressed.

5.2.3. Continuation versions of some of the direct operators from Section 2 can now be given.

$$\begin{aligned}\textbf{do}\ (\textbf{assign}\ a)\ \kappa\ v\ s &= \kappa(s[v/a])\\ \textbf{do plus}\ \kappa\ u\ v &= \kappa(+\ u\ v)\\ \textbf{do}\ (\textbf{fetch}\ a)\ \kappa\ s &= \kappa(s\ a)s\\ \textbf{do swap}\ \kappa\ u\ v &= \kappa\ v\ u\end{aligned}$$

5.3. *Continuation counterparts of pipes.* In order to connect functions that expect continuations, a family of combinators $\&_i$ closely related to $\dagger_i$ will be used. Informally, when & is used to connect continuation style operators then the operational intuition of $f\&g$ will be "do f and then do g". However this intuition depends on conventions regarding the form of continuation style operators. Pipes were introduced to eliminate the reliance on conventions and to make the operational intuition more secure.

5.3.1. *Definition.*

$$(\ f\ \&_i\ g\ )\ y_1 \cdots y_i = f(g\ y_1 \cdots y_i)$$

& is just $\&_0$.

5.3.2. We assume that $\&_i$ is right associative:

$$f\ \&_i\ g\ \&_j\ h = f\ \&_i\ (\ g\ \&_j\ h\ )$$

and that $\&_i$ has lower precedence than juxtaposition, so $e\,f\,\&_i g\,h$ is $(e\,f)\&_i(g\,h)$.

5.3.3. $\&_0$ is just function application, while $\&_1$ is the composition of single argument single result functions. $\&_1$ is the **B** combinator of Schönfinkel, with the generalization to $\&_i$ being due to Abdali [abd76]. He uses a prefix $\mathbf{B}_i$ instead of the infix $\&_i$ used here.

5.3.4. As with pipes, there is an associative identity that allows trees of &s to be linearized:

PROPOSITION 6. [wan80a] $(\ f\ \&_i\ g\ )\ \&_j\ h = f\ \&_{i+j-1}\ (\ g\ \&_j\ h\ )$.

5.4. *Relating $\&_l$ and $\dagger_l$.* Here we will construct continuation semantic rules by starting with the direct operators connected by $\dagger$ as in Section 4.

5.4.1. The technicalities involved in relating &s and pipes have to do with keeping track of the numbers of arguments. The functions I_d and κ in the following proposition ensure that the first and last functions in the pipe "touch all elements in the sequence". The term ***do*** f & κ is parsed (***do*** f) & κ.

PROPOSITION 7. *Let* $d \geq m+l$, *and let* κ *be a function of* $d-m+n$ *arguments. Then,*

$$I_d \ \dagger_l \ f \ \dagger \ \kappa \quad = \quad \textbf{do} \, f \ \ \&_l \ \kappa$$

5.4.2. Proposition 7 can now be generalized to take care of a sequence of functions connected by †.

PROPOSITION 8. *Define* $d_i = d_{i-1}-m_i+n_i$, $1 \leq i \leq k$. *Let* $d_{i-1} \geq m_i+l_i$ *for all* i, $1 \leq i \leq k$. *Let* κ *be a function of* d_k *arguments. Then,*

$$I_{d_0} \ \dagger_{l_1} f_1 \cdots \dagger_{l_k} f_k \ \dagger \ \kappa \quad = \quad \textbf{do} \, f_1 \ \&_{l_1} \cdots \textbf{do} \, f_k \ \&_{l_k} \ \kappa$$

Note that the subscript l_i appears before f_i with † and after f_i with ***do***-&.

5.5. *Example.* Together with Proposition 5, the above proposition relates pipes in Section 2-3 with continuation style semantics. We illustrate by considering **let** expressions again.

5.5.1. Some of the operators used in [wan80b] are related to the operators of Section 2 as follows.

store *a*	=	***do*** (***assign*** *a*)
add	=	***do plus***
load *a*	=	***do*** (***fetch*** *a*)
exchange	=	***do swap***

Starting essentially with (2.2)

$$I \mid \textbf{fetch} [\![id]\!] \mid [\![exp_1]\!] \mid \textbf{assign} [\![id]\!] \mid [\![exp_2]\!] \mid_1 \textbf{swap} \mid \textbf{assign} [\![id]\!] \mid \kappa$$

we use Proposition 5 to get (4.1) (with a leading ***I*** †)

$$I \ \dagger \ \textbf{fetch} [\![id]\!] \ \dagger_1 \ [\![exp_1]\!] \ \dagger_1 \ \textbf{assign} [\![id]\!] \ \dagger_1 \ [\![exp_2]\!] \ \dagger \ \textbf{swap} \ \dagger_1 \ \textbf{assign} [\![id]\!] \ \dagger \ \kappa$$

Proposition 8 now yields the following continuation style term

$$\textbf{load} [\![id]\!] \ \& \ [\![exp_1]\!]_c \ \&_1 \ \textbf{store} [\![id]\!] \ \&_1 \ [\![exp_2]\!]_c \ \&_1 \ \textbf{exchange} \ \& \ \textbf{store} [\![id]\!] \ \&_1 \ \kappa$$

where $[\![exp]\!]_c = \textbf{do} [\![exp]\!]$.

The transformation from one form into another can clearly be mechanized.

6. Discussion of basic combinators

The symmetric counterpart of the ***do*** combinator is

$$\textbf{on} \ x \ y \ z \quad = \quad y(z \ x)$$

Recall that $\textbf{do}_{1,1}$ is given by

$$\textbf{do} \ x \ y \ z \quad = \quad y(x \ z)$$

Together with ***W***, given by $W \, x \, y = x \, y \, y$, ***on*** and ***do*** can be used to eliminate bound variables.

Consider for example the semantics of the assignment $a{:=}b$.

$$\lambda s. \ \textbf{assign} \ a \ (s \ b) \ s \tag{6.1}$$

The following steps show the elimination of the bound variable s.

$$= \ W \ \& \ \lambda s'. \ \lambda s. \ \textbf{assign} \ a \ (s' \ b) \ s$$

$$= \ W \ \& \ \textbf{on} \ b \ \& \ \lambda v. \ \lambda s. \ \textbf{assign} \ a \ v \ s$$

$$= \ W \ \& \ \textbf{on} \ b \ \& \ \textbf{assign} \ a$$

Note that the operator ***load*** in Section 5 is just ***W*** $\&_2$ ***on***.

do and ***on*** perform bottom up elimination of bound variables, as opposed to the usual top down approaches [cur58, abd76, tur79] which map (6.1) to final terms like[7]

$$S(\ S(\ S(K\textbf{assign})(Ka) \ )(\ SI(Kb) \ ) \ )I \tag{6.2}$$

[7] The combinators ***B***, ***C***, ***I***, ***K***, ***S***, and ***W*** are as in [cur58]. A simple algorithm for eliminating bound variables uses $Ix = x$, $Kyz = y$, and $Sxyz = xz(yz)$: replace $\lambda x.x$ by ***I***; $\lambda x.y$ by Ky; and $\lambda x.E_1E_2$ by $S(\lambda x.E_1)(\lambda x.E_2)$. This algorithm yields (6.2) from (6.1). ***B*** and ***C*** are specialized versions of ***S*** that apply if x is in either E_1 or E_2, but not both. The definitions are: $Bxyz = x(yz)$ and $Cxyz = xzy$. Using ***B*** and ***C*** we get (6.3) from (6.1).

$S(\ B(assign\,a)(CIb)\ )I$ (6.3)

However these terms are not close to conventional machine code since a state has to be passed down to the leaves.

Appendix. Properties of pipes

Since similar statements can be made for the connectives | and †, in Sections 3 and 4, results that apply to both can be proved axiomatically. A number of the proofs will be omitted to save space.

Axioms. Let $F = \{f_1, f_2, \cdots\}$ be a set of *function symbols*. Associated with each function symbol f are two integers $m \geqslant 0$ and $n \geqslant 0$, called the numbers of *arguments* and *results*, respectively, of f. Included in F are distinguished symbols $I_0, I_1, \cdots$, where I_d has d arguments and d results.

Rules. The symbol ! is used in place of | or †.

R1. For $d \geqslant m+j$, $I_d\ !_j\ f$ has d arguments and $d-m+n$ results.

R2. For $d' \geqslant m+j$ and $d \geqslant d'+i$, $I_d\ !_i\ (\ I_{d'}\ !_j\ f\ )\ =\ I_d\ !_{i+j}\ f$.

R3. For $d \geqslant m_1+j$ and $m_2 = n_1$, $I_d\ !_j\ (\ f_2 \circ f_1\ )\ =\ (\ I_{d-m_1+n_1}\ !_j\ f_2\ ) \circ (\ I_d\ !_j\ f_1\ )$.

R4. For $m = \max(m_1, m_1+m_2-n_1+j)$, $f_1\ !_j\ f_2\ =\ (\ I_{m-m_1+n_1}\ !_j\ f_2\ ) \circ (\ I_m\ !\ f_1\ )$.

R5. $I_m\ !_0\ f\ =\ f$.

Convention. ! associates to the left.

LEMMA 1. *The function* $f_1\ !_j\ f_2$ *has* $m = s+m_1-n_1$ *arguments and* $n = s-m_2+n_2$ *results, where* $s = \max(n_1, j+m_2)$.

Remark. With the notations of Lemma 1, $m-n = (m_1-n_1)+(m_2-n_2)$. □

PROPOSITION 1. *Consider the function* $f\ =\ f_1\ !_{j_2} \cdots !_{j_k}\ f_k$. *Given any* d_0, *define* $d_i = d_{i-1}-m_i+n_i$, $1 \leqslant i \leqslant k$, *and let* $j_1 = 0$. *Then*

(i) $d_0\ -\ m\ =\ d_k\ -\ n$, *and*

(ii) $d_0 \geqslant m$ *if and only if* $d_{i-1} \geqslant m_i + j_i$, *for all* i, $1 \leqslant i \leqslant k$. *Moreover,* $d_0 = m$ *if and only if* $d_{i-1} \geqslant m_i + j_i$, *for all* i, $1 \leqslant i \leqslant k$, *and for some* i', $1 \leqslant i' \leqslant k$, $d_{i'-1} = m_{i'} + j_{i'}$.

Proof. We prove the result by induction on k.

Basis, $k=1$. In this case, $f = f_1$, $m = m_1$, and $n = n_1$. The definition of d_1 implies that $d_0 - m = d_k - n$. Since we are given $j_1 = 0$, $d_0 \geqslant m_1 + j_1$ if and only if $d_0 \geqslant m_1$.

Inductive step, $k>1$. Since ! is assumed to associate to the left, $f = f'\ !_{j_k} f_k$, where $f' = f_1 !_{j_2} \cdots !_{j_{k-1}} f_{k-1}$. The definition of d_k is,

$$d_k = d_{k-1} - m_k + n_k \tag{A.1}$$

From the inductive hypothesis, $d_{k-1} - n' = d_0 - m'$, so

$$d_{k-1} = d_0 - m' + n' \tag{A.2}$$

For $s = \max(n', m_k + j_k)$, Lemma 1 gives

$$m = s + m' - n' \tag{A.3}$$

$$n = s - m_k + n_k \tag{A.4}$$

Hence by eliminating the differences $m' - n'$ and $m_k - n_k$ in (A.1-4) and (A.2-3)

$$d_0 - m = d_k - n = d_{k-1} - s$$

which already proves (i). Assertion (ii) will follow from the equivalence of $d_0 \geqslant m$ if and only if $d_{k-1} \geqslant s$. From the definition of s, $d_{k-1} \geqslant s$ if and only if $d_{k-1} \geqslant m_k + j_k$ and $d_{k-1} \geqslant n'$. From the inductive hypothesis, $d_{k-1} \geqslant n'$ if and only if $d_{i-1} \geqslant m_i + j_i$ for all i, $1 \leqslant i \leqslant k-1$. As for the limiting case, $d_0 = m$ if and only if $d_{k-1} = s$; this last condition is true if and only if either $d_{k-1} = m_k + j_k$ or $d_{k-1} = n'$, which in turn implies the result from the inductive hypothesis. □

LEMMA 2. *Let* $f\ =\ f_1\ !_j\ f_2$ *and* $d \geqslant m+i$. *Then,*

$$I_d\ !_i\ (\ f_1\ !_j\ f_2\ )\ =\ (\ I_d\ !_i\ f_1\ )\ !_{i+j}\ f_2$$

LEMMA 3. *The functions* $f_1\ !_i\ (\ f_2\ !_j\ f_3\ )$ *and* $(\ f_1\ !_i\ f_2\ )\ !_{i+j}\ f_3$ *have the same number of arguments.*

PROPOSITION 2. $f\ !_i\ (\ g\ !_j\ h\ )\ =\ (\ f\ !_i\ g\ )\ !_{i+j}\ h$.

Proof. Let f_1, f_2, f_3 stand for f, g, h, respectively. Let m_{12} and $m_{(12)3}$ be the number of arguments of $f_1\ !_i\ f_2$ and $(\ f_1\ !_i\ f_2\ )\ !_{i+j}\ f_3$, respectively. Similarly, let m_{23} and $m_{1(23)}$ be the number of arguments of $f_2\ !_j\ f_3$ and $f_1\ !_i\ (\ f_2\ !_j\ f_3\ )$, respectively. Let $m = m_{1(23)} = m_{(12)3}$, where the latter equality follows from Lemma

3.

Let $d_0=m$, $d_1=d_0-m_1+n_1$, and $d_2=d_1-m_2+n_2$. Proposition 1 applied to $(f_1 !_i f_2) !_{i+j} f_3$, ensures that $d_1 \geq m_2+i$ and $d_2 \geq m_3+i+j$.

From Rule R4, using $d_0=m$ and $d_1=m-m_1+n_1$,

$$f_1 \,!_i\, (\, f_2 \,!_j\, f_3 \,) \;=\; [\, I_{d_1} \,!_i\, (\, f_2 \,!_j\, f_3 \,)\,] \circ [\, I_{d_0} \,!\, f_1 \,] \tag{A.5}$$

From Proposition 1, $d_2 \geq m_3+i+j$, so $d_1 \geq m_2+m_3-n_2+j+i$. Also, $d_1 \geq m_2+i$ subsumes $d_1 \geq m_{23}+i$, and the right hand side of (A.5) can be reassociated using Lemma 2:

$$=\; [\, (\, I_{d_1} \,!_i\, f_2 \,) \,!_{i+j}\, f_3 \,] \circ [\, I_{d_0} \,!\, f_1 \,] \tag{A.6}$$

As above, $d_1 \geq m_2+i$, so $I_{d_1} !_i f_2$ has d_1 arguments and d_2 results. Since $d_2 \geq m_3+i+j$, $(I_{d_1} !_i f_2) !_{i+j} f_3$ has d_1 arguments. From Rules R4 and R2, (A.6) becomes

$$=\; [\, (\, I_{d_2} \,!_{i+j}\, f_3 \,) \circ (\, I_{d_1} \,!_i\, f_2 \,)\,] \circ [\, I_{d_0} \,!\, f_1 \,]$$

From the associativity of $\circ$:

$$=\; (\, I_{d_2} \,!_{i+j}\, f_3 \,) \circ (\, I_{d_1} \,!_i\, f_2 \,) \circ (\, I_{d_0} \,!\, f_1 \,) \tag{A.7}$$

With less fuss (because it is associated differently) $(f_1 !_i f_2) !_{i+j} f_3$ can also be shown equivalent to (A.7) so the result must be true. □

LEMMA 4. *Consider function* $I_{d_0} !_{j_1} f_1 \cdots !_{j_k} f_k$ *of* d_0 *arguments. Define* $d_i = d_{i-1}-m_i+n_i$, $1 \leq i \leq k$. *Then,*

$$I_{d_0} \,!_{j_1}\, f_1 \cdots !_{j_k}\, f_k \;=\; (\, I_{d_{k-1}} \,!_{j_k}\, f_k \,) \circ \cdots \circ (\, I_{d_0} \,!_{j_1}\, f_1 \,)$$

PROPOSITION 3. *Consider function* $f = f_1 !_{j_2} \cdots !_{j_k} f_k$. *Define* $d_0=m$ *and* $d_i = d_{i-1}-m_i+n_i$, $1 \leq i \leq k$. *Let* $j_1=0$. *Then,*

$$f_1 \,!_{j_2} \cdots !_{j_k}\, f_k \;=\; (\, I_{d_{k-1}} \,!_{j_k}\, f_k \,) \circ \cdots \circ (\, I_{d_0} \,!_{j_1}\, f_1 \,)$$

Proof. Apply rule R5, and then repeatedly apply the associativity rule to prove that

$$f_1 \,!_{j_2} \cdots !_{j_k}\, f_k \;=\; I_{d_0} \,!\, f_1 \,!_{j_2} \cdots !_{j_k}\, f_k$$

One application of Lemma 4 concludes the proof. □

The proof of Proposition 7 is included here since it illustrates the joint roles of **do** and $\&_l$. The term **do** f & κ is parsed (**do** f) & κ.

PROPOSITION 7. *Let* $d \geq m+l$, *and let* κ *be a function of* $d-m+n$ *arguments. Then,*

$$I_d \;\dagger_l\; f \;\dagger\; \kappa \;=\; \textbf{do}\, f \;\&_l\; \kappa$$

Proof. Let $(x_1, \ldots, x_n) = f\ v_1 \cdots v_m$. From the definition of $\dagger$,

$$(\, I_d \;\dagger_l\; f \;\dagger\; \kappa \,)\ u_1 \cdots u_l\ v_1 \cdots v_m\ w_1 \cdots w_{d-m-l}$$

$$=\; \kappa\ u_1 \cdots u_l\ x_1 \cdots x_n\ w_1 \cdots w_{d-m-l} \tag{A.8}$$

On the other hand, consider

$$(\, \textbf{do}\, f \;\&_l\; \kappa \,)\ u_1 \cdots u_l\ v_1 \cdots v_m\ w_1 \cdots w_{d-m-l} \tag{A.9}$$

From the definition of $f \&_l g$, g is applied to the first l arguments, so (A.9) equals

$$(\, \textbf{do}\, f \;\&\; \kappa\ u_1 \cdots u_l \,)\ v_1 \cdots v_m\ w_1 \cdots w_{d-m-l} \tag{A.10}$$

From the definition of **do** f, in (A.10) f is applied to $v_1, \ldots, v_m$, and then $\kappa\ u_1 \cdots u_l$ is applied to the n results of f, so (A.10) equals

$$(\, \kappa\ u_1 \cdots u_l\ x_1 \cdots x_n \,)\ w_1 \cdots w_{d-m-l} \tag{A.11}$$

Note that the function within parentheses in (A.11) expects exactly $d-m-l$ arguments, so (A.11) equals (A.8), thereby proving the result. □

LEMMA 5. *Let* $f = f_1 !_{j_2} \cdots !_{j_k} f_k$. *Let* $d_{i-1} = m$ *and let* $d_i = d_0-m_i+n_i$, $1 \leq i \leq k$. *Then,*

$$f_1 \,!_{j_2} \cdots !_{j_k}\, f_k \;=\; f_1 \,!\, (\, I_{d_1} \,!_{j_2}\, f_2 \cdots !_{j_k}\, f_k \,)$$

PROPOSITION 8. *Define* $d_i = d_{i-1}-m_i+n_i$, $1 \leq i \leq k$. *Let* $d_{i-1} \geq m_i+l_i$ *for all* i, $1 \leq i \leq k$. *Let* κ *be a function of* d_k *arguments. Then,*

$$I_{d_0} \dagger_{l_1} f_1 \cdots \dagger_{l_k} f_k \dagger \kappa \;=\; \textbf{\textit{do}}\, f_1 \;\&_{l_1} \cdots \textbf{\textit{do}}\, f_k \;\&_{l_k}\; \kappa$$

Proof. By induction on k. The basis $k=1$ follows from Proposition 7, so consider $k>1$. First apply Lemma 5 to get the left hand side into the form $(I_{d_0} \dagger_{l_1} f_1) \dagger \kappa'$. Then Proposition 7 transforms this term into $\textbf{\textit{do}}\, f_1 \;\&_{l_1} \kappa'$. The inductive hypothesis applied to κ' finishes the proof. □

References

abd76. S. K. Abdali, "An abstraction algorithm for combinatory logic," *J. Symbolic Logic* **41**(1), pp. 222-224 (March 1976).

bac57. J. W. Backus *et al.*, "The FORTRAN automatic coding system," *Western Joint Computer Conference*, pp. 188-198 (1957).

bjo78. D. Bjorner and C. B. Jones, *The Vienna Development Method: The Meta-Language*, Lecture Notes in Computer Science 61, Springer Verlag, Berlin (1978).

bur77. R. M. Burstall, J. S. Collins, and R. J. Popplestone, *Programming in POP-2: Revised Edition*, Dept. of Artificial Intelligence, Univ. of Edinburgh (1977).

chu41. A. Church, *The calculi of lambda conversion*, Annals of Math. Studies, No. 6, Princeton University Press, Princeton NJ (1941).

cur58. H. B. Curry and R. Feys, *Combinatory Logic*, North-Holland, Amsterdam (1958).

gor79. M. J. C. Gordon, *The Denotational Description of Programming Languages*, Springer-Verlag, New York NY (1979).

mor73. F. L. Morris, "Advice on structuring compilers and proving them correct," *ACM Symposium on Principles of Programming Languages*, Boston MA, pp. 144-152 (October 1973).

mos79. P. D. Mosses, "SIS – semantics implementation system: Reference manual and user guide," DAIMI MD-30, Department of Computer Science, University of Aarhus, Denmark (August 1979).

mos80. P. D. Mosses, "A constructive approach to compiler correctness," pp. 449-469 in *Automata, Languages and Programming, 7th Colloquium, Noordwijkerhout*, Lecture Notes in Computer Science 85, Springer-Verlag, Berlin (July 1980).

mos81. P. D. Mosses, "A semantic algebra for binding constructs," pp. 408-418 in *Formalization of Programming Concepts, Intl. Colloquium, Peniscola, Spain*, Lecture Notes in Computer Science 107, Springer-Verlag, Berlin (April 1981).

rit80. D. M. Ritchie, "The evolution of the Unix time sharing system," pp. 25-35 in *Proc. Symp. Language Design and Programming Methodology, Sydney, September 1979*, ed. J. M. Tobias, Lecture Notes in Computer Science 79, Springer-Verlag, Berlin (1980).

sch24. M. Schönfinkel, "On the building blocks of mathematical logic," pp. 355-366 in *From Frege to Gödel*, ed. J. van Heijenoort, Harvard University Press, Cambridge MA (1967). Written up for publication by H. Behmann in March 1924 under the title, "Über die Bausteine der mathematischen Logik".

set81a. R. Sethi, "Circular expressions: elimination of static environments," pp. 378-392 in *Automata, Languages and Programming, 8th Colloquium, Acre*, Lecture Notes in Computer Science 115, Springer-Verlag, Berlin (July 1981). The final version will appear in Science of Computer Programming.

set81b. R. Sethi, "Control flow aspects of semantics directed compiling," TR 98, Bell Laboratories, Murray Hill NJ (September 1981). For a summary see *SIGPLAN 82: Symposium on Compiler Construction*,Boston, (June 1982).

tha81. J. W. Thatcher, E. G. Wagner, and J. B. Wright, "More on advice on structuring compilers and proving them correct," *Theoretical Computer Science* **15**, pp. 223-249 (1981).

tur79. D. A. Turner, "A new implementation technique for applicative languages," *Software – Practice and Experience* **9**(1), pp. 31-49 (January 1979).

wan80a. M. Wand, "Deriving target code as a representation of continuation semantics," TR 94, Computer Science Department, Indiana University, Bloomington IN (July 1980).

wan80b. M. Wand, "Different advice on structuring compilers and proving them correct," TR 95, Computer Science Department, Indiana University, Bloomington IN (September 1980).

wan82. M. Wand, *Ninth ACM Symposium on Principles of Programming Languages*, Albuquerque NM, pp. 234-241 (January 1982).

ON THE POWER OF PROBABILISTIC CHOICE IN SYNCHRONOUS PARALLEL COMPUTATIONS

John H. Reif*

Aiken Computation Laboratory
Division of Applied Science
Harvard University
Cambridge, Massachusetts

ABSTRACT

This paper introduces probabilistic choice to synchronous parallel machine models; in particular parallel RAMs. The power of probabilistic choice in parallel computations is illustrated by parallelizing some known probabilistic sequential algorithms. We characterize the computational complexity of time, space, and processor bounded probabilistic prallel RAMs in terms of the computational complexity of probabilistic sequential RAMs. We show that parallelism uniformly speeds up time bounded probabilistic sequential RAM computations by nearly a quadratic factor. We also show that probabilistic choice can be eliminated from parallel computations by introducing nonuniformity.

1. INTRODUCTION

Probabilistic choice is the use of randomly chosen moves in an otherwise deterministic computation given a fixed input. The introduction of probabilistic choice in *sequential computations* (see the landmark paper of Rabin, 74]) leads to considerable improvement to the computational complexity of various number theoretic problems [Berlekamp, 70], [Rabin, 74], [Solovay and Strassen, 77]; [Adleman, Manders, and Miller, 79], [Rabin, 80], [Zippel, 79] to combinatorial problems on graphs and matroids [Lovász, 80], to testing polynomial identities [Schwartz, 80], and testing program equivalence [Ibarra and Moran, 80].

Recently, [Rabin, 80], [Lehman and Rabin, 80], [Francez and Rodeh, 80], [Reif and Spirakis, 81, 82A and 82B] have utilized probabilistic choice in *synchronization algorithms* for asynchronous multiprocesses systems.

This paper investigates the use of probabilistic choice in *synchronous parallel machines*. Section 2 provides the relevant definitions.

In Section 3 we provide some concrete examples of probabilistic parallel algorithms for combinatorial problems. We give an $O(\log n)^2$ time algorithm for testing if a graph of n vertices has a perfect matching. We give an $O(\log n)$ time, $n^2/\log n$ processor algorithm for testing the product of $n\times n$ matrices. Also, we give an $O(n)$ time test for irreducibility of a polynomial of degree n finite field $GF(p^n)$. (NOTE: All these algorithms are simply derived by parallelizing known sequential algorithms; and are merely examples of the power of probabilistic choice in parallel computations. Later sections of our paper give deeper and more substantive theoretical results.)

Probabilistic choice has also recently been used in parallel algorithms for sorting. [Reischuk, 81] has shown that a probabilistic RAM can sort in time $O(\log n)$ with n processors, and [Reif and Valiant, 82] give an $O(\log n)$ time algorithm for sorting in constant valence, fixed connection networks with n processors.

We present in Section 4 a pair of simulation results (Theorems 4.1 and 4.2) which relate probabilistic sequential and probabilistic parallel computations on RAMs. By parallel simulation of previously known probabilistic sequential algorithms [Aleliunas, *et al.*, 79], our Theorem 4.1 immediately yields as corollaries $O(\log n)$ time probabilistic parallel algorithms for a variety of combinatorial problems such as testing if there exists a path between two vertices of a undirected graph and testing if graph is bipartite. Both these probabilistic parallel algorithms use $O(n^3 \log n)$ processors. [Reif, 82A] describes related $O(\log n)$ time, $n^{O(1)}$ processor probabilistic parallel algorithms for constructing minimum spanning forests, k-connectivity, k-connected components, and recognizing chordal graphs, comparability graphs, interval graphs, split graphs, permutation graphs, and constant valence planar graphs. Previously the fastest known parallel algorithms for any these problems required $\Omega(\log^2 n)$ time.

We have an interesting theoretical result (Theorem 5) for speeding up a log-cost (unit-cost, respectively) probabilistic sequential RAM computation of time $T(n)$, by simulation on a probabilistic parallel RAM in log-cost time $O(T(n)^{1/2}\log T(n))$ (in unit-cost time $O(T(n)(\log T(n))\log(T(n)I(n)))^{1/2}$, respectively, where $I(n)$ is the maximum integer operated upon the simulated unit-cost probabilistic RAM). Our simulation result also holds for deterministic computations. Previously, [Dymond, 80] proved a quadratic speedup of deterministic multitape Turing machines; however he considered the simulation of neither probabilistic machines nor RAMs.

---

*This work was supported in part by the National Science Foundation Grant NSF-MCS82-00269 and the Office of Naval Research Contract N00014-80-C-0674.

[Adleman, 78] has previously proved that probabilistic choice can be eliminated in sequential computation if there is no error of acceptance. Theorem 6 of Section 6 proves that probabilistic choice can be eliminated from probabilistic parallel RAMs with both errors of acceptance and errors of rejection by introducing nonuniformity, with some increase of time and processor bounds which may be traded off. For example, this implies there exists nonuniform deterministic parallel RAMs which can in unit-cost time $O(\log n)$ test if a graph of n vertices is connected, and in time $O(\log n)^2$ test if a graph of n vertices has a perfect matching.

At the end of this paper we provide an extended list of references to literature on probabilistic and parallel algorithms which may aid further research in this area.

2. DEFINITIONS OF PROBABILISTIC MACHINES

2.1 Abstract Machine Types

Before describing our probabilistic parallel machines, it is useful to define probabilistic (and also deterministic and nondeterministic) machine types abstractly, without reference to the particular details of operation of the machines.

Let M be a fixed machine. A *configuration* of M is a finite string I over a fixed finite alphabet describing the current state and storage contents of M. Let $\mathcal{I}$ be the set of configurations of M. Let $\mathcal{I}_A \subseteq \mathcal{I}$ be the set of *accepting configurations* of M. Let Σ be the finite input alphabet of M. Given an input string $\omega \in \Sigma^*$, let $I_0(\omega) \in \mathcal{I}$ be the corresponding *initial configuration* of M. Let $\vdash \subseteq \mathcal{I} \times \mathcal{I}$ be the *next move relation* for M; for each $I \in \mathcal{I}$, $\text{NEXT}(I) = \{I' | I \vdash I'\}$ is the set of possible configurations derived from I by a single move of M. (We assume there is no next move from an accepting configuration.) In a *nondeterministic* machine, any $I' \in \text{NEXT}(I)$ may be chosen nondeterministically. In a *probabilistic machine*, each $I' \in \text{NEXT}(I)$ is chosen with equal probability, independently of previous and succeeding choices. In a *deterministic machine* M, $|\text{NEXT}(I)| \leq 1$ for all $I \in \mathcal{I}$.

Given a fixed input string $\omega \in \Sigma^*$, a *computation sequence* of M is a maximal length sequence of configurations $I_0, I_1, \ldots$ such that $I_0 = I_0(\omega)$ and $I_{i-1} \vdash I_i$ for $i = 1, 2, \ldots$. The computation sequence is *accepting* if it is finite and the last configuration is accepting. In a deterministic or nondeterministic machine, M accepts ω iff there exists an accepting computation sequence from $I_0(\omega)$. In a probabilistic machine, M *accepts* ω iff $\text{Prob}(\text{COMP}(\omega)$ is accepting$) > 1/2$, where $\text{COMP}(\omega)$ is a random computation sequence from $I_0(\omega)$ (generated by random next moves as defined above). Let the *language accepted* by M be $L(M) = \{\omega \in \Sigma^* | M$ accepts $\omega\}$.

2.2 Error Restricted Probabilistic Machines

Let M be a probabilistic machine which accepts language $L(M)$. Let the *acceptance error* $\varepsilon_A(n)$ and the *rejection error* $\varepsilon_R(n)$ be the minimum functions such that for all $n \geq 0$, $\omega \in \Sigma^n$,

(i) if $\omega \notin L(M)$ then $\text{Prob}\{\text{COMP}(\omega)$ is accepting$\} \leq \varepsilon_A(n)$

(ii) if $\omega \in L(M)$ then $\text{Prob}\{\text{COMP}(\omega)$ is accepting$\} \leq \varepsilon_R(n)$.

Note that by definition $\varepsilon_A(n) \leq 1/2$ and $\varepsilon_R(n) \leq 1/2$.

For deterministic or nondeterministic machines M, M' let $M \approx M'$ if $L(M) = L(M')$. For two probabilistic machines M, M', let $M \approx M'$ if both M and M' have the same error of acceptance and the same error of rejection.

Let M be a BP-*probabilistic machine* if there exists a constant $\varepsilon < 1/2$ such that for all $n \geq 0$, $\varepsilon \geq \max(\varepsilon_A(n), \varepsilon_R(n))$. Thus a BP-probabilistic machine has a constant upper bound, which is less than 1/2, on errors of acceptance and rejection.

Let M be a R-*probabilistic machine* if there exists a constant $\varepsilon < 1/2$ such that for all $n > 0$, $\varepsilon \geq \varepsilon_R(n)$, and M never has an accepting computation on any input string $\omega \in \Sigma^* - L(M)$.

2.3 Probabilistic Sequential Machines

A nondeterministic Turing machine may be made a *probabilistic Turing machine* by allowing next moves to be chosen randomly with equal probability, as described in Sec. 2.1. See [Simon, 75] for a discussion of probabilistic Turing machines with unrestricted errors and see [Adleman, 78] for some results for R-probabilistic Turing machines. [Bennett and Gill, 81] discuss these and various other classes of probabilistic Turing machines.

Our principal sequential machine model is the probabilistic Random Access Machine (RAM), which is defined here similarly to [Aho, Hopcroft and Ullman, 74], except we allow the RAM probabilistic choice. A *probabilistic RAM* consists of

(1) an infinite sequence of memory locations $m_0, m_1, \ldots$ each of which are indexed by and contain a non-negative integer

(2) a fixed set of registers R each of which contains a nonnegative integer

(3) a probabilistic finite state control which allows the following operations:

(a) for any registers $r_1, r_2 \in R$, *store* (or *read*) the contents of r_1 into (or from, respectively) the contents of global memory location m_i, where i is the current contents of register r_2.

(b) for any registers $r_1, r_2, r_3 \in R$, apply an addition, subtraction, multiplication, or division operation on the contents of registers r_1, r_2 and load the result into register r_3.

(Note: We round noninteger rationals to the next lower integer. Also, we substitute 0 for the result of a subtraction which is negative.)

A *unit cost* RAM is charged 1 step for each of the above operations; a *log-cost* RAM is charged $\lceil \log(x+2) \rceil$ steps for each of the above operations which are on integers of size x.

We assume a binary input alphabet $\{0,1\}$. Given an input string $\omega \in \{0,1\}^*$, each memory location m_{i-1} initially contains the i-th bit of ω for $1 \leq i \leq |\omega|$, m_n contains 2, and all other memory locations and registers are initially 0. The memory locations $m_0, \ldots, m_n$ are read-only, and cannot be stored into. Also, we assume the finite control has distinguished *initial* and *accepting* states. A configuration is accepting if the machine is in the accepting state. The probabilistic RAM *accepts* input ω if with probability $> 1/2$ a random computation sequence is accepting. The probabilistic RAM has *time bound* $T(n)$ (*space bound* $S(n)$, *integer bound* $I(n)$) if on all inputs of length n and accepting computation sequences, the machine takes $\leq R(n)$ steps (uses $\leq S(n)$ space, operates on integers $\leq I(n)$, respectively). Note that we have defined steps differently for unit-cost and log-cost RAMs. Furthermore, a log-cost RAM (unit-cost RAM, respectively) is charged $\log(x+2)$ (1, respectively) units of space for each noninput memory location and register utilized in an accepting computation, where x is the largest integer stored in that memory location or register.

2.4 Probabilistic Parallel RAMs

Our principle parallel machine model is the Parallel Random Access Machine (P-RAM), similar to that defined in [Fortune and Wyllie, 78] and [Wyllie, 79]. However, we allow these machines probabilistic choice. Initially, given an input string $\omega \in \{0,1\}^*$, a probabilistic P-RAM consists of a single probabilistic RAM initialized as defined in 2.3, with an additional operation: *fork* which allows the original RAM to create a new "clone" RAM sharing the same memory, with copies of the original RAM's registers with the same contents, with an identical finite state control, and initialized at some given state. Any new RAMs may also create new RAMs by the fork operations. All these RAMs operate synchronously with the original RAM. Furthermore, their probabilistic choices are assumed to be independent. RAMs are allowed to simultaneously read the same memory location. However, if two distinct RAMs simultaneously store into the same memory contents, then the entire computation of the P-RAM fails. If on a particular computation sequence the original RAM enters its accept state and there have been no such simultaneous memory store conflicts then this computation sequence is considered to be accepting. The probabilistic P-RAM accepts an input string $\omega \in \{0,1\}^*$ if with probability $> 1/2$ a random computation sequence is accepting. (See 2.2 for definitions of errors of acceptance and rejection.) The probabilistic P-RAM has *time bound* $T(n)$ (*space bound* $S(n)$, *integer bound* $I(n)$, *processor bound* $P(n)$) if on all inputs of length n and accepting computation sequences, the machine taken $\leq T(n)$ steps, (uses $\leq S(n)$ space, operates on integers $\leq I(n)$, uses $\leq P(n)$ processors, respectively). Note that space and time are charged in units depending on whether the machine is unit-cost or log-cost as defined in 2.3.

3. SOME FAST PROBABILISTIC PARALLEL ALGORITHMS

This section describes some time efficient algorithms for probabilistic P-RAMs which we easily drive by parallelizing known probabilistic sequential algorithms. (For more substantive theoretical results the reader should read later sections; for example, Section 4 gives a uniform method for parallelizing any probabilistic sequential algorithm.) All the algorithms described here can be made R-*probabilistic* (with rejection error $< 1/2$ and no errors of acceptance) if the probabilistic trials are made twice.

THEOREM 3.1. *There are unit-cost* R-*probabilistic* P-RAMs *with time bound* $O(\log n)$ *and processor bound* $O(n^3 \log n)$, *which given a graph* G *with* n *vertices,*

(a) *can test if* G *has a path between two given vertices, and*

(b) *can also test if* G *is bipartite.*

Proof. [Aleliuneas, *et al.*, 79] give for these problems R-probabilistic sequential algorithms which can be implemented on a probabilistic RAM in $O(1)$ space (using integers size $\leq n^2$ for representing edges) and $O(n^3)$ time. Our probabilistic parallel algorithms are derived immediately by applying Theorem 4.1.

Note that the fastest known deterministic P-RAM algorithm for testing undirected connectivity requires $\Omega(\log n)^2$ time [Hirschburg, Chandra, and Sarwate, 78].

THEOREM 3.2. *A unit-cost* R-*probabilistic* P-RAM *with time bound* $O(\log n)^2$ *and processor bound* $O(n^{3.31})$ *can test if a graph of* n *vertices has a perfect matching.*

Proof. Let $G = (V,E)$ be a simple graph with vertices $V = \{1,\ldots,n\}$. [Lovász, 80] gives a probabilistic sequential algorithm which chooses an $N = n^{O(1)}$ and constructs a symmetric $n \times n$ matrix $B = B_{ij}$ where for $1 \leq i,j \leq n$

(a) B_{ij} is a random element of $\{1,\ldots,N\}$ if $i < j$ and $(i,j) \in E$.

(b) $B_{ij} = -B_{ji}$ if $i > j$ and $(i,j) \in E$.

(c) $B_{ij} = 0$ otherwise.

G has a perfect matching if the determinant of any such B is not 0. If G has no perfect matching, then for n sufficiently large, the determinant of B is 0 with probability $\geq 1/2$. The parallel matrix inversion algorithm of [Csanky, 76] as improved by [Praparata and Sarwate, 78] can be used to compute the determinant in time $O(\log n)^2$ and $O(n^{3.31})$ processors on a P-RAM. □

THEOREM 3.3. *A unit-cost* R*-probabilistic* P-RAM *with* $O(n)$ *time bound and* $(n+m)^{O(1)}$ *processor bound can test if a polynomial* $f(x)$ *of degree* m *has a root in* $GF(p^n)$*, where* p *is a fixed prime.*

Proof. We parallelize the probabilistic algorithm of [Rabin, 80] (this algorithm can be implemented on a unit-cost probabilistic sequential RAM in time $O(n^2m)$) which generalized and proved validity for a previous algorithm of [Berlekamp, 70] for $GF(p)$. First, compute $f_1(x) = GCD(f(x), x^{p^n-1} - 1)$. If $f_1(x) = 1$ then $f(x)$ has no roots over $GF(p^n)$. Otherwise, choose a random $\delta \in \{0,1,\ldots,p^n-1\}$ and compute $f_\delta(x) = GCD(f_1(x), (x+\delta)^{(p^n-1)/2})$. Let d_1, d_δ be the degrees of polynomials $f_1(x)$, $f_\delta(x)$ respectively. If $0 < d_\delta < d_1$ then $f(x)$ has a root in $GF(p^n)$ (in this case $f(x)$ has factor $f_\delta(x)$ if $2d \leq d_1$ and factor $f_1(x)/f_\delta(x)$ if $2d_\delta > d_1$), and otherwise $f(x)$ is irreducible in $GF(p^n)$ with probability $\geq 1/2$. The required polynomial GCD computations can be done in parallel time $O(\log(nm))^2$ with $(n+m)^{O(1)}$ processors by using the algorithm of [Borodin, von Gather, and Hopcroft, 81]. The exponentiations can be computed in $O(n)$ parallel time by repeated exponentiation. □

(Note that the fastest known deterministic sequential algorithms [Adleman, 80] and [Adleman and Odlyzko, 81] for testing if a polynomial of degree n has a root over $GF(p^n)$ require time $O(\log n)^{\log(\log(\log n))}$. These algorithms be speed-up by our Theorem 5 to $O(\log n)^{1/2 \log(\log(\log(n)))+1}$ parallel time on a deterministic P-RAM, but the resulting parallel algorithms remain very slow in comparison to those provided by Theorem 3.3.

THEOREM 3.4. *A unit-cost* R*-probabilistic* P-RAM *with time bound* $O(\log n)$ *and processor bound* $O(n^2/\log n)$ *given* $n \times n$ *integer matrices* A, B, C *can test* $A \cdot B \neq C$.

Proof. Choose a random column vector $x \in \{-1,1\}^n$ and test $A(Bx) \neq Cx$. This test can be done by a probabilistic P-RAM within time $O(\log n)$ and processor bound $O(n^2/\log n)$ by forming $n/\log n$ binary trees of processors, each of size $2n$ and depth $O(\log n)$, and pipelining the required dot products. [Freivalds, 79] shows that if $A \cdot B \neq C$ then $\mathrm{Prob}\{A(Bx) = Cx\} < 1/2$. □

Note that the naive pipelining algorithm for testing $A \cdot B \neq C$ in time $O(\log n)$ on a deterministic P-RAM requires $\Omega(n^3/\log n)$ processors, and requires time $\Omega(n \log n)$ given only $n^2/\log n$ processors.

4. SIMULATION RESULTS BETWEEN PROBABILISTIC RAMs AND PROBABILISTIC P-RAMs

[Fortune and Wyllie, 78] and [Wyllie, 79] characterize the computational complexity of their deterministic P-RAMs in terms of the complexity of deterministic complexity classes. It is the aim of this section to do the same for our probabilistic P-RAMs. Our simulation methods are similar, except for the use of probabilistic choice to insure the probability of errors of acceptance and rejection are preserved.

4.1 Simulation of a Probabilistic RAM by a Probabilistic P-RAM

THEOREM 4.1. *Let* M *be a probabilistic* RAM *with constructible time bound* $T(n) \geq n$*, space bound* $S(n) \geq \log n$*, and integer bound* $I(n)$*. Then there is a probabilistic* P-RAM M' *such that* $M \approx M'$ *(see 2.2 for definition of the equivalence relation* $\approx$ *and note that if* M *is deterministic, then* M' *is also deterministic); if* M *is unit-cost then* M' *has unit-cost time bound* $O(S(n)\log I(n) + \log T(n))$*, and processor bound* $O(I(n)^{S(n)}T(n))$*; if* M *is log-cost then* M' *has log-cost time bound* $O(S(n) + \log T(n))^2$ *and processor bound* $O(4^{S(n)}T(n))$.

(Note: Theorem 4.1 gives a speed-up for unit-cost RAMs only if $S(n)\log I(n) < T(n)$; Theorem 5.1 provides a uniform quadratic speed-up even if $S(n) = T(n)$.)

Proof. Fix some input string $\omega \in \Sigma^n$ and let $I_0(\omega)$ be the initial configuration of M. Let $\mathcal{I}$ be the set of configurations of M with space $S(n)$. Let $p = |\mathcal{I}|(T(n)+1)$. Let each $I \in \mathcal{I}$ and each t, $0 \leq t \leq T(n)$ be encoded as a distinct integer $i = \langle I,t \rangle$, where $1 \leq i \leq p$. We can assume that the encoding and its decoding are computed in $O(\log p)$ steps on a P-RAM.

Our simulating probabilistic P-RAM M' will begin by a series of fork operations yielding RAMs $M_1,\ldots,M_p$. Each RAM M_i, $1 \leq i \leq p$, has a local register r_i and an associated global memory location $NEXT_i$ which is initialized as follows: suppose $i = \langle I,t \rangle$ then if I has any immediate successor I', let M_i randomly choose some such I' and store $\langle I',t+1 \rangle$ into $NEXT_i$ and otherwise if I has no successors then let M_i store i into $NEXT_i$. After this initialization, each M_i, for $1 \leq i \leq p$, synchronously:

(1) reads the contents of $NEXT_j$ into register r_i where j is the contents of $NEXT_i$, and

(2) then stores $NEXT_i$ with the contents of r_i.

This is repeated $\lceil \log p \rceil$ times. We can assume $\langle I_0(\omega),0 \rangle = 1$ and M_1 is the original RAM of M'. We let M_1 enter the accepting state (so M' accepts) if $NEXT_1$ ever contains integer $\langle I,t \rangle$ where I is an accepting configuration of M.

If M' accepts on a particular computation, then there must be a sequence of memory locations $NEXT_{\langle I_0,0 \rangle},\ldots,NEXT_{\langle I_{t-1},t-1 \rangle}$ is initialized to $\langle I_1,1 \rangle,\ldots,\langle I_t,t \rangle$ where $I_0(\omega) = I_0, I_1,\ldots,I_t$ is an accepting computation sequence of M, and $t \leq T(n)$. Thus the memory essentially forms a path from $NEXT_{\langle I_0,0 \rangle}$ to $NEXT_{\langle I_t,t \rangle}$ decreases by a factor of $1/2$. Thus after $\lceil \log p \rceil$ iterations, $NEXT_{\langle I_0,0 \rangle}$ contains $\langle I_t,t \rangle$.

Suppose $I_0, I_1, \ldots$ is an execution sequence of M, derived from a particular sequence of probabilistic choices ρ. Suppose also that the RAMs of M' make a sequence of probabilistic choices ρ' such that $M_{<I_t,t>}$ initially loads $NEXT_{<I_t,t>}$ with $<I_{t+1},t+1>$ for $t=0,1,\ldots,T(n)-1$. Then M errors on acceptance (rejection, respectively) of ω when making probabilistic choices ρ iff M' errors on acceptance (rejection, respectively) of ω when making probabilistic choices ρ'. Since ρ and ρ' are chosen randomly, it follows that $M \approx M'$. If M is unit-cost $|\mathcal{I}| \leq I(n)^{S(n)}$; so if M' is also considered to be unit-cost the time and space bound is $O(\log p) = O(S(n)\log I(n) + \log T(n))$ and the processor bound is $p = O(I(n)^{S(n)}T(n))$. If M is log-cost $|\mathcal{I}| \leq 2^{2 \cdot S(n)} = 4^{S(n)}$; so if M' is also considered to be log-cost its time bound is $O(\log p)^2 = O(S(n) + \log T(n))^2$ and processor bound is $p = O(4^{S(n)}T(n))$. □

4.2 Simulation of a Probabilistic P-RAM by Probabilistic RAM

THEOREM 4.2. *Let* M *be a probabilistic* P-RAM *with time bound* $T(n)$, *space bound* $S(n)$, *and processor bound* $P(n)$. *Then there is a probabilistic* RAM M' *with space bound* $O(S(n)+P(n))$ *such that* $M \approx M'$. *Furthermore, if* M *is unit-cost then* M' *has unit-cost time bound* $O(T(n)P(n))$; *and if* M *is log-cost then* M' *has log-cost time bound* $O(T(n)P(n)\log P(n))$.

Proof. The simulating probabilistic RAM will have only 5 registers; the first register of M' will store an integer p giving the total number of RAMs currently being executed, and the second register of M' will store an integer designating the RAM currently being simulated; the other 3 registers of M' will be used for arithmetic operations and indirect addressing of memory locations. Suppose each RAM of M has r registers. The registers of the simulated RAMs of M will be stored in a special block of memory locations, which is increased by r+1 on every fork operation. The simulation of M' by M is straightforward; on each move of M, M' must simulate a move by each of the currently active RAMs of M. This requires $O(P(n))$ steps if M' is unit-cost, and $O(P(n)\log P(n))$ steps of M' is log-cost. By storing two copies of the memory of M, it is easy to detect simultaneous store conflicts. M' is allowed to enter its accepting state just when the original RAM of M enters its accepting state and there are no simultaneous store conflicts. Since the probabilistic choices taken by the individual probabilistic RAMs are assumed to be independent, and the simulating probabilistic RAM M' takes independent probabilistic choices, the probability of errors of acceptance and rejection of M and M' are identical, so $M \approx M'$. □

5. PARALLEL SPEED-UP OF PROBABILISTIC RAMs

THEOREM 5.1. *Let* M *be a probabilistic* RAM *with constructible time bound* $T(n) \geq n$ *and integer bound* $I(n)$. *Then there is a probabilistic* P-RAM M' *such that* $M \approx M'$ *and if* M *is unit-cost then* M' *has unit-cost time bound* $O(T(n)(\log T(n))\log(T(n)I(n)))^{1/2}$ *and if* M *is log-cost then* M' *has log-cost time bound* $O(T(n)^{1/2}\log T(n))$.

Proof. Let $\omega \in \{0,1\}^*$ be on input string of length n.

There is a constant $c \geq 1$ such that M has at most c choices for next moves at each step. Thus the choices can be represented by a sequence $\rho = \rho_0, \ldots, \rho_{T(n)-1}$ where $\rho_t \in \{1,\ldots,c\}$. The parallel simulation of M by M' begins by probabilistically choosing $\rho_0, \ldots, \rho_{T(n)-1}$ in $O(\log T(n))$ parallel time, and storing these choices in distinct memory locations.

The fundamental idea (previously used in [Hopcroft, Paul, and Valiant, 75] and [Dymond, 80] for speed-up of deterministic Turing machines) is to partition the $T(n)$ steps into consecutive intervals of length L, $1 \leq L \leq T(n)$ to be determined below.

Let q be the number of states in the finite control of M. Suppose in the following that M is unit-cost. Then M can read from and store into at most 3L registers and memory locations within a time interval Δ of length L. Furthermore, we can encode by a positive integer $\leq r = q(T(n)I(n))^{3L}$ the current state and the contents and addresses of the registers and memory locations read from (or stored into) during Δ. (If M is log-cost, M can read from and store into at most 3L bits of registers and memory locations with a time interval Δ of length L. Thus we can encode this by a positive integer $\leq r$, where $r = q(T(n)4)^{3L}$ in the case M is log-cost.)

Let $H = \lceil T(n)/L \rceil - 2$. For each $t = 0, L, 2L, \ldots, HL$ the simulating M' constructs in global memory a table $PREDICT_t$ whch given a positive integer $i \leq r$ encoding a possible state of M and contents and addresses of all registers and memory locations to be read during time interval $\Delta_t = \{t, t+1, \ldots, t+L-1\}$ $PREDICT_t(i)$ is a positive integer $\leq r$ encoding the contents and addresses of all registers and memory locations to L stored into during Δ_t using the predetermined choice sequence $\rho_t, \rho_{t+1}, \ldots, \rho_{t+L-1}$. However, let $PREDICT_t(i) = 0$ if this choice sequence requires reading a register or memory location whose contents are not defined by i, or if the contents of a register or memory location are provided by i but are not read from. These tables can be constructed in parallel by M' in time $O(L + \log r)$.

$T(n)$ distinguished global memory locations of M' are used to store the contents of the memory of M. Also, a special register is used to store the state of the finite control of M. These are initialized as in the initial configuration of M. The simulation of M by M' will then proceed sequentially in H phases, each corresponding to a time interval Δ_t, for $t = 0, L, 2L, \ldots, HL$.

Suppose at the start of the phase corresponding to interval Δ_t, M' is currently storing (as described above) the configuration I_t of M, where $I_0, I_1, \ldots, I_t$ is the sequence of configurations of M induced from $I_0 = I_0(\omega)$ by the choice sequence $\rho_0, \rho_1, \ldots, \rho_{t-1}$ chosen by M' at the start of the simulation. Then there is a unique sequence of configurations $I_t, I_{t+1}, \ldots, I_{t+L}$ induced by the predetermined choice sequence $\rho_t, \rho_{t+1}, \ldots, \rho_{t+L-1}$. Hence there is a unique i_t, $1 \leq i \leq r$, such that $PREDICT_t(i_t) \neq 0$ and i_t encodes contents of registers and memory locations consistent with I_t. $PREDICT_t(i_t)$ is encoded and is used to update the memory of M' to store the configuration I_{t+L}. After the phase associated with time interval Δ_{HL},

M' simulates M step by step sequentially for $t=(H+1)L,(H+1),\ldots,T(n)$. Let the original RAM of M' enter the accepting state if the simulated M does. Since the choice sequence $\rho_0,\ldots,\rho_{T(n)-1}$ is chosen randomly by M', it induces a random computation sequence of M from $I_0(\omega)$, so $M\approx M'$.

In the case M is unit-cost, we let M' be unit-cost. The unit-cost time for initialization and computation of the PREDICT tables is $O(L+\log r)=O(L\log(T(n)I(n)))$. The unit-cost time for each phase is $O(\log\log r)=O(\log(L\log(T(n)I(n))))$ since encoding and decoding of elements of the PREDICT tables is done in parallel. There are $<T(n)/L$ phases. Thus the total unit-cost time is

$$O(L\log(T(n)I(n)))+(T(n)/L)O(\log(L\log(T(n)I(n))))+L = O(T(n)(\log T(n))\log(T(n)I(n)))^{1/2},$$

for
$$L = (T(n)(\log T(n))/\log(T(n)I(n)))^{1/2}.$$

In the case M is log-cost, we similarly let M' be log-cost. To allow for $O(\log\log r)$ parallel log-cost time access of the PREDICT tables, the $\log r$ bits of each element of a PREDICT table must be stored in distinct contiguous memory locations, instead of a single memory location. The log-cost time for initialization and computation of the PREDICT tables is $O(L+\log r)+O(L\log T(n))$. The log-cost time for each phase is $O(\log\log r)=O(\log(L\log T(n)))$. Thus the total log-cost time is

$$O(L\log(T(n)))+(T(n)/L)\log(L\log T(n)))+L = O(T(n)^{1/2}\log T(n))$$

for
$$L = T(n)^{1/2}$$ □

6. ELIMINATION OF PROBABILISTIC CHOICE IN PARALLEL COMPUTATIONS

Let M be a (uniform) probabilistic P-RAM with time bound $T(n)$ and processor bound $P(n)$. Let $Z(n)$ be the maximum number of probabilistic choices made by all the RAMs of M on any input of length n. (Note that $Z(n)\leq T(n)P(n)$). Let $\varepsilon_A(n),\varepsilon_R(n)$ be the acceptance and rejection error functions for M, and let $\varepsilon(n)=\max(\varepsilon_A(n),\varepsilon_R(n))$. Also, let $\lambda(n)=(1+2n)/\log(1/(4\varepsilon(n)(1-\varepsilon(n))))$. We assume $\varepsilon(n)<1/2$ so $\lambda(n)$ is finite.

The following theorem states that we can eliminate the probabilistic choice in M by introducing *nonuniformity with advice bound* $A(n)$: i.e., we allow the nonuniform P-RAM to have in the initial configuration for each input length $n\geq 0$, a distinguished sequence of $A(n)$ memory locations each initialized to either 0 or 1 and fixed for all inputs of length n.

THEOREM 6. *For any* $\tau(n)$, $1\leq\tau(n)\leq\lambda(n)$, *there is a deterministic nonuniform* P-RAM $\hat{M}$ *which accepts* L(M) *with time bound* $O(T(n)\tau(n)+\log(\lambda(n)/\tau(n)))$, *processor bound* $O(P(n)\lambda(n)/\tau(n))$, *and advice bound* $O(\lambda(n)Z(n))$.

(Note: Thus to eliminate probabilistic choice we have a trade-off between an increase in time bounds and an increase in processor bounds. However, if $\varepsilon(n)$ decreases exponentially, then neither the time bound nor the processor bound are asymptotically increased.)

Theorem 6 will be proved as follows: first we show that we can eliminate probabilistic choice from M if $\varepsilon(n)$ is sufficiently small; then we show how to make $\varepsilon(n)$ sufficiently small.

We can assume a constant $c\geq 1$ such that M has $\leq c^{P(n)}$ choices of moves next from any configuration. Fix some input length $n\geq 0$. A parallel *choice sequence* ρ is of the form $\rho_0,\rho_1,\ldots,\rho_{T(n)-1}$ where $\rho_i\in\{1,\ldots,c^{P(n)}\}$ for $i=0,1,\ldots,T(n)-1$. Let $R_{T(n)}$ be all choice sequences of length $T(n)$. Given an input $\omega\in\{0,1\}^n$, a choice sequence in $S_{T(n)}$ induces a computation sequence of M. Let $R_{T(n)}(\omega)=\{\rho\in R_{T(n)}\,|\,(\omega\in L(M)$ and M has an accepting computation sequence on input ω and choice sequence $\rho)$ or $(\omega\notin L(M)$ and M has a nonaccepting computation sequence on input ω and choice sequence $\rho)\}$.

LEMMA 6.1. *If* $\varepsilon(n)<2^{-n}$, *then there is a deterministic nonuniform* P-RAM $\hat{M}$ *which accepts* L(M) *with time bound* $O(T(n))$, *processor bound* $P(n)$ *and advice bound* $O(Z(n))$.

Proof. It suffices to show (*):

(*) if $\varepsilon(n)<2^{-n}$ then there exists some choice sequence $\rho^*\in R_{T(n)}$ such that for all $\omega\in\{0,1\}^n$, $\rho^*\in R_{T(n)}(\omega)$.

Our proof is by contradiction (and thus is not constructive). For each $\rho\in R_{T(n)}$ let $f(\rho)=|\{\omega\in\{0,1\}^n|\rho\in R_{T(n)}(\omega)\}|$ and let $r=|R_{T(n)}|$. Suppose (*) does not hold, so $2^n>f(\rho)$ for all $\rho\in R_{T(n)}$. Hence

$$2^n > \frac{1}{r}\sum_{\rho\in R_{T(n)}} f(\rho) = \frac{1}{r}(r/\varepsilon(n)) = 1/\varepsilon(n) > 2^n, \quad \text{a contradiction.}$$ □

LEMMA 6.2. *For any* $\tau(n)$, $1\leq\tau(n)\leq\lambda(n)$, *there is a probabilistic* P-RAM M' *which accepts* L(M) *with acceptance and rejection errors* $\varepsilon_A'(n)$, $\varepsilon_R'(n)$ *where* $\max(\varepsilon_A'(n),\varepsilon_R'(n))<2^{-n}$, *and time bound* $O(T(n)\tau(n)+\log(\lambda(n)/\tau(n)))$ *and processor bound* $O(T(n)\lambda(n)/\tau(n))$.

Proof. Let $\omega\in\{0,1\}^n$ be the input string, for some $n\geq 0$. Our probabilistic P-RAM M' will simulate M on input ω a total of $\lambda(n)$ times; these simulations will be done by $\lceil\lambda(n)/\tau(n)\rceil$ groups of $P(n)$ probabilistic RAMs, with each group simulating M $\tau(n)$ times. M' is allowed to enter an accepting configuration only if M enters an accepting configuration on at least $\lambda(n)/2$ of the $\lambda(n)$ trials. (This technique of determining the consensus of a series of trials is due to [Bennett and Gill, 81].) The count of successful trials can be computed in $\log(\lambda(n)/\tau(n))$ parallel time. The acceptance error of M' is

$$\varepsilon'_A(n) = \sum_{i=\lambda(n)/2}^{\lambda(n)} \binom{\lambda(n)}{i} \varepsilon(n)^i (1-\varepsilon(n))^{\lambda(n)-i}$$

$$\leq (4\varepsilon(n)(1-\varepsilon(n)))^{\lambda(n)/2} \quad \text{by bounds of [Chernoff, 52] also given in [Feller, 57]}$$

$$< 2^{-n} \quad \text{for given } \lambda(n) > 2n/\log(1/(4\varepsilon(n)(1-\varepsilon(n)))).$$

Also we can similarly show the error of rejection $\varepsilon'_R(n) < 2^{-n}$. Hence $\max(\varepsilon'_A(n), \varepsilon'_R(n)) < 2^{-n}$ as claimed. □

Theorem 6 follows immediately by applying to Lemma 1 the probabilistic P-RAM M' derived by Lemma 6.2. By applying Theorem 6 to Theorems 3.1-3, we have:

COROLLARY 6.1. *There exists unit-cost nonuniform deterministic* P-RAMs *with time bound* $O(\log n)$, *processor and advice bound* $O(n^4 \log n)$, *which given a graph* G *with* n *vertices, can test* (a) *whether* G *has a path between two given vertices and can also test* (b) *whether* G *is not bipartite.*

COROLLARY 6.2. *There exists a unit-cost nonuniform deterministic* P-RAM *with time bound* $O(\log n)^2$, *processor and advice bound* $n^{O(1)}$ *which can test if a graph of* n *vertices has a perfect matching.*

COROLLARY 6.3. *There exists a unit-cost nonuniform deterministic* P-RAM *with time bound* $O(n)$ *and with processor and advice bound* $n^{O(1)}$ *which can test: given a polynomial of degree* $O(n)$, *does it have a root in* $GF(p^n)$?

7. CONCLUSION

This paper has primarily considered the power of probabilistic choice for parallel RAMs. Theorems 3.2-5 also hold for fixed connection parallel networks with probabilistic processors. Theorems 4.1 and 4.2 can be extended to similar simulation results for other probabilistic parallel machines, such as the hardware modification machines (HMMs) of [Cook, 80] augmented with probabilistic choice (see [Reif, 81]). Also Theorem 6 easily generalizes to other probabilistic parallel machines such as HMMs and circuits with probabilistic choice.

ACKNOWLEDGMENTS

The author was informed by Larry Russo of the consensus technique previously used by [Bennett and Gill, 80] for decreasing errors of probabilistic choice. Steven Cook and Paul Spirakis gave helpful comments on a reading a preliminary draft of this paper. Renate D'Arcangelo is sincerely thanked for an excellent typing of this paper.

REFERENCES

Adleman, L., "Two theorems on random polynomial time," Proceedings of the 19th IEEE Symposium on the Foundations of Computer Science, Ann Arbor, MI, 1978, pp. 75-83.

Adleman, L., "On distinguishing prime numbers from composite numbers," Annual Symposium of Foundations of Computer Science, 1980.

Adleman, L. and K. Manders, "Reducibility, randomness and intractability," Proceedings of the 9th ACM Symposium on the Theory of Computing, 1977, pp. 151-153.

Adleman, L., Manders, K., and G. Miller, "On taking roots in finite fields," IEEE Symposium on the Foundations of Computer Science, 1977, pp. 175-178.

Adleman, L. and Odlyzko, A., "Irreducibility testing and factorization of polynomials," 22nd Annual Symposium on Foundations of Computer Science, 1981, pp. 409-420.

Aho, A.V., J.E. Hopcroft, and J.D. Ullman, *The Design and Analysis of Computer Algorithms*, Addison-Wesley Pub. Comp., Reading, Mass., 1974.

Aleliunas, R., R.M. Karp, R.H. Lipton, L. Lovasz and C. Rackoff, "Random walks, universal traversal sequences, and complexity of maze problems," Proc. 20th Annual Symposium on Foundations of Computer Science, 1979, pp. 218-223.

Barzdin, A.M., "On computability by probabilistic machines," Dokl. Akad. Nauk SSSR, 189 (1969), pp. 699-702, = Soviet Math. Dokl., 10 (1969), pp. 1464-1467.

Bennett, C.H. and Gill, J., "Relative to a random oracle A, $P^A \neq NP^A \neq coNP^A$ with probability 1," *SIAM J. Comput.* vol. 10, No. 1 (Feb. 1981), pp. 96-113.

Berlekamp, E.R., "Factoring polynomials over large finite fields," *Math. Comp.* 24 (1970), pp. 713-735.

Borodin, A., j. von zur Gothen, and J. Hopcroft, "Fast parallel matrix and gcd computations," preliminary draft, 1981.

Cook, S.A., "Towards a complexity theory of synchronous parallel computation," Presented at Internationales Symposium über Logik und Algorithmik zu Ehren von Professor Horst Specker, Zürich, Switzerland, Feg. 1980.

Csanky, L., "Fast parallel matrix inversion algorithms," *SIAM J. Comput.* 5 (1976), pp. 618-623.

Chernoff, H., "A measure of asymptotic efficiency for tests of a hypothesis based on the sum of observations," *Ann. of Math. Stat.* 23 (1952), pp. 493-507.

Dymond, P.W., "Speedup of multi-tape Turing machines by synchronous parallel machines," Technical Report, Dept. of EE and Computer Science, Univ. of California, San Diego, California.

Dymond, P., and S.A. Cook, "Hardware complexity and parallel computation," IEEE FOCS Conference, 1980.

Feller, W., *An Introduction to Probability Theory and its Applications.*, John Wiley, New York, 1957.

Freivalds, R., "Fast Probabilistic Algorithms," 8th MFCS, 1979.

Fortune, S. and J. Wyllie, "Parallelism in random access machines," In Proc. of the 10th ACM Symposium on Theory of Computation, 1978, pp. 114-118.

Francez, N. and Rodeh, "A distributed data type implemented by a probabilistic communication scheme," 21st Annual Symposium on Foundations of Computer Science, Syracuse, New York, Oct. 1980, pp. 373-379.

Gill, J., "Complexity of probabilistic Turing machines," *SIAM J. of Computing*, 6(4), 675-695 (1977).

Goldschlager, L., "A unified approach to models of synchronous parallel machines," In Proc. 10th Annual ACM Symposium on the Theory of Computing, San Diego, California, 89-94 (1978).

Hirschburg, D.S., A.K. Chandra, and D.V. Sarmate, "Computing connected components on parallel computors," *CACM* 22(8), Aug. 1978.

Hopcroft, J.E., and Karp, R.M., "An $n^{5/2}$ algorithm for maximum matchings in bipartite graphs," *SIAM J. Comp.* 2(4), (Dec. 1973), pp. 225-231.

Hopcroft, J.E., W. Paul, and L. Valiant, "On time versus space and related problems," *IEEE* 16 SWAT, 1975.

Iberra, O.H., and S. Moran, "Probabilistic algorithms for deciding equivalence of straight-line programs," Computer Science Dept., University of Minnesota, Tech. Report 80-12 (March 1980).

Lehman, D. and M. Rabin, "On the advantages of free choice: A symmetric and fully distributed solution to the dining philosophers' problem," to appear in 8th ACM Symp. on Principles of Program Languages, Jan. 1981.

Lovasz, L., "On determinants, matchings, and random algorithms," to appear, 1980.

Rabin, M.O., "Probabilistic algorithms," *Algorithms and Complexity, New Directions and Recent Results*, edited by J. Traub, Academic Press, 1974.

Rabin, M.O., "Probabilistic algorithms in finite fields," *SIAM J. Comp.* 9(2), (May 1980), pp. 273-280.

Rabin, M.O., "N-process synchronization by a 4 $\log_2 N$-valued shared variable," 21st Annual Symposium on Foundations of Computer Science, Syracuse, New York, Oct. 1980, pp. 407-410.

Reif, J.H., "Symmetric complementation," 14th Annual ACM Symposium on Theory of Computing, San Francisco, May 1982.

Reif, J.H. and P. Spirakis, "Distributed algorithms for synchronizing interprocess communication within real time," 13th Annual ACM Symposium on the Theory of Computing, Milwaukee, Wisconsin, 1981.

Reif, J.H. and P. Spirakis, "Unbounded speed variability in distributed communication systems," 9th ACM Symposium on Principles of Programming Languages, Albuquerque, New Mexico, Jan. 1982.

Reif, J.H. and L.S. Valient, "Flashsort: An $O(\log n)$ time sorting algorithm for n process fixed connection networks," to appear 1982.

Reischuk, R., "A fast probabilistic parallel sorting algorithm," 22nd Annual Symposium on Foundations of Computer Science, Nashville, Tenn., Oct. 1981.

Preporata, F.P. and D.V. Sarwate, "An improved parallel process-bound in fast matrix inversion," *Information Processing Letters* V7(3), 1978, pp. 148-150.

Schwartz, J.T., "Fast probabilistic algorithms for verification of polynomial identities," *JACM* 27(4), Oct. 1980, pp. 701-717.

Simon, J., "On some central problems in computational complexity," TR75-224, Dept. of Computer Science, Cornell Univ., Ithaca, N.Y., 1975.

Solovay, R. and Strassen, V., "A fast Monte-Carlo test for primality," *SIAM J. of Computing* 5(1), 1977, pp. 84-85.

Valiant, L.G., "A scheme for fast parallel communication," Technical Report, Computer Science Dept., Edinburg University, Edinburg, Scotland, July 1980.

Wyllie, J.C., "The complexity of parallel computations," Ph.D. Thesis and TR-79-387, Dept. of Computer Science, Cornell University, 1979.

Zippel, R., "Probabilistic algorithms for sparse polynomials," EUROSAM Proceeding, 1979.

BIPREFIX CODES AND SEMISIMPLE ALGEBRAS

Christophe Reutenauer
LITP Institut de Programmation.
4 place Jussieu
75005 Paris

Abstract We show here that there exists a close connection between the language-theoretic concept of biprefixity and the classical algebraic concept of semisimplicity. More precisely, the main result is that, under suitable hypothesis, a (variable-length) code is biprefix if and only if its syntactic algebra is semisimple.

1. Introduction

Let A be a finite alphabet. Recall that a language $L \subset A^*$ is prefix if for any words u and v

$$u, uv \in L \text{ implies } v = 1$$

where 1 stands for the empty word.

A language L is suffix if it satisfies the symmetric condition

$$v, uv \in L \text{ implies } u = 1$$

A language that is simultaneously prefix and suffix is called biprefix or bifix .

Examples Let $A = \{a,b\}$ a fixed alphabet. Biprefix codes exist in great profusion as A, $\{a^2, b^3\}$, $\{w\}$ (for any word w) : but these examples are more or less trivial. More interesting are the maximal biprefix codes, as for instance

$$a \cup ba^*b = \{a, bb, bab, baab, baab, \dots\}$$

If you ask moreover that the code be finite, you will find the homogenous codes, that is : $A^n = \{$ words of length $n \}$; but if you ask for another example, it becomes difficult : however non homogeneous finite maximal biprefix codes exist, they were discovered by Schützenberger [9]. An example is

$$\{ a^3, a^2ba, a^2b^2, ab, ba^2, baba, bab^2, b^2a, b^3 \}$$

These codes are fascinating objects : they have many combinatorial, algebraic, and probabilistic properties as shown by Schützenberger, Perrin, Césari ; see the forthcoming book of Berstel and Perrin [1]. See also the paper of Perrin in the present book.

A code is a language that is the basis of a free submonoid of A^*. Equivalently, $C \subset A^*$ is a code if for any words $u_1, \dots, u_n, v_1, \dots, v_p$ in C, one has :

$u_1 \ldots u_n = v_1 \ldots v_p$ implies $n = p$ and $\forall i,\ u_i = v_i$.

It is easily verified that a prefix (or suffix) language, different from $\{1\}$, is a code (see e.g. prop. IV.5.1 in [3]). We call it a prefix (or suffix) code.

Let k be a field. Let $k\langle A\rangle$ denote the algebra of noncommutative polynomials in A over k. Each element P of $k\langle A\rangle$ is a (finite) linear combination of words

$$P = \sum_{w \in A^*} (P,w)w$$

where (P,w) is the coefficient of w in P ; the (P,w)'s are all but a finite number equal to zero.

$k\langle A\rangle$ is a k-algebra : the product is the unique product extending the one of A^* (A^* may evidently be embedded in $k\langle A\rangle$).

If L is a language over A, we define a linear mapping

$$\varphi : k\langle A\rangle \rightarrow k$$

by

$$\varphi(P) = \sum_{w \in L} (P,w)$$

Let $\mathcal{J}$ be the sum of all (two-sided) ideals of $k\langle A\rangle$ contained in $\operatorname{Ker}\varphi$: we call $\mathcal{J}$ the <u>syntactic ideal</u> of L and the <u>syntactic algebra</u> of L is the quotient $\mathcal{M} = k\langle A\rangle/\mathcal{J}$.

<u>A language is regular if and only its syntactic algebra is finite dimensional</u> : to see this, let L be a regular language and $\mathcal{A} = (Q, q_o, Q_f)$ a deterministic automaton recognizing L. Let $\mu : k\langle A\rangle \rightarrow k^{Q\times Q}$ the k-algebra morphism (where $k^{Q\times Q}$ is the algebra of $Q\times Q$ matrices over k) defined for each $a \in A$ by

$$(\mu a)_{p,q} = \begin{cases} 1 & \text{if } p.a = q \text{(i.e. } p \xrightarrow{a} q) \\ 0 & \text{otherwise} \end{cases}$$

Then for each word w one has

$$(\mu w)_{p,q} = \begin{cases} 1 & \text{if there is a path } p \xrightarrow{w} q \\ 0 & \text{otherwise} \end{cases}$$

Let $\lambda \in k^{Q\times 1}$, $\gamma \in k^{1\times Q}$ be defined by

$$\lambda_{q_o} = 1$$
$$\lambda_q = 0 \text{ if } q \neq q_o$$
$$\gamma_q = 1 \text{ if } q \in Q_f$$
$$\gamma_q = 0 \text{ if } q \notin Q_f$$

Then $\lambda\, \mu w\, \gamma = 1$ if $w \in L$ and $= 0$ if not.

Letting φ be the linear form on $k\langle A\rangle$ defined above, we have $\varphi(P) = \lambda \mu P \gamma$. Hence $\operatorname{Ker}\mu$ is contained in $\operatorname{Ker}\varphi$. But $\operatorname{Ker}\mu$ is of finite codimension, hence the syntactic ideal of L is of finite codimension, too.

For the converse ($\mathcal{M}$ finite dimensional implies L regular), see [6] where it is shown that a formal power series is rational if and only if its syntactic algebra is finite dimensional, and [7] where it is shown that a language is regular if and only if its characteristic series is rational. We shall not need this here.

2. Results

Let k be of characteristic zero. We call, by a slight abuse of language, syntactic algebra of a code C the syntactic algebra of the submonoid C^* generated by C.

Theorem 1

Let C be a biprefix and regular code. Then its syntactic algebra is semisimple.

Recall that a finite dimensional $\mathcal{M}$ is semisimple if it contains no non zero nilpotent ideal (that is, an ideal $\mathfrak{J} \neq 0$ such that for some n, each product of n elements in $\mathfrak{J}$ vanishes). By a theorem of Wedderburn, such an algebra $\mathcal{M}$ is isomorphic to a direct product of a finite number of simple algebras (an algebra is simple if it has no nontrivial ideal). Another theorem of Wedderburn asserts that a finite dimensional simple k-algebra is isomorphic to a matrix algebra $K^{n\times n}$ where K is a (skew) field containing k in its center and of finite dimension over k. All this staff shows that semisimplicity implies many properties : a semisimple algebra $\mathcal{M}$ behaves a little bit like a field ; for instance, each submodule of an $\mathcal{M}$-module admits a supplementary submodule. For this and other classical properties, see e.g. [4].

Proof Let C be a biprefix and regular code. We may suppose $C \neq A$.

(i) Recall that the syntactic congruence of the language $L = C^*$ is the congruence of A^* defined by

$$u \sim v \text{ iff for any words } x \text{ and } y$$

$xuy \in L \Leftrightarrow xvy \in L$ see [3]. Note that C^* is a union of classes for $\sim$.
The syntactic monoid M of L is the quotient $A^*/\sim$. As L is regular, M is finite (Kleene's theorem).

Let $\mu : A^* \to M$ be the natural morphism. Let J be an ideal in M of cardinality ≥ 2. Then $\mu C^* \cap J \neq \emptyset$: to see this note that if $\mu C^* \cap J = \emptyset$, then for $u,v \in \mu^{-1}(J)$ and any words x,y you have $xuy, xvy \in \mu^{-1}(J)$ hence $xuy, xvy \notin C^* \Rightarrow u \sim v$ and J would be of cardinality one, contrary to assumption.

We fix now such an ideal J in M : if M has no zero, we choose J = the minimal ideal of M ; it has not cardinality one, otherwise it would be a zero. If M has a zero then $M \neq \{0\}$ and we take J as to be a minimal element of the family of ideals in M containing 0 properly (a so-called 0-minimal ideal) ; we have $|J| \geq 2$ trivially.

In the first case, J is a finite simple semigroup (that is, a semigroup with only one ideal) and in the second, a finite 0-simple semigroup (that is, with a zero and with only two ideals).

Let $e \in \mu(C^*) \cap J$; we may suppose that e be idempotent : $e^2 = e$. We shall use the important fact (due to Suschkewitsh) that eMe is a group G if M has no zero, or the union $G \cup 0$ of a group with a zero if M has a zero, see [5].

(ii) Let $\mathcal{J}$ be the syntactic ideal of C^* and φ the linear form on $k\langle A\rangle$ defined by C^*. One has

$\mathcal{J} = \{P \in k\langle A\rangle \mid \forall x,y \in A^* \ \varphi(xPy) = 0\}$ as is easily verified (see [6] §2).

Hence for any words u and v

$$u \sim v \quad \text{iff} \quad u-v \in \mathcal{J}.$$

This means that the image of A^* in the syntactic algebra $\mathcal{M}$ of C^* is isomorphic to M ; that's why we may still denote μ the natural algebra morphism $\mu : k\langle A\rangle \to \mathcal{M}$ and identify M and μA^*. Moreover if M has a zero, it is the zero of $\mathcal{M}$: indeed let w a word such that μw is the zero of M ; then $xwy \sim w$ for any words x and y.

It suffices to show that $w \notin C^*$ (because then $xwy \notin C^*$ by definition of $\sim$, and $\varphi(xwy) = \varphi(w) = 0 \Rightarrow w \in \mathcal{J} \Rightarrow \mu w = 0$). Now C^* contains no ideal of A : otherwise there exists a word u such that $A^* u A^* \subset C^*$; then for any letter a, au and ua are in C^* hence $a \in C$ (see [5] prop. V. 2.2) and $C = A$ contrary to assumption. If $w \in C^*$, μC^* contains the zero 0_M of M, hence C^* contains $\mu^{-1}(0_M) \cap A^*$ which is an ideal of A^*.

(iii) Consider $e \mathcal{M} e$: it is an algebra contained in $\mathcal{M}$, with e as neutral element. We show that it is semisimple. Indeed, $e \mathcal{M} e$ is equal to the linear hull of the finite group G : first, $k\langle A\rangle$ is generated (as a vector space) by A^*, hence $\mathcal{M}$ is generated by M and $e \mathcal{M} e$ by $e M e = G$ or $G \cup 0$; in both cases, $e \mathcal{M} e$ is the linear hull of G. By Maschke's theorem, it follows that $e \mathcal{M} e$ is semisimple and has therefore no nonzero nilpotent ideal [4].

(iv) Let x_o be a word in C such that $\mu x_o = e$ (it exists by (i)). As C is prefix, one has for any u in C^* :

$$w \in C^* \Leftrightarrow uw \in C^*$$

(see [5] prop. V.2.5).

Because C is also suffix, one has finally

$$w \in C^* \Leftrightarrow x_o w x_o \in C^*$$

Hence $\varphi(x_o P x_o) = \varphi(P)$ for any polynomial P.

(v) Let N be a nilpotent ideal in $\mathcal{M}$. Then eNe is a nilpotent ideal of $e\mathcal{M}e$. Hence $eNe = 0$. But if P is a polynomial such that $\mu P \in N$, then $\mu(x_o P x_o) = e \mu P e = 0$ hence $x_o P x_o \in \operatorname{Ker}\mu \subset \operatorname{Ker}\varphi$. Thus $\varphi(P) = \varphi(x_o P x_o) = 0$. This shows that $\mu^{-1}(N)$ is contained in $\operatorname{Ker}\varphi$; as it is an ideal, it is therefore contained in the syntactic ideal $\mathcal{J} = \operatorname{Ker}\mu$ of C^*, hence $N = \mu(\mu^{-1}(N)) = 0$. □

Remarks

1. The proof uses the theorem of Maschke (the algebra over k of any finite group is semisimple). Actually, theorem 1 contains this result : indeed if G is a finite group, let A be an alphabet and $\mu : A^* \to G$ a surjective morphism. Then $\mu^{-1}(1)$ is a free submonoid of A^* generated by a biprefix code C, because u, uv = 1 implies v = 1 hence C is prefix, and symmetrically C is suffix. Furthermore, it is easily verified that the syntactic algebra of C is k[G], the k-algebra of G.

2. It is not true in general that the algebra of the syntactic monoid of a regular biprefix code is semisimple. It is possible only if the minimal ideal J is a group (see [2] cor. 5.24).

Theorem 2

Let C be a regular and maximal code the syntactic algebra of which is semisimple. Then C is biprefix.

Proof

(i) We shall use the following theorem of Schützenberger : if C is a maximal code, then C^* meets each ideal in A^* (see [5] prop. V.3.1)
It shows that the syntactic monoid of C^* has no zero (see part (i), (ii) and (iii) of the preceding proof ; the assumption "biprefix" is not used there).
By the Rees-Suschkewitsch theorem, J is a finite union of disjoint groups $(G_{i,\lambda})_{i \in I, \lambda \in \Lambda}$ such that each $R_i = \bigcup_{\lambda \in \Lambda} G_{i,\lambda}$ is a minimal right ideal of M (and similarly for left ideals). Moreover, if $m \in G_{j,\mu}$ then $m\, G_{i,\lambda} = G_{j,\lambda}$ (see [5] chapter 3).

(ii) If $E \subset J$, denote $\bar{E}$ the element $\sum_{m \in E} m$ of $\mathcal{M}$. The above shows that for any $m \in G_{j,\mu}$ one has $m \bar{R}_i = \sum_{\lambda \in \Lambda} \bar{G}_{j,\lambda}$.
Hence for any i,i' in I, one has $m(\bar{R}_i - \bar{R}_{i'}) = 0$.

Let $\mathcal{J}$ be the linear hull of J. It is an ideal in $\mathcal{M}$. One has $\mathcal{J}(R_i - R_{i'}) = 0$, hence $\bar{R}_i - \bar{R}_{i'}$ generates a nilpotent ideal of $\mathcal{J}$.

If $\mathcal{M}$ is semisimple, $\mathcal{J}$ is also semisimple (being an ideal in a semisimple algebra) hence has no non zero nilpotent ideal. Thus $\bar{R}_i = \bar{R}_{i'}$.

(iii) Let ψ be the linear form on $\mathcal{M}$ induced by φ (because $\mathcal{I} \subset \operatorname{Ker}\varphi$). Then for any word w in A^*, $\varphi(w) = \psi(\mu w)$, hence for any m in M, $\psi(m) = 1$ if and only if $m \in \mu(C^*)$.
Now $\psi(\bar{R}_i)$ is equal to the number of $m \in R_i \cap \mu(C^*)$. This number is independant of i, hence nonzero because μC^* meets $J = \bigcup_i R_i$. This shows that μC^* meets all minimal right ideals in M. Thus C^* meets all right ideals in A^*. To conclude, we

use the following theorem (see [5] prop. VI.4.2) : if C^* meets all right ideals in A^* then C is prefix.
Symmetrically C is suffix. □

Corollary Let C be a regular and maximal code. Then C is biprefix if and only if its syntactic algebra is semisimple.

Remarks.

1. All these results are still true if the characteristic of k does not divide the order of the Suschkewitsch group of the code (see [5] chapter 8 for the definition of this group).

2. Theorem 2 is not true without the assumption "maximal"; indeed the syntactic algebra of the code $\{a, ab\}$ is $k^{2\times 2}$, hence simple, but this code is not prefix.

3. Examples and problems

The syntactic algebra of the code $a \cup ba^*b$ is $k \times k$.
The syntactic algebra of the non-homogeneous finite and maximal code given in §1 is $k \times k^{3\times 3}$.
For these examples, it was possible to express each algebra as a product of simple algebras (recall that a matrix algebra is always simple), as tells us the theorem of Wedderburn cited in § 2.

In general, it is always possible to compute the syntactic algebra of a given rational power series, hence of a regular biprefix code ; indeed, the syntactic algebra of a rational power series is directly related to its reduced linear representation ([6] th. II.1.3) and this is calculable ([8] B).
However I don't know if it is always possible to express it as a direct product of simple algebras. It would be interesting to know if the simple components correspond to a combinatorial properties of the code, especially for finite and maximal codes.

For homogeneous codes, it is possible : the problem is reduced to compute the syntactic algebra of a code of the form $\{a^n\}$ (where a is a letter). In this case, this algebra is $k[a]/(a^n-1)$, which is isomorphic to k^n if $k = \mathbb{C}$, and to $k[a]/\phi_d(a)$ when $k = \mathbb{Q}$ (where $\phi_d(a)$ is the cyclotomic polynomial of order d ; as ϕ_d is irreducible in $Q[a]$, $Q[a]/\phi_d$ is a field, hence simple).

Other examples are given by the one element codes $\{w\}$: if w is primitive of length $|w|$, then the syntactic algebra is $k^{|w|\times|w|}$ and if $w = u^n$ where u is primitive it is $(k[a]/a^n-1)^{|u|\times|u|}$.

Aknowledgements

Many discussions with Pr Betréma and Perrin were helpful to simplify the proofs presented here.

A first version of this result is to appear in Semigroup Forum.

Références

[1] J. Berstel, D. Perrin, M.P. Schützenberger : the theory of codes, to appear.

[2] A.H. Clifford, G.B. Preston : the algebraic theory of semigroups, A.M.S.(61).

[3] S. Eilenberg : automata, languages and machines, vol. A, Acad. Press (1974)

[4] I.N. Herstein : noncommutative rings, Carus mathematical monograph (1969).

[5] G. Lallement : semigroups and combinatorial applications, John Wiley (1979)

[6] C. Reutenauer : séries formelles et algèbres syntactiques, J. Algebra 66, 448-483 (1980).

[7] A. Salomaa, M. Soittola : automata-theoretic aspects of formal power series, Springer Verlag (1977).

[8] M.P. Schützenberger : on the definition of a family of automata, Information and Control 4, 245-270 (1961).

[9] M.P. Schützenberger : on a special class of recurrent events, Annals of Math. Stat. 32, 1201-1213 (1961).

ALGORITHMIC THEORIES OF DATA STRUCTURES

Andrzej Salwicki
Institute of Informatics
University of Warsaw
PL-00-901 Warsaw PKiN p.o.box 1210

ABSTRACT

We are arguing that main problems of data structures i.e.

- specification,
- implementation,
- verification,

can be approached and solved by developping and studying theories of data structures which are based on algorithmic logic AL. We propose to specify a data structure by a proper set of algorithmic axioms. Then verification of a corresponding property of a program consists in proving the formula which expresses the property. The proof making use of axioms of the data structure.

We present a case study of the algorithmic theory of priority queues ATPQ. We show that the axiomatization of ATPQ is proper by proving the representation theorem. Namely, every model of the theory is isomorphic with the two-sorted model of a linearly ordered set of elements and the family of all finite subsets of the given set of elements. Next, we prove the correctness of an implementation of priority queues in binary search trees. We relate theoretical results to corresponding modules of software written in LOGLAN programming language. Remarks on dynamization of abstract theories of data structures by adding notion of reference, also axiomatizable in AL, are given. Finally, we compare our approach with others known in the literature.

1. INTRODUCTION

Every programmer is aware that his work on software can be , in a natural way, factorized onto two stages:

(i) specification and implementation of data structure

(ii) design, verification and debugging of an algorithm.

The methodological advice listed above was pointed by Hoare [8]. According to this advice we can and should abstract from details of implenentation, instead, we should utilize only those properties of data structures which are listed in the specification or can be deduced from the specification.

During the synthesis and analysis of an algorithm we are to prove correctness of the algorithm, to estimate its complexity and to compare it with the lower bound of the problem to be solved(if possible). Here we shall not deal with computational complexity. Our main interest will be in proving semantical properties of programs and data structures.

The point of view on data structures we wish to present here can be stated in a few lines:

1. <u>many sorted structures</u>. We as many others, conceive data structures as many sorted algebraic systems (cf. [5,6,7,8,10,12,17,18,19]).

2. <u>specification</u>. We propose to develop algorithmic theories of data structures. Specification in this case will consists of a set of algorithmic formulas. Below, we shall quote examples showing that in many cases algorithmic axioms specify a data structure up to isomorphism (categoricity property). In many other cases where we are interested in a class of data structures (cf. parametrized abstract data type) we can supply a maximal set of axioms specifying exactly the desired class.

3. <u>implementation</u>. Implementation of adata structure within another data structure creates problems similar to implementation of an algorithm. We wish to be able to analyze correctness of an implementation by formal tools similarly to those offered by logics of programs [2] Here we propose to utilize the notion of interpretation among (algorithmic) theories of data structures as a formal counterpart of the notion of implementation among data structures.

4. <u>verification</u>. The processes of developping akgorithmic theories and of proving properties of programs are mutually convoluted.

we use our knowledge of a data structure i.e. the theory of it when proving properties of programs. On the other hand once we have it proved, the theorem stating, say, the correctness of a discussed algorithm, enlarges our knowledge of data structure and can be used in the proof of other properties of other programs.

From now on we shall use the notion of formalized theory which differs from the intuitive one used above.

An algorithmic theory of a data structure is defined whenever we are given three elements:

a/ an algorithmic language,

b/ a logical deductive system,

c/ a set of specific nonlogical axioms.

We base our considerations of theories of data structures on algorithmic logic AL. There are many kinds of algorithmic logics depending on the collection of program connectives allowed in the construction of programs. In this paper we shall give examples not exceeding the standard collection

begin ... end	composition
if ... then ... else ... fi	branching
while ... do ... od	iteration

of program connectives. All theories will have their languages defined in a common way. The class of algorithmic languages discussed here follows one general pattern. The difference between languages lies in different sets of functional and relational symbols. The set of wff s can be split onto three parts: terms, formulas and programs. The structure of the set of terms is as usual. Programs are built from atomic programs(assignments) by means of program connectives. Formulas contain quantifier-free formulas, are closed with respect to the usual formation rules and moreover we agreed that whenever an expression K is a program and α is a formula then the expression of the form

$$K\alpha$$

is also a formula. The semantical meaning of $K\alpha$ is as follows: given a realization R of functional and relational symbols and a state v (here we shall conceive it as a valuation of variables) the meaning of $K\alpha$ at R and v is truth iff the computation of K at the initial state v is finite and its resulting state, denote it by v′, satisfies the formula α, in the remaining cases the value of $K\alpha$ is false.

Examples

Formulas of the form

$$\alpha \Rightarrow K\alpha$$

are expressing total correctness of the program K with respect to the precondition α and the postcondition β .
Let α , β , K be the expressions:

α : $f(a) \cdot f(b) < 0 \wedge (b - a) > \mathcal{E} > 0$

β : $f(a) \cdot f(b) < 0 \wedge (b - a) < \mathcal{E}$

K : <u>while</u> $(b - a) > \mathcal{E}$ <u>do</u> x := (a + b)/2 ;
<u>if</u> f(x) · f(a) < 0 <u>then</u> b := x <u>else</u> a := x <u>fi</u>
<u>od</u>

Now, the formula $(\alpha \Rightarrow K\beta)$ is true iff the bisection algorithm K terminates with an approximation of a zero of the function f. This formula can be deduced from the following axiom

$$x > y > 0 \Rightarrow (z := y;\ \underline{\text{while}}\ z < x\ \underline{\text{do}}\ z := z + x\ \underline{\text{od}})\ \text{true}$$

of Archimedean fields. □

Algorithmic logic has enough expressive power to specify semantical properties of programs and data structures. Notice, that the language of AL is the minimal extension of a given programming language such that algorithmic properties can be expressed in it.

The problem of axiomatic definition of semantics of program and logical connectives has been succesfully solved (cf.[14,15]). The logical cinsequence operation is defined by means of the set of schemes of logical axioms and inference rules. The set of axioms contains all formulas arising from the schemes of classical propositional calculus by substitutions and of formulas of other schemes e.g.

$$K(\alpha \vee \beta) \Leftrightarrow K\alpha \vee K\beta$$

$$(\underline{\text{while}}\ \gamma\ \underline{\text{do}}\ K\ \underline{\text{od}})\alpha \Leftrightarrow (\neg\gamma \wedge \alpha) \vee (\gamma \wedge K\ \underline{\text{while}}\ \gamma\ \underline{\text{do}}\ K\ \underline{\text{od}}\ \alpha) .$$

Among inference rules let us quote modus ponens and

$$\frac{\{(\underline{\text{if}}\ \gamma\ \underline{\text{then}}\ K\ \underline{\text{fi}})^i(\neg\gamma \wedge \alpha) \Rightarrow \beta\}_{i\in\omega}}{(\underline{\text{while}}\ \gamma\ \underline{\text{do}}\ K\ \underline{\text{od}})\alpha \Rightarrow \beta} \qquad \frac{\alpha \Rightarrow \beta}{K\alpha \Rightarrow K\beta}$$

In the sequel we shall present a case study of the algorithmic theory of priority queues. We shall discuss the problem of its specification and of implementation of priority queues in binary search trees. We would like to call the attention of the reader to the included pieces of software and their closeness to the presented theory. They are written in LOGLAN universal programming language. LOGLAN has been designed and impmented by the group of theory of computing in the Institute of Informatics, University of Warsaw[3] .

The last section contains remarks comparing the other approaches to data structures with the one proposed here.

2. ALGORITHMIC THEORY OF PRIORITY QUEUES ATPQ

Priority queue is a data structure for finite sets with operations: insert, delete, min, member. Priority queues appear frequently in many programs and systems. There are many various implementations of priority queues(cf.[1,11]). Hence, we shall think of a class of priority queues, similarly as one thinks of class of groups, of rings. Below, we shall give a specification of the class of priority queues by means of an axiomatic system.

An algebraic structure is called a priority queue whenever its carrier consists of two disjoint subsets

$$E \text{ and } S$$

called sorts and has the following operations and predicates

insert:	$E \times S \to S$	
delete:	$E \times S \to S$	
min:	$S \to E$	
member:	$E \times S \to B_o$	; B_o is the two-element Boolean algebra
empty:	$S \to B_o$	
$\leqslant$	$E \times E \to B_o$	

and such that the following axioms are valid in the structure

A1 E is linearly ordered by the relation

A2 (<u>while</u> $\neg$ empty(s) <u>do</u> s := delete(min(s), s) <u>od</u>) true

A3 $\neg$ empty(s) $\Rightarrow \forall e$ member(e,s) $\Rightarrow$ min(s) $\leqslant$ e

A4 member(e,insert(e,s)) $\wedge$ [e' $\neq$ e $\Rightarrow$ {member(e',insert(e,s)) $\Leftrightarrow$ member(e',s)}]

A5 $\neg$ member(e,delete(e,s)) $\wedge$ [e'$\neq$e $\rightarrow$ {member(e',delete(e,s)) $\Leftrightarrow$ member(e',s)}]

A6 member(e,s) $\Rightarrow$
```
begin s1 := s; bool := false;
   while ¬ empty(s1) ∧ bool do
      e1 := min(s1) ;
      bool :=(e1 = e);
      s1 := delete(e1,s1)
      od
end bool
```

and the usual axioms of identity = .

Now, consider programs making use of priority queues. We base analysis of the programs on those properties of priority queues which were listed as axioms or can be deduced from axioms. It is not necessary to know how the operations min,insert etc. are performed. The question: is there enough axioms in our specification? becomes the crucial one. The positive answer to it is supplied by the following

<u>The representation theorem</u>
Every model $\mathfrak{M}$ of algorithmic theory of priority queues ATPQ is isomorphic to a standard one, that is

$$\langle E \cup Fin(E) , f_1, f_2, f_3, r_1, r_2, =, \leq \rangle$$

where Fin(E)is the family of all finite subsets of E,

$f_1(e,s) = s \cup \{e\}$ $\qquad$ $r_1(e,s) \Leftrightarrow e \in s$

$f_2(e,s) = s \setminus \{e\}$ $\qquad$ $r_2(s) \Leftrightarrow s = \emptyset$

$f_3(s)$ = the least element of s.

This result indicates that really we have managed to gather all necessary axioms. There are many corollaries and consequences of the representation theorem. The most important says that any property of priority queues which is expressible in the language of algorithmic logic and is valid in the class of all priority queues has a proof from axioms of ATPQ. Hence, we have a choice between formal proofs and semantical validation and we shall choose what is easier in given circumstances.

It is not astonishing that ATPQ is not a complete theory, it has too many different models. Let us see an example of a formula independent of axioms of ATPQ

$$(\exists s_0)(\forall e)\ eq(s_0, insert(e,s_0)) .$$

Here eq stands for the predicate of equality of priority queues.

3. ALGORITHMIC THEORY OF BINARY SEARCH TREES

Let $(E, \leqslant)$ be a set linearly ordered by the relation $\leqslant$
A binary search tree is a labelled binary tree in which each vertex w is labelled by an element $e(w) \in E$ and such that

a. for each vertex q in the left subtree of w $e(q) < e(w)$

b. for each vertex q in the right subtree of w $e(w) < e(q)$.

Binary search trees are usually implemented with the help of the following type declaration

```
unit N : class(v : E) ;
   var l,r : N
end N
```

which is related to the following signature

$$\langle E \cup N, v, l, r, node, ul, ur, isnone, =_E, \leqslant_E \rangle$$

where node : $E \to N$; it is a counterpart of new N operation

v : $N \to E$

l : $N \to N$ r : $N \to N$

ul : $N \times N \to N$ ur : $N \times N \to N$

isnone : $N \to B_0$

$=_E$ and $\leqslant_E$ are relations of identity and linear order in E.
For the operations v, l, r we shall use notation n.v, n.l, n.r instead of v(n) , l(n), r(n). This shows our intention to keep closely to the conventions of programming languages. Similarly the operations ul and ur are corresponding to .l:= and .r:= and we shall replace instruction n:= ul n′,n by n.l := n′.

Any algebraic structure of the above signature will be called a binary search tree if it satisfies the following axioms B1 - B8.

B1 node(e).v = e

B2 isnone(node(e).l)

B3 isnone(node(e).r)

B4 $n.v < n.r.v \vee isnone(n) \vee isnone(n.r)$

B5 $n.l.v < n.v \vee isnone(n) \vee isnone(n.l)$

B6
```
isnone(n′)∨(n′:= n;
            while ¬ isnone(n′)do
               if isnone(n.l) then n′:=n′.r
                              else n1 := node(n .l.v);
                                   n1.l := n′.l.l;
```

```
                                    n2 := node(n´.v);
                                    n2.l:=n .l.r; n2.r := n´.r;
                                    n1.r  := n2    fi
                n´:= n1    od) true
B7   (n.r=n" ∧ n.v=e ∧ [ isnone(n´)∨(n2 := n´;
                        while  ¬ isnone(n2.r)do n2 := n2.r od ;
        if n2.v > n.v then bool:= true else bool :=false fi) bool]
     => (n.l :=n´) { n.r =n"∧ n.v=e ∧ n.l =n´ }
B8   (n.l =n" ∧ n.v=e ∧ [isnone(n´)∨(n2 := n´;
                        while ¬ isnone(n2.l)do n2 := n2.l od;
        if n2.v < n.v then bool :=true else bool := false fi) bool]
     =>(n.r := n´){n.l =n" ∧ n.v =e ∧ n.r = n´ } .
```

The set of axioms B1 - B8 is consistent since

Theorem 3.1

Algorithmic theory of binary search trees ATBST has a model.

P r o o f. Indeed, let us consider a set of expressions over the set E such that for every $e \in E$

1° the expression (( )e( )) is in S,

2° if two expressions ν and τ are in S and if
 for every element f occurring in ν, $f \prec e$
 for every element f occurring in τ, $e \prec f$
 then the expression

$$(\nu\ e\ \tau) \quad \text{is in S,}$$

3° S is the least set of expressions containing ( ) and closed with respect to 1° and 2°.

Now, it is easy to give an interpretation to v, l, r, ul, ur, isnone operations in S such that all axioms B1 - B8 will be valid. S will be called a standard model of ATBST. □

Moreover, we can prove

Theorem 3.2 (representation theorem)

Every model of algorithmic theory of binary search trees is isomorphic to a standard one. □

Let us conclude this section with the remark that the standard model of ATBST can be described by the following declarations

```
unit Bnode : N class ;   readonly l,r;
  (* outside Bnode the operations .l:=, .r:6 are forbidden *)
   unit ul : procedure n´: N ;    var n2 : N ;
```

```
        begin   if n′= none then l := n′ else n2 := n′fi ;
          while n2.r =/= none do n2 := n2.r od ;
          if n2.v < v then l := n′ else ALARM fi
      end ul;
     unit ur : procedure n′: N ...(*similar to ul*) end ur;
   end Bnode
```

Notice that this declaration of type Bnode is concatenated (prefixed) with the declaration of type N.

4. AN INTERPRETATION OF THE THEORY OF PRIORITY QUEUES

In this and the followingsection we shall discuss the question of correctness of an implementation of priority queues. We shall start by extending the algorithmic theory of binary search trees with algorithmic definitions of member, insert, delete, min operations. Next, we observe that the extended theory is strong enough to prove that algorithmic theory of priority queues is interpretable within the theory of binary search trees since axioms A1 - A5 of priority queues are provable in the extended theory of binary search trees.

Let us consider the following definitions

Definition 4.1

```
min(n) =df ( if isnone(n) then ALARM else  n1 := n;
                       while ¬ isnone(n1.l)do n1 := n1.l od;
                       result := n1.v ) result
```

Definition 4.2

```
member(e,n) =df  (n1 := n; result := false;
                  while ¬ result ∧ ¬ isnone(n1) do
                    if e = n1.v then result := true else
                    if e < n1.v then n1 := n1.l else n1 := n1.r
                  fi fi od ) result
```

and similarly we construct definitions of insert and delete [1,11].

Theorem 4.1

All axioms of priority queues are provable from the axioms of ATBST augmented with definitions of insert, delete, member, min, empty.□

It means that given a model of ATBST we can define a model of ATPQ. Its construction is effective since all definitions are algorithmic.

5. AN IMPLEMENTATION

Making use of the theorem 4.1 we see that the following declaration is a proper implementation of priority queues.

```
unit BST : class type E ; function less e,e' : E : Boolean ;

   unit node : class  v : E ;
      var  l,r : node
   end node;
   unit min : function n : node  : E ;
      begin
       while n.l =/= none do n := n.l od;
       result := n.v
   end min;
   unit member : function  ...        end member;
   unit empty : function  ...         end empty;
   unit insert : function  ...        end insert;
   unit delete : function  ...        end deletee;
end BST
```

There exists another posssibility in which one can avoid making E a parameter of type BST . In order to do so we apply concatenation of type declarations and virtual procedure.

```
unit BST' : class
   unit E : class;  end E ;
   unit less : virtual function e,e':E : Boolean ; end less;
   unit node : class v : E ;
      var l,r : node
   end node;
   unit min ...
   unit member ...
   unit insert ...
   unit delete ...
   unit empty ...
end BST'
```

Units BST and BST' are two different implementaions of a problem oriented language. The difference between them lies in different environments needed to apply problem oriented languages BST and BST'. LOGLAN allows parametrized type declarations like BST. Notice that concatenation of type declarations is another solution of the problem of generic type declarations. BST′ can be conceived as a description of a whole family of data structures. It represents a pattern which is to be completed by a user. Namely, the declaration

```
unit myBST : BST' class;
   unit Elem : E class ... end Elem ;
   unit less : function e,e': Elem : Boolean ... end less;
end myBST
```

represents an extension of BST′ by one′s concrete set Elem and ordering relation less.

In order to apply such a problem oriented language we write

```
pref my BST block
              declarations
            begin
              instructions
            end
```

6. DYNAMIZATION OF ALGORITHMIC THEORIES

One can observe that theories ATPQ and ATBST both lack of proper notion of identity of objects appearing as priority queues and nodes. Both theories can be called abstract or static since they are not sufficiently rich in order to explain phenomena like

new node(e) =/= new node(e)

and

$$(p1 := \text{new node}(e);\ p2 := p1;\ p2.l := p3)\ p1.l = p3$$

Wishing to dynamize our theories we have to add the notion of reference to our picture. Here we would like to call the attention of the reader to the algorithmic theory of reference [16].

The theory of references deals with two sorts FR of frames and St of states of reservation of memory. The specific signs of the language of the theory are: insert, delete, newfr, none, free, member. Letters f,f′ etc. will be used to denote frames, letters s,s′ will serve as St-variables.

insert: $(Fr \setminus \{none\}) \times ST \longrightarrow St$	; reserve f in s result is s′
delete: $Fr \times St \longrightarrow St$	; free f in state s
newfr: $St \longrightarrow Fr$	; supply new frame in the state s

```
  none :->Fr                              ; distinguished frame
  free :->St                              ; distinguished state
  member : Fr × St —— B_o                 ; check whether f is reserved in s
```

Axioms

```
ATR1  (begin s':= free; while s =/= free do
           f := newfr s' ; if member(f,s) then s := delete(f,s) fi
           s' := insert(f,s') od end ) true
ATR2  member(f,insert(f,s)) ∧ {f'=/=f⇒[member(f',s)⇔ member(f',insert(f,s))
ATR3  ¬ member(f,delete(f,s)) ∧{f≠f' ⇒[member(f',s) ⇔ member(f',delete(f,s))
ATR4  newfr(s)=/= none
ATR5  ¬ member(newfr(s), s)
ATR6  ¬ member(f,free)
ATR7  ¬ member(none ,s) .
```

Theorem 6.1 [16]
The theory of references ATR has a model (hence it is consistent). □

Theorem 6.2 [16]
Every two models of ATR are isomorphic if we disregard the operations newfr . □

A standard model of ATR consists of the family of all finite subsets of the set of natural numbers. Two standard models can differ in the realizatmion of newfr operation. Theorems 6.1 and 6.2 convince us that the axioms of ATR theory adequately describe the notion of reference.

Now, we shall introduce the notion of dynamic objects. Suppose we are given a formalized algorithmic theory T which specifies properties of "abstract" objects i.e. elements of a model of T. Making use of the notion of reference we shall deal with "dynamic" objects to be conceived as ordred pairs

$$\langle \text{reference, static object} \rangle$$

Example. For nodes of ATBST we have staic objects being triples

$\left\langle \begin{array}{c|c|c} v & l & r \\ \hline e & n_1 & n_2 \end{array} \right\rangle$ and dynamic objects being pairs $\left\langle \text{ref}, \begin{array}{c|c|c} v & l & r \\ \hline e & n_1 & n_2 \end{array} \right\rangle$

It is not difficult to observe that interpretation of new node operation as composition of operation node of ATBST and instruction
s := insert(newfr(s), s) enables us to explain why

new node(e)=/= new node(e) □

Let us consider a few simple properties of dynamic objects and states of computations.

1° Every state of a computation contains a finite number of dynamic objects (cf 6.2).

2° In every state s of a computation, if two dynamic objects have equal references then they are identical.

3° No operation can update reference in an existing dynamic object.

These and other properties of dynamic objects can be deduced in a new theory which arises by putting together a theory T of abstract objects and ATR theory of references. In addition the new theory requires axioms specifying operation new T of creating new dynamic object of static type T and others. Once again we can study problems of consistency and represntation of the resulting theory.

7. FINAL REMARKS

We have observed that algorithmic theories allow to specify data structures. We have seen axiomatic systems defining classes of structures and it is not difficult to find axioms which define one data structure up to isomorphisms e.g. the formula

$$(x := 0\ ;\ \underline{\text{while}}\ x \neq y\ \underline{\text{do}}\ x := s(x)\ \underline{\text{od}})\,\text{true}$$

makes all models of algorithmic arithmetic isomorphic (categoricity).

Proving properties of programs in algorithmic theories is relatively easy (cf. [17,18]) since axioms are already algorithmic formulas. In most cases there is no need for induction. Proofs can be carried on by means of inference rules in a way resembling stepwise refinment of programs. Notice, however, that the rules like the following ones

$$\frac{\alpha \Rightarrow \beta}{(\text{while } \beta \text{ do K od})\,\text{true} \Rightarrow (\text{while } \alpha \text{ do K od})\,\text{true}}$$

and

$$\frac{(\text{while } \alpha \text{ do K od})\ \text{true},\ \ \text{L true},\ \ \text{M true}}{(\text{while } \alpha \text{ do M; K; L od})\,\text{true}}$$

where L and M do not change the variables of K and α

do not preserve any equivalence relation among programs. It seems important to collect useful inference rules which are used in proofs. For examples of proofs in algorithmic theories see [17,18].

Here, we have proposed to study the notion of interpretation among algorithmic theories as a formal counterpart of the notion of implementation. Another suggestion, also based on algorithmic logic has been proposed by L. Banachowski [2].

One can compare our approach with the denotational semantics DS and abstract data types ADT. Both DS and ADT are similar in the sense that they use first order formulas (usually equalities) as axioms. As a result we have many models and an additional tool like the least fixed point or initial algebra is needed in order to pick up a unique algebra to be the meaning of axioms. Observe that initial algebra has more properties than it can be deduced from the original set of axioms. The set of all sentences valid in the initial algebra is much more complicated than the set of axioms. One can ask whether there exists a method for complementing the original axioms with new truth. It is not difficult to see that this is a hopeless goal. Moreover, there are questions of consistency and completeness of a specification. In algorithmic logic they are approached by the theorem stating that every consistent theory has a model and by numerous examples showing that , in contrast with the first order logic, we are able to give adequate axiomatizations of data structures. The same questions translated to the languages of DS and ADT would read: is there any method of checking whether the least fixed point or initial algebra will be not a trivial one? is there any method of checking whether a specification is maximal and can not be extended?

Finally, we would like to mention the close relationship between software and algorithmic theories and the promising possibility of putting theories together which corresponds in a way to concatenable type declarations prefixing in SIMULA and LOGLAN.

REFERENCES

[1] Aho,A.,Hopcroft,J.,Ullman,J., The design and analysis of computer algorithms, Addison-Wesley,1974

[2] Banachowski,L., On proving program correctness by means of stepwise refinement method, to appear in Proc. Symp. Algorithmic Logic and LOGLAN in Lecture Notes in Computer Science

[3] Bartol,W.M.,et al.,Report on the LOGLAN programming language Müldner,T., ed University of Warsaw 1981

[4] Dańko,W., A criterion of undecidability of algorithmic theories, in Proc. MFCS'80 P.Dembiński ed. LNCS Springer Vlg vol.88

[5] Engeler,E., Algorithmic properties of structures, Math. Systems Theory 1(1967), 183-195

[6] Goguen,J.A.,Thatcher,J.W.,Wagner,E.G., An initial algebra approach to the specification,correctness and implementation of abstarct data types, IBM Rep. RC 6487(1977)

[7] Guttag,J., Abstract data types... CACM 20(1977), 396-404

[8] Hoare,C.A.R., Proof of correctness of data representation, Acta Informatica 1(1972),271-281

[9] Kfoury,D., Comparing algebraic structures up to algorithmic equivalence in Proc 1-st ICALP'72 . North-Holland 1972

[10] Kreczmar,A., Programmability in fields, Fundamenta Informaticae 1(1977), 195-220

[11] Knuth,D., The art of computer programming, vol.3 Addison-Wesley 73

[12] Liskov,B.M., Zilles,S.N., Programming with abstract data types Proc ACM SIGPLAN Symp. on Very High Level Languages, SIGPLAN Notices 4(1974), 50-59

[13] Mazur,S., Computable analysis, Dissertationes Mathematicae 33 (1963 PWN)Publ. Warsaw

[14] Mirkowska,G., Algorithmic logic and its applications in the theory of programs,Fundamenta Informaticae1(1977),1-17, 147-167

[15] Mirkowska,G.,Algorithmic logic with nondeterministic programs, Fundamenta Informaticae 1(1980), 45-64

[16] Oktaba,H., On algorithmic theory of reference, Ph.D. Thesis University of Warsaw 1981

[17] Salwicki,A., On algorithmic theory of stacks in Proc.MFCS78 J.Winkowski ed. Lecture Notes in Comp.Sci. v. 64, 452-461

[18] Salwicki,A., On the algorithmic theory of dictionaries, in Proc Logic of Programs E.Engeler ed. LNCS vol.125, 145-168

[19] Scott,D., Data types as lattices, SIAM J.Comp. 5(1976),522-587

IMPLEMENTATION OF PARAMETERISED SPECIFICATIONS

-- Extended Abstract* --

Donald Sannella

Department of Computer Science
University of Edinburgh

Martin Wirsing

Institut für Informatik
Technische Universität München

Abstract

A new notion is given for the implementation of one specification by another. Unlike most previous notions, this generalises to handle parameterised specifications as well as loose specifications (having an assortment of non-isomorphic models). Examples are given to illustrate the notion. The definition of implementation is based on a new notion of the simulation of a theory by an algebra. For the bulk of the paper we employ a variant of the Clear specification language [BG 77] in which the notion of a data constraint is replaced by the weaker notion of a hierarchy constraint. All results hold for Clear with data constraints as well, but only under more restrictive conditions.

We prove that implementations compose vertically (two successive implementation steps compose to give one large step) and that they compose horizontally under application of (well-behaved) parameterised specifications (separate implementations of the parameterised specification and the actual parameter compose to give an implementation of the application).

1. Introduction

Algebraic specifications can be viewed as abstract programs. Some specifications are so completely abstract that they give no hint of a method for finding an answer. For example, the function inv:matrix->matrix for inverting an nxn matrix can be specified as follows:

```
inv(A) x A = I
A x inv(A) = I
```

(provided that matrix multiplication and the identity nxn matrix have already been specified). Other specifications are so concrete that they resemble programs. For example:

```
reverse(nil) = nil
reverse(cons(a,l)) = append(reverse(l),cons(a,nil))
```

(this specification of the reverse function on lists amounts to an executable program in the HOPE functional programming language [BMS 80]).

It is usually easiest to specify a problem at a relatively abstract level. We can then work gradually and systematically toward a low-level 'program' which satisfies the specification. This will normally involve the introduction of auxiliary functions, particular data representations and so on. This approach to program development is related to the well-known programming discipline of stepwise refinement advocated by Wirth [Wir 71] and Dijkstra [Dij 72].

---

*The full version of this paper is available as Report CSR-103-82, Department of Computer Science, University of Edinburgh.

A formalisation of this programming methodology depends on some precise notion of the *implementation* of a specification by a lower-level specification. Previous notions have been given for the implementation of non-parameterised ([GTW 78], [Nou 79], [Hup 80], [EKP 80], [Ehr 82]) and parameterised ([Gan 81], [Hup 81])** specifications, but none of these approaches deals fully with 'structured' algebraic specifications (as in Clear [BG 77] or CIP-L [Bau 81]) which may be constructed in a hierarchical fashion and may be *loose* (with an assortment of non-isomorphic models). We present a definition of implementation which agrees with our intuitive notions built upon programming experience and which handles such loose hierarchical specifications, based on a new (and seemingly fundamental) concept of the *simulation* of a theory by an algebra. We show how this definition extends to give a definition of the implementation of parameterised specifications. An example of an implementation is given and several other examples are sketched.

We work within the framework of the Clear specification language [BG 77] which allows large specifications to be built from small easy-to-understand bits. For most of the paper we employ a variant of Clear in which the notion of a *data constraint* is replaced by the weaker notion of a *hierarchy constraint*. The result is still a viable specification language, although specifications tend to be somewhat longer than in ordinary Clear. We later show that all results hold for 'ordinary' Clear (with data constraints), but only under more restrictive conditions.

The 'putting-together' theme of Clear and the ideas incorporated in CAT [GB 80] (a proposed system for systematic program development using Clear) lead us to wonder if implementations can be put together as well. We prove that if P is implemented by P' (where P and P' are 'well-behaved' parameterised specifications) and A is implemented by A', then P(A) is implemented by P'(A').

We prove that implementations compose in another dimension as well. If a high-level specification A is implemented by a lower-level specification B which is in turn implemented by a still lower-level specification C (and an extra compatibility condition is satisfied), then A is implemented by C. These two results allow large specifications to be refined in a gradual and modular fashion, a little bit at a time.

2. Preliminaries -- Clear and data/hierarchy constraints

This section is devoted to a very brief review of the notions underlying Clear along with a discussion of data and hierarchy constraints. See [BG 77] for an informal description of Clear, [San 81] and [BG 80] for its formal semantics, and [WB 81] for more about hierarchy constraints. For the usual notions of *signature* Σ, *signature morphism* (*inclusion*) $\sigma=\langle f,g\rangle$ (f maps sorts, g maps operators), *Σ-algebra* $\underline{A}=\langle A,\alpha\rangle$ (A_s is the carrier for sort s, $\alpha(\omega)$ is the function associated with operator ω), *homomorphism*, *Σ-equation*, and *satisfaction* of a set of Σ-equations by a Σ-algebra see [BG 80]. The following less conventional definitions are taken (with minor changes) from the same source.

Def: If $\sigma=\langle f,g\rangle$ is a signature morphism $\sigma:\Sigma\rightarrow\Sigma'$ and $\underline{A}'=\langle A',\alpha'\rangle$ is a Σ'-algebra, then the *Σ-restriction* of $\underline{A}'$ (along σ), written $\underline{A}'|^{\sigma}_{\Sigma}$ is the Σ-algebra $\langle A,\alpha\rangle$ where $A_s=A'_{f(s)}$ and $\alpha(\omega)=\alpha'(g(\omega))$. Normally σ is obvious from context, in which case the notation $\underline{A}'|_{\Sigma}$ may be used.

Def: A *simple Σ-theory presentation* is a pair $\langle\Sigma,E\rangle$ where Σ is a signature and E is a set of Σ-equations. This is *simple* because no constraints (see below) are included.

Def: A Σ-algebra $\underline{A}$ *satisfies* a simple theory presentation $\langle\Sigma,E\rangle$ if $\underline{A}$ satisfies E. Then $\underline{A}$ is called a *model* of $\langle\Sigma,E\rangle$. A theory presentation $\underline{T}$ *specifies* a set of

**Also [EK 82] which we discovered while writing the final version.

algebras, namely the set of its models denoted Models(T). A theory is called satisfiable if it has at least one model.

Def: If E is a set of Σ-equations, let E^* be the set of all Σ-algebras which satisfy E. If M is a set of Σ-algebras, let M^* be the set of all Σ-equations which are satisfied by each algebra in M. The closure of a set E of Σ-equations is the set E^{**}, written $\overline{E}$. E is closed if $E=\overline{E}$.

Def: A simple Σ-theory T is a simple theory presentation $\langle\Sigma,E\rangle$ where E is closed. The simple Σ-theory presented by the presentation $\langle\Sigma,E\rangle$ is $\langle\Sigma,\overline{E}\rangle$.

Def: A simple theory morphism (inclusion) $\sigma : \langle\Sigma,E\rangle \rightarrow \langle\Sigma',E'\rangle$, where $\langle\Sigma,E\rangle$ and $\langle\Sigma',E'\rangle$ are simple theories, is a signature morphism (inclusion) $\sigma:\Sigma\rightarrow\Sigma'$ such that $\sigma(e)\in E'$ for each $e\in E$.

Note that any algebra satisfying a simple theory (presentation) is a model of that simple theory. This is in contrast to the 'initial algebra approach' of ADJ [GTW 78] in which only the initial algebra of a theory is accepted as a model. Clear permits us to write loose specifications such as the following:

```
const ApproxSqrt = enrich Nat by
                       opns sqrt : nat -> nat
                       eqns x - (sqrt(x))^2 ≤ x/2 + 1  = true    enden
```

This specifies an approximate square-root function on the natural numbers. Any function with at least the specified accuracy will do (for example, sqrt(100) may be 7, 8, 9 or 10). Under the initial algebra approach such a specification yields a single model with extra values of sort nat.

Even in Clear, we often want to restrict the class of models. For instance, if no restriction is present in the above example then trivial models (where all natural numbers are equal to 0) and models with extra values of sort nat (other than $succ^n(0)$ for $n\geq 0$) are allowed. This facility is provided by Clear's data operation, which may be applied when enriching a theory by some new sorts, operators and equations. Each application of the data operation contributes a data constraint to the theory which results from the enrichment. Unfortunately, implementations (section 3) do not seem to have nice properties in the presence of data constraints. Accordingly we use for the bulk of this paper a variant of Clear in which data constraints are replaced by hierarchy constraints, contributed by the 'data' operation (see [BDPPW 79] and [WB 81]). Hierarchy constraints are weaker than data constraints so specifications tend to be somewhat longer than in ordinary Clear (as in the terminal algebra approach, it is sometimes necessary to add extra operators to avoid trivial models). We show later that all results hold for Clear with data constraints, but only under more restrictive conditions. We now give some definitions concerning data and hierarchy constraints; note that in most respects the two kinds of constraints are identical.

Def: A Σ-data (hierarchy) constraint c is a pair $\langle i,\sigma\rangle$ where $i:T\hookrightarrow T'$ is a simple theory inclusion and $\sigma:signature(T')\rightarrow\Sigma$ is a signature morphism.

A data (hierarchy) constraint is a description of an enrichment (the theory inclusion goes from the theory to be enriched to the enriched theory) together with a signature morphism 'translating' the constraint to the signature Σ.

A signature morphism from Σ to another signature Σ' can be applied to a Σ-constraint, translating it to a Σ'-constraint, just as it can be applied to a Σ-equation to give a Σ'-equation.

Def: If $\sigma':\Sigma\rightarrow\Sigma'$ is a signature morphism and $\langle i,\sigma\rangle$ is a Σ-data (hierarchy) constraint, then σ' applied to $\langle i,\sigma\rangle$ gives the Σ'-data (hierarchy) constraint $\langle i,\sigma.\sigma'\rangle$.

A data (hierarchy) constraint imposes a restriction on a set of Σ-algebras, just as an equation does. The only difference between a data constraint and a hierarchy constraint is in this restriction; compare the "no confusion" and "no crime" conditions in the following definitions.

Def: A Σ-algebra $\underline{A}$ satisfies a Σ-data constraint $\langle i:\underline{T}\hookrightarrow\underline{T}',\sigma:sig(\underline{T}')\rightarrow\Sigma\rangle$ if (letting $\underline{A}_{target} = \underline{A}|^{\sigma}_{sig(\underline{T}')}$ and $\underline{A}_{source} = \underline{A}|^{i.\sigma}_{sig(\underline{T})}$) $\underline{A}_{target}$ is a model of $\underline{T}'$ and:

- "No confusion": $\underline{A}_{target}$ does not satisfy any sig($\underline{T}'$)-equation e with variables only in sorts of $\underline{T}$ for any injective assignment of variables to $\underline{A}_{source}$ values unless e is in $\overline{eqns(\underline{T}')\cup\underline{A}^{*}_{source}}$.

- "No junk": Every element in $\underline{A}_{target}$ is the value of a $\underline{T}'$-term which has variables only in sorts of $\underline{T}$, for some assignment of $\underline{A}_{source}$ values.

Without loss of generality we assume that every theory contains the theory Bool (with sort bool and constants true and false) as a primitive subtheory.

Def: A Σ-algebra $\underline{A}$ satisfies a Σ-hierarchy constraint $\langle i:\underline{T}\hookrightarrow\underline{T}',\sigma:sig(\underline{T}')\rightarrow\Sigma\rangle$ if (with $\underline{A}_{target}$ and $\underline{A}_{source}$ as above) $\underline{A}_{target}$ is a model of $\underline{T}'$ and:

- "No crime": $\underline{A} \models$ true≠false.

- "No junk": As above.

Since data (hierarchy) constraints behave just like equations, they can be added to the equation set in a simple theory presentation to give a data (hierarchical) theory presentation.

Def: A data (hierarchical) Σ-theory presentation is a pair $\langle\Sigma$,EC$\rangle$ where Σ is a signature and EC is a set of Σ-equations and Σ-data (hierarchy) constraints.

The notions of data (hierarchical) theory, satisfaction (of a data or hierarchical theory), closure and data (hierarchical) theory morphism follow as in the 'simple' case. The denotation of a (hierarchical) Clear specification is a data (hierarchical) theory $\langle\Sigma$,EC$\rangle$, specifying all Σ-algebras which satisfy the equations and data (hierarchy) constraints in EC. For the remainder of the paper (except where noted at the end of section 5) all discussion will concern only hierarchical Clear. We will use terms like 'theory' in place of longer terms like 'hierarchical theory'.

Def: A sort or operator of a theory is called constrained if it is in $\sigma(sig(\underline{T}')-sig(\underline{T}))$ for some constraint $\langle i:\underline{T}\hookrightarrow\underline{T}',\sigma:sig(\underline{T}')\rightarrow\Sigma\rangle$ in that theory.

Lack of space permits only a single brief example to illustrate data and hierarchy constraints. Consider the following specification:

```
const Triv = enrich Bool by
                 sorts element   enden

const T = enrich Triv by
              data sorts newelem
                   opns f : element -> newelem   enden
```

T includes a data constraint $\langle Triv\hookrightarrow T, id\rangle$. Given a sig(T)-algebra, we can check if it satisfies this constraint. For example:

$A_{element}$ = {0,1,2} $A_{newelem}$ = {a,b,c} f(0)=a f(1)=b f(2)=a

(with the usual interpretation of Bool). This fails to satisfy the "no confusion" condition (consider the equation f(x)=f(y) under the injective assignment $[x\mapsto 0, y\mapsto 2]$). It also violates the "no junk" condition (the element c is not the value of any term). But if the function f is altered so that f(2)=c then the constraint is satisfied. In general, any algebra satisfying this data constraint will have both carriers of the same cardinality with f 1-1 and onto.

Changing *data* above to *'data'* changes the data constraint to a hierarchy constraint. The following algebra is then a model of T, although it does not satisfy the "no confusion" condition:

$A_{element} = \{0,1,2\}$ $\quad A_{newelem} = \{a\}$ $\quad f(0) = f(1) = f(2) = a$

(again with the usual interpretation of Bool). It is necessary to add some new operators (e.g. ==:element,element->bool and ==:newelem,newelem->bool) and equations (e.g. f(x)==f(y) = x==y) to retain the original class of models.

The data constraints described here are a special case of those discussed in [BG 80], where the theory inclusion is replaced by an arbitrary theory morphism; essentially the same concept is described by Reichel [Rei 80] (cf. [KR 71]). General data constraints never actually arise in Clear. The definition of data constraint satisfaction given above is an attempt to capture, in this special case, the definition of [BG 80] using a different approach.

A consequence of the inclusion of data or hierarchy constraints in Clear theories is that no complete proof system can exist for Clear (see [MS 82]). This means that the model-theoretic closure of a set of equations and constraints (as defined above) is not always the same as its proof-theoretic closure.

For later results we need a generalisation of Guttag's notion of sufficient completeness [GH 78] and of the classical notion of conservativeness from logic:

Def: A theory T is *sufficiently complete* with respect to a set of operators Σ, sorts S, a subset Σ' of Σ, and variables of sorts X (where $S,X \subseteq sorts(T)$, $\Sigma \subseteq opns(T)$) if for every term t of an S sort containing operators of Σ and variables of X sorts, there exists a term t' with variables of X sorts and operators of Σ' such that $T \vdash t=t'$.

Def: A theory T is *conservative* with respect to a theory $T' \subseteq T$ if for all equations e containing operators only of T', $T \vdash e \Rightarrow T' \vdash e$.

Sufficient completeness means that T does not contain any new term of an old sort which is not provably equal to an old term (where 'new' and 'old' depend on Σ, S, Σ' and X). Conservativeness means that old terms (from T') are not newly identified in T. Instances of these general notions guarantee that all models of a theory possess a convenient hierarchical structure.

3. A notion of implementation

A formal approach to stepwise refinement of specifications must begin with some notion of the *implementation* of a specification by another (lower level) specification. Armed with a precise definition of this notion, we can prove the correctness of refinement steps, providing a basis for a methodology for the systematic development of programs which are guaranteed to satisfy their specifications. But first we must be certain that the definition itself is sound and agrees with our intuitive notions built upon programming experience.

Suppose we are given two theories $T=\langle\Sigma,EC\rangle$ and $T'=\langle\Sigma',EC'\rangle$. We want to implement the theory T (the *abstract* specification) using the sorts and operators provided by T' (the *concrete* specification). Previous formal approaches (see [GTW 78], [Nou 79], [Hup 80], [EKP 80], [Gan 81], [Ehr 82]) agree that T' implements T if there is some way of deriving sorts and operators like those of T from the sorts and operators of T'. Each approach considers a different way of making the 'bridge' from T' to T. We will require that there be a more or less direct correspondence between the sorts and operators of T and those of T'. Each sort or operator in Σ must be implemented by a sort or operator in Σ' -- this correspondence will be embodied by a signature morphism $\sigma:\Sigma\rightarrow\Sigma'$. Note that two different sorts or operators in Σ may map to the same Σ' sort or operator, and also that there may be some (auxiliary) sorts and operators in Σ' which remain unused. This is a simplification over previous approaches, which generally allow some kind of restricted enrichment of T' to T" before matching T with T". But the power is the same; we would say that T" implements T and leave the enrichment from T' to T" to the user. As a consequence of a later theorem (see section 5) our results extend to more complex notions.

Given a signature morphism $\sigma:\Sigma\rightarrow\Sigma'$, what relationship must hold between T and T' before we can say that T' implements T? One might suspect that $\sigma(EC) \subseteq EC'$ is required -- i.e. that for any model A' of T', $A'|^{\sigma}_{\Sigma} \in$ Models(T) -- but this condition is too strong. Roughly speaking, T' implements T if the Σ-restriction of each model of T' simulates T. A (Σ-restricted) T' model need not be a model of T, but need only have the appearance of a model of T. In particular, values of the T' model must 'represent' the values of the corresponding Σ-terms, but the carriers of the T' model need not match the carriers of any T model. Some flexibility is necessary in order to approximate our intuitive notion of an implementation:

- A subset of the values of a T' sort may be used to represent all the values of a T sort. Example: implementing the natural numbers using the integers -- the negative integers are not needed.

- More than one T' value may be used to represent the same T value. Example: implementing sets by strings -- the order does not matter, so "1.2.3" = "3.2.1" (as sets).

Now T' implements T if (and only if) the Σ-restriction of any model of T' is a model of T after these two considerations have been taken into account. This ensures that corresponding operators will yield the same result (modulo data representation) which is intuitively the decisive criterion for a correct implementation.

Our definition of implementation will proceed in two steps. First we define the simulation of a theory by an algebra, making precise the vague and informal ideas outlined above. The notion of simulation is then used to give a simple definition of implementation. We chose to highlight the notion of simulation because it seems to be a fundamental concept which may be useful outside the present context. The following diagram shows how the definitions given below fit together to give notions of simulation and implementation:

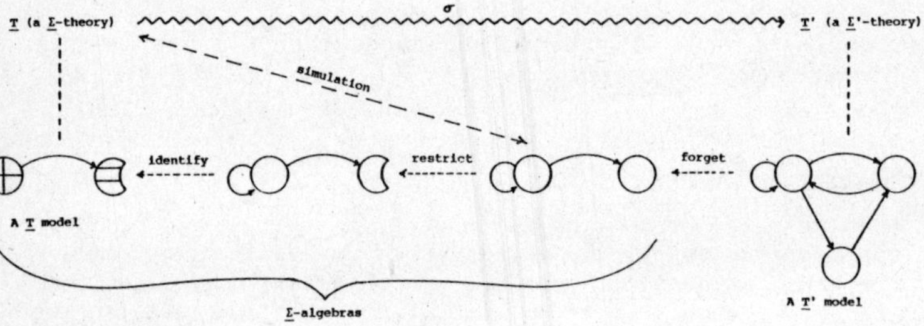

An implementation $T \overset{\sigma}{\rightsquigarrow} T'$

For the definition of simulation we need an auxiliary notion. As mentioned above, a subset of the available 'concrete' values may be used to represent all 'abstract' values. Restricting the carriers of the concrete algebra to the values which are actually used yields an intermediate algebra which plays an important role in the definition of simulation. We do not want to restrict the carrier for every sort, but only for those sorts of Σ which are constrained by hierarchy constraints in T (for unconstrained sorts we do not know which values are unused). This is where we depart from the usual practice of restricting to 'reachable' values (see for example [EKP 80]). We want the subalgebra which has been reduced just enough to satisfy the "no junk" condition for each of these constraints.

Def: If Σ is a signature, A is a Σ-algebra and T is a Σ-theory, then $restrict_T(A)$ is the largest subalgebra A' of A satisfying the "no junk" condition (section 2) for every hierarchy constraint $\langle i:T' \hookrightarrow T", \sigma:sig(T") \rightarrow \Sigma \rangle$ in T.

Note that the subalgebra A' does not always exist. Consider the following example:

```
const T = let Nat = enrich Bool by
                    'data' sorts nat
                           opns 0 : nat
                                succ : nat -> nat    enden in
          enrich Nat by
            opns neg : nat    enden
```

Let Σ be the signature of T. Suppose A is the Σ-algebra with carrier {-1,0,1,...}, the usual interpretation for the operators 0 and succ, and neg=-1. Now $\text{restrict}_T(A)$ does not exist because every subalgebra of A must contain -1 (the value of neg) and hence fails to satisfy the "no junk" condition for the constraint of T.

A Σ-algebra A simulates a Σ-theory T if it satisfies the equations and constraints of T after allowing for unused carrier elements and multiple representations.

Def: If Σ is a signature, A is a Σ-algebra and $T=\langle\Sigma,EC\rangle$ is a Σ-theory, then A *simulates* T if $\text{restrict}_T(A)/\equiv_{EC}$ (call this RI(A)) exists and is a model of T.
[$\equiv_{EC}$ is the Σ-congruence generated by EC -- i.e. the least Σ-congruence on $\text{restrict}_T(A)$ containing the relation determined by the equations in EC]

RI stands for restrict-identify, the composite operation which forms the heart of this definition. To determine if a Σ-algebra A simulates a Σ-theory T, we *restrict* A, removing those elements from the carrier which are not used to represent the value of any Σ-term, for constrained sorts; the result of this satisfies the "no junk" condition for each constraint in T. We then *identify* multiple concrete representations of the same abstract value by quotienting the result by the Σ-congruence generated by the equations of T, obtaining an algebra which (of course) satisfies those equations and also continues to satisfy the "no junk" condition of the constraints. If this is a model of T (i.e. it satisfies the "no crime" condition for each constraint in T) then A simulates T. Note that any model of T simulates T. It has been shown in [EKP 80] that the order restrict-identify gives greater generality than identify-restrict.

Most work on algebraic specifications concentrates on the specification of abstract data types, following the lead of ADJ [GTW 78] and Guttag *et al* [GH 78]. As pointed out by ADJ, the *initial* model (in the category of all models of a theory) best captures the meaning of "abstract" as used in the term "abstract data type", so other models are generally ignored (there is some disagreement on this point -- other authors prefer e.g. final models [Wan 79] -- but in any case some particular model is singled out for special attention). This is not the case in Clear (the ordinary version or our variant); although the *'data'* operation may be used to restrict the set of models as discussed in section 2, no particular model is singled out so in general a theory may have many nonisomorphic models (as in the Munich approach). Such a *loose* theory need not be implemented by a theory with the same broad range of models. A loose theory leaves certain details unspecified and an implementation may choose among the possibilities or not as is convenient. That is:

- A loose theory may be implemented by a 'tighter' theory. Example: implementing the operator choose:set->integer (choose an element from a set) by an operator which chooses the smallest.

This is intuitively necessary because it would be silly to require that a program (the final result of the refinement process) embody all the vagueness of its original specification. This kind of flexibility is already taken into account by the discussion above, and is an important feature of our notion of implementation. Previous notions do not allow for it because they concentrate on implementation of abstract data types and so consider only a single model for any specification.

Now we are finally prepared to define our notion of the implementation of one theory by another. This definition is inspired by the notion of [EKP 80] but it is not the same; they allow a more elaborate 'bridge' but otherwise their notion is more restrictive than ours. Our notion is even closer to the one of Broy *et al* [BMPW 80] but there the 'bridge' is less elaborate than ours. It also bears some resemblance to a more programming-oriented notion due to Schoett [Sch 81].

Def: If $\underline{T}=\langle\Sigma,EC\rangle$ and $\underline{T}'=\langle\Sigma',EC'\rangle$ are satisfiable theories and $\sigma:\Sigma\to\Sigma'$ is a signature morphism, then $\underline{T}'$ implements $\underline{T}$ (via σ), written $\underline{T}\overset{\sigma}{\rightsquigarrow}\underline{T}'$, if for any model $\underline{A}'$ of $\underline{T}'$, $\underline{A}'|^{\sigma}_{\Sigma}$ simulates $\underline{T}$.

Note that any theory morphism $\sigma:\underline{T}\to\underline{T}'$ where $\underline{T}'$ is satisfiable is an implementation $\underline{T}\overset{\sigma}{\rightsquigarrow}\underline{T}'$. In particular, if $\underline{T}'$ is an enrichment of $\underline{T}$ (e.g. by equations which 'tighten' a loose theory) then $\underline{T}\rightsquigarrow\underline{T}'$.

A simple example will show how this definition works (other implementation examples are given in the next section). Consider the theory of the natural numbers modulo 2, specified as follows:

```
const Natmod2 = enrich Bool by
                  'data' sorts natmod2
                         opns 0, 1 : natmod2
                              succ : natmod2 -> natmod2
                              iszero : natmod2 -> bool
                         eqns succ(0) = 1           succ(1) = 0
                              iszero(0) = true      iszero(1) = false     enden
```

Can this be implemented by the following theory?

```
const Fourvalues = enrich Bool by
                     'data' sorts fourvals
                            opns zero, one, zero', extra : fourvals
                                 succ : fourvals -> fourvals
                                 iszero : fourvals -> bool
                                 eq : fourvals, fourvals -> bool
                            eqns succ(zero) = one        succ(one) = zero'
                                 succ(zero') = one       succ(extra) = zero
                                 iszero(zero) = true     iszero(one) = false
                                 iszero(zero') = true    iszero(extra) = false
                                 eq(zero,one) = false    eq(zero,zero') = false
                                     . . .                    . . .
                                 eq(p,q) = eq(q,p)       eq(p,p) = true     enden
```

The iszero operator of Natmod2 and the eq operator of Fourvalues are needed to avoid trivial models.

All models of Fourvalues have a carrier containing 4 elements, and all models of Natmod2 have a 2-element carrier. Now consider the signature morphism σ:sig(Natmod2)$\to$sig(Fourvalues) given by [natmod2$\mapsto$fourvals, 0$\mapsto$zero, 1$\mapsto$one, succ$\mapsto$succ, iszero$\mapsto$iszero] (and everything in Bool maps to itself). Intuitively, Natmod2$\overset{\sigma}{\rightsquigarrow}$Fourvalues (zero and zero' both represent 0, one represents 1 and extra is unused) but is this an implementation according to the definition? Consider any model of Fourvalues (e.g. the term model -- all models are isomorphic). 'Forgetting' to the signature sig(Natmod2) eliminates the operators zero', extra and eq. Now we check if this algebra (call it $\underline{A}$) simulates Natmod2.

- 'Restrict' removes the value of extra from the carrier.

- 'Identify' identifies the values of the terms "succ(1)" (=zero') and "0" (=zero).

The "no crime" condition of Natmod2's constraint requires that the values of true and false remain separate; this condition is satisfied, so $\underline{A}$ simulates Natmod2 and Natmod2$\overset{\sigma}{\rightsquigarrow}$Fourvalues is an implementation.

Suppose that the equation succ(zero')=one in Fourvalues were replaced by succ(zero')=zero. Forget (producing an algebra $\underline{B}$) followed by restrict has the same effect on any model of Fourvalues, but now identify collapses the carrier for sort natmod2 to a single element (the closure of the equations in Natmod2 includes the equation succ(succ(p))=p, so "succ(succ(0))" (=zero') is identified with "0" (=zero), and "succ(succ(1))" (=zero) is identified with "1" (=one)). Furthermore, the carrier for sort bool collapses; "iszero(succ(succ(1)))" (=true) is identified with "iszero(1)" (=false). The result fails to satisfy the "no crime" condition of the constraint, so B does not simulate Natmod2 and Natmod2$\overset{\sigma}{\leadsto}$Fourvalues is no longer an implementation.

Implementation of parameterised theories

Parameterised theories in Clear are like functions in a programming language; they take zero or more values as arguments and return another value as a result. In Clear these values are theories. Here is an example of a parameterised theory (usually called a theory procedure in Clear):

```
meta Ident = enrich Bool by
               sorts element
               opns eq : element,element -> bool
               eqns eq(a,a) = true
                    eq(a,b) = eq(b,a)
                    eq(a,b) and eq(b,c) --> eq(a,c) = true    enden

proc Set(X:Ident) =
  let Set0 = enrich X by
               'data' sorts set
                      opns Ø : set
                           singleton : element -> set
                           U : set,set -> set
                           is_in : element,set -> bool
                      eqns Ø U S = S
                           S U S = S
                           S U T = T U S
                           S U (T U V) = (S U T) U V
                           a is_in Ø = false
                           a is_in singleton(b) = eq(a,b)
                           a is_in S U T = a is_in S or a is_in T    enden in
  enrich Set0 by
         opns choose : set -> element
         eqns choose(singleton(a) U S) is_in (singleton(a) U S) = true    enden
```

Ident is a metatheory; it describes a class of theories rather than a class of algebras. Ident describes those theories having at least one sort together with an operator which satisfies the laws for an equivalence relation on that sort.

Ident is used to give the 'type' of the parameter for the procedure Set. The idea is that Set can be applied to any theory which matches Ident. Ident is called the metasort or requirement of Set. When Set is supplied with an appropriate actual parameter theory, it gives the theory of sets over the sort which matches element in Ident. For example

```
Set(Nat[element is nat, eq is ==])
```

gives the theory of sets of natural numbers (assuming that Nat includes an equality operator ==). Notice that a theory morphism (called the fitting morphism) must be provided to match Ident with the actual parameter. The result of an application is defined using pushouts as in [Ehr 82] (see [San 81] and [BG 80] for this and other aspects of Clear's semantics) but it is not necessary (for now) to know the details. In this paper we will consider only the single-parameter case; the extension to multiple parameters should pose no problems.

Note that parameterised theories in Clear are different from the parameterised specifications discussed by ADJ [TWW 78]. An ADJ parameterised specification works at the level of algebras, producing an algebra for every model of the parameter. A Clear parameterised theory produces a theory for each parameter theory. The result P(A) may have 'more' models than the theory A (this is the case when Set is applied to Nat, for example). Since ADJ parameterised specifications are a special case of Clear parameterised theories, all results given here hold for them as well.

Since a parameterised theory $\underline{R} \hookrightarrow \underline{P}$ (that is, a procedure with requirement theory $\underline{R}$ and body $\underline{P}$ -- $\underline{R}$ will always be included in $\underline{P}$) is a function taking a theory $\underline{A}$ as an parameter and producing a theory $\underline{P}(\underline{A})$ as a result, an implementation $\underline{R}' \hookrightarrow \underline{P}'$ of $\underline{R} \hookrightarrow \underline{P}$ is a function as well which takes any parameter theory $\underline{A}$ of $\underline{P}$ as argument and produces a theory $\underline{P}'(\underline{A})$ which implements $\underline{P}(\underline{A})$ as result. But this does not specify what relation (if any) must hold between the theories $\underline{R}$ and $\underline{R}'$. Since every actual parameter $\underline{A}$ of $\underline{R} \hookrightarrow \underline{P}$ (which must match $\underline{R}$) should be an actual parameter of $\underline{R}' \hookrightarrow \underline{P}'$, it must match $\underline{R}'$ as well. This requires a theory morphism $\mu:\underline{R}' \to \underline{R}$ (then a fitting morphism $\rho:\underline{R} \to \underline{A}$ gives a fitting morphism $\mu.\rho:\underline{R}' \to \underline{A}$).

<u>Def</u>: If $\underline{R} \hookrightarrow \underline{P}$ and $\underline{R}' \hookrightarrow \underline{P}'$ are parameterised theories, $\mu:\underline{R}' \to \underline{R}$ is a theory morphism and $\sigma:sig(\underline{P}) \to sig(\underline{P}')$ is a signature morphism, then $\underline{R}' \hookrightarrow \underline{P}'$ <u>implements</u> $\underline{R} \hookrightarrow \underline{P}$ (via σ and μ), written $\underline{R} \hookrightarrow \underline{P} \overset{\sigma}{\underset{\mu}{\rightsquigarrow}} \underline{R}' \hookrightarrow \underline{P}'$, if for all theories $\underline{A}$ with fitting morphism $\rho:\underline{R} \to \underline{A}$, $\underline{P}(\underline{A}[\rho]) \overset{\hat{\sigma}}{\rightsquigarrow} \underline{P}'(\underline{A}[\mu.\rho])$ where $\hat{\sigma}$ is the extension of σ from $\underline{P}$ to $\underline{P}(\underline{A}[\rho])$ by the identity id (i.e. $\hat{\sigma}|_{sig(\underline{P})-sig(\underline{R})} = \sigma$ and $\hat{\sigma}|_{sig(\underline{A})} = id$).

Ordinarily $\underline{R}$ and $\underline{R}'$ will be the same theory, or at least the same modulo a change of signature. Otherwise $\underline{R}'$ must be <u>weaker</u> than $\underline{R}$.

Sometimes it is natural to split the implementation of a parameterised theory into two or more cases, implementing it for reasons of efficiency in different ways depending on some additional conditions on the parameters. For example:

- Sets: A set can be represented as a binary sequence if the range of possible values is small; otherwise it must be represented as a sequence (or tree, etc) of values.

- Parsing: Different algorithms can be applied depending on the nature of the grammar (operator precedence, LR, context sensitive, etc).

- Sorting: Distribution sort can be used if the range of values is small; otherwise quicksort.

In each instance the cases must exhaust the domain of possibilities, but they need not be mutually exclusive.

Our present notion of implementation does not treat such cases. We could extend it to give a definition of the implementation of a parameterised theory $\underline{R} \hookrightarrow \underline{P}$ by a collection of parameterised theories $\underline{R}'+\underline{R}_1' \hookrightarrow \underline{P}_1'$, ..., $\underline{R}'+\underline{R}_n' \hookrightarrow \underline{P}_n'$ (where for every theory $\underline{A}$ with a theory morphism $\sigma:\underline{R} \to \underline{A}$ there must exist some i>1 such that $\sigma':\underline{R}'+\underline{R}_i' \to \underline{A}$ exists). But we force the case split to the <u>abstract</u> level, rather than entangle it with the already complex transition from abstract to concrete:

$$
\begin{array}{lll}
\underline{R} \hookrightarrow \underline{P} & \dashrightarrow & \underline{R}+\underline{R}_1 \hookrightarrow \underline{P}_1 = \underline{P}(\underline{R}+\underline{R}_1) \\
 & & \quad \cdots \\
 & \dashrightarrow & \underline{R}+\underline{R}_n \hookrightarrow \underline{P}_n = \underline{P}(\underline{R}+\underline{R}_n)
\end{array}
$$

This collection of n parameterised theories is equivalent to the original $\underline{R} \hookrightarrow \underline{P}$, in the sense that every theory $\underline{P}(\underline{A}[\sigma])$ with $\sigma:\underline{R} \to \underline{A}$ is the same as the theory $\underline{P}_i(\underline{A}[\sigma'])$ with $\sigma':\underline{R}+\underline{R}_i \to \underline{A}$ for some i>1. (A theory of the transformation of Clear specifications is needed to discuss this matter in a more precise fashion; no such theory exists at present.) Now each case may be handled separately, using the normal definition of parameterised implementation:

$$
\begin{array}{l}
\underline{R}+\underline{R}_1 \hookrightarrow \underline{P}_1 \rightsquigarrow \underline{R}'+\underline{R}_1' \hookrightarrow \underline{P}_1' \\
\quad \cdots \\
\underline{R}+\underline{R}_n \hookrightarrow \underline{P}_n \rightsquigarrow \underline{R}'+\underline{R}_n' \hookrightarrow \underline{P}_n'
\end{array}
$$

4. Examples

Sets (as defined in the last section) can be implemented using sequences. We must define sequences as well as operators on sequences corresponding to all the operators in Set. We begin by defining everything except the choose operator:

```
meta Triv = theory sorts element    endth

proc Sequence(X:Triv) =
  enrich X + Bool by
    'data' sorts sequence
           opns empty : sequence
                unit : element -> sequence
                . : sequence,sequence -> sequence
                head : sequence -> element
                tail : sequence -> sequence
           eqns empty.s = s
                s.empty = s
                s.(t.v) = (s.t).v
                head(unit(a).s) = a
                tail(unit(a).s) = s    enden

proc SequenceOpns(X:Ident) =
  enrich Sequence(X) by
    opns is_in : element,sequence -> bool
         add : element,sequence -> sequence
         U : sequence,sequence -> sequence
    eqns a is_in empty = false
         a is_in unit(b) = eq(a,b)
         a is_in s.t = a is_in s or a is_in t
         add(a,s) = s  if a is_in s
         add(a,s) = unit(a).s  if not(a is_in s)
         empty U s = s
         unit(a).t U s = add(a,t U s)    enden
```

The head and tail operators of Sequence and their defining equations are needed to avoid trivial models; they serve no other function in the specification.

Before dealing with the choose operator, we split Set into two cases:

```
meta TotalOrder = enrich Ident by
                    opns ≤ : element,element -> bool
                    eqns a≤a = true
                         a≤b and b≤a --> eq(a,b) = true
                         a≤b and b≤c --> a≤c = true
                         a≤b or b≤a = true    enden

Ident↪Set  ------→ Ident↪Set
              ----→ TotalOrder↪Set' = Set(TotalOrder)
```

These two cases may be handled separately. The choose operator can select the minimum element when the element type is totally ordered; otherwise we can leave the precise choice unspecified as before.

```
proc SequenceAsSet(X:Ident) =
  enrich SequenceOpns(X) by
    opns choose : sequence -> element
    eqns choose(unit(a).t) is_in (unit(a).t) = true    enden

proc SequenceAsSet'(X:TotalOrder) =
  enrich SequenceOpns(X) by
    opns choose : sequence -> element
    eqns choose(unit(a)) = a
         choose(unit(a).unit(b).s) = choose(unit(a).s) if a≤b
                                     else choose(unit(b).s)    enden
```

Now Ident$\hookrightarrow$Set $\xrightarrow[\mu]{\sigma}$ Ident$\hookrightarrow$SequenceAsSet and TotalOrder$\hookrightarrow$Set' $\xrightarrow[\mu']{\sigma}$ TotalOrder$\hookrightarrow$SequenceAsSet', where σ = [element$\mapsto$element, eq$\mapsto$eq, set$\mapsto$sequence, Ø$\mapsto$empty, singleton$\mapsto$unit, U$\mapsto$U, is_in$\mapsto$is_in, choose$\mapsto$choose] (and everything in the signature of Bool maps to itself), and μ and μ' are the identity morphisms on Ident and TotalOrder respectively. Note that choose is not specified for empty sets and sequences -- although the same notion of implementation should work for error theories and algebras, we prefer to avoid the issue of errors for now. Also note that an incorrect implementation results if choose in SequenceAsSet is changed to select the <u>first</u> element; Set contains an equation choose(singleton(x) U singleton(y))=choose(singleton(y) U singleton(x)), so the identify step would collapse the parameter sort (and consequently bool).

This example illustrates all of the features of our notion of implementation. Not all sequences are needed to represent sets -- sequences with repeated elements are not used. Each set is represented by many sequences, since the sequence representation of a set keeps track of the order in which elements were inserted. Set is split into two theories before implementation, and finally SequenceAsSet' is 'tighter' than Set' because the choose operator (select an element) is implemented by an operator which chooses the minimum element.

A nonparameterised example is obtained by applying Set or Set' and SequenceAsSet or SequenceAsSet' to an argument, for example:

Set(Nat[element <u>is</u> nat, eq <u>is</u> ==]) $\xrightarrow{\sigma}$ SequenceAsSet(Nat[element <u>is</u> nat, eq <u>is</u> ==])

where σ is the same as σ above except that element$\mapsto$element is replaced by nat$\mapsto$nat.

Two additional examples:

- Lists can be implemented using arrays of (value,index) pairs, where the index points to the next value in the list (and where some distinguished index value denotes nil). There are many representations for the same list (the relative positions of cells in the array are irrelevant, for example) and circular structures are not needed to represent the value of any list.

- The specification of matrix inversion in the Introduction can be implemented by a specification of matrix inversion using the Gauss-Seidel method. Conversely, this specification can be implemented by the specification in the Introduction (enriched by some auxiliary functions).

The matrix inversion example shows that the expectation that A$\leadsto$B should imply that B is 'lower level' than A is not always justified. This is because the definition of implementation is concerned with classes of models rather than with the equations used to describe those classes. In this case both theories will have the same class of models except that the Gauss-Seidel method will probably require auxiliary operators.

5. Horizontal and vertical composition

Large specifications are needed to solve large problems. But a large monolithic specification of a compiler (for example) would be impossible to understand because of the sheer numbers of interacting operators and equations. The value of a specification depends on the ease with which it was written and can be understood; a large number of pages full of equations are not of much use to anybody.

The Clear [BG 77] and CIP-L [Bau 81] specification languages were invented to combat just this problem. Clear and CIP-L are languages for writing <u>structured</u> specifications; that is, they provide facilities for combining small theories in various ways to make large theories. A large specification can thus be built from small easy-to-understand bits. Following [GB 80] this shall be called <u>horizontal</u> structure.

Likewise, the implementation of a large specification is not done all at once; it is good programming practice to implement and test pieces of the specification separately and then construct a final system from the finished components. If the theories which make up a Clear or CIP-L specification are implemented separately, it should be possible to put together (*horizontally compose*) the implementations in the same way that the theories themselves are put together, yielding an implementation of the entire specification.

Although the problem of developing a program from a specification is simplified by dividing it into smaller units, the step from specification of a component to its implementation as a program is still often uncomfortably large. A way to conquer this is to break the development of a program into a series of consecutive refinement steps. That is, the specification is refined to a lower level specification, which is in turn refined to a still lower level specification, and so on until a program is obtained. Again following [GB 80], this is called the *vertical* structure (of the development process). If a specification A is implemented by another specification B, and B is implemented by C, then these implementations should *vertically compose* to give an implementation of A by C. Goguen and Burstall [GB 80] propose a system called CAT for the structured development of programs from specifications by composing implementations in both the horizontal and vertical dimensions.

The vertical composition of two implementations is not always an implementation. For example, consider the following theories:

```
const T = enrich Bool by
              opns extra : bool   enden

const T' = enrich Bool by
               opns extra : bool
               eqns extra = true   enden

const T" = theory 'data' sorts three
                         opns tt, ff, extra : threevals   endth
```

Now $T \leadsto T'$ and $T' \leadsto T''$ but $T \not\leadsto T''$ (consider the model of T" where tt≠ff≠extra). The theories must satisfy an extra condition.

Def: A theory $\underline{T}$ is *reachably complete* with respect to a parameterised theory $\underline{R} \hookrightarrow \underline{P}$ with $\underline{P} \subseteq \underline{T}$ if $\underline{T}$ is sufficiently complete with respect to opns($\underline{P}$), constrained-sorts($\underline{P}$), constrained-opns($\underline{P}$), and variables of sorts($\underline{R}$) $\cup$ unconstrained-sorts($\underline{P}$). A theory $\underline{T}$ is reachably complete with respect to a nonparameterised theory $\underline{A}$ if it is reachably complete with respect to $\emptyset \hookrightarrow \underline{A}$.

In the example above T" is not reachably complete with respect to T because extra is not provably equal to either tt or ff.

Vertical composition theorem

1. [Reflexivity] $\underline{T} \overset{id}{\leadsto} \underline{T}$.

2. [Transitivity] If $\underline{T} \overset{\sigma}{\leadsto} \underline{T}'$ and $\underline{T}' \overset{\sigma'}{\leadsto} \underline{T}''$ and $\underline{T}''$ is reachably complete with respect to $\sigma.\sigma'(\underline{T})$, then $\underline{T} \overset{\sigma.\sigma'}{\leadsto} \underline{T}''$.

Corollary

1. [Reflexivity of parameterised implementations] $\underline{R} \hookrightarrow \underline{P} \underset{id}{\overset{id}{\leadsto}} \underline{R} \hookrightarrow \underline{P}$.

2. [Transitivity of parameterised implementations] If $\underline{R} \hookrightarrow \underline{P} \underset{\mu}{\overset{\sigma}{\leadsto}} \underline{R}' \hookrightarrow \underline{P}'$ and $\underline{R}' \hookrightarrow \underline{P}' \underset{\mu'}{\overset{\sigma'}{\leadsto}} \underline{R}'' \hookrightarrow \underline{P}''$ and $\underline{P}''$ is reachably complete with respect to $\sigma.\sigma'(\underline{R}) \hookrightarrow \sigma.\sigma'(\underline{P})$, then $\underline{R} \hookrightarrow \underline{P} \underset{\mu'.\mu}{\overset{\sigma.\sigma'}{\leadsto}} \underline{R}'' \hookrightarrow \underline{P}''$.

In the absence of constraints (as in the initial algebra [GTW 78] and final algebra [Wan 79] approaches), reachable completeness is guaranteed so this extra condition is unnecessary.

To prove that implementations of large theories can be built by arbitrary horizontal composition of small theories, it is necessary to prove that each of Clear's theory-building operations (combine, enrich, derive and apply) preserves implementations. We will concentrate here on the application of parameterised theories and the enrich operation. Extension of these results to the remaining operations should not be difficult.

For the apply operation our object is to prove the following property of implementations:

<u>Horizontal Composition Property</u>: $\underline{R} \hookrightarrow \underline{P} \rightsquigarrow \underline{R}' \hookrightarrow \underline{P}'$ and $\underline{A} \rightsquigarrow \underline{A}'$ implies $\underline{P}(\underline{A}) \rightsquigarrow \underline{P}'(\underline{A}')$.

But this is <u>not</u> true in general; in fact, $\underline{P}'(\underline{A}')$ is not even always defined. Again, some extra conditions must be satisfied for the desired property to hold.

<u>Def</u>: Let $\underline{R} \hookrightarrow \underline{P}$ be a parameterised theory.

- $\underline{R} \hookrightarrow \underline{P}$ is called <u>structurally complete</u> if $\underline{P}$ is sufficiently complete with respect to opns($\underline{P}$), sorts($\underline{R}$) $\cup$ constrained-sorts($\underline{P}$), opns($\underline{R}$) $\cup$ constrained-opns($\underline{P}$), and variables of sorts($\underline{R}$) $\cup$ unconstrained-sorts($\underline{P}$). A nonparameterised theory $\underline{A}$ is called structurally complete if $\emptyset \hookrightarrow \underline{A}$ is structurally complete.

- $\underline{R} \hookrightarrow \underline{P}$ is called <u>parameter consistent</u> if $\underline{P}$ is conservative with respect to $\underline{R}$.

If $\underline{R}' \hookrightarrow \underline{P}'$ is structurally complete, parameter consistent and reachably complete, and $\underline{A}'$ is structurally complete and a valid actual parameter of $\underline{R}' \hookrightarrow \underline{P}'$, then the horizontal composition property holds.

<u>Horizontal composition theorem</u>: If $\underline{R} \hookrightarrow \underline{P}$ and $\underline{R}' \hookrightarrow \underline{P}'$ are parameterised theories with $\underline{R}' \hookrightarrow \underline{P}'$ structurally complete and parameter consistent, $\underline{P}'$ is reachably complete with respect to $\sigma(\underline{R}) \hookrightarrow \sigma(\underline{P})$, $\underline{R} \hookrightarrow \underline{P} \overset{\sigma}{\underset{\mu}{\rightsquigarrow}} \underline{R}' \hookrightarrow \underline{P}'$ and $\underline{A} \overset{\sigma'}{\rightsquigarrow} \underline{A}'$ are implementations with $\underline{A}'$ structurally complete, and $\rho: \underline{R} \to \underline{A}$ and $\rho': \underline{R}' \to \underline{A}'$ are theory morphisms where $\rho' = \mu . \rho . \sigma'$, then $\underline{P}(\underline{A}[\rho]) \overset{\hat{\sigma}.\tilde{\sigma}'}{\rightsquigarrow} \underline{P}'(\underline{A}'[\rho'])$, where $\tilde{\sigma}'|_{sig(\underline{P}(\underline{A}[\rho]))-sig(\underline{A})} = id$ and $\tilde{\sigma}'|_{sig(\underline{A})} = \sigma'$.

<u>Corollary</u> (Horizontal composition for <u>enrich</u>): If $\underline{A} \overset{\sigma}{\rightsquigarrow} \underline{A}'$ is an implementation, $\underline{B}$ = <u>enrich</u> $\underline{A}$ <u>by</u> <stuff> and $\underline{B}'$ = <u>enrich</u> $\underline{A}'$ <u>by</u> σ<stuff>, $\underline{A}' \hookrightarrow \underline{B}'$ is structurally complete and parameter consistent, $\underline{B}'$ is reachably complete with respect to $\sigma(\underline{A}) \hookrightarrow \sigma(\underline{B})$ and $\underline{A}'$ is structurally complete, then $\underline{B} \overset{\tilde{\sigma}}{\rightsquigarrow} \underline{B}'$, where $\tilde{\sigma}|_{sig(\underline{B})-sig(\underline{A})} = id$ and $\tilde{\sigma}|_{sig(\underline{A})} = \sigma$.

A consequence of this corollary is that our vertical and horizontal composition theorems extend to more elaborate notions of implementation such as the one discussed in [EKP 80]. Again, reachable completeness is guaranteed in the absence of constraints.

The vertical and horizontal composition theorems give us freedom to build the implementation of a large specification from many small implementation steps. The correctness of all the small steps guarantees the correctness of the entire implementation, which in turn guarantees the correctness of the low-level 'program' with respect to the high-level specification. This provides a formal foundation for a methodology of programming by stepwise refinement. CAT's 'double law' [GB 80] is an easy consequence of the vertical and horizontal composition theorems. This means that the order in which parts of an implementation are carried out makes no difference, and that our notion of implementation is appropriate for use in CAT.

Our notions of simulation and implementation extend without modification to ordinary Clear (with data constraints rather than hierarchy constraints); all of the results in this paper then remain valid except for the horizontal composition theorem and its corollary. These results hold only under an additional condition.

Def: A data theory $\underline{T}$ is _hierarchical submodel consistent_ if for every model M of $\underline{T}$ and every hierarchical submodel M^- of M (i.e. every submodel of M satisfying the constraints of $\underline{T}$ when viewed as hierarchy constraints), M^- satisfies the data constraints of $\underline{T}$.

Horizontal composition theorem (with _data_): In Clear with _data_, if $\underline{R} \hookrightarrow \underline{P}$ and $\underline{R}' \hookrightarrow \underline{P}'$ are parameterised theories with $\underline{R}' \hookrightarrow \underline{P}'$ structurally complete and parameter consistent, $\underline{P}'$ is hierarchical submodel consistent and reachably complete with respect to $\sigma(\underline{R}) \hookrightarrow \sigma(\underline{P})$, $\underline{R} \hookrightarrow \underline{P} \underset{\mu}{\overset{\sigma}{\leadsto}} \underline{R}' \hookrightarrow \underline{P}'$ and $\underline{A} \overset{\sigma'}{\leadsto} \underline{A}'$ are implementations with $\underline{A}'$ structurally complete, and $\rho : \underline{R} \to \underline{A}$ and $\rho' : \underline{R}' \to \underline{A}'$ are theory morphisms where $\rho' = \mu . \rho . \sigma'$, then $\underline{P}(\underline{A}[\rho]) \overset{\hat{\sigma}.\hat{\sigma}'}{\leadsto} \underline{P}'(\underline{A}'[\rho'])$.

The horizontal composition theorem for _enrich_ extends analogously.

This result is encouraging because ordinary Clear is easier to use than our 'hierarchical' variant. However, the extra condition on the horizontal composition theorem is rather strong and it may be that it is too restrictive to be of practical use.

Acknowledgements

We are grateful to the work of Ehrig, Kreowski and Padawitz [EKP 80] for a start in the right direction. Thanks: from DS to Rod Burstall for guidance, from MW to Manfred Broy and Jacek Leszczylowski for interesting discussions, to Burstall and Goguen for Clear, to Bernhard Möller for finding a mistake, and to Oliver Schoett for helpful criticism. This work was supported by the University of Edinburgh, by the Science and Engineering Research Council, and by the Sonderforschungsbereich 49, Programmiertechnik, München.

REFERENCES

Note: LNCS n = Springer Lecture Notes in Computer Science, Volume n

[Bau 81] Bauer, F.L. _et al_ (the CIP Language Group) Report on a wide spectrum language for program specification and development (tentative version). Report TUM-I8104, Technische Univ. München.

[BDPPW 79] Broy, M., Dosch, W., Partsch, H., Pepper, P. and Wirsing, M. Existential quantifiers in abstract data types. Proc. 6th ICALP, Graz, Austria. LNCS 71, pp. 73-87.

[BMPW 80] Broy, M., Möller, B., Pepper, P. and Wirsing, M. A model-independent approach to implementations of abstract data types. Proc. of the Symp. on Algorithmic Logic and the Programming Language LOGLAN, Poznan, Poland. LNCS (to appear).

[BG 77] Burstall, R.M. and Goguen, J.A. Putting theories together to make specifications. Proc. 5th IJCAI, Cambridge, Massachusetts, pp. 1045-1058.

[BG 80] Burstall, R.M. and Goguen, J.A. The semantics of Clear, a specification language. Proc. of Advanced Course on Abstract Software Specifications, Copenhagen. LNCS 86, pp. 292-332.

[BMS 80] Burstall, R.M., MacQueen, D.B. and Sannella, D.T. HOPE: an experimental applicative language. Proc. 1980 LISP Conference, Stanford, California, pp. 136-143; also Report CSR-62-80, Dept. of Computer Science, Univ. of Edinburgh.

[Dij 72] Dijkstra, E.W. Notes on structured programming. _Notes on Structured Programming_ (Dahl O.-J., Dijkstra, E.W. and Hoare, C.A.R.), Academic Press, pp. 1-82.

[Ehr 81] Ehrich, H.-D. On realization and implementation. Proc. 10th MFCS, Strbske Pleso, Czechoslovakia. LNCS 118.

[Ehr 82] Ehrich, H.-D. On the theory of specification, implementation, and parameterization of abstract data types. JACM 29, 1 pp. 206-227.

[EK 82] Ehrig, H. and Kreowski, H.-J. Parameter passing commutes with implementation of parameterized data types. Proc. 9th ICALP, Aarhus, Denmark (this volume).

[EKP 80] Ehrig, H., Kreowski, H.-J. and Padawitz, P. Algebraic implementation of abstract data types: concept, syntax, semantics and correctness. Proc. 7th ICALP, Noordwijkerhout, Netherlands. LNCS 85, pp. 142-156.

[Gan 81] Ganzinger, H. Parameterized specifications: parameter passing and implementation. TOPLAS (to appear).

[GB 80] Goguen, J.A. and Burstall, R.M. CAT, a system for the structured elaboration of correct programs from structured specifications. Computer Science Dept., SRI International.

[GTW 78] Goguen, J.A., Thatcher, J.W. and Wagner, E.G. An initial algebra approach to the specification, correctness, and implementation of abstract data types. Current Trends in Programming Methodology, Vol. 4: Data Structuring (R.T. Yeh, ed.), Prentice-Hall, pp. 80-149.

[Grä 79] Grätzer, G. Universal Algebra (2nd edition), Springer.

[GH 78] Guttag, J.V. and Horning, J.J. The algebraic specification of abstract data types. Acta Informatica 10 pp. 27-52.

[Hup 80] Hupbach, U.L. Abstract implementation of abstract data types. Proc. 9th MFCS, Rydzyna, Poland. LNCS 88, pp. 291-304.

[Hup 81] Hupbach, U.L. Abstract implementation and parameter substitution. Proc. 3rd Hungarian Computer Science Conference, Budapest.

[KR 71] Kaphengst, H. and Reichel, H. Algebraische Algorithmentheorie. VEB Robotron, Zentrum für Forschung und Technik, Dresden.

[MS 82] MacQueen, D.B. and Sannella, D.T. Completeness of proof systems for equational specifications. In preparation.

[Nou 79] Nourani, F. Constructive extension and implementation of abstract data types and algorithms. Ph.D. thesis, Dept. of Computer Science, UCLA.

[Rei 80] Reichel, H. Initially-restricting algebraic theories. Proc. 9th MFCS, Rydzyna, Poland. LNCS 88, pp. 504-514.

[San 81] Sannella, D.T. A new semantics for Clear. Report CSR-79-81, Dept. of Computer Science, Univ. of Edinburgh.

[Sch 81] Schoett, O. Ein Modulkonzept in der Theorie Abstrakter Datentypen. Report IFI-HH-B-81/81, Fachbereich Informatik, Universität Hamburg.

[TWW 78] Thatcher, J.W., Wagner, E.G. and Wright, J.B. Data type specification: parameterization and the power of specification techniques. SIGACT 10th Annual Symp. on the Theory of Computing, San Diego, California.

[Wan 79] Wand, M. Final algebra semantics and data type extensions. JCSS 19 pp. 27-44.

[WB 81] Wirsing, M. and Broy, M. An analysis of semantic models for algebraic specifications. International Summer School on Theoretical Foundations of Programming Methodology, Marktoberdorf.

[Wir 71] Wirth, N. Program development by stepwise refinement. CACM 14, 4 pp. 221-227.

ALGEBRAIC SEMANTICS OF RECURSIVE FLOWCHART SCHEMES

Hartmut Schmeck
Institut für Informatik und Praktische Mathematik
Christian-Albrechts-Universität Kiel

1. Introduction

As is well known in case of recursive tree schemes this paper derives algebraic semantics of recursive schemes over reducible flowcharts. The results of this paper heavily depend on the algebraic characterization of reducible flowcharts as given by Elgot and Shepherdson [ES1], [ES2] and Schmeck [S1], [S2]. Based on Elgot's investigations into structured flowcharts [E1], [E2] the former showed the class of finite accessible reducible flowcharts to be freely generated from a set of elementary flowcharts by means of three basic operations: composition, sum, and scalar iteration. In [S1], [S2] Elgot and Shepherdson's results are extended to the class of finite or infinite almost accessible reducible flowcharts.

In case of Σ-trees the freeness and ω-continuity of CT_{Σ} allow the definition of algebraic fixpoint semantics of recursive tree schemes [N], [G2], [G4]. Analogously the freeness results obtained for reducible flowcharts lead to algebraic semantics of recursive flowchart schemes.

Reducible flowcharts are of interest with respect to certain code optimization techniques. This is demonstrated by Hecht and Ullman [HU1] [HU2] who give a graph theoretic characterization of this class and show it to be exactly the class of flowcharts amenable to the intervall analysis technique of Allen and Cocke [AC]. Furthermore it is easily seen that the class of reducible flowcharts is sufficient to serve as the target language of the compiler in the paper by Thatcher, Wagner, and Wright on compiler correctness [ADJ6].

2. Γ-Flowcharts

Let Γ be a one-sorted signature, i.e. $\Gamma=\{\Gamma_i\}_{i<\omega}$ where Γ_i is the set of all i-ary symbols. For each ordinal number n define $[n]:=\{i+1 \mid i<n\}$. As usual A^* denotes the free monoid generated from A.

A <u>Γ-flowchart with n begins and p exits</u> (or <u>Γ-flow from n to p</u>) then is a quadrupel $f=(s,b,\tau,\ell)$ where $n,p<\omega$, s an ordinal number, the <u>weight</u> of f,

[s] the set of <u>interior vertices</u> of f,

$b:[n]\to[s+p]$ the <u>begin function</u> of f,

$\tau:[s]\to[s+p]^*$ the <u>graph</u> of f, and

$\ell:[s]\to\Gamma$ the <u>labeling</u> of f

such that for all $i\in[s]$ we have $i\ell\in\Gamma_{|i\tau|}$. The vertices $1b,\ldots,nb$ are the <u>begins</u> of f, the unlabeled vertices $s+1,\ldots,s+p$ are the <u>exits</u> of f. The set of all Γ-flowcharts with n begins and p exits is denoted by $\mathrm{Flo}_\Gamma(n,p)$. The set of all Γ-flowcharts from n to p of finite weight is denoted by $\mathrm{FFlo}_\Gamma(n,p)$.

<u>Example 1:</u>
The Γ-flow $f=(2,b,\tau,\ell)\in\mathrm{Flo}_\Gamma(1,1)$ with $1b=1$, $1\tau=32$, $2\tau=1$, $1\ell=\pi$, and $2\ell=\gamma$ looks as follows

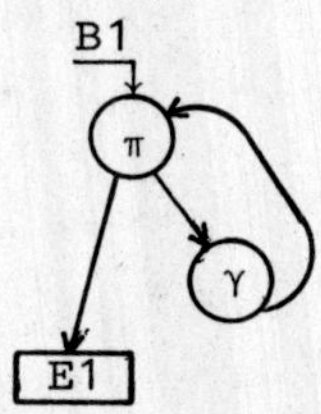

Figure 1

Let MAP denote the category having nonnegative integers as objects and mappings from [n] to [p] as morphisms from n to p. There is a natural embedding of MAP and Γ into Flo_Γ :

Each $f:[n]\to[p]$ determines the <u>trivial Γ-flow</u> $\hat{f}:=(0,f,0_{[p]}*,0_\Gamma)$. Each $\gamma\in\Gamma_k$ determines the <u>atomic Γ-flow</u> $\hat{\gamma}:=(1,b,\tau,\ell)\in\mathrm{Flo}_\Gamma(1,k)$ where $1b=1$, $1\tau=2\cdots k+1$, and $1\ell=\gamma$. The trivial and atomic Γ-flows are also called <u>elementary</u>. If the context allows, we usually write f and γ instead of $\hat{f}$ and $\hat{\gamma}$.

A vertex j of a Γ-flow f from n to p of weight s is <u>accessible</u> iff there is a path from a begin vertex to j. f is <u>accessible</u> iff every vertex of f is accessible. f is <u>almost accessible</u> iff every interior vertex of f is accessible. f is <u>acyclic</u> iff the graph of f does not contain any cycles. f is <u>reducible</u> iff every strongly connected subset C of [s+p] contains a unique vertex j such that every path from a begin into C enters C through j. If F is a class of Γ-flows, then F^{ac} and F^{red} denote the subclasses of all acyclic and of all reducible Γ-flows, and AF and AAF denote the subclasses of all accessible and of all almost accessible Γ-flows respectively. Thus $\mathrm{AAFFlo}_\Gamma^{red}$ is the class of all reducible almost accessible finite Γ-flowcharts. In the same way as accessible Γ-flowcharts from n to p may be viewed as generalized surjective mappings from [n] to [p] the almost accessible Γ-flowcharts from n to p may be viewed as generalized mappings from [n] to [p]. They differ from the biaccessible flowcharts of Bloom and Tindell [BT] in that there need not be a path from every interior vertex to an exit and in that there may be exits which are not accessible.

In the following informal definition of the basic operations on Γ-flows a Γ-flow f from n to p is represented as

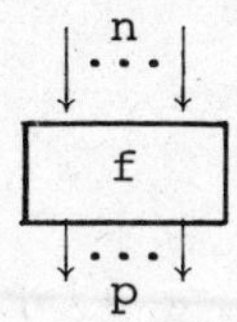

Figure 2

The <u>composition</u> of $f \in Flo_\Gamma(n,p)$ and $g \in Flo_\Gamma(p,q)$ identifies the exits of f with the begin vertices of g:

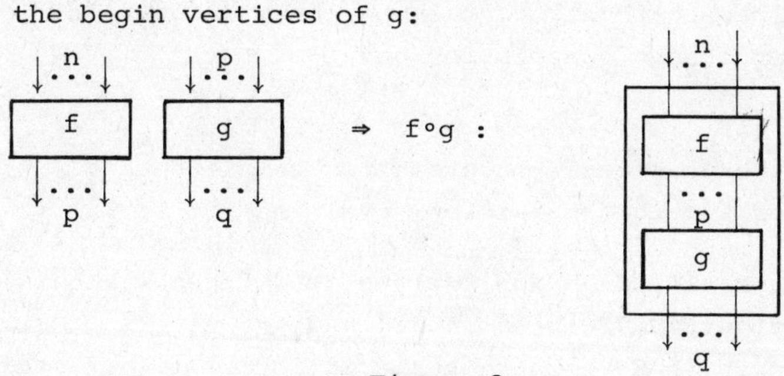

Figure 3

The <u>strong composition</u> f*g furthermore deletes all the interior vertices of f∘g which are not accessible, thus producing an almost accessible Γ-flow.

The <u>sum</u> of $f \in Flo_\Gamma(n,p)$ and $g \in Flo_\Gamma(m,q)$ disjointly lays f and g side by side:

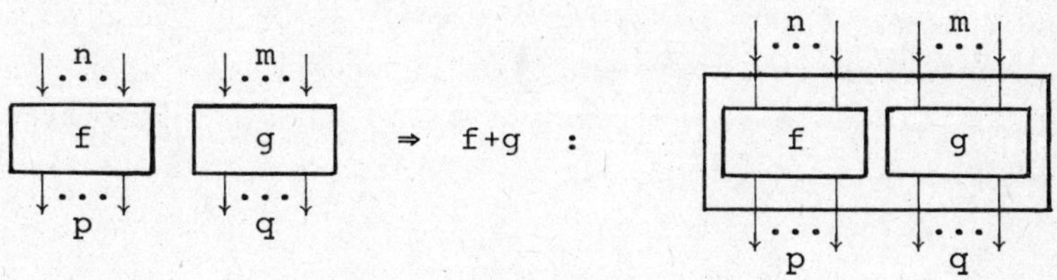

Figure 4

Finally the scalar iteration of a Γ-flow $f \in Flo_{\Gamma}(1,p+1)$ identifies exit p+1 with the begin :

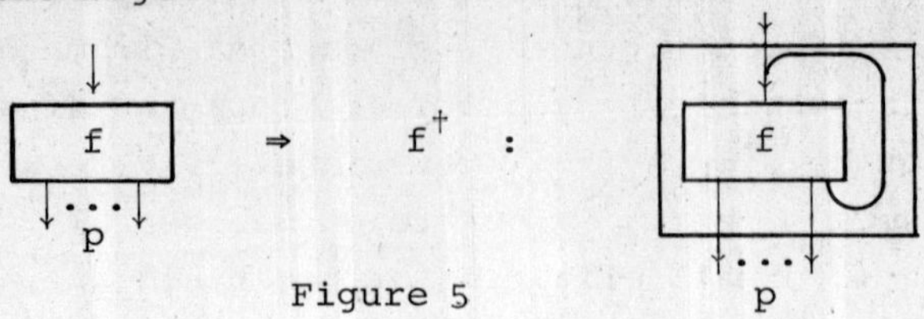

Figure 5

If the begin vertex is equal to the exit p+1, this vertex becomes a new interior vertex labeled with the distinguished nullary operator ⊥.

The formal definition of these operations may be found in [S1] [S2] as well as in [ADJ6] or [ES1].

Based on results of [ES1] the following theorems are obtained in [S1] [S2]:

Theorem 1
$AAFFlo_{\Gamma}^{ac}$ is the least category containing the elementary Γ-flows and being closed under strong composition and sum.

Theorem 2
$AAFFlo_{\Gamma}^{red}$ is the least category containing the elementary Γ-flows and being closed under strong composition, sum, and scalar iteration.

In [S1] [S2] a partial order on Γ-flows is defined which is close to corresponding notions for Σ-trees [ADJ2] and graphs [G1] [G3]. But in contrast to the case of Σ-trees this partial order is not strict, i.e. there is no least element. Let us call a partially ordered set weakly strict (weakly ω-complete) iff it is strict (ω-complete) up to isolated elements. The least element of the maximal strict subset of a weakly strict set M is called the least element of M.
These definitions allow the following extension of theorems 1 and 2:

Theorem 3
$AAFlo_{\Gamma}^{ac}$ is the least category with weakly ω-complete sets of morphisms containing the elementary Γ-flows and being closed under strong composition and sum.

Theorem 4
$AAFlo_{\Gamma}^{red}$ is the least category with weakly ω-complete sets of morphisms containing the elementary Γ-flows and being closed under strong composition, sum, and scalar iteration.

Other important results with respect to the partial order on Γ-flows are

Theorem 5

Composition, strong composition, sum and scalar iteration are ω-continuous operations.

Theorem 6

Every element of Flo_Γ is the least upper bound of an ω-chain of finite Γ-flows.

An analogous algebraic characterization is known in case of Σ-trees [ADJ2]

The main result of [S2] is the freeness of $AAFlo_\Gamma^{red}$ in the category CIFlM having all ω-continuous scalar iteration flow theories over MAP as objects. CIFlM is defined below:

A flow theory over MAP is a strict monoidal category [ML] $(T,\circ,+)$ extending MAP and satisfying the block permutation axiom

$$\forall\, f_1\in T(n_1,p_1)\ \forall\, f_2\in T(n_2,p_2) \quad (f_1+f_2)\circ\pi(p_1,p_2)=\pi(n_1,n_2)\circ(f_2+f_1)$$

(where $\pi(n_1,n_2)$ is the permutation of $[n_1]$ and $n_1+[n_2]$ in $[n_1+n_2]$) and the injection axiom

$$\forall\, i\in[2]\ \forall\, f_i\in T(n_i,p_i) \quad \iota_{(i)}^{n_1,n_2}\circ(f_1+f_2)=f_i\circ\iota_{(i)}^{p_1,p_2}$$

(where $\iota_{(i)}^{n_1,n_2}$ is the injection of $[n_i]$ into $[n_1+n_2]$).

If in addition $T(1,0)$ contains a distinguished element ⊥, and if T is equipped with an operation †, called scalar iteration, satisfying

(I1) $\forall p\in\mathbb{N}_0 \quad {}^\dagger : T(1,p+1) \to T(1,p)$

(I2) $\forall f\in T(0,p) \quad (f+1_1)^\dagger=f+\bot$

(I3) $\forall f\in T(1,p) \quad (f\circ\iota_{(1)}^{p,1})^\dagger=f$

(I4) $\forall f\in T(1,p+2) \quad f^{\dagger\dagger}=(f\circ(1_p+\langle 1_1,1_1\rangle))^\dagger$

(I5) $\forall f\in T(1,p+1)\ \forall g\in T(p,q) \quad f^\dagger\circ g=(f\circ(g+1_1))^\dagger$

then T is a scalar iteration flow theory over MAP.

T is called ω-continuous iff each $T(n,p)$ is weakly ω-complete with least element $\bot_{n,p}$ and if the operations ∘, + and † are ω-continuous. If T_1 and T_2 are ω-continuous scalar iteration flow theories over MAP, then every ω-continuous mapping $\phi: T_1\to T_2$ respecting ∘, +, and † is called a CIFlM-morphism. Finally we call a mapping φ from Γ into an ω-continuous scalar iteration flow theory T over MAP strict iff Γφ does not contain any isolated elements.

Since Elgot and Shepherdson only consider accessible flowcharts their flow theories only have to satisfy the block permutation axiom.

Now we can state the main result of [S2] saying that $AAFlo_\Gamma^{red}$ is a free ω-continuous scalar iteration flow theory over MAP.

Theorem 7

If T is an ω-continuous scalar iteration flow theory over MAP, then every strict mapping $\phi:\Gamma\to T$ has a unique extension to a CIFlM-morphism $\bar{\phi}:AAFlo_{\Gamma}^{red}\to T$.

3. Recursive Flowchart Schemes

Let X be a one-sorted signature of variables for nontrivial Γ-flows where $x\in X_n$ is a variable for a Γ-flow from 1 to n.
As usual define for each $u\in\mathbb{N}_o^*$ of length k $X^u:=\{x_1^u,\dots,x_k^u\}$ such that for each $i\in[k]$ $x_i^u\in X_{u_i}$.

Following [ADJ1] and [G2] [G4] we define a recursive Γ-flowchart scheme from $u\in\mathbb{N}_o^*$ to $v\in\mathbb{N}_o^*$ to be a strict mapping $\alpha:X^u\to AAFlo_{\Gamma\cup X^v}^{red}$ such that for all $i\in[|u|]$ we have

$$x_i^u\alpha\in AAFlo_{\Gamma\cup X^v}^{red}(1,u_i)$$

If for all $i\in[|u|]$ $x_i^u\alpha$ is a finite Γ-flow, then α is called finite. Let $RFS_\Gamma(u,v)$ denote the set of all recursive Γ-flowchart schemes from u to v, and let $FRFS_\Gamma(u,v)$ denote the set of all finite schemes.

Example 2

Let $\alpha\in RFS_\Gamma(112,112)$ be as follows

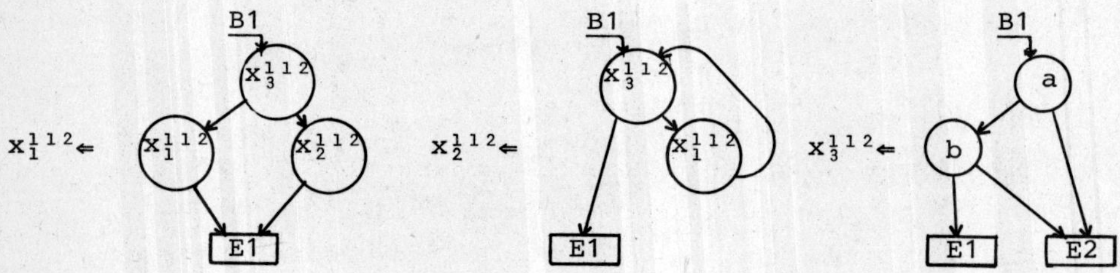

Figure 6

Theorem 7 implies that every $\alpha\in RFS_\Gamma(u,v)$ has a unique extension to a CIFlM-morphism

$$\bar{\alpha}:AAFlo_{\Gamma\cup X^u}^{red}\to AAFlo_{\Gamma\cup X^v}^{red}$$

Thus the composition of $\alpha\in RFS_\Gamma(u,v)$ and $\beta\in RFS_\Gamma(v,w)$ (or substitution of α into β) can be defined by $\alpha\lhd\beta:=\alpha\circ\bar{\beta}$ where ∘ is the composition of mappings. Figure 7 illustrates this definition.

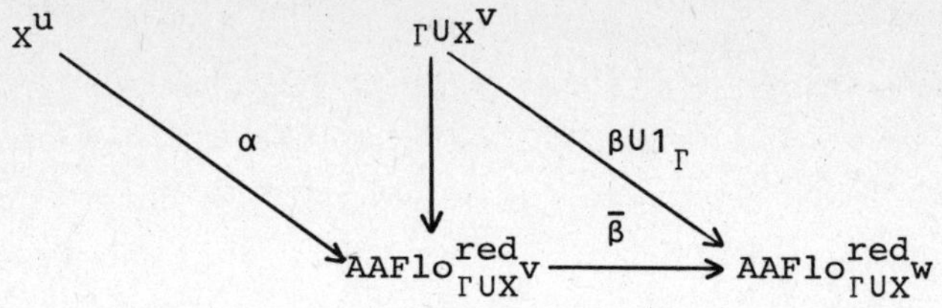

Figure 7

The associativity of $\lhd$ is an obvious consequence of the associativity of the composition of mappings and of the uniqueness of the extensions to morphisms.

For $\alpha \in RFS_\Gamma(u,v)$ and $\beta \in RFS_\Gamma(u',v)$ $<\alpha,\beta> \in RFS_\Gamma(uu',v)$, the <u>pairing</u> of α and β, is defined by

$$x_i^{uu'} <\alpha,\beta> := \begin{cases} x_i^u \alpha, & \text{if } i \in [|u|] \\ x_{i-|u|}^{u'} \beta, & \text{if } i \in |u| + [|u'|] \end{cases}$$

For $u \in \mathbb{N}_o^*$ there is an obvious definition of the identity scheme $1_u \in RFS_\Gamma(u,u)$ and for each $i \in [|u|]$ the i-th injection $\iota_i^u \in RFS_\Gamma(u_i,u)$ is defined by $x^{u_i} \iota_i^u := x_i^u$.

Obviously we have for all $\alpha \in RFS_\Gamma(u,v)$, $\beta \in RFS_\Gamma(u',v)$

$$\iota_{(1)}^{u,u'} \lhd <\alpha,\beta> = \alpha \quad , \quad \iota_{(2)}^{u,u'} \lhd <\alpha,\beta> = \beta,$$

and for all $\alpha \in RFS_\Gamma(uu',v)$ $\quad <\iota_{(1)}^{u,u'} \lhd \alpha, \iota_{(2)}^{u,u'} \lhd \beta> = \alpha$

where $\iota_{(i)}^{u,u'}$ is the i-th generalized injection ($i \in [2]$).

Thus RFS_Γ is an $\mathbb{N}_o$-sorted algebraic theory [ADJ5].

Looking for interpretations of recursive Γ-flowchart schemes (or "generalized interpretations" in the sense of [G2]) we have to introduce "functional theories":

Let T be an ω-continuous scalar iteration flow theory over MAP.

For each $n<\omega$ define $T_s(1,n) := \{t \in T(1,n) \mid \bot_{1,n} \leq t\}$, i.e. $T_s(1,n)$ is the set of all nonisolated elements of $T(1,n)$ or the maximal strict subset of $T(1,n)$. For $u \in \mathbb{N}_o^*$ with $|u|=k$ define

$T_s^u := T_s(1,u\ ) \times \cdots \times T_s(1,u_k)$ and $T^\varepsilon := \{\varepsilon\}$. Then define $CF(T)(u,v) := [T_s^v \to T_s^u]_c$, the set of all ω-continuous mappings from T_s^v to T_s^u. For $\alpha \in CF(T)(u,v)$ and $\beta \in CF(T)(v,w)$ define the <u>composition</u> of α and β $\alpha \square \beta \in CF(T)(u,w)$ by $\alpha \square \beta := \beta \circ \alpha$ where $\circ$ is the usual composition of mappings. Now the <u>ω-continuous functional theory over T</u> is the category CF(T) with sets of objects $\mathbb{N}_o^*$, sets of morphisms $CF(T)(u,v)$ and composition $\square$.

The <u>i-th injection</u> $\iota_i^u \in CF(T)(u_i,u)$ may be defined by $(t_1,\ldots,t_k)\iota_i^u := t_i$, where $|u|=k$ and $(t_1,\ldots,t_k)\in T_s^u$. Furthermore define the pairing of $\alpha\in CF(T)(u,v)$ and $\beta\in CF(T)(u',v)$ for all $t\in T_s^v$ by $t<\alpha,\beta> := (t\alpha,t\beta)$. Now it is easily verified that CF(T) is an $\mathbb{N}_o$-sorted algebraic theory.

Paralleling the results which have been obtained e.g. in [G2] [G4] in case of recursive tree schemes the following theorem is derived in [S1], making heavy use of results of section 2 especially of theorem 7:

<u>Theorem 8</u>

If T is an ω-continuous scalar iteration flow theory over MAP, then every strict interpretation $I:\Gamma\to T$ uniquely defines a morphism of algebraic theories $I^{\#}: RFS_\Gamma \to CF(T)$.

Thus to interpret a recursive flowchart scheme we only have to know the interpretation of Γ.

4. Fixpoint Semantics

In this section we show how to obtain fixpoint semantics of recursive Γ-flowchart schemes.

Let α be a recursive Γ-flowchart scheme from u to uv. Then $\beta\in RFS_\Gamma(u,v)$ is a <u>fixpoint</u> of α iff $\beta=\alpha\lhd\!<\beta,1_v>$ (compare [ADJ1]). As usual we are interested in deriving a least fixpoint of α. Thus we define a partial order on RFS_Γ by extending the partial order of Flo_Γ, i.e. for each $\alpha,\beta\in RFS_\Gamma(u,v)$ we have $\alpha\le\beta$ iff for each $i\in[|u|]$ $x_i^u\alpha \le x_i^u\beta$. Further let $\bot_{u,v}\in RFS_\Gamma(u,v)$ be defined by $x_i^u\bot_{u,v} := \bot_{1,u_i}$ where $\bot_{1,u_i}$ is the least element of the weakly strict set $A\dot{A}Flo_\Gamma^{red}(1,u_i)$ as illustrated by figure 8.

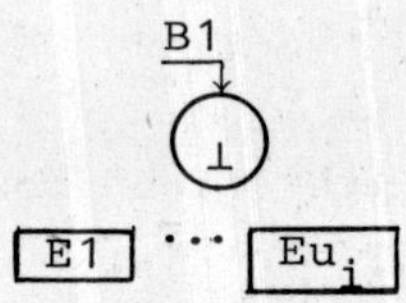

Figure 8

Since all the Γ-flows occuring in recursive Γ-flowchart schemes are nontrivial, $RFS_\Gamma(u,v)$ is a strict set. As demonstrated in [S1] we even have

<u>Theorem 9</u>

RFS_Γ is an ω-continuous algebraic theory.

Analogously a partial order on CF(T) can be defined where T is an ω-continuous scalar iteration flow theory over MAP.

For $\alpha,\beta\in CF(T)(u,v)$ define $\alpha\leq\beta$ iff for all $t\in T_s^v$ we have $t\alpha\leq t\beta$. Further let $\perp_{u,v}\in CF(T)(u,v)$ be defined by

$$t\perp_{u,v}:=(\perp_{1,u_1},\ldots,\perp_{1,u_k})\in T_s^u$$

where $|u|=k$ and $t\in T_s^v$. Analogously to theorem 9 we get

<u>Theorem 10</u>

If T is an ω-continuous scalar iteration flow theory over MAP, then CF(T) is an ω-continuous algebraic theory.

As an extension to theorem 8 we get

<u>Theorem 11</u>

If T is an ω-continuous scalar iteration flow theory over MAP, then every strict interpretation $I:\Gamma\to T$ uniquely defines an ω-continuous morphism $I^{\#}:RFS_{\Gamma}\to CF(T)$.

In order to obtain least fixpoints of recursive Γ-flowchart schemes we look at the well known fixpoint construction in ω-continuous algebraic theories [ADJ1] [ADJ4] [G2] [G4]:

Let S be an arbitrary set, CT an S-sorted ω-continuous algebraic theory. For each $u,v\in S^*$ and $\alpha\in CT(u,uv)$ an ω-chain $(\alpha^{(i)})_{i<\omega}$ is defined by

$$\alpha^{(0)}:=\langle\perp_{u,v},1_v\rangle$$

$$\alpha^{(i+1)}:=\langle\alpha,\iota_{(2)}^{u,v}\rangle\circ\alpha^{(i)}$$

Then for all $i<\omega$ $\alpha^{(i)}\leq\alpha^{(i+1)}$. Define $\alpha^{\nabla}:=\bigsqcup_{i<\omega}\alpha^{(i)}\in CT(uv,v)$ and $\alpha^{+}:=\iota_{(1)}^{u,v}\circ\alpha^{\nabla}\in CT(u,v)$. Then α^{+} is the least fixpoint of the equation $\eta=\alpha\circ\langle\eta,1_v\rangle$ and we get the following result:

<u>Theorem 12</u>

If CT_1 and CT_2 are S-sorted ω-continuous algebraic theories, then every ω-continuous morphism $\phi:CT_1\to CT_2$ respects ∇ and $^+$, i.e. for each $u,v\in S^*$ and $\alpha\in CT_1(u,uv)$ we have

$$\alpha^{\nabla}\phi=(\alpha\phi)^{\nabla}\quad,\quad\alpha^{+}\phi=(\alpha\phi)^{+}$$

and for all $i<\omega$ $\qquad \alpha^{(i)}\phi=(\alpha\phi)^{(i)}$.

By means of theorems 9, 10, and 11 we thus get

<u>Theorem 13</u>

If T is an ω-continuous scalar iteration flow theory over MAP, then every strict interpretation $I:\Gamma\to T$ uniquely defines an ω-continuous morphism of ω-continuous algebraic theories

$$I^{\#}: RFS_{\Gamma} \to CF(T)$$

such that for all $u,v \in N_0^*$ and $\alpha \in RFS_{\Gamma}(u,uv)$ we have

$$\alpha^{\nabla} I^{\#} = (\alpha I^{\#})^{\nabla} \quad , \quad \alpha^{+} I^{\#} = (\alpha I^{\#})^{+}$$

and for all $i<\omega$ $\qquad \alpha^{(i)} I^{\#} = (\alpha I^{\#})^{(i)}$.

Thus in case of recursive Γ-flowchart schemes we get the same "Mezei-Wright"-result as is well known in case of recursive tree schemes.

Example 3

Let $\alpha \in RFS_{\Gamma}(112,112)$ be as in example 2. Then we have

$\alpha^{(0)}$:

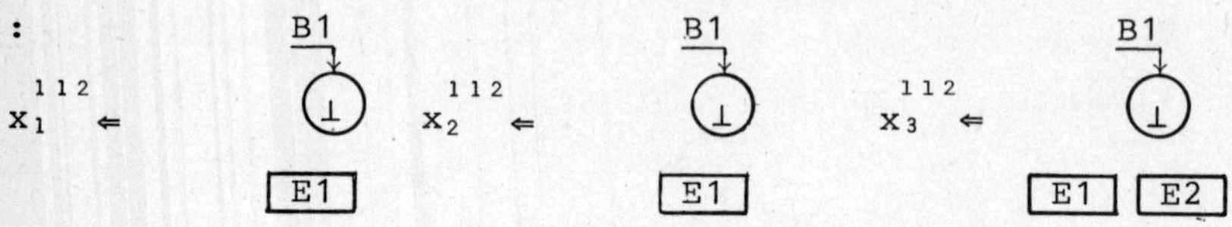

Figure 9

$\alpha^{(1)}$:

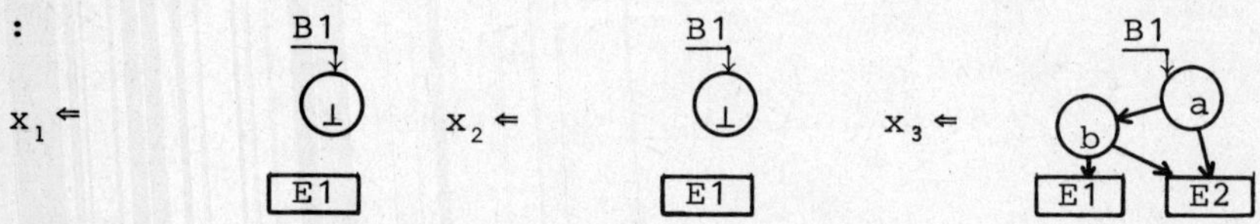

Figure 10

$\alpha^{(2)}$:

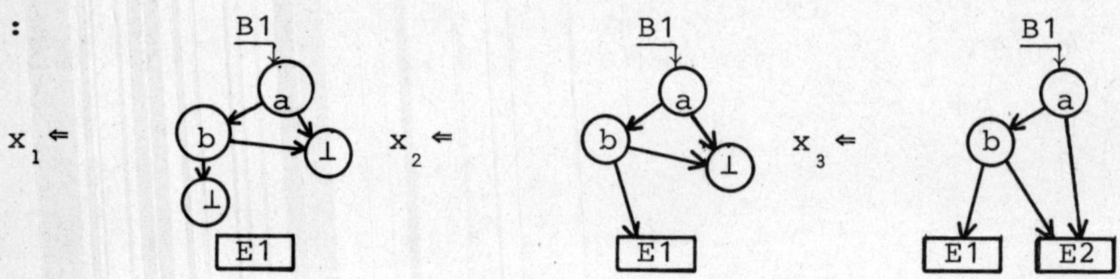

Figure 11

$\alpha^{(3)}$:

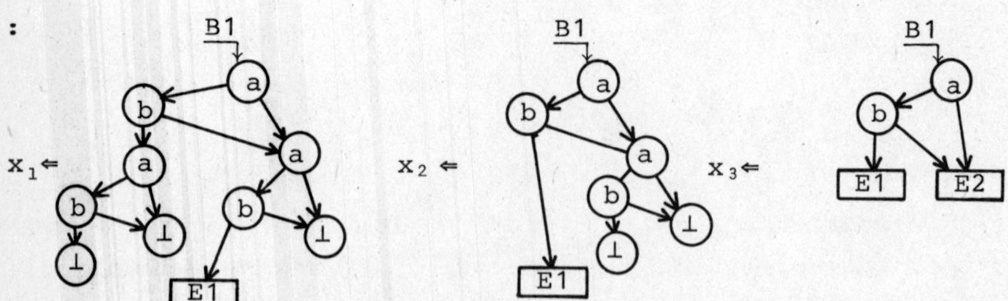

Figure 12

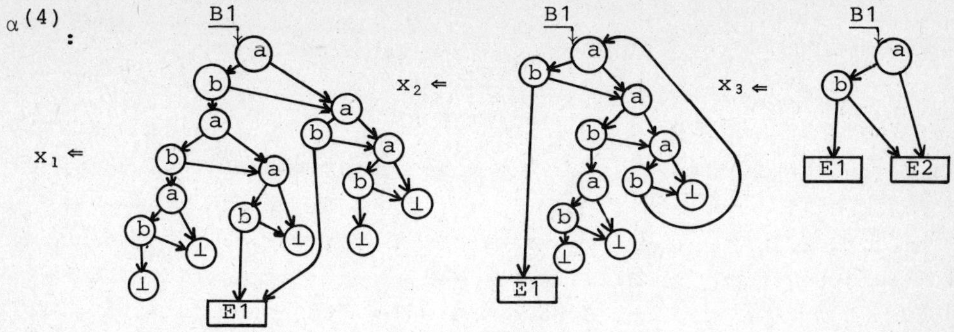

Figure 13

and $x_1^{112}\alpha^{\nabla}=x_1^{112}\alpha^{+}$ is shaped as follows

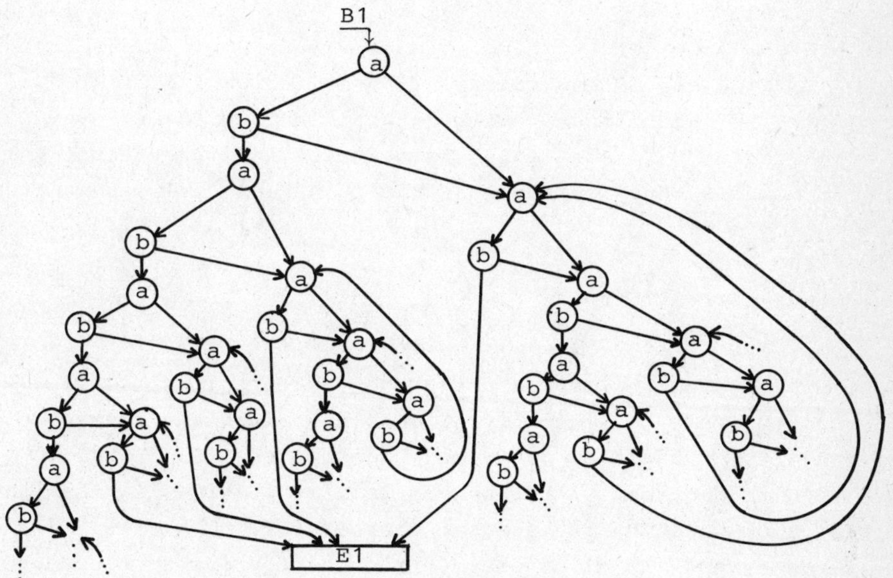

Figure 14

Theorem 13 naturally leads to fixpoint semantics of recursive Γ-flowchart schemes:

Let $u \in \mathbb{N}_o^*$ and $\alpha \in RFS_{\Gamma}(u,u)$. If T is an ω-continuous scalar iteration flow theory over MAP, and if $I:\Gamma \rightarrow T$ is a strict interpretation of Γ, then the <u>(T,I)-semantics</u> of α is defined to be $(\alpha I^{\#})^{+}$.

Since for all $\alpha \in RFS_{\Gamma}(u,u)$ we have $\alpha^{\nabla}=\alpha^{+}$, this could be rewritten as:

$$(\alpha I^{\#})^{+}=\alpha\nabla_{I}^{\#}$$
$$=(\bigsqcup_{i<\omega}\alpha^{(i)})I^{\#}$$
$$=\bigsqcup_{i<\omega}(\alpha^{(i)}I^{\#})$$

Thus the (T,I)-semantics of α is the least upper bound of an ω-chain of approximating semantics of α.

Let us call $\alpha,\beta\in RFS_{\Gamma}(u,u)$ <u>equivalent</u> ($\alpha\sim\beta$) iff for all ω-continuous scalar iteration flow theories T over MAP and for all strict interpretations I of Γ in T α and β have the same (T,I)-semantics, i.e. iff $(\alpha I^{\#})^{+}=(\beta I^{\#})^{+}$. We get the following result:

<u>Theorem 14</u>

For all $\alpha,\beta\in RFS_{\Gamma}(u,u)$ we have $\alpha\sim\beta \Leftrightarrow \alpha^{+}=\beta^{+}$.

<u>Proof</u>

From theorem 13 we get $\alpha\sim\beta \Leftrightarrow (\alpha^{+})I^{\#}=(\beta^{+})I^{\#}$.

Thus $\alpha^{+}=\beta^{+}$ implies the equivalence of α and β. On the other hand $AAFlo_{\Gamma}^{red}$ is an ω-continuous scalar iteration flow theory over MAP, and the embedding of Γ into $AAFlo_{\Gamma}^{red}$ is a strict interpretation. The equivalence of α and β thus implies that their ($AAFlo_{\Gamma}^{red}$, 1_{Γ})-semantics is the same, whence $\alpha^{+}=\beta^{+}$. □

5. Conclusion

In this paper we have shown how algebraic semantics can be defined for recursive Γ-flowchart schemes using the freeness results for reducible Γ-flowcharts. This considerably extends the algebraic characterization of flowcharts as begun by Elgot and Shepherdson [ES1][ES2].

Our results contrast with those of Gallier [G1][G3] in that they are derived independent of the special choice of Γ.

In [S2] an example is given where Γ-flowcharts represent nondeterministic programs on a stack machine thus providing an extension of the target language used by Thatcher, Wagner, and Wright in [ADJ6]. The results of this paper might lead to an extension of their compiler correctness results to programming languages incorporating recursive structures.

References

[AC] Allen, F.E., Cocke, J.: Graph Theoretic Constructs for Control Flow Analysis. IBM Research Report RC3922, 1972

[ADJ1] Goguen, J.A., Thatcher, J.W., Wright, J.B.: Rational Algebraic Theories and Fixed Point Solutions. Proc. 17th Symp. Found. of Comput. Sci., Houston, Texas, 147-158(1976)

[ADJ2] Goguen, J.A., Thatcher, J.W., Wagner, E.G., Wright, J.B.: Initial Algebra Semantics and Continuous Algebras. J. Assoc. Comput. Mach. 24, 68-95(1977)

[ADJ3] Wagner, E.G., Thatcher, J.W., Wright, J.B.: Free Continuous Theories. IBM Research Report RC6906, 1977

[ADJ4] Thatcher, J.W., Wagner, E.G., Wright, J.B.: Notes on Algebraic Fundamentals for Theoretical Computer Science. Lect. Notes, 3 rd Advanced Course Found. of Comput. Sci., Amsterdam, 1978

[ADJ5] Wagner, E.G., Wright, J.B., Thatcher, J.W.: Many-Sorted and Ordered Algebraic Theories. IBM Research Report RC7595, 1979

[ADJ6] Thatcher, J.W., Wagner, E.G., Wright, J.B.: More on Advice on Structuring Compilers and Proving Them Correct. Theor. Comput. Sci. 15, 223-249(1981)

[BT] Bloom, S.L., Tindell, R.: Algebraic and Graph-Theoretic Characterizations of Structured Flowchart Schemes. Theor. Comput. Sci. 9, 265-286(1979)

[E1] Elgot, C.C.: Monadic Computation and Iterative Algebraic Theories. Proc. Logic Colloquium 1973, North-Holland, 175-230(1975)

[E2] Elgot, C.C.: Structured Programming With and Without GOTO Statements. IEEE Trans. Soft. Eng., Vol. SE-2, 41-53(1976)

[ES1] Elgot, C.C., Shepherdson, J.C.: A Semantically Meaningful Characterization of Reducible Flowchart Schemes. Theor. Comput. Sci. 8, 325-357(1979)

[ES2] Elgot, C.C., Shepherdson, J.C.: An Equational Axiomatization of the Algebra of Reducible Flowchart Schemes. IBM Research Report RC8221, 1980

[G1] Gallier, J.H.: Semantics and Correctness of Classes of Deterministic and Nondeterministic Recursive Programs. Ph. D. Dissertation, UCLA, 1977

[G2] Gallier, J.H.: Recursion Schemes and Generalized Interpretations. Proc. 6th ICALP, Graz, 1979, Lect. Notes Comput. Sci. 71, 256-270(1979)

[G3] Gallier, J.H.: Nondeterministic Flowchart Programs With Recursive Procedures: Semantics and Correctness I, II. Theor. Comput. Sci. 13, 193-224, 239-270(1981)

[G4] Gallier, J.H.: Recursion-Closed Algebraic Theories. J. Comput. Syst. Sci. 23, 69-105(1981)

[HU1] Hecht, M.S., Ullman, J.D.: Flow Graph Reducibility. SIAM J. Comput. 1, 188-202(1972)

[HU2] Hecht, M.S., Ullman, J.D.: Characterization of Reducible Flow Graphs. J. Assoc. Comput. Mach. 21, 367-375(1974)

[ML] MacLane, S.: Kategorien. Springer Verlag, 1972

[N] Nivat, M.: On the Interpretation of Recursive Polyadic Program Schemes, Symposia Mathematica, Vol. 15, Academic Press, 225-281(1975)

[S1] Schmeck, H.: Zur algebraischen Charakterisierung reduzierbarer Flußdiagramme. Bericht 3/81, Inst. f. Inform. u. Prakt. Math., Universität Kiel, 1981

[S2] Schmeck, H.: Algebraic Characterization of Reducible Flowcharts. Submitted for Publication, 1981

THE COMPLEXITY OF PROMISE PROBLEMS

Alan L. Selman[1] and Yacov Yacobi[2]

ABSTRACT

A "promise problem" is a formulation of a partial decision problem. Complexity issues about promise problems arise from Even and Yacobi's work in public-key cryptography [1]. Using a notion of Turing reducibility between promise problems, this paper disproves a conjecture made in [1].

---

1 Computer Science Department, Iowa State University, Ames, Iowa 50011. This paper was written while the author visited the Computer Science Department, Technion, Haifa, Israel, with funds provided by the United States-Israel Educational Foundation (Fulbright Award). This research was supported in part by the National Science Foundation under grant MCS77-23493 A02.

2 Electrical Engineering Department, Technion, Haifa, Israel. Part of this research was done while the author visited the Electrical Engineering and Computer Sciences Dept., University of California at San Diego, La Jolla, CA, U.S.A.

1. INTRODUCTION

This paper is concerned with several complexity issues about certain kinds of partial decision problems. The nature of these partial decision problems can be best explained by contrasting them with ordinary decision problems. A decision problem is given as a predicate $P(x)$. The question, of course, is to determine whether there exists an algorithm A that solves the problem, i.e., such that $A(x)$ converges for all meaningful input instances x and such that

$$\forall x[A(x) = \text{"yes"} \leftrightarrow P(x)].$$

In practice, one often encounters problems for which only a subclass of the domain of all instances is of concern. Such problems are here called promise problems. Informly, a promise problem has structure

input x ,

promise $Q(x)$,

property $R(x)$,

where Q and R are predicates. Formally, a promise problem is a pair of predicates (Q,R). The predicate Q is called the promise. A deterministic Turing machine M solves the promise problem (Q,R) if

$$\forall x[Q(x) \rightarrow [M(x)\downarrow \wedge (M(x) = \text{"yes"} \leftrightarrow R(x))]].$$

If a Turing machine M solves (Q,R), then the language $L(M)$ accepted by M is a solution to (Q,R).

The study of problems with this format is certainly not new. For partial recursive functions one wants a program that computes correctly on its domain. And, techniques for establishing correctness of a program are typically distinct from halting issues. Problems of this kind have also arisen in context-free language theory [4].

Complexity issues about promise problems arise from Even and Yacobi's work in public-key cryptography [1]. In [1], a public-key cryptosystem is described and the basic question of whether there exist systems with NP-hard cracking problem is raised. The cracking problem is describable as a promise problem (Q,R), with the additional added feature that both (Q,R) and the complementary problem $(Q, \sim R)$ have solutions in NP. They then introduce a new hypothesis that extends the popular conjecture that NP is not closed under complements, and observe on the basis of this hypothesis that there exist no public-key cryptosystems with NP-hard cracking problem.

We show here that this hypothesis is false. Related results are obtained also. These results indicate that complexity classes of promise problems have different structural properties than do complexity classes of decision problems.

2. BASIC CONCEPTS

We require notation for promise problems that have solutions in NP. One possibility is to extend the definition of NP to include promise problems. However, in order to keep NP sacrosanct for decision problems (encoded as languages), the following notation is introduced instead.

Definition 1: NPP is the class of all promise problems (Q,R) such that (Q,R) has a solution in NP. Co-NPP is the class of all promise problems (Q,R) such that (Q, ~R) is in NPP.

A promise problem (Q,R) belongs to co-NPP if and only if (Q,R) has a solution in co-NP. Also note that a language L is a solution to (Q,R) if and only if ~L is a solution to (Q, ~R). Thus, L is a solution in NP to (Q,R) if and only if ~L is a solution in co-NP to (Q, ~R).

Every set S in NP may be considered to be a promise problem (Σ^*,S) with the trivial promise Σ^*, where S is a language over the finite alphabet Σ. In this way, NPP is a proper extension of NP, co-NPP is a proper extension of co-NP, and NPP ∩ co-NPP is a proper extension of NP ∩ co-NP.

Let $\leq_m^P$ and $\leq_T^P$ denote polynomial-time many-one and Turing reducibilities, respectively. Recall that a language L is NP-complete if L is in NP and every set in NP is $\leq_m^P$-reducible to L. A language L is NP-hard if every set in NP is $\leq_T^P$-reducible to L.

Definition 2: A promise problem (Q,R) is NP-hard if every solution L of (Q,R) is NP-hard.

It follows from the definition that if an NP-hard promise problem has a tractable solution (i.e., in P), then P = NP. For an oracle Turing machine M with oracle set A, let L(M,A) denote the language accepted by M with oracle A. According to Definition 2, (Q,R) is NP-hard if and only if, for every set S in NP and for every solution A of (Q,R), there is an oracle Turing machine M that operates in polynomial time so that S = L(M,A).

Definition 3: A promise problem (Q,R) is uniformly NP-hard if, for every set S in NP, there is an oracle Turing machine M that operates in polynomial time such that, for all solutions A of (Q,R), S = L(M,A).

Uniformly NP-hard obviously implies NP-hard. The converse can be expected to be false but no proof is yet known. In any case, the main results of the next section will hold for both notions.

The concepts thus far defined can now be used as bases for definitions of reductions and uniform reductions between promise problems.

Definition 4: A promise problem (Q,R) is Turing reducible in polynomial time to a promise problem (S,T), in symbols, $(Q,R) \leq_T^{PP} (S,T)$, if, for every solution A of (S,T), there is an oracle Turing machine M that operates in polynomial time such that M with oracle A solves (Q,R).

Definition 5: A promise problem (Q,R) is uniformly Turing reducible in polynomial time to a promise problem (S,T), $(Q,R) \leq_{UT}^{PP} (S,T)$, if there is an oracle Turing machine M that operates in polynomial time such that, for every solution A of (S,T), M with oracle A solves (Q,R).

Lemma 1:

(i) $\leq_T^{PP}$ and $\leq_{UT}^{PP}$ are transitive relations.

(ii) $(Q,R) \leq_{UT}^{PP} (S,T)$ implies $(Q,R) \leq_T^{PP} (S,T)$.

(iii) (Q,R) is NP-hard if and only if, for every set S in NP, $(\Sigma^*,S) \leq_T^{PP} (Q,R)$.

(iv) (Q,R) is uniformly NP-hard if and only if, for every set S in NP, $(\Sigma^*,S) \leq_{UT}^{PP} (Q,R)$.

Whether $\leq_{UT}^{PP}$ implies $\leq_T^{PP}$ is an open question.

3. ELEMENTARY RESULTS

Since we are focusing on polynomial time complexity issues, let us assume henceforth that, for all promise problems (Q,R) mentioned, both Q and R are recursive predicates. Furthermore, if M is a Turing machine that solves (Q,R), then M halts on every input. Therefore, every solution to a promise problem is a recursive set. The solution criterion becomes

$$Q(x) \rightarrow (M(x) = \text{"yes"} \Longleftrightarrow R(x)).$$

The recursive solutions to a promise problem (Q,R) can be completely characterized set theoretically: A is a recursive solution to (Q,R) if and only if $A = (Q \cap R) \cup B$, where $Q \cap B = \emptyset$ and B is recursive. In particular, $Q \cap R$ and R are both solutions, and $Q \cap R$ is the smallest solution. If (Q,R) is an NP-hard promise problem, then R and $Q \cap R$ are NP-hard sets.

Promise problems with tractable promise can be analyzed rather completely. First of all, R is NP-hard and Q is in P does not imply that (Q,R) is NP-hard. (Take Q to be empty or finite and observe that $Q \cap R$ is either empty or finite.) To obtain a non-trivial example, use Ladner's result [2] to obtain an NP-complete set R and a set Q in P such that $Q \cap R$ is not NP-hard (although $Q \cap R$ is in NP-P assuming $P \neq NP$). Thus, (Q,R) is not NP-hard.

Theorem 1: If R is NP-hard, Q is in P, and (Q,R) has a solution in P, then $(\sim Q,R)$ is NP-hard.

Proof: Let R be NP-hard, Q in P, and let A in P be a solution to (Q,R). Let B be an arbitrary solution to $(\sim Q,R)$. To show that $(\sim Q,R)$ is NP-hard, it suffices to show $R \leq_T^P B$. This is accomplished by the following algorithm with oracle set B.

```
input x;
if Q(x)
   then if  x ∈ A then accept else reject
            {Q(x) → (x ∈ A <-> R(x))}
   else if  x ∈ B then accept else reject
           {~Q(x) → (x ∈ B <-> R(x))}.
```

□

Lemma 2: If Q is in P and A is a solution to (Q,R), then $Q \cap R \leq_T^P A$.

Proof: Let Q belong to P and let A be any solution to (Q,R). The reduction is given by the following algorithm:

```
input x;
if Q(x)
   then if  x ∈ A  {Q(x) → (x ∈ A <-> R(x))}
                then  accept
                else  reject
   else reject.
```

□

As an immediate consequence we have the following theorem:

Theorem 2: If Q is in P and $Q \cap R$ is an NP-hard set, then (Q,R) is an NP-hard promise problem.

Theorem 2 can be used to generate many interesting examples of NP-hard promise problems in NPP. The technique is this: let R be any known NP-complete problem and let $Q \cap R$ be a refinement that is still NP-complete, where Q belongs to P. Then, (Q,R) is NP-hard. For example, let SAT be an encoding of the satisfactory formulas of propositional logic, and let $\underset{\sim}{3}$ be an encoding of all formulas with three literals per clause. $\underset{\sim}{3} \cap$ SAT is the well-known NP-complete set 3SAT. Since $\underset{\sim}{3}$ is in P, Theorem 2 applies. Hence, $(\underset{\sim}{3}, \text{SAT})$ is an NP-hard promise problem in NPP.

Theorem 3: If Q belongs to P and (Q,R) is an NP-hard promise problem, then (Q,R) is uniformly NP-hard.

Proof: Since (Q,R) is NP-hard, $Q \cap R$ is an NP-hard solution. Let M be an oracle Turing machine that operates in polynomial time and that implements the algorithm given in the proof of Lemma 2. Let S be any set in NP. Then, the machine which $\leq_T^P$-reduces S to $Q \cap R$ followed by M uniformly reduces S to each solution of (Q,R). □

4. ON THE CLASS NPP ∩ co-NPP

It is well-known that NP ∩ co-NP contains an NP-hard set if and only if NP is closed under complements. Hence, the former property is unlikely to be true. It is hypothesized in [1] that there exist no NP-hard promise problems in NPP ∩ co-NPP. By the following lemma it is certainly reasonable to conjecture that NPP ≠ co-NPP.

Lemma 3: NPP = co-NPP if and only if NP = co-NP.

Proof: Since NPP and co-NPP are extensions of NP and co-NP, respectively, the proof from left to right is trivial. The converse implication follows from the observation that if A is a solution to (Q,R), then $\bar{A}$ is a solution to (Q, ~R). □

However, we now provide an example of an NP-hard promise problem in NPP ∩ co-NPP. Let ⊕ denote the logical operator "exclusive or". Let SAT denote the NP-complete satisfiability problem. We will take the liberty also of writing SAT as a predicate, so that SAT(x) asserts that x is satisfiable. Let EX denote the predicate defined by EX(x,y) <-> SAT(x) ⊕ SAT(y). Define SAT1(x) = $\lambda x\, \lambda y$ SAT(x).

Theorem 4:
(i) (EX, SAT1) ∈ NPP ∩ co-NPP.
(ii) (EX, SAT1) is NP-hard.

Proof: (i) Let x and y be input words and suppose the promise EX(x,y) is true. Then, ~SAT(x) is equivalent to the predicate SAT(y). Thus, it is evident that both (EX, SAT1) and (EX, ~SAT1) belong to NPP.

(ii) Let A be any solution to (EX, SAT1). (Technically, A is a language consisting of encoded ordered pairs; we will write <x,y> ∈ A to denote membership in A.) If SAT(x) ⊕ SAT(y), then <x,y> ∈ A <-> SAT(x). To show that A is NP-hard it suffices to show that SAT $\leq_T^P$ A, by the following iterative algorithm with oracle A.

Let ψ be a program variable that ranges over propositional formulas. Let $\varphi(\sigma_1,\ldots,\sigma_n)$ be an input formula with Boolean variables $\sigma_1,\ldots,\sigma_n$.

```
ψ := φ(σ_1,...,σ_n);
for i := 1 to n do
    {ψ has free variables σ_i,...,σ_n}
    if <ψ(0,σ_{i+1},...,σ_n), ψ(1,σ_{i+1},...,σ_n)> ∈ A
        then ψ := ψ(0,σ_{i+1},...,σ_n)
        else ψ := ψ(1,σ_{i+1},...,σ_n);
{ψ is a variable-free Boolean expression}
if ψ has value 1
    then accept {φ is satisfiable}
    else reject {φ is not satisfiable}.
```

The algorithm clearly operates in polynomial time. If the accept state is reached, then a satisfying assignment for φ has been found. Conversely, suppose φ is satisfiable. We claim that the loop preserves satisfiability of ψ. At each execution of the loop body, if $\psi(\sigma_i,\ldots,\sigma_n)$ is satisfiable, then $\psi(0,\sigma_{i+1},\ldots,\sigma_n)$ is satisfiable or $\psi(1,\sigma_{i+1},\ldots,\sigma_n)$ is satisfiable. If exactly one of these is satisfiable, then the promise is true and the oracle query provides correct information. If both of these are true, then ψ remains true independent of the value of the oracle query. Hence, the algorithm correctly reduces SAT to the solution A of (EX, SAT1) in polynomial time. □

Since the algorithm just given does not depend on choice of solution, we have the following corollary.

Corollary 1: (EX, SAT1) is uniformly NP-hard.

Corollary 2: For each promise problem (Q,R) in NPP, $(Q,R) \leq_T^{PP}$ (EX, SAT1).

Proof: Let (Q,R) ∈ NPP. Let L be a solution in NP to (Q,R). Let A be an arbitrary solution to (EX, SAT1). Let M be an oracle Turing machine that operates in polynomial time such that L = L(M,A). By definition, M with oracle A solves (Q,R). □

Whereas NP ∩ co-NP probably does not contain a set that is complete for NP ∩ co-NP [3], we see here that NPP ∩ co-NPP does contain the complete promise problem (EX, SAT1).

Open Question: Does there exist an NP-hard promise problem (Q,R) in NPP ∩ co-NPP with promise Q belonging to NP? The reader may verify that if no such promise problems exist then the conclusions of [1] still hold.

REFERENCES

1. Even, S. and Yacobi, Y., Cryptocomplexity and NP-completeness, Proc. of ICALP-80, Springer-Verlag Lecture Notes in Computer Science, Vol. 80, 195-207.

2. Ladner, R.E., On the structure of polynomial time reducibility, J. ACM 22 (1975).

3. Sipser, M., On relativization and the existence of complete sets, this conference.

4. Ullian, J.S., Partial algorithm problems for context free languages, Information and Control, Vol. 11, 1967, 80-101.

GLOBAL AND LOCAL INVARIANTS IN TRANSITION SYSTEMS

by Joseph SIFAKIS
IMAG, BP53X, 38041 Grenoble Cedex, France

Abstract :

Given a transition system and a cover P of the set of its states, a set of local invariants with respect to P is defined as a set of predicates in bijection with the blocks of P and in such a way that a local invariant be true every time the system is in a state belonging to the corresponding block of the cover.

This definition is proved to be sufficiently general in the sense that any proof made by using global invariants can be also made by using sets of local invariants. The same result is proved for two more restrictive definitions of the notion of local invariant by using well-known properties of connections between lattices.

Finally, it is shown how the theory of connections can provide a general frame for tackling the problem of decomposing a global assertion into a logically equivalent set of local assertions.

I. INTRODUCTION

The difficulty in comparing the different methods for proving programs, is due on the one hand to the big variety of the formalisms used to represent them and on the other hand to the diversity of the approaches followed.

Carrying out a proof consists in searching and proving a set of assertions about the program under study. Several classifications of proof methods can be made according to different criteria concerning the way of generating assertions, the way of establishing their truth, the type of the assertions etc... Concerning the type of the assertions used in proof methods at least two classification criteria can be considered.

- The first, concerns the nature of the properties expressed by the assertions. For example, an assertion can express an <u>invariant property</u> [PNUE 79] [SIF 79] i.e. a statement which remains always true or a <u>non-invariant</u> one i.e. a statement which can or should become true in some future.
- The second, concerns the locality or the globality of the assertions. In some methods, assertions are associated with subsets of program states (for example, with labels representing control points as in [FLO 67]) while in other methods global assertions are used (as in [KEL 76]).

The different kinds of properties which are necessary for expressing the correction of programs, especially of the concurrent ones, have been the object of some studies [LAM 80] [MAN 81] [PNU 79] [QUE 81] [SIF 79]. However, although the distinction between local and global assertions is quite easy to apprehend, there exists no study, to our knowledge, establishing in a formal manner relations between these two notions. Such a study could allow the comparison of the different proof methods as far as their efficiency and limitations are concerned and also the study of general problems such as,

- How to decompose a global assertion into a set of logically equivalent local assertions expressing a property of the same type ?
- Among all the possible decompositions are there someones leading to simpler proof methods ?
- Finally, are the two approaches by global and local assertions equivalent, i.e. can, for any proof method using global assertions, a proof method using local assertions be found and conversely ?

The aim of this paper is to answer these questions in the case of transition systems, when assertions express invariant properties, and also to propose a general approach for studying this problem in the case of non-invariant properties. The choice of transition systems as a working model has been motivated by the desire to obtain results simple to formulate and of general application.

Proof methods using global assertions seem to be more general since for any local assertion it is possible to find an equivalent global assertion (maybe, after introducing some labels or auxiliary variables to characterize control points). Thus, a main problem to be studied is the existence, for any global assertion, of equivalent sets of local assertions. Tackling this problem in the case of invariants requires first, a definition of the notions of global and local invariant for transition systems.

If for global invariants a generally accepted definition exists (see, for example, [KEL 76] [MAZ 74] [SIF 79]), this is not the case for local invariants for which a (hopefully) sufficiently general definition must be devised. This is made in part II where, given a cover P of the state set Q of a transition system, a set of local invariants with respect to P is defined as a set of unary predicates on Q the elements of which are in bijection with the blocks of P and such that a local invariant be true every time the system is in a state belonging to the corresponding block of the cover. Also, it is provided a characterization of both local and global invariants as fixed points of monotonic predicate transformers built from one and the same basic predicate transformer. In part III, it is shown that the proposed definition of local invariants is sufficient in the sense that for any unary predicate X and any given cover of the set of states there exists a set of predicates Y in bijection with this cover such that X is a global invariant if and only if Y is a set of local invariants with respect to P. Furthermore, two more restrictive definitions for local invariants are proved to be sufficient by using well-known results on the connections between lattices. These results can be applied for the decomposition of global assertions other than invariants. In part IV, it is shown that the notion of invariant assertion, commonly used for proving programs, can be deduced from the definition of local invariant when a transition system represents a program. In this case, the fixed point equations characterizing local invariants can be simplified to obtain semantical equations of programs.

II. THE NOTIONS OF GLOBAL AND LOCAL INVARIANT

II.1 Transition Systems

A transition system [KEL 72] is defined by a doublet $S = (Q,\rightarrow)$ where Q is a set of states and $\rightarrow$ is a transition relation on Q ($\rightarrow \subseteq Q\times Q$).

The relation $\rightarrow$ represents the transitions or actions of S : $q\rightarrow q'$ means that there exists an action executable from the state q and after its execution the resulting state is q'. The behaviour of a transition system from a given state q is represented by the set of the state sequences $q_0,..,q_i,q_{i+1}...$ such that $q=q_0$ and $q_i\rightarrow q_{i+1}$.

Transition systems are a very primitive model making use of few notions, such as those of state and transition which are at the base of every discrete model. They are a sequential non-deterministic model: sequential in the sense that only one transition can be executed at a time and non-determinstic in the sense that generally more than one transitions are executable from a given state. Clearly, every sequential discrete system can be represented, at some level of abstraction, by a transition system. Futhermore, in so far as concurrency in the functioning of a system can be represented by global non-determinism (as in [ASH 75] and [KEL 76]), transition systems can be considered as a primitive model for concurrent systems too.

II.2 Invariants as fixed points of monotonic operators

II.2.1 Definitions

Given a set Q, we identify a unary predicate on Q with its characteristic set. Thus, for a unary predicate P the following three notations are equivalent : $P(q)=\underline{true}$, $P(q)$, $q\in P$.

$L=(2^Q,\cup,\cap,-)$ represents the lattice of unary predicates on Q with the operations of disjunction, conjunction, complementation and $[L\rightarrow L]$ the set of the internal mappings (predicate transformers) of L. For $f,g\in[L\rightarrow L]$, $f\cup g$, $f\cap g$, $\bar{f},\tilde{f}$ and Id_L represent the functions $\lambda X\ .\ f(X)\cup g(X)$, $\lambda X\ .\ f(X)\cap g(X)$, $\lambda X\ .\ \overline{f(X)}$, $\lambda X\ .\ \bar{f}(\bar{X})$ and $\lambda X\ .\ X$.

Definition :

Given a transition system $S = (Q,\rightarrow)$, a (global) invariant of S is a predicate X on Q such that, $\forall q,q' \in Q$ (X(q) and $q \rightarrow q'$ implies X(q'))
i.e. X is a set of states containing all its possible sucessors.

Definition :

Let $S = (Q,\rightarrow)$ be a transition system and $P = (P_1,\ldots,P_s)$ be a tuple of predicates on Q such that $\bigcup_{i=1}^{s} P_i = Q$. A set of local invariants (SLI) with respect to P is a tuple of predicates $Y = (Y_1,\ldots,Y_s)$ such that $\forall q,q' \in Q$, $\forall i,k \in [1,s]$:
($Y_i(q)$ and $P_i(q)$ and $q \rightarrow q'$ and $P_k(q')$) implies $Y_k(q')$
i.e. if a state q satisfies P_i and the local invariant Y_i associated with P_i, then for every successor q' of q : $P_k(q')$ implies $Y_k(q')$.

II.2.2 The predicate transformer pre

Given a transition system $S = (Q,\rightarrow)$, pre denotes a predicate transformer ($pre \in [L \rightarrow L]$) defined by : pre $\overset{def}{=} \lambda X \, \lambda q \, . \, (\exists q' \, (q \rightarrow q'$ and $X(q')))$, i.e. pre (X) represents the set of the states from which it is possible to reach some state of X by executing one transition. Also, we denote by post the predicate transformer : post $\overset{def}{=} \lambda X \, \lambda q$. $(\exists q' \, (q' \rightarrow q$ and $X(q')))$, i.e. if $\overset{-1}{\rightarrow}$ is the inverse of $\rightarrow$, then the post predicate transformer for $(Q,\rightarrow)$ is the pre predicate transformer for $(Q,\overset{-1}{\rightarrow})$.

The following are well-known properties of the predicate transformer pre [HOA 78] [SIF 79].

Properties 1 :

For every transition system $S = (Q,\rightarrow)$,

a) pre $(\emptyset) = \emptyset$ and dually $\widetilde{pre}(Q) = Q$

b) for every sequence of predicates $\{X_i\}_i$

$pre(\bigcup_i X_i) = \bigcup_i pre(X_i)$ (distributivity w.r.t. to disjunction)

$\widetilde{pre}(\bigcap_i X_i) = \bigcap_i \widetilde{pre}(X_i)$

c) $X_1 \subseteq X_2$ implies $pre(X_1) \subseteq pre(X_2)$ (monotonicity)

$X_1 \subseteq X_2$ implies $\widetilde{pre}(X_1) \subseteq \widetilde{pre}(X_2)$

d) $pre(X) \cup pre(\bar{X}) = \overline{SINK}$, where $SINK = \{q \mid \nexists q'(q \rightarrow q')\}$

Properties 2 :

For every transition system $S = (Q,\rightarrow)$,

a) $pre \circ \widetilde{post} \subseteq Id_L$ and dually, $Id_L \subseteq \widetilde{pre} \circ post$

b) $post \circ \widetilde{pre} \subseteq Id_L$ and dually, $Id_L \subseteq \widetilde{post} \circ pre$

c) For X_1, X_2 predicates on Q,

$$pre(X_1)\cap pre(X_2)\cap[\widetilde{pre}(X_1)\cup\widetilde{pre}(X_2)] \subseteq pre(X_1\cap X_2)\subseteq pre(X_1)\cap pre(X_2) \quad \text{and dually,}$$

$$\widetilde{pre}(X_1)\cup\widetilde{pre}(X_2)\subseteq\widetilde{pre}(X_1\cup X_2) \subseteq \widetilde{pre}(X_1)\cup\widetilde{pre}(X_2)\cup pre(X_1)\cap pre(X_2)$$

Proposition 1 :

For a transition system S the following propositions are equivalent :

a) X is a global invariant of S

b) $post(X)\subseteq X$

c) $X\subseteq\widetilde{pre}(X)$

Proof : In [SIF 79].

Proposition 2 :

Let $S = (Q,\rightarrow)$ be a transition system, $P = (P_1,\dots,P_s)$ a tuple of predicates on Q such that $\bigcup_{i=1}^{s} P_i = Q$. The following propositions are equivalent :

a) $(Y_1,\dots,Y_s)$ is a set of local invariants with respect to P.

b) For $i\in[1,s]$, $Y_i\subseteq\bar{P}_i\cup\widetilde{pre}(\bigcap_{j=1}^{s}(\bar{P}_j\cup Y_j))$

c) For $i\in[1,s]$, $P_i\cap post(\bigcup_{j=1}^{s} P_j\cap Y_j) \subseteq Y_i$

Proof :

a) is equivalent to b) : We obtain successively the following equivalent statements,

$\forall i,k\in[1,s]$, $\forall q,q'\in Q$ $[Y_i(q)$ and $P_i(q)$ and $q\rightarrow q'$ and $P_k(q')$ implies $Y_k(q')]$

$\forall i,k\in[1,s]$, $\forall q\in Q[Y_i(q)$ implies $\bar{P}_i(q)$ or $\forall q'\in Q$ (non$(q\rightarrow q')$ or $\bar{P}_k(q')\cup Y_k(q'))]$

$\forall i\in[1,s]$, $\forall q\in Q[Y_i(q)$ implies $\bar{P}_i(q)$ or $\forall k\in[1,s]$ $\widetilde{pre}$ $(\bar{P}_k\cup Y_k)(q)]$

And by distributivity of $\widetilde{pre}$ with respect to $\cap$: $\forall i\in[1,s], Y_i\subseteq\bar{P}_i\cup\widetilde{pre}\bigcap_{k=1}^{s}(\bar{P}_k\cup Y_k)$.

b) implies c) :

$\forall i\in[1,s]$ $Y_i\subseteq\bar{P}_i\cup\widetilde{pre}\bigcap_{k=1}^{s}(\bar{P}_k\cup Y_k)$ implies successively,

$\forall i\in[1,s]$ $P_i\cap Y_i \subseteq P_i \cap \widetilde{pre}\bigcap_{k=1}^{s}(\bar{P}_k\cup Y_k)$, $\bigcup_{i=1}^{s} P_i\cap Y_i \subseteq (\bigcup_{i=1}^{s} P_i) \cap \widetilde{pre}\bigcap_{k=1}^{s}(\bar{P}_k\cup Y_k)$,

$\bigcup_{i=1}^{s} P_i\cap Y_i \subseteq \widetilde{pre}\bigcap_{k=1}^{s}(\bar{P}_k\cup Y_k)$.

By application of property 2b), $post(\bigcup_{i=1}^{s} P_i\cap Y_i) \subseteq post\circ\widetilde{pre}\bigcap_{k=1}^{s}(\bar{P}_k\cup Y_k) \subseteq \bigcap_{k=1}^{s}(\bar{P}_k\cup Y_k)$.

The relation $post\bigcup_{i=1}^{s} P_i\cap Y_i \subseteq \bigcap_{k=1}^{s}(\bar{P}_k\cup Y_k)$ is equivalent to $\forall k\in[1,s]$, $P_k \cap post\bigcup_{i=1}^{s} P_i\cap Y_i\subseteq Y_k$.

c) implies b) :

$\forall k\in[1,s]$ $P_k\cap post\bigcup_{i=1}^{s} P_i\cap Y_i \subseteq Y_k$ is equivalent to, $post(\bigcup_{i=1}^{s} P_i\cap Y_i) \subseteq \bigcap_{k=1}^{s}(\bar{P}_k\cup Y_k)$.

This implies, $\widetilde{pre}\circ post(\bigcup_{i=1}^{s} P_i\cap Y_i) \subseteq \widetilde{pre}\bigcap_{k=1}^{s}(\bar{P}_k\cup Y_k)$.

By the dual of property 2a) we have, $\bigcup_{i=1}^{s} P_i\cap Y_i \subseteq \widetilde{pre}\bigcap_{k=1}^{s}(\bar{P}_k\cup Y_k)$ which is equivalent to $\forall i\in[1,s]$, $Y_i \subseteq \bar{P}_i \cup \widetilde{pre}\bigcap_{k=1}^{s}(\bar{P}_k\cup Y_k)$.

III. CORRESPONDENCES BETWEEN LOCAL AND GLOBAL INVARIANTS

In this part we always refer to the same transition system $S = (Q,\rightarrow)$ with predicate lattice L and the same tuple $P = (P_1,\ldots,P_s)$ such that $\bigcup_{i=1}^{s} P_i = Q$.

III.1 More restrictive definitions for SLI's

The following notations are used :

- $(Y_i)_1^s$ represents a tuple, element of the lattice L^s, whose i-th component is Y_i ; we simply write $(Y_i)_i$ for a tuple whose number of elements is irrelevant or understood by the context. Moreover, $(X)_i$ represents a tuple having all its elements equal to X.
- For A, B elements of a given lattice we represents by [A,B] the sublattice (if there exists any) having as supremum A and as infimum B.
- f and g represents the function $f\in[L\rightarrow L^s]$, $g\in[L^s\rightarrow L]$:

$$f \stackrel{def}{=} \lambda X \,.\, (P_1\cap X,\ldots,P_s\cap X) = \lambda X \,.\, (P_i\cap X)_1^s$$

$$g \stackrel{def}{=} \lambda(Y_1,\ldots,Y_s) \,.\, \bigcap_{i=1}^{s} (\bar{P}_i\cup Y_i) = \lambda(Y_i)_1^s \,.\, \bigcap_{i=1}^{s} (\bar{P}_i\cup Y_i).$$

Notice that by using these notations the results of proposition 2 can be expressed by :

$Y\in L^s$ is a set of local invariants iff $Y\subseteq\tilde{f}\circ\widetilde{pre}\circ g(Y)$ iff $f\circ post\circ\tilde{g}(Y)\subseteq Y$.

The following properties of the functions f and g can be easily proved :

<u>Properties</u> 3 :

a) f is distributive with respect to both $\cup$ and $\cap$.

b) g is distributive with respect to $\cap$.

c) $g\circ f = Id_L$ and dually, $\tilde{g}\circ\tilde{f} = Id_L$.

d) $f\circ g \subseteq Id_{L^s}$ and dually, $Id_{L^s} \subseteq \tilde{f}\circ\tilde{g}$.

e) $g\circ\tilde{f} = Id_L$ and dually, $\tilde{g}\circ f = Id_L$.

f) $f \subseteq \tilde{f}$

g) $g \subseteq \tilde{g}$

<u>Proposition</u> 3 :

a) If $X\in L$ is a global invariant then f(X) anf $\tilde{f}(X)$ are two sets of local invariants.

b) If $Y\in L^s$ is a set of local invariants then g(Y) and $\tilde{g}(Y)$ are global invariants.

<u>Proof</u> :

a) If $X\subseteq\widetilde{pre}(X)$ then $\tilde{f}(X)\subseteq\tilde{f}(\widetilde{pre}(X))$ and by property 3e), $\tilde{f}(\widetilde{pre}(X)) = \tilde{f}(\widetilde{pre}(g\circ\tilde{f})(X))$ Thus, $\tilde{f}(X)$ satisfies the inequality $Y\subseteq\tilde{f}\circ\widetilde{pre}\circ g(Y)$.

Also, if $post(X)\subseteq X$ then $f(post(X))\subseteq f(X)$ and by property 3e), $f(post(X)) = f(post(\tilde{g}\circ f)(X))$. Thus, f(X) satisfies the inequality $f\circ post\circ\tilde{g}(Y)\subseteq Y$.

b) If $Y\subseteq\tilde{f}\circ\widetilde{pre}\circ g(Y)$, then $g(Y)\subseteq g\circ\tilde{f}\circ\widetilde{pre}\ g(Y)$ and by property 3e), $g(Y) \subseteq \widetilde{pre}\circ g(Y)$.

Also, if $f\circ post\circ\tilde{g}(Y) \subseteq Y$, then $\tilde{g}\circ f\circ post\circ\tilde{g}(Y) \subseteq \tilde{g}(Y)$ and by property 3e),

$post \circ \tilde{g}(Y) \subseteq \tilde{g}(Y)$.

Properties 4 :

a) f is one-to-one

b) g is surjective

Proof :

These properties follow immediately from property 3c).

According to proposition 3 and properties 4, given an invariant X it is possible to associate with X via f or $\tilde{f}$ two SLI's and given a SLI Y it is possible to associate with it via g or $\tilde{g}$ two invariants (in principle, the same invariant can be obtained from different SLI's as g and $\tilde{g}$ are not one-to-one). The question arises whether it is possible to find a bijection b, $b : L \to L'$, where L' is a sublattice of L^S, such that : $b(X) = Y$ if and only if "X is an invariant" is equivalent to "Y is a SLI". If such a bijection exists then every proof made by using invariants can be made using SLI's. The following proposition gives an answer to this question.

Proposition 4 :

a) For any X element of L, X is an invariant if and only if f(X) is a SLI.

b) For any X element of L, X is an invariant if and only if $\tilde{f}(X)$ is an SLI.

Proof :

a) If X is an invariant then f(X) is a SLI according to proposition 3a). Conservely, if for some $X \in L$, $f(X) \subseteq \tilde{f} \circ \tilde{pre} \circ g(f(X))$, then $g \circ f(X) \subseteq g \circ \tilde{f} \circ \tilde{pre} \circ g(f(X))$ and by properties 3c) and 3e), $X \subseteq \tilde{pre}(X)$.

b) A similar proof can be carried out.

The preceding proposition proves the existence of bijections between the global invariants of L and the SLI's of the sub-lattices defined by Im(f) (image of f) and Im($\tilde{f}$). It is easy to prove that they are respectively identical to $[(\emptyset)_i, (P_i)_i]$ and $[(\bar{P}_i)_i, (Q)_i]$. The following proposition gives a characterization of the SLI's of these two lattices and suggests two different, more restrictive but sufficient definitions for local invariants.

Proposition 5 :

a) Y is a SLI, $Y \subseteq (P_i)_i$ if and only if $Y \subseteq f \circ \tilde{pre} \circ g(Y)$

b) Y is a SLI $(\bar{P}_i)_i \subseteq Y$ if and only if $\tilde{f} \circ post \circ \tilde{g}(Y) \subseteq Y$.

Proof :

a) By property 3f), $f \circ \tilde{pre} \circ g(Y) \subseteq \tilde{f} \circ \tilde{pre} \circ g(Y)$. Thus if Y satisfies $Y \subseteq f \circ \tilde{pre} \circ g(Y)$ then it is a SLI and in addition $(Y_i)_i \subseteq (P_i)_i$. If $(Y_i)_i \subseteq (P_i)_i$ and $(Y_i)_i \subseteq \tilde{f} \circ \tilde{pre} \circ g(Y_i)_i$ then, $(Y_i)_i \subseteq (P_i)_i \cap \tilde{f} \circ \tilde{pre} \circ g(Y_i)_i = f \circ \tilde{pre} \circ g\ (Y_i)_i$.

b) A similar proof can be carried out.

III.2 Using the results on connections between lattices

A big part of the presented results are obtained by observing that f, g and their duals can be used to define connections between the lattices L and L^s and by applying well-known properties of them [ORE 44]. Nevertheless, we have not adopted such a presentation fearing that it would be too abstract and hide the approach followed in the study of the different notions of local invariant.

Connections are a very useful tool for studying correspondences between partially ordered sets. In the domain of program verification, they have been used in [COU 80] to compare different program proof methods. Hereafter we recall some results on connections and representations between lattices and show how they can be applied in order to establish correspondences between invariants and SLI's. Most of the results given have been proved in the original paper of Ore. Our presentation follows that of Sanchis [SAN 77].

Definitions and notations :

Given two lattices L and L', we represent by $[L \overset{m}{\to} L']$ the set of the monotonic functions from L into L'

A retraction of L is a function $h \in [L \overset{m}{\to} L]$ such that $h \circ h = h$. A retraction h of L is said to be an upper (lower) closure of L if $Id_L \subseteq h$ ($h \subset Id_L$).

A connection between L and L' is a pair of functions (h,j) such that $h \in [L \overset{m}{\to} L']$, $j \in [L' \overset{m}{\to} L]$, $h \circ j \circ h = h$ and $j \circ h \circ j = j$.

Notice that by properties 3c) and 3e) the pairs of functions $(\tilde{f},g)$, (f,g), $(f,\tilde{g})$ and $(\tilde{f},\tilde{g})$ are connections between L and L^s.

Proposition 6 :

Let (h,j) be a connection between L and L'. Then,

a) h restricted to Im(j) is an isomorphism from Im(j) onto Im(h) and j restricted to Im(h) is an isomorphism from Im(h) onto Im(j).

b) $j \circ h$ and $h \circ j$ are retractions of L and L' respectively.

Proposition 7 :

Let (h,j) be a connection between L and L'. The following conditions are equivalent:

a) $h \circ j = Id_{L'}$, ($j \circ h = Id_L$)

b) j is surjective (h is one-to-one)

c) h is one-to-one (j is surjective)

Proposition 3 can be considered as an application of the following proposition.

Proposition 8 :

Let (h,j) be a connection between L and L' such that $j \circ h = Id_L$ and $f \in [L \to L]$.

a) If $X \subseteq F(X)$ then h(X) qatisfies the inequality $Y \subseteq h \circ F \circ j(Y)$

b) If $Y \subseteq h \circ F \circ j(Y)$ then j(Y) satisfies the inequality $X \subseteq F(X)$

Definition :

A representation between two lattices L and L' is a pair of functions (h,j) such that

$h \in [L \overset{m}{\to} L']$, $j \in [L' \overset{m}{\to} L]$, $Id_L \subseteq j \circ h$ and $h \circ j \subseteq Id_{L'}$.

Obviously, if (h,j) is a representation then it is a connection while the converse is not necessarily true. It can be easily verified that among the connections $(\tilde{f},g)$, (f,g), $(f,\tilde{g})$, $(\tilde{f},\tilde{g})$ only the pairs (f,g) and $(\tilde{f},\tilde{g})$ define representations.

<u>Proposition</u> 9 :

Let h and j be two functions such that $h \in [L \overset{m}{\to} L']$ and $j \in [L' \overset{m}{\to} L]$. The following conditions are equivalent :

a) (h,j) is a representation between L and L'.

b) $\forall X \in L\ \forall Y \in L'\ (h(X) \subseteq Y \iff X \subseteq j(Y))$.

c) h is distributive w.r.t. $\cup$ and $j = \lambda Y.\ \cup\{X \mid h(X) \subseteq Y\}$.

d) j is distributive w.r.t. $\cap$ and $h = \lambda X.\ \cap\{Y \mid X \subseteq j(Y)\}$.

As an application of this proposition the results of proposition 4 can be obtained. In particular, a consequence of 9d) and 9c) is that f(g(Y)) is the least SLI corresponding (via g) to the same global invariant g(Y) and that $\tilde{f}(\tilde{g}(Y))$ is the greatest SLI corresponding (via $\tilde{g}$) to the same global invariant $\tilde{g}(Y)$.

Relations between the three different definitions of SLI's are given in [SIF 81]. The pairs $(\tilde{f} \circ g, f \circ g)$, $(f \circ \tilde{g}, \tilde{f} \circ \tilde{g})$ are connections of L^s and $(f \circ \tilde{g}, \tilde{f} \circ g)$ is a representation of L^s. Thes three pairs establish correspondences between the solutions of the inequalities defining the different notions of local invariants (for example, if $U \subseteq f \circ \widetilde{pre} \circ g(U)$ then $\tilde{f} \circ g(U)$ is a solution of $\tilde{f} \circ post \circ \tilde{g}(Z) \subseteq Z$).

III.3 <u>Generalization of this approach</u>

This approach seems to be quite general. It can be applied for decomposing global assertions in an equivalent set of s local assertions provided that a connection (h,j) be given between the lattice of global assertions L and a product lattice $L_1 \times L_2\ \times L_s$ such that $j \circ h = Id_L$ (the i-th local assertion belongs to L_i). Clearly, tackling this problem requires a preliminary study concerning the definition of the lattice of global assertions and the choice of the lattices L_i. We do not intend to treat the general problem in this paper. Nevertheless, we show by an example how it is possible to decompose trajectoires in transition systems.

<u>Example</u> :

A trajectory W of a transition system $S = (Q,\to)$ is a unary predicate on Q such that

$W = \lambda q.\ (W(q)$ <u>and</u> $q \in \overline{SINK}$ <u>implies</u> $\exists q'\ (q \to q'$ <u>and</u> $W(q')))$

i.e. a trajectory characterizes the set of the states visited by the system when a computation sequence is executed.

Trajectories can be used to express non-invariant properties. It has been shown in [SIF 79] [QUE 81] that the verification (by evaluation) of assertions expressed as formulas of a temporal logic, can be made by computing invariants and/or trajectories.

A trajectory W can be characterized by the following inequality [SIF 79] : $W \subseteq (pre \cup \widetilde{pre})(W)$

As for invariants, the connections (f,g), $(\tilde{f},g)$, $(f,\tilde{g})$ and $(\tilde{f},\tilde{g})$ can be used to define different decompositions of a trajectory into a set of "local trajectories" by considering the inequalities : $Y \subseteq f\circ(pre \cup \widetilde{pre})\circ g(Y)$, $Y \subseteq \tilde{f}\circ(pre \cup \widetilde{pre})\circ g(Y)$, $Y \subseteq f\circ(pre \cup \widetilde{pre})\circ \tilde{g}(Y)$, $Y \subseteq \tilde{f}\circ(pre \cup \widetilde{pre})\circ \tilde{g}(Y)$. Clearly, in this case the approach followed for the study of the relations between invariants and SLI's can be applied too.

IV. SLI'S WITH RESPECT TO A PARTITION

In this part we show how the relation $Y \subseteq f\circ \widetilde{pre}\circ g(Y)$ and $\tilde{f}\circ post\circ \tilde{g}(Y) \subseteq Y$ can be simplified when Y is a SLI defined with respect to a partition.
The approach followed is inspired from [BLI 73]. The aim is to show that the notion of invariant assertion, commonly used for proving programs, can be deduced from our definition of local invariants when additional hypotheses concerning the structure of a transition system are adopted. In particular, the given results are applied to the case of finite control schemata which is an abstract model for sequential flowchart programs. It is shown that the canonical set of equations [BLI 73] or the semantical equations [COU 78] of a program can be obtained from the fixed point equations characterizing SLI's.

IV.1 The general case

Let $S = (Q,\rightarrow)$ be a transition system and $P = (P_1,\dots,P_s)$ a partition of Q. This partition induces a partition P_R of $s\times s$ blocks on $\rightarrow$:

$P_R = (R_{ij})_{i,j=1,1}^{i,j=s,s}$ with $R_{ij} = \rightarrow \cap (P_i \times P_j)$, i.e. $R_{ij} = \{(q,q') \in Q\times Q \mid q\rightarrow q'$ <u>and</u> $P_i(q)$ <u>and</u> $P_j(q')\}$

In the sequel we denote by pre[R] the predicate transformer pre associated with the transition system (Q,R).

<u>Proposition</u> 10 :

Let $S = (Q,\rightarrow)$ be a transition system, $P = (P_i)_{i=1}^{s}$ a partition of Q and $P_R = (R_{ij})_{i,j=1,1}^{i,j=s,s}$ the induced partition on $\rightarrow$. Then, $U = (U_i)_{i=1}^{s}$ is a SLI such that $U \subseteq P$ if and only if $\{U_i \subseteq P_i \cap \bigcap_{j=1}^{s} \widetilde{pre}[R_{ij}](U_j)\}_{i=1}^{s}$.

<u>Proof</u> :

According to proposition 5, $U = (U_i)_{i=1}^{s}$ is a SLI such that $U \subseteq P$ iff $U \subseteq f\circ \widetilde{pre}[\rightarrow]\circ g(U)$.
We have, $\widetilde{pre}[\rightarrow]g(U) = \widetilde{pre}[\bigcup_{i}\bigcup_{j} R_{ij}](g(U)) = \bigcap_{i}\bigcap_{j} \widetilde{pre}[R_{ij}](g(U)) =$

$$\bigcap_{i}\bigcap_{j} \widetilde{pre}[R_{ij}](\bigcap_{k}(\bar{P}_k \cup U_k)) = \bigcap_{i}\bigcap_{j}\bigcap_{k} \widetilde{pre}[R_{ij}]\,(\bar{P}_k \cup U_k)$$

By the dual of property 2c) $\widetilde{pre}[R_{ij}](\bar{P}_k \cup U_k) = \widetilde{pre}[R_{ij}](\bar{P}_k) \cup \widetilde{pre}[R_{ij}](U_k)$ because

$pre[R_{ij}](\bar{P}_k) \cap pre[R_{ij}](U_k) = \emptyset$. Given that $U_k \subseteq P_k$ one can easily deduce that if $j \neq k$ then $pre[R_{ij}](U_k) = \emptyset$ and if $j=k$ then $pre[R_{ik}](\bar{P}_k) = \emptyset$.

Futhermore, if $k=j$ then $\tilde{pre}[R_{ij}](\bar{P}_k) \cup \tilde{pre}[R_{ij}](U_k)$ is equal to $\tilde{pre}[R_{ij}](U_j)$ because in this case $\tilde{pre}[R_{ij}](\bar{P}_j) \subseteq \tilde{pre}[R_{ij}](U_j)$.

By noticing that for $k \neq j$, $\tilde{pre}[R_{ij}](U_j) \subseteq \tilde{pre}[R_{ij}](P_j) \subseteq \tilde{pre}[R_{ij}]\ (\bar{P}_k \cup U_k)$, one can obtain :

$\bigcap_k \tilde{pre}[R_{ij}](\bar{P}_k \cup U_k) = \tilde{pre}[R_{ij}](U_j)$. Thus, $\tilde{pre}[\rightarrow] \circ g(U) = \bigcap_{i\,j} \tilde{pre}[R_{ij}](U_j)$ and $U \subseteq f \circ \tilde{pre}[\rightarrow] \circ g(U)$ is equivalent to the set of the inequalities,

$$\{U_r \subseteq P_r \cap \bigcap_{i\,j} \tilde{pre}[R_{ij}](U_j)\}_{r=1}^{s}.$$

If $i \neq r$ then $P_r \subseteq \bar{P}_i \subseteq \tilde{pre}[R_{ij}](U_j)$. So the preceding inequalities can be simplified :

$$\{U_i \subseteq P_i \cap \bigcap_{j=1}^{s} \tilde{pre}[R_{ij}](U_j)\}_{i=1}^{s}$$

The converse can be shown by proceeding up this proof.

<u>Proposition 11</u> :

Let $S = (Q,\rightarrow)$ be a transition system, $P = (P_i)_{i=1}^{s}$ a partition of Q and $P_R = (R_{ij})_{i,j=1,1}^{i,j=s,s}$ the induced partition on $\rightarrow$. Then $Z = (Z_i)_{i=1}^{s}$ is a SLI such that $\bar{P}_i \subset Z_i$, $i \in [1,s]$ if and only if $\{\bar{P}_j \cup \bigcup_{i=1}^{s} post[R_{ij}](Z_i) \subseteq Z_j\}_{j=1}^{s}$.

<u>Proof</u> : Given in [SIF 81].

IV.2 <u>Application : Finite Control Schemata</u>

The following definition is obtained by simplication of that of finite control algorithm given in [BLI 73].

<u>Definition</u> :

A <u>Finite Control Schema</u> (FCS) is a triple (D,V,INS) where,

- D is an arbitrary set of <u>data</u> ,
- V is a finite set of <u>labels</u> representing control points, $V \cap D = \emptyset$; for convenience we take $V = \{1,\ldots,s\}$,
- INS is a finite set of triples called <u>instructions</u>. An instruction is an element of $V \times R \times V$ where R is the set of binary relations on D.

An FCS is considered to be a transition system $S = (Q,\rightarrow)$ with $Q \subseteq V \times D$ and $(v,d) \rightarrow (v',d')$ if and only if there exists an instruction (v,R',v') such that $dR'd'$. Clearly, sequential flowchart programs (deterministic or not) can be modelled as finite control schemata.

Given a FCS, consider the partition $P = (P_v)_{v \in V}$ on $V \times D$ defined by $P_v = \{(v',d) \in V \times D \mid v'=v\}$ i.e. two states belong to the same block of this partition if they have the same control component. Let $P_R = (R_{ij})_{i,j \in V}$ the partition induced by P on $\rightarrow$. That is,

$$R_{ij} = \{((i,d),(j,d')) \mid \exists\ R'\ (i,R',j) \in INS \text{ and } dR'd'\}.$$

Denote by r_{ij} the relation on D obtained from R_{ij} by dropping the control compenents

$$r_{ij} = \{(d,d') \mid ((i,d),(j,d'))\in R_{ij}\}.$$

Consider a SLI, $U = (U_i)_{i\in V}$ with respect to P such that $U \subseteq P$.
According to proposition 10, $\{U_i \subseteq P_i \cap \bigcap_{j=1}^{s} \widetilde{pre}[R_{ij}](U_j)\}_{i=1}^{s}$.

Suppose that, for $i\in V$, U_i is of the form $U_i = P_i \cap A_i$ where A_i is a unary predicate on D. Since $pre[R_{ij}](\bar{P}_j) = \emptyset$ we find,
$\widetilde{pre}[R_{ij}](P_j \cap A_j) = \widetilde{pre}[R_{ij}](P_j) \cap \widetilde{pre}[R_{ij}](A_j) = Q \cap \widetilde{pre}[R_{ij}](A_j) = \widetilde{pre}[r_{ij}](A_j)$.

By substituting $P_i \cap A_i$ for U_i the preceding inequalities become, $\{P_i \cap A_i \subseteq P_i \cap \bigcap_{j=1}^{s} \widetilde{pre}[r_{ij}](A_j)\}_{i=1}^{s}$. Thus, the A_i's must satisfy the inequalities $\{A_i \subseteq \bigcap_{j=1}^{s} \widetilde{pre}[r_{ij}](A_j)\}_{i=1}^{s}$.

A similar development can be made for a SLI $Z = (Z_i)_{i=1}^{s}$ of a transition system, associated with a given FCS, such that, $\{\bar{P}_j \cup \bigcup_{i=1}^{s} post[R_{ij}](Z_i) \subseteq Z_j\}_{j=1}^{s}$, by supposing that Z_i is of the form $Z_i = \bar{P}_i \cup B_i$, where B_i is a unary predicate on D. In this case the B_i's must satisfy the inequalities $\{\bigcup_{i=1}^{s} post[r_{ij}](B_i) \subseteq B_j\}_{j=1}^{s}$.

The following proposition shows that the approaches consisting in propagating invariant assertions on data, backward or forward are equivalent.

<u>Proposition 12</u> :

For a given finite control schema,

$$\{A_i \subseteq \bigcap_{j=1}^{s} \widetilde{pre}[r_{ij}](A_j)\}_{i=1}^{s} \text{ iff } \{\bigcup_{i=1}^{s} post[r_{ij}](A_i) \subseteq A_j\}_{j=1}^{s}$$

<u>Proof</u> : Given in [SIF 81].

V. CONCLUSION

Starting from a definition of the notion of set of local invariants, it has been shown that this definition is sufficiently general in the sense that any invariant property can be proved by using local invariants.

Throught this study the results on connections between lattices have been proved very useful. They allowed the discovery of two more restrictive definitions for local invariants. Furthemore they provide a general frame for studying the problem of decomposing global assertions into an equivalent set of local assertions.

REFERENCES

[ASH 75] E.A. ASHCROFT "Proving assertions about parallel programs" Journal of Comp. and System Sciences 10, (1975), pp. 110-135.

[BLI 73] A. BLIKLE "An algebraic approach to mathematical theory of programs" Polish Academy of Sciences, Report n° 119, Warszawa, 1973.

[COU 78] P. COUSOT "Méthodes itératives de construction et d'approximation de points fixes d'opérateurs monotones sur un treillis, analyse sémantique des programmes" Thèse d'Etat, Grenoble, March 1978.

[COU 80] P. COUSOT and R. COUSOT "Constructing program invariance proof methods" International Workshop on Program Construction, Château de Bonas, INRIA (Ed.) Sept. 1980, pp. 13-21.

[FLO 67] R.W. FLOYD "Assigning meaning to programs" Proc. Symp. on Applied Mathematics, Vol. 19, I.T. Schwartz (Ed.), A.M.S., 1967, pp. 19-32.

[HOA 78] C.A.R. HOARE "Some properties of predicate transformers" J.A.C.M., Vol. 25, n° 3, July 1978, pp. 461-480.

[KEL 72] R.M. KELLER "Vector replacement systems : a formalism for modeling asynchronous systems" Princeton University technical report n° 117, December 1972.

[KEL 76] R.M. KELLER "Formal verification of parallel programs" Comm. ACM, Vol. 19, n° 7, July 1976, pp. 371-384.

[LAM 80] L. LAMPORT "Sometime" is sometimes "not never"-On the temporal logic of programs" Proc. of the 7th Annual ACM Symp. on Principles of Programming Languages, Las Vegas, Jan. 1980, pp. 174-185.

[MAN 78] Z. MANNA and R. WALDINGER "Is "sometime" sometimes better than "always" ?" Comm. ACM, Vol. 21, n° 2, Feb. 1978, pp. 159-172.

[MAN 81] Z. MANNA and A. PNUELLI "Verification of concurrent programs : the temporal framework" Int. Summer School Theoretical Foundations of Programming Methodology, July 28 to August 9, 1981, Munich.

[MAZ 74] A. MAZURKIEWICZ "Proving properties of processes" Algorytmy, XI, n° 19, 1974, pp. 5-22.

[ORE 44] O. ORE "Galois connexions", Trans. A.M.S., 55 (1944), pp. 493-513.

[PNU 79] A. PNUELLI "The temporal semantics of concurrent programs" LNCS Vol. 70, Springer Verlag, July 1979, pp. 1-20.

[QUE 81] J.P. QUEILLE and J. SIFAKIS "Specification and verification of concurrent systems in CESAR : An example" Research report RR 254. IMAG, Grenoble, June 1981.

[SAN 77] L.E. SANCHIS "Data types as lattices : retractions, closures and projectiores" RAIRO Informatique Théorique, Vol. 11, n° 4, 1977, pp. 329-344.

[SIF 79] J. SIFAKIS "A unified approach for studying the properties of transition systems" Research report RR 179, IMAG, Grenoble, December 1979 (Revised December 1980) ; to appear in Theoretical Computer Science 1982.

[SIF 81] J. SIFAKIS "Global and local invariants in transition systems" Research report RR n° 274, IMAG, Grenoble, November 1981.

On Relativization and the Existence of Complete Sets

Michael Sipser
Mathematics Department
Massachusetts Institute of Technology
Cambridge, Massachusetts 02139

I Introduction

A member of a complexity class is called a complete set if all other members can be efficiently transformed into it. Complete sets have been useful in elucidating the structure of the complexity classes, partially because in some sense they are examples of "hardest" members. Many classes have been shown to have complete sets such as NL, P, NP, PSPACE, and EXPTIME, though not others such as NP $\cap$ co-NP and R [Adleman, 1978]. Adleman [1978] gives a set having some properties of an R-complete set and asks if such a set does exist. Kannan [1979] asks if there is a set complete for NP $\cap$ co-NP.

All currently known complete sets enjoy this property for essentially the same reason: they can represent the simulation of Turing machine computations. Since such simulation arguments are preserved by relativizations [BGS, 1977] this implies that any class currently known to have a complete set also has complete sets under any relativization. The technique introduced in this paper is to show that the classes NP $\cap$ co-NP and R do not always have complete sets under relativization and hence in the unrelativized case do not have sets that can be shown by current methods to be complete. Note also that there are relativizations collapsing these classes down to P [BGS, Rackoff] and hence for which these classes trivially do have complete sets.

II Relativization of classes having complete sets

For the following definitions, let X be an oracle (set of strings), S and U be languages, and C^X be a relativized complexity class, which for the purposes of our discussion may be taken to be a collection of languages under downward reducibility, i.e. $L \in C^X$ and $K \leq_p L \Rightarrow K \in C^X$ and which furthermore are all recognized by Turing machines operating with oracle X.

Definition: S is a complete set for C^X iff, $S \in C^X$ and every language $L \in C^X$ can be reduced to S via a polynomial time reduction.

Definition: S is an X-complete set for C^X iff $S \in C^X$ and every language $L \in C^X$ can be reduced to S via a reduction that operates in polynomial time and which may access oracle X .

Definition: U is universal for C^X iff $U \in C^X$ and U is a collection of triples $(i, 1^{|s|^i}, s)$ such that for any $L \in C^X$ there is an k such that $L = U^k$ where

$$U^k = \{s \mid (k, 1^{|s|^k}, s) \in U\}.$$

Theorem: The following three statements are equivalent:

i) C^X has a complete set

ii) C^X has an X-complete set

iii) C^X has a universal set

Proof: The only slightly nontrivial case is (ii) → (iii). Let $p_1, p_2, p_3, \ldots$ be an enumeration of the polynomial time reducibilities, each appearing infinitely often. If S is X-complete then let $U = \{(i, 1^{|s|^i}, s) \mid p_i(s) \in S$ and

$p_i(s)$ halts in $|s|^i$ steps. Clearly $U \leq_p S$ and hence $U \varepsilon C^X$.

<u>Theorem</u>: For any oracle X, NP^X has a complete set.

Proof: Let $n_1, n_2, \ldots$ be an enumeration of nondeterministic polynomial time Turing machines operating with oracle X, where each machine appears infinitely often. The set $U = \{(i, 1^{|s|^i}, s) \mid n_i$ accepts s within $|i| + |s|^i$ steps$\}$ is universal for NP^X.

This theorem can be generalized to other classes having complete sets in the unrelativized case.

III Relativization of NP $\cap$ co-NP.

Theorem: For some oracle X, $NP^X \cap$ co-NP^X does not have a complete set.

Proof: Construct an oracle X so that $NP^X \cap$ co-NP^X does not have a universal set. Let $E_1, E_2, \ldots$ be an enumeration of the nondeterministic polynomial time oracle Turing machines and $A_1, A_2, \ldots,$ be an enumeration of the co-nondeterministic polynomial time (sometimes called π_1) oracle Turing machines. Let $\langle E_i, A_j \rangle$ be an enumeration of all pairs of NP and co-NP machines. Say such a pair <u>accepts</u> a language L if both members of the pair accept L. Clearly, any language in $NP^X \cap$ co-NP^X is accepted by some such pair. Our goal is to construct an oracle X such that no pair accepts a universal set.

Specifically, X will have the property that for each i,j if $L(A_i) = L(E_i)$, (machines are implicitly assumed to be running under an oracle which should be clear from the context) then there is a language $B \in NP^X \cap co\text{-}NP^X$ such that for every k, $B \neq L^k(E_i)$. Here, L(M) is the language accepted by M and $L^k(M) = (L(M))^k$. We decompose X into countably many sets $X_{ij} = \{s \mid 1^i 0 1^j 0 s \in X\}$ where X_{ij} is used to attack the pair $\langle E_i, A_j \rangle$. The following construction proceeds in parallel for all pairs i,j. For simplicity denote E_i by E and A_j by A.

To construct X_{ij} so that the pair $\langle E,A \rangle$ does not accept a universal set we need to show one of two things: either the set accepted by $\langle E,A \rangle$ is not universal or the machines E and A do not accept the same set. Assume that both E and A run within time p(n). Let:

$$L_e = \{s \mid \exists t \quad |s| = |t| \text{ and } 0st \in X_{ij}\}$$

$$L_a = \{s \mid \forall t \quad |s| = |t| \text{ implies } 1st \in X_{ij}\}$$

Clearly $L_e \in NP^X$ and $L_a \in co\text{-}NP^X$. Observe that for any X, if L_e and L_a differ only finitely then they are both in $NP^X \cap co\text{-}NP^X$. The X we construct will have this property. The construction proceeds in stages, each stage placing some strings into or out of X. Initially X is everywhere undefined. The kth stage ensures that either $L^k(E) \neq L_e$ or that E and A accept different sets. Begin at stage 1.

<u>Stage k</u>: Let m be minimal so that $2^m > p(2m^k)$ and that X_{ij} is as yet undefined on all strings of length $n = 2m+1$. Let $X_1, \ldots, X_{n'}$ be the $n' = 2^{2^n}$ extensions of X_{ij} obtained by defining X_{ij} on all strings of length n in the n' possible ways. Say that such an extension is <u>consistent</u> if it preserves that $L_e = L_a$ i.e. for each s of length m: $\exists$ t of length m where $0st \in X_{ij}$ iff $\forall$t of length m, $1st \in X_{ij}$. For each oracle X_ℓ run E on the string $v = (k, 1^{m^k}, 1^m)$ (resolving undefined oracle calls in the standard way). If for any consistent extension X_c, exactly one of "E accepts v" and "$1^j \in L_e$" is true, then we have found an extension of X_{ij} ensuring that $L^k(E) \neq L_e$. Redefinine X_{ij} to be X_c and proceed with stage k + 1.

The primary difficulty occurs when E behaves correctly on all consistent extensions. We then find an inconsistent extension on which E and A behave differently and thus accept different sets. Let $s_1, \ldots, s_{2^m}$ be the 2^m strings of length m. For $c = 1, \ldots, 2^m$ let Y_c be the extension of X_{ij} where $01^m s_c \in Y_c$ and for all d, $11^m s_d \in Y_c$, and all other strings of length n are not in Y_c. Similarly let Z_c be the extension of X_{ij} where for all d, $01^m s_d \notin Z_c$ and $11^m s_c \notin Z_c$, and all other strings of length n are in Z_c. Note that for every c, both Y_c and Z_c are consistent extensions and that if for some c, $X_{ij} = Y_c$ then $v \in L_e$ but if $X_{ij} = Z_c$ then $v \notin L_e$. Let $\overline{Y}_c$ be the set of those strings of length n that are queried by E with oracle Y_c in any one of the accepting computations on input v and let $\overline{Z}_c$ be the set of those strings of length n that are queried by A with oracle Z_c in any one of the rejecting computations on input v. Define a bipartite graph with 2^m left nodes and 2^m right nodes. If $d \in \overline{Y}_c$ say that Y_c <u>spoils</u> d and draw a red edge between the cth left node and the dth right node. If $d \in \overline{Z}_c$ say that $\overline{Z}_c$ spoils d and draw a blue edge between the cth right node and the dth left node. By the following lemma there must be a pair c,d such that neither Y_c spoils d nor Y_d spoils c. We use the fact that the cardinality of $\overline{Y}_c < 2^m$.

<u>Lemma</u>: Let G be a bipartite graph with ℓ left nodes and ℓ right nodes.and red or blue edges between left and right nodes. Each right node has $<\ell$ attached blue edges and each left node has $<\ell$ attached red edges. Then there is a left node and a right node with no edge between them.

Proof: There are $<k^2/2$ blue edges and $<k^2/2$ red edges but k^2 edge slots.

Let W be the inconsistent extension of X_{ij} containing the strings $01^m S_c$ and the strings $11^m S_b$ for all $b \neq d$, and no other strings of length n. Then because W agrees with Y_c on $\overline{Y}_c$, E with oracle W accepts v, and because W agrees with Z_d on $\overline{Z}_d$, A with oracle W rejects v. Hence E and A accept different sets and the pair $<E,A>$ does not accept a universal set. Let $X_{ij} = W$.

On the other hand if this case never arises then we have constructed X_{ij} so that for each k, $L^k(E) \neq L_e$. Yet $L_a = L_e \in NP^X$ co-NP^X. Hence $<E,A>$ does not accept a universal set.

IV Relativization of R

Definition of R: A language L is in R iff there is a deterministic polynomial time Turing machine M which <u>randomly accepts</u> L, $(L = L_R(M))$. This means that there is a polynomial f such that $L = \{s \mid \; r \in \{0,1\}^{f(n)}$ M accepts $<s,r>$ where $n = |s|\}$ and furthermore M has the <u>threshold property</u>, for every $s \in L$ M accepts $<s,r>$ for at least one half of the strings $r \in \{0,1\}^{f(n)}$. We say that M uses f(n) bits of randomness.

<u>Theorem</u>: For some oracle X, R^X does not have a complete set.

Proof: Let $M_1, M_2, \ldots$ be an enumeration of the deterministic polynomial time Turing machines. Construct X so that none of the M_i randomly accept a universal set. As in the previous proof we decompose X into $X_1, X_2, \ldots$ and use X_i to attack M_i. We describe this step. Let:

$$L = \{s \mid \exists t \; |s| = |t| \text{ and } st \in X_i\}$$

Observe that if, for all but finitely many s, $s \in L \rightarrow st \in X$ for more than one half of the t's, then $L \in R^X$. The oracle will be constructed so that L has this property. The kth stage of the construction extends the definition of X_i in such a way that either $L \neq L^k(M_i)$ or M_i fails to have the threshold property. Say that M_i runs in p(n) time and uses f(n) bits of randomness.

<u>Stage k:</u> Let m be minimal so that $2^m > p(m^{3k})$ and X_i is as yet undefined on all strings of length $n = 2m$. Let $Y_1, \ldots, Y_{n'}$ be the $n' = 2^{2^n}$ possible extensions of X_i by defining X_i on all strings

of length n in all possible ways. Say that such an extension Y_i is consistent if for each S of length m, either, for every t of length m, st $\not\in Y_j$ or for at least one half of the t's of length n, st εY_j. If on any consistent extension Y_j exactly one of the following is true: "M_i randomly accepts v" and "$1^m \varepsilon L$" where $v = (k, 1^{m^k}, 1^m)$ then extend X_i to Y_j and we have ensured that $L \neq L_R^k(M_i)$.

If M_i behaves correctly on all consistent extensions, then we find an inconsistent extension on which it fails to have the threshold property. Say $\ell = |v|$ and M_i runs for at most $p(\ell)$ steps on inputs of the form <v,r> for $r \varepsilon \{0,1\}^{f(\ell)}$. Let Y_1 be the consistent extension on which M_i randomly rejects v, i.e. for all $t \varepsilon \{0,1\}^m$, $1^m t \not\in Y_1$. Letting $r_1,\ldots,r_{2^{f(\ell)}}$ be the members of $\{0,1\}^{f(\ell)}$ this means that M_i rejects all the inputs < ,r_j>. Let S_j be the set of queries that M_i makes on input < ,r_j> when run on oracle Y_1. Let $Z = \{1^m t \mid t \varepsilon \{0,1\}^m\}$. For each $z \varepsilon Z$ define the weight of z, w(z) = the number of S_j containing z, and for each $S \subseteq Z$ define $w(S) = \sum_{z \varepsilon S} w(z)$. Then

$w(Z) \leq p(\ell) \cdot 2^{f(\ell)}$ since each of the $2^{f(\ell)}$ sets S_j contributes at most $p(\ell)$. Let Z' be the $2^{m/2}$ elements of Z of smallest weight. The extension of X_i containing Z' is a consistent extension, and hence M_i on this randomly accepts v . Thus for some r_j, M_i accepts < v,r_j> on this extension. Thus there is a smaller extension X' of X_i containing a set $S' \subseteq Z'$ of size at most $p(\ell)$

on which M_i accepts $<v, r_j>$. It is easy to see that $w(S') \leq p(\ell)\cdot(p(\ell)\cdot 2^{f(\ell)}/2^m) = (p(\ell))^2 \cdot 2^{f(\ell)-m}$ since the elements of Z' have weight $\leq p(\ell)\cdot 2^{f(\ell)}/2^m$. It also follows that M_i on oracle X' accepts $<v, r_j>$ for at most w(S') j's because X' and X_1 differ only on S' and at most this many inputs $<v, r_j>$ make oracle calls within S'. Hence since $(p(\ell))^2 < 2^m/2$ then $w(S') \leq 2^{f(\ell)-1}$ and M_i on X' fails to have the threshold property. Therefore, letting X_i be X' M_i does not randomly accept a universal set.

V Question for Further Research

Can one prove analogous results using polynomial bounded Turing reducibility rather than many-one reducibility?

VI References

Adleman, L. "Two theorems on random polynomial time", 19th Annual Symposium on Foundations of Computer Science, 1978.

Baker, Gill, Solovay, "Relativizations of the P = ? NP question," SICOMP 1977.

Kannan, Unpublished.

Rackoff, Relativized questions involving probabilistic algorithms, JACM V. 29, 1982, p. 261.

SEMANTICS OF INTERFERENCE CONTROL

R. D. Tennent
Computing and Information Science
Queen's University
Kingston, Canada

1. Introduction

Hoare [1], Brinch Hansen [2], Wirth [3], Reynolds [4], and others have argued that programming languages should be designed to allow programmers and compilers to determine easily that two program phrases are *non-interfering*; i.e., that executing or assigning to either of them cannot possibly affect the outcome of the other. The motivations for syntactic control of interference include implementation flexibility [5], determinacy of concurrent execution [2], and easier reasoning to establish program correctness using axiomatic methods [6].

J. C. Reynolds [4] described simple syntactic constraints that permit easy detection of non-interference, and a "collection" construct that allows useful forms of interference which otherwise would be disallowed by the constraints. In this paper, we use a semantic model to validate this approach to interference control. Because of space limitations, we must assume that the reader is familiar with [4] and with the concepts of denotational semantics [7,8,9].

A "standard" denotational semantic definition of his language is presented in Section 2. However, this description is too abstract to allow formulation of the necessary properties. A less abstract (but still denotational) semantic model is presented in Section 3 and shown to be congruent (i.e., equivalent in effect) to the standard semantics. In Section 4, predicates are defined to test for "non-reachability" of locations and the non-standard model is used to prove that the language has certain properties. Then, in Section 5, the three principles stated in [4] are formalized and verified relative to the semantic model.

The abstract syntax of the language to be considered is given in Table 1. It is essentially the "core" language in [4], but for simplicity (and to avoid the syntactic problems discussed by Reynolds) all type (and scope) constraints have been omitted from the

---

$I \in$ **Ide** identifiers
$P \in$ **Phrase** phrases

$$
\begin{aligned}
P \; ::= \; & \lambda I.P \mid \text{new } I.P \mid \langle \ldots ; I{:}P; \ldots \rangle \\
\mid \; & I \mid P(P) \\
\mid \; & \textbf{noaction} \mid P := P \mid P ; P \mid \textbf{while } P \textbf{ do } P \\
\mid \; & \textbf{if } P \textbf{ then } P \textbf{ else } P \\
\mid \; & P.I \\
\mid \; & \mathbf{Y}(P)
\end{aligned}
$$

Table 1 Abstract Syntax

syntax. A minor difference between the languages is that the variable declaration block **new** I **in** P has been replaced by an additional abstract (i.e., "lambda expression") **new** I.P which provides the call-by-value form of parameter. The combination (**new** I.P_1)(P_2) then gives the effect of declaring I to denote a new variable in P_1 with the initial value obtained by evaluating P_2.

2. The Standard Semantics

A "standard" Scott-Strachey semantic description of the language of Table 1 is given in Table 2. The notation used is summarized in the Appendix. Domains here are complete partial orders with least element $\perp$. The domain of locations, L, is assumed to be an infinite flat domain. The domain of storable values, R, is also flat and contains the truth values, but is otherwise unspecified. Denotable values are functions of stores in order to model the call-by-name parameter mechanism.

Domains

$t \in T = \{true, false\}_\perp$	truth values
$l \in L$	locations
$r \in R = T + \ldots$	storable values
$p \in P = D \to D$	procedures
$c \in Cv = U$	collection values
$u \in U = Ide \to [D + \{undefined\}_\perp]$	environments
$s \in S = L \to [R + \{unused\}_\perp]$	stores
$d \in D = S \to A$	denotable values
$e \in E = L + R + P + Cv$	expressible values
$a \in A = E + S + \{error\}_\perp$	answers

Auxiliary functions

$$deref : D \to S \to A$$
$$deref(d)(s) = (a \,?\, L \to s(a),\ a) \quad \text{where } a = d(s)$$

$$arid : U$$
$$arid[\![I]\!] = undefined$$

$$fix : [D \to D] \to D$$
$$fix(g) = \mathrm{lub}\{g^i(\perp) \mid i = 0,1,2,\ldots\}$$

Table 2 Standard Semantics

Valuation function

$$P : \mathbf{Phrase} \to \mathbf{U} \to \mathbf{S} \to \mathbf{A}$$

$P[\![\lambda \mathrm{I}.\mathrm{P}]\!]us = p$ where $p(d) = P[\![\mathrm{P}]\!](u[\mathrm{I} := d])$

$P[\![\mathbf{new}\ \mathrm{I}.\mathrm{P}]\!]us = p$
where $p(d)(s) = (a_1 ? \mathrm{R}\ \&\ a_2 ? \mathrm{S}) \to a_2[l := unused],\ error$
where $a_2 = P[\![\mathrm{P}]\!](u[\mathrm{I} := \lambda s.l])(s[l := a_1])$
where $s(l) = unused$ and $a_1 = deref(d)(s)$

$P[\![<\mathrm{I}_1 : \mathrm{P}_1 ; \ldots ; \mathrm{I}_n : \mathrm{P}_n>]\!]us = arid[\mathrm{I}_1 := P[\![\mathrm{P}_1]\!]u] \ldots [\mathrm{I}_n := P[\![\mathrm{P}_n]\!]u]$

$P[\![\mathrm{I}]\!]us = u[\![\mathrm{I}]\!] ? \mathrm{D} \to u[\![\mathrm{I}]\!](s),\ error$

$P[\![\mathrm{P}_1(\mathrm{P}_2)]\!]us = a ? \mathbf{P} \to a(d)(s),\ error$
where $a = P[\![\mathrm{P}_1]\!]us$ and $d = P[\![\mathrm{P}_2]\!]u$

$P[\![\mathbf{noaction}]\!]us = s$

$P[\![\mathrm{P}_1 := \mathrm{P}_2]\!]us$
$= (a_1 ? \mathrm{L}\ \&\ a_2 ? \mathrm{R}) \to s[a_1 := a_2],\ error$
where $a_1 = P[\![\mathrm{P}_1]\!]us$ and $a_2 = deref(P[\![\mathrm{P}_2]\!]u)(s)$

$P[\![\mathrm{P}_1 ; \mathrm{P}_2]\!]us = (a_1 ? \mathrm{S}\ \&\ a_2 ? \mathrm{S}) \to a_2,\ error$
where $a_2 = P[\![\mathrm{P}_2]\!]ua_1$
where $a_1 = P[\![\mathrm{P}_1]\!]us$

$P[\![\mathbf{while}\ \mathrm{P}_1\ \mathbf{do}\ \mathrm{P}_2]\!]u = fix(g)$
where $g(d)(s) = a_1 \to (a_2 ? \mathrm{S} \to d(a_2),\ error),\ s$
where $a_1 = deref(P[\![\mathrm{P}_1]\!]u)(s)$ and $a_2 = P[\![\mathrm{P}_2]\!]us$

$P[\![\mathbf{if}\ \mathrm{P}_0\ \mathbf{then}\ \mathrm{P}_1\ \mathbf{else}\ \mathrm{P}_2]\!]us = a \to P[\![\mathrm{P}_1]\!]us,\ P[\![\mathrm{P}_2]\!]us$
where $a = deref(P[\![\mathrm{P}_0]\!]u)(s)$

$P[\![\mathrm{P}.\mathrm{I}]\!]us = (a ? \mathbf{Cv}\ \&\ a[\![\mathrm{I}]\!] ? \mathrm{D}) \to a[\![\mathrm{I}]\!](s),\ error$
where $a = P[\![\mathrm{P}]\!]us$

$P[\![\mathrm{Y}(\mathrm{P})]\!]us = a ? \mathrm{P} \to fix(a)(s),\ error$
where $a = P[\![\mathrm{P}]\!]us$

Table 2 (Continued)

3. A Non-Standard Semantic Model

The semantic description of Section 2 is quite satisfactory as an "abstract" specification of the language under consideration. However, it is not suitable for reasoning about interference control because of the need to establish properties of the environments for procedure bodies and actual parameters. In the standard semantics these become inaccessible when the mathematical functions that model procedures and call-by-name parameters are defined.

One approach that can be used [10] is to adopt a form of operational semantics in which such functions are represented by "closures", finitary data structures with components representing environments. However it is then invalid to use structural induction over the language to prove properties of such valuations, because they are not defined structurally. Furthermore, it is quite complex to verify that an operational semantics is congruent with a denotational semantics; separate inductions must be used to prove that each approximates the other [9,11].

To establish similar properties of more powerful languages, Milne [11,12] has used a "non-standard" form of denotational semantics he termed store semantics. Here, we can take advantage of the Algol 60-like nature of the language discussed by Reynolds and use a simpler form of non-standard denotational semantics. A procedure is modelled by a (code,environment) pair, where the code component is a function of environments as well as the usual argument. Then the "abstract" procedure represented by such a pair may be obtained by applying the code component to the environment component.

Formally, we re-define the domain of procedures as follows:

$p \in P = Q \times U$	procedures
$q \in Q = U \to D \to D$	procedure code

and define a de-representation function $apply: P \to D \to D$ as

$$apply(q,u)(d) = q(u)(d)$$

A similar approach may be taken for denotable values, but there is a slight complication: not all denotable values have a "hidden" environment. We therefore adopt the domains

$d \in D = E + W$	denotable values
$w \in W = Z \times U$	thunks
$z \in Z = U \to S \to A$	thunk code

and a de-representation function $eval: D \to S \to A$ such that

$$eval(e)(s) = e$$
$$eval(z,u)(s) = z(u)(s)$$

The non-standard semantics is specified in Table 3. Domains and functions not defined explicitly are as in Table 2. An auxiliary valuation function S is used to abbreviate the semantic description of phrases whose "answer" can depend on the store. Function *rend* is used to obtain "minimal" environments in the representations of procedures and thunks to simplify the definitions of the predicates to be used in subsequent sections.

Proposition 1 For all P and u, $P[\![P]\!](rend[\![P]\!]u) = P[\![P]\!]u$.

Domains

$p \in P = Q \times U$	procedures
$q \in Q = U \to D \to D$	procedure code
$d \in D = E + W$	denotable values
$w \in W = Z \times U$	thunks
$z \in Z = U \to S \to A$	thunk code

Auxiliary Functions

$apply : P \to D \to D$

$apply(q,u)(d) = q(u)(d)$

$eval : D \to S \to A$

$eval(d)(s) = (d = (z,u) \to z(u)(s),\ d|E)$

$deref : D \to S \to A$

$deref(d)(s) = a\,?\,L \to s(a),\ a$ where $a = eval(d)(s)$

$rend : Phrase \to U \to U$

$rend[\![P]\!](u)[\![I]\!] = (I \text{ is free in } P) \to u[\![I]\!],\ undefined$

Valuation Functions

$P : Phrase \to U \to D$

$S : Phrase \to Z$

$P[\![\lambda I.P]\!]u = (q, rend[\![\lambda I.P]\!]u)$ where $q(u)(d) = P[\![P]\!](u[I := d])$

$P[\![\mathbf{new}\ I.P]\!]u = (q, rend[\![\mathbf{new}\ I.P]\!]u)$
where $q(u)(d) = (z,u)$
where $z(u)(s) = (a_1\,?\,R\ \&\ a_2\,?\,S) \to a_2[l := unused],\ error$
where $a_2 = eval(P[\![P]\!](u[I := l]))(s[l := a_1])$
where $a_1 = deref(d)(s)$ and $s(l) = unused$

$P[\![\langle I_1 : P_1; \ldots; I_n : P_n \rangle]\!]u = arid[I_1 := P[\![P_1]\!]u] \ldots [I_n := P[\![P_n]\!]u]$

Table 3 Non-Standard Semantics

For all of the remaining forms of phrase,

$$P[\![\mathrm{P}]\!]u = (S[\![P]\!], rend[\![\mathrm{P}]\!]u)$$

where

$$S[\![\mathrm{I}]\!]us = u[\![\mathrm{I}]\!]\,?\,\mathrm{D} \rightarrow eval(u[\![\mathrm{I}]\!])(s),\ error$$

$$S[\![\mathrm{P}_1(\mathrm{P}_2)]\!]us = a\,?\,\mathbf{P} \rightarrow eval(apply(a)(P[\![\mathrm{P}_2]\!]u))(s),\ error$$
$$\text{where } a = eval(P[\![\mathrm{P}_1]\!]u)(s)$$

$$S[\![\mathbf{noaction}]\!]us = s$$

$$S[\![\mathrm{P}_1 := \mathrm{P}_2]\!]us = (a_1\,?\,\mathrm{L}\ \&\ a_2\,?\,\mathrm{R}) \rightarrow s[a_1 := a_2],\ error$$
$$\text{where } a_1 = eval(P[\![\mathrm{P}_1]\!]u)(s) \text{ and } a_2 = deref(P[\![\mathrm{P}_2]\!]u)(s)$$

$$S[\![\mathrm{P}_1 ; \mathrm{P}_2]\!]us = (a_1\,?\,\mathrm{S}\ \&\ a_2\,?\,\mathrm{S}) \rightarrow a_2,\ error$$
$$\text{where } a_2 = eval(P[\![\mathrm{P}_2]\!]u)(a_1)$$
$$\text{where } a_1 = eval(P[\![\mathrm{P}_1]\!]u)(s)$$

$$S[\![\mathbf{while}\ \mathrm{P}_1\ \mathbf{do}\ \mathrm{P}_2]\!]us = eval(fix(g))(s)$$
$$\text{where } g(d) = (z, rend[\![\mathbf{while}\ \mathrm{P}_1\ \mathbf{do}\ \mathrm{P}_2]\!]u)$$
$$\text{where } z(u)(s) = a_1 \rightarrow (a_2\,?\,\mathrm{S} \rightarrow eval(d)(a_2),\ error),\ s$$
$$\text{where } a_1 = deref(P[\![\mathrm{P}_1]\!]u)(s) \text{ and } a_2 = eval(P[\![\mathrm{P}_2]\!]u)(s)$$

$$S[\![\mathbf{if}\ \mathrm{P}_0\ \mathbf{then}\ \mathrm{P}_1\ \mathbf{else}\ \mathrm{P}_2]\!]us = a \rightarrow eval(P[\![\mathrm{P}_1]\!]u)(s),\ eval(P[\![\mathrm{P}_2]\!]u)(s)$$
$$\text{where } a = deref(P[\![\mathrm{P}_0]\!]u)(s)$$

$$S[\![\mathrm{P}.\mathrm{I}]\!]us = (a\,?\,\mathbf{Cv}\ \&\ a[\![\mathrm{I}]\!]\,?\,\mathrm{D}) \rightarrow eval(a[\![\mathrm{I}]\!])(s),\ error$$
$$\text{where } a = eval(P[\![\mathrm{P}]\!]u)(s)$$

$$S[\![\mathrm{Y}(\mathrm{P})]\!]us = a\,?\,\mathbf{P} \rightarrow eval(fix(apply(a)))(s),\ error$$
$$\text{where } a = eval(P[\![\mathrm{P}]\!]u)(s)$$

Table 3 (Continued)

This semantic description is less abstract than the standard semantics, but it is still structurally-defined: the meaning of every syntactic construct is expressed only in terms of the meanings of its immediate syntactic constituents. As a result, it is quite straightforward to verify the congruence of the two descriptions using the binary predicates defined in Table 4. The acute accents (´) indicate values and domains from the standard semantics of Table 2; grave accents (`) indicate values and domains from the non-standard semantics of Table 3. The existence and inclusivity (also known as "directed-completeness" or "admissability for fixed-point induction") of these recursively-defined predicates (and others to be defined later) may be established using the methods of Milne [11,12] and Reynolds [13]; see also Stoy [9].

$$
\begin{aligned}
envs(\acute{u},\grave{u}) &= \forall I.\ \acute{u}[\![I]\!]\ ?\ \acute{D} \vee \grave{u}[\![I]\!]\ ?\ \grave{D} \\
&\qquad \rightarrow \acute{u}[\![I]\!]\ ?\ \acute{D}\ \&\ \grave{u}[\![I]\!]\ ?\ \grave{D}\ \&\ dens(\acute{u}[\![I]\!]|\acute{D},\grave{u}[\![I]\!]|\grave{D}), \\
&\qquad\ \ \acute{u}[\![I]\!] = \grave{u}[\![I]\!]
\end{aligned}
$$

$$
dens(\acute{d},\grave{d}) = \forall s.ans(\acute{d}(s),eval(\grave{d})(s))
$$

$$
\begin{aligned}
&ans(\acute{a},\grave{a}) \\
&\quad = (\acute{a}\ ?\ \acute{E} \vee \grave{a}\ ?\ \grave{E}) \rightarrow \acute{a}\ ?\ \acute{E}\ \&\ \grave{a}\ ?\ \grave{E}\ \&\ exps(\acute{a}|\acute{E},\grave{a}|\grave{E}), \acute{a} = \grave{a}
\end{aligned}
$$

$$
\begin{aligned}
&exps(\acute{e},\grave{e}) \\
&\quad = (\acute{e}\ ?\ \acute{P} \vee \grave{e}\ ?\ \grave{P}) \rightarrow \acute{e}\ ?\ \acute{P}\ \&\ \grave{e}\ ?\ \grave{P}\ \&\ procs(\acute{e}|\acute{P},\grave{e}|\grave{P}), \\
&\qquad (\acute{e}\ ?\ \acute{Cv} \vee \grave{e}\ ?\ \grave{Cv}) \rightarrow \acute{e}\ ?\ \acute{Cv}\ \&\ \grave{e}\ ?\ \grave{Cv}\ \&\ envs(\acute{e}|\acute{U},\grave{e}|\grave{U}), \\
&\qquad\qquad \acute{e} = \grave{e}
\end{aligned}
$$

$$
procs(\acute{p},\grave{p}) = \forall \acute{d},\grave{d}.dens(\acute{d},\grave{d}) \Rightarrow dens(\acute{p}(\acute{d}),apply(\grave{p})(\grave{d}))
$$

Table 4 Congruence Predicates

Theorem 1 For all P, $\acute{u}$ and $\grave{u}$, $envs(\acute{u},\grave{u}) \Rightarrow dens(\acute{P}[\![P]\!]\acute{u},\grave{P}[\![P]\!]\grave{u})$.

The proof is a straightforward structural induction over the language, with subsidiary fixed-point inductions for the **Y** operator and the **while** loop.

In subsequent sections, only the non-standard semantics will be used, and so accents will be omitted.

4. Unreachable Locations

Our approach to the semantics of interference control avoids having to deal with state sequences and interleavings [6]. If a location is unreachable from some program phrase, then it cannot be a "channel of interference" for that phrase. The following predicates will be used to test whether a location l is unreachable in, respectively, an environment u, a denotable value d, or an expressible value e:

$$
l \# u = \forall I.u[\![I]\!]\ ?D \Rightarrow l \# u[\![I]\!]|D
$$

$$
\begin{aligned}
l \# d = \ & d\ ?E \rightarrow l \# (d|E), \\
& d = (z,u) \rightarrow l \# u, \\
& \qquad\qquad true
\end{aligned}
$$

$$
\begin{aligned}
l \# e = \ & e\ ?L \rightarrow l \neq (e|L), \\
& e\ ?\ Cv \rightarrow l \# (e|U), \\
& e = (q,u) \rightarrow l \# u, \\
& \qquad\qquad true
\end{aligned}
$$

We use the symbol # to denote these predicates (and others to be defined later) because they are the semantic counterparts of the syntactic predicates defined by Reynolds.

Proposition 2 For all P, u, and l, $l \# u \Rightarrow l \# P[\![P]\!]u$.

An easy proof by structural induction.

We are now able to verify some important "Algol 60-like" properties of the language. These are expressed in terms of the predicates on domains U, U x S, D, E, Q and Z, respectively, defined in Table 5. Theorem 2 following will show that all semantic entities arising during the execution of any program in Reynolds's language will satisfy these predicates. The most significant constraints are the conditions

$$\forall l.(l \# u \Rightarrow l \# (a|E)), \qquad \text{when } a\,?\,E$$

and

$$\forall l.(l \# u \Rightarrow (a|S)(l) = s(l)), \qquad \text{when } a\,?\,S$$

in the definition of *tcode*. They state that if a location is updateable in an environment or reachable in any value expressible in an environment, then the location must already be reachable in that environment. Another important property (in the definition of *state*) is that a reachable location cannot contain *unused*; that is, "dangling references" are not possible.

$$env(u) = \forall I.(u[\![I]\!]\,?\,D \Rightarrow den(u[\![I]\!]|D))$$

$$state(u,s) = env(u)\ \&\ \forall l.(s(l) = unused \Rightarrow l \# u)$$

$$\begin{aligned} den(d) = {} & d\,?\,E \rightarrow exp(d|E),\\ & d = (z,u) \rightarrow tcode(z)\ \&\ env(u), true \end{aligned}$$

$$\begin{aligned} exp(e) = {} & e\,?\,Cv \rightarrow env(e|U),\\ & e = (q,u) \rightarrow pcode(q)\ \&\ env(u), true \end{aligned}$$

$$\begin{aligned} pcode(q) = {} & \forall u,d.env(u)\ \&\ den(d) \Rightarrow den(d')\ \&\ \forall l.(l \# u\ \&\ l \# d \Rightarrow l \# d')\\ & \quad \text{where } d' = q(u)(d) \end{aligned}$$

$$\begin{aligned} & tcode(z)\\ & = \forall u,s.state(u,s)\\ & \quad \Rightarrow a\,?\,E \rightarrow exp(a|E)\ \&\ \forall l.(l \# u \Rightarrow l \# (a|E)),\\ & \quad\ \ a\,?\,S \rightarrow state(u,a|S)\ \&\ \forall l.(l \# u \Rightarrow (a|S)(l) = s(l)), true\\ & \qquad \text{where } a = z(u)(s) \end{aligned}$$

Table 5 Semantic Predicates

Theorem 2 For all P and u, $env(u) \Rightarrow den(P[\![P]\!]u)$.

Lemma For all P,

$$\text{if } \forall u.(env(u) \Rightarrow den(P[\![P]\!]u), \text{ then } tcode(z),$$
$$\text{where } z(u) = eval(P[\![P]\!]u).$$

To prove the lemma, consider any u and s such that $state(u,s)$, and let $a = z(u)(s)$.

If $P[\![P]\!]u\,?\,E$, then $a = P[\![P]\!]u|E$ by the definition of $eval$. But the assumed property of $P[\![P]\!]u$ implies that $exp(a|E)$, and $\forall l.(l \# u \Rightarrow l \# (a|E))$ by Proposition 2, and so $tcode(z)$.

If $P[\![P]\!]u = (z',u')$, then $a = z'(u')(s)$. By the assumed property of $P[\![P]\!]u$, $tcode(z')$ & $env(u')$, and by Proposition 2, $\forall l.(l \# u \Rightarrow l \# u')$. Thus $state(u',s)$, and it follows that $tcode(z)$. This completes the proof of the lemma.

The theorem may be proved by structural induction:

Case λI.P

Suppose $env(u)$ and let $u' = rend[\![\lambda I.P]\!]u$. Then $env(u')$ and to complete a proof of $exp(P[\![\lambda I.P]\!]u)$, we must show that $pcode(q)$ where $q(u)(d) = P[\![P]\!](u[I:=d]) = d'$. Suppose $env(u)$ and $den(d)$. Then $env(u[I:=d])$. By the induction hypothesis on P, $den(d')$, and by Proposition 2, $\forall l.(l \# u[I:=d] \Rightarrow l \# d')$. Thus, $\forall l.(l \# u \;\&\; l \# d \Rightarrow l \# d')$ and so $pcode(q)$.

Case new I.P

The proof is similar to that for λI.P, except that we must show $tcode(z)$, where

$$z(u)(s) = (a_1 ?R \;\&\; a_2 ?S) \rightarrow a_2[l := unused], \quad error$$
$$\text{where } a_2 = eval(P[\![P]\!](u[I:=l])(s[l:=a_1])$$
$$\text{where } a_1 = deref(d)(s) \text{ and } l = new(s)$$

Suppose $state(u,s)$, $a_1 ?R$ and $a_2 ?S$. Then $state(u[I:=l], s[l:=a_1])$. By induction and the lemma, $state(u[I:=l], a_2)$ and

$$\forall l'.(l' \# u[I:=l] \Rightarrow a_2(l') = s[l:=a_1](l'))$$

But then $state(u, a_2[l:=unused])$ and

$$\forall l'.(l' \# u \Rightarrow a_2[l:=unused](l') = s(l')),$$

and so $tcode(z)$.

Case $P_1(P_2)$

It is sufficient to show $tcode(S[\![P_1(P_2)]\!])$. Suppose $state(u,s)$ and let $d = P[\![P_2]\!]u$. By induction and Proposition 2 we know that $den(d)$ and $\forall l.(l \# u \Rightarrow l \# d)$. Suppose $eval(P[\![P_1]\!]u)(s) = (q,u')$. Then, by induction and Proposition 2 $pcode(q)$ & $env(u')$, and $\forall l.(l \# u \Rightarrow l \# u')$. By the definition of $pcode$, $den(d')$ and $\forall l.(l \# u' \; \& \; l \# d \Rightarrow l \# d')$ for $d' = q(u')(d)$. Then, by a proof similar to that of the lemma, it can be shown that $tcode(S[\![P_1(P_2)]\!])$.

Case Y(P)

Suppose $state(u,s)$ and $eval(P[\![P]\!]u)(s)?P$. Then fixed-point induction may be used to show $den(d) \; \& \; \forall l.(l \# u \Rightarrow l \# d)$ for $d = fix(apply(eval(P[\![P]\!]u)(s)))$.

The remaining cases are straightforward.

5. Three Principles of Interference Control

Reynolds describes his first principle as requiring all "channels of interference" to be named by identifiers. It may be proved that the illustrative language under consideration has this property by using the following obvious corollary of Proposition 2:

$$\text{if, for all I free in P } l \# u[\![I]\!], \text{ then } l \# P[\![P]\!]u$$

that is, if a location is reachable in the meaning of a phrase in some environment, then it must be reachable via some free identifier of the phrase. If we define

$$d_1 \# d_2 = \forall l.(l \# d_1 \vee l \# d_2),$$

then we can prove

$$\text{if } \forall I_1 \text{ free in } P_1, I_2 \text{ free in } P_2 . \; u[\![I_1]\!] \# u[\![I_2]\!], \\ \text{then } P[\![P_1]\!]u \# P[\![P_2]\!]u$$

To show this, suppose that $u[\![I_1]\!] \# u[\![I_2]\!]$ for all I_1 free in P_1 and all I_2 free in P_2, but that, contrary to the above, there is a location l reachable in both $P[\![P_1]\!]u$ and $P[\![P_2]\!]u$. Then, by the corollary to Proposition 2, there are identifiers I_1 and I_2 free in P_1 and P_2 respectively such that l is reachable in both $u[\![I_1]\!]$ and $u[\![I_2]\!]$. But this is a contradiction, and so $P[\![P_1]\!]u \# P[\![P_2]\!]u$.

The second principle requires any channel of interference to be *uniquely* named in any context where it is used. This disallows aliasing of channels of interference, including "higher-order" aliasing involving procedure names. To achieve this for the illustrative language, Reynolds suggested the following syntactical constraints:

(i) for any phrase of the form $P_1(P_2)$, no identifier may be free in both P_1 and P_2;

(ii) for any phrase of the form **Y**(P), the sub-phrase P may not have any free identifiers.

To verify that these restrictions are sufficient, Theorem 2 may be proved with two of the predicates re-defined as follows:

$$env(u) = \forall I.(u[\![I]\!]\ ?\ D \Rightarrow den(u[\![I]\!]|D) \\ \& \forall I_1 \neq I_2.\ u[\![I_1]\!]|D \ \#\ u[\![I_2]\!]|D$$

$$pcode(q) = \forall u\, d.env(u)\ \&\ den(d)\ \&\ d \# u \\ \Rightarrow den(d')\ \&\ \forall l.(l \# u\ \&\ l \# d \Rightarrow l \# d') \\ \text{where } d' = q(u)(d)$$

where we define

$$d \# u = \forall l.(l \# d \vee l \# u)$$

The additional constraints specify that channels of interference are uniquely named in any environment, and that procedures do not interfere with their arguments.

For the case λI.P, we must prove that $pcode(q)$, where $q(u)(d) = P[\![P]\!](u[I:=d])$. We may assume $d \# u$ as well as $env(u)$ and $den(d)$, so that $env(u[I:=d])$, and the remainder of the proof can proceed as before.

For the case $P_1(P_2)$, suppose $state(u,s)$, and let $(q\,\mu') = eval(P[\![P_1]\!]u)(s)$ and $d = P[\![P_2]\!]u$. We will prove by contradiction that $d \# u'$. Suppose that l is reachable both in d and in u'. Then, by the corollary to Proposition 2, there are identifiers I_1 and I_2 free in P_1 and P_2, respectively, such that l is reachable in $u[\![I_1]\!]$ and in $u[\![I_2]\!]$. But $env(u)$ requires that $I_1 = I_2$, and this violates the first syntactic constraint. So, $d \# u'$, and the remainder of the proof can proceed as before.

For the case Y(P), the second syntactic constraint ensures that $\forall l.l \# u'$, where $(q\,\mu') = eval(P[\![P]\!]u)(s)|P$, allowing a proof by fixed-point induction that $den(d)\ \&\ \forall l.l \# d$, for $d = fix(q(u'))$.

The third principle of interference control suggested by Reynolds is to take into account that certain identifier occurrences are *passive* (called "expression-like" in [6]) and cannot cause interference. To model the distinction between active and inactive identifier occurrences, we add a Boolean "tag" to each denoted value in an environment:

$$u \in U = Ide \rightarrow [(D \times T) + \{undefined\}_1] \qquad \text{environments}$$

If the tag for an identifier is *true*, then this indicates that all uses of that identifier are in phrases of passive type (as defined in [4]), and so cannot cause interference. The semantic description of Table 3 may be modified in obvious ways to define these tags appropriately. The following predicates may then be defined to test whether a location l is *inactive* in, respectively, an environment u, a denoted value d, or an expressed value e:

$$l \not{e} u = \forall I.(u[\![I]\!]\ ?\ D \times T \Rightarrow l \not{e} d \vee t) \\ \text{where } (d\ t) = u[\![I]\!]$$

$$l \not{e} d = d\ ?\ E \rightarrow l \not{e} (d|E), \\ d = (z\,\mu) \rightarrow l \not{e} u, \\ true$$

$$
\begin{aligned}
l \notin e = {} & e\,?\,\mathrm{L} \rightarrow l \neq (e|\mathrm{L}),\\
& e\,?\,\mathrm{Cv} \rightarrow l \notin (e|\mathrm{U}),\\
& e = (q,u) \rightarrow l \notin u,\\
& \quad\quad\quad \mathit{true}
\end{aligned}
$$

Stronger versions of Proposition 2 and Theorem 2 may be then be proved, and by re-defining

$$d_1 \# d_2 = \forall l.[(l \# d_1 \vee l \notin d_2) \;\&\; (l \# d_2 \vee l \notin d_1)]$$

it may be verified that the weaker syntactic constraints described by Reynolds are sufficient to ensure the correctness of the more complex definition of $P_1 \# P_2$.

6. Discussion

In this paper we have defined a "non-standard" semantic model for an illustrative language, verified that it is congruent with a "standard" semantic model, and used it to justify three principles of interference control described by Reynolds [4]. These techniques are applicable to other languages with an "Algol 60-like" approach to storage management. For example, jumps can be modelled using continuation semantics as usual [7,8,9], but exits from blocks or procedures must de-allocate local storage.

An important problem that has not yet been solved is to verify the following implementation suggestion [4]:

> When an expression is a single parameter to a procedure, as opposed to a component of a collection which is a parameter, then its repeated evaluation within the procedure must yield the same value (though non-termination is still possible). This suggests a possible application of the idea of "lazy evaluation" [14,15].

It would appear that no rigorous proof has ever been published for the correctness of implementing call-by-name by call-by-need (the term originally used by Wadsworth [16] for "lazy evaluation"), even in a language with no assignments at all. It should be possible to adapt such a proof to apply to the language discussed here.

It would also be desirable if the results proved here could be verified more directly. Reynolds [17] has recently outlined a form of denotational semantics for which the "Algol 60-like" properties of a language are immediately apparent from the form of its description. In this paper these properties were proved in Proposition 2 and Theorem 2. It would be interesting to see whether more economical proofs of the results in Section 5 can be obtained by adopting a form of semantic description even more closely tailored to the properties of Algol 60-like languages.

Another possibility for simplification (suggested by Robert Milne) would be to replace the recursively-defined predicates used to express the various versions of Theorem 2 by appropriate retracts of the semantic domains. This would make it feasible to develop proofs of similar results within LCF [18].

Finally, it is possible that the location-unreachability semantics for # used here is applicable to validation of proof rules in "specification logic"[6,19]. It is easy to prove the following converse of Proposition 2: for all P, u and l, $l \# P[\![P]\!]u \Rightarrow l \# rend[\![P]\!]u$, and similarly with $\not\!@$ replacing #. These facts should make it possible to validate the "questionable" rule of Non-interference Composition[19]. However, conventional beta reduction may reduce location reachability, and so some restriction on the use of beta reduction is required to prevent inconsistency with the rule of Inference by Equivalence. For example, it should not be possible to infer $(\lambda k.\mathbf{noaction})(k) \# k$ from $\mathbf{noaction} \# k$. This seems to be closely related to the syntactic problems described at the end of [4].

Acknowledgements

I have benefitted from discussions with Robert Milne, William O'Farrell and John Reynolds. Jennifer O'Farrell helped type the manuscript. The research was funded by the Natural Sciences and Engineering Research Council of Canada, grant A8990.

References

1. C.A.R.Hoare, *Hints on Programming Language Design*, technical report CS-403, Computer Science Dept., Stanford University, Stanford, California (1973).

2. P.Brinch Hansen, "Structured multiprogramming", *Comm. ACM* 15, 7, pp. 574-8 (1972).

3. N.Wirth, "On the design of programming languages", in *Proc. IFIP Congress 74* (ed., J.L.Rosenfeld), North-Holland, Amsterdam (1975).

4. J.C.Reynolds, "Syntactic control of interference", *Conf. Record Fifth ACM Symp. on Principles of Programming Languages*, pp. 39-46, ACM, New York (1978).

5. C.A.R.Hoare, "Procedures and parameters, an axiomatic approach", in *Symposium on Semantics of Algorithmic Languages* (ed., E.Engeler), Lecture Notes in Mathematics, vol. 188, Springer, Berlin (1971).

6. J.C.Reynolds, *The Craft of Programming*, Prentice-Hall International, London (1981).

7. R.D.Tennent, *Principles of Programming Languages*, Prentice-Hall International, London (1981).

8. M.J.C.Gordon, *The Denotational Description of Programming Languages*, Springer, New York (1979).

9. J.E.Stoy, *Denotational Semantics: The Scott-Strachey Approach to Programming Language Theory*, MIT Press, Cambridge, Mass. (1977).

10. J.E.Donahue, "Locations considered unnecessary", *Acta Inf.*, 8, pp. 221-242 (1977).

11. R.E.Milne and C.Strachey, *A Theory of Programming Language Semantics*, Chapman and Hall, London, and Wiley, New York (1976).

12. R.E.Milne, *The Formal Semantics of Computer Languages and their Implementations* (thesis), University of Cambridge (1974); also Technical Microfiche PRG-13, Programming Research Group, University of Oxford.

13. J.C.Reynolds, "On the relation between direct and continuation semantics", pp. 141-56, *Proc. Second Int. Coll. on Automata, Languages, and Programming*, Saarbrucken, Springer, Berlin (1974).

14. P.Henderson and J.H.Morris, "A lazy evaluator", *Conf. Record Third ACM Symp. on Principles of Programming Languages*, pp. 95-103, ACM, New York (1978).

15. D.P.Friedman and D.S.Wise, "CONS should not evaluate its arguments", *Third Int. Coll. on Automata, Languages and Programming*, pp. 257-84, Edinburgh University Press (1976).

16. C.P.Wadsworth, *Semantics and Pragmatics of the Lambda Calculus* (thesis), University of Oxford (1971).

17. J.C.Reynolds, "The essence of Algol", *Int. Symp. on Algorithmic Languages*, Oct. 26-29, 1981, Amsterdam, (de Bakker and van Vliet, eds.), North-Holland, Amsterdam (1982).

18. M.Gordon, R.Milner and C.Wadsworth, *Edinburgh LCF*, Lecture Notes in Computer Science, vol. 78, Springer, Berlin (1979).

19. J.C.Reynolds, *Idealized Algol and its Specification Logic*, technical report, School of Computer and Information Science, Syracuse University, Syracuse, N.Y. (1981).

Appendix Summary of Semantic Notation

1. Semantic domains

(a) $s \in S = \ldots$ indicates that s (possibly with subscripts or primes) is a meta-variable for stores.

(b) Four domain constructions are used:

$A+B$	(coalesced) sum
$A \times B$	Cartesian product
$A \to B$	function space
$A_\perp$	lift

2. Semantic functions

(a) For $e \in E = \ldots + L + \ldots$,

$$e?L = \begin{cases} \perp, & \text{if } e=\perp; \\ \mathit{true}, & \text{if } e \text{ has been injected into E from L;} \\ \mathit{false}, & \text{otherwise.} \end{cases}$$

(b) $e|L$ is the projection of e into L; if $e?L = \mathit{false}$, then $e|L = \perp$. Explicit injections (and projections when no confusion can arise) are omitted.

(c)
$$r \to a_1, a_2 = \begin{cases} \perp, & \text{if } r=\perp \\ \mathit{error}, & \text{if } r?T = \mathit{false} \\ a_1, & \text{if } r|T = \mathit{true} \\ a_2, & \text{if } r|T = \mathit{false} \end{cases}$$

(d) $u[I:=d]$ is the function that is like u except that it maps I into d.

(e) Double brackets "⟦" and "⟧" enclose syntactic operands.

EFFICIENT SIMULATIONS OF MULTICOUNTER MACHINES*)

(Preliminary version)

Paul M.B. Vitányi
Mathematisch Centrum
Kruislaan 413
1098 SJ Amsterdam
The Netherlands

ABSTRACT

An oblivious 1-tape Turing machine can on-line simulate a multicounter machine in linear time and logarithmic space. This leads to a linear cost combinational logic network implementing the first n steps of a multicounter machine and also to a linear time/logarithmic space on-line simulation by an oblivious logarithmic cost RAM. An oblivious $\log^* n$-head tape unit can simulate the first n steps of a multicounter machine in real-time, which leads to a linear cost combinational logic network with a constant data rate.

1. INTRODUCTION

In many computations it is necessary to maintain several counts such that, at all times, an instant signal indicates which counts are zero. Keeping k counts in tally notation, where a count is incremented/decremented by at most 1 in each step, governed by the input and the set of currently zero counts, is formalized in the notion of a k-counter machine [2]. Multicounter machines have been studied extensively, because of their numerous connections with both theoretical issues and more or less practical applications. The purpose of this paper is to investigate the dependence of the required time and storage, to maintain counts, on storage structure and organization and the cost required by a combinational logic network. To do this, we use a notion of auxiliary interest: that of an oblivious Turing machine. An oblivious Turing machine is one whose head movements are fixed functions of time, independent of the inputs to the machine. The main result obtained here shows that an oblivious Turing machine with only *one* storage tape can simulate a k-counter machine on-line in linear time and in storage logarithmic in the maximal possible count. These bounds are optimal, up to order of magnitude, also for on-line simulation by nonoblivious machines.

It is obvious that, for any time function T(n), given a k-counter machine, or a k-pushdown store machine, which operate in time T(n), we can find a time equivalent k-tape Turing machine. However, such a Turing machine will, apart from using k tapes, also use $\mathcal{O}(T(n))$ storage. In [7] it was shown that for the pushdown store, of which

---

*) Registered at the Mathematical Centre as Report.

the contents can not be appreciably compacted, the best we can do for on-line simulation by an oblivious Turing machine is 2 storage tapes, $\Theta(T(n) \log T(n))$ time and $\Theta(T(n))$ storage. For the multicounter machine, [2] demonstrated a linear time/logarithimic space simulation by a 1-tape Turing machine. [9, Corollary 2] showed how to simulate on-line a T(n) time-, S(n) storage-bounded multitape Turing machine by an oblivious 2-tape Turing machine in time $\mathcal{O}(T(n) \log S(n))$ and storage $\mathcal{O}(S(n))$. Combining the compacting of counts in [2] and the method of [9] we achieve the best previously known on-line simulation of a k-counter machine by an oblivious Turing machine: 2 tapes, $\mathcal{O}(T(n) \log\log T(n))$ running time and $\mathcal{O}(\log T(n))$ storage. It is somewhat surprising to see that we can restrict a Turing machine for on-line simulation of a k-counter machine to 1 storage tape, logarithmic storage, oblivious head movements and still retain a linear running time.

In Section 2 this result is derived and connected with a linear cost combinational network for doing the same job. This network processes the inputs in sequence and may incur a time delay of $\Theta(\log n)$ between processing and input and producing the corresponding output followed by the processing of the next input. Since we would like to obtain a constant data rate, i.e., a constant time delay between processing the i-th input at the i-th input port and producing the i-th output at the i-th output port, $1 \le i \le n$, we show in Section 3 how to real-time simulate n steps of a multicounter machine by an oblivious $\log^* n$-head tape unit and use this to obtain a linear cost combinational network with such a fast response time. It is not our purpose here to introduce an odd machine model with a variable number of access pointers. One should rather think of it as an expedient intermediate step to derive the desired result for fixed n. Subsequently we note that cyclic networks (or VLSI where the length of the wires adds to the cost) can real-time simulate a multicounter machine in logarithmic (area) cost.

In Section 5 we analyse the cost of on-line simulation of a multicounter machine by a logarithmic cost RAM. This turns out to be $\mathcal{O}(n)$ time and $\mathcal{O}(\log n)$ space on the oblivious version, which is optimal, also for nonoblivious RAMs. For the relevant definitions of multicounter machines [1,2], multitape Turing machines [8], combinational logic networks [7], real-time and linear time on-line simulation [7] and oblivious computations [7,9,10] we direct the reader to these references. The present paper is a preliminary draft; the results in Sections 2 and 4 appeared in Techn. Report IW 167, Mathematical Centre, Amsterdam, May 1981.

2. LINEAR-TIME ON-LINE SIMULATION BY AN OBLIVIOUS ONE-HEAD TAPE UNIT WITH AN APPLICATION TO COMBINATIONAL LOGIC NETWORKS

We first point out one of the salient features of the problem of simulating k-CM's on-line by efficient oblivious Turing machines. Suppose we can simulate some abstract storage device S on-line by an efficient oblivious Turing machine M. Then we can also simulate a collection of k such devices $S_1, S_2, \ldots, S_k$, interacting through a common finite control, by dividing all tapes of M into k tracks, each of which is a duplicate of the corresponding former tape. Now the same head movements do the same job on k collections of tracks as formerly on the tapes of M, so the time and storage complexity of the extended M are the same as those of the original. While the problem of, say, simulating a k-counter machine in linear time by a k'-tape Turing machine $k' < k$, stems precisely from the fact that k' is less than k, the problem of simulating a k-counter machine by a k'-tape oblivious Turing machine in linear time is the same problem as that of simulating a 1-counter machine in linear time by a k'-tape oblivious Turing machine. Hence, for a proof of feasibility it suffices to look for the simulation of 1 counter only. (For a proof of infeasibility we would have the advantage of knowing that the head movements are fixed, and are the same for all input streams. Besides, we could assume that we needed to simulate an arbitrary, albeit fixed, number of counters.)

In [2] it was shown that a 1-TM can simulate a k-CM on-line in linear time. This simulation uses $\mathcal{O}(\log n)$ storage, for n steps by the k-CM, which is clearly optimal. It is a priori by no means obvious that an oblivious multitape TM can simulate one counter in linear time. We shall show that the result of [2] can be extended to hold for oblivious Turing machines.

In our investigation we noted that head-reversals are not necessary to maintain counters. We did not succeed in getting the idea below to work in an oblivious environment, and include it here as a curiosity, possibly folklore, item.

Suppose we want to simulate a k-CM C with counts $x_1, x_2, \ldots, x_k$ represented by the variables n_1 through n_k. The number of simulated steps of C is contained in the variable n. For $i = 1,2,\ldots,k$ if count x_i is incremented by $\delta \in \{-1,0,+1\}$ then

$$n_i \leftarrow n_i + 2 \quad \text{for } \delta = +1$$
$$n_i \leftarrow n_i + 1 \quad \text{for } \delta = 0$$
$$n_i \leftarrow n_i \quad \text{for } \delta = -1$$

Let, for $i = 1,2,\ldots,k$, $\hat{x}_i$ denote the current count on the i-th counter of C.

PROPOSITION 1. *For* $i = 1,2,\ldots,k$, $\hat{x}_i = 0$ *iff* $n_i = n$.

PROOF. Let n be the number of steps performed by C, p_i be the number of +1's, r_i be the number of 0's, and q_i be the number of -1's, added to the i-th counter, $1 \le i \le k$, during these n steps. Hence $p_i+q_i+r_i = n$ for all i, $1 \le i \le k$. By definition we have $n_i = 2p_i + r_i$. Suppose $n_i = n$. Then it follows that $p_i = q_i$ and therefore $p_i - q_i = \hat{x}_i = 0$. Conversely, let $\hat{x}_i = p_i - q_i = 0$. Then $p_i = q_i$ and $n_i = p_i + q_i + r_i = n$. □

Hence we obtain:

COROLLARY. *A one-way* k-CM C *can be simulated in real-time by a* (k+2)*-head one-way non-writing finite automaton* F *of which the heads can detect coincidence. Hence, four heads without head reversals suffice to accept all recursively enumerable sets.*

(Hint: 1 head reads the input from left to right, 1 head keeps the count of n by its distance to the origin, and the remaining k heads so keep the counts n_1 through n_k. It was shown in [4] that 2-CMs can accept all recursively enumerable sets. We assume that the tape is unbounded, whatever the input may be.)

After this digression we show:

THEOREM 2. *If* C *is a* k-*counter machine, then we can find an oblivious* 1-*tape Turing machine* M *that simulates* C *on-line in time* $O(n)$ *and storage* $O(\log n)$ *for* n *steps by* C.

Following [7], we note that in the above theorem "machine" can be replaced by "transducer" and the proof below will still hold.

PROOF. It shall follow from the method used, and is also more generally the case for simulation by oblivious Turing machines (cf. above), that if the theorem holds for 1-CM's then it also holds for k-CM's, $k \geq 1$. Let C be a 1-CM. The simulating oblivious 1-TM M will have one storage tape divided into 3 cannels, called the *n-channel*, the *y-channel*, and the *z-channel*. If, in the current step of C its count c is modified to $c+\delta$, $\delta \in \{-1,0,+1\}$, then:

$$\delta = +1 \Rightarrow n \leftarrow n+1; \quad y \leftarrow y+1; \quad z \leftarrow z,$$
$$\delta = 0 \Rightarrow n \leftarrow n+1; \quad y \leftarrow y \ ; \quad z \leftarrow z,$$
$$\delta = -1 \Rightarrow n \leftarrow n+1; \quad y \leftarrow y \ ; \quad z \leftarrow z+1,$$

where n is the count contained on the n-channel, y is the count contained on the y-channel and z is the count contained on the z-channel. Hence, always (1) $c = y-z$, and (2) $y+z \leq n$. The count n on the n-channel is recorded in the usual binary notation, with the low order digit on the start square and the high order digit on the right, see Figure 1. At the start of the cycle simulating the i-th step of C, $i = p.2^j$ and p is odd, squares 0 through j-1 on the n-channel contain 1's and square j contains a 0. So in this cycle, M's head, starting from square 0, travels right to square j and deposits a 1 there. It turns all 1's on squares 0 through j-1 into 0's during this pass. The head then returns to square 0. This maintenance of the count n completely fixes M's head movement, so M is oblivious. The representation of y and z is in a redundant binary notation. If y is denoted by $y_0y_1\ldots y_i$, y_j in square j of the y-channel, then $y_j \in \{0,1,2\}$, $0 \leq j \leq i$, and $y = \Sigma_{j=0}^{i} y_j 2^j$. Similarly for the count z. So the representation of y[z] over {0,1,2} is not unique. Finally, the head covers 2 squares on the tape, and shifts 1 square in 1 step of M, like a mask covering 2 tape-squares. So it has a look-ahead of 1. See Figure 1.

We now explain the operation of M. The intuitive idea behind a 2 in square j of the y[z]-channel is an, as yet unprocessed, carry from the j-th to (j+1)-th position of the binary representation of y[z]. During the left-to-right sweeps of its head, governed by the moves indicated for the updating of n, M maintains invariants (1) and (2). During the corresponding right-to-left sweeps back to the start square, M maintains also invariant (3): if $y_j[z_j] > 0$ is the contents of square j on the y[z] channel then z_{j-1}, z_j, z_{j+1} $[y_{j-1}, y_j, y_{j+1}]$ are 0 or blank. Moreover, every square right of a blank square, on that channel, contains blanks and no square containing a 0 has a blank right neighbour in that channel. This latter condition gets rid of leading 0's.

The validity of the simulation is now ensured if we can show the following assertions to hold at the end of M's cycle to simulate the i-th step of C, $i \geq 0$.

(a) For all i, $i \geq 0$, M can always add 1 to either channel y or z in the cycle simulating step i+1 of C.

(b) M can maintain invariants (1), (2) and (3) to hold at the end of each simulation cycle.

(c) The fact that (1), (2) and (3) hold at the end of the i-th simulation cycle of M ensures that the count of C is 0 subsequent to C's i-th step iff both the y-channel and z-channel contain blanks on all squares subsequent to the completion by M of simulating C's i-th step.

CLAIM 1. Assertion (a) holds at the start of each simulation cycle.

PROOF SKETCH. In the process of simulating the i-th step of C, M takes care of (a) during its left-to-right sweeps by propagating all unprocessed carries on squares 0,1,...,j on both the y-channel and z-channel to the right, leaving 0's or 1's on squares 0,1,...,j and depositing a digit d, $0 \leq d \leq 2$, on square j+1 of the channel concerned, for $i = p.2^j$ and p is odd. Assuming that M has adopted this strategy, we prove the claim by induction on the number of steps of C, equivalently, number of simulation cycles of M. □□

CLAIM 2. Assertion (b) holds at the start of each simulation cycle.

PROOF SKETCH. As we saw in the proof of claim 1, assertion (a) is implemented during the left-to-right sweeps. During the right-to-left sweeps assertion (b) is implemented.

1	1	1	1	1	-	-	-	-	-	} n-channel
0	0	0	0	1	-	-	-	-	-	} y-channel
1	2	-	-	-	-	-	-	-	-	} z-channel

read-write head

Figure 1. The configuration on M's tape after it has simulated 31 steps of C, consisting of, consecutively, 16 "add 1"'s, 11 "add 0"'s, and 5 "add -1"'s. The head has returned to the start position.

Clearly, assertion (b) holds at the start of the 1-th cycle. During its right-to-left sweeps, at each step M subtracts the 2-digit numbers covered on the y- and z-channel from each other, leaving the covered positions on at least one channel containing only 0's. M also changes (by marking the most significant digits) leading 0's on either channel into blanks during its right-to-left sweeps. Suppose the claim holds at the start of simulation cycles 1,2,...,i. We show that it then also holds at the start of simulation cycle i+1. It is obvious that M's strategy outlined above maintains invariants (1) and (2). It is left to show that it also maintains invariant (3). Again this is done by induction on the number of simulation cycles of M. □□

CLAIM 3. Assertion (c) holds at the start of each simulation cycle.

PROOF OF CLAIM. That a square on a channel can only contain a blank if all squares right of it, on that channel, contain blanks, and that the representations of y and z have no leading 0's, at the start of each simulation cycle, is a consequence of the proof of claim 2. That y-z = c at the conclusion of the i-th simulation cycle of M, where c is the count of C after i steps, follows because in the left-to-right sweep we add the correct amount to a channel according to claim 1, and in the right-to-left sweep we subtract equal amounts from either channel. It remains to show that as a consequence of the maintainence of condition (3) assertion (c) holds under these conditions.

Suppose that, at the end of the i-th simulation cycle of M, not both the y- and z-channel contain but blanks and that, by way of contradiction, y-z = 0. Then there is one channel, say y, which has a leading digit in position j, $j > 0$, while the digits on the positions j and j-1 on the z-channel are blank. So the count represented by y is greater or equal to 2^j while the count on z is smaller or equal to $2\sum_{j=0}^{j-2} 2^i = 2^j-2$. So $y-z \geq 2$ which contradicts the assumption. (For j = 0, $y-z \geq 1$.)

It remains to show that if $c \neq 0$ then not both channels y and z contain only blanks. Since always, at the start of a cycle, c = y-z holds, if $c \neq 0$ then $y \neq z$; so in that case at least one of the y-channel and z-channel must contain a count $\neq 0$. Hence there must be a square which contains a digit $d > 0$ on one of these channels.□□

By claims 1, 2 and 3 the on-line simulation of C by M is correct as outlined. It is easy to see that the simulation uses $\mathcal{O}(\log n)$ storage for simulating n steps by C. We now estimate the time required for simulating n steps by C. In the i-th simulation cycle M needs to travel to square j, for $i = p.2^j$ and p is odd. Therefore, M needs 2j steps for this cycle. For $i = p.2^j$ and p is even, i.e., i is even, M needs 1 step. Hence, for simulating 2^{h+1} steps by C, M needs all in all:

$$T(2^{h+1}) = \Sigma_{j=1}^{h} 2^{h-j}.2j + 2^h = 2^{h+1}.\Sigma_{j=1}^{h} j.2^{-j} + 2^h < 2^{h+1}.\Sigma_{j=1}^{\infty} j.2^{-j} + 2^h$$

$$\leq 2.2^{h+1} + 2^h = 5.2^h.$$

Now, given n, choose $h = \lfloor \log n \rfloor$ so that $2^h \leq n < 2^{h+1}$. Then $T(n) \leq T(2^{h+1}) \leq 5.2^h \leq 5n$.

Since the movement of M's head has nothing to do with the actual counts y and z, but only with the number of steps passed since the start of C, we observe that a k-CM can be simulated on-line by an oblivious 1-tape TM M_k, which is just like M, but equipped with y_i- and z_i-channels, $1 \leq i \leq k$, and therefore with a total of 2k+1 channels. Just like M, M_k uses $\Theta(\log n)$ storage and $T(n) \leq 5n$ steps to simulate n steps of C_k, the simulated k-CM, which proves the Theorem.

The covering of 2 or 3 tape squares by the head of M can be simulated easily by cutting out 1 or 2 squares of the storage tape and buffering it in the finite control. The swapping to and fro, from tape to buffer, according to the storage head movement, is easily handled in the finite control, of which the size is blown up a bit. This is similar to the way to achieve the speed-up in [3]. □

It is well-known that oblivious Turing machine computations correspond to those of *combinational logic networks* [7,9]. The networks we consider are acyclic interconnections of *gates* by means of *wires* that carry signals. It will be assumed that there are finitely many different types of gates available and that these form a "universal" basis, so that any input-output function can be implemented by a suitable network. Each type of a gate has a *cost*, which is a positive real number, say 1 for each. The *cost* of a network is the sum of the costs of its gates. The method used above can be used to construct a combinational logic network that implements the first n steps of the computation by a k-CM. Such a network will have n inputs carrying suitable encodings of the symbols read from the input terminal and n outputs carrying encodings of the symbols written on the output terminal, where we assume, for technical reasons, that the k-CM is a transducer. If the input- and output-alphabets have more than two symbols, the inputs and outputs of the network will be "cables" of wires carrying binary signals. Using standard techniques, [7,9], it is easy to show, by imitation of the oblivious Turing machine constructed in the proof of Theorem 2, that:

<u>COROLLARY</u>. *If* C *is a* k-CM *transducer, then we can construct a combinational logic network implementing* n *steps of* C *with cost* $O(kn)$.

3. REAL-TIME SIMULATION BY AN OBLIVIOUS $\log^* n$-HEAD TAPE UNIT AND A CORRESPONDING COMBINATIONAL LOGIC NETWORK

In the simulations of the previous section we may incur a time delay of $\Theta(\log n)$ between the processing of an input and the production of the corresponding output. For the combinational logic network with n input ports and n output ports this is interpreted as follows. The (i+1)-th input port is enabled by a signal of the i-th output port. Between this enabling and the production of the (i+1)-th output $\Theta(\log n)$ time may pass. Note that we can only process the (i+1)-th input after the i-th output is produced, since the set of zero counts at step i influences the translation of the j-th input to incrementing/decrementing the various counters for $j > i$. To eliminate the unbounded time delay we construct as an intermediate step, for each n, a real-time simulation by an oblivious $\log^* n$-head tape unit. While this doesn't solve the problem of simulating an arbitrary multicounter machine in real-time by a Turing machine with a fixed number of tapes [1,2], it turns out that with respect to the resulting combinational logic network this gives as good a result as could be expected from simulating an arbitrary multicounter machine in real-time by an oblivious Turing machine with a fixed number of tapes. In the sequel we call a combinational network with $\Theta(1)$ time delay, between enabling the i-th input port and the production of the i-th output, a *constant data rate* network.

For the $\log^* n$-head simulation we use basically that of the previous section with the tape divided into $\log^* n$ blocks of increasing sizes, each with a resident head. The size of the 0-th block is $x = s(0)$ for some constant x, of block 1, $s(1) = 2^{x-1}$ and of block i, $i > 1$, $s(i) = 2^{s(i-1)}$. Since we need $\Theta(\log n)$ length tape to simulate n steps, we need less than $\log^* n$ blocks, where $\log^* n$ is the number of consecutive iterations of taking the logarithm to get a number less or equal to 1 when we start from n. The 0-th block is maintained in the finite control and, assuming the blocks are marked, all heads can travel around on local information alone. Only the head on block 1 needs to be connected with the finite control to exchange information regarding the counts. See Figure 2.

Each head covers four squares, like a window, and is said to be scanning the leftmost square it covers. Each head, on information which is put in the first square of its block by the head on the previous block, makes a sweep from left-to-right over its block until it scans the end cell and then back from right-to-left until it scans the first cell. There it waits until the next sweep is due. Hence such a complete sweep over block i by the resident head takes $2s(i)$ steps. We maintain three invariants.

At all times $t > 0$ holds:

(1) $\quad y+z \le t$

(2) $\quad y-z =$ current count

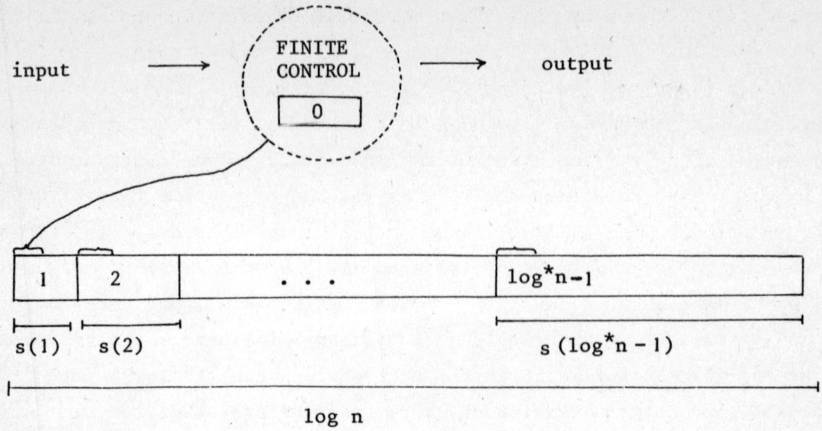

Figure 2.

(3) for all positions j on blocks 0 through $\log^* n$:

$$y_j > 0 \Rightarrow z_{j-1}, z_j, z_{j+1} \in \{0,-\} \ \&$$

$$z_j > 0 \Rightarrow y_{j-1}, y_j, y_{j+1} \in \{0,-\} \ \&$$

$$(y_j = - \Leftrightarrow z_j = -) \ \& \ \neg(y_j = z_j = 0 \ \& \ y_{j+1} = z_{j+1} = -).$$

(For j = 0 the obvious allowances are made.) The movements of the heads are governed by the count on the n-channel. Here this count may contain 2's representing unprocessed carries. This does not occur on the segment of n maintained on block 0, which is incremented by 1 in each step. When that count reaches 0 again (modulo 2^x steps) a carry is sent to the head on block 1 which then resides on the first square. Upon receiving a carry from block 0, the head on block 1 makes a full sweep over block 1 processing the carry and returning to the first square. Since this takes $2 \cdot s(1) = 2^x$ steps, it is in position to receive the next carry. When the segment of the n count on block 1 reaches 0 again (modulo $2^{s(1)}$ sweeps), at the right extreme of this last sweep a carry is propagated to the first square of block 2, starting a sweep of the resident head. In general, each cycle of $2^{s(i)}$ sweeps over block i produces a carry to the first square of block i+1 starting a sweep by the resident head. Since this sweep takes $2 \cdot s(i+1)$ steps, and a carry is produced each cycle of $T(i) \geq 2 \cdot s(i) \cdot 2^{s(i)}$ steps, the head on block i+1 is in position to start its sweep upon receiving the carry if

$$(*) \qquad 2 \cdot s(i+1) \leq 2 \cdot s(i) \cdot 2^{s(i)}, \quad \text{for } i \geq 1.$$

Block 0 is instantly updated, and therefore we need $2\, s(1) \leq 2^{s(0)}$. Since the inequalities are satisfied by the chosen block sizes, each propagated carry to a block is processed immediately. Having fixed the oblivious head movements, by starting a sweep over block i+1 each time a carry arrives from block i on the n channel, it remains to prove that invariants (1) - (3) can be maintained at all times during the real-time simulation. (Before proceeding, we remark that it is not necessary to assume that the blocks are delimited on the tape initially. Using four extra counters we can, as soon as we have the size of block i on one of them, determine s(i+1) before the first sweep over block i+1 is due. Determining the size of block 1 by the finite control, we can *bootstrap* the simulation of these four counters in the main simulation itself, which will be able to simulate an arbitrary number of counters, and so successively determine the blocks as they are needed. However, for the present objective of eventually producing a combinational logic network, there is no advantage in amplifying on this construction.)

We have to show:

(a) Each block can always receive incoming carries on the first square of its y-[z-] channel, and, in particular, block 0 receiving the inputs never overflows. I.e., (1) and (2) are maintained at all times.

(b) Invariant (3) holds at all times.

From (a) and (b) it follows, by the same reasoning as in the last section, that the current count y-z = 0 iff both y = z = 0 iff both y- and z-channel currently contain blanks only. The finite control, containing block 0, therefore knows instantly when the count is zero.

CLAIM 1. (a) can be maintained.

PROOF SKETCH. By induction on the consecutive blocks i.

Base case. A sweep over block 1 takes $2\,s(1) = 2^{s(0)}$ steps. Since a channel y, z on block 0 can accomodate a count of $2\cdot(2^{s(0)}-1)$, subsequent to propagation of a carry to block 1 (signifying a count of $2^{s(0)}$) block 0 contains at most $2^{s(0)} - 1$ on either channel. In the next $2^{s(0)} - 1$ steps the count may rise to $2\cdot(2^{s(0)}-1)$, but at the $2^{s(0)}$-th step a new carry is propagated to block 1, resulting from the current count on the channel plus the current input to that channel, restoring a count of at most $2^{s(0)} - 1$.

Induction. During its left-to-right sweeps, the head on block i, i > 0, processes a 2 deposited in the first square of the y,z-channels by propagating it as far as possible on the left two squares covered. So a 2 in the first square of a channel of block i may increment the contents of the first square of that channel on block i+1 by 1. Assume that the first square of a channel on block j, $1 \le j \le i$, is not incremented by more than 1 in between the starts of two consecutive sweeps over that block. Identifying 0's and blanks, and considering only one channel, let block i contain 00...0 or 10...0 at the start of the t_1-th sweep. By assumption, if block i contains

211...1 at the start of the t_2-th sweep, then $t_2 - t_1 \geq 2^{s(i)} - 1$. So sweep t_2 causes an increment of 1 on the first square of block i+1, by propagating the 2 right leaving 0's. Also by assumption, at the start of the $(t_2 - t_1 + 1)$-th sweep block i contains 00...0 or 10...0 again. Since block i contains only blanks initially, and $t_2 - t_1 + 1 \geq 2^{s(i)}$, while a sweep over block i+1 takes less time than $2^{s(i)}$ sweeps over block i, the assumption holds for block i+1. The assumption holds for block 1 by the base case.

So no channel on a block i, i > 0, ever contains more than $2^{s(i)} + 1$ which, together with the base case, proves the claim. □□

CLAIM 2. (b) can be maintained.

PROOF SKETCH. Contrary to the simulation in the previous section, we preserve invariant (3) while going from left-to-right on a block in propagating a carry. Going from right-to-left nothing is changed, so invariant (3) will hold at all times. We do so by subtracting the 3 bit pieces of the y- and z-count, covered by the left three positions of the head while going from left to right. If a nonzero digit replaces a 0 or a blank on a channel this is in the middle position of the three positions covered and the three positions covered on the other channel are replaced by 0's (or blanks). This still allows us to propagate a 2 as far as the central position of the 3 covered, so to the first square on the next block at the right extreme of the sweep. From the proof of the previous claim we have seen that a carry to the first square of the next block was sufficient. The rightmost (fourth) square covered by the head serves to detect adjacent blanks so as to return created leading 0's to blanks immediately. Due to the fact that invariant (3) holds and 2's occur only on the first square of a block and underneath a head, only one new leading 0 can be created per channel in a sweep on the rightmost nonblank block. □□

Hence we have:

THEOREM 3. *We can simulate the first* n *steps of a multicounter machine by an oblivious* $\log^* n$*-head tape unit in real-time and logarithmic space. (Similarly we can directly construct an oblivious* $\log^* n$*-tape Turing machine for the same job.)*

Just as argued in the previous section, we can construct a corresponding combinational logic network. Since only squares which are being rewritten need to be represented by logic components, and the time to make a sweep on block i+1 is $2 \cdot s(i+1)$ while there is only one such sweep in each cycle T(i), $T(i) \geq 2 \cdot s(i) \cdot 2^{s(i)} = 2 \cdot s(i) \cdot s(i+1)$ steps, the cost of this network is reduced from the expected $O(n \log^* n)$ by not representing squares covered by a head which does no rewriting.

THEOREM 4. *We can implement the first* n *steps of a* k*-counter machine on an* $O(kn)$ *cost combinational logic network with constant data rate.*

PROOF. The network has a constant data rate, i.e. a time interval $O(1)$ between enabling the i-th input port by the (i-1)-th output and producing the i-th output, $1 \le i \le n$, since it is derived from a real-time simulation. Each piece of logic circuitry, representing four squares covered by a head which is moving, has cost c(k), depending only on the number k of counters simulated but not on the number of steps n. The state of the finite control (containing block 0) is represented by cost d(k) pieces of logic connected to the input ports. In each cycle $T(i) \ge 2\, s(i) \cdot 2^{s(i)}$ steps, the head on block i+1 is active for only $2 \cdot 2^{s(i)}$ steps. Hence such a head is active for only $O(n/s(i))$ steps out of n, $1 \le i < \log^* n$. Summing this for all blocks i, $1 \le i \le \log^* n$, and adding the cost for the blocks 0 connected to the input ports we obtain a total cost C(k,n):

$$C(k,n) = \Big(\Big(\sum_{i=1}^{\log^* n-1} n \cdot c(k)/s(i)\Big) + n(c(k)+d(k))\Big)$$

$$= O(n \cdot k). \qquad \square$$

4. SIMULATION BY CYCLIC NETWORKS (AND VLSI)

When we are not restricted to acyclic logic networks, but are allowed cyclic logic networks, or work in the framework of the VLSI model of computation recently advanced in [5], it is not difficult to see that:

THEOREM 5. *If* C *is a* k-CM *transducer, then we can construct*
(i) *a cyclic logic network simulating* n *steps of* C *with cost* $O(k \log n)$ *in real-time;*
(ii) *a* VLSI *simulating* n *steps of* C *in real-time with area* $O(k \log n)$.

PROOF. We prove (ii), and (ii) clearly implies (i). The VLSI circuit realizing the claimed behaviour could look as follows:

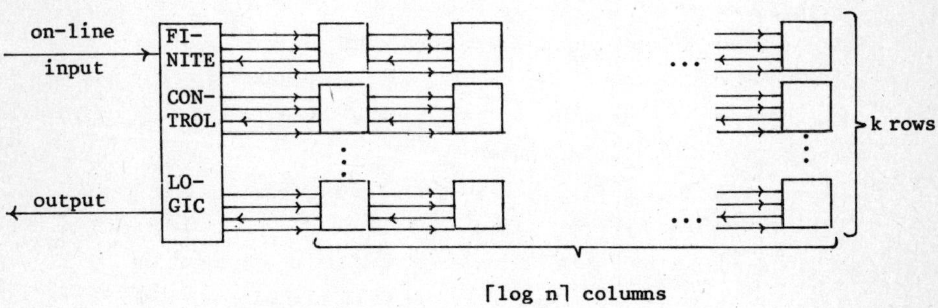

Figure 3. VLSI circuit simulating k-CM.

Each row stores a count in ordinary binary notation, with the low digit contained in the left block. Each block stores two bits: one for the binary digit of the count, and one to indicate whether the count digit contained is the most significant bit of that count. Carries are propagated along the top wire of each row, borrows along the bottom wire. The middle wires of each row transport information concerning the most significant bit in that row. Each block contains the necessary logic to process and transmit correctly carries, borrows and information concerning the most significant bit. The finite-control-logic rectangle processes the input signals and the information from the first blocks of each row, whether they contain a most significant bit 0 of the corresponding count, to issue carries or borrows to the first block of each row and to compute the output signal. We leave it to the reader to confirm that, subsequent to receiving the input signal, the corresponding output signal can be computed in time $O(\log k)$, which corresponds to the bit length of an input signal for driving k counters. Hence the VLSI circuit simulates the k-CM in real-time. Since the area occupied by the wires emanating from each block can be kept to the same size as the area occupied by the block itself, the blocks take $O(k \log n)$ area. The finite control logic structure contains some trees of depth log k, so its area can be kept to $O(k \log k)$. Under the assumption that $k \in O(n)$ this yields the required result. □

To fit a long thin rectangle in a square, as often is necessary to implement the structure on chip, we can fold it without increasing the surface area significantly. Note that the structure contains no long wires, and that it does not have to be overall synchronized: local synchronization is all we need. Hence it is a practicable design.

5. SIMULATION BY RAMs

For simulation with a uniform cost RAM it is clear that we can simulate a multicounter on-line with constant delay and constant storage. Constant delay is the RAM analogue for real-time, i.e. if T(n) is the time for simulating n steps by the multicounter then the RAM simulates on-line with constant delay if $T(n+1) - T(n) < c$ for some constant c and all n. It is easy to see, that a logarithmic cost RAM cannot simulate a counter machine on-line with constant delay, since it can only address registers of bounded index and bounded contents.

At first glance it seems that we can do no better than $O(n \log n)$ time for simulation of a countermachine by a logarithmic cost RAM. If we simulate with a tally mark in each register, we have to use indirect addressing to maintain the top of the counter requiring $O(n \log n)$ time and $O(n)$ storage to simulate n steps. Using a binary count we need only k registers for a k-counter machine, but need again $O(n \log n)$ time and $O(\log n)$ storage. Define an *oblivious RAM* as one in which the sequence of executed instructions, as well as the sequence of accessed storage locations, is a function of time alone. Due to the usual restrictions of the arithmetic operations of RAMs to +

and -, as well as to the needed translation of input commands with respect to the set of currently zero counters into counter instructions, we need to augment the RAM with some constant bit length boolean/arithmetic instructions in order not to be artificially precluded from obtaining the following result by imitation of the simulation in Section 2. (If we do not add these extra operations the Theorem below might only hold for nonoblivious RAMs by purely irrelevant definitional reasons.) Since we view the RAM as an abstract storage device performing a transduction we also assume it is connected to the input and an output terminal and dispense with the usual 'accept' instruction. Using the simulation in Section 2 we obtain:

THEOREM 6. *We can simulate a k-counter machine on-line by an oblivious logarithmic cost RAM in* $O(k \cdot n)$ *time and* $O(k \log n)$ *storage.*

PROOF. Do the simulation of Section 2 with the RAM, storing the head position of the 1-tape Turing machine in register 1 and the j-th square contents in register j+1. Then the sequence of executed instructions in the RAM program, and the sequence of accessed registers can be made a function of time alone. So the RAM is oblivious. The time for simulating sweeps of length j on the RAM is $O(k\ \Sigma_{i=2}^{j+1} \log i) = O(kj \log j)$. So if $T(2^{h+1})$ is the time needed to execute the first 2^{h+1} steps of the multicounter we obtain:

$$T(2^{h+1}) \in O\Big(\sum_{j=1}^{h} k \cdot 2^{h-j} \cdot j \log j + k \cdot 2^{h}\Big)$$

$$= O(k \cdot 2^{h+1}).$$

So $T(n) \in O(kn)$ and the storage used is $O(k \log n)$. □

This simulation is optimal in both space and time, even for nonoblivious RAMs.

6. FINAL REMARKS

Comparing our solution of the linear time simulation of a k-CM with the nonoblivious one in [2], the reader will notice that our average time complexity is the same as the worst case time complexity in [2]. So in actual fact, the solution in [2] runs faster in most cases than the one presented here. In [1] it was shown that the Origin Crossing Problem: "report when all k counts simultaneously reach 0" admits a real-time one-tape Turing machine solution. Contrary to the linear time simulation of [2], the method in [1] seems to contain inherently nonoblivious features, preventing us from turning it into an oblivious version. It has been a classic question [1,2], whether or not the Axis Crossing Problem: "report when one out of k counters reaches 0" or more generally "on-line simulate a k-counter machine" can be done in real-time by a (nonoblivious) k'-tape Turing machine for k' < k. A reasonable approach may seem to show that, anyway, a real-time simulation of multicounter machines by *oblivious* one-head tape units is impossible. In the event, intuition is wrong. We have noticed, cf. Section 2, that if we restrict the simulating device to its oblivious counterpart we have the advantage that if 1 counter is simulatable then k counters can be simulated in just the same way. This key observation has led us in the meantime, by augmenting the ideas presented here with an involved tape manipulation technique, to a real-time simulation of multicounter machines by *oblivious* one-head tape units, thus solving the above problem with a considerable margin [11]. Although superficially it would seem that this farther reaching result obviates the present ones we like to point out that:

- The present results are far simpler to derive and will suffice for many applications, as will some of the distinctive techniques.
- To derive the linear cost constant datarate combinational logic network the present route by way of a $\log^* n$-head tape unit suffices.
- The RAM simulation result seems difficult to derive, if at all, from the simulation in [11] without regressing to the simulation given here.

REFERENCES

[1] FISCHER, M.J. & A.L. ROSENBERG, *Real-time solutions of the origin-crossing problem*, Math. Systems Theory 2 (1968), 257-264.

[2] FISCHER, P.C., A.R. MEYER & A.L. ROSENBERG, *Counter machines and counter languages*, Math. Systems Theory 2 (1968), 265-283.

[3] HARTMANIS, J. & R.E. STEARNS, *On the computational complexity of algorithms*, Trans. Amer. Math. Soc. 117 (1965), 285-306.

[4] MINSKY, M., *Recursive unsolvability of Post's problem of tag and other topics in the theory of Turing machines*, Ann. of Math. 74 (1961), 437-455.

[5] MEAD, C.A. & L.A. CONWAY, *Introduction to VLSI Systems*, Addison-Wesley, New York, 1980.

[6] PATERSON, M.S., M.J. FISCHER & A.R. MEYER, *An improved overlap argument for on-line multiplication*, SIAM-AMS Proceedings, Vol. 7, (Complexity of Computation) 1974, 97-112.

[7] PIPPENGER, N. & M.J. FISCHER, *Relations among complexity measures*, Journal ACM, 26 (1979), 361-384.

[8] ROSENBERG, A.L., *Real-time definable languages*, Journal ACM 14 (1967), 645-662.

[9] SCHNORR, C.P., *The network complexity and Turing machine complexity of finite functions*, Acta Informatica 7, (1976), 95-107

[10] VITÁNYI, P.M.B., *Relativized Obliviousness*, in *Lecture Notes in Computer Science* 88 (1980), 665-672, Springer Verlag, New York. (Proc. MFCS '80).

[11] VITÁNYI, P.M.B., *Real-time simulation of multicounters by oblivious one-tape Turing machines*, Proceedings 14th ACM Symp. on Theory of Computing, 1982.

EVENT STRUCTURE SEMANTICS FOR CCS AND RELATED LANGUAGES

Glynn Winskel
Computer Science Department
Aarhus University, Aarhus
Denmark

Introduction

We give denotational semantics to a wide range of parallel programming languages based on the idea of Milner's CCS [M1], that processes communicate by events of mutual synchronisation. Processes are denoted by labelled event structures. Event structures represent concurrency rather directly as in net theory [NT]. The semantics does not simulate concurrency by non-deterministic interleaving.

We first define a category $\mathbb{E}$ of event structures ([NPW1, 2], [W]) appropriate to synchronised communication. The category bears a natural relation to a subcategory of trees through an interleaving functor; so results transfer to trees neatly. Then we introduce the concept of a synchronisation algebra (S.A.) on labels by adopting an idea of Milner [M2]. An S.A. specifies how two processes synchronise via labels on their events. From each S.A., L, we derive a category $\mathbb{E}_L$ of labelled event structures with natural operations for composing labelled event structures. In particular the parallel composition Ⓛ is derived from the product in $\mathbb{E}$. We obtain semantics for a class of CCS-like languages by varying the S.A.. Synchronisation algebras are very general so the class is very broad, handling synchrony and asynchrony in a common framework.

As a corollary we get an event structure semantics for CCS. When interleaved our semantics is Milner's synchronisation/communication tree semantics [M1]. However our semantics distinguishes more terms as it reflects concurrency. Event structure semantics is at a rather basic level of abstraction but should support all abstract notions of equivalence (see [M1] for examples), including those which take concurrency into account.

Here we omit proofs which will appear in a computer science report at Aarhus University.

1. Event structures

Processes are modelled by event structures. An event structure consists of a set of possible event occurrences together with a family of configurations; a configuration is a set of events which occur by some stage in the process, possibly after infinite time. To define operations on event structures neatly we modify the definition of [NPW1, 2] so that an event can occur in several incompatible ways. The definition is motivated further in proposition 1.5.

Notation Let F be a family of subsets of a set E. Let $X \subseteq F$. We write $X\uparrow^F$ for $\exists y \in F \forall x \in X. x \subseteq y$ and say X is compatible. When $x,y \in F$ we write $x\uparrow^F y$ for $\{x,y\}\uparrow^F$.

1.1 Definition An event structure is a pair (E,F), where E is a set of events and $F \subseteq P(E)$ is a family of configurations, which is:

(i) coherent $\forall X \subseteq F. (\forall x,y \in X. x\uparrow^F y) \Rightarrow \bigcup X \in F$

(ii) stable $\forall X \subseteq F. X \neq \emptyset$ & $X\uparrow^F \Rightarrow \bigcap X \in F$

(iii) coincidence-free $\forall x \in F\ \forall e,e' \in x. e \neq e' \Rightarrow (\exists y \in F. y \subseteq x$ & $((e \in y$ & $e' \notin y)$ or $(e \notin y$ & $e' \in y))$

(iv) finitary $\forall x \in F\ \forall e \in x\ \exists y \in F.\ e \in y$ & $y \subseteq x$ & $|y| < \infty$

1.2 Example Let E = {0,1,2} and F be

{0,2} {0,1} {1,2}

{0} {1}

$\emptyset$

or equivalently 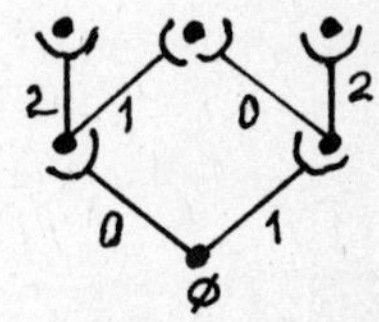

where $\prec$ is the covering-relation representing the occurrence of one event. Then (E,F) is an event structure. The events 0 and 1 are concurrent, neither depends on the occurrence or non-occurrence of the other to occur (see [NPW1, 2] and [NT]). The event 2 can occur in two incompatible ways, either through event 0 having occurred or event 1 having occurred. This possibility makes event structures of 1.1 easier to work with than those of [NPW1,2].

1.3 Example "A ticking clock". Let Ω consist of events ω and configurations the sets $\emptyset, \{0\}, \{0,1\}, \ldots, \{0,\ldots,n\}, \ldots \omega$. Then Ω is an event structure which models a clock ticking 0,1,2,... .

The next proposition motivates the axioms of 1.1. It shows that event structures possess an intrinsic causal dependency relation local to each configuration. The stability axiom ensures that when an event is in some configuration its occurrence has depended on a unique set of events. The set on which the event depends will be finite because of the finitary axiom and the dependency relation will be a partial order because of coincidence freeness. The ways in which events can occur correspond to complete primes of configurations ordered by inclusion; they form a subbasis making the domain of configurations prime algebraic [NPW1, 2].

<u>1.4 Definition</u> Let $(D,\sqsubseteq)$ be a partial order. Let $p \in D$. Say p is a <u>complete prime</u> iff for all $X \subseteq D$ when the lub $\bigsqcup X$ exists and $p \sqsubseteq \bigsqcup X$ then $p \sqsubseteq x$ for some $x \in X$. Say D is <u>prime algebraic</u> iff

$$\forall x \in D.\ x = \bigsqcup \{p \sqsubseteq x \mid p \text{ is a complete prime}\}.$$

<u>1.5 Proposition</u> Let E be a set and $F \subseteq P(E)$. Then

(i) (E,F) is coherent according to 1.1 iff $(F,\subseteq)$ is a coherent cpo such that for all $X \subseteq F$ if the lub of X exists it is $\bigcup X$. (Thus $\emptyset \in F$). For $x \in F$ define the <u>causal dependency relation</u> $\leq_x$ on x by $e \leq_x e' \iff \forall y \in F. y \subseteq x \Rightarrow (e' \in y \Rightarrow e \in y)$ and for $e \in x$ define $[e]_x = \{e' \in x \mid e' \leq_x e\}$. Then $[e]_x = \bigcap \{z \in F \mid e \in z \subseteq x\}$, and we have

(ii) If (E,F) is coherent then
(E,F) is stable according to 1.1 iff $\forall x \in F \forall e \in x. [e]_x \in F$
and $\forall x,y \in F \forall e \in x \cap y. x \uparrow^F y \Rightarrow [e]_x = [e]_y$

(iii) (E,F) is coincidence-free according to 1.1 iff
$\leq_x$ is a partial order for all $x \in F$.

(iv) If (E,F) is stable then
(E,F) is finitary according to 1.1 iff $\forall x \in F \forall e \in x. |[e]_x| < \infty$.

Suppose (E,F) is coherent and stable. Then $(F,\subseteq)$ is a coherent prime algebraic partial order [NPW1,2]; the complete primes are of the form $[e]_x$ for $x \in F$ and $e \in x$. Further (E,F) is finitary iff each isolated element of the domain $(F,\subseteq)$ dominates only a finite number of elements.

Proposition 1.5 suggests a subclass of event structures for which each event can occur and always causally depends on the same set of events, no matter in what configuration it occurs, so events correspond to complete primes.

<u>1.6 Definition</u> Let (E,F) be an event structure. Say (E,F) is <u>prime</u> iff $\forall e \in E \exists x \in F. e \in x$ and $\forall x,y \in F \forall e \in x \cap y. [e]_x = [e]_y$.

For prime event structures the local causal dependency relations ($\leq_x$ for configurations x) are restrictions of one global causal dependency ($\leq$) and incompatibility of configurations stems from a pairwise incompatibility, or conflict (#), between events.

<u>1.7 Proposition</u> Let (E,F) be a prime event structure. Define the relations $\leq$ (called the <u>causal dependency</u> relation) and # (called the <u>conflict</u> relation) on E by

$e' \leq e$ iff $\forall x \in F. e \in x \Rightarrow e' \in x$

$e \# e'$ iff $\forall x \in F. e \in x \Rightarrow e' \notin x$

Then $\leq$ is a partial order s.t. $[e] =_{def} \{e' \in E \mid e' \leq e\}$ is finite for all $e \in E$ and # is a binary irreflexive symmetric relation s.t. $e \# e' \leq e'' \Rightarrow e \# e''$ for all $e, e', e'' \in E$. Further the configurations F are precisely the left closed consistent subsets of E w.r.t. $\leq$ and # (i.e. $x \in F$ iff $x \subseteq E$ & $\forall e, e'. e' \leq e \in x \Rightarrow e' \in x$ & $\forall e, e' \in x. \neg(e \# e')$).

1.8 Example We show the configuration of a prime event structure alongside its causal dependency $\leq$ and conflict relation #. Its events are $\{0,1,2\}$.

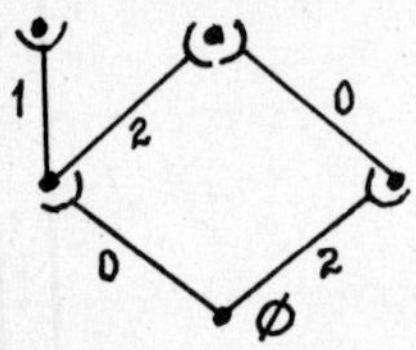

Consequently prime event structures are in 1-1 correspondence with structures $(E, \leq, \#)$ which consist of a set of events with causal dependency and conflict relations satisfying simple axioms. They give a simple, intuitive model of concurrent processes related to net theory in [NPW1,2] and [W]. In fact any event structure of 1.1 determines a prime event structure with an isomorphic domain of configurations - take the complete primes as the new events (see 4.2 for details). We work with more general event structures because it is difficult to define parallel composition directly on prime event structures; for prime event structures events correspond to the ways they can occur so to compose them in parallel we must duplicate as many copies of an event as there are ways introduced for it to occur. In the more general class we avoid a messy inductive naming of events, and can "tap out" prime event structures by the construction in 4.2.

Trees are another simple kind of event structure.

1.9 Definition An event structure (E, F) is a pre-tree iff $\forall x, y \in F. x \uparrow^{F} y \Rightarrow x \subseteq y$ or $y \subseteq x$. A tree is an event structure which is prime and a pre-tree.

The reader may check that the configurations of a pre-tree are isomorphic to sequences of events ordered by extension - so configurations correspond to partial and maximal branches - and that for a tree the events correspond to arcs. For this reason we shall often write a tree as (A,B) consisting of events A - for "arcs" - and configurations B - for "branches".

To sum up we have a class of event structures which includes trees and those event structures of [NPW1, 2] which satisfy a simple finiteness restriction.

2. A "cpo" of event structures

By restricting the configurations of an event structure (E,F) to those inside a subset E' of E a new event structure is formed.

2.1 Definition Let (E,F) be an event structure. Let $E' \subseteq E$. Define the restriction $(E,F)\upharpoonright E'$ to be (E',F') where $F' = \{x \in F \mid x \subseteq E'\}$.

Such restriction accompanies an idea of substructure - the relation $\trianglelefteq$ below.

2.2 Definition Let (E_0,F_0), (E_1,F_1) be event structures. Define

$$(E_0,F_0) \trianglelefteq (E_1,F_1) \text{ iff } E_0 \subseteq E_1 \;\&\; F_0 \subseteq F_1 \;\&\; \forall x \subseteq E_0.\, x \in F_1 \Rightarrow x \in F_0.$$

2.3 Lemma Let (E_0,F_0), (E_1,F_1) be event structures. Then $(E_0,F_0) \trianglelefteq (E_1,F_1)$ iff $E_0 \subseteq E_1$ and $(E_0,F_0) = (E_1,F_1)\upharpoonright E_0$.

Our semantics for recursively defined processes is based on the relation $\trianglelefteq$. Event structures ordered by $\trianglelefteq$ almost form a cpo. The ordering is not a cpo merely because event structures form a class and not a set. (The same kind of situation occurs in [S] and [BC].)

2.4 Theorem The relation $\trianglelefteq$ is a partial order on event structures with least event structures $(\emptyset,\{\emptyset\})$. Let $(E_0,F_0) \trianglelefteq \ldots \trianglelefteq (E_n,F_n) \trianglelefteq \ldots$ be an ω-chain of event structures. Then it has a lub with respect to $\trianglelefteq$. The lub is (E,F) where $E = \bigcup_{n\in\omega} E_n$ and

$$x \in F \text{ iff } (x \subseteq E \;\&\; (\forall n \in \omega.\, x_n \in F_n) \;\&\; x = \bigcup_{n\in\omega} x_n), \text{ in which}$$

$$x_n =_{def} \bigcup\{z \in F_n \mid z \in x\}.$$

The naturalness of $\trianglelefteq$ and its lubs is easier to see on prime event structures. It follows that on trees $\trianglelefteq$ is just the subtree-relation.

2.5 Proposition Let (E_0,F_0), (E_1,F_1) be prime event structures. Then $(E_0,F_0) \trianglelefteq (E_1,F_1)$ iff $F_0 \subseteq F_1$ & $\forall x \in F_1.\, x \cap E_0 \in F_0$. Let $(E_0,F_0) \trianglelefteq \ldots \trianglelefteq (E_n,F_n) \trianglelefteq \ldots$ be an ω-chain of prime event structures. Its lub is (E,F) where $E = \bigcup_{n\in\omega} E_n$ and $x\in F$ iff $\forall n\in\omega.\, x\cap E_n \in F_n$.

The recursive definition of a process will be associated with an operation continuous w.r.t. $\trianglelefteq$. The denotation of the recursively defined process will be the least fixed point of the operation.

<u>2.6 Definition</u> Let op be a unary operation on event structures. Say op is <u>$\trianglelefteq$-continuous</u> iff it preserves lubs of ω-chains ordered by $\trianglelefteq$. If op is an n-ary operation say it is $\trianglelefteq$-continuous iff it is $\trianglelefteq$-continuous in each argument.

3. A category of event structures

We define a rather basic class of morphisms on event structures. They are partial functions between event-sets which respect events and configurations. An event is imagined to synchronise with its image event whenever this is defined. One notable example of morphism will be a projection from the compound process of an event structure put in parallel with another back to the original event structure - see the product of event structures 3.4. Refer to the appendix for our treatment of partial functions - we use $*$ to represent undefined - and a formal definition of the $\hat{}$ operator which extends a function on events to a function on subsets.

<u>3.1 Definition</u> Let (E_0,F_0), (E_1,F_1) be event structures. A <u>(partially synchronous) morphism</u> $\theta: (E_0,F_0)\to(E_1,F_1)$ is a partial function $\theta: E_0 \to_* E_1$ such that

(i) $\forall x\in F_0.\, \hat{\theta}(x)\in F_1$

and (ii) $\forall x\in F_0 \forall e,e'\in x.\, \theta(e)=\theta(e')\neq * \Rightarrow e=e'$.

A morphism θ is <u>synchronous</u> iff θ is a total function.

Note that condition (ii) above says no two distinct events are together synchronised with a common image event. Notice if we have $(E_0,F_0)\trianglelefteq(E_1,F_1)$, for two event structures (E_0,F_0) and (E_1,F_1), then the inclusion map $i: E_0 \hookrightarrow E_1$ is a morphism, in fact a rather special one, so $\hat{i}$ is a rigid embedding in the sense of Kahn and Plotkin [KP].

<u>3.2 Example</u> Let (E_0,F_0), (E_1,F_1) be event structures with $E_0 = \{a_0,a_1,b_0,b_1\}$, $E_1 = \{a,b\}$ and configurations

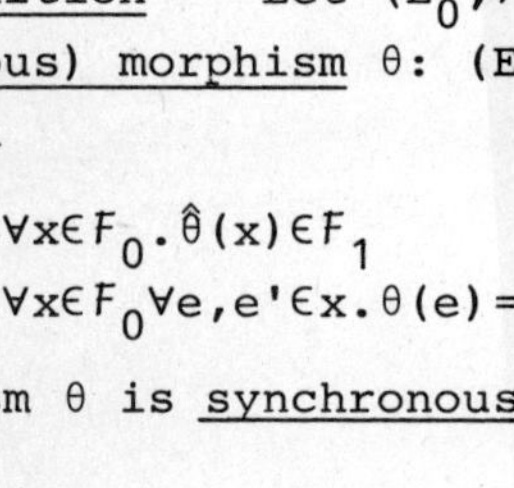

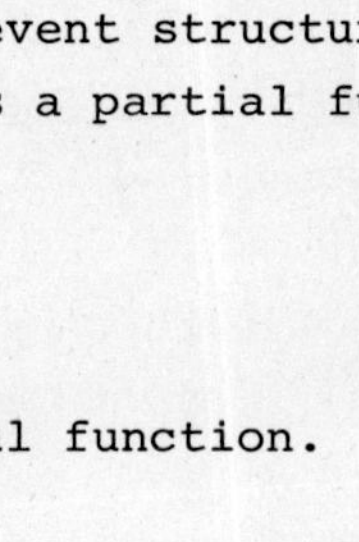

Then θ defined so $\theta(a_0)=\theta(a_1)=a$ and $\theta(b_0)=\theta(b_1)=b$ is a (synchronous) morphism. (Incidentally this morphism, although total, cannot be induced on event structures by a net morphism on Petri nets - see [NT], [NPW1, 2].)

It is easy to check that the morphisms defined above give a category of event structures with composition that of partial functions (see appendix) and identity morphisms the identity functions on sets of events.

<u>3.3 Definition</u> Define $\mathbb{E}$ to be the category of event structures with morphisms as defined in 3.1. Define $\mathbb{E}_{syn}$ to be the subcategory with synchronous morphisms.

The category $\mathbb{E}$ has products and coproducts characterised, to within isomorphism, by the following constructions. They provide a basis for defining, and proving relations between, different semantics for CCS and its variants.

The parallel composition of two processes will be denoted by a restriction of the product. The product corresponds to a very loose synchronisation discipline between processes; any event of one may or may not synchronise with an event of the other. A configuration of the product of two event structures E_0 and E_1 may contain events of synchronisation between E_0 and E_1 and must project to configurations of E_0 and E_1 by morphisms.

<u>3.4 Definition</u> <u>(Partially synchronous) product</u>
Let (E_0,F_0), (E_1,F_1) be event structures. Define their <u>product</u> $(E_0,F_0)\times(E_1,F_1)$ to be (E,F) where $E=E_0 \times_* E_1$, the product in $\underline{\underline{Set}}_*$ with projections π_0,π_1, and F is given by:

$$x\in F \quad \text{iff } x\subseteq E_0 \times_* E_1$$
$$\& \text{ (a) } \hat{\pi}_0(x)\in F_0 \ \& \ \hat{\pi}_1(x)\in F_1$$
$$\& \text{ (b) } \forall e,e'\in x.\ \pi_0(e)=\pi_0(e')\neq * \text{ or } \pi_1(e)=\pi_1(e')\neq * \Rightarrow e=e'$$
$$\& \text{ (c) } \forall e,e'\in x.\ e\neq e' \Rightarrow \exists y\subseteq x.\ \hat{\pi}_0(y)\in F_0 \ \& \ \hat{\pi}_1(y)\in F_1 \ \& \ ((e\in y \ \& \ e'\notin y) \text{ or } (e\notin y \ \& \ e'\in y)).$$
$$\& \text{ (d) } \forall\ e\in x\exists y\subseteq x.\ \hat{\pi}_0(y)\in F_0 \ \& \ \hat{\pi}_1(y)\in F_1 \ \& \ e\in y \ \& \ |y|<\infty$$

Note how (a) and (b) express that the projections are morphisms while (c) and (d) say the structure (E,F) is coincidence-free and finitary respectively.

3.5 Example (product) Let (E_0,F_0) be $(\{0\},\{\emptyset,\{0\}\})$ and (E_1,F_1) be $(\{1\},\{\emptyset,\{1\}\})$. Then their product $(E_0,F_0)\times(E_1,F_1)$ consists of events $E_0 \times_* E_1=\{(0,*),(0,1),(*,1)\}$ with configurations

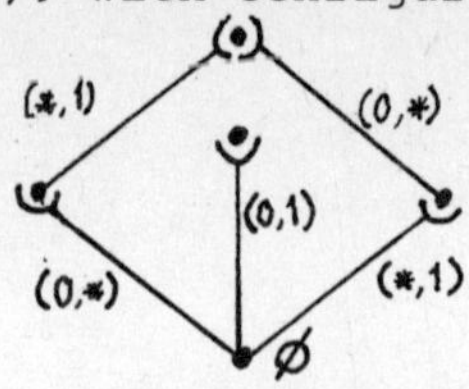

Intuitively (E_0,F_0), (E_1,F_1) can proceed asynchronously or alternatively communicate through synchronising events 0 and 1 to form the event (0,1) (c.f. $(\alpha\ NIL|\bar{\alpha}NIL)$ in Milner's CCS - see §5).

It is useful to also define a product in the category $\mathbb{E}_{syn}$ of event structures with synchronous morphisms, induced by just total functions. We define it as a restriction of the product above though there is an equivalent definition exactly analogous to that above with events and projections based on Set instead of Set_*.

3.6 Definition Synchronous product

Let (E_0,F_0), (E_1,F_1) be event structures. Define their synchronous product $(E_0,F_0)\otimes(E_1,F_1)$ to be the restriction $(E_0,F_0)\times(E_1,F_1)\upharpoonright E_0\times E_1$, where $E_0\times E_1$ is the product in Set of the sets E_0,E_1. (Note the obvious projections $\pi_i:E_0\times E_1\to E_i$ which are restrictions of those in 3.4.)

Notice how in the above definition an event of E_0 must synchronise with some event of E_1 if it is to occur. We use the synchronous product to define an interleaving operator on event structures. The operator synchronises occurrences of events one at a time with the ticking of a clock.

3.7 Proposition Let Ω be the event structure of example 1.3 - "the ticking clock". Let (E,F) be an event structure. The synchronous product $(E,F)\otimes\Omega$ is a pre-tree which consists of events $E\times\omega$ and configurations all finite or infinite sequences $\{(e_0,0),(e_1,1),\ldots,(e_n,n)\ \ldots\}$ such that $\{e_0,e_1,\ldots,e_n\}\in F$ for all n at which e_n is defined.

A simpler construction is that of coproduct which is essentially the disjoint union of event structures.

3.8 Definition Coproduct

Let $(E_0,\mathcal{F}_0)$, $(E_1,\mathcal{F}_1)$ be event structures. Define their coproduct $(E_0,\mathcal{F}_0)+(E_1,\mathcal{F}_1)$ to be $(E,\mathcal{F})$ where $E=\{0\}\times E_0 \cup \{1\}\times E_1$ and $\mathcal{F}=\{\{0\}\times x \mid x\in\mathcal{F}_0\} \cup \{\{1\}\times x \mid x\in\mathcal{F}_1\}$. (Note the evident injections $i_0:E_0\to E$ and $i_1:E_1\to E$.)

3.9 Example (coproduct) Let $(E_0,\mathcal{F}_0)=(\{a\},\{\emptyset,\{a\}\})$ and $(E_1,\mathcal{F}_1)=(\{b\},\{\emptyset, b\})$. Then $(E_0,\mathcal{F}_0)+(E_1,\mathcal{F}_1)$ has events $\{(0,a),(1,b)\}$ and configurations

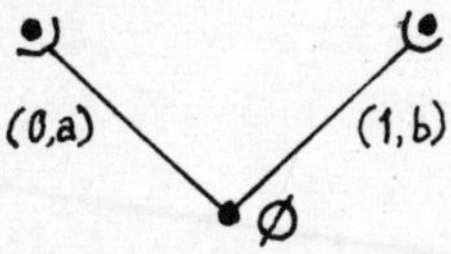

The following theorem shows the above constructions were already determined to within isomorphism by our choice of morphism. However our rather concrete constructions do give continuous operations on event structures ordered by $\trianglelefteq$, so they can be used in recursive definitions.

3.10 Theorem Let $(E_0,\mathcal{F}_0)$, $(E_1,\mathcal{F}_1)$ be event structures. Then

(i) $(E_0,\mathcal{F}_0)\times(E_1,\mathcal{F}_1),\pi_0,\pi_1$ as defined in 3.4 is their categorical product in $\mathbb{E}$.

(ii) $(E_0,\mathcal{F}_0)\otimes(E_1,\mathcal{F}_1),\pi_0,\pi_1$ as defined in 3.6 is their categorical product in $\mathbb{E}_{syn}$.

(iii) $(E_0,\mathcal{F}_0)+(E_1,\mathcal{F}_1)$ as defined in 3.8 is their categorical coproduct in $\mathbb{E}$ and $\mathbb{E}_{syn}$.

Further each operation $\times$, $\otimes$ and $+$ is continuous w.r.t. $\trianglelefteq$.

4. Two subcategories, prime event structures and trees

Importantly our work transfers over to the two subcategories of $\mathbb{E}$ with objects the prime event structures, and trees. In particular this means we can relate event structure semantics to semantics based on trees using interleaving.

4.1 Definition Define $\mathbb{P}$ to be the full subcategory of $\mathbb{E}$ with objects the prime event structures. Define $\mathbb{T}\mathrm{r}$ to be the full subcategory of $\mathbb{E}$ with trees as objects.

The inclusion functor $\mathbb{P}\hookrightarrow\mathbb{E}$ has a right adjoint Pr which to an event structure associates a prime event structure with an isomorphic domain of configurations. Intuitively the operation Pr renames events of a process so each event has a unique causal history. Similarly the inclusion functor $\mathbb{T}\mathrm{r}\hookrightarrow\mathbb{E}$ has a right adjoint I which is an interleaving operation defined with the synchronous product $\otimes$ and "ticking clock" Ω of 3.7. These adjunctions determine the form of products and coproducts in $\mathbb{P}$ and

$\mathbb{T}r$ (see [Mac]). Both operations Pr and I are $\trianglelefteq$-continuous so a fixed-point semantics based on event structures will image under Pr to a semantics based directly on prime event structures, or under I to one based directly on trees.

<u>4.2 Proposition</u> Let (E,F) be an event structure.

(i) Define $\Pr(E,F)$ to consist of events $P=\{[e]_x \mid e\in x\in F\}$ and configurations F_p where $z\in F_p$ iff $\exists x\in F. z=\{[e]_x \mid e\in x\}$. Then $\Pr(E,F)$ is a prime event structure. There is a morphism $ev_{E,F}:\Pr(E,F)\to(E,F)$ given by $ev_{E,F}([e]_x)=e$ for $e\in x\in F$. In fact $\Pr(E,F), ev_{E,F}$ is cofree over (E,F) i.e. for any morphism $\theta:(E',F')\to(E,F)$ with (E',F') a prime event structure, there is a unique morphism $\psi:(E',F')\to\Pr(E,F)$ such that $\theta=ev_{E,F}\psi$.

(ii) Define $I(E,F)=\Pr((E,F)\otimes\Omega)$. Then $I(E,F)$ is a tree. There is a morphism $\pi_{E,F}:I(E,F)\to(E,F)$ given by $\pi_{E,F}=\pi_0 ev_{(E,F)\otimes\Omega}$ where $\pi_0:(E,F)\otimes\Omega\to(E,F)$ is the projection morphism. In fact $I(E,F)$, $\pi_{E,F}$ is cofree over (E,F).

Further, both operations Pr and I are $\trianglelefteq$-continuous.

<u>4.3 Corollary</u> (i) Let (E_0,F_0), $(E_1,F_1)\in\mathbb{P}$. Their product in $\mathbb{P}$ is $\Pr((E_0,F_0)\times(E_1,F_1))$. Their coproduct in $\mathbb{P}$ is $(E_0,F_0)+(E_1,F_1)$.

(ii) Let $(A_0,B_0),(A_1,B_1)\in\mathbb{T}r$. Their product in $\mathbb{T}r$ is $I((A_0,B_0)\times(A_1,B_1))$. Their coproduct in $\mathbb{T}r$ is $(A_0,B_0)+(A_1,B_1)$.

(Note $\times$ and $+$ stand for product and coproduct in $\mathbb{E}$.)

Another characterisation of product $\times_{\mathbb{T}r}$ in $\mathbb{T}r$ relates it to Milner's parallel combinator on synchronisation trees [M1]. When labels are introduced his combinator is just a restriction of the product of trees.

<u>4.4 Definition</u> Let $(E,F)\in\mathbb{E}$ and $\varepsilon\notin E$. Define $\varepsilon(E,F)=(E\cup\{\varepsilon\},F_\varepsilon)$ where $z\in F_\varepsilon$ iff $z=\emptyset$ or $(\varepsilon\in z$ & $z\setminus\{\varepsilon\}\in F)$.

<u>4.5 Proposition</u> Let the trees T, S be coproducts $T=\sum_{a\in A} a\, T_a$ and $S=\sum_{b\in B} b\, S_b$. Then

$$T \times_{\mathbb{T}r} S \cong \sum_{a\in A} (a,*)\, T_a \times_{\mathbb{T}r} S + \sum_{(a,b)\in A\times B} (a,b)\, T_a \times_{\mathbb{T}r} S_b + \sum_{b\in B} (*,b)\, T \times_{\mathbb{T}r} S_b$$

<u>4.6 Example</u> Let a, b, c be distinct events. Let T be the tree $ab(\emptyset,\emptyset)$ and S the tree $c(\emptyset,\emptyset)$. We show their products in $\mathbb{E}$, $\mathbb{P}$ and $\mathbb{T}r$. We label coverings and events to show how they project to T and S.

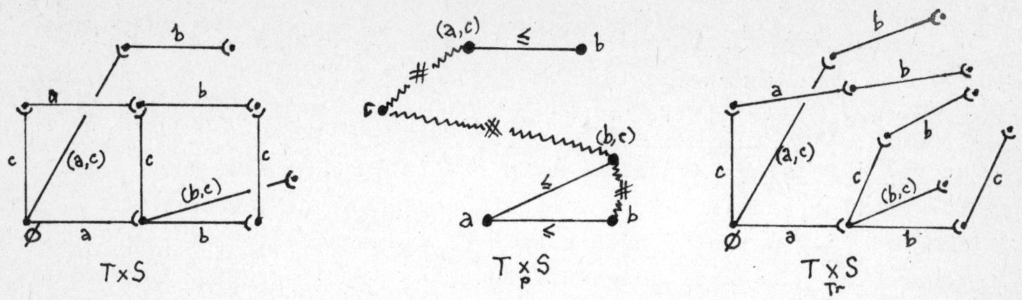

5. A semantics for communicating processes

Now we label the events of processes. Possible synchronisations between two processes set in parallel are determined by a synchronisation algebra (S.A.). An S.A. specifies how, depending on their labels, pairs of events are combined to form synchronised events and what labels such combinations carry. We adopt an idea from [M2] and present an S.A. as a binary operation $\cdot$ on labels. Unlike [M2] our algebra is not necessarily a monoid (it may not have 1) and has two distinguished constants * and a zero 0.

The constant * still represents undefined, exactly as it does for morphisms and is important for handling asynchrony. No real event is ever labelled *. However when two processes are set in parallel, an event of one process may be left to occur asynchronously, unsynchronised with any event of the other. Then it is enormously convenient to pretend, mathematically, that the event is synchronised with the unreal "event"* labelled by * - just as we did in the product 3.4.

The constant 0 is another fictitious label; no real event is labelled 0. We have $\lambda\cdot\lambda'=0$, for two labels λ,λ', when two events labelled λ and λ' cannot be synchronised. The introduction of 0 saves us from a partial operation on labels.

5.1 Definition A synchronisation algebra (S.A.) is a quadruple $(L,*,0,\cdot)$ where L is a set of labels, containing * and 0 with $L\setminus\{*,0\}\neq\emptyset$ and $\cdot$ is a binary associative, commutative operation on L which satisfies

(i) $\forall\lambda\in L.\quad \lambda\cdot 0=0$

(ii) $*\cdot *=*$ and $\forall\lambda,\lambda'\in L.\lambda\cdot\lambda'=*\Rightarrow\lambda=*$.

An S.A. determines a "divides" relation as follows. It says when one label is a divisor, or factor, of another.

5.2 Definition Let $(L,*,0,\cdot)$ be an S.A. For $\alpha,\beta\in L$ define α div $\beta \Leftrightarrow (\alpha=\beta$ or $\exists\gamma\in L.\alpha\cdot\gamma=\beta)$.

Thus condition (ii) in the definition of an S.A. says * is the unique divisor of *.

5.3 Example The S.A. for CCS

Without value passing: Recall that in CCS [M1] there are three kinds of (non*,0) labels; labels $\alpha,\beta,\ldots$, their complementary labels $\bar{\alpha},\bar{\beta},\ldots$ and the label τ. Only pairs of events with complementary labels can synchronise to produce a τ-labelled event. Thus the S.A. for CCS satisfies the axioms of 5.1 and rules of the form $\alpha\cdot *=\alpha$, $\bar{\alpha}\cdot *=\bar{\alpha}$, $\tau\cdot *=\tau$ and $\alpha\cdot\tau=\alpha\cdot\beta=0$ where $\alpha\neq\beta$. Note all non-0 labels divide τ.

With value passing: Suppose values $v\in V$ are passed during synchronisation. Take labels of the form $*,0,\alpha v$ (receiving the value v labelled by α), $\bar{\alpha}v$ (sending of value v labelled by α), with an S.A. like above but with $\bar{\alpha}v$ the complement of αv.

An S.A. determines a category of labelled event structures. Morphisms are event structure morphisms such that the label of the image of an event divides the event's label.

5.4 Definition Let $(L,*,0,\cdot)$ be an S.A. Define the category $\mathbb{E}_L$ to consist of objects (E,F,l) where $(E,F)\in\mathbb{E}$ and $l:E\to L\setminus\{*,0\}$, and morphisms $\theta:(E_0,F_0,l_0)\to(E_1,F_1,l_1)$ where $\theta:(E_0,F_0)\to(E_1,F_1)$ is a morphism of $\mathbb{E}$ and $\forall e\in E_0.\, l_1\theta(e)\,\mathrm{div}\, l_0(e)$; composition is that of partial functions $\underline{\underline{\mathrm{Set}}}_*$.

Note in the above definition that the composition $l_1\theta$ is understood to be in $\underline{\underline{\mathrm{Set}}}_*$. If $\theta(e)=*$ for some e in E_0 then $l_1\theta(e)=*$. Then for θ to be a morphism in $\mathbb{E}$ we would require $*\ \mathrm{div}\ l_0(e)$. Thus an S.A. can specify whether morphisms are partial or total functions. For example the categories $\mathbb{E}$ and $\mathbb{E}_{syn}$ arise from very simple S.A.s.

5.5 Example The S.A.'s for $\mathbb{E}$ and $\mathbb{E}_{syn}$

Take the S.A.'s A, S to be given by

A: ·	*	T	0
*	*	T	0
T	T	T	0
0	0	0	0

S: ·	*	T	0
*	*	0	0
T	0	T	0
0	0	0	0

Notice how morphisms in $\mathbb{E}_A$ may be partial functions as *divT. We get $\mathbb{E}_A\cong\mathbb{E}$. However morphisms in $\mathbb{E}_S$ must be total functions as * does not divide T. We get $\mathbb{E}_S\cong\mathbb{E}_{syn}$.

We now define the <u>parallel composition</u> of two labelled event structures as a restriction of the product in E. (See definition 3.4 of product; π_0, π_1 below are the projection morphisms.)

<u>5.6 Definition</u> Let L be an S.A. Let $(E_0,F_0,l_0),(E_1,F_1,l_1)\in\mathbb{E}_L$. Define their <u>parallel composition</u> $(E_0,F_0,l_0) \, Ⓛ \, (E_1,F_1,l_1)=((E_0,F_0)\times(E_1,F_1)\restriction E,l)$ where $E=\{e\in E_0 \overset{*}{\underset{*}{\times}} E_1 \mid l_0\pi_0(e)\cdot l_1\pi_1(e)\neq 0\}$ and $l(e)=l_0\pi_0(e)\cdot l_1\pi_1(e)$.

<u>5.7 Example</u> Let L be the S.A. for CCS without value passing - refer to 5.3. Suppose $(E_0,F_0,l_0),(E_1,F_1,l_1)\in\mathbb{E}_L$. Then their parallel composition is their product in $\mathbb{E}$ restricted to the events $\{(e_0,*)\mid e_0\in E\}\cup$ $\{(*,e_1)\mid e_1\in E_1\}\cup\{(e_0,e_1)\in E_0\times E_1 \mid l_0(e_0),l_1(e_1)$ are complementary$\}$ with a subsequent labelling $l(e_0,*)=l_0(e_0)$, $l(*,e_1)=l_1(e_1)$, $l(e_0,e_1)=\tau$.

<u>5.8 Example "Broadcasting"</u> Let L be the S.A. with labels $*,0,\alpha,\tau$ satisfying laws of the form $\alpha\cdot\alpha=\alpha$, $\alpha\cdot *=\alpha\cdot\tau=0$ and $\tau\cdot *=\tau$. Then the parallel composition of several processes must synchronise on α while τ-labelled events occur asynchronously (such multiway synchronisation is used in [H], [Mi], [LST] - see [M2] too).

Before giving the programming language based on an S.A. we present a few extra much simpler operations on labelled event structures based on [M1, 2].

<u>Definitions</u>
Let L be an S.A. Define the following operations on $\mathbb{E}_L$. Let (E,F,l), $(E_i,F_i,l_i)\in\mathbb{E}_L$ for $i=0,1$.

<u>5.9 Lifting</u> Suppose $\lambda\in L\smallsetminus\{*,0\}$. Define $\lambda(E,F,l)=(E',F',l')$ where $E'=\{0\}\cup\{1\}\times E$ and

$x\in F' \Leftrightarrow x\subseteq E'$ and $x=\emptyset$ or $(0\in x$ and $\{e\mid (1,e)\in x\}\in F)$
$l(e')=\lambda$ if $e=0$, $l(e)$ if $e'=(1,e)$ for $e'\in E'$.

<u>5.10 Sum</u> Define $(E_0,F_0,l_0)+(E_1,F_1,l_1)=((E_0,F_0)+(E_1,F_1),l)$ where $+$ is the coproduct of 3.8 and $l((0,e))=l_0(e)$ and $l((1,e))=l_1(e)$.

<u>5.11 Restriction</u> Let $\lambda\in L\smallsetminus\{*,0\}$. Define $(E,F,l)\smallsetminus\lambda=((E,F)\restriction E',l')$ where $E'=\{e\in E\mid l(e)\neq\lambda\}$ and $l'=l\restriction E'$.

<u>5.12 Relabelling</u> Let S be an endomorphism on L (i.e. S preserves $*$, 0 and $\cdot$ and $\forall\lambda\in L.\ S(\lambda)=0\Rightarrow\lambda=0$ & $S(\lambda)=*\Rightarrow\lambda=*$). Define $(E,F,l)\langle S\rangle=(E,F,Sl)$.

Apart from restriction, the above operations extend to functors on $\mathbb{E}_L$ in an obvious way. They are all continuous with respect to $\trianglelefteq_L$ the labelled version of $\trianglelefteq$. Thus we can take fixed points of them and their compositions.

5.13 Proposition Let L be an S.A. For $(E_0,F_0,l_0),(E_1,F_1,l_1)\in\mathbb{E}_L$ define $(E_0,F_0,l_0)\trianglelefteq_L(E_1,F_1,l_1)$ iff $(E_0,F_0)\trianglelefteq(E_1,F_1)$ and $l_0=l_1\restriction E_0$. Then

(i) $\mathbb{E}_L$ has lubs of all countable chains ordered by $\trianglelefteq_L$.

(ii) Each operation above is continuous with respect to $\trianglelefteq_L$ i.e. they preserve lubs of ω-chains ordered by $\trianglelefteq_L$.

(iii) Let Γ be a continuous operation on $\mathbb{E}_L^r\to\mathbb{E}_L$. Let $\bot=((\emptyset,\{\emptyset\},\emptyset),\dots,(\emptyset,\{\emptyset\},\emptyset))\in\mathbb{E}_L^r$. Define fix$\Gamma$ to be the lub of $\bot\trianglelefteq_L\Gamma\bot\trianglelefteq_L\dots\trianglelefteq_L\Gamma^n\bot\trianglelefteq_L\dots$. Then $\Gamma(\mathrm{fix}\Gamma)=\mathrm{fix}\Gamma$.

Given L, an S.A., we define a language for communicating processes called Proc_L. Each term of Proc_L denotes an event structure in $\mathbb{E}_L$.

5.14 The syntax of Proc_L

Assume an infinite set of process-variables $x\in X$. Define a term of Proc_L by:

$t::=\underline{\mathrm{NIL}}\,|\,x\,|\,\lambda t\,|\,t+t\,|\,t\setminus\lambda\,|\,t\langle S\rangle\,|\,t\,Ⓛ\,t\,|\,x\ \underline{\mathrm{isrec}}\ t$, where $x\in X,\lambda\in L\setminus\{*,0\}$ and S is an endomorphism of L.

5.15 The semantics of Proc_L

Define an environment to be a function $\rho:X\to\mathbb{E}_L$ from process-variables to labelled event structures. For a term t and an environment ρ, define $[\![t]\!]\rho$, the event structure t denotes with respect to ρ, by the following structural induction. (Note, that syntactic operators occur on the left and their semantic counterparts, operations on $\mathbb{E}_L$, on the right.)

$[\![\mathrm{NIL}]\!]\rho = (\emptyset,\{\emptyset\},\emptyset)$ $\qquad [\![t\setminus\lambda]\!] = [\![t]\!]\rho\setminus\lambda$

$[\![x]\!]\rho = \rho(x)$ $\qquad [\![t\langle S\rangle]\!]\rho = [\![t]\!]\rho\langle S\rangle$

$[\![\lambda t]\!]\rho = \lambda([\![t]\!]\rho)$ $\qquad [\![t_1 Ⓛ t_2]\!]\rho = [\![t_1]\!]\rho\,Ⓛ\,[\![t_2]\!]\rho$

$[\![t_1+t_2]\!]\rho = [\![t_1]\!]\rho+[\![t_2]\!]\rho$ $\qquad [\![x\ \underline{\mathrm{isrec}}\ t]\!]\rho = \mathrm{fix}\ \Gamma$ where $\Gamma:\mathbb{E}_L\to\mathbb{E}_L$ is given by $\Gamma(E)=[\![t]\!]\rho[x\leftarrow E]$

A structural induction shows that Γ is indeed continuous so the above definition is justified by proposition 5.13. We automatically derive semantics for Proc_L in prime event structures and trees by composing the above semantics with the operation Pr_L given by $\mathrm{Pr}_L(E,F,l)=(\mathrm{Pr}(E,F),\mathrm{lev}_{E,F})$ to get denotations as labelled prime event structures $\mathbb{P}_L$ and with the interleaving operation I_L given by $I_L(E,F,l)=(I(E,F),l\pi_{E,F})$ to get denotations as labelled trees $\mathbb{T}\mathrm{r}_L$ - refer to 4.2.

When L is the S.A. for CCS our interleaved semantics agrees with Milner's synchronisation/communication tree semantics - see 4.5. (Our treatment of recursion is more general than Milner's so our denotations as trees may be $\aleph_0$-branching when recursion is not "guardedly well-defined".)

Isomorphism in each category $\mathbb{E}_L$, $\mathbb{P}_L$, $\mathbb{T}r_L$ induces a congruence on closed terms of $Proc_L$, where L is an S.A.; for instance define $t \sim_P t'$ iff $Pr_L[\![t]\!]\rho \cong Pr_L[\![t']\!]\rho$ for environment ρ and closed terms t,t'. The congruences will express for example the associativity of Ⓛ. Generally because the event structures of $\mathbb{E}_L$ and $\mathbb{P}_L$ reflect concurrency, their congruences are strictly included in that for $\mathbb{T}r_L$. This strict inclusion fails in an interesting special case where communication is purely synchronous, when no asynchrony is allowed because L satisfies the strict <u>synchronous law</u>: $\forall\lambda\in L\setminus\{*\}.\lambda\bullet *=0$. Then the congruences induced by $\mathbb{P}_L$ and $\mathbb{T}r_L$ are the same. The synchronous law on S.A.s has two equivalents (cf. [M2]): firstly that parallel composition distributes over sum, t_0Ⓛ$(t_1+t_2)\sim t_0$Ⓛt_1+t_0Ⓛt_2, and secondly that NIL is a Ⓛ-zero, t Ⓛ NIL~NIL, where ~ is any of the above congruences - the synchronous law means Ⓛ inherits these properties from the product in <u>Set</u>. This illustrates how assumptions on L determine laws and proof rules for congruences on terms.

<u>5.16 Example</u> <u>The synchronous calculi of [M2]</u>
Any Abelian monoid $(M,\bullet,1)$ extends to an S.A. $(L,*,0,\bullet)$ simply by adjoining elements * and 0 to M and extending composition so $*\bullet*=*$ and $*\bullet\lambda=0$ for all $\lambda\neq*$ in L and $0\bullet\lambda=0$ for all $\lambda\in L$. The language $Proc_L$ includes the synchronous calculus associated with the monoid M in [M2] . In the parallel composition E_0ⓁE_1 every event e_0 of E_0 is synchronised with an event e_1 of E_1; the event may be labelled by 1 when it represents a delay or idle action. Denotations of closed terms of $Proc_L$ are pre-trees in $\mathbb{E}_L$ and trees in $\mathbb{P}_L$.

<u>Appendix</u> We take <u>Set</u> to be the category of sets with usual function-composition. To cope with partial functions, we take $\underline{Set}_*$ to have sets as objects but morphisms are now functions which may take the value * (representing "undefined"). A morphism in $\underline{Set}_*$ is drawn as $\theta:X\to_* Y$. The morphisms $X \overset{\theta}{\underset{*}{\to}} Y$ and $Y \overset{\varphi}{\underset{*}{\to}} Z$ compose to $\varphi\theta(x)=\varphi(\theta(x))$ if $\theta(x)\neq*$, and * otherwise. Morphisms in <u>Set</u> (total functions) correspond to those morphisms of $\underline{Set}_*$ which never yield *. For $\theta:X \to_* Y$ and $A\subseteq X$ define $\hat{\theta}(A) = \{\theta(e) \mid e\in A \ \&\ \theta(e)\neq*\}$.

For us, a notable fact about $\underline{Set}_*$ is the nature of its products. If X and Y are sets their <u>categorical product</u> in $\underline{Set}_*$ takes the form $X \times_* Y =_{def} \{(x,*) \mid x\in X\}\cup\{(*,y) \mid y\in Y\}\cup\{(x,y) \mid x\in X \ \&\ y\in Y\}$ with the obvious projections.

Acknowledgements

I am grateful for discussions with Mogens Nielsen. Mogens has previously given a prime event structure semantics to CCS. Thanks to Gordon Plotkin for encouraging morphisms even when they were quarter-baked. The stability axiom is essentially Gérard Berry's "deterministic" condition [BC]. Related ideas appear in [F] and [MS]. Thanks to Karen Møller for typing a symbol-laden paper. The work was supported in part by an SRC grant directed by Robin Milner and Gordon Plotkin and in part by the Royal Society.

References

[BC] G. Berry, P.L. Curien, "Sequential algorithms on concrete data structures", to appear in TCS.

[F] T. Fogh, "En semantik for synkroniserede parallelle processer", Master's Thesis, Aarhus University, 1981.

[H] C.A.R. Hoare, "A Model for Communicating Sequential Processes", Programming Research Group, Oxford University, 1978.

[KP] G. Kahn, G. Plotkin, "Structures de Données concrètes", IRIA-Laboria Report 336, 1978.

[LTS] P.E. Lauer, P.R. Torrigiani, M.W. Shields, "COSY: A System Specification Language based on Paths and Processes", Acta Informatica 12, 1979.

[Mac] S. Maclane, "Categories for the working mathematician", Springer-Verlag, 1971.

[Mi] G.J. Milne, "Synchronised Behaviour Algebras: a model for interacting systems", Dept. of Comp. Sc., University of Southern California, 1979.

[M1] R. Milner, "A Calculus of Communicating Systems", LNCS 92, 1980.

[M2] R. Milner, "On relating Synchrony and Asynchrony", Dept. of Comp. Sc., University of Edinburgh, 1980.

[MS] U. Montanari, C. Simonelli, "On distinguishing between concurrency and nondeterminism", Proc. Ecole de Printemps on Concurrency and Petri Nets, Colleville, 1980 (to appear).

[NPW1] M. Nielsen, G. Plotkin, G. Winskel, "Petri nets, event structures and domains", Proc. Conf. on Semantics of Concurrent Computation, Evian, LNCS 70, 1979.

[NPW2] M. Nielsen, G. Plotkin, G. Winskel, "Petri nets, event structures and domains, part I", TCS 13, 1981.

[NT] W. Brauer (ed.), "Net Theory and Applications", LNCS 84, 1980.

[S] D.S. Scott, "Lectures on a Mathematical Theory of Computation", Lecture notes in mathematics, University of Oxford, 1980.

[W] G. Winskel, "Events in Computation", Ph.D. Thesis, Dept. of Comp. Sc., University of Edinburgh, 1980.

DOMAINS FOR DENOTATIONAL SEMANTICS

by

Dana S. Scott

Department of Computer Science

Carnegie-Mellon University

Pittsburgh, Pennsylvania 15213

Abstract. The purpose of the theory of domains is to give models for spaces on which to define computable functions. The kinds of spaces needed for denotational sematics involve not only spaces of higher type (*e.g.* function spaces) but also spaces defined recursively (*e.g.* reflexive domains). Also required are many special domain constructs (or functors) in order to create the desired structures. There are several choices of a suitable category of domains, but the basic one which has the simplest properties is the one sometimes called *consistently complete algebraic cpo's.* This category of domains is studied in this paper from a new, and it is to be hoped, simpler point of view incorporating the approaches of many authors into a unified presentation. Briefly, the domains of elements are represented set theoretically with the aid of structures called *information systems.* These systems are very familiar from mathematical logic, and their use seems to accord well with intuition. Many things that were done previously axiomatically can now be proved in a straightfoward way as theorems. The present paper discusses many examples in an informal way that should serve as an introduction to the subject.

1. Introduction. I would like to begin with some personal remarks. When I think of the number of headaches I have caused people in Computer Science who have tried to figure out the mathematical details of the Theory of Domains, I have to cringe. The difficulty in the presentation of the subject is in justifying the level of abstraction used in comparison with the payoff: too often the effort needed for understanding the abstractions does not seem worth the trouble—especially if the notions are unfamiliar or excessively general.

For example, Category Theory, which is much used in discussions of the Theory of Domains, seems far too abstract to many people. On the other hand, Automata Theory—which has often benefited from some use of Category Theory—is quite abstract and, in many aspects perhaps, quite useless, but the level of abstraction is fairly low and the reasons for the definitions are usually evident. Thus, the subject has become by now a standard topic even for undergraduate courses. I believe that Michael Rabin and I had much to do with influencing the subsequent development of the theory by formulating some years ago some basic concepts (many previously known) in a way that made sense to anyone who had been exposed to a little Abstract Algebra, Logic and Set Theory. This expository part of our paper did not require originality, but rather a certain frame of mind and a certain style of writing to put the ideas and problems in sharp relief. (The original paper is Rabin–Scott [1959]; see the excellent historical review of the subject in Greibach [1981].)

Domain Theory has fared less well. I feel I made a mistake in 1969 in using Lattice Theory as a mode of presentation—a mistake as far as Computer Science is concerned. Lattices are very familiar to logicians and those interested in Universal Algebra, and I liked very much the structures I found. But it takes some time to learn the special terminology and to become comfortable with the necessary examples. Indeed, without a stock of examples, it is impossible to have sufficient intuition for making the required constructions. True, some people took to the approach, and the lattice-theoretic definitions were simple enough to motivate. But a much greater percentage of people I came in contact with found the large number of things to learn a definite roadblock to understanding. And the Lattice Theory was only partly standard, since this approach to the theory has to employ complete lattices and topological notions in order to explain *limits* and *continuity* adequately. In fact, Topology of a rather mathematically simple set-theoretical kind could have been used as the whole foundation much as in Scott [1972], but that kind of mathematics seems even less attractive to computer scientists. Again, it is a matter of background, I think, and it is unreasonable to expect people to know everything. Nevertheless, the lattice-theoretic approach has great consistency and coherence; it has been carried out in full detail in Gierz, *et al.* [1980], which also gives the topological connections. That book contains a large number of references to the mathematical literature to show the connections of the theory to many other topics. What we had to miss out there is a clear hook-up with computability theory, owing simply to a lack of space and time to be able to cover everything.

In Scott [1981], I tried out another, different presentation (which is also explained in Scott [1982].) However, I have found that the use of *neighborhood systems* causes confusion in people not used to thinking in terms of sets of sets of sets of sets . . . , even though the set theory required is quite simple. My purpose in the present lecture, then, is to go back once more to the very beginning to try out another plan for making the story easy and natural. The notion to be used I call an *information system.* This is a "static" notion appropriate to bodies of information about coherent groups of elements. The "dynamic" ideas enter in the ways different systems can be related and in the semantical definitions about meanings of programming language constructs. (For discussions of semantical definitions see Stoy [1977], Gordon [1979], and Tennent [1981].) Neighborhood systems are, in a precise sense, equivalent to information systems, but there seems to be an interesting trade-off between what properties of structures are *axiomatized* and what are *implicit* in the form of the structure. Perhaps, despite their simplicity, neighborhoods leave too much implicit, too much to be extracted by definition; information systems, on the other hand, do seem to be more flexible in doing several of the important constructions. It all comes down to just where one imposes the closure conditions on the structures. I have a feeling that I now have found just about the right mix of axioms *vs.* definitions.

Another word about Category Theory: I actually feel that it is particularly significant and important for the theory and for the whole area of semantics. But it must be approached with great caution, for the sheer number of definitions *and* axioms can try the most patient reader. It seems to me to be especially necessary in discussing applications of abstract mathematical ideas to keep the motivation strongly in mind. This is often hard to do if the categories get too thick, but of course it all depends on the writer. Category Theory is especially useful in stating *general* properties of structures and in *characterizing* constructions uniquely; however, there often is a problem actually justifying the *existence* of certain constructions, and a direct approach can be quicker than quoting lots of theorems. But, man cannot live by construction alone: theorems have to be proved in order to get the proper value out of the work. Domain Theory must also be convenient for demonstrating the soundness of various proof rules for properties of recursively defined objects and recursively defined domains, and I think that Category Theory can be helpful here. A step in the right direction has been made in the LCF system (see Gordon-Milner-Wadsworth [1979]), which, however, does not take advantage of general Category Theory; but the whole area needs much more development in my opinion.

The main purpose of the Theory of Domains in Denotational Semantics, as I see it, is to give a mathematical model of a system of *types*—including function-space types—and to explain a notion of *computability* with respect to these types. There are many possible theories of types, but the construction of domains is meant to justify *recursive definitions* at all types, and—most essentially—to justify recursive definitions *of* types. Pursuing these goals has certain consequences, as we shall see. The model presented here is only one approach, and some comparisons with other methods will be made in Section 8. Again some help from Category Theory would be welcome in comparing the different kinds of modelling.

One benefit of Domain Theory is that it is possible to make sense of types containing *infinite* elements. The cost required seems to be that the domains therefore have to contain *partial* elements as well as *total* elements. And this is where the lattice-theoretic definitions entered in the earlier presentations: the partial ordering with relations like $x \sqsubseteq y$ was used to express the fact that the element x was "less defined" (*i.e.* more partial) than y but "contained in" y. The relation $\sqsubseteq$, however, must be subjected to many axioms to have a theory suitable to the desired applications. Instead of such a big group of axioms, I wish to put forward here a construction where the "skeleton" (or better: "backbone") of a domain is introduced by just a few axioms. Then the domain itself is *defined* as a certain construct from the backbone in order to define the appropriate notion of element. There are several advantages I can see to the new approach:

- *Simple* definitions of the basic concepts can be given.
- Detailed properties are *proved* as theorems rather than assumed as axioms.
- Emphasis can be given to the *constructive* nature of the definitions.
- Domains can be made more *visible*.
- The theory of domains is made more available for *applications*, because it is easier to produce the needed complex domains.

It is to be hoped that the reader can judge the validity of these claims from the perhaps too brief exposition to follow.

2. Information systems. Intuitively, an *information system* is a set of "propositions" that can be made about "possible elements" of the desired domain. We will assume that sufficiently many propositions have been supplied to distinguish between distinct elements; as a consequence, an element can be constructed abstractly as the *set* of all the propositions that are true of it. Partial elements have "small" sets; while total elements have "large" sets (even: maximal). To make this somewhat rough idea precise, we have to explain—by a suitable, but small choice of axioms—how the collection of all propositions relevant to the domain hangs together, or better, is structured as a set of abstract propositions. Fortunately, the axioms for this structure are very simple and familiar, which is a great help in making up examples.

DEFINITION 2.1. An *information system* is a structure

$$(\mathcal{D}, \Delta, \mathrm{Con}, \vdash),$$

where $\mathcal{D}$ is a set (the set of *data objects* or *propositions*), where Δ is a distinguished member of $\mathcal{D}$ (the *least informative* member), where Con is a set of finite subsets of $\mathcal{D}$ (the *consistent* sets of objects), and where $\vdash$ is a binary relation between members of Con and members of $\mathcal{D}$ (the *entailment relation* for objects). Concerning Con, the following axioms must be satisfied for all finite subsets $u, v \subseteq \mathcal{D}$:

(i) $u \in \text{Con}$, whenever $u \subseteq v \in \text{Con}$;

(ii) $\{X\} \in \text{Con}$, whenever $X \in \mathcal{D}$; and

(iii) $u \cup \{X\} \in \text{Con}$, whenever $u \vdash X$.

Concerning $\vdash$, the following axioms must be satisfied for all $u, v \in \text{Con}$, and all $X \in \mathcal{D}$:

(iv) $u \vdash \Delta$;

(v) $u \vdash X$, whenever $X \in u$; and

(vi) if $v \vdash Y$ for all $Y \in u$ and $u \vdash X$, then $v \vdash X$.

In words we may say of Con that, as a set of sets, (i) it is closed under subsets, (ii) it contains all singletons, and (iii) adjunction of an entailed object to a consistent set preserves consistency. Concerning $\vdash$, which should be viewed as a "multiary" relation, we may say that (iv) Δ is entailed by anything, (v) $\vdash$ is reflexive, and (vi) $\vdash$ is transitive. (The last two properties are both expressed in a way appropriate to a multiary relation on members of $\mathcal{D}$.) ∎

The best advice is to think of the members of $\mathcal{D}$ as consisting of *finite* data objects, some of which are more informative than others. The word "finite" should be taken here in the sense of "fully circumscribed"—as regards what is given in **A** these data objects can be comprehended in "one step." It is of course possible to introduce information systems where the data objects are infinite sets, but *relative* to **A** they are finite as data objects.

The member that provides *zero information* is Δ. Data objects are intended to give information about possible *elements* of the domain to be constructed, so if we were to use Δ alone, we would be describing the the least defined element usually written as $\perp$.

Not just any combination of data objects will describe a possible element, however; hence, the need for the notion of *consistency.* If $u \in \text{Con}$ is false, then the "propositions" in u cannot all be applied to the same element at the same time. Finally we have to agree that, in general, the propositions to be allowed are rarely mutually independent. It follows that an entailment relation must be imposed to record the dependencies that do hold among the propositions. With these informal understandings, the axioms chosen should all be self-evident.

A first example. Suppose we let $\mathcal{D}$ be the set of non-negative integers, where we think of an integer n as an abbreviation of the proposition $n \leq x$. Here x is a yet-to-be-determined element, about which one proposition gives only a little information. We can identify Δ with 0, and take Con to be the set of all finite subsets of $\mathcal{D}$. The entailment relation can be defined formally in the way suggested by the intuitive reading of the data objects:

$$\{n_0, \ldots, n_{k-1}\} \vdash m \text{ iff either } m = 0 \text{ or } m \leq n_i \text{ for some } i < k.$$

(Remember to think of the same possible x on both sides of the $\vdash$.) That $\vdash$ is an entailment relation in the sense of our axioms is clear. ∎

A second example. The first example is possibly misleading because all (finite) sets of data objects were allowed to be consistent. The example can be modified in a natural way so this is not so; of course, quite a different system will be obtained. The idea is to let $\mathcal{D}$ be the set of all *pairs* (n, m) of integers with $n \leq m$, where such a pair stands now for the proposition $n \leq x \leq m$. Clearly the two data objects (0,2) and (3,7) taken together are *inconsistent.* (Why?)

Oh, I see, I have left out Δ from $\mathcal{D}$; we must therefore include the somewhat artificial pair $(0, \infty)$ with the obvious interpretation. When I say "obvious interpretation" here I mean that $u \in$ Con can be defined by saying that there must be an integer satisfying all the "propositions" in u. Further, $u \vdash X$ can be defined by saying that *whenever* an integer satisfies all the propositions in u, *then* it must satisfy X. The notion of "satisfy" really should be obvious from the intuitive reading given to the data objects, and the reader can verify easily that all the axioms hold for this example of an information system. ∎

A third example. Let A and B be two fixed sets, and let $\mathcal{D}$ as a set consist of the ordered pairs (a, b), with $a \in A$ and $b \in B$, plus the extra object Δ. Here the "information" contained in (a, b) is that a is mapped to b by a yet-to-be-determined *function.* With this thought in mind, we will know that a finite set of data objects is consistent just in case it is possible that they can all belong to the *same* function. Formally, we can assert:

$$\{(a_0, b_0), \ldots, (a_{k-1}, b_{k-1})\} \in \text{Con iff for all } i, j < k \text{ whenever } a_i = a_j, \text{ then } b_i = b_j.$$

It is something of a bother having to throw in Δ in this case, but all we have to say is that if u is consistent under the above rule, then so also will $u \cup \{\Delta\}$; and these are the only consistent sets of data objects for this example. Perhaps it would make more sense to use $\{(a, b)\}$ in place of the simpler (a, b), and then we could set $\Delta = \emptyset$ more naturally. From this point of view we can regard each data object as a (very small!) fragment of the graph of a function; the consistent sets then point to larger fragments of graphs.

The definition of the entailment relation is the minimal one:

$$u \vdash X \text{ iff either } X = \Delta \text{ or } X \in u.$$

These examples show that sometimes the main part of the structure is in Con, sometimes it is in $\vdash$, and sometimes it is in the interplay between the two notions. The object Δ is not in itself very important, but it is sometimes useful to have an object there that can always be counted upon to act in the same way in every system. ∎

Already in formulating the axiom about the transitivity of $\vdash$ a relation between sets in Con was suggested; we now make this official.

DEFINITION 2.2. For $u, v \in$ Con we write $u \vdash v$ to mean that $u \vdash X$ for all $X \in v$. ∎

PROPOSITION 2.3. *For all* $u, v, w, u', v' \in$ *Con, we have*:

(i) $\emptyset \vdash \{\Delta\}$;

(ii) $u \vdash v$ *implies* $u \cup v \in$ Con;

(iii) $u \vdash u$;

(iv) $u \vdash v$ *and* $v \vdash w$ *imply* $u \vdash w$;

(v) $u' \supseteq u, u \vdash v$, *and* $v \supseteq v'$ *imply* $u' \vdash v'$; *and*

(vi) $u \vdash v$ *and* $u \vdash v'$ *imply* $u \vdash v \cup v'$.

Proof. Obvious. ∎

Remark. It is not worth formulating a formal result at this point, but it should be clear that the properties in 2.3 could have been used as axioms. That is to say, we could have taken $\vdash$ as a binary relation on the set Con, used 2.1 (i)–(ii) and 2.3 (i)–(vi) as axioms. (Actually, 2.3(ii) is redundant.) The old-style entailment relation would then be definable by:

$$u \vdash X \text{ iff } u \vdash \{X\}.$$

The previous axioms in 2.1 are then easily proved from the new ones. ∎

Some notation. As it is not always clear what structure is meant if we refer to a domain simply by naming its underlying set of data objects, it will be better if we use a letter to refer to an information system *as a whole*. We shall therefore write:

$$\mathbf{A} = (\mathcal{D}_{\mathbf{A}}, \Delta_{\mathbf{A}}, \mathrm{Con}_{\mathbf{A}}, \vdash_{\mathbf{A}}),$$

and say that $\mathbf{A}$ is an information system—with its parts as indicated. For a more informal discussion, the notation without subscripts can suffice, but there can be problems when several different systems are involved. ∎

So much for the definition of what a system is as a mathematical structure. The next question is: What is it good for? More precisely, if information systems are the backbones of domains, then where are the elements? That is the topic of the next section.

3. The elements of a system. Let $\mathbf{A}$ be an information system, and suppose we already had a concept of being an element of $\mathbf{A}$. The data objects are meant to be propositions about elements, so if X is in $\mathcal{D}_{\mathbf{A}}$ and if x is an element, then we can be expected to know what it means to say that X is *true* of x. Since all we are given is the set of data objects $\mathcal{D}_{\mathbf{A}}$, we have to assume that it contains enough objects to distinguish between distinct elements. (If there were not enough of them, we would have to change the set $\mathcal{D}_{\mathbf{A}}$.) Formally, we can write of two elements x and y:

$$x = y \text{ iff all } X \in \mathcal{D}_{\mathbf{A}} \text{ which are true of } x \text{ are also true of } y, \text{ and conversely.}$$

If this principle is accepted, then the elements can be *identified* with the sets of propositions true of them; formally we can assert:

$$x = \{X \in \mathcal{D}_{\mathbf{A}} \mid X \text{ is true of } x\}.$$

There can be no confusion injected here in identifying elements that ought to be distinct, since we are *assuming* that there are enough data objects in the system. If for some reason we felt we ought to have more of them to distinguish between more elements, then we would have to pass to a larger and *different* information system. By agreement, then, the above equation is a tautology.

So, for the sake of simplicity, elements can be taken to be *sets* of data objects. But, we hasten to ask, which sets? The question is really: What are the properties of truth? The answers are well known, and, in fact, we have already used them in our examples in the last section. In words, the set of true propositions about a possible element must be (i) consistent in itself, and (ii) closed under entailment (or *deductively closed*, for short). Condition (i) is clear because we are talking about a *possible* element, not an impossible one. Condition (ii) is acceptable, because, by the very meaning of the word, entailment should be truth preserving. In addition, we are also saying the converse: *any* set having properties (i) and (ii) corresponds to a (partial) element. Here is the formal statement:

DEFINITION 3.1. The *elements* of the information system $\mathbf{A} = (\mathcal{D}_{\mathbf{A}}, \Delta_{\mathbf{A}}, \mathrm{Con}_{\mathbf{A}}, \vdash_{\mathbf{A}})$ are those subsets x of $\mathcal{D}_{\mathbf{A}}$ where:

(i) all finite subsets of x are in $\mathrm{Con}_{\mathbf{A}}$; and

(ii) whenever $u \subseteq x$ and $u \vdash_{\mathbf{A}} X$, then $X \in x$.

We write $x \in |\mathbf{A}|$ to mean x is an element of the system. This set of elements is the *domain* determined by the given system. An element that is not included in any strictly larger element in the domain is called a *total* element; the set of total elements is denoted by $\mathrm{Tot}_{\mathbf{A}}$. ∎

Remarks. Any subset of $\mathcal{D}_{\mathbf{A}}$ satisfying 3.1 (i) can be called consistent, and every consistent set generates an element by closing it under entailment. Note, too, that every element contains $\Delta_{\mathbf{A}}$ as a member, because the least informative proposition is true of all elements. Moreover, every domain has a least element contained in all other elements. We call it $\perp_{\mathbf{A}}$ and write formally:

$$\perp_{\mathbf{A}} = \{X \in \mathcal{D}_{\mathbf{A}} \mid \{\Delta_{\mathbf{A}}\} \vdash_{\mathbf{A}} X\}.$$

In the above we could just as well have used the empty set $\emptyset$ in place of $\{\Delta_{\mathbf{A}}\}$; and often we can write simply $\vdash_{\mathbf{A}} X$.

The element $\perp_{\mathbf{A}}$ is often called the *bottom* element of the domain. There need be no *top* or maximal element, $\top_{\mathbf{A}}$. Such an element is possible if, and only if, *all* finite subsets of $\mathcal{D}_{\mathbf{A}}$ are consistent, in which case, as a set, $\top_{\mathbf{A}} = \mathcal{D}_{\mathbf{A}}$. The possibility is not excluded—rather, it is not required. In case $\top_{\mathbf{A}}$ exists, it is the unique total element of the domain, and conversely. ∎

Returning to our question of the balance between axiomatizaton and construction, what we have done is first to axiomatize the properties of $(\mathcal{D}_{\mathbf{A}}, \Delta_{\mathbf{A}}, \mathrm{Con}_{\mathbf{A}}, \vdash_{\mathbf{A}})$, then to construct the domain $|\mathbf{A}|$ from this structure. The principal claimed advantages are that the axioms for consistency and entailment are already essentially familiar, and that the definition of elementhood is direct and natural from our understanding of the properties of truth.

The examples. Let us look again at the three examples of information systems of the last section. (1) In the first we see that the elements, by the formal definition, are either the finite sets $\{n \mid n \leq m\}$ or the whole set (*i.e.* $\top$). Intuitively, this corresponds to the fact that the chosen propositions only give *lower* bounds on a possible element; thus, no element is "finished" until it becomes infinite. (2) In the second example there is no top, and the elements are the sets of the form:

$$\{(n, q) \mid n \leq m \leq p \leq q\},$$

where $m \leq p$ are given, and where $q = \infty$ is allowed. The total elements here correspond to the (non-negative) integers, and the partial elements to situations where the lower and upper bounds have not come exactly together. (3) In the third example, the elements are just the graphs (*i.e.* sets of ordered pairs) of partial functions from A into B (with the object Δ adjoined to the graph). Total elements correspond to total functions (*i.e.* functions well defined on *all* of the set A). ∎

The reader should be able to obtain some more examples of information systems from his own experience and should then consider what the corresponding domain is like. Examples are really quite easy to make up. Needless to say, Mathematical Logic provides a host of information systems, but logicians do not often consider the domains determined by the the systems they know to be worthy of study *in themselves.* In particular, it does not seem to be widely recognized that the domains obtained from information systems form a rich category, as we shall show later. The word "category" is definitely being used here in the precise technical sense of Category Theory, and the application of the notion is very appropriate since the category of domains has very good closure properties.

4. Domains as lattices and as topological spaces. I will attempt to keep this section as informal as possible—especially as Sections 2 and 3 were quite formal (*i.e.* mathematical) enough. The main purpose of the discussion of this section is to relate the new presentation of the Theory of Domains to previously published ones. (Some alternatives are discussed at the end of the paper.)

Lattice-theoretic considerations. Let $\mathbf{A}$ be an information system. Because the elements of $|\mathbf{A}|$ are introduced as sets, these elements can be given structure from what we know already about ordinary sets. For instance, the set-theoretic inclusion relation between sets can certainly be applied to elements. The question is: What does $x \subseteq y$ mean intuitively? In fact, we have already mentioned this relationship before. It means that every proposition (among the ones given by the information system) true of x is also true of y (though not necessarily conversely). In other words, x is perhaps only partially determined, while y is more fully determined in a way that includes everything true of x. Clearly, then, if we grant the interest of partial elements, then this relation is a natural and basic one. We often read "$x \subseteq y$" as "*x approximates y*".

Now here is one of the main points of the new exposition: Because $x \subseteq y$ is *defined* in terms of a familiar mathematical notion, then as a relation between elements it inherits all the well-known properties of the set-theoretical relation. It should not be necessary to write them out, for everyone who can read this far knows that $\subseteq$ is in particular reflexive and transitive. We say that the domain $|\mathbf{A}|$ is a *partially ordered set under inclusion.* We note that this (trivial) result is *proved* from the definition rather than assumed as an axiom.

Let us try out another notion. Elements are consistent, deductively closed sets of data objects. Right? Every subset of a consistent set is consistent, but not every subset is closed under entailment, in general. Right? But suppose that x and y are two elements. It can easily be seen that their intersection $x \cap y$ is again consistent and deductively closed (by a 2 nanosecond proof). Therefore, the set of elements of a domain is closed under intersection. This means that, as a partially ordered set, $|\mathbf{A}|$ is an *inf semilattice.*

Well, the exact terminology is quite unimportant, but the properties of $\cap$ when combined with the properties of $\subseteq$ are pleasantly "algebraic" (and run to several lines when written out). We all know them: $\cap$ is idempotent, commutative, and associative. The element $\perp$, being the smallest element of the domain, is a zero element for $\cap$. The operation $\cap$ is monotonic with respect to $\subseteq$, and we have the connection:

$$x \subseteq y \text{ iff } x \cap y = x.$$

What has just been alluded to in words is the standard mathematical axiomatization of the properties of an infimum (or meet) operation in a partially ordered set. (Remember, however, to have an operation well defined within a set it is necessary also to have *closure* under that operation.)

What about infs of subsets? No problem. For any *non-empty* subfamily of $|\mathbf{A}|$, it is just as easy to prove that the set-theoretical intersection of all the elements in the subfamily is again an element of the domain. This makes $|\mathbf{A}|$ a (conditionally) complete inf semilattice. Even if you do not have any idea what I am talking about, it does not matter because the properties of the domain are built in by the very definition; you do not have to worry *at the start* about their formulation, for you can prove them when you need them (if ever).

What about suprema (or sups or joins)? Here there is a slight problem, because in the way we set things up they *do not* always have to exist. Consider what happens with just two elements x and y. The set-theoretical union of the two elements as subsets of $\mathcal{D}_{\mathbf{A}}$ need be neither consistent nor deductively closed; and even if $x \cup y$ is consistent, it need not be closed under entailment. So if we want sups *within* $|\mathbf{A}|$, we cannot get by as cheaply as we can with a domain of arbitrary sets for which the simple union is the answer.

Let us write the sup (supposing it exists in $|\mathbf{A}|$) as $x \sqcup y$. What do we have when we actually have it? By the lore of partially ordered sets, $x \sqcup y$ must be the *least element* in $|\mathbf{A}|$ which includes (in the sense of $\subseteq$) both x and y. Now we have just spoken about infs of families of elements: they exist if the family is non empty. This indicates that $x \sqcup y$ exists exactly when there is at least one element z in $|\mathbf{A}|$ such that $x \subseteq z$ and $y \subseteq z$. This turns out to be a way to say—entirely inside $|\mathbf{A}|$—that $x \cup y$ is consistent. In other words (and more generally) a sup of a subfamily exists if, and only if, the union of the family is consistent. (And in that case the sup is just the deductive closure of the union—that is, it is generally larger than the simple set-theoretical union.) This has an axiomatic version, but it is slightly complicated by the fact that sups do not always exist. In case $\top_{\mathbf{A}}$ exists, then we always have all the sups, and $|\mathbf{A}|$ is a *complete lattice.* (This is discussed in full axiomatic splendor in Gierz, *et al.* [1980].) But, let it hasten to be added, not every complete lattice is isomorphic to a domain. The lattices that correspond to domains are the so-called *algebraic lattices.* (See the discussion *loc. cit.* for the additional axiomatics required.) When the top is missing, the partially ordered structures corresponding to domains are called *conditionally complete, algebraic cpo's.*

There is, however, an important case in $|\mathbf{A}|$ where the union is consistent and is, in fact, the sup in the domain. Suppose we have a sequence of elements such that

$$x_0 \subseteq x_1 \subseteq x_2 \subseteq \cdots \subseteq x_n \subseteq x_{n+1} \subseteq \cdots.$$

As n increases, we can say that the elements x_n are getting "better and better"; thus, they must be approaching something even more desirable *in the limit.* Let

$$y = \bigcup_{n=0}^{\infty} x_n,$$

then there is no question that y is a subset of $\mathcal{D}_{\mathbf{A}}$. But is it an element? Consistency, recall, means that every *finite* subset is in $\mathrm{Con}_{\mathbf{A}}$. The trick is that a finite subset of y must be a subset of one of the x_n, because the sequence of elements x_n is increasing. But all the terms of our given sequence are elements, and so, consistent; therefore, every finite subset of y is consistent.

The same argument also shows that the set y of data objects is closed under entailment, because $\vdash_{\mathbf{A}}$ is defined as a relation between finite (consistent) sets and data objects. It follows that since each x_n is a set closed under $\vdash_{\mathbf{A}}$, then so is y. In other words, y is indeed an element. Otherwise said, the domain $|\mathbf{A}|$ is closed under the formation of unions of increasing chains of elements, and the union is, of course, the sup in the sense of the partial ordering. Again we have proved closure rather than assuming it, and the necessary properties of the sup follow from its definition as a union.

This last argument can be generalized—as is well known to mathematicians—to the case of *directed* families of elements. The word "directed," or better "upward-directed," means that every finite number of elements in the family is included in some further element of the family; chains always have this property. A good example of the use of directed sets of elements figures in the discussion of the *finite* elements of the domain.

As we have remarked several times, any consistent set of data objects *generates* an element by closing it up under the entailment relation; thus, in particular, any set $u \in \mathrm{Con}$ generates an element. Let us write

$$\overline{u} = \{X \in \mathcal{D}_{\mathbf{A}} \mid u \vdash_{\mathbf{A}} X\}$$

for the *closure* of u under entailment. (This notation could be used for any consistent subset of $\mathcal{D}$, but the case of finitely generated elements is especially important.) Such a $\overline{u}$ is always an element of $|\mathbf{A}|$; the totality of such elements form, by definition, the *finite elements* of the domain. The notation $\overline{u}$ should of course be decorated with a subscript $\mathbf{A}$, but, as there is no good place to write it in, we leave it out.

We have for all elements x of the domain the basic formula:

$$x = \bigcup\{\overline{u} \mid u \in \mathrm{Con}_{\mathbf{A}} \text{ and } u \subseteq x\}.$$

This can be read intuitively as saying that *every element of the domain is the limit of its finite approximations.* And, having used the word "limit" so often, we ought now to say something about how to make the meaning of this word correct mathematically. Note that in the limit representation for x, the union is a directed one. (Why?)

Topological considerations. Geometrically speaking, a topological space is a collection of "points" which group themselves in various "neighborhoods" providing thereby a sense of "nearness." More specifically, a neighborhood of a point in a *metric* space consists of all those points within a certain positive "distance" from the given point; that is, nearness is limited, but it is not pushed to *zero.* The major reason for leaving some "breathing space" around the point comes out in defining *continuity* of functions.

A function f from one topological space to another is said to be *continuous* provided that, for every point x of the first space, and for every neighborhood in the second space around $f(x)$, it is possible to find—in the first space—a neighborhood around x with the following property. If the function is restricted to this neighborhood, then its values lie entirely in the given neighborhood around $f(x)$. In the metric case we can say that if we do not want the function to wander any great distance from $f(x)$, then there is a restricted distance around x giving a neighborhood over which the function values stay as close to $f(x)$ as specified. This keeps the function from jumping around wildly, since small variations in x lead to only small variations in $f(x)$.

The intuition about continuity is no doubt very clear in the more geometric examples, and gometric intuition can carry us quite far. But the spaces obtained from domain theory are not really geometric spaces, so we need to make some shifts in our metaphors. The geometric notion of a point usually implies that two points are perfectly distinguishable: if x and y are different, then they have *disjoint* neighborhoods. This is certainly true in the metric case, where, if two points are different, then they are at a positive distance apart. Early on in the study of topological spaces, however, it was found that not all spaces were metric, and weaker separation properties of pairs of distinct points were uncovered. One of the very weak versions of such a condition is called the "T_0–axiom." The best way to put it is that if two points have the *same* neighborhoods, then they are the same. The contrapositive statement sounds odd: if two points are distinct, then there is a neighborhood that contains one but not the other. The oddity of this statement lies in the feeling that you cannot make up your mind over which is the better point.

In our domains there is already a notion of "betterness" which proves to be very closely related to the implicit neighborhood structure. The reason why our domains, as spaces of points, are not "geometric" in the familiar sense is that they contain *partial elements.* A geometric point on the other hand is "perfect" or totally determined; it cannot be made better than it already is. The metric in common spaces is measuring something other than betterness, for there are competing notions of approximation afoot here. Thus, we must keep our special goals in defining domains clearly in mind to avoid confusion.

Consider an information system **A**. For each $u \in \mathrm{Con}_{\mathbf{A}}$, we define a corresponding *neighborhood* of $|\mathbf{A}|$ by the equation:

$$[u]_{\mathbf{A}} = \{x \in |\mathbf{A}| \mid u \subseteq x\}.$$

The neighborhoods *of* an element x are all those sets $[u]_{\mathbf{A}}$ where $u \subseteq x$. Note that this is the same as saying $\overline{u} \subseteq x$ or $\overline{u}$ approximates x. Indeed, the neighborhoods are in a one-one correspondence with the finite elements of $|\mathbf{A}|$. A neighborhood collects together all those elements sharing the same finite amount of information.

If both $u \subseteq x$ and $v \subseteq x$, then it is easy to see that the intersection of the two neighborhoods is again a neighborhood of x by virtue of the formula:

$$[u]_{\mathbf{A}} \cap [v]_{\mathbf{A}} = [u \cup v]_{\mathbf{A}}.$$

In case u and v are inconsistent with each other, then the intersection will be the empty set $\emptyset$. Because every element of our domain $|\mathbf{A}|$ is the union of the finite elements it contains, it is trivial to prove that two elements with exactly the same neighborhoods are the same. For these reasons, then, it follows that $|\mathbf{A}|$ is a T_0–topological space. The immediate reaction to this intelligence is: So what?

The answer to this scepticism will appear in the best light when we discuss in the next section the notion of *function* or *mapping* appropriate to our domains. The argument will be based on the extremely elementary form of the definition that characterizes the general continuous function together with the fact that the geometric intuition is suggestive of theorems to prove. In Section 6 we will find that the space of all continuous functions between two given domains is also a domain, a most useful result that is interesting topologically. But further interest for Domain Theory comes from the circumstance that there is a connection between geometry and domains. We cannot go into the full details here, but I can make some brief remarks.

Before continuing that discussion, though, it should be remarked that once the topology of the domain has been uncovered, then the unions of chains of elements (or directed sets of elements) *are* topological limits according to accepted general definitions. Thus, what we felt intuitively was a limiting process (the getting better and better up to the union) is in fact a limit formation in a precise mathematical sense. This helps convince us that we are on the right track.

Total elements as a space. In any domain it can be proved that any element x can be extended to a *total* element t, which is characterized by the property that it is a *maximal* element of the partial ordering. (Perhaps there are many such t, but there is always at least one with $x \subseteq t$.) Recall that the set of all total elements of $|\mathbf{A}|$ is denoted by $\mathrm{Tot}_{\mathbf{A}}$. Because the set $\mathrm{Tot}_{\mathbf{A}} \subseteq |\mathbf{A}|$, it is a topological space itself. Suppose s and t are two distinct total elements, then they must be inconsistent with each other—but we shall prove more. If every finite consistent $u \subseteq s$ also satisfied $u \subseteq t$, then $s \subseteq t$ would follow. But this is impossible, because s is maximal. Let, then, $u \in \mathrm{Con}$ with $u \subseteq s$ be chosen so that $u \subseteq t$ fails. Now u must be inconsistent with t, since otherwise there would be an element containing them both. It follows that u must be inconsistent with some $v \in \mathrm{Con}_{\mathbf{A}}$ with $v \subseteq t$. In this way we show that the neighborhoods $[u]_{\mathbf{A}}$ and $[v]_{\mathbf{A}}$ are disjoint.

This argument proves that $\mathrm{Tot}_{\mathbf{A}}$ is a *Hausdorff space* (or T_2–space). We cannot go further into the details here, but it is also a totally disconnected, compact Hausdorff space. (These spaces—well known from studies of Logic and the Theory of Boolean Algebras—are also zero-dimensional.) Assuming the countability of $\mathrm{Con}_{\mathbf{A}}$, which is not such a bold assumption, all such spaces can be conveniently embedded into the real line so as to preserve the topological structure. Perhaps this does not seem so surprising, but it shows that the topological nature of $\mathrm{Tot}_{\mathbf{A}}$, the uppermost level of the T_0 space $|\mathbf{A}|$, is indeed quite geometric. And it can also be shown that any arbitrary continuous function on $\mathrm{Tot}_{\mathbf{A}}$ into *any* topological space can be extended to a continuous function on $|\mathbf{A}|$, so the whole domain proves to be quite a "roomy" space with many good connections to more usual topological spaces.

A note on neighborhood structures. Topological spaces can be defined in several ways, and in general they do not carry a preferred neighborhood structure. (For example,there is no topological significance to the the usual rational intervals we use to define neighborhoods for the real line: any similarly dense set of points would do in place of the rational numbers.) Domains, the way we have defined them, however, do have preferred neighborhoods. The set of finite elements of $|\mathbf{A}|$ can be defined topologically, and as we have seen they determine a convenient set of neighborhoods. (The reason for all this is the so-called zero-dimensonal character of the domains. There is a higher-dimensional theory, but this leads to continuous lattices and can only be explained using the kind of presentation in Gierz, *et al.*[1980]. It is too long-winded a story for the present paper. The higher-dimensonal domains do not have a preferred set of neighborhoods, however.)

Having realized this, it is a short step to giving an algebraic axiomatization of the neighborhood structure. Smyth [1975] contains a presentation in terms of the equivalent notion of finite element. Scott [1981] turns the story around and defines a set-theoretical representation of a neighborhood as just a family of sets containing a largest "neighborhood" and closed under forming the intersection of any two sets in the family that contain a third. The set-theoretical form of this definition is very simple, and Scott [1981] spells out the details of how the theory of domains can be based on this starting point. Subsequent investigation, however, has convinced the author that the present approach through information systems is even simpler and better for a number of the essential constructions. The theory introduced by Ersov [1970] of F-spaces is another axiomatization somewhat intermediate between the topological and the lattice theoretic. Domains in the present sense then become *complete* F-spaces. There are many interesting aspects to this method, but the author feels that information systems are about as elementary and familiar as we can get, and they are therefore more suggestive of new constructions.

5. Approximable mappings between domains. Once a general notion of set or domain has been defined mathematically, the next major issue is: How are the different domains to be related one to another? The answer to this important question can many times be given by defining an appropriate concept of *mapping* between domains. The answer need not be unique; the same collection of domains may support more than one idea of function depending on the special aspects of the domains that need to be brought out. In the case of the kinds of domains being studied here, there are two principal answers, one of which is to be explained in this section.

In order to understand an appropriate notion of a mapping or a function between domains constructed from information systems, we have to refer back to the way in which elements are introduced. As we have seen in Section 3, an element is a consistent, closed set of data objects. To generate an element, one has to generate more and more of the finite consistent subsets of the element. Note that the separate data objects have to be grouped into these finite consistent sets, because the entailment relation may require a finite set of arbitrary size on the left in making the necessary entailments for closure. It is this kind of passage from a finite set to its closure that is to be generalized in defining mappings.

Consider two domains. To map from one to another, some information about a possible element of the first is presented as *input* to the function f. Then as *output* the function f starts generating an element. If the input were u, a consistent set of the first domain, then *part* of the output in the second domain might be a consistent set v. We could say that there is an input/output relationship set up by f, and indicate by $u\ f\ v$ that this relation holds going from u in the first domain to v in the second. Of course to get the full effect of f, it is necessary to take *all* the v's related to a given u, because even a small finite amount of input may cause an infinite amount of output. But every element of a domain is just the sum total of its finite subsets (finite approximations), so it is sufficient to make the mapping relationship go between finite sets. Here is the formal definition with the exact conditions that the relation f must satisfy.

DEFINITION 5.1. Let $\mathbf{A}$ and $\mathbf{B}$ be two given information systems. An *approximable* mapping $f : \mathbf{A} \to \mathbf{B}$ is a binary relation between the two sets $\mathrm{Con}_{\mathbf{A}}$ and $\mathrm{Con}_{\mathbf{B}}$ such that:

(i) $\emptyset\ f\ \emptyset$;

(ii) $u\ f\ v$ and $u\ f\ v'$ always imply $u\ f\ (v \cup v')$; and

(iii) $u' \vdash_{\mathbf{A}} u, u\ f\ v$, and $v \vdash_{\mathbf{B}} v'$ always imply $u'\ f\ v'$.

We say that **A** is the *source* of f and **B** is the *target*. ∎

Intuitively the relationship $u\ f\ v$ is an input/output passage which can be read informally as: *"if you are willing to give at least u amount of information about the argument, then the mapping f is willing to give at least v amount of information about the value (and possibly even more—if you are patient)."* Condition (i) means that *no* (non-trivial) information about the input merits no information about the output. Condition (ii) implies that all the contributions to the output from a fixed input are consistent, and in fact the union of two of the output sets is again an output set. Output corresponding to a fixed input is *cumulative.* Condition (iii) assures us that the mapping relation f works in harmony with the two entailment relations: if a certain relationship holds, and if the left-hand side is strengthened while the right-hand side is weakened, then the mapping relation must continue to hold. What we must discuss next is what this means for elements.

Before defining the notion of function value, however, it is useful to remark that in the definition of approximable mapping the form of the statement could be simplified by reducing sets on the right to their elements. Specifically, we note the equivalence:

$$u\ f\ v \text{ iff } u\ f\ \{Y\} \text{ for all } Y \in v.$$

In other words an approximable mapping is completely determined by the relation set up between consistent sets on the left and single data objects on the right.

DEFINITION 5.2. If $f : \mathbf{A} \to \mathbf{B}$ is an approximable mapping between information systems, and if $x \in |\mathbf{A}|$ is an element of the first, then we define the *image* (or *function value*) of x under f by the formula:

$$f(x) = \{Y \in \mathcal{D}_{\mathbf{B}} \mid u\ f\ \{Y\} \text{ for some } u \subseteq x\}.$$

Alternatively, we could use the equivalent formula:

$$f(x) = \bigcup\{v \in \mathrm{Con}_{\mathbf{B}} \mid u\ f\ v \text{ for some } u \subseteq x\}. \quad ∎$$

Note that, under Definition 5.2, it has to be *proved* that the image of an element in $|\mathbf{A}|$ lies in $|\mathbf{B}|$ in order to justify the use of the ordinary function-value notation. But both the consistency and the closure under entailment of $f(x)$ are direct consequences of the properties in the definition of approximable mapping.

PROPOSITION 5.3. *Let $f, g : \mathbf{A} \to \mathbf{B}$ be two approximable mappings between two information systems. Then*

(i) *f always maps elements to elements under Definition 5.2;*

(ii) $f = g$ *iff* $f(x) = g(x)$ *for all* $x \in |\mathbf{A}|$; *and*

(iii) $f \subseteq g$ *iff* $f(x) \subseteq g(x)$ *for all* $x \in |\mathbf{A}|$.

Moreover, the approximable mappings are monotone in the sense that

(iv) $x \subseteq y$ *in* $|\mathbf{A}|$ *always implies* $f(x) \subseteq f(y)$ *in* $|\mathbf{B}|$.

All these results follow from the observation that

(v) $\quad u\, f\, v \quad$ *iff* $\quad \overline{v} \subseteq f(\overline{u})$,

for all $u \in \mathrm{Con}_{\mathbf{A}}$ *and all* $v \in \mathrm{Con}_{\mathbf{B}}$. ∎

The proof is straightforward, and it completely justifies the use of the function-value notation. Consequently, the question arises as to whether the characterization of approximable mappings could not have been given in terms of elements in the first place. The answer is yes. Indeed, approximable mappings correspond exactly to functions on elements preserving unions of chains (this, in the case of countable information systems; directed unions must be used in general). This characterization has also been called "continuity," because it is equivalent to saying that the mappings between elements are continuous mappings *in the topological sense*, when $|\mathbf{A}|$ and $|\mathbf{B}|$ are regarded as topological spaces, as explained in the last section. The reason for the word "approximable" is explained in Section 7.

Having justified the idea of an approximable mapping as a transformation on elements, the next step is to combine mappings. It is hardly surprising to learn that *compositions* of approximable mappings are approximable, which in mathematical terms means that the domains together with the approximable mappings form a *category*. The interesting part starts when we want to combine *domains*. But, to fix ideas, it is useful to spell out how compositions take place on the level of the data objects and consistent sets. For instance, it was noted that in any information system $\vdash$ is transitive on Con, and in Definition 5.1 a transitivity condition comes in. There is a perfectly good reason for the parallelism, for, as we see next, the first idea (entailment) is a special case of the second (approximable mapping).

PROPOSITION 5.4. *Let* $\mathbf{A}$ *be an information system. Then the following formula defines an approximable mapping* $\mathrm{I}_{\mathbf{A}} : \mathbf{A} \to \mathbf{A}$:

(i) $\quad u\, \mathrm{I}_{\mathbf{A}}\, v \quad$ *iff* $\quad u \vdash_{\mathbf{A}} v$,

for all $u, v \in \mathrm{Con}_{\mathbf{A}}$. *And we have*:

(ii) $\quad \mathrm{I}_{\mathbf{A}}(x) = x$,

for all $x \in |\mathbf{A}|$. ∎

In other words, the given entailment relation itself defines the identity function on the domain in question; and of course, the identity function is an approximable mapping.

PROPOSITION 5.5. *Let* $f : \mathbf{A} \to \mathbf{B}$ *and* $g : \mathbf{B} \to \mathbf{C}$ *be two approximable mappings. Then the following formula defines an approximable mapping* $g \circ f : \mathbf{A} \to \mathbf{C}$:

(i) $\quad u\,(g \circ f)\,w \quad$ *iff* $\; u\, f\, v$ *and* $v\, g\, w$ *for some* $v \in \mathrm{Con}_{\mathbf{B}}$,

for all $u \in \mathrm{Con}_{\mathbf{A}}$ *and* $w \in \mathrm{Con}_{\mathbf{C}}$. *And we have*:

(ii) $\quad (g \circ f)(x) = g(f(x))$,

for all $x \in |\mathbf{A}|$. ∎

In other words, composition of input/output relations is effected by putting the input into the first, getting some output, and then putting that in as input to the second. The correctness of this recipe on elements (*i.e.* formula 5.5(ii)) follows from the basic formula 5.3(v). Because the class of *all* sets and *arbitrary* mappings forms a category—in the formal meaning of the word—the above three propositions show that the totality of information systems and approximable mappings also forms a category: a sub-category of the category of sets. We have given a special representation to the category by our use of data objects and consistent sets, and we have thereby put the elements into a secondary position—for a good reason. But the elements are there to use. The axioms for a category could also be verified *directly* using the basic definitions like 5.4(i) and 5.5(i); the details are bland. The more interesting topic is: what are the closure conditions on our domains; how do we construct new domains given old ones?

Before we go on to the first basic constructs of sums and products of domains, we remark on some other easy examples of approximable mappings: *constant maps.*

PROPOSITION 5.6. *Given information systems* $\mathbf{A}$, $\mathbf{B}$, $\mathbf{C}$, *and* $\mathbf{D}$, *and given a fixed element* $b \in |\mathbf{B}|$, *then there is a unique approximable mapping* $\mathrm{const}\, b : \mathbf{A} \to \mathbf{B}$ *such that:*

$$\text{(i)} \qquad (\mathrm{const}\, b)(x) = b,$$

for all $x \in |\mathbf{A}|$. *Moreover, we have:*

$$\text{(ii)} \qquad f \circ (\mathrm{const}\, b) = \mathrm{const}\, f(b),$$

for all approximable mappings $f : \mathbf{B} \to \mathbf{C}$; *and*

$$\text{(iii)} \quad (\mathrm{const}\, b) \circ g = \mathrm{const}\, b,$$

for all approximable mappings $g : \mathbf{D} \to \mathbf{A}$. ∎

The proof is immediate, since we need only interpret the input/output relation $u\,(\mathrm{const}\, b)\, v$ as meaning $v \subseteq b$. We note that our notation is somewhat ambiguous since, for example, in 5.6(iii) we are using $\mathrm{const}\, b$ in two senses: once as a mapping from $\mathbf{A}$, and once as a mapping from $\mathbf{D}$. In fact, we should hang *two* subscripts on the thing to fix *both* the source *and* the target of the mapping. This is too painful, however, and we generally rely on context to make the meaning clear. (Formal rules of type checking can be given, so on a computer-based system all the necessary subscripts could be put back in. Thus, the kind of ambiguity we are dealing with here is not very serious.)

6. Products and sums of domains. In the category of sets, the product (the cartesian product) of two sets is by definition just the set of ordered pairs of elements. We could use the same definition in the category of domains—provided we worked in terms of the elements of the domains. The disadvantage is that the determination of the product domain from data objects is lost, or at least pushed into the background. We shall therefore give a construction of products directly in terms of the given data objects, and then show how to prove that the product is just the one expected when we look at the elements.

The idea for the definition is a simple one. Think of two domains $\mathbf{A}$ and $\mathbf{B}$. A data object $X \in \mathcal{D}_{\mathbf{A}}$ can be giving information about a possible element $x \in |\mathbf{A}|$, and a data object $Y \in \mathcal{D}_{\mathbf{B}}$ can be giving information about a possible element $y \in |\mathbf{B}|$. How do we wish to give information about the pair (x, y)? The first piece of advice is not to say all that is known all at once. For example, if pressed, we can say we know X about the first coordinate of the pair; only later, if really pressed, we can say we also know Y about the second coordinate. The point is that data objects provide only partial information, and it does not matter if it takes several of them to give fairly complete information about the whole element. This attitude motivates, then, the particular form of our official definition.

DEFINITION 6.1. Let $\mathbf{A}$ and $\mathbf{B}$ be two information systems. By $\mathbf{A} \times \mathbf{B}$, the *product system*, we understand the system where:

(i) $\mathcal{D}_{\mathbf{A}\times\mathbf{B}} = \{(X, \Delta_{\mathbf{B}}) \mid X \in \mathcal{D}_{\mathbf{A}}\} \cup \{(\Delta_{\mathbf{A}}, Y) \mid Y \in \mathcal{D}_{\mathbf{B}}\}$;

(ii) $\Delta_{\mathbf{A}\times\mathbf{B}} = (\Delta_{\mathbf{A}}, \Delta_{\mathbf{B}})$;

(iii) $u \in \mathrm{Con}_{\mathbf{A}\times\mathbf{B}}$ iff $\mathrm{fst}\, u \in \mathrm{Con}_{\mathbf{A}}$ and $\mathrm{snd}\, u \in \mathrm{Con}_{\mathbf{B}}$;

(iv′) $u \vdash_{\mathbf{A}\times\mathbf{B}} (X', \Delta_{\mathbf{B}})$ iff $\mathrm{fst}\, u \vdash_{\mathbf{A}} X'$; and

(iv″) $u \vdash_{\mathbf{A}\times\mathbf{B}} (\Delta_{\mathbf{A}}, Y')$ iff $\mathrm{snd}\, u \vdash_{\mathbf{B}} Y'$;

where, in (iii), u is any finite subset of $\mathcal{D}_{\mathbf{A}\times\mathbf{B}}$, in (iv′) and (iv″), $u \in \mathrm{Con}_{\mathbf{A}\times\mathbf{B}}$, and we let:

$$\begin{aligned} \mathrm{fst}\, u &= \{X \in \mathcal{D}_{\mathbf{A}} \mid (X, \Delta_{\mathbf{B}}) \in u\}, \text{ and} \\ \mathrm{snd}\, u &= \{Y \in \mathcal{D}_{\mathbf{B}} \mid (\Delta_{\mathbf{A}}, Y) \in u\}. \quad \blacksquare \end{aligned}$$

Note that in 6.1(i) the two sets in the union are just two copies of $\mathcal{D}_{\mathbf{A}}$ and $\mathcal{D}_{\mathbf{B}}$, respectively. There is a shared member, however, the object $(\Delta_{\mathbf{A}}, \Delta_{\mathbf{B}})$, which is indeed the least informative data object—whether it is looked at from the point of view of $\mathbf{A}$ or of $\mathbf{B}$. We could have used all the pairs (X, Y), but if we did, the consistent set $\{(X, Y)\}$ would be deductively equivalent to the set $\{(X, \Delta_{\mathbf{B}}), (\Delta_{\mathbf{A}}, Y)\}$ according to the definition of $\vdash_{\mathbf{A}\times\mathbf{B}}$, and so there is not much point in having this redundancy. Strictly speaking, we should not make these remarks until we have actually verified that 6.1 is indeed a proper definition.

PROPOSITION 6.2. *If* $\mathbf{A}$ *and* $\mathbf{B}$ *are information systems, then so is* $\mathbf{A} \times \mathbf{B}$*, and we have mappings*

$$\mathrm{fst} : \mathbf{A} \times \mathbf{B} \to \mathbf{A} \quad \textit{and} \quad \mathrm{snd} : \mathbf{A} \times \mathbf{B} \to \mathbf{B},$$

such that, for approximable mappings

$$f : \mathbf{C} \to \mathbf{A} \quad \textit{and} \quad g : \mathbf{C} \to \mathbf{B},$$

there is **one and only one** *approximable mapping* $\langle f, g \rangle : \mathbf{C} \to \mathbf{A} \times \mathbf{B}$ *such that*

$$\mathrm{fst} \circ \langle f, g \rangle = f \quad \textit{and} \quad \mathrm{snd} \circ \langle f, g \rangle = g.$$

Proof. Checking that 6.1 does indeed define an information system is straightforward, but there are six things that must be proved according to Definition 2.1. We have to leave the details to the reader. Next using the notation of 6.1, where fst and snd were applied as operations on consistent sets $u \in \mathrm{Con}_{\mathbf{A}\times\mathbf{B}}$, we redefine matters to have approximable mappings, where, for $v \in \mathrm{Con}_{\mathbf{A}}$ and $w \in \mathrm{Con}_{\mathbf{B}}$,

(1) $u \,\mathrm{fst}\, v$ iff $\mathrm{fst}\, u \vdash_{\mathbf{A}} v$;

(2) $u \,\mathrm{snd}\, w$ iff $\mathrm{snd}\, u \vdash_{\mathbf{B}} w$; and

(3) $s \,\langle f, g\rangle\, u$ iff $s\, f\, (\mathrm{fst}\, u)$ and $s\, g\, (\mathrm{snd}\, u)$.

Because we defined $\mathbf{A} \times \mathbf{B}$ so that consistency and entailment worked independently on the two halves of the set of data objects, it is easy to check that (1)–(3) define approximable mappings having the desired properties.

The uniqueness of $\langle f, g\rangle$ comes out of the observation that, if z and z' are two elements of $\mathbf{A} \times \mathbf{B}$ for which

$$\mathrm{fst}(z) = \mathrm{fst}(z') \text{ and } \mathrm{snd}(z) = \mathrm{snd}(z'),$$

then $z = z'$. The reason is that fst and snd just divide elements into the two kinds of data objects, and then strip off the parentheses. (Look back at Definition 6.1.) No information is lost, so if z and z' are transformed into the same elements both times, then they have to be the same.

That lemma treats one pair of elements at a time, but $\langle f, g\rangle$ is a function. But if $\langle f, g\rangle'$ were another function satisfying the conditions of the above proposition, then the two functions would be pointwise equal. We could then quote 5.3 to assure ourselves that they are the same function. ∎

Ordered pairs. By using the definition

$$(x, y) = \langle \mathrm{const}(x), \mathrm{const}(y)\rangle(\bot_{\mathbf{C}}),$$

which invokes 6.2 on any convenient fixed domain $\mathbf{C}$, it is easy to prove that $|\mathbf{A} \times \mathbf{B}|$ is in a one-one correspondence with the set-theoretical product of $|\mathbf{A}|$ and $|\mathbf{B}|$. Indeed, it can be shown that for $x \in |\mathbf{A}|$ and $y \in |\mathbf{B}|$,

(1) $(x, y) = \{(X, \Delta_{\mathbf{B}}) \mid X \in x\} \cup \{(\Delta_{\mathbf{A}}, Y) \mid Y \in y\} \in |\mathbf{A} \times \mathbf{B}|$;

(2) $\mathrm{fst}(x, y) = x$;

(3) $\mathrm{snd}(x, y) = y$;

and, for all $z \in |\mathbf{A} \times \mathbf{B}|$,

(4) $z = (\mathrm{fst}\, z, \mathrm{snd}\, z)$.

Also, using the notation of 6.2, we can say that

(5) $\langle f, g\rangle(t) = (f(t), g(t))$,

for all $t \in |\mathbf{C}|$.

There are also remarks that could be made about the pointwise nature of the partial ordering of $|\mathbf{A} \times \mathbf{B}|$, but we will not formulate them here. We do remark, however, that there is also a trivial product of *no* terms, $\mathbf{1}$, called the *unit* type or domain. It is such that $\mathcal{D}_{\mathbf{1}} = \{\Delta_{\mathbf{1}}\}$, and that equation determines it up to isomorphism. The domain **1** has but one element, namely $\perp_1$. Note also that all approximable mappings $f : \mathbf{1} \to \mathbf{A}$ are *constant*, which shows how Definition 5.1 is a generalization of Definition 3.1. Note finally that there is but one approximable mapping $f : \mathbf{A} \to \mathbf{1}$, namely $f = 0 = \text{const}(\perp_1)$. ∎

We turn now to the definition and properties of sums of domains.

DEFINITION 6.3. Let **A** and **B** be two information systems. By $\mathbf{A} + \mathbf{B}$, the *separated sum system*, we understand the system where, after choosing some convenient object Δ belonging neither to $\mathcal{D}_\mathbf{A}$ nor to $\mathcal{D}_\mathbf{B}$, we have:

(i) $\mathcal{D}_{\mathbf{A}+\mathbf{B}} = \{(X,\Delta) \mid X \in \mathcal{D}_\mathbf{A}\} \cup \{(\Delta, Y) \mid Y \in \mathcal{D}_\mathbf{B}\} \cup \{(\Delta,\Delta)\}$;

(ii) $\Delta_{\mathbf{A}+\mathbf{B}} = (\Delta,\Delta)$;

(iii) $u \in \text{Con}_{\mathbf{A}+\mathbf{B}}$ iff either $\text{lft}\, u \in \text{Con}_\mathbf{A}$ and $\text{rht}\, u = \emptyset$ or $\text{lft}\, u = \emptyset$ and $\text{rht}\, u \in \text{Con}_\mathbf{B}$;

(iv′) $u \vdash_{\mathbf{A}+\mathbf{B}} (X', \Delta)$ iff $\text{lft}\, u \neq \emptyset$ and $\text{lft}\, u \vdash_\mathbf{A} X'$;

(iv″) $u \vdash_{\mathbf{A}+\mathbf{B}} (\Delta, Y')$ iff $\text{rht}\, u \neq \emptyset$ and $\text{rht}\, u \vdash_\mathbf{B} Y'$; and

(iv‴) $u \vdash_{\mathbf{A}+\mathbf{B}} (\Delta,\Delta)$ always holds.

where, in (iii), u is any finite subset of $\mathcal{D}_{\mathbf{A}+\mathbf{B}}$, in (iv′)–(iv‴), $u \in \text{Con}_{\mathbf{A}+\mathbf{B}}$, and we let:

$$\text{lft}\, u = \{X \in \mathcal{D}_\mathbf{A} \mid (X,\Delta) \in u\}, \text{ and}$$
$$\text{rht}\, u = \{Y \in \mathcal{D}_\mathbf{B} \mid (\Delta, Y) \in u\}. \quad ∎$$

The plan of the sum definition is very similar to that for product, except that (1) for reasons to be made clear in examples, the parts *do not* share the least informative element (*i.e.* the data objects $(\Delta_\mathbf{A}, \Delta)$, $(\Delta, \Delta_\mathbf{B})$, and (Δ,Δ) are inequivalent in this system), and (2) instead of defining consistency and entailment in a conjunctive way, these notions are defined disjunctively. The effect of these changes over Definition 6.1 is to produce a system $\mathbf{A} + \mathbf{B}$ whose elements divide into disjoint copies of those of **A** and **B** (*plus* an extra element $\perp_{\mathbf{A}+\mathbf{B}}$). These remarks can be made more precise in the following way:

PROPOSITION 6.4. *If* **A** *and* **B** *are information systems, then so is* $\mathbf{A} + \mathbf{B}$, *and we have approximable mappings*

$$\text{inl} : \mathbf{A} \to \mathbf{A} + \mathbf{B} \quad \textit{and} \quad \text{inr} : \mathbf{B} \to \mathbf{A} + \mathbf{B},$$

such that, for approximable mappings

$$f : \mathbf{A} \to \mathbf{C} \quad \textit{and} \quad g : \mathbf{B} \to \mathbf{C},$$

there is **one and only one** *approximable mapping* $[f, g] : \mathbf{A} + \mathbf{B} \to \mathbf{C}$, *such that*

$$[f,g] \circ \text{inl} = f\,, \quad [f,g] \circ \text{inr} = g\,, \textit{ and } \quad [f,g](\perp_{\mathbf{A}+\mathbf{B}}) = \perp_\mathbf{C}.$$

Proof. The proof that 6.3 defines a system satisfying the basic axioms of 2.1 has to be left to the reader. Next using the notation of 6.1, where lft and rht were applied as operations on consistent sets $u \in \mathrm{Con}_{\mathbf{A}+\mathbf{B}}$, we redefine matters to have approximable mappings, where, for $v \in \mathrm{Con}_{\mathbf{A}}$ and $w \in \mathrm{Con}_{\mathbf{B}}$,

(1) $v \text{ inl } u$ iff $\{(X, \Delta) \mid X \in v\} \vdash_{\mathbf{A}+\mathbf{B}} u$;

(2) $w \text{ inr } u$ iff $\{(\Delta, Y) \mid Y \in w\} \vdash_{\mathbf{A}+\mathbf{B}} u$; and

(3) $u\ [f, g]\ s$ iff either $\vdash_{\mathbf{C}} s$, or $\mathrm{lft}\, u \neq \emptyset$ and $\mathrm{lft}\, u\ f\ s$, or $\mathrm{rht}\, u \neq \emptyset$ and $\mathrm{rht}\, u\ g\ s$.

Because we defined $\mathbf{A} + \mathbf{B}$ so that consistency and entailment worked on the two halves of the set of data objects just as they worked on **A** and **B**, respectively, it is easy to check that (1)–(3) define approximable mappings, and that the desired properties hold.

The uniqueness of $[f, g]$ comes from the fact that the elements of $\mathbf{A} + \mathbf{B}$, apart from the bottom element of the domain, are just the elements in the ranges of inl and inr. Since the function $[f, g]$ takes bottom to bottom (in the indicated domains), it will be uniquely determined by what it does on the two halves of the sum. The last equations of the theorem just say that the function *is* completely determined on these elements. ∎

It can also be shown that Propositions 6.2 and 6.4 uniquely characterize the domains $\mathbf{A} \times \mathbf{B}$ and $\mathbf{A} + \mathbf{B}$ up to isomorphism, and they give us the existence of additional mappings that are needed to show that product and sum are *functors* on the category of domains. We can also show from these results that the domain

$$\mathbf{BOOL} = \mathbf{1} + \mathbf{1}$$

has two elements true and false, such that any mapping on **BOOL** is uniquely determined by its action on true, false and $\perp_{\mathbf{BOOL}}$, and the values on the first two elements may be arbitrarily chosen.

7. The function space as a domain. Functions or mappings between domains are of basic importance for our theory, since it is through them that we most easily transform data and relate the structures into which the elements defined by the data objects enter. There are many possible functions, and large groups of them can be treated in a uniform manner. For instance, if the source and target domains match properly, any pair of functions can be composed—composition is an operation on functions of general significance. Now, if in the theory we could combine functions into domains themselves, then an operation like composition might become a mapping *of* the theory. Indeed, this is exactly what happens: suitably construed, composition is an approximable mapping of two arguments. Of course, for each configuration of linked source and target domains, there is a separate composition operation.

In order to make approximable mappings elements of a suitable domain, we have to discover first what their appropriate data objects are. In Section 5 this was hinted at already. To determine an approximable mapping $f : \mathbf{A} \to \mathbf{B}$, we have to say which pairs (u, v) with $u \in \mathcal{D}_{\mathbf{A}}$ and $v \in \mathcal{D}_{\mathbf{B}}$ stand in the mapping relation $u\ f\ v$. One such pair gives a certain (finite) amount of information about the possible functions that contain it, and an approximable mapping is completely determined by such pairs. Therefore, if there are appropriate notions of consistency and entailment *for these pairs*, we will be able to form a domain having functions as elements. Let us try out a formal definition first, and then look to an explanation of how it works.

DEFINITION 7.1. Let **A** and **B** be two information systems. By $\mathbf{A} \to \mathbf{B}$, the *function space*, we understand the system where:

(i) $\mathcal{D}_{\mathbf{A}\to\mathbf{B}} = \{(u,v) \mid u \in \mathrm{Con}_{\mathbf{A}} \text{ and } v \in \mathrm{Con}_{\mathbf{B}}\}$;

(ii) $\Delta_{\mathbf{A}\to\mathbf{B}} = (\emptyset, \emptyset)$; and where,

for all n and all $w = \{(u_0, v_0), \ldots, (u_{n-1}, v_{n-1})\}$, we have:

(iii) $w \in \mathrm{Con}_{\mathbf{A}\to\mathbf{B}}$ iff whenever $I \subseteq \{0, \ldots, n-1\}$ and $\bigcup\{u_i \mid i \in I\} \in \mathrm{Con}_{\mathbf{A}}$, then $\bigcup\{v_i \mid i \in I\} \in \mathrm{Con}_{\mathbf{B}}$; and

(iv) $w \vdash_{\mathbf{A}\to\mathbf{B}} (u', v')$ iff $\bigcup\{v_i \mid u' \vdash_{\mathbf{A}} u_i\} \vdash_{\mathbf{B}} v'$,

for all $u' \in \mathrm{Con}_{\mathbf{A}}$ and $v' \in \mathrm{Con}_{\mathbf{B}}$. ∎

We have already explained the choice of data objects in (i) above, and the least informative pair in (ii) is clearly right. Remember that as a data object (u, v) should be read as meaning that if the information in u is supplied as input, then at least v will be obtained as output. It is pretty obvious that one such data object by itself is consistent (they make constant functions, don't they?), but a *set* of several of these pairs may not be consistent. Hence, the need for part (iii) of the definition. It can be read informally as follows: Look for a selection I of the indices used in setting up w where the u_i for $i \in I$ are jointly consistent. Since the pairs in w are meant as correct information about a *single* function, then the combined input from all these selected u_i must be allowable. The function will then be required to give as output at least all the v_i for $i \in I$, owing to the fact that we are given that w is true of the function we have in mind. As a consequence, the set $\bigcup\{v_i \mid i \in I\}$ has got to be consistent, because it comes as output from consistent input for a single approximable function. What we are arguing for is the *necessity* of (iii)—the word "consistency" should mean that the data objects in the set are all true of at least one function.

Finally we have to argue that (iv) must give the right notion of entailment for these data objects. This can be seen by noting that for a fixed consistent w the set of pairs (u', v') satisfying the right-hand side of (iv) *defines* an approximable function. In checking this we have to remark that, for each $u' \in \mathrm{Con}_{\mathbf{A}}$, the set $\bigcup\{v_i \mid u' \vdash_{\mathbf{A}} u_i\}$ is consistent, so the definition makes sense. The transitivity properties needed for proving that we have an approximable mapping are easy to establish. This shows in particular that w is true of at least one approximable function, since the separate pairs (u_i, v_i) all satisfy the definition. But it is also simple to argue that for *any* approximable function, if w is true of it, then so is any pair (u', v') satisfying the definition of (iv). Consequently, what we find in (iv) is the definition of the *least* approximable function generated by w. The argument we have just outlined thus shows that the relationship $w \vdash_{\mathbf{A}\to\mathbf{B}} (u', v')$ means exactly that whenever w is true of an approximable mapping then so is (u', v'). It follows at once that $\vdash_{\mathbf{A}\to\mathbf{B}}$ is an entailment relation, and that the elements of $\mathbf{A} \to \mathbf{B}$ are just the approximable mappings, as we indicate in the next theorem.

THEOREM 7.2. *If* $\mathbf{A}$, $\mathbf{B}$, *and* $\mathbf{C}$ *are information systems, then so is* $\mathbf{A} \to \mathbf{B}$, *and the approximable mappings* $f : \mathbf{A} \to \mathbf{B}$ *are exactly the elements* $f \in |\mathbf{A} \to \mathbf{B}|$. *Moreover we have an approximable mapping* apply : $(\mathbf{B} \to \mathbf{C}) \times \mathbf{B} \to \mathbf{C}$ *such that whenever* $g : \mathbf{B} \to \mathbf{C}$ *and* $y \in |\mathbf{B}|$, *then*

$$\mathrm{apply}(g, y) = g(y).$$

Furthermore, for all approximable mappings $h : \mathbf{A} \times \mathbf{B} \to \mathbf{C}$, *there is* **one and only one** *approximable mapping* curry $h : \mathbf{A} \to (\mathbf{B} \to \mathbf{C})$ *such that*

$$h = \mathrm{apply} \circ \langle(\mathrm{curry}\, h) \circ \mathrm{fst}, \mathrm{snd}\rangle.$$

Proof. We have already remarked on the essentials of the proof above. Definition 7.1 was devised to characterize exactly in $\mathrm{Con}_{\mathbf{A}\to\mathbf{B}}$ the finite subsets of approximable functions, which, as binary relations, are being regarded as sets of ordered pairs. If $f : \mathbf{A} \to \mathbf{B}$ and if $w \subseteq f$, then from the properties of approximable functions, it can be checked directly that w satisfies the right-hand side of 7.1(iii). Conversely, if $w \in \mathrm{Con}_{\mathbf{A}\to\mathbf{B}}$, then, as we have said, the relation which is defined by 7.1(iv) and may be notated by:

$$\overline{w} = \{(u', v') \mid w \vdash_{\mathbf{A}\to\mathbf{B}} (u', v')\},$$

is an approximable mapping, as can be proved using the right-hand side of 7.1(iv) and the usual properties of $\vdash_{\mathbf{A}}$ and $\vdash_{\mathbf{B}}$. Since $w \subseteq \overline{w}$, we see that $w \vdash_{\mathbf{A}\to\mathbf{B}} w'$ if, and only if, for all approximable $f : \mathbf{A} \to \mathbf{B}$, $w \subseteq f$ implies $w' \subseteq f$. (This is also the same as $w' \subseteq \overline{w}$, of course.) From these considerations it follows that not only is $\mathbf{A} \to \mathbf{B}$ an information system, but all approximable mappings are elements. Finally, if $f \in |\mathbf{A} \to \mathbf{B}|$, then—as a binary relation —it must be an approximable mapping, because the properties of Definition 5.1 are built into 7.1.

The construction of the special mapping apply as an approximable mapping also uses the idea of 7.1(iv). The consistent sets of the compound space $(\mathbf{B} \to \mathbf{C}) \times \mathbf{B}$ are essentially pairs of consistent sets, say $w \in \mathrm{Con}_{\mathbf{B}\to\mathbf{C}}$ and $u' \in \mathbf{B}$. Now the relation we want from such pairs to consistent sets $v' \in \mathrm{Con}_{\mathbf{B}}$ is just nothing more or less than $w \vdash_{\mathbf{B}\to\mathbf{C}} (u', v')$. Our discussion in the previous paragraph hints at why apply does in fact reproduce functional application when we evaluate apply(g, y).

The definition of curry h uses the same trick of regarding a binary relation with one term in a relationship being a pair as corresponding to another relation with one coordinate of the pair shifted to the other side. Specifically, we can think of an approximable mapping $h : \mathbf{A} \times \mathbf{B} \to \mathbf{C}$ as a relation from pairs (u, v) of consistent sets for $\mathbf{A}$ and $\mathbf{B}$, respectively, over to consistent sets w for $\mathbf{C}$. What we want for curry h is the relationship that goes from u to the pair (v, w). Of course (v, w) is just *one* data object for $\mathbf{B} \to \mathbf{C}$, but the input/output passage from the consistent sets of $\mathbf{A}$ to these objects is sufficient to determine curry h as an approximable mapping. The exact connection between the two mappings is given in terms of function values as follows:

$$h(x, y) = (\mathrm{curry}\, h)(x)(y),$$

for all $x \in |\mathbf{A}|$ and $y \in |\mathbf{B}|$. From this equation it follows that curry h is uniquely determined. But, from what we know about apply, this is actually the same equation as that stated at the end of the theorem. ∎

Approximations to functions. Why have approximable functions been given this name? In general, elements of domains are the limits of their finite approximations. We have just indicated why the approximable mappings from one domain into another do form the elements of a domain themselves. We have explicitly shown how to construct the *finite* approximable mappings $\overline{w}$. A closer examination of the definitions would emphasize the very constructive nature of this analysis. It follows that the approximable mappings can therefore be approximated by simple functions. It *does not* follow that all approximable mappings are simple or constructive, since what takes place in the limiting process can be very complex. But the result does show how we can start to make distinctions once a precise sense of approximation is uncovered. ∎

Higher-type functions and the combinators. In the above discussion we have already combined the function-space construction with other domains by means of products. But there is nothing now stopping us from iterating the arrow domain constructor with itself as much as we like. This is how the so-called *higher types* are formed. In certain categories, such as the category of sets, this is a non-constructive move leading to the higher cardinal numbers. In the category of domains, however, the construct *is* constructive, because we have shown how to define all the parts of $\mathbf{A} \rightarrow \mathbf{B}$ in terms of very finite data objects (assuming, it need hardly be added, that $\mathbf{A}$ and $\mathbf{B}$ are constructively given).

Once the higher types have been formed as spaces, it must be asked what we are to do with them. The answer is that there are many, many mappings between these spaces that can be defined in terms of the simple notions we have been working with. These mappings are useful for the following reason: the higher types provide remarkabe scope for modelling notions (as those needed in denotatonal semantics for example), but the various aspects of the models have to be related—and this is where these mappings come into play. We have already seen a preliminary example in the last theorem, which can be interpreted as saying why the two domains shown are *isomorphic*:

$$\mathbf{A} \times \mathbf{B} \rightarrow \mathbf{C} \cong \mathbf{A} \rightarrow (\mathbf{B} \rightarrow \mathbf{C}).$$

We have neither the time nor the space to present a full theory of higher-type operators here, so some further examples will have to suffice. First, we have already made use of constant mappings. Since the construction of them is very uniform, there ought to be an associated operator. In fact, we have already been using it notationally. We have the approximable mapping $\mathrm{const} : \mathbf{B} \rightarrow (\mathbf{A} \rightarrow \mathbf{B})$ that takes every element of $\mathbf{B}$ to the corresponding constant function. (It has to be checked that this is an approximable mapping.) Note that there is a different mapping for each pair of domains $\mathbf{A}$ and $\mathbf{B}$, because the resulting types of const are different.

As another example, take the pairing of functions explained in Proposition 6.2. We can think of the operator in this case being

$$\mathrm{pair} : (\mathbf{C} \rightarrow \mathbf{A}) \times (\mathbf{C} \rightarrow \mathbf{B}) \rightarrow (\mathbf{C} \rightarrow (\mathbf{A} \times \mathbf{B})),$$

where for functions of the proper type we have:

$$\mathrm{pair}(f, g) = \langle f, g \rangle.$$

There will be a similar operator for the construct of Proposition 6.4.

Of course the most basic operator of function composition is also approximable of the appropriate type. We can write:

$$\mathrm{comp} : (\mathbf{B} \to \mathbf{C}) \times (\mathbf{A} \to \mathbf{B}) \to (\mathbf{A} \to \mathbf{C}),$$

where for functions of the right types we have:

$$\mathrm{comp}(g, f) = g \circ f.$$

The approximability has to be checked, of course. But once a number of the more primitive operators have been established as being approximable, then others can be proved to be so by writing them as combinations of previously obtained operators. ∎

Categories again. All of what we have been saying about operators ties in with category theory very nicely—as the category theorists have known for a long time. The technical term for what we have been doing in part is *cartesian closed category*—that is a property of the category of domains. Without going into details, that is essentially what 6.2 and 7.2 show of our category. But domains have many other properties beyond being a cartesian closed category. For example the possibility of forming sums is an extra (and useful) bonus, and there are many others. Nevertheless, the categorical viewpoint is a good way of organizing the properties, and it suggests other things to look for from our experiences with other categories. The next result gives a particularly important notion that can be expressed as an operator. ∎

THEOREM 7.3. *Let* **A** *be an information system. Then there is a unique operator,* **the least fixed-point operator**, *such that*

(i) $\mathrm{fix} : (\mathbf{A} \to \mathbf{A}) \to \mathbf{A}$; *and,*

for all approximable mappings $f : \mathbf{A} \to \mathbf{A}$, *we have:*

(ii) $f(\mathrm{fix}(f)) \subseteq \mathrm{fix}(f)$; *and*

(iii) *for all* $x \in |\mathbf{A}|$, *if* $f(x) \subseteq x$, *then* $\mathrm{fix}(f) \subseteq x$.

Moreover, for this operator, condition (ii) *is an equality.*

Proof. This is a well-known result—especially the fact that the conditions above uniquely determine the operator. The only question is the existence of the operator. The inclusion of condition (ii) gives the hint, for $\mathrm{fix}(f)$ is the least solution of $f(x) \subseteq x$. Suppose x is any such element, then if $u \subseteq x$ and $u\ f\ v$ hold, it follows that $v \subseteq x$. Now, since $\emptyset \subseteq x$ always holds, if we wish to form the least x, we start with $\emptyset$ and just follow it under the action of f.

Specifically, we define $\mathrm{fix}(f)$ to be the union of all $v \in \mathrm{Con}_{\mathbf{A}}$ for which there exist a sequence $u_0, \ldots, u_n \in \mathrm{Con}_{\mathbf{A}}$ where:

(1) $u_0 = \emptyset$;

(2) $u_i\ f\ u_{i+1}$ for all $i < n$; and

(3) $u_n = v$.

Because f is approximable, it is clear that fix f is closed under entailment. To prove that it is consistent, suppose both v and v' belong to the sets thrown into the union. We have to show that $v \cup v'$ is consistent and also is thrown in. Consider the two sequences $u_0; \ldots, u_n \in \mathrm{Con}_{\mathbf{A}}$ and $u_0', \ldots, u_n' \in \mathrm{Con}_{\mathbf{A}}$ that are responsible for putting v and v' in. It is without loss of generality that we assume they are of the same length, since we can always add lots of $\emptyset$'s onto the front of the shorter one and still satisfy (1)–(3). Now one just argues by induction on i that the sequence of unions $u_i \cup u_i'$ satisfies (1)–(3) with respect to $v \cup v'$.

But why is fix approximable? The method of proof is to replace f by $\overline{w}$ in (2) above, and to use the condition that there exists a sequence satisfying (1)–(3) as *defining* a relation between sets $w \in \mathrm{Con}_{\mathbf{A}\to\mathbf{A}}$ and sets $v \in \mathrm{Con}_{\mathbf{A}}$. It is not difficult to prove that this is an approximable mapping in the sense of the official definition. Clearly this relation determines fix as an operator. ∎

The result above not only proves that every approximable mapping of the form $f : \mathbf{A} \to \mathbf{A}$ has a fixed point as an element of $\mathbf{A}$, but that the association of the *least* fixed point is itself an approximable operator. The formulation makes essential use of the partial ordering of the domains, but Gordon Plotkin noticed as an exercise that the characterization of the operator can be given entirely by equations.

PROPOSITION 7.4. *The least fixed-point operator is uniquely determined by the following three conditions:*

(i) $\mathrm{fix}_{\mathbf{A}} : (\mathbf{A} \to \mathbf{A}) \to \mathbf{A}$, *for all systems* $\mathbf{A}$;

(ii) $\mathrm{fix}_{\mathbf{A}}(f) = f(\mathrm{fix}_{\mathbf{A}}(f))$, *for all* $f : \mathbf{A} \to \mathbf{A}$; *and*

(iii) $h(\mathrm{fix}_{\mathbf{A}}(f)) = \mathrm{fix}_{\mathbf{B}}(g)$, *whenever* $f : \mathbf{A} \to \mathbf{A}$, $g : \mathbf{B} \to \mathbf{B}$, $h : \mathbf{A} \to \mathbf{B}$, *provided that* $h \circ f = g \circ h$ *and* $h(\bot_{\mathbf{A}}) = \bot_{\mathbf{B}}$. ∎

Remarks on the space of strict mappings. In 7.4 and many other places we have had occasion to make use of mappings that take the bottom element of one domain over to the bottom element of the other domain. Such mappings are called *strict* mappings because they take a strict view of having empty input. As notation we might write

$$f : \mathbf{A} \to_{\mathbf{s}} \mathbf{B}$$

to mean that f is a *strict* approximable mapping (*i.e.* $f(\bot_{\mathbf{A}}) = \bot_{\mathbf{B}}$). The totality of domains and strict mappings forms an interesting category in itself, but it is best used in connection with the full category of all approximable mappings.

The collection of strict mappings forms a domain, too. The way to see this is to refer back to Definition 7.1 and add an additional clause ruling out non-strict mappings as inconsistent. What has to be added to 7.1(iii) is the conjunct on the right-hand side to the effect that if the condition $\emptyset \vdash_{\mathbf{A}} \bigcup\{u_i \mid i \in I\}$ holds, then $\emptyset \vdash_{\mathbf{B}} \bigcup\{v_i \mid i \in I\}$ holds too. By the same arguments we used before, it follows that this is the appropriate system for the domain of strict mappings. We can denote it by $(\mathbf{A} \to_{\mathbf{s}} \mathbf{B})$

There is also a useful operator

$$\mathrm{strict} : (\mathbf{A} \to \mathbf{B}) \to (\mathbf{A} \to_{\mathbf{s}} \mathbf{B})$$

defined by the condition that for $f : \mathbf{A} \to \mathbf{B}$ we have:

$$u \ \mathrm{strict}(f)\ v \quad \text{iff} \quad \text{either } \emptyset \vdash_{\mathbf{B}} v \text{ or } \emptyset \not\vdash_{\mathbf{A}} u \text{ and } u\, f\, v,$$

for all $u \in \mathrm{Con}_{\mathbf{A}}$ and $v \in \mathrm{Con}_{\mathbf{B}}$. This operator converts every approximable mapping into the largest strict mapping contained within it.

Since every strict mapping *is* an approximable mapping, there is also an obvious operator going the other way. The pair of operators shows that $\mathbf{A} \to_s \mathbf{B}$ as a domain is what is called a *retract* of $\mathbf{A} \to \mathbf{B}$. There is an interesting theory of this kind of relationship between domains, but we cannot enter into it here.

As a very small application of the use of strict mappings, we remark that the following two domains are isomorphic:

$$\mathbf{A} \times \mathbf{A} \cong (\mathbf{BOOL} \to_s \mathbf{A}).$$

The mapping from right to left is called the *conditional* operator, cond, and we have for all elements $x, y \in |\mathbf{A}|$ and $t \in |\mathbf{BOOL}|$

$$\mathrm{cond}(x,y)(t) = \begin{cases} x, & \text{if } t = \mathrm{true}, \\ y, & \text{if } t = \mathrm{false}. \end{cases} \quad \blacksquare$$

8. Some domain equations. Having outlined the theory of several domain constructs, the final topic for this paper will be the discussion of the *iteration* of these constructs in giving *recursive*, rather than direct definitions of domains. These recursively defined systems have often been called "reflexive," because the domains generally contain copies of themselves as a part of their very structure. The way that this self-containment takes place is best expressed by the so-called *domain equations*, which are really isomorphisms that relate the domain as a whole to a combination of domains—usually with the main domain as a component. This description is rough, since recursion equations for domains can be as complex as recursion equations for functions. We will not enter into a full theory of domain equations now but will just review some preliminary examples to illustrate how the new presentation makes the constructions more explicit.

A domain of trees or S-expressions. This is everyone's favorite example. And a very nice example it is, but we should not think that it contains all the meat of the theory of domain equations. Even if we generalize the kinds of equations to contain all iterations of the domain constructs $+$ and $\times$, the full power of the method has not been exploited. We will try to make this clear in the further examples.

Let a domain (information system) $\mathbf{A}$ be given. What we want to construct is a domain $\mathbf{T}$ of "trees" built up from elements of $\mathbf{A}$ as "atoms". For simplicity we consider unlabelled binary trees here, but more complex trees are easy to accommodate. The domain equation we want to "solve" is this one:

$$\mathbf{T} \cong \mathbf{A} + (\mathbf{T} \times \mathbf{T}).$$

If such a domain exists, then we can say that (up to isomorphism) the elements of the domain **T** are either bottom, or elements of the given domain **A**, or *pairs of elements* from the domain **T** itself. And these are the only kinds of elements that **T** has.

To prove that such a domain exists it is only necessary to ask what information has to be given about a prospective element. The answer may involve us in a regress, but the running backwards need not be infinite—at least for the finite elements. As we shall see, the infinite elements of **T** can be self-replicating; but, to define a domain fully, all we have to do is to build up the finite elements out of the data objects in a systematic way. Fortunately, in order to satisfy the above equation, the required closure conditions on data objects are simple to achieve.

In the first place, we need copies of all the data objects of **A** to put into the sum. The easy way to do this is to take an object Δ not in $\mathcal{D}_{\mathbf{A}}$ and to let, by definition,

$$\Delta_{\mathbf{T}} = (\Delta, \Delta).$$

That gives us one member of $\mathcal{D}_{\mathbf{T}}$, the one we always have to have in any case. The copy of an $X \in \mathcal{D}_{\mathbf{A}}$ is just going to be (X, Δ). The other members of $\mathcal{D}_{\mathbf{T}}$ will be of the form (Δ, U), where U gives us information about the other kind of elements of **T**. The point is that **T** has to be a sum, and we are using just the scheme of Definition 6.3 to set this up.

Next we have to think what kind of information the U above should contain. Because we want a product, we refer back to Definition 6.1 and imagine we have already defined $\mathcal{D}_{\mathbf{T}}$. What 6.1(i) suggests is that we throw in a bunch of other data objects into $\mathcal{D}_{\mathbf{T}}$. The only point that needs care is that the data objects for the product must be *copied* into the overall sum. With this in mind, the following clauses give us the inductive definition of $\mathcal{D}_{\mathbf{T}}$:

(1) $\Delta_{\mathbf{T}} \in \mathcal{D}_{\mathbf{T}}$;

(2) $(X, \Delta) \in \mathcal{D}_{\mathbf{T}}$ whenever $X \in \mathcal{D}_{\mathbf{A}}$; and

(3) $(\Delta, (Y, \Delta_{\mathbf{T}})) \in \mathcal{D}_{\mathbf{T}}$, and $(\Delta, (\Delta_{\mathbf{T}}, Z)) \in \mathcal{D}_{\mathbf{T}}$ whenever $Y, Z \in \mathcal{D}_{\mathbf{T}}$.

Of course,when we say "inductive definition," we mean that $\mathcal{D}_{\mathbf{T}}$ is the *least* class satisfying (1)–(3). By standard arguments it can be shown that $\mathcal{D}_{\mathbf{T}}$ satisfies this set-theoretical equation:

$$\mathcal{D}_{\mathbf{T}} = \{\Delta_{\mathbf{T}}\} \cup \{(X, \Delta) \mid X \in \mathcal{D}_{\mathbf{A}}\} \cup \{(\Delta, (Y, \Delta_{\mathbf{T}})) \mid Y \in \mathcal{D}_{\mathbf{T}}\} \cup \{(\Delta, (\Delta_{\mathbf{T}}, Z)) \mid Z \in \mathcal{D}_{\mathbf{T}}\}.$$

In fact, with some very mild assumptions about ordered pairs in set theory, $\mathcal{D}_{\mathbf{T}}$ is the *only* solution to the above equation.

Defining the data objects is but part of the story: the same data objects can enter into quite different information systems. Data objects are just "tokens" and are only given "meaning" when $\mathrm{Con}_{\mathbf{T}}$ and $\vdash_{\mathbf{T}}$ are defined. Let us consider the problem of consistency first. We already understand the notion as it applies to sum and product systems, so we must merely copy over the parts of the previous definitions in the right position for the definition of $\mathrm{Con}_{\mathbf{T}}$. There are two forms we could give this definition; perhaps the best is the inductive one. We have:

(4) $\emptyset \in \mathrm{Con}_{\mathbf{T}}$;

(5) $u \cup \{\Delta_{\mathbf{T}}\} \in \mathrm{Con}_{\mathbf{T}}$ whenever $u \in \mathrm{Con}_{\mathbf{T}}$;

$$(6)\quad \{(X,\Delta) \mid X \in w\} \in \mathrm{Con}_{\mathbf{T}} \ \text{ whenever } w \in \mathrm{Con}_{\mathbf{A}};$$

$$(7)\quad \{(\Delta,(Y,\Delta_{\mathbf{T}})) \mid Y \in u\} \cup \{(\Delta,(\Delta_{\mathbf{T}},Z)) \mid Z \in v\} \in \mathrm{Con}_{\mathbf{T}} \ \text{ whenever } u, v \in \mathrm{Con}_{\mathbf{T}}.$$

Conditions (4)–(7) certainly make the inductive character of $\mathrm{Con}_{\mathbf{T}}$ clear—again, let us emphasize, the set being specified is the least such. Also clear from the definition is the fact that a consistent set of **T**—aside from containing $\Delta_{\mathbf{T}}$—is either a copy of a consistent set of **A** or a copy of a consistent set of $\mathbf{T} \times \mathbf{T}$. We could thus state a set-theoretical equation for $\mathrm{Con}_{\mathbf{T}}$ similar to the one for $\mathcal{D}_{\mathbf{T}}$.

It remains to define entailment for **T**. Here are the inductive clauses which are pretty much forced on us by our objective of solving the domain equation:

$$(8)\quad u \vdash_{\mathbf{T}} \Delta_{\mathbf{T}} \ \text{ always;}$$

$$(9)\quad u \cup \{\Delta_{\mathbf{T}}\} \vdash_{\mathbf{T}} Y \ \text{ whenever } u \vdash_{\mathbf{T}} Y;$$

$$(10)\quad \{(X,\Delta) \mid X \in w\} \vdash_{\mathbf{T}} (W,\Delta) \ \text{ whenever } w \vdash_{\mathbf{A}} W;$$

$$(11)\quad \{(\Delta,(Y,\Delta_{\mathbf{T}})) \mid Y \in u\} \cup \{(\Delta,(\Delta_{\mathbf{T}},Z))\} \vdash_{\mathbf{T}} (\Delta,(X,\Delta_{\mathbf{T}})) \ \text{ whenever } u \vdash_{\mathbf{T}} X \text{ and } v \in \mathrm{Con}_{\mathbf{T}}; \text{ and}$$

$$(12)\quad \{(\Delta,(Y,\Delta_{\mathbf{T}})) \mid Y \in u\} \cup \{(\Delta,(\Delta_{\mathbf{T}},Z))\} \vdash_{\mathbf{T}} (\Delta,(\Delta_{\mathbf{T}},X)) \ \text{ whenever } u \vdash_{\mathbf{T}} X \text{ and } u \in \mathrm{Con}_{\mathbf{T}}.$$

Inductive definitions engender inductive proofs. It now has to be checked that consistency and entailment for **T** satisfy the axioms of 2.1. The steps needed for this check are mechanical. (The proof may be aided by noting that the cases in (4)–(7) and in (8)–(12) are disjoint—except for a trivial overlap between (8) and (9). The cases get invoked typically by asking, when confronted with an entailment to prove, for the nature of the data object on the right of the turnstile.)

Having defined and verified that **T** is an information system, the validity of the domain equation for **T** is secured by forming the right-hand side and noting that **T** is *identical* to $\mathbf{A} + (\mathbf{T} \times \mathbf{T})$. The reason is that we carefully chose the notation to match the official definitions of sums and products. (In general, in solving domain equations some transformation might have to take place to "re-format" data objects if things are not set up to be literally the same.)

It should be remarked that the sense can be made precise in which **T** is the *least* solution of the given domain equation. (It is an initial algebra in a suitable category of algebras and algebra homomorphisms.) It is pretty obvious that it is minimal in some sense, because we put into it only what was strictly required by the problem and nothing more.

It is also fairly obvious that there are *many* solutions to this domain equation. A non-constructive way to obtain non-minimal solutions is to interpret the whole construction of **T** in a non-standard model of set theory. Though, in the definition of $\mathcal{D}_{\mathbf{T}}$, it looks like we are only working with very finite objects, everything we did could be made abstract and could be carried out in some funny universe. The result would be a system of "finite" data objects having all the right formal properties but containing things not in the standard minimal system. We would then take the notions of consistency and entailment that also exist in the funny universe and restrict them to sets of data objects that are actually finite in the standard sense. It can be seen from the formal properties of the construction that the resulting notions satisfy our axioms for an information system and that the domain equation holds—BUT the system would have many different elements beyond what we put into the original **T**. To make this construction work, by the way, we would have to force **A** to be absolute in the model: if it is actually finite (say, $\mathbf{A} = \mathbf{BOOL}$), then there is no problem. (Constructive methods for introducing "nonstandard" data objects can also be given.)

Finally, we must remark on why we called T a domain of *S-expressions.* The answer becomes clear when we structure **T** as an algebra. First, there is an approximable mapping

$$\text{atom} : \mathbf{A} \to \mathbf{T},$$

which injects **A** into **T** making the elements of **A** "atoms" of **T**. Then there is a truth-valued predicate on **T** which decides whether an element is an atom:

$$\text{isatom} : \mathbf{T} \to \mathbf{BOOL}.$$

Finally, since $\mathbf{T} \times \mathbf{T}$ is a part of **T**, we can redefine the paring functions so that:

$$\text{pair} : \mathbf{T} \times \mathbf{T} \to \mathbf{T}, \;\; \text{fst} : \mathbf{T} \to \mathbf{T}, \text{ and } \;\text{snd} : \mathbf{T} \to \mathbf{T}.$$

In LISP terminology, these operations are the same as the familiar cons, car, and cdr. This makes **T** into an algebra where, starting from atoms, elements—expressions—can be built up by iterated pairing.

But why is our system different from the usual way of regarding S-expressions? The answer is that by including partial expressions (those involving $\perp_{\mathbf{T}}$) and by completing the domain with limits, *infinite* expressions are introduced. For instance, if $a \in |\mathbf{T}|$, then we can solve the fixed-point equation:

$$x = \text{pair}(\text{atom}(a), x),$$

which is an infinite list of a's. This is but one example; the possibilities have been discussed in many papers too numerous to mention here.

As is common to remark, S-expressions can also be thought of as trees: the parse tree that gives the grammatical form of the expression. What we have added to the idea of a tree is possibility of having infinite trees, and having all these trees as elements of a domain. ∎

A domain for λ-claculus. A lengthy discussion with many references on λ-calculus models can be found in Longo [1982]. All we wish to remark on here is how the method of construction by solving a domain equation can be fit into the new presentation. What I have added to the previous ideas (that in any case came out of an analysis of finite elements of models) is the general view of information systems. In particular the models obtained this way are *not* lattices—hence, the need for the calculations with Con. I hope that the presentation here makes it clearer how "pure" λ-calculus models can be related to other domains having other types of structures—for instance, those needed in denotational semantics.

The domain equation we wish to solve is:

$$\mathbf{D} \cong \mathbf{A} + (\mathbf{D} \to \mathbf{D}).$$

We proceed in much the same way we did for **T**, except we must now put in data objects appropriate to the function space. Here is construction, where again Δ is chosen outside $\mathcal{D}_{\mathbf{A}}$ and $\Delta_{\mathbf{D}} = (\Delta, \Delta)$:

(1) $\Delta_{\mathbf{D}} \in \mathcal{D}_{\mathbf{D}}$;

(2) $(X, \Delta) \in \mathcal{D}_{\mathbf{D}}$ whenever $X \in \mathcal{D}_{\mathbf{A}}$;

(3) $(\Delta, (u, v)) \in \mathcal{D}_{\mathbf{D}}$ whenever $u, v \in \mathrm{Con}_{\mathbf{D}}$;

(4) $\emptyset \in \mathrm{Con}_{\mathbf{D}}$;

(5) $u \cup \{\Delta_{\mathbf{D}}\} \in \mathrm{Con}_{\mathbf{D}}$ whenever $u \in \mathrm{Con}_{\mathbf{D}}$;

(6) $\{(X, \Delta) \mid X \in w\} \in \mathrm{Con}_{\mathbf{D}}$ whenever $w \in \mathrm{Con}_{\mathbf{A}}$; and

(7) $\{(\Delta, (u_0, v_0)), \ldots, (\Delta, (u_{n-1}, v_{n-1}))\} \in \mathrm{Con}_{\mathbf{D}}$ provided $u_i, v_i \in \mathrm{Con}_{\mathbf{D}}$ for all $i < n$ and whenever $I \subseteq \{0, \ldots, n-1\}$ and $\bigcup\{u_i \mid i \in I\} \in \mathrm{Con}_{\mathbf{D}}$, then $\bigcup\{v_i \mid i \in I\} \in \mathrm{Con}_{\mathbf{D}}$.

What is different here from the definition of **T** is the fact that the concepts $\mathcal{D}_{\mathbf{D}}$ and $\mathrm{Con}_{\mathbf{D}}$ are *mutually recursive* because the data objects are themselves built from consistent sets. The scheme is based on a combination of the sum construct and the function-space construct, but the mutual recursion allows "feedback" to occur.

To complete the definition we have to give the clauses for the inductive definition of entailment. They are:

(8) $u \vdash_{\mathbf{D}} \Delta_{\mathbf{D}}$ always;

(9) $u \cup \{\Delta_{\mathbf{D}}\} \vdash_{\mathbf{D}} Y$ whenever $u \vdash_{\mathbf{D}} Y$;

(10) $\{(X, \Delta) \mid X \in w\} \vdash_{\mathbf{D}} (W, \Delta)$ whenever $w \vdash_{\mathbf{A}} W$;

(11) $\{(\Delta, (u_0, v_0)), \ldots, (\Delta, (u_{n-1}, v_{n-1}))\} \vdash_{\mathbf{D}} (\Delta, (u', v'))$ whenever $\bigcup\{v_i \mid u' \vdash_{\mathbf{D}} u_i\} \vdash_{\mathbf{D}} v'$ and the set on the left is in $\mathrm{Con}_{\mathbf{D}}$.

Obviously these definitions are much shorter if we have a domain in which all sets are consistent, but there are many reasons for retaining the consistency concept throughout. The check that **D** is an information system and satisfies the domain equation is mechanical. We cannot detail here how this construction provides a λ-calculus model.

It is clear that these definitions are constructive, and that, with a suitable Gödel numbering of the data objects, the predicates for consistency and entailment are recursively enumerable. However, the recursion used builds up the predicates by going from less complicated data objects to more complicated ones; therefore, the predicates must be *recursive*, because, for a certain size data object, the derivation that puts it into the predicate is of a bounded length. This observation helps in the discussion of the computability of the operators defined on these domains—another topic we cannot discuss here. ∎

A universal domain. As a final example of building up domains recursively, we give a construction of a "universal" domain **U**. (The reason for the name will be explained presently.) The best way to define **U** seems to be to define a domain **V** with a top element first,and then to remove the top.

The recursion for **V** is remarkably simple. We begin with two distinct objects Δ and ∇ that give information about the top and bottom of **V**, respectively. Thus, $\Delta_{\mathbf{V}} = \Delta$ by definition. We assume that these two special data objects are "atomic" in the sense that they are not equal to any ordered pair of objects. For the definition of $\mathcal{D}_{\mathbf{V}}$ we have these clauses:

(1) $\Delta, \nabla \in \mathcal{D}_{\mathbf{V}}$;

(2) $(X, \Delta) \in \mathcal{D}_{\mathbf{V}}$ and $(\Delta, Y) \in \mathcal{D}_{\mathbf{V}}$ whenever $X, Y \in \mathcal{D}_{\mathbf{V}}$.

In other words, we begin with two objects and close up under two flavors of copies of these objects. (A product result is involved here, so that is the reason for structuring the flavors the way we have.)

For **V** all subsets of $\mathcal{D}_{\mathbf{V}}$ are consistent, so all we have left is to define entailment for this domain. The clauses are:

(3) $u \vdash_{\mathbf{V}} \Delta$ always;

(4) $u \vdash_{\mathbf{V}} \nabla$ whenever either $\nabla \in u$ or $\{X \mid (X, \Delta) \in u\} \vdash_{\mathbf{V}} \nabla$ and $\{Y \mid (\Delta, Y) \in u\} \vdash_{\mathbf{V}} \nabla$;

(5) $u \vdash_{\mathbf{V}} (X', \Delta)$ whenever either $\nabla \in u$ or $\{X \mid (X, \Delta) \in u\} \vdash_{\mathbf{V}} X'$; and

(6) $u \vdash_{\mathbf{V}} (\Delta, Y')$ whenever either $\nabla \in u$ or $\{Y \mid (\Delta, Y) \in u\} \vdash_{\mathbf{V}} Y'$.

The proof that **V** is an information system proceeds as before. Note that, under the above definition of entailment, the data objects $\Delta, (\Delta, \Delta), ((\Delta, \Delta), \Delta)$, *etc.* are all equivalent. There is, however, no other data object equivalent to ∇. The domain equation satisfied by **V** is:

$$\mathbf{V} \cong \mathbf{V} \times \mathbf{V}.$$

Of course, there are an unlimited number of solutions to this equation, so the fact that **V** satisfies it tells us very little.

Because ∇ entails everything, we can regard it as a "rogue" object that ought to be banned from polite company: the only element of **V** it gives any information about is the top element, which is as unhelpful as any element could be. We should simply throw it out as being "inconsistent." What remains is the domain **U**. Formally we have:

(7) $\mathcal{D}_{\mathbf{U}} = \mathcal{D}_{\mathbf{V}} - \{\nabla\}$;

(8) $\Delta_{\mathbf{U}} = \Delta_{\mathbf{V}}$;

(9) $\mathrm{Con}_{\mathbf{U}} = \{u \subseteq \mathcal{D}_{\mathbf{U}} \mid u \text{ finite and } u \not\vdash_{\mathbf{V}} \nabla\}$; and

(10) $u \vdash_{\mathbf{U}} Y$ iff $u \in \mathrm{Con}_{\mathbf{U}}$, $Y \in \mathcal{D}_{\mathbf{U}}$ and $u \vdash_{\mathbf{V}} Y$.

The same style of definition would work in any situation when an information system has a rogue data object that entails everything: there always is a system that results from eliminating all those objects that entail everything. Indeed, we could have always included such an object in any domain and altered the definition to take as elements those deductively closed sets of data objects that do not have the rogue object as a member. We did not do this for the reason that superfluous elements cause lots of exceptions in constructs such as product, where there is a temptation to let them enter into various combinations.

Now in **U** we *do* allow ∇ to enter into combinations—and this is part of the secret of the construction. The consequence is, however, that the domain equation which **U** satisfies is not too easy to state since it involves an unfamiliar functor. So it is not through such equations that we will understand its nature in a direct way. But it is possible to explain how it works by reference to the steps in the construction.

Imagine the full (infinite) binary tree. The data objects of **U** are giving information about possible paths in the tree. We think to the tree starting at the root node at the top of the page and growing down. The object Δ gives no information—so no paths are *excluded.* (If we would have allowed ∇, then the information it would have been giving is that *all paths are excluded.*) The data object (X, Δ) tells us about a path that *either* it is unrestricted on the right half of the tree, *or* on the left, when we start at the node directly below the root, the paths that are excluded from the subtree are those excluded according to X. This makes sense because the subtrees of the binary tree look exactly like the whole tree, so information can be relativized or translated to other positions. With (Δ, Y) the rôles of right and left are interchanged. We could have introduced data objects of the form (X, Y) which tell us information about both halves of the tree at the same time, but the consistent set $\{(X, \Delta), (\Delta, Y)\}$ does the same job. In general consistent sets should be thought of as *conjunctions*; while, in this example, the comma in the ordered pair should be thought of as a *disjunction* when "reading" information objects.

We can now see that a single data object (if it contains ∇) looks down the tree along a finite path to some depth and then *excludes* the rest of the tree below that node. A consistent set of data objects leaves at least one hole, so at least one path is not excluded. The maximal consistent sets of information objects are those giving true information about one single (infinite) path—the total elements of the domain **U** correspond exactly to the infinite paths in the binary tree. The partial elements are harder to describe geometrically, however. In accumulating information into a consistent set, holes can be left all over the tree. A partial object is therefore of an indeterminate character, since the "path" we are describing might sneak through any one of the holes. (There is, by the way, a precise topological explanation of what is happening. The total elements of **U** form a well-known topological space, the so-called Cantor space, and the partially ordered set of elements of **U** is isomorphic to the lattice of *open* sets of the space—save that the whole space is not allowed.)

This is all very well, but what, we ask, is the good of this domain, and why is it called "universal". The proof cannot be given here, but the result is as follows. As a consequence of standard facts about countable Boolean algebras, it can be proved that every "countably based" domain is a subdomain of **U**. More specifically, if **A** is an information system, and if $\mathcal{D}_{\mathbf{A}}$ is countable, then there exists a pair of approximable mappings

$$a : \mathbf{A} \to \mathbf{U} \text{ and } b : \mathbf{U} \to \mathbf{A},$$

such that

$$b \circ a = I_A \text{ and } a \circ b \subseteq I_U.$$

This makes **A** a special kind of retract of **U**. The mappings a and b are far from unique, but at least there is one way to give a one-one embedding of the elements of **A** into the elements of **U**.

The universal property of **U** can be applied quite widely. For example, since $(\mathbf{U} \to \mathbf{U})$ is a system with only countably many data objects (by explicit construction!), this system is a retract of **U**. Fixing on one such retraction pair as above, makes **U** also into a model of the λ-calculus. Whether different retractions give essentially different models I do not know. But the point of the remark is to show that domains can contain their own function spaces for a variety of interesting reasons. ▮

A domain of domains. Not many details can be presented here, but we would also like to remark that even domains can be made into a domain. One way of getting an idea of how this is possible is to note that since subdomains of **U** correspond to certain kinds of functions on **U**, and since the function space of **U** is also a subdomain of **U**, it might be suspected that the subdomains of **U** form a single subdomain of **U**.

That is a fairly sophisticated way of reaching the conclusion (and many details have to be worked out). A more elementary approach would be just to ask what it means to give a finite amount of information *about a domain.* For the sake of uniformity, suppose that the data objects of the possible domain are drawn from the non-negative integers, and that we conventionally use 0 for Δ. Then to give a finite amount of information about a domain is—roughly—to specify a finite part of Con and a finite part of $\vdash$. To make the formulation easier, we will reserve for 1 a rôle like the one recently played by ∇. What the specifications will boil down to is pairs (u, v) of finite sets of integers used as data objects to convey one piece of information about an entailment relation.

But hold, entailment relations are very closely connected to approximable mappings. Indeed, we remarked before that the identity function as an approximable mapping on a domain is just represented as the underlying entailment relation itself. Suppose we take as our domain the domain of all sets of integers. It is a powerset, so call it **P**. That is to say, the integers are the data objects, all finite sets are consistent, and the entailment relation is the minimal possible one. (As far as elements go, an arbitrary set of integers is equal to the union of all its finite subsets, which means that the elements of the domain are in a one-one correspondence with the arbitrary sets of integers.) The question is: which approximable mappings on **P** into itself correspond to entailment relations on the integers as data objects?

The answer can be expressed most succinctly using our standard notation. If we think of $r : \mathbf{P} \to \mathbf{P}$ as a relation between finite sets in the usual way, then to say that r is reflexive is to say:

(1) $\quad I_P \subseteq r.$

To say that r is transitive is to say:

(2) $\quad r \circ r = r.$

To say that for r the object 0 plays at being Δ is to say:

$$(3) \quad \overline{0} \subseteq r(\bot),$$

where in general $\overline{n}$ is short for $\overline{\{n\}}$ in the domain $\mathbf{P}$. Then, to say that 1 plays at being a rogue object is to say:

$$(4) \quad \top = r(\overline{1}).$$

Finally, to say that 1 is an inconsistent object that has to be excluded is to say:

$$(5) \quad \overline{1} \not\subseteq r(\overline{0}).$$

That's it. The collection of approximable mappings satisfying (1)–(5) gives us all the entailment relations we need. Condition (5) is a consistency condition, and for r the consistent finite sets u are those such that $\overline{1} \not\subseteq r(\overline{u})$. What we are asserting is that the totality of r satisfying (1)–(5) forms the elements of a domain—one that has been derived from $(\mathbf{P} \to \mathbf{P})$ in a way similar to the way we derived $\mathbf{U}$ from $\mathbf{V}$ above.

Having made domains into a domain, the next step is to see how constructs on domain (*i.e.* functors) can be made into approximable mappings. But the retelling and development of that story will have to wait for another publication along with the very interesting chapter on powerdomains. I only hope the ground covered here makes the theory of domains seem more elementary and more natural. ∎

BIBLIOGRAPHY

BARENDREGT, H.P.

1981 **The Lambda Calculus: Its Syntax And Semantics.** Studies in Logic, vol. 103, North Holland, New York (1981), xiv+615pp.

BERRY, G. and CURIEN, P.L.

1981 *Sequential algorithms on concrete data structures.* Report of Ecole Nationale Supérience des Mines de Paris, Centre de Mathematiques Appliquées, Sophia Antipolis (1981).

ENGELER, E.

1979 **Algebras and combinators.** Berichte des Instituts fur Informatik, Nr. 32, ETH Zurich, 12pp.

GIERZ, G., HOFMANN, K. H., KEIMEL, K., LAWSON, J. D., MISLOVE, M. and SCOTT, D.S.

1980 **A Compendium of Continuous Lattices.** Springer-Verlag (1980), 371 pp.

GORDON, M. J., MILNER, A.J.R. and WADSWORTH, C.P.

1979 **Edinburgh LCF.** Springer-Verlag Lecture Notes in Computer Science, vol. 78 (1979), 159 pp.

GORDON, M.

1979 **The Denotational Description of Programming Languages, An Introduction.** Springer-Verlag (1979).

GREIBACH, S. A.

1981 *Formal languages: origins and directions.* Annals of the History of Computing, vol. 3 (1981), pp. 14–41.

KAHN, G. and PLOTKIN, G.

1978 *Domaines Concrètes.* Rapport IRIA-LABORIA, No. 336 (1978).

LONGO, G.

1982 *Set-theoretical models of lambda-calculus: theories, expansions, isomorphisms.* Preprint, Pisa (1982), 46pp.

MEYER, A. R.

1981 *What is a model of the lambda calculus?.* (Expanded version) Preprint, MIT (1981), 40 pp.

NIELSEN, M., PLOTKIN, G. and WINSKEL, G.

1981 *Petri nets, event structures and domains.* Theoretical Computer Science, vol. 13(1981), pp.85–108.

PLOTKIN, G.D.

1972 *A set-theoretical definition of application.* Memorandum MIP-R-95, School of Artificial Intelligence, University of Edinburgh, 32pp.

1978 *The category of complete partial orders: a tool for making meanings.* **In: Proc. Summer School on Foundations of Artificial Intelligence and Computer Science.** Instituto di Scienze dell' Informazione, Universita di Pisa (June 1978).

RABIN, M. O. and SCOTT, D. S.

1959 *Finite automata and their decision problems.* IBM Journal Research and Development, vol. 3 (1959), pp. 114–125.

SCOTT, D.S.

1972 **Continuous lattices.** Springer Lecture Notes in Mathematics, vol. 274 (1972), pp. 97–136.

1976 *Data types as lattices.* **SIAM Journal on Computing.** vol. 5 (1976), pp. 522–587.

1980a *Lambda calculus: some models, some philosophy.* **The Kleene Symposium.** Barwise, J., et al., eds., Studies in Logic 101, North Holland (1980), pp. 381–421.

1980b *Relating theories of the λ-calculus.* **To H. B. Curry: Essays on Combinatory Logic, Lambda Calculus and Formalism.** Seldin, J. P. and Hindley, J. R., eds., Academic Press (1980), pp. 403–450.

1980c *Lectures on a mathematical theory of computation.* Oxford University Computing Laboratory Technical Monograph PRG–19 (1981), 148pp.

1982 *Some ordered sets in computer science.* **In: Ordered Sets.** I. Rival, ed., D. Reidel (1982), pp. 677–718.

SMYTH, M. and PLOTKIN, G. D.

1981 *The categorical solution of recursive domain equations.* **SIAM Journal on Computation..** To appear (1981).

STOY, J.E.

1977 **Denotational Semantics: The Scott–Strachey Approach to Programming Language Theory.** M.I.T. Press, Cambridge, Mass., xxx+414pp.

TENNENT, R.D.

1981 **Principles of Programming languages.** Prentice–Hall (1981), 271 pp.6.

WADSWORTH, C.

1976 *The relation between computational and denotational properties for Scott's D_∞–models of the lambda–calculus.* SIAM Journal of Computing, vol. 5, pp. 488–521.

WINSKEL, G.

1980 **Events in Computation.** Ph.D thesis, University of Edinburgh (1980).

Author Index